IT Governance Policies & Procedures
2015 Edition

by Michael Wallace and Larry Webber

The role of IT management is changing even more quickly than information technology itself. The 2015 Edition of *IT Governance Policies & Procedures* is an updated guide and decision-making reference that can help you to devise an information systems policy and procedure program uniquely tailored to the needs of your organization. Not only does it provide extensive sample policies, but this valuable resource also gives you the information you need to develop useful and effective policies for your unique environment. For fingertip access to the information you need on IT governance, policy and planning, documentation, systems analysis and design, and much more, the materials in this ready-reference desk manual can be used by you or your staff as models or templates to create similar documents for your own organization.

Highlights of the 2015 Edition

The 2015 Edition brings you:

- New chapter (Chapter 3) describing the use of metrics in IT governance including:

    - why monitoring process metrics is important to IT governance;

    - how to focus on the critical few metrics;

    - basic metric analysis; and

    - managing a governance metric program.

- Guidance and policy for determining when and how local administrative rights should be given to local users (Chapter 30).

- How to create a software deployment policy that helps you keep your in-house developed software up-to-date efficiently, including a new software deployment checklist (Chapter 17).

- The latest information on how to manage "Bring Your Own Network—(BYON)" and protecting your corporate assets (Chapter 27).

- A new Requirements Traceability Matrix and information on its use (Chapter 13).

- How to implement an Install/Move/Add/Change policy to more effectively manage your IT assets (Chapter 26).

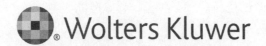

- Updated information and policy on managing Web-based collaboration and social media use by your employees (Chapter 22).

- New policy on properly archiving IT project records (Chapter 16).

- Over eighty IT policies that you can use right away to better govern your IT processes.

- Actual sample policies on the enclosed CD that you can modify for your own use to enforce proper governance of IT within your organization.

- New and updated worksheets on the enclosed CD that you can use for planning and documentation of your critical processes.

- Proposal templates, checklists, tally sheets, worksheets, tables, logs, questionnaires, and agreements for quick reference and adaptation to your particular needs.

- An updated glossary with the latest IT and business terms.

9/14

For questions concerning this shipment, billing, or other customer service matters, call our Customer Service Department at 1-800-234-1660.

For toll-free ordering, please call 1-800-638-8437.

IT
GOVERNANCE
POLICIES
& PROCEDURES

2015 EDITION

Michael Wallace ◆ Larry Webber

Wolters Kluwer

Copyright © 2014 CCH Incorporated. All Rights Reserved.

No part of this publication may be reproduced or transmitted in any form or by any means, including electronic, mechanical, photocopying, recording, or utilized by any information storage or retrieval system, without written permission from the publisher. For information about permissions or to request permissions online, visit us at *http://www.wklawbusiness.com/footer-pages/permissions*, or a written request may be faxed to our permissions department at 212-771-0803.

Published by Wolters Kluwer in New York.

Wolters Kluwer serves customers worldwide with CCH and Kluwer Law International products.

Printed in the United States of America

ISBN 978-1-4548-4266-8

1 2 3 4 5 6 7 8 9 0

About Wolters Kluwer Law & Business

Wolters Kluwer Law & Business is a leading global provider of intelligent information and digital solutions for legal and business professionals in key specialty areas, and respected educational resources for professors and law students. Wolters Kluwer Law & Business connects legal and business professionals as well as those in the education market with timely, specialized authoritative content and information-enabled solutions to support success through productivity, accuracy and mobility.

Serving customers worldwide, Wolters Kluwer Law & Business products include those under the Aspen Publishers, CCH, Kluwer Law International, Loislaw, ftwilliam.com and MediRegs family of products.

CCH products have been a trusted resource since 1913, and are highly regarded resources for legal, securities, antitrust and trade regulation, government contracting, banking, pension, payroll, employment and labor, and healthcare reimbursement and compliance professionals.

Aspen Publishers products provide essential information to attorneys, business professionals and law students. Written by preeminent authorities, the product line offers analytical and practical information in a range of specialty practice areas from securities law and intellectual property to mergers and acquisitions and pension/benefits. Aspen's trusted legal education resources provide professors and students with high-quality, up-to-date and effective resources for successful instruction and study in all areas of the law.

Kluwer Law International products provide the global business community with reliable international legal information in English. Legal practitioners, corporate counsel and business executives around the world rely on Kluwer Law journals, looseleafs, books, and electronic products for comprehensive information in many areas of international legal practice.

Loislaw is a comprehensive online legal research product providing legal content to law firm practitioners of various specializations. Loislaw provides attorneys with the ability to quickly and efficiently find the necessary legal information they need, when and where they need it, by facilitating access to primary law as well as state-specific law, records, forms and treatises.

ftwilliam.com offers employee benefits professionals the highest quality plan documents (retirement, welfare and non-qualified) and government forms (5500/PBGC, 1099 and IRS) software at highly competitive prices.

MediRegs products provide integrated health care compliance content and software solutions for professionals in healthcare, higher education and life sciences, including professionals in accounting, law and consulting.

Wolters Kluwer Law & Business, a division of Wolters Kluwer, is headquartered in New York. Wolters Kluwer is a market-leading global information services company focused on professionals.

WOLTERS KLUWER SUPPLEMENT NOTICE

This product is updated on a periodic basis with supplements and/or new editions to reflect important changes in the subject matter.

If you would like information about enrolling this product in the update service, or wish to receive updates billed separately with a 30-day examination review, please contact our Customer Service Department at 1-800-234-1660 or email us at: *customer.service@wolterskluwer.com.* You can also contact us at:

Wolters Kluwer
Distribution Center
7201 McKinney Circle
Frederick, MD 21704

Important Contact Information

- To order any title, go to *www.wklawbusiness.com* or call 1-800-638-8437.

- To reinstate your manual update service, call 1-800-638-8437.

- To contact Customer Service, e-mail *customer.service@wolterskluwer .com*, call 1-800-234-1660, fax 1-800-901-9075, or mail correspondence to: Order Department—Wolters Kluwer, PO Box 990, Frederick, MD 21705.

- To review your account history or pay an invoice online, visit *www .aspenpublishers.com/payinvoices.*

Wolters Kluwer

ABOUT THE AUTHORS

Michael Wallace has more than 30 years of experience in the information systems field. He began his career as a mainframe operator for Super Food Services and then moved to a programming position at Reynolds & Reynolds developing financial applications for automotive dealers.

He became a consultant after graduating magna cum laude from Wright State University (Dayton, Ohio) with a Bachelor of Science degree in Management Science. For eight years he was president of Q Consulting, a custom application development firm. Mr. Wallace has been an application developer, a business analyst, and a technical and business consultant and has assisted the state of Ohio in developing statewide IT policies.

Mr. Wallace has served on the board of directors of various information technology user organizations and is active in the local technical community. He is past President of the Columbus Chapter of the International Association of Microsoft Certified Partners (IAMCP), is a Competent Toastmaster and Competent Leader with Toastmasters International, and graduated from the Executive MBA program at the Fisher College of Business at The Ohio State University.

After working as a practice manager and director for the last few years, Mr. Wallace is now a Senior Consultant at FortyAU, providing software development and project managing consulting services to customers. He has also taught in the graduate programs at The Ohio State University and DeVry University Keller Graduate School of Management and has published several articles and books on business and technology topics.

Mr. Wallace can be reached by e-mail at *michaelw269@gmail.com*, on his blog at businesstechbooks.wordpress.com, or on Twitter@MichaelWallace.

Larry Webber has more than 30 years of experience in the information services field. He began his career in the U.S. Marine Corps as a digital network repairman and then moved to a position as a COBOL programmer supporting the Marine Corps's Logistics traffic management systems.

After his release from active service, he worked in Kansas City as a COBOL programmer, systems analyst, and IT manager at Waddell & Reed, Temperature Industries, United Telecommunications, and the law offices of Shook, Hardy & Bacon.

For the next 12 years, Mr. Webber held various systems engineering and data processing management positions with International Truck and Bus in Springfield, Ohio, where, among other achievements, he authored an extensive Disaster Recovery plan for the manufacturing facility. He is currently a Senior Project Manager working at a major manufacturer in the Columbus, Ohio area.

Mr. Webber has an Associate in Science degree from Darton College in Albany, Georgia, in Data Processing; a Bachelor of Science degree in Business Administration and an MBA both from Rockhurst College in Kansas City, Missouri; and an Associate in Science degree in Industrial Engineering from Sinclair Community College in Dayton, Ohio. He also completed a Master of Project Management degree from West Carolina University.

Mr. Webber is retired from the U.S. Army Reserve as a First Sergeant in the Infantry. He is a certified Project Management Professional by the Project Management Institute, Certified in Production and Inventory Management by APICS, Master of Business Continuity Planning by DRII, Six Sigma Black Belt, and ITIL Service Manager. Mr. Webber is a Visiting Professor at DeVry University Keller Graduate School of Management, and has published several articles on disaster recovery topics. His published works include disaster recovery/business continuity, quality control, project management, and veteran's benefits.

Mr. Webber can be reached by e-mail at *ljwljw88@hotmail.com*.

Your comments and suggestions for improving this book are welcome.

CONTENTS

A complete table of contents for each chapter is included at the beginning of the chapter.

FOREWORD

Confucius is quoted as saying, "A man who does not plan long ahead will find trouble at his door." As information technology matures and becomes more ubiquitous, we who provide IT services must also grow up and work proactively to improve our craft. Many must agree with that statement, because methodologies, frameworks, and "best practices" are emerging almost as quickly as the technologies they attempt to support.

Even as resources abound, many IT leaders struggle with trying to manage real-world IT projects of all kinds, never getting their arms around why their infrastructure continually fails, their applications are never deployed on schedule, and security risks lurk around every corner. The answer? As CIO of a quickly growing healthcare company, I knew developing sustainable processes and reliable procedures was our only hope for keeping our fast-moving freight train of technologies on the proverbial rails. That, for us, meant supporting immediate, reliable access to terabytes of patient data to all of the right people—but not a single record to the wrong person. *Ever.* So we set a target of developing a solid policies and procedures manual.

As I am sure you have guessed, and perhaps experienced, the adage "easier said than done" does not begin to describe the challenge that simple concept introduces. Few IT professionals, even those deeply knowledgeable in their area of expertise, are able to assemble processes and procedures for every aspect of their professional space—much less have the skill to record and formalize them. Add to that the lack of governance background to know precisely what to include, with which protections, and with what appropriate verbiage, and any internal approach to writing policies and procedures will likely fall far short if not fail outright.

Consider too that the vast majority of economic activity in America and throughout the world is generated by small, struggling, understaffed businesses. They are often led by well-meaning experts in that business's product or service, and are not at all equipped to build sustainable processes for the technology supporting their business.

Enter *IT Governance Policies & Procedures*. It is *Robert's Rules of Order* for the IT professionals. This book assembles the best content from various IT governance models and frameworks, collecting their strengths into a practical, usable, virtually copy-and-paste-able format. The documents are professional and complete, making them available to anyone at a fraction of the cost of both the terribly expensive experience-based approach as well as the "nuclear option" of acquiring them from attorneys.

If you think writing thorough and actionable policies and procedures is hard, try convincing the top levels of leadership that it is worth the enormous effort to construct and implement them. To make life easier, each well-organized section of *IT Governance Policies & Procedures* provides insights as to why each is so important, providing much-needed talking points for winning executive management approval for supporting governance initiatives. It just might help explain the same to the reader, especially in sections concerning perilous subjects such as:

- BYOD ("Bring Your Own Device")
- IT metrics—measuring IT customer service success
- Managing virtual/remote IT teams
- Anticipating and mitigating risk
- Creating and reaching reasonable Service Level Agreements (SLAs)
- Relocating technology safely, with minimal downtime
- Maintaining a healthy service desk
- Managing the unexpected

Those sections, and many others, have proven enormously helpful in many thousands of IT leaders' work toward optimizing and protecting their valuable technical resources through robust but reasonable controls.

As an aside, most protective governance laws require annual review of all of a company's policies and procedures. This assumes both that you have them and that you are able to effectively modify them to support all of the latest laws, rulings, and methodological improvements in the prior year. Fortunately, this book is revisited annually by its authors. For as long as that is the case, I highly recommend a fresh copy of this volume be at the top of your IT budget.

Enjoy, and with the wisdom of Confucius and thousands of proactive, well-prepared IT leaders, plan now.

Kenny Wyatt, entrepreneur, IT consultant, CIO

PREFACE

While many of the basic principles of superior IT operations have not changed over the years—we still have to do backups, service business users, and so on—the Internet and an explosion of connectivity options have added new challenges to running an effective IT organization. Writing *IT Governance Policies & Procedures, 2015 Edition*, has been a challenge because of the explosion of IT technology. By the time you finish this book, technology changes are already being developed for the next edition.

WHAT THIS MANUAL WILL DO FOR YOU

No two information systems operations are alike, but many do share some basic elements, such as hardware, software, and personnel. This manual defines the common threads that link all information systems operations, providing for a variety of situations—not as a one-size-fits-all model but, instead, as an updated guide and decision-making reference that can help you devise an information systems policy and procedure program uniquely tailored to the needs of your organization. Rather than simply providing sample policies that will not encompass what is unique to your organization, this manual gives you the information you need to develop useful and effective policies for your unique environment.

ORGANIZED FOR QUICK ACCESS

"Simplicity is the ultimate design." Often, a multitude of forms are included in policies and procedures handbooks. This manual, however, provides a minimum of forms with the understanding that a well-written memo or e-mail message can take the place of a form and reduce the complexity of an IT operation. As an operation grows in complexity, the challenge to keep it running smoothly grows, and thus the need for a formal system of operations becomes a necessity. IT operations that have a formal systems and procedures manual in place are more efficient.

ADDED STRATEGIC VALUE

The role of IT management is changing even more quickly than information technology itself. Today the IT operation is no longer found in some obscure corner of the corporate organization. Instead, it plays an interactive role in global systems. This manual will help you to formalize policies and procedures that are needed to formally document the IT operation. Doing so will save both time and effort. This manual will help you identify standard operations and procedures, documenting as needed, but still allowing for special needs.

Reality check: End-user computer systems will grow with or without the guidance of corporate IT, but the two working together will provide synergistic dividends. This manual updates the policies and procedures that can expedite your objective.

Our research discovered many well-run information systems operations and some real disasters. The better ones had noticeably good management and practical documentation. Expensive consultants, fad innovations, and cutting-edge technology did not always produce the desired IT results.

IT Governance Policies & Procedures is a compilation of systems policies and procedures—the best practices within the industry—in current use. This manual is a process development tool that any seasoned information systems manager, working in a large or small IS operation, will find useful.

SAVING YOU TIME

In addition to the background information, you need to create policies specific to your organization, sample policies are included with each chapter that you can use as a starting point for developing your own resource, by copying the sample policies from the included CD. Of course, you can also make needed changes and post the manual on a local area network or even a company intranet site.

ACKNOWLEDGMENTS

Michael dedicates this book to his teacher and mentor, George Jenkins, whose encouragement and support have been invaluable over the years, and to his wife and best friend, Tami, for all her support during his many projects.

Larry gratefully acknowledges the assistance of his wife, Nancy, in preparing this project.

Part I

OPERATING AND ORGANIZING THE BUSINESS

1

IT GOVERNANCE: ALIGNING IT WITH THE BUSINESS

§ 1.01 OVERVIEW

[A] Purpose and Scope

Information Technology (IT) departments have long struggled with providing the level of service that the "business" side of the organization has demanded. IT exists but to serve the rest of the organization, and yet customers always demand more. In addition, IT consumes a large share of the company's operating budget and has a voracious appetite for ever more resources.

To make matters worse, how often have IT users and business executives complained that the various IT teams seem to work at cross-purposes? How often has one team completed something, "tossed" it to another IT group, and walked away? How often has one IT team "slipped in" a change that no one else knew about, and that brought important IT systems to a halt?

Managing IT complexities, while maintaining customer satisfaction, is a difficult task. Companies typically do a few things well, a few things poorly and the rest falls somewhere in the middle. IT is not the core competency of most companies, yet the very survival of the company may depend on how well its IT operation supports the goals and objectives of the business. Most companies turn to IT governance to close the difference between what they expect from their IT function and the value that it is delivering.

IT governance applies structure and control over how IT is managed within the organization. It includes proper controls over how resources are allocated, how change is managed, and how services are delivered. While IT has its own unique problems, applying basic management and governance principles to how IT is delivered allows the organization to get the most return for its investment in IT. IT governance can include the following activities:

A. Defining how money should be spent. It ensures that spending aligns with company priorities.
B. Justifying and prioritizing the investments in IT. Efforts are based on return on investment rather than on personal preference.
C. Defining the controls on spending. Spending for capital investments and ongoing expenses is appropriately approved and monitored.
D. Managing and controlling projects. Projects are selected based on alignment with company strategies and monitored for the early detection of out of control budget and schedule.
E. Deploying IT staff. Staff is reassigned as needed to support evolving business needs.
F. Using service level agreements (SLAs) to define appropriate levels of service from IT. SLAs set expectations with service providers on what they are to deliver and for the receiver on what they should expect.
G. Managing the change control process. Changes to IT system are controlled events that occur after all parties are informed and approve.
H. Complying with regulatory requirements such as Sarbanes-Oxley. IT governance verifies that applicable laws are followed.

While there are several different IT governance models to choose from, they all attempt to bring order to the chaos of IT by some combination of the following activities:

A. Measurement of results
B. Justification of resources used
C. Accountability and transparency
D. Control of the work being performed
E. Coordination of work being done in different areas
F. Compliance with internal and external policies or regulations
G. Ensuring that IT meets the needs of the organization

IT governance sometimes forces companies to take those actions that they say they want to but that are often omitted by middle management. For example, business resiliency is required to ensure that vital business functions are always available, as their absence will cause financial hardships. This may involve parallel processing, multiple sites that can perform the same function, or IT resilience such as mirrored disk and automatic server failover. Tied to this is an ongoing documented and tested disaster recovery program.

IT governance becomes reality with the creation of the appropriate policies and procedures to ensure that the IT governance model used by your organization is being followed. With the right IT governance model and well thought out policies and procedures in place, you can properly control and manage IT to ensure that it brings the maximum value to the business.

[B]   Critical Policies to Develop Based on This Chapter

Using the material discussed in this chapter, you will be able to create the following policies:

A. IT governance model to be followed by the organization.
B. Developing a strategic plan.

Policies should always be developed based on the local situation. Successful managers cannot issue appropriate guidance if the policies are written with another company's situation or location in mind.

§ 1.02   IT GOVERNANCE MODELS

[A]   Overview of Governance Models

There are several different IT governance models that have been developed, some driven from a strategic viewpoint and others developed from tactical processes such as project management. Each has its strengths and weaknesses; the business and IT management must select the appropriate governance model based on the unique needs of the business. The following sections are a brief overview of the most widely used governance models.

§ 1.02[C]

Introducing a governance model into an organization takes a long time. Compliance can be mandated but cultural changes typically require several years to change personal habits. During this time, a strong executive sponsorship is required to emphasize and support the new approach.

[B]   COSO

COSO (the Committee of Sponsoring Organizations) was originally formed in 1985 to sponsor the National Commission on Fraudulent Financial Reporting, which was a private sector initiative to study the causes of fraudulent financial reporting by public companies. In 1992, COSO established a framework for the proper authorization, recording and reporting of transactions. The Securities and Exchange Commission (SEC) officially recognizes the COSO framework as adequate for establishing internal controls over financial reporting. COSO is the basis for COBIT's professional standards for internal controls and auditing.

COSO's financial origins are apparent in its approaches to governance. In COSO's framework, an internal control is a process. Internal controls only provide some assurance that something will occur, and not an absolute guarantee. Each internal control addresses a specific objective. Controls are implemented by people and people can make mistakes. Therefore, a COSO control only provides a level of assurance (not 100% certainty) to the company's board of directors that something has been correctly monitored.

COSO internal controls are measured in terms of:

A.   Control environment. Processes for developing controls and a control-conscious workforce. The control environment sets a company-wide tone of ethical business practices and personal integrity.

B.   Risk assessment. Identification and analysis of risks of fraud and inaccurate financial reporting. Managing a business is essentially the management of risk in all activities.

C.   Control activities. Policies and procedures for execution of management directives, such as management oversight, separation of duties, and audits by external organizations. Control activities occur throughout all levels of the organization.

D.   Information and communication. Effective operation and control of the business through the appropriate level of information sharing.

E.   Monitoring. Ongoing activities or separate evaluations. Includes the feedback loop of reporting discrepancies and then promptly addressing them.

[C]   COBIT

COBIT™ (Control Objectives for Information Technology™) is a framework of IT management best practices. It was originally released by the Information Systems Audit and Control Association (ISACA) in 1992 as an IT process and control framework for linking IT to business requirements. In 1998, "Management Guidelines" were added to COBIT providing management tools such as maturity models and metrics, making it more appropriate as a framework for IT governance. In 2012, COBIT 5 was created, which combined COBIT 4.1 with

Val IT 2.0 and Risk IT frameworks, and aligns with other frameworks and standards such as ITIL, PMBOK, TOGAF, PRINCE2, and ISO.

COBIT utilizes controls that provide management and audit functions for IT departments and business process owners. Every company is unique and faces unique marketplace challenges. COBIT identifies what should be done rather than how to do it. This enables each company to be compliant with the COBIT framework while applying their unique solutions. COBIT 5 consists of five principles and seven enablers. The five principles are:

A. Meeting stakeholder needs
B. Covering the enterprise end-to-end
C. Applying a single integrated framework
D. Enabling a holistic approach
E. Separating governance from management

The seven COBIT 5 enablers are:

A. Processes
B. Organizational structures
C. Culture, ethics, and behavior
D. Principles, policies, and frameworks
E. Information
F. Services infrastructure applications
G. People, skills, and competencies

Many companies use COBIT to fulfill Sarbanes-Oxley's 404 legal compliance requirements. It provides a proven solution to the current climate of corporate accountability and control. Rather than try to invent something new, they adopt portions of COBIT that fit their industry and situation. It also provides an entity-wide model of best practices to manage IT's contribution to the business. COBIT helps non-IT managers understand their IT systems and set the level of security and control necessary to protect their company's assets.

[D] ITIL

ITIL™ (Information Technology Infrastructure Library) is a collection of IT service management best practices developed by the government of the United Kingdom. It began as an effort to collect the best IT practices used by the most successful companies into one guideline for efficient IT operations. An important aspect of this framework was that it be independent of any particular vendor.

ITIL contains nothing new. It is a collection of the proper way to do such things as change control, service delivery, running a service desk, etc. Most companies already do these things (or know that they should do them, and still do not). What is new is how ITIL integrates these functions and clarifies the best way to conduct these processes. ITIL's power is the way its framework glues these various functions into one coherent strategy.

The current version, ITIL 2011, changed the emphasis from an operationally focused process to service management guidance. It also includes an emphasis on continual service improvement.

[E] CMMI

The Capability Maturity Model® Integration (CMMI) is a process improvement approach developed by the Software Engineering Institute at Carnegie Mellon University. It provides organizations with guidelines for developing effective processes at the project level, by a division, or by an entire organization. CMMI helps connect business and IT functions, provides guidance on setting process improvement goals and priorities, offers advice for improving the quality of processes, and provides a mechanism for evaluating current processes. CMMI consists of the following models:

A. CMMI for Development
B. CMMI for Acquisition
C. CMMI for Services

CMMI's main value is in providing guidance on integrating functions within the organization, setting process improvement goals and priorities, defining quality processes, and in providing a point of reference for appraising current processes. CMMI uses a maturity model to determine the current state of the organization's processes and as a roadmap to improvement. The five levels of the maturity model are:

A. Level 1—Initial. The process is ad hoc.
B. Level 2—Managed. The process is controlled at the project level.
C. Level 3—Defined. A set of standards is defined and followed at the organizational level.
D. Level 4—Quantitatively Managed. Results are measured and repeatable.
E. Level 5—Optimizing. Continuous improvements are being made to the process.

This idea of a maturity model can also be applied to the operation of the IT function as a whole. This can provide management with a measure of how well IT is meeting the needs of the business.

[F] PMBOK

PMBOK (Project Management Body of Knowledge) was developed by the Project Management Institute (PMI) as "the sum of knowledge within the profession of project management." PMBOK documents and describes the current best practices for managing projects. While not specific to IT projects, it is heavily used in IT as a guide for managing complex IT projects.

Companies have long struggled with completing projects on time and on budget. This struggle comes from a variety of causes but in most cases, it was from a lack of a methodical approach to project planning and execution. The

PMBOK represents the accumulated project knowledge of thousands of project managers accumulated over many years. The outcomes are not guaranteed as projects are estimated by people and managed by people. However, a thorough understanding of the PMBOK will result in significantly better results than managing the effort day to day.

PMBOK describes five basic process groups and ten knowledge areas that are typical for almost all projects. The basic concepts are applicable to projects, programs, and operations. The five basic process groups are:

A. Initiating
B. Planning
C. Executing
D. Controlling and Monitoring
E. Closing

The ten knowledge areas are:

A. Project Integration Management
B. Project Scope Management
C. Project Time Management
D. Project Cost Management
E. Project Quality Management
F. Project Human Resource Management
G. Project Communications Management
H. Project Risk Management
I. Project Procurement Management
J. Project Stakeholders Management

Following the best practices as outlined in the PMBOK can help ensure that projects will be completed effectively and efficiently. Most IT governance models require effective project managements and usually turn to the PMBOK as the standard.

[G] PRINCE2

PRINCE2 (Projects IN Controlled Environments) is a project management methodology that provides a structured method for project management. It was initially developed in 1989 by the Central Computer and Telecommunications Agency (CCTA) of the United Kingdom government as a standard for information systems project management. Most companies that have adopted ITIL have also adopted the PRINCE2 methodology.

PRINCE2 breaks projects down into the following four components:

A. Method. How will the project be organized and planned?
B. Procedures. Instructions on exactly what is to be done.
C. Techniques. The skills needed to get the work done.
D. Tools. Aids to completing the project.

PRINCE2 is a process-driven project management method that defines 45 separate sub-processes and organizes these into seven processes as follows:

A. Starting Up a Project
B. Initiating a Project
C. Directing a Project
D. Controlling a Stage
E. Managing Product Delivery
F. Managing Stage Boundaries
G. Closing a Project

The primary complaint about PRINCE2 is that it involves a considerable amount of overhead making it unsuitable for small projects. However, this same amount of mandatory planning (such as approvals at every project phase) provide structure for large projects and keep the many stakeholders engaged throughout the project's execution.

[H] TOGAF

TOGAF (The Open Group Architecture Framework) provides a detailed method and a set of supporting tools for developing an enterprise architecture. Developed by The Open Group in 1995, TOGAF is based on work done by the US Department of Defense. IT architecture is an integral part of every business function and must support the goals of the entire enterprise. An enterprise wide view enables companies to begin interconnecting their many fragments processes and policies toward more efficient operations.

TOGAF is a top down methodology. It starts with the enterprise wide view and then breaks it down into its components. Some companies then link the overall TOGAF architecture with existing processes. TOGAF is not a framework. It is a process for designing one.

TOGAF defines four separate architectures that must be considered for the benefit of the organization:

A. Business (or Business Process) Architecture. The business strategy, governance, organization, and key business processes.
B. Data Architecture. The structure of an organization's logical and physical data assets and data management resources.
C. Applications Architecture. Defines how the individual application systems are to be deployed, their interactions, and their relationships to the core business processes of the organization.
D. Technology Architecture. The software infrastructure intended to support the deployment of core, mission-critical applications. This type of software is sometimes referred to as "middleware."

TOGAF 9.1, the current version, builds on previous versions by adding more examples to illustrate solutions and templates for creating it. It also provides guidance for developing an information security architecture.

[I] TICKIT

TickIT is a software quality assessment system developed primarily by the software industry in the United Kingdom and Sweden. Its purpose is to improve the effectiveness of the quality management process used to create quality software. TickIT is designed to improve quality of software by improving the effectiveness of auditors working in IT through training and subsequent certification. Software development organizations seeking TickIT Certification are required to show conformity with ISO 9001:2000. It is compatible with the other ISO standards for IT.

A major objective of TickIT is to provide the software industry with a practical framework for the management of software development quality by developing more effective quality management system certification procedures. These include:

A. Publishing guidance material to assist software organizations in interpreting the requirements of ISO 9001.
B. Training, selecting, and registering auditors with IT experience and competence.
C. Establishing rules for the accreditation of certification bodies involved in the software sector.

Unlike the other IT governance methodologies previously described, TickIT is focused entirely on software quality and does not have a business performance improvement component. Such improvement will be an outgrowth of improved software quality. For this reason, TickIT is normally used in conjunction with one of the major governance schemes such as ITIL or CMMI.

The current version is known as TickITplus. This builds on the TickIT approach by including covering a wider range of organizational areas. TickITplus includes 40 processes and defines five levels of organizational maturity.

See Policy ITP-01-1 Establishment of IT Governance Model as an example.

POLICY ITP-01-1. Establishment of IT Governance Model

Policy #:	ITP-01-1	Effective:	01/19/13	Page #:	1 of N
Subject:	Establishment of IT Governance Model				

1.0 PURPOSE

This policy establishes the IT governance model that will be followed by the organization.

2.0 SCOPE

The policy applies to all users of information technology within the company.

3.0 POLICY

The CIO must establish and provide governance for information technology policies, procedures, and best practices for the company's technology infrastructure in order to secure all IT assets and promote the most efficient use of technology resources.

The CIO will submit a report to the Board of Directors at its first meeting of each calendar year, and submit interim reports at the request of the Board, on the current status of the company's technology policies and procedures.

All operating units within the company that use information technology (IT) are responsible for:

A. Adhering to the IT policies issued by the CIO.
B. Developing and implementing, when appropriate, additional IT policies and procedures specific to their operating units.
C. Promoting IT policy adherence.
D. Complying with the requirements of the IT governance model adopted by the organization.
E. Ensuring the security of the IT systems and the network to which they are connected.
F. Informing the CIO if there are any problems with a policy or if inputs from other sources do not comply with the defined policies.
G. Providing new employees with instruction and/or documented procedures that relate to their job descriptions.
H. Providing an annual "refresher" for current employees highlighting the changes made or problem areas during the previous year.
I. Maintaining the functionality of the IT systems within their area.
J. Facilitating training and the dissemination of information.
K. Preventing unauthorized access to company information, personal files, and e-mail.
L. Developing and maintaining a plan for recovery of mission critical data and systems if a loss is sustained.

The head of each business unit must designate an "Information Technology (IT) Coordinator" to ensure that these responsibilities are carried out and to serve as a contact person for that business unit with the CIO. This policy recognizes that different business units have different needs, IT resources, and levels of internal expertise. Hence, the needs and resources of a given business unit may not require the IT Coordinator to have an extensive technical background. Many business units also have "Technical Managers" who are responsible for the operation of the IT systems and with whom the IT Coordinator may share the responsibilities in this policy. Technical Managers are expected to have the technical expertise required to ensure the safe and reliable operation of their respective business unit's IT systems.

4.0 REVISION HISTORY

Date	Revision #	Description of Change
03/18/12	1.0	Initial creation.
01/19/13	1.1	Added support for IT governance model.

5.0 INQUIRIES

Direct inquiries about this policy to:

George Jenkins, CIO
Our Company, Inc.
2900 Corporate Drive
Columbus, OH 43215

Voice: 614-555-1234
Fax: 614-555-1235
E-mail: gjenkins@company.com

Revision #:	1.1	Supersedes:	1.0	Date:	01/19/13

§ 1.03   IT STRATEGIC PLANNING PROCESS

[A]   Overview

The IT strategic plan is the major vehicle for articulating the information systems needs of the business and the associated resource requirements. It reflects how the IT organization will support the company's long-term and short-term business strategies. The entire business must be involved in the creation of the IT plan, as it will shape the IT resources available for supporting their individual objectives. If left solely to the IT organization without business unit input, it will not provide maximum value to either part of the organization. The plan must reflect the evolving business drivers, the relationship of those drivers to the intended IT activities, and the resources required to support those activities.

The head of the firm's corporate computer and/or desktop computing operations takes responsibility for developing an effective IT plan for the organization. Division-level plans also must be created, showing how the corporate objectives will be carried out. The head of the firm's corporate computer and/or desktop computing operations reviews the division plans, ensuring these objectives are met, and provides support. Plans also will be reviewed to evaluate their technical feasibility and assess achievability of the planned benefits.

[B]   Policy and Procedures to Submit a Strategic Plan

Each division within your organization prepares an annual information technology strategic plan including strategies, goals, objectives, and performance measures. The division's plan must integrate with the overall business strategies, goals, and objectives. The plan also must consider the overall IT plan, developed at the corporate level if appropriate.

Submittal schedule. Department/division-level IT plans must be submitted at the beginning of each fiscal year to the head of the firm's corporate computer and/or PC operations. Each division reviews its plan's status quarterly and updates corporate every six months.

Submittal procedure. The plan must be submitted to the head of the firm's corporate computer and/or desktop computing operations in electronic format, PDF version, with one unbound paper copy.

The sections described below are required, with subsections or appendixes added, if necessary.

A. **Executive summary.** This 1- or 2-page summary provides a general understanding of the division's IT plan and a frame of reference for understanding the overall objectives of the plan. It also includes information on who developed the plan and how the plan was created.

B. **Division mission.** This section discusses the mission of the division and how it fits into the organization. Each major functional area of the division and its role in fulfilling the division's mission should be discussed.

C. **Goals and objectives.** This section describes the major goals and objectives of the division and how they will be achieved. *Goals* are the long-term results that the organization will achieve as it fulfills its mission. *Objectives* are the near-term results that are attained as the organization meets its goals. Measurements used for determining whether or not the goals and objectives are met should be included in this section.

D. **External factors.** This section discusses the division's business drivers. The division's business drivers are derived from the mission, goals, and objectives and define how the division operates. Identify the external forces such as the economy, technology changes, and political environment and so on that drive the business.

E. **Internal factors.** This section identifies the factors internal to the division that affect the division's IT activities. This may include organizational structure, personnel capabilities, management strength, facilities, training needs, and financial resources. Describe the organization's strengths and weaknesses and how they affect IT programs and management. Include an IT organizational chart and personnel factors such as recruitment, retention, and training.

F. **IT architecture.** This section discusses how the division's IT planning supports its business drivers. A diagram showing the division's current architecture, including internal and external linkages, should be included. If there are plans to significantly change the architecture during the current year, a diagram of the proposed changes should be included. This section also should describe how the division's architecture fits in with the overall corporate architecture.

G. **Technology initiatives.** The major technology initiatives of the division are described in this section. Examples might include e-commerce programs, ERP implementations, wireless initiatives, etc.

H. **Business resumption plans** and the division's project management methodology are included in this section.

I. **Project plans.** A high level project plan for each major new or maintenance project should be presented in this section. Minor projects may be grouped together into one or more general support projects. Each project plan should include the following information:

1. A brief statement of the project purpose.
2. A reference to the goal or objective from the section above that the project supports. This section should describe the scope of the project, the expected benefits, the implementation time frame, the resource requirements for the project, and the expected impact the project will have on the organizational goals. Also, describe the impact on the organization if the project is not undertaken.
3. Describe the success criteria for the project. What metrics (return on investment, service level, system performance, and so on) will be used to measure the success of the project?
4. Describe the technical approach employed on this project. Include hardware needs, software to be used (including operating system and development tools), and any telecommunications requirements.
5. List any additional concerns about the project, such as staffing and training needs, schedule, integration with other divisions, etc.
6. Document the estimated costs by fiscal year for staffing, hardware, telecommunications, etc., needed to complete the project.
7. Estimate any future maintenance costs for the life of the system once the project is completed.

J. **Project summary.** Document a summary of each project planned by the division in this section. This should list the project name, estimated costs, projected start and completion dates, and the estimated benefit in dollars.

2

BUSINESS PROCESS MANAGEMENT: DEFINING YOUR BUSINESS

§ 2.01 OVERVIEW

[A] Purpose and Scope

IT departments are either results-oriented or process-oriented. Results-oriented departments emphasize completing the job. Anything to get the task completed, "take care of the customer," and then move on. A process-oriented department focuses on establishing and applying processes to situations. Tasks are documented and best practices are applied to improve effectiveness and efficiency. This requires time to establish and maintain these processes.

Most IT departments fall into the results-oriented model as they tumble from crisis to crisis with periods of blissful quiet in between. As soon as one customer requirement is fulfilled, the overworked team jumps on the next one. This works well for small teams where everyone understands how to perform the basics of each other person's job.

However, as IT departments grow, the team begins specializing in various functions. Now few people understand all of the department functions. Where the IT Director could monitor processes, now there is a dependence on local supervisors. The larger the department, the less control is exercised. One question constantly arises; is the department operating efficiently, or are there individuals who appear to be very busy but accomplish little (or less than they could)?

Business Process Management (BPM) is a "big picture" view of how a company conducts business. It ensures that processes are in alignment with the company's current strategy. BPM focuses on processes that deliver products and services to customers. These value streams are linked back to the company's strategic objectives. Each process has metrics that indicate their effectiveness and efficiency.

As basic as this concept is, few IT executives will claim that their department's processes are as effective or efficient as they could be. This is due to several factors. First, processes represent a solution to a problem at a point in time. The business environment constantly evolves but processes change slowly. Second, changing a process introduces uncertainty into the work environment. A fix for one problem may create another issue elsewhere.

In most companies, each work team develops their own series of steps for completing a task. These steps may not be the most effective or efficient way to accomplish something. Some people using a process either ignore the approved steps or make unauthorized changes to it. Processes may contain additional steps "just because that is how we have always done it." The result is a process at odds with the company's internally published statements of direction and policies.

BPM is not a one-time action. It is more of a journey of continuous improvement. The business environment that every company exists within is constantly changing. New products, new competitors, and new laws constantly influence the company in many ways. As company executives react to these changes, BPM helps the organization to identify processes that must be changed to meet the new direction.

Management processes is an integral part of managing a business. It:

- specifies goals
- communicates targets
- approves task steps
- monitors performance
- motivates staff

[B] How BPM Works

A process is a localized view of how to perform a task. It provides workers with a list of actions, materials, and equipment to complete a specific organizational goal. BPM is the "Big Picture" view of the company's critical processes. It ensures that all of the company's processes remain focused on achieving the company's strategies.

Managing processes on the entire company level enables the identification of the company's "best practices." Those found in one team can be applied across the organization. This spreads hard-learned lessons across the organization and helps to break down internal business "silos" that inhibit this effort. BPM also smooths the interface points between processes.

Important business events occur in their own time. Often, the speed with which a company responds to an event can make the difference between capitalizing on an opportunity and minimizing risk exposure. A detailed knowledge of company processes enables agility in meeting customer requirements to continue satisfying customers as their requirements shift.

[C] Why BPM Is Important to IT

In most companies, IT departments consume a significant share of the company's operating budget. Even with this budget, it rarely satisfies the never-ending requests for additional services. In the ongoing competition for funds between IT and the other company departments, it is essential that the IT department is run efficiently.

IT Managers are a cross between business leader and technical specialist. The focus is so intensely on the processing of data, often with inadequate resources, that process management is an afterthought. Yet this is a significant cost savings opportunity. If processes can be made more efficient, then they require less labor that frees time to work on other things.

Consider how many people in the IT department are necessary to support its many administrative processes. Asset management, service utilization chargeback, budget monitoring, access control, telephone bill review—the list goes on and on. Would it be possible to tighten these processes, rebalance the workload, and free a single person to address urgent technical issues?

BPM is a technique for an IT Director to synchronize the day-to-day processes within an IT organization. This includes both the processes necessary to maintain the internal requirements of the IT department as well as to provide services to the rest of the company.

[D]   Critical Policies to Develop Based on This Chapter

Using the material discussed in this chapter, you will be able to create the process documentation policies. Policies should always be developed based on the local situation. Successful managers cannot issue appropriate guidance if the policies are written with another company's situation or location in mind.

COMMENT

If there is a technique worth knowing, there must be a certification for it! All IT governance models require formal process management. Process management certification is a fragmented marketplace. There are numerous organizations and training companies that offer BPM certificates and the latest techniques.

§ 2.02   BUILDING YOUR BPM PROGRAM

[A]   Overview

Companies have long sought ways to improve their processes. From an executive's view, the easiest way to reduce costs without sacrificing customer service is by improving a process' performance. The trick is to accomplish this without upsetting the internal organizational equilibrium.

If you have ever been assigned to develop an IT process, you may have felt rushed to action, plagued with incomplete specifications, and that your manager really did not care how you completed your job—just finish it! The result is what you thought was needed at the time, combined with some vital additional information provided at the last minute. Once the process is written and approved, there is no incentive for anyone to change it.

This is more or less the way that IT administrative processes are created. Once a process is in place, people accept it as "the way it is" and are reluctant to change it. Add in a few team members who habitually file every document they touch or document every conversation, and the "extra" steps in the process build more time. A one-hour-per-day task turns into a full-time job. Other people will prefer to do one particular process instead of others and will extend it until it fills their entire day. So, when an IT Director is denied expanding their staff, often the answer is to better utilize what is available.

An organization's process management program evolves through several stages of maturity. In any given company, different departments will be in different stages of process management maturity. The payoff of a mature process management is greater efficiencies, fewer defects, increased consistency of product or service delivery, and greater customer satisfaction. The stages are:

A. **Initial.** Processes are performed in an ad hoc fashion. There is little documentation. Costs and quality vary significantly based on when and by whom the process is executed.

B. **Repeatable.** Management has implemented basic process metrics and begins tracking internal defects from inspection and customer complaints. Basic quality measurements are in place. The quality of incoming material is inspected.

C. **Defined.** Processes are clearly defined and relevant to specific company strategies. All processes are documented and managed to the company standard. Employees are trained and supplier quality is monitored.

D. **Quantitatively Managed.** Continuous improvement through statistical analysis of inputs, outputs, and process performance. Best practices are shared across the company. Fresh ideas are sought from competitors by benchmarking against "best in class" companies.

[B] Align IT Processes to the Company's Strategies

Processes are tools for implementing a company's strategy. Strategies are an executive's way of establishing priorities for employee actions. The company strategy that a process supports in some significant way should be identified or they are a candidate for deletion. If the company strategies seem vague, then the IT Director can create their own.

Typical company goals include:

- Always take care of the customer
- Reduce costs with no reduction in customer service
- Maintain current software and technology levels

The IT department may stand around waiting for executives or the IT Director to identify strategies to fulfill each of these goals. Each strategy should be supported by IT department processes; for example, closely managing IT equipment through the asset management process to reduce the number of items under maintenance.

Each process that supports a strategy should be reviewed and optimized. All others should be reviewed for potential elimination. It is possible that a process (or process step) existed only to support an IT strategy that is no longer in play.

Every company implements BPM in their own way because every business environment is unique. Implementation can be broken down into the following key steps:

A. **Identify the critical few processes.** A company has many processes from debt collection to processing payroll checks to issuing the company newsletter. Perhaps 20 percent of these are critical to the company's operation. The rest are useful but their absence would not threaten the company's survival. A significant improvement to a critical process will have a visible impact on company operations. Performing a business impact analysis can identify these processes.

B. **Validate customer requirements.** The business environment is ever changing. It is possible that the customer's requirements have shifted but the process remains the same as before. (This is common when a significant customer has dropped your company.) Periodically validating requirements realigns processes with their reason for being. Detail all assumptions and customer requirements to explain the context in which the process was created or last modified.

Customer requirements can be found in documents such as a statement of work, purchase order details, or you can even ask them. A source of unfulfilled customer needs should be in your file of customer complaints and product returns. These requirements may be undocumented but still exist in the customer's mind. Processes start and end with people.

Whenever tinkering with a process, beware of the people side of the issue. People interact with processes in many ways. Someone initiates the process, they receive the benefit, they approve specific action, or they participate in completing the process. Each of these people has their own expectations as to what the process must deliver, what this final product should look like, and how quickly it should be completed.

Even if the people working on the process find it annoying, it is still a known process and preferable to a change that might increase their irritation. What incentive does the worker have to perform the process to simplify or to shorten the task since it introduces uncertainty into their workday? In most cases, these changes must be initiated by someone outside of the team.

C. **Model the process.** Imagine how a new process will work. Implementing a new process is a gamble. Purchasing machinery, training people, and running electrical connections is time consuming and expensive. Processes are created based on the experience of the people creating it. Often, the team has little or no experience with the new procedure. Modeling is a method for reducing the risk of implementing a poorly designed process. It illustrates how a process will function by varying the combinations of inputs.

To create a model, list the various inputs expected to be applied, and inputs that should not be applied but may be. Step through the process to see how it would react, varying everything that is not constant. Using software provides even greater insight to throughput based on varying different inputs.

D. **Process costing.** Each process has direct and hidden costs to operate. The direct cost for labor, materials, and machinery can be easily collected. Understanding the cost of a process is essential when seeking out new business. It is not unusual for a company to unwittingly underbid a job and then scramble to fulfill it while drastically cutting costs.

The hidden costs include delays built into the larger processes due to processing work in batches, an excessive number of approvals, and bottlenecks at shared machines. Costing a process provides valuable information when considering optimization. A process cost may provide excellent results but requires expensive material to do so. Inexpensive materials may still provide adequate results for a greatly reduced price.

E. **Develop process measures.** Metrics measure a process' performance and identify areas of improvement. This data illustrates the cost and complexity of operating a process. Review the critical deliverables for the process and develop measurements to determine effectiveness and efficiency:

1. Stability (consistent performance)
2. Effectiveness (meets customer needs)
3. Efficiency (minimal resource use)

Process metrics enable managing processes at the lowest practical level in the organization. Metrics provide a continuous feedback loop to the process operator. On a basic level, metrics can measure if something works or not. However, the real power of metrics is the "how much" of the measurement. This identifies factors that are drifting toward the limits of acceptable performance.

COMMENT

Reducing the cycle time to complete a task improves customer satisfaction. Everyone wants it cheap, fast, and right.

[C] Commit Processes to Paper

Often when a supervisor wants to know something specific about a task that is completed, they seek out the person who executes the process and asks them. This provides the latest information, but is this process operating in the way that it was approved by management? Is it effective or efficient? An important management step is to convert from a verbal process description to written directions.

Process documentation anchors work steps to a point in time. Once it is on paper it cannot be altered without management approval. Approved changes are added to the existing documentation and the people executing the process become responsible for the change's implementation.

Written documentation is a valid training tool. As new people are assigned to work on a process, it tells them what to do. It also saves the IT Manager from problems when the usual worker is absent due to illness or vacation.

[D]   Cross-Functional Approval

Processes are usually linked to one another. Optimizing one process may disrupt those that feed into it or that use its output. Before a process change is finalized, it must be approved by the various departments of the organization. This reduces the chance of overlooking an important linkage.

For example, imagine a change to a warehouse pick and ship order fulfillment process. This must be approved by various departments:

- Accounting to ensure they can capture any billing information
- Human Resources to ensure that it does not violate any company labor policies
- Warehouse manager to ensure that it can meet its cycle times
- Traffic manager to ensure it will be completed in time to make the delivery trucks
- IT Manager to approve expected system changes

COMMENT

IT Managers are in a quandary. They lack time to attend all of the meetings held within the company, and if they do not attend, they are tasked to support a process change that may be technically inadvisable.

§ 2.03   PROCESS ANALYSIS TOOLS

[A]   Overview

Serious practitioners of BPM will insist that the only way to properly manage an organization's processes is to use simulation software to model the behavior of processes based on changing inputs. Simulations can be time consuming to set up and are based on assumptions known at that time. However, they can be a useful tool for fine tuning processes in the design phase. The negative side is the expense to purchase simulation software and the time to learn how to use it.

Companies embark on BPM to save money. Obtaining approval for an expensive software package can be difficult. Instead, consider using the following basic tools to examine processes for the easier to find problems.

[B]   SIPOC

This tool is a way to break down a process into its significant components. Often when examining a process, people focus on the main elements of it and overlook the subtle aspects that may be the primary drivers for the process. A SIPOC identifies the many inputs that alter a process' outputs.

SIPOC means:

- **Suppliers.** Organizations that provide information or materials to the process. For an IT department, this could be the supplier of the database management system software, the network hardware, an outsourced service provider, or anything else that provides a process input.
- **Inputs.** Materials, tools, and things provided by the supplier for use by the process.
- **Processes.** The steps taken to transform the inputs into the outputs.
- **Outputs.** Key deliverables, reports, products, and services that result from this process.
- **Customers.** Who or what receives the outputs from this process.

Consider the many inputs that feed a process. Varying an input or a particular combination of inputs can change the output of a process. Typical inputs include labor, equipment, materials, work instructions, training, or even the management attention. If a slow server was used instead of a fast server, then processing could take longer. If cheap toner was used in a high-speed laser printer, the result may be streaked or difficult to read reports. Outputs include both the desired and undesired results of a process. Undesired outputs may include rework, defects, cycle time, and equipment utilization.

Exhibit 2-1 is a SIPOC of someone contacting the IT Help Desk to request a user ID. Typically, the person must fill out a form so that there is a pen and ink signature on the company's accessible use policy. Therefore, this process begins when the person fills out the form and ends when the requestor has the new user ID in hand.

EXHIBIT 2-1. SIPOC

Suppliers	Inputs	Processes	Outputs	Customers
Linux Support Company	SysAdmin permissions	Submits a pre-printed user ID request	User ID	All departments
Talltree Paper and Toner company	Pre-printed user ID request	Help Desk logs request	Temporary password	
	Spreadsheet software	Help Desk validates request	Log of ID requests	
		Help Desk creates user ID with one-time password		
		Help Desk passes user ID and password to requestor		

§ 2.03[C]

[C]   Flowcharts and Swim Lanes

It is true that a picture is worth a thousand words. Process documentation can result in a dry text where the poorly selected words result in ambiguous meanings. Using a flowchart to illustrate the flow of a work product through the process presents data in an easily understood format. The advantage of the flowchart approach is simplicity (see Exhibit 2-2). It is a tradeoff between providing a high-level display without attempting to detail every step. The work product flows from top to bottom. Each block identifies a sub process of multiple discrete steps.

EXHIBIT 2-2.   Sample Flowchart

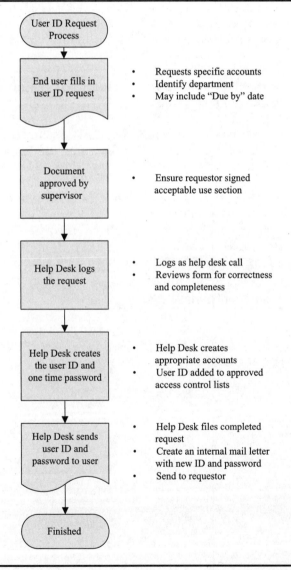

IT systems have long used flowcharts to explain the flow of data through its logical processes. It is not such a big step to apply the same visual explanation to manual processes instead of automated ones. However, to keep the process on a single page, flow charts tend to be high level with notes adjacent to specific process steps to explain key action to be accomplished.

Establish basic rules for creating flowcharts:

A. Each process has an action that initiates action and one that signals the end of the process.
B. Create processes with a small group and validate in a large group.
C. Arrows indicate the flow of work product. Ideally, they flow to the right and down.
D. If practical, make all of the decision flows (YES or NO) move in the same direction, such as always right or down.
E. Use the X-axis (horizontal) to indicate time.

In this example, someone is requesting a user ID from the Help Desk. The requestor fills out the request form that includes a signature agreeing to the company's acceptable use policy. Since the document contains a signature, it must be handled manually.

Once the request arrives at the supervisor's desk, it sits until Friday since the supervisor only reviews documents for signature on Fridays. Once it is approved, it is forwarded via interoffice mail to the IT Help Desk.

At the Help Desk, it is reviewed for completeness and correctness, and then logged into the Help Desk ticket service request tracking system. The Help Desk technician establishes a user profile (usually copied from someone with a similar position in the same department), establishes the user ID, and sets a one-time password. All of this is recorded into a new user ID notification document which is addressed to the user and sent via interoffice mail in a sealed envelope.

EXHIBIT 2-3.   Example of Swim Lanes in a Flowchart

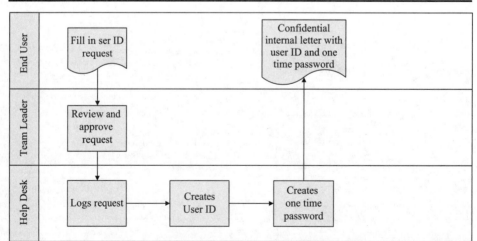

"Swim lanes" remind you of the lines painted along the bottom of a swimming pool. Each swimmer stays within their lane for an entire race (see Exhibit 2-3). In a flowchart, each swim lane represents a functional area or the person who will be doing the work. This might be a single person or a group. This eliminates some of the clutter in a flowchart by removing the need to identify in the flowchart who is doing what. A person working in the process can focus on their own role in the activity by concentrating on the actions located in their "swim lane."

[D]   RACI Charts Clarify Responsibility

A RACI chart details the relationship between stakeholders and actions in a process. It illustrates the dimension of who is responsible for doing what in a single document (see Exhibit 2-4). When analyzing a process, this can clarify who on the team contributes what for process success. RACI charts can also be useful for illustrating to new people their role in the context of the process.

EXHIBIT 2-4.   Sample RACI Chart

Help Desk User ID request	End User	End-User Supervisor	Help Desk Technician	Help Desk Supervisor
Fill in ID request	R	A		
Supervisor approval	I	R		
Log request	I		R	C
Create ID/password			R	C
Send to user		I	R	A

legend

R   Responsible
A   Accountable
C   Consulted
I   Information

The acronym RACI means:

- **Responsible.** Typically the person who must perform this action.
- **Accountable.** The manager that ensures the task is completed accurately and on time. There can only be one of these per task.
- **Consulted.** The person or persons who must be asked for advice or information prior to beginning the process.
- **Informational.** People who do not control the task but want to know about its performance and quality of execution.

A RACI chart is built by listing the steps in the process down the left-most column. Use an action term to describe each task, such as perform, records, operate, decide, etc. Avoid generic activities like status meetings. Across the top of the chart's horizontal axis, list the people involved. Often this is a position title rather than a name.

Another advantage of a RACI chart is to clarify the roles of each person involved in a process. This helps to minimize "turf battles" by clarifying who is responsible for what. This improves performance since everyone can readily see what everyone else is expected to complete.

A RACI can raise other issues. Once everyone sees who is executing which process actions, the question may arise if that person is qualified to do so. Sometimes it is not obvious where in a process the delays and problems occur. A RACI chart quickly shows if there are a high number of approvals. Often these approvals (A) can be changed to informed (I).

COMMENT

Simple processes are always the most stable and error-free. At every process step, ask everyone if it can be eliminated.

[E] Process Mapping

A process map is a visual representation of the flow of a process (see Exhibit 2-5). At a high level it illustrates the process steps and the way that specific actions align. It can be quite complex or it can stick to the basics. Process maps can be assembled for each department at a very high level and then worked down to the individual processes. The high-level map highlights boundaries where handoffs occur as these interfaces are often a source of friction between teams.

Once the individual processes are drawn, add in the cycle time required to complete each one. This type of flow is useful when looking for ways to reduce the process' cycle time. People execute a process to resolve something or to solve a problem. The quicker that it executes, the quicker that they can proceed with their normal work. Each idle time is an opportunity to eliminate the delay

EXHIBIT 2-5. Process Map

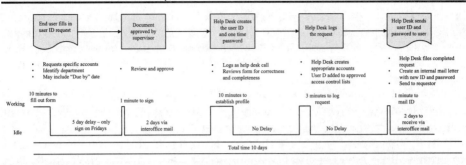

and reduce the processes overall cycle time. Each step where the work product is touched is another opportunity to eliminate or consolidate a step.

Next, identify pain points—those places where problems occur. Often these are the causes of customer complaints. Make these data collection points for process metrics and for problem resolution.

§ 2.04 SIMPLIFYING A PROCESS

[A] Overview

Processes are often put in place in a rush. As the company gains experience with it, the participants may make informal changes to the workflow. Over time, short-term urgent requirements become ingrained in the steps of the process even though they are no longer needed. On and on the business environment changes but the process does not. Participants do things merely because "that is our process."

A process is a snapshot in time. The best opportunity to implement efficiencies is during process development. Unfortunately, in the very beginning, you know the least about how the process will function in practice. Once in place, it becomes difficult to change as that is how people are used to it.

Some companies try to keep their processes weeded out by reviewing them from top to bottom at least every three years. However, managers do not willingly jump into this. Every action in a process exists because at some point, there was a reason to do this. Every action taken in a process is another opportunity for the process to fail. Few people have the time to fully research why something is done. This is why processes are left alone. IT Directors fear a short-term improvement will later be shown to cause long-term problems.

No process is ever perfect. After a process has run for some time, call the people involved together and simply ask them what they would like to see changed. Often, this will reveal simple changes to approve or further research. The people who are closest to it often have ways to reduce cycle time and cost. They also have an interest in simplifying the effort. The key is to tap into this support.

[B]   Opportunities for Failure

Processes consist of a series of actions. Each action alters the work product in some way (which may be a physical object, a logical object, or a service). It might add a piece of information, it might be an approval, or even connect it to a piece of code. Each of these actions is an opportunity to complete the task correctly, or to make an error.

The goal in optimizing a process is to reduce the likelihood of an error occurring. We all want to work with processes that deliver the same correct solution every time. The biggest improvement to a process is to eliminate steps within it. This reduces the cycle time for a given task and also the chance that an error will be made. This is why simple processes always have the fewest errors.

When optimizing a process, ask the people who work in or with a process:

- What steps in the process do you skip or work around?
- In which steps of the process do you spend most of your time, and why?
- What step in the process creates repeat work? How often does this occur and why do you think it happens?

Count the opportunities to make an error. Everything that a process does or could do is an opportunity to do something correctly or incorrectly. These are opportunities for failure. The fewer opportunities there are to fail, the fewer defects will result from a process.

[C]   Investigate Mistake Proofing

Repeatable processes provide predictable results. However, many processes are not reliably repeatable. They depend on people to take the correct action and to always make the right choice. To avoid errors is far from foolproof or reliable. A mistake proofed item includes simple steps to ensure that everything is in place.

For example, a software edit is a mistake proof step. Ensuring all critical fields are on a data entry field is a start. Ensuring that only valid entries have been made in each field is another level of checking, while an even deeper level of checking is to ensure that the valid entries all make sense in context to each other. (This last step is expensive to develop and maintain.)

[D]   Ensure Clean Process Interfaces

Every process has a point where it starts and ends. Often the results of one process are handed to the next. These hand-off points (process interfaces) become sources of delays and quality defects. Clean handoffs are not automatic. Some processes run infrequently. Also, if the regular workers are not available at either side of the interface then progress on the work product may stop.

Often people are the significant obstacle at process interfaces. Different work priorities and misunderstandings between the people involved can lead to delayed processes. The exchange of work product (document, Help

Desk call, outage resolution, etc.) must be explained in both the process producing the product and the process using it as input for further processing.

There are times when linked processes seem to work against each other. Observers will wonder if these people even work for the same company! This is understandable given that different people optimize their work environment to meet their personal goals and work style. A person who does as little as possible in one process might hand work product over to someone who runs a "tight ship." Whenever people are involved, there will always be a measure of personal friction. If the personalities are very different, then the sparks fly.

[E] Is Modeling Software the Answer?

BPM purists will tell you that modeling software is an essential tool for controlling processes. This software is powerful but expensive to purchase and time consuming to learn. However, if the time and financial resources are available, then modeling can be used not only to predict the performance of processes in the design phase but to also uncover process input variations (or combination of inputs) that hurt process performance.

BPM applications illustrate business processes end to end so that process managers can reduce costs, improve productivity, and bring efficiency to their business. A successful implementation of BPM systems requires clear understanding of an organization's business processes and business rules. Typically, the process flow is entered. Next, each decision point is estimated for how often each branch is taken. There may also be entries for the percent of time that specific inputs occur or has errors. Finally, any other business rules governing the process flow are included. Now the team can vary inputs and business rules to see what the result will be.

The biggest negative for modeling software is the danger that executives believe the expensive software is the silver bullet itself. Once purchased and installed, the company's processes are as good as optimized and management is off to solve other problems. A piece of software without the supporting methodology and executive support is just an expensive tool. Modeling results depend on the quality of the data analyzed and how the model is configured. Defects in either will provide incorrect results.

COMMENT

Business process modeling software vendors can be found by searching the Internet. Some of these packages are offered as Open Source or free use (read the license carefully).

See Policy ITP-02-1 IT Process Management Procedures as an example.

POLICY ITP-02-1. IT Process Management Procedures

Policy #:	ITP-02-1	Effective:	04/01/13	Page #:	1 of N
Subject:	IT Process Management Procedures				

1.0 PURPOSE

This policy defines the process documentation and maintenance of IT processes.

2.0 SCOPE

The policy applies to all processes within the IT department to include applications development and management, system administration, IT administrative processes, Data Operations, networks, outsourced labor or services, and all other areas under the IT Director's direction. This does not apply to IT processes that are one time or only needed for a short duration.

3.0 POLICY

A written explanation is required for all IT processes except for one-time or short duration activities. The following guidelines will be followed for managing IT processes:

A. Process Creation
The person with the greatest expertise in the process area will be assigned to lead the process development team. This team must include representatives from each department that feeds into the process or that receives its work products. Each team will, at a minimum, invite representatives from the following departments:

- Accounting
- Human Resources
- Information Security
- Business Continuity
- Information Technology team that supports that area

The process will be documented in the standard Quality Management format. The draft process will be reviewed in a meeting with all department representatives present. After one week, another meeting will be held to address any concerns. If all concerns have been addressed, then the process will be approved.

Once the process is approved, training will be scheduled for everyone involved with the process. A process review will be conducted with teams that feed into the process or who receive its work product.

§ 2.04[E]

There are times when a process must be implemented prior to the creation of a proper process design. In this case, the approved process documentation process must be completed within 30 days after the process has begun.

B. Process Documentation

The process documentation is a step-by-step narrative explaining how to complete the task. If practical, photographs and screen images are used to illustrate specific points. All text is easy to understand with a minimum of technical or internal company jargon. The processes include:

1. The company's standard desktop products must be used to create the documentation. Other products are not permitted.
2. The footer on every page indicates that the document is "Company Confidential."
3. A flowchart of the process steps must accompany the narrative. This can be a flow chart, a Swim Lanes chart, or a process map.
4. A RACI chart is required for all processes. The process owner must verify this chart and ensure that each person understands his or her role in the process execution.

Every process will include measures of its effectiveness and efficiency. These metrics will be posted where they will be visible to process team members and reported at least monthly to the next higher level supervisor/ manager. These measures must be retained by the team leader for at least the previous 12 months.

C. Process Maintenance and Sunset

All new processes are reviewed after 90 days with the people who use it or are affected by it. This review is intended to identify obvious problems and opportunities for improvement.

Once every year, the designated process owner must review every process. This is to ensure that the documented process accurately reflects the current process steps. The process owner verifies this review by signing the process revision tables at the beginning of each process.

Every three years, the process is completely redesigned. The analysis verifies the current customer requirements, the current process capability to meet these requirements, and asks team members for their ideas on improving it. Also considered are best practices as learned across the company.

D. Process Library

Approved process documentation is maintained in the process documentation library in their electronic form. Once every month the process librarian will review processes to identify those that are due for an annual review. These processes will be sent to the manager in charge of that area.

The process librarian ensures that only approved processes and changes are maintained in the library and also that the process documentation are available to the appropriate people. The process library is a restricted area since some processes detail the handling of confidential data.

4.0 REVISION HISTORY

Date	Revision #	Description of Change
04/01/13	1.0	Initial creation.

5.0 INQUIRIES

Direct inquiries about this policy to:

George Jenkins, CIO
Our Company, Inc.
2900 Corporate Drive
Columbus, OH 43215

Voice: 614-555-1234
Fax: 614-555-1235
E-mail: gjenkins@company.com

Revision #:	1.0	Supersedes:	N/A	Date:	04/01/13

3

IT GOVERNANCE METRICS: MEASURING YOUR SUCCESS

§ 3.01 OVERVIEW

[A] Purpose and Scope

Ask an IT team leader how his or her team is performing today and they will likely reply, "Alright." What they mean is that at that moment no one is calling to complain. This is a classic application of the GO/NO-GO metric. There are only two states. "Alright" means no complaints and "bad day" means there are urgent issues to resolve. If the IT team's objective was to just tread water, then this may be a satisfactory response. However, no IT department can stay static and still remain relevant to its company amidst a dynamic swirl of legal changes, customer preference shifts, introduction of new technologies, etc. The business environment is in constant change and which requires the same of IT processes.

Using a simple GO/NO-GO approach ignores the department's key performance indicators. It may be that the group is drifting toward a performance crisis and the team leader does not know. What if a key team member leaves the department? How can you detect the degree of change in the group's performance and its adjustment to the absence?

IT Governance promotes the use of pro-active management. During lulls between crises, there is an opportunity to proactively address performance issues that are trending in the wrong direction even if they are still in acceptable bounds. Metrics are the essential indicators for these improvement opportunities. Metrics are used to:

A. Understand something about a process input
B. Monitor the performance of the process efficiency
C. Control a process output for prompt action
D. Predict an impending failure through trend analysis

An old management rule is that you cannot manage what you cannot measure. This means that effective governance requires that the most important characteristics of the most important business processes are monitored to see how much of something they are doing. Given that the business environment is subject to many pressures from trade issues, customer preferences, time of year, legal challenges, etc., it is important to watch for adverse trends in critical areas. Gathering and analyzing metrics identifies trends before they become serious problems.

The basic business metrics are income and expenses. These two simple measurements indicate if the company is gaining profit or losing money. In the long term, they indicate if the company will remain in business. Of course, both the income and expenses are made up of many things and any one of these can make many good inputs look bad a high level.

Of the many things that could be measured, we try to identify the critical few that seem to make the biggest difference. These are known as "key" indicators. Key indicators are values that drive higher values.

Metrics can mislead as easily as they inform. Metric collected on an insignificant action can be used for a decision to take incorrect action. Also, metrics that are incorrectly collected will likewise indicate a situation that is not true. Careful validation of data and its collection method must be done prior to taking action.

Some companies use metrics solely as a part of their quality program. This is understandable yet it tends to confine them to the quality department. Every person in the organization should be a part of its continuous improvement program. Metrics are valuable tools for that. In a quality program, metrics normally relate to a physical item. However, in IT governance, metrics are typically applied to processes.

Measuring the same thing over and over again leads to "metric fatigue" where the numbers are collected but no one cares about them after that. To combat this apathy, periodically change some of your metrics to monitor other areas of your operation. A good time to change is when the process under measurement seems to be running predictably with a steady acceptable level of effectiveness and efficiency.

COMMENT

Metric analysis generally involves the application of statistical techniques. Some people love statistics and other run away as quickly as possible. This chapter discusses a few simple ways to analyze data. Some companies employ Six Sigma training which can wring the greatest amount of information out of your metric data.

[B] Compare to Stakeholder Expectations

Key performance indicators (KPI) are the vital signs of an IT team. Just as a doctor assesses a patient's overall health by checking the patient's vital signs (heart rate, pulse, temperature, blood pressure, etc.), the IT department's KPIs indicate the health of its performance.

In IT governance, metrics typically describe the performance of an important process. Just because the process still seems to work does not mean it is running well or not needing improvement. These process metrics are commonly referred to as KPIs. The process can be manual or automated. The metric may describe one aspect of the process or the end-to-end performance.

IT department KPIs should be aligned with stakeholder expectations. Sources of KPIs are:

A. Customers are interested in the value they derive from a product or service. In this case, the metrics should monitor the primary service satisfiers to keep them high and the problem areas to keep their occurrence low.

   B. KPIs are found in service level agreements (SLAs) to demonstrate that IT is fulfilling its service commitments.

   C. KPIs can be found in the Business Impact Analysis (BIA) rating of business processes.

   D. KPIs can be identified by the IT department strategies to monitor primary processes to identify opportunities for improvements to reduce the occurrence of problems.

Service level agreements detail expectations by IT customer and the IT department. Over times, both groups depend on these agreements to provide a normal part of their business. Each SLA must include metrics of the key support elements. Monitoring these metrics ensures that the appropriate level of support is being provided. During the annual SLA review, these statistics may indicate places to increase support or reduce it based on changing business needs.

COMMENT

Collecting, analyzing, and trending metrics is not free. It takes someone's time to collect, record, analyze, and communicate what has been found. Multiply this across a large number of potential data collection points and it is easy to see how this could become an expensive program. Another cost is a loss in employee confidence in the company leaders. Papering the walls with metrics collected and then taking no action on the trends means they are only superficial efforts.

[C] Importance to IT Governance

Metrics help managers to understand how well something is working. The easiest metric is if something is broken or is not broken. This information is useful but there is so much more that it could be. Could the process failure be detected before it occurred? For example, is there a trained replacement to step in to support a critical system?

The collection and analysis of process metrics moves the IT department from an "I feel things are this way" to data driven decisions. A strong business case backed up by data makes it easier to obtain approval for process changes, or to build the leader's confidence for making decisions.

Metrics help individual IT team members to participate in the department's continuous improvement program. Metric monitoring engages the IT staff to improve their daily work processes. Instead of helplessly struggling through a bad process, they can use metric data to demonstrate problem areas and make changes. Metrics also provide a way to uncover undesirable trends in system performance before they become a serious problem.

[D] Critical Policies to Develop Based on This Chapter

Using the material discussed in this chapter, you will be able to create the following policies:

A. Identify key process indicators for metric monitoring.
B. Annually review and eliminate metric collection where no longer needed.
C. Ensure that SLA performance metrics are monitored to demonstrate IT's fulfillment of the agreed service level.
D. Every vital business function (as defined by the Business Continuity Plan's business Impact Analysis) must be measured to ensure compliance.
E. All metrics collection is to be approved by IT management.

Policies should always be developed based on the local situation. Successful managers cannot issue appropriate guidance using policies written with another company's situation or location in mind.

§ 3.02   BASICS OF IT GOVERNANCE METRICS

[A] Overview

On a typical workday, do you walk into the office hoping that no one will call to complain, request service, or to request status of an open request? If no one calls, is it considered to be a good day? If many calls arrive, is it a bad day at the office? This is reactive management and at times, it can seem that the entire team is buried under requests from others. The proper IT governance approach is to begin measuring the critical few department performance metrics to identify the root cause of problems and resolve them. Over time, these improved processes may save manpower as well as improve service quality.

IT departments are full of processes. There are processes to request a user ID, to purchase hardware, to request a project, etc. The list seems endless. Each of these processes consumes staff time and hopefully provides some benefit. A continuous improvement program, such as Total Quality Management (TQM) requires that processes are constantly monitored for opportunities to improve them.

The first step in process governance is to document all processes and then approve the resources for continuing them. Once there is a firm idea of what the department's processes are (and the list may be quite long), the more important question may be:

A. Is each process still relevant?
B. Are your processes running effectively providing a high quality result?

C. Are your processes running efficiently with a minimal waste of resources?

Monitoring metrics are like checking the vital sign indicators for your body (temperature, blood pressure, pulse, etc.). They provide an initial indication that something may need attention. They provide the same benefit to IT department processes. If a metric indicates that something is operating outside of its target values, then attention is needed. Do you have an approved metric for the cycle time to complete something such as a new ID request, to build a project ROM estimate, to replace a PC to repair a PC, etc.?

COMMENT

For most companies, the quality program is centrally managed and applied to objects. The continuous improvement of processes is managed at the team level as a component of their Total Quality Management (TQM) program. Always engage the team member closest to the process being measured to collect the data.

A metric is a measurement that describes some characteristic of something. Metrics help you to understand a characteristic about something. To describe a structure, you could say it is an apartment building. The same object could be described as having three floors and it is 1,200 yards long. Each of these metrics helps to build a more accurate image in the mind of the listener. The more metrics that you can collect on an object, the clearer the picture of it in your mind.

Metrics are descriptive. They help you to understand how much of something is being used or how effectively that a process delivers something. An example of this might be the number of calls into the service desk. The count of calls may be used to determine staffing levels. If this same information was matched to the time of day and day of week that calls are received, then staffing can be precisely assigned. In the first instance, there would not be enough people for the peak times and too many for the slow times. In the second instance, adequate staff can be assigned for the peak times and reassigned for the off periods.

Metrics are essential for identifying trends before they become problems. For example, Storage Area Network (SAN) engineers use metrics to monitor the trends of disk usage. Based on the speed at which databases are growing, additional disk drives can be purchased and installed before they are required. Also, based on usage, rarely used files can be identified for movement to less expensive offline storage.

A properly constructed metric must be understood by everyone involved in its collection and analysis. Its management should be assigned to an individual who is closest to the process and most knowledgably of its components. Metrics are most meaningful to management when they are connected to a company strategy or an identified problem.

[B] Selecting a Metric

The proper selection of a metric is the foundation of its success. A metric should have a compelling reason to exist. Poorly selected metric will be expensive to support, and provide marginally useful or even useless data. They waste scarce resources with little to show for the work. In short, they provide nothing but expense and a demoralized staff.

Careful selection of metrics ensures that the greatest benefit is received for the least effort. It also demonstrates IT management's commitment to focus on the things that matter most.

Some things are more valuable to monitor than others are. Some people use the "squeaky wheel" approach where the departments that shout the loudest seem to receive the most IT attention. However, applying scare resources to collecting the wrong things will result in the wrong answers. There is another way. The Pareto principle is the 80/20 rule. This says that 80 percent of your problems will be caused by 20 percent of your processes.

Start the data collection process by selecting which processes to monitor. This may be "pain points" such as service calls that take longer to resolve than desired, this might be the number of customer orders that exceed a resolution time through order entry. Easy areas include:

- Recent customer complaints
- Problem tickets for the same thing
- Loudly complaining customers

Metrics can be internally focused for process improvement. They may also be customer focused for better service or for problem resolution focused to determine the root cause of process problems.

Over time, the easy to identify problem areas may have been resolved. At that point, pull together an ongoing process for selecting areas to monitor:

A. Calendar of SLA renewal dates, begin collecting 90 days prior to demonstrate compliance.
B. Review service desk tickets for frequency of problems by device, by user, by department, by time of day, by day of week, etc. The goal is to identify and resolve the root cause of problems. This increases user satisfaction and reduces staff time on repetitive calls.
C. Problems with Vital Business Functions as identified by the BIA.
D. Support areas for critical business strategies or customers.

E. Seek out the Voice of the Customer:
  1. Periodic surveys of customers to identify problem areas.
  2. Attend department meetings to explain the IT department and ask for feedback.

[C] Planning

Collecting data requires a bit of formal planning. What is very clear to you may be a complete fog to the person collecting the data. Also, a poorly planned data collection effort wastes a lot of time in trial and error. Always engage the team member closest to the process being measured to collect the data.

Even if there is a good idea of what you are investigating, it may require sampling a few different places in the process to identify the one that will provide the most relevant data. The process documentation will help as will a map of the steps in that process.

Creating a plan to monitor a metric begins by asking relevant questions:

A. Why is this metric being collected? Does it address a problem or demonstrate team performance? This clear statement will anchor the rest of the plan.
B. What to measure? Each process has multiple inputs and outputs. Which inputs have the greatest impact on the outputs; and which outputs are of most concern to the customer?
C. What is the process capable of? The metric must be within the process's ability to deliver. For example, if the metric is to record a service desk ticket within three minutes and the computer is old and slow; then this may not be possible, no matter how many things are measured.
D. Where will the measurement be made? Pinpoint the place in the process to record data.
E. Who will make it? Identify the persons as they become responsible for correct data collection.
F. How is the data collected? Briefly document how each measurement is made, with what tool, etc. This is important as the person, who was carefully trained to collect data, may move to another position, go on vacation, etc.
G. What gage is being applied? Describe the tool.
H. What precision is needed? It should be at least one level of discrimination less than the measurement made.
I. How is it recorded? Often there is some sort of data collection form to fill in with each reading.
J. How is it submitted? What to do with the data collection sheets when they are ready for processing.
K. What process will be used to analyze it?
L. Reporting—frequency, format, audience.

Worksheet 03-1 is an example Metric Collection Approval Form. Each site will use something similar based on its local needs.

WORKSHEET 03-1. IT Metric Collection Approval Form

IT Metric Collection Approval Form	
Submitted by:	Metric owner:
IT Process name:	Metric name:
Objective:	
Metric goal:	
Collection	
What is to be measured	Who will measure it
Where will it be measured	Tools used
How will it be measured	When will it be measured
Who will collect the data sheets for analysis	
Dates for initial and quarterly review of Gage R&R studies	
Analysis	
How often will the data be analyzed	
What formulas are used to create the report	
What type of chart will be used to illustrate results	
How often will the report be issued	
Storage location for metric documents	
Publication of Results	
Bulletin Board for Printed results	
Frequency of reporting	
Duration of posting	
Video Reporting locations	
Approval	
Approved By:	Date:
Attach data collection form	
Attach example Metric Report	

[D] Costs

Data collection is never free. Therefore, each metric that is monitored should be approved by the department manager. Always select metrics collection points carefully. They should be the critical inputs or outputs of a process. For each metric measured, data collection involves an expense to:

- Plan for it
- Create or purchase metric collection tools
- Train someone on what to collect and when
- Collect the data
- Receive and store the data
- Periodically analyze it
- Act on it

Other costs of data collection may include:

- Labor (cost of time to collect and potentially the lost opportunity to work on a more valuable effort)
- Materials (such a data measurement tooling, a data tallying program)
- Process delays to collect data
- IT costs (to collect, store, and analyze data)

Automated data collection is cheaper than manual data collection, but there is still an expense. This type of data is usually IT transactional data. Often automatic data collection can be implemented easily as the data already exists. Examples are date/time stamps on files on data collection. This might be the date-time automatically added as a service request ticket is entered, to a purchase order approval, or even whenever someone logs into a server. Three immediate benefits of automatic data collection are that the data is already entered into the computer; you know the criteria for collecting that data item, and potential data entry errors are avoided. Of course, in large volume processes, collecting date-time data adds to processing time and data storage costs.

Automated data collection costs include:

- Time to alter software to add (and later remove) data elements such as date/time fields
- Data storage space
- Data archive space
- Data processing time to collect, store, retrieve, and archive

COMMENT

It is nice to collect data to improve a process but not mentally challenging. Automated data collection has a side benefit in that it reduces the amount of menial labor in a workday.

§ 3.03 DATA COLLECTION

[A] Overview

Every metric must have a goal that indicates for that dimension, the process is running optimally. Metrics are used to determine current process performance against its stated goals. Therefore, the first step in using goals is to determine what is to be measured. For the resources applied, what is the optimal value for that measurement?

Perfection is an elusive goal. The nearer you come to it, the more that a small problem appears to be large. This is similar to cutting in half, over and over again, the distance between where we are and perfection. We come quite close to the goal but never achieve it. The closer to perfection that a process nears, the greater the incremental cost of additional improvements. Each process change should be balanced between cost and benefit.

Goals must be set for "good enough." In the case of service desk staffing, setting the goal of always answering every call within two rings would mean staffing for the peak times and most of the people sitting idle the rest of the work week. Instead, by matching the time of day and day of week to demand, an approximate staffing level can be set. This means that, at some times, the goal will not be reached. The acceptable level is normally described in the SLA for that function.

Goals can also be set as expected operating levels. For example, disk drive storage may have a maximum of 80 percent utilization. Any disk using more than this amount for data storage must be reconfigured to keep the load beneath that threshold. Also, disk storage is monitored to detect the utilization trend velocity and amount so to provide early warning of pending problems.

When it comes to picking a metric's goal, most companies take the easy way out. They research the subject until they find an "industry standard" value for that type of metric. After collecting data for a metric for a period of time, it becomes easier to modify the goal to something that suits the local business need. One of the advantages of using the industry standard is that it has already been worked out by many other companies. It also makes benchmarking your performance against other companies in your industry much easier. An example of this might be the industry standard (for your company's industry) ratio of PC techs to users. This is useful if your desk side support response time seems too long.

[B] Goals Must Be Within the Process's Capability

A process's goal must be something that it is physically possible of achieving. Trying to obtain sub-second response time while pushing a very large number of transactions through an old and overburdened server will not happen, no matter how many changes are made. Before selecting a goal, ensure that it is within the process's capabilities.

For example, a goal to achieve 100 percent first-time acceptance on purchase orders is possible. However, it may require that each user is provided with extensive training prior to receiving his or her user access to that system.

§ 3.03[C]

Given the expense of training, it may make more sense to make the user interface as fool proof as possible and then deal with the few that still fail.

> ## COMMENT
>
> Pushing the team to achieve unrealistic goals creates resentment. In some cases, it may motivate the team to manipulate the data to give the desired outcome.

Another requirement before collecting metrics is that the process must be stable. New or recently changed processes must have time for their operators to settle in. Allow time for the initial problems to be resolved and for everyone to master their tasks. Otherwise, instead of collecting metrics with process problems, you care collecting metrics on the challenges of learning a new process.

[C] Types of Metrics

A measurement is a tradeoff between accuracy and precision. Accuracy is the degree that the measurement made is close to the true measurement. For example, if a person is using a tool such as a ruler to measure something, then how straight that person holds the ruler, and how directly the person is positioned in front of it may result in recording a value that is less than 100 percent accurate.

Precision is the number of digits used to express a number. Too little precision may lose useful data. An example of this is using the date/time stamp on a transaction. If only the hours and minutes are recorded, then many thousands of transactions will have the same time value. If more information was needed, then the time field would be expanded to include more digits to show the hundredths of a second. Ensure that the precision of any measurement tool is at least one degree of discrimination greater than the value to be measured. For example, a metric that is expressed in inches should be measured by something that has a precision of tenths of inches.

Unless the data is automatically collected, there is a cost tradeoff between accuracy and precision. The degree of both that are required in a metric must be decided when the metric is formalized.

A. GO/NO-GO. The fastest and easiest type of metric is GO/NO-GO. This is a metric that indicates if something exists or not. The YES/NO is the easiest metric to establish and to verify. This type of metric is normally counted as the number of YESs to the number of NOs. In some cases, the NOs must never occur (such as an aircraft engine stopping while in flight).

Examples of where this metric is important:

1. Security software (and the key hardware components required for its use)
2. Legally mandated monitoring systems
3. Customer critical system availability (without which the company cannot sell its products)
4. Critical manufacturing systems (without which manufacturing of products must cease)

The advantage of the GO/NO-GO metric is its speed and simplicity. It is easy to count and easy for the data collector to understand. Collection is easy to learn as it consists of a count of the number of occurrences of pass or fail. However, it does not indicate how close the measurement was to passing. An example might the electrical voltage on the power line. If a value falls below a threshold, then the power line may still be active but is too weak to perform as desired.

GO/NO-GO indicates fulfilling a specification but does not indicate the degree that it missed fulfilling the desired amount. It also does not collect why something did not meet its target (important information for mitigating the problem).Therefore, most companies use GO/NO-GO to monitor many processes as a way to identify where a problem area may be for future action.

COMMENT

GO/NO-GO? 99.9 percent uptime for an IT system is still 876 hours of downtime per year.

B. How Much. Counting defects does not include details. Further analysis is not possible on the same data. The YES/NO test provides some useful information but is more suited to detecting where a problem might exist. It is most valued due to its low cost to implement and analyze. A more useful type of metric to collect is the value of some process characteristic. A GO/NO-GO test may be applied to multiple dimensions of a process. Any one of them may fail it. However, which one failed, and by how much? Was it close to the standard or missing altogether?

A more important measurement is to quantify the measurements of the critical dimensions of a process. For example, submitting a purchase requisition for IT equipment:

1. Time for the request to advance through each step of the approval and order placement process

2. The number of errors on each request
3. Location (data field) of each error
4. Number of times a request was rejected (a GO/NO-GO measurement)
5. The reasons that a request was rejected

Using these examples, there is a lot of potential data to gather from a single requisition. Given that there is a cost for every data collection and analysis, only the few critical areas will be monitored.

Consider an example of the total time for requisition processing from beginning to end, and a metric for the number of rejected requisitions. If either of these metrics exceeds a specific threshold, then additional analysis and remedial action is needed. In this example, the threshold for the number of rejected purchase requests may be as high as 20 percent before the department experiences significant delays. It may be as low as one single rejection if the application involved legal compliance, such as a failed transaction attempt to the company's treasury account.

[D] Gage R&R

It is a shame when a lot of effort is spent collecting data that is unreliable and must be discarded. Before taking action on the data, in fact before even collecting the first piece of data, ensure that your data collection process is valid.

Many things could go wrong. The measuring tool could be inaccurate, the operator's technique could be poor, and they may not collect a representative sample. In most data collection processes, there is some amount of personal judgment and personal data collection technique. Defects that are counted may not be defects at all, or real defects may slip by unrecorded. This may be caused by the angle at which someone holds his or her head when reading a meter, the time of day that a measurement is made, or even which standard is applied to a process.

A Gage Repeatability and Reliability (Gage R&R) is a process for validating the process and measurement data collection tools. A Gage R&R is a statistical technique that determines the amount of variation in a measurement process. Repeatability refers to the defect measurement tooling used. This shows that the tool is capable of providing an accurate reading in multiple tests. Reproducibility describes the people making the measurement. This proves that their technique will provide a consistent result every time.

A Gage R&R study is not a one-time action. It should be performed for every new person collecting the data, every new data collection tool, and whenever the data being collected is changed.

To perform a Gage R&R, ask someone who is considered to be the expert in the data and its collection to collect a sampling of the data. The sample should be about 30 items. Perform this test three times on the same set of items and average the results. Multiple examinations of the same items should indicate the amount of repeatability in the process.

Next, instruct the people who will be routinely collecting the data on the proper way to collect the data and ask them to evaluate the same set of data items. Observe how they do this. How close were the various operators to the "expert"? Did the normal workers arrive at the same conclusion as the "expert"? How consistent were their measurements?

Next, check for the measurement stability by performing the same test at a later time. For example, if the data volumes or origins vary significantly over the month, run the test again during that time to determine the process stability.

COMMENT

Data is valuable because it is factual information about your business function. It is not unusual for decisions to be based on anecdotal evidence rather than facts. Basing decisions on facts leads to better outcomes than basing decisions on a desire or wish.

[E] Tools

If process improvement is the goal, then there are a number of ways to identify troubled processes. The first is from a tally of customer complaints. This may be collected by the service desk from people calling with problems, from conversations with customers, and from comments gathered by the IT team.

Another way is to create a customer satisfaction survey. Do not despair if most of the responses are negative. Many people will ignore the survey request. However, someone who is upset with the service will often release his or her pent up frustrations in an anonymous survey. This is important. Others may think the same way but are too polite to speak their minds.

In some cases, simple tally sheets can collect data. The IT service desk typically receives many calls that can be resolved in less time than it takes to enter a trouble ticket. In those cases, data can be collected on a tally sheet, which also indicates call volumes. Consider breaking the tally sheet into categories to identify which areas are generating the most calls.

[F] Sampling the Few

Metric monitoring is normally a statistical exercise. It would be nice to collect metrics from every transaction that passes through the process. Unfortunately, this is time consuming and expensive. However, it may not be necessary. Where using every transaction will give your metric 100 percent certainty, the same result may be obtained by using a small subset of the overall population.

Sampling is using a small number of items of a group to represent the entire group. A statistical sample for each metric can be calculated. However, a shortcut is to use 30 samples out of the total population. These samples should be made at irregular times throughout the day to detect variations to the process inputs.

An exception to sampling is automatic data collection (such as the date/time stamp on a transaction).In this case, it is common to collect 100 percent of the data for analysis.

§ 3.04 ANALYZING

[A] Overview

After the data is recorded, drop by daily and pick up the collection sheets. Sometimes dropping in to pick up the sheets is your first inkling that the person you so carefully trained has just left on a four-week medical leave! This ensures that:

- Data is being captured as requested
- Data sheets are not lost
- The person collecting the data sees that you are serious about collecting metric data
- The person collecting the data can ask questions
- You have a good opportunity to thank them for their help

Collecting data is the necessary first step. However, understanding what this data is trying to tell you needs some interpretation. The data is shouting something about the process, but you must translate it to hear the message. This translation is the data analysis. Charts are the best way to do this, as people can understand the meaning of pictures more quickly than text.

There are many ways to analyze data that dig deeper into its meaning. For most situations, the statistical functions in a spreadsheet are adequate. Many people find statistics somewhat difficult to understand; so here are two basic ways to present metric data:

A. Bar charts tell how many of something. By comparing the bars, the most frequently occurring data is identified.
B. Trend charts takes bar charts a bit farther by showing changes in data values over time.

COMMENT

Data analysis assumes that all of the data was collected according to the approved process. As always, bad data creates incorrect results.

[B]   Bar Charts

A basic bar chart illustrates the frequency of values in the data. This is a good way to illustrate the magnitude of a metric category. GO/NO-GO metric work well with bar code charts. They show the number of measurements that passed the measurement goal and that failed. Bar charts can be used to compare metrics on inputs to outputs to help identify places for further investigation.

Exhibit 3-1 Origin of Requests is an example using bar charts to identify problems. In this case, a large organization has a problem with the number of user access requests rejected by the service desk. The goal of collecting these metrics is to identify the cause and resolve it for greater user satisfaction.

Number accepted vs. rejected

EXHIBIT 3-1.   Origin of Requests

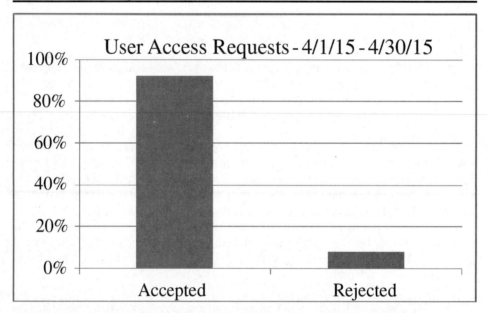

Exhibit 3-2 Originating Department is the "Rejected": items broken down by the department that submitted them. This would be used to identify departments that require additional training.

Exhibit 3-3 Cause for Rejection is the "Rejected": items broken down by what caused them to be rejected. Note that one defect rejects the entire form. This count does not reflect that there may be multiple reasons on the same form to reject it.

This second example is for the number of pages printed every day by an office laser printer. The company is pressing for "greener" operations through a reduced waste stream. You have been asked to track printer usage to determine which days use the most paper so that those processes can be moved to online viewing.

EXHIBIT 3-2. Originating Department

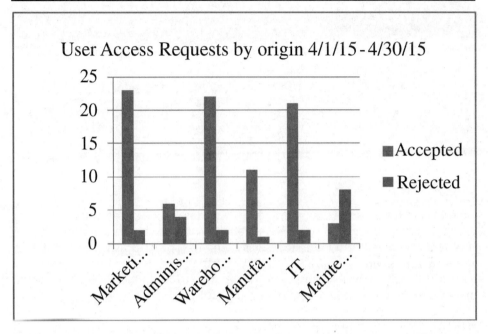

EXHIBIT 3-3. Cause for Rejection

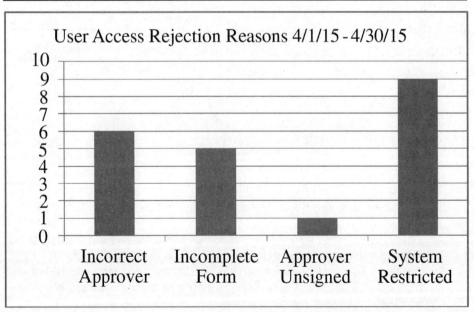

COMMENT

Metric collection and analysis depends on people. For their own reasons, people may provide the data that you want to see rather than what it really was. Also, if they feel the data is detrimental to their job, they may alter it before submitting.

[C]   Trend Charts

Trend charts are useful for seeing how the data is trending over time. For example, if the operators were given refresher training, did the incidence of problems decrease? After a change was made to a process, is it more stable or still providing widely erratic results? A change may also be in operators as a more experienced person moved to another position. It may also be before and after the introduction of a new material or form.

EXHIBIT 3-4.   Example Trend Chart

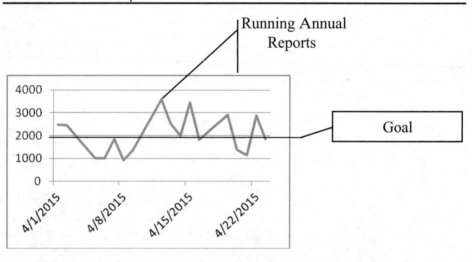

Trend charts have the following advantages:

A. There are many enhancements that can be added to a basic trend chart.
B. Mark the average value over the previous reporting period.
C. Note any extraordinary events that are driving the metric. In the case of the chart in Exhibit 3-4, it is the printing of annual reports. Notations could also be made for data points on the low side of the chart, such as days when the printer was out of service.

EXHIBIT 3-5. Bar and Trend Charts Illustrating the Same Data

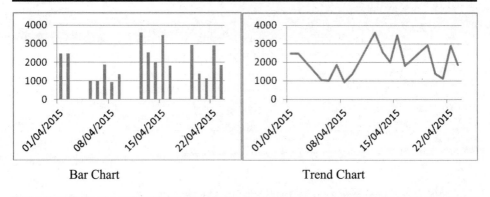

Bar Chart   Trend Chart

Both bar and trend charts illustrate the same data (see Exhibit 3-5). Each bar or data point is for a weekday. If the goal is to reduce the daily usage to below 2000 pages per day, then the team can focus on those days that exceed the goal.

[D] Run Charts

A more sophisticated type of trend chart is a run chart. A run chart adds several components that help a manger to see if the reported value is within normal variation or extraordinary and requiring investigation. These three items are:

A. Recent average—recalculated every time the run chart is updated. In this case, it is monthly.
B. Upper control limit—plus three standard deviations above the average.
C. Lower control limit—minus three standard deviations below the average.

The area between the control limits should contain 99.9 percent of the expected data values. Any data point above or below the control limits is a special event. Each special event must be investigated to identify what caused this significant change. The more consistently the process output, the narrower the limits.

Also, count the number of data points in a row above or below the line. If there are three or more in the same direction, this is a trend.

Example Control Chart (see Exhibit 3-6) is another view of the lines of pages printed by a department's laser printer during workdays.

EXHIBIT 3-6. Example Control Chart

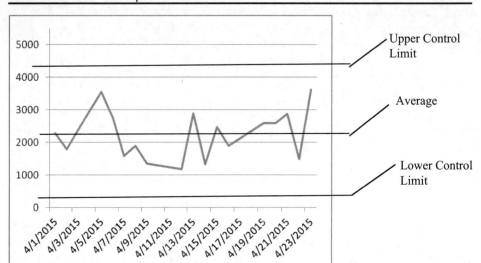

§ 3.05 REPORTING

[A] Overview

Metric analysis is a feedback mechanism from a process to its operators. Collecting and analyzing data is a start. The business benefits come from publishing the data to all interested parties.

In the past, various charts were posted around the office indicating results. No one knew what they meant, where they came from, who managed them, or even how old the chart data was. In short, they were to be snapshots of data without the time and place context necessary to figure out what they meant. A part of this came from the time necessary to build the charts and then scurry around posting them. If the same person was responsible for multiple metrics, the person was more concerned with posting them instead of explaining them.

Today, large screen TVs connected to the company Intranet can display this information around the department in a visually appealing way. Posting a chart to the Intranet Web page makes it available along with the other metric charts for the department. This saves paper, bulletin board space, and a lot of running around. The data is also available to anyone with a company workstation.

A classical explanation of metrics is that there are three kinds of lies: lies, damn lies, and statistics. Metric reporting is easy to manipulate. Lying is not necessary. You can arrive at the desired result by cherry-picking the metrics you chose to report (and the ones you chose to omit). If more people are wanted in the help desk, the performance of the call center is shown to require an additional person. Similarly, you can manipulate metrics to show the need for a better communication tool to dispatch PC techs instead of them returning to their desk for their next ticket.

[B] Visual Management

Visual management is a technique where a manager can walk through a department and see the volume of products passing through the processes. This may be the size of items in the "in box," the "out box," or sitting at a desk of an absent worker. By visually gaging the size of the piles, it is easy to assess the workflow of the process without disturbing anyone. If the data is all online, then the length of the queues in and out can also be checked. The information can also be available electronically.

Sharing the metric data reports can be done many ways. Traditionally, this was through charts posted on a company bulletin board. However, updates to these charts were not always timely and the analysis process not explained. When the employees see a problem area, it is so far in the past that they shrug and walk on.

Many companies have shifted metric reporting to large video displays. Large screen monitors can be set up in work areas to see break areas so that workers can see their performance against the standard. For example, the average hold time for an incoming call to customer service desk, the number of service tickets closed so far that day, and even the percentage of server utilization of the online product catalog. This feedback enables the IT team to make immediate process adjustments to remain within performance objectives.

Visual management engages the IT personnel in real time process improvement. They can try something, see the difference, and then suggest a minor process improvement. They can offer suggestions for new metrics to track, old ones to drop, and ideas that may lead to the root cause of problems. This environment moves the metrics off an ignored printed page and into the hands of the team.

[C] Executive Reporting

The classical purpose of metric reporting is to demonstrate the department's performance to company executives. Use these reports to build their confidence in your management skills.

A common metric is to collect the number of times that a particular company department or line of business is calling the service desk. Even though the department's SLA describes the amount of resources it may use, its urgent requests for services may reduce service levels for others. An example might be the problems with the use of third-party hardware and software that was sold as "trouble free." Since many companies only renegotiate SLAs as a run up to the annual budget cycle, nothing will be done about it.

As with any executive reporting, be prepared to back up metrics with the raw data. If the report indicates a problem external to the IT department, this data will be requested prior to any action.

[D] Team Motivation

Metrics indicate to management the performance of a product or process. They can also be used to focus team behaviors in positive ways. A truism of data gathering is that managers get what they measure. The trick is to measure the right things. There are only so many hours in a workday. Focus metric reporting on the critical few measurements for each team to encourage them to increase their performance in these areas.

When selecting a metric to measure, take time to explain it to the work team involved. If the goal is to reduce cost, or to reduce errors, then explain what that means. The validity of any metric program can be diminished through employee non-participation. IT Team members each have a stake in a positive outcome only if it is properly explained to them.

COMMENT

Sometimes, the person collecting the data may be suspected of skewing the numbers toward an outcome the person desires. If this is the case, temporarily assign someone else to collect the data (call it rotating the responsibility) or even collect a day's worth of data samples yourself.

§ 3.06 MANAGING A GOVERNANCE METRICS PROGRAM

[A] Overview

Once the data is collected and analyzed, the next step is to act on it. Small variations may just be monitored for the short term. However, if there is a significant spike in the data, it must be investigated. One-time situations are easily identified. Something that might occur again should be addressed. However, if the data indicates a trend toward further problems, then take prompt action.

Collecting and analyzing metrics does not impress the team (for long). Action is what marks a leader. Taking action on the metrics results might include:

A. Do not over react to small changes. Some variation is natural based on a wide range of causes.

B. Time of month (at a rush to complete some things at the end, no hurry in the beginning).

C. Weather—severe weather may cause some workers to stay home and for stores to be less busy. However, online activity may increase.

    D. End of accounting quarter—closing down activities and budgeting for the next term.

    E. Allow for seasonal variations on data.

[B] Annual Metric Sunset Review

All good things come to an end. Review each metric at least annually to determine if the reasons that justified its adoption are still valid. It is not unusual for a business to shift its focus from year to year. Also, if a process seems to be consistently stable, then spend your limited time monitoring a different process to identify potential changes to it.

Sometimes staff turnover give metrics a life of their own. Once the people who knew the reason driving the collection of a metric are no longer around, no one knows why the metric is important. Therefore, the new people keep on doing it without any idea of anyone even reviews it. They believe that it is just a part of the job. If they stop monitoring the metric, they may be scolded but if they keep on collecting and reporting, no one will say anything bad about them.

Such an attitude is understandable but for lack of individual initiative, the company continues to waste resources. Be sure that any metric whose current value cannot re-justify its existence is promptly cancelled.

[C] Track the Value

Metrics can convey negative news or positive news. Good news at times can be in short supply in a workplace. If the process is working well, then reporting the metrics will demonstrate the team's good performance. One technique is to determine the company benefits from the improvements made based on the metrics collected and post it on the bulletin board. These benefits may be calculated in time saved (which was used for other purposes).

One technique is to post the current week's metrics chart on top of the previous week's report. This enables anyone interested to thumb through the process performance over time (and hopefully see the improvement).

COMMENT

Always recognize the team members for their assistance in collecting and analyzing metric reports. One way is to place a block in the corner of the chart that identifies everyone who assisted in the development of the report.

[D]   Avoid the Traps

Measuring the same thing over and over again leads to "metric fatigue" where the numbers are collected but no one cares about them after that. To combat this apathy, periodically change some of your metrics to monitor other areas of your operation. A good time to change is when the process under measurement seems to be running predictably with a steady acceptable level of effectiveness and efficiency.

Collecting data for "show" rather than for action is a waste of scarce resources. Think of the times where management has requested someone to collect data and plot it for a wall chart that no one ever reviewed or acted upon. This is a waste of valuable labor and processing to build the graphs. However, the larger cost is the loss of employees' confidence in their managers' judgment. If the data is manually collected, then, since it is not believed to be seriously used, the numbers may contain errors as the person doing the collection feels no one cares.

COMMENT

The classic problem with metrics is that you will get the most of what you are measuring. A PC manufacturer's warranty help desk began measuring the length of talk time per call. Technicians were pressed to keep calls to 4 minutes or less. In response, the help desk technicians would provide the callers with a few tests to try and ask them to call back if the problem persisted.

Later, the metric was changed to first call resolution. In this case, if a caller needed to reboot his or her PC to return to the point where the problem occurred, the caller was told to call back and the trouble ticket was closed as resolved on the first call.

The company's goal was to have short calls that solved the problem in the shortest time. The difficulty was it was only working on one factor of the problem.

Perhaps, if the metric was used to identify and address the causes of long calls that drive to the solution (measures of both effectiveness and efficiency), the company might achieve its goals. In that case, it is focusing on minimizing the causes and not on the result.

4

ITIL: MEETING THE NEEDS OF BUSINESS

§ 4.01 OVERVIEW

[A] Purpose and Scope

ITIL™ (Information Technology Infrastructure Library) was an effort sponsored by the United Kingdom's government to collect the best IT practices used by the most successful companies into one guideline for efficient IT operations. It describes procedures and artifacts to provide a measurable level of IT competence. It also provides a process for measuring improvement in all areas of IT performance. An important aspect of this framework was that it be independent of any particular vendor.

ITIL contains nothing new. It is a collection of the proper way to do such things as change control, service delivery, running a service desk, etc. Most companies already do these things (or know that they should do, and still do not). ITIL adds and clarifies the best way to conduct these processes. However, its power is the way the ITIL framework glues these various functions into one coherent strategy.

ITIL is primarily used by IT executives to rein in some of the chaos that echoes around a large IT shop and refocus it on customer service. Successfully applied, ITIL makes an IT team less reactive by addressing both current and persistent problems toward providing a measurable level of customer service. It also forces these various IT teams to work together to achieve these service goals.

COMMENT

"ITIL," "IT Infrastructure Library," and "PRINCE2" are registered trademarks held by the United Kingdom government.

[B] ITIL History

ITIL began as a simple idea. How can the UK government improve its IT operations efficiency and perhaps share this "best way" with all companies? In the mid-1980s, the Central Computer and Telecommunications Agency (CTTA), an agency of the UK government, gathered the best IT management practices used in major companies. This was intended to standardize government IT operations as well as the many companies providing IT services to it. Another goal was to avoid making the same mistakes over and over again throughout the organization.

Over time, the success of this effort grew. In 2001, CCTA was merged into the Office of Government Commerce (OGC) who promotes a wide range of best business practices (such as PRINCE2™ for Project Management). OGC managed the copyright for ITIL and the trademark for the name. It also promoted use of best practices while maintaining control of them to ensure a high quality. This control guarantees that ITIL remains independent of any one company. OGC has since been absorbed by the UK government.

ITIL is called a library because it consists of a series of books explaining how it works. At one point, there were over 30 books in the set. ITIL version 3 consolidated these volumes into five volumes. These five volumes were most recently updated in 2011. These volumes are:

A. ITIL Service Strategy
B. ITIL Service Design
C. ITIL Service Transition
D. ITIL Service Operation
E. ITIL Continual Service Improvement

ITIL has evolved through several versions. ITIL version 2 was replaced by ITIL version 3 in 2007. A basic premise introduced in ITIL version 3 was continuous improvement. Version 3 provides a more comprehensive big picture of IT services and how the many components interrelate.

Following through on the premise of continuous improvement, ITIL 2011 was published. The five ITIL books were updated to make them more consistent and to include current best practices. Also, a new certification scheme was implemented that includes a new "ITIL Master" level.

[C] ITIL Processes Are Artifact-Centric

ITIL uses a series of processes and tools (artifacts) to tie the various practice areas together. For example, a key ITIL artifact is a configuration management database. This artifact contains information about everything in the IT organization that must be controlled. Some of the information in the configuration database might include:

A. Software versions
B. Hardware standards
C. Every significant IT hardware item
D. Service Level Agreements with customers
E. Versions of internally generated documentation
F. About anything else that must be controlled to ensure the current version is always available and only changed by authorized persons!

Today, IT departments use a variety of homegrown forms, processes, terminology, and business policies that are implemented at the whim of a manager and quickly modified by that person's replacement. ITIL provides a standard set of terminology across the organization to ease the flow of information between the various functions.

> ## COMMENT
>
> ITIL does not come with a set of forms. It describes the information that is needed and how it will be used. The creation of forms and their exact content is left to the company implementing it.

[D] ITIL as a Published Standard

Most ITIL users are in the UK and the British Commonwealth. ITIL has made some progress in the United States, but its acceptance has suffered from its foreign origins. Also, each company, intentionally or not, applies its own twist to ITIL to accommodate its own business climate.

To standardize ITIL for wider acceptance, ITIL was formalized into the British Standard 15000 (BS 15000). This published standard was useful for countries in the British Commonwealth, but full international acceptance was still lagging. ITIL version 3 has been codified into ISO 20000, which focuses on IT Service Management.

ITIL is sometimes implemented alongside of other frameworks such as Capability Maturity Model (CMM) and Control Objectives for Information and related Technology (COBIT). Microsoft's Operations Framework is based on ITIL. CMM is primarily focused on software and COBIT on regulatory compliance.

[E] Critical Policies to Develop Based on This Chapter

Using the material discussed in this chapter, you will be able to create the following policies:

A. Operating the service desk
B. Managing incidents
C. Creating a configuration management database
D. Change management
E. ITIL certification

Policies should always be developed based on the local situation. Successful managers cannot issue appropriate guidance if the policies are written with another company's situation or location in mind.

§ 4.02 ITIL'S FIVE BOOKS

[A] Service Strategy

Service strategy looks at a company's IT service requirements and service capabilities. It then proceeds to the development of a strategy to fulfill those requirements. The strategy assembles a gap analysis to identify additional capabilities to acquire and a path to develop them.

Service strategy has five significant sections:

A. **Strategy Management for IT Services.** Analyzes current customer service capabilities, benchmark against other organizations to identify areas for improvement, and develop a strategy to improve capabilities.

B. **Service Portfolio Management.** Manages the IT service mix to ensure it fulfills business requirements within its budget.

C. **Demand Management.** Meets current customer needs, looks ahead to see what future needs may be required, and works with customers to shape their view of the services available now.

D. **Financial Management for IT Services.** Provides guidance on the proper accounting and budgeting for IT services and support.

E. **Business Relationship Management.** Recognizes that users of IT services are customers and works to build a positive relationship with them.

[B] Service Design

To fill in the gaps of service capabilities identified by the service strategy, Service Design guides their creation and changes to existing offerings.

A. **Design Coordination.** Ensures that changes to any IT service are effective and coordinated across the organization. All services, new or existing, must include measurements of their key process indicators.

B. **Service Catalog Management.** To create and maintain an IT service catalog of all IT services, their related support contact information, and a description of the agreed service levels with various customers.

C. **Service Level Management.** The negotiation of service level, operational level, and underpinning agreements to support IT customer agreements.

D. **Risk Management.** To identify and mitigate threats to company IT assets to provide a more reliable level of service.

E. **Capacity management.** Planning to ensure that IT assets have the capability to meet current and pending service levels.

F. **Availability Management.** Ensures that IT systems are available when needed (according to the service level agreement).

G. **IT Service Continuity Management.** Planning to mitigate the risk of a disaster or a less severe IT service interruption from negatively impacting service levels.

H. **Information Security Management.** Planning and actions to ensure the confidentiality and integrity of company information.

I. **Compliance Management.** Planning to ensure IT complies with company directives and regulatory requirements.

J. **Architecture Management.** Planning for an overall IT architecture for the current, medium-term, and long-term future.

K. **Supplier Management.** Planning to ensure that contracts fulfill their intended purpose and that contractors fulfill their obligations.

[C] Service Transition

Change is a common IT event. Service transition facilitates change, ensuring that all interested parties are aware and approve of the change(s), the risk of unintended results is evaluated, etc. Complex or important changes should be implemented through the application of a formal project management program.

A. **Change Management.** Ensure IT changes cause minimal service level interruption.
B. **Change Evaluation.** The careful and coordinated evaluation of a planned change on the various IT domains prior to making it.
C. **Application Development.** The planned development and maintenance of internally developed software and customized package software.
D. **Release and Deployment Management.** The controlled implementation of IT system releases to ensure minimal customer impact.
E. **Service Validation and Testing.** Verification that planned releases meet customer requirements and are appropriately tested.
F. **Service Asset and Configuration Management.** The collection, storage, and maintenance of IT asset configuration and their interrelationships.
G. **Knowledge Management.** Provision of a central site for the collection and storage of IT information.

[D] Service Operation

Service Operation is the heart of IT support. It provides a single face to the people it serves and uses continual improvement to ensure that IT services keep pace with customer requirements. It includes techniques for receiving service requests, prioritizing their resolution, and for dealing with long-term problems.

A. **Event Management.** Monitoring of events to determine the appropriate action for each.
B. **Incident Management.** Management of incidents from their report through to their resolution, and follow-up.
C. **Request Fulfillment.** Efficient and effective resolution of all requests made to the IT team.
D. **Access Management.** Application of policies and procedures created by the Information Security team, to requests for all types of IT access.
E. **Problem Management.** Resolution of long-term service problems. Proactively, it reviews service requests for problem trends that can be resolved before impacting users.

F. **IT Operations Control.** Effective control of the many day-to-day tasks such as process monitoring, ensuring backups are properly completed, scheduling and managing routing maintenance, etc.
G. **Facilities Management.** Management of the environmental systems for the data center, IT offices, and access to different IT security spaces.
H. **Application Management.** Details appropriate management of software creation and careful implementation of changes to it.
I. **Technical Management.** Details management of technical resources for support of IT infrastructure.

[E]   Continual Service Improvement

The IT landscape is ever evolving from new technologies to changing business environments. This book provides techniques to analyze processes for improving their effectiveness and efficiency. It also looks at learning from adverse events through reviews of lessons learned.

A. **Service Review.** The periodic review of IT processes to identify areas for performance improvement.
B. **Process Evaluation.** The establishment and analysis of process metrics to identify areas for improvement.
C. **Definition of CSI Initiatives.** The definition of process improvement efforts.
D. **Monitoring of CSI Initiatives.** The ongoing oversight of process improvement efforts to ensure they reach a timely conclusion, and to verify that completed improvements remain in service.

§ 4.03   ITIL SERVICE OPERATION

[A]   Service Desk

Most companies already have some variation of a service desk. It is a place to call for IT support on just about anything. Service desks run the gamut from an on-site staff, knowledgeable about local operations, to a call center in a remote corner of the world that takes messages and dispatches help. The goal is to provide a single point of contact for all users.

There are many types of "desks" that receive calls of IT system users and dispatch help. ITIL advocates a full service single point of contact for the IT department through a service desk. (Nothing new about that—they have been around for years.) However, an ITIL service desk provides assistance based on a catalog of service offerings. This catalog lists every IT service offered, the promised response times, the users it is offered to, the times of service covered, etc.

Service catalog creation and maintenance is controlled by Service Management. Its content is based on negotiated service level agreements (SLAs) between the IT department and the people IT supports. Internally within the IT departments, an SLA is supported by Operational Level Agreements which acts as an internal SLA. It may also include underpinning contracts with external service providers.

An SLA provides the details of what the users want to "pay" for. It will clearly describe the service wanted, and the cost for providing that service. The description includes the times of coverage (9 am to 5 pm, Monday through Friday or all day, every day).

The SLAs are then reviewed by the supporting IT organizations that agree to provide that service using either current resources or the cost to meet the requirements. For example, if a customer wanted a four-hour response time to recover a lost PC file, during normal working hours and workdays, then that may already be covered. However, if they want the same service and same response time 24 hours a day—seven days a week—including holidays (which they will ask for)—then they must bear the cost for someone to sit around all of those hours just in case they are needed (which they normally will not agree to pay for).

This exchange between IT and the rest of the company establishes an expectation of service level. Once the agreements are in place, then as long as IT meets the required times, they are fulfilling their part of the bargain. Over time, an SLA can be refined to reflect the true business need.

Previously, service desk calls were roughly assigned priorities (such as low, medium, and high). Calls were generally handled as First In–First Out. While this is simple to understand, user service delivery was uneven. Where one day a call was resolved in five minutes, on another the same problem took five days (due to other service issues).

Under ITIL, priority of calls is established in the SLAs. For example, if the SLA for password resets is four hours, then doing so anytime within those four hours is a success. If the users want to pay for someone to sit and wait for calls to come in—so a higher level of service is available—then, that option is available to their management also. Even if there is an "IT Technical Emergency," the four-hour requirement must be met to fulfill the agreed service level.

[B] Incident Management

Any reported service disruption within the SLA is known as an "incident." The service desk resolves whatever they can (within their local guidelines). If the problem still exists, then they refer to the SLA for a list of questions to ask the user that gathers initial diagnostic information.

Under ITIL, the analysis of reported problems is handled by the Incident Management team. The guiding focus of Incident Management is the prompt, cost-effective resolution of the problem. The Incident Management process begins by ensuring the problem is properly (and clearly) recorded. It is sometimes difficult for the service desk to gather the appropriate information into a clear document when users are adding information as it springs to mind. Also, if the phone lines are busy, there isn't time to step back and clean up the description.

The incident is matched to an SLA to verify that the user is entitled to this service. If not, then a change request is sent to Service Management to investigate a change to the service catalog. If the user is entitled to the service, then the SLA indicates how priority is assigned.

The incident is checked against other incidents to see if there is a pattern emerging in the problem reports. After that, the incident is assigned to some-one to investigate. The result could be:

A. The problem is repaired and full service restored.
B. Problem resolution disrupts other IT services or cannot be immediately repaired. The incident is passed over to Problem Management for res-olution. Meanwhile, a work-around is created and made available through the Known Error database.
C. The problem is not considered cost effective to address (such as in a one-time process).

As the incident progresses to resolution (or work-around for a known error), Incident Management, through the service desk, keeps the user informed about progress. This reduces the number of calls to the service desk requesting updates.

COMMENT

ITIL version 3 was introduced in 2007. It shifts some of ITIL's emphasis from Service Delivery and Support to an integrated Service Management lifecycle. It also promotes planned, continual improvement in IT processes.

[C] Problem Management

Incident Management is focused on the quick restoration of service and all that is needed for many service disruptions. However, the root causes of some pro-blems are not so obvious—and the solution is not so soon to appear. These incidents are passed over to Problem Management.

Similar to Incident Management, Problem Management prioritizes the incoming work load to work on the most urgent, highest value tasks first. The incident tracking database is checked for similar problems in the past and possible connection to other recently reported incidents.

Problem Management will bring together the necessary technical skills to trace back the incident to its source. One tool commonly used is a fault tree analysis that details all the sequence of actions necessary to complete a tech-nical task. The goal is to identify where the chain of events is broken. Another common tool is a fishbone analysis that details all of the factors required for something to work. This indicates what was missing that may have caused the failure.

Once the root cause of the incident is located, its classification is changed to "Known Error." If the problem can be easily repaired, then it is resolved.

However, if the problem will impact customer service levels, then a temporary work-around process is created and provided to Service Management. The incident report is added to the Known Error Database (KED). Problem Management then submits a Request For Change (RFC) to Change Management to resolve the problem. Problem Management tracks the incident until the requested change is successfully completed.

The proactive portion of Problem Management is to address emerging trends before they impact customer service. An example might be a recurring problem that is quickly repaired by Incident Management, or a hardware item that is drifting toward an out of tolerance situation. Once reported or recorded by Problem Management, they are resolved in the same manner as requests from Incident Management, according to their priority.

[D] Configuration Management

Configuration Management supports the cost effective control of IT assets. (Historically, an IT asset was a chunk of hardware. Under ITIL, it is anything of value to the IT department.) It encompasses all aspects of IT to ensure that everything remains in sync.

The following are issues to address for support configuration management:

A. Configuration Management Database. Information about IT assets is gathered and maintained in the Configuration Management Database (CMDB). This database provides a significant amount of control for IT systems.

IT has long had an asset-tracking problem. The tools it uses are expensive, are spread across the organization and they require regular maintenance or replacement. In the beginning, a configuration database began as a way to track hardware items (asset management). Many companies have these today to facilitate the maintenance of equipment. These same companies know how tedious it is to keep this database current.

Eventually, this tool was expanded to track software and its many versions. The logical extension was to tie the hardware and software files to a telephone listing. Now when someone calls the service desk, information on that person's equipment and software is available to anyone helping to resolve the problem.

ITIL takes the Configuration Management Database further. ITIL loads the database with *everything* used to govern IT. It includes:

1. Service Level agreements and version control.
2. End User documentation version control.
3. Change requests, active and historical.
4. Problem reports tied to the hardware or software that caused them.
5. Versions (and information about how that version is unique) for all mainframe/server and PC software.

The problem with this database is to know when to quit adding to it! Sure, it is nice to know where all of the documentation (supposedly) is, so that in a version change it can all be collected and replaced, but is that necessary for every product?

B. Keeping the Database Current. Everything contained in the CMDB is called a Configuration Item (CI). A CI can be a single component (such as a telephone instrument) or an entire system (the PBX unit). Every configuration item is managed to a lifecycle. Initially, this is tied to the actual item. For example, a PC software package may have a useful life of three years. It is first entered into the database when it is purchased. The next entry might be when it is installed (which is linked to the hardware item where it resides) along with a maintenance agreement, if one was purchased. Every time it is patched, there is another entry for the last known good configuration (copies of both the old software and the updated module), etc.

Carrying this idea forward, a PC package typically creates and stores data. Given that different types of corporate data have different retention rates, it is conceivable that a company must maintain all of the various versions of its many software packages to ensure it can read archived data at some future point to defend itself in a legal suit. In theory, companies already do this.

COMMENT

Retention time for data depends on its content. Tax information must be retained for seven years, SEC information for a different time and then, medical records may have an indefinite retention. Always refer to your company's retention plan. One issue that can occur is if the data is retained for a computer type, OS version, and application software format that is no longer available, has the company fulfilled its retention requirements?

There is a cost for each element in the configuration database (and for that matter in any database). The costs include acquiring the data, entering it, storing it, and keeping it current. The more items there are to maintain, the higher the cost—the fewer items maintained, the less value the database adds to the organization! The key is to find the balance between costs and benefits.

C. CMDB Holds the Last Working Configuration. One benefit of the CMDB is that it contains the before and after images of software upgrades. This assists in rolling back failed patches and upgrades. Again, it is also useful for reloading software at a particular point. For example, some software is only used once per year for special tax generation, such as the program to print W-2 statements.

COMMENT

A new area in ITIL v3 is Application Management. This combines the old software asset management techniques with the proper management of applications development, roll out and follow up.

D. **Relationships.** A particularly time-consuming task is to identify, implement, and maintain connections between the various configuration items in the database. Example relationships to track include:

1. User documentation that supports a specific generation of locally written mainframe software. When an upgrade is made to the software, it is easy to determine who needs copies of the new documentation.
2. When someone calls for assistance, the connection between his or her workstation, its software and that person's server applications and authorization provides everything needed to address a wide range of problems.
3. Relationships between all of the hardware items supporting a specific application. For example, if a specific database server required an emergency shutdown, which applications use it and which users must be notified?

E. **Creating a Configuration Management Database.** Many brave technical experts have tried to create their own database from scratch. However, as they worked through its many complex levels, they discovered how much easier it is to purchase one. There are several major vendors in the marketplace—and this software is not cheap.

1. The process for building a CMDB begins with developing a detailed implementation plan. Decisions must be made as to what is going into the database, what relationships will be tracked, etc.
2. Next comes locating and tagging everything. (If your asset database already includes asset tags, then this is the same process, except it covers many other things to track.) Given the wide range of items to tag, decisions must be made as to where tags go on a type of object (hardware, software media, software in storage, etc.).
3. After everything is loaded, additional complexity comes from establishing access rights so that only authorized personnel can change the configuration items. Further, a process is set in place to record all changes that are made.
4. Expect an immediate inflow of ongoing updates. As new configuration items arrive, they must be added to the database. As they are moved to (perhaps) a person's desk, another update is needed, etc. Software patches, new versions, repairs to hardware all require database updates.

5. Despite the team's best efforts, there will be something missed or incorrectly entered. An ongoing audit program samples data and identifies errors. A simple way to do this for something like hardware is to ask the caller the asset tag on his computer, etc. whenever he reports an incident.

See Policy ITP-04-1 IT Configuration Management Database Policy as an example policy to create and maintain a CMDB.

POLICY ITP-04-1. Configuration Management Database Policy

Policy #:	ITP-04-1	Effective:	04/01/13	Page #:	1 of N
Subject:		Configuration Management Database Policy			

1.0 PURPOSE

This policy defines the creation and maintenance of the ITIL Configuration Management Database (CMDB).

2.0 SCOPE

The policy applies to all services within the IT department, to include applications development and management, system administration, IT administrative processes, Data Operations, networks, outsourced labor or services, and all other areas under the IT Director's direction. This does not apply to IT processes that are one time or only needed for a short duration.

3.0 POLICY

The IT Director will acquire a database management system adequate to function as the company's ITIL CMDB. This database will be the single repository for all of the IT department's information, to include explanations of which elements link to another.

The Service Desk Manager will manage the CMDB on a day-to-day basis.

A. CMDB Implementation
The Service Manager will determine what will go into the CMDB. Each section will be assigned to the managers most familiar with it. Examples of what this might include:

1. Service Desk Manager
   a. IT service catalog
   b. All SLAs and underpinning agreements supporting the service catalog
   c. Service desk procedures
2. Applications Manager
   a. All application technical, service desk, and end-user documentation
   b. All third-party documentation for IT tools and its locations
3. IT Operations
   a. Capacity projections

      b. Performance reports
      c. Scheduled changes
      d. Business continuity plan
      e. Disaster recovery plan
   4. Information Security Manager
      a. IT security plan
      b. IT systems risk assessment
      c. Security access approvals
   5. IT Director
      a. All IT policies
      b. IT training records
      c. All approved IT forms

Once per month, each IT manager checks the age of documents in the CMDB. Once per calendar year, every policy and procedure must be updated or approved as current for the year. Application documentation should be recertified by the applications manager annually as still current.

B. Content Sunset

Once per year, the Service Desk Manager reviews which IT hardware, software, and system tools have been retired. Once removed from the premises, their documentation should have been removed from the CMDB. However, this annual review ensures that all components and links to those components have been removed to avoid future confusion.

4.0 REVISION HISTORY

Date	Revision #	Description of Change
04/01/13	1.0	Initial creation.

5.0 INQUIRIES

Direct inquiries about this policy to:

George Jenkins, CIO
Our Company, Inc.
2900 Corporate Drive
Columbus, OH 43215

Voice: 614-555-1234
Fax: 614-555-1235
E-mail: gjenkins@company.com

Revision #:	1.0	Supersedes:	N/A	Date:	04/01/13

[E] Change Management

IT systems are massive, interlinked, and complex. There are servers, networks, applications, and workstations all interacting in many different ways. Individual IT items (hardware and software) may seldom change. However, when this is multiplied over the large number of items, the effect is a steady flow of changes and new installations across the entire technology spectrum (security, applications, hardware, software, etc.). Each change has the potential to disrupt customer service. The task of Change Management is to minimize the service disruption caused by installing these "improvements."

COMMENT

Change Management encompasses all changes to controlled items in the Configuration Management Database. However, each IT department must decide where to draw the line between a minor change (such as adding a person to the access list of a database) and a significant change that must be controlled.

To do this, Change Management works with everyone else to ensure that all changes to controlled items are made in a tightly controlled manner. Even those emergency changes that must go in *NOW* can be accommodated by the Change Management process. Change Management supports the organization by:

A. **Ensuring that the Change Package Is Complete.** The Change Manager verifies that the package for implementing the change is complete before it is offered for approval. The CMDB identifies relationships between CIs to ensure that everything touched by the change has been addressed in the package.

The Change Manager ensures that the change package has been tested to verify that it alters what it is supposed to alter and nothing else. This may be done along with the package submitter or in a separate environment.

A Change Back-Out Plan is created and tested so that the change can be reversed if problems arise. The back-out plan must also be tested. This is the Change Manager's primary tool for minimizing the service impact of a change gone wrong.

The Change Manager's recommendation for approval of the change includes an analysis of the change's risk of failure or negative impact on IT service. It also includes a review of the resources required and a recommended slot in the change calendar.

B. **Ensuring that Changes Are Scheduled.** Routine changes are scheduled in a published calendar known as the Forward Schedule of Changes (FSC). This plan is approved by both the various IT departments and the business it supports. Based on required availability, the calendar provides time windows for applying changes. As these windows fill up, everyone can see when a change can next be implemented. This involves the supported business in the discussion about priorities and change impact on availability (rather than IT making the call in a back room).

C.   **Ensuring that Changes Are Properly Approved.** Every change must be approved by either the Change Advisory Board (routine changes) or the Change Advisory Board Executive Committee (emergency or high impact changes). This board is an important hurdle for any change to pass.

Change Advisory Board members include business managers as well as the various technical disciplines. Everyone gets a chance to review the change package and comment on risks it might raise. This also provides advance warning to users so they are prepared for the change.

COMMENT

Configuration items to be changed should be tied to SLAs, which indicate which business managers must approve the change.

D.   **Performing a Past Change Review.** After a change is implemented, the Change Manager reviews the results. The first check is to verify that the change provided the desired result. Inputs may be customer complaints (the service desk can provide this data), resource contention, adequacy of the back-out plan (if used), etc. The driving issue is to learn from every change ways to improve and streamline the change management process.

COMMENT

Change Management is an area where IT has consistently stumbled. It may be possible to sneak in 100 changes without the supported business realizing it was done—but that one change that flops will be the one remembered and repeated in meetings for months. This isn't idle complaining—business managers are trying to tell IT management just how important stability is to their operations.

[F]   Release Management

Release Management, as the name implies, controls the release of approved changes. It is closely linked to Change Management and, in some companies, is accomplished by the same team. However, in that case, care must be taken to ensure it does not dilute Release Management's role for ensuring that the change package is correct and ready for installation. It also works closely with Configuration Management to ensure that the released package's software is properly licensed and the CMDB is updated. Release Management ensures that changes to the production environment are completed with minimal disruption to existing service.

Release Management's testing procedures and pre-implementation checklists are IT's last defense against a poorly designed change. Procedures set up each release like its own small project. The details of Release Management include:

A. **Resources.** The resources required to ensure that people with the right skills are on hand or on standby as needed. For example, a network expert, a systems administrator, security technician, desktop repairman, etc. This includes contact information and information about whether they will work on site or remotely.

B. **Task List.** A list of release implementation tasks to ensure that everything is completed in the correct sequence.

C. **Timing.** Times required for each task can be gathered during the release package testing.

D. **Education.** An explanation of the changes made and how the service desk should handle calls concerning the changes (errors, complaints about the way the interface looks, etc.).

Release Management controls access to two important repositories:

A. The "Definitive Software Library" (DSL) of last known good copies. Release Management holds software licenses for purchased packages and validates licenses before installation. It is also the physical storage location of all software. The definitive copies of the software may be secured in the configuration management database.

B. The "Definitive Hardware Store" (DHS) is a secure area for storing emergency hardware spares. Items are used based on approved releases.

COMMENT

Release Management publishes a policy so that the IT department and the business users understand how the release of new systems (hardware, software, or a combination of the two) will be managed. The policy details various situations and how they will be addressed, such as emergency changes, required testing and documentation, how versions will be identified, etc.

[G] Continual Service Improvement

Companies operate within an ever changing business and regulatory environment. For IT departments, this is further complicated by evolving technologies, which replace or complement current IT capabilities. Continuous improvement is a process for the IT staff to evolve.

Originally, continuous improvement was a process for learning from our mistakes. We planned an action, performed it, evaluated it and then planned an improvement. Then the cycle was repeated. Whenever someone in IT made a significant mistake, or a major system failed, the team was gathered after the recovery to review what happened in order to plan what will be changed for future situations. The continual service improvement function formalizes this requirement.

It is not necessary to sit and wait for something to break. Every vital business function should include performance metrics that are routinely monitored and analyzed. This improves business resilience by identifying problems as they build but before they strike. This ranges from the ever-shrinking available disk space to lengthening response time on important customer entry screens.

Continual Service Improvement involves every member of the IT team. A successful program trains everyone on how to break down a problem situation to uncover the root cause of the situation. Often cross-functional teams from the various IT disciplines are necessary to capture all dimensions of a situation.

§ 4.04 ITIL SERVICE DELIVERY

[A] Service Level Management

Service Level Management is the primary interface between the customer and IT. It negotiates cost effective service level agreements with customers and then works within the IT organization and external vendors to ensure the desired level can be provided. The agreed services and support levels are detailed in the service catalog which is created and maintained by Service Level Management.

COMMENT

A customer is the person who has authority to describe and approve services to be provided to that business group. Users are the workers who use the services negotiated.

The Service Level Manager stands with one foot in the customer's world and one in IT. This person must speak both "business language" and "IT jargon." Service Level Management uses three different types of agreements to match requirements to resources:

A. **Service Level Agreements** (SLAs) are negotiated with customers to provide the level of service they desire, at a cost they can afford. By discussing these agreements in advance, the customer's service expectations can be set. SLAs are written using nontechnical terms. They contain the "what" that will be provided and not the "how."

B. **Operational Level Agreements** (OLAs) are agreements between the various IT departments and Service Level Management to provide the types and levels of service requested by the customer. This might be response times, hours of support, etc. If the requested support involves additional cost (for example, Saturday support for a specific application), then that cost is provided to the customer to pay or to drop that requirement.

C. **Underpinning Agreements** are made with external vendors to provide specific services, at a set cost, and within specified time frames. Typical examples are hardware repair, external network repair, pre-negotiated "best price" hardware purchase agreements, etc.

Service Level Management monitors the performance of the IT organization for meeting these promised levels to demonstrate to the customer how well IT is meeting its obligations and to demonstrate how well the IT internal organization provides its promised support. Reports on service quality are periodically reviewed with customers along with things that could be added or changed to improve service support.

[B]   Financial Management for IT Services

IT is an expensive part of any business. Every aspect of its organization is expensive: equipment, technician salaries, maintenance agreements and a never-ending requirement to purchase upgrades. Without the proper level of funding, IT cannot operate. Without accountability for its expenses, there is no incentive to improve service and drive down costs. ITIL addresses this important area through the Financial Management for IT Services (FMITS) function. FMITS includes the following:

A.   Budgeting. IT departments have long maintained budgets. A budget has many important uses:

1. Projects financial requirements for future periods. An approved budget sets a management limit on spending per time period (usually a month).
2. Provides a baseline for gauging performance (budget versus actual).
3. Ensures adequate funding will be available when it is needed.
4. Projects major future purchases, such as mainframe software license renewal or major item replacement.

COMMENT

Budgets are a reflection of an operating plan. Once an IT department completes its annual operating plan, then the budget represents the cost to implement that plan. Sometimes, the cost is too high and the operating plan must be reduced to a financially acceptable level.

The IT budget funds support of its service levels. Based on the SLAs in place, the budget can be built from the ground up. Add in overhead expenses, salaries, and long-term commitments. The result is a month-by-month annual operating budget.

B. Auditable Results. Once the budget is approved, the planned expenses are compared to actual expenditures. If something costs more than planned, then an analysis must determine if it was incorrectly estimated or if the cost exceeds expectation. ITIL emphasizes cost effective service. Over budget items may indicate a service issue that the IT Manager was not aware of.

Tracking of actual costs provides:

1. A process for generating financial reports, since the data to track actual versus budget is already maintained.
2. A historical tool for estimating future expenses.

C. Cost Recovery. "To charge, or not to charge. THAT is the question!" Some IT departments charge the departments that they support for everything they do—and others do not. The value of charging is that those who use it pay for it. This rewards those who economize and use it the least. Charging for service implies there is a way to collect data on usage and a chart of how much each service charges. The hurdle for most organizations is building this data collection process.

Charging for services is a cost recovery issue. IT only exists to support the company and some departments use it heavily. Others do not. Some demanding executives can drive costs up by requiring services that help them but whose costs far outweigh the benefits. However, if they paid for what they requested, the hope is they would moderate their demands.

Some companies implement an internal chargeback process without the intention of collecting any cash. It is used to demonstrate where the IT expenses are applied.

The ability to charge for a service can shape customer demand for it. Imagine a customer demanding service desk support on Sunday mornings. If two workers are scheduled to work in the office, should a service desk technician sit idle for most of eight hours just in case they are needed? Should the departments who do not work weekends pay for this person to wait for the telephone to ring?

[C] Availability Management

Availability Management focuses attention on ensuring IT services are active and available as required by approved SLAs. It works closely with the Change Advisory Board to minimize service availability impact whenever changes are implemented.

However, Availability Management is so much more. In addition to scheduling changes, it proactively roots out anything that reduces availability. It works closely with other ITIL teams to review technologies to make them quicker to change in a crisis or easier to maintain. Availability Management includes:

A. **System Resiliency.** Availability Management constantly scans the performance of systems to detect any that are drifting out of compliance. This might be a software application or piece of hardware that was designed for far fewer users than seem to be using it now. It might be the addition of a significant amount of online disk storage that requires longer to backup and is now encroaching on required uptime.

An important part of Availability Management is to review reports about problems that resulted in downtime. Availability Management may apply various tools to dig into recurring issues to identify the root cause of problems, such as Component Failure Impact Analysis.

Whenever new systems are proposed, Availability Management reviews the technical architecture for potential problems. This might be identification of single points of failure, the amount of load applied to equipment, and the types of tests to be used prior to implementation.

Another systems resiliency issue is to improve the speed at which problems are detected. It is possible to detect and repair problems that result in downtime, but that have no impact to the customer. The key is to discover them before the customer does, and repair them promptly.

B. **New Technology.** Availability may be enhanced by the introduction of new technology. The Availability Manager constantly scans the press looking for new technology that can improve the existing systems, in particular new technology that reduces costs, increases availability, or improves ease of maintenance. However, this should be primarily proven new technology. Otherwise, it will only introduce more instability into IT systems.

C. **Maintainability.** A well-designed IT system is built to be easily maintained. It follows published IT department standards and only uses approved technologies. The involvement of the Availability team early in the system development lifecycle enables them to point out areas to avoid or to include in the design. This enables faster problem resolution and improved system uptime.

[D] Capacity Management

Capacity Management is based on the concept of "enough"—will there be enough IT resources to meet demand? Capacity Management assists in the proper sizing of resources to meet desired service levels.

Capacity Management requires the constant monitoring of resource usages. Usage can be segmented by shift, by day of week, time of year, location in the company's business cycle, etc. It also monitors usage trends to detect threats to maintaining an adequate resource buffer. All of this information is maintained in the Capacity Database.

Capacity Management creates the Capacity Plan, which includes resource utilization for existing and planned systems. The Capacity Plan assists in the timely (and cost effective) purchase of additional resources (rather than a panic purchase when resources run out).

Demand for resources is rarely level. An important aspect of Capacity Management is to determine the peak usage times for each system and to encourage users to spread out their work. Demand Management seeks to reduce peak loads by shifting users to off-peak times. One way is to raise user rates for peak time (if internal chargeback is in place). The best way is to work with customers to demonstrate how the cost of their SLA will be lower by assisting in reducing the peak capacity requirements.

COMMENT

IT vendors and some applications developers demand the allocation of extensive hardware resources to their product. This may provide it with better performance. It may also result in large amounts of expensive idle resources. An important tool for Capacity Management is to performance test every application prior to its implementation. This ensures that it will have adequate resources for its anticipated workload based on need instead of arbitrary estimates.

[E] IT Service Continuity Management

Despite the best planning efforts, something will go wrong. The fault may be due to human error, sabotage, severe weather, hardware failure—any number of things. To maintain service credibility, ITIL specifies IT Service Continuity Management (ITSCM). ITSCM includes:

A. **Business Impact Analysis.** Different IT systems provide different degrees of benefit to the company. A Business Impact Analysis is conducted with the business departments to identify their critical business functions, and the financial (or legal) impact of an outage over an hour, four hours, 24 hours, two days, one week, and two weeks. The goal is to identify the true IT Vital Business Functions that ITIL focuses its efforts on supporting.

In most organizations, this will be approximately 25 percent of their IT systems. This small set must be protected from interruption. If the remaining IT systems are interrupted, customers are annoyed but damage to the company is minimal.

B. **Disaster Recovery.** IT shops have long maintained some sort of disaster recovery plan—even if it was just a set of data backup tapes. Disaster recovery is a subset of ITSCM. Disaster recovery is activated after a disaster occurs whose damage is so extensive that the data center must be moved elsewhere (to another room or another town). This is a serious service disruption. Disaster recovery strives to keep the business alive (at a cost of additional labor, additional errors, and reduced performance) until a permanent solution can be implemented. It is rarely invoked and therefore considered by many IT executives to be of minimal importance.

Disaster recovery is the cheapest plan to implement but it is all cost since the benefits are not realized until there is a disaster. There are several ways to recover a destroyed data center:

1. Do nothing in advance and figure it out later. This is a CIO gambler's position—it may never occur while I am in charge of IT, so why do it?

2. Cold site—renting a prepared data center shell (no computers) that is ready on request. The company must provide its own equipment to activate it.

3. Hot site—an expensive safety net where a data center and equipment is standing by for use when needed. This provides the quickest recovery.

C. **Business (Service) Continuity.** Business Continuity is the activity that most people think of when they say Disaster Recovery. Business Continuity risk reduction actions minimize interruptions from the many small disasters that occur in a typical workday. Examples are Uninterruptible Power Supplies (UPS) to avoid short-term power outages, locks on the data center doors to prevent sabotage, and RAID disks to recover if a disk drive fails.

A Business Continuity Plan contains a disaster recovery plan as one part of its recovery options. ITSCM works closely with Availability Management to keep vital systems running whatever the disruption may be.

D. **Keeping the plan current.** Keeping ITSCM plans current can be quite time consuming. The key is to be involved with project and resource expansions during the proposal stage to ensure that vital business system expansions include funds for the Business Continuity program. Otherwise, this funding must come later and creates considerable ill will in the organization.

E. **Testing.** Whatever plan is chosen, it is important that the plan is tested at least annually. Since it is unlikely that a data center or a significant amount of its resources can be turned off for a simulated disaster, testing is normally accomplished on related subsets of equipment. Testing not only debugs the continuity/disaster plans (pointing out unreported upgrades, errors and omissions) but it also trains the participants.

COMMENT

Much of an IT department's business continuity instructions are spread across the file cabinets and sticky notes on team member desks. Collecting all of these into one place is a quick way to begin the document creation process.

§ 4.05   ITIL CERTIFICATION

[A]   Training and Exams

Mastering ITIL, like anything else, requires study. The surest way to learn about it is to attend formal training class and study the books available. Ideally, companies adopting ITIL will seed their organization with experienced, certified professionals who can mentor their coworkers and help them understand the ITIL study materials.

[B]   Foundations

The Foundations certification demonstrates a familiarity with ITIL practice areas, guiding concepts and terminology. IT professionals can self-study for this certification or attend a training session which provides a deeper explanation. Passing the certifying exam is one way to measure the effectiveness of the training. It is also worth 2 ITIL credits toward the 17 total credits required to be eligible for the IT Expert rating.

A Foundations certification is an excellent way to introduce all IT staff members to the ITIL way, as it touches on all service areas. Many companies send their entire IT staff to Foundations training so they will understand the basic terminology of ITIL and the different service management areas.

COMMENT

Foundations' training is also beneficial to end users who work closely with their IT department.

There are no prerequisites to sitting for Foundations exam, but experience working in IT makes the concepts much easier to understand. Foundations' training is also recommended for business staffs who work closely with IT technicians.

[C]   Intermediate Level

The Intermediate Level certification program focuses on single areas of ITIL Service Lifecycle or Service Capability. There is one Intermediate Level exam for each ITIL Service Delivery or Service Support area.

Service Lifecycle—3 ITIL credits each toward ITIL Expert

- Service Strategy Qualification—techniques, guidelines for designing and implementing IT Service management for an organization.
- Service Design Qualification—designing and implementing service processes.
- Service Transition—organizing and implementing the transition to IT Service management.
- Service Operation Qualification—an understanding of the four main service areas: service desk, technical management, IT operations management, and application management.
- Continual Service Improvement—the tools and processes for continuously improving service management.

Service Capability—4 ITIL credits each toward ITIL Expert

- Service Offerings and Agreements—managing the portfolio of services in the company catalog.
- Release, Control, and Validation—managing controlled change, configurations, and deployment of technology.
- Operational Support and Analysis—management of incidents, events, and problems in a service management environment.
- Planning, Protection, and Optimization—planning, capacity planning, service continuity, and information security.

The prerequisites to sit for an Intermediate Level exam are:

A. Possess an ITIL Foundations certificate.
B. Recommended two years' general experience in an IT service management area.
C. Attend a course by an accredited training organization (self-study is not an option).

[D]   ITIL Expert Level

In the ITIL version 2 certification program, the highest level was ITIL Service Manager. Under version 3, this is now known as ITIL Expert. An ITIL Expert has demonstrated a broad understanding of a significant portion of the ITIL areas as well as how they all work together.

§ 4.05[E]

There are several steps to the certification. First, an adequate number of the intermediate certifications must be earned. Next there is a required training class and examination on "Managing Across the Lifecycle" which integrates the various Intermediate Level certifications into a coherent overall service management approach. The prerequisites for certifying as an ITIL Expert are:

A. Possess an ITIL Foundations certificate—two ITIL credits.
B. Possess at least 15 credits from Intermediate Level certifications.
C. Pass the "Managing Across Lifecycles" examination.
D. Five years' general experience in an IT service management area, with two of those years in a supervisory position.
E. Attend a course by an accredited training organization (self-study is not an option). During the training, the candidate must receive a positive assessment by the instructor for completion of class assignments.

[E]   ITIL Master Level

The highest level of ITIL certification is the ITIL Master Level rating. Unlike the other levels, the examination for this level is to explain and justify how the ITIL principles, techniques, and artifacts are applied to a given business situation. The candidate develops a detailed proposal for applying ITIL to a situation, conducts the work, and then submits a package detailing what happened.

The proposal must follow the defined outline of the certifying agency. It can address an existing problem and how the ITIL practitioner will address it, or can refer to a previous assignment. However, the application process must be completed within 24 months unless an extension is granted.

Once the proposal document has been accepted, the candidate proceeds to develop a package detailing the work. Examples are provided that demonstrate the application of ITIL principles. The solution applied is described along with the benefits to the organization. As the work package is the substance of the application for Master rating, it must address every one of the ITIL areas described in the proposal.

Once the work package is approved, the candidate is invited for an interview by a panel of experts. The panel asks probing questions about the project and ITIL in general. The goal is to ensure that the work was truly done by the candidate. The candidate can also answer any questions about those parts of the work package that the panel considers to be weak.

There are two eligibility requirements for the ITIL Master rating. The candidate must possess the ITIL Expert rating and possess five years' of experience in a managerial or leadership role.

See Policy ITP-04-2 ITIL Training Program as an example policy relating to training of IT personnel in ITIL processes.

POLICY ITP-04-2.   ITIL Training Program

Policy #:	ITP-04-2	Effective:	04/01/13	Page #:	1 of N
Subject:	ITIL Training Program				

1.0 PURPOSE

This policy requires the training of all IT personnel in the appropriate ITIL processes.

2.0 SCOPE

The policy applies to all personnel within the IT department, to include applications development and management, system administration, IT administrative processes, Data Operations, networks, outsourced labor or services, and all other areas under the IT Director's direction. This does not apply to IT contractors brought in for less than four months.

3.0 POLICY

Formal training in the ITIL processes is required for all personnel.

A. ITIL Training Administrator

The IT Director will appoint a staff member to act (either full- or part-time) as the ITIL Training Administrator. That person is responsible for implementing this policy and for recommending changes to it.

B. Training Required

Once per quarter, the IT Training Administrator will conduct an onsite class on ITIL Foundations. This three-day class of no more than 15 students at a time will review the ITIL Foundation's curriculum and the way it is implemented at this company. The course will include exercises to assess the student's understanding of the material.

The day after the course is completed, the Foundations exam will be given. Any student who fails the exam will sit in the next Foundations class. Any student who fails the examination twice will be dismissed from the company as not technically qualified to hold his or her position.

C. Optional Training Is Encouraged

Intermediate level certification is encouraged for all employees. All IT Operations personnel are encouraged to train for and pass the ITIL exams pertaining to their area within two years of employment.

The ITIL Training Administrator will assess the need and employee interest for each class. If at least five students can attend, the ITIL Training Administrator will arrange to conduct the class on site.

If fewer than five students is anticipated for a class, then the ITIL Training Administrator will select a training provider and negotiate the best rate.

Students attending one of the Intermediate level courses are required to take the exam. Any employee passing one of the Intermediate Exams will receive an extra five days' vacation to be used within 12 months. If the employee fails it twice, then he or she is ineligible to attend any future company-sponsored ITIL Intermediate training classes.

§ 4.05[E]

The Intermediate ITIL classes are:

1. Service Lifecycle—3 ITIL credits each toward ITIL Expert
   a. Service Strategy Qualification—techniques, guidelines for design-ing and implementing IT Service management for an organization.
   b. Service Design Qualification—designing and implementing service processes.
   c. Service Transition—organizing and implementing the transition to IT Service management.
   d. Service Operation Qualification—an understanding of the four main service areas: service desk, technical management, IT opera-tions management, and application management.
   e. Continual Service Improvement—the tools and processes for con-tinuously improving service management.
2. Service Capability—4 ITIL credits each toward ITIL Expert
   a. Service Offerings and Agreements—managing the portfolio of ser-vices in the company catalog.
   b. Release, Control, and Validation—managing controlled change, configurations, and deployment of technology.
   c. Operational Support and Analysis—management of incidents, events, and problems in a service management environment.
   d. Planning, Protection, and Optimization—planning, capacity plan-ning, service continuity, and information security.

For the ITIL Expert Level, the ITIL Training Administrator will select a train-ing provider and negotiate the best rate. Employees achieving the ITIL Expert Level will be rewarded with a $5,000 bonus (assuming they remain with the company for at least one year thereafter). They will also be occasionally tasked with teaching the company's ITIL Foundations classes.

D. Training Reporting
The ITIL Training Administrator will maintain records on:

1. training provided
2. training required
3. copies of all employees' ITIL certifications

Based on these records, the ITIL Training Administrator will budget and schedule refresher training as needed. As the ITIL program continues to evolve, the training program will be updated.

The ITIL Training Administrator will post a certification chart indicating which IT employee has achieved which ITIL certification(s).

E. Reference Library
The ITIL Training Administrator will establish and maintain a library of ITIL reference materials (preferably online). Other useful materials in the library may include company best practices summaries, self-paced training materials,

and case studies of similar companies' ITIL experiences. Access to this library will be controlled by the ITIL Training Administrator.

4.0 REVISION HISTORY

Date	Revision #	Description of Change
04/01/13	1.0	Initial creation.

5.0 INQUIRIES

Direct inquiries about this policy to:
George Jenkins, CIO
Our Company, Inc.
2900 Corporate Drive
Columbus, OH 43215

Voice: 614-555-1234
Fax: 614-555-1235
E-mail: gjenkins@company.com

Revision #:	1.0	Supersedes:	N/A	Date:	04/01/13

§ 4.06 ITIL AS AN OFFICIAL STANDARD

[A] Standards—Why Bother?

Companies engage in an ongoing struggle with their competitors. One area is in delivery credibility to their customers. How can a new customer without boundless time to investigate a company gauge if a supplier has the expertise and efficiency to reliably handle its business?

Conversely, how can companies stand out from among the crowd? What independent proof can they show that they are well managed, efficient, and dependable?

The concept of a standards organization is to identify the most effective and efficient way to run some aspect of the business and then to live up to that high mark. Further, an outside organization inspects the company to identify areas of improvement and to certify that they essentially meet the published standards.

[B] British Standard

ITIL's wide acceptance in the UK and British Commonwealth led to its adoption as the basis for the official British Standard (BS 15000). BS 15000 was an attempt to establish an idea of what an efficient and effective IT organization would do. It focuses on:

A. Service Delivery Processes
B. Relationship Processes
C. Resolution Processes
D. Release Processes
E. Control Processes

[C] International Standards Organization

Manufacturing companies have long sought ISO 9000 certification to demonstrate to prospective customers that they may be relied upon to deliver high quality products. But what about a company that sells data processing services? Or what if a company's products depend heavily on data systems? How may they demonstrate to prospective customers the high quality of such an intangible thing as IT service?

COMMENT

The International Organization for Standards can be located on the Internet at *www.ISO.org*.

Over the years, ITIL's appeal expanded worldwide to countries that do not recognize the British Standards within their own countries. (This may sound silly to some people, but to others it must be important! After all, a good idea is a good idea.) So BS 15000 was used as the basis for ISO 20000.

ISO standards have long been used as an indication of a well-run company. Many organizations have seen the benefits of adopting ISO practices to improve their operating efficiencies and product quality. However, there was a gap in the data processing part of the business—a part that drives the performance of the rest of the company.

An ISO audit begins with an initial assessment that provides a baseline from which to measure progress, and some ideas of where the greatest effort is needed. After a company has implemented all of the requirements, the auditors come through for a certifying inspection. This is a pass/fail review. Even companies who pass may have a long list of things that must be promptly addressed. To maintain their ISO certification, the organization must be re-inspected at least every three years thereafter.

Also, companies may not demonstrate their expertise by certifying as "ITIL compliant" since no such company certification program exists. However, companies may now be certified as ISO 20000 compliant. ISO certification requires an examination by a third party to certify the degree of conformance.

Preparing for an ISO examiner forces a company to review and improve its internal processes to obtain or maintain certification.

ISO 20000 was recently updated to emphasize continuous improvement as an integral part of any IT activity. Often seen as after action reviews or "post mortems" after a serious incident, continuous improvement requires companies to examine and learn from their mistakes.

Conformance tells customers and company executives that the IT organization follows industry best practices.

§ 4.07 IMPLEMENTING ITIL

[A] ITIL Changes Everything IT

ITIL is a unique way of running a business. Many companies do some aspect of it in some places, so some of the concepts are not new. What is new is how ITIL forces these disparate pieces to work together toward a common goal. Introducing ITIL is recognition that ad hoc processes of the past must give way to mature IT processes in the future.

IT departments evolve over time. There are people who were there from the first day to people who were just hired. Each person has their own collection of ideas, motivations, and practices that worked successfully for him in the past. Implementing ITIL means overcoming the reluctance of many key IT participants to work closely together. Yet these same people will acknowledge the benefits if asked individually. Therefore, to overcome team members' reluctance, strong executive leadership is necessary. (A weak leader will lead the ITIL rollout project to ruin in a few months.)

The first step is a clear vision of what you hope to achieve from implementing ITIL. Begin with an honest assessment of how the IT department provides services today.

A. How is the IT department functionally organized?
B. What does each function do?
C. What are each function's responsibilities to technology management, to customer service, to supporting internal IT processes?
D. What benefits does each functional group provide?
E. What service level agreements (SLAs) are in place?
F. What databases exist that describe IT assets, processes, or knowledge?

[B] ITIL Implementation Leader

Implementing a change in an organization requires overcoming the reluctance of the people within it. A heavy-handed approach may provide quick results but generate long-term animosity for the implementation leader and the new process. As soon as the pressure is off, all of the disliked changes are discarded. The concept of leadership is to guide people in the desired direction and to gain their willing cooperation.

The ITIL implementation leader provides the vision (used at the many decision points), provides encouragement, and breaks down the barriers to progress. The ITIL leader also acts as the team's cheerleader when the opposition seems to be insurmountable. IT executives can keep this person focused by tying his or her future bonuses and raises to that project's progress.

Some companies feel that the internal battles will be too bruising and damaging for an internal project manager to survive. Therefore, they bring in a consultant to manage implementation. This external resource lacks institutional knowledge and must refer to internal team leaders for information when adjusting ITIL concepts to local situations.

The leader must overcome reluctance through constant dialogue, listen to concerns, and address them promptly. Overcoming these concerns will remove some of the "fear of change" from the team.

COMMENT

An ITIL rollout may take up to two years depending on the size of the organization, its commitment to change, etc. An efficient rollout should proceed with minimum customer disruption. However, the longer a project takes to complete, the more likely it is to drift off course or to be cancelled uncompleted.

[C]   Configuration Management Database (CMDB)

A considerable amount of time is spent selecting a configuration management database. This tool can be expensive to purchase, load with data, and maintain. Many companies offer one, or a standard database tool currently in use can be adapted. However, establishing the many interlocking views of the data may make purchasing an already configured tool the best choice.

There are several important collections of data to load into this database. This is where the detailed analysis of existing databases, processes, and SLAs pay off. First, load all of the asset information into the database, including capacity planning information, information of the applications run on each server, and so on. There is quite a lot of information that likely must come from several sources.

Next, create the tables necessary to begin using the CMDB's service management module for the service desk. To this, add the SLAs with connections to the assets. This tells the service desk the priority for service calls as it includes the impact and severity for each item.

Creating a complete CMDB can take years. Each company must identify the point of diminishing returns and cut off adding more data elements. Each element has its own costs in maintenance to keep the data current, cost for disk storage, etc.

COMMENT

IT departments are heavily dependent on outside suppliers. Consider, who provides hardware maintenance for servers? Who provides patches for purchased software? The list can be extensive. For IT to meet its service-level objectives, these critical suppliers must meet theirs. Include key suppliers in the ITIL rollout process to ensure they do not become the weak link.

[D]   Introduce ITIL to One Area at a Time

For many companies, ITIL rollout begins at the service desk. They likely already have a Help Desk of some sort so this transition will seem easy at first. Also, better customer service is an easy sell to executives.

Rollout changes in a series of small tasks. Select the first few carefully for a series of quick successes. This helps to justify the ongoing expense and to build momentum for the changes. Carefully publicize ITIL's business alignment at every opportunity.

Training is essential to a successful rollout. Training for the IT staff tells them what needs to be done and how to do it. Training for IT executives helps them to identify decision points and make the trade-off decisions necessary to implement this process. Training for key end users is also necessary if they are to understand their role in a successful operation.

Ideally, training is completed just before it is needed and provided in a classroom for all affected staff. In reality, this is very expensive both for the instructor and for the lost labor of the participants. Therefore, training is usually provided to a key few participants with the rest picking up their skills through reading, in-house newsletters, and one-on-one coaching.

5

IT QUALITY MANAGEMENT: THE KEY TO PREDICTABLE RESULTS

§ 5.01 OVERVIEW

[A] Purpose and Scope

Quality is one of those things that everyone agrees is good but never seem to find the time to implement. It will not be applied to the IT department unless the IT Director takes a personal interest in launching a coordinated effort and then sustaining it through ongoing team emphasis.

People purchase a product or service to solve a business problem. In exchange for money and a bit of their time, the product relieves them of a problem. The extent that the product provided aligns with their desired outcome is the degree of customer satisfaction. Quality is always defined from the customer's perspective. Doing an excellent job on something the customer does not value is an aspect of poor quality (inefficient use of resources).

IT's internal customers are the other IT groups whose collective success is the success of the IT department. Applications development needs prompt and accurate service from the Systems Administrators. The network team needs accurate problem reports from the Help Desk, and so on. It is essential that these services add to the department's agility and speed of completion and not hinder it.

IT's external customers have nowhere else to turn to for their IT support. They must come to the IT department for essential services. They highly value prompt and effective solutions to their problems and dread multiple calls to accomplish the same basic tasks. This illustrates a basic requirement of IT services. Everyone wants predictable outcomes that provide what they need, when they need it.

Predictability reduces problems requiring management attention. If the Help Desk always answers the telephone within two rings, then the only management issue is when the calls ring to the backup support desks. Management by exception is a significant way to save time. It works best when a process provides reliable outcomes. In this example, callers prefer an answer within two rings to the Help Desk. In addition, they prefer talking to a person over voice mail. This is an example of "good enough" versus perfect. We can always make "good enough" into excellent, but given resource constraints, most IT departments focus on fixing what is broken before improving on what works.

The question becomes how the IT Manager can gauge the true quality of the department's services. One source is the volume of customer complaints. Another source is the number of software crashes or equipment outages (downtime) during working hours. Each indicates a process failure of some type. Some of these may have been detectable prior to failure through the collection and monitoring of process metrics. The collection of process performance metrics moves process monitoring from success or failure to trending performance toward either result, along with potential early failure warning.

The next logical step is how the IT Director can resolve the department's quality problems. Obvious solutions can be quickly implemented but what about solutions that are not clear to anyone? What basic techniques can be applied?

Two important characteristics of a process are its effectiveness and its efficiency. Effectiveness is how closely the outcome conforms to the expected result. Efficiency indicates that minimal resources were expended to obtain the intended result. Performance measurements should indicate both of these dimensions so that, as required, processes can be improved. IT departments whose processes are both effective and efficient will be judged to be, "well run."

Leaders set the tone for process quality efforts through their actions. If they pay close attention to the steps for ensuring quality, then so will the IT team. A proactive quality management program can bring significant savings by identifying serious errors in products or services prior to their release. A quality program that maintains a high standard for products or services is profitable because it brands the company as highly competent.

IT Managers have long complained about the small size of their staff in relation to the workload. Requests for additional people are frequently rejected. Before trying to justify additional people, the IT Manager must ensure that the existing staff is effectively utilized.

Never assume that because a process exists that it is efficient. Never assume that because the IT staff looks busy that they are focused on the department's priorities. People naturally reshape their workflows for their own convenience. They may skip steps, change the workflow, and schedule activities according to their personal preference instead of the department's priority. Without oversight of process execution, no one ever knows! IT Managers must ensure that their team is effectively assigned to the highest department priorities.

As the leader, the IT Manager must develop a program to assure that all IT products and services remain aligned with customer requirements. As their wants and needs change as the company's customer's desires change, it is not unusual to realign IT deliverables. Every IT work team must determine what local quality of service they intend to provide.

[B] Basic Terms

Like all technical disciplines, quality management has its own terminology. This enables quality professionals to exchange information with specific understanding:

A. **Quality assurance** includes the many things done to ensure the success of an effort before it begins.
B. **Quality control** addresses actions after the process is complete to identify and correct problems before the product or service is delivered to the customer.
C. A **metric** is a quantifiable characteristic of a process. It may be an input, an output, or something that occurs during processing.
D. **Effectiveness** is the correct solution to the problem.
E. **Efficiency** is the use of minimal resources to solve a problem.

[C] Critical Policies to Develop Based on This Chapter

Using the material discussed in this chapter, you will be able to:

A. Define the process for managing the IT department's Quality Program.

    B. Create a policy requiring that all documented processes include verifiable measurements of effectiveness before implementation.

    C. Create a policy for the collection and tracking of reported defects and early detection.

    D. Create a policy for reporting compliance to approved process.

    E. Determine root cause of critical or systemic problems.

Policies should always be developed based on the local situation. Successful managers cannot issue appropriate guidance if the policies are written with another company's situation or location in mind.

§ 5.02 START WITH A QUALITY MANAGEMENT PLAN

[A] Overview

Quality is not an all or nothing effort. It begins with a framework that is fleshed out as the program progresses. The first step is to recognize the need for a coordinated quality effort. A look around the current team may find areas where individual groups have created their own informal quality efforts.

The whole is always more powerful than the sum of the individuals, so pulling everything together into a coherent program will increase its benefit to the company. The goal is to obtain consistently excellent results through the use of best practices. Some parts of the plan will be applicable to everyone in the department—some will be specific to a team. However, without a formal program in place, the results will be uneven.

Appointing someone in the IT department as the "Quality Manager" establishes responsibility for someone to coordinate the program. However, this step does not absolve anyone of their individual responsibilities of ensuring quality in their individual efforts.

[B] Measuring Process Effectiveness

Each process provides some service to a department or to the company. Before a process can deliver "quality," we must know what quality for that particular task would be. Quality is measurable. Every technical specification in the scope of work must include a description of how to measure it. Measurement indicates the degree of conformity of the delivered product. Quality analysis is based on metrics.

The easiest evaluation to make is the GO/NO GO where the delivered product works or it does not. An example is a software program that is either working or is inoperable. When a customer uses the product, they validate functionality against product specifications (it suits their needs or not). Analysis can determine the degree of success.

For example, if the specification says to include a way to securely enter credit card information into a Web page, this might be measured with a Yes/No answer (the feature exists or it does not). However, if the specification is to validate the credit card number (as not stolen) within 1.25 seconds after the customer submits their information, then there is a measurable deliverable.

The quality delivered is the degree to which it achieves or surpasses the 1.25 seconds during peak usage.

There are two basic types of quality measurements:

A. **Objective measurements (the preferred type).** Objective measurements are finitely measurable in some way. When an objective measurement is assigned to a product specification, a description of how it is to be measured should be included. It is easiest to obtain customer agreement on how to measure something during its definition. An example of an objective measurement is a "GO/NO GO," or a number on a scale, such as the response time example mentioned previously.

B. **Subjective measurements (opinion based).** IT Managers avoid these since a person's opinion can vary from day to day. How can a measurement be created for a task whose completion is subject to a whim? An example of this type of measurement is a requirement to provide a "visually pleasing" Web page.

When possible, ensure that each task's quality measurements are objectively measured. This reduces arguments with the end users. As processes change, the corresponding quality measurement must also be updated. Example software metrics include the following:

A. **Availability**. Number of minutes in a day the software system is operational. Non-available time would be when it is down for data backups, service to hardware, service to intervening network devices, etc.

B. **Recoverability.** How long it takes to reload the software and data in case of a disaster. Software can be designed for recoverability through frequent database checkpoints, by journaling the data to an off-site location, or by identifying the minimal components for operation that restore basic service until the full system is reloaded. This is important when designing company-critical systems.

C. **Usability.** How much time is required for a user to learn how to use the system? Is it intuitively obvious or must a manual always be within reach? A data entry screen can be quickly thrown together, but one that is easy to understand where the data is logically linked and that provides clear messages of edit failures, takes a long time to complete.

COMMENT

The management maxim is that you get what you measure. Take care when selecting a metric as it may distort a department's performance.

Some example IT process metrics might be Help Desk number of calls per hour, response time for desktop hardware support, size of the applications backlog per team, or print room number of lines of print per day. This can break down further. The Help Desk calls could be tracked by type of call, originating department, or even day of the week.

The quality program in most IT departments is patchy. There may be a strong program for the testing of new application software but not a lot beyond that. Not that there is any lack of interest, but it never seems to rise to the top of the department's priorities. This will never change unless the IT Director takes a personal interest and mandates the program.

The first step is the creation of a quality policy. The policy sets the high-level goals and expectations for the program. The Quality Plan provides the details for achieving each of those goals. In most cases, the quality plan is updated annually with the funded goal for the fiscal year.

[C] Quality Policy

The quality policy is always signed by the highest level executive that will support your program. Often this is the leader of your company. This signature demonstrates the highest level of support and breaks down some of the internal barriers to its implementation.

Next is a statement about how the top executives support the quality program. Something like, "The XYZ Company has a total commitment to the delivery of high quality, and low cost goods and services to our customers." The IT Director can sign this but often the top business leaders like to issue a written policy governing the company's IT program.

The quality policy describes some broad objectives for the IT department. Team members can review these specific objectives and submit plans for fulfilling them in their own area. Some examples of this are:

- Consistently exceeding our customer's expectations for product quality and performance
- Ensure the efficient use of IT resources
- Timely delivery of products and services to meet our customer's requirements
- Continuous improvement of our processes and systems
- Ensuring our personnel are properly trained so they are better able to serve our customers
- Controlling processes with tools and techniques to achieve sustainable growth

[D] Quality Plan Requirements

The IT quality plan implements the quality policy. It draws on existing customer (internal and external) expectations for specific requirements. Quality standards may be the customer's policies, industry standards, or some mutually agreed to standards. The plan defines quality assurance, quality control, and continuous improvement aspects as they apply to the process.

The process's quality plan does not end on paper. It makes no difference to the customer if fault was due to a contractor or an employee. The quality plans for all critical contractors or suppliers must also be considered in the final plan—or each must adopt the same one as used by the process. If a contractor has its own quality plan, then review it to ensure that it essentially conforms to the process's plan or better.

[E] Quality Audits

Randomly audit portions of the IT department. A quality audit is an independent review of a process that verifies how closely it conforms to the published quality plan and company policies. The focus of an audit must be on identifying and correcting those actions, which will save money and time. They should never be punitive. If they are, then time will be wasted while team members raise defenses against them.

The quality audit also verifies that:

- The process uses approved tools and practices. Any new tools (such as forms or tracking documents) created or modified to address specific situations should be reviewed for use across the department.
- The accuracy and completeness of metrics used.
- The quality of the product created as compared to the current scope and criteria for success. Did the Process deliver the form, fit, and function requested?

Plan audits carefully. They may create delays in an otherwise on-schedule effort. A random audit detects problems before they become major issues. Remember to lavish praise twice as readily as condemnation. When well-running processes are found, be sure to recognize them as such.

[F] Process Documentation

A high quality process provides repeatable predictable results. To achieve this process documentation, begin with a description of what they do and how they do it. This description provides process stability. The goal is repeatability. At this point, changes can be introduced and their impact of the process determined. Quality measurements are also important for providing feedback on the accuracy of process documentation. Often processes are documented and then forgotten. A poorly performing process may not be executing as designed.

A process provides a particular service for someone. In the beginning, it is designed and approved by IT management for use. It reflects the tradeoff between resources available and the desired output at that point in time. For a process to be formally approved by the IT Manager, it must be described as written action steps. These steps describe what must be done in sequence to complete this service.

Say what you do, then do what you say. Simply the process of writing it down forces the IT team to examine what a process accomplishes and the resources required to run it. Documenting a process anchors it. Over time, there will be approved and unsanctioned changes to meet customer needs or more likely to meet the needs of the person performing the process. These changes may improve the process or they may make it less efficient. For each step of the process ask yourself, "would my customers pay me to do this?"

Documented processes tend to be stable processes. A stable, documented process allows the IT Manager to improve it. Since it is stable, any change made by the IT Manager will be the cause of any change in output. This enables experimenting with various mixtures of resources to obtain the optimal result. To document the team's processes:

A. **Create a standard format.** This enables everyone to quickly find the desired information in any work instruction since they are all organized in the same fashion. A standard format also speeds auditing of processes.

B. **Pilot it on your administrative process.** Everyone is in a hurry. The theory is to rush something in now and fix it later after we know more about it. "Later" never seems to come. Time spent documenting a few processes and working with the authors will result in consistent and complete documentation.

C. **Roll out to team leaders.** Ask each team leader to create a list of their most common processes and when the documentation will be ready.

D. **Peer review of processes.** Most processes touch other people. Reviewing in a team raises issues.

E. **Review at least annually.** Processes represent the business needs at a moment in time. As the weeks roll past, these specific needs may slowly change.

§ 5.03   QUALITY ASSURANCE OR QUALITY CONTROL

[A]   Overview

Quality has been defined by some people as "conformance to specification." Another way to state this is that it seeks to minimize performance errors. Quality efforts also strive to ensure the final product is fit for use. The two basic types of quality programs are assurance and control. In most processes, the same team member who is dedicated to the quality analysis program evaluates both. In a large team, there will be a different person for each function because the focus is different.

Quality inspection exists only because there are defects in the product or process. The real goal is to eliminate the need for expensive inspection and rework. If specifications were complete and the design was thoroughly reviewed prior to beginning the effort, then the quality is built in instead of added on later.

Work-product quality focuses on three areas:

A. **Prevention.** Evaluate processes and design them to avoid errors before they occur.

B. **Inspection.** Test and peer reviews to catch a problem with the product before the customer sees it. Inspection locates problems and tracks them until they are resolved.

C. **Lessons learned.** Conduct periodic reviews to spread the solution to issues among the rest of the IT team to prevent similar errors elsewhere.

[B]   Quality Assurance

Quality assurance encompasses all of the things done to ensure that a process has the best tools, utilizes a well-understood and tested process, and include tested materials and a clear description of the deliverables before it begins. In essence, quality assurance means that it takes good things into the process to get good things out of it. Its goal is to anticipate and prevent problems before they occur. An effective quality assurance program saves money by minimizing the rework of completed products. Quality assurance principles are applied to every task throughout the process even before it begins. Some of the areas where quality assurance is applied include:

A. **Tools**. Ensure that the team's tools (such as compilers, workstations, or even work areas) are reliable and suitable for the purpose allows for the work to flow smoothly. Reliable means that unstable software development tools or hardware are not passed to the team "just because they are convenient." Suitable to the purpose means that the team's tools provide adequate performance and are easy to use. Again, just because surplus Pentium III desktop PCs are "free" to the department (saving expense), does not mean that they should be used for time critical and calculation intensive applications.

B. **Processes**. Providing the team with efficient processes means that work flows smoothly. This defines performance standards, and the process for measuring and evaluating performance against these standards. Processes must be understood by those using them. This implies training for familiarization and time to develop expertise in their use.

C. **Design and analysis**. The greatest savings from quality is in the process's design. Design verification is the key to minimizing product rework:

   1. Ensuring the customer and/or process sponsor fully understands what problem they are trying to solve.

   2. Verifying the process scope, including everything necessary to solve that problem.

   3. Ensuring that all deliverables are clearly defined and objectively measurable.

   4. When appropriate, using prototyping of customer interfaces to verify everything required is in the process definition.

   5. For many processes, problems arise where they interface with other processes. To avoid conflicts, obtaining written agreement where subsystems integrate, on passing control, data, and any other process dependencies.

[C]   Quality Control

Verifying the results of completed work is the duty of quality control. Quality control compares the product or service created to the documented scope and specifications to ensure it meets the stated customer expectations. Errors are always cheaper to repair closest to where they occur. The quality control function minimizes the negative budget impact of errors.

Quality control inspection acts as the process's gatekeeper. Before delivering a task as complete, the quality control technician verifies that the finished piece meets all of the deliverables identified for it. Errors that evade detection here will be much more difficult to repair once they are embedded deep within a product.

Inspecting quality into a product is a long and expensive process. The person inspecting something must have the same or greater expertise with the object under review than the person who created it. Given the broad range of products and services used and provided by IT, this is a difficult position to fill. Usually it is a peer checking the work of another team member.

Inspection adds cost to a process that was likely never included in its original cost. Inspection should be used to gather data on performance. Problems found should be addressed. A process that needs constant inspection must be changed. The exception is for critical processes where any problem with their output must be promptly detected.

COMMENT

As soon as a new process has been debugged, switch from 100 percent inspection to sampling based on ANSI standards.

[D] Effectiveness vs. Efficiency

The effectiveness of IT actions is a key concern of both internal and external customers. Effectiveness deals with "getting it right" the first time. Although everyone feels that their efforts accomplish this, it is the customer's opinion— the opinion of the person using the product or service provided—that counts the most. To ensure that a quality result is provided, it must be measured from that person's perspective.

There are two basic measures of each process. The first is effectiveness, or does the process successfully provide the product or service it is expected to provide. For example, does the software correctly calculate the accounting ledgers? Is a user ID created with the appropriate system accesses? Is the IT work estimate accurate?

An efficient process uses the minimum amount of resources (time, people, consumables, machine time, etc.) to complete its result. For example, how archive data is packed onto the fewest backup media cartridges, an order entry program that runs very quickly, or even a new e-mail server that uses less electricity than its predecessor. An inefficient process will overrun its timelines and budget. Both of these circumstances irritate customers. If a process is not effective, it does not matter how efficient it is.

COMMENT

Consider for a moment, your daily commute to work. You could drive an economy car or an 18-wheeled semi-truck. Both will eventually carry you to your destination. That makes both of them effective solutions. However, the economy car burns far less fuel to complete the task and would be considered the more efficient of the two choices.

Processes address a business need at a particular point in time. Processes developed for the use of keypunch machines are no longer relevant no matter how effective or efficient they may be. Similarly, the everyday processes in use in an IT department may be less effective or efficient than they once were.

Examples of process outputs:

- Accuracy of the time and budget estimates
- Ability to issue timely reports and notices
- Speed with which issues are resolved
- Speed with which software change requests are addressed
- Efficient use of budget—is money wasted on express deliveries or late charges?

COMMENT

System and data recoverability may not be high on the designer's list but is an important quality criterion to the IT Manager.

[E]   IT Quality and ISO

The International Organization for Standardization (ISO) is a consortium that sets quality standards in a variety of areas. ISO standards provide an internationally recognized collection of best practices dedicated to customer satisfaction. (The ":2008" following each standard is the year of the standard's approval.)

ISO's purpose is to facilitate international trade by providing a single set of standards that people everywhere would recognize and respect. ISO focuses on:

A. **The customer.** Understand the customer's requirements and strive to exceed them.

B. **Company leadership.** Identify a unity of purpose and set the direction for the organization. Create a positive work environment that helps people to achieve the company's goals.

C. **Involve the team.** Help people to develop and use their abilities. Involve all management levels in the quality process in everything they do.

D. **Use a process approach.** Examine, document, and improve the processes throughout the organization.

E. **Use a systems approach.** Most company processes are interrelated, yet are managed separately. ISO encourages ignoring internal organizational boundaries and managing systems as a unit.

F. **Encourage continual improvement.** Businesses are pressured by a wide range of environmental forces.

G. **Get the facts before deciding.** Gather and analyze data about processes and their results. Use the data to identify the root cause of problems and address them.

H. **Work with suppliers.** The business between a company and its suppliers binds them together. Work as partners to improve customer satisfaction, to everyone's mutual benefit.

ISO provides standards for just about anything. There are many standards that apply to various aspect of IT. The most common standards used by companies are:

- ISO 9000:2008 is a quality system standard for any product, service, or process.
- ISO 9001:2008 is a quality system standard for design, production, and installation of a product or service.
- ISO 9004:2008 is a set of quality management guidelines for any organization to use to develop and implement a quality system.
- ISO 27001 is a set of standards for the proper implementation of Information Security (formerly ISO standard 17999).
- ISO 14001 a set of standards for the proper implementation of environmental management, of which IT is usually a significant contributor.

COMMENT

Two other important sources for IT quality assurance and control information are:
- Institute of Electrical and Electronics Engineers (IEEE) at *www.ieee.org*
- American Society of Quality (ASQ) at *www.asq.org*

§ 5.04 CONTINUOUS IMPROVEMENT

[A] Overview

Quality actions cannot be viewed as one-time measures that are "someone else's" responsibility. They must be a part of the IT team's culture. Nurturing a culture of quality falls squarely on the shoulders of the IT Director. If the IT Director displays a positive attitude toward efforts to identify and improve problem areas then so will the rest of the team. Then again, if the quality checks are the first thing discarded when times are tight, the IT team will notice and follow that example as well!

The best ideas for improving a process usually come from the people who execute the process. Some people will bubble forth with a steady stream of suggestions and others will sit quietly assuming their ideas have already been thought of before and discarded. Ensure that the entire team has an opportunity to participate. The IT Director must encourage a steady stream of process critiques to uncover those "critical few" time-saving suggestions.

Documentation provides an opportunity to review processes for problems. The closer that multiple processes are reviewed, the more that best practices are identified. Spreading best practices across the IT department enables the company to learn from past problems without paying to learn something a second time. For example, a simple tool for tracking customer requests or setting a destruction date for all department records (and freeing up online storage space for productive uses).

COMMENT

Carefully word process-improvement suggestions to ensure they are never misunderstood as personal attacks.

[B] Process Team Members Are the Key

Continuous improvement means every team member assists in improving the product or service's quality and the quality of the process's execution. If the team member's opinion is valued, then it will be offered. If it is ignored or berated, then a valuable source of continuous improvement information will be lost.

The following are used to evaluate the process.

A. **Critique processes.** What process tools have been provided to the team and are they adequate for the job? Are the tasks burdened with work that adds no value? Are there ways to meet work requirements while reducing time and expense?

B. **Critique process metrics.** Although the workers may have been involved with creating the original metrics, over time, they may feel differently about them now. These should be considered for revision during process reviews.

C. **Critique problems and incidents.** Based on the team's experience and customer complaints, what could have been done differently?

[C]   Open Discussions Are Valuable

Beyond the traditional quality assurance and control group is the use of peer reviews. Team members examine deliverables and process issues to offer recommendations. Peer reviews can be quickly coordinated and provide issue-specific suggestions for improvement.

Team meetings focused on production improvements can be very useful for surfacing obstacles and hindrances. Topics such as the flow of work into and out of the team, ready availability and quality of materials, and the availability of essential information when it is needed are all good topics.

[D]   Continuous Improvement Has Its Critics

Continuous improvement is based on identifying and implementing incremental changes to a process. Almost all of these changes are small. The idea is that many, many small changes can add up to significant process improvements. This is based on the assumption that the process remains focused on what the customer desires. In some cases, the process may result in doing a better and better job at the wrong thing. Continuous improvement shifts the employee's focus onto the process and if not properly managed, may cause the process to drift away from the value it adds to the customer.

Another criticism is that continuous improvement takes time away from break-through improvements (a Six Sigma improvement specialty). So many people have so much "personal capital" tied up in maintaining the status quo that they resist significant changes.

COMMENT

Reworking something requires that the company spend twice as much to accomplish the same objective. Rework and a process that generates scrap material are prime areas for an IT Director to seek quality improvement.

§ 5.05   MAJOR QUALITY TECHNIQUES

[A]   Overview

There are several proven techniques to improving the quality of processes. Each has its own strengths. They all begin with documented processes and a recent set of process performance metrics. Metrics and process documentation are the baseline form which process improvement is measured.

[B] Lean: Eliminate the Seven Wastes

Lean is based on the identification and elimination of process waste. It believes first that complex processes have more opportunities to fail and therefore fail more often. Applying Lean principles to existing processes is a way for IT Directors to identify and eliminate the obsolete actions embedded with their team's work tasks. From a business continuity perspective, simple processes are easiest and fastest to recover.

The seven types of waste are:

A. **Overproduction.** Most common type of waste. Sometimes people focus on the time required to "set up" a task for work. They group the work together and complete all of it in a single batch. If this is to make something, then more is created than needed. The logic is that the set-up time is spread over more units. An example is ordering printer paper by the truckload instead of small quantities. This excess production sits and occupies space, and may shrink due to decay and poor handling.

B. **Waiting.** This is where inputs sit idle before processing. An example of this might be where purchase orders for the IT department are collected throughout the week and then only processed on Thursday mornings, or even that the IT Director only responds to e-mail in the evenings. Other examples of waiting waste include a caller to the Help Desk who is on hold awaiting a chance to report an issue, someone waiting for a repair to a program before they can continue work, or a database administrator waiting for the system administrator to provide some service. Waiting waste (lost time) is all around us.

C. **Unnecessary transportation.** It takes time to create something, move it to an intermediate location, and then pick it up from there and pull in later. For example, consider the many materials consumed in a busy print room. Paper is received in bulk and moved to a storage area. Then as paper is needed, someone goes to the storage area to fetch it. Ideally, paper is only ordered in the amounts needed for one or two days. It comes from the delivery truck right into the print room where it is used. This eliminates the labor to fetch paper and to share it. It also wastes expensive floor space. Material can be lost to theft, environmental damage, etc.

COMMENT

Collecting service requests of any kind and then processing them all at once may reduce the amount of time lost in "setting up a job" for an IT staff member, but it forces everyone to wait until that person is ready. This bottlenecking of work slows the steady flow of services to the customer.

D. **Unneeded process steps.** These are found in older and established processes. At one time, a report may have been required to support a temporary requirement or one of the people operating a process may have added "make-work" tasks to seem busier. Another common problem is when a business process was discontinued but the supporting IT processes were never eliminated. Every process should be reviewed at least annually to identify and eliminate unneeded steps.

E. **Excess inventory.** Can be found everywhere in IT. Some of it is used as a cushion against unanticipated demand. It might be a stack of old CRT monitors that lingers on just in case they are needed. Other examples might be new toner cartridges for obsolete equipment or under-utilized servers that sit idle most of the day. This is often caused by rewarding the procurement team for lowest per unit cost ignoring the expense to warehouse and shuffle excess material about.

F. **Unnecessary motion.** This may be an online form that requires users to move around the screen in search of needed fields. It might also be the storage of commonly used documents in an archived format, etc.

G. **Defective product.** Every defective result delivered to an end user is another disappointed person. Each process failure may cost the IT team many hours. Therefore, each defective process result is a significant time waster for both the IT department and the end user who requested it.

[C] Six Sigma: The Cure for Deep Problems

Six Sigma is a valuable analytical process for determining the root cause of problem processes. Any process that fails to perform reliably and everyone says, "that is just the way it is," is a good candidate for a Six Sigma analysis. Six Sigma's audacious goal is a breakthrough that dramatically improves the effectiveness and efficiency of a process.

The Six Sigma process is heavily dependent on data. Processes are analyzed and people interviewed to identify the critical places to gather data on process inputs and outputs. The results are analyzed through various statistical methods to identify the causes and the correlation between causes that result in a given output. A Six Sigma problem analysis can be very time consuming. A project may require months to finally ask the right question and identify the source of the problem.

Six Sigma uses a five-step process:

A. **Define.** Clearly understand what the problem is. A succinct problem statement is essential, as are the data that describes the impact of this problem to the company. This impact may be in delays (waste employee time), required rework, or may even result in a product whose errors are only caught by the customer. Develop a process map to better understand the inputs and outputs.

B. **Measure.** Identifies the essential deliverable of a process and measures the inputs that might change the outputs. Determine what the process results should be compared to what they are.

C. **Analyze.** Review data on the various process inputs and statistically determine if there is a correlation between one or more inputs to the output. Develops alternative solutions to the problem.

D. **Improve.** Develop a hypothesis of what may resolve the problem and test the potential solutions. The best solution is selected and applied to the process. The result is monitored over time to ensure it truly repairs the process.

E. **Control.** Ensure that what has been repaired remains so. People are creatures of habit and after a short while may return to their old and familiar ways of doing things. The control phase establishes performance triggers which alert the IT Manager that the process is again drifting toward problems.

COMMENT

Companies have learned the hard way that Six Sigma by itself is too slow and expensive to solve all of their problems. It is best applied to stubborn problems that no one believes will ever be fixed. Lean analysis will solve most process issues while TQM is very useful for day-to-day improvements.

[D] TQM: Common Sense Approach

Total Quality Management (TQM) is a broad-based program where quality is instilled in an organization from top down. In terms of IT, TQM requires that every part of the department is involved in quality improvement from the administrative team to the network technicians to the print room. TQM recognizes that the success of the various teams is interrelated.

TQM begins with visible executive support. It requires a climate of integrity where every employee can speak up about quality issues. Training (that oft-cut budget item) is required for employees on a regular basis.

TQM is best known for its four-step cycle of quality

A. **Plan.** Identify the desired outputs from the process.
B. **Do.** Implement the new process.
C. **Check.** Compare the actual output to the planned output.
D. **Act.** Initiate actions to modify the process to eliminate the differences between the planned and actual outputs.

Every company implements TQM to address their unique quality requirements. This enables IT departments to emphasize different areas according to their industry or corporate culture. The key to any IT quality program is the attitude of its leaders (see Policy ITP-05-1 IT Quality Program as an example).

§ 5.05[D]

No matter what they say, their actions tell the team what to do. When times are tough, if the first thing they drop are the quality steps, then so will the team—a short-term gain exchanged for a long-term problem.

POLICY ITP-05-1. IT Quality Program

Policy #:	ITP-05-1	Effective:	04/01/13	Page #:	1 of N
Subject:	IT Quality Program				

1.0 PURPOSE

This policy defines the process for managing the IT department's Quality Program.

2.0 SCOPE

The policy applies to all IT processes and personnel.

3.0 POLICY

The following guidelines will be followed for ensuring that:

A. Documentation
All IT processes will be documented except those created for one-time or limited duration use. Each process will include target service levels (both planned and included in customer service level agreements).

B. Metric Collection
Every documented IT process will provide for the collection and analysis of measurements of its effectiveness and efficiency. Every process exists to provide some product or service. Each of these results has one or more measure of quality. These measurements must be tracked to ensure that the service is still meeting the customer's requirements. Metrics may be collected for 100 percent of the outcomes (very expensive) or for a representative sampling of the outcomes.
   Each metric will include:

1. Customer approved statement critical to quality features for this process
2. Time period for collection
3. Collection method
4. Collection point in the process
5. Position title of who will collect the data and analyze it
6. When the data must be reported to IT management
7. Format for the report to indicate current situation and trending

C. Root Cause of Problems
Repetitive problems drain the IT department's limited time. Each customer complaint deserves a review to determine the cause of the issue. The root cause

5-19

of the problem means that the cause of the problem has been identified and a resolution to eliminate it has been implemented. Every reported customer complaint is recorded in a customer complaint log to track the issue through to completion.

Every customer complaint is documented on an IT Customer Service Request form. Every other week, the IT Director reviews with all team supervisors each of the open issues to discuss their resolution. Also discussed are the issues closed since the last meeting.

4.0 REVISION HISTORY

Date	Revision #	Description of Change
04/01/13	1.0	Initial creation.

5.0 INQUIRIES

Direct inquiries about this policy to:

George Jenkins, CIO
Our Company, Inc.
2900 Corporate Drive
Columbus, OH 43215

Voice: 614-555-1234
Fax: 614-555-1235
E-mail: gjenkins@company.com

Revision #:	1.0	Supersedes:	N/A	Date:	04/01/13

[E]   Common Tools

Companies implementing a quality program constantly collect data about their performance. Unfortunately, some companies only collect it and then file for future reference. This is expensive and wasteful. Data has a limited "shelf life." What is the point of spending work time to collect something unless it will be used to improve service?

Stating that something has a problem can generate some management interest. However, if the solution requires significant changes or the investment of funds, nothing speaks louder than data. Clear and well-documented process performance data demonstrates the severity of an issue and illustrates recent performance trends.

Data can point detect problems or trends toward problems. Here are a few easy to apply data collection tools:

EXHIBIT 5-1. Tally Sheet

	Monday	Tuesday	Wednesday	Thursday	Friday	Saturday
Reset password		III	IIIIIIII	II		
Internet site blocked	I	I			III	I
Hardware failure		I	I		I	
Network slow		I	III			I
Accounting software	I		I	II		
Materials software	II	I				II
Time and attendance system	IIII	II	I			II

A. **Tally Sheets.** Tally sheets are data collection forms designed for collecting data about a specific "something." For example, the number of password reset calls to the Help Desk, the number of failed hacking attempts for a specific user ID over a period of time, or even the number of Help Desk calls from a specific user.

We have all used tally sheets at some time. They are the simplest tools to set up and can be adapted to anything. Yet this simple tool can collect data across two dimensions. In this example (Exhibit 5-1), it is a Help Desk sheet to count the number of calls for different areas of IT. In this case, it indicates which days a particular area has the most calls. This data is useful in establishing staffing to promptly answer questions (Some types of questions take longer to resolve than others.) In another direction, it illustrates the problem areas to focus on improving system resiliency.

The problem with a tally sheet is that it depends on the person keeping score to do so fairly. If they desire, they can mark some items twice for a single call or not at all if they wish. Also, if times are busy, they may forget to mark the sheet.

B. **Scatter Diagrams.** A scatter diagram helps to illustrate the range of a problem as well as its trends. The X-axis is typically over time and the Y-axis is for the frequency. In this example (Exhibit 5-2), an applications programmer has been tracking how long it takes for a customer service screen to accept a new transaction. A scatter plot can also be used to illustrate the relationship between two variables.

Another way to use a scatter diagram is to force into the data a trend line. This might show the average value over time, the least value, or the

EXHIBIT 5-2. Scatter Plot

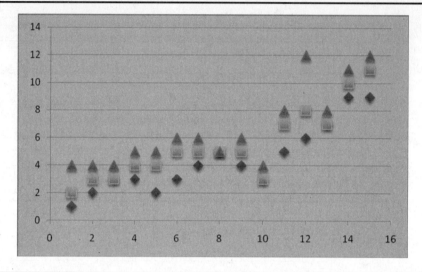

greatest. The purpose of a trend chart is to see if over time something is increasing or decreasing in frequency or severity.

C. **Pareto Charts.** Pareto charts illustrate the principle that 20 of the factors create 80 percent of the problems. Pareto chart is a frequency bar chart where the values are sorted from greatest to least, from left to right. A Pareto chart is another way to analyze the results of a check sheet. Typically, the chart will have eight or fewer vertical bars. Sometimes the bars must include a final "others" category.

Tackling the highest bar on the Pareto chart should provide the greatest benefits for the least results. Often the largest bar must be itself broken down into more finite definitions. Such as the password resets might be reviewed in terms of the IT system where passwords need to be reset or the department that calls the most. Refer to Exhibit 5-3.

D. **Cause and Effect Diagrams.** When the cause of a problem is obvious, just fix it! However, for those times where the cause is not obvious, pick the situation apart until something points toward the problem. One way to do this involves identifying all of the input factors. A visual tool for this is also commonly called a Fishbone chart (after its shape) or an Ishigawa diagram (after the person who created it).

To build a fishbone diagram, assemble a small team for a brainstorming session. Each person identifies pertinent factors that may cause the problem. Sometimes, one of the fish's "bones" becomes too crowded and must be analyzed separately. This is good since it is caused by many ideas from the team.

A concern about a fishbone diagram is that it deals with listing things but not quantities or time. Another issue is that it does not consider the inter-relationship of factors. The team leader must ensure that these factors are considered using other analytical tools.

Refer to Exhibit 5-4. This diagram identifies the many factors of a problem. The first step leads to deeper analysis using other tools. Identifying the individual factors may point to the significant causes. In most cases, however, it identifies input as to the process to monitor.

EXHIBIT 5-3. Pareto Plot

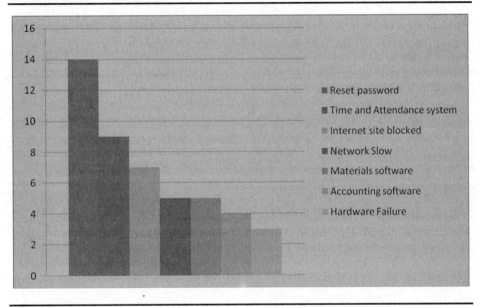

EXHIBIT 5-4. Cause and Effect Diagram

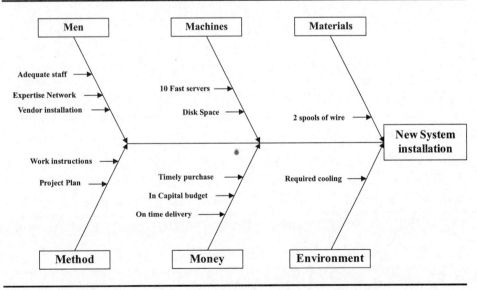

6

POLICIES AND PROCEDURES: SETTING THE FRAMEWORK

§ 6.01 OVERVIEW

[A] Purpose and Scope

IT governance becomes reality with the creation of the appropriate policies and procedures necessary to implement the IT strategy of the organization. Comprehensive policies and procedures are critical for ensuring that your investment in IT is best used to support the overall strategy of the enterprise. They help ensure that all areas of IT are working toward the shared goal of supporting and enabling the mission of the organization. This chapter will show you the mechanics of creating effective IT policies and procedures. Each of the remaining chapters offers you examples using this format and templates to guide you in the establishment of comprehensive policies and procedures vital to the success of your IT organization. The goal of the remainder of this book is to suggest ways of developing, adopting, and distributing uniform IT policies and procedures that support the selected IT governance model.

The guidelines for policies and procedures contained in this book are appropriate for information systems functions at the corporate, division, local area network, and device levels. The guidelines are not intended to replace instructions by various vendors in the operation of their software or hardware. Although the examples used here can be adapted to fit your unique circumstances, there is no "one size fits all" solution.

A policy and procedures manual must be kept current, ideally by reviewing every section at least once a year. An out-of-date manual or one with too many gaps in it will not hold employee interest. After its review, the company executives should approve it and ensure it is properly presented to the relevant employees through presentations explaining its changes and by providing printed copies or online access.

The number of policies in effect should be minimal. The thicker the policy binder is, the less it will be read. However, there are times when it is necessary to include formal policies to inform employees and protect the company from legal entanglements.

[B] Policies vs. Procedures

Policies are general statements of direction. They provide guidance so employees understand the boundaries within which they must operate. Well-written policies provide freedom of action, promote initiative, and facilitate the delegation of authority throughout an organization. They also promote the efficient use of resources in the organization. Policies explain *what* and *why* things are done. They are not, however, a substitute for sound judgment and common sense.

Policies have the following characteristics:

A. Have widespread application
B. Change infrequently
C. Describe major operational issues
D. Usually are expressed in broad terms

Policies represent management's guidance in the way that a situation is to be addressed. This framework empowers workers to make decisions and act on them without constantly referring to a higher authority.

Policies are effective only if they are enforced. If a policy no longer fits your business situation, cancel it. If it still fits, enforce it. All management personnel must know what the policies are and enforce them throughout their teams. If the managers do not understand them, they will be unable to explain them to others. Credibility is a powerful tool for managers. It permits issuing orders without reference to coercion. If credibility is lost, then only negative action will obtain results.

Policies must be applied equally to everyone. Selective enforcement damages the credibility of the policies and the management team as a whole. The few policies you fail to enforce will effectively cancel the remaining policies in the eyes of your employees.

Some policies are probably already in place through your human resources department. Where possible, do not overlap with any of them. Ambiguity between competing policies confuses the people they are supposed to be guiding.

Procedures, on the other hand, are specific statements designed to provide direction in actions necessary to support the policies of the organization. Procedures explain *how* things are done. They have the following characteristics:

A. Have a narrow application
B. Are prone to change as new systems are made operational
C. Describe process
D. Are usually very detailed

[C] Critical Policies to Develop Based on This Chapter

Using the material discussed in this chapter, you will be able to create the following policies:

A. Document the lines of policy authority
B. Policy approval process
C. Policy to Submit a Strategic Plan

Policies should always be developed based on the local situation. Successful managers cannot issue locally correct guidance if the policies are written with some other company's situation or location in mind.

§ 6.02 ORGANIZING A MANUAL

[A] Manual Organization

A fundamental step to assigning structure is to develop a policies and procedures manual for quick reference and easy updating. This is true whether you create a paper version or post an electronic version to your corporate intranet. Building such a volume can be very time-consuming. The extent to which your company will benefit will be determined by how it is used. If the managers refer to it, so will the employees. If the managers ignore it, so will the employees. (Do you see a pattern here?)

If your organization does not already have a policies and procedures numbering and formatting policy, consider using the format of the chapters in this book. This book is divided into chapters as a "living example" of manual organization and style. Remember that, unlike a novel, a manual is not intended to be read from front to back. A manual must be organized for the quick location of pertinent information. Fortunately, this is made much simpler with word processing software, which can automatically build tables of contents and indices for you. Electronic and Web-based versions can make searching for the appropriate information quick and easy. Make sure you use language that is appropriate for your organization to facilitate the use of automated search tools in finding suitable policies in a given situation.

A "chapter" in your policies and procedures manual might represent a subject area under which related policies are grouped. For example, all policies related to security should be grouped together in a "chapter." Each separate policy within a "chapter" is then numbered sequentially just as are the sections in a chapter of this book. The sections are subdivided into subsections, organizing the details of each policy. The manual opens with a table of contents displaying the chapters, sections, and subsections (just like this book). Contact information for the person responsible for the policies should be included in the front of the manual so users may request updates or get clarification, if needed.

Many organizations will use a two or three letter prefix for each corporate policy to denote the area responsible for the policy—"IT" or "ITP" are popular prefixes to use for IT policies. An example of the reference index for your policy manual (the format used for this book) is below:

> N. CHAPTER NUMBER
>   N.N SECTION NUMBER
>   N.N.N. Subsection number
>   A. First-level subdivision
>   1. Second-level subdivision
>   a. Third-level subdivision
>   (1) Fourth-level subdivision
>   (a) Fifth-level subdivision

Using this format, a policy on covering the acquisition of peripheral devices might be designated ITP-12-1; "ITP" being the prefix you decide to use for all IT-related policies, "chapter" 12 containing all policies concerning non-PC devices, and '1' signifying that this was the first policy created in this "chapter."

[B] Type Styles and Page Numbering

Most manuals use type styles to aid in fast information retrieval. For example:

[**CHAPTER** titles will be uppercase and bold.]

[**Section** titles will be bold.]

[The subsequent text's first character will be uppercase.]

Pages can be numbered sequentially, or can be numbered within each section as page x-x, like this book. For example, if the last page of section six is four, it would be numbered 6-4. Whatever page numbering scheme you use, the placement of page numbers, headers, and footers needs to be consistent from section to section.

[C] Printing Policies and Procedures

If the policies and procedures manual is printed, use 20-lb. white paper. Temporary policies or procedures should be printed on colored paper—light blue is a good choice—and should show the duration time in the "effective date" box at the top of each page (MM/DD/YY-MM/DD/YY).

[D] Page Layout

A clean, uncluttered layout encourages one to read the material. Experiment with different formats to find the one that works best for you. Exhibit 6-1 shows some possible header and footer formats to use.

You should also develop standards for the sections to be contained within each policy. Determine whether all sections are required, or whether some are required and some are optional. Some sections you may want to include are:

A. **Purpose**. This section is where you document the purpose of this policy.
B. **Scope**. Document not only what this policy covers but also what it does not cover in this section.
C. **Reference**. If this policy references any other existing policies, document it here.
D. **Background**. This section is for background information on what brought about the creation of this policy.
E. **Policy**. The actual policy is documented in this section.
F. **Procedures**. Any procedures that were created specifically to support this policy are documented here.
G. **Revision history**. Document the lifespan of this policy.

EXHIBIT 6-1. Headers and Footer

Headers

Policy and Procedure Manual		Page:	2 of 3
Chapter:	1. Organizational Responsibility	Issued by:	
Section:	2. Manual Organization	Approved:	
Effective Date:	03/01/2003	Supersedes:	

Subject:	Organizational Responsibility	Policy #:	1–2
		Page #:	2 of 3
Covers:	Manual Organization	Effective:	03/01/2004

Footers

Revision #: Revision Date:	Issued by:

Revision #:	Supersedes:	Date:

H. **Inquiries**. This section tells the reader where to go for additional information on this policy.

I. **Appendices**. Any material necessary to support the policy can be placed in this section.

You may need to add additional sections based on your individual situation. Exhibit 6-2 is a sample policy with suggested sections.

EXHIBIT 6-2. Sample Policy Format

Policy #:	ITP-99-9	Effective:	03/18/13	Page #:	1 of N
Subject:	The Title or Subject of the Policy				

1.0 PURPOSE

This is where you document the purpose of this policy.

2.0 SCOPE

The Document not only states what this policy covers but also what it does not cover here.

3.0 REFERENCE

If this policy references any other existing policies, document it here.

4.0 BACKGROUND

This section is for background information on what brought about the creation of this policy.

5.0 POLICY

The actual policy is documented in this section.

6.0 PROCEDURES

Any procedures that were created specifically to support this policy are documented here.

7.0 REVISION HISTORY

Document the lifespan of this policy using a table like the one here.

Date	Revision #	Description of Change
03/18/13	1.0	Initial creation.
08/12/13	1.1	Modified section X.4 to include new regulations.

8.0 INQUIRIES

This section tells the reader where to go for additional information on this policy.

9.0 APPENDICES

Any material necessary to support the policy can be placed here.

Revision #:	1.1	Supersedes:	1.0	Date:	08/12/13

§ 6.03 SETTING THE STANDARDS FOR RESPONSIBILITIES

[A] Who Has Management Authority?

Information systems policies typically flow top-down from the highest level of authority in the organization affected by the computer procedures. This person should designate a policy manager or team to develop and oversee the implementation of the policies. Note that imposing policies "from on high" without involving those affected can inhibit acceptance and compliance.

For consistency, it is important to designate a single corporate IT executive (usually the Chief Information Officer) with the authority to implement all company-wide computer systems policies. This person will receive policy mandates from the firm's delegated operations policymakers. These policies will be defined in writing and dated, signed, and forwarded to the corporate operations manager who will incorporate these policies into the corporate operational policies.

COMMENT

The first policies developed for the organization should be to designate the authority for the establishment of IT policies and procedures. These policies should outline who has the authority, from what that authority is derived, explain the importance of compliance with the policies that are issued, and describe how policies are created and revised. They should be issued by the Chief Executive Officer and designate the top IT executive within the organization, the Chief Information Officer (CIO) as the person responsible for the care of all IT assets within the facility. This will include any assets purchased outside of the normal IT channels. See Policy ITP-06-1 Establishment of Policy Authority as an example.

Financial aspects of the firm's computer systems may require the co-approval of the firm's auditors, both in-house and outside, if applicable. The responsibilities of the corporate IT executive are defined in the corporate policies and procedures manual.

The structure of the IT operation determines how local authority is derived and the scope of responsibility for the manager of the IT operation at the local level. Below are several common scenarios and the appropriate policy management structure.

A. **Local network manager within corporate IT.** The manager of a business unit using a local area network within a corporate information system operation is typically the authority for such systems. If the company has a corporate system with a network or PC policies and procedures manual in place, its maintenance will be the responsibility of the corporate information systems management. Policy enforcement will come under the authority of the manager of the business unit whose responsibilities are defined in the corporate information systems policies.

   Where the manager of a local area network receives only policy guidance from the head of corporate information systems, he or she needs the flexibility to adapt these policies, as needed, into the PC policies and procedures manual.

B. **Local network manager outside corporate IT.** Managers of local area networks that are not part of the corporate system are the authority for the systems in their area. The company must create a combined policies and procedures manual formulated to carry out the firm's policies for the company network and any local area networks. The manager of local area networks will be responsible for the procedure development, maintenance, and enforcement within his or her area of authority. The respective responsibilities for the PC policy and procedure manuals will be documented in the Corporate Policy and Procedures Manual. Any financial transactions or data access of the company's computer database systems via local area networks or individual devices may require the co-approval of the firm's auditors, both in-house and outside, if applicable.

C. **Local network manager with no corporate IT.** Managers of local area networks in a firm that has no corporate information system will be the sole authority of the systems in their area. They are responsible for policy and procedure development, maintenance, and enforcement. The person approving will be so noted at the top right-hand side of each section's first page in the manual. This will be the same person who provides the policies or his/her designated representative.

POLICY ITP-06-1. Establishment of Policy Authority

Policy #:	ITP-06-1	Effective:	01/19/13	Page #:	1 of N
Subject:	Establishment of Policy Authority				

1.0 PURPOSE

This policy recognizes the authority and responsibility of the Chief Information Officer (CIO) to establish and govern technology policies, procedures, and best practices for the company's technology infrastructure in order to support the company's business and IT strategies.

2.0 SCOPE

The policy applies to all users of information technology within the company.

3.0 POLICY

The CIO must establish and provide governance for information technology policies, procedures, and best practices for the company's technology infrastructure in order to secure all IT assets and promote the most efficient use of technology resources.

The CIO will submit a report to the Board of Directors at its first meeting of each calendar year, and submit interim reports at the request of the Board, on the current status of the company's technology policies and procedures.

All operating units within the company that use information technology (IT) are responsible for:

A. Adhering to the IT policies issued by the CIO.
B. Developing and implementing, when appropriate, additional IT policies and procedures specific to their operating units.
C. Promoting IT policy adherence.
D. Complying with the requirements of the IT governance model adopted by the organization.
E. Ensuring the security of the IT systems and the network to which they are connected.
F. Informing the CIO if there are any problems with a policy or if inputs from other sources do not comply with the defined policies.
G. Providing new employees with instruction and/or documented procedures that relate to their job descriptions.
H. Providing an annual "refresher" for current employees highlighting the changes made or problem areas during the previous year.
I. Maintaining the functionality of the IT systems within their area.
J. Facilitating training and the dissemination of information.
K. Preventing unauthorized access to company information, personal files, and e-mail.
L. Developing and maintaining a plan for recovery of mission critical data and systems if a loss is sustained.

The head of each business unit must designate an "Information Technology (IT) Coordinator" to ensure that these responsibilities are carried out and to serve as a contact person for that business unit with the CIO. This policy recognizes that different business units have different needs, IT resources, and levels of internal expertise. Hence, the needs and resources of a given business unit may not require the IT Coordinator to have an extensive technical background. Many business units also have "Technical Managers" who are responsible for the operation of the IT systems and with whom the IT Coordinator may share the responsibilities in this policy. Technical Managers are expected to have the technical expertise required to ensure the safe and reliable operation of their respective business unit's IT systems.

4.0 REVISION HISTORY

Date	Revision #	Description of Change
03/18/12	1.0	Initial creation.
01/19/13	1.1	Added support for IT governance model.

5.0 INQUIRIES

Direct inquiries about this policy to:

George Jenkins, CIO
Our Company, Inc.
2900 Corporate Drive
Columbus, OH 43215

Voice: 614-555-1234
Fax: 614-555-1235
E-mail: gjenkins@company.com

Revision #:	1.1	Supersedes:	1.0	Date:	01/19/13

[B] Policies and Procedures Responsibility

The top IT executive for a company must be responsible for all computer operations, software, supplies, and supporting hardware for the firm. The authority to create and enforce policies and procedures should be defined in the manual. This person has the responsibility to approve and sign all issued and temporary policies and procedures and his or her name will be noted at the top right-hand side of each section's first page in the manual. The person writing the policies and procedures will be designated by the head of the company's information systems or he or she may elect to write it him-or herself. The writer is identified at the top right-hand side of each section's first page after the word "By" and under the name of the person noted as approving.

COMMENT

The higher up the approval authority, the more likely the policies will be followed. In addition, "buy-in" from users will help policies take root quickly. If the IT executive does not assign responsibility for enforcing a policy to someone, then it will not be enforced, as being the naysayer to someone is never a popular or rewarding task.

[C]   Implementation

All corporate and business unit managers using information technology are responsible for ensuring that the provisions set forth in the Information Technology Policies & Procedures Manual are complied with. These management persons:

A. Ensure that all application standards are followed in their respective areas.
B. Inform the person in charge of approving the procedures if there are any problems with a procedure or if inputs from other sources do not comply with the defined procedures. This should be done in writing.
C. Provide new employees with instruction and/or documented procedures that relate to their job descriptions.
D. Provide an annual "refresher" for current employees highlighting the changes made or problem areas during the previous year.

All stand-alone device operations will be covered by a user's procedure manual provided by the supervisor. This manual will contain all procedure information needed for the authorized device user to be in compliance. Also, the service desk contact will be identified for any needed assistance.

§ 6.04   IT POLICY APPROVAL PROCESS

[A]   Overview

An official policy creation, review, acceptance, and update process should be created so that everyone in the organization understands and participates in the policy process. The life cycle of a policy is:

A. A policy need is identified
B. A draft is created and reviewed
C. The appropriate level of management approves the new policy

D. The policy is distributed
E. The policy may be revised
F. The policy may be rescinded

See Policy ITP-06-2 Policy Approval Process as an example.

POLICY ITP-06-2.   Policy Approval Process

Policy #:	ITP-06-2	Effective:	03/18/13	Page #:	1 of N
Subject:	Policy Approval Process				

1.0 PURPOSE

This policy defines the policy approval process.

2.0 SCOPE

The policy applies to all users of information technology within the company.

3.0 POLICY

The following steps define the process for creating and approving a new policy:

A. A policy suggestion is made. Policy suggestions may originate from the policy manager, users, or management mandates.
B. The policy manager works with management to determine whether there is a need for a new policy (see § 6.04[C], "Policy Acceptance Criteria"). If the suggestion is rejected, the requestor is notified of the reasons for rejection. Alternatives to a new policy should be suggested to the person making the request.
C. The policy manager assigns a priority to the policy. The policy manager works with management's input to assign a priority to the development of the new policy.
D. The policy manager or an assigned policy analyst researches the requirements for the new policy. This research includes reviewing existing policies, obtaining examples from outside the company, and conducting interviews with stakeholders affected by the new policy.
E. A draft policy is created. The draft policy is reviewed by others in the policy department, if applicable.
F. The draft policy is reviewed by management. The draft policy is sent to upper management and important stakeholders for review.
G. Revisions are made to the draft, if necessary. Revisions may be made after input is received from upper management and important stakeholders.

H. Is this a mandated policy? If management mandated the new policy, then go to Step N. Mandated policies are typically those required by law or requested by upper management.

I. The draft policy is sent to all affected stakeholders for review and comment. This can be done by hardcopy, e-mail, or placement on the corporate intranet. The quality of the final policy can depend on the number of people who review the proposed policy.

J. Stakeholder comments are incorporated into the draft, if appropriate. Incorporating as many suggestions as possible from users will help in gaining acceptance of the new policy.

K. Determine if additional research is required. A large percentage of negative comments may suggest additional research is required.

L. Revised policy draft is sent to management for review.

M. The policy manager makes any revisions suggested by management.

N. Send the new policy to the CIO for signature.

O. The new approved policy is sent to stakeholders. This should include anyone affected by the existence of the policy.

P. Update the master policy manual.

4.0 REVISION HISTORY

Date	Revision #	Description of Change
03/18/13	1.0	Initial creation.

5.0 INQUIRIES

Direct inquiries about this policy to:

George Jenkins, CIO
Our Company, Inc.
2900 Corporate Drive
Columbus, OH 43215

Voice: 614-555-1234
Fax: 614-555-1235
E-mail: gjenkins@company.com

Revision #:	1.0	Supersedes:	N/A	Date:	03/18/13

Policy additions or revisions are communicated using the form shown in Exhibit 6-3, either as a hardcopy form or as a Web page on the corporate intranet. If a Web page is used, a link to a Web page showing the acceptance criteria should be included.

EXHIBIT 6-3. Policy Suggestion Form

Policy Suggestion Form		
Name/Title:		
Department:		Date:
Manual Area:		
Chapter:		☐ New Policy
Section:		☐ Change Existing Policy
Page(s):		
Suggested Policy/Changes:		
Write the proposed needed revision. Attach any necessary details, along with supporting documentation.		
Rationale:		
Describe the problem and how it is affecting the current operation or will affect future operations. How will the proposed revision resolve the problem?		
Signed:		Date:
Approved By:		Date:
Approved/Disapproved:		Date:
Revision Completed By:		Date:
Comments:		

[B] Policy Creation Process

The policy manager identified above is responsible for developing and following a standard process for creating new policies. This policy should define:

- Who can originate a policy suggestion?
- How the need for a new policy is determined.
- How is a priority assigned to the policy?
- Who develops the initial policy?
- The review process for the suggested policy (some firms have a formal policy review committee for review and change control; for others, this is ad hoc).
- How revisions are handled.
- Is this a mandated policy?

- Who approves the policy?
- How is the master policy manual updated?

[C]   Policy Acceptance Criteria

Policy suggestions are made either by filling out the Policy Suggestion Form (Exhibit 6-3) and delivering it to the policy manager or by filling out a form on the corporate intranet. The form must be filled out completely in order for the policy to be considered. The policy manager will use the following criteria to determine if a suggestion is accepted and a new policy is written or changes made to an existing one. Few suggestions will meet all criteria; the policy manager must balance strengths against shortcomings in evaluating each suggestion. Any of the following criteria may provide an overwhelming reason to accept or reject a specific suggestion. Policy suggestions made by upper management will be automatically accepted.

A. **Purpose.** The purpose of the policy suggestion must be stated clearly and be relevant to the mission, goals, and operations of the organization.

B. **Audience.** The suggestion must address and identify the intended users of the policy, and satisfy some real or perceived need of this audience.

C. **Authority.** The policy manager must have the authority to issue policy for the area in question.

D. **Currency.** The suggested policy must apply to current and/or future activities.

E. **Scope.** The scope of the suggestion must match the expectations of the intended audience.

F. **Uniqueness.** To avoid needless duplication of effort, the information contained in a new policy should not already be covered in any existing policy.

G. **Organizational impact.** A new policy suggestion should have a positive impact on the operations of the organization. Suggestions with a greater impact will have a higher priority than those with a lower impact. Impact assessments must address cost-benefit and forecast return on investment.

H. **Urgency.** Suggestions with a higher degree of urgency will have a higher priority than those with a lower one. Policy requests mandated by law or upper management will have a higher priority.

[D]   Manual Maintenance

Permanent manual revisions will be sequentially identified, after the word "Rev.," at the top right-hand side of each section's first page. Temporary policies or procedures supersede permanent policies and procedures. The permanent policies will remain in the manual; they can only be replaced by the issuance of replacement policies and/or procedures. In the event a policy and/or procedure is to be discontinued, an order will be issued by the person who originally approved the policy and/or procedure or by a successor or agent in writing. Requests for temporary or permanent policy and/or procedures will be handled as follows:

A. Any user, management person, information technology person, work-group head, or manual holder may submit a request for a temporary policy and/or procedure or for a permanent revision to the Information Technology Policies & Procedures Manual.

B. Revision requests will be handled in the following manner:
1. Request a revision using the Policy Suggestion Form in Exhibit 6-3.
2. Submit one copy to the approving authority (or successor) for the policy and/or procedure.
3. The final authority will review the request and approve or deny it, providing a reason for any action taken. The person assigned to investigate the request will be identified. The person assigned to determine the course of action necessary might also be the approval authority. The recommended course of action may result in a feasibility study if the required undertaking is large or expensive enough.
4. If the initial request is denied, the person requesting the change may move up the chain of command to the appropriate level needed for resolution.

C. Revised documentation will be issued simultaneously to all affected manual holders using print or electronic means. The person responsible for maintaining the manual and any local area network or stand-alone device policies will keep a current list of all manual holders with a partial or complete manual. Partial manual holders, who will have identified which sections they receive, will be cross-indexed by those sections. When a particular section is replaced, a list of appropriate manual holders may be provided for distribution. The lists may be maintained in a database and distribution lists printed as needed.

When permanent revisions are issued, all pages for the given section will be reissued. If corrections to current procedures are required and numbering is not affected, only the affected pages need be distributed. This applies to both temporary and permanent policies and/or procedures. All releases will have a cover memo noting:

A. The person issuing the release
B. The effective date(s) of the release
C. The reason for the release

[E] Annual Policy Review

Once per year, all policies will be reviewed by management for updating. These changes will follow the same review process as normal change requests except that they may be reviewed all at once. Following these updates, all policies will be reviewed annually with the IT employees. Some policies, especially those with legal ramifications, will be reviewed in their entirety (such as conflict of interest), while others will be reviewed by summarizing them in a simple paragraph.

[F]   Sunset Clause

Every policy has its day, and eventually, that day will pass. After a policy has been in effect for five years (or whatever time period you feel is appropriate for your organization), it should be closely examined as to its currency. Technology changes, people change, and business objectives change. Policies should also change. After five years, the policy should be rewritten to reflect current business needs.

7

BUSINESS IMPACT ANALYSIS: MEASURING RISK

§ 7.01   OVERVIEW
    [A]   Purpose and Scope
    [B]   What Is a BIA?
    [C]   Key Points in a BIA
    [D]   Critical Policies to Develop Based on This Chapter

§ 7.02   MANAGING A BUSINESS IMPACT ANALYSIS (BIA)
    [A]   A BIA Is a Project
    [B]   Senior Executive Sponsorship
    [C]   Building the Team

§ 7.03   BIA DATA COLLECTION PROCESS
    [A]   The Basics
    [B]   Develop a BIA Glossary
    [C]   What to Collect?
    [D]   Data Collections Planning

§ 7.04   CRUNCHING THE DATA
    [A]   Gathering the Data
    [B]   Build Initial Reports

§ 7.05   BIA RESULTS AND THE IT DEPARTMENT
    [A]   Overview
    [B]   Recovery Priority
    [C]   Recovery Time Objective
    [D]   Recovery Point Objective
    [E]   Risk Analysis

§ 7.06   UPDATES
    [A]   Business Updates
    [B]   IT Updates

§ 7.01 OVERVIEW

[A] Purpose and Scope

IT executives face a basic problem. Their data systems encompass numerous programs, databases, and devices that span the company. If two data systems are dead at the same time, which one must be addressed first? What is the cost of downtime per system? Intuitively, some of these must be more valuable than others, but what is that value? How can this value be measured? In a time of scarce resources, which systems should be nurtured and which ones left to wither on the vine? In a major disaster, which systems are essential for the company's survival?

All of these questions are pertinent. Often, decisions are based on the perceived value of a particular data process when comparing two competing issues and the resources for only one of them is available. Capital spending, major improvement projects, and of course, support staff training often are decided by the perceived value that a data system provides the company. But what is this value based on? Where is the data that supports this value? How old is this data? Has the value provided by a process changed over time?

The problem with the business-as-usual approach to this is that it is based on a limited understanding or personal whim—not on the facts. A new IT Manager lacks the "institutional knowledge" of which system failures in the past have caused the greatest damage. Another caveat is that the business impact of a technology changes over time. Companies compete in an ever-shifting business environment. Yesterday's cash cow may be today's cash drain. Yesterday's cash drain may be today's regulatory compliance requirement and must be retained to keep the government at arm's length!

Unfortunately, few executives fully appreciate which of their technologies are truly critical. They draw on personal experience, but that is limited to the areas with which they are familiar. They can ask their peers, but each person sees the world through the narrow view of his own situation. The accounting department will identify all of their applications as critical since they handle the money. The materials management team will identify its technologies as critical since the company's assets are reflected in a fragile collection of materials. The engineering department will think this is the most critical since their technology holds the company's valuable intellectual property. To some extent, all of these people are right!

To determine where the true benefits lie, conduct a detailed analysis that breaks the business down by its major functions, and assigns value to each function in terms of cash flow and regulatory obligations. Then the data systems that support these functions are identified and the functions rolled up. Based on this data—based on these facts—an IT executive can more efficiently assign resources for the greater benefit of the organization.

[B] What Is a BIA?

A Business Impact Analysis (BIA) is a systematic analysis of a company or business unit to identify its critical business functions and the impact to the company if these functions ceased to function. These business functions are linked to the IT systems that support them (lose the IT system, and that function cannot continue). Risks to the most valuable processes are identified along with mitigation actions to reduce the likelihood or impact of these risks. In the event of a disaster, the BIA indicates how much is lost per hour or per day for the length of the outage.

COMMENT

A BIA is a snapshot of what is currently in place. A major shift in business operations requires conducting a new BIA.

An organization's critical functions depend on its primary mission. For a charity, a BIA would focus on the key services provided to its target audience. For a factory, this might be the primary products created. A bank might identify the various services offered. An online store would value availability of its Web page, speed of processing, and security of customer data.

[C] Key Points in a BIA

A BIA provides many benefits:

A. Identifies critical business functions.
B. Quantifies the financial and intangible costs of loss of a critical business function.
C. Identifies the Recovery Time Objective (RTO)—the length of time the organization can afford for that function to be disabled before severe financial damage is experienced.
D. Identifies the people, technology, and vital records necessary for the function to recover.
E. Through analysis, identifies the most critical functions to protect, which is input to a risk assessment.
F. Identifies the sequence that IT functions must be recovered during an outage.
G. Identifies vital records (including non-electronic ones) and the impact of their loss.

Financial costs of an outage might include:

A. Lost revenue.
B. Loss of shareholder confidence in company's executive management.
C. Spoiled materials or finished goods.
D. Penalties to customers for late shipments or lost services.
E. Legal penalties for missed or inadequate reporting.

Intangible losses include:

A. Loss of customer good will.
B. Loss of marketplace confidence in delivery credibility.
C. Impact to employees.
D. Loss of local "good neighbor" image.

Based on the BIA report, the IT Director can determine:

A. **Maximum Acceptable Outage (MAO).** The length of time that a system can be down before the company's finances are seriously harmed. In the case of a localized disaster, this is further broken down by application.
B. **Recovery Time Objective (RTO).** The amount of time before a company is seriously financially damaged. This drives the disaster recovery strategy.
C. **Recovery Point Objective (RPO).** The amount of data that can be lost before serious consequences. It is measured in time. This drives the data protection strategy.

[D] Critical Policies to Develop Based on This Chapter

Using the material discussed in this chapter, you will be able to create the following policies:

A. Business Impact Analysis policy
B. Collect data for a Business Impact Analysis
C. Identify critical records and data
D. Determine Recovery Time Objective/Recovery Point Objective

Policies should always be developed based on the local situation. Successful managers cannot issue appropriate guidance if the policies are written with another company's situation or location in mind.

§ 7.02 MANAGING A BUSINESS IMPACT ANALYSIS (BIA)

[A] A BIA Is a Project

A BIA is best run as a formal project. The project definition and budget is approved at the highest company levels. With so many parts of the organization to talk to and people to meet with, a published project plan is essential.

In most companies, the Board of Directors is the authority ordering the study. Even if the BIA request originates in the IT department, its scope is so all-encompassing that it must have board or executive management approval to proceed.

A BIA must be a carefully coordinated effort. It is visible across the company. A well-run project builds credibility where a blundered effort raises defenses in every department. The key in any project's success is the selection of a skilled Project Manager.

The BIA Project Manager has a tough job. He must follow up and insist that the BIA questionnaires are promptly returned. He must moderate discussions among executives as to the true value of internal processes. He will touch on areas normally discussed behind closed executive doors. It is very easy for this person to bruise some executive egos and endanger his own long-term career possibilities.

Therefore, companies choose one of two paths:

A. **Internal.** An employee is appointed as the Project Manager. This person already understands the corporate structure, knows the personalities involved, where to find people, etc. This approach builds internal expertise.
B. **External.** An outside organization is brought in to lead the project. This brings in someone without the internal ties and whose loyalty is to the executive paying their bill. The problem is that the company's inner business processes, finances, and problems will be exposed to this third party.

The Project Manager is responsible for planning the BIA and executing the plan. In a large company, there are a lot of people to meet with. Meetings must accommodate executives' busy schedules. The Project Manager provides status reports to the executive sponsor.

[B] Senior Executive Sponsorship

A BIA touches every part of a business. It asks probing questions that make many executives and managers nervous. They are concerned that the data may indicate that their work is not vital and that they may be cut from the company. They are concerned that the data may be misused in department infighting. They are concerned that the entire affair is a smokescreen for something nefarious that they cannot even guess at. Consequently, they will try to avoid the study or inflate their own importance.

To overcome the reluctance to participate, a senior executive is appointed. This person:

A. Appoints the Project Manager.
B. Approves the project's budget.
C. Issues executive directives mandating participation.
D. Addresses all objections raised by the various departments.
E. At the end, approves the project's final report.

[C] Building the Team

A typical BIA project team consists of several business analysts. The analysts manage the data collection process to include:

A. Tuning the questionnaire to the local organization (many companies start with a standard form and modify for local use).

   B. Providing training to small groups (usually a department at a time) on how to fill out the questionnaire.
   C. Following up when data entered is illegible or incomplete.
   D. Compiling the BIA data into a format for review by the various organizational levels.
   E. Conducting peer review meetings with the participants to discuss the responses gathered by an entire department.

§ 7.03   BIA DATA COLLECTION PROCESS

[A]   The Basics

The goal of a Business Impact Analysis is to identify the most critical company processes. If ten different managers were asked what this might be, they would likely provide ten different answers—each slightly skewed toward their own departments. In the data collection phase of the analysis, the leaders of each important business function are asked for their opinion as to what is most critical. These functions are then reviewed in terms of financial and legal impacts.

A data collection plan addresses what to collect and from whom. Many other variables can be added to these basic items, such as when to collect, who must respond, etc. The guiding principle is that data should only be collected *once*. Time spent in preparation is saved later by only doing it one time.

The data collection plan is to:

   A. Identify who will contribute information (based on the organization chart).
   B. Create a questionnaire that reflects information required for the final report.
   C. Roll out the questionnaires in a series of meetings.
   D. Aggregate returned questionnaires into business units.
   E. Review the aggregated data in meetings with the business units.
   F. Review the total roll up with executive management.

COMMENT

Anyone who has been tasked with collecting data from a number of people knows the problem. The requirement seems so clear, just go find out the information from the various people. As the collection proceeds, each manager uses a slightly different term for the same thing. Each sees things differently and often throws in additional items or factors to consider. If accepted, these additional factors must be recollected from the people interviewed earlier, etc.

[B]   Develop a BIA Glossary

The purpose of collecting data is to combine it into reports. It is important that responses are consistently described in the same way in every questionnaire. This speeds reporting, improves reporting consistency, and makes obvious when something new (and unexpected) is encountered.

Electronic forms are very useful for this. Drop-down boxes confine the customer's answers to a set of categories or range of numbers to ease the consolidation of the data. However, always leave an "other" category where they can describe something and enter its value. Each of the other entries must be investigated but this keeps an analysis moving forward without pausing constantly to answer questions.

A glossary must be made readily available to all participants. This helps to standardize terminology across the study. When each department is briefed prior to filling in their questionnaires, the glossary can be reviewed with them.

[C]   What to Collect?

The easiest way to identify data elements to collect is to identify what will be used to create the final report. Start by defining what the result should be. Create a questionnaire that collects the data needed to answer these questions.

COMMENT

The BIA focus is on processes. A business process typically involves trained people, business records, and technology.

For example, consider the process of receiving material into a factory. The receiving clerk reviews the manifest and locates the purchase order number. Next, a data connection is made to the materials management software so that the shipment can be checked against the order to ensure everything was received. Then it can be marked as complete and undamaged which connects to the accounts payable system. Meanwhile, the person handling the material follows local procedures for storing it.

In this example, the manifest is a critical document (for claiming hidden damage), the software supporting the process is important along with the equipment used to run it.

A simplistic BIA questionnaire is found on the CD (Worksheet 07-1 Business Impact Analysis Questionnaire). It is presented here to explain its various parts. The sections of a BIA are as follows:

A. Identification Block. A questionnaire begins with an identification block that indicates who filled in the data and when. It also explains how to contact the respondent with further questions by telephone or e-mail. The function number is used by the BIA team to control the questionnaires and ensure they are all returned.

An important entry is the department name. Each department can have many business functions to report. Therefore, each department numbers its forms according to how many functions it is reporting. This reduces the chance of missing a report.

Department: _____	Function # _____
Filled in by: _____	Date: _____
Phone: _____ E-mail: _____	

B. Describe the Business Function. The process name must be the one that it is most commonly known as. When the final report is reviewed, executives will question high values for something that no one can recognize. The process owner field will be used by the IT department as the contact person if any of this process's IT systems fail.

Business Process Name: _____
Business Process Description: _____
_____
_____
Process Owner: _____

C. Impact if This Business Function Is Lost. This matrix lists five categories across the top and a time scale along the vertical axis. It is the heart of the analysis and must be tuned to the local requirements. The impact categories for this business function are:

	Cumulative Financial Loss (Revenue lost plus costs incurred)	Legal Compliance Impact	Loss of Customer Confidence	Loss of Supplier Confidence	Damaged Public Image
1 hour					
4 hours					
1 day					
2 days					

	Cumulative Financial Loss (Revenue lost plus costs incurred)	Legal Compliance Impact	Loss of Customer Confidence	Loss of Supplier Confidence	Damaged Public Image
3 days					
4 days					
5 days					
2 weeks					

1. Cumulative Financial Loss (Revenue lost plus costs incurred)—measured in dollars. This might include:
   a. Lost revenues
   b. Lost sales
   c. Financial penalties
   d. Wages paid for no work
   e. Overtime wages paid to catch up
   f. Spoiled materials and finished goods
2. Legal Compliance Impact—Yes or No. Space is provided later for an explanation.
3. Loss of Customer Confidence—answers can be Low, Medium, or High. Space is provided later for an explanation.
4. Loss of Supplier Confidence—answers can be Low, Medium, or High. Space is provided later for an explanation.
5. Damaged Public Image—answers can be Low, Medium, or High. Space is provided later for an explanation.

Rate each of the impact categories according to its impact over time. For example, what is the Cumulative Financial Loss for one hour of outage?

Example #1:
   If this was a busy online catalog, then a one-hour outage might have a significant financial impact since buyers may look elsewhere for their goods.
Example #2:
   If this was the shipping department for a factory, then a one-hour outage would mean that shipments would leave the dock late that day. A four-hour outage might involve shipments arriving late to the customer. Beyond four hours, late shipments would be widespread and, depending upon the purchasing stipulations, may be refused by the customer. There may even be penalties for late deliveries. Also, at some point, the rest of the factory is shut down since finished goods are piled up with nowhere to go.

Example #3:
> If the payroll department was down for an hour, then the clerks can tidy up around the office or even leave early for lunch, and the cost is minimal.

However, if the same payroll department was inoperable for a week, the company may not have lost revenue but the employees definitely would be angry. If the employees belonged to a union, they might walk off the job.
Other categories to consider adding to the questionnaire include:

1. Shareholder Confidence
2. Loss of Financial Control
3. Employee Morale
4. Customer Service
5. Employee Resignations
6. Vendor Relations
7. Potential Liability
8. Competitive Advantage
9. Health Hazard
10. Additional Cost of Credit
11. Additional Cost of Advertising to Rebuild Company Image and Reliability
12. Cost to Acquire New Software and to Recreate Databases
13. Damage to Brand Image
14. Potential Reduction in Value of Company Stock Shares

D. Explain How the Non-Dollar Issues Will Impact the Company. The goal is to confine the answers within an easy to aggregate indicator, such as Low, Medium, or High. Provide space so that the respondent can explain the factors that drove their answer.

What Legal Compliance issues would be created: _____
Describe the Loss of Customer Confidence created: _____
Describe the Loss of Supplier Confidence created: _____
Describe Damage to the Company's Public Image: _____

E. Vital Records. Data retention and protection is vital. Departments that originate, use, or store vital business records must be identified. This information can be used to develop protection plans for this data. It can also identify documents that should be properly destroyed instead of stored on site.

> What critical documents are created, used, or stored by this business
> function:
>
> _____   _____
> _____   _____
> _____   _____

F. Vital Equipment. A BIA can identify weakness in processes that could bankrupt a business. In this section, respondents are asked to identify critical devices that may be difficult or impossible to replace. This can spawn a project to modify the project to eliminate these unique devices (and thereby reduce the chance of a business function outage due to a special machine).

> List the non-IT equipment vital to this business function:
>
> _____   _____
> _____   _____

G. IT Applications Supporting This Process. This data is important for the IT department to determine the required recovery time for each application. For example, if a department claims that a one-hour outage costs the company $10,000, then that is financial justification to purchase redundant equipment to reduce the likelihood or duration of an outage.

To ensure consistency among the answers, the IT department provides a list of all applications on all platforms (desktop, server, mainframe, on-line). The list is included in the instructions accompanying the form. Be sure to include both the official name and the commonly used name (if one is better known). Respondents can select from this list to minimize variation of system names.

COMMENT

This is one place where an electronic BIA data collection form is handy. An electronic form enables providing a list of all applications on all platforms (desktop, server, mainframe, on-line) in a drop-down box. Be sure to include both the official name and the commonly used name (if one is better known). This ensures consistency of data collection.

Tools	Impact							
	1 hour	4 hours	1 day	2 days	3 days	4 days	5 days	2 weeks

[D]   Data Collections Planning

With the questionnaire complete, the plan turns to how to contact the various departments. The Project Manager must carefully sequence the BIA rollout and coordinate times to work with each department that minimizes disruption to its normal operations.

   A. **Who Will Receive a Questionnaire?** Obtain a current company organizational chart. This will be used to identify who will receive a survey and to break the organization into Business Units. Business Units are work groups with complementary functions that can be brought together for validating the data. Often, questionnaires are provided to the lowest level team leader in each department. Although it is nice to give everyone a voice in the BIA, it takes time to brief participants on the process, to review their responses, etc.

   B. **Stratify the Respondents.** Some people will expect more hand-holding than others. An effort to establish and maintain executive support in each department saves time in the long run. Enlist their support in their department's prompt return of completed forms.
   Provide an advance copy of the questionnaire to the higher level executives (typically, the vice presidents). Meet with them to discuss its purpose and methods. They do not fill it out—just need to understand it. Their role comes later on when validating the data.

   C. **Run a Trial with a Single Department.** Before sending the form out to everyone, use one department to test. Walk through the entire process with them looking for places where the form is missing something or where the instructions are not clear. Often what is clear as day to the BIA team is obscure or has dual meaning to people who are less familiar with the material.

D. **Issue the Questionnaires.** Meet with each of the department leaders and help them to draft a list of the major business functions within their domain. Provide a numbered stack of questionnaires. Assign a number to each person the department leaders indicate should receive one. An important management tool is a log of which form number went to which person. This is used to verify that all of the forms are returned.

Along with the questionnaire, provide written instructions. Explain how every field on the form will be used and what the respondent should fill in there. Ideally, include a telephone number for someone on the BIA project team to quickly answer questions. (The quicker questions are resolved, the greater the respondents will cooperate.)

COMMENT

Before issuing the questionnaires, be sure that person is not on vacation or a business trip—or about to leave on one.

E. **Conduct Department Meetings.** Passing out questionnaires to a list of people is not a good data collection plan. It will be stonewalled and sidetracked due to many questions as to what means what, etc. The best approach is to coordinate a series of meetings with the various work groups and departments. Yes, this takes time. Try to keep the groups smaller than 20 people. This provides opportunities to ask questions. During these meetings:

1. Explain the purpose of the BIA and how it will help the company—sell the concept to them!
2. Provide copies of the executive support letter. This puts everyone on notice that they are expected to cooperate. If possible, ask this executive to drop by the meetings for a brief word of "encouragement."
3. Provide copies of the questionnaires along with a printed explanation of what each item means.
4. Walk through every item in the questionnaire and provide examples of how they might be filled in.

F. **Special Handling.** A few departments, such as the legal team, may be small and the workers all highly paid. In those cases, the BIA team may use interviews to fill in the questionnaires. Selecting who gets a questionnaire (refer to the organization chart in Exhibit 7-1):

EXHIBIT 7-1. Example Organization Chart

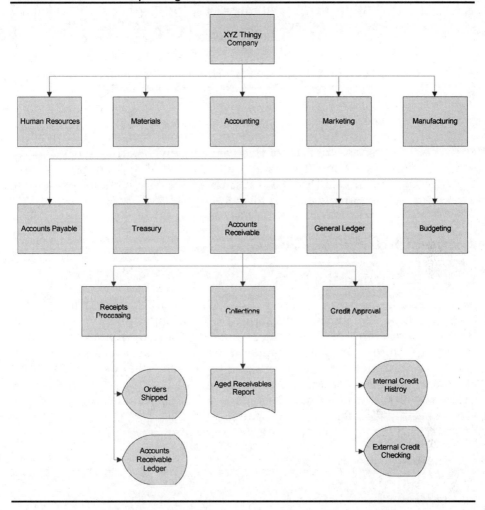

1. Traversing the hierarchy
   a. Start with the company on top. This is the CEO.
   b. The next level is for each Vice President.
   c. In this example, we enter the Accounting Department, and then Accounts Receivable.
2. Within Accounts Receivable, there are three Business Functions. A form is filled out for each of these functions.
3. Roll Up the numbers
   a. 1st Level
      (1) Within the Accounts Receivable team, the Manager reviews the reports for each of the three functions.
      (2) As a team (facilitated by the BIA Project Manager), the three function workers and their manager discuss and agree on the recovery time required and costs for non-availability.

b. 2nd Level
    (1) Within the Accounting Department, the Vice President of Accounting reviews the reports for each of the five accounting teams.
    (2) As a team (facilitated by the BIA Project Manager), the five teams and their Vice President discuss and agree on the recovery time required and costs for non-availability.

c. 3rd Level
    (1) All of the Vice Presidents, along with the CEO, review the reports for each of the five company departments.
    (2) As a team (facilitated by the BIA Project Manager), the five teams and the CEO discuss and agree on the recovery time required and costs for non-availability.

§ 7.04   CRUNCHING THE DATA

[A]   Gathering the Data

Most companies allow one work week to fill out BIA questionnaires. As the forms come in, be sure to check them off the questionnaire log. At the announced deadline, begin visiting anyone who has not submitted his form.

At first, this is a friendly reminder. Most people just get busy and forget about it amidst their many daily crises. A few others won't do anything until the questionnaire becomes the daily crisis! After a few extra days, the crisis is created by alerting the various managers as to who has not complied with the data collection requirements. For the final few forms, a list must be sent to the sponsor who can reset their priorities.

COMMENT

Another way to improve the prompt return of questionnaires is to visit the respondents several days after handing them the form. Make it a friendly visit to see if they had any questions about the form, the process, etc. This reminds them about the due date. It also provides a one-on-one opportunity to answer questions.

As the forms come in, review them carefully. Look for:

A. **Readability.** Handwriting can be a challenge to decipher.
B. **Completeness.** Incomplete forms must be returned with a request to complete the information. If only a few things are missing, the

respondent likely did not know what to enter. A quick meeting can often fill in the gaps.

C. **Use of Other.** Review and address anything entered into an "Other" category. Some of the "Others" may fit into existing categories. Some of them may be unique situations that can become their own category.

COMMENT

There are two primary ways to analyze data:

A. Qualitatively—represents the important but intangible values of something that is not easily measured.
B. Quantitatively—or how many. Quantitative analysis presents summary data in terms of quantities, percentages or other mathematical terms.

To simplify data analysis, strive to frame qualitative questions such that they can be replied to quantitatively.

[B] Build Initial Reports

Data from the questionnaires is compiled into a hierarchy of reports:

A. Work Group. Groups of managers, supervisors, or team leaders who work in the same area. Each business function has a single form completed. As soon as all of the forms have been received from a department, proceed to create the department's roll-up reports. This example shows a rollout for a work group. Each business process is listed along the left side and along the top is the time range. This shows the impact of an outage of each function over time. In some cases, a financial loss is not listed since at that point, the facility is shut down. There could be a financial loss value for that event—or just the idea of a forced shutdown may be serious enough to urge the group to do something.

COMMENT

Any business function that is required to fulfill legislative requirements is automatically treated as a high cost outage. In many cases, the daily fines could be used for the cost of outage.

Work Group Report

Business Process	Cumulative Impact								
	1 hour	4 hours	1 day	2 days	3 days	4 days	5 days	2 weeks
Collections				$5k	$10k	$15k	$20k	$50k
Accounts Receivable	0	$1k	$5k	$20k	$40k	$80k	$160k	$500k
Sales-Major Accounts	$10k	$40k	$100k	$200k	$300k	$400k	$500k	$1.5M
Sales-Other Accounts	$1k	$40k	$80k	$160k	$240k	$320k	$400k	$800k
Shipping		$5k			shutdown	shutdown	shutdown	shutdown
Accounts Payable							$10k	$50k

B. **Department.** The work groups are merged into a single entry. Conduct a meeting with everyone in a work group that completed a questionnaire—and their next level manager. The BIA analyst provides copies of the reports to all participants. If possible, project the spreadsheet so everyone can see it. One line at a time, the BIA analyst reads the business function title and asks the *entire group* if these numbers are valid. The BIA analyst is non-judgmental and only guides the discussion.

The group debates the data. In this way, the collective knowledge can point out existing manual processes and other efforts available to reduce potential losses and to lengthen the amount of time before the company incurs serious financial losses. The discussion may also point out overlooked business functions.

The amount of time a vital business function can tolerate downtime determines the disaster recovery strategy. The less tolerant that a business function is to an outage, the more expensive the disaster recovery strategy must be and more urgent that business continuity mitigation is implemented.

Every line in the report should be either validated or updated. In this way, the BIA report is the product of both the team and that work area's boss. The entire discussion is important, because this manager must defend the work group's consensus at the next level of data validation.

C. Business Unit. The results of the departments are aggregated into a business unit-wide report. After all of the work group reviews are completed and the data approved, it is time to move up a level. Repeat the work group review at each level of the organization. As the teams meet, expect a lot of heated discussion as to what is vital, and how long the company can tolerate an outage of that function. For many executives, the discussion is an eye opener. An executive may discover important responsibilities and works areas under his control that he may not have been aware of.

COMMENT

When reviewing the data with higher levels of management, it takes too long to go through everything. Focus on the shortest time as these will drive the cost of the business continuity strategy. At the top level, the discussion may only hit on the impact of the first day's outage.

Executives are often surprised at the quantity of documents critical to a business function. Expect to uncover a lack of backups for these documents and unmarked containers. This becomes an action item for those work areas to coordinate off-site storage for archives, on-site data security, and a recovery plan if the on-site documents are destroyed. Be sure to pass all of this information to the company's Document Management Program.

See Policy ITP-07-1 Business Impact Analysis Policy as an example policy.

POLICY ITP-07-1.   Business Impact Analysis Policy

Policy #	ITP-07-1	**Effective**	04/18/13	**Page #**	1 of N
Subject:	Business Impact Analysis Policy				

1.0 PURPOSE

This policy establishes the requirements evaluating the business processes within the organization and determining the criticality of each process to the overall operation of the business. A business impact analysis is a detailed analysis that breaks the business down by its major functions and assigns value to each function in terms of cash flow and regulatory obligations. The data systems that support these functions are also identified. Based on this data, management can more efficiently assign resources for the greater benefit of the organization.

2.0 SCOPE

This policy applies to all business functions that impact the mission of the organization.

3.0 POLICY

Each business unit within the organization must perform a business impact analysis (BIA) on all critical functions and their supporting information systems to determine the criticality of those functions to the operation of the organization. The BIA must also include a determination of the financial and operational impacts to the organization if those operational functions and processes were to be interrupted.

A BIA Project Manager must be approved by executive management and given the authority to carry out the tasks required to complete the BIA. The BIA Project Manager will provide to each business unit:

A. Overall guidance and support.
B. A vetted process to be followed by each business unit and its departments that helps to determine the criticality and impact of each business function.
C. A questionnaire tuned to the local organization (many companies start with a standard form and modify for local use).
D. Training to small groups (usually a department at a time) on how to fill out the questionnaire.
E. Follow up when data entered is illegible or incomplete.

F. The BIA data compiled into a format for review by the various organizational levels.
G. Peer review meetings with the participants to discuss the responses gathered by an entire department.

The BIA Project Manager will develop a data collection plan to address what to collect and from whom. Many other variables can be added to these basic items, such as when to collect, who must respond, etc. The guiding principle is that data should only be collected *once*. Time spent in preparation is saved later by only doing it one time.

The data collection plan is to:

A. Identify who will contribute information (based on the organization chart).
B. Create a questionnaire that reflects information required for the final report.
C. Roll out the questionnaires in a series of meetings.
D. Aggregate returned questionnaires into business units.
E. Review the aggregated data in meetings with the business units.
F. Review the total roll up with executive management.

The BIA Project Manager is responsible for compiling the information provided by the business units for presentation to executive management. The report must include an executive summary, a determination of the criticality, and impact of critical business functions and recommendations for protecting these functions. The BIA becomes an integral part of each business unit's disaster recovery planning process.

4.0 REVISION HISTORY

Date	Revision #	Description of Change
04/18/13	1.0	Initial creation.

5.0 INQUIRIES

Direct inquiries about this policy to:

George Jenkins, CIO
Our Company, Inc.
2900 Corporate Drive
Columbus, OH 43215

Voice: 614-555-1234
Fax: 614-555-1235
E-mail: gjenkins@company.com

Revision #:	1.0	Supersedes:	N/A	Date:	04/18/13

§ 7.05   BIA RESULTS AND THE IT DEPARTMENT

[A]   Overview

Once the business functions and amount of time an outage can be tolerated have been determined, the next step is to link that information to the application that supports those business functions. This provides the IT Director with an idea of how long a data system outage for a particular application can be tolerated.

[B]   Recovery Priority

For every business function, create a matrix that ties the IT systems required to support that function to a time frame. In this example, the applications are listed on the vertical axis and the timeline is across the top. Since different business applications have different times that they are critical, enter a number in the appropriate square for the number of applications. In this example, e-mail will impact three business functions on the first day, but one other will be seriously impacted within an hour.

Application	Impact							
	1 hour	4 hours	1 day	2 days	3 days	4 days	5 days	2 weeks
E-mail	1		3	1	6	2	2	
Web Catalog	2	5	2	1				
EDI	4	1	2	4			2	
Sql Database	1	1	3	2		3		1
Payroll			1	1				
Remedy	3	1	2		2		4	

This information can be used by the Service Desk to identify restoration priorities when addressing multiple outages at the same time. Now, based on customer requirements, it is easy to see which system must be restored first.

[C]   Recovery Time Objective

Based on the required recovery time, the IT Business Continuity Manager can determine a Recovery Time Objective (RTO). This is the target time within which the IT department must have specific systems operational after a disaster. In their reviews of the BIA data, company executives settle on the required RTO. The IT department's task is to develop a strategy for fulfilling it.

In time long past, a set of backup tapes stored off-site were considered the essential tool for data center recovery. However, with so much of a company's business stuffed away on computer disks, this is no longer practical. Consider, for a moment, how long it would take just to read a full set of data backups onto new disks. Added together to the unlikelihood that identical hardware would be available on short notice, the magnitude of the problem becomes obvious.

Leave the data center recovery discussion for the Business Continuity Manager. The point is that the IT staff must determine a strategy to fulfill management's mandated RTO. However, once they see the cost, they tend to soften how critical some business functions are.

[D]   Recovery Point Objective

The Recovery Point Objective (RPO) is the quantity of data that must be reloaded, or whose loss is acceptable in a disaster. This is a difficult concept to explain to end users.

Most companies make a full back up of all disk drives every weekend. Every weeknight, they make backup copies of what has changed that day, called incremental backups.

So, if a disaster occurred in the night after the backups were made and sent off-site for storage, no data is lost. But if the disaster occurs in the mid-afternoon, then all of the data entered or calculated during that day must be re-entered or skipped over. This can be a significant amount.

COMMENT

Given today's internet ordering and many real-time systems, companies have invested in off-site data replication. This might be off-site journaling of data (similar to an incremental backup) or mirroring data at off-site locations. These expensive solutions are justified by the executives' RPO requirements.

[E]   Risk Analysis

With the BIA results in hand, the IT Director can initiate studies of the most critical systems, searching for ways to make them more resilient. Disaster Recovery is for recovering from a major disaster. However, a more common situation is a system outage. This analysis is to examine each critical system from end to end looking for:

A. Single points of failure.
B. Persistent problems with a piece of code or hardware.
C. Old equipment that should be replaced.

D. Critical third-party software that is close to losing vendor support.
E. Technologies where the IT staff lacks expertise.
F. Quality of technical documentation.

Each of these can initiate a number of actions. These studies can provide input to the IT department's:

A. Items for the upcoming capital budget to replace major hardware items.
B. People and training for the upcoming training schedule and budget.
C. Project proposals to rework unreliable software.

The risk analysis can also be general, such as the loss of electrical service or external network connection to the outside world. If the IT Department has a Business Continuity Manager, he should already have these worked out.

§ 7.06 UPDATES

[A] Business Updates

After the BIA is completed, do not just toss it on the shelf. Although it is just a snapshot of the company, it can be updated whenever there is a major shift in the business. The BIA can drive so many parts of the IT department that it should be referred to regularly. In a dispute with an end user over priority, the BIA is the neutral expert that both can point to.

However, businesses change constantly. To keep the BIA in line with the business, perform mini-BIAs whenever a significant business change occurs. This might be the purchase of a new branch office, introduction of a new product line, replacement of a major IT system, etc.

COMMENT

BIAs should be completely redone every two years.

[B] IT Updates

One of the more difficult parts of a BIA is keeping it in sync with IT changes. If the BIA identifies a data system as critical, and business continuity plans are created to support it, these plans must be updated whenever a significant IT change occurs. The best time to uncover these changes is during a project proposal. For example, if a new database server and additional disk is purchased to expand the company's ERP system, then this should be included in the project during the proposal stage, and not just prior to implementation.

8

BUSINESS CONTINUITY PLANNING: STAYING IN BUSINESS

§ 8.01   OVERVIEW

[A]   Purpose and Scope

Business continuity planning (BCP) is a lot like car insurance. If it is not in place when needed, then it is too late to get it. Most executives are optimists by nature. There are so many urgent, exciting, or challenging things to work on that it is hard to find time for something as doom-and-gloom as BCP.

Over the years, business continuity planning has evolved as the business environment has changed. Thirty years ago, it was primarily concerned with disaster recovery planning (DRP). DRP focused on recovery from catastrophic problems such as how to rebuild a flattened facility. An IT DRP was only activated if the damage required the displacement of the data center to another site. A DRP contained its own dirty little secret—that it was sometimes easier and cheaper to take the insurance check and walk away from the business rather than rebuild the facility. Examples of this might be a department store roof collapse, a factory fire, or even an accusation of selling less-than-wholesome foods.

COMMENT

Law mandates disaster recovery planning for financial institutions. It assumes that financial institutions hold assets belonging to others and closing up is not an option. Hospitals also have tested plans since a major crisis could open them to a slew of lawsuits. However, most industries do little disaster planning and only apply it to their data processing operations.

A major problem with DRP was testing the adequacy of the plans. Testing is expensive and company funds are always under pressure to address the day's immediate issues rather than a pessimistic future that may never happen. Testing, if ever done, usually occurred when the crisis was at hand with no time left to repair flaws in the plan. Still, the DRP concept survived.

Eventually disaster recovery planners recognized how important a company's customers and suppliers were to a long-term recovery. What good was recovering a facility if, in the process, neglected suppliers and customer relationships withered away? This led to the addition of BRP to the disaster recovery plan. A BRP addresses customers' concerns and explains to them any delays in their orders. It might also include explaining to customers where to find other suppliers in the interim. Supplier cooperation includes requests to help by taking back delivered goods not immediately required. A BRP keeps suppliers informed as the recovery progresses. BRPs made these two critical groups participants in the recovery efforts.

EXHIBIT 8-1. Planning Scope Relationships

Time marches on and companies recognize the huge expense of holding materials inventories and large queues of work-in-process material. Impressed by the results of Japanese automakers, many companies have adopted lean production practices. Under the previous model, a factory might hold a 30-day supply (safety stock) of a key material to protect against interruptions to the supply chain. The assumption was that carrying extra inventory was necessary to protect the continuous flow of goods down the production lines. Multiply this carrying cost across all materials company-wide and the corporations were paying a lot of money to buy, store, and handle safety stock.

COMMENT

It should be a company policy that every critical business tool and process has a written and tested business continuity plan. The exercise of writing this plan will reap major business benefits as it forces managers to examine their processes and drive out their weak links.

Under lean production methods, companies realized this was not necessary and drastically cut their safety stock. In return, they became dependent on the reliability of their suppliers to deliver quality goods on demand. Many customers now rate their suppliers on the credibility of delivery promises. Late goods may idle in their own factory. On the other hand, keeping delivery promises in the face of adversity can be a major competitive weapon!

Taking this on-demand requirement even further, the Internet has made most companies 24/7 (24 hours a day, 7 days a week) sales centers. Interruptions to a company's operations cause customers to go elsewhere. Every company has charts that show the longer their customers must wait for their goods, the more the cancellation rate increases. Few companies can afford this.

So out of lean production and the around-the-clock world arose a need for BCP. BCP acts as the outer shell of disaster recovery planning. It addresses not only major tragedies such as burned warehouses but also the occasional major disruption such as severe weather, loss of electrical power, and even loss of a key machine. It is more than a set of dusty plans; it is a continuous proactive process of examining business processes to drive out problems and maintain workflow.

COMMENT

We all use business continuity every day. Consider a car. There is the risk of an accident. In this case, transfer the risk of loss to someone else (insurance company). This could be similar to disaster recovery if the insurance money was used to buy another car. If the car was severely damaged and there were difficulties making the journey to work every day on time until repairs were finished, a mitigation plan would inform your employer, family, and any other outside parties of potential delays. If a small, inexpensive "commuter car" was used for driving to work and a larger car for family outings, then the business continuity plan is to drive the larger car to work until the commuter car is repaired.

BCP is a broad topic. The goal of this chapter is to provide ideas for assembling a basic plan useful to an IT Manager. Start with the "Ten Steps to a Basic Recovery Plan" in Section 8.04[A]. If planning stops after completing this list, then the plan is off to a good start. To obtain the full benefits, continue and write a full plan. If this appears to be too large a challenge, consider hiring a professional BCP consultant to develop it.

There is an even more important reason for IT Managers to develop a business continuity plan—keeping their jobs. Companies without plans waste time fighting crisis after crisis and never seem to run smoothly. This translates into higher cost of goods through overtime pay, airfreight for critical materials, and delayed customer shipments. Perhaps some people enjoy the chaos. Those companies are costly to operate and gradually fall by the wayside.

[B]   Critical Policies to Develop Based on This Chapter

Using the material discussed in this chapter, you will be able to create the following policies:

A. Conduct a business impact analysis bi-annually.
B. Assemble plans for every critical business function.

Policies should always be developed based on the local situation. Successful managers cannot issue appropriate guidance using policies written with another company's situation or location in mind.

§ 8.02   PREPARE TO PLAN

[A]   Overview

A BCP is not a know-all book of how to recover from any potential problem. Such a tome would be far too large to be useful. Instead, it consists of a series of smaller plans that address specific risks. Each plan provides an overview of the technologies involved and guidance that can be applied to the problem at hand.

A disaster is an anticipated or unanticipated event that seriously disrupts critical business operations. Has the facility ever lost electrical power or telephone service? Has the data center ever run with half of the normal number of employees with the other half trapped by a major snowstorm? Most companies have muddled through these problems, so a lot of the plan already exists in the collective memory of the managers and workforce. ***Write it down!***

A plan could contain many things. At a minimum, it explains the basic steps to take while waiting for key support staff to arrive. This immediate action (similar to the concept of first aid) addresses most of the common problems or stops the spread of the damage.

COMMENT

Disaster recovery is something of a misleading title. These plans do not detail how to rebuild a burned out data center, which would be a full recovery. Rather they explain immediate action steps to restore a business function to *minimal* usefulness so the company can resume its cash flow. (A minimal plan provides critical business functions at a labor, throughput, and/or quality penalty. It is "limping along.")

Therefore, if a data center was burned out, the recovery plan, in this sense, would be to set up a temporary data center somewhere, with the minimal required equipment, as quickly as possible. The full recovery of a rebuilt room with new data center equipment, built for the long-term, etc., is beyond the scope of these plans.

[B]   Hire an Expert

Creating a business continuity program requires expertise. Like learning anything else new to the company, a subject matter expert is essential to kick off and run a program. Some companies hire someone with this experience and others hire a consultant and then develop someone on their team to take over the program. An on-site expert ensures success and speeds the program over the small obstacles that regularly rear their ugly heads.

COMMENT

Cynical managers say that consultants must be dragged kicking and screaming to the door. Include an end date and exit plan in the consultant's scope of work so that, by the end of the engagement, they have trained someone in the company to carry on leading the program.

[C]   Why Bother for Something That Will Never Happen

There are many reasons to build Business Continuity plans. First, they are simply good business. Parts of them are likely already in place, such as a UPS electrical support system. Business continuity planning forces an examination of processes to determine the risks to their ongoing operation. As these risks are mitigated, business continuity is more ensured. As mitigation steps are prepared for catastrophic events, the Business Continuity plan takes shape.

However, there are other reasons. Disaster recovery plans are specifically required or strongly implied in a number of legal mandates:

A. The Health Insurance Portability and Accountability Act of 1996 (HIPAA) implies the need for a business continuity plan as personal health information must be readily available. A disaster recovery plan may delay availability for many days. In a crisis, a business continuity plan would make the information available within hours.

B. SEC Rule 17a-4 for records preservation. Without an adequate data system backup and recovery capability, this rule is violated.

C. Sarbanes-Oxley section 404 implies the need for a disaster recovery plan.

IT Governance models that require a documented, tested business continuity program include:

A. Information Technology Infrastructure Library (ITIL) standard for continuity management.

B. Control Objectives for Information and related Technology (COBIT).

C. BCP is mandated by the ISO 17799 standard for data security.

[D] Basic Planning Assumptions

A list of assumptions to include in the plan:

A. **The primary objectives of all plans are the safety of people, and then the protection of company assets.** Always state that people come first, for both legal and ethical reasons.

B. **Problems arise in their own good time.** It could be in the middle of the day or in the dead of night on a holiday weekend. If a problem arises while key staff is on site, then they will take care of it. However, if it occurs in the middle of the night, or while they are away on vacation, would the staff on site have something to consult? What would the company do if the key people suddenly resigned?

C. **Major problems create major chaos.** Imagine the confusion caused by a loss of electricity in the building. Ideally, the support staff would know what to do, but just the loss of lights is enough to bring work to a standstill. Since their workstations are dead, employees will shuffle off to break rooms or congregate anywhere there is light. This reaction is normal. However, is it what the executives want?

D. **People are prone to inaction.** When problems arise, most people will just sit down to await the arrival of the "experts" as if there is nothing to do until they restore operations to normal. Is that what they should be doing? Is it true that these people are helpless?

[E] The Local Expert

Most departments have someone that everyone turns to in a crisis—and it is rarely their boss. The "local expert" is often a long-time employee who has seen or worked through the most common forms of problems that arise in the department. Whatever the crisis, managers always consult this person.

The problem with the local expert approach is that everyone sits around until this expert appears on the scene. In addition, despite his air of confidence, the local expert's experience tends to be spotty and often the solution is something that others in the staff could have pulled together. It is time for a change.

There are many problems with the local expert approach.

A. What will the team do if the expert is not available?
B. It assumes this person is "all knowing" of business processes and technologies, including the latest ones.
C. It makes the staff (and the IT Manager) dependent on one person (a single point of failure).

If an IT Manager would watch the local expert in action, he would witness someone with an informal continuity plan. He would have telephone numbers for vendors, help sheets for resolving problems (perhaps given to him by the original developers), and his own notes from over the years for what to do. A local expert has a mental index of where to find these fragments of information. A cynic would say that the local expert keeps the information dispersed to protect his status as the department's "wise one."

Rather than bet the company, and the IT Manager's job on this person, begin a plan by moving all of this information out of his area, off of the "sticky notes," and into a central department document. This provides at least something to act on in a crisis.

COMMENT

Most business initiatives begin with the assignment of an executive sponsor. This makes funding for the plan easier to obtain. However even without executive backing, IT Managers have a responsibility to the company and to their coworkers to develop a plan on their own initiative. Few modern companies can exist for long if their data system is out of service for an extended period. Reverting to manual processes or trying to rebuild everything from scratch is not an economically viable alternative.

§8.03 BUSINESS CONTINUITY PLANNING BASICS

[A] Overview

Assembling a plan is a long but valuable process. It will uncover weaknesses in processes to address before an actual problem occurs. Basic BCP involves three steps:

A. Identifying what is critical to the organization.
B. Identifying what risks (threats) these critical functions face.
C. Developing action plans to reduce these risks.

The IT recovery plan does not stand alone. It exists alongside of the Facilities Recovery Plan and the Security/Safety department's emergency plans. By coordinating with these groups, the IT plans can focus on the technologies and leave those areas to the people who know them best.

For example, if a fire occurred in two offices, which also consumed the wire closet between them, the IT Manager would require quick access to determine the extent of the damage. Any recovery (and even access to the damaged area) must be coordinated with the facilities team. Therefore, knowledge of the facilities plans will help the IT Manager to establish coordinate points in the recovery process.

[B] Identify the Critical Processes

What are the essential few functions of the business? For some companies, delivering a high level of customer service is critical. For an electrical power supplier, it might be a high level of service. For a factory, it may be the on-time shipment of promised material to customers. In a crisis, there is not enough time to restore everything. Avoid diverting scarce resources to restoring low value functions. To focus resources and reduce the recovery time required, companies zero in on the essential few functions that keep the cash flowing in the doors.

COMMENT

Pareto's law indicates that roughly 20 percent of the business's effort (the critical tasks) provides 80 percent of its value.

These critical elements are the foundation of a continuity plan. They are what the company is trying to protect. Any functions that do not directly support these activities may still have a plan but are secondary in a recovery. It is an executive management responsibility to identify these critical few. If any critical function is having problems, then an IT Manager must expend whatever effort is necessary to resolve the problem.

COMMENT

The authors have worked for companies whose critical functions were "To build, ship, and invoice product on time." Another company's vital few functions were "To maintain 24 by 7 customer services, the ability to receive orders, and the timely shipment of goods."

In a small company, the executives identify critical business functions based on their experience. Larger enterprises conduct a business impact analysis (BIA) which identifies critical business functions based on their cash flow impact and their legal necessity.

A BIA involves a series of interviews with company executives to identify:

A. The origins of the company's cash flows, and the impact of losing them, over time. This might indicate that after one day's loss of a specific business function, the company would not lose any money at all. However, by the third day, the daily loss would be some large amount of money.

B. Potential negative impacts to the company, such as a contractual performance penalty for failing to perform a customer service. Another example is an inability to perform customer support or to deliver goods on time.

C. Actions required demonstrating legal compliance, such as air pollution monitoring systems.

D. The IT systems that support each of the critical business functions. This prioritizes them for IT recovery and drives the data center recovery planning. (Most plans assume that, in a crisis, office space could be found but the IT systems will be the most complex thing to restore.)

Taken together, the BIA quantifies the impact to the company of a total outage—or a partial outage affecting numerous business functions. The quantified impact is used to make trade-offs between the risk of the loss versus the cost of mitigating actions. Therefore, the BIA justifies the BCP budget.

COMMENT

Beware of the "whining executive" who tries to inflate his importance by declaring all of his business functions as critical. It is up to the C level executives to arbitrate among the departments what is truly essential.

Sometimes executives demand to restore everything immediately. Once they see the cost for immediate failover of just a few of the larger systems, they withdraw the request.

The BIA tracks the losses to the company over time. This is important as some companies cannot tolerate a single day of total outage (such as an online service) while others can tough it out with little more than some lost productivity and salary wages. The duration of a *tolerable* outage is the Recovery Time Objective (RTO) and drives the strategy of the data center recovery plan.

BIAs are time consuming and expensive to conduct but are valuable to the company in many ways. They benefit not only IT analysis but also the company's strategic planning processes. Based on the revenue loss of a disabled business function, the IT can rationally set system recovery priorities.

Most business managers lack a big picture perspective of their company. Even executives with long company tenure typically have a narrow view of departments other than the ones through which they advanced. BIA results are useful for allocating future capital and highlight the costs/revenues of marginal operations.

COMMENT

After the BIA identifies the critical functions, the IT Manager can review the staff's skills for supporting them and use any knowledge gaps to justify team training.

[C] Identify Risks (Threats)

Every day the company's critical few functions face a series of risks. The first step is to identify these threats. The second step is to raise defenses against the more likely or damaging risks. To evaluate these risks, build a spreadsheet to sift through the threats and help identify the key ones to address. An example is found in Worksheet 08-1.

WORKSHEET 08-1.   Risk Assessment Form

Risk Assessment Form					
Date:			Likelihood	Impact	Restoration Time	Score
Grouping	**Risk**	0-10	0-10	0-10	
Natural Disasters					
	Earthquake				
	Tornadoes				
	Severe thunderstorms				
	Hail				
	Snow / ice / blizzard				
	Extreme temperatures				
	Floods / tidal surges				
	Forest or brush fires				
	Landslides				
	Sinkholes				
	Sand storms				
Man-made Risks					
	Highway access				
	Railroad				
	Pipelines				
	Airports				
	Harbors				
	Industrial areas				
	Chemical users				
	Dams				
	Rivers				
Civil Issues					
	Riot				
	Labor stoppage / picketing				
Key Suppliers					
	(list your suppliers here)				

A risk, or threat, is the *potential* that something may happen. Although risks can be positive as well as negative, business continuity planning focuses on the damaging risks, or those that can go wrong. Risks have many dimensions.

The main four dimensions are impact, likelihood, warning, and recovery time.

A. **Impact.** First, examine risks based on their impact to company operations if they occurred. Impact is typically measured by lost revenue, and the time and resources required to restore normal function.

For example, if the facility were located in Minnesota, the impact of a blizzard would be high due to problems of shipping raw materials in and finished goods out. Contrast the snowstorm with a department store fire. Damage from the flames is small. However, there is now an odor of smoke on all of the goods in the store. Recovery time to clean out all the smoke-damaged clothes and refill the building with fresh goods can be quite long.

A bank has a risk for robbery. The impact is high but the recovery is quick. The police are usually finished within a day and with a fresh stock of money the bank can reopen.

B. **Likelihood.** This leads to the second dimension of risk—likelihood. Many horrible things *might* happen, but realistically, what is the chance that they will? If the chance is very, very small, then ignore it. Yes, the sun might quit shining tomorrow, but its likelihood is too small to address. What is the likelihood that a crazed employee with a gun will rampage through the offices? What is the likelihood of an electrical outage? What is the likelihood that severe weather will shut the facility down for more than one day?

C. **Warning.** The third dimension of risk is warning. A weather report will warn about incoming severe weather. This allows some time to prepare. However, the theft of a server or a fire in the UPS unit arrives without any prior indication. Therefore, threats that can be anticipated allow more time to react. Threats that emerge suddenly allow no time to mitigate and are more damaging.

D. **Recovery Time.** The fourth dimension is recovery time. For example, a critical device in a remote part of the facility may be susceptible to lightning strikes. Any outage of that device is a critical emergency. However, the recovery time is quick by exchanging it with an on-site spare. Another example is a server. If a server is physically destroyed, the recovery time is how long it takes to bring in a spare server and then reload it.

Refer to Worksheet 08-1 for some ideas of risks to consider. Use this example just to get the plan started. This process works best as a team exercise to gain many points of view. Change the list to address the local situation. Replace the section on natural risk with the ones in the local area. Carry on with this throughout the chart. Then working with other managers, assign scores (1 through 10) for likelihood (10 means almost certain), impact, and restoration time. The score for the warning column is 1 for the most warning and 10 for no warning at all. Multiply the scores together and sort them (descending) with the highest scores on top. Address these top risks. At some point, draw a line across the list and ignore anything below it.

A look at the risks shows that some of them would have the same recovery actions, such as a fire that gutted a building or a tornado that wiped it away. Two different risks, but essentially the same recovery plan.

[D]   Other Risk Considerations

Some risks are local. If a branch bank is robbed, that location will be out of service for the day, but the rest of the company's banking branches are still operational. A bad day for that one branch office but the company as a whole experienced no disruption. Another localized risk is a tornado—terrible where it hits, but generally, the rest of the area is fine.

COMMENT

It is essential that a company review the BCPs of its critical vendors. Otherwise, the vendor's disaster may become your own.

The opposite of a local risk is a wide area risk, such as the snowstorm in Minnesota. This risk may close roads across the state, keep employees away, and prevent the movement of materials on the highways. The factory is intact and may still be churning out goods but nothing is moving outside the facility's four walls. No fresh materials come in and no finished goods flow out until the highways reopen. Other wide area risks to consider are floods, hurricanes, and earthquakes. Wide area risks often hurt customers and suppliers.

Man-made threats come in many forms. There could be a terrorist threat against the company, a truck carrying toxic chemicals could crash outside of the facility and force evacuation, or an angry person with a gun could be looking for victims. Man-made threats tend to be localized.

Infrastructure threats would include problems with the things essential for the company to continue operating. Electrical power is an essential part of any company. Without it, there are no lights for the offices, desktop workstations fall dark, and the heating and air conditioning stop. Everyone has experienced electrical outages. Another infrastructure threat is to the telecommunications lines outside the building. These lines also carry data traffic, so this risk is a double whammy.

Possible subsets to the previously mentioned infrastructure risks are associated with the facilities. This includes roof collapses, interior electrical failures, etc. Many things can cause leaking water pipes and water damages spread quickly.

A very common risk facing companies involves the security of their assets and employees. Computers make attractive theft targets as do a wide number of things within a company's walls. The risk to this can be high as the PC stolen may be full of company secrets, confidential legal files, or the only copies of accounting records. A comprehensive internal security program is a key part of any business continuity plan.

COMMENT

In 2010, the Veterans Affairs Department reported that a laptop computer stolen from an unidentified contractor contained personal information of 644 veterans, including data from some VA medical centers' records. Although the contractor had certified to the VA that it had encrypted laptops that stored department data, the data on the stolen laptop was unencrypted.

Most companies have at least one disgruntled employee. As an insider, this person knows company processes and what would hurt operations the most if damaged. Employee sabotage may be difficult to stop. Alongside of this is employee theft. Sometimes a thief will try to cover his crime by setting a fire to destroy evidence. Address all of this through the company's security plan and policies.

[E]   Develop Action Plans to Reduce These Risks

After spreading "doom and gloom" to depress the brightest optimist, let's begin fighting back. Once we have stripped away the element of surprise from these risks, take steps to address them. There are three basic strategies to consider:

A. **Avoidance.** Are there any actions that can be taken to avoid the risk? If hurricanes interrupt operations, could the company move to Wisconsin? This move avoids the threat to the flow of work from hurricanes. Avoidance actions often introduce new threats to the company.

B. **Mitigation.** Unavoidable risks require steps to reduce the likelihood or impact of the threat. Examples of mitigation actions are all around. Consider the fire sprinkler system in the offices. A sprinkler does not stop a fire from starting. It requires the heat from a fire to activate it. A fire sprinkler contains and slows the fire's spread—reducing the damage, it can cause. To reduce the likelihood of losing electrical power, some companies install instant-on generator systems. Another example is a car's spare tire. If needed, it reduces the delay caused by a flat tire by providing a way to return mobility to the car.

C. **Transference.** After trying to avoid and mitigate a problem, the third option is to transfer the risk to someone else. Transfer losses from a threat to insurance policies. For example, product liability insurance can protect a company in case someone was hurt using one of their products. Since a company cannot stop people misusing products, transfer that risk to an insurance policy. Reduce insurance rates through the introduction of well-written and tested business continuity plans. Insurance companies will often provide advice for writing a plan since it reduces their risk.

With these three strategies in mind, reexamine the list of threats to the company and see which strategy is best suited to each threat. The steps required to carry these actions out become the continuity planning action items. Some of these steps may have already been taken, such as the installation of fire sprinklers.

This third step of planning includes the development of specific plans to address threats to the critical few company activities. Start by comparing the risks to the list of solutions found in the notes of the local expert. Discussing this list in a staff meeting may also bring out some solutions used in the past.

To keep the planning efforts focused, constantly refer to:

A. What are my critical processes and the critical assets that enable them to work?
B. What threatens them?
C. What actions reduce the likelihood of a threat becoming reality?
D. What will minimize the damage if the risk does occur?
E. What does the team do if a problem occurs?
F. Where can more information be found on this?

COMMENT

"If you cannot describe what you are doing as a process, you don't know what you're doing."

—W. Edwards Deming

[F] Executives' Business Continuity Plan

In a crisis, most IT Managers want executives to be as far away as possible. However, they have a role to play. Rather than leaving them to their own imagination in a crisis, write an executive annex to the IT plan. This annex, a small plan in itself, describes the roles that executives must play during the crisis.

The executives' first responsibility is to assemble in a safe area as near to the disaster as practical. Practical means a room with telephones and data communication lines. Hotel rooms serve this purpose nicely. The executives will need this capability to communicate with customers, suppliers, news media, and shareholders.

During a disaster, these executives will receive the initial damage assessment from the facility manager and the security manager. If the IT Manager could safely enter the structure, then a quick damage assessment to the data system will be included. At this point, the executives must decide to restore service in a patched together structure or to restore IT services in another location. If this company has a hot site contract, they could declare a disaster and relocate to the hot site. Relocating a data center or activating a hot site is expensive, so executive involvement is essential.

The next executive action is to appoint someone to oversee the disaster management. The CEO and other top executives will be busy addressing external communications. This "Disaster Master" must be empowered to make purchasing decisions and to slice through paperwork to press the recovery forward rapidly.

See Policy ITP-08-1 Business Continuity Planning Policy as an example for starting the process at your organization.

POLICY ITP-08-1. Business Continuity Planning Policy

Policy #:	ITP-08-1	Effective:	03/18/13	Page #:	1 of N
Subject:	Business Continuity Planning Policy				

1.0 PURPOSE

The purpose of this policy is to create and maintain a Business Continuity Plan (BCP) for the IT support of critical company processes. An effective plan allows the company to minimize the adverse effect of emergencies that arise. The Company has an ethical obligation to the organization's workforce, shareholders, and customer stakeholders to protect the continuing operations of the business.

2.0 SCOPE

This policy encompasses all IT processes and technology that supports critical business functions.

3.0 POLICY

The IT Manager is responsible for creating, maintaining, and testing the IT Business Continuity Plan. The following activities must be performed:

A. Identify Critical Processes.
To identify the business processes critical to the company's financial and legal well-being, a bi-annual Business Impact Analysis (BIA) is conducted. The result is a Recovery Time Objective—that point at which company losses become intolerable (Recovery Time Objective—RTO). The IT Business Recovery Plan must ensure that critical IT processes (equipment and software) can be recovered at a remote site within the RTO.

The CEO initiates and sponsors the BIA. The BIA will:
1. Encompass all departments and areas of the company.
2. Identify the point in time that the financial and legal issues seriously threaten the company's survival.
3. Identify the processes required to meet all regulatory requirements.
4. Include a risk assessment of natural and man-made risks to the critical processes.

B. Business Continuity Planning.

The IT manager will assemble plans for every identified critical business function.
1. Develop the plan.
   a. Develop plans for the recovery IT processes, equipment, and software for all critical business processes identified by the BIA. These plans must address steps necessary to reestablish the IT functions at an emergency recovery location.
   b. Based on the BIA, publish a restoration priority list of all critical technologies.
   c. Create an emergency notification program to ensure the prompt notification of executive management in a crisis.
2. Maintain the plan.
   a. Perform a technical, natural, and man-made risk assessment annually.
   b. Identify mitigation actions to ensure the easiest and most timely recovery.
   c. Establish and maintain off-site storage of copies of all vital IT records, including a full backup of the disk storage media, updated daily. Ensure that the transportation and storage of media conforms to the company's data security policies.
   d. Update the IT Business Continuity Plan as technology supporting critical processes is changed.
3. Exercise the plan.
   a. Test all IT Business Continuity Plans at least bi-annually to demonstrate the ability to achieve the BIA determined Recovery Time Objective. Conduct a lessons-learned session with all participants to capture and incorporate improvements into the plans.
   b. Report all test results to the CEO within 30 days of the test's completion.
4. Training.
   a. Train all members of the IT department in their roles in supporting the BCP.
   b. Train all new employees on their roles within 30 days of joining the department.
5. Coordinate with other company disaster plans. The IT manager will coordinate the IT BCP with:
   a. The Facilities Disaster Recovery plan and the Security/Safety department's crisis plan.
   b. The various business recovery plans of other departments.

4.0 REVISION HISTORY

Date	Revision #	Description of Change
03/18/13	1.0	Initial creation.

5.0 INQUIRIES

Direct inquiries about this policy to:

George Jenkins, CIO
Our Company, Inc.
2900 Corporate Drive
Columbus, OH 43215

Voice: 614-555-1234
Fax: 614-555-1235
E-mail: gjenkins@company.com

Revision #:	1.0	Supersedes:	N/A	Date:	03/18/13

§ 8.04 PLANNING—THE NEXT STEP

[A] Use What Is Already Available

Before writing the plan, check around to see what information is already available. Writing a plan can be time-consuming and yet much of the source material isn't far away. Assemble a basic community plan with a few calls and a notebook. *In most crises, three keys are needed—key people, keys to the doors, and key support contract information.* Be sure to label the origin of any information collected, as there may be a need to go back for further clarification later.

Ten steps to a basic recovery plan:

A. **Start with the basics—whom do I call.** Obtain a current organization chart for the facility. This will show who works in what areas. Now get an organization chart for the entire company—specifically the key technical areas and executives. In a crisis, their help may be useful. For example, if there was a severe crisis with the data network, the IT Manager could call on the network experts from other company sites to come in on short notice and help for a few days.

B. **With these names in hand, match them to three telephone numbers.** This is very important for people directly supporting the facility and less so for people at other sites. Try to obtain the 24-hour contact information for at least one contact person for each of the other company sites (usually this is their IT Manager). For each person on the contact list, find their:

1. Office telephone number.
2. Home telephone number.
3. Cellular telephone number.

C. **Check with the security staff to see if they keep a key to every door in a secure key locker.** Keys are easy to copy. It is impossible to know who has a key to what doors. If possible, use electronic locks on the critical doors. A report can be generated by the server controlling the electronic locks listing who has access to which doors protected by electronic locks. A part of this step is the identification of doors the individual IT staff members need access to.

D. **Build a spreadsheet of service contract information.** The sheet should indicate who to call for which items, the terms of service (24/7, Monday through Friday, etc.), how to call for help, and the contract expiration date. This could be a long list. A copy should reside at the service desk.

E. **Build a vendor list of anyone who supplies critical materials or who provides critical services.** This could be the company that prints IT's special forms (such as invoices and checks), the place from which the company buys backup media, etc. Service companies could be hardware repair services, the company that provides off-site storage of backup tapes, or companies that support software tools.

F. **Take a walk around asset inventory.** Walk around the entire facility and note every major piece of equipment and its location on an asset list. Which device is important to critical operations? Which device must always be available? Compare the asset list to the service contract list. Are all of the critical devices covered? Is the service coverage adequate?

G. **Talk to the systems administrators and make a list of software assets.** This includes purchased software as well as homegrown code. Do the purchased packages have service support agreements? Are these agreements included on the service contract list? Are the software licenses securely stored off-site?

H. **Identify the various business functions that IT supports.** Make a list of them and then fill in the technologies that are necessary to support them. (This information is in the BIA report.) This is a big list.

I. **Establish a list of restoration priorities.** Base it on the list of critical business functions. Later on, review this list with executive management so planning efforts coincide with their expectations. In a crisis, the recovery team will use this to guide their actions.

J. **Build an employee skills matrix for the IT department.** This will give some idea of who to call on for emergency backup on a specific technology. It can also be matched against the critical equipment list and software asset lists to develop a staff-training plan. Identify the skills gaps now and begin training the IT staff!

To complete these ten basic steps, the IT Manager probably spent a couple of days pulling the information together. However, now the staff has a lot of information for the service desk and other key people in this organization. Much more is needed, but this forms the nucleus of a formal continuity plan.

COMMENT

The essential ingredient for an IT recovery is the ready availability of readable backup media. Back up *all* files onto other media as often as possible, and store this media off-site in a secure location. As media is rotated back to the data center, verify that it is still readable.

One way to see how ready the staff is (and to uncover any more hidden caches of information) is to make an unannounced visit to the support people and ask for their critical information. Some will reference the sticky notes that encircle their monitor; some will dig deep back into an address book for bypass codes, and some will bring out the cheat sheets. Others will give a condescending blank stare. Imagine the ball of energy they would become fumbling for this same information in a real emergency! Be sure to copy all of this information into the files, as it will be useful later.

COMMENT

Some people will declare that they already have a plan. Ask for a copy. In most cases, it will lack many of the essential details. This shows they have already bought into the recovery plan concept. Make sure that the plan is executable by someone familiar with the technology, but who has not worked on that business process.

After organizing what has been collected so far, begin validating it with people other than those who provided the information. Crosscheck the accuracy, to see which employees are better organized than others. It is especially important if the notes copied were rather old and out of date. All information should be neatly typed (or copied) and placed in a three-ring binder, broken down by subjects with tabs to identify the sections. In an emergency, the tabs allow quick access to needed information without fumbling through a lot of pages.

Be sure to mark the binder and all sheets as "company confidential." Much of what is in the business continuity plan will be useful to mischievous people.

[B]   Distributing Interim Copies

There is now enough of a plan to make copies and distribute them to key people. This is an important step, as the project has now progressed from a one-person show to a team effort. Ask each of these people to help improve the book by filling in the gaps and commenting on what has been collected so far. The minimal number of copies is:

A. One copy of the book at the plan administrator's office desk. (Use this when problems arise.)
B. One copy at the plan administrator's home to address problem calls when they come in (and in case something happens to the copy at work!).
C. One copy to the IT Manager.
D. One copy at the IT Manager's home.
E. One copy at the IT service desk.

At this stage it is best to keep the number of copies in circulation to a minimum since there will be many updates as the plan evolves. The IT Manager's copy and the service desk's copy may be skipped if they are stored on a CD and on the network as a read-only file.

[C]   Adding to the Plan—More Contact Information

During normal work hours, it is easy to find people when problems arise. Rather than chase them down, obtain a facility telephone directory. The company's telephone technician likely has one. This list provides the daytime telephone numbers. However, emergencies have a habit of arising in the middle of the night, on holiday weekends, etc. Using the telephone list and the company organization chart, identify the key managers to call in the event of an after-hours emergency. Ask these people for their home telephone and cell phone numbers.

These numbers are useful for advising people of IT problems during off hours. This forewarns them so when they come into work in an emergency, they are prepared for the situation. This might be to inform the materials managers that the warehouse management system has failed and will take many hours to repair. By calling them in the wee hours of the night, they can decide if their staff needs to come in early and work around the problem. The same situation holds for about every department: accounting, payroll, human resources, engineering, etc.

Respect the personal privacy of these home telephone numbers and never give them out to anyone. These personal numbers will likely be covered by the company's privacy policy, so do not leave them lying around. While on the subject, draft guidelines explaining the circumstances that are severe enough to call someone at home.

[D]   Keys

An important step in BCP is keeping people away from critical equipment. Some people are curious, like to push buttons, and are intrigued about what will happen next. There is the occasional discontented person who wants to express his outrage by turning off a server or unplugging a network hub. It could be almost anything. So wherever possible, limit the ability of anyone to disturb the operation of equipment. Keep critical equipment in locked closets, hard wired into the electrical outlet, and away from the wondering masses.

After keeping everyone else out, make sure the IT staff can get in! Problems can arise at any hour of the day or night. If technical support staff is called in to work on something, can they get in? If there is a company security force, they should have a copy of the key to every door. If not, then establish an IT key cabinet. A key cabinet holds one copy of every key to every door or cabinet the IT staff needs to access. Be sure to attach a label to every key because in a small pile, they all look alike!

Some people are certain that the world is out to get them, and they will attach their own locks to doors and tool lockers. They typically forget to pass a copy to the key locker. Fortunately, a well-stocked key locker includes a master key named "Mr. Bolt Cutter." Whenever encountering a personal lock on one of the equipment room doors, introduce that lock to Mr. Bolt Cutter. If this is not done, valuable time will be lost in a crisis looking for someone to open a $2.00 lock that did not belong there.

COMMENT

The company's security policy should require the security office to stock and provide approved locks for doors and cabinets, or a process for the security office to obtain two keys to each. The same policy must prohibit the use of personal locks on anything other than company lockers. This together with an employee orientation should greatly reduce the use of personal locks on company equipment.

It is easy to copy physical keys without anyone knowing about it. No one knows for sure how many copies of a particular key are floating around. The security office should always sign out keys to people for ease of retrieval when the employee leaves the company. Otherwise, these keys may wind up with people who should not have them.

Physical keys can effectively keep out most people, but by far the best approach is the use of electronic locks. These are common in hotels. Instead of turning a key, an electronic key checks the database to see if that key should have entry through that door. It also maintains a log of who unlocked what door, and when. In addition, a record is available of who has propped it open.

Electronic keys allow the IT Manager to grant or remove access easily. Over time, some people forget their pass card and ask for a "temporary" one for the day. Then they forget to turn it back in. Some people will go through this frequently. It is doubtful they lose their car keys so often! When issuing a temporary card, always limit its access to one day. Otherwise, it is like the copies of physical keys floating around. It is impossible to be sure of who is walking through what door and what they might be carrying out!

Passwords are the logical keys to IT equipment. Just like a master key, a system administrator password is the golden pass to anywhere and anything on a computer system. Guard passwords closely. The problem is that, in a crisis, the support staff may need specific passwords to shut down or restart servers, mainframes, computers, etc. Establish a secure place to store them so they are available in an emergency.

[E] Service Contracts—HELP!

The company probably pays a princely sum every month for someone to be on call to repair its vital equipment. This is a common practice. However, paying someone to come in at any hour to fix something is useless if the support staff does not know how to contact him/her! Take the time to pull information on all service contracts and put it in the BCP book. This is important information for the service desk to have too.

Ask everyone in the department for a copy of their service contract information. This would include:

A. **Vendor's name.**
B. **What is covered.** Sometimes this is specific equipment (by serial number); sometimes the agreement is for everything on the premises.
C. **Hours of coverage.** The company pays one rate for service to cover normal working hours, and a higher rate for around-the-clock coverage. If the company pays for 24-hour coverage, do not let the service company off the hook if they try to defer until morning. Around-the-clock coverage is double the cost of normal service.
D. **Whom to call during normal working hours and after hours.** Every agreement must include a 24-hour number. Try to get an after-hours telephone number even for the companies only providing 8:00 a.m. to 5:00 p.m. service. It will be expensive to bring them in on a Saturday to help with a repair, but it might be worth it.
E. **When the contract expires.** This information should go on a calendar to reevaluate the service level before the contract expires. Reevaluate the importance of the covered equipment, its incidence of repair, and if the current service level is adequate.

F. **Any limitations or extra cost provisions.** Sometimes the agreement covers parts and labor; sometimes it only covers the labor cost of "best effort." Know what this is in case an emergency purchase order is required.

G. **Contract number.** The larger companies will check to see if the caller has paid his bills before sending anyone out. They will look up the contract number in their database to see if the item in question is covered. In some cases, they want the unit serial number as well.

H. **Company-appointed contact person.** Usually, a company designates one or two people the person(s) who can make the call. It helps to know who they are. Often, these are people who know how to make minor adjustments to the equipment and avoid service calls.

I. **Guaranteed response time.** How long will it be before they show up? Usually this is something like four hours or eight hours. If they do not show up on time, start escalating the requests!

There are five basic types of service agreements. Select the one that best suits that piece of equipment's failure rate, the degree of criticality of the equipment, and the availability of alternate devices until that machine is operational.

A. **Cold call for service.** This is where the IT Manager's fingers do the walking through the phone book and find someone to come out. The result will be a long service call since they know nothing about the site or its equipment. They may also take several days to get around to coming out.

B. **Time and materials.** The service vendor will come out for a set rate per hour and work until the machine is operational. They will also charge for the parts. Although the hourly rate is expensive, this may be cheaper than a service contract. This approach is good for equipment that rarely breaks and for equipment where there are on-site spares. Under the time and materials arrangement, there is an existing business arrangement so the service company should be somewhat familiar with the company's equipment and its business processes.

C. **Normal working hours.** This is usually 8:00 a.m. until 5:00 p.m. Under this agreement, the service company will do what they can during these hours. If the job will run past 5:00 p.m., they will go home and pick up where they left off during the next business day.

D. **Full service.** This is 24/7 service. Unlimited calls at any time of day, for any day of the week. The contract includes all costs. Always use this type of service contract for mission critical equipment.

E. **Exchange.** This is a good approach for smaller items like bar-code scanner guns. Keep some spares on site and send in the broken ones for repair—usually at a set rate. However, it may take weeks to get the device back.

With this service contract information in hand, walk around and look at all of the critical equipment. Is it on the service contract list? Did someone forget to mention something or is there a gap in the service agreements? Does each critical device have the appropriate level of coverage? Business requirements change and often the service contracts do not keep pace with them.

After collecting all of this information into a spreadsheet, provide a copy to everyone who has the BCP book. The service desk will find this all very handy.

To ensure that everyone knows what to do, make up small cards with the service contract information on them. Attach the cards to the major devices like large printers, servers, etc. If possible, put it somewhere inside the machine where it is easy to find, such as under the dust cover of a printer. Be sure to remove any old service information. If there is a lot of equipment in a room, just post the collective information on the wall.

[F] Vendor Contacts

Like service contracts, the support staff needs to know who to call for a particular service or material. This is not an all-inclusive list. It should only include current vendors or someone the team may need to contact in an emergency. This list will do more than help in a major crisis; it can help with the more mundane emergencies that pop up every day. Has an off-brand printer ever run out of toner at a critical business time? Knowing who to call could get the ball rolling.

A vendor list provides a single point of reference for everyone in the department who needs materials. (Of course, they would still need to work through the usual approval process.) In addition, this list reduces the time required looking for vendors to bid on projects.

Include for each vendor the company name, account manager's name, daytime and after-hours telephone number, fax number, e-mail address, the company's address, and a description of what they supply. The vendor list should also contain every company on the service contract list.

When drafting the list, remember the "other" vendors such as the electric company, telephone company, water company, waste removal service, and local ambulance. These numbers may become very handy in a crisis. See Worksheet 08-2 Critical Vendor List.

[G] Walk-Around Asset Inventory

Grab a pad and pencil and walk around the company areas. Begin in the IT department. Make a note of every major item found, like a server, network hub, major printer, etc. Do not try to do this from memory. In particular, look for equipment that has popped up in user departments. Indicate which of these items support critical company processes. Walk everywhere. Be curious and open cabinets and every closet.

Look everywhere—especially where equipment does not belong.

WORKSHEET 08-2. Critical Vendor List

Critical Vendor List

Company Name	Contact Position	Name	Telephone Numbers				Email	Street Address
			Office	Cell	Fax	Home		
	Sales							
	Support							
	Sales							
	Support							
	Sales							
	Support							
	Sales							
	Support							
	Sales							
	Support							
	Sales							
	Support							
	Sales							
	Support							

COMMENT

In a large factory, one of the authors found:

- Modems connected to antifreeze coolant tanks so someone could remotely monitor the contents!
- Old 8088-based PCs used to monitor PLCs!
- A copper pipe bender that used 8-inch floppy disks!
- IBM network controllers that used a 5-inch floppy for storage—a floppy so worn you could almost see through it!
- 8088-based PCs with a custom communications board!

At a different site, there was:

- A time clock server stashed under a desk in the payroll department!
- An electronic lock server in the security office!

When walking through, note the location of disconnected equipment. Send someone out to pick it up for potential reissue. Likely some pockets of new equipment will be uncovered that someone keeps as a personal emergency spare parts stash. Check every closet! Arrange to have all of this equipment collected into one spot and lock it up. Repair and reissue the good material and scrap the broken ones.

Compare the asset inventory to the list of service contracts. Are all the critical devices covered? Is the level of coverage adequate? Sometimes the machine itself will have a sticker saying who to call for service. When in doubt, ask the operators whom they call with questions.

Include supporting equipment that enables other devices to work on the list. This might be an uninterruptible power supply or critical air conditioning unit. It may also include electronic time clocks or electronic door lock servers. An important goal is to identify "non-standard" equipment that is essential to a critical operation. (Often this equipment is too old to find replacement parts to repair.) The trouble with one-off equipment is that it can be impossible to replace in a crisis.

[H] Software Asset List

With the easy part out of the way, move on to backup copies of software and data. A look around will reveal a vast proliferation of computers from departmental servers, to special client software that interfaces with other companies, to shop floor equipment controllers. Inside each of these is valuable and potentially irreplaceable software and data. The BCP must ensure that someone makes a periodic backup, or safety, copy of this data, clearly labeled and stored off site.

For each critical piece of equipment, make a list of its critical software. It is often easier to replace the hardware than the software. Some software is unique and almost all software has settings to customize it to the situation. The scariest machines are the ones that no one will shut off since they are not sure if they will ever start again.

Ensure that every device has more than one backup copy of its software and that they are stored separately (preferably off site). For equipment not maintained in the computer room (such as in offices or on the shop floor), store one copy off site and one copy in the data center's tape library room.

Some devices to include:

A. Telephone PBX, automated attendants, and voice mail system—these are simply special-purpose computers requiring data backup in the same manner as a mainframe computer.
B. Programmable network devices.
C. Shop floor control systems, such as PLCs, robots, CNC devices, etc.
D. Special-purpose PCs that perform critical but highly specialized functions such as clearing credit cards.
E. Servers that control electronic door locks.
F. Copies of software source code locally developed.
G. Licenses for purchased software.

COMMENT

If the search uncovers software where the source code is lost, mark that system for replacement. If the source code cannot be found and that machine dies, then it may not be possible to use the replacement hardware without recompiling the software—which is kind of hard without the source code.

[I] Restoration Priorities

With the list of the critical processes in hand (as identified by the BIA or by the company executives), the next logical step is to develop restoration priorities for specific technical systems around the facility. Keep this list in the service desk area so that they know which problem to dispatch a technician to first. Discuss it during departmental meetings so everyone knows what is expected. Now everyone knows which system outages require all hands to drop everything and run to the rescue.

For example, if the accounting system was dead and the network was dead, address the network first since it enables all other critical systems to function. Another example would be if both the e-mail system and the materials management system were down. Which system should the service desk dispatch a repair technician to first?

A valuable use for this list is to identify ways to keep these systems running even in the face of adversity. It might mean adding small UPS units to departmental servers or specific workstations. Another possibility is installing failover servers along with the active ones. If the primary system fails, then the shadow system automatically activates.

Use this list to identify areas where manual workaround instructions are needed until normal operations resume. Recovery from manual processing (which usually involves keying in all the data that was not captured) can be tedious but the facility can keep moving forward!

[J] Toxic Material Storage

For safety's sake, everyone on the IT staff should know where toxic materials are stored and used within the facility. Technicians should take precautions in case whatever damaged the equipment also damaged the toxic materials containers.

Move or safely isolate equipment found in or adjacent to toxic materials storage areas. If moving this equipment is expensive, include it in the upcoming year's capital budget. This becomes a future planning item to isolate or move the equipment far away from the toxic storage area.

[K] Employee Skills Matrix

If a key support person is on vacation in a far-off place, who will be called to fix the problems? The IT Manager can guess or ask around, but in the meantime, the problem is simmering and so is the boss. Save time by building an employee skills matrix before problems arise.

Begin with a list of the critical processes supported. Each of these processes uses a set of technologies (hardware and software) to accomplish their mission. Technologies exist within a business reference, so a degree of understanding of how they fit in the customer's operations is useful. The skills matrix breaks the critical system down into its components to identify support requirements. The components might be a programming language, specific hardware knowledge, and an understanding of the database management system. This list of components translates into a list of skills required to support them.

A spreadsheet makes an easy-to-use tool for building the matrix. The skills matrix lists the technologies along the vertical axis (which can be a very long list) and the staff names along the top (column headings). Rate each person according to skills at using each of these technologies.

Add a few more rows to this list to identify other useful expertise, such as who is emergency medical technician (EMT) qualified, who is a volunteer firefighter, etc. As an important added benefit, use this list to identify people for training over the upcoming year.

§ 8.05 WRITING A PLAN

[A] Overview

Some people are reluctant to write recovery plans because they do not know where to start. Writing a plan is as simple as stating the basics of any story: who, what, where, when, why, and how. Base the format on what to do first, what to do second, etc. If the plan addresses these basic points, then it should be sufficient. The goal is to develop a set of instructions so that employees can take the right actions in a disaster. BCPs are intended as guidelines and advice. The technician on the scene should review the plan and then proceed as the circumstances dictate.

If there is a good risk analysis, then everyone has an idea of the various things that could go wrong. No one can predict exactly what will happen. However, a set of generalized actions fit in most situations. When working through the risk analysis, it is apparent that most plans contain the same details. Recovering a destroyed office is the same whether burned out in a fire or a snow-packed roof collapsed.

A plan is not a complete set of instructions to rebuild something. Typically, there are specific actions to repair something or contain the spread of damage to operations. Full recovery plans are created while the containment effort is still under way. When writing, always remember the target audience. Emergencies affect people in different ways. Emergencies are chaotic. A good plan reduces this confusion by providing guidance on what to do. Once the team is working on the problem, they will feel more in control and the chaos will diminish.

COMMENT

Cynics will say that a disaster will occur at the worst possible moment. For an accounting system, this might be when closing the year-end books, etc. Write plans as if the crisis erupted at the worst time in the annual business cycle, usually during the busy season.

Write each plan as if explaining the matter to someone. Think of the person likely to come in after hours to react to the emergency and imagine explaining it to him. Perhaps begin with a short overview paragraph that explains the business purpose of the process and essentially how it accomplishes this. Another way is to imagine the room during the emergency. What is the clearest way to address the problem?

A picture is worth a thousand words. Include pictures of hard to describe locations or drawings of how the major pieces work together. Use digital cameras to include some photos in the plan. Pictures can also shorten the narrative since who has time to read more than a few pages in a crisis?

[B] What to Write About

Every department should have a plan that addresses natural and infrastructure risks. People should not sit helplessly waiting for things to happen; they should be active participants in forcing the results they want. All department processes depend on some basic infrastructure support to be in place for them to be successful. This includes electricity, telecommunications, data communications, and data systems. Therefore, the facility-wide continuity plans should begin with supporting these areas.

Each plan should include three major sections:

A. **Immediate actions.** The first section is the "first aid" to be applied by the technician on the spot. This includes things like shutting off the sprinkler valve once the fire is out to minimize the amount of water damage to clean up. Another immediate action is to use employees' cell phones for communications during a telephone system outage. Many things are possible if thought out in advance.

B. **Containment.** The next section describes containment actions to reduce the spread of the damage until the primary support people arrive. This is not busy work. These are the same actions the "experts" would take when they arrive. In the fire sprinkler example, it would be to contain the water on the floor, picking up items from the floor to minimize water damage, etc.

C. **Establish minimal service levels.** The third major section of the plan contains the actions to return the process to a *minimal* level of service. A company cannot sit idle until a full recovery is completed. This could involve establishing a temporary office, shifting this process to a different company site, implementing manual procedures, etc.

With these three sections in mind, formulate a basic plan format. In this way, all plans at the facility will have a similar "look and feel."

[C] Contents of a Typical Plan

Base the plan's terminology and the level of explanation on the assumed audience. These plans are not targeted at the process expert who might use the plan to gather some ideas in the midst of chaos; an expert would typically just act. The plans are for others in the department who either were on site during the emergency or were the first ones in. Assume they are familiar with the technology but not with that particular business system.

Begin with how obvious the problem is. A building hit by a tornado is obvious. Magnetic damage to backup tapes is not. Hard to detect problems require detailed step-by-step instructions.

How much warning may there be before a problem hits? Some natural disasters, such as a hurricane, provide extensive warnings before they hit. Other disasters, like a lightning strike or blue smoke wafting from the back of a computer provide little advance warning. Emergencies that have a warning time can trigger containment actions before they begin. Again, a hurricane is an excellent example of an emergency where action is warranted. This can range from covering all of the windows with wood to testing the emergency power generator.

The second consideration in writing a plan is how long the reader must hold out before expert help arrives. If they are fighting to contain a problem, can the expert be on site within one or two hours? They will need enough information to contain the problem and fight it until the expert arrives.

Finally, if a key process is dead, is there anything that can be done to keep the facility running? Could materials be shipped out of the front of the building until the network is restored to the shipping docks? Can the factory manually perform the processes that the dead machine used to accomplish? Can the payroll office issue "40 hour" paychecks until the payroll system is restored?

So in each plan, remember:

A. The target audience
B. How obvious the problem is
C. How much warning you will have
D. How long until expert help arrives
E. Are there any manual workarounds?

[D]   Which Processes Need a Plan?

It is not practical to write a plan to cover every eventuality for every item. A plan is only required for critical processes (although a prudent IT Manager has a plan for recovering every process). The facilities department should have a plan to address all natural disasters and man-made disasters (as described in the previous risk analysis section). Other departments are also involved in these areas, such as human resources.

All infrastructure risks should also have a plan. This includes electrical service, data processing, and telecommunications. Even if the facilities department is handling the loss of electrical power, the IT department needs a plan for managing the UPSs for maximum availability, a power-shedding plan to relieve pressure on the UPS by turning off low value equipment, etc.

Most companies have a few other critical processes outside of the infrastructure area for which they should also plan. It might be an expensive and unique machine in the factory. It might be special equipment to route incoming calls to individual salespersons or even a very old machine that manages the finished goods inventory. Whatever specific critical processes are, they need a plan.

Even in our mechanical world, there are still some manual critical processes. They need recovery plans too!

Ensure that the manual processes are clearly documented.

[E]   Testing

Testing is a vital part of recovery planning. Often business managers view testing as time consuming, expensive, and a nonessential activity. This is completely wrong. An untested plan is a risk. Such a plan may provide a false sense of security if it misses the mark and no one takes the time to validate its contents.

Testing provides many valuable benefits:

A. **Testing a plan validates that it works**. It uncovers any gaps in the document. The author may have known what was meant by a passage but anyone reading the document would come to a quick halt.

8-34

B. **Testing ensures the document is up to date with the latest process it is supporting**. Keeping recovery plans in sync with process changes is a major challenge. With so much to do, busy people leave changes to the plan for last. Testing catches and updates plans with this problem.

C. **Testing trains the participants in their roles during a crisis**. It is one thing to read a plan but something different to do it. Involving people in a test helps to debug a plan as others interpret it. It builds confidence in the participants that they could fulfill their responsibilities in a crisis.

Preparing for a test requires considerable planning. People and materials must be gathered. A test scenario is required to provide a backdrop for the exercise. The primary types of tests are:

A. **Walkthrough.** The plan's author walks peers through the plan step by step. The goal is to identify omissions and difficult to understand passages.

B. **Tabletop exercise.** The plan is talked through by both the IT support team and the department they are supporting (such as Payroll). A disaster scenario is provided to make the plan more "real." An example might be a fire in the server room, a data security breach, or a multi-day electrical blackout.

C. **Simulation.** The IT team and the supporting departments act as if a real disaster has occurred. A good simulation places the teams in separate rooms (to complicate communications) and feeds information in a bit (or complication) at a time. Simulations require considerable preparation and many companies hire a consultant to develop and run the test.

D. **Wide area simulation.** A company-wide exercise. A worthwhile effort but rarely done due to expense. A simple example is a fire drill.

Few companies can afford to shut down their operations to conduct testing. Often it is accomplished in "slices," such as for an entire department, or a subset of it. The exception is for hot site testing. IT departments must test this at least annually. It is also a good idea to rotate the IT staff through the hot site. In a crisis, the team will be more familiar with the new location, its limitations, and rules of operation.

[F] Keeping the Plan Current

This is an ongoing struggle, especially in a large IT shop. There are several common approaches:

A. BCP documentation must be updated within 30 days of upgrade installation.

B. Additional hardware for the host site must accompany every request for system expansion (such as additional CPUs or disks).

C. Make BCP updates a step in the formal change control process.

D. Whenever a crisis erupts, check to see if someone pulls out the plan for reference. Whatever happens, after the emergency passes, require the team to review and update the plan with what worked the best during the recent problem.

The key to keeping the plan up to date is to train the team on the importance of current information in a crisis, and to require the various IT supervisors to enforce this requirement. In essence, push the responsibility as close to the source of the change as possible. IT supervisors tend to support this since they are the ones who scramble to repair systems when the primary support person is far away on vacation.

The support team must review plans not tested in the previous 12 months. The IT supervisor for that team will also review it and sign it as correct.

§ 8.06   SOURCES OF ADDITIONAL INFORMATION

[A]   Publications

There are many books concerning this subject. Most of them are general in nature and a great place to start. As the planning program matures, look for something that is specific to your industry.

Some publications include a regular column about disaster recovery, such as Computerworld™ (*www.computerworld.com*). Two popular and free periodicals dedicated to Business Continuity are:

A. Disaster Recovery Journal—*www.drj.com*
B. Continuity Insights—*www.continuityinsights.com*

[B]   Training and Certification

Several organizations offer formal training on the concepts of Disaster Recovery and Business Continuity. Some colleges offer degrees and others only a few classes. These schools can be located by searching the Internet, and through the FEMA site (*www.fema.gov.*)

The most popular training organizations offering classes, certification, and ongoing professional information are:

A. Disaster Recovery International—*www.DRII.org*
B. Business Continuity Institute—*www.BCI.org*

[C]   Web Sites

The most comprehensive Web site on disaster recovery is run by the U.S. government's Federal Emergency Management Agency (FEMA) at *www.fema.gov.* This site contains information on training, developing plans, and links to many other useful sites. Take time and explore because the deeper into this site a person goes, the more interesting it becomes. It is the best site for all around (and free) information.

Another useful Web site for developing the risk assessment for your locations is also run by the U.S. government's National Oceanic & Atmospheric Administration at *www.NOAA.gov*. This site provides information about severe weather for your area, based on historical data.

[D]   Business Continuity Plan Checklist

A. Is there a published policy assigning responsibility and guidelines for creating and maintaining a Business Continuity Plan?
   1. Does it designate a person responsible for writing the plan?
   2. Has an executive been assigned to oversee the planning effort? (Ultimately, the CEO is responsible for the plan.)
B. Was a Business Impact Analysis conducted within the last two years? Does it identify:
   1. Critical business functions
   2. Critical IT systems
   3. Recovery Time Objective
C. Was a risk assessment conducted to identify threats to the critical systems?
D. Are mitigation actions assigned to the most serious risks?
E. Does every IT technology that stores data have a current safety copy stored securely off site?
   1. Data
   2. Software
   3. Configuration tables
F. Is there a crisis communications plan for alerting the appropriate employees and executives at the appropriate time during a disaster?
G. Is there a designated separate facility for the recovery of the IT department, such as a hot site?
H. Does the BCP cover the prompt shipment of equipment in the event of an emergency?
 I. Is there a work area recovery plan for the business departments to continue work?
   1. Has this plan been tested within the last two years?
   2. Did the test include a sampling of departments?
J. Are vital records securely stored on site, with safety copies securely stored off site? Usually this involves paper documents.
K. Are there manual "workarounds" for every critical IT data system?
L. Is there a crisis management plan in place for executive leadership?
M. Is every plan tested at least every other year?
   1. Has every critical system been recovered at the alternate site?
   2. Does each critical system have its own set of recovery instructions?
   3. Can all of these technologies be recovered within the Recovery Time Objective?
N. Is every person who might execute a plan trained in his role? Does this include new employee orientation?
O. Is there a reliable process in place to update the BCP as the IT and business functions change?

9

IT AUDITS: STAYING IN COMPLIANCE

§ 9.01 OVERVIEW

[A] Purpose and Scope

"The auditor is coming!"—words that strike fear into the hearts of IT Managers everywhere. Employee attitudes toward audits depend on how the company uses audits. Well-run audits are not "witch hunts" devised to dig up real or imagined shortcomings with the IT department. They provide insights into departmental performance and suggestions for improvement. Only the incompetent fears these audits.

Audits are executive management's verification that the departments in their company follow proper management and financial practices. Most people are familiar with accounting audits—a review of financial transactions and procedures to ensure that money is not stolen or misused. This type of audit also verifies that appropriate checks and balances are in place to remove the likelihood or temptation to steal. An IT audit applies a similar approach to test and verify that funds are properly spent, appropriate process checks are in place, and resources are properly utilized.

An important aspect of an audit is to identify and address risks to the organization. Data systems are the heart of a company. IT audits look for risks that may be due to management or technical errors. More recently, audits have verified that IT departments are aware of and abide by laws concerning the management and retention of critical company information. The auditor must understand the workings of an IT department if he is to examine both aspects.

Auditors are best known through their military counterparts, Inspectors General, or IGs. The IG serves as an alternate conduit of information from members of the service upward (for reporting problems) and from the commander downward (by inspecting units). Anyone in the military can bypass commanders and obtain fast action by reporting a situation to the IG who answers only to the top unit commanders.

COMMENT

Department of the Navy Inspector General Web Site
"We are agents of change for the Department. We will highlight practices which deserve emulation and publicize pitfalls when we find them. We will help all DoN (Department of the Navy) activities and commands raise readiness while improving their business operations to ensure responsible stewardship of the resources of the DoN." (*www.ig.navy.mil*)

Executives in large companies have the same problems as their military counterparts. How can they gauge the true effectiveness of a department?

They lack the time and the expertise to evaluate each one. Often layers of middle management filter out negative but important information as it moves up the reporting chain. Bad news causes upset executives and occasional loss of positions. The executives may think that reported problems mean the manager is incapable of handling the job and will replace him. Soon, everyone knows to tell them what they want to hear.

Unfortunately, this minimization of problems delays executive recognition until they are too big to hide. By that time, something simply solved in an earlier stage now requires a lengthy and expensive process.

To bypass the filtering of information by middle management, executives employ agents (called auditors) who report directly to them. The auditors inspect and evaluate company processes to ensure they provide the best return for the company's investment. Auditors sidestep the middle layers by speaking directly to the workers and examining their equipment. Audit reports go straight to top executives or the board of managers—making many a middle manager uneasy. A full audit of every practice in a department is a monumental task and a serious disruption to business. Typically, audits sample practices in a department based on their criticality, previous audit findings, or emerging risks to the company. These practices reflect priorities set by executive management and by changes in the business environment.

Auditors use personal expertise, checklists, and published policies and procedures to examine existing practices. A department's policy and procedure manual detail how employees are supposed to address specific issues. The auditor compares these documents to industry models to ensure that all of the appropriate steps are in place. Next, these documents are compared to employee interviews to determine how work is *actually* accomplished. Discrepancies between the policies and work practices are noted in the audit report.

Audits are necessary to ensure that IT departments operate on a solid foundation of policies and procedures. Careers sometimes advance by installing the latest software or cutting costs. Sometimes these changes are made at the expense of executive mandated business practices such as maintaining a current disaster recovery plan, shortcutting prudent security steps, or skipping technical support training. Audits ensure that these shortcuts do not occur behind the scenes.

Audits can be a bit disruptive but useful. If funding for important activities such as security upgrades has not been forthcoming, the auditor can report this as a potential problem. If funds are lacking for the replacement of antiquated critical hardware, or the funds diverted for other uses, this also is reported. On the other hand, if lazy IT Managers ignore their own policies, and generally run a halfhearted security program, then this also will be reported.

[B] Types of Audits

Corporate audits come in two flavors: management audits and technical audits. Management audits examine practices that are commonly used in all departments. The auditors are looking to see if the IT department is following company and commonly accepted management practices. Some of the areas examined might include:

    A. Adherence to company policies concerning expense accounts, personnel management, performance evaluation, hiring/firing, and compliance with legal requirements.

    B. Planning, both tactically and strategically.
1. Is an IT technology strategy in place and current?
2. Do the plans support stated company strategic directions?
3. Are plans published (where appropriate)?
4. Does the IT staff know and understand the plans?

    C. Budgeting
1. Do the head count, capital, and operating budgets reflect the plans they are designed to support?
2. Are funds spent on what was appropriated?
3. Are financial records retained and easy to find?
4. Are all funds accounted for?

    D. Are appropriate IT vital records maintained, such as software license files, purchase receipts for hardware, personnel records, etc.?

Technical audits examine technical aspects of the IT service offering. They include all sections of the department: management, operations, programming, systems programming, security, networking, and telephony. Often technical audits focus on system controls and audit trails.

Specific technical audit items sometimes reflect emerging threats such as virus protection and data security. Technical audits typically examine a few critical areas and a sampling of other areas. Most IT auditors have expertise in some aspect of technology and have checklists to examine the others. Some technical audit points will include:

    A. Security review to include firewall and virus protection and the timely inclusion of updates. It may also include logs of intrusion attempts and actions taken.

    B. Programming documentation and testing to ensure that proper controls are used to validate formulas used in financial reports.

    C. Completeness of the department's business continuity plan and records of tests conducted.

[C] Critical Policies to Develop Based on This Chapter

Using the material discussed in this chapter, you will be able to create the following policies:

    A. IT practices during an audit
    B. IT Manager responsibilities after an audit
    C. Ongoing IT practices

Policies should always be developed based on the local situation. Successful managers cannot issue appropriate guidance if the policies are written with another company's situation or location in mind.

§ 9.02 IT MANAGEMENT AUDIT

[A] Purpose

A management truism is to "inspect what you expect." If executives expect that specific practices are to be followed, then auditors will be eventually dispatched to verify that they are.

[B] IT Organization

IT personnel are a major company expense. Proper utilization of personnel resources is important if the company is to receive the full benefit for its investment. Proper generally means that the level of expertise is equal to the assigned tasks—not too high or too low. The IT audit will verify that the company is receiving the maximum benefit for the money spent.

IT organizational charts should specify the following:

A. Structure and the appropriate segregation of duties.
B. Detailed job descriptions written for each type of position and reflecting the actual assignments and not a generic situation. Compare job descriptions to local job markets to gauge if the staff is over or under paid for the local economy.
C. Maintenance of current employee resumes and employment records. The auditor can compare these to the job descriptions to verify that employee skills are properly employed.
D. Positions that support critical data systems or infrastructure. Verify the resumes and employment records for the primary and backup support personnel to ensure they possess the expertise to support them.
E. Provision of adequate continuing management and technical training, based on identified staff deficiencies and incoming technologies.
F. Maintenance of an adequate staffing level, based on published service levels and industry norms.
G. An adequate compensation program is in place for attracting and retaining qualified personnel.

Without a plan, an IT department is like a mob wandering the company's countryside without a road map. They may arrive somewhere but it will not be where their paymasters wanted them to be. The company's strategic plans are the road map that all departments are expected to follow. The IT department bases its strategic plans on the requirements it derives from the company strategy. This is broken down into technology updates, capacity planning, and support of changes to the various department plans. Identify future staffing level requirements by position and key skills to support these changes.

The IT department regularly participates in short- and long-term planning with its user community. The auditor verifies that the IT plans support the company's strategic directions and customer department improvement plans.

[C]   IT Controls

IT management requires controls ensuring the operation maintains adequate safeguards at all times.

- A. **Management standards and procedure controls.**
    1. Secure personnel administration records, physical and electronic, to prevent compromise of company or personal data.
    2. Trace systems development audit trails to ensure that problems or system interruptions can be traced to their approximate source.
    3. Computer operations have adequate segregation of duties and limited access to file information. Only authorized personnel perform activities or obtain company confidential forms (e.g., checks).
    4. Networking operations permit only authorized personnel access to firewalls and network security systems.
    5. Contingency planning and disaster recovery procedures are current, published, enforced, and tested. Documentation of test efforts is available for examination.
    6. Logs are maintained and reviewed daily to ensure that backups are properly completed and stored, that intrusion attempts have been investigated, and that system errors are promptly addressed, etc.
- B. **Reports on the effectiveness of IT.**
    1. Management performance metrics including employee turnover, budget performance, project budget, and schedule performance are gathered and tracked.
    2. Performance of critical company systems to include systems utilization and data accuracy.
    3. Performance and problem reports prepared by user groups. Items cited in these reports are reviewed for action.
    4. Internal and external audit reports of IT activities.
    5. Major hardware performance and load balancing to ensure maximum practical utilization of resources.
    6. Comparable performance norms available from similar sized companies in the same industry.
- C. **Project performance reports.** To ensure control of projects, performance reports of selected projects are audited for management. These reports compare actual performance with project plans. Reasons for variances are determined and reported.
- D. **Vital records management.** In the course of business, the IT department creates and utilizes vital records, both physical and electronic.
    1. **Identification.** Identify all records essential to the IT organization to include software licenses (mainframe and workstation) and warranties. Many of the vital IT records are electronic (e.g., security logs) and must be maintained to meet legal requirements.
    2. **Documents are properly completed.** Equipment warranties require identification of the date purchased to validate the warranty

coverage. Incomplete personnel records may result in legal action and accusations of unfair discharge.

3. **Document storage.** Documents of all type are stored for easy access (by the proper authorities) and safeguarded against the effects of heat, humidity, and insects.

[D] Financial Analysis

Audits of IT financial records ensure that funds are properly requested and spent only for the equipment or services approved. This includes a comparison of IT operating costs to industry norms for a similar size and type of institution. Things to look for:

A. Ensure that documents used to request funds clearly state the intended purpose with a link to the company's strategic business plan.

B. Sample completed appropriations to ensure that funds were only used for the approved purposes and not diverted to other equipment or services.

C. Prices paid are appropriate.

D. Receipt of goods purchased. Often this involves inspecting the items and matching the serial numbers of the items to the receiving document.

COMMENT

When internally charging users for IT services, compare these costs with bids from outsourcing companies.

E. Obtain the credit ratings of critical vendors. Note those in danger of financial collapse so appropriate contingency steps can be prepared.

F. Ensure that vendor services include a written contract that specifies the type and level of service to be provided. The auditor verifies that the employees who can call for service understand what the vendor has agreed to provide.

G. Determine there is no conflict of interest between any IT employee and vendor. Company policies concerning conflict of interest and gifts from vendors are enforced.

H. Check vendor invoices against work done ensuring correct billing.

See Policy ITP-09-1 IT Audit Policy as an example.

POLICY ITP-09-1.   IT Audit Policy

Policy #:	ITP-09-1	Effective:	03/18/13	Page #:	1 of N
Subject:	IT Audit Policy				

1.0 PURPOSE

This policy describes IT support for executive management mandated audits.

2.0 SCOPE

This policy encompasses all aspects of the IT department. Audits may be required to meet internal requirements or legal requirements. The IT Manager is responsible for implementing all aspects of this policy.

3.0 POLICY

This policy mandates IT management support to include:

A. IT practices during an audit.
   1. IT Manager will brief all IT staff members on their conduct during the audit.
      a. Require honesty—employees are required to provide prompt, honest, and factual answers to all questions by the auditors.
      b. Opinion versus facts—employees will identify those answers that are their opinion and those answers they can substantiate as facts.
   2. IT Managers will support all requests made by auditing officials.
      a. Making key employees available for auditors within a reasonable time.
      b. Providing records requested. If records are nonexistent, they will obtain whatever is available.
B. IT responsibilities after an audit.
   1. IT Managers will carefully review the auditor's report and comment, within 5 working days, on each negative point:
      a. Concurrence—Include any clarifying facts and an action plan for resolving the point.
      b. Objection—Include reasons why the audit point is incorrect.
   2. Follow up the report after 6 months identifying:
      a. Audit points resolved—how they were satisfied.
      b. Outstanding audit points—must include an action plan for prompt resolution.
C. Ongoing IT practices.
   1. Establish and maintain audit trails for critical functions, such as user ID authorizations.
      a. Identify records essential for auditing critical functions and all financial transactions.
      b. File critical records in secure storage.

2. Conduct IT Manager audit of policies to ensure compliance.
   a. Critical record completion and accuracy.
   b. Critical records storage.
   c. Critical files are complete.

4.0 REVISION HISTORY

Date	Revision #	Description of Change
03/18/13	1.0	Initial creation.

5.0 INQUIRIES

Direct inquiries about this policy to:

George Jenkins, CIO
Our Company, Inc.
2900 Corporate Drive
Columbus, OH 43215

Voice: 614-555-1234
Fax: 614-555-1235
E-mail: gjenkins@company.com

Revision #:	1.0	Supersedes:	N/A	Date:	03/18/13

§ 9.03 IT LEGAL MANDATES AND RECORDS RETENTION

[A] Overview

The IT department is, by far, the largest records custodian in the company. Accounting records, personnel records, mail, and a host of other records all reside under the control of the IT Manager. Numerous government regulations govern the control and retention of each of these record types. In the event of a legal action, the IT Manager must ensure that he is not personally liable for missing information.

This is not an area for IT Managers to "go it alone." The IT auditor can provide a wealth of information concerning the mandatory records retention for each type of data as well as prudent actions that can demonstrate "due diligence" by IT management. Do not hesitate to ask for assistance in this area. If "due diligence" compliance requires additional capital budget funding, then the auditor's opinion will speed executive approval.

COMMENT

In November 1986, Lt. Col. Oliver North, USMC, a national security advisory aid to President Ronald Reagan, began systematically deleting more than 5,000 e-mail messages from his account on the White House data systems. What he did not realize is that all of these electronic records were on backup media. Investigators later used these copies to reconstruct the Iran-Contra scandal.

[B]   Public Laws

Many regulatory agencies place requirements on data management and retention. Some of these are specific to types of business but most touch every company in some way. Always refer to the company's legal counsel for a complete list. Examples of this are:

- The Sarbanes-Oxley Act ensures the integrity of the company's financial documents through the control and security of the financial system. The IT audit ensures that financial systems are accurate so that executives can certify their financial statements as reliable.
- Occupational Safety and Health Administration (OSHA)—records pertaining to company accidents and safety.
- Environment Protection Agency (EPA)—records pertaining to emissions and discharge monitoring and compliance.
- SEC—Securities and Exchange Commission's regulations governing the handling of non-public company information to guard against insider trading.
- Gramm-Leach-Bliley Act of 1999 concerning the safeguarding of customer information.
- Department of Labor and the Walsh-Healey Act concerning payroll data.
- Health Insurance Portability and Accountability Act of 1996 (HIPAA)—regulations covering the handling of medical records.

COMMENT

Whenever making decisions about complying with legal issues, always consult your company's legal counsel. Do not waste time guessing—ask the people who should know!

[C] Records Retention

IT Managers must be aware of the various types of data on their active and backup data systems and ensure they comply with all legal requirements. This will require some forethought when developing data backup strategies. Backup media automatically falls under the longest retention period of its contents. For example, to retain a single record on a tape indefinitely means retaining the entire tape.

Practically speaking, some segregation of backup data on media will create a need for more media but ease system restoration time. For example, if the accounting system lost a specific database or set of files, they may be quicker to locate. Some managers address retention requirements by backing up and retaining every bit of data indefinitely. This may seem the simplest answer but creates its own problems. Issues to keep in mind include:

- The more data the company retains beyond its useful life, the greater the storage space requirements and costs.
- The more media that must be purchased but not reused.
- The more data that must be searched if the company is required to provide information during a legal "discovery" order.
- Retained media must be readable by current equipment. At some point, this mountain of data must be copied onto new media since backup tapes and microfiche decay over decades.

Retained records have many characteristics:

- The type of media, including tape, microfiche, paper, optical disk—both on-site and off-site.
- The length of time that a record has legal or historical value.
- The length of time that the record must be maintained in active storage.
- The method and proof of a record's destruction.

COMMENT

In December 2000, the Securities and Exchange Commission imposed fines of $1.65 million per firm against five major broker-dealer organizations for violations of SEC, NYSE, and NASD rules for failing to preserve electronic records for the mandated amount of time. Specifically mentioned is the retention of electronic communications.

[D]   Types of Records

IT Managers should always refer to their company's legal counsel when establishing legal retention periods for records. Update these legal recommendations annually. File each written recommendation in a safe place to protect the IT Manager against potential legal action. It is important that the IT Manager knows which data elements are contained in each data system so he can determine the appropriate retention time. Examples of documents and data elements that require retention periods include:

- Personnel records
- Insurance records
- E-mail and internal memos
- Instant messenger communications
- Accounting and finance records
- Tax records
- Payroll records
- Facilities and real estate documents
- Research notes, patents, and copyrights
- Customer credit applications

§ 9.04   RESOURCE MANAGEMENT

[A]   Scope

IT is one of the most expensive departments in any company. The people are expensive, the equipment is expensive, and there never seems to be enough of either! The IT Manager can be sure that, to some extent, the auditor will examine the resource management records of the department to ensure that expenditures are in accordance with company guidelines.

[B]   Technical Resources

Technical resources encompass hardware, software, and all of the miscellaneous items required to keep them in operation. In essence, this includes all of the IT assets except the people. Technical resources are often long-term commitments. To guide purchases, the IT Manager develops a long-term strategy for hardware and software directions that minimizes the number of different technologies and maximizes their benefits. Items to track include:

A. **Software inventory.** The software coordinator is responsible for developing and maintaining a list of active (in-house-developed and purchased) software.
   1. A strategy to maximize the benefit of software products and minimize the variety of products supported. This is often based on functionality and interoperability.

    a. An overall plan that displays the "fit" for each product based on capabilities. Apply this to application development tools such as databases and programming languages.

    b. A process to identify obsolete products and then retire them. Adding new technologies without retiring the lesser used ones increases the expertise demands of the IT staff and increases costs.

    c. A strategy to eliminate products that duplicate functionality that is found in the "standard" company software products. The fewer products there are to support, the fewer the experts that are required and the lower the department's personnel costs.

    d. Publishing software development/acquisition method.

2. Purchased software information includes:

    a. Information protecting the company's licenses and proof of ownership to include the dates of purchases, the vendor's name, version number, and purchase price. License information must be organized for ready access according to the platform it runs on.

    b. Information on contractual vendor support both from the original purchase and for ongoing service agreements.

    c. Any internal audit reports that reconciled software licenses to the number of copies in use.

3. In-house-programmed software information includes:

    a. Information identifying when and by whom a data system was created. This includes the name of the authors, the date it was implemented, and references to design documents used in its development.

    b. Major revision dates and explanations.

    c. User and technical documentation.

    d. Names of current support persons and their trained backup team.

B. **Hardware inventory.**

1. A detailed technology strategy outlining the useful life of technologies in general and major installed items in particular.

2. A listing of current hardware and attached components is maintained and grouped as follows:

    a. Mainframe or server computers and peripheral devices.

    b. Workstations and peripheral devices.

    c. Network devices.

    d. Telecommunications equipment.

    e. Expected future purchases of hardware.

3. Identification and implementation plan to retire old hardware by migrating applications to other equipment over the next five years. Adding new technologies without retiring the lesser used ones increases hardware service expense and increases the potential of a forced hardware upgrade in a disaster.

COMMENT

Carefully designed technology strategies are seriously challenged by changes in technology that sometimes burst onto the scene. Stand-alone PDAs became PDAs with wireless Internet, which became cell phone PDAs and, more recently, smartphones and tablets with built-in cameras. All of this occurred in a few short years. From out on the fringe the simple PDA has evolved into a mainstream workstation with all of the security issues that go along with it. Auditors verify that IT strategies keep pace with technological change.

[C]   Personnel Resources

Maintain a published organizational chart of the IT department, both with names and with general responsibilities of each person. Identify lines of authority to ensure that responsibilities align with the authority to control them. This indicates an efficient use of delegation and improved productivity of the staff.

IT personnel expenses relate to the relevant expertise of the staff. To verify this, the auditor may follow a five-step process:

A. Identify the critical systems supported by the department.
B. Identify the technologies that these critical systems depend upon.
C. Identify the skills required by the IT staff to adequately support these technologies.
D. Compare the skills required to the skills found on the IT staff.
E. Note deficiencies in the audit report.

The auditor might check for an active training program based on the skills requirement data. The IT Manager should have a personnel skills inventory on file for each person. Compare these profiles to the job descriptions to identify training requirements for the staff. Personnel records should include:

A. Stated job descriptions.
B. Additional duties assignments.
C. Primary/backup persons identified for all critical systems.
D. Staff training plan, to include training for technical skills refresh.
E. Skills assessments for each person completed by the individual and his or her supervisor.
F. Salaries aligned to contribution to the department.
G. Market check of salaries based on levels and types of expertise.

§ 9.05 PROGRAMMING ACTIVITIES CONTROL

[A] Overview

In the absence of an official policy, technicians will make decisions they feel are most appropriate. Where policies have been created, a periodic audit ensures that these policies still serve the best interests of the organization.

Correct methodologies must be used to guide software management:

A. **Preliminary analysis.** The analyses required for a proposed system must state the business case for the system (or change) and the approximate cost to implement it.

B. **User service request evaluation.** The current system operation, including cost to user, has been assessed. Potential tangible and intangible benefits are detailed and ultimate objectives of requested services assessed. Demonstration that cost/benefit analysis is used to prioritize requests.

C. **Requirements and objectives.** Detailed definitions are assembled and descriptions of requirements and objectives are identified by the users. Requirements are approved by end users before work begins.

D. **System design.** System design is based on IT standard processes and software tools.

E. **User nomenclature.** Explain customer specific terminology. Typically, these are terms unique to their field of business, such as accounting, material management, etc.

F. **Computer programming standards.** Following standards permits others to maintain the systems.

G. **Documentation.** Technical, operations, and user manuals are current and easily understood.

H. **Implementation.**
   1. **Program testing.** Maintain test scripts in technical documentation along with sample data test cases.
   2. **User, service desk, and operations training.** All of this must be documented.
   3. **A contingency plan.** Be prepared for a system rollback if the implementation fails.

[B] Standards for Systems Development and Programming

Adequately define and follow standards for systems development, programming functions, systems development methodology, and program and system documentation. Controls should be implemented to ensure orderly software changes. The segregation of duties into application program development, cataloging of programs for production, and operating systems programming activities are in place.

An audit of the systems development area should look for the following items:

A. Written programming standards cover coding techniques, documentation, testing, acceptance, and data conversion and include:
   1. Systems design and development.
   2. Software package selection.
   3. Program testing.
   4. Systems implementation.
   5. Systems and programming documentation.
   6. Program change controls.
   7. Quality assurance and cataloging.
B. Application systems design development standards including:
   1. Project feasibility studies.
   2. Project cost-benefit analysis.
   3. Predetermined progress milestones and follow-up review of progress reports.
   4. Documented user approval of systems design, program tests, user documentation, and user's final acceptance.
   5. Documented post-implementation performance studies.
C. Programming standards such as:
   1. Use of control totals, programmed audits, and validation checks of input before processing starts.
   2. Audit trails and exception reports of uncommon transactions.
   3. Standardized routines and modular coding.
   4. Standards for reusable coding practices.
   5. Involvement of users in major decisions affecting input, logic flow, and output.
   6. Test plans that include all conceivable error conditions.
   7. Documentation of user training before systems implementation.
D. Technical documentation standards that include:
   1. Systems narratives.
   2. Program narratives.
   3. File layout schematics and output formats.
   4. Database dictionary listings.
   5. Descriptions of edit checking and programmed controls.
   6. A chronological listing of program changes explaining what was charged, by whom, why, and when.
   7. Naming conventions for data elements, software modules, files, etc.
E. Distribute current user manuals to all appropriate departments in the quantity required.
   1. Program documentation library procedures are employed ensuring adherence to systems/programming standards.
   2. Program documentation, including program changes, is complete.
   3. Distribution of documentation to authorized parties.

[C] Programming Activities Control

To control programming activities and ensure uniformity and conformity, consider these guidelines:

A. Documents generated for new programs and after-program changes are reviewed and documentation contains the following:
1. A description of problem or reasons for change.
2. Name of programmer and date of change.
3. Signature and date of supervisor who reviewed and approved program change.
B. Sufficient numbers of persons with training and experience are available to provide support and backup for critical systems and programming functions.
C. Application programmers are denied access to:
1. Documentation and source listings for operating system.
2. Production program libraries.
3. Live data files.
D. Records of temporary program changes using patches or system utilities are maintained and periodically reviewed by supervisory personnel.

[D] Database Management

The database management system adequately meets audit standards when:

A. There is an appointed database administrator with a trained secondary support person.
B. Written procedures are employed for maintaining a data dictionary file.
C. Transaction logs and procedures effectively allow for recovery of the database.
D. Data security measures are employed to prevent unauthorized access of data and/or changes to it.

[E] Management Post-Implementation Reviews

Determine whether the IT management maintains post-implementation reviews and continued reviews of existing systems. Post-implementation reviews should compare the original time and cost estimates to the actual requirements to improve future project planning.

Compare the performance and benefits from the new system to the benefits used as a basis to approve the work. Inconsistencies may point out where unreliable data is used as the basis for expensive financial decisions.

Reviews should adequately determine that:

A. The resultant system designs are consistent with original objectives.
B. Audit trails and controls are satisfactory.
C. Program and system testing plans are satisfactory.
D. System and program documentation is adequate.
E. Users are informed of changes in a timely manner and provided with revised user operation manuals.
F. User training is adequate and timely.
G. Synchronized source and object programs.

§ 9.06 COMPUTER OPERATIONS

[A] Objective

Data center operations are the enablers of the IT organization. Responsibilities vary between organizations, but in general, they encompass all of the routine efforts, such as backing up data, running a central print room, staffing the service desk, vital records storage, workstation and peripheral repairs, user IDs administration, security, etc. The primary goal of operations is stability—not optimal processes. A stable, predictable environment is more valuable to end users than an optimal but erratic service. Computer operations provide the environment in which the more complex tasks can run in the background.

The data center operations manager is the "landlord" for all of the central computer and network rooms and has control over the equipment within them. This control includes physical security, logical security access, environmental controls, fire safety, operator training, and anything else necessary to keep the back room stable. This enables the manager to control items placement and to ask people to leave the area.

[B] Computer Operations

Computer operations procedures auditing points may include:

    A. Performing equipment maintenance and maintaining records of equipment problems.

    B. Maintaining controls over access to information systems hardware, files, and production program libraries.

    C. Maintaining a proper separation of duties among input batches, computer operations, and output distribution.

    D. Ensuring business continuity and disaster recovery plans are documented, tested, and in effect. Training the staff on the individual roles for contingency actions addressing anticipated problems such as loss of electrical power, loss of data networks, loss of a key-shared system, loss of air conditioning, etc.

[C] Computer Room Controls

Control the computer room environment to ensure safe computer operation. The following safeguards are appropriate for a wide range of room sizes:

    A. Establish adequate procedures ensuring only authorized persons are permitted in the computer room.

    B. Restrict operation and repair of computer hardware to authorized personnel.

    C. Adequately protect the computer room facility with:

        1. Housekeeping procedures to minimize the accumulation of paper and other flammables in and around the computer room.

        2. Heat, smoke, and water detectors.

3. A suitable fire control system with the appropriate type of fire extinguishers.
4. Temperature and humidity control equipment.
5. Alternate power supply and emergency lighting.

D. Adequate on-call personnel and maintenance agreements covering all equipment are up to date.
1. Recall rosters for critical personnel are readily available.
2. Instructions for summoning service for each item covered by a service agreement are readily available.

E. Perform preventive maintenance according to a posted schedule based on the manufacturer's instructions. Maintain a log of all maintenance performed.

[D]   Computer Operations Management Reporting

Computer operations reporting for feedback and control might include:

A. Detailed hardware problem logs.
B. Computer-generated reports that include:
1. Proper program identification
2. Job processing times
3. Rerun times
4. Downtimes
5. Operator identification
C. Machine utilization and performance reports.
D. Review console logs for unusual activity such as reruns, halts, and failed accesses.

[E]   Data Library Controls

The data library (also known as the tape vault) requires its own audit readiness procedures. Some of the core duties/procedures requirements are as follows:

A. Librarians' responsibilities are prohibited to anyone with conflicting duties.
B. Only authorized personnel have library access.
C. Use external labels to identify removable data storage media.
D. A removable media locator database includes:

COMMENT

A major expense during the Year 2000 conversion was the lack of source code at many sites. Organizations could not find the current version of code to change, forcing major rewrites of programs.

    1. File name or description of contents
    2. Storage location
    3. Volume serial number
    4. Creation and expiration dates

E. Live media in off-site storage is never used to restore data. Copies must be made by the off-site storage facility and the copy sent to the data center. This reduces the chance of losing the backup copy in transit or during the restoration process.

F. Periodically test backup media in the library to ensure that each type of media can be read.

G. Store data storage media in a closed, fire-resistant, and limited-access vault.

H. Provide controlled storage for blank payroll and accounts payable checks. Maintain a beginning and ending control number log.

[F] Input Data Controls

Control input data for any computer operation. The systems and operations audit must ensure that the following procedures are followed:

A. Reference manuals, including examples (copies) and illustrations (drawings) of source documents, are available for each data entry operator.

B. All data received by the data entry unit is accompanied by pre-numbered transmittal batch forms and posted control totals.

C. A log is maintained of input received by source.

D. Retain batch control documents received with the input data in an orderly and logical manner for final balancing.

E. All transactions, such as item counts, are subject to controls similar to those used for monetary transactions.

F. Require monetary totals and item counts for data entry systems.

G. Supervisory personnel regularly review exception and reconciliation items.

[G] Output Controls

Output controls cover physical materials created by IT operations, such as CDs, printed, network-accessible, and microfiche output. Typical procedures that the auditor might follow include:

A. Review all reports for print quality prior to distribution.

B. Control procedures are in place to ensure reports are produced and delivered as scheduled.

C. Procedures are published for the control of signature stamps.

D. Locked output distribution boxes for pickup of company-controlled documents, such as checks.

§ 9.07   DATA NETWORKS

[A]   Overview

Data networks are the lifeblood of modern computer systems. Through them, programs exchange information, customer orders are received over the Internet, and long distance telephone communications is economically provided. A single malicious person who penetrates a network can undo all of these wonderful things.

IT auditors will verify that the company's data traffic is secure from intrusion, interruption, or interception. As with other IT areas, the auditor will check that policies and procedures are in place, that they are adequate, and that they are enforced.

People from both inside and outside of the company threaten networks. Outsiders may be attempting entry simply to say they have accomplished it—or to access confidential company data. Disgruntled employees or competitors may attempt to disable a competitor's network and temporarily paralyze the company.

All network security plans should address:

A. **Physical security.** Barriers that separate unauthorized people from the network equipment, such as locked rooms and wire closets.
B. **Network security.** Isolate network segments, packet encryption, and password protection.
C. **Platform security.** Isolate and control administrator functions, intrusion protection, and detection monitoring tools.
D. **Application security.** Authentication, privilege management, electronic commerce.

[B]   Security Issues

The network team is the linchpin of a company's data security effort. Intruders bypassing their defenses can roam at will among the files and programs. To be effective, the network security team must diligently examine every potential entry point and apply the appropriate security measures to screen incoming traffic.

The primary threat against the network is from inside the company offices. Company insiders commit 80 percent of computer crime. Insiders may be motivated by malicious intent or financial gain. They know exactly where to look for specific data or how to gain access. Insiders may be familiar with the network defenses and know how to bypass them. Even adequately defended systems may be attacked through the misuse of access authorization. An insider criminal's situation is analogous to a fox running loose inside the hen house. Once past the exterior defenses of the walls and bolted doors, he can easily lay hands on many things of value—unless there are adequate internal safeguards.

IT auditors will be looking for several basic internal management practices. Typical internal defenses are network segmentation through virtual LANs and firewalls, a vigorous program of password management with regular changes, and the tight control of internal access to data. Unfortunately, such measures will face internal resistance. Executives must balance the degree of threat and possible harm against the inconvenience required to adequately secure their data systems. Items auditors look for include:

A. Separation of duties divides critical steps in a process among several people, often in different departments. Just as employees processing incoming funds are separated from those who audit these accounts, network security administrators are separate from system administrators who control file access and separate from programmers. Although separated duties can be defeated by a conspiracy, it is much harder to disguise.

B. "Least privilege" restricts users to the minimum functions required to perform their duties. This includes physical access to special data center items such as signature stamps or blank checks. Server restrictions include the ability to read, write, or delete files. Managing an effective "least privilege" program is time consuming and auditors will be checking for ill-advised short cuts, such as blanket privileges to classes of users.

An adjunct to this defense is to educate users about securing their data files. Many users (including executives) leave confidential data unsecured in shared network directories unaware of how many employees surf the systems looking for files of interest.

Individual accountability is most effective when it is continually publicized. User IDs leave traces in transaction and system logs. Attempts to bypass network security can be detected and traced back to the originator. By publicizing this capability, end users with security access will be less likely to leave their workstations logged in and unattended since they will be blamed for the access attempts.

A great deal of the network defenses are focused against external threats. Given the global nature of the Internet and data networks, the potential number of attackers is immense. In general, network attackers look for weaknesses in systems and exploit them. Companies should identify the threats to their systems and tailor defenses to address them.

Defenses against external attacks depend on layers. The first layer is access to the network. If a company's networks are internal, and not physically connected to the "external world," then an attacker must find a way to tap into the physical network connection. This does not always require cutting into a wire. Improperly secured wireless networks make this as simple as sitting with a wireless notebook in a car outside of a building.

The second layer is to isolate the networks into segments so that access to one does not automatically open the door to everything. Few companies can afford to isolate themselves from the Internet and easy access by their customers. Firewalls must separate services intended for external use from those intended exclusively for internal use.

A third level of security is to restrict the access to data files. Do this at the server, directory, or file level. By admitting only specific user IDs, some external attackers are excluded.

A fourth level is the security to execute specific programs, such as to print checks or to read payroll records. Some programs contain code granting the authority to access secured files and must not be available for general use.

In addition to screening out undesired users, firewalls often screen out undesirable traffic. Computer viruses arrive in a variety of guises and the firewall must be ready to screen all of them out. Message attachments, browser controls, and applets all have the potential to harbor virus software. Malicious denial-of-service attacks have also blocked Internet commerce for extended periods of time.

[C] Network Audit Points

Data network audit procedures ascertain that the following are in place:

A. Publish a thorough written data security policy covering all telecommunications and network systems hardware and software.
B. Network firewall systems are in place and updated at least daily.
C. Configure firewalls to protect the company by filtering undesirable Internet sites such as pornography.
D. A strong password program that forces password changes at least quarterly. All passwords must contain a combination of letters, numbers, and uppercase letters. This includes any system that uses password protection—especially network devices.
E. Data systems that access funds also use a double authentication process such as an access card along with a password (something you own and something you know). This improves security since knowledge of a password will not provide access.
F. Virtual private network (VPN) access to servers and services are tightly controlled.
G. Authentication of dial-in access through hardware tokens or dial-back technology.
H. User access to critical data is periodically reviewed to determine if it is still warranted.
I. Tightly controlled temporary employee access through unique ID identifiers and an ID expiration date.
J. The human resources office promptly notifies the IT department when someone leaves the company so that all access can be immediately disabled.
K. Control access to network systems.
L. Control physical access by locking doors and closets.
M. Control digital access to network control programs by identification and passwords.
N. Maintain logs for all transactions performed remotely.
O. Monitor and record unauthorized access attempts to all critical systems. Logs gather sufficient data to track the attempt back to the source. Review logs daily.
P. Incorporate alternate processing procedures into disaster recovery plans.

[D] Security Policies

Security policies guide the network staff in the proper way to approach given situations. They must contain sufficient detail to provide clear staff guidance but not enough to aid an attacker. Policies must be published and periodically reviewed with the staff to ensure they are aware of them and to provide information on improving them. Policies should be in tune with the network's topology and capabilities.

A. **System logs.** A proactive security policy guides installation and use of technology to prevent intrusions and to detect attempts. The investigation of entry attempts will require specific data elements to place the attempt into context. Policies must identify what these data elements will be, such as date, time, user ID, etc. Collect data into secure system logs. The handling, review, and retention period of system logs must be detailed in the policy along with their proper storage location. Data from logs may be used in litigation so advice from the company's legal advisor on data collection and handling will be useful.

Safeguard system logs since they may contain sensitive company data. They must be properly stored and destroyed.

B. **System administration.** This policy guides the people who are watching everyone else. It details the circumstances and required approvals before a network or system administrator can examine a user's account, monitor a person's network traffic, read his or her files, or open his or her mail.

C. **Successful break-in.** This policy and accompanying procedures detail actions to take when an intruder has successfully breached security. Often this is detected after the intruder has departed. The policy will guide whom to inform, information to gather for potential prosecution, etc. It must specify the point at which law enforcement agencies are to be notified.

§ 9.08 DISASTER RECOVERY/CONTINGENCY PLANNING

[A] Overview

An essential audit point is the adequacy of the IT department's business continuity and disaster recovery preparations. The terror attacks on September 11, 2001 not only destroyed several large buildings, but also interrupted a great number of surrounding businesses in the New York City area. This event forced companies to scrutinize their own disaster contingency plans and many were severely lacking. Few auditors today will pass through an IT department without carefully reviewing portions of their plans.

There are two distinctly different plans to review:

A. Disaster recovery involves actions to contain and recover from a major disaster, such as the loss of a data center or a portion of a building.

IT plans tend to focus on the data center but must also look at the company's use of technology as a whole. IT disaster recovery plans include the ability to restart the data center at a distant "hot site" using backup media. The key to a rapid recovery is the availability of complete and readable system backups.

B. Business continuity plans address the more common but shorter duration problems, such as loss of electricity, loss of data network, loss of a server, etc. These plans identify risks and detail mitigation plans to reduce the likelihood of an occurrence and its impact if it occurs.

[B] Data Center Contingency Planning

The data center disaster and recovery contingency plans should include:

A. Complete data and software file backups according to a published schedule.
   1. Critical data systems are identified. Few companies can afford to deal with everything in a crisis. Critical systems are identified by executives and typically involve cash flow and regulatory requirements.
   2. Restoration instructions are tested and available for rapid use at the hot site.
   3. The recovery team tests portions of the recovery process annually at the hot site.
   4. All backup media is tested periodically to ensure it is still recording properly.
   5. Off-site storage location should:
      a. Closely control access to stored media.
      b. Provide a stable environment for maximum media life.
      c. Be organized to rapidly locate specific backup media for quick dispatch.
B. A method of transporting materials to and from the off-site storage facility with the same high level of environmental and physical security as employed at the data center.
C. A written emergency plan addresses:
   1. Physical security of the computer installation.
   2. Actions to be taken in specific emergency situations, such as the loss of electrical power, the loss of external network communications, etc.
   3. Contingency procedures required to recover from a disaster or server failure.

[C] Plan Updates

Data systems evolve over time. They emerge and eventually they fade away. In between are changes to the software, to the technical documentation, and even to the platforms used. It is critical that when new systems are implemented or changed, the impact on their disaster recovery processing be considered. In some cases, this will require a modification to the hot site support contract.

An important part of a systems analysis will be the impact on the system's recovery plans. The subsequent change control meeting must ensure that as system changes are implemented, the recovery plans are likewise adjusted. Auditors must verify this process and compare sample recovery plans to system changes.

In a crisis, time is in short supply. Under the best of circumstances, it may take days to reestablish a data center in a hot site. Incomplete or inaccurate plans will increase recovery time. Issues that may arise include:

A. The upgrading or addition of servers to the computer room means that additional servers must be available at the hot site.
B. Reflecting changes in network access at the recovery site.
C. Plans for restoring retired systems will delay the recovery effort by working on something no longer needed.
D. Security measures may have changed inhibiting the recovery team's ability to restore an application.

§ 9.09   WORKSTATION AUDIT ISSUES

[A]   Objective

Workstations have changed dramatically over time—from shared terminals to PCs and now include Web-enabled cell phones. IT auditors will ensure that workstation policies and control have kept pace with these changes.

[B]   Workstation Standards

Policies and procedures for the appropriate control and use of company workstations must be in place. To be effective, orientation sessions with end users must be conducted to explain workstation policies. The goal is compliance rather than punishment.

To control workstation assets, the IT department will maintain an inventory of hardware and software owned by the company. This will aid in the detection of theft and unauthorized copying of software. Standards to consider include:

A. Hardware and software relocation will be controlled by the IT department. This will assist in maintaining asset database accuracy.
B. Neither software nor hardware shall leave the facility without an approved pass by the IT department. Anything removed without this pass is theft.
C. Company workstations shall only be used to conduct company business and not for personal use. This includes the Internet.
D. The IT department will maintain an organized and accessible software license file in a fireproof environment.
E. The loading of software by anyone other than the IT department is prohibited (and restricted by the operating system if possible).

F. The IT department will approve all purchases of workstation hardware and software to ensure compliance with published standards.
G. Employees using company owned notebook PCs, tablets, or cell phones outside of the facility:
    1. Are responsible for the safe return of company property. If these items are lost, the employee must promptly file a theft report with the local police authorities. Otherwise, the employee will be suspected of theft and the cost of the replacement item deducted from his pay.
    2. Shall only use these items for company business.
    3. Shall obtain a properly approved property pass before the item can leave the facility.

Policies governing the proper use of workstations:

A. All company critical files are stored on network drives and not on personal workstations.
B. Restriction of network access to Internet and e-mail to business use only.
C. Software developed on company time and/or using company assets is company property.

[C] Workstation Environment

Environments where workstations are used do not require the same degree of control needed by IT computer operations. However, their users are usually unfamiliar with IT operation requirements and must learn those that are applicable. The following are standard environment requirements:

A. Workstation security
    1. Physical security maintained by key locks on the hardware.
B. Access controls required
    1. Passwords for access.
    2. Encryption of classified data.
    3. Use of password protected screen savers.
C. Power supply
    1. Computer hardware must not share its power outlets with any other devices.
    2. Plug all hardware into surge protectors.
    3. Areas that may have power supply problems must have uninterrupted power supply (UPS) backup supply units capable of providing power for the full time required to bring down the system properly.

§ 9.10 STRATEGIES FOR SURVIVING AN AUDIT

[A] The Auditor Is Your New Friend

Audits are unavoidable. The more managers squirm to avoid them, the more the auditor believes that there is something to uncover. "If you can't beat them—join them!" Take advantage of the auditor's visit to improve the department's operations. Yes, there will be deficiencies noted for the department, but that is to be expected. If nothing is reported, the auditor's boss will think he did not do his job. Make the auditor's job easy by assisting him in uncovering and reporting problems.

This is not as radical as it sounds. Again, the auditor must report *something* is wrong to justify his existence. The key is to influence what is reported and how it is reported. Is something a sweet-smelling long-stemmed rose, or is it a dead red thing on a green stick with thorns? The difference is all in the wording! Most auditors will appreciate some assistance with the specific technical details.

By guiding the audit, the IT Manager is less likely to be stuck with the worst curse imaginable—the vague audit point. Every citation in an audit must be resolved before the next audit—maybe immediately. A vaguely worded audit citation may require unnecessary extraordinary effort to satisfy. Ensure that all citations are clear and as specific as possible.

[B]   Steps for a "Successful" Audit

The rest of this chapter explains what an audit is and how it functions. Audits are useful tools for both the company's executives and the IT Manager. Do not hide in an office! Dodge the bullet by managing the audit to everyone's benefit.

Step 1—Did anyone pay attention to the last auditor? Begin with the last several audit reports.

A. Has everything cited on the reports been resolved? If this involves a report, pull it out and read it. If this involves equipment, find it and personally verify that changes were made and are still in effect. Do not take someone else's word for it.

B. Can anything from previous reports that has not been addressed be resolved before the upcoming audit? It is never too late to address an open issue. If the task is too large, but will be attempted, then an in-process effort will often satisfy the audit point.

C. Is there an audit point that is impossible or a very bad idea to do? Write an explanation of what the audit point is *really* asking for and why it is impossible or illogical to attempt. It is possible that the audit point was poorly written. This will verify the citation. Auditors make mistakes too! When the audit begins, discuss this issue with the auditor to clarify or satisfy the citation as misguided.

Step 2—Prepare for the visit. Appearance of records is half of the battle.

A. If the policy manual looks ragged and dusty, it will be closely scrutinized.
   1. Ensure the document shows dates from within the last 12 months.
   2. Ideally, review, update, and re-authorize each policy.

    B. If the financial documents are occasionally missing or the signatures are illegible, the auditor may dig deeper.

    C. If documents are difficult to find or take a long time to produce, the auditor may suspect sloppy bookkeeping practices. Clean up all file systems and ensure that all financial and performance records for the period being audited, and the period before, are readily available.

    D. Pull the department together to explain what an IT audit is and why it is important to the team. Do not assume that they understand the purpose or process of the audit. State your expectations to them.

        1. Treat requests from the auditor as high priority.

        2. Require everyone to answer questions truthfully. (It is too difficult for an entire department to remember the same lie.)

        3. Explain the importance of providing information the auditor requests and no more. Excessive information is like a half truth that raises more questions than it solves.

        4. Separate opinions from facts. Label opinions as such. If they become audit points, much time may be wasted to prove that a problem did not really exist.

        5. Attempting to slip personal attacks into data as a fact may result in disciplinary actions.

        6. Identify important but under-funded activities. Sometimes prudent technology purchases are sidetracked by middle managers for more career enhancing activities.

    E. For an IT department, audits can be a bit disruptive but useful. If funding for important activities such as security upgrades has not been forthcoming, the auditor can report this as a potential problem. If replacement of antiquated critical hardware has not been funded, or the funds diverted for other uses, this also is reported. On the other hand, if the IT Manager is lazy, ignores his own policies, and generally runs a halfhearted security program, then this will also be reported.

Step 3—Perform a pre-audit audit. Walk around and play auditor. See what can be found and cleaned up before the "real article" arrives.

    A. Make a list of things to check in each IT department.

    B. Ask the managers for each department to verify the accuracy of their policies and procedures, and that the appropriate workers know and follow them. After the managers confirm that this is done, play auditor and verify this is done.

    C. Check all security procedures, system logs, maintenance logs, inventory records, management metrics, etc. for completeness, currency, and accuracy.

    D. Check records for previous executive mandates over the past two years. Ensure they are in place.

    E. Ask the legal department for an updated chart of legally mandated data retention periods.

Step 4—During the audit. Appearance is the other half of the battle.

A. Be candid. It is far easier to provide honest answers than to try and remember a string of lies. Remember that part of an audit is to meet individually with the IT staff members—away from the management. If their story does not match the manager's, then everything the manager says may become suspect.

B. Show an interest in the audit process. Like most people, auditors are overworked and under-appreciated.

C. Open records freely. Hiding information at worst raises suspicion and at best indicates incompetence at critical recordkeeping. If the auditor later learns of intentional obstruction, the IT Manager's credibility will be shattered.

D. Stay close to the auditor and write down comments—pro and con. Openly take notes and allow the auditor to read them at any time. If the auditor requests a copy, provide one at every request. Use these notes to identify items that will appear on the report.

E. As the audit proceeds, the auditor may mention or communicate in some fashion points that are below standard. If any of these items can be resolved quickly—immediately do so. This saves time later and may keep them off the report. Track all of these quick changes to ensure they are permanent.

F. Do not be shy about clarifying audit points! Any audit point should be clear enough that action can be taken or a response provided. It is possible that the auditor is mistaken. A vague audit point will be very difficult to address later.

G. If an audit point cannot be quickly satisfied, find out why. It may be possible to form a reasonable action plan for addressing the problem before the auditor leaves—even if the solution will not begin for some time.

H. Explain why a situation is as it is, but never argue with the auditor. No matter how the argument ends, they have the last word in their report!

I. Ask the auditor's opinion about the department's toughest problems. An outsider's perspective may be very insightful.

Step 5—After the audit. Answering the audit citation is the rest of the fight.

A. Begin preparing for the audit report to hit the executive council. Immediately follow up on any items cited in the report. Do not wait for publication of the final report. Report small tasks as they are finished. Either large tasks should begin or a proposal should be developed for the next capital funding cycle.

B. Begin preparation for next year's audit. Analyze the IT audit process. Write down what went well during the year and what went poorly with the audit. Bring together everyone who participated in the audit.

C. Which records were requested but were hard to find? Change the filing system to capture this data and make it easy to find.

[C] Using the Audit to Your Advantage

Sometimes urgent requests for technology go nowhere. If the old equipment is still running, then purchasing the newer models is just an exercise in "computer envy." This may be the accounting manager's opinion but is not always the case. Properly maintained data systems can run for decades—far longer than their reasonable useful life.

Sometimes the purchase of essential technology is shuttled aside by middle managers pursuing their own objectives. The auditor can provide executive support for these purchases if they can be included in the audit report.

The auditor will decide to include or exclude an item from his report based on the description the IT Manager provides to him of the items in question. If their purchase is tied to compliance with a legally mandated action, it will be difficult for the purchase to be rejected. It is all in how it is described. Once an item is included in an audit as critical to legal compliance, no manager will sign on as the one who obstructed it. Use this logic to:

A. Drive out obsolete equipment, such as servers, printers, and punch card equipment.
B. Improve data backup equipment (which may reduce staff and storage expenses).
C. Support additional staffing or training requests in key areas.

10

RISK MANAGEMENT: MANAGING THE UNEXPECTED

§ 10.01 OVERVIEW

[A] Purpose and Scope

Nothing is certain. Every endeavor has an element of uncertainty. This uncertainty represents variance from the expected outcome both positive and negative. This uncertainty can be considered as the possibility of an undesired outcome or a "risk" of an outcome other than the planned one.

A risk is an event that threatens the predictable outcome of some endeavor. It manifests itself as an event, such as a blizzard that shuts all physical commerce for a week, an extended power outage, or the extended illness of a key technician. The risk that has become an actual event then has consequences, either positive or negative. Risks sometimes arise in multiples. Taken individually, they may be minor but when all occur together, the consequences are significantly greater.

Risk management is the process that IT uses to address this issue. Risk management is a natural instinct that we use every day. A toddler's fear of falling is an early risk assessment that we all performed. Eventually the legs feel strong enough to stand. With the next handhold in sight, the first steps are taken despite the risk of falling. Risk assessments are often accomplished without any conscious thought. However, it is this management of risk that separates the brave (calculated risk) from the foolhardy (ignoring the risk).

Good risk management can improve the quality of products produced and the financial returns of a business. It reduces the likelihood of delay or failure. Others may look upon it as good fortune but it is really a reflection of the IT leader's management skill. Effective risk management helps to fulfill management objectives by improving accountability, decision-making, transparency, and visibility of decisions. It executes change more effectively and efficiently. It also controls expenditure and delivers a cost-optimal control environment.

Risk management implements processes, methods, and tools to deal with the consequences of events you have identified as significant threats to your business. This could be something as simple as ensuring effective data backups to IT support procedures for dealing with a systems failure.

Someone with perfect knowledge of all things that could possibly happen will select a course of action that provides the greatest return. The reality is that no one can control every factor that can alter an outcome. Guesses can be made about many things but something will be overlooked, or be unknown to the person estimating the situation. Inaction is not an option. Leaders must make decisions under uncertainty and trust to "luck" (random events that permeate our existence) that unforeseen problems do not arise.

Executives deal in risk management but as optimists, they do not like to think about it. When an IT Manager shares a discussion with them about the risks of a particular action, they may be labeled as alarmist, or as someone who is passing their difficult decisions to their superiors.

[B]   Defining Risk

Risk is the possibility that something in the future will not work out as we wished. The undesired outcome could be positive or negative. A risk is only the potential of a problem occurring. It does not mean that it will occur; only that it might. The key is to identify likely risks in advance and then manage them. Ignoring risks is to assume a business process and the environment are perfect, predictable, and unchangeable.

A positive risk is an opportunity to increase the positive outcomes. This could be a piece of off-the-shelf software, purchased for one reason, which includes other features valuable to the company. It might be a special price reduction for an expensive server. It could also be an existing employee, hired for one technical skill that also possesses other critical technical expertise.

A negative risk is something that will diminish the likelihood of success or its value even with success. This is what we normally associate with risks. This might be the late delivery of critical materials to the print room or a critical support person absent with the flu. It may also be a blade server chassis that had many empty slots when a new blade was ordered but was full when the blade arrived. (Now whose budget will pay for the new chassis?)

Risk is evaluated by its dimensions. The first dimension is its likelihood of occurrence. There are an infinite number of risks (for example, you could be hit by a meteorite while reading this page). However, the likelihood is so small that the risk is ignored. Most risks are so unlikely that they are not considered. Risk management focuses on likely risks.

A second dimension of risk is its impact should it occur. The impact is the "how much" should the risk occur. It may be slight or massive. Risks are rarely all or nothing of something so impact is rated as the most likely impact if something occurs—not automatically the most serious.

The third dimension is the amount of warning before it strikes. There may be no warning or a lot of warning. For example, there may be no warning of a power outage on a day with a clear sky, or an approaching severe thunderstorm may warn that it is more likely than normal.

Risks are cumulative. Image an endeavor with three steps in it, and each step has a 95 percent chance of success. If you multiply the likelihood of step one's 95 percent likelihood of success times step two's 95 percent likelihood of success, and finally step three's 95 percent likelihood of success, you have an 85.7 percent chance that these three steps will complete successfully. The more steps there are in the process, the less likely its success.

To be successful, an IT leader proactively manages risk. "Risk management" is the ongoing action of identifying, assessing, and monitoring risks, and then proactively addressing them before they occur. It is an essential part of business management. Successful managers try to resolve risks before they occur. It is a daily activity.

COMMENT

Some managers are uncomfortable examining risks as they are by nature optimistic people. It is as if they are dwelling on the negative "could be(s)" instead of focusing on the work at hand. However, ignoring risks is like driving a car on a dark night with the headlights off, dealing with obstacles only as they are struck.

[C] Risk Is Proactive Management

Companies either manage their risks or manage by crisis. Crisis management is the opposite of risk management as it is only invoked after an incident occurs. It is similar to running full speed through a dark room until you stumble over something or hit a wall. Only during a crisis is planning action taken to resolve the issue. Then it is back to waiting for the next crisis to arise. These managers seem like firefighters, always rushing here and there to resolve an emergency.

Managers can sit back and complain about risks or they can take control of the situation and address it. Risk is managed by taking action to reduce the likelihood, increase the warning, or minimize the impact of an adverse event. If your company has power outages, purchase alternate power sources. If your order entry server dies and halts business, then buy a second one, build a cluster, and mirror the data. Recognize the risks and then shrink them to a manageable size.

Risks are managed through four steps:

A. Identify the significant risks.
B. Create proactive mitigation plans to minimize these risks.
C. Monitor risks to see if they are about to occur.
D. Regularly repeat the first three steps because situations change.

When investigating a mitigation action, most companies require a return on investment (ROI) study or a risk versus reward review. The reward can be the avoidance or minimization of a negative outcome (such as failing to fulfill a legal requirement). It can also be the realization of a rewarding opportunity (stable systems attract new customers).

The concept of risk versus reward is the underlying principle in most business decisions. Businesses apply their limited resources in a quest for the certainty of greater returns. To entice someone to invest in a venture that may fail (and result in loss of investment), the potential reward must be comparatively greater than for a safer investment.

[D]   Critical Policies to Develop Based on This Chapter

A risk management policy describes your business's approach to and tolerance for risk and how it will be managed. It clearly assigns responsibility for it to chosen employees. The risk policy must be approved and enforced at the CIO level.

Using the material discussed in this chapter, you will be able to create a risk management policy that includes:

A. Risk Identification
B. Risk Evaluation
C. Risk Mitigation
D. Risk Monitoring

Policies should always be developed based on the local situation. Successful managers cannot issue appropriate guidance if the policies are written with another company's situation or location in mind.

COMMENT

The formal standard for documenting and managing risk is ISO 31000:2009. It is a useful tool for organizations requiring Sarbanes-Oxley compliance. This standard may also establish a reliable basis for decision making and planning, identify opportunities and threats, and encourage proactive management.

§ 10.02   RISK MANAGEMENT IS A PROCESS

[A]   Overview

Risk can be broken into two general categories. *Business risk* identifies the profit and loss from uncertain outcomes. It also uses ROI to assess whether a risk's potential benefits are worth the gamble of its potential negative outcomes. The second risk is referred to as *pure risk*. It addresses only the potential negative outcome or loss, such as lost workdays due to a blizzard.

Operational risks, an example of a business risk, arise during the execution of normal IT functions. Operational risks are usually local in nature; that is, confined within the IT department. They typically involve a single function, such as the network, a critical server, a database product, etc. Strategic risks, which impact the well-being of the entire organization, are managed by top executives. Ideally, risk management for the organization should be addressed as a company-wide effort. Without risk assessment, an unfortunate but avoidable event could blindside the organization.

Companies manage operational risks as a part of their daily business functions. This is the risk of loss resulting from inadequate or failed internal processes, employee actions, IT systems, or from external events. Anticipating potential causes of failure can improve the chances of survival and success through improved preparedness.

Operational risk is influenced by the forces of corporate culture, quality of leadership, state of the marketplace, changes in the legal environment, and changes in technology. Its management tends to be conservative and risk adverse as failures can end a career. Managing risk is often informally done, so it should be no surprise that the results are uneven. However, a formal risk management program should not consume much time once the entire IT department is trained in its execution.

Companies manage risk through a process based on its internal best practices. It evaluates the potential positive and negative outcomes of a situation. Each potential risk is further defined by an assigned score in terms of the likelihood of occurrence, the impact if it occurs, and the amount of warning before it occurs. After risks are evaluated using these three criteria, they are ranked with the highest scoring ones on top. The biggest risks are mitigated and the lesser ones are accepted. Risks can be:

- Eliminated by not taking the action that would cause this risk to arise.
- Mitigated through actions taken to reduce the likelihood of occurrence, the impact should it occur, or to increase the warning before it will occur.
- Transferred to someone else, such as through insurance.
- Ignored as something we can do nothing about, such as the weather.

Most company-wide risks are addressed through business continuity plans. For example, if the seasonal influenza sweeps through the workforce, which business functions will receive the bulk of the remaining workforce and which ones will lie unattended? These contingency plans provide a starting point for addressing the situation and should not be interpreted as the only available course of action.

Risk assessment is a component of understanding a process or project in depth. It enables introduction of mitigation actions such as mistake-proofing steps in the process to eliminate likely problems.

Risks that may occur within a few weeks, or where the team has extensive experience, are easy to project. For example, based on the IT team's experience of working in a particular building, they can estimate the likelihood of a power outage, severe weather, etc. Likewise, for the immediate future, based on experience and the current business climate, they can estimate the likelihood of material shortages, labor issues, etc.

The farther into the future you predict, the greater is the uncertainty of your predictions. Agile project management is a technique for breaking a larger project into a series of smaller projects that each delivers some part of the overall project. As each of the small projects is completed, the next one is planned. This keeps the planning horizon short (typically less than two months) so that the risk assessment reflects the current situation instead of a hypothetical one imagined a year before.

COMMENT

The risk for IT projects change as the project progresses. Risks for a process tend to remain stable and change in response to the work environment.

[B] Identifying Risk

The first step is to identify all of the things that could go wrong with a process or project. A touch of paranoia helps. The usual approach is to list every possible thing that could go wrong and then pare the list down. However, skip risks that seem remote and stand little likelihood of remaining on the list. This focuses limited resources on the significant few risks instead of the trivial many. Consolidate some of the risks triggered by the same event or controlled in the same fashion.

Managers can only calculate the risks for those things that they know or are aware of, and they cannot plan for things that they do not know. Often, people do not know what it is that they do not know. To gather a wide range of potential risks, use a small team of no more than seven people in a brainstorming session. This team should include people working on the process, those who supervise it, those who use its output, and those who provide its inputs. This provides an all-around view of potential risks.

COMMENT

Risk can be broken down many different ways. Traditionally, we focus on the known risks with known likelihood. These are usually within our personal experience. Another type of risk is those that we know about, but the likelihood, impact, and amount of warning are unknown to us. For example, we know that our car needs gas but we do not know exactly how much it will cost to fill the tank. The third type of risk is something that we do not know about and therefore cannot gauge its impact.

Risk identification usually begins with the assets that are at risk. Examples might be service level agreements, critical systems, and any threats to providing a high level of ongoing services. Each of these categories is then broken down into major components and the risks identified for each. This list of risks is then consolidated where practical.

Another source of assets to be protected can be found in your business plan. These risks are the events that could arise and diminish or eliminate the success of individual plan objectives.

Risk analysis is more effective as a team rather than as a solo effort. If there are too many people to conduct an orderly analysis, then appoint representatives from each organizational component. The team's collective experience will provide a well-rounded perspective on what to address, and the most effective way to do it.

Most risks are only pertinent to a particular part of the IT department. For example, if the print room ran out of paper or data operations ran out of blank backup media. However, some risks are applicable across the entire department. For example:

- Legal compliance risk.
- Technical risk, such as hardware or software failures, information security vulnerabilities, product delivery delays, or errors in reports.
- Changes in the marketplace such as dramatically rising energy costs.
- Worker safety.
- Keeping the business continuity plan current and tested.
- Power outage or brownout.
- Disease outbreak such as seasonal influenza or pandemic.
- Labor risks such as a work stoppage or epidemic.
- Environmental issues such as the weather or from nature.

On the CD is a matrix (Worksheet 08-1 Risk Assessment Form) that can be used to organize your risks assessment. The recommendation is to make one matrix and analysis for the department as a whole and then one for each critical process or IT team.

[C] Analyzing Risk

Risk analysis is a technique for assessing the impacts of potential risks. It applies a value to the primary characteristics of each risk to generate a score. This analysis indicates which risks are to be managed closely and which risks are to be acknowledged without taking further action.

Risk analysis is a big field. Some companies spend a considerable amount of time shuffling numbers to quantify a risk. IT Managers do not have time to do that. They must analyze risks by using the broad-brush factors of likelihood, impact, and warning time.

Review the department's list of risks for commonality and overlap. Some risks will logically appear in multiple categories such as the risk of a server failure due to loss of electrical power or due to the loss of a network connection. The concern is if the mitigating actions for the overlapping risks begin to conflict and complicate oversight of the risk management.

One way to categorize risk is to make a separate risk plan spreadsheet for each service level agreement (SLA) and vital business function supported. This focuses managers on areas for improving service and areas to closely monitor for changes. A risk evaluation determines the significance of risks to the business and decides to accept the specific risk or take action to prevent or minimize it.

COMMENT

Chaos Theory

Some people are adamant that astrology is cheaper than trying to predict business futures and is just about as accurate. There are too many variables and correlations influencing an issue to identify and track them all. Chaos theory looks for the underlying order in apparently random data.

For example, in terms of financial markets, chaos theory believes that price is the last thing to change for a stock, bond, or some other security. Price changes can be determined through stringent mathematical equations based on a trader's own personal motives, volume changes, acceleration of the changes, and momentum behind the changes.

The first step in performing a risk evaluation is to determine your risk evaluation criteria. No one has time to monitor every potential risk and not all of them are worth the effort. A common practice is to develop a risk importance score to focus your limited resources on the most important ones. However, the farther into the future that you try to look, the less accurate the predictions. The three primary criteria for evaluating risks are:

A. **Likelihood.** The chance that this risk will occur. There are many, many risks that could occur but most are very unlikely. Focusing on the most likely risks improves your chances of success rather than spreading limited resources over all risks equally.
B. **Impact.** The amount of damage that will occur if a particular risk occurs. In this case, consider the most likely amount of damage that could occur instead of the very worst possible damage.
C. **Warning.** This is the amount of warning available before the risk occurs. For example, a hurricane should be well announced in weather reports days before it strikes. However, a critical server failure or network outage will strike without advance notice.

Each of these criteria is scored by a scale and then sorted so that the highest scores are at the top of the sheet. Based on the resources available, the IT leader draws a line somewhere down the list. Everything above the line will be mitigated in some fashion. Everything below the line will be "accepted risks" and only addressed as they appear or become imminent.

The second step is to create a risk evaluation spreadsheet. You can use Worksheet 10-1 Risk Management Plan Form. It should contain a list of risks

WORKSHEET 10-1. Risk Management Plan Form

Risk Management Plan Form

Risk	Quantification			Damage		Trigger	Risk Event	Mitigation	Assigned		Comments	Actual
	Likelihood	Impact	Warning	Score	Cost	Outage		Status	Actions	To	Date		Results
				0									
				0									
				0									
				0									
				0									
				0									
				0									
				0									
				0									
				0									
				0									
				0									

identified, grouped according to whatever categories chosen by the Project Manager. In this step, add values under the "Quantification" section. The quantification section is where a "score" is developed to determine which risks require improvement plans and which ones can be accepted but do nothing about. The quantification section has four columns:

A. **Likelihood.** This is an estimate of the probability that the risk will become a reality. Some risks are very real but very unlikely to occur. A risk of lightning striking a key team member is real but extremely low.
B. **Impact** is how badly the event would damage the asset's quality; incur a cost or the amount of downtime until it is resolved.
C. **Warning** is how much warning the IT leader would have before this event occurred.
D. **Score** is a numeric risk score based on the previous three values.

The scales for Likelihood and Impact are from 1 to 10, with 1 as extremely unlikely and 10 as a sure thing. Use any consistent numbering system for the scores, but if a zero is used as a value, then that entire risk may be scored as zero. Some companies establish a range for each value:

A. **Impact (to the scope, budget, or timeline)**
    1 to 3 is little negative impact—a nuisance
    4 to 5 is some negative impact—a disruption
    6 to 8 is definite negative impact—serious impact
    9 to 10 is severe negative impact—a project-threatening crisis
B. **Likelihood**
    1 to 3 is very unlikely
    4 to 5 is unlikely
    6 to 8 is possible
    9 to 10 is very possible
C. **Warning (signals the risk is about to occur)**
    Score the Warning column the reverse from the other two. It is also rated from 1 to 10. A risk typically accompanied with a lot of warning would be rated very low. Rate a risk that would occur with little or no warning as high since the IT leader would not have time to react. Some companies establish a warning range for each value:
    1 to 3 gives lots of warning—can see it coming far off
    4 to 5 builds over time—sufficient notice to attenuate the issue
    6 to 8 gives little warning—short notice before it strikes
    9 to 10 is a sudden event—no notice before the risk strikes

Now move the risk analysis from dealing with the many, to addressing the critical few. A risk's score is determined by multiplying the three columns together. The higher the score is, the greater the attention that must be paid to that risk. The score is the key to the analysis. After scoring the risks, sort the entire spreadsheet on this column in descending order. This brings the risks with the highest score to the top.

Review the sorted risks. At some point in the list, draw a line across it. Monitor anything scoring below this point, but take no further action about it. This focuses attention toward addressing the key risks. Periodically review the risks below the line to see if they should be moved up the list or dropped all together.

There are several ways to establish a score for the impact, likelihood, and warning fields for each risk. The group may range from a small IT team of a few technicians who normally work together to an entire department.

A. Do it yourself. The easiest way is to fill in whatever values the situation warrants. This is quick, but depends on a single person's perspective. Leading an IT group is a team effort and if the team does not participate in its development, they may lack ownership in its execution.

B. Use previous risk assessments to see the score for these risks and how closely it conformed to reality. Although this point in time has a different business and legal climate, there may be enough similarities to be useful.

C. Use team scoring along with a review of historical information. Assemble the IT team and discuss the list of risks along with any pertinent historical data. Distribute a score sheet listing each risk item to the team members and ask them to score each one as to its impact, likelihood, and warning. This step typically raises many questions about the risk descriptions for clarification. Clear risk descriptions are important since many of the stakeholders may later refer to this list.

Next, collect the sheets and average the scores for each item. Redistribute the sheets for the participants to score again, but this time around, indicate the average value from the first pass through. Average the values for the second pass, and then average the average value from both passes together.

Redistribute the risk sheets with the revised numbers and ask the participants to speak up for any value they feel is more than 10 percent too high or too low. The discussion will either answer the person's questions or allow them to raise issues about a risk's score that the others may not have considered before.

[D]   Mitigating Risk

IT leaders can implement controls to deal with the consequences of an adverse event. These controls are called "mitigation" plans. Mitigation plans are proactive. They are intended to reduce a risk's likelihood of occurring, its impact if it does occur, or to increase the amount of warning before it strikes. There are four primary mitigation strategies. You can:

A. **Eliminate** it by eliminating the task or object at risk. For example, an IT department may have a risk of a very old software system failing with no one on hand to repair it. If that software system was replaced or deleted, then the risk of a failure without anyone skilled to repair it goes away.

B. **Mitigate** the risk through actions that reduce the likelihood that it will occur, the impact if it does occur, or that provides additional warning. The likelihood of a disk drive hardware failure stopping a system is reduced through the use of RAID. The impact of a server failure is reduced if several servers are clustered together to share the workload. The amount of warning from adverse weather may be increased by monitoring long-range weather projections.

C. **Accept** it as nothing can be done to avoid it. This is often the course of action for very unlikely risks. For example, an IT department has no practical control over the cost of the energy to power the data center. There is a risk that the cost may rise rapidly and severely impact the department's budget. You may accept a risk as something that is too expensive to be funded. Many of the accepted risks may be mitigated over time with imagination but few companies bother to try.

D. **Transfer** it to someone else. This normally involves purchasing insurance of some kind so that if the event occurs, the company is protected against financial loss. Another example of this is to use a fixed bid contract versus a cost plus agreement. With a fixed bid, the cost for the product or service cannot exceed the agreed amount.

Mitigation plans are both proactive and reactive. Proactive plans are actions taken before a risk is a reality to minimize it. Examples are mirrored data systems, technicians trained as backup support, data backup programs, fire sprinklers (in the ceiling), etc. Proactive plans require the application of resources to a problem that does not yet exist. However, it does provide increased confidence in the organization's ability to continue to meet its service-level agreements. Proactive plans are often documented as policies, such as all critical IT systems must be clustered, that technicians supporting critical systems have designated and trained backup personnel, etc. Positive risks rarely are as urgent to address as negative risks and plans for managing them are rarely documented.

A reactive plan is something that can only be executed after the adverse event has occurred. Reactive plans include both process work-around plans (manually processing the work previously done by an automated system) and business continuity plans.

IT departments use a wide range of risk mitigation strategies. For example:

- Background checks prior to engaging new employees.
- Segregation of duties.
- Server clustering.
- Data mirroring.
- Locked doors with electronic keys, with different rooms grouped into zones.
- Onsite spares of critical hardware devices.

COMMENT

Some risks are unavoidable and you can only take steps to reduce their impact. If a facility is located on the seashore with a view of the ocean, defenses can be built against a tidal surge or hurricanes, but these risks cannot be prevented. The damage can only be minimized. Another unavoidable risk is when an important team member cannot be prevented from leaving the company in the middle of a project, but all work can be well documented, so that the next person will be able to pick up the work faster.

[E]   Monitoring Risk

Risk management is not a one-off exercise. Businesses operate amidst a swirl of changing marketplaces, technology, and legislation. Continuous monitoring is crucial for ongoing success. This monitoring validates the accuracy of risk assessments to date and ensures that emerging risks are addressed.

Risk management requires a regular review of the identified risks. It should be a topic in every staff meeting when discussing future plans. Risks no longer relevant need to be shuttled aside to prevent obscuring the ones requiring attention. Keeping all risks on the "active" list can make processes lengthy. The risk plan is easier to use if risks are categorized in some fashion. Group risks according to any common characteristic.

Risk assessments can be improved through the basic quality improvement process of plan, do, act, and check. Essentially, whenever creating the next department risk assessment, review previous assessments to see how well they helped to predict and mitigate problems.

Metrics are a valuable tool for monitoring processes. This is data collected from the vital few steps in a process to detect performance problems. These values will normally vary within an acceptable range. If they begin trending in a negative direction, they should be addressed before crossing a threshold of unacceptable performance. Performance data such as this is typically analyzed using "statistical process control" (SPC).

COMMENT

"And if you look into an abyss, the abyss also looks into you."
   —Nietzsche

§ 10.03 WHY RISK MANAGEMENT FAILS

[A] Overview

Risk management is such a simple concept yet for many people contemplating how some activity may fail runs against their positive nature. It also fails because people tend to dwell on the most unlikely events that dilute their efforts to address the more likely risks.

In most cases, IT Managers do not think very far into the future. Risk management is not used by people who live in the here and now and do not contemplate the future. Their time is so consumed with addressing pressing immediate issues that they have little inclination to think about what may occur in the future. However, these same people practice risk management in their daily personal life. When driving in traffic, they assess the driving performance of the people in front, behind, and next to them. The likelihood of their actions forms the driver's actions. The challenge is to transfer this personal risk management process that they find so useful into a business practice.

For example, they watch the weather report (which is almost entirely speculation) to see if it might rain or snow, so they can plan to leave early. Yet the sky may be clear and the roads dry. They use experience to anticipate places on the highway that may be crowded or where driving is tricky. Yet these places may be empty or the traffic flowing smoothly.

Risk management is not a one-time-and-it-is-done event. It is an ongoing process. It often fails because management performs it only to fulfill a requirement and not because they believe in it. Consequently, it is not kept current and becomes a meaningless exercise.

COMMENT

> Current thinking is that since we cannot predict these events with any accuracy, IT systems must be made resilient enough to withstand whatever may hit them.

[B]   Never Saw It Coming

A primary risk management failure is through not identifying all of the significant factors to consider. This goes back to the quandary that you cannot ask the question about something you are unaware (you do not know what you do not know). This unknown may emerge suddenly to upset the planned outcome.

A common way to address this problem is to first use a team. A team provides different perspectives of the same situation. Some managers discuss risks as an agenda item in their team meetings. Everyone can offer their perspective even if the topic is not in their technical field. An alternative is to establish an online discussion area to review and add to the potential risks for a particular area.

Another problem with identifying and assessing risks is that it builds false confidence. The risk that is overlooked or incorrectly assessed can suddenly occur to the IT department's detriment.

[C]   Did the Wrong Thing with the Right Result

Another failure is through the incorrect application of risk management and somehow resulting in positive results. This provides a false sense of security and sets a company up to be later blindsided by an unknown risk. (This is analogous to superstitious behavior. For example, I carried my lucky charm to my annual performance review and I was given a pay raise. Therefore, my lucky charm works.)

Incorrectly applying risk management will sooner or later result in a serious problem and a loss of confidence in the process. This is why risk management should be administered at the corporate level with training audits of the various departments. The auditor verifies that the process is correctly followed and mentors groups that need clarification on the identification, analysis, and mitigation steps.

COMMENT

Military history is full of successful attacks that came from the place where it could not possibly originate (overlooked or a discounted risk). Examples are the Trojan Horse from Greek history and the poor risk assessment that lead to Custer's attack at the Little Bighorn river. Business has similar paradigm shifting events such as the portable MP3 players killing off other portable music formats and digital photography eliminating the development of photographic film.

[D]   Black Swan Events

A term specific to risk management is the "black swan," which means a perceived impossibility that should not occur. This term reaches back to the Romans who never saw a black swan and used the term to describe something that did not exist (they have since been found in Australia). A black swan risk is a significant event that appears out of nowhere and changes everything. These events are rare and difficult to predict. They are beyond the realm of normal expectations in history, science, finance, and technology. In some cases, there are psychological biases that make people blind to uncertainty and unaware of the massive role of the rare event.

One example was when Hurricane Ike swept through Ohio in 2008. With the force of a Category 1 hurricane, the sustained high winds (they roared for hours) felled trees, which cut electrical power across the state for up to several weeks. Like many black swan events, looking back, this was a predictable risk yet no one was prepared for it.

Military history is full of examples where an attacker took advantage of the route that was impossible (Hannibal across the Alps) or who attacked when all military logic said to retreat (Chamberlain at Gettysburg). An Israelite shepherd named David used a sling to slay the mighty Goliath. These unexpected actions provided game-changing positive results to the perpetrator.

Black swan events can also be positive. For example, a sudden rise in fuel prices and availability such as in the 1973 Arab Oil Embargo provided a significant market demand for bicycles and for fuel-efficient cars. There are often warnings of impending black swan events, if you are looking for them.

Sometimes, these events could have been predicted as rare occurrences by studying history. In other cases, the people making the risk assumption cannot conceive of such a thing occurring so they never consider the possibility (it could never happen here). When examining risks to a given situation, the benefit of suing a group with different backgrounds is that what one person is confident is impossible may be very possible to someone else. The discussion is useful for identifying "black swan" events.

Black swans may be really poor risk identification. In the earlier example of Hurricane Ike sweeping through Ohio with sustained high winds, this has occurred before, but not in the personal memories of the people of Ohio. Since they had not experienced it, they could not consider the risk as credible.

§ 10.04 BUSINESS CONTINUITY PLANNING AS A MITIGATION TECHNIQUE

[A] Overview

Companies encounter problems all of the time. These isolated challenges make the day difficult for a particular manager but the corporation's operations continue. For example, a machine failure, seasonal influenza sweeping though a call center, or an electrical outage. These localized disasters can be worked through more quickly if a plan for their resolution is in place. Business continuity plans detail what to do if a certain event occurs. You cannot avoid all risk, but business continuity plans can minimize the disruption to your business.

> ## COMMENT
>
> Disaster recovery plans generally refer to relocating a significant portion of the business to an alternate facility. For example, a major fire in the computer room or in the offices may require that function to be temporarily moved somewhere else. However, a localized fire, such as in a single computer server or office can cause a lot of disruption but not require relocating anyone. In this case, the business continuity plan would be used.

§ 10.04[C]

Business continuity plans can be strategic, such as customer service must answer all calls within 30 seconds, no matter what the situation. In this case, plans must accommodate a wide range of potential situations. However, most business continuity plans are localized. They address risks that may arise when a particular process fails. For example, the failure of the e-mail server may upset many people; but the company is still in business and providing its products and services, albeit without an important communications channel.

A business continuity plan should be provided for:

- Every IT process supporting an internal or external service level agreement.
- Every vital business function and its IT support.
- Every "politically sensitive" function (even if it fails the vital business function test).
- Every legally mandated IT function.

Some SLAs are specified in customer contracts. In those cases where the SLA is not met, then the company may be required to pay a financial penalty. However, the company's financial situation may not provide funds for redundant systems or machinery. In those cases, the IT leader must implement metrics to monitor if the process is trending toward non-compliance. For example, an early morning verification that the process support team is onsite or that the existing staff is focusing on the essential services and not "business as usual."

[B] Keeping Pace with Change

Business processes change (officially and unofficially). Often in the hectic confusion of day-to-day business, no one updates the business continuity plan to reflect process changes. Sometimes these changes introduce new risks into the process. Unless they are reviewed and minimized in some way, the process again is susceptible to interruption.

Some changes are a result of external forces. Changes in materials suppliers or changes in personnel sourcing can change a process's output. Legislative requirements (which evolve as companies try to implement them) can change a process's required outputs and may require extensive audit trails.

Another common change comes from changes in the information security environment. As new exploits are discovered, processes may need to be changed on short notice. This quick implementation will often defer documentation updates to a never-to-come date.

[C] Audit the Plans

Written plans often suffer from neglect. Processes are changed but plans not updated. When an issue arises and someone reaches for the incident management plan, it is very disruptive when it no longer reflects the current process. There are several ways to ensure that plans remain in sync with reality.

A. Require the manager responsible for that area to verify every quarter that the plans are still valid. Requiring a signature will make them pause before making a blanket statement.

10-19

B. Require (at a minimum) semiannual tests to demonstrate the plan. This will also train the participants in their roles during a problem.

C. Periodically audit the plans. Randomly select plans and review them with the process participants.

COMMENT

Everyone wishes that risk could be managed through some tool. Unfortunately, there are so many factors to consider (legal, business climate, time of year, public opinion, etc.) that attempting such a model would be far beyond most IT departments. Models are intended to predict an outcome based on inputs. The problem is to include all of the necessary inputs and to understand their interactions. Some risks may only occur when a combination of risks are present or absent.

Some companies use quantitative models to predict the potential outcome of a risk. This supposes that you know of all of the potentially significant inputs to calculate a reliable output (this is why weather forecasts are rarely useful more than a week out). It looks for correlations between input variables and emerging variables that seem to influence the outcome for potential correction of the model.

Typical process metrics that an IT department might use include failure rates for hardware, reported problems by users, and capacity utilization rates. Another source of data is the service desk problem database, which may indicate troublesome technologies that were previously stable.

The term "model risk" means that a model can only contain the factors that you are aware of. It does not include interactions you are not aware of nor does it include potential risks that are unknown to you.

§ 10.05   IMPLEMENTING IT RISK MANAGEMENT

[A]   Overview

Every company has its own threshold of acceptable risk. Usually it is quite conservative. Executives may speak about rewarding risk but middle management never accepts the potential of a failure slowing their career. To change this, company leadership at all levels must teach employees how to identify the risks in a given situation and evaluate them. Then acceptable risks can be taken and unacceptable ones avoided.

Risks evolve as changes in the business climate change over time and the seasons of the year pass. Processes to manage business risks should be regularly reviewed to ensure continued relevancy. This takes time that does not create anything of value that the company can sell so it tends to be pushed to the back of the work list.

People are the key to a successful risk management program. They are close to the situation and in the best place to assess risks. The problem is that most companies discourage this sort of action. Even if the line supervisor sees a reasonable risk of success, the line supervisor's own supervisor may deny the action as he/she is risk averse. Over time, this erodes personal initiative and then quashes the idea.

People are a risk. They prefer the known to the unknown. People over-estimate unfamiliar risk and discount the ones familiar to them. They are uncomfortable with a lack of control and tend to react emotionally when the unexpected occurs. If they do not believe in the values of risk management, they will only embrace it when its application is public and will discard it if they believe they can do so.

[B]   A Reasonable Risk

Managers in general are risk averse. This is due to the typical career climate in most companies. If a risk is taken and the result is a success, then they are just considered to be doing their job. However, if a risk is taken and the situation fails, then they are viewed as rash and their career prospects may be significantly diminished. Therefore, the safest approach is to do nothing that may fail.

This addresses the manager's personal security issue but does nothing to advance the company's prosperity. Companies wishing to improve their productivity must be willing to take reasonable chances. A reasonable chance is where risks have been assessed and the likelihood of success is high (note that it is not 100 percent).

In a given situation, the potential reward of taking a risk must be defined, and usually quantified. For example, if we buy another drill press, we can build 100 more parts per day, with additional revenue of $1,500. However, there is a risk that adding this tool may create another bottleneck somewhere else in the process.

Project managers deal with risk in every project. The project plan and budget are both estimates and have a risk of being insufficient. It is very difficult to accurately estimate the exact amount of time and cost of something that may take a year to complete. Therefore, project managers create a time and budget contingency amount to absorb the likelihood of a small overrun.

[C]   Teach the Team

Risk management is essentially a trade-off between risk and reward. The reward can be the avoidance or minimization of a negative outcome (such as paying your bills on time). It can also be the realization of a rewarding opportunity (such as finding that a new IT process takes half the time of its predecessor). The concept of risk versus reward is the underlying principal in the securities market. To entice someone to invest in a venture that may fail (and result in loss of investment), the potential reward must be comparatively greater than for a safer investment.

A technique with positive results is to teach the team how to estimate risks through repetition. Use Worksheet 10-1 Risk Management Plan Form to walk through several of the common risks in the IT department. By applying, identifying, and assessing these risks, the team begins to see how the scale for likelihood and impact can be applied. (Some people will always grade high and others low.) By identifying, rating, and then prioritizing risks the team can see how the tool can be used to focus on the most pressing risks at hand and how to incorporate the mitigation plans into future capital and operating plans.

Make risk planning a part of the normal staff process. It can be during staff meetings or in dedicated risk management meetings. It is easier to assess risks that may occur within the next month or so than to assess all potential risk for the upcoming year. This also enables the benefit of timely feedback between estimated risks and the actual events.

Specific risks should be assigned to those people who are in the best position to monitor them. For example, the person addressing network complaints may be in the best position to detect an increasing trend of specific problems rather than the network manager who is tied up in administrative details.

§ 10.06 PROCESS RESILIENCE THROUGH RISK MANAGEMENT

[A] Creating an FMEA

There are many tools that will help you analyze the risk of a given process. One of these is the failure modes and effects analysis (FMEA). This tool examines a process in detail to identify potential problems and their resolutions. Once an FMEA is in place, it becomes a part of that process's operator documentation for immediate reference. Refer to Worksheet 10-2 Failure Mode and Effects Analysis.

An FMEA is a different approach to a basic risk assessment already discussed. It begins by detailing the steps in the process, and then examining all of the things that can go wrong. The FMEA then assigns a score to the error based on the likelihood, impact, and how easily it is detected. This list is sorted to bring the most important risks to the top, and then a list of mitigation actions is identified along with an action list of who is going to do what.

Creating an FMEA is typically a group effort, consisting of the people who work with the process every day. It begins by drawing a process flow or process map illustrating the movement of product (or services) through the process. The team then examines each step of the process. This is very useful, but time consuming, so it is either applied to small processes or to segments of larger processes. For example, a team could be assembled to analyze "receiving help desk calls," "using a form used to collect end user software specs," or to debug the company's IT performance evaluation and pay raise program.

WORKSHEET 10-2. Failure Mode and Effects Analysis

Failure Mode and Effects Analysis Worksheet

Problem Description			Impact				Action Recommended	Resolution					Risk X Score	Implementation			
Part/ Process	Failure	Failure Impact	Failure Effects	SEV	OCC	DET	SCORE		SEV	OCC	DET	SCORE	Risk		Responsible Person	Schedule Date	Action Taken	Completion Date
							0					0		0				
							0					0		0				
							0					0		0				
							0					0		0				
							0					0		0				
							0					0		0				
							0					0		0				
							0					0		0				
							0					0		0				
							0					0		0				

[B]   Rating the FMEA Categories

FMEAs are usually built using spreadsheets. The cells in the example in Worksheet 10-2 Failure Mode and Effects Analysis are shrunken to fit the page. In actual use, the cells expand as needed to contain the text. This version of the FMEA has four main sections:

A.   **Problem Description.** Describes and categorizes the problem. Later analysis can group problems with similar characteristics. Each problem can have more than one failure. For example, a process for entering data into a screen can have multiple issues, each with several possible resolutions.

1.   **Part/Process.** Name the process step, such as "enter help desk ticket" or "establish user ID."
2.   **Failure.** What caused the problem, such as "a paper jam," "file contention," or "duplicate IP addresses."
3.   **Failure Impact.** This describes what occurred, such as "ID did not work," "tape did not load," etc.
4.   **Failure Effects.** Notes the "damage" that was done, such as a "report was late" and "missed a required deadline."

B.   **Impact.** Establish a score for how terrible this event would be should it occur.

1.   **SEVERITY.** The degree of damage caused by the error, usually on a 1–10 scale with 10 being the worst.
2.   **OCCURRENCE.** How often the error occurs, usually on a 1–10 scale with 10 being the most often.
3.   **DETECTION.** How obvious the error is when it occurs, generally on a 1–10 scale with 10 being the hardest to detect (not obvious).
4.   **SCORE.** The product of severity times the frequency times the detection. The results are sorted in descending order to bring the most serious issues to the top for action, and push the least likely and least damaging ones to the bottom.

C.   **Resolution.** This section identifies potential resolutions to an issue and evaluates the anticipated impact on the severity, frequency, and detection of the problem once the resolution is applied. Use the same scoring scale as before.

1.   **Action Recommended.** Explain the proposed solution. In project management, this is a mitigation action.
2.   **SEVERITY.** After the solution is applied, what is the anticipated severity of the mitigated problem?
3.   **OCCURRENCE.** After the solution is applied, what is the anticipated frequency of occurrence of the mitigated problem?
4.   **DETECTION.** After the solution is applied, how obvious will future errors be?
5.   **SCORE.** The product of severity times the frequency times the detection. The results can be compared to the earlier score to determine a magnitude of improvement.

6. **Risk.** Proposed solutions are nice, but what is the likelihood they will improve the process without hurting it? A solution that requires major changes, such as reconstructing the Help Desk office just to see if it really helps, is rather risky. This factor acknowledges the cost and effort required just to test the solution.

7. **Risk × Score.** Multiply the anticipated improvement score by the risk value to identify which solutions to try, and in what sequence.

D. **Implementation.** This section assigns tasks and responsibilities for implementing these changes. There is no need to detail these fields—they are just typical project assignment tasks!

1. Responsible person
2. Schedule date
3. Action taken
4. Completion date

One of the more powerful uses of an FMEA is as a quick process-debugging tool long after the process is in place. The FMEA form can be sorted by the "Failure" or even the "Failure Impact" columns. So, in this example, if the paper in a high-speed laser printer is jamming, then sorting the "Failure" column would bring together all of the potential causes for jamming (as identified by the team during process implementation) along with their mitigation steps.

When a process is evaluated for improvement or replacement, its FMEA highlights areas for process improvement and pitfalls to avoid. FMEAs should be reviewed and updated whenever a significant change is made to a process. They should also be reviewed and updated annually to reflect the processes' current usage.

See Policy ITP-10-1 IT Risk Management Policy as an example.

POLICY ITP-10-1. IT Risk Management Policy

Policy #:	ITP-10-1	**Effective:**	01/19/13	**Page #:**	1 of N
Subject:	IT Risk Management Policy				

1.0 PURPOSE

This policy defines the IT department's risk management program. Risk management encourages the prudent application of risks to improve company performance and to minimize the likelihood, impact, or to increase the amount of warning before the occurrence of an adverse event.

2.0 SCOPE

The policy applies to risk management in the IT department. It includes all projects, processes, and routine IT activities. This policy includes the ongoing training of personnel in risk management techniques and the auditing of team efforts to ensure that risk management is included in all significant activities.

3.0 POLICY

Risk is the possibility that something in the future will not work out as we wished. The undesired outcome could be positive or negative. Risks are managed through four steps:

A. **All Projects Shall Use a Formal Risk Assessment Plan.** Every IT project must include a formal risk assessment, using Worksheet 08-1 Risk Assessment Form. The assigned project manager is responsible for the creation and maintenance of this document.

   The contents of this form are to be reviewed informally during project team meetings. At the conclusion of every project milestone, the risks to the project from that point to completion are re-evaluated, and the project plan is adjusted to include appropriate mitigation actions.

   At the conclusion of the project, the risk assessment forms are collected. Each must be updated as to whether the risk occurred or not, and to what degree. The leader of the company's Project Management Office will ensure these forms are completed and filed.

B. **Every Significant IT Process Shall Include an FMEA Analysis.** The IT department uses many routine processes to complete its required work. Each of these processes possesses multiple opportunities for failure to deliver on time, within budget, or the desired product. To minimize the likelihood of this occurring, each process will include a documented Failure Modes and Effects Analysis (FMEA) study.

   The FMEA procedure is described in Worksheet 10-2 Failure Modes and Effects Analysis. This process must be repeated annually to catch any changes and to focus the IT department members on continuous process improvement.

C. **Risk Management Training Plan.** It is a rare decision that does not include some element of uncertainty or risk of failure. To ensure the IT staff knows how to identify and evaluate the risk in a given situation, the IT Director shall provide an annual training class in how to identify, evaluate, and report risk.

D. **Department-Wide Formal Risk Reviews.** During staff meetings, the risks involved with ongoing processes and projects will be reviewed. These discussions will enable risk reviews by a wider cross-section of the organization with the goals of educating them on current activities and to obtain their perspective of these activities.

   Whenever a new technology is considered for use within the organization, the IT director will assemble a team from each of the IT areas to evaluate the risks of its adoption. This meeting is intended to identify and report on any significant negative or positive impacts of introducing this technology into the company. If the technology is accepted for use, then the same team will assemble to identify mitigation plans for these risks.

4.0 REVISION HISTORY

Date	Revision #	Description of Change
01/19/13	1.0	Initial creation.

5.0 INQUIRIES

Direct inquiries about this policy to:

George Jenkins, CIO
Our Company, Inc.
2900 Corporate Drive
Columbus, OH 43215

Voice: 614-555-1234
Fax: 614-555-1235
E-mail: gjenkins@company.com

Revision #:	1.0	Supersedes:	N/A	Date:	01/19/13

Part II

OVERSEEING AND DIRECTING PROJECTS AND PEOPLE

11

HUMAN RESOURCES: IT'S POOREST MANAGED ASSET

§ 11.01 OVERVIEW

[A] Purpose and Scope

Imagine purchasing a new server for the IT department. It would be a large powerful server that might cost somewhere in the range of $90,000. What would an IT Manager do to prepare for this major investment? Ensure there was an outlet on the UPS? Find rack space or even buy a new rack? Assign an administrator to set up and ensure the machine runs smoothly? Purchase an equipment maintenance agreement to cover required repairs for the next four years? Create a project plan to ensure that everything was done to make the device quickly available and productive? Likely they would do all of these things—and more.

So why when it comes to staffing an IT department is so much left to chance? The salary and overhead for the average IT professional is about $90,000 (salary plus 50 percent for overhead). Yet how often are new employees haphazardly introduced to an IT department? The ongoing maintenance of these people is only an afterthought. Their work environment is based on whatever is available—even if it is noisy and distracting.

The old saying that an IT staff is the department's most valuable resource is quite true. A quick look at the department's budget will show where the costs are. Staffing is always near the top of the budget of most IT departments. For an IT Manager to be effective, this resource must be carefully nurtured.

Management of the IT department's human assets must be a proactive effort. Through daily conversations, staff meetings, and performance reviews, the IT Manager must strive to identify and address issues before they become major problems. People don't want a manager. They want a leader. Leaders know that they set an example in all they do—good and bad.

Human Resources policies governing IT personnel are focused on:

A. Obtaining the best workers with the required skills.
B. Continually motivating the workers for high productivity.
C. Improving skills sets through training.
D. Retaining employees through fair treatment and fair compensation.

IT personnel policies only augment corporate personnel policies. On close examination, they are simply good management practices. The difference between IT and other departments is that highly skilled technical people are expensive and difficult to find. They can more readily depart for other companies if they believe they are not fairly treated.

It is time consuming to train a replacement for a competent employee in any department. Training requires both the new person and a skilled person to teach him or her. Replacements must be trained and allowed time to learn their new responsibilities. This may delay scheduled projects. New personnel often cost more than current employees creating a pay imbalance in the department.

IT jobs attract a certain personality type. Studies indicate that IT workers are motivated more by personal fulfillment and growth than money or job titles. Other research indicates they tend to be more loyal to their profession than to their firm. IT personnel policies and procedures must accommodate these differences for the department to function effectively and to minimize turnover.

[B]   Critical Policies to Develop Based on This Chapter

Using the material discussed in this chapter, you will be able to create the following policies:

A. Recruiting
B. Performance reviews
C. Training for new employees
   1. Orientation policy
   2. Mentoring policy
D. Developing staff
E. Nontraditional working arrangements
   1. Working from home
   2. Flextime
   3. Job sharing
   4. Rehiring workers

Policies should always be developed based on the local situation. Successful managers cannot issue locally correct guidance if the policies are written for some other company's situation.

§ 11.02   RECRUITING, REASSIGNMENTS, AND PROMOTIONS

[A]   Overview

Recruiting is the responsibility of the Human Resources department. Based on the information provided by the IT Manager, the Human Resources recruiters attempt to match resumes with an open position. However, without a detailed understanding of IT technologies and local requirements, this is a poor way to find people. If the IT department cannot obtain a dedicated Human Resources recruiter to learn about their specific needs, then they must screen all incoming resumes themselves.

Workers vary widely in productivity and their inclination to work harmoniously with others. Through its experience in hiring and disciplining workers, the Human Resources department strives to ensure that new employees are as "trouble free" as possible. Human Resources professionals know that less than 5 percent of the employees cause over 95 percent of the problems. It is essential that the company's interviewing and screening processes identify problem people before they join the organization.

COMMENT

IT management professionals also learn over time that the most productive 5 percent of all IT people get 95 percent of the work done. Corporate compensation plans rarely take this into account.

A common pitfall of recruiting is hiring relatives of valued company workers. In theory, this becomes a further reward for successful service. In practice, it can lead to a wide range of problems. Because of the controls needed for an IT operation, hiring relatives causes nothing but problems. Relatives tend not to abide by the same rules as nonrelatives. They tend to cover up more errors and have higher rates of orchestrated thefts. Very large companies can successfully overcome this by requiring large separation in facilities, subsidiaries, or other company subdivisions between related workers.

[B] Creating a Clear Job Description

It all begins with a clear idea of the job. A job description, as the name implies, describes a job. Some managers try to shortcut the process and substitute vague boilerplate descriptions that are generic and not specific to the actual job. This is a big mistake. A well-written job description details the type of tasks that the employee is expected to perform. It communicates an expectation from the employer to the worker as to the skills and duties expected for that position. Job descriptions are the foundation for setting a position's pay range.

How detailed should a job description be? Some will argue that more than a page is too much detail. Much of the description can be "standard" but some must be specific. For example, the "standard" part might be a description for a C++ programmer. Essentially, all of this class of workers has about the same technical requirements. The "specific" part of the description is that this person will be supporting the materials management department and must understand the business side of that department.

Some managers do not like detailed job descriptions. They feel it hinders their flexibility when assigning work. This is not true. Work is assigned as required. Well-written job descriptions include a final statement that the person will perform any additional duties as assigned. A well-written job description includes:

A. **Primary responsibilities.** These are the expectations that justify the existence of this staff position. This list is used to determine who will be chosen for this position, so it must be carefully written. The primary responsibilities detail what is wanted and how much. Any candidate that does not meet *each* of the primary responsibilities is automatically excluded from consideration. Since the list of primary responsibilities narrows the list of potential candidates, it should be 10 items or less.

An example of a primary responsibility might be a requirement that the candidate possess at least "5 years of project management experience." Just asking for project management experience would open the position to someone with insufficient background. Often the requirement would even more specifically require "web software design project management."

Technical skills may be the same as with other positions within the department. An example might be two Java programmers sitting side by side with different business knowledge requirements. When listing skill requirements, think specifically about what this person will be assigned to do rather than sticking to generic tasks. This person's software application might include coding access to a non-standard database, it may interface with some antique equipment or software, or it might require extensive travel.

Sometimes skill levels are indicated by professional certifications, such as PMI's Project Manager Professional or Microsoft Certified Systems Engineer. Certifications indicate an understanding of technical specific principles but are not a reliable indicator of the person's ability to translate these principles into action.

COMMENT

Project Management Institute (PMI)'s Project Management Professional certification can be found at *www.pmi.org*.
Microsoft's MCSE (Microsoft Certified Systems Engineer) can be found at *www.microsoft.com*.

B. **Secondary responsibilities.** These are the non-critical functions assigned to this person. Candidates are evaluated by how well they fulfill these requirements. However, not meeting a secondary responsibility will not disqualify them from consideration. This might be expertise with technology outside of their normal responsibility but would be handy for the department. It might be knowledge of a specific foreign language or experience working for the government.

C. **Standard boilerplate.** This is a list of company-wide expectations that are sometimes tacked onto the bottom. This runs the gamut from "supports company EEO initiatives" to "works well with others." Usually these are already covered in company policies and are stated here to highlight them to all applicants.

Job descriptions can be misused. They can be tailored to only fit a single person or to require an inflated salary. Examples of how job descriptions can be misused include:

A. **Tailored job descriptions.** These are written in such a way as to exclude as many people as possible (usually all internal candidates). An alternative is to write in such a way that only one person could plausibly qualify. Both will backfire on the IT Manager. It exposes the job posting system as a phony management practice and not fairly applied for promotions or transfers. The implication is that, to be promoted or transferred, the employees must leave the company.

B. **Inflated job descriptions.** These add nonessential requirements and technical skills to inflate the position's pay scale. Examples would be to require a Masters degree, expert level expertise in a technical area, or a significant number of years experience.

C. **Hiring someone who lacks the primary requirements.** This applies a standard for excluding some employees and not others. Like the tailored job description, this one is hard to disguise and demoralizes the rest of the employees.

COMMENT

It is always interesting to see an advertisement in the newspaper asking for more years of experience working with a hot new technology than that technology has been in existence.

[C] Establishing Clear Selection Criteria

All new cars are nice. The same goes for interviewing job applicants—they all seem so suited for the position. To select the best candidate for a position, and to be fair to all applicants, the hiring IT Manager must establish the criteria for rating all candidates before speaking to the first one. These criteria become the "yard stick" against which all candidates are measured.

The criteria should be written and are usually maintained in a "score sheet" form created just for filling this position. The first section is for primary responsibilities. Each of these is weighted according to its importance. Candidates may barely meet a requirement or be an expert in that skill. Their degree of compliance should be indicated. Any candidate that does not minimally fulfill all of the primary requirements is automatically disqualified.

COMMENT

One trick to help keep your biases in check is to force yourself to be harder on candidates you immediately like, and to give those you don't like at first the benefit of the doubt.

Secondary requirements include: education, industry experience, personal characteristics, and future growth potential. They reflect characteristics of present employees who are happy and successful in the same type of position. Again, the degree to which someone meets these skills should be noted.

[D]   Internal Opportunity Posting

One of the most difficult things to gauge is an IT professional's degree of institutional knowledge. An understanding of how a company actually works is not available from any textbook—it must be gained through experience. Personal relationships built over time make implementing technical change much easier. For these reasons, it is preferable to fill open positions with qualified internal candidates.

Most companies post job openings internally for at least two weeks before looking outside of the company. This allows time for people to return from business trips and vacation to see them. However, this is also abused by posting for only one week during holidays or peak summer vacation season. When an exciting opportunity appears, some employees will see that they lack a primary requirement and not apply for it. Imagine the discontent when someone else lacking the same skill is hired! (If a primary responsibility is moved to the secondary column because sufficient candidates cannot be found, then the job *must* be reposted internally.)

A major benefit of internally posting jobs is to open opportunities for all and to break up some of the "buddy" system of promotions. Using a "buddy" system to select people opens the door to a discrimination lawsuit. Posting positions may reveal latent talent and skills within the department. Whenever hiring or promoting people, management is open to accusations of gender or race bias. An open posting of positions makes them equally available to all.

Managers get what they reward. If "friends" are rewarded with promotions that their performance does not rate, then the hard-working employees will shift their efforts from technical results to being the manager's "buddy," since that is what is rewarded. Other workers will become demoralized by their unfair exclusion from consideration and "retire on the job."

Some large companies rate their IT Managers on the number of positions filled internally. Although it is not possible to find someone internally, that is a good fit for every job, a high internal fill rate is indicative of managers "growing" their staff and improving their skills. Managers who "protect" their team by preventing anyone from leaving need to be replaced—before everyone on their team does!

[E] External Opportunity Posting

Locating the right person for a position is an expensive and time-consuming process. There are many places to post open position notices and many ways to receive resumes. Unfortunately, the ones most used by IT professionals are the ones that are the hardest to make effective. The most used external posting opportunities are:

A. **Employment agencies.** Using an employment agency hands the responsibility of finding good candidates to a third party. An employment agency is not cheap and typically charges a fee that is equal to 20 percent or more of the candidate's first year salary.

Employment agencies have the advantage of disguising the company that has an opening. Sometimes a company does not wish its employees to know a search is underway, such as when they are replacing a key employee, or if all internal candidates are obviously not suited for the position.

An agency is most useful if hiring someone whose expertise is not already in-house. Without knowledge of the subject, the hiring company cannot ask pertinent questions to determine the depth of a candidate's knowledge. A well-selected agency assumes the task of validating the candidate's technical qualifications.

B. **Employee referral.** A popular program is to pay a bonus to employees who recommend someone from outside of the company for an open position. Proven personnel usually recommend qualified persons like themselves. The person recommending someone has a personal stake in "bringing in a winner."

An immediate benefit is that the company saves time and money over using an employment agency. Other expenses saved include newspaper advertisement and Internet posting costs. Bonuses for finding a candidate who is hired should be no less than $1,000. Smaller bonuses will result in fewer recommendations. See Policy ITP-11-1 Recruiting Bonus Policy as an example.

POLICY ITP-11-1. Recruiting Bonus Policy

Policy #:	ITP-11-1	Effective:	03/18/13	Page #:	1 of N
Subject:	Recruiting Bonus Policy				

1.0 PURPOSE

This policy is designed to encourage employees to recommend someone from outside of the company for an open position within the IT department. Proven personnel usually recommend qualified persons like themselves. The person recommending someone has a personal stake in "bringing in a winner." An immediate benefit is that the company saves time and money over using an employment agency or using other recruiting methods.

2.0 SCOPE

This policy applies to all IT staff members.

3.0 POLICY

Subject to the conditions described below, it is corporate policy to compensate employees that recommend someone from outside of the company for open positions within the IT department. Employees will be compensated in the amount of $1,000 for each referred employee under the following conditions:

A. The referred candidate cannot have at any time been employed by the company or any of its subsidiaries.
B. Payment will be made on the pay period following the 3-month anniversary of the new employee.
C. The new employee must remain employed in good standing with no reprimands during the initial 3 months of employment.
D. The referring employee must be employed at the company and in good standing at the time, the referral bonus payment is due.

4.0 REVISION HISTORY

Date	Revision #	Description of Change
03/18/13	1.0	Initial creation.

5.0 INQUIRIES

Direct inquiries about this policy to:

George Jenkins, CIO
Our Company, Inc.
2900 Corporate Drive
Columbus, OH 43215

Voice: 614-555-1234
Fax: 614-555-1235
E-mail: gjenkins@company.com

| Revision #: | 1.0 | Supersedes: | N/A | Date: | 03/18/13 |

C. **Internet posting and search.** Posting jobs on the Internet has been a valuable tool for human resources staff. Prior to the Internet, just getting the word out about an open position was difficult. Creating advertisements for newspapers had to hit certain deadlines and were expensive. If the best candidates did not read the paper that weekend, then they would not know of the opportunity. Cost is based on newspaper space, and small ads may fail to adequately describe the opportunity and how exciting it is.

Posting open positions on the Internet makes them immediately available to a wide audience. Job applicants near and far can learn about openings, qualifications desired, and in some cases, the salary range offered. There is usually space for including the entire job description, plus information on the company.

Unfortunately, this openness has led to abuses. In days gone by, candidates would print their resumes and mail them to individual companies. Even if they tried to send resumes to all companies within an area, it was time consuming and expensive to create the letters and post them. The ease with which the Internet can create and mail resumes has changed this entirely. There are now companies that will blast resumes to hundreds of companies at once for little cost and irrespective of the candidate's qualification. This in turn has inundated companies with more resumes than they could possibly review. (Large companies could receive hundreds of resumes per day.) As a defense, most human resources departments now use text databases to receive and store resumes. Candidates are screened through key word searches.

The result is that resumes are now peppered with "buzzwords" that indicate some specific skill. Supposedly, these buzzwords will fool the search process long enough for the resume to be read by someone. Unfortunately, this means that many valuable resumes are never reviewed since they did not use the appropriate phrase.

COMMENT

Popular Internet job sites for technical professionals include *www.monster.com*, *www.dice.com*, and *www.computerjobs* *.com*.

D. **Temporary-to-permanent hiring.** Some companies prefer a "try before you buy" approach where open positions are first filled with temporary employees. The company then evaluates their performance over time and determines if they are suitable candidates for employment. If they do not work out, then their contract (usually six months) is allowed to expire, and a replacement is brought in. This approach sounds safe but it is also expensive.

First, time is required to orient the new person to the duties required, the peculiarities of the local operations, who on the team does what, etc. This requires the efforts of an existing employee. Second, the person's temporary agency will charge a fee in addition to that person's salary. Finally, the temporary employee may be offered a permanent position elsewhere and leave on short notice.

[F]   Using Offshore Staffing

For years, companies have been "outsourcing" work to other companies. These companies submit either fixed bid or time-and-materials contracts and deliver whatever service is desired. Service desk support and PC repair were some of the first services to be widely outsourced. The idea was that by using a company focused on delivering this type of service, they could do it better and sometimes cheaper.

A natural follow-up was the still cheaper labor overseas. Offshore companies can be located anywhere in the world. Labor overseas can be cheap and, with inexpensive worldwide telecommunications, it makes little difference if the contractor is down the street or around the globe.

This type of arrangement works well with some IT tasks and is a failure in others. Work that is clearly defined, such as the specifications for programming a new accounting system, is well suited for offshoring. However, tasks that require interaction with customers have had mixed results.

Companies feel a greater sense of security for their trade secrets and program code if it is within the same borders. Some of the pitfalls or important considerations when offshoring include:

A. Poorly defined work can result in extended times to complete it. Tasks must be clearly understood—even through the filters of language and culture.
B. Language/cultural interpretation differences. English is a highly nuanced language. An understanding of proper English may not help when speaking to someone with a thick regional dialect.
C. Contracts may be interpreted under the laws and customs of the off-shore country. This is important in terms of who owns the code, who owns the design and other intellectual property rights.
D. Contract workers may be more inclined to test the company's security limits and, if they are weak, download confidential material.
E. Sending work offshore adds the complications of communicating across multiple time zones, cultural, and language barriers.
F. Some of the more technical offshore companies have high employee turnover.
G. The technical infrastructure of these countries may not be as stable as in western countries. Electrical and telecommunications outages, civil

unrest, and disrupted communications due to natural disaster are factors that make offshore contracting more complex than hiring someone down the street.

COMMENT

One author worked for a company that offshored individual technical support positions. At one point, they tried to offshore a project manager position. Unlike a technical support person who dealt primarily with machine issues, project managers deal primarily with people and normally face-to-face since 80 percent of communication is nonverbal. Problems immediately arose with time zones, cultural communications, and a lack of understanding about the client's product. It was not long before the job was brought back into the building.

Like all things, offshoring must be the right tool for the right job and is not always the correct answer.

[G]   College Recruiting

Colleges are an excellent source of entry-level IT employees. A degree in computer science is just that—training in the use of computers. Graduates know how to code a program but not how to convert business requirements into usable code. Hiring graduating students implies a requirement to train them in common business processes.

Hiring new graduates into the department can be something of a culture shock. The new employees will be bright, energetic, and highly enthusiastic. It is important to harness and direct this energy into positive directions and not let it be crushed by cynics. All newly hired graduates need their own mentor. Some companies prefer mentors of nearly the same age (big brother/sister), while others go for a generational difference, sort of a father/mother figure.

Keep in mind that most new graduates have few of the domestic obligations that "force" other employees to stay. If they are not challenged by their work and reasonably well compensated—or advanced as they improve—then they will quickly depart for another company.

College recruiting requires a person with the enthusiasm to match that of the candidates. Often the IT department is tasked to send "someone" to explain their programs and technology to graduating seniors. Be sure to pick someone knowledgeable about the company, its processes, and who can tell a positive, compelling story about its technological environment and achievements.

[H] Student Interns

A common "try before you buy" approach is to hire college students as part-time employees, generally referred to as interns or co-ops. These students schedule their work around their classes and are usually available for a few hours a day, several days each week. They may also work full-time during their school breaks.

Internships enable a company to get to know the prospective candidate. The student not only has to perform, but also "fit in." If hired by the firm after graduation, they will already know the IT operation and corporate culture. A student intern program is an excellent recruiting tool. However, it must be properly managed. Unlike experienced employees, interns require a structured work situation and should not be assigned to work without a mentor. Assign an intern to shadow and assist a senior worker who will take the time to explain what is happening and why.

A successful intern program requires planning. Interns are very useful for assisting the IT department with many routine tasks—once they are trained on how to do them. However, to gain the full benefit from the program, interns should be attached to major projects where they can observe and learn how the IT team works.

Including interns in interesting projects that tax their skills is important for the company's recruiting efforts. Interns do not automatically accept a company's offer upon graduation. Some interns reject offers if they felt the IT team was boring, dysfunctional, or a dead-end opportunity.

[I] Notes on Interviewing

Interviewing candidates is a very important responsibility. The demeanor and professionalism of the interviewers will be the candidate's primary impression of how desirable a company is to work for. In this sense, the interviewers are "selling" the company as a great place to work. It would be unfortunate if the style and actions of the interviewers scared away the best person for the position.

Whenever speaking to candidates, there should always be two interviewers in the room. This provides multiple perspectives on the candidates and their answers. It also reduces the likelihood of a candidate claiming improprieties during the discussion. Sometimes a representative of the company's human resources department wants to be present to ensure that the questioning follows company and legal requirements.

A consistent way to collect interview data is through use of a standard form. This form is filled out by each interviewer when meeting with the candidates. Record all impressions, since sometimes nonverbal responses expand on the candidate's verbal answers. At the conclusion of each interview, the hiring manager collects all forms and keeps them secured until time to select someone for the job. After the position is filled, the forms are retained by the hiring manager or forwarded to the human resources department according to company policy. *Never* throw these forms or interview notes away. Disgruntled candidates have been known to file lawsuits months later claiming all sorts of discrimination. See Worksheet 11-1 IT Candidate Interview Rating Form as an example.

WORKSHEET 11-1. IT Candidate Interview Rating Form

IT Candidate Interview Rating Form			
Applicant Name:			
Position:		Date of Interview:	
Interviewer:		Total Score:	

Response Rating Scale:
    1–Candidate's response is below expectations
    2–Candidate's response mostly meets expectations
    3–Candidate's response fully meets expectations
    4–Candidate's response exceeds expectations
    5–Candidate's response far exceeds expectations
    NA–Not applicable/unable to determine			

Technical Questions			1–5 or NA
Please discuss your experience in our industry.			
Please discuss your experience with (technology).			
Describe how you would (technical activity).			
Discuss how you solved a difficult technical problem.			
Describe a situation where the technology failed and how did you handle it.			
Non-technical Questions			1–5 or NA
What do you do to maintain and expand your technical skills?			
Describe a situation where you helped someone with a difficult technical problem.			
Describe your ideal workday.			
Describe how you handled a difficult situation with a customer or user.			
Competencies			1–5
Candidate is expected to demonstrate the following technical competencies based on the requirements of the position.			
Enter competency #1			
Enter competency #2			
Enter competency #3			
Notes:			
Adding the score from each rating and dividing the sum by the number of ratings assessed will provide the candidate's rating.			
This form should be submitted to the Human Resources department when completed.			

During the screening process, there was something on the candidate's resume that stood out as a reason to interview this person. Discuss it in detail. Never accept a claimed skill at face value. If they claim to have written Java programs, ask them to describe the programs and the systems. When they touch on a technology or process that the hiring company also uses, ask them to explain in fuller detail. Take time to drill down to a level of detail that illustrates the depth and breadth of their knowledge.

The goal of these questions is not to find someone who can answer 100 percent of the technical questions. Often interviewers optimistically take claimed skills at face value and do not gauge if these skills are at novice, expert, or nonexistent levels.

For software developers, a good way to determine their overall skill level is to have them bring sample code that they have written to the interview (this could be done on a phone interview). Have them explain what the code does and why they coded it the way they did. Another good screening process is to create a simple programming problem to be completed at the interview. This can be basic tasks such as simple looping problems, conditional statements, or recursion. This helps to screen out candidates that may know the language syntax but do not have good programming skills.

COMMENT

When discussing a candidate's work experience, make sure to ask for specific details such as who else worked on the team, the candidate's specific role, what worked well and what didn't on projects, etc. Asking for specifics makes it more difficult for the candidate to embellish his experience.

[J] Some Prudent Checks

Sometimes it becomes necessary to discharge an employee. This can be a long-term, time-consuming process. There isn't much to be done with the people already on the team, but the IT Manager must take care when inviting a new person to join the team. The likelihood of future problems can be reduced by thoroughly checking the candidates before they are hired.

IT personnel, by the nature of their work, have many opportunities to play havoc with company information. They might be able to expose personal information, company confidential information, or even steal money from the company. They can poke around company confidential files and reveal information that may breach legal disclosure regulations.

Prior to extending an offer, verify:

A. Any claim of formal education that was a qualifier for this position, such as college degrees.

B. Comments by previous employers.
C. References provided by the applicant.
D. Character by running a criminal background check to ensure there have been no felony convictions.
E. Character through a drug screening (at the company's expense).
F. Judgment, by running a credit check to determine if the candidate employs good judgment in his or her own affairs.

COMMENT

The best advice when dealing with employees is to be slow to hire and quick to fire. What that means is to be diligent in the hiring of new employees, and realize that problem employees rarely turn into desirable team members.

§ 11.03   NEW EMPLOYEE ORIENTATION

[A]   First Impressions

First impressions are lasting, and in time, those employees reacting negatively may depart for another firm. To create a positive, lasting impression during the employee's first few days, the IT department follows two simple procedures. First, designate a mentor. Second, give the employee a "welcome aboard" education package.

COMMENT

An insurance company in Ohio thinks so highly of this training that they developed and carefully follow a detailed procedure for new employee indoctrination and education.

[B]   IT Orientation Package

This package is a compilation of useful information for the new IT employee. It should contain the following information:

A. **Organization description.** At a minimum, the organization description includes an explanation of each unit's function and identifies those in charge. An organizational chart is useful for large departments. Include a short chronological history of the information systems operation. This provides the new employee with information about promotion tracks, areas of vested interest, and fast-track employees. Note IT's position within the organization.

B. **Equipment and facilities.** List all the hardware in use and its locations. Identify personnel authorized to use the equipment. A facilities map should include the locations of the restrooms, dining areas, and restricted facility areas.

C. **Telephone numbers.** Provide an up-to-date telephone directory of the firm. Include a supplementary list of numbers for frequently called IT units, personnel, and services.

D. **E-mail listing.** Indicate the proper way to address e-mail to other employees.

E. **Mail.** Note when and how the employee will receive his or her mail. This covers both interoffice and outside mail (U.S. Postal Service, UPS, FedEx, etc.).

F. **Forms.** Include a listing of all important forms required by IT personnel, providing the name and number of each form, its source and destination(s), purpose, and any other special information. Include samples used by the new employee's unit. The needs of computer operators are not the same as systems analysts, so packages for new employees may contain different forms.

G. **Schedules.** Include schedules of operations in the procedure package. These can be daily, weekly, or monthly. For daily schedules include begin and end times of normal activities, such as breaks and lunch hours. The weekly, monthly, and annual schedules contain paydays, holidays, vacation scheduling, and meetings. Some IT departments publish monthly listings of employees' birthdays.

H. **Glossary and practices.** This section contains a list of common terms and acronyms used by IT and the firm. Note practices that are extremely important or different from the industry norm.

I. **Unit procedures.** This section contains a listing of all IT procedures and where they are explained. Use a checklist for each type of IT procedure. Check off and date as new employees read the material.

COMMENT

A firm in Michigan, for its own reasons, does not run a slash through the character zero. They place the slash through the alpha character O. There were problems because a new programmer was unaware of this practice. Emphasize unusual department practices to minimize difficulties.

J. **IT project descriptions.** New programmers, systems analysts, and other staff personnel should be provided a list of current and pending IT projects. Note a short description of the objective, as well as target dates, along with the Project Managers' names.

[C]   Mentor Assignment

Joining a company can be a personally traumatic situation. New employees feel disoriented since they do not know where basic services in the facility are located or how to make requests for simple support. At the same time, they are striving to make a good first impression on the new coworkers.

New IT personnel require a "personal touch." Each new employee is assigned a mentor, someone to give a permanent positive impression of the firm. The selected mentor should be personable, someone who the new employee feels comfortable about asking questions concerning procedures.

The mentor must also be patient. Often a simple question answered calmly by a mentor is critical for a new employee. The mentor should not be condescending, which only makes the new IT employee nervous and doubtful about his or her future. A mentor program allows new employees to become productive much more quickly since all of the new employee's questions can be answered directly.

The mentor is responsible for ensuring that the new employee is given a tour of the facility to see where basic services are located, and is properly introduced to his or her coworkers. The mentor ensures that a work area is ready when the employee arrives for the first day of work. The work area should include a telephone, a workstation, a desk containing basic office supplies, log-on passwords, voice-mail password, and in some cases, the employee's new business cards.

Remember that first impressions are lasting. A new IT employee joins the department with high hopes, and a mentor's positive attitude can become infectious, reinforcing these high expectations. Make the new employee feel welcome and a member of the team. See Policy ITP-11-2 New Employee Mentoring Policy as an example.

POLICY ITP-11-2.   New Employee Mentoring Policy

Policy #:	ITP-11-2	**Effective:**	03/18/13	**Page #:**	1 of N
Subject:	New Employee Mentoring Policy				

1.0 PURPOSE

This policy mandates that all new IT employees shall be assigned a mentor during their probationary period.

2.0 SCOPE

This policy covers all new IT employees and any rehires that have been gone over 24 months. The IT Manager is responsible for implementing all aspects of this policy.

3.0 POLICY

Every new IT employee will be assigned a mentor during his or her probationary period by the IT Manager. The mentor is charged with doing the following:

A. Give the new employee a positive impression of the firm.
B. Make the new employee feel comfortable about asking questions concerning procedures.
C. Be patient and answer questions calmly.
D. Take care not to be condescending, which only makes the new IT employee nervous and doubtful about his or her future.
E. Give the new employee a tour of the facility to see where basic services are located, and to be properly introduced to his or her coworkers.
F. Ensure that a work area is ready when the employee arrives for the first day of work. The work area should include a telephone, a workstation, a desk containing basic office supplies, log-on passwords, voice-mail password, and in some cases, the employee's new business cards.
G. Make the new employee feel welcome and a member of the team.

The mentor must report weekly to the IT Manager on any issues or concerns with the new employee throughout the new employee's probation period.

4.0 REVISION HISTORY

Date	Revision #	Description of Change
03/18/13	1.0	Initial creation.

5.0 INQUIRIES

Direct inquiries about this policy to:

George Jenkins, CIO
Our Company, Inc.
2900 Corporate Drive
Columbus, OH 43215

Voice: 614-555-1234
Fax: 614-555-1235
E-mail: gjenkins@company.com

Revision #:	1.0	Supersedes:	N/A	Date:	03/18/13

§ 11.04 PERFORMANCE REVIEW

[A] Overview

Performance reviews are an important management tool for adjusting employee behaviors and productivity before these issues become major problems. Managers who do not properly use this tool invariably complain about the people on their team not cooperating or being disruptive.

In our culture, it is considered discourteous to mention people's shortcomings or to recommend ways to improve unless they first ask. However, a good leader knows that this "fine tuning" is an essential part of a team member's development. Performance reviews open a channel of communication between the manager and the team members.

There are many fine books available on the subject of conducting employee performance reviews. Your company may have specific details on how they want the program to be conducted. Points provided here only highlight some of the basics. The key is to open and maintain a flow of feedback between the team members and the manager so that issues can be resolved before they turn into a crisis.

[B] Conducting a Review

Before beginning the interview, be aware of your own state of mind. If it has been a bad day, it is not a good time to review team members. The same is true for the person to be reviewed. However, many people "steel" themselves for a slew of bad news at these reviews so in most cases, the reviewer has a slight psychological advantage at the beginning of the review. Take care not to waste it!

A performance review is a *two-way* conversation that takes place within the supervisor/worker context. The manager must be aware of this and choose his or her comments carefully. It is important that (in most cases) these reviews be held in a nonconfrontational manner. They must be conducted in a quiet place and completely out of hearing of others.

It is a rare employee who has not earned some positive feedback to begin the conversation with. A bit of well-directed praise does much to place people at ease. If the employee has no positive actions since the last review, then the manager must be at fault for assigning him or her to tasks beyond the employee's ability.

The performance conversation flows two ways—the manager's appraisal of the worker and the worker's appraisal of the manager. Both people must be open to discussing performance and behaviors. It is possible that the problem is with something done by the manager. Often it is easier for the person to absorb some of the recommended improvements if the manager also acknowledges his or her own faults and asks the worker how he or she can improve.

Some pitfalls of performance reviews are:

A. Saving up everything negative and dumping it all at once on someone who was unaware there was a problem. If something needs corrective action, bring it up at that time and do not "sit on it." Reviews are not a time to spring surprises.

B. Arguing, as it indicates people are taking defensive positions and are resistant to change.

C. Allowing the discussion to sink into a "battle of wits," which, like arguing, is more focused on winning than on learning from the conversation.

D. Manager nitpicking and micromanaging minor details.

E. The worker manipulating the wording to try to push all faults on the manager and none onto him or herself to address.

Performance reviews should end on a positive note. Last impressions are the most enduring ones. Many managers leave training, new assignments, and career discussions for the end of the conversation. This is a good time to look ahead with positive expectations of what is to come.

[C] Periodic Performance Reviews

In this context, performance is a comparison of what has been accomplished to what was expected to be accomplished. Performance reviews compare assignments to results. Therefore, the review begins with a recap of the assignments made at the previous review and any interim changes. This is another chance to emphasize the positives. It is easy to judge something long past and ask why it took two weeks to accomplish it—but without the context of the situation, the judgment may seem flawed. During this session, time must be set aside to identify the manager's expectations for worker performance during the upcoming review period. This can be specific tasks to be accomplished and any actions that would improve this person's interaction with the rest of the team.

A good starting place for discussing technical expectations is the job description. The incumbent should be working toward mastering all of the requirements. The second step is the job description of the next level up so that the person is working toward promotion. (Not everyone will want to do this, but it should be offered.) By stepping through each assigned responsibility and discussing performance, the workload on a particular person can be evaluated and adjusted. It also indicates which skills need improvement.

Keeping the review positive does not mean that the manager should avoid offering constructive criticism. This should be worded carefully and clearly. "Hinting" at a problem may seem polite to the manager but is ambiguous to the team member. Speak plainly, discuss the problem with the team member until you are sure he or she understands and then move on and do not belabor the point.

At times during a discussion, assignments will have been delayed due to lack of tools or training. If valid, these act as performance reviews of the manager's results in providing everything needed for success. Take note of these and set a performance goal of when they will be delivered to the team.

> ## COMMENT
>
> A variation on the performance review is a monthly one-on-one meeting between the manager and the team members. These half-hour meetings are free form and provide an uninterrupted conversation.

[D] Peer Performance Reviews

Some companies use Peer or 360-degree reviews. This allows critiques by coworkers as well as the supervisors. These must be conducted so that they do not cross any company guidelines for "personal comments." Peer review can be valuable because team members interact in a manner differently than when the manager is present. This also allows team members to vent their interpersonal frustrations before they become too deeply held.

Peer reviews are time consuming. They must be carefully controlled or they can turn into outright fights. After all, the people are evaluating someone they are competing with for pay raises and promotion. When they think there is money at stake, objectivity may suffer. If a peer review sinks into personal attacks, then cut it off immediately. See Policy ITP-11-3 Peer Performance Review Policy and Worksheet 11-2 IT Staff Peer Performance Form to help develop your peer review process.

POLICY ITP-11-3. Peer Performance Review Policy

Policy #:	ITP-11-3	Effective:	03/18/13	Page #:	1 of N
Subject:	Peer Performance Review Policy				

1.0 PURPOSE

The peer input policy is a mechanism for IT staff members to receive important feedback from their team members about their performance. Peer input is to be obtained through a means that it is both fair and respectful of IT staff members. Peer Performance Reviews must occur annually and should be completed before the end of the fiscal year. Peer is defined as an employee's coworkers or individuals other than the employee's supervisor who are familiar with the employee's performance, work products, and/or services. Peer input should be done independently of the evaluation being conducted by the employee's supervisor.

2.0 SCOPE

The policy applies to all IT staff members within the IT department.

3.0 POLICY

The following steps define the process for performing a peer evaluation:

A. Peer selection is made using the following steps:
1. Employee selects one peer.
2. Supervisor selects one peer.
3. Employee and Supervisor jointly select one peer.
B. For purposes of peer input, the employee will be rated on demonstrated values and customer service utilizing the following rating scale:
1. 1—Employee's performance is consistently below expectations.
2. 2—Employee's performance sometimes meets expectations and needs.
3. 3—Employee's performance consistently achieves expectations improvement.
4. 4—Employee's performance often exceeds expectations.
5. 5—Employee's performance far exceeds expectations.
6. NA—No longer applicable/unable to determine.
C. Each of the selected peers will evaluate the employee using the appropriate form.
D. The evaluation forms are turned into Human Resources for scoring and aggregation of comments.
E. Human Resources delivers the evaluation results to the employee's supervisor.
F. The supervisor reviews the results with the employee.

4.0 REVISION HISTORY

Date	Revision #	Description of Change
03/18/13	1.0	Initial creation.

5.0 INQUIRIES

Direct inquiries about this policy to:

George Jenkins, CIO
Our Company, Inc.
2900 Corporate Drive
Columbus, OH 43215

Voice: 614-555-1234
Fax: 614-555-1235
E-mail: gjenkins@company.com

Revision #:	1.0	Supersedes:	N/A	Date:	03/18/13

WORKSHEET 11-2. IT Staff Peer Performance Form

IT Staff Peer Performance Form		
Employee Name:		
Position:	Evaluation Period:	

Performance Rating Scale:

       1–Employee's performance is consistently below expectations
       2–Employee's performance sometimes meets expectations and needs
       3–Employee's performance consistently achieves expectations improvement
       4–Employee's performance often exceeds expectations
       5–Employee's performance far exceeds expectations
       NA–No longer applicable/unable to determine

Value Expectations

Employee will demonstrate, model, and reinforce the company values listed below. The employee should demonstrate these values in interactions with co-workers, supervisors, and customers; in personal contributions to work assignments and projects; and when representing the IT department or the company.

Personal Values	1–5 or NA
Honesty—displays integrity in work and interactions with others	
Fairness—treats others equitably	
Attitude—maintains a professional attitude	
Respect—is considerate of others	
Business acumen—demonstrates proper business behavior	

Team Values	1–5 or NA
Excellence—strives to create a high performing work environment	
Cooperation—participates and shares information within the department and the company	
Commitment—performs in accordance with the vision and mission of the organization	
Teamwork—willing to collaborate with other team members	

Competencies	1–5
Employee is expected to demonstrate the following technical competencies based on the requirements of the position.	
Enter competency #1	
Enter competency #2	

WORKSHEET 11-2. (Continued)

Enter competency #3	
Notes: Adding the score from each rating and dividing the sum by the number of ratings assessed will provide the employee's annual peer rating. This form should be submitted to the Human Resources department when completed.	

[E] Documentation

Comments made during every review must be carefully documented. In the event that an employee must be formally disciplined or terminated, these contemporary accounts make the action easier to arrange. To ensure that the essential information is captured during these sessions, many companies use a standard form. Copies of review documentation must be filed with the human resources department promptly after the session.

Notes made during performance reviews must remain confidential (as must the conversation). Failing to do this will result in some very reticent team members.

Notes made during previous performance reviews make an excellent starting point for the next review. Any commitments made by either party can be evaluated and discussed. Using notes in this way provides continuity between the sessions.

[F] Preparing the Way for Employee Termination

Discipline and termination policies fill a special need in every department. Discipline should not jeopardize any future relations between employees and the firm, and must be fair.

Discipline establishes the boundary of acceptable behavior. Although unpleasant, it is preferable to leaving a festering problem that may erupt into a crisis. IT workers are free thinkers and will not be productive in a restrictive environment. However, from time to time, someone's behavior may create a negative imbalance in the team. The IT Manager owes it to the company and to the other team members to firmly and fairly establish the boundaries of acceptable behavior.

Termination of an IT employee requires careful treatment. Procedures must be in place and followed precisely ensuring no further trouble from a departing employee. Security access must be severed and company property recovered. Worksheet 11-3 is a termination checklist you can use to make sure all procedures are followed.

Terminations send ripples of uncertainty through a department as people pause to consider whether their own employment is in jeopardy. It is critical the IT Managers use this as a last resort and, when practical, explain to the remaining employees why termination was required.

WORKSHEET 11-3. Employee Termination Checklist

Termination Checklist			
Date:		Department:	
Employee Information			
Name:		Number:	
Department:		Business Unit:	
Last Official Day:		Last Day Onsite:	
Physical Access			
Access		Date Access Terminated	
Building Access			
Office Access			
Desk/Cabinet Keys			
Software Applications			
Application		Date Access Terminated	
Accounting System			
CRM			
Payroll			
Remote Access			
E-mail			
Instructions for Existing and New E-mails:			
Office Equipment			
Equipment		Date Recovered	
Office Phone			
Voice Mail			
Long Distance Access			
Calling Card			
Conference Call Access			
Pager			
Cell Phone			
Laptop			
Home Equipment			
PDA			

WORKSHEET 11-3. (Continued)

Electronic Communications	
Medium	Date Terminated
Dialup Account	
VPN Access	
LAN/WAN Account	
Access to Special Files	
Home Internet Access	
IT Employees	
Item	Date Terminated
Access to Computer Room	
Access to Hosting Facility	
Access to Development Servers	
Passwords	
Servers	
Routers	
Systems	
Listed as Technical Contact	
Applications	
Network Management	
Remote Monitoring	
Software Distribution	
Other	
Item	Date
Non-compete Agreement	
Confidentiality Agreement	
Notice to Security	

To protect the company, information systems managers use special termination procedures. Departing IT employees have many opportunities for destructive activities. As the termination process gets underway, the IT Manager must remove the person from the potential of harming company systems and reassign him or her to an area of low risk—usually as a "special assignment."

§ 11.05   EMPLOYEE DEVELOPMENT

[A]   Overview

An important management responsibility is to prepare team members for new technologies and their next promotion. Selfish managers try to build walls around their most valuable people and prevent them from advancing, since if they leave the team, the manager would be forced to train a replacement.

The flip side of this is "stagnant" and passive people. Often they have retired on the job. They know just how little they need to do to get by. Such departments are typically led by weak leaders who complain they must do everything themselves.

Training must be tied to an assignment. Classes only provide familiarity—not expertise. Expertise only comes with experience. Since classes are "shallow," they must be immediately followed by several assignments to reinforce the knowledge gained.

[B]   IT Skills Inventory

Information technologies are never static. Programming languages more in tune with current requirements seem to appear every four years or so. In the interim, many other skills emerge and recede—from batch oriented procedural languages to event driven programming to Artificial Intelligence to database systems. All of these have emerged, shot to popularity, and gradually became an ordinary part of the IT landscape. Unless IT management prepares the team for these changes, the company will be burdened with low productivity legacy team members and paying a premium to bring in new workers with the latest skills.

To establish and maintain a correlation between employee skills and the skills required by the department, a "Skills Assessment" is done. This compares the skills in the team to the skills required by the department. The gap then becomes the training requirements for the IT department. Skill assessments are normally scheduled to be completed in time for adding training costs into the early stages of the annual budget cycle.

The department's skill set is the sum of the team members. A skills inventory is maintained for each employee and updated at least annually. A file of this type might contain:

  A. Person's name and ID number.
  B. Date the person started with IT.
  C. List of technical skills and their skill rating on a scale of 1 (novice) to 5 (expert).
  D. Formal education received.

    E. Other training received.
    F. Certifications received.
    G. Current job title.
    H. Future education plans.
    I. Future training plans.
    J. Hobbies or interests that could benefit firm.
    K. Next goal/promotion objective within firm.

[C] Continuing Education and Training

Many IT departments assign to someone the part-time duty of coordinating the team's education and training. Often this is the same person who maintains the skills inventory since the two responsibilities are clearly related. This person is both an advisor to and an information source for those seeking education or training information. He is familiar with the company's policies and paperwork involved in training. The coordinator must also know the various sources of training available.

[D] Plan for the Future

Refer to the asset management list of hardware and software. List every hardware and software tool used by the company. Add to this list every critical process. Use the department roster and build a spreadsheet. (See Worksheet 11-4 Employee/Process Matrix as an example.)

Using Worksheet 11-4, list the names down the left side of the page and the technologies across the top. Rate each employee from 1 to 5 (5 being an expert) on how skilled he is in each area. Do the same thing on a different spreadsheet for critical processes. Are there any gaps? Are there two (preferably three) people in a high skill level for every technology or critical process? If not, then assign someone as the backup person for the technology and schedule him for training.

Combine this information with whatever new technologies are anticipated for the upcoming year and a complete set of data necessary to build a training plan is at hand.

Repeat this same evaluation process, but this time let the team members rate themselves. Compare how they rate themselves to how their manager rates them as additional input into the training plan.

[E] Training and Consultants

The development or installation of a major new technology is always an exciting time in an IT department. Often, temporary technical employees (consultants) are brought in since no one in the company has experience with this technology. It is a prudent policy to match one employee to every one or two consultants. This allows the employee to gain valuable experience with the new product and provides a path for the eventual departure of the consultants. Otherwise, the consultants could become a permanent fixture.

For this to be effective, the IT Manager must monitor and ensure this training is being accomplished. Eventually, a "stake in the ground" is set—a date

WORKSHEET 11-4. Employee/Process Matrix

Employee/Process Matrix								
AS/400					Shop Floor Systems			
OS		Applications						
Queue Mgmt	Admin	Order Entry	Payroll	Warehouse System	VOC Tracking	Waterjet Cutter	Paint Line Robots	Tank Farm
Abraham Lincoln								
William McKinley								
Theodore Roosevelt								
Ronald Reagan								
Bill Clinton								

when the consultants will leave. The person being trained will see that he will soon be on his own and must gather as much understanding as he can before the experts depart.

COMMENT

> IT Managers at a major truck manufacturer complained that their ERP consultants often cost $200 per hour, and that many were needed to support the product. When asked why they didn't train their own employees to support the product, they said that if they did, the employees would just leave to be consultants!

§ 11.06 MANAGING IT TRAINING

[A] Developing a Training Strategy

A training strategy is not hard to develop. The purpose of training in an IT department is to prepare someone to provide a level of support for a technology. Strategy development involves identifying areas of weak or nonexistent expertise and then preparing someone to fill that gap. The basic steps for developing a training strategy include:

A. Identifying the expertise gaps.
B. Identifying training requirements for projects planned over the upcoming year.
C. Identifying nontechnical training essential for the department to function optimally.

Identifying the expertise gaps. The first step is to identify existing gaps between the requirements to support existing systems and the IT department's current expertise. To accomplish this, we will assemble a matrix that compares the technologies to be supported to the employees on staff. To do this:

A. Begin with an inventory of the hardware and software necessary to be supported. The foundation of your training plan is an understanding of what skills the department should possess to effectively maintain the existing hardware and software. These skills may be confined to how to use it (hardware—we do not repair the circuitry) or how to repair it (such as Java or SQL training classes). Create a list of every hardware model and variation you support. This can be quickly obtained from your asset management database if one exists. If not, then talk to the various people in the IT department and create a list. If you have a service desk, their problem-tracking database could be a resource to identify hardware items. Only include model variations on the list if they are significantly different from the base model. When creating your hardware list, be sure to include hardware supported by every team in the IT department. This includes the mainframe computer, the network components, desktop units, engineering workstations, data collection devices such as scanners, printers, notebook PCs, etc.

B. Remove from the list any hardware items that may not require any team training. Some hardware categories such as monitors may not be a training issue because they are normally repaired by exchanging them for new units. Other hardware categories such as mainframe computers are serviced by the manufacturer and we do not intend to change that. The goal in building the hardware list is not to train people to repair the equipment but rather to show them how to determine if it is broken or misused. Enter the list of hardware supported along the left side of a spreadsheet. We will be doing more with this later.

C. With the hardware list in hand, create a similar list for software. Some software will be obvious, such as the programs that run on your desktop PC. Some software may require some digging, such as the specialized programs used in network routers. List all of the software you can find in all of the various computers and technologies supported. Next, identify the programs that are purchased and the ones developed in-house. Purchased programs are usually supported by the company that created them. Their in-house support component is often the system administrator. Many of the mainframe programs are purchased but they should still be on the training list. There could be some fine tools available for use that only a few people understand how to use. The program's author usually supports in-house developed programs, although in some cases, that person may have moved on and a different person is saddled with the job. The list of in-house developed programs can be quite long. Refer back to the spreadsheet created for the hardware. Open a second workbook in the same spreadsheet. Enter the list of software supported along the left side of a workbook using the same format as was used for the hardware.

D. Identify which of these products support critical business functions. The IT Manager must identify which hardware and software items are used to support the facility's critical business functions. To do this, refer back to the critical systems identified in the IT business continuity plan or base this on experience in the department. Mark each of the critical items by shading in their columns on the spreadsheet.

E. Identify the basic technical skills required by everyone in the department. These are the fundamental technical skills that the IT Manager expects everyone in the department to possess. Ask the IT Manager to mark the hardware and software with which everyone should be proficient. Use a different-colored column. This might include the company standard word processing program, the standard desktop PC operating system, etc.

F. Identify the basic skills required for everyone on a specific team (applications development, operations, network support, etc.). Each of the functional teams within the IT department depends on its own basic technologies that each person on the team should know. Schedule a meeting with the IT Manager and the team leader for each section to identify these skills.

G. Survey employees to determine their expertise for supporting each of these functions. Create a survey form for the employees to use. Along the left side, list each of the hardware and software technologies. Do not mention anything about the technologies identified as essential. Ask each person to evaluate their skills for each technology in terms of zero to five: 0–No experience with the product at all. 1–Novice—has started the product and reviewed some documentation. 2–Familiarity—has successfully used the product but would need some time to prepare before using it again. 3–Competent user—has successfully used the product before and ready to use it again. 4–Expert user—has used the product a number of times and explored many of its options. 5–Complete mastery of the product. This is a great time for the team members to also indicate those technologies for which they have primary or secondary support responsibilities. When the surveys are complete, enter them into the spreadsheet. An optional exercise is to ask the team leaders to fill out their own skill assessments for each team member. Later the team leader can compare them with the team member's self-evaluation to better understand the team's perception of itself.

H. Identify those areas where support is required but employees are not at the expert level. Identify training required.

1. Based on the items on the matrix that are required, are there any team members who are not at least rated as "competent"? Make a list of these people and the technologies involved. If someone indicates that they are a key support person for a technology and they do not rate themselves at least "competent," then their training should be scheduled immediately. If a critical technology does not have anyone listed as its primary or secondary support technician, then the IT Manager must designate someone. Again, check to see if they are at least competent at supporting that technology. Identify potential instructors.

2. Anyone claiming to work at the expert or master level of a product is a likely instructor for that technology. Before asking for their assistance, verify this competency claim with their supervisors.

I. Develop training plans to fill these gaps. Review your list of technologies. Make a note of how each item will be trained now and in the future. Some tools are easily taught one-on-one between the new employee and his or her mentor. Other tools must be taught in off-site classes. Each technology should have a training strategy for instructing IT employees on how to maximize its value. Based on the matrix of technologies supported and the skills in-house, develop a training plan to bring each person in the IT department up to the desired technical level.

Identify training requirements for projects planned over the upcoming year. Every year, companies plan their operating and capital budgets for the upcoming year. A part of this process is to identify new initiatives to be undertaken. The training manager must be involved in this planning to identify technologies that are not covered in the current skills assessment and to project training required.

Often the technologies to be used are not clearly defined this far in advance. The training manager is at the same disadvantage as the people lined up to support these projects. Maintain open communications with the facility planning staff so that as a project prepares to begin, the training manager can begin lining up the requisite training.

Identify nontechnical training essential for the department to function optimally. There is more to an IT department than bits and bytes. Other job skills are important for the department to function smoothly. The training manager must keep these training objectives equally to the front of the planning discussion to prevent them from becoming lost in the shuffle of programming classes.

A. Time management. Technical people are generally not the best practitioners of time management. If an IT Manager wants to improve the productivity of the department, he or she should schedule training for the employees to optimize the use of their workdays.

B. Project management. This is an important part of information technology management. Just about everyone in the department can benefit through improved skills at organizing their work and coordinating with others to complete tasks. On a larger scale, this becomes a stepping-stone for developing people for increased responsibilities.

C. Organizing and running effective meetings. No person or system in IT exists in a vacuum. We all interact with our peers and end users to maximize benefit to the company. A common method of this is through meetings. Meetings can be useful events or boring wastes of time. Well-organized and productive meetings do not occur by accident. Training the IT staff to effectively plan and execute meetings will not only provide improved productivity but also raise the end user's opinion about the competence and professionalism of your entire operation.

D. Stress management. The IT staff can be worked hard and under immense pressure when critical systems fail. Stress management training involves teaching techniques for relaxation to avoid IT burnout. Technicians working in high stress environments tend to make more mistakes and take risks they would not normally consider.

E. Effective writing. Some technicians are quite articulate and some can barely write their own name with a crayon. Effective writing again improves the productivity of the author, the reader, and raises the company's opinion of the IT department as a whole.

F. Negotiation skills. Some IT people would be very happy if left to themselves in the corner. Unfortunately for them, IT is a service department that must interact with the people who use its services. Effective communications with these people often involves tradeoffs between the work necessary to accomplish something technical and the benefit to be derived. It also involves obtaining cooperation during times of short deadlines. Negotiation skills help the IT technician to identify areas of agreement so they can focus on areas to resolve for quick results.

G. Training presentation. The IT staff represents a ready team of instructors (whether they know it or not). They know their users, they know their technologies, and they are often called on for impromptu instruction for using one feature or another. In this class, teach them how to teach. You explain how to break complex thoughts and processes down into bite-sized pieces of information and explain it to others.

[B] End-User Training

The need for computer operation training is not limited to the IT department. Make company-wide training available to all computer users. This not only provides needed training, but also helps to create goodwill between IT and the rest of the firm. The charge-back for these services depends on corporate cost accounting procedures.

Request for training may be initiated by a user or an IT project leader. A user's request should be in the form of a memo from the user's management, directed to the IT trainer. If a project leader desires the service, make it part of the formal project effort.

Furnish a list of users completing each course to the employee's supervisor(s) by a memo from the manager of the IT training unit. All persons completing the program receive certificates of completion forwarded to the employee's supervisor for presentation.

End-user training is critical for the success of any business system. Without proper training, the benefits planned from the system will not be realized. End user training is appropriate for:

A. **New System Rollout.** Implementing new technology is an exciting part of working with computer systems. But all computer systems depend on human interaction to reach their maximum potential. People must be trained on ways to maximize the effectiveness of a tool. Without this training, the best tools in the world will sit and not be used.

The training department should become involved with a new system project well before it is ready for installation. The training department's role is to present the system to the users and explain how to make it work. To do this, the trainer must become familiar enough with the tools to be installed to write an explanation of them. This explanation becomes the outline for the training class.

Training for new systems should be completed and tested prior to presenting the technology to the users. The training can be provided immediately before the product rollout. Developing booklets with explanations of what to do in a given situation can provide a ready reference for the occasional user and the service desk. It can also be used later to train new end users.

B. **Ongoing Training.** Another source of end-user training requirements comes from the service desk problem logs. The service desk can identify problems that seem to generate multiple calls. Information on how to address these issues can go into the next training class (and immediately in the facility's newsletter). The service desk can also identify individuals who seem to be struggling with using a product. This can be addressed by one-on-one instruction or by offering them the next class scheduled. This training will reduce end-user frustration and reduce the number of calls to the service desk.

A well-stocked technical library is an important adjunct to your training room. Often technical staff members need to know how to do a specific action using your company's technical tools. A library provides a central source for them to research problems. In addition to the library, provide a list of the manuals that different people keep in the work areas. This will maximize the use of manuals, many of which the company must purchase.

[C] Keeping Records of Training

Each IT employee file contains education and training information, including training the employee brings to the department and recommendations for future training. All additional training received is posted to a file that is part of the IT skill inventory. (See § 11.05, "Employee Development" for more procedure information.) Starting a file is simple; keeping it up to date is a more challenging task. Do not neglect this.

IT employee training files contain the following information.

A. **Education and training before joining the IT department**
   1. Degrees received, courses taken, dates, and grades.
   2. Dates of noncredit courses taken.
   3. Type of work-related material read.
   4. Dates of certifications received.
   5. Listing of professional memberships and any offices held.
   6. The hardware type and software used if the employee owns a personal computer.
B. **Future education and training benefiting the employee.** Establish the training needs of each employee. This information can justify a training program and give the people on record first choice. Priority is as follows:
   1. Training or education that helps develop personnel for current positions:
      a. Areas of weakness.
      b. Areas that require training to stay current with new technology.
   2. Training or education needed for promotion.
C. **New education or training received**
   1. Upon completion of training not provided in-house, each employee forwards to the IT department a memo containing the following to be included in the employee's file:

      a. What training was received.
      b. Who provided the training.
      c. What grade was received, if any.
      d. When the training was received.

2. Upon completion of in-house programs, the overseer of IT training programs forwards the necessary information for inclusion in the training record files. For non-IT people, a memo will be sent to each supervisor listing which of their employees has completed the training and indicating the following:
      a. What training was received.
      b. When the training was conducted.
      c. Personnel who are to receive credit for completing the program.

[D] Employee Recognition

When an employee completes an in-house course, his or her supervisor should present a certificate for course completion. Certificate forms are available from most office supply firms and should be completed and signed by the manager of training and also the IT Manager.

Certificates provide a visual acknowledgement of achieving the course completion and are often found decorating a person's work area with pride. They also provide backup proof of course completion if training records are not properly kept.

[E] Education Information Booklet

The IT education unit provides an "education information booklet" to all new IT employees as part of an orientation package. Revised editions are distributed to all current IT employees. It should contain the following information:

A. **IT outside education policy and procedures.** Outline the type of support the firm provides for outside education and training, and the procedures required to apply for sanctioned education outside the firm. Copies of any required reimbursement forms are included.

B. **Scheduled courses offered by the training unit.** Detail the courses offered, including dates and times, requirements for admission, and procedure for enrolling in courses and/or programs.

C. **A list of self-paced training packages available.** This list is available from the IT training unit and includes videotapes, self-teaching texts, and PC self-instruction programs. Include an explanation of how to request this material.

D. **Publications available.** A list of books and journals should be available in the IT training department and/or computer store.

[F] Outsourced Training

Because not all information systems departments have resources available for in-house IT training, it is common to use outsourcing firms for professional IT training at the firm's location. (See Chapter 24, "Vendors: Getting the Goods," for more information.)

Recordkeeping of outsourcing personnel training is still done by the IT department for IT personnel. A person delegated by the manager of IT provides user training. Costs will be paid from the IT training budget. User training can be charged back to the user's budget and prorated if need be. This is all dependent on the internal accounting practice of the company.

Training evaluation is performed by a person from the IT department at the end of the course or program. Payment may be governed by the results of the evaluation. If so, inform accounts payable of this procedure before the outside firm bills for the service. The follow-up three- to six-month evaluation, also performed by the IT training department, is particularly important to alter future training if needed. The evaluation also is an effective way to judge the provider of the outsourced training.

[G]   Annual Reporting

The IT training unit should submit an annual report of activities, including cost. Cost justification (relating dollars to return on investment) of training dollars spent can be a problem because most of the returns are intangible. Any input from user management can help. However, intangible items contribute to the company's bottom line and should be listed in the annual report. There is a worldwide fast-food chain known for its training programs and even more for its success story.

Time required to produce instruction packages is often more than anticipated. Preparation time rule of thumb for a lecture presentation with simple slides can be as much as 15 hours for each lecture hour. Producing a 30-minute video presentation can take up to 200 hours. General planning, setup, reporting, and equipment repair will consume time. All these hours are reported. Treat each new program as a project with individual cost of materials and time cost reported. Compute time cost as hourly cost plus benefits.

COMMENT

Be aware that training and education evaluations can be subjective. People tend to give higher appraisals when they are entertained.

Both students' and trainers' time is a cost factor. With new technology, training and preparation time can be reduced. Therefore, the training department should house an array of software and hardware tools to be effective. Drop ineffective resources. Include plans for the coming year, as well as current year results, in the annual report. The report also should contain activities of the training unit for the year. The following items are reported:

A. Number and size of classes conducted.
B. Number of self-study programs completed.
C. Number and purpose of new programs developed.
D. Total number of people served by training unit.
E. List of participant evaluation comments with any supervisor's comments or memo information.

§ 11.07 EMPLOYEE COMMUNICATIONS

[A] Overview

A common complaint from employees is that they find out more about what is happening in their own department from other groups than they hear from their managers. Use all available tools to push a steady stream of information to employees. They will feel more like a team and less like isolated islands. This will also reinforce the manager's authority as the primary source of information about the department.

There are many avenues for employee communications: e-mail, memos, newsletters, rumor boards, telephone, voice mail, information meetings, and work meetings. More than one method should be used to communicate important employee information. The best tool for the job depends on how dispersed the team members are.

[B] Staff Meetings

The best way to pass and receive information to and from the team is a regularly scheduled staff meeting. Team members may have heard a rumor about this or that, but a statement by the manager about the same issue makes it an official announcement.

Preparation is the key to a successful meeting. Staff meetings should be kept to one hour or less and follow a standard agenda. One approach is to hold the meeting the day after the team submits status reports. In this way, only exceptions need to be discussed. Any discussion that runs more than five minutes must be set aside for a later meeting so that it does not derail the meeting. Focused meetings are appreciated, rambling time wasters will be avoided!

[C] E-Mail and Memos

When the IT Manager has a message to get out fast, or even routine announcements, an e-mail sent to every team member is an easy way to do it. Written messages allow everyone to see the same message worded the same way. They can be drafted in advance and sent when the time is right.

However, written announcements must be carefully worded. Unlike face-to-face communications, the reader cannot see any body language that accompanies the message. They will fill that in based on their own experience. For this reason, the message must be clear and not ambiguous.

Written communications are a great way to maintain the flow of communications to the team. Did someone do a great job that everyone should know about? Has a new employee joined the team? An e-mail is a great way to introduce a new employee to the team.

[D]   Rumor Board

In times of uncertainty, rumors can sweep through a department and disrupt productivity. To minimize their impact and reassert the department's leaders as the primary source of factual information, IT Managers must address rumors immediately. Rumors often reflect the deepest fears of a group and will grow in magnitude on their own. Rather than wishing them away, the IT Manager can eliminate this distraction to the workday by decisively and clearly answering with the true situation.

If rumors are a factor in a company, establish a rumor control box where anonymous messages can be left. A rumor control box works as follows:

A. A person concerned about a rumor writes it on a slip of paper and places it in a locked box attached to the department bulletin board.
B. Management reads the slip of paper and places a response on the bulletin board.

Rumor boards require judgment on the IT Manager's part to ensure that veiled personal attacks are not treated as legitimate questions. The anonymity of the locked box encourages participation but may be used for negative purposes.

§ 11.08   EMPLOYEE BURNOUT

[A]   Responsibility

IT support requirements can place a great deal of pressure on skilled and caring team members. It is the manager's responsibility to watch for signs of overwork (or burnout) and address the problem immediately. Exhausted employees make mistakes both with the company's systems and in their own personal safety. Overworked employees are a sign of failed IT leadership.

There are times when a great deal of time and stress are a part of a project. Major product rollout, year-end closing, flash cutovers of major changes all can be stressful times. However, in these cases, IT Managers can anticipate the upcoming events and rest the team before the major effort begins. After it is over, time should be allowed for the team to decompress.

No employee should suffer from burnout. Any supervisor responsible for pressure and time demands resulting in an employee's experiencing burnout should be reprimanded, and the details of the reprimand placed in their personnel folder. This will also include Project Managers or project leaders.

[B]   What Causes Burnout?

Often, employees bring burnout on themselves. Some people just cannot say "no" to a request. Some spend hours building a paperwork jungle around their assigned work—all work not assigned or desired by the manager. Some feel that if they show any sign of weakness, their position with the company may be eliminated.

Sometimes, unknowingly, the IT Manager asks for more than workers can reasonably deliver and they scramble to fulfill the request by working long hours. If a worker is susceptible to making major projects out of simple assignments, the IT Manager must take the time to ensure the person understands the true assignment before starting. The worker must understand that in the eyes of the IT Manager, a lot of activity does not equal a lot of value or productivity.

[C] Company Assistance

It is in the company's best interest to care for burned out employees. They should first be given paid time off. When they return, the IT Manager must determine how they ended up in the state they were in and address it. Did they take on too much work? Were they over-assigned by the manager? Did the worker misunderstand the scope of a simple project?

Other actions to address the issue include:

A. Providing the person with someone to share the workload.
B. Encouraging the person to take a seminar somewhere that will reduce the strain and include a weekend "on the house" for some fun time. No contact between company and employee will be allowed during this time.
C. Periodically rotating IT tasks.
D. Allowing for telecommuting and more flexible work hours.
E. Limiting overtime.
F. Limiting on-call demands.
G. Reassigning workloads.
H. Encouraging feedback.
I. Scheduling team social activities for meeting project milestones.

[D] Signs of Burnout

The signs of burnout are everywhere—if the IT Manager is inclined to look. Irritability, a harried look, and late assignments are all signs that something is not right. Other signs include:

A. Extreme dissatisfaction with work.
B. Notice of drinking or substance abuse during lunch or after work.
C. Reduced productivity.
D. Panic attacks.
E. Marital problems.
F. Problems with coworkers.
G. Persistent eating, sleeping, and fatigue disorders.
H. Noticeable signs of depression.

§ 11.09 IT EMPLOYEE PRODUCTIVITY

[A] Overview

Productivity is the goal of every IT team. Managers spend hours trying to identify ways to improve it. New IT tools are purchased, training is provided, incentives handed out, and even a few sharp rebukes. Still, it seems as if nothing can force the lethargic mass of IT flesh to move one way or the other!

IT productivity requires both management and leadership skills. A leader works with the team members to identify problem areas as early as possible and deals with them before they become irretrievable disasters.

[B] IT Management Productivity

There are several indicators of good management: low employee turnover and absenteeism, no employee sabotage, good productivity, and a reliable employee suggestion system. The signs may look good but must be confirmed. Some ways to confirm this in information systems are:

A. Projects are finished when planned.
B. Completed projects are finished within budget.
C. End users have faith in information system reports.
D. Most IT job promotions are filled from within the company.

IT Managers must actively work outside their offices. Do not depend on memos and the telephone to understand IT productivity. Leadership is a people business, and there is no better way than face-to-face. Some things the IT Manager can do to help actively promote IT production:

A. Encourage participatory management.
B. Ask what can be done about problems, and listen.
C. Set realistic norms and goals.
D. Use real quality circles.
E. Employ time management.
F. Delegate and follow up.
G. Learn when to say no.
H. Set deadlines.
 I. Finish what is started.
J. Do difficult jobs during the more productive time of day.
K. Make a daily timetable.
L. Do unpleasant things first.
M. Realize employee behavior may be due to weak supervisors or disruptive coworkers.

[C] IT Employee Productivity

It is more difficult measuring IT personnel's productivity than production jobs. Areas particularly hard to monitor are systems and programming. Programmers are too often measured on how hard and long they work, and how many lines of code they write. The ignored programmer is often the one who could do the same program in much less time with half the lines of code and no test data errors.

To discover the level of a programmer's productivity, survey other programmers about how they would rank their colleague's skills. Do this at employee review time. The feedback could be informative. Other ways to get feedback are:

A. End users speak well of the service desk and other IT assistance by programs and systems. The flip side of this is when users specifically ask that a certain person not be sent to their department again.
B. Use work simplification studies for programmers and systems people.
C. Compare performance with other projects and tasks.
D. Have all project work effort ranked regarding each member's contribution to the project's completion.
E. Notice who is the most helpful and who people go to for help.
F. Review how systems conversions are made. Are the end users satisfied with the assistance, training, service desk response, and the presence of project members during and after the conversion?
G. Find ways to have employees work together in teams—they will quickly discover who is productive and who is not.

§ 11.10 NONTRADITIONAL WORKING ARRANGEMENTS

[A] Telecommuting Policy

Telecommuting is an alternative to the traditional office-bound work practice. Telecommuting benefits both the employee and the employer. Given the low cost of high-speed Internet lines, it is now practical for more people to work from home.

Telecommuting, however, brings its own set of problems. There could be problems with hourly workers' time records and overtime problems, but none with salaried personnel. Work with human resources management to craft policies and procedures that protect the company when using telecommuters.

Some of the benefits of telecommuting include:

A. Marked employee productivity
B. Greater job satisfaction
C. Less job turnover
D. Lower absenteeism
E. Lower company worksite expense due to:
   1. Annual office floor space cost
   2. Reduced employee parking requirements
   3. Reduced janitorial service costs
   4. Less need for utilities

§ 11.10[C]

Some workers with physical challenges would prefer to work at home. Others could work from remote sites or even out of the country. Employees could benefit from the following:

A. Lower day-care costs
B. Lower transportation costs
C. Less travel time and fighting traffic
D. Less time spent getting ready for work
E. Reduced eating-out costs
F. Reduced wardrobe investment
G. Less need for a second car
H. More flexible lifestyle
I. Can have the radio on while working

[B] Job-Sharing Policy

Job sharing can benefit both parties. Two different skill levels, not necessarily equal, can fill one full-time position. It does not require each to have half of the same job. Divide this position as flextime responsibilities or even telecommuting. Flexibility can attract higher skilled talent than more traditional routes for IT specialties. Fill the position with salaried employees.

Pay for job-shared positions will not require equal pay for equal time. The employee benefits package may not be the same for both parties. The cafeteria benefit plan provides for a more equitable distribution of benefits. Paid vacation time as part of the benefit program should resolve the vacation question. Policy about taking unpaid vacation time should be determined in advance for this arrangement.

This policy attracts better talent to the IT department. It assures a backup is available. It is better to lose a half-person specialty than a whole, if that position is the only one IT has. This provides for safer backup than if that talent is being vested in one person. Depending on the responsibility, the job sharing may be done by related people, as long as one of the individuals, upon giving notice of leaving the firm, would not affect the other member, too.

[C] Flextime Policy

Flextime is commonly used as a "free" company benefit. It is free since flextime is valued by the employees and it costs companies nothing to implement it. Flextime is defined as open windows of time to arrive or leave work provided an 8-hour day is completed. It also applies to telecommuting and job-sharing positions.

Most companies establish a core time when all employees are required to be present: for meetings, training, etc. This is normally no less than a 4-hour window. Core time is sometimes at the discretion of the IT Manager. Anyone abusing this will be placed back on the standard work hours the IT operation maintains. See Policy ITP-11-4 IT Staff Flextime Policy as an example.

POLICY ITP-11-4. IT Staff Flextime Policy

Policy #:	ITP-11-4	**Effective:**	03/18/13	**Page #:**	1 of N
Subject:	IT Staff Flextime Policy				

1.0 PURPOSE

This policy is intended to respond to the needs of full-time IT staff members for whom the standard corporate work schedule is not ideal. Some of the reasons that an individual may wish to work an alternative schedule include:

A. Need for before or after hours system maintenance.
B. Carpooling arrangements with spouse or fellow employees.
C. Avoiding traffic congestion problems.
D. Coordinating schedules with a working spouse.
E. Child care issues.
F. Coordinating work schedule with a limited bus schedule.

2.0 SCOPE

This policy applies to all IT staff members for whom there are no business requirement to adhere to the standard work hours.

3.0 POLICY

Within the guidelines described below, it is corporate policy to provide all full-time IT staff members the opportunity to request the hours of work that consistently suit their individual needs. However, it is recognized that it will not be possible to accommodate all such requests for alternative schedules.

The standard corporate schedule is from 8:00 a.m. to 5:00 p.m. Monday through Friday, and it is expected that all offices will be open during regular corporate hours. The following guidelines should be followed:

A. Under flexible working hours, daily hours totaling 8.0 per day, 5 days per week, may be selected during the time 7:00 a.m. through 7:30 p.m.
B. A fixed schedule should be selected for at least three months at a time.
C. Some departments may be unable to offer flexible hours for some positions and/or during certain times of the year.
D. All employees must take at least half an hour for lunch each day.
E. A request for an alternative schedule (i.e., other than 8:00 a.m. through 5:00 p.m. with one hour lunch) must be discussed and confirmed in writing with the individual's supervisor and any others who are directly affected by the individual's work.
F. The individual selecting an alternative schedule must see that at least one other person is available to handle issues that arise during his or her absence from standard working hours.

G. Hours actually worked must be recorded on each non-exempt employee's time reporting form.
H. Staff members in their first six months in a new job may expect to be asked to work the standard 8:00 a.m. to 5:00 p.m. schedule to ensure appropriate training and interaction with others in the department.
I. Flexible working hours are not available to bargaining unit employees unless it is so stated in the governing labor agreement.

4.0 REVISION HISTORY

Date	Revision #	Description of Change
03/18/13	1.0	Initial creation.

5.0 INQUIRIES

Direct inquiries about this policy to:

George Jenkins, CIO
Our Company, Inc.
2900 Corporate Drive
Columbus, OH 43215

Voice: 614-555-1234
Fax: 614-555-1235
E-mail: gjenkins@company.com

Revision #:	1.0	Supersedes:	N/A	Date:	03/18/13

[D]   Rehiring Former Employees

Many organizations have a firm policy against the rehiring of former employees, usually citing security concerns about still angry laid-off employees. For IT Managers, there are many good reasons to consider rehiring ex-employees. These reasons include:

A. Lower training costs. Former employees have already been trained in the technologies used, and may have picked up additional valuable skills while at another firm.
B. Shorter learning curve. Former employees are already familiar with the company's systems and processes.
C. Return of vital expertise. When senior people leave, they take valuable experience and skills with them.
D. Possibly greater loyalty. If the employee left voluntarily due to feeling that "the grass is greener on the other side of the fence," he or she may appreciate more what the firm has to offer upon returning.

Any rehire policy must be clearly documented and understood by all employees. The policy must clearly state:

A. Who the policy applies to. Does it apply only to full-time staff, or also to part-time employees and consultants?
B. Guidelines on when the former employee will not be considered for rehire. This typically is applied to employees terminated for serious offenses, such as theft, workplace violence, breach of security, felony conviction, etc.
C. The period of time from the employee's separation for which they are eligible to return without going through the normal hiring procedures.
D. How severance pay is handled when the employee returns.

The exit interview is a great place to identify departing employees who would be eligible to return. See Policy ITP-11-5 IT Staff Rehire Policy as an example.

POLICY ITP-11-5.   IT Staff Rehire Policy

Policy #:	ITP-11-5	Effective:	03/18/13	Page #:	1 of N
Subject:	IT Staff Rehire Policy				

1.0 PURPOSE

This policy outlines the process and conditions for the rehiring of IT employees. Some of the reasons that the IT department may wish to rehire a former employee include:

A. Lower training costs. Former employees have already been trained in the technologies used, and may have picked up additional valuable skills while at another firm.
B. Shorter learning curve. Former employees are already familiar with the company's systems and processes.
C. Return of vital expertise. When senior people leave, they take valuable experience and skills with them.
D. Possibly greater loyalty. If the employees left on their own due to feeling that "the grass is greener on the other side of the fence," they may appreciate more what the firm has to offer when they return.

2.0 SCOPE

This policy applies to all IT staff members that have previously worked for the company and wish to be rehired. It covers former fulltime employees, part-time employees, and individuals who have worked at the company as consultants.

3.0 POLICY

Within the guidelines described below, it is corporate policy to allow for the rehiring of IT staff who has previously worked for the company:

A. Only employees who left in good standing are eligible for rehire. Employees who were terminated for violation of any corporate policy or for illegal activity are not eligible for rehire.
B. Previous employees who have been separated from the company for more than 6 months must go through the normal hiring procedures. This includes background and credit checks and drug screening.
C. If the employee is rehired for a different position than the one held previously, the rehired employee must go through the standard pro-bationary period for the new position.
D. An employee who has received severance pay and who returns to work in a position with the company at the same or higher salary as the position held at the time of separation shall repay to the company any portion of severance pay received that is in excess of the time the employee was separated from the company.

4.0 REVISION HISTORY

Date	Revision #	Description of Change
03/18/13	1.0	Initial creation.

5.0 INQUIRIES

Direct inquiries about this policy to:

George Jenkins, CIO
Our Company, Inc.
2900 Corporate Drive
Columbus, OH 43215

Voice: 614-555-1234
Fax: 614-555-1235
E-mail: gjenkins@company.com

Revision #:	1.0	Supersedes:	N/A	Date:	03/18/13

12

VIRTUAL TEAMS: REMOTE CONTROL MANAGEMENT

§ 12.01 OVERVIEW

[A] Purpose and Scope

A virtual worker is someone who is virtually in the office. Virtual workers work on their assignments, meet objectives, and participate in meetings. Virtual workers can meet with customers, create software, and even troubleshoot technical problems. They can do all of this without ever physically being there.

Previously, these workers were called "telecommuters" because they used telephones to connect to their office. Instead of driving to the office, they set up a work area in their home. Telecommuting is one tool companies used to retain their talent with conflicting family responsibilities. Today, it is not unusual for an office worker to occasionally work remotely from home during bad weather or perhaps one day per week to eliminate the commute. All of this has been made possible by modern data and telephonic communications.

Company culture plays a significant role in the success or failure of a virtual workforce. If the company respects its employees as skilled workers motivated to succeed and complete their assigned tasks promptly, then virtual workers may be the answer. If the company believes workers are lazy and untrustworthy, and must be watched at all times, then virtual workers are not for them.

COMMENT

Long ago, "virtual" was something that a computer did. For example, virtual memory was where the computer's Random Access Memory (RAM) was artificially expanded to a portion of a fixed disk. If more RAM was needed, some of the code in RAM was "rolled out" onto a special area of disk and managed by the CPU as if it were a part of the computer's RAM. Virtual teams are similar to this. People working from home—nearby or far way—act is if they were in the office, laboring alongside everyone else to accomplish the company's goal. Given how glued people are to their office's monitor and telephone, their coworkers may as well be miles away!

[B] Policies and Objectives

Virtual team policies provide guidance to everyone involved with the program. The objectives may be to reduce company costs and improve team member satisfaction while reducing the amount of greenhouse gases emitted by workers (as they no longer commute daily to work). These policies must be well considered, approved, and distributed to everyone affected by them.

Working out-of-sight of the boss makes companies uneasy. Companies that determine that virtual teams are appropriate to their business situation must establish measurable goals so that even though no one sees the team working, its results validate the team's efforts. Typical work includes data entry or program development, both of which provide tangible results.

[C] Critical Policies to Develop Based on This Chapter

Using the material discussed in this chapter, you will be able to create the following policies:

A. The appropriate type of work for virtual workers.
B. Support policy for virtual work teams.
C. Conduct guidance for virtual team members' conduct.

Policies should always be developed based on the local situation. Successful managers cannot issue appropriate guidance if the policies are written with another company's situation or location in mind.

§ 12.02 THE VIRTUAL COMPANY

[A] What's in it for the Company?

Traditionally, a company hires people, provides them with tools and a place to work, and assigns them things to accomplish. Throughout the workday, supervisors walk about the office to see who shows up for work, who is working hard, who is working little, and so on. Managers can see the progress and gauge how close a task is to completion. A virtual workplace changes all of this.

Companies that use a large virtual workforce may realize other savings. As location becomes of secondary importance to the labor pool, smaller offices can be closed and their servers merged into the primary data center. Workers all connect to the central office via high-speed Internet. Alternatively, smaller offices can be opened far from the large (expensive) cities. This may provide a pool of lower-cost virtual workers. Benefits to the company include:

A. **Avoid the high cost of office space.** In the early days, a prime driver for data processing was the way it decreased costs by automating massive manual processing. Once considered a radical idea, data processing today is the norm. So what about the high cost of office space? Just the cost of floor space alone can run $50 per square foot, per month (depending on location). Add in office furniture/cubicle walls for several thousand dollars, plus parking, networking, telephone equipment, utility costs, and more—and it is easy to see that providing employees an adequate place to work is expensive. Imagine cutting this cost to almost nothing!

Just as computers eliminated many manual jobs, why not use them to dramatically reduce the high expense of office space required by a company? Virtual teaming is a money saver.

B. **Scalable workforce.** Virtual workers enable a company to scale its labor pool. Instead of limiting the amount of attempted work by the number of local workers, a temporary work surge can be shared with a virtual workforce from across the entire enterprise. As work increases, virtual workers are assigned from the various locations. As it is reduced, virtual workers are turned to other tasks.

People prefer to reside where they wish rather than where the centers of employment are located. For example, consider the situation where Colorado has an excess of expert Java programmers while Boston is critically short. In years gone past, the only way to use these Java programmers was to move them to where the work was (or move the work to them). However, if they did not want to move, then the out-of-balance situation remained. Using a virtual work arrangement, the Colorado workers can be employed in Boston while still enjoying the western mountain sunsets.

COMMENT

Using virtual teams around the globe permits rapidly developing software. A team in one time zone writes the code and the team on the other side of the world tests it that same day—feeding results back to the coding team the next morning.

[B] What's in it for the Worker?

Workers have a lot to like about working virtually. It simplifies their life and saves them money. However, it trades these advantages for other complexities that the typical worker never needed to deal with. Benefits to the workers include:

A. **Think green—no daily commute.** Imagine all of the hours spent every workday driving to and from the office? How many hours is this per week, per month, per year? Imagine recapturing all of that time for other uses. Instead of leaving at 7:00 a.m. to arrive at work before 8:00 a.m., just be seated at the virtual work place by 8:00 a.m.—another precious hour of life is recaptured! The same benefit arises again at the end of the workday.

Not driving to work also means savings in fuel. How much is saved by not filling a car just to drive to work? This is like an immediate pay raise as daily expenses visibly drop. Does it cost to park near the office? Not anymore. Wear on vehicles is also saved, making them last longer and stretching the time between required mechanical services. When cars last longer, fewer are needed and you are even greener than ever.

COMMENT

Is it snowing outside? Is a major storm raging? No problem—it is warm and dry inside! Start work on time, safe at home.

B. **At home to handle simple issues.** Working from home improves employee attendance. Often, domestic issues and responsibilities combine to pull workers away from work and back into the home. If people normally worked out of their homes, these issues could be resolved without missing work and disrupting the efforts of all who depend on them. For example:
   1. Let a repairman in. Sounds simple, but it requires a round trip from the office or, just as frequently, skipping a day of work altogether because repair services rarely say when they will drop by.
   2. A mild illness that makes it too uncomfortable to be in an office with others but fine to work from home.
   3. Staying home to tend sick children or children homebound by a school "snow day."
C. **Save on business attire.** Typically, women are more fashion minded than men and tend to spend more on clothes for work. Yet, an office that requires all men to wear suits incurs the daily cost for pressed and starched white shirts. In short, some jobs require the purchase and maintenance of expensive clothing. This is not an issue when working from home where you can wear a robe and fuzzy slippers.

[C] What's in it for Society?

Some people have a lot to contribute but have physical mobility difficulties, child care responsibilities, elder care requirements, or any number of reasons. Virtual jobs enable these people to do to work around their home responsibilities (or limitations). Companies that reach out to homebound people may find loyal and dependable employees.

[D] Virtual Pitfalls

With such a rosy outlook, why would anyone want to tramp through rain and snow to work in an office? There are several reasons:

A. Lack of direct contact with boss. Many find it harder to be promoted without daily personal contact with their managers—daily contact lets them know that everything is okay.
B. Consciously and subconsciously, people use a considerable amount of nonverbal communication. Without visual contact during

conversations, communications are not complete and part of the message is lost.

C. It is more difficult to find quick answers to simple questions. Remote workers trying to contact someone in an office spend more time trying to establish communications—especially if the individual they are trying to contact will not respond to electronic requests. Who hasn't worked with someone who screened all of their calls and ignored most of their e-mail?

D. Virtual workers may feel socially isolated because their coworkers are just a disembodied voice. They may spend a considerable amount of working time trying to find out "what is going on" in the virtual workspace, rather than working. There are many visual cues found in an office—on bulletin boards, the way people decorate their work areas, etc., that are missing when working from home.

E. There are too many distractions when working at home. Dogs want out, family members want errands run, and other domestic responsibilities may lure the worker away from their employer's assigned tasks.

F. Absence of a coworker support network make taking the tough times more difficult.

G. It is more difficult for companies to cultivate a corporate culture and loyalty.

§ 12.03   BECOMING A VIRTUAL WORKER

[A]   Overview

Working at home takes more than a telephone line and a corner of the kitchen table. A home office requires essentially the same floor space and furniture as an office cubicle. Office workspaces are configured as they are because that is the optimal layout for that type of work. Before volunteering to work from home, be sure enough dedicated space is available.

COMMENT

Virtual workers maintaining a home office incur expenses normally borne by the employer in a traditional setting. A prime example is office supplies—pads of paper, paper for a printer, toner, etc. Companies may provide each virtual worker an allowance to cover these expenses—or should not be surprised when virtual workers refuse to pay for these things with a corresponding loss of productivity.

[B] Work Area

A typical office cubicle is about six feet wide by eight feet deep—about the size of a crypt vault. Minimally, the desktop space must provide room for a keyboard, a monitor (and computer if it must sit on top), a telephone, and a writing area. Ideally, there will be enough room for several writing areas to accommodate the paperwork sprawl, as well as some shelves to hold reference manuals. Because no one is at hand to answer quick process questions, reference manuals are important for working through problems.

The work area must be in a quiet part of the house. If no one else is home all day, then this is easier. If children come home from school, they may be disruptive for the last few hours of work unless a door can keep their noise out. Other interruptions to avoid:

A. Noise from outside such as busy streets, railroad crossings, noisy neighbors, etc.
B. "Sounds of the home," such as chiming clocks, cuckoo clocks, squeaky chairs or doors, sounds from televisions in adjacent rooms, etc.
C. Demanding pets such as barking dogs, cats who must sit on keyboards, loud birds, etc.

The work area must include storage for files. These documents provide background materials and cross-references to business issues. If the worker is someone who must see things on paper, he or she must also obtain a laser printer (cheaper to use than an inkjet printer) to print documents and drawers for filing these documents. Ideally, the virtual workers store documents electronically, which minimizes the need for file cabinets.

COMMENT

A quick way to gain weight is to sit all day. In a normal office, there are regular ups and downs out of the chair to attend meetings, discuss things, etc. In a home office, the work effort is to sit by the PC and telephone (with the occasional trip to the refrigerator). Home workers must plan exercise into their day the same as they plan their work.

[C] Communications

Teamwork is based on communications. In the office, this is through spoken words, gestures, memos, meetings, casual encounters, and so on. For the virtual worker, the two main vehicles of communication are data and voice (telephonic). If either of these is out of service, then the virtual worker is "speechless."

COMMENT

Companies employing virtual workers should always provide them a complete electronic setup: a workstation loaded with software, a cell phone (with the bill paid by the company), and ready access to high-speed Internet. Companies must also devise a process to rapidly replace broken hardware.

Critical communications tools required by the virtual worker include:

A. **Personal computer and software.** Some companies provide tele-commuting workers with computers and network connection devices. The advantage of this is that they know what is on the working desktop and can provide prompt tech support for issues. The company's VPN (virtual private network) client can be included with the basic workstation image. This standard office setup ensures that documents can be easily exchanged among team members. Telecommuters using their own personal computers may introduce problems with virus transmission, inconsistent software, software version interfering with document exchange, and so on.

Providing company-owned PCs also enables the company to control its software efficiently. All patching is accomplished by the home office to ensure seamless data exchange.

However, many companies dislike spreading their hardware assets all over the country. It is too easy to lose them. It is hard to ensure that the equipment is properly safeguarded and easy to recover when someone separates from the team. An alternative is to require virtual team members to purchase their own equipment. These workers should be provided applications over the Web, such as Software as a Service (SaaS). However, this only works for employees with the financial resources to do so before receiving their first paycheck.

Workers using their own equipment must be required to have an approved antivirus application installed and operating on their device at all times. The antivirus software must be configured as follows:

1. The antivirus definitions must be updated at least once per day.
2. Complete scans of the device for viruses must be done at least weekly.
3. The product should scan applications in real time as they are accessed.

COMMENT

Home workers' PCs also require an Uninterruptible Power Supply (UPS) to filter electrical power, and protect it from data losses and damage during a power outage. Because data are stored on the local workstation, some method of backing up the workstation's disk storage is also essential. Backing up local data to a server in the company's data center also provides control of documents in case an employee must be separated.

B. **Broadband network connection.** The primary enablers of virtual workers are the widespread availability of broadband communications and cheap long-distance telephone service. Dial-up data communications (similar in function and speed to a dumb terminal) can be used for data entry or e-mail but lack strong security and are limited by telephone equipment speeds. Dial-up communications barely keep up with the pace of work. Broadband is the enabler of video conferencing, Webinar training, and groupware to share documents. Access to a high-speed data connection must be a qualification when hiring virtual workers (just as reliable transportation to work is a requirement for office-bound workers).

A high-speed data connection enables the use of video. This allows you to mount a camera on your PC and exchange live video with the other members on your team. A high-speed line also opens the opportunity to use Voice over IP (VOIP) and save on long-distance connection charges.

C. **Virtual Private Network (VPN).** A virtual worker's PC requires a secure connection to the company's network. The most common approach is a VPN connection through the Internet. A VPN connection encapsulates and encrypts the data that travels between the user's device and the company's network. This safeguards the company's data from interception. A VPN requires software and some authentication mechanism for the operator. VPN software may use a client program on the device or establish the connection through a sign-on screen over the Web.

A VPN connection uses "something you know and something you own." This is a combination of an authentication device, such as a number-generating token or fingerprint reader and a password. Successfully logging on through the VPN authenticates someone as the real thing. Once the VPN connection is established, that device acts as if it were located within the company's office walls. See Policy ITP-12-1 Remote Access Policy as an example of a policy covering connections to the organization's network from the outside.

D. **Groupware for team collaboration.** Many documents are the result of collaboration between team members. Groupware provides a virtual workplace for sharing team documents, sharing ideas, and

12-10

submitting ideas or prototypes for team review. For example, the "team description" document is drafted by the virtual team manager and then passed around to virtual team members who each add to it or correct some part of it. By posting it in a shared area, each team member can update it without playing round-robin with the e-mail.

Groupware is also a valuable way to collect all of a team's files into a central repository. When a new person joins the team, he or she can review the files to learn about the team's issues and progress to date. If someone leaves the team, his or her documents are still in storage. Also, all company data stored in the repository are backed up.

E. **Telephone.** Most homes use a single telephone line. Transforming a simple home phone to a business line takes a bit of effort:

1. A virtual worker is heavily dependent on reliable telephone service. Because calls can come in at any time, it is not advisable to use the family's home number as your official business number. If family members tie up the line with local calls, some of the workday may be lost. Consider using the family telephone line only for outgoing calls.

2. A second telephone line is useful for incoming calls. This is the number that will be spread around the company for anyone to contact you. A cell phone is handy for this as it usually comes with a voice mail feature to catch missed calls. Some companies provide virtual workers with a cell phone and pay for all of the charges. This provides an added benefit to the team in that this person's replacement will have the same telephone number.

3. A connection for low-cost, outbound, long-distance calls is essential. These can be purchased by the month for a standard telephone line or included on a cell phone account.

4. The home worker's telephone needs a speakerphone (and/or headset) and a mute button. The speakerphone or headset reduces the fatigue of holding a telephone handset to an ear (many meetings will last an hour or more). The mute button reduces the amount of noise passed over the line when listening to a meeting over a bridge number. It is also nice to have hands free to look things up on the computer or to shuffle documents during the call.

F. **Telephone bridge number.** Companies frequently provide a "bridge" number for team meetings. This is a toll-free number (available from the telephone companies) where anyone can dial in and join a virtual conversation. Issue a bridge number to each virtual worker. Documents can be distributed by e-mail prior to the meeting or an online Web service can be used where everyone can log into and see the documents under discussion as they are changed.

COMMENT

Because the bridge number is toll free, consider dialing out on the house line and save the cell phone minutes for other calls.

G. **Electronic mail.** Electronic mail delivers documents and memos to team members. It allows for quick distribution of the same message to many people. Many companies maintain their telephone directories in the same place as their e-mail addresses. E-mail provides a way to fill in forms, pass on friendly notes—and many other things that an office worker takes for granted but that are vital to a virtual worker.

Most e-mail systems also include a calendar function for scheduling meetings. This is very important for virtual workers who may be assigned part time to various assignments. Rather than trying to catch someone by telephone in their free moment, time can be set aside on everyone's calendars for a quick chat.

H. **Instant messaging.** Instant messaging is the virtual worker's prized tool. It is the vehicle for informal communications with coworkers and acts as the quick question over the cubicle wall. Many people can respond to a quick instant message when they don't have the time to answer a telephone. For instance, a virtual worker sitting in on a long telephone meeting and listening to the discussion can respond to a quick question that appears at his or her workstation—without ever leaving the meeting.

POLICY ITP-12-1. Remote Access Policy

Policy #:	ITP-12-1	Effective:	03/18/13	Page #:	1 of N
Subject:	Remote Access Policy				

1.0 PURPOSE

This policy defines how remote workers access the organization's network and the security standards that must be met when remotely accessing the organization's network. It is designed to prevent unauthorized access to the organization's network and to prevent damage to the network and loss of data.

2.0 SCOPE

The policy applies to all users that access the organization's network from outside locations. This policy also applies where the employee is not physically working in company-owned offices, and also includes remote workers, part-time remote workers, and contract labor.

3.0 POLICY

All workers connecting to the organization's network from outside the firewall must use the standard VPN connection. Workers using their own equipment are required to have an approved antivirus application installed and operating on their device at all times. The antivirus software must be configured as follows:

§ 12.03[D]

A. The antivirus definitions must be updated at least once per day.
B. Complete scans of the device for viruses must be done at least weekly.
C. The antivirus program must scan applications in real time as they are accessed.

The device must also include a firewall that is installed and operating while connected to the organization's network. The operating system must be properly configured and have all of the latest security updates.

Company-owned equipment that is used to access the organization's network from the outside must have installed the standard VPN software and meet the antivirus and firewall conditions stated above.

All workers and devices that access the organization's network remotely are subject to all policies that apply to those using the network locally.

VPN users will be automatically disconnected from the organization's network after 30 minutes of inactivity; the user is required to logon again to reconnect to the network. Use of pings or other processes to prevent the connection from being terminated due to inactivity are prohibited.

4.0 REVISION HISTORY

Date	Revision #	Description of Change
03/18/13	1.0	Initial creation.

5.0 INQUIRIES

Direct inquiries about this policy to:

George Jenkins, CIO
Our Company, Inc.
2900 Corporate Drive
Columbus, OH 43215

Voice: 614-555-1234
Fax: 614-555-1235
E-mail: gjenkins@company.com

Revision #:	1.0	Supersedes:	N/A	Date:	03/18/13

[D]   Home Office Security

If you work in an office building, security is provided for all workers. Doors are locked, entrances monitored, equipment safeguarded against theft. Not so a home office! All of this security is now the responsibility of the virtual worker. Managers of virtual teams must provide a new-hire orientation that explains:

A. **Safeguarding equipment.** Sorry if a burglar carries off the hardware, but no work can be done until it is replaced. So, if no work is done, should a salary be provided? Not only must the virtual worker report theft of the equipment to the police, but also they must promptly report theft of the data to the company!

B. **Communication connections must be secure at all times.** This requires use of a VPN.

C. **Company documents no longer needed on site must be shredded.** This reduces the likelihood of the company's documents scattering across the lawns when a trash can is accidentally overturned.

D. **CDs containing company data must be shredded.** Be sure to purchase a shredder that chews up CDs as well as paper.

E. **Data backups of the virtual worker's PC must be protected as well as the computer.** Stealing a backup provides a criminal the same information as stealing the computer and its data.

[E] It Takes a Special Person

Working virtually is quite different from sitting in the midst of a sea of cubicles. It is easy to be distracted when the work is tedious or boring. Virtual workers must be self-disciplined to focus on their assignments without constant supervision. Even people who work well by themselves feel adrift without the traditional office boundaries.

Virtual workers must be skilled communicators. Without visual cues from others on the team, they must pick up conversational nuances and react appropriately. The tone of voice and rhythm of the conversation fills in somewhat for the lack of body language. They must also not read dark inferences into hasty or poorly worded messages. Virtual work is a tough job for pessimists.

Finally, virtual team members must not require a lot of social interaction during their workdays. Telephones, e-mail, and instant messaging all provide some sense of community to the isolated worker and a chance to build friendships. However, people need more than a distant voice to feel accepted within the team and to take the drudgery of work to a higher level.

[F] Career Management Is Just a Bit Different

Virtual careers must be managed slightly differently than in-office careers. Virtual workers may have multiple bosses as assignments roll in. This makes it difficult to build a track record of solid performance. Ask for a performance evaluation whenever working on an assignment for someone for more than 80 hours. Things you might do to help your career along include:

A. Provide an online resume that details the types of work successfully completed in previous projects.

B. Volunteer for specific projects that would benefit most from your skills.

C. When work is slow, take some time to develop your contacts with coworkers. A wide support network of coworkers is one way to learn more about the inner workings of the company's virtual organization.

D. Send a monthly status report to your many bosses—but send all of them the same one. It lets them know what you are working on to show what you are capable of in the future.

§ 12.04 VIRTUAL WORKFORCE STRATEGY

[A] Places Where Virtual Workers Fit Best

Successful virtual workforces are the result of careful planning. Companies considering a virtual workforce must allow adequate time and money for planning and implementation. These costs are easily offset by the savings in floor space, furniture, and so on. Prior to embarking on this journey, develop a strategy of how this workforce will be created, supported, and applied to available work.

Virtual workers are ideal for assignments that have a definable deliverable, such as a code module, a document, or a users' manual. When an assignment is made, a time estimate to completion is also submitted. This approach allows virtual workers to set their own deadlines.

Virtual work is also suitable for data entry. This works well with the local workforce. A Web-enabled screen with VPN access is provided for all workers. This removes the variability of the equipment used at home and minimizes company investment. Virtual workers can be compensated by the page or the hour.

Another successful virtual strategy is for companies with many offices across the country (or even around the world). Typically, as work tapers off in one region of the country, it usually picks up in another. This allows rapid scaling of resources according to the local requirements, while still maintaining control over workers in the offices.

COMMENT

Virtual workers are more successful if their efforts do not require close coordination with others. Save those jobs for a traditional work environment.

[B] Organizing Your Business for Virtual Workers

A successful virtual worker program requires the establishment of a support structure. The following steps are critical for the success of your virtual worker program:

A. **Select a leader.** Even if it is only part time, someone must be assigned responsibility for the proper use of virtual workers. Companies that outsource projects or an entire segment of their organization must assign a single person to monitor the results. The virtual workforce leader ensures that everyone keeps up with their administrative tasks, such as submitting timesheets, properly submitting expenses, and so on. The leader also provides performance reviews for each person.

If virtual teams are something new for your company, make the first virtual team leader someone who has virtual teamwork experience. This may avoid some of the learning problems of new teams.

B. **Human resources support.** Assign a human resources clerk as an advisor to the virtual workforce manager. Sooner or later, some issue will arise where the manager must deal with poor performance (not everyone can handle working at home).

C. **Technical support.** Arrange for technical support for virtual workers. They may have a special line into the service desk to provide quick answers. If company equipment is provided, it may be necessary to quickly ship a replacement workstation to the virtual worker's home.

[C] Acquiring Virtual Workers

Virtual workers can be found in many places:

A. Company sites that are closing
B. Freelance contract technicians
C. Employees who are unable to come into the office
D. Employees who want to work from home several days per week

A great place to find virtual workers is by asking other virtual workers to locate them. This type of work is not suitable for everyone, but current virtual workers may know of others who have worked well in the past. Also, the team will come together quicker if some of the people are already acquainted.

[D] Not Suitable for Virtual Work

Sending work outside the office to employees working at home is not always a good idea. Critical business functions should not be assigned to virtual workers. The key to work that must be kept on-site lies in the types of virtual workers you use. If they are long-time employees, they can be trusted with more. If they are hired off the street to work from home, their motivations may be less aligned with those of the company.

Consider this when selecting work to distribute off-site:

A. Keep the responsibility for the effectiveness and overall success of a business function in the office where it can be closely monitored.
B. Prior to assigning a process to virtual workers, ensure that the process is operating effectively and efficiently. Sending a broken process off-site can, at best, provide no better results than it does using on-site staff.
C. Never use virtual workers for any part of your company's unique business processes. Once these processes are off-site, they are easier for a competitor to learn about.

12-16

D. The IT department should always own the customer relationship with either in-house or external customers. Much valuable feedback information is lost when passing this off to others.

E. IT legal compliance and security controls must stay in-house.

§ 12.05 LEADING A VIRTUAL TEAM

[A] Virtual Team Manager

The challenge in leading a virtual team is in the increased reliance on verbal and written communication. Trust is the basis for all communications. Workers and managers lacking trust in their coworkers will be defensive, will be less willing to share their ideas, and may withhold information.

Leading a virtual team takes patience and trust. Patience is needed because virtual tasks may take more time to complete than to do the same work in an office where advice and assistance are readily available. Trust is needed in that the manager is confident that team members will meet their assignments.

Virtual team members need more "care and feeding" than a typical team. In a traditional setting, a manager might walk around and visit each team member sometime during the day to quickly see if there are any issues or obstacles with their assignment. Without the nonverbal communications, they feel uncomfortable about their status in the team and the team manager's true attitude toward them. In a virtual team, the same thing can be done with short instant messages. The difference is that when this is done in person, there is the personal message, "we're both OK." An instant message must be cheerful and carefully worded not to sound mechanical or micromanaging.

Everyone, whether sitting in an office or working from the beach, has a preferred way to receive electronic information. This may be through an instant messenger service, by e-mail, by telephone, and so on. Managers who can determine the best way to communicate with each individual team member will encounter fewer problems. Some options are:

A. **Make frequent, short visits.** As team members are out of direct contact with their boss and teammates, they may feel out of touch with the organization and peer opinions (which might be more obvious in body language were they standing before you). During conversations, the manager must determine if a virtual worker is struggling and needs some assistance. The tone of voice and rhythm of the conversation fills in somewhat for lack of body language.

COMMENT

A sense of isolation is the primary reason people drop out of virtual teams and return to traditional office positions.

B. **The online break room.** Create an online message board and open chat room where virtual workers can swap ideas and stories and generally learn more about others in their virtual workspace. The team manager uses this space to ensure that all pertinent company information—both big and small—is provided to everyone. Include a knowledge base for addressing the administration problems of virtual workers. Permit anyone to add to it.

However, managers must monitor everything posted to these spaces for inappropriate comments or confidential company information. Otherwise, it is a wide-open exchange between virtual and office-bound workers.

C. **Managing someone you will never meet.** It can be uncomfortable for managers working within a tight deadline to depend on someone when they cannot even see if that person is working or playing. One approach is to break deliverable results into one-week increments. Organize and specify work in terms of results so that it can be accomplished without detailed management supervision. In this way, the results validate the work time required.

COMMENT

When someone has a computer problem in the office, he or she calls the local service desk. However, a virtual team member generally does not have anyone local to turn to. The virtual team manager must have a plan for supporting virtual team member equipment. If the company owns the equipment, then keep a spare cell phone and a PC loaded with software and ready for immediate shipment. In a crisis, it can be sent out for overnight delivery to exchange for a broken unit. Otherwise the worker sits and waits while time drags on.

If virtual team members provide their own equipment, ensure they have prearranged for local tech support including hardware repair.

Leading a virtual workforce of independent-minded IT experts is a demanding task. It is made easier by establishing a framework for data collection and sharing through a set of standard forms and processes. Use Worksheet 12-1 Virtual Team Checklist to help manage your virtual team.

[B] Virtual Team Members

A strong focus on goals and task completion keeps virtual teams working without someone nagging them for action. Team members prefer that the virtual team manager clearly define their assignments and reward them according to their performance.

WORKSHEET 12-1. Virtual Team Checklist

Virtual Team Checklist	
Manager's Checklist	**Date Completed**
Create a place to share team documents	
Standardize document naming conventions	
Company policies and forms for reference	
Create, update, and frequently publish up-to-date contact lists for team members, support staff, and key customers	
Document procedures to	
Submit expense statements	
Submit time sheets	
Submit status reports and the standard format	
Ordering office supplies	
Publish updated contact information monthly	
How to report data loss to the company	
Document practices to	
Reply to all team messages within 24 hours	
Availability during published working hours	
Virtual Team Member Checklist	
Data	
Workstation	
Standard office software	
Standard communications software	
High speed data line	
Camera for video conferencing	
Laser printer	
Telecommunications	
Outbound line with unlimited long distance time (usually a cell phone)	
Inbound line	
Fax machine	
Voice mail	
Headset & mute button	

WORKSHEET 12-1.   (Continued)

Work area	
Desktop, chair	
Office supplies	
Shredder for paper and CDs	
Publish work hours	
Publish resume with work skills	
Supporting a Virtual Team	
Always keep a back-up workstation loaded with software and ready to ship.	
Use a national carrier for company supplied cell phones so that repairs and exchanges can be completed locally.	
Arrange a process and time for online patching of company-owned workstations used by virtual team members.	
Create an online repository for team documents and require its use. Reference material can be stored here for team use.	
Create a standard document naming convention for the team to facilitate the exchange of documents.	
International Issues	
Pick an official language	
Research local business cultures	
Project Leader:	**Date:**

A. **New team members.** New virtual team members require time to orient themselves to their new surroundings. Bring them into the virtual team support office to pick up their equipment, learn how to use the tools and to walk through the team processes. This also allows them to meet the support staff—putting faces to the voices.

New employees should clearly understand what is expected from them. Use a checklist to review such things as availability during working hours, submission of timesheets, document requirements, and so on. Break in new virtual employees with a few easy assignments until they become accustomed to the company's processes and software tools.

B. **Team etiquette.** Virtual teams develop their own social rules governing communications. Team managers can force the issue early in team forming by providing simple guidelines for communications.

Because the team is dependent on messaging and prompt responses, the manager must ensure that the team promptly responds to requests from other team members. (In an office, a person can check to see if someone is on the telephone. Virtual workers cannot see that far, so they leave their message and move on.) Team members slow to respond (for whatever reason) to a question will cause the team progress to lag. Further, if the slow responder is intentionally delaying an answer, the team will develop mistrust and considerable dissention. Disaffected team members can choose to ignore messages or leave them for other times. This increases team stress. Other guidelines to follow include:

1. Carefully prepare all participants for meetings. Distribute documents for advance review. These meetings will result in fewer follow-up discussions.

2. Always debate points over the telephone and not through e-mail. If more than three e-mails are exchanged to clarify a point, it is easier to call and explain it than to write pages explaining things in detail.

3. If something someone says rubs you wrong, wait a while and then call him. Don't let misunderstandings fester. Be sensitive of others. It is easier to work patiently with someone courteously than to fight and create enemies.

4. Respect the normal working hours of others. Keep time zones in mind when scheduling meetings or calling. However, emergencies take priority.

5. Always return messages promptly. Do not build delays into the team.

6. There is no shame in not knowing how to do something—but there is in not asking for help. Never hesitate to ask other team members for help but spread out the requests to various team members because everyone is busy.

7. Be careful when using humor, as the body language aspect is not present. Also, humor does not translate well across cultures.

C. **Meeting minutes.** Virtual meetings are a bit different from the typical business meeting. The meeting leader cannot look around to see who is attentive and who is sleeping. Be sure that the high points of the discussions are recorded and passed out to the participants. Meeting minutes are a valuable source of information to managers for the early detection of problems. Also place a copy in the central team document store as a historical record of what did (or did not) happen, and when.

Schedule regular meetings to assess needs, give feedback, discuss problems, and just catch up. If you hold regular meetings to set time-tables and assess progress, employees will have deadlines to keep them on target. Every meeting must be formally documented because, unlike a face-to-face discussion, no one can see if anyone else is writing anything down. Also, without eye contact around the room, the team manager may experience difficulty bringing a meeting to an emotional conclusion.

COMMENT

If practical, bring all virtual team members into the home office quarterly for a day or more of face-to-face discussions. This goes a long way in building team cohesion as faces are added to the voices.

[C]   Administrative Assistance

Virtual teams need administrative assistance to complete their assignments. Assign a core group of administrators in the virtual workforce office to provide advice and answer questions. This might be assistance with routine clerical tasks, expediting purchase orders through the approval process, following up on nonresponsive team members or customers, or fulfilling requests for materials and supplies. Sometimes, they might just need a friendly voice to chat with.

If the virtual team is supporting a customer, either place one of the team members on-site with the customer or arrange for the customer to provide a "go-to" person to assist the team. This "feet on the street" can chase down answers, look at things, and represent the team to the customer. A motivated on-site team member can make the toughest assignment seem (somewhat) easy.

[D]   Virtual Support Processes

The virtual workforce office must have clearly documented and published processes. This reduces confusion when virtual team members are working part time for multiple managers. Processes to support your virtual workers include:

A. **Store all documents in a central repository.** Virtual teams have a higher attrition rate than normal teams. To ensure a smooth transition, require that copies of all key documents are sent to the virtual workforce office for storage in a central server. This includes:
   1. Design notes explaining trade-offs considered and the reason for the one selected.
   2. Customer contact reports.
   3. Status reports—like any office, the customer will expect performance metrics. Ensure that status reports contain the essential information that can be rolled up into a summary report.
   4. Meeting minutes.
   5. Customer approvals—provide contact lists so that workers don't lose time trying to find out how to contact someone. Provide up-to-date contact lists in a central location.

12-22

B. **Standardize document naming conventions.** Provide a standard document naming convention to reduce confusion. Typically, this is the time charge account number, followed by the official team name, followed by the title of the document. If the document is revised, then a version number is appended onto the end. For example:

QC-1234 Team Manager's Compensation Study—Meeting Minutes 1 Apr 09 v13.0

1. Time charge account number: QC-1234
2. Team name: Team Manager's Compensation Study
3. Document title: Meeting Minutes 1 Apr 09
4. Version number: 13

C. **Communications and response.** Communications overload can be an issue. Set a standard priority for communications among the team. The sender of a message is responsible for setting its priority and including it in the first part of the message title line. Each level of priority corresponds to the number of business hours within which it must be replied to. Example levels:

1. Hot! Must have an immediate response.
2. Urgent—answer within four hours.
3. (No urgency listed) two days.

Always use e-mail subject lines that describe the subject. Then place the key part of your message in the first few lines of the message. Skip slang as it may mean different things in different regions of the country—or to international team members. When in doubt, be more formal rather than less.

COMMENT

Everyone has experienced arguing through e-mail. The results satisfy no one. The virtual team leader must carefully chose comments to avoid accidental offense, especially when pressing an issue on a reluctant team member.

D. **Create a common virtual workforce vocabulary to minimize misunderstanding.** The meaning and intent of communications are easier if everyone uses the same terms in a consistent manner. Definitions must be clear and understood by the entire team. This is particularly important for cross-cultural teams. Any two people can disagree about the same term. Complicate this with regional or international cultural backgrounds and avoidable problems can be addressed.

COMMENT

Another communications issue is to ensure that messages are sent within their context. A simple way to do this is to forward responses to messages that include the original questions. Another way is to repeat the question along with the response.

E. **Team members must post their normal working hours on the contact list.** Team members must be readily available at agreed-upon times. In the United States, this is normal working hours for the local time zone. International workers must be available for at least half of the normal U.S. working hours, even if it forces them to work the night shift. European workers are usually available early in the North American morning.

By posting hours, it is easier to separate work time from family time. There will be times when workers will cut into their normally off-work hours to attend a meeting, but the manager must ensure these times are few. Otherwise, team members may stop accepting virtual assignments.

[E] "Pumping Up" the Virtual Team

Take time to celebrate the team's successes at milestones. Everyone can use a pat on the back sometimes. With a virtual workforce, it just requires some new ideas. One way is to plan a virtual team party. Schedule the event in advance. Send out gift cards for national restaurants and ask the local team to pick up something to share at the same time (lunch is tough to schedule across many time zones).

The manager can help to reduce team member stress by instituting a continuous improvement program. Team members note the top things that get in the way of completing their work. The manager strives to eliminate these obstacles—even if it means standing up to the customer (something many managers seems afraid to do). Progress is reported to the team every other week. As one of the tasks is completed, the team can nominate another for that spot.

The second part of the continuous improvement program is a list of things impossible to change. In the long run, nothing is impossible. The manager must also whittle away at this list, although successes here take much longer.

[F] International Issues

Communications between people sitting together are sometimes challenging, but communicating across time zones, educational backgrounds, and cultures complicates this significantly. Language nuances, different holidays, or even different workdays can disrupt team communications. The way that team members relate can be drastically different. Even the meaning of basic terms such as when a task is "finished" can mean different things to different cultures. In some cultures, it is shameful to admit when someone is unsure of the task or how to complete it—so workers from such cultures may not ask for help.

English is the modern language of business, so finding someone who can communicate with you is not the trick. The issue is to ensure that the meaning of what you are asking for, and what is being said to you, is the same as if talking to someone across the room. Different cultures have different rules of etiquette. Violating these local norms may create ill will where none was intended. Also, different cultures have different expectations of what a normal workday should be, how hard to drive tasks to completion, and how to handle interpersonal conflict.

The key to minimizing your cultural missteps is doing your homework. Where possible, have an advisor who is well versed in the business customs of the country you are using, to include the regional nuances.

A. **Offshore workers.** Some virtual teams include members from outside North America. This is an extension of the idea that virtual workers can live anywhere. Whoever engages these workers must make clear to them the hours they must be available for communication with the customer and the team. Typically this is 8:00 a.m. to 5:00 p.m. wherever the customer is located.

Depending on their origins and cultural background, it may be difficult to understand what the various team members are saying. Accents, language skills, and possession of a technical vocabulary are important requirements of offshore team members. As with all team members, the use of graphics helps to share ideas.

Take time to carefully interview prospective team members. Are they claiming an expertise that they know little about? Do they speak English but lack a technical vocabulary? Do they have experience working with North Americans and therefore understand something of the local business culture and customs?

B. **Cultural sensitivity.** We are all a product of our cultural background. It is reflected in our values, our customs, our habits, and our language. Much of what we do is a product of this culture and we don't even think about it. Someone from a different culture can easily understand some things ("do unto others as you would have others do unto you," for example, is universal). Other business customs are neither so obvious nor easily discovered from books.

Some cultures hold corporate position and age in high respect and feel it is rude or unacceptable to question higher-ups. This can stifle team discussions. If technical discussions seem to lack usefulness, it may be that some of the participants have a problem expressing a contrary opinion to those offered by others.

Even if they do not understand, foreign team members may say "yes" to whatever you tell them. In their culture this may mean "I am listening to you" (but do not understand a thing you have said), whereas you culturally filtered this to mean acceptance and understanding of what was said. After explaining something to foreign team members, engage them in a conversation of its finer points or choices to gauge their depth of understanding.

C. **Building a cross-cultural team.** Building a cross-cultural team is a lot like building any other team. It begins by finding some neutral topic that everyone can join in with, taking sides, and expressing opinions without offense. Sports are a great international topic. Pick up information on local or national teams for every participant. Toss it out as an icebreaker to get the conversation started. Stand by to rein in the discussion if it gets too heated.

Another important tip is to take the time to clearly pronounce basic terms, such as "thank you," "please," "good work," "excellent," "I do not understand," and so on, in each international member's home language. Also learn about international members' foreign nuances, as their language may not translate exactly into what they mean in your own location.

D. **Pick the team's official language.** Usually, the official team language is the one spoken by the sponsoring organization. However, if a significant number of team members speak a different language, consider using that one for meetings. Discussions will run faster and smoother. If you do this, select a group leader to report back with a translation of meeting results.

Using translators is expensive and prone to problems. Words must be translated within their context as well as by their literal meaning. Always meet with a translator prior to a meeting. Discuss with the translator what will be covered and the message you want to convey to the team. This will allow the translator some time to work the message into the correct context.

See Policy ITP-12-2 Virtual Workforce Policy as an example of a policy covering virtual workers.

POLICY ITP-12-2. Virtual Workforce Policy

Policy #:	ITP-12-2	**Effective:**	03/18/13	**Page #:**	1 of N
Subject:	Virtual Workforce Policy				

1.0 PURPOSE

This policy creates the IT department's Virtual Workforce program. It ensures the consistent, efficient, and effective implementation of virtual workers across the organization.

2.0 SCOPE

The policy applies to all information technology departments within the company that want to employ virtual workers. This program encompasses all employee programs where the employee is not physically working in company owned offices, to include remote workers, part-time remote workers, and contract labor.

3.0 POLICY

The type of work sent out of the office depends to a great degree on who the virtual workers are. If they are long-time employees, or employees at remote sites, then more sensitive work can be assigned to them. If the virtual workers are new to the company or contracted labor, then their work must not reveal sensitive internal company processes.

A. **Types of work suitable for virtual workers**. Virtual work is ideal for assignments that have a definable deliverable, such as a code module, a document, or a users' manual. It can also be used to provide data entry of documents (which also has measurable results). Virtual work can be assigned to under-utilized company employees in remote offices. They can remain in their offices while supporting other company sites. Also, ensure that a process is working optimally prior to assigning it to virtual workers.

B. **Types of work not suitable for virtual workers**. Critical business functions should not be assigned to virtual workers. Other things to consider:
   1. Keep the responsibility for the effectiveness and overall success of a business function in the office where it can be closely monitored.
   2. Never use virtual workers for any part of your company's unique business processes. Once these processes are off-site, they are easier for a competitor to learn about.
   3. Customer facing processes must remain in house and only use virtual workers for selective assignments. All customer contact must be handled by the IT staff.
   4. IT legal compliance and security controls must stay in house.

C. **Virtual workforce leader duties.** Duties of the leader include:
   1. Is responsible for implementing this policy.
   2. Create a Mission Statement that outlines the virtual workers' roles and responsibilities within the IT department. It also establishes the scope of the policy.
   3. Identify the primary strategies on how the virtual workforce will fulfill its mission statement and align with company business strategies.
   4. Establish and maintain the tools and processes for use by the IT department's virtual workers.
   5. Establish processes for prompt technical support of virtual worker issues.
   6. Manage the IT department's portfolio of pending virtual assignments:
      a. Create a standard form for requesting virtual worker support. This ensures every request has the same "look and feel."
      b. Monitor contents of portfolio to combine assignments where practical.
   7. Standardize virtual worker tools.
      a. Set processes
      b. Create tools
      c. Establish ground rules

8. Resource management.
    a. Coordinate the use of virtual resources to optimize utilization and minimize cost.
    b. Develop and maintain a positive working relationship with internal resource suppliers.
    c. Identify external virtual resources required and pre-qualify major suppliers (internal and external).
    d. Assign and reassign resources.
9. Establish training and mentoring program.
    a. Identify and train mentors for assisting new virtual workers.
    b. Coordinate peer reviews for troubled assignments.
10. Establish a virtual worker document repository.

D. **Worker responsibility.** Responsibilities of the worker includes:
1. Posts his or her normal working hours (as approved by the Virtual Workforce Leader).
2. Promptly responds to communications by telephone, electronic mail, and instant messaging.
3. Provides a high-speed data connection and telephone line into the work area.
4. Provides physical security for company equipment and data.
5. Provides a weekly status report for every current virtual assignment in process.

4.0 REVISION HISTORY

Date	Revision #	Description of Change
03/18/13	1.0	Initial creation.

5.0 INQUIRIES

Direct inquiries about this policy to:

George Jenkins, CIO
Our Company, Inc.
2900 Corporate Drive
Columbus, OH 43215

Voice: 614-555-1234
Fax: 614-555-1235
E-mail: gjenkins@company.com

Revision #:	1.0	Supersedes:	N/A	Date:	03/18/13

13

REQUIREMENTS ANALYSIS: PLANNING FOR SUCCESS

§ 13.01 OVERVIEW

[A] Purpose and Scope

Business requirements analysis and project management are complementary processes. Business systems requirements identify the "what" that is to be accomplished. They include the system's logic flow and all of the elements that must be included. Project management details "how" the project will be done, by whom, for how much, and by when.

A project plan is the most efficient way to focus resources toward solving a business problem. It provides a "roadmap" to the journey toward project completion. Without a good map, you will not know where you are or where to turn next. Moving from a vague idea to a final product requires careful analysis. Projects begin with a vague idea. The process of translating a vague idea into specific needs is requirements analysis. The clear description of requirements, to include their quantifiable attributes, is essential for efficient project execution. Poorly defined requirements result in the loss of time and money due to rework and discarded features.

Gathering requirements requires collecting various personal perspectives on the project vision and synthesizing them down to their essential features. For example, if three different people were asked to provide 10 characteristics of the same elephant, a few of them may be the same. Some of these will be variations on the same requirement but explained in different ways. Collecting all of this into a single description is the essence of requirements analysis.

[B] Policy Objectives

To ensure that the company's best practices are always applied to its business problems, establish policy guidelines for requirements analysis. Establishing a policy to guide the standard development of project requirements allows others to pick up a project if the business analyst moves on, as everyone uses the same basic approach. This policy should incorporate the company's unique experiences and lessons learned from previous projects. Every analysis deals with unique circumstances so guidelines must be broad enough to allow for flexible execution but narrow enough so that the final product is consistently excellent.

Requirements must be traceable from their origin through any "child" requirements. For example, a requirement from an executive that a Web site accept customer payments implies additional features for safeguarding credit card data. If this high-level requirement is later canceled, then so are the dependent "child" requirements. Ensure that requirements include advice from all critical stakeholders. More discussion on "child" requirements comes later in this chapter.

Every requirement must include adequate descriptive criteria, such as physical dimensions, actions it must perform, etc. These criteria are approved by the project sponsor along with the project descriptions, for the validation test criteria.

The policy objectives governing requirements development should include:

A. Ensuring that IT projects have correctly identified the project's purpose, benefits, and objectives so that it will deliver what the customer is requesting.
B. Determining when solution prototyping is appropriate due to its cost and time requirements.
C. Providing traceability of requirements from first request to final delivery.

[C] Critical Policies to Develop Based on This Chapter

Using the material discussed in this chapter, you will be able to create the following policies:

A. Proper collection of requirements.
B. IT system prototyping.

Policies should always be developed based on the local situation. Successful managers cannot issue appropriate guidance if the policies are written with another company's situation or location in mind.

COMMENT

Project planning is reviewed in greater detail in Chapter 14, "Project Management: Getting It Out on Time."

§ 13.02 STAKEHOLDERS HOLD THE ANSWERS

[A] Overview

IT technicians are reluctant to ask their customers a lot of questions. Some feel this indicates that they are not the masters of their subject. Others lack the conversational skills to lead a group discussion. The result is technical solution to a business problem, which was created by a technician with minimal customer advice. It also results in significant project rework when technicians deliver something that they wanted to create instead of what the customer wanted to use. This is why companies use semi-technical business analysts to translate "business speak" into its associated technical IT terms.

Companies create a project to solve a business problem or to take advantage of a business opportunity. Upon completion, it delivers a completed product or service for someone. Usually the person running the project is different than the person requesting it (project sponsor). The transfer of the mental picture of what is needed from the project sponsor to the business analyst is called the project vision. A business analyst develops a written description of this vision for approval by the project sponsor. This narrative is then further defined as the project's objective and the basis for all project decisions.

The project sponsor begins with a basic idea and then shapes it to the point where it is passed to someone else for execution. But how does someone effectively convey something as intangible as an idea? A general verbal description might pass a vague idea from one person to another. However, vague descriptions leave a considerable amount of latitude for product creators to make what they wish instead of what was requested. To ensure the final product is the same as what is desired, a set of written requirements is created and approved as a detailed description of the project vision.

Part of the problem lies with the speaker's perspective. Project sponsors typically deal with issues at a high level and can only describe what they want in general terms. They may know it if they see it but cannot describe it in sufficient detail to create it. To ensure a complete transfer of the idea, the business analyst develops a clear set of descriptive characteristics of the desired result. Each characteristic is described in measurable, finite terms. At the end of the project, each of these characteristics is demonstrated to exist within the final product.

Gathering requirements takes time. Anxious executives press for projects to start as soon as possible and do not appreciate the importance of this step. Requirements gathering may be seen as a paperwork exercise. However, any project plan built on incomplete specifications is doomed to schedule and budget overruns. When encountering a project that is out of cost and time control and where chaos reigns, it is usually started with poor specifications and casually adding new requirements throughout its existence.

COMMENT

Each requirement exists in a project plan in at least three places: where it is created, unit testing, and system testing. It may also need a step to purchase materials needed to create it.

[B] Identifying Stakeholders

Anyone whose workday is potentially altered by the existence of a project or by its final product is a potential stakeholder. In a sense, every employee of a company is automatically a stakeholder because every project consumes a portion of the company's limited resources from other uses. The result is an unmanageable number of people to interview. However, most of them would have little new information to contribute to your understanding of its details.

To make this process manageable, stakeholders are broken into the categories of "vital" and "casual."

Vital stakeholders are those who are directly impacted by a project's result or existence. Stakeholders also include "politically" powerful individuals whose actions can alter the project's requirements or courses of actions. Vital stakeholders may also include union representatives, corporate auditors, the human resources department, and always the accounting department. Casual stakeholders are all other interested parties.

Stakeholders see a project through the lens of their own experience. Some know what they want in the final product; some just like to hear themselves talk. A business analyst who proactively seeks these people out during the requirements gathering phase will reduce the number of changes mandated later in the project and increase corporate support. Useful documents for identifying stakeholders include:

A. Company organizational chart as it shows the official lines of authority.
B. Geographic maps if the company sites are dispersed, especially internationally.
C. Data flow diagrams indicating which data system elements may need to be accessed or require an interface; this implies that the organizational entities that control the use of these requirements must be contacted for access and permissions.
D. Technology architecture diagrams showing where the final product will sit in the overall company system. This may imply staff members who possess valuable information for the project requirements.

COMMENT

Prioritize the stakeholder list to ensure the most valuable ones have an opportunity to participate in project requirements gathering before time runs out.

IT project stakeholders always include:

A. Senior management who provide the business context of the project—how it will return benefit to the company for the resources expended.
B. Users—stakeholders whose work processes will change when the project is completed. They describe the input/output interfaces on paper and on a display screen. These ideas also explain how this IT component fits into their processes. These requirements may be at odds with the sponsor's requirements. Sometimes "users" are the company's customers.

C. The project sponsor who provides resources (time, people, materials, etc.) for the project, and is the approving authority for changes.
D. Project team, which includes anyone assisting with completing the project's final product. They uncover many of the unstated requirements.
E. Ongoing support organization—people who will provide ongoing maintenance to the finished product once it is delivered. They focus on ease of maintenance.
F. Facilities department that provides floor space, tables, electricity, network connections, etc., required to install new devices. The physical reality of an installation site sometimes constrains the final product.
G. IT department
   1. Server administration—user ID and access authorizations, CPU, and disk sizing.
   2. Applications Development and Maintenance teams—identifies company processes and policies relating to the technologies needed to assemble this code.
   3. Network management—security, access, and capacity requirements and constraints.
   4. Information security, business continuity planning, etc.

[C]   Second Time Around

There is more information about a company in circulation than is found in IT documentation. This includes information about who really runs certain departments and examples about project successes and failure. Patient interviewing of stakeholders will uncover the institutional knowledge stored in the memories of long-term employees. This information may point out pitfalls to avoid and identify key stakeholders whose support is essential.

Pay close attention to comments that the project has been tried before. This could be a valuable source of information about things to avoid, stakeholders to be pleased, etc. An understanding of where a previous project went wrong can help you to avoid it. As your project executes, draw a clear distinction between it and the failed project. Fend off the comparisons with facts. As the initial milestones are completed, showcase the early successes. Soon the comparisons will fade from the conversation as irrelevant.

[D]   You Can't Please Everyone

When meeting with stakeholders, always take a few minutes to establish a context for the conversation by explaining the requirements collection, validation, and approval process. Describe how changes to the requirements will be handled during the course of the project in case something else comes to mind. Stakeholders can use this process later if they wish to add features to the project's scope after it is approved.

Most people will base their expectations about the project on their own work environment. In the absence of information to the contrary, they may expect certain functions or features that are beyond the scope of the project. Not every good idea can be accommodated in the final design. Stakeholders may misunderstand the purpose of the requirements-gathering interviews. Ensure that they understand that your discussion is not a commitment to add any particular requirement to the final product. Only the project sponsor, the person who is paying for the work, can decide on the final specifications. See Policy ITP-13-1 Requirements Gathering Policy as an example.

POLICY ITP-13-1. Requirements Gathering Policy

Policy #:	ITP-13-1	Effective:	04/01/13	Page #:	1 of N
Subject:	Requirements Gathering Policy				

1.0 PURPOSE

This policy establishes the minimal information that must be gathered about a project before it begins. The intention is to minimize the amount of project rework required due to incomplete or inaccurate project requirements.

2.0 SCOPE

The policy applies to all information technology projects within the company with a project budget of $20,000 or more.

3.0 POLICY

The CIO will ensure that all IT projects with a project budget of $20,000 or more will be based on documented project requirements.

A. **Requirements Collection.** Documented requirements, approved by the project sponsor, are required of all IT projects prior to the start of their execution. This ensures that the project's purpose, benefits, and objectives have been clearly identified.
   1. Mandatory requirements to collect include:
      a. Identification of critical stakeholders. This is a list of all stakeholders who have a significant interest in the successful outcome of this project whether they will use it, it will alter their work environment, or they must support it. Each critical stakeholder must be interviewed for his or her project requirements.
      b. Statement of the problem or opportunity to be addressed.
      c. A list of benefits anticipated from a successful project.
   2. Mandatory requirements reporting:
      a. A Work Breakdown Schedule illustration that identifies all of the explicit and implied project specifications. A final list of every requirement for the project, broken into "must have" and "desired" categories. The desired category is further broken into a group of "accepted desired requirements" and "not-accepted desired requirements."

       b. A report on each stakeholder interview to include the key elements that the stakeholder requires to be in the project and those that the stakeholder would "like" to see in it.

       c. Requirements traceability table, which indicates the requestor for each requirement, if it is derived from a higher-level need, and if it is further broken down into more granular requirements.

       d. Every requirement must include the test that validates that the requirement is achieved. This might be that the feature exists or not, has quantifiable criteria such as length, color, etc.

       e. Enter all requirements into a requirements tracking tool that holds all requirements. This may be a simple spreadsheet or a complex database.

B. Requirements Approval. The company manager who is sponsoring the project is the final approver for IT requirements. Prior to submitting the requirements for approval, the IT project manager must submit the requirement to the IT "special teams" to ensure the project is aligned with company practices. Requirements are submitted to these groups at the beginning of the project any time there is a significant change and along with the final product at the end. Including these mandatory changes in the beginning of the project minimizes their cost.

    1. The business continuity manager ensures that this project does not change the recoverability of a vital business function. If it does, or if it creates a new vital business function, the business continuity plans become an additional requirement.

    2. The information security manager ensures that any software (purchased or written) adheres to approved coding standards. The information security manager also ensures that all data collection, retention, and use conforms to company standards and meets all legal requirements for the jurisdictions where it is collected or used.

    3. The environmental/Green manager ensures that all incoming equipment conforms to the company's Green equipment acquisition and disposal policies, and that the plan includes retaining the device's energy savings settings. In addition, the requirements include the proper disposal of any excess equipment.

    4. The ergonometric and safety department considers the impact of the project's product or service on how people work. The goal is to minimize such things as repetitive injuries.

    5. The help desk needs information, procedures, and training to ensure that staff can address basic problems that arise during installation and ongoing maintenance.

    6. The capacity-planning group verifies that existing equipment is used to an optimal level prior to purchasing additional devices or licenses.

C. Requirements Change Control. The longer a project exists, the greater the likelihood that its requirements will change, due to an ever-evolving business climate, executive preferences, shifts in the company's strategic direction, and advances in technology. The proposal detailing the project requirements that is submitted to the project sponsor must include a process for managing changes.

1. Requests for changes to the approved requirements must be made in writing. The business analyst reviews the requirements and reports the impact to the budget and timeline on the change request form.
2. The IT "special teams" (business continuity, information security, etc.) will be provided copies and at least two business days to reply to the request. They need only respond if there is a problem.
3. The project sponsor is the only person authorized to approve a change. Approval also applies to the changes in the schedule and project budget associated with this change.

4.0 REVISION HISTORY

Date	Revision #	Description of Change
04/01/13	1.0	Initial creation.

5.0 INQUIRIES

Direct inquiries about this policy to:

George Jenkins, CIO
Our Company, Inc.
2900 Corporate Drive
Columbus, OH 43215

Voice: 614-555-1234
Fax: 614-555-1235
E-mail: gjenkins@company.com

Revision #:	1.0	Supersedes:	N/A	Date:	04/01/13

[E] Speak the Same Language

Many technical departments have a glossary of terms unique to their industry. If a written glossary is not locally available, look for one on the Internet. Whenever an unfamiliar technical term is used, verify it with the glossary entry. This is a case in which a bit of awkwardness is better than misunderstanding a requirement. Besides, people like to talk about their job. Asking for a clarification of a term can reduce the tension of the discussions.

In addition to industry-wide terms, work teams often develop their own terminology to reflect their unique work processes. Language is an imprecise tool. To ensure that the complete message was received containing the same information as when it was created, we use specific words, often technically unique to the subject. It may be necessary to create an extended glossary of local technical terms unique to the work team. (Attach this glossary to all future requirements documentation.)

§ 13.03   DESCRIBING A REQUIREMENT

[A]   Overview

Requirements analysis breaks the project vision down into its various functions. The business analyst guides the discussion from the big picture to the major components to the specific details. Each of the smaller refinements continues to be broken down until the specific requirement is clear to the people who must fulfill it.

Therefore, when digging out requirements, begin with stakeholders whose view of the project is most general, such as executives, the project sponsor, and other senior stakeholders. As the interviews are extended to the technical staff, the details will become more specific. The big-picture requirements define the boundaries while the technical discussions describe individual activities.

[B]   Specific Requirements

Specific requirements are product functions or characteristics requested by a stakeholder, which must be included in the final product. The ideal requirement includes a finite physical description. Even software can be described finitely with some patience. Specific requirements exist in a project plan in at least four places: where it is initially created, where a test is created to ensure that it exists, where it is tested by itself (unit test), and when it is tested in the final product as a whole (system test).

A finitely described requirement enables its existence in the final product to be demonstrated. Where one person may describe a project's product height as "kind of short," another may identify a product's height as somewhere around an inch. Strive for clear measurements, such as that the product provides five blank lines on a data entry screen for customer address entry, or that it is made of SAE 201 steel that is 1/32-inch thick. Unambiguous measurements enable quick testing during product acceptance and reduce reliance on a technician's judgment.

Explicit requirements take many forms. Some are legal mandates, such as this specific information element must be reported monthly, or that project must complete by April 1. Legal mandates usually carry their own detailed requirements. Other explicit requirements may be to follow all published company processes and policies (very important to know if you are a contractor working inside a company). A specific requirement may also be a high-level requirement, which will require lower-level managers or engineers to provide the detailed characteristics.

[C]   Inferred Requirements

Inferred requirements are characteristics that must be included in the final product but are not specifically requested by the customer. For example, if someone was describing a Web page that would accept customer credit card payment, then an inferred characteristic is a secure way to receive the credit card number. Where a business manager thinks in terms of accepting orders, the project team knows that without a secure connection, no one will use the site. This inferred requirement adds time and cost to the project.

Inferred requirements are the bane of the business analyst. The proposed project sounds so straightforward that sponsors cannot accept delays for tasks they do not think are needed. Inferred requirements represent, "Before this can begin, you must do this first." These issues often arise during the development of IT systems. For example, someone else uses hardware that was thought to be available surplus before the business analyst can secure it, thereby raising the cost of the project. Another IT issue is network bandwidth. Everyone assumes it is a limitless pipeline when it is actually a finite resource.

Digging out hidden requirements before the project budget is finalized is an area where good business analysts really shine. Each hidden requirement represents a potential budget- and schedule-busting task. Examples of inferred requirements include:

- Additional software licenses required for supporting system components.
- Dramatically higher fuel costs (or surcharges) for deliveries or business travel.
- Inadequate environmental support in the data center for hosting additional equipment.
- Maintenance contracts for new hardware and software—or for additional software coverage.
- Key infrastructure components undergoing a version upgrade during your project.
- Documenting user support information and the technical structure of the solution.
- Ensuring that all existing devices and software used in the solution possess the required revision level of software and firmware.

[D] Functional Requirements

Functional requirements describe something the product does rather than a physical characteristic. It could be an off/on switch or even an alarm buzzer. The characteristics of functional requirements are easy to identify; however, they may vary significantly. Capturing this data is important as different stakeholders may set conflicting requirements.

Each functional requirement results in a series of lower-level, more detailed requirements. Adding a data entry field to a Web-based customer ordering system can be further broken into validation edits for that field: adding a field to the database, adding that data to reports, processing instructions for that field, operator training for that field, technical and user documentation changes, etc. Each item in this example requires conversations with the various tech staffs (database, programming, technical writers) to gather further details.

[E]   Non-Functional Requirements

In a sense, all requirements are functional. Non-functional requirements simply "exist." It can also be argued that their existence is functional. Non-functional requirements tend to be the aesthetic characteristics of the final product. They might be the color of a computer case, the specific layout of a Web page, or the texture of the cover of the end-user documentation. They are essential to the final product but do not enable the final product to perform additional work.

Non-functional requirements must be described as clearly as functional requirements. A clear description is the only way to validate that they fulfill the customer's request. IT professionals tend to focus on the functional issues and neglect the "dressy" aspects of the project. Appearance of the final product is what people will see first, so these requirements—although non-functional—are still important. Always consider the value of non-functional requirements from the end user's perspective.

[F]   Requirements Vary Widely

Some of the many types of requirements include:

A. Time of day for some systems, the time of day that an IT system is needed may drive its requirements. For example, a data system supporting racetrack gambling has some critical times of day when it must be fault tolerant. Systems supporting time clocks for employees entering and leaving the factory every day will have a few hours of heavy use and then a lot of idle time. Seasonality is a variation on time of day as days of the year may require different function or performance standards than others. Annual closing of a company's financial statements is a classic example.

B. Validation of critical fields, such as transaction keys. All data must be validated before acceptance. A capability is implied for someone (ideally in a business department) to maintain the contents of each of the validation tables.

C. Input—specific data collection capabilities beyond those provided by the operating system, such as a bar code reader, RF ID, or a material handling proximity switch.

D. Output—the result of calculations, accumulations, and other data processing that is provided to end users as displays, printed documents, flashing lights, etc.

E. Legal mandates—this requirement is necessary to comply with an existing or anticipated law. Sometimes the specific requirements are not known until some standard emerges or a judicial decision is published. Multinational companies must track laws that apply to the various places where their systems will be used.

F. Performance requirements—peak transaction volumes by type and origin for the server, the workstation, the storage area network (SAN), and the network.

G. Interfaces to existing systems (flowing data in and out) whose contents and controls are beyond the scope of this project, such as the computer servers owned by supply chain partners, functions within commercial software, etc.

H. Company policies, standards, processes. Often company standards will restrict the final product to using specific software tools in the interest of future maintainability, such as our standard operating system is Linux, and the company prohibits all others (to save on support costs).

I. Testing criteria used to demonstrate that a particular project function exists.

§ 13.04 ASSEMBLING SPECIFICATIONS

[A] Overview

With all of the stakeholder's requirements in hand, it is time to organize them into a comprehensive picture of what is needed. Collecting them in one volume minimizes conflicting requests and allows the project sponsor to select those they desire (or can afford) in the final product.

Specifications can be assembled into a hierarchy from general to specific. These are referred to as parent/child requirements relationships. A high-level requirement (parent) might be to include EDI exchange between a proposed materials management system and the company's suppliers. Child requirements under that category will further expand on the idea of adding required details and features. If the EDI requirement is later discarded by the project sponsor, then all child requirements under it are also eliminated, similar to cutting the main branch of tree also brings down its attached smaller branches.

[B] Tracing Customer Requirements

Traceability is the ability to follow a requirement back to its source, and to understand its relationship to other requirements. It is easy to provide if data about customer wants and needs are collected from the very beginning. There may be multiple sources for a single requirement if people interviewed at different times all mentioned that it was needed.

Assigning each requirement a unique requirement tracking number facilitates tracing. "Backward traceability" is a term for tracing a requirement back to its source. "Forward traceability" enables tracing requirements from general to specific or from parent to child. In both cases, it is accomplished by recording the requirement numbers of the originating and child requirements.

Requirements must be traceable from the document of approved requirements to the project plan. This ensures that everything in the specifications is included in the project plan to be added onto the final product. The final step in traceability is ensuring that the testing actions for each requirement are included in the project plan. This demonstrates that the requirement exists in the final product. By including the requirement number with the project plan task, actions to cut cost or time by eliminating specific features can be quickly traced to ensure all tasks are removed.

One tool for tracing customer requirements is the Requirements Traceability Matrix. An example of such a matrix can be found in Worksheet 13-1 Requirements Traceability Worksheet. This matrix ensures that every customer requirement is accounted for in the system design, is coded, and is properly tested. The columns on the worksheet should map to the individual project documents that are created by your team, and trace each item in each document back to the original requirement.

For larger projects, you may want to track the requirements in a requirements repository database. This tool holds all of the many requirements in one container along with its origin and characteristics. Fields in a requirements repository might include:

A. **Record key.** Requirement number unique to this entry.
B. **Stakeholder name.** Identifies the origin of a requirement so further questions can be raised if later some part of the description seems ambiguous. There may be multiple stakeholders requesting a particular requirement.
C. **Date.** Date requested by each stakeholder.
D. **Description of the requirement.** A narrative of what this requirement is, the value it adds to the final product, etc.
E. **Characteristics of the requirement.** These are the measurable aspects of the requirement so we know when it is completed and if it can be proven to exist in the final product. It might be that something is 14 inches long, that it supports 35 simultaneous users and 1,000 online transactions per minute, etc.
F. **How will it be tested.** Actions taken at the end of the project to prove that the requirement is fulfilled. This includes a description of the testing process and required measurement tools.
G. **Constraints.** Anything that limits this requirement or the project's creation of the result of this requirement, such as company policies, standardized IT products, etc.
H. **Risks.** Potential pitfalls of implementing this requirement. Mitigation actions may be added as "children" to this requirement.
I. **Alignment with business strategies.** A list of the businesses strategies that this requirement supports.
J. **Importance.** 0 for weak nice-to-have; up to a 10 for a strong need.
K. **Parent requirement number.** The higher-level requirement that this requirement further defines in greater detail. There may only be one of these.
L. **Child requirement number.** The lower-level requirements that further define this requirement in greater detail. There may be many of these.

To ensure that all of these data are collected with each requirement, a form reflecting each field is created. Use this form when conducting stakeholder interviews to reduce the number of return visits to gather information.

WORKSHEET 13-1. Requirements Traceability Matrix

Requirements Traceability Matrix

Project Name:

Project Number:

Requirements						
ID	Short Description	Architecture Reference	Technical Specification	Code Reference	Test Plan	Comments
1.1	Search by name	1.1	3.2	2.1	3.5.1	
1.2	Search by city	1.1	3.3	2.1	3.5.2	

[C]   Focus on Key Needs

Not all requirements may be possible, practical, or affordable. If two specifications conflict, then which one should survive? The project sponsor—the person paying for this project—must make all decisions. However, when interviewing stakeholders, ask them how important a requirement is to the success of this project. Some requirements are just "nice to have" and not essential. Successful projects strive for simplicity in the final product to reduce the opportunities for errors. Use the nice-to-have requirements as added features in later versions of the product.

Some requirements will be requested by multiple stakeholders. In those cases, record both the average and highest importance rating. Be sure to indicate which stakeholder applied the highest rating for later discussions. Often desires of key executives trump those of all other stakeholders.

In the end, it is up to the project sponsor to decide the final priority for each requirement. It is not unusual to have more requirements than there is time or money to create them. By prioritizing requirements, the project scope can be fine-tuned to the available resources.

[D]   Prepare for Changes

Eventually the requirements gathering phase must close and project planning should begin. After the project sponsor formally approves the requirements, stakeholders will keep adding ideas on to the project. These suggestions must be approved or denied by the project sponsor. The business analyst's role is to gather relevant information for the project sponsor to consider and then present it for review.

The project sponsor must approve all changes to the project scope. This is because every scope change has a corresponding change to the project's cost and timeline. If the business analyst becomes the person who makes these decisions, then he or she will receive the brunt of internal "political" pressure to make changes—something that few people can successfully fend off. After all, the executive pushing for a change today might be your boss tomorrow. Also, in this way, if the project sponsor presses changes without adjustments to budget or schedule, it will be on record when the project runs too long and over budget.

[E]   Risk Assessment

All IT projects involve some degree of risk. To manage risk proactively, identify and analyze risk continuously in the normal course of the project. The following steps can be used to manage the risk in a project:

A. Identify the risk. Discuss risks during the requirements gathering process. Look for opportunities to avoid or mitigate risks. The sooner risks are identified, the sooner solutions can be found.

B. Analyze the risk. Determine how risk can impact the project. What effect will the risk have on cost, project duration, or the ability of the project to satisfy the user's requirements?

C. Prioritize risks to determine which ones deserve the most attention and which risks can be safely ignored.
D. Add mitigation steps to the project plan to reduce the likelihood of the threat occurring, or to increase the amount of warning that it is about to occur or its impact if it is unavoidable.
E. Follow up. Track risks and what is being done to mitigate them.

Several risk areas can influence requirements during collection and later during project execution:

A. Economic fluctuation can change the value of the project to the firm or affect funding available for the project.
B. Changes in government regulations can impact the cost or utility of the project.
C. Marketplace shifts can occur due to changes in customer requirements and preferences.
D. A project's technology may not work as advertised or may change during the course of a long project.
E. Lukewarm management support, changes in management, unrealistic expectations, etc., can all adversely affect the project.

For more information on risk analysis, please see Chapter 10.

§ 13.05 STAKEHOLDERS INTERVIEWS

[A] Overview

Stakeholders have their own opinion of what belongs in a project's final product. Some will wish you well, and others will wish that you would just go away. Some will speak right up and others will sit quietly lost in their own thoughts. Whatever the stakeholders' personal motivations, their requirements must be uncovered before their expectations can be included in the final project results.

[B] Just Ask Them

The most time-consuming and effective way to gather requirements is through one-on-one interviews with stakeholders. This is a good way to identify specific requirements of the project. Executives tend to provide high-level, general requirements while individual technicians will describe details pertinent to their profession. Before asking questions, begin by setting the context for the conversation. Begin each interview with a(n):

A. General description of the project's objectives as described by the sponsor.
B. Explanation of the requirements gathering process.

Individual interviews are that person's perspective of the issue. We all see the world through the filters of our personal experiences. Most individuals lack the big-picture view of an issue. Once the requirements from various stakeholders are combined, the individual, narrowly focused requests are blended together much like the individual instruments in an orchestra combine to make a happy tune.

Open-ended questions keep the conversation flowing but the interviewer must keep it on target, taking care not to steer the stakeholders' responses. Keep the discussion open to any ideas that come up. The weaker points will be screened out later.

People deal in emotions and intuition as well as in facts. They may express a concern or doubt as to the potential for success for some aspect of the project. The person being interviewed may also oppose the existence of a project as that may prevent something the stakeholder wants from the beginning. There are only so many resources in a company and resources used on your project deplete those available for their own. Also, if your project requires an infrastructure different from that which they discuss, then they might also oppose it.

The ability to resolve stakeholder concerns can turn a naysayer into a cheerleader. Listen carefully to them and craft a win/win situation to gain their support. Sometimes concerns are not spoken and must be determined from careful investigation. No matter how far afield it seems from your project, list each concern as a project constraint or requirement. By pointing out flaws in the project, stakeholders identify risk areas to avoid or mitigate.

[C]   Gathering Techniques

Interviews are the traditional approach. It is easy to arrange a meeting of just two people. However, some people are reluctant to participate in one-on-one meetings and a small group meeting may be necessary to bring them on board. Also, some people are reluctant to speak about something in which they lack complete knowledge. Additional techniques to help gather requirements include:

A.   **Cross-functional team meeting.** Sometimes it is quicker to bring a small team of stakeholders to gather their thoughts at the same time. There are advantages to this approach. The idea of one person may inspire another person to build on it—often in a new direction. Cross-functional teams (network, systems administration, applications, information security, business continuity, Green Initiative, etc.) can raise and quickly resolve questions that touch on multiple technical areas.

Cross-functional team meetings may also be known as a "requirements workshop." They work well when sifting through the many project requirements collected through individual stakeholder interviews. They can quickly provide detailed requirements and resolve many issues. Provide a list of all requirements to participants prior to the meeting. Each person can then comment on requirements as they relate to their technical area and interact with other teams. However, facilitated groups must be carefully moderated to avoid bickering over the fine points. They can quickly provide detailed requirements and resolve many issues. It is also expensive to place so many high-paid people in one room to work on the same thing. Keep the attendee list to a manageable seven or less participants.

B. Understanding needs through use cases. A use case is a way to gather requirements, based on how the final product will be used. The user's interactions with the product are observed to derive the project's requirements. Assembling a use case involves customers envisioning what the system will do and then writing down every step of the process of how they use it.

A use case description is a more thorough view of the task to be accomplished. It begins with the primary flow of events—the normal interaction with the system. Added to this are all of the alternate flows of events. This might be handling of error messages, incorrect operator data collection, etc. It also includes any logic branches the user may select.

Sometimes a "typical user," known as an "actor," acts out the interactions. Each use case description describes one interaction between the actor and the system. When a use case list seems to be fairly exhaustive, convert the contents into requirements and prioritize by investment (time and money) and impact of failure (low to high).

Separate the optional user interactions from the essential. For example, a person must be able to check e-mail. He may also want to have the text displayed in orange font on a gray background. The difference between these requests is that the ability to check e-mail is a functional requirement since picking a custom color scheme is an aesthetic requirement.

C. Observation. IT projects begin and end with people. People interact with the result of an IT project to start it (usually by collecting data) and by how they use the data that come out of it. Sometimes these processes are difficult to describe. A common issue is that process documentation does not reflect how the work is actually accomplished.

To ensure that the project's product meshes with existing processes, the business analyst observes both the existing upstream and downstream manual processes and compares them to the published process steps. This ensures that the project's data collection process fits in with existing capabilities. If stakeholders have difficulties describing how a process works, observation is one way the business analyst can gather this information.

Watching how something is used uncovers differences between the documented and actual process steps. Documented processes represent a snapshot of the process steps at the time the explanation was written.

Updating documentation is sometimes overlooked when patching a process. Over time, the documentation no longer reflects reality.

While observing the process, discuss the steps with the operators. They can identify the types and frequency of problems that they must resolve. They often offer insightful ways to simplify the process.

[D] Turn Off Your Technical Filters

We all filter the words we hear. These filters are a combination of our experience, culture, preconceived ideas, educations, and a wide range of other factors—including the context of the conversation. The problem is that these filters shape how the stakeholder's words are interpreted. It is a natural action that must be suppressed. For example, if the business analyst's background is as a Unix system administrator, then the requirements will be measured as to how they conform to the capabilities and strengths of that single technology instead of fairly gathering the requirements and then aligning them with the appropriate technology. So, in this sense, the less the business analyst knows about the technologies to be applied, the more open the analyst is to the requirements without the technical filters.

Another aspect of filters is the stakeholder's opinion of the person gathering requirements. If that person is known as deeply favoring one type of technology or another, then the stakeholder may hold back his or her ideas because he or she feels the solution has already been selected.

§ 13.06 VALIDATING PROJECT REQUIREMENTS

[A] Overview

Collecting requirements is a race against time. There is always a lot of detail to sift through. Every project specification must be checked for completeness, consistency, and accuracy and organized into some priority for the sponsor to decide what is in and out of scope.

[B] Is It All Here?

Trace all of the requirements from high level down to low level. Is the lowest level requirement clear and finitely expressed? If not, there may be some missing requirements that need to be hashed out before project planning begins. Every high-level requirement must have lower-level requirements providing details that describe or test it.

Normalizing data means ensuring they only exist in one place. Sift through all of the requirements and combine duplicate entries. With so much information, some items may be mutually exclusive. The business analyst eliminates the obvious ones, but it is up to the project sponsor to select what stays in and what comes out of a project. Before the final specifications are approved, the business analyst should discuss the excluded requirements and explain why they were removed. This minimizes the risk of incorrectly categorizing an important product need.

Next, organize the requirements logically from the most general requirement down to the detailed specifications. This will make pruning the requirements easier when, at some point later in the project, the budget must be trimmed.

Requirements must be easy to understand and clearly understood by all stakeholders. Well-defined specifications are:

A. **Verifiable.** They can be proven through inspection, analysis, or demonstration.

B. **Feasible.** It is possible to build within the limited project budget, schedule, and available technical resources.
C. **Valuable.** An explanation of the value that requirement provides.
D. **Well thought out.** An explanation of the risk to the project's success of including this requirement.

[C] Context Diagram to Show Relationships

People think in images. Context diagrams are a picture of how requirements relate to one another and in IT systems—they can show the flow of transactions, inter-relations between modules, interactions between data tables, and a wide range of things. Large systems may need several diagrams to show the different views of the final product. Context diagrams are useful for identifying implied requirements (see Exhibit 13-1).

EXHIBIT 13-1. Context Diagram

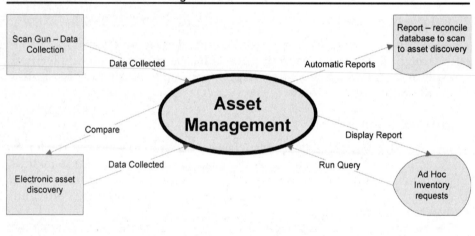

When walking stakeholders through the diagrams, discuss each requirement and how they all relate to one another. The context diagram may mislead some stakeholders by simplifying the challenges offered by protocols and interfaces. The diagrams should indicate the many assumptions and constraints that apply to each module along with the data flows.

[D] Try a Requirements Breakdown Schedule

A picture can be used to illustrate the relationship between requirements much better than words on a page. Validate your requirements by showing them to stakeholders in a picture, such as a hierarchical Work Breakdown Structure (WBS), where the project description is visually decomposed into individual tasks (see Exhibit 13-2). The pictorial image of all of the requirements at one place helps to identify what may be missing.

COMMENT

It is not unusual for someone to ask for a feature with no personal appreciation of the complexity of delivering it. Use illustrations to educate project sponsors on the complexity of some requests. It could be that upon examination, the requested feature was not worth the effort.

Apply a hierarchical numbering system to each module for later cross-reference to the project plan and the requirements gathering database. A significant problem with this approach is that relationships between requirements are only shown as parent/child, and not cross-functionally. For example, the requirement "3122 EDI Interface" will relate to a requirement under "4000 transition to new system" to set up the EDI interface and to "5000 User Training" to show someone how to configure EDI transactions.

EXHIBIT 13-2. Hierarchical Work Breakdown Structure

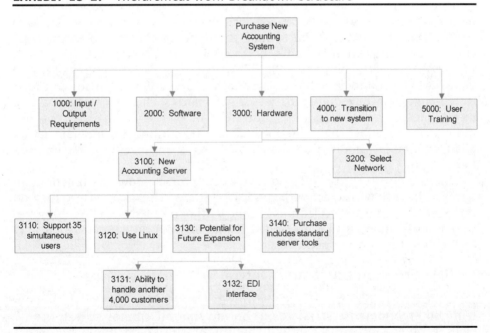

§ 13.07 IT SPECIAL TEAMS ROUND OUT THE SPECS

[A] Overview

Once the requirements are ready for customer review, the last step is to ensure they comply with the company's best IT and business practices. It is time for the IT department's "special teams" to move in. IT specialists must review the requirements to ensure that they include the necessary action or that they do not conflict with current company practices. It is always cheaper to build them in rather than add them later. This review can be time consuming, but it saves a lot of rework later in the project.

[B] Business Continuity Impact

Any process that the company depends on to conduct its business should have a written and tested business continuity plan. Does the project's final product expand on an IT system already identified as a vital business function, or will it create a new vital business function? If so, then requirements must be added to provide emergency support for any key components not already adequately covered in the disaster recovery or business continuity plans.

[C] Information Security

Ask the information security experts to review the data created, accessed, or reported by the project in terms of legal compliance, privacy, or company secrets. Does this data system include the required controls to ensure legal compliance for all financial laws, best practices, or privacy legislation? Is it in compliance with company policies? Are controls over the object code and data files in place and does the new product avoid weakening existing controls?

Changes may be required to provide safeguards such as encrypting backup media, limiting user access to specific areas, or even changing the programming design to reduce the likelihood of data entry crashing the program. Other changes may be required of the firewalls to open specific ports for user interaction.

Information security will also review the project product's functions in terms of how they interact with other IT systems. This is to ensure they do not open any security "back doors" to allow other problems to enter. Information security changes that are added to the original design can be cheaply included in the development.

[D] Ergonometric and Safety

Does the new system incorporate within its input and output the company-required ergonometric standards to ensure that all employees can use it? Does it involve repetitive motions that might cause permanent injuries? Is user-operated equipment placed at the optimal height and angle to avoid awkward reaching? Is the project solution designed to avoid repetitive motions?

[E] Help Desk

The help desk's requirements for the project reflect the tools and training required to support this product from the first day it is installed. Ensure there are instructions for the help (service) desk so they can support it during implementation and eventual end-user operation. They may also have suggestions to improve the flow of information on end-user displays. The help desk needs copies of all end-user documentation and must attend each of the end-user training classes. The IT team supporting this new product will provide technical tips for repairing the most common end user errors.

[F] Capacity Planning

This team seeks to slide new IT systems into available servers, SANs, and data communication networks without purchasing new equipment. It is not always possible, but someone must ensure the proper utilization of resources. Once the final product is completed, the capacity planners must again examine it to determine its expected resource requirements during its peak utilization. For example, financial software's peak utilization may be during the annual closing of the company's accounts.

Does the project use energy-efficient CPUs (central processing units) and help to soak up any existing excess CPU capacity? Does it provide for the archiving of data to reduce the amount of online storage required? Does it use a virtualized CPU instance? Do the data have a retention or archive date to avoid clogging disk storage with rarely used data?

If any equipment is replaced, is its proper disposal included in the plan? Is new equipment acquired with an eye toward its eventual disposal?

§ 13.08 MODELING YOUR REQUIREMENTS

[A] Overview

Sometimes words fail to adequately convey an idea. A prototype provides the look and feel of how the requirements shape up in the final product. As something tangible, it will stimulate discussion with everyone involved with the requirements process. A prototype is a hollow shell with the user interfaces mocked-up. It is a visual rough draft that communicates or validates one or more important concepts in a project. Prototypes help to break the ice with stakeholders, verify that a task is either possible or working as intended, or just used to help muck through confusing requirements.

Prototypes are a risk reduction tool. By assembling the "first" of something, a lot can be learned about customer requirements and the resources to create the project's object. As with every other tool, it has its advantages and drawbacks.

Prototypes take time and technical expertise to construct, and they sometimes seem to take on a life of their own. There is a point when it seems "real enough" to show to stakeholders. The temptation is to add too many working features. This defeats the purpose, which is to build something that can be discarded because once stakeholders see it they may want something entirely different.

COMMENT

A problem with prototypes is that stakeholders see the mock-up and believe the project is close to completion. This illusion pressures the project timeline to decrease because "so much is already completed." Often the code to create the prototype shell must be discarded as the way it is structured violates good programming standards.

[B] How Prototypes Aid Requirements Gathering

Prototypes clarify the expectations of stakeholders when developing requirements or demonstrating project progress. They can clear up misunderstandings and enable stakeholders to better understand the nature of the work being done. This provides several benefits:

A. Prototypes can demonstrate that a particular requirement is feasible. They also help to determine how long it takes to create the product or how much it may cost (resources required).
B. A prototype can be used to verify vague requirements with the project sponsor by stating, "Is this what you meant?"
C. Prototyping enables a team to verify project progress. For example, building a temporary structure that simulates all of the required interactions between software modules verifies that a requirement is fulfilled.
D. Prototyping helps to ferret out requirements that exist in the mind of stakeholders but haven't been communicated to the business analyst or team members.

However, the primary drawback of prototyping is the time and expenses of creating a prototype. Project sponsors are anxious for the project to begin. They may see prototyping as an unnecessary delay and waste of precious money. See Policy ITP-13-2 Prototyping IT Projects Policy as an example.

POLICY ITP-13-2.   Prototyping IT Projects Policy

Policy #:	ITP-13-2	**Effective:**	04/01/13	**Page #:**	1 of N
Subject:	Prototyping IT Projects Policy				

1.0 PURPOSE

This policy establishes guidelines for those instances where prototyping of an IT project may be appropriate.

2.0 SCOPE

The policy applies to IT project prototypes requiring more than 20 hours to create and/or more than $5,000.

3.0 POLICY

Prototyping is best suited for sharpening system requirements that are not well defined by the project sponsor, or for choosing between competing alternatives. It allows for the visualization and discussion required for quick systems development. All too often users request something they cannot define, or cannot see how changes will satisfy their needs. It is also useful for selecting aesthetic requirements since it is difficult to imagine how they will fit until seen as they will be presented to the customer.

Prototypes are valuable tools for demonstrating what the technical team believes the sponsor wants. However, large or extensive prototypes are expensive to create. Also, they are built to illustrate a point and are not suitable for incorporation into an IT production system. Project managers must be aware that people will confuse a prototype with a final product review. They must be constantly reminded that they are looking at a mock-up intended for better understanding project requirements. Therefore, the project team must expect that most or all of a prototype will be discarded.

   A. **Prototype Guidelines.** Use prototypes:
      1. As a tool for determining the cost to accomplish something. For example, the time and materials required to replace an existing desktop computer with a new unit and the latest software. This provides a standard for estimating the time and cost to replace every desktop unit in the company. The same could be true for patching existing units.
      2. To create examples of a user interface for project sponsor approval.
        a. Report mock-ups
        b. Web pages examples (for approval of "look and feel")
        c. Data entry screens (for logical flow)
      3. To model aesthetic requirements to judge their appearance once they are all sitting together.
   B. **Prototype Approval.** The CIO approves all project prototypes requiring more than 20 hours to create and/or more than $5,000. The cost and time required to build IT prototypes must be included in the project budget.
   C. **Prototype Justification.** Four types of prototype are approved for requirements collection:

1. Prototypes to demonstrate that a particular requirement is feasible. They can also be used to determine how long it takes to create the product or how much it may cost (resources required).
2. A prototype to improve communications, such as creating a model and then asking the project sponsor, "Is this what you meant?"
3. Prototyping that enables a team to verify project progress. For example, building a temporary structure that simulates all of the required interactions between software modules to verify that a requirement is fulfilled.
4. Prototyping that helps to ferret out requirements that exist in the mind of stakeholders but haven't been communicated to the project manager or team members.

4.0 REVISION HISTORY

Date	Revision #	Description of Change
04/01/13	1.0	Initial creation.

5.0 INQUIRIES

Direct inquiries about this policy to:

George Jenkins, CIO
Our Company, Inc.
2900 Corporate Drive
Columbus, OH 43215

Voice: 614-555-1234
Fax: 614-555-1235
E-mail: gjenkins@company.com

Revision #:	1.0	Supersedes:	N/A	Date:	04/01/13

[C] Prototype Techniques

Prototypes take many shapes and forms. Some tools could be labeled as prototypes that aren't necessarily perceived that way normally, such as screen shots or screen sketches. Several of the prototype tools are:

A. **Storyboard.** The least expensive and quickest prototype to make is a storyboard. Storyboards use a series of pictures to present a flow of events to a stakeholder. They request stakeholder feedback as to a program's function. This can be done differently at various stages of the product's life cycle. Several methods are:

At the initial meeting between the business analyst and the stakeholder, the basic vision of the project's objective can be created by talking through the functionality of the product, which can be sketched briefly by the business analyst. As the design team's work progresses, a more formal storyboard can be created. This time, the flow will be provided by the design team and the client will use the storyboard as a meaningful way to understand the features proposed for the project.

After completing each milestone, update the storyboard to display completed panels, as they will appear in the final user interface. For the Web browser example, the same set of Web pages could be utilized with screen shots substituted for concept art or text.

1. Drawing on a white board.
2. Sketch on one or more pages of paper.
3. A simple set of linked html pages.

B. **First Article in a Run.** Another method of prototyping is the unit test. This is a subset of the tests written to validate software requirements. Unit tests can be part of a rolling acceptance test, or a confirmation that a certain part of the software is indeed working as the project sponsor intended.

Consider this scenario: a client is coming in to see how well your new imaging software displays .ppm files. Your team members have done such a great job that .png, .jpg, and .gif files are all loading without a problem on each of their individual computers. All of the codes could be combined and demonstrated all at the same time. However, if a code has not been tested working together, it is likely that one piece will break the others, and your client will end up seeing a large number of problems.

C. **Simulation.** A simulation is where the business analyst creates something that has the appearance and basic functionality of the final product but lacks its inner working. An example might be an accounting system, which would show the layout of the various user interactions screens and examples of reports. However, there is little logic behind the scenes. The goal of this simulation might be to assist the project sponsor in visualizing what the finished product may look like. Through the sponsor's interactions with the simulation, product features may be further identified.

Simulations are time consuming to create. They also are expensive through their use of resources. They are best suited to the introduction of a new product where the sponsor does not have any experience with similar items, or where the sponsor cannot adequately communicate his or her requirements.

A Web browser simulation could be accomplished on internal servers verifying each unit test and then more complex tests run by team members. Being off the Internet frees it from disconnections, page errors, and other problems—until, of course, the simulation or unit test calls for it.

14

PROJECT MANAGEMENT: GETTING IT OUT ON TIME

§ 14.01 OVERVIEW

[A] Purpose and Scope

Project management is the management of uncertainty. It begins with a series of analyses and progresses through decomposing large tasks into their component parts, which are analyzed and shaped into a plan. Project management is to a great degree the art of people management, as people are a project manager's primary tools. If someone moves a lever on a machine tool, they are a machinist. However, if they direct the people who work the tools in concert, they are a manager.

Project management is something everyone practices whether we realize it or not. Imagine planning a vacation. There was a destination to select and, for most people, a limit of how much could be spent. There was a time set to arrive at the airport, specific items to pack (a parka is not needed at the beach!), hotel and car reservations at the destination, and on and on. This scenario has all of the elements of a basic project plan.

The destination was the project's "goal," the budget was a resource constraint on activities, and traveling was a part of the action steps. With the goal in mind, a series of actions was identified, sequenced, and executed to successfully arrive at the vacation spot and to return. Resources, such as money and vacation time from work, were allocated and used to complete the project. An alternative to this scenario would be to decide at this moment to take a vacation, put everyone in the car, and drive off. Given the lack of preparation, it is doubtful that this would be a very happy experience.

Project management is something that everyone encounters every day. Have you ever driven past a construction site? Are the workers busy or idle? Idle workers cost the builder money. How is the structure completed without bankrupting the builder's company in the process? If the workers are present and there are not any materials to use, they still must be paid for the day. If the materials are there but the workers are not, the materials may be damaged by the weather.

Another big user of project management is the military. They frequently organize the movement of large amounts of equipment and people, ensuring fuel, food, and water are available along the route. They station mechanics and tow trucks so that vehicles may be fueled or repaired at various points along the journey. As an added challenge, this movement may be through mountains or a jungle, or alongside a hostile population.

In short, project management is nothing new and quite widely used in government and business. From these examples, the essential elements can be identified:

A. **Sponsor.** Someone is authorizing this work and has a stake in its success. The sponsor is the project's "protector," keeping others from pulling it too far off course. The sponsor (or customer) is the one who "hired" the project manager, provides funding, and approves the bills.

The sponsor ensures that the project has the resources necessary for success. The sponsor is kept informed of the project's progress and of any major decisions made about the project. Some sponsors seek to be actively involved with the project and others want to be left alone until it is finished.

B. **Goal.** What is this project trying to achieve? A clear vision of the project's goal makes it easier for everyone involved in the project to participate in its success. In the case of the vacation, the family can visualize the fun they will have at the beach and pack their own suitcases accordingly. Establishing a clearly defined goal is an important step in planning a project. A project creates *something*, such as a product or service. If the Project Manager cannot visualize the goal, it will be hard for him to explain it to others. Goals must be specific and measurable.

Often the goal is expanded as a list of success factors or requirements that must be achieved. For a data processing project, this might include reducing response time by half a second, the ability to search a specific Web site, or requiring all technical documentation to be submitted before payment. A list of specific, measurable criteria is essential for clarifying what is often a vaguely worded goal.

C. **Scope.** Project scope defines the specific who's, what's, where's, and timing of the project to the best knowledge of the project team. The project team must take into account constraints when defining the scope. How broad is this project? What are its boundaries? What departments are affected? For the vacation, one boundary and constraint was the amount of money available to pay for it. Other boundaries include the number of vacation days available and the capacity of the suitcases. All projects have boundaries whether they are obvious or not.

Establishing project boundaries reduces the likelihood of the project drifting off course and costing more than expected. Having a good handle on scope is necessary when estimating project resources and project schedules.

D. **Assumptions and Risks.** It is rare for a decision to be made with all of the necessary information at hand. This is especially difficult when writing plans for future action. Throughout the planning process, decisions are made based on assumptions. Often an assumption must be made as to when a specific resource will be available or how something will work in order to continue with the planning process. Maintain a list of each assumption and the decisions it affects. Review the list periodically with the sponsor. The project plan will be more realistic if errors in the assumptions are caught early.

Every project has risks. It is important to identify and periodically review the significant project risks. When identifying risks, include with each risk the conditions that trigger the risk, any risk mitigating actions that can be taken, and when the risk no longer affects the project.

E. **Start date and time.** Every project has a point in time where it begins. Sometimes it is considered started when the boss says to set up a project to do something. Sometimes the start date is set in advance (e.g., beginning the project on the first day of the next fiscal year). However it is established, a project has not been properly launched until it has written goals and scope statements approved by the project sponsor. They act as anchors to keep a project from drifting off course.

F. **End date and time.** A project must have an end. Sometimes the end is when the goal is achieved. Other times, an end is declared and whatever is completed must be delivered. There are two ways to establish an end date. The first (and often unrealistic) way is for the executives to mandate a completion date. However, sometimes this date is selected to meet a legal requirement and is out of their control. The second way is to develop a project plan that, based on the tasks, resources, and time estimates, indicates when the project should be completed and present that plan to executives for approval. Like most things in life, a project "takes as long as it takes," no matter what date executives may select.

G. **Resources.** Projects use resources to achieve their goals. Resources may be skilled workers for a construction company or cash for the vacation. Resources may be vehicles, fuel, food, and water for the military exercise. Resources are any item or person used to complete a project task. Identifying, quantifying, and coordinating resources is an important part of project planning. Resource requirements overlooked in planning will not be in the budget or project timeline. Such a project will assuredly go "off course."

COMMENT

Each resource has its own level of efficiency. Be specific when describing a resource. Using highly skilled resources, like master carpenters, will shorten a project but will add cost. Using an apprentice carpenter on a non-critical task may take longer, but be more cost effective.

H. **Predecessors.** Predecessors are tasks that must be completed before another task can begin, similar to prerequisite courses in school. Students cannot sign up for Algebra II until they complete Algebra I. A PC technician cannot load software onto a computer before it is purchased and delivered. The chain of tasks and their predecessors make up the length of time a project is expected to last.

COMMENT

It is recommended that the Project Manager use some sort of project management software to organize project tasks into a plan. This software will automatically draw Gantt and CPM network charts, level resources, and recalculate the project schedule every time a date changes or a task is completed.

[B]   Critical Policies to Develop Based on This Chapter

Using the material discussed in this chapter, you will be able to create the following policies:

A. Project plan requirements
B. Project documents used to manage a project
C. Policy on frequency and format of project meetings
D. Project execution procedures
E. Project close out procedures

Policies should always be developed based on the local situation. Successful managers cannot issue appropriate guidance if the policies are written with another company's situation or location in mind.

§ 14.02   PROJECT MANAGEMENT FUNDAMENTALS

[A]   Project Definition

Start at the beginning, the project's origination. Someone might think that an activity as expensive and important to a company as a project would include a formal beginning. Someone might think that, but often it is not the case. In many companies, a project is verbally assigned by the sponsor—no formal goals are established; no clear description of the end product is given; no discussion identifying the resources required. There is just a single sentence directive to make it happen.

However a challenge is assigned, the first thing to do is to ensure that the project manager's vision of the project is the same as the sponsor's. To do this, the project manager recaps notes concerning the project into a statement of the project's goals, scope, budget, start time, end time, and authority. All management parties involved must agree to these items, including user management and the project manager.

COMMENT

> Projects are created to solve a business problem or to implement a business strategy. A project description should state the problem, how it harms the company, how it will be solved, and the benefits derived from solving it.

A clear definition of a project's goal is essential. Sometimes the sponsor is intentionally vague. The sponsor may not be sure what the result should look like. In this situation, the project manager should help the sponsor to shape ideas and clearly define what the project is to achieve. Often, the sponsor is trying to solve a specific business problem. Keep asking the sponsor about the functions and features required in the product. Ask questions that begin with general subjects and then gradually narrow down to specific issues. Dig out the details. From this conversation, develop a list of requirements or "criteria of success" that describes the end object in some detail. It may help the sponsor to visualize the result if the project manager creates mock-up floor plans, computer screens, and reports.

All projects have boundaries. The project scope helps to define what is within the bounds of a project. Everything not detailed in the project scope is outside of the boundaries and should not be included in the project. For example, a data entry program is not intended to manage the controls on a building's air conditioning. It is not intended to run the monthly accounting reports that reconcile all accounts. Its only intended purpose is to enable the entry of data into a specific system.

Project scope should include such things as:

A. This program is to support the Dayton Assembly Plant. (No other facility.)

B. The data entry system will support the entry of Department 69's scrap material information. (No other department's requirements need to be accommodated.)

C. The data entry program will be written in Java, for use on PCs running LINUX. (This precludes using other languages or operating system versions.)

D. The data entry program will connect to the AIX-based server via the corporate intranet. (This means the program will not use any other server or connection methodology.)

E. Systems installation will be transparent to users. (No downtime during normal working hours will be permitted.)

The project goals describe how the project's end product will look and function. Remember, *goals must be specific and measurable*. The project manager should create a memo of understanding that summarizes the project goals, including the criteria for success and the project scope, and then present it to the sponsor for approval. Before doing anything on this project, the project manager must clearly understand what the objective is and is not. This document synchronizes the project manager's vision of the project with the sponsor's vision. As the project progresses, "scope creep" will appear—where executives want to add features to the project, gradually spinning it out of control. The signed memo acts as the anchor to reduce the likelihood that this will happen.

[B] What a Project Is Not

A project is used to create something that is unique. Milking a cow three times a day is not a project. It is an ongoing operation. Yes, the changes in the weather, the cow's attitude, the farmer's attitude, and the smell of the barn all make each milking a unique experience; however, essentially the same resources are used repeatedly to achieve the same goal.

If someone wanted to be argumentative, the discussion of what is or is not a project could go on for hours. In an IT setting, this means that making backup tapes is not a project. Answering the service desk telephone is not a project, but developing a new data entry program is a project because it has unique tasks with start and end dates.

Projects do not have a defined size. For example, the department's annual barbeque may only take one person to plan and execute, but it still is a project. Some of the tasks include making a shopping list, starting the coals at the right time, etc. It has distinct start and end dates. The next time there is a barbeque; likely different resources will be used. "Personal" project planning is primarily a way to reduce the likelihood of missing an important item or appointment.

For most IT people, a project is something larger than a family cookout. It involves creating something that is complex, requires assistance from others, and is completed within a set time frame. Well-run projects add value to the company and poorly run projects drain cash with little return.

Overall, a project consists of four major areas:

A. **Project definition.** The goals, scope, resource availability, assumptions, and risks define the project. The project definition phase lays the foundation on which the project plan is built.
B. **Project planning.** An action plan is assembled to create what was described in the project definition. A good plan can be executed by a mediocre project manager—a bad plan is living hell from day one!
C. **Project management.** A military maxim is that all well-made battle plans go out the window after the first bullet is fired. Plans may look easy on paper, but bringing them to fruition is difficult. This phase involves executing the project plan and ensuring the end product is true to its defined requirements. Executing a plan requires agility, good

information, and the ability to work through adverse situations on short notice.

D. **Project closeout.** When the project is completed, the resources must be reallocated, the budget closed, and the project documentation gathered for later reference.

[C]   The Project Manager

A project's success depends on many factors, but the key element is the careful selection of a project manager. Project managers wear many hats:

A. Leader of team (not a manager—a project manager must be a leader).
B. Negotiator with team members' home department managers.
C. Part-time accountant to track project budget.
D. All-around cheerleader and advocate of project's success. If the project manager does not believe in the project's success and work to convince others of it, then everyone will know the project is doomed. Workers will abandon a doomed project.

A project manager does not succeed by writing the code or turning a screwdriver. Success is achieved by coordinating the efforts of others to accomplish these tasks. A project manager lost in the minutia of details will not have the time to focus the efforts of others. Most technical professionals lack the administrative and interpersonal skills needed to function effectively in this position. With a bit of mentoring, they can rise to the challenge.

Selecting a project manager is the joint responsibility of the sponsor and the IT Manager. Choosing a candidate requires knowledge of attributes that have been proven to be universally successful. The only testimonial a person really needs is a successful track record with the company. However, a person selected as project manager for the first time requires special consideration.

[D]   Creating the Project Plan

With a top-notch project manager assigned and a clear vision of the project's objective, it is time to begin charting a course for the project's completion. Based on the criteria for success, the project manager has an idea of what is required to get from where the company is to where it wants to be. Based on an evaluation of the project goals, determine the technical expertise necessary to successfully complete the project and invite representatives from affected areas to a project-planning meeting. Included with the invitation should be a copy of the project's approved goals and scope. The people invited may be the ones who will work on the project or they may be subject experts who will help to define the skill set needed for the project. A representative of the people who will be using the final product should always be invited.

The planning meeting follows a simple format. First, the project's goals should be discussed to determine whether there are any major implied tasks that have not been foreseen. These could extend the project's timeline. Next, the scope should be discussed to ensure it is in line with the goals and addresses potential problem areas.

Now is the time to build a plan! It is a long journey from a blank piece of paper to a well-considered project plan. The first step is to draft an initial plan to build a framework for action and to fill in as many steps as possible. Once the initial plan is on paper, the remaining details can be identified. There are many ways to do this. Consider these basic approaches to drafting an initial project plan:

A. **Brainstorming.** This is a useful approach when the project flow is not immediately obvious. It is most useful when major parallel efforts obscure a clear vision of the plan, or the project is something the company has never done before.

   One effective brainstorming method is to use "sticky notes" and a large whiteboard. Each sticky note is equal to a task on the project plan. Anyone can call out an action necessary to the plan, such as "build the data entry screen," "identify field edits," or "coordinate with the database administrators." The tasks do not need to be in any particular order. One person is assigned to capture the ideas onto large sticky notes and attach them to the whiteboard as they are called out. A second person moderates the discussion and keeps the conversation focused and flowing. All ideas are posted and no idea is criticized.

   The team next selects group names and then indicates in which group each task logically belongs. Duplicate or overlapping tasks are consolidated or clarified. Group names might include "planning," "testing," "coding," and "documentation."

   Finally, the tasks and groups are organized into a logical process flow from the beginning of the project to the end. The flow specifies which processes are predecessors to what tasks and represents the initial project plan. All of this information should then be written down and/ or entered into project management software.

B. **Left to right, block diagram.** If the project is for something the team is familiar with, a list of tasks from start to finish can be made. A whiteboard should be used since there will be some modifications as the planning progresses. Left to right means that the tasks will be iden-tified in the approximate order in which they will appear on the plan. It is not unusual for additional tasks to come to mind that are in previous sections. Capture all of this detail to side step as many problems during development as possible.

C. **Top down.** This approach starts with a very general task overview and then breaks each task down repeatedly until the lowest level tasks are identified. When dealing with a new idea, start by breaking the goals down one level at a time. Consider a five-block diagram where each block represents a phase of the project: "Define, Analyze, Code, Test, and Implement." Under each block, list the actions required to achieve these project goals. Next, break each block into its major components. On the lowest level of the breakdown (use as many as needed), identify any additional tasks. Then, organize the tasks into a logical flow and eliminate overlapping actions.

D. **Straw man.** Based on the project manager's experience, draft the project plan including as many tasks as the project manager can identify. Use previous project plans to help flesh it out. Present this plan to the group and ask them to critique its overall flow, content, etc. This approach is not for the thin-skinned as its purpose is to generate discussion by questioning every inch of the plan. It works best if the project manager already has a long-term positive project management relationship with the group.

For some people, this is the quickest way to develop a plan. When confronted with a blank page, many people simply stare at it unsure where to begin. On the other hand, if the team does not feel a personal stake in the project's success, they may rubber stamp the plan without suggesting any improvements.

With the tasks formed into a basic plan, the project manager should write a brief paragraph about each task to describe the meaning of the task name. For instance, if the task is to "build a data entry screen," it might be described as:

Write a Java program to build a visual screen to accept the 10 data fields on the Order Entry form. Edit every field for length and format, and validate against a table of acceptable values as required.

The project manager includes as much detail as necessary to describe the goals and scope for the desired task. These time consuming narratives will come in handy later when assigning tasks to team members. Some tasks, like the example on Order Entry, will highlight additional requirements. If the Order Entry screen is to validate against a table of acceptable values (such as in a drop-down box), then a way for someone to update the table must be provided. How is this table to be originally populated? When the narratives have been written, they should be sent with the plan to the planning team members, and a meeting scheduled to discuss it.

At the next meeting, each task should be discussed and validated. Discuss where the tasks most logically fit on the chart. This exercise, while tedious, should weed out most of the overlapping requirements and fill in any requirements that have been overlooked.

COMMENT

Ideally, each task should result in a deliverable object. It should be something that can be examined such as a document, piece of code, or the installation of equipment. Also, each task should be fit within a project reporting period such as one week or less. Too finite of task breakdown will diminish the individual's creativity and morale.

[E] Adding Resources to the Plan

Up to this point, the project planning has been all theoretical. Adding resources to the plan throws the cold water of reality right into its face! A lack of resource availability when it is needed is a common factor in project delays. Highly technical resources are scarce. Often they are lined up at the beginning of the project and asked to be available for certain days. As the project moves forward, a small delay here and a brief setback there and pretty soon the entire resource plan will be askew.

Before estimating time on the project, detail the technical and business expertise level expected from each position. Technical skills can be identified by job title, such as "programmer." Level of expertise can be indicated by a title modifier, such as "senior" and "junior." (Some people prefer the suffixes I, II, III, or IV since being identified as a "junior" might be viewed negatively.) Assigning a task to an unqualified person can create delays and mistakes, while assigning the same task to an overqualified person wastes resources. When time permits, the manager should consider using project tasks to develop or enhance team members' skills.

Together with the team, add a time estimate and the resources required for each task. Break tasks into their components until they are small enough to estimate the time and resources required. When allocating task worker-hours, the project manager should note the worker's past record for finishing in the time allowed. The project manager should check with the assigned worker to confirm that the time allowed is reasonable. If not, a different time allowance should be negotiated. In addition, contingency time should be added, if needed, based on the worker's past performance record. If there is no previous record, time allowed should be more liberal. Ten percent above the original estimate is not unreasonable. The project manager should recalculate the project time based on this new information, rearranging the schedule as needed. When the project management software has analyzed this data, the project manager should complete the final staffing plans for the project.

[F] Essential Estimating Factors

Estimating completion dates and the work-hours required become more accurate as the project advances. Unfortunately, it is most helpful to have this level of accuracy early in the project. If the organization has previously completed a similar project, the actual times required to complete tasks should be used to build time estimates.

COMMENT

Time Estimation Pitfalls

- Research has shown that project members who estimate their own performance for completion times are consistently optimistic. Add 30 percent or more as contingency time to address problems that arise.
- If a worker perceives that a task assigned to take three weeks will only require one week, then he is more likely to do something else for the first two weeks and then address the task. If the worker then realizes that the one-week estimate was too low, he will blame the project manager!
- To reduce the likelihood of workers misjudging the time required for a task, always schedule tasks tightly. If a task has slack time, move the due date that much closer and remove the slack. Only allow the worker the time required to perform the task.

Factors that affect the estimate accuracy and ways to minimize this distortion are:

A. **Project size.** The project size can affect the time and effort needed for completion. This in turn can affect the amount of calendar time needed and the final cost. Businesses exist in a very fluid environment. The longer the project takes, the more likely it is that the business sponsor will require additional changes. Changes that will be required for a usable product will also take additional time to install, which can justifiably lead to more changes. This is called the "snowball effect."

To reduce this possibility, projects should be as small as possible. Changes made after project completion will then be maintenance changes to a tested system already in operation. This is preferable to making the same changes to a yet-to-be-debugged product. Large projects should be completed in phases with each phase ending in a working part of the product. Projects do not need to be an all-or-nothing affair.

B. **Project complexity.** The more project variables there are to manage, the more time and effort the project will take to complete. Complex projects are more difficult to estimate. They should be cut down into smaller modules for easier and more accurate estimation. Complex projects should have a large contingency budget to compensate for the uncertainty.

C. **Personnel productivity.** This is a universal problem with IT departments. In the IT data entry unit, the output minus the errors defines the person's productivity. If the source documents are simply input, the system for judging a worker's output is simple and fairly accurate. This is not the case with the systems and programming production estimates.

A systems analyst's past performance can be a gauge for estimating future performance for similar tasks. The difference in the output of programmers has been estimated to be as high as 20:1 between the best and the worst. A person's activity level should never be confused with his or her results.

When using in-house employees on the team, the project manager must take a hard look at their expertise. Some companies are willing to pay for good contract programmers, but not willing to pay competitive wages for better in-house programmers. A poorly performing programmer can reduce the group's total output. Consider contract programmers to help raise the expertise of company employees by mixing in-house and contract programmers in the project.

D. **Resources available.** Resources must have quality, but they must also be available in quantity. There is no assurance that the people promised for the project will be available when needed. The longer the duration of the project, the greater this problem can become. People leave, retire, are promoted, or are reassigned to other higher-priority projects.

If possible, the project manager should make sure funds are budgeted to hire outside contractors. It is better to have this money in reserve than to ask for it mid-project and be rejected.

E. **Resource technology.** The physical and technical resources available to the project team affect the time estimate as well. These items can include:

1. **Work area.** The team's work area can affect the productivity estimate. Is the project team housed together in a private area or spread out into different locations in noisy offices?

2. **Programming tools.** Are the programming tools familiar to the staff? If the tools are new, will training be available in time to be effective? Are upgrades or new versions planned during the project development?

3. **Computer hardware.** Are the team's workstations fast and efficient or old and slow? Are notebook computers needed? Will everything be in place and ready to use when the notebooks arrive? What about e-mail and voice mail accounts?

4. **Project management software.** Always use project management software. It will reduce the amount of administrative time and effort required.

When working through the project plan development process, the project managers should determine the level of detail desired in the plan. Should there be a single item for "Develop a Data Entry Program" or should it be a heading with task items under it for "Analyze," "Code," "Test," "Document," and "Deliver the Completed Package"?

Estimating time is tough. If possible, use the experience from past projects to estimate how long a step might take. Time estimates often depend on the resource. The difference in time it takes to accomplish tasks with specific resources can be compared to the time it takes to walk, run, or swim a quarter mile. Moving a person a quarter mile may be the task, but what a difference the resource of "movement choice" makes.

Create a resource calendar to indicate the availability of each resource. Be sure to include all company holidays. Ask prospective team members about their vacation/time-off plans. Include this information on the resource calendar for that person. Unfortunately, at the time the calendar is being established, some vacation plans may not yet have been scheduled and key people may already be lined up for other projects. The longer the project will be, the harder this factor will be to control. So again, the plan at this stage is still theoretical. Add to the growing list of assumptions the names of the resources expected to be available for this project and how much of their time will be needed. They may be full-time, half-time, or available on demand to help with a "spot" issue or whatever is needed.

At this point, tasks have been identified, resources assigned to each one, and an estimation has been made of the time required to complete each task. Assumptions have been stated as to which resources will be available and when.

Unfortunately, really good workers can be in short supply. It is not unusual for managers to "overbook" their best people to conflicting tasks. To smooth out the plan based on resource availability, use the resource leveling function in the project management software. This function will review every task and identify the resources overcommitted on the project. This will help the project manager to change work assignments, rearrange the sequence of events, or change their durations to smooth out the conflicts. This capability however depends on an accurate resource availability calendar.

Print the project plan diagram and highlight the time required to complete the longest path through the plan. This is the critical path. Most project management software will identify the critical path automatically. Reducing the time spent on tasks along the critical path will reduce the length of time required for the project—unless the changes create a new critical path!

Once again, review the plan with the project team. Review every assumption used to resolve resource conflicts and to reduce the critical path. Are they all still valid? This is the last review before meeting with the sponsor again. Make it good.

Next, roll up the costs identified with each task in terms of hardware, software, consultants, etc. These costs should be detailed on a month-by-month projection to show the cash flow necessary to sustain the project.

[G]   Hardware and Software Delivery

Identify the required dates for the project's software and hardware delivery. Use backward planning to place orders in time to have the items in-house when needed. Contact the vendor a week before the due date to ensure the material will arrive on time. Take appropriate action if it will be late. Key items should have extra lead-time planned to avoid project delays.

COMMENT

Backward planning means to assign due dates to tasks starting with the last task in the chain and working back to the first one. For example, if a company needs PCs ready to install software on the 30th of the month, then they must be in place on the 28th. Therefore, since they must be unpacked the week before (21st), they must be ordered two weeks before that (7th) and the purchasing document must be sent to the sponsor the week before that (1st of the month).

Delays may be caused for any of the following reasons:

A. Custom-fabricated hardware.
B. Custom-purchased software.
C. Shipping problems because of distance (delays are more likely when items are imported).
D. Items that have to be scheduled for processing (e.g., custom-printed forms).
E. Plants closed for vacation, holidays, or because of a strike.
F. Seasonal availability (such as buying new servers at the beginning of the calendar year when many budgets are open for the new year).
G. New model popularity, which may lead to scarcity and full price purchases.

Items should not be delivered too far in advance. If bulky items come in before they are needed, there could be a storage problem, incurring an unnecessary expenditure. IT hardware ordered too far in advance could become obsolete before installation or their costs could be lowered. IT hardware often comes with a manufacturer's warranty. This limited time normally starts when it is delivered. Also, there may be a monthly hardware or software maintenance fee that likewise begins after delivery.

> ### COMMENT
>
> One nervous project manager was so afraid that his project budget would be cut that he purchased all the equipment the project required as soon as the project was approved. Due to programming delays, it was 18 months before the timekeeping project systems were ready for rollout to the customer. Meanwhile, the one-year warranty had expired on the equipment that had yet to be unpacked! The project budget had to assume the burden for repair costs for any dead-on-arrival equipment. Even worse, most of the equipment consisted of PCs. By waiting 18 months to purchase the PCs, the equipment's capabilities would have almost doubled!

[H] Sponsor's Sign-off

Prepare a project review packet for the sponsor's approval. Schedule a team meeting where the project plan and budget are reviewed with the sponsor. Walk through the plan step by step and the budget item by item. Obtain written approval and a start date (which is usually dictated by resource availability).

The packet should contain a:

A. Cover sheet with an executive summary explaining how long the project will take and how much it will cost. A recap of the project's goal and scope should be included.
B. Printed project plan with Gantt chart.
C. Budget to complete the project.
D. List of assumptions made when developing the project plan and budget.
E. List of the internal resources required to finish the project plan within the time stated.

With a bit of good luck, the sponsor's adjustments to the plan will be minor and the project can begin. With bad luck, the sponsor will slash the budget, slash the timeline, and threaten the project manager if the project is late. Such is a project manager's lot!

§ 14.03 IMPORTANT ELEMENTS OF THE PROJECT PLAN

[A] Overview

There are tools that will help to identify and avoid the various management pitfalls that may plague a project as the plan unfolds. These adjunct plans are very useful for small project plans but are essential for large projects. No project flows smoothly. The best of them are roller-coaster rides of problems and successes. The rest of them start as a disaster and speed rapidly downhill from there.

[B]   Risk Assessment

A risk assessment looks at the project plan and identifies those areas where something might go wrong. It could be an incorrect assumption. It could be a resource that is not available until weeks after its scheduled availability date. It could be overlooked systems requirements that mean additional tasks for the schedule not in the budget or timeline.

A risk assessment is a review of the project in light of what could go wrong, how likely it is to occur, and how damaging it would be if it did happen. Based on these factors, a numerical score is assigned to identify those risks that should be reduced through a mitigation plan.

Certainties are things we know will happen. The sun will rise tomorrow. The risk of this not happening is zero percent. Risks dwell in the area of uncertainty. Risks are things that may or may not occur. Although anticipating good things is very uplifting personally, a project's risk plan mostly focuses on the risk of negative events. Making a risk assessment is easier for a pessimistic person.

COMMENT

Positive risks are "opportunities." An opportunity is realized when the project manager takes steps for it to occur. For example, saving project time and cost by purchasing a software component instead of the team creating it. Opportunities are evaluated similarly to negative risks with rating the potential benefit, the likelihood it will be realized, etc.

Risks have their own characteristics, such as the likelihood of occurring. A meteor may one day fall from the sky and hit someone on the head, but the likelihood of that is very, very small. The likelihood of someone attempting to add on to the project's scope is fairly high. The likelihood of a risk occurring must be viewed within the context of the project.

A second risk characteristic is the impact of an event if it actually occurs. In the case of the meteor, the impact would be catastrophic. Normally something this dangerous would make someone want to walk around with a steel plate on his or her head to ward off falling space rocks. But given its low likelihood, the person would soon tire of the plate and it would be discarded.

COMMENT

Some risks are global, such as a project that is executing during the annual influenza season, will execute across a fiscal year boundary or that underlying software (such as compilers or database management systems) may change. Some risks are specific, such as the possibility of late delivery of urgent equipment.

[C]   Organizing a Project Risk Analysis

The Risk Assessment form in Worksheet 14-1 is a good place to start building a project's risk analysis. This form will be the basis of the following discussion. The form consists of the following sections:

A. Identification section
    1. **Task**. This is the name or identifier of the task under evaluation. This also may refer to a group of tasks or to all tasks under a milestone.
    2. **Risk**. This is a description of the risk associated with the task.
B. Quantification section
    1. **Likelihood.** An estimate of the probability that the risk will become a reality. Some risks are very real, but very unlikely to occur.
    2. **Impact.** How badly the event would damage the project's scope, budget, or timeline if it occurred.
    3. **Warning.** How much warning the team would have before this event occurred. In the case of a hurricane, someone could monitor the weather reports for days and plan accordingly. In the case of an earthquake, the team would likely have no warning before it struck.
    4. **Score.** A numeric risk score based on the previous three values.

The scales for Likelihood and Impact are from 1 to 10, with 1 as extremely unlikely and 10 as a sure thing. Any consistent numbering system can be used for the scores, but if it includes a zero as a value, then that entire risk will be scored as zero.

The Warning column is scored the reverse from the other two. It is also rated from 1 (a lot of warning) to 10 (no warning). A risk typically accompanied with a lot of warning should be rated very low. A risk that could occur with little or no warning should be rated high since the project team would not have time to react.

A risk's Score is determined by multiplying the three columns (Likelihood, Impact, and Warning) together. The higher the score, the greater the attention that must be paid to that risk.

The Score is the key to the analysis. Once all of the risks are scored, the entire spreadsheet should be sorted based on this column in descending order. This brings the risks with the highest score to the top. At some point in the list,

WORKSHEET 14-1. Project Risk Management Plan

Project Risk Management Plan

WBS # / Description	Quantification				Damage		Trigger	Risk Event Status	Mitigation Actions	Assigned To	Date	Comments
	Likelihood	Impact	Warning	Score	$ at Stake	Time at Stake						
				0								
				0								
				0								
				0								
				0								
				0								
				0								
				0								
				0								
				0								
				0								

draw a line across it. Anything below this point will be monitored, but no further action taken. As the project progresses, review the risks below the line every milestone or monthly to see if they should be moved up the list or dropped all together.

C. Damage section

If this risk became reality, what would its impact be on the project? Damage is divided into two types: financial impact and timeline impact.

1. **Money at stake.** How severely would this risk damage the project budget? For example, if the risk was that the task might overrun its schedule and incur additional costs for contracted programmers, how much would this be? Are there legal fines to pay or bonuses lost for being late?

2. **Time at stake**. How long would this risk delay the project's completion? Use the same unit of time as used by the project plan (e.g., days, weeks).

These two factors describe the damage in various ways. For example, if a task is not on the critical path and it is late, it may not damage the project in either category, unless a change in the plan suddenly elevates that task onto the critical path. Some companies establish a risk guideline that the most a risk can put at stake financially is the budgeted cash outlay for that task.

D. Risk containment section

1. **Trigger.** The "Trigger" column describes events that would enable this risk to occur. The trigger column alerts the Project Manager that the conditions are right for this risk to arise. For example:

    a. A task becomes at risk of being late only after it has begun.

    b. The implementation phase of a project may be at risk of delay if the project is approaching the company's annual busy season.

    c. The project may be at risk of losing a sponsor's support if that executive is replaced or if the project falls significantly behind the plan.

    d. The project may be at risk if the company releases a financial report indicating excessive losses, which may signal an upcoming budget cut.

2. **Risk Event Status.** The Risk Event Status column indicates if this risk is past, pending, or in the future. This column is useful for a quick review of risks looming on the horizon. The Risk Analysis spreadsheet is a valuable historical tool to review whenever new projects are started, and this column allows valid risks to remain on the document even after they pass. Valid values for this column are:

    a. Past—The task at risk is completed.

    b. Pending—The task at risk is in process or about to start.

    c. Future—The task at risk is in the future.

3. **Actual Results.** These are the outcomes of the risk once it has occurred or passed. Valuable project documentation for lessons learned and historical purposes can be pulled from this column. Did

the risk occur? Were the triggers useful or incorrect? What was the impact? Which mitigation steps were the most effective? The least? Make the column as large as needed or use it to refer to a detailed document in the files.

4. **Mitigation Actions.** These are the steps to take to eliminate a risk or reduce its impact. Mitigation actions are key steps in proactive management of the project. Primary mitigation actions are avoidance, diminishment, transference, and acceptance. It is always cheaper to mitigate a risk than to repair the damage after it occurs.

E. Responsibility section

1. **Assigned To.** This is the name of the person assigned to monitor this risk. Instead of the project manager scurrying from desk to desk trying to monitor risks, he or she can be assigned to team leaders or the person working on the corresponding task. Although the project manager has the ultimate responsibility for the project, effective delegation spreads the workload around the team. The team member working on the task is close enough to it to see if the risk is becoming reality. If the team member is too close to the work to see the problems, the risk should be assigned to the team leader.

2. **Date Assigned.** This is the date the risk was assigned to this person to monitor.

3. **Comments.** Anything that would clarify the risk, its triggers, or its mitigation actions. When the risk is added to the list and analyzed, many details can be captured. Adding notes in this section will be useful when monitoring the tasks weeks later. This also provides valuable historical information for future projects. If the spreadsheet cell is too small to hold the pertinent comments, then refer to a detailed document.

[D] Mitigation Plans

Identifying what could go wrong is only the first step. Project management is not a passive job. It involves action! With the project risks identified, plans should be developed to eliminate them. These actions are called mitigation plans and fall into three primary categories:

A. Avoidance
B. Reducing the impact/likelihood
C. Transferal

COMMENT

The alternative to mitigation is acceptance of a risk, where the project manager does nothing about it. An example is to not provide UPS support for developer PCs in an area that rarely experiences power outages.

Mitigation plans avoid the likelihood of a problem by planning around it. If the project involves accounting systems, consider scheduling the project to begin after the fiscal year books are closed and avoid the accountants' busy season. If the project depends on a new radio frequency (RF) network to support scan guns, avoid the impact of the RF network shakeout by waiting until it is installed and stable before beginning that portion of the project.

A second aspect of mitigation is to take steps to reduce the amount of damage should the risk occur. For example, if a network expert is not available to work on the project, consider hiring one earlier than needed to avoid being short one person at the last minute. This may cost more than necessary, but it reduces the likelihood of that risk occurring. Another example is with critical hardware. If one computer is crucial to a system's development, then arrange for a second one to be available on short notice or pay to have it available all of the time.

The third mitigation method is to transfer the risk to someone else. This is usually through insurance. Two easy examples come to mind:

A. A life insurance policy on the project manager or key technician could cushion the financial blow of a project delay because a replacement must be found and trained.
B. If the project depends on the timely arrival of new hardware at the facility, transfer the financial risk of freight damage by insuring the shipment.

[E] Stakeholder Analysis

Project stakeholders are people who will be directly or indirectly impacted by the existence of a project. They may try to influence a project's outcome or course of action based on their perception of how threatening the project is to them. To preclude these people from derailing the project, the project manager must identify who these people are and guide their perceptions toward the project in a favorable direction.

Stakeholders live in their own world in which the project may intrude. By understanding something about their work environment, their interests, and motivations, a plan can be charted for a win-win strategy between the project and each stakeholder.

The following are some of the project's stakeholders:

A. **Sponsor.** This person is normally very interested in seeing the project succeed unless he is transferred in the middle of the project and his successor hates him! In general, the sponsor is the project's guardian against executive interference. The sponsor also ensures that critical resources are available for the project. He often smooths the way with other stakeholders.
B. **Executive management.** Typically, business executives view the project plan and budget as an agreement with the project manager as to when the project will be completed and at what cost. They cannot

fathom why their meddling would ever change the completion date or the budget.

C. **Workers.** Will the result of this project cause them more work? Make their lives easier or a living hell? No matter how much they complain about their jobs, at least it is a known factor. They fear the unknown of the new project more.

D. **Team members.** Team members appreciate challenging assignments, working with new technology, etc. Do they view assignment to the project as an opportunity or a punishment?

E. **Union officials.** Represented labor is not automatically against change. However, they may have other issues on their agenda and want to use cooperation with this project as a bargaining chip for something else.

F. **Project Manager.** Well, you'll just have to work on yourself.

G. **Accounting department** (if the project has a budget). Will they work with the project manager or complain about every nickel? They deal in future financial needs and appreciate advance information of cost overruns.

H. **Human resources.** This department provides the project with personnel. Are they forced to bring in technical consultants while, at the same time, they are laying off forklift drivers? The more notice they have, the lower their labor costs.

I. **Vendors.** Those who are providing contract programmers or making the result a showcase if they are installing their equipment.

J. **Shareholders.** If this project opens important new markets or results in major economies, then the shareholders will be very interested. If the project is a long-term or very expensive effort, then the shareholders will likewise be concerned.

K. **General public.** Will the end-product negatively or positively impact the company's public image? Does it have a minimal environmental impact?

L. **Regulatory agencies.** Does this project involve information or products regulated by the government, e.g., securities, taxes, employee information, patient records, etc.?

Managing stakeholder expectations is a difficult task. Each person exists in his own world with his own pressures and motivations. Accounting managers may push for the cheapest materials, the programmers may press for the latest exotic technologies, and some of the team members may enjoy the project more than their regular assignments and stretch everything out! The project manager must reconcile the differences between all of these influences and keep the project on track. It is not possible to make everyone happy, but you do try.

Determining which stakeholder to mollify and which one to stand tough against can be a difficult decision. Some people do not even want what they are asking for! When in doubt, decisions should be based on what is best for the customer. Accounting managers may be upset, but they may have to purchase the more expensive, but more reliable, hardware. The programmers may not be happy, but the project must be based on tried and true technologies, not the latest technology fashion.

To correctly gauge the impressions and attitudes of the stakeholders, meet with them separately. Review those parts of the project that most affect their workspace. It takes time for them to relax and hopefully spill what is on their mind about the project. Typical questions to ask:

A. What do you think about this project?
B. How do you envision the end product?
C. What features are important to include?
D. How long should this take?
E. Will this project interfere with the department's operations?

Organize this into a single document; consider using the Stakeholder Analysis Form in Worksheet 14-2. This form has the following fields:

A. **Role.** What role does this person play in the project? Typical roles are sponsor, team member, manager of customer department, union steward, and IT quality manager.
B. **Stakeholder.** List his or her name here.
C. **Goals, Motivations, and Interests.** What is his interest in this project? Did he suggest it? Will it reduce his operating budget? List all of his concerns (public and private) about the project here. Ask him what he thinks of the goals and assumptions. Ask his opinion about the timeline and listed tasks.
D. **Power and Influence.** This is a numeric score of 1 to 10. What is each stakeholder's ability to influence others for and against the project? What is her ability to speed along or hinder the project?
E. **Importance to the Project.** This is a numeric score of 1 to 10. How important is her active support to the project?
F. **Impact on the Project.** This is a numeric score of 1 to 10. He may or may not be powerful, but how badly could he delay or hurt the project if he chooses to? On the other hand, how valuable is his active support of the project?
G. **Stakeholder Score.** This is the product of the Power and Influence, Importance and Impact scores multiplied together. Sort this column in descending sequence to bring the most critical players to the top.
H. **Role on Project.** Are they cheering (or jeering) from the sidelines or players on the team? Stakeholders can be important to a project but indifferent to it. A stakeholder can have a small part on the team or be there from start to finish.
I. **Win-Win Strategies.** What can be done to address this person's concerns and still complete the project on time? Some people just want to be heard. Often, they have a single issue they feel is serious and must be addressed. The win-win strategy is the project manager's mitigation plan to keep this stakeholder on the team.

WORKSHEET 14-2. Stakeholder Analysis Form

Stakeholder Analysis Form

Role	Stakeholder	Goals, Motivations, and Interests	Power and Influence	Importance to the Project	Impact on the Project	Stakeholder Score	Role on Project	Win-Win Strategies
Sponsor								
Data Processing Manager								
Controller								
Plant Manager								
Employees								
Telephone Systems Manager								
Security Manager								
Facilities Manager								
Purchasing Manager								

As is very obvious from the potential for personal opinions, this document is not for general distribution.

[F]   Communications Plan

For a team to operate effectively it must communicate. Otherwise, it is just a collection of individuals. The communications plan should go beyond a weekly team meeting and determine the best way to keep each stakeholder apprised of the project's progress. If stakeholders do not hear what is going on from the project manager, they may make their own assumptions that are based more on their worst fears than on the facts.

Drafting reports may not sound like much fun, but it is an important way to mold stakeholders' opinions. "Information is power" and no one has a better handle on what is occurring on a project than its manager. Keep the message simple and clear. Ambiguity is the enemy.

A good time to find out what the stakeholders want to hear about is when the project manager meets with them to gauge their views on the project. Ensure that the status of their specific concern is included in the status reports.

All projects have successes and setbacks. Accurate reporting should include all of this. The project manager was hired to detect and resolve problems. Normally, setbacks do not belong in status reports if they are under control and if they will not materially delay the project. On the other hand, if there is a serious threat to the timeline or budget, be sure to inform the sponsor and summarize the details for others. Follow up on the issue in later reports until it is resolved. Stakeholders may not enjoy the bad news, but they would prefer to hear it from the project manager rather than through office rumors.

Through all of this, remember that all reports must be truthful. The first time the project manager is caught in a lie, credibility is forever tarnished. Ambiguous statements are open to interpretation and can be considered as an untruth where no lie was intended.

When building the stakeholder communication plan, the following should be considered:

A. **Executives.** Business executives may want a monthly summary indicating progress, budget performance, and any major issues. Some executives may want this face to face while others might be looking for an e-mail memo. If the reports include notification of problems, they may perceive that the project manager is asking for guidance or that the issues are beyond his ability to control.

B. **Sponsor.** The project's sponsor will want to be able to answer questions from his peers about the project. He may want a brief weekly summary along with a detailed monthly update.

C. **Workers in the department.** They will be interested in the final product's features and encouraged by how it will make their working environment easier. If workforce cutbacks are an intended result of the project, leave any information about this to the department manager.

WORKSHEET 14-3. Stakeholder Reporting Matrix

Stakeholder Reporting Matrix

Role	Stakeholder	Reports to Receive	Amount of Detail	Frequency of Reporting	Best Format	Delivery Mechanism
Sponsor						
Data Processing Manager						
Controller						
Plant Manager						
Employees						
Telephone Systems Manager						
Security Manager						
Facilities Manager						
Purchasing Manager						

14-28

D. **Team members.** They will want to know the progress of the project. This is important if their part of the project is coming up so they can prepare accordingly.

E. **Union officials.** They will want to know the project's progress. In some companies, this report is given to the human resources department who passes it on to them.

F. **Accounting department.** The accounting staff will want to chart the progress of the project in terms of overall cost and monthly cash flow. They may want to juggle the expenses a bit, paying something here and there in advance or a bit late. The project manager's job is to ensure accounting knows what is coming and what is pending.

G. **Human resources.** The human resources team will be primarily interested from a labor perspective. If the project needs more people or is releasing people, they will need to know in advance so they can plan accordingly.

H. **Vendors.** Companies providing the project with goods or services appreciate advance notice of materials requirements.

I. **General public.** If the project is highly visible, the project manager must pass project progress information through the corporate communications office and often the legal office as well.

To assemble a communications plan, refer to Worksheet 14-3, Stakeholder Reporting Matrix.

A. **Role.** What role does this person play in the project? Typical roles are sponsor, team member, manager of customer department, union steward, and IT quality manager.

B. **Stakeholder.** Name of the person to receive the report.

C. **Reports to Receive.** Some people may receive multiple reports. The sponsor may want the accounting report, the progress report, risk assessment report, etc. Others may want only a brief summary.

D. **Amount of Detail.** Brief or detailed? Summary or show how all of the numbers add up?

E. **Frequency of Reporting.** Weekly, monthly, at every milestone?

F. **Best Format.** Bullet points, narrative, Gantt chart?

G. **Delivery Mechanism.** Should this be delivered by e-mail, verbally, in an updated Gantt chart?

§ 14.04 EXECUTING THE PROJECT

[A] Managing the Project

The project plan is a road map for how the project should unfold. In reality, it is a rather fluid document that shows a general direction, but tasks can be completed early or late, the budget overrun, tasks omitted, etc. Even with these changes, the project plan represents the best communications tool to guide the team's expectations of what lies ahead. The team will use the project plan for a guide if the project manager refers to it and they will ignore the project plan if the project manager ignores it.

Project management is people management. Meet with the team at least weekly. Let them speak about the obstacles they have encountered and concerns about what is to come. The project manager can pass on information concerning the project's progress and any alterations to the plan. Remember that communications flow from bottom up (the team to the project manager), top down (the project manager to the team), and laterally (among the team members).

The project manager has a responsibility to use the resources of the project team in the most effective manner. This means that team members should be assigned according to their strengths and technical expertise, not on availability or the project manager's whim.

Project management requires that three important variables be in control: cost, quality (or scope), and time (or speed of completion). A project manager must have control over at least two of these variables to ensure project completion. Altering any one variable will affect the others. Generally, to improve quality (or to expand the scope), higher cost and, possibly, more time will be incurred. For example, a software project can be completed more quickly (time) if there is more money for overtime or to hire more contract programmers (money). Or, the project manager could cut the quality (scope) to increase the speed.

[B] Scope Change

The scope of the project is set by the sponsor before the project plan is drafted. All time and cost estimates should be based on the approved scope. Altering the scope will automatically alter both the timeline and the cost. As the project unfolds, some of the uncertainty will fall away and there may be pressure to adjust the project scope to better fit the current reality. This is where the project manager must stand firm.

Changes in the budget and the timeline are normally worked out between the sponsor and the project manager. The same holds true for the scope, except that sometimes it is changed by business executives without either the project manager or the sponsor being aware of it!

In their work on the project or in their contacts with the end users, programmers may sometimes make side agreements to include additional features to the system or alter the product design. They also may neglect to mention it to the project manager. This is known as "scope creep." Taken alone, each change may seem minor, but taken in aggregate, the changes can alter the project by loading it with additional code to test and maintain. Simple changes may prove more difficult than initially estimated with considerable time lost attempting to repair code that is not in the plan.

These unofficial agreements may be difficult to repudiate later. To contain scope creep, a formal process must be established to control all project scope changes. This should include a form to request the change and a log sheet to track it.

The change request form can be a basic memo stating what is wanted and why. The form should be presented to the project manager who will then analyze the request and identify its impact to the project in terms of time and money. This information is passed to the sponsor who should have the final authority to approve or deny the change. Approving the change also approves the project manager's estimated changes to the project timeline and budget.

COMMENT

Do not try to fight change requests. Often they are the result of late arriving requirements. Instead, manage these requests. Promptly assess the impact on time and cost and then pass them straight to the project sponsor to approve. In this way, there will be fewer end runs around you to press changes in.

[C]   Basic Rules for Managing Projects

The following are basic rules for managing projects:

A. Plan the work—work the plan.
B. Resolve all issues brought to the project manager's attention as soon as possible. If the project manager delays, so does the project. If the project manager hesitates to make a decision or to raise an issue with the sponsor, so will the team.
C. Working with people takes time. Do not be in a rush when talking to the project team members.
D. At every milestone, update the assumption list, risk analysis, and stakeholder communications plan.

[D]   Task Completion

Projects that fall more than 15 percent behind schedule rarely finish on time. The project manager must press the project forward from the first day. As task milestones are reached, update the project plan. Assess completed tasks for quality, completion effort required, and effect on the project schedule. The hours estimated to complete a task effort should be compared with the actual hours, and the information retained for future estimates.

This task completion information will be used to identify the project status at different points in time, and will be discussed in status meetings. The following are some solutions that can be used to take care of project slippage:

A. **Overtime.** Working overtime, or hours in excess of the standard work day, should only be used to complete critical path tasks and only for a short time. If the need for overtime becomes routine, it can affect the personnel turnover rate. The best time for paid overtime is right after Christmas and the worst time is during the summer months.

B. **Assign more people.** Assigning people to the start of a project is less of a problem than adding more people later. The worst time to add team members is near the end of the project. As more people are added, the communications required between project members will reduce the output per worker. Using a skilled worker to break in a new coworker will further slow progress. The project effort may be less effective than if no additional people had been added.

COMMENT

Adding more people does not automatically speed up the result. The time for communications between new team members and existing team members consumes much of the benefit of additional staff.

C. **Pass on a task to a vendor.** This action has merit if the vendor has reliable skills in the appropriate area. For the best results, the vendor should be given advance notice to expect work from the project.

D. **Reduce the project scope.** If the sponsor is willing to reduce the project scope, this may be an effective solution to project slippage, helping to keep the quality of remaining project tasks intact.

E. **Reschedule module delivery.** Modules that may not be required for the finish date can be delayed. This can be a better solution than reducing the project scope; however, it can complicate resource planning.

F. **Request additional funds.** If the project is over budget, then a change request for more money must be submitted. The sooner this is done, the better, because as the end of the fiscal year approaches, money will become less available. If the dollars represent people cost, this is not so much of a problem. Salaried employees do not require overtime pay.

[E] Progress Measurement

Items that must be controlled and managed should be monitored for both quantity and quality. It is harder to measure the quality of output than quantity at the time the work is being done, since the quality of the effort appears only when the end product is tested and debugged. Therefore, testing should begin as soon as a major component is completed.

Employee time is usually the greatest cost of the project, and it should be closely monitored to gauge the results for effort exerted. Everyone must report the time spent working on the project—including the project manager. Some of the project management packages collect this data online and summarize it in a weekly report, automatically applying the time and dollar values to relevant project tasks.

To minimize the time and aggravation spent collecting this data, the project manager should:

A. **Explain why the data is needed**. Demonstrate the process used to record task time. Encourage the use of real numbers, not estimates. Stress that the information collected is for their benefit too.

B. **Simplify the recording**. Do not require too much detail. Let people know they may receive a telephone call from a spouse or go to the restroom. Typically allow workers 15 percent of their work day for personal time.

COMMENT

Enter time sheets into the project accounting system daily. Efforts expended on Monday morning are difficult to remember by Friday afternoon.

C. **Confirm time estimates**. Inform employees that the time estimates on which the project is constructed need to be confirmed. Estimates are only approximations and should be corrected if wrong. This cannot be done without keeping track of the actual time.

§ 14.05 PROJECT CLOSEOUT

[A] Overview

Projects end for various reasons. Ideally, the project ends because the project's goal has been achieved and is ready to hand over to the customer. Sometimes executive management will decide that a project needs to stop. However the end of the line arrives, there are some steps the project manager should take to properly close out the project.

Planning to close a project is like planning for any other phase of a project. The only difference is that the goal is to end the project by closing off the various areas that support it. The project manager identifies the tasks to be completed, assigns resources, adds durations, and creates the plan. The projected financial requirements for the project closeout should be rolled into a budget for the sponsor's approval.

The project manager coordinates a planning meeting with the key stakeholders to identify tasks to be completed to close their involvement in the project. The key stakeholders for this phase are:

   A. **Sponsors.** Hand over what has been completed and obtain their sign-off.

   B. **Accounting department.** Assist in closing the project's budget accounts.

   C. **Customer.** Gather product documentation and provide training for usable products.

   D. **Team members.** Reassign to company departments.

   E. **Contract employees.** Release back to their companies.

   F. **Program office.** Gather the project's records for storage and later use in research.

The closeout plan should include a document that identifies all company material purchased to support the project team and its location. The project sponsor should reassign these assets before they get lost.

[B] Sponsor

When the project is completed, the project manager obtains a written acceptance of the results from the customer. If the project ended before the goal was reached, the project manager should obtain formal written notice from the sponsor to close the project.

Designate a point of contact for any future project issues and transition key information to this liaison. This is usually the manager who will pick up support responsibilities for the product.

The project manager coordinates a closeout meeting with the sponsor to compare the statement of work and project scope against actual project performance. Identify any shortcomings and determine if they can be resolved prior to the project's end. Review the final project closeout plan and the timeline with the sponsor. After the sponsor has approved the closeout plan, publish it to all stakeholders.

[C] Accounting Department

Most projects have a budget to close at the end of the project. There are three major areas to address with the accounting department before the project can close:

   A. Performance of the project—a comparison of the amount budgeted for the project to the amount actually required.

   B. Projection of budget requirements to implement the approved project closeout plan.

   C. A list of all pending invoices and open purchase orders. The list of pending invoices must include contract employees who are to be retained through the last days of the project.

[D] Customer

A clean handover of the products completed is critical to customer satisfaction. Coordinate training on finished products to acquaint users with their proper functions. Include a handbook to which users can refer and use to train new employees.

Coordinate the continued maintenance and support of the project product to include hardware servicing and service desk support. Both departments may require technical documentation as well as a copy of the users' manual.

This is an opportune time to gather some idea of the end users' impression of the project. Solicit and analyze feedback regarding project performance from business representatives, project team members, suppliers, customers, and management. Some companies create a customer satisfaction survey for distribution to pertinent stakeholders. If used, specify a deadline for its completion and return.

[E] Clean Handoff to Support

The new IT system will someday need someone to address problem reports or to upgrade its components. In either event, before the project team departs, a written approval of a clean handoff must be made to the:

A. **Service desk.** So they know who to call and any immediate action steps to take in an emergency.
B. **Workstation support team**. So they know what software to load on a replacement unit and how to configure it.
C. **Applications support.** So they can quickly research the system architecture to debug issues.

[F] Team Members

Taking care of the project team at closeout will have many benefits. As soon as project closeout planning begins, meet with the human resources department to discuss the redeployment of employees. The team members are counting on the project manager to "sell" their good work on the project to obtain desirable positions in the company. Word can get around a company pretty fast. If a project manager is known as someone who "takes care" of his team members, it will be easier to recruit people for future projects.

Schedule performance reviews for each person on the team. Discuss their involvement in the project to date, how well they performed to plan, and any new skills they acquired. Performance reviews completed during the project can be used to show trends of improvement. The result of these reviews can be used as justification for project bonuses or pay raises. Forward the individual's performance appraisal to the human resources department and the employee's new manager.

The project manager must try to keep people from jumping off the project early. Establish a range of release dates for team members based on the closeout plan. Add a week or two to the plan to ensure they will be available to address last minute questions. Do not let anyone leave the project early as it may start a stampede for the door!

When a project closes, it is important to take some time to celebrate its completion. Project closeout is a time of transition for many people—friendships as well as jobs are ending. To aid in this transition, most project managers throw a party where the contributions of the various team members can be recognized.

The event should be held off site and hosted by the project's sponsor or even the person to whom he or she reports. Disperse individual rewards such as gift certificates, bonuses, additional vacation days, trips, plaques, personalized certificates of accomplishment, items with company logo, and other tokens of appreciation. Do not forget to personally thank each person!

[G]   Contractual Issues and Contract Employees

Review all open contracts to identify terms that must be addressed before the agreement can be closed. There may be clauses concerning the number of days of notice required before releasing contractor-supplied employees back to their companies. There may be penalty clauses if the proper amount of notice is not provided to them. If in doubt, include the legal department in the contract reviews.

If the project ended early, look for penalty clauses for canceling materials. Common goods can be resold by the manufacturer, but custom materials often require the buyer to pay for at least a portion of the unit's price.

Review all work to date to ensure compliance with the current project plan and requirements documentation. This may require a review of all communications with the vendor, any work schedules, accounting data (invoices and payment), and inspection results. Audit completed work to ensure that it complies with the task specifications. Obtain written warranties from all subcontractors and vendors for completed work orders.

Complete updated performance evaluations for contract employees and forward them to their companies. Detail their accomplishments, task descriptions, strengths, and areas of improvement. Include letters of recommendation detailing their performance to assist them in securing their next engagement.

[H]   Final Project Report

An important part of closing a project is to gather all of the records and information about the project and file it with the Project Management Office (PMO). This information will be useful when planning for similar products or for making major changes to the end product.

Compose a project completion report that highlights the achievements of the project and underlying reasons for any problems. Specify areas that added value for the customer. The report should:

A. Identify which goals and objectives were fully or partially achieved.
B. Identify which goals and objectives were not achieved and their impact.
C. Identify any expected benefits that were not achieved and their impact.
D. Indicate major milestones achieved with actual dates vs. planned dates and explain the reasons for any differences.
E. Include guiding factors (objectives and constraints) that affected the project from the start.

14-36

F. Include team members' opinions and perspectives of project successes and weaknesses as reported in the post-project review.
G. Include documentation of the final scope, work breakdown structure, and the stability of the project's requirements.
H. Include customer feedback and comments on the project as well as feedback from suppliers and other third-party suppliers.

A valuable section in the project report is a review of the lessons learned during the project. This section should review the challenges the team faced and how they were overcome. A "lessons learned" section can guide future project managers around the pitfalls of working with this type of product or in working with a specific department.

§ 14.06 PROJECT MANAGEMENT PITFALLS

When everything is running smoothly, project management can seem a very easy job. Typically, in the beginning of the project, there seems to be a lot of extra time and money. Of course, the exact opposite is felt at the other end of the project. The transition from plenty to scarcity is the result of many things.

[A] Team Issues

Teams are made up of people, and people are a highly variable resource. The same person can go from happy to angry to sad to productive all within the same day (or in some cases, in the same hour). Where they feel free to change at will, all expect the project manager to be calm, caring, and all-knowing of the technology. This variability is more so in an IT team where many people with minimal social skills seem to congregate.

People take a lot of time. Time is needed to discuss project issues, and even to exchange regular pleasantries. Time is spent to listen to people express frustrations, and sometimes to just discuss the weather. Many project managers feel they are too busy to do this on a regular basis or only do this with a few favorite workers. The end result will be problem team members. Time invested establishing and maintaining good relations with every team member will pay off in fewer problems along the way. Some things to look out for when dealing with people on your project include:

A. **Inaccurate information.** Some team members are content to tell you what they think you would like to hear instead of the truth because it makes you happier (and go away). For example, when you ask how much of a task is completed, and you say 85 percent, then the project manager is happy. However, depending on that number can cause serious problems for the project manager.
B. **Team member apathy.** Team member apathy leads to low productivity and constant excuses. This is a long battle to fight but requiring written acceptance of the project plan for the next 60 days minimizes their efforts at throwing up roadblocks to success. The project manager

is ultimately responsible for the project but closely tie the team member to ownership of tasks, their estimates, and completion.

C. **Sponsor apathy.** Project sponsor apathy can make altering a project scope, timeline, or budget a significant problem. In the early phases of the project, they may try to add scope without budget or to cut the budget as excessive. However, the significant expense is during the development and testing phases—those funds will be essential then.

[B] Scope Creep

The scope of a project must be carefully managed. When the project manager submits the project plan (timeline) and project budget, it is based on completing the assigned tasks. As end users try to change the project requirements, the project manager ensures that through change control, there is a corresponding increase in time and budget. However, other things can occur:

A. Project sponsor tells you to take the cost of a scope change out of the project's contingency funds.

B. Helpful team members add features to the product without approval (aka gold plating). A variation to this is when they decide by themselves to add work or cost to ensure product stability. Unfortunately, none of this effort or expense is in the project plan or budget.

[C] Poor Budgeting

The budget of a project must be carefully managed. When the project manager submits the project plan (timeline) and project budget, it is based on completing the assigned tasks. As end users try to change the project requirements, the project manager ensures that through change control, there is a corresponding increase in time and budget. However, other things can occur:

A. IT professionals are proud of their technical skills and are not shy about demonstrating that. They will sometimes provide optimistic estimates for task completion. If a bit of this is included in every task, pretty soon you have a project that quickly trends out of control for labor hours.

B. Most time and cost estimates are made assuming that everything will work out fine on the first attempt. Little time is allowed for problems that invariably arise—some of them serious. The extra time to address these problems should be included in the project's contingency time and cost.

C. Tasks missing from the project plan will automatically add time and cost. Ensure the project team assists fully in the project plan development and ongoing modification.

[D] Poor Project Selection

Project Management Offices have a backlog of work to choose from. Some of these projects have an obvious urgency to the company. Others are considered routine updates or new technology migration action—both of which may be unpopular with project customers. Examples of poorly selected projects include:

A. Projects for a customer who really does not want them can be an uphill battle for the project manager. The project sponsor may want the project completed but the business people who must assist with the project may not. For example, a project to move an unauthorized server sitting in a business department into the data center where it can be properly supported. The server works fine where it is and the user provided only grudging assistance with the project. Even bringing them into a meeting was an ongoing struggle.

B. Projects that are started only because they are the oldest ones in the backlog. Many of the assumptions in that project proposal may no longer be true or the project itself may lack customer urgency.

C. Small projects are started because they are quicker to conclude than a larger one that may have greater payback to the company. This enables the PMO to claim a large number of projects to be completed but also causes big projects to stack up and their budgets to expire.

D. Projects that require new technology, without anyone in the company to support it or money to hire someone with those skills.

E. Projects that will eliminate the jobs of the users who must assist you with completing it.

See Policy ITP-14-1 Project Management Policy as an example of a policy for successfully managing projects.

POLICY ITP-14-1. Project Management Policy

Policy #:	ITP-14-1	Effective:	03/06/14	Page #:	1 of N
Subject:	Project Management Policy				

1.0 PURPOSE

This policy requires that any organized effort recognized by the IT Department as a "Project" shall include the appropriate level of formal planning, progress tracking, and documentation. Project documentation is essential for the effort to be completed on time and within budget.

2.0 SCOPE

The policy applies to all information technology projects conducted within the company, using company resources. Projects conducted entirely under a contract using an external organization are not covered by this policy.

3.0 POLICY

Projects managed under this policy will, at a minimum include the following artifacts:

A. Project Charter—approved by the project customer and the IT Director—to document
1. Project vision—what the final result of the successful project will look like.
2. Specific deliverables and how they will be validated.
3. Specific requirements in finite, measurable terms.
4. Estimated timeline with a contingency amount that reflects the timeline's uncertainty.
5. Estimated budget with a contingency amount that reflects the budget's uncertainty.
6. Assumptions concerning the project's execution and product's features.
7. Risks reflecting potential positive and negative events that alter the project's timeline and expenses.
8. Roles and responsibilities of all team members to include the project manager, project sponsor, and team members.

B. Project plan—providing a list of sequenced tasks
1. A list of tasks needed to create each of the project deliverables and to fulfill specific requirements.
2. Each task will have people, tools, and materials identified that are necessary for the task's completion. Each task should conclude with the creation of some sort of a deliverable that can be examined by the project manager to verify task completion.
3. The time duration planned for each task in the project plan will add up to indicate the project's estimated completion date.
4. The expense required to complete each task (labor rates, tools, external support, and materials) will be added up to form the project's budget, by month.

C. Risk Assessment—results stored in a Risk Register
1. A list of potential negative actions that might delay the project or create extra costs along with Mitigation plans for each risk are details to reduce the impact or likelihood of an adverse event.
2. A list of potential opportunities that will shorten the timeline, reduce expense, or improve product quality, along with a plan to exploit them if they occur.
3. Each risk in the Risk Register is rated according to its likelihood and impact. The impact and likelihood score are multiplied together and sorted in descending order to determine the most serious risks to be addressed.
4. The Risk Register must be updated at least every milestone.

D. Issues Tracking log
1. A list of actions necessary to keep the project on time. These "tasks" are in addition to the project plan list.

    2. Each issue is assigned a due date and a team member to resolve it.
    3. The issues log regularly has new issues added and completed issues moved are a "Completed issues Log."
- E. Meeting Notes—Notes are taken during each team meeting to record
  1. Meeting notes include project decisions made, task accomplishments, and upcoming events.
  2. Updates to the issues log and risk log.
  3. Any team member planned absences.
- F. Weekly Status reports—Every week the project status is recapped for the project sponsor
  1. Current project completion timeline, compared to original estimate.
  2. Current project expenses compared to original budget estimate.
  3. Any obstacles, current or pending, that will hinder the project's progress.
- G. Change Control Process
  1. A published process for how scope, timeline, and/or budget changes are proposed. It also explains how they will be evaluated for approval or denial by the project sponsor.
  2. All proposed changes are recorded in a Change Request log.

4.0 REVISION HISTORY

Date	Revision #	Description of Change
03/06/14	1.0	Initial creation.

5.0 INQUIRIES

Direct inquiries about this policy to:

George Jenkins, CIO
Our Company, Inc.
2900 Corporate Drive
Columbus, OH 43215

Voice: 614-555-1234
Fax: 614-555-1235
E-mail: gjenkins@company.com

Revision #:	1.0	Supersedes:	N/A	Date:	03/06/14

15

PROJECT MANAGEMENT OFFICE: OPTIMIZING THE ORGANIZATION

§ 15.01 OVERVIEW

[A] Purpose and Scope

A Project Management Office (PMO) manages a company's (or department's) projects. In times past, each department of the company might include in its strategic plans various types of projects to meet one business objective or another. To realize these strategies, projects were conducted. These isolated efforts were rarely coordinated to maximize resources. Sometimes they worked at cross-purposes or consumed resources for non-strategic objectives.

A PMO brings all pending and current projects together under a single office's control. By examining all projects side by side, the PMO is able to identify and resolve areas of overlap to the company's advantage. This framework optimizes the use of resources and minimizes mutually exclusive project goals.

The shift to a PMO eases workloads all around. Instead of dealing with individual project managers, each supporting department (e.g., accounting, purchasing, facilities, and human resources) can refer to a single place when providing services. Instead of creating separate status reports for each concerned executive, project managers can submit a single document to the PMO who distributes consolidated reports for all projects to the interested parties.

[B] Project Management Office Basics

A new PMO develops several fundamental documents to establish the scope of its actions and its strategy for implementing the office. Properly written, these documents will set an expectation of where the PMO fits into the organization and the value it adds to the bottom line.

A. **Mission Statement.** A general statement that outlines what the PMO does, how it is to be done, and who the customers are. It establishes the scope of the PMO's authority within the company, such as IT-only, company-wide or support for a particular site.

B. **Strategies.** High-level directions on how the PMO will fulfill its mission statement and align the PMO with the company's business strategies. Strategies provide an overall framework for creating objectives as well as an anchor for PMO policies and procedures.

C. **Objectives.** A clear statement of what the PMO intends to achieve over the upcoming year. Objectives should be specific, measurable, achievable, and include estimated completion dates. Typical objectives are:
   1. To hire and manage qualified project managers and support staff.
   2. Ensure that all customer commitments are documented and tracked to completion.
   3. On a bi-weekly basis, to track and maximize the use of resources (labor, cash, time, and equipment) for the greatest benefit of the company.
   4. To provide clear, summary information on all project status in a timely manner, on a scheduled basis or upon request from senior management.

5. To provide mentoring, training, and assistance in the career development of the PMO's project managers.

D. **Deliverables.** Products and services created or offered by the PMO. Products are tangible "things" the PMO will deliver. Services are actions taken for the benefit of others. PMOs add value to the company through the combined application of their products and services.

[C]   Critical Policies to Develop Based on This Chapter

A project management office needs a few basic policies. Using the material discussed in this chapter, you will be able to create policies for:

A. Establishing the project management office.
B. Defining the portfolio management process.
C. Mandating the quality review of executing projects.

Policies should always be developed based on the local situation. Successful managers cannot issue appropriate guidance if the policies are written with another company's situation or location in mind.

§ 15.02   PROJECT MANAGEMENT OFFICE RESPONSIBILITIES

[A]   Overview

A Project Management Office increases a company's project management administrative overhead by adding a PMO Manager, perhaps an administrative assistant and process steps to manage the project portfolio. In exchange for this cost, some benefits are expected. A rational approach to selecting projects that maximizes the company's limited resources is required. Project excellence is enhanced through identification and propagation of best project management practices. Also, the PMO minimizes project manager administrative load by consolidating and minimizing project reporting requirements.

[B]   Determining a Basic Tool Set

Watch a group of five project managers and you will find five different sets of tools used to manage projects. The challenges in this situation are clear. If one of the project managers must be replaced due to illness or leaving the company, the next project manager cannot easily step in since everyone is doing things to suit their own tastes. It means that personal preferences instead of best practices are used. It also means that shared team members must learn the processes used by each project manager they support.

The heart and soul of the project management office is its standardized tools and processes. These are variously called its toolkit, methodology, or standard operating procedures. They include a set of processes and basic tools that ease the execution of projects through the organization. These processes are regularly reviewed to add into them recently identified best practices. Some of the tools commonly used are:

A. Estimation guides for judging the time and expense for completing a task.
B. Resource/requirement projections to reserve technical resources for specific periods of time.
C. Standards for project scheduling and management to ensure others can assist with or take over a project.
D. Simplified equipment acquisition steps to reduce administrative overhead for the project manager.
E. Scope and budget change control processes to ensure control of these critical functions remains with the project manager.
F. Consolidated status reporting to present one "face" to executive management.

Standardized project management processes also make it easy for the PMO to provide oversight and mentoring of project managers. By using the same processes and tools for every project, team members spend less time orienting to a new project. Team meetings, project management document formats, ways to request support are all the same. If a project manager is unavailable for an extended period of time, the PMO can arrange for a substitute since all projects use the same tools and processes.

[C] Resource Management

Ensuring that the right people will be available when needed is an important ingredient for project progress. Project managers use resources (e.g., skilled people, special tools, and cash) to move a project to completion. The more scarce or expensive these resources are, the more difficult they become to schedule since the company cannot afford to leave them idle. Also, the longer that a project requires to complete, the more difficult it is to accurately estimate when a resource will be required later in the project. The PMO provides tools for project managers to estimate the timing of their resource requirements, consolidate them into a central requirements file, and resolve conflicts between projects.

When project managers operate independently, they each must negotiate with every resource manager for the resources they need. Not only is this a nuisance for the project managers, but imagine the resource managers who must meet repeatedly throughout the week with individual project managers, each pressing that his or her project is the most urgent and important effort!

To optimize resource utilization, the PMO is established as the primary customer of these services—not the individual projects. This allows the PMO to request specific units of resources to support all projects and ensure their proper utilization. For example, the PMO might request 60 hours per week of Java programming support for project development. Instead of bombarding the Java programming team leader with requests from various projects, the team leader can identify the resources available to support projects in advance and better plan work for the rest of the team. The PMO then can allocate the programmers to the projects that need them.

In addition, the project manager can smooth out resources needed versus what is available. The PMO Manager reviews all projects and predicts the resources demanded for the upcoming month. In the case of conflicts, the PMO Manager allocates scarce resources to projects the IT Director has designated as highest priority.

When dealing with external resource providers, such as temporary agencies, the PMO Manager is a single contact point. This saves time for individual project managers from meeting with and negotiating with multiple temporary services agencies. A single contact point provides negotiating leverage for best price and service.

At the end of a project, there may be furniture, computers, or skilled people to reallocate or send on their way. The PMO leader's view over all projects makes the reallocation of resources easier and more efficient. Leaving this action to the very end of a project, skilled resources and expensive equipment may be idled, creating additional company costs.

Various project management principles are defined by numerous accrediting organizations. Given that each company has a unique corporate culture and business situation, the PMO selects and emphasizes those principles that provide the most benefit for the least effort.

An example process might be to break projects into five different levels based on their complexity, benefit, and urgency to the company. The projects with the lowest levels have the least stringent project management administrative requirements and the projects rated the highest value, such as a "5" (typically very large and important efforts), receive the greatest PMO attention.

[D] Centralize Reporting

Stakeholders need information about projects. This information may need to be in written reports, oral reports, monthly presentations, or any number of formats. These administrative reports are important but can be very time consuming for the project manager to assemble. The other side of the issue is that each of the individual project managers may deliver this information in different formats with different nuances to the data.

To simplify this for everyone, the PMO Manager receives weekly status reports from every project. This report is always in the same format for all projects. The data is all defined in the same way. Taken together, the PMO Manager can provide a single face for all projects to the IT Director and other interested parties.

From this data, the PMO Manager can assemble reports as required for:

A. **Financial.** The current financial needs for each project and projected out by month through the scheduled project completion.
B. **Human Resources.** Labor requirements (both internal and external) by month and skill type.
C. **Portfolio Progress.** Reports showing the timeline for all projects (in a single Gantt chart) through to completion.
D. **Risks.** Significant issues hindering project progress.

COMMENT

An important PMO responsibility is to minimize the amount of administrative overhead required of project managers. At times, requests for information seem to come from all directions. However, the PMO Manager must turn away the low value requests and refer other requestors to existing reports. Otherwise, valuable project hours are wasted.

For example, one company's PMO Manager wanted to measure the amount of time between 36 distinct steps in a project (when it started, when requirements gathering began, when requirements gathering ended, when implementation planning began, etc.). The result was useless numbers since it did not include a measure of a project's size or complexity and combined all projects (large and small) into a single pool. However, all Project Managers were mandated to gather and report on this information so that the PMO Manager could look like she was addressing the quality of project delivery.

See Policy ITP-15-1 Project Management Office Policy as an example for creating a PMO at your organization.

POLICY ITP-15-1.   Project Management Office Policy

Policy #:	ITP-15-1	**Effective:**	03/01/14	**Page #:**	1 of N
Subject:	Project Management Office Policy				

1.0 PURPOSE

This policy creates the IT department's Project Management Office (PMO). This office is to ensure the consistent, efficient, and effective implementation of projects across the IT department.

2.0 SCOPE

The policy applies to all users of information technology within the company. The PMO is responsible for managing all IT projects of more than 40 hours, or that involve the purchase of hardware of more than $5,000.

3.0 POLICY

The following individuals will perform the duties outlined below:

A. PMO Sponsor
   1. Create a Mission Statement that outlines the PMO's roles and responsibilities. The mission statement establishes the scope of the PMO's authority within the company.
   2. Identify the primary strategies on how the PMO will fulfill its mission statement and align the PMO with the company's business strategies.
   3. Develop a list of objectives for the PMO to achieve over the next 12 months.
   4. Together with the IT Manager, appoint a person as the IT department's PMO leader. This person is delegated to be responsible for implementing this policy.
B. PMO Leader
   1. Establish and maintain the tools and processes for use by the IT department's project managers.
   2. Standardize project management methodology by consolidating status requests to flow through the PMO.
   3. Manage the IT department's portfolio of pending projects.
      a. Create a standard form for requesting and analyzing projects. This ensures every proposed project summary has the same "look and feel" with a standardized format.
      b. Monitor contents of portfolio to combine projects where practical.
      c. Identify project goals that conflict with strategies or objectives of other projects.
      d. Develop guidelines for determining project costs and savings (tangible and intangible).
   4. Standardize project management tools.
      a. Determine the strategy for selecting the PMO's toolset.
      b. Create a process for updating the toolset to meet changing situations.
      c. Ensure that the PMO staff is trained in their use.
      d. Publish a standard process for managing the changes to a project's scope.
   5. Resource management.
      a. Coordinate the use of resources by the PMO to optimize utilization and minimize cost.
      b. Develop and maintain a positive working relationship with internal resource suppliers.
      c. Identify external resources required by the PMO and pre-qualify major suppliers (internal and external).
      d. Assign and reassign resources to projects.
   6. Establish training and mentoring program.
      a. Identify and train mentors for assisting new project managers.
      b. Coordinate peer reviews for troubled projects.

7. Establish a project historical library.
    a. Establish a library that contains the planning documents, status reports, and final report of all projects.
    b. Publish rules for accessing the data.
    c. Create guidelines for what is to be collected from each completing project.
    d. Ensure that company confidential data is secured from unauthorized access.

4.0 REVISION HISTORY

Date	Revision #	Description of Change
03/01/14	1.0	Initial creation.

5.0 INQUIRIES

Direct inquiries about this policy to:

George Jenkins, CIO
Our Company, Inc.
2900 Corporate Drive
Columbus, OH 43215

Voice: 614-555-1234
Fax: 614-555-1235
E-mail: gjenkins@company.com

Revision #:	1.0	Supersedes:	N/A	Date:	03/01/14

§ 15.03 MANAGING THE PROJECT PORTFOLIO

[A] Overview

It is a rare company that does not have more projects proposed than it has time to complete them. In fairness, many of the proposed projects should not be attempted. Some are not financially justified; others may be an executive's pet project with little alignment to company directions. Still others may be a blind push of a new-and-exciting technology into a place where it is not suitable. The PMO organizes all projects (pending and in process) into one view so that executives can select for execution those projects that most closely align with their strategic objectives. In most companies, the final decision on the IT Project Portfolio is made by the IT Director.

The PMO creates a standard format for gathering the essential elements of a project. This includes a clear business case, a concise scope statement, a list of success criteria, anticipated costs and benefits, required completion dates, and a list of actions required to complete the project. Taken together, a reasonable bottoms-up cost estimate can be made for completing the project. However, the longer the project runs, the wider the tolerance for resource estimation must be. Estimates supporting a 90-day project should vary much less than estimates for a year-long project. This variance is represented by the project's contingency time and budget.

[B]   So Many Projects, So Little Time

The collection of all projects in process and pending execution is known as the PMO's Project Portfolio. The portfolio is managed to achieve company goals. This may be to lower operating costs, to increase revenues, to maximize resource utilization, etc. Normally, the PMO uses a scoring system to select projects to begin execution. This score reflects the degree to which a project aligns with current company strategies. In some cases, a project's portfolio score may also halt lower value projects already in progress, to free resources to address projects with a higher return.

All project proposals must pass through the PMO's project proposal process. This ensures a consistent data basis for IT Director review and same-to-same comparison with other projects. The PMO Manager tracks incoming project requests either using a service request tracking system or a simple spreadsheet. The intent is to ensure that requests are not lost. Such a tool also provides visibility to project requestors as to the status of their submission.

[C]   Project Portfolio Prioritization

A common PMO challenge is selecting which project to work on next, and which ones to stop. To do this, the PMO regularly evaluates all projects, pending and active, to determine priority of execution. Business climates and marketplaces change. Projects already in action must be reviewed to reva-lidate the reasons for their approval.

Portfolio management seeks to maximize the value of the projects in the portfolio. (Note that a company may value several different things in a project.) Not every project is worth doing. Each PMO must determine how it will eval-uate projects to select the best mix to work on. Some of the various selection goals might include:

- Support of the company's strategic initiatives.
- Provide the maximum financial payback.
- Ensure optimum use of available resources.
- Balance risk among projects (such as 25% for high-risk projects and 75% for medium to low-risk projects).
- Allocate project funds to different goals (25% for cost reduction, 40% for new product development, 15% for equipment replacement and 20% for new product research and concept development).

There are several easy-to-set-up tools that support portfolio management. See Worksheet 15-1 Project Portfolio Ranking. This matrix creates a weighted score for each project in the portfolio, active and pending. To build this matrix:

A. Identify the criteria used to evaluate the projects. In this example, the criteria are categorized as "Strategic, Technical, Financial." Under each category are several areas to rate projects.

B. For each of the rating criteria, assign a weight for its importance. For example, if the company's cash flow is low for this time of year, then use a low weight for project cost, or a high weight for cost reduction.

C. List each project along the top of the matrix as column headings.

D. Rate the projects according to each of these criteria from 0 to 10 in terms of the following areas:

    1. **Strategic alignment.** How well do this project's goals align with the company's stated strategies?

    2. **Marketplace enhancement.** Does this project improve an existing product, or create a new product that protects or enhances market share?

    3. **Core competencies.** Does this project emphasize core competencies or does it require new expertise?

    4. **Business risk.** Overall, how uncertain is this project's outcome? Does it involve a new market segment, a new technology, or even something outside of the company's traditional business?

    5. **Resource utilization.** How well does this project maximize use of the company's resources, and minimize reliance on external resources?

    6. **Technical risk.** How risky is the technology involved? Is the technology proven but new to the company, or is it leading edge? Some companies prefer a mix of high-risk and low-risk projects.

    7. **Project cost.** How expensive is the project?

    8. **Financial payback.** What is the potential payback for the investment? This may be return on investment (ROI) or net present value.

    9. **Cost reduction.** Does this project reduce operating costs?

E. To calculate the score, multiply each criterion's rating of 0 to 10 by its weight, and sum the scores across that row. Sort the scores in descending order so the highest scores move to the left of the list.

There are some limitations to this matrix.

- It assumes that the financial projections for cost and payback are reliable. Often, such estimates are within +25 or −10 percent.
- The true risk of each project is a guess, especially if it is a new technology or product.
- Projects such as legal compliance or contractually required efforts are "trumped" to the top of the list.

Sometimes it is easier to restate the project portfolio visually. A common tool is a bubble chart, as shown in Exhibit 15-1.

WORKSHEET 15-1. Project Portfolio Ranking

Project Portfolio Ranking

	Project	Weight	Project 1	Project 2	Project 3	Project 4			
Strategic	Strategic Alignment								
	Core Competencies								
	Marketplace Enhancement								
	Business Risk								
Technical	Resource Utilization								
	Technical Risk								
	Project Cost								
Financial	Financial Payback								
	Cost Reduction								
	Score		0	0	0	0	0	0	0

EXHIBIT 15-1. Portfolio Bubble Chart

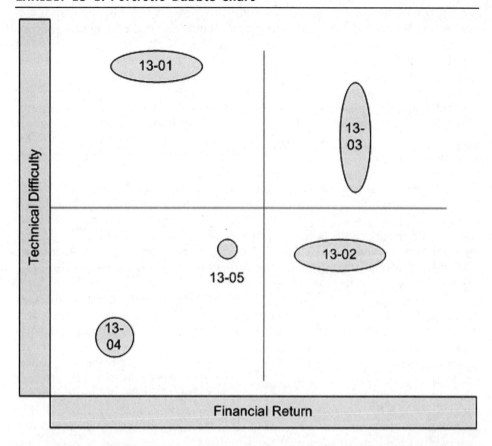

In this visual report for management, the horizontal axis indicates the estimated payback for a project, and the vertical axis is the technical difficulty. Each project is labeled (for example, 13-XX for 2013, and project number XX). The size of the bubble indicates the potential estimation error. A bubble that is oval shaped from left to right indicates that the financial return estimate has a high degree of uncertainty, while the estimate of technical difficulty is relatively certain.

In this example, Project 13-01 has a high estimated technical difficulty for an uncertain, but low payback; Project 13-02 looks like a project with moderate technical difficulty with a high payback. Given a choice between the two, Project 13-02 would win.

Bubble matrices can be in any format. The axis can reflect project score versus risk, or any desired combination. Often the portfolio management matrix and the bubble chart are used together when discussing portfolio options.

[D] Project Benefits—Fact or Fiction

When a project request is received from a competent authority (generally someone authorized to spend the company's money), the PMO assigns a

Project Manager to review the proposal's costs and benefits. Few people requesting a project have a clear idea of how long an IT project will take or what it will cost to implement. In general, their experience has been to see or use the external aspects of the result, with little experience of the essential background effort or materials required. (If the project already has a complete and approved feasibility study, then base the ROI analysis on that information.)

At this point, a minimal amount of time has been spent obtaining specific cost information. This analysis approximates a project's costs since most equipment and services quotes expire in 30 days. A complete costing of the project requires considerable analysis and that will be lost if the project is not promptly approved. Cost estimates at the "approximate cost" stage should be within ±25 percent.

With the cost estimate in hand, conduct an analysis of the project's benefits. As described by the project requestor, the project benefits can be inflated as much as the costs are deflated. Verify claims of project benefits. Labor savings are a particularly difficult area to calculate. The final estimate of project benefits must be approved by the project requestor. If project benefits include savings for staffing or equipment, the project requestor must commit to making these changes when the project completes.

If labor savings are included, they must adhere to the company's labor accounting practices. For example, in most companies, a project cannot save one-half of a person. In this situation, either someone is removed from the company's payroll or not. If no one leaves the company, then no payroll savings can be claimed—even though hours in the week are now available for other uses.

Project savings claimed for equipment departing the company is a different issue. Leased equipment may incur a penalty for early return. Equipment freed up as the result of one project does not become a "free" asset available for use elsewhere in the company. For a project to claim a savings for eliminating a device, that equipment must exit the premises.

Along with proposed ROI, the analyst will assess the risks surrounding the project. The risk of failure, that resource costs will skyrocket, of technical obsolescence, and all other risk dimensions must be included in the report. Some PMOs detail specific environmental and resource risks that must be addressed in proposals.

COMMENT

A variation of ROI is the cost of non-investment (CONI). CONI measures how much not doing a project will cost the company. This is common with legal compliance issues, such as mandatory environmental controls for air pollution, water pollution, or disposal of toxic wastes. In some instances, the cost is measured in time instead of dollars—jail time!

[E]   Rate Backlogged Projects

An important function of the PMO is the control of projects. In times past, each department of the company might include in its strategic plans various types of projects to meet its business objectives. These isolated projects were rarely coordinated to maximize resources. Sometimes, they worked at cross-purposes or consumed resources for non-strategic objectives.

A PMO brings all pending and current projects together under a single office's control. The PMO leader can then examine all projects side-by-side to identify and resolve areas of overlap to the company's advantage. This framework optimizes the use of resources and minimizes mutually exclusive project goals.

Today's non-urgent project can become tomorrow's hot topic. The PMO consolidates new project requests into a single file. Each request is periodically reviewed to determine if changes in its critical factors alter its payback time or its urgency.

The PMO monitors the projects in the backlog for opportunities to combine any of them with new projects. This provides additional resource economies and potentially meets the company's ROI "hurdle rate." After a project's costs and benefits appear to meet historically acceptable levels, the project can be added to the PMO's pending project list.

See Policy ITP-15-2 Project Portfolio Management Policy as an example for managing the portfolio of projects at your organization.

POLICY ITP-15-2.   Project Portfolio Management Policy

Policy #:	ITP-15-2	**Effective:**	03/01/14	**Page #:**	1 of N
Subject:	Project Portfolio Management Policy				

1.0 PURPOSE

This policy creates the IT department's Project Management Office's (PMO's) portfolio management process. Project portfolio management is mandated to ensure the consistent, efficient, and effective implementation of projects across the IT department.

2.0 SCOPE

The policy applies to all users of information technology within the company. The PMO is responsible for managing all IT projects of more than 40 hours, or that involve the purchase of hardware of more than $5,000.

3.0 POLICY

Each proposed project will be submitted on a form designed by the PMO Manager. This form will include, at a minimum:

A.   Description of the proposed project.

B. Estimated benefit (showing all calculations), if this is mandated for legal compliance or the potential loss if this is not done.
C. Alignment with stated company strategies.
D. Requestor contact information.

Every project description item is assigned a score. For example, one point per thousand dollars of anticipated Company savings. A project's "total score" determines its place in the portfolio. If the project has a significantly higher (25% or more) total score than a project already in execution, then the executing project is paused until the higher project is completed.

The PMO Leader has primary responsibility for maintaining the project portfolio. All incoming proposals are verified as complete and then added to the portfolio. The final decision on which projects to pause and which ones to start rests with the IT Director.

A. Ensure all incoming project requests are properly completed.
B. Calculate the total score for each project proposal.
C. Present the entire project portfolio to the IT Director every two weeks to determine which projects are next for execution, and if any existing project should be paused.

4.0 REVISION HISTORY

Date	Revision #	Description of Change
03/01/14	1.0	Initial creation.

5.0 INQUIRIES

Direct inquiries about this policy to:

George Jenkins, CIO
Our Company, Inc.
2900 Corporate Drive
Columbus, OH 43215

Voice: 614-555-1234
Fax: 614-555-1235
E-mail: gjenkins@company.com

Revision #:	1.0	Supersedes:	N/A	Date:	03/01/14

§ 15.04 ENSURING PROJECT MANAGEMENT QUALITY

[A] Overview

Every project is a unique endeavor. It may have a different project leader, a different goal, and different risks but even if it seems to be the same effort as the last, it is still unique. Also, the way it is managed can likewise be unique. The PMO reduces the likelihood of a project exceeding its budget or timeline by auditing its execution for adherence to PMO policies.

A project audit provides many company benefits. Most projects do not appear to run out of money or time until near their end. Yet the signs were all there during execution that either inadequate amount of both was provided or that they were being wasted away. A project audit will estimate a project's true estimate to completion (ETC). That number is used to determine the project's financial and time requirements given its performance to date.

[B] Project Audits

PMOs add value by auditing projects in process or recently completed. This audit verifies how closely the project conformed to PMO processes. The degree of conformance (quality) provides feedback on the effectiveness of processes.

Sometimes an audit is needed because a project has experienced major problems with the end-product development, the project schedule, or the project budget. Since a project is already troubled, most of the audit is spent identifying where the problems arose, what actions the sponsor and project manager took, and what steps to take to correct the problem. The PMO project audit also verifies that:

A. The project used approved PMO tools and practices. Review any new tools created or modified to address specific situations for acceptance by the PMO.

B. The accuracy and completeness of project metrics. These metrics guide future PMO actions and their accuracy is important. Knowledge of a potential audit inhibits a project manager from disguising project problems by misreporting metrics.

C. The quality of the product created as compared to the current scope and criteria for success. In essence, did the project deliver the form, fit, and function requested?

D. How well the project manager's actions conformed to the published schedule, and how effectively the project manager utilized assigned resources.

E. The project as a whole, and individual tasks within it, along with the actions taken by the project manager, for the likelihood, or impact, of adverse events.

Another PMO function is to randomly audit projects in process to ensure proper management. Do this carefully since the time taken to address an audit may create delays in an otherwise on-schedule effort. The goal of a random audit is to detect problems before they become major issues. Narrowly focus random audits on such things as issues tracking, financial reporting, or risk management. This helps to determine the quality of the project management effort with a minimum of disruption.

[C] Project Metrics

A popular management maxim is that a person cannot manage what cannot be measured. Create a consistent set of project performance metrics for executive oversight. Project metrics provide performance visibility to management in a common and consistent manner. They also permit the comparison of current project performance to historical levels.

There are two primary types of project metrics:

A. Product metrics pertain to the result or product created by the project. How closely does the result conform to the published specifications; how much better is it in identified key quality areas, etc.? How does the customer rate the final product's quality?

B. Project management metrics deal with how effective and efficient the project was in creating the result, usually by comparing the current timeline and budget to the baseline. Were unnecessary steps included? Were resources efficiently utilized or were expensive people left sitting around idle?

Metrics provide a source of feedback into the PMO's performance and customer satisfaction. They ensure decisions are based on facts and not emotion. Metrics illustrate the result of changes made to processes and areas of potential improvement. Since metrics use numbers instead of pass/fail, smaller changes can be detected and monitored, such as a trend toward greater resource efficiency. Examples of metrics to track include:

A. Schedule performance.
   1. The number of tasks completed on time.
   2. The estimated hours to complete the project (as a percentage over or under run).
B. Financial performance—Actual expenses compared to budgeted expenses (as a percentage over or under run).
C. Customer satisfaction as measured by end-of-project or end-of-milestone surveys.
D. Percentage of tasks completed on time, sequenced by the resource used.

See Policy ITP-15-3 Project Quality Review Policy as an example for measuring project quality at your organization.

POLICY ITP-15-3.   Project Quality Review Policy

Policy #:	ITP-15-3	Effective:	03/01/14	Page #:	1 of N
Subject:	Project Quality Review Policy				

§ 15.04[C]

1.0 PURPOSE

This policy requires the IT department's Project Management Office (PMO) to perform quality reviews on all projects of more than 2,000 hours or $100,000. This quality review is to ensure the consistent, efficient, and effective implementation of approved PMO policies and practices in all projects.

2.0 SCOPE

The policy applies to all information technology projects conducted within the company, using company resources. Projects conducted entirely under a contract for external support are not covered by this policy. The PMO is responsible for auditing all IT projects of more than 2,000 hours at the completion of each project phase, or at their conclusion for projects less than 2,000 hours.

3.0 POLICY

3.1 Reporting
The PMO Manager will create a standard project audit scorecard to ensure that every essential component of the project is reviewed.

Any executing project that is found to be out of compliance for either the timeline or budget must immediately submit a project change request to the project sponsor to update the estimate to completion for both categories.

The written results of all project audits must be reported to the IT Director within 5 working days of the audit.

Project managers of audited projects will have 10 working days from the day of the audit to respond to all negative findings.

3.2 Auditing During Project Execution
Project audits during execution are typically scheduled during milestones or at the completion of a project phase. Their purpose is to ensure the project is taking the essential steps early in the project to ensure its timely conclusion. For example, poor requirements definition will result in a muddle Execution phase since task objectives will be unclear. This will also lead to running over budget and timeline. Example documents to review are customer approval of deliverables, requirements, and high-level solution. For these same documents, ensure that supporting IT departments such as Security, Business Resilience, Capacity Planning, Operations, and Architecture all concur.

The auditor makes an estimate to completion from this point in the project to its end. This is done by comparing the project's baseline schedule and budget to the actuals. For example, if the project timeline is already running at 13 percent over schedule, then this is projected through to the end to determine a likely completion date. This likely completion date is compared to the customer promise date.

Likewise, an estimate completion for the project budget must be completed so the sponsor will verify that the project's timeline is on track for completion by the date promised to the project sponsor. Project spending to date is compared to the work completed to date. The result is used to estimate the cost at completion.

3.3 Auditing at Project Conclusion

When a project manager declares a project to be ready to close, the PMO Manager schedules a project audit. This audit verifies:

A. Project sponsor's written acceptance of deliverables.
B. An end of project report is compiled that accurately reflects the estimated to actual timeline and budget.
C. Team member's assessment of project—how it was conducted, efficiency of resource utilization, project manager's performance.
D. Project sponsor's assessment of project.

3.4 PMO Manager's Responsibilities

A. Create a scorecard for evaluating at each phase of the project, to include at a minimum:
  1. Initiation
     a. Statement of project goals and objectives
     b. Statement from project originator detailed anticipated benefits
     c. High-level description of project deliverables, requirements, and solution approved by project sponsor
     d. High-level estimate of cost and timeline approved by project sponsor
  2. Design
     a. Statement of project goals and objectives
  3. Execution
     a. Statement of project goals and objectives
  4. Conclusion
     a. Signed sponsor acceptance of each deliverable
B. Train a staff of project auditors in proportion of one for every five IT Project Managers to be used for project audits. This pool of auditors will be rotated so that auditors do not become too familiar with the project managers they will be auditing.

4.0 REVISION HISTORY

Date	Revision #	Description of Change
03/01/14	1.0	Initial creation.

§ 15.04[C]

5.0 INQUIRIES

Direct inquiries about this policy to:

George Jenkins, CIO
Our Company, Inc.
2900 Corporate Drive
Columbus, OH 43215

Voice: 614-555-1234
Fax: 614-555-1235
E-mail: gjenkins@company.com

Revision #:	1.0	Supersedes:	N/A	Date:	03/01/14

16

PROJECT PHASE REVIEWS: KEEPING EVERYTHING ON TRACK

§ 16.01   OVERVIEW

[A]   Purpose and Scope

Projects can be expensive and complex. Approving their budget and use of company resources often requires multiple executive approvals. If the project creates something tangible, such as erecting a building, progress would be obvious. However, much of an IT project product is intangible. It may involve purchasing expensive equipment and its installation can be seen but the progress toward the creation of software is not something easily verified.

Phase reviews are an integral part of a well-run IT governance program. Each review provides valuable feedback to the project team as to how well they performed to expectations. They confirm to IT and business management that a project is under control in the areas of scope, budget (to include estimate to completion), and timeline. The review ensures that the project is still relevant to business, that the goals are clearly understood, and that best practices are followed. Unlike a milestone review, at the conclusion of a phase review, a project is approved to continue or cancelled.

COMMENT

Approvals of critical documents will be by written signature rather than by e-mail. Some people may shoot off a quick e-mail approval to make a request go away but they are hesitant to sign their name without first reviewing the document.

Company executives have limited time yet their oversight of projects is expected. Reviewing the project progress at the conclusion of each phase, using a standardized format, enables them to sift through the essential information in a short time. Knowing that a project's execution will be scrutinized at set points during its execution forces the project manager to adhere to approved best practices.

Phase reviews are about communications—conversations between the project customer, the project manager, and company management. Everyone can see how the project is progressing at this point in time and contribute one's suggestions for improving it. Customer requirements shift with changing business needs. An excellent IT system that meets all of yesterday's business needs may no longer benefit the company. If a project runs for more than a few months, it is not uncommon for executives to add scope or consider combining several projects for greater benefit.

COMMENT

The management rule is to "Inspect what you expect." Phase reviews are a necessary management action. Where project managers may know what they are supposed to do, sometimes tight timelines, team dysfunction, customer haste, personal preference, or even laziness will lead them to cut corners in the project. The negative results of this are most apparent during implementation.

Every company has its own approach for phase reviews. Some use fewer reviews or in the case of a critical project, more frequent sub-phase reviews. The review process follows a waterfall approach.

A. Phase I begins with a basic idea and sharpens it through a business case analysis that examines the potential costs against its expected benefits. It includes a high level analysis of the proposal including detailed requirements, rough order of magnitude estimates, resources required, risks involved, etc.

B. Phase II is the detailed design. It reaffirms and expands the requirements. A Work Breakdown Structure and project plan are created to arrive at a project budget within plus or minus 10 percent estimate of cost and time. This phase locks in the requirements and includes a detailed risk assessment.

C. Phase III begins project development. Company resources are committed, equipment is ordered, and the IT product is assembled. This phase review verifies that the project manager maintained a proper level of control over the scope, timeline, and budget. Long or critical projects may have multiple Phase III reviews to oversee execution.

D. Phase IV examines if the completed project is ready to implement. Is the product suitable for the intended purpose and most importantly, does the intended purpose still exist? At this point, the project may be assigned additional scope to fine-tune the final result.

E. Phase V is a follow-up after some period of time to validate claimed benefits against actual. It reviews the number and type of trouble tickets created after the product was installed and asks project sponsor's opinion of the finished product's quality.

Phase reviews are a quality assurance check that projects are addressing the relevant issues at each phase of execution. They are intended to minimize the confusion at the end of a project where appropriate planning was not done and everything is in chaos. Each project phase has its unique project management artifact deliverables. A successful phase review results in the Project Management Office (PMO) Manager's approval to continue with the project.

COMMENT

The phases in a project review are of unequal length. They represent significant changes in the project effort rather than a consistent timeline.

An executing project can seem to be all in order until it is time to install the product it has created. Then mass chaos reigns. Disagreements may arise with the customer over the basic requirements. Performance of the new software product "appears" to the customer to be inadequate yet seems fine to the IT team. No one consulted the security engineer and the intended access method is no longer acceptable to the company. The list of things that could go wrong is endless and almost all of them are avoidable.

Phase reviews provide several immediate benefits:

A. The project manager is forced to properly complete the required project artifacts for the review.
B. Customers cannot later claim ignorance about project's requirements or design decisions made during development.
C. Requirements are adjusted to track changing business needs.
D. Fresh perspectives are added to the risk assessment.
E. Fewer surprises for PMO management later in the project.
F. Brings IT and business management together for a focused conversation about a particular project.

COMMENT

Use a standard format for the phase review presentations. This makes it easy for the reviewers to find what they are looking for and minimizes guessing for what should go into a particular presentation slide.

[B] Critical Policies to Develop Based on This Chapter

Using the material discussed in this chapter, you will be able to create the following policies:

A. Establishing a project phase review process.
B. Retention of project documents.

Policies should always be developed based on the local situation. Successful managers cannot issue appropriate guidance if the policies are written with another company's situation or location in mind.

§ 16.02 PHASE I—BUSINESS CASE PHASE REVIEW

[A] Overview

The business case phase review is a conversation between the IT department and the customer to ensure that everything needed is understood and recorded. This phase transforms the customer's vague needs into detailed and specific requirements. Some of these requirements may significantly drive the cost beyond what was approved in the original business case. It is typically performed by an IT business analyst.

The business case review is normally completed within a few weeks. It sharpens vague business objectives so that a time and cost estimate can be developed. In essence, given the expected cost, should this project continue? It also quantifies the tangible and intangible benefits that the successful project will deliver. At this stage, we are beginning with a concept and ending with a high level design. Its time and cost estimates are at a rough order of magnitude (typically of plus or minus 50%). Any criteria used for portfolio analysis should also be included, such as the anticipated payback period for the project. Phase deliverables may include:

A. Specific requirements approved by the project sponsor.
B. Statement of project benefits from the project's requestor.
C. Initial risk assessment, in priority order with mitigation for top risks.
D. Significant obstacles to be addressed.
E. Identification of key resource requirements.
F. High level project budget.
G. High level timeline illustrating which resources are needed, and when.
H. A score sheet that includes all of the PMO's project portfolio evaluation criteria.

The business case review ensures that the project is based on a firm planning foundation and that all of the requirements and project benefits have been identified. It is common for additional technical requirements to be identified during the detailed project planning in Phase II.

[B] Inspect What You Expect

Phase reviews are an executive's opportunity to review a project's critical information. They are formal reports to management about the project's scope, budget, and timeline. The project's sponsors are an important part of these discussions to demonstrate that the project's features are still what they expect.

The project manager must demonstrate that he or she is following approved PMO practices without shortcuts. To eliminate guesswork (and to provide for consistent products), the project management office provides a list of the documents to be included in each type of review. Typically, these documents are recapped in a deck of presentation slides for the review discussion. Examples are proof of customer approval of detailed requirements, an ongoing risk assessment program, cost management reports, etc. If everything is in order, approval is given to progress to the next step.

Phase reviews are time consuming for the project manager to prepare. They represent a significant effort by the company. There is also the cost for many managers to sit in the room to critique the effort. Phase reviews may be reserved for large or company-critical projects in terms of hours or overall cost. For example, an abbreviated review for projects more than a $50,000 budget, a medium detailed review for projects over $150,000, and a full review for all projects over $250,000. This scale may also be adjusted based on the timescale involved or criticality of the project to company operations.

COMMENT

Project Management Offices typically oversee phase reviews. Yet these are the same people charged with vigorously rooting out wasteful administrative work from project management. The tradeoff is to ensure the phase reviews focus on the minimal essential information and not devolve into massive PowerPoint exercises. If a minimal phase review raises questions on a specific point, then the project manager can provide follow-up information instead of trying to cover every possible subject.

[C] Tips on Conducting Phase Reviews

Phase reviews should not contain surprises. A well-managed project should be resolving issues and informing management of significant projects (such as over schedule or over budget conditions) well in advance of the review. If this is not possible, acknowledge the conflict early in the discussion and set it aside until the presentation is completed.

Use your project team as a knowledge resource. To conserve time, the information presented is a high level statement about each dimension. If the conversation proceeds into the underlying details, then turn to that technician for help. Do not try to be an expert in every aspect of the project.

Presentation slides with endless lists of bullet points can quickly put the most hyper person into a deep sleep. Use illustrations and pictures to describe the topics and add in the narrative description. However, some things such as a list of requirements must be listed.

Limit the number of attendees at the review to the essential few (this will still be a large number). The fewer people present means the less likely someone will derail the meeting. It also makes finding an open meeting time much easier.

At the end of each phase review, the project needs an answer to either "continue execution" or "stop the project." It is not unusual for the go ahead to be conditional on something. In either case, IT and business management must sign the decision.

[D] Project Product Requirements

Dimensions of the business functions are further described by detailed requirements. Techniques for gathering detailed requirements are detailed elsewhere in this book. In this phase, the customer's requirements are grouped according to the project objectives that they support. Each requirement includes a description for how it will be validated as completed.

The conversation to gather requirements often adds new features as the customer fills in gaps in the vision of the final product. Characterize each requirement as mandatory or optional. To meet time and financial limits, it may be necessary to trim the desired requirements from this project and apply them to future versions.

One of the project requirements is the acquisition of critical or scarce resources required to complete the project. In some cases, the company may lack these tools (or skilled technician) and not wish to pay a premium to acquire them, thereby ending the project.

COMMENT

Many companies conduct feasibility studies to analyze a concept to see if the company should even attempt it. The result is a report that explains the risks and issues involved along with a rough (high uncertainty of accuracy) estimate and timeline to complete it. Sometimes the project proceeds directly to execution but often the result is to place the project into the upcoming fiscal year's capital budget.

[E]   Technical Solution Design

With the requirements in hand, draft an overall technical solution design. The high level design will identify the databases, program logic, system resiliency, network connections, equipment, software, etc. needed to complete the project. The solution design applies company policies against the approved requirements to determine what will be required. This "big picture" design demonstrates that the project is achievable. It also determines an approximate cost and timeline.

For example, if a company policy requires all business critical databases to be mirrored on another server, then the cost for an additional server and database software will increase the project budget. If the project creates a service that people access from off-site, then additional security measures may include hardware and software. All of this is apparent to the IT team but not so to the manager requesting this system.

[F]   Business Process Benefits

A company does not receive benefits from IT systems alone. The IT solution must exist within a business process to provide value. Use a drawing to illustrate the business processes that this IT system will support. Discuss how the IT solution supports the process. This illustration facilitates a discussion between the IT and business managers as to the problem to solve and the IT system to solve it.

Most business cases are based on benefit versus cost. This benefit is identified by the business manager requesting the IT support. Rather than try to verify the requestor's assertions, request a written statement from the system requestor that details the tangible and intangible benefits to the company from this system. Since any benefits (such as labor savings, expense saving, etc.) are usually found in the business process, the business manager is the appropriate person to certify them.

Some benefits are obvious such as the removal of obsolete equipment. However, other benefits may not be so obvious. Explain how each of the anticipated benefits will be measured after the project concludes.

[G]   High Level Deliverables

At this early stage of the project, the "big picture" deliverables can be identified. These are IT functions or equipment that must be created to fulfill the business process requirements. The description for these deliverables includes an explanation of how they will be demonstrated as completed.

One of the results of the business case phase review is a realignment of the project budget. Often project proposals are optimistic as to their costs. This phase provides an approximate understanding of the IT hardware and software development costs. Comparing this cost to the anticipated project benefits may sink the proposal. The challenge is that while the PMO understands the variability of estimates and that the final cost may be significantly higher, the business executives will (conveniently for them) consider this estimate a commitment.

Cost estimates for this phase should be a rough order of magnitude or potentially plus or minus 50 percent. This reflects the uncertainty of a simple analysis versus a detailed analysis and that unless the project is undertaken immediately, vendor quotes will expire before execution. Most projects are not normally started immediately. They are added to the PMO's project portfolio based on the portfolio rating scale.

Budgets and timelines are only estimates—guesses of what is needed. These guesses are based on assumptions about business and IT technical variables. Include a list of assumptions with every estimate. The more the uncertainty about these assumptions, the greater the contingency in time and budget required for the project. The approved project budget and schedule becomes the project baselines against which performance is measured.

Phase reviews usually show the budget and timeline as two trending lines. One line represents the baseline and the other the actuals. The actual value line is extended to show the projects' estimate to completion time and cost.

[H]   High Level Risks

Every project is faced with a wide range of risks to its budget and timeline. During the Phase I review, explain a team assessment of the likelihood and potential impact from:

- Legal environment (existing or pending)
- Technical challenges (technology too new or too old)
- Financial uncertainty (adequate funding available)
- Social/cultural environment (will this project damage our public image)
- Information security impact
- Data privacy concerns for data involved

[I]   Phase I Review Results

The high level analysis will uncover the significant costs and risk for a project. This enables a high level cost, time, resources, and benefit review. Often what sounds like a great idea is not practical given existing technology or company resources. Projects passing the Phase I review are added to the company's pending project portfolio. The results will also verify that the appropriate signatures are on artifacts such as required deliverables, project requirements, and anticipated benefits.

COMMENT

The PMO's project portfolio represents a company's wish list of its many pending projects. Not all of these projects will see the light of day. Some have minimal payback. Others represent a half-formed idea that has no payback at all. By aggregating all of the projects onto one list, company executives can apply limited resources to the critical few efforts that further company strategies and avoid spending resources for minimal payback. It will also facilitate the appropriate combination of projects working in the same technical area.

§ 16.03 PHASE II—PLANNING PHASE REVIEW

[A] Overview

Once a project is released by the PMO Manager for execution, it begins the planning phase. For most people, this indicates the official start of the project since it empowers the project manager to apply company resources toward its completion. The planning phase updates requirements with anything that may have changed between the end of Phase I and approval to execute starting Phase II. Planning further develops project requirements at a more detailed level.

Based on these revised requirements, the project team drafts a technical solution design. This big picture narrative illustrates the overall solution. It includes sections on data management, security, architecture, and business resilience.

The solution design describes what is to be done. This is decomposed into a Work Breakdown Structure (WBS). The WBS is then organized into a detailed project timeline and budget that should be within plus or minus 10 percent of actual performance. Many of the artifacts required for the planning phase review are to ensure that interruptions to the timeline and budget are anticipated and mitigated.

Often the detailed review uncovers significant technical obstacles to the project's completion. This might be an invalid assumption about available server resources and new equipment must be purchased. Skilled technicians may no longer be available when needed. There may also have been a change in some database or security policy, which will require additional effort to satisfy. The result is a request for additional project funding to address these needs.

This phase is concluded by a formal phase review by IT and business management. Details in the expanded project requirements are often a surprise to business managers. This initiates a valuable conversation between IT management and business managers about expanding the project to provide additional functions or to interact with existing systems. This can lead to additional analysis and another Phase II review. If further requirement are presented, then the phase is stopped until the customer's requirements are fully understood.

COMMENT

Overhead should be in proportion to benefit and phase reviews take a long time to prepare. If the project is less than 200 hours, then perhaps only a simplified review is necessary. Otherwise, the administrative burden will overshadow the time the project manager spends leading the project team.

Some of the Phase II artifacts are updated versions of documents from Phase I. Phase deliverables may include:

A. **Deliverables.** A description of what this project is to deliver to the project sponsor, described in finite details.
B. **Business requirements.** From the business perspective the benefits to provide.
C. **Technical requirements.** Each of the business requirements is broken down further into the technical requirements necessary to create the function.
D. **Work Breakdown Structure.** A high level overview of the major tasks to accomplish to deliver the technical requirements.
E. **Use cases and test cases.** If the project involves the creation of software, then it should also include:
   1. Use cases describing the project's function within the business process.
   2. Test cases of how each requirement will be verified for the project sponsor's acceptance.
F. **Updated risk assessment.** This may include a process Failure Modes and Effects Analysis (FMEA)—at this stage, the mitigation actions for each risk can be considered for inclusion in the project scope and budget.
G. **Project timeline.** Based on known requirements and available resources, the points in time when the project's milestones are estimated to be ready.
H. **Project budget.** This is the budget based on the work breakdown structure and performance to date. It also includes the project's estimate to completion. With the completion of detailed planning, additional funds may be required or project scope trimmed (features pushed out to a Phase II).

COMMENT

Beware of business managers adding requirements during the phase reviews. This not only delays phase approval but encourages the same people to throw in additional requirements as the project progresses. A well-managed scope change management process ensures that these "simple" scope expansions increase the budget and extend the timeline as appropriate.

[B]   Requirements and Approvals

Few business managers or their staffs have a detailed idea of the IT effort necessary to create a specific function. They describe what business value they want the system to provide. Each of these business requirements is further described by the technical requirements that the new IT system must fulfill. These technical requirements can then be expanded to include the hardware, software, and labor needed to fulfill them.

Speaking confidently about topics is a business manager trait—even if they know little about the subject. Beware of business managers speaking confidently about a specific technical solution. They may sound knowledgeable but are usually repeating something they heard elsewhere.

With the business functions in hand, the technical team decomposes them to identify the technical requirements. Requirements must be clear, measurable, and tied to specific business functions. Tasks necessary to fulfill these requirements result in the project's timeline and budget. Skipping one of these steps increases the uncertainty of the budget and timeline (but that never seems to stop anyone). Once approved, all additional requirements must pass through the change control process.

[C]   IT Architect's Diagram

IT architects provide high-level system designs that solve business problems within the company's IT policies and best practices. They provide consistency across projects to minimize the effort necessary to support the company's technical infrastructure. Depending on the company's size, there may be separate architects for software, network, security, operations, and infrastructure.

The architect reviews the technical requirements and provides a high level image of how the various components will work together. This might be a list of the database tables to be used, the time of day for batch processing to minimize conflicts with other systems and to ensure the brand and model of equipment to be purchased is consistent with other company devices.

The architect's solution design is then approved by various IT functions. Every company is different but these are typically:

A. **System Administrators.** Verifying the CPU and disk load and in some cases, selecting the server to share
B. **Information Security.** Ensuring that company confidential and legally confidential data is properly protected or accessed, minimize openings in the firewall, creation of user access groups, etc.
C. **Database Administrators.** For appropriate data structures, indices, stored procedures, and performance
D. **Network Planners.** For capacity planning, appropriate logical isolation
E. **Capacity Planner.** Ensuring there is adequate system-wide resources set aside to support the final solution.

COMMENT

Once all of the requirements and solution designs are completed, they are formed into a single document and each IT discipline provides a written signature to approve them. This validates that each area was appropriately consulted and agrees with the solution. This reduces the likelihood of someone balking at implementation time.

[D] Detailed Technical Solution

Based on the business and technical requirements, a technical solution to fulfill the requestor's needs must be created. This includes a detailing of the problems to solve and how they will be addressed (at a high level). It is based on the architect's diagram of the servers, database tables, firewalls, etc. and how they all relate together.

For example, additional servers may need to be purchased (adding tasks to check for rack space, to arrange for electrical and network connections, etc.). A common requirement is to establish the necessary information security authorizations for applications and users to communicate with the servers and databases.

The solution design uncovers many of the non-obvious IT costs. It examines where the data comes from and where it is stored at. It describes how data is stored to include tables, indices, and security. A section describing a security analysis reviews the sensitivity of the data involved. Required hardware configuration requirements are estimated. There is normally a section on business resilience and the environmental impact of the system solution. If the process is graphics intensive, a network load analysis may be required.

The technical solution design provides the big picture description of the project's product. To assure IT management that this solution is technically sound, the document is signed by:

A. IT Technical Architect
B. IT Security Manager
C. Database Administrator
D. IT Operations Manager
E. Network Administrator
F. Application's subject matter expert

[E] Budget Approval and Timeline

The solution design is decomposed into a Work Breakdown Structure (WBS). The WBS is then organized into a detailed project timeline and budget that should be within plus or minus 10 percent. Many of the artifacts required for the planning phase review are to ensure that development of the timeline and budget followed the company's guidelines.

Once all of the work required to complete the project is detailed in the project plan, it is possible to determine the true estimated cost of the project. It is not unusual to request additional funds to pay for work that was not anticipated during the initial project analysis.

With the budget and project schedule approved, the finance department will provide funds to cover the month-by-month expenditures. A significant problem arises if the detailed budget exceeds the amount in the feasibility study in Phase I. In that case, either scope must be reduced or the budget increased. This situation is not unusual and should be resolved prior to the phase review.

[F] Resources

Over the years, the term "resources" has been used to identify the workers on a project. Resources may also be the materials and tools needed to complete the assignment. The skill level and availability of technical team members is the most common reason that IT projects are delayed. During this phase review, the team members' assignments are confirmed for this project through its completion.

The review is an opportunity for IT and business management to confirm the purchase of expensive development tools required by the team. Examples of this are the purchase of software or virtual servers, renting of workstations, or the assignment of office space. Management can also review the technical skills required and "reserve" their use for the team.

[G] Team Communications

IT engineers seem to prefer to sit off in a corner and create their IT magic. This can lead to good work on the wrong things. Communications are a basic part of project team management. However, human nature being what it is, some project managers, team members, and project sponsors are more communicative than others. The project's communications program is explained in the phase review for the IT executives. Evidence of regular project team meetings and project status reports to the PMO and project sponsor is required.

Team communications can be explained by:

A. Location, day of week, and time of weekly team meetings
B. Link to directory containing meeting minutes
C. Link to the directory of status reports.

[H] Risks and Issues

There are various processes for identifying the risks faced by a project. On the macro level, these are in common with many projects. Detailed risks are based on the project plan, requirements, and technical solution design.

Each can indicate an aspect of the project that is significantly less than a certainty.

During the phase review, significant project issues and risks must be reviewed. PMOs will sometimes review the project artifacts to ensure that the project manager is looking ahead to mitigate risks and is tracking open issues. Either can significantly impact the project on budget and on time delivery.

[I] Phase II Review Results

In the early stages of a project, there may be a rush to "do something." This leads to the early purchase of expensive resources or to start coding immediately. Often the result is wasted time and money. A well performing project depends on proper preparation. This phase review ensures that all of the essential project foundations for a successful project are in place. Skipping steps during planning will not cause immediate problems but will result in waste and chaos later in the project.

§ 16.04 PHASE III—EXECUTION PHASE REVIEW

[A] Overview

The project execution phase converts the project solution design into an IT solution. During project execution, expenditures climb to their peak, materials are ordered, and expensive technical staff engaged. Technical problems are encountered and overcome. Schedule delays disrupt resource and roll planning. All of these things are normal to project execution. The Phase III review examines how the project manager anticipated and mitigated these issues.

Every project (by definition) is unique, so its management is likewise unique. However, some basic rules (best practices) must still be followed. Scope must be managed, cost contained, and the timeline met. Additionally, the customer must remain involved in the project to understand its progress, help resolve issues, and advice on design decisions.

Phase III artifacts may include:

A. Budget and timeline comparison of baseline to actual
B. Status reports
C. Issues log
D. Risk register
E. Written scope control process
F. Customer acceptance testing
G. Defect tracking
H. Business resiliency plan

[B] Scope Control

Project scope changes are a normal part of project execution. Scope changes may be submitted by any team member. Commonly, as the IT solution takes shape, additional requirements may come from the project sponsor. Shifts in the business environment may also alter the project.

Project scope changes impact the timeline and budget. These estimates indicated how much time and expense was needed to provide a specific result. Changes to this result will also change the timeline and budget. Project changes are a normal occurrence.

COMMENT

At the Phase III review, the project manager explains the process for making changes and recaps changes requested, both accepted and denied. The point is not what was accepted or was not accepted, but rather that the change process is working.

[C]   Budget Control

To a project manager, a budget is a cost estimate that over time is proven to be relatively accurate or not. However to an Accounting manager, it is a flow of cash that must be provided to the project. That which is an educated guess to a project manager is a commitment to the Accounting Department. Therefore, remaining within the limits of the budget is more than a guideline.

During the phase review, the project manager details the project actual costs compared to the project budget. The actuals versus budget analysis must include a Cost Performance Index analysis to determine the extent of cost variance and to calculate the estimate to completion. Significant cost variances must be explained in terms of cause, and steps taken to avoid future occurrence.

[D]   Schedule Control

How does the current project schedule compare to the original? Is this due to scope creep, poor estimates, or external factors? Accurately estimating projects is as much an art as a science. By definition, an estimate is a guess. However, to the business community, the project delivery date is a commitment.

During the phase review, the project manager compares the project actual schedule with the project baseline. The actuals versus baseline analysis must include a Schedule Performance Index analysis to determine the extent of schedule variance and to calculate the estimate to completion. Timeline discussions usually focus on the estimate to completion rather than on a list of problems encountered in the past.

[E]   Customer Acceptance Testing

When the product is ready for delivery, the customer will run its own tests to verify that the product fulfills the customer's requirements. Now is the time to describe these functional tests. The tests must be aligned with the project's business requirements and deliverables. Understanding the sort of tests the customer will perform help the project team to ensure the product is ready for delivery prior to calling the customer.

[F]   System Testing Results

Recap the results of the system testing of the many project components. This recap may discuss the number and types of defects found and in some cases, how they were overcome. To ensure that the hardware capabilities are appropriately sized for the anticipated load, performance testing may be required. Some companies avoid this additional expense but it demonstrates the number of simultaneous users that can access a system at the same time. The result may be to alter the data flows of the software or to increase the size of the target production system.

Depending on the type of data to be handled, information security tests may be required. This is typically penetration testing of the user interface. It examines the code to ensure it follows best software security practices and is not vulnerable to hacking attacks.

[G]   Business Resiliency Plans

With the IT solution firmly in mind, now is the time to include appropriate business resiliency elements into the solution design. Based on the financial impact to the organization, what actions are prudent in the event that this IT solution fails? Should disk storage be mirrored? Are redundant servers needed? Should a disaster recovery server be prepared in the hot site?

COMMENT

> Most companies use virtual servers for hot site spares. This reduces the number of physical servers wasting away on the racks in a hot site that may never be used.

[H]   Phase III Review Results

Phase III is usually the time when the greater amount of project resources are expended. During the phase review, the IT and business managers are checking to ensure that prudent steps were taken to keep the cost within the budget and the project delivery on time. Most of the artifacts concentrate on project management best practices. Actions such as periodic risk assessments, the tacking of project issues, monitoring cost in a timely fashion, customer communications are all important.

§ 16.05 PHASE IV—PROJECT IMPLEMENTATION PHASE REVIEW

[A] Overview

Once the IT product is completed and ready to install, there is one final check. This is to verify that the product has been properly completed and tested. It also verifies that the customer still needs it.

IT projects typically start at a leisurely pace, as there seems to be plenty of time and money for what is needed. Even if this is true in the beginning, the team's tone gradually changes the deeper they submerge into the project work and the "hidden" requirements seem to surface. Typically near the end of the development, the work is rushed and sometimes not as complete as the IT and business management would like to see it. In short, the focus is on meeting the deadline rather than ensuring everything is ready to go.

The product implementation review ensures that the project is truly ready for installation. It ensures that:

A. The team providing ongoing maintenance is ready to pick up the task.
B. Adequate testing has been completed to minimize the defects discovered after users begin.
C. The customer has accepted that the product fulfills the requirements approved at the beginning of the project.

Phase deliverables may include:

A. Testing results.
B. Written approval of customer acceptance testing.
C. A review of implementation plans.
D. Verification of acceptance by the team who will support the product in daily use.
E. Service Level Agreements detailing limits of IT support responsibilities.
F. Verification of a successful disaster recovery test.
G. Customer's comments on the product's quality and the project team's execution.

[B] Customer Acceptance Test Results

Once all of the technical testing is completed, the product is demonstrated for the customer. Each of the business requirements must be proven to function as approved during the project planning stage. At the conclusion of this demonstration, the project sponsor signs the Customer Acceptance Test document.

Often during customer acceptance testing, the project sponsor asks for additional features and functionality. A common statement is that "this is what I was really asking for." The best defense for the project team is the signed requirements statement from the planning phase. (The requirements document includes a description of how the function will be demonstrated.) Changes are not a problem but must flow through the change control process.

[C]   Technical Testing Results

A high level description of the testing performed on the new system is a way for the IT Manager to ensure that an appropriate level of testing was completed. This will reduce the likelihood of the project team rushing the installation of a defect riddled system. The test results of each function are described. One technique is to develop test cases based on the software planning USE cases. In this case, the tests prove that each course of action ("happy case" and alternate data flows) works as planned. (The presentation slide on test results is at a high level, with low level data available on request.)

The purpose of testing is to uncover problems. That defects exist is not an issue. It is the thoroughness of the testing and the tracking of problems through resolution. Open defects will be categorized as "cosmetic," "resolve later," or "prevents installation."

[D]   Implementation Plans

Moving a new system from testing into production can be a ticklish operation. Implementation plans describe the detailed steps for doing this. These plans should be in proportion to the complexity of the installation and the importance of the system. Implementation planning is based on the identification and mitigation of risks to a successful roll out.

Implementation plans have four stages:

A. **Pre-implementation stage.** The many things to do before the roll out date arrives. Notify the users, obtain agreement for the date, line up users to test immediately after the system is turned on, etc. Of course, the project technicians must be ready to work that day (usually on a weekend).

B. **Roll out stage.** Often a minute by minute timeline for the system installation. Example tasks include ensuring that the original data tables and files have been copied to other media (in case we must back out the change). Sometimes data files must be converted to another format. New programs must be activated and pointers installed on user desktops.

A part of the roll out is a risk assessment of what may go wrong and mitigation steps to avoid it. For example, checking with team members the day before the roll out to verify they will be available as previously agreed.

C. **Roll back plan.** Unfortunately not all new system installation are successful. If there are problems with the new system, then a decision must be jointly made with the project sponsor as to whether the new IT solution should be pulled out for repair or left in place since the problems may be minor. The roll back plan must be tested prior to the implementation, both to work out problems and to train the team in their duties. The length of time required to perform the roll back determines when the go/no go decision must be made on the implementation.

D. **Post implementation stage.** Actions performed to smooth the new IT system into use. This includes assisting the new users on the morning of the system's first use and providing "tip sheets" for what to do in given circumstances. Also a post roll-out survey (perhaps two weeks later) to determine how closely the new solution fits their needs.

[E]   Transition to Support Team

In most organizations, the team that develops the solution is not the same one as will provide its long-term support. If a project is already long past its requested completion date, there is a tendency for the development team to drop the new IT system into production and run off to the next project. Of course, this creates support issues if the understanding of the system's inner working is lost.

Prior to the installation date, a sign off is required from the support team that they are ready to assume support for the new system. This signoff signifies that the system's technical documentation is up to date and understandable. It also indicates that the support team will be involved in the system roll out to better identify problem areas.

[F]   Customer Concerns About This Implementation

This is the last chance for the project sponsor and users to speak up prior to system installation. They can voice concerns over the installation timing or testing demands upon their team's time. At this point, any issue is fair game. However, most project managers resolve any concerns prior to the phase review.

[G]   Service Level Agreements (SLAs)

Everyone has expectations when a new IT system is installed. If only the user's and IT staff's expectations were the same! A Service Level Agreement (SLA) defines the level of system support to expect after the initial roll out period. More importantly, the SLA may identify any unique equipment or software provided by the user that will be the user's responsibility to support. For example, if the new IT system depends on user supplied third-party software (for example, to run the building's air conditioning systems), then support of that product would be the user's responsibility.

COMMENT

Working through the details of SLAs is an excellent way for an IT Manager to learn about a business process's IT needs.

[H]   Training and User Guides

Prior to implementation, the people who will be using this new IT solution need to be taught about its features. Beyond that, some sort of users' guide must be distributed. This will help to reduce the likelihood that the IT solution will be pulled out of production due to user resistance to its use. During the phase review, explain who will teach the classes and who will write and maintain the users' guide.

[I]   Disaster Recovery/Business Continuity Test

One of the common places for a project team to cut corners is for a new system's disaster recovery instructions. The solution's recovery plan is best written at this time while the development team is still together. For the review, the plan should have been approved by the company's business resilience coordinator.

An important step is a test recovery of the system. This can be a tough sell to a development team who are racing just to complete the project on time. The goal of the test recovery is to determine how long is necessary to complete it. This time is important to the overall company recovery timeline. Of course, the test recovery also validates the recovery instructions.

[J]   Budget and Timeline Status

In the beginning of the project, there seems to be plenty of time and money, but as the project nears its end, both appear to be in short supply. As with the other review phases, the project manager must provide a high level status of the project's budget and timeline. Both also provide an estimate to completion, based on their current status.

During this discussion, the status of high level risks and important project issues are discussed. Obstacles to project completion are discussed. This late in the game, the emphasis is on the estimate to complete time and expense.

[K]   Phase IV Review Results

The results of this phase are either an approval to install the IT solution, to defer it, or to cancel the project. The timing of an installation is important. Most businesses have key dates when no interruption is permitted (such as year-end closing for the accounting department). During the Phase IV review, the business management team agrees to a roll out date and to the back out steps in case the installation fails.

§ 16.06   PHASE V—POST IMPLEMENTATION PHASE REVIEW

[A]   Overview

At some point, perhaps 60 days or so after roll out, business management, IT management, and the project manager meet again to discuss the quality of the delivered IT product. For the company funds expended, this is everyone's opportunity to identify what went well with the project and what could be improved. This valuable feedback is used to improve future projects.

Specific areas are examined during the review. They begin with the intangible impressions of the quality of the final product. This is measured by the customer's impressions of value provided. From the technical side, the number of service desk tickets is an indicator of product quality and stability.

One area of ongoing contention is the statement of project benefits used in Phase I to justify the project's expense. Now that the IT solution is in place, have these benefits been realized? If machinery was replaced, has the old equipment left the premises? If jobs were to be eliminated, has the payroll been reduced? Business manager's promises of cost reductions are evaluated to see if they have occurred or were just something said so a pet project can begin.

Critiquing the work may make the project manager uncomfortable, but there may be much to learn. Shortcuts that "no one knew about" may now be obvious. Many times, after all of the confusion and tension of the project roll out are past, project sponsors grow to appreciate the project manager's efforts.

Phase V artifacts include:

A. Recap of service desk calls since implementation
B. Customer comments on the product's functions and reliability
C. IT's impression of the product quality and user acceptance
D. Benefits realization review

[B] Service Desk Tickets

All project managers try to provide trouble free IT solutions. Time spent planning and testing software are steps in that direction. From the customer's perspective, is the IT solution stable? Does it crash or provide unpredictable results?

For the Phase V review, provide a recap of the trouble tickets submitted on this IT solution since its installation. Problem reports can be categorized into system defects (these should have been caught in testing) or operator mistakes (these should have been covered in training or eliminated through a mistake proofed user interface). Another dimension is the trend of service desk tickets over time. Hopefully the call frequency has declined over time.

Not everything can be tested in a development environment. Given an unlimited budget and timeline, an exact duplicate of the production environment can be created. However, this is often not practical. IT test environments are only as accurate as budgets will allow. Therefore, the final tests for complex systems that have many connections or connections to large IT entities may conduct their final tests during roll out.

[C] Customer Impressions

This is the customer's opportunity to sound off about all of the cost and time spent for the IT solution provided to them. Customer impressions can be collected in a brain storming session or an online survey.

Does the solution provided fulfill the original vision? Does it solve the customer's business problem? Are there additional changes needed to make it easier to use or to add time saving features? It is not unusual to want more of a successful solution. Just the suggestion of expanding the delivered solution is a compliment to its value and stability.

[D] IT Impressions

The Phase V review is also for the IT management to review how well the project flowed. Was the work load fairly spread? How well did the design decisions play out? Were all appropriate project management steps followed or did what seemed like prudent shortcuts diminish the quality of the final product?

[E] Benefits Review

Business managers have been known to promise many things if IT would just start the project. Based on these promised benefits, the project's funding is approved. When the project is completed, are the benefits realized? The realization of benefits is a business (non-IT) issue. It is usually addressed between the project sponsor, business management, and the Accounting Manager.

Some common tricks include promised staff reductions that are used to fill other positions. Equipment to be removed is used for another purpose and never leaves. Typical savings to demonstrate include:

A. Increased throughput
B. Equipment simplified
C. Staff reductions
D. Reduced defects
E. Savings by ending leases or maintenance contract

[F] Phase V Review Results

After a successful implantation, everyone smiles and is off to his or her next assignments. However, the real test of the IT solution is how well it performs over time. Despite all of the fine assurances up to this point, how well did the final product perform? The Phase V review will reflect this to management.

The other significant point is the realization of project benefits. These benefits were the basis of a business decision. This review discusses whether they have come to pass or are still pending.

See Policy ITP-16-1 Project Phase Reviews Policy as an example for performing phase reviews at your organization.

POLICY ITP-16-1. Project Phase Reviews Policy

Policy #:	ITP-16-1	**Effective:**	01/19/14	**Page #:**	1 of 3
Subject:	Project Phase Reviews Policy				

1.0 PURPOSE

This policy requires that any organized effort recognized by the IT Department as a "Project" shall include the appropriate level of formal planning, documentation, and management oversight. This documentation is essential for a project to be completed on time and within budget.

2.0 SCOPE

The policy applies to all information technology projects conducted within the company, using company resources. Projects conducted entirely under a contract for external support are not covered by this policy.

The administrative overhead of a project should be proportionate to its size. Project phase reviews are applied as follows:

A. Very small projects of less than $75,000 in total expense will perform Phase I.
B. Small projects of less than $75,000 only will perform Phases I and V.
C. Projects larger than $75,000 will perform all five phases.

3.0 POLICY

Based on industry standards, there are five phases to a project. At the conclusion of each phase, a formal review shall be held with (at a minimum) the project manager, the project sponsor, and the IT Manager. The five phases are:

A. Phase I—Business Case Phase Review
B. Phase II—Planning Phase Review
C. Phase III—Execution Phase Review
D. Phase IV—Project Implementation Phase Review
E. Phase V—Post Implementation Phase Review

Phase reviews are presentations which highlight critical aspects of a project. If any of these project "vital signs" indicate a project execution problem, then additional information can be provided by the project manager.

Phase reviews consist of both standard information and specific information for that phase. This information touches on the critical elements of a project and is presented at a high level. Details must be provided on request. Standard information to include in each review are:

A. Project objectives in clear, simple, and measurable terms. This reminds everyone present of the project's purpose.
B. Budget showing the baseline budget versus actual charges to the project. The estimate to completion is calculated (using the cost performance index) and shown on the chart. A contingency amount that reflects the budget's uncertainty.
C. Project schedule showing the baseline schedule versus actual time required for the project. The estimate to completion is calculated (using the schedule performance index) and shown on the chart. A contingency amount that reflects the timeline's uncertainty.
D. High level risks that will hinder the project.
E. Issues and obstacles that currently delay the project or increase costs.

F. Customer comments on project progress—their chance to focus the presentation on their concerns.

Unique information in each phase includes:

A. Phase I—Business Case Phase Review
  1. Statement of Planned Benefits.
  2. Statement of the problem to solve.
  3. Rough Order of Magnitude estimate (plus or minus 50%) of expense and time required.
  4. Specific deliverables.
  5. Assumptions concerning the project's execution and product's features.
  6. Risks to the project's success.
B. Phase II—Planning Phase Review
  1. Resolution of reviewer reservations from approval of previous phase.
  2. Recap of approved project charter.
  3. Specific business and technical requirements.
  4. High level project product solution with signed approval of the entire project team and project sponsor.
  5. High level work breakdown structure (details available on request).
  6. Detailed project budget and timeline (plus or minus 10%).
  7. Specific technical risks.
  8. Project organization to include the roles and responsibilities of team members.
  9. Customer written approval of user screens and reports.
  10. Statement of required system performance.
C. Phase III—Execution Phase Review
  1. Resolution of reviewer reservations from approval of previous phase.
  2. Demonstrated linkage of project requirements to USE cases to Test cases.
  3. Review of change control process with the number of requested changes.
  4. System test process and results.
  5. Performance testing results.
  6. Security testing results and approval of final version.
  7. Approval of final product by each.
D. Phase IV—Project Implementation Phase Review
  1. Implementation Plan, approved by project sponsor.
  2. Organization of team providing ongoing support.
  3. Proof of completed product acceptance test.
  4. Proof of successful disaster recovery test.
  5. Approved service level agreement.
  6. Acceptance of the new product by the team who shall take on ongoing support.

E. Phase V—Post Implementation Phase Review
    1. Statement of Planned Benefits versus realized.
    2. Product users' comments.
    3. Review of service desk problem tickets, to include a trend over time.
F. Phase review presentations will include:
    1. Phase reviews must include, at a minimum the IT Manager, PMO Manager, project manager, Business sponsor, Line Manager who will be using the new product.
    2. The PMO manager will approve the quality of the presentation before scheduling the full review meeting.
    3. Prior to the review, all relevant project documentation will be posted to the team's file share.
G. Project documents used to manage a project.

4.0 REVISION HISTORY

Date	Revision #	Description of Change
01/19/14	1.0	Initial creation.

5.0 INQUIRIES

Direct inquiries about this policy to:

George Jenkins, CIO
Our Company, Inc.
2900 Corporate Drive
Columbus, OH 43215

Voice: 614-555-1234
Fax: 614-555-1235
E-mail: gjenkins@company.com

Revision #:	1.1	Supersedes:	1.0	Date:	01/19/14

[G] Archiving Project Documents

Once the project is ready to close, take some time to clean up the many project documents for the archive. These documents should include anything that was used to make design changes, agreements with suppliers and the project sponsor, and anything that pertain to the internal design. All of these could be useful in the future, if this project's objective is ever updated or replaced.

The first step is to sift through the documents and delete all earlier drafts of a final document. For example, there may be multiple versions of the solution design that were developed over the course of multiple team meetings. However, the design of the product should be reflected in the final version of that document. Retaining the many drafts in the archive will only add clutter to the files.

Meeting minutes may be useful however; they can represent a considerable pile of documents to search through. If retained, be sure to read them to remove any comments of a personal nature. The same is for the retained personal correspondence.

See Policy ITP-16-2 IT Project Records Archive Policy as an example for archiving project records at your organization.

POLICY ITP-16-2. IT Project Records Archive Policy

Policy #:	ITP-16-2	Effective:	04/01/15	Page #:	1 of 2
Subject:	IT Project Records Archive Policy				

1.0 PURPOSE

This policy defines the IT project records archive program. Documents created during the life of a project contain many items of decisions made, agreements achieved and implementation problems. All of this is valuable information for the team maintaining the project product and when the objects created by the project are upgraded or replaced.

2.0 SCOPE

This policy applies to all projects managed through the IT department. It includes all documents created during the execution of the project creation, planning, execution, implementation, and follow up. The IT Director is responsible for establishing and maintaining the project archive.

This archive shall be held in online data storage with appropriate access security control. Documents with written signatures will be scanned into online document for storage.

3.0 POLICY

The following guidelines will be followed for the project management document archive program:

3.1 What to retain
Documents are retained to assist people with the ongoing product maintenance as well as for the design for future upgrades. Useful documents include:

- Decisions made during the design process. Most designs are tradeoffs between potential actions. These decisions and the logic supporting them are useful to future engineers proposing changes.

- User interface agreements with the project sponsor may show the evolution of the customer's desires.
- Project plans comparing the original estimates and task flow to the final may assist future project estimation.
- User and system technical documentation delivered with the final project product.
- Project team rosters to indicate who has expertise in various aspects of the final product.
- Product test plans and user acceptance plans.
- Risks and issues identified during the project.

Some IT projects are small or routine. In these cases, the benefit from retaining them may be outweighed by the hassle and storage costs. This determination can be made when approving the project's formal closure.

3.2 Purge documents
Before adding documents to the archive, sift through them and only include the latest versions. Old versions may confuse someone over what was included in the final product. Place yourself in the role of someone looking through the files to find something. Large or long projects may generate quite a pile to wade through. However, time spent doing this now when some idea of the project is fresh makes it easier for later archive researchers.

3.3 Retention
At some point, these documents will have little value. For example, if the product is upgrades annual, then after several upgrades, the original document might be candidate for deletion.

The IT Director will ensure that the company's record retention program on document retention is applied to these documents as appropriate. Where that program does not apply, the IT Director shall provide guidance on which types of documents to retain and for how long.

4.0 REVISION HISTORY

Date	Revision #	Description of Change
04/01/15	1.0	Initial creation.

5.0 INQUIRIES

Direct inquiries about this policy to:

George Jenkins, CIO
Our Company, Inc.
2900 Corporate Drive
Columbus, OH 43215

Voice: 614-555-1234
Fax: 614-555-1235
E-mail: gjenkins@company.com

Revision #:	1.0	Supersedes:	N/A	Date:	04/01/15

17

SOFTWARE DEVELOPMENT: SOLID PRACTICES

§ 17.01 OVERVIEW

[A] Purpose and Scope

A company's software is a reflection of its ever changing and complex operations. Creating or buying software is more than a question of resources and cost; it is also a question of remaining competitive. Software and the services it provides can give a company a competitive advantage; poorly designed software acts as a drag on the business. IT policies covering software development and acquisition help ensure that the organization receives the desired benefits from its software.

Creating computer software is expensive, and a company that employs its own programming staff has invested a considerable amount of money into processes to support its business. Ideally, this provides the company with an operating efficiency or other business advantage. To protect this investment, the company must have clearly defined policies that document how software is created, deployed, and maintained, and stipulate that all programs written using company resources (such as time, equipment, utility software, books, and so on) are the company's property. Without such policies, a company may find its software impossible to maintain or being used by a competitor or generally available in the marketplace.

[B] Critical Policies to Develop Based on This Chapter

Using the material discussed in this chapter, you will be able to create the following policies:

A. The company possesses title to all software created using its resources.
B. Version control and authorized upgrades.
C. Purchasing software.
D. Beta and test software.
E. Uniform coding practices.
F. Adequate documentation must be provided whenever implementing a major software change.
G. Software deployment.
H. Use of non-standard programming languages and software tools.
I. Unlicensed software.

Policies should always be developed based on the local situation. Successful managers cannot issue appropriate guidance if the policies are written with another company's situation or location in mind.

§ 17.02 SOFTWARE DEVELOPMENT PROCESS

[A] Why IT Is Important

Proper policy guidance makes the software development process more efficient: the longer it takes to develop software, the greater the chance that problems will occur. Creeping user requirements are the result of trying to build software to meet dynamic and ever-changing business requirements. It is simple; a company's business environment (competitive, legal, and environmental) is constantly changing.

Anyone who has been involved with software development for any length of time knows that the majority of all software development projects run over budget or are cancelled before completion. Even those that are completed rarely totally meet the user's original requirements.

COMMENT

Research by the Standish Group in 2012 finds that 18 percent of IT projects will be cancelled; 43 percent of projects will be late, over budget, and/or with less than the required features and functions. Only 39 percent are completed on time and on budget. Large projects have twice the chance of being late, over budget, and missing critical features than their smaller project counterparts. A large project is more than 10 times more likely to fail outright.

Capers Jones, in his book *Assessment and Control of Software Risks* (Prentice Hall PTR, 1994), identified no fewer than 50 major problems affecting software development. While technology has advanced since this book was published, our ability to complete projects successfully has not. He notes, "Few projects have more than 15 software risk factors at any time, but many projects have half a dozen simultaneously." He points out the "five most frequently encountered risk factors for large IT shops":

1. Creeping user requirements
2. Excessive schedule pressure
3. Low quality
4. Cost overruns
5. Inadequate configuration control

Application project overload and the deterioration of programming quality play havoc with programmer productivity. The prudent IT Manager not only has effective programming policies and procedures in place, but also makes certain they are observed.

COMMENT

All developers are encouraged to read *Code Complete, A Practical Handbook of Software Construction* by Steve McConnell. The sections on commenting code and code reviews are particularly important.

[B]   Ownership of Computer Software

Policy should be created to ensure that employees understand that all software developed by employees during the hours they are being paid by the company and/or using company equipment is the exclusive property of the employer. Many companies cover this under their employment agreement concerning development of patentable items. Be sure software ownership rights are specifically included in company employment agreements. Employees must also be aware of their responsibilities in honoring the terms of the license agreement for purchased software.

Purchased software. Purchased software and software documentation may only be copied as specified by the vendor. No versions of any purchased software are permitted beyond the number the firm has purchased. This applies to everyone in the company.

COMMENT

Purchased software provides only a license or permission to use a product under the conditions detailed in the license. The terms of this license will be violated if the purchaser makes more than the stipulated number of copies of the software. If the agreement is violated, the copyright holder may file a lawsuit for damages. The copyright holder may also reclaim all of the licenses purchased from him or her.

Unauthorized software. Personnel may not purchase or write their own software for use in the organization without authorization. They may not bring into the organization any software, in any form, that is not the property of the organization. The downloading of any unauthorized software to company-owned hardware at any company site also is not permitted.

See Policy ITP-17-1 Ownership of Computer Software Policy as an example.

POLICY ITP-17-1.   Ownership of Computer Software Policy

Policy #:	ITP-17-1	Effective:	03/18/13	Page #:	1 of N
Subject:	Ownership of Computer Software Policy				

1.0 PURPOSE

This policy defines the ownership of computer software developed using the company's time and resources.

2.0 SCOPE

The policy applies to all software applications developed at the company. It applies both to applications developed by the IT staff and to software developed using end-user tools such as Microsoft Excel or Access by non-IT staff.

3.0 POLICY

All software developed by employees or contractors during the hours they are being paid by the company and/or using company equipment is the exclusive property of the company. Salary-exempt personnel have no proprietary interest in programs they develop. All programming effort and documentation is the exclusive property of the employer as long as the hardware/software used belongs to the firm.

Personnel may not purchase or write their own software for use in the organization without authorization. They may not bring into the organization any software, in any form, which is not the property of the organization. The downloading of any unauthorized software to company-owned hardware at any company site also is not permitted. Any violation of this policy subjects the offender to immediate discharge and/or the reimbursement of all costs associated with such action.

4.0 REVISION HISTORY

Date	Revision #	Description of Change
03/18/13	1.0	Initial creation.

5.0 INQUIRIES

Direct inquiries about this policy to:

George Jenkins, CIO
Our Company, Inc.
2900 Corporate Drive
Columbus, OH 43215

Voice: 614-555-1234
Fax: 614-555-1235
E-mail: gjenkins@company.com

Revision #:	1.0	Supersedes:	N/A	Date:	03/18/13

COMMENT

Computer technicians appreciate the difficulties of keeping all the loaded systems software in "agreement" so that one program does not "crash" another. The introduction of additional software not previously tested and approved for company use exposes stable systems to a potentially destabilizing influence. Other issues include the ability for the unapproved software to exchange files with other systems as well as the ability of the company to provide cost-effective support to users.

[C] Review of Software Specifications

The initial step in program development is a review of the system's software specifications to ensure there is no misunderstanding of specification requirements between the business analyst, the requesting business sponsor, and the programmer(s). The following steps should be taken before any software is written:

A. **General review.** With the purpose and scope of the programs understood, the next step is to determine their relationships in the total system. When reviewing each program:
   1. Review the program's place in the system.
   2. Check the functions of programs preparing input for programs under review. Include the sequence of input elements and contents

of element sets. In addition, check the purposes of the program(s) that will use the output of this program.

3. Resolve any questions regarding system or programming requirements.

B. **Detailed review.** To ensure a complete understanding of the requirements for the program(s), consider the following items:

1. Data element specifications determine the precise record formats for files and the data dictionary specifications for database systems. For example, are the "year" data elements four-numeric character fields, or is there some other solution that was used to resolve the Y2K problem?

2. Data element flexibility to handle impending or likely field expansions. Examples of this are the size of currency fields, foreign currency conversions, additional tax requirements, or even an expansion of the Social Security number field.

3. Processing specifications determine calculations and comparison tests of data.

4. Systems specifications are reviewed to resolve any ambiguities or problems.

[D] Reusable Component Identification

Reusable components are those having identifiable commonalities across programs of a given project. The project must be large enough or consist of several smaller projects in the same general domain to justify a reuse strategy. For reuse to pay off, a specific plan must be developed before coding starts. Reuse planning prior to coding a new system will help organizations avoid the error of thinking about reuse too late.

A taxonomy system is needed to identify modules or objects for reuse. No single taxonomy system will apply to all reusable component libraries.

Program module commonalities include common data, common constants, common formula process, common tables, and/or reiteration processes. Because models are built prior to coding the actual program modules, potential reuse is greater.

One word of caution: Make sure the module or object works. There is nothing worse than having reusable code that has a bug placed into your library. A list should be maintained of each object location in case errors are detected later, as well as for future update requirements. At some installations, a comment line is added to the top of each object identifying each program that uses it. When the object is changed, these programs must also be updated and tested.

§ 17.03 PROGRAMMING METHODOLOGIES

[A] Systems Development Methodologies

A software development methodology (also known as a systems or software development life cycle, or SDLC) is a set of rules and practices used to create computer software. It describes the stages involved in a software development project, beginning with the initial feasibility study through the maintenance of the completed application. Various methodologies have been developed over the years to guide the processes involved, including the waterfall model, rapid application development (RAD), joint application development (JAD), agile, code and fix, spiral, and many others. Most software teams will use a combination of these models, using the attributes from each that work best in their particular environment. In many cases it is not so much the particular model that is used that is important for project success, but more that the chosen model is followed consistently.

Most practitioners divide the various software development methodologies into one of two camps: heavyweight and lightweight. A heavyweight methodology has many rules, practices, and documents. It requires discipline and time to follow correctly. A lightweight methodology has only a few rules and practices or ones that are easy to follow. Whatever methodology is used, most follow the steps below:

A. The existing business process or system is evaluated. This is usually done by interviewing users of the existing process.
B. The requirements of the new system are documented.
C. The new system is designed. The design should take into account the hardware and operating system requirements, security issues, and communication processes.
D. The new system is developed. Users of the system are trained. Any adjustments due to user requirements or performance issues are made.
E. The new system is implemented and integrated into the existing processes.
F. The system is maintained and modified as needed.

Popular development methodologies are described in the following sections. You must create policies that ensure that whatever methodology you use, it is consistently followed by all members of your development team.

[B] Waterfall

The Waterfall methodology is one of the oldest software development processes. It looks at a software project as a sequential series of phases, which each then consists of a series of activities and tasks. Each phase must be complete and accurate before the next phase can begin. The phases typically consist of the following:

A. System concept
B. System requirements definition
C. Software design
D. Detailed design
E. Code and unit test
F. Integration and system test

While all software development projects consist of these phases in one form or another, the Waterfall methodology treats each phase as distinct and separate. The project progresses in an orderly fashion from one phase to the next, much like water flowing downstream from one waterfall to the next. It provides an orderly sequence of development steps, which helps ensure that documentation and design reviews are completed before coding begins. This helps to guarantee the quality, reliability, and maintainability of the developed system.

Most software development teams today do not follow a strict Waterfall methodology, as it is seen as having too much overhead and being too slow for today's fast moving environment. But the Waterfall process does illustrate the steps necessary to successfully complete a software development project, with many of the basic concepts living on in the newer methodologies.

[C] Spiral

The demands for reducing the time to develop a usable software system make it difficult to strictly follow the Waterfall methodology. The Spiral methodology allows for multiple deliveries of usable software to the user by compressing the phases of the Waterfall method to deliver some portion of the ultimate system to the user while then working on the next portion.

Rather than attempting to deliver a complete system all at once, the desired user functionality is broken up into portions that can be incrementally delivered to the user. Each portion is then developed in turn using the basic Waterfall process and delivered as completed. User feedback from delivered portions of the system can then be incorporated into portions yet to be developed. In this way, the user gets his hands on usable software early in the process, which helps to ensure that the system being developed is what the user required.

The Spiral methodology also benefits from the fact that most users really do not know what they want until they see it, and many times ask for features they really do not need. By delivering the system in smaller pieces with minimal functionality, the user can provide valuable feedback to the developers early in the process. The Spiral method should still be planned methodically, with tasks and deliverables identified for each step in the spiral.

[D] Rapid Application Development

Rapid Application Development (RAD) is a systems development methodology created to radically decrease the time needed to design and implement information systems. RAD relies on extensive user involvement, Joint Application Design sessions, prototyping, integrated CASE tools, and code generators. The RAD approach is most appropriate for projects that do not have to be 100 percent right the first time, but that can be refined as the software is used. Project scope, size, and circumstances all determine the success of a RAD approach. RAD is appropriate for projects with the following attributes:

A. The scope of the project is narrow and well defined.
B. There are a limited number of people that are involved in design decisions.

    C. Users are available for questions at all times.

    D. The data for the project is well defined and already exists.

    E. The technical architecture is defined and in place.

    F. The project team is small; preferably six people or less.

    G. The technical requirements of the system are reasonable and well within the limits of the technology being used.

The major difference between RAD and other development methodologies is in the management techniques used. These techniques are:

    A. **Rapid prototyping**. Software usable by the user is created as quickly as possible to enable the user to provide feedback. This requires close cooperation between the developers and the users, with emphasis on relationship management and change management. Knowing when to start prototype development is an important skill.

    B. **Iteration**. There must be a commitment to make changes often based on user feedback. Development becomes an incremental process based on constant refinement.

    C. **Time boxing**. This is a management technique that forces delivery on a set schedule. The scope can be changed for an iteration but the delivery schedule cannot.

RAD works well when the user community and the software development team have established an environment of mutual respect and trust.

[E]   Agile

The term "Agile" is used to describe a number of related lightweight software development methodologies that are all based on incremental and iterative development. Formalization of what has become Agile software development started with the publishing of the *Manifesto for Agile Software Development*, which can still be found at *www.agilemanifesto.org*. The manifesto defines the priorities of practitioners of Agile software development, which are as follows:

    A. Individuals and interactions over processes and tools;

    B. Working software over comprehensive documentation;

    C. Customer collaboration over contract negotiation; and

    D. Responding to change over following a plan.

There are numerous software development methodologies that are considered to be Agile; Extreme Programming (XP), Scrum, Kanban development are a few of the more popular ones.

All Agile processes are intended to improve the efficiency of software development. They do this by delivering solutions early and often, keeping things simple, and recognizing that change is an inevitable part of the process. The fundamental characteristics of Agile are:

A. **User Stories**. The planning process in Agile is a joint effort of the customer and the developers. User stories are written on 4×6 cards and are used to communicate the desired outcome. Each user story is given a name and an overall description of what the customer wants. The development team then estimates the amount of time and effort required to deliver the requirements of the story. Each story must fit within the iteration time frame established by the team.

B. **Simple Design**. The design of any part of the system must be as simple as possible and still get the job done. Nothing is added that does not meet the requirements of the current story. No planning for the future is done, as the future is difficult to predict with accuracy.

C. **System Metaphor**. A consistent, organizing metaphor must be developed using a common terminology so that communication between the development team and the customer is error free.

D. **Coding Standards**. Coding standards are enforced to ensure consistency throughout the system. Two other Agile practices, pair programming and refactoring, help to enforce coding standards.

E. **On-Site Customer**. An on-site customer ensures that the development team stays on track. The rapid nature of an Agile development process requires that a customer be available at all times to answer questions and provide feedback.

F. **Small Releases**. Small releases allow the development team to put the system into production early, and to update it frequently. Each update cycle adds a few new features, and allows the team to get feedback from the customer much sooner.

G. **Continuous Testing**. Programmers using Agile develop customer approved test plans before writing any code. The developer then knows when they are done—when the test plan executes cleanly, the code is complete. Once that is done, future changes can be more easily validated using these test plans. The use of automated testing tools greatly improves this process.

H. **Refactoring**. Refactoring is the process of continuously improving existing code. The goal is to keep the code as clean and simple as possible, most often by removing any duplicate code. By using the test plans completed for each part of the system, you can ensure that any changes made by refactoring do not introduce errors.

I. **Pair Programming**. In some versions of Agile, especially XP, all production coding is done in pairs with two developers using a single machine. This causes all code to be reviewed while it is being written, which is much more effective than trying to review code after the fact. Pair programming also encourages the sharing of best practices throughout the team.

J. **Collective Code Ownership**. Work on the various sections of the application is reassigned on a regular basis. This ensures that no one person "owns" any part of the system, and it allows changes to be made without waiting for any one person.

K. **Continuous Integration**. All changes are integrated into the complete system. This helps eliminate integration problems since they are caught earlier in the process.

L. **Forty-Hour Work Week**. Tired programmers tend to make more mistakes. Agile considers overtime to be a sign of a poorly managed project.

The following characteristics of Agile are derived from software development principles that have been proven to work and are strongly emphasized in Agile:

A. **Communication**. Communication and interaction between the customer and the developers is good. Therefore, an Agile team should have a customer on-site that answers questions and helps to prioritize the work.

B. **Learning**. Learning is good, so have the developers work together in pairs or switch between functions to more easily spread the group knowledge. As a manager, you also get quicker feedback on new team members.

C. **Simple Code**. Simple code is more likely to work. Therefore, in Agile, you only write the code you need today to meet the customer's requirements. You also rewrite any code that becomes too complex.

D. **Code Reviews**. Reviewing code is a good practice. By working in pairs or by having different people working on each area of the project, code gets reviewed by multiple team members.

E. **Testing**. Testing code is good. In Agile, tests are written before the code is written. The code is considered complete when it passes the tests. The system is tested regularly using all automated tests to ensure that it works.

COMMENT

Excellent sources of additional information on Agile include the *Manifesto for Agile Software Development* (*www.agilemanifesto.org/*), Ron Jeffries' Web magazine at *Xprogramming.com—an Extreme Programming Resource* (*www.xprogramming.com/*), and the *Scrum Alliance* at *www.scrumalliance.org*.

Two of the more controversial aspects of Agile from a project manager's perspective are the concepts of pair programming and refactoring. To a project manager experienced with other software development methodologies, pair programming looks like two people doing the job of one; and refactoring looks like fixing something that is not broken.

Pair Programming. Pair programming is probably the most controversial practice in Agile. The typical reaction of management is that two people are getting paid to perform one job. Pair programming is—as the name implies— two programmers at a single workstation. One programmer is at the keyboard "driving," while the other is helping to solve problems and review the code as it is being written. The programmers take turns at each task. The pair collaborates on the design, coding, and testing of every line of code written.

Objections by management include:

A. Having two people at one workstation cannot be very cost effective.
B. If two people are doing the work of one, it is going to take twice as long.
C. That is not the way we have always done things around here.

Programmers who have never tried pair programming are not usually excited about trying it. Most programmers have been trained to work alone. Objections by programmers include:

A. Working with another person will slow me down.
B. I am used to working by myself; I need peace and quiet to think.
C. That is not the way we have always done things around here.

While all of these objections seem intuitively obvious, studies that have looked at pair programming have shown numerous benefits for the Project Manager and the members of the team. Benefits for the Project Manager include:

A. Improved team training.
B. Knowledge sharing is built into the process as pairs are switched.
C. Positive peer pressure increases productivity and rate of learning.
D. Quality is improved through greater defect prevention and defect removal.
E. All production code has been tested and reviewed.
F. Improved design, coding, and testing.
G. Faster and more accurate feedback on new team members.

Benefits for the team members include:

A. Less time is wasted being stuck on a problem.
B. Feedback on ideas is immediate.
C. Better able to solve problems due to the synergy created by working in pairs.
D. Greater exposure to different parts of the application.
E. Empowered to try new things without worrying about breaking the system.

In order for pair programming to work, each person must understand his or her role and responsibilities to make the pairing a success. In an Agile pair, the person using the keyboard is called the "driver," and the other member of the pair is called the "observer." Both have to do their job correctly to make the pair work. The role of the driver is to:

    A. Control the keyboard and mouse to actually enter the code or design.
    B. Discuss options and ideas with the observer.
    C. Brainstorm as required with the observer and others.
    D. Think tactically about how to implement the solution.

The role of the observer is to:

    A. Actively observe the work of the driver.
    B. Watch for defects.
    C. Discuss options and ideas with the driver.
    D. Think strategically about the direction the solution is going.

While the benefits of pair programming are many, it can be difficult to introduce the practice within an existing team. Some of these difficulties include:

    A. Resistance from team members.
    B. Personality conflicts within pairs.
    C. Egos getting in the way.
    D. Driver not accepting advice.
    E. Observer not actively participating.
    F. Selling the idea to management.
    G. Negative attitudes from team members such as:
        1. Not wanting to be a team player.
        2. Being defensive toward suggestions.
        3. Cowboy mentality.
        4. Impatience with less knowledgeable teammates.
        5. Fear of others discovering your lack of knowledge.

So how do you get started using pair programming with your team? The first step is to educate all of the team members on the process and the benefits it can provide. A small initial project works best, where a few members of the team can get their feet wet with pairing. It will take some time before the team becomes comfortable with pair programming, but 90 percent of programmers who have tried pair programming actually prefer it to other methodologies.

Some keys to successfully using pair programming include:

    A. Play nice
    B. Check your ego at the door
    C. Do not take criticism too seriously

  D. Clean up your mess
  E. Share everything with your partner

Refactoring. To the uninitiated, refactoring looks a lot like fixing things that are not broken. But the reality is that as a system evolves, changes made to the code at least indirectly affect all the code in the system. Refactoring is taking the time to review code that has not been changed recently to ensure that it is still the most appropriate code to support the current state of the system. When a change is made to the code, refactoring does not just look at what needs to be changed, but also looks at how the code can be improved or simplified. Constant refactoring improves the design of existing code, and helps to prevent unintended side effects from causing problems later.

  One of the main goals of refactoring is to keep the code as simple as possible. Nothing is added to the code that is not needed *now*. Code should be refactored when:

  A. A new function or object is added.
  B. Code is reviewed.
  C. A bug is being fixed.
  D. There is redundant code.
  E. The code becomes complex.
  F. New functionality is added.

§ 17.04 PROGRAMMING CONVENTIONS

[A] Coding Conventions

There may be a different format coding convention for each programming language used. RAD and CASE tools conventions, depending on the vendor, may not be similar to other language tools. In any case, conventions should be used consistently. Some suggestions for creating policies specific to your environment are listed below:

  A. Program coding.
    1. Coding format is restricted by compiler language specifications.
    2. All program source code should have programmer's name, program title, page number, and date at beginning of each source module or object.
  B. Character representation.
    1. Special care should be exercised in coding to distinguish alphabetic uppercase O and numeric zero (0). To avoid confusion, never use a zero in a field name—only as a number.
  C. Comments or notes.
    1. Comments or notes should be used to explain special mathematical or programming techniques at that point in the program where these techniques appear. Use them freely—especially before each major section of code.

> ## COMMENT
>
> One popular naming convention is "Hungarian notation," invented by Microsoft's chief architect Dr. Charles Simonyi, and is widely used by Microsoft. It became known as Hungarian notation because Simonyi is originally from Hungary and the prefixes give the variable names a non-English look. Documentation on the use of Hungarian notation can be found on Microsoft's Web site at *http://msdn.microsoft.com/en-us/library/aa260976(VS.60).aspx*. This notation ties the data element to its originating field making it easy to trace data elements back to their source.

D. Names used in programming.
   1. Data element names and variable names should be related to the type of data being stored.
   2. Size of names used is limited by the naming conventions of the language.
   3. Procedure names used for programming should correspond to names of those procedures used in program flowcharts.
E. Error messages embedded within a program should clearly describe what the problem is and *where* in the program it occurred. You should also include instructions to the user as to what to do. For example, to troubleshoot this error, the PC must be left as-is until the programmer examines the program, or it could direct the user to reload the data file, etc. This assists the user because he or she knows if and how to proceed.

[B] Controls

It is the programmer's responsibility to incorporate into a program the controls specified by the program supervisor, systems analyst, or auditor. Programmers should identify any additional controls necessary for the proper processing of data through the system. These controls may focus on such details as:

A. Specifying the use of standard labels.
B. Sequence checking input files.
C. Validating vital input elements not checked by a previous program.
D. Showing specific control totals to be accumulated within program.

§ 17.05 SOFTWARE ACQUISITION

[A] Overview

The decision to purchase software is typically made when in-house development cost is prohibitive or programming talent is unavailable in the timeframe required. It is a waste of money to write software already available as an off-the-shelf, shrink-wrapped package. One type of packaged software, known as horizontal software, is widely available for PCs, such as word processors, spreadsheets, or personal database programs. The other type of packaged software, vertical software, has a much more limited market. It is used for specific procedures by organizations that have common needs, such as a billing system for hairdressers.

If a shrink-wrapped program is not available, you can contact outside software contractors for bids. Contractors can work at their facilities or yours. How much control the company wants over product development will govern where the contractors work. Different procedures for requesting a purchasing order and for payment of the invoice will be required, depending on where the work is done.

[B]   IT Purchased Software

The IT Manager should delegate the job of coordinator of IT software purchasing. This person is responsible for ensuring that all software requested is on the approved software list. The coordinator is also responsible for ensuring that the software inventory is kept current and that all licenses are accounted for. He or she should generate a periodic report informing the IT Manager of all purchases, budget status, and software license status. See Policy ITP-17-2 Acquisition of Computer Software Policy as an example.

POLICY ITP-17-2.   Acquisition of Computer Software Policy

Policy #:	ITP-17-2	**Effective:**	03/18/13	**Page #:**	1 of N
Subject:	Acquisition of Computer Software Policy				

1.0 PURPOSE

This policy defines the process for purchasing computer software.

2.0 SCOPE

The policy applies to all software applications purchased by the company. It applies both to the IT department and to software purchased by end users.

3.0 POLICY

The IT Manager will designate an IT staff member to be the coordinator of IT software purchasing. This person will oversee the purchasing of all software used at the company. The following procedures must be followed when purchasing new software.

    A. **IT software requisition procedure.** The coordinator of IT software purchasing is sent a memo listing the software requested, the reason for

17-18

the request, and the date by which the software is needed. The coordinator checks the approved software purchasing lists by name and kind of software. The coordinator then prepares a purchase requisition. If the coordinator can approve the requisition, information will be extracted for the monthly software report before the requisition is sent to purchasing. If not, it will be forwarded to the IT Manager for his or her approval.

The IT Manager will approve or deny the request, note the decision on the requesting memo, sign and date it, and return it to the software coordinator.

The coordinator will take the approved requests and issue purchase requisitions. Information will be extracted for the monthly software report before the purchase requisitions are sent to purchasing. The IT Manager must sign the requisitions before they are sent on to purchasing. The IT Manager, providing any information as to why the request was denied, will answer the unapproved requisitioning memos. The original requesting memos, requisition copies, and reply memos will be filed in the form of hardcopies or scanned and saved.

B. **IT monthly software report.** The software coordinator should report the following information to the IT Manager by memo on a monthly basis:
1. Cumulative expenditures to date for software.
2. Balance of budget to date.
3. Name and cost of software purchased.
4. Total amount spent to date by kind of software purchased.
5. Name of software purchased by each organizational unit and dollars spent.
6. Total spent to date by each unit.
7. Monthly license maintenance fee per product (if any).
8. Expiration date for each software license (if applicable).

C. **Payment of invoice.** For purchase orders to be paid, the IT software coordinator has to confirm the software has been received. If there are any problems, the coordinator should notify accounts payable to hold up payment to the vendor. If the software is returned, purchasing and accounts payable should be notified. If the vendor will not accept the returned software, and there is a problem with it, this information should be given to the IT Manager. If the vendor requires a rewrapping charge, the original purchase order is canceled and a new requisition written for the rewrapping charge, which will have to be applied to the software expense list and identified as such.

4.0 REVISION HISTORY

Date	Revision #	Description of Change
03/18/13	1.0	Initial creation.

5.0 INQUIRIES

Direct inquiries about this policy to:

George Jenkins, CIO
Our Company, Inc.
2900 Corporate Drive
Columbus, OH 43215

Voice: 614-555-1234
Fax: 614-555-1235
E-mail: gjenkins@company.com

Revision #:	1.0	Supersedes:	N/A	Date:	03/18/13

COMMENT

The addition of new software technology to an IT department increases the technical requirements on an IT staff. Each new tool comes with an implied requirement for software maintenance support, staff training, documentation, etc. This may be easier to say than to do. One CIO made a rule that for every new tool added to the data center, one had to leave. Despite this, four years later the number of software tools had risen by 10 percent.

[C]   Other Unit Software Requisition Procedures

Other business units that have their own budget for software should use the same procedures as for other purchases. The information systems unit should publish a list of approved software they support. Training costs time and money. There is far more software in the world than there is time to learn it. If someone sneaks around and installs non-standard software, it will be difficult for the IT staff to assist him or her. If the person calls for help, there is no point in denying the request, but it will not be a high priority. In these cases, IT may purchase some service desk support time from the vendor, but funds from the customer's department should be used.

The small print on a software package lists restrictions in force unless the vendor guarantees something else in writing. License restrictions should be reviewed before the seal is broken on the program disk container since it is usually impossible to return opened software. If the seal is broken and the software does not perform as expected, ask the purchasing department to contact the vendor. Send a memo to accounts payable instructing a hold on payment of the invoice until the problem is resolved.

[D]   Contract Programming

Purchasing contract software is governed by the organization's policy for contracting outside services. The purchase order should contain a statement describing an acceptable program as noted in § 17.05[G], "Beta Software Testing and Evaluation." In addition, if this software is written exclusively for your company, a clause should be included in the purchase that specifies the company will have complete ownership of the software copyright. (It is unsettling to see a contract programmer selling on the open market the software you paid to have him develop. When in doubt, refer to your legal counsel concerning copyright ownership.)

The vendor must provide the source code that will be converted to executable code and tested, as well as the software documentation. These results will be compared with the vendor's test output to ensure it is the same. The vendor will be provided with test data that has been approved and/or generated by the user, and a copy will be used for the final (in-house) source code test.

Once the software has been purchased, there is little leverage to get corrections made (assuming the firm is still in business when corrections are needed). Therefore, the prudent IT Manager sends the contract and/or purchase order specifications to the organization's legal department before signing any commitments.

[E]   Contract Programmers

Contract (temporary) programmers may or may not work in-house, but are paid by the hour to work on assigned projects. When contract programmers start, the person they are reporting to should give them a short introduction to the staff, a tour of the facilities, and information about the company's established policies and procedures for programming and documentation. Giving them samples of previous project efforts to review would be helpful. Contract persons working at the firm's IT site should be provided with a desk and required tools. Other information about working with contract programmers is provided in Chapter 24, "Vendors: Getting the Goods."

The contract person should be monitored closely during the first week or two to ensure proper job performance, in addition to the regular progress reports filed weekly by all programmers. Any personality problems with staff or users also should be noted and addressed promptly.

[F]   Evaluation of Packaged Software

There are some major issues to address when purchasing packaged software that can apply to almost any type of software supplier. Use the list below to develop policy specific to your organization on how packaged software is to be evaluated.

A. Will the vendor be in business next year?
B. What warranty will be provided?
C. Will the software integrate with other software used by the company?
D. Will the software adapt to the company's information systems standards?
E. How flexible is the software package?
F. Is current company hardware compatible with the proposed software?
G. Will documentation provided be user-friendly?
H. What type of training is offered?
I. What other expenses will be required?
J. Can the vendor provide modifications to the software?
K. Is there an upgrade planned in the near future?
L. Is there a vendor service desk?
M. What is the vendor's reputation?
N. How many will use software?
O. Is there a users' support group?
P. Will the vendor supply names of current users? If answer is yes, contact him or her and ask for names of other users to contact.
Q. What is the major business focus of the vendor?

To discover how difficult or easy it will be to implement the proposed software, the following issues should be addressed:

A. How complex is the installation procedure, including the initial data load?
B. Will the vendor provide installation assistance?
C. How easy is the software to maintain?

To evaluate vendor-supplied software, ask current or former users the following:

A. Would they buy from the same vendor again?
B. Did the software perform as promised?
C. Was the training of value?
D. Was the documentation easy to follow and complete?
E. Were there any implementation problems?
F. Did installation or operation have any hidden costs (to find real cost of installation and data conversion)?
G. Would the referenced user allow a visit to his or her site to see how the software is working and talk to operations personnel?

New packaged software must be evaluated, whether for new applications or for placement on the "approved purchase list," especially if this purchase commits the company to buy in volume. Depending on the software being evaluated, consider using the following procedures.

General use software evaluation. A person or formal committee will be responsible for general-use packaged software evaluation. A request for such evaluation can come from a user, a systems analyst, information systems management, or the party performing the evaluation. The person or committee responsible will be a source for packaged software information consulting services. Worksheet 17-1 is a sample form used for software evaluation.

Whenever possible, more than one vendor should be evaluated for the same kind of software. Computer publications and Web sites, as well as their advertisements, are good sources of evaluation information. Keep an information folder for each type of packaged software evaluated.

Client/server and vertical software evaluation. Client/server and vertical packaged software will require a preliminary operations hands-on test followed by controlled client/server prototype operations testing. Users' evaluation also will be required. The time required for each controlled group prototype test will vary with the complexity of the software operation and the number of planned future users. The more users, the safer the software should be (e.g., free of bugs). The time required for testing also would be limited by the vendor, the time limit on returning the software, or when the invoice has to be paid.

[G] Beta Software Testing and Evaluation

In their quest for a competitive advantage, some companies reach out to the leading edge of technology. Often, this involves assisting in the testing of products that are still in development. This is known as beta testing (alpha testing is done by the programmers). Beta testing agreements commit the company to apply some of its hardware and personnel resources to further debug a product. The advantage to the company is to gain in-depth knowledge of a leading-edge product or technology and how to best use it before it is released to the general marketplace.

WORKSHEET 17-1. Software Evaluation Worksheet

Software Evaluation Worksheet						
Software Title:			Version:			
Vendor:		Description:				
Vendor Address:						
Contact Person:			Phone #:			
PO #:			Date:			
Date(s) Software Tested:				By:		
Copied to Server:				Date:		
Rights Are Assigned/Flagged (list rights):						
Software Copied to Other Servers (list):						

WORKSHEET 17-1. (Continued)

Software Evaluation (attach extra pages and documents):
Documentation Evaluation (attach extra pages and documents):

However, the cost to a company can be high. One or more technical people must be dedicated for a considerable amount of time to learn a product that is still changing. The product being tested can crash at any time, corrupt company files, and even lock up the hardware platform it is running on. There is no guarantee that the final commercial version of the product will even possess the key functions the company desires.

In general, IT policy should discourage beta testing products. Technical people by nature enjoy working with the latest technologies and tend to quickly volunteer for such programs. A firm policy against this will inhibit the flow of beta requests. The policy also must strictly forbid the installation of any beta products without the IT Manager's approval.

Any beta commitments should require the prior approval of the head of information systems or a designated agent. Any commitments to use beta testing should be limited to pilot operations not part of the corporate information systems operation. No beta operations should be planned beyond the time limit specified by the vendor.

Beta testing should not have access to the corporate system or database at any time but will be limited to a segregated portion of the network or on a stand-alone PC. It should not have contact with any processing or database that is under the domain of the auditors.

All costs associated with a beta testing operation should be monitored and reported monthly to the head of information systems. In addition, a final report should be submitted after beta testing is complete. The following should be reported:

A. **Personnel time.** Personnel time used should be kept for IT staff, user employees, and other workers. The total time for each group should be reported. If required by the head of IT, the dollar cost by each group, the total cost, and any overtime incurred because of beta testing should be listed and identified in the report.

B. **Other costs.** Costs, other than personnel, also should be reported. This covers such items as: supplies, postage, telephone calls, costs of outside services rendered, any chargeback services (computer, copies made, etc.), and expense account reimbursements.

C. **Beta operating problems.** Any beta testing and/or operating problems occurring during the month should be reported, with the estimated total cost of each occurrence. It should be noted if any problem has occurred before and, if so, how often.

D. **Vendors' contact documentation.** Copies of correspondence sent to vendors, telephone call notes, and e-mail sent or received should be attached to the report. The person writing the report should summarize comments addressing these issues.

E. **User reports.** Copies of beta testing memos or e-mail concerning the project should be attached to the report. The person writing the report should summarize comments addressing these issues.

F. **Report summary.** The person writing the report should summarize the status of the beta testing. Any changes the vendor plans to make that would benefit the future use of the software should be noted. Any recommendation as to continuing or discontinuing the beta testing or any other comments worth noting should be included. Also, the question of whether the beta shut-down date will create any problems should be addressed.

G. **Final report.** A final report should be submitted after beta testing has been completed. Attached to the final report should be a copy of all completed Software Evaluation Worksheets (see Worksheet 17-1). Benefits derived from the beta test project should be reported in detail. The report also should include a summarized cost-benefit analysis and what final action was taken based on the beta testing.

§ 17.06 PROGRAM TESTING

[A] Test Planning

Software written by IT programming staff or contract programmers, or contracted with an outside firm, will require program testing according to the procedures presented here. All new and updated programs require testing, the magnitude and complexity of which may be determined by the auditors. User acceptance should not be overlooked. Everyone concerned in the company may be happy with the test results, but unless the user is satisfied, operation problems may occur later. A formal test plan should be composed of the following:

A. **General information.** This section contains pertinent information needed to identify a program and the project with which it is associated. The following information is included:
   1. Project number
   2. Programmer(s)
   3. Program identifier(s)
   4. Scheduled completion date

    5. Date

    6. Language in which program is written

B. **Test plan.** This section describes the steps required for testing individual segments of each program's logic. The information includes:

    1. Program identifier

    2. Function to be tested

    3. Test number

    4. Test priority

C. **Approval.** This section contains the signature blocks required to approve the test plan and authorize the testing. The program supervisor or Project Manager also will use this part of the program test to indicate the type of testing to be conducted.

    1. **Unlimited.** The programmer may test until completion without additional review and/or approval.

    2. **Limited.** A specific number of tests is permitted before approval expires and a review to approve further testing is required.

D. **Test results.** This section reflects the progress of the program during testing, including date of the first test, systems tests, and volume test. If tests are run for the auditors, the date the auditors' presence is required will be noted.

[B] Test Preparation

To ensure test data is representative, all conditions shown in the program flowcharts must be included. The flowchart can be reduced to a decision tree, showing only the decision points and the conditions for the decisions. This makes it easy for users or auditors to follow the decision conditions.

WORKSHEET 17-2. Decision Table Worksheet

Decision Table Worksheet								
TITLE	DECISION RULES							
	1	2	3	4	5	6	7	8
CONDITION STUB	CONDITION ENTRY							
ACTION STUB	ACTION ENTRY							

Another tool for test preparation is a decision table. (See Worksheet 17-2 for a Decision Table Worksheet.) The box labeled "title" contains the procedure title. The area labeled "condition stub" lists all possible conditions tested. The "action stub" area lists all actions that can take place. Under "decision rules" are listed "condition entries," the actual conditions that determine how the data will be treated, and "action entries," the actions that determine which course to follow predicated on the entry conditions. A sample procedure for credit approval is shown in Exhibit 17-1. A decision table with an "else" rule is shown in Exhibit 17-2. For best results, someone other than coding personnel should prepare the test data. ***Never use live data for testing!*** Make a copy of it and, if possible, run all tests on similar but separate platforms. The developer may conduct preliminary testing, as long as someone else does the final test development. This procedure and use of the decision table enhance the potential for detecting errors.

Test material is retained and kept current for later use in testing systems and program specifications. Following are specifications for preparing test data:

A. The requirements outlined in the system specifications must be clearly understood.
B. The logic and major routines requiring testing must be reviewed and the findings documented.

EXHIBIT 17-1.   Sample Decision Table

Decision Table Worksheet								
CREDIT APPROVAL	DECISION RULES							
	1	2	3	4	5	6	7	8
ON APPROVED LIST	Y	N	N	N	N			
PAST EXPERIENCE OK	—	Y	N	N	N			
APPROVED CO-SIGNER	—	—	Y	N	N			
SPECIAL APPROVAL RECEIVED	—	—	—	Y	N			
APPROVE ORDER	X	X	X	X	—			
RETURN ORDER	—	—	—	—	X			
GO TO TABLE A5	X	X	X	X	—			
END OF PROCEDURE	—	—	—	—	X			

EXHIBIT 17-2. Sample Decision Table With Else Rule

Decision Table Worksheet		
EMPLOYMENT	**DECISION RULES**	
	1	ELSE
COLLEGE DEGREE	YES	—
3 YEARS EXPERIENCE	VISUAL BASIC	—
APPLICATION FORM	GET ONE	—
INTERVIEW	SCHEDULE	—
DISPOSITION	—	REJECT

C. The test data must be filed in the library or project folder. This material is considered part of the documentation and must be maintained during the life of the program.

The analyst or program supervisor responsible must review all system modifications to determine if any changes are required in the test data. When a change is made, the programmer or test preparer conducts tests with the pertinent data to ensure the modifications are correct and have not affected other processing areas.

[C] Test Analysis

Once the test cases have been prepared you are ready to test the software. Your testing policy should include the following items that should be carefully checked to avoid testing errors:

A. Input/Output
 1. Proper heading format, line spacing, spelling, and punctuation of reports.
 2. Correct data element size and content.
 3. Report output matches expected specifications.

    4. Correctly keyed-in data.
B. Problem Analysis
    1. Original specifications are understood.
    2. Flowcharting does not have logic errors.
    3. Coding errors are not present.
    4. No software revision errors exist.

[D] Operating Program Maintenance

Only maintenance programmers should have access to the software and be allowed to copy it for maintenance. The maintenance of running programs should be forbidden without the approval of the operations manager, and auditor if required. A violation of this procedure is grounds for dismissal.

After the required maintenance is completed, the program(s) should be tested. The procedures described in § 17.07[C], "Review and Acceptance of Test Results," should be repeated in order for the changes to become part of the production system.

[E] Testing

The purpose of testing a coded program is to detect syntax and logic errors. Syntax errors are detected while compiling a source program into an executable program and commonly occur when program-coding rules for the language being used are not followed. The compiler will identify the statement that contains the error by producing syntax error messages. In some cases, an executable program is not generated because of syntax errors. After all syntax errors are corrected, the compiler generates an executable program.

Use the test data prepared in desk checking (reviewing your code) to generate input data to test the program's functions. Several types of errors often are made by programmers and can be detected and corrected with the proper testing procedures. These errors are classified as:

A. Clerical errors.
B. Logical errors.
C. Interpretation or communication errors (these occur due to misinterpretation or misunderstanding of program requirements).
D. Data type errors.

There are tools available to automate testing. Some automated testing environments include:

Junit	Open source	*www.junit.org*
Test Studio	Telerik	*www.telerik.com/teststudio*
TestComplete	SmartBear	*www.smartbear.com*

Maintain a copy of the test plan with the program documentation. This will be handy the next time a quick change is made and a test is needed to verify the software.

COMMENT

Just how expensive can bad software be? In December 2005, the Tokyo Stock Exchange reported that a bug in its trading system software contributed to a trade mistake that caused an investment bank to lose $346 million. A trader entered an order to sell 610,000 shares at 1 yen each, when what he meant to do was sell 1 share at 610,000 yen. When he tried to cancel the order, he discovered that the system was not designed to allow a sell order to be cancelled while processing buy orders.

[F]   Audit Review

Rare indeed is the company that is not heavily dependent on computer technology. As business objectives and processes evolve, so must the data systems. Data systems audits are necessary to ensure that the computer systems in use continue to run properly and accurately.

Management bears the ultimate responsibility for having an IT audit policy that can assure them of the validity and integrity of financial and reporting programs. Auditors determine the actual audit procedures, and either internal or external auditors perform the actual audit.

Computer-related fraud is now an everyday possibility. Because of the disturbing rise in unauthorized access to databases, computer fraud, mismanagement, and lawsuits, IT Managers and auditors have to be more security-minded than ever before.

Auditors approve and oversee financial programs. They also are very concerned with data's accuracy. IT Managers should seek the auditor's approval to confirm reliability of financially related systems and programs. Audits are intended to:

A. Review all corporate computer programs under development or have maintenance performed to ensure that adequate and reliable audit controls are built into the system and program software.
B. Determine that specified controls are reliable within operational system programs.
C. Confirm that access to operating programs and databases by remote or network access is continually governed by security policies and technologies to prevent unauthorized access.
D. Confirm that established accounting standards have been met and employed by all information systems using them.

§ 17.07 SOFTWARE DEPLOYMENT

[A] Overview

Deploying a software application from developmental to operational status follows standard review and approval procedures. These procedures apply to programs developed by IT programming staff or contract programmers, or contracted with an outside firm. Purchased or completed beta tested software will follow the same procedures whenever possible. The deployment can begin only after the software or system passes all testing procedures.

Deployment is the placing into operation of the tested software or system, which either replaces existing applications or is completely new. When discontinued software is replaced by a new system, the options are:

A. **Phased.** The new system can be deployed in modular fashion or in phases. When one phase is identified as operational and accepted, the next part of the deployment can begin.

B. **Direct.** Direct deployment can be a complete, one-time conversion or deployment. The old system will be replaced completely by the new. Operations has to be totally involved with the deployment and operation of the new system software.

C. **Pilot.** The new system can be deployed as a prototype operation in one safe location. After this operation is running properly, it may be deployed to other locations. This type of deployment is ideal for workgroups or independent PC operations.

D. **Parallel.** This type of deployment is most often used with corporate IT computer operations. It is the safest and most preferred method of deploying a new software system, but also the most costly as it requires the business user to enter data twice—once into each system. If, after comparing output results and the database status of both systems, the results are compatible, the new deployment is considered complete.

When no existing software is being replaced, new software deployment can occur as phased, direct, or pilot deployment. These procedures for software deployment are the same whether a new system is replacing an old one or not.

[B] Deployment Strategy

The deployment of an enhancement to an existing system or of a new system is a significant milestone in the completion of an IT project. It is critical that a deployment strategy be developed and documented before the new software in placed into production to ensure minimal disruption to the business. Your deployment strategy should consider the following:

A. **Proposed deployment date and time.** Are there business or systems considerations for determining the appropriate date and time for deployment?

B. **Checkpoints identified.** Are there steps in the deployment process where a decision to continue or roll back are desirable?

C. **Dependencies.** Are there any dependencies that could impact the deployment? This might include the status of other systems, user training, availability of hardware, etc.

D. **Communication plan.** How will the deployment be communicated to both the technical and user teams? Will the availability or performance of other systems be impacted? If so their users should be notified.

E. **Who will perform the deployment?** Larger organizations will have a dedicated deployment team; in small organizations, members of the development team typically perform deployments.

F. **Staging environment.** Is a staging environment available to test the deployment?

G. **What members of the business should be involved?** Include members of the user community to ensure their input and support of the deployment plan.

H. **Risk mitigation plan.** It is critical to document the risks involved in performing the deployment and have a plan for avoiding or mitigating the risks.

I. **Rollback plan.** Not all deployments will be successful; you must have a plan to roll back all changes to systems and data made by deployment to their pre-deployment state.

J. **Post deployment activities.** Are there tests that need to be executed or other items that need to be reviewed once the deployment is complete?

See Worksheet 17-3 for a Software Deployment Checklist.

WORKSHEET ITP-17-3.   Software Deployment Checklist

Software Deployment Checklist		
	Responsible Person	**Date Completed**
QA Team		
All test plans completed successfully		
Test results documented		
All remaining defects documented		
User acceptance of test results		
Development Team		
Security requirements reviewed with security team		
Installation and configuration scripts have been created		

WORKSHEET 17-3. (Continued)

Risk assessment and roll back plan has been completed		
All source code saved and versioned		
Release Team		
Staging environment configured		
Create and distribute communications plan		
Documentation		
System requirements documented and approved		
System design documented and approved		
Requirements traceability matrix completed		
Training of users completed		
Approved by:	**Date:**	

[C] Review and Acceptance of Test Results

To ensure that correct results are obtained from extended program testing, a review should be conducted with users and auditors, if they are involved. Now is the time to bring to everyone's attention any concerns by the people who will be using this product. If a Requirements Traceability Matrix was created, it should be reviewed to ensure that testing covered all of the user requirements.

Acceptance should be confirmed by memo from involved users and/or auditors directed to the system Project Manager or the program supervisor. If a change tracking or service management system is being used, then this approval must be stored there. A vendor who is involved with the project should receive this information from the system manager and/or programming supervisor.

[D] Selection of a Deployment Day

The first day that the revised or new program is to be run is very important. Some companies have a policy that all changes will go in on the same night of the week, such as a Thursday. Then, on Friday, they are on alert to any problem arising from the change. This also allows time to alert the service desk so they can promptly call the development team if anything unusual or unexpected is reported for that system during the rollout day.

A very good business policy is for the development team to walk through the program with the business department who uses the code to obtain first-hand information of any start-up problems and to explain to the business users how to benefit from system changes.

[E] Review and Acceptance of Documentation

Technical and end-user documentation should be prepared according to established specifications. Any changes or additions should be conveyed by e-mail or hardcopy memo to the appropriate person in charge of documentation approval. Its acceptance should be conveyed by memo to the heads of programming and systems.

Documentation should be approved by the intended audience. The end users should verify that the instructions are clear and understandable by the technical level of their workers. Technical documentation will be accepted by the program manager if it is complete and conforms to the staff's normal document flows. Computer operations and service desk documentation focus on actions these teams must perform to support this product.

[F] Acceptance of Contracted Software

The deployment of contracted software should follow the same deployment procedures as in-house developed software programs. Acceptance of purchased software as operational includes informing accounts payable via memo or e-mail that the invoice can be paid. The note should contain the vendor's name, item name and description, and purchase order number. If, on the other hand, the software does not meet the standards specified in the purchase order, a memo or e-mail is sent to the purchasing and/or accounts payable departments so informing them; the purchasing department will then inform the vendor.

[G] Deployment Sign-off

After the deployment of the software is completed and accepted, the software development team will no longer have access to the production system software. The source and object code is archived in the source code control system. The code cannot be changed without performing the routine change control turnover process. Access to this code is usually restricted to the maintenance programmers.

See Policy ITP-17-3 Software Deployment Policy as an example.

POLICY ITP-17-3. Software Deployment Policy

Policy #:	ITP-17-3	**Effective:**	03/18/15	**Page #:**	1 of 2
Subject:	Software Deployment Policy				

§ 17.07[G]

1.0 PURPOSE

This policy is designed to ensure that updates to software developed by corporate IT are properly deployed to production.

2.0 SCOPE

This policy encompasses all software developed by corporate IT that supports critical business functions.

3.0 POLICY

The IT Manager will designate a release coordinator who ensures that all software deployments are done following the approved deployment checklist. The deployment checklist must contain at a minimum the following:

A. **Proposed deployment date and time.** Are there business or systems considerations for determining the appropriate date and time for deployment?

B. **Checkpoints identified.** Are there steps in the deployment process where a decision to continue or roll back are desirable?

C. **Dependencies.** Are there any dependencies that could impact the deployment? This might include the status of other systems, user training, availability of hardware, etc.

D. **Communication plan.** How will the deployment be communicated to both the technical and user teams? Will the availability or performance of other systems be impacted? If so their users should be notified.

E. **Who will perform the deployment?** Larger organizations will have a dedicated deployment team; in small organizations, members of the development team typically perform deployments.

F. **Staging environment.** Is a staging environment available to test the deployment?

G. **What members of the business should be involved?** Include members of the user community to ensure their input and support of the deployment plan.

H. **Risk mitigation plan.** It is critical to document the risks involved in performing the deployment and have a plan for avoiding or mitigating the risks.

I. **Rollback plan.** Not all deployments will be successful; you must have a plan to roll back all changes to systems and data made by deployment to their pre-deployment state.

J. **Post deployment activities.** Are there tests that need to be executed or other items that need to be reviewed once the deployment is complete?

4.0 REVISION HISTORY

Date	Revision #	Description of Change
03/18/15	1.0	Initial creation.

5.0 INQUIRIES

Direct inquiries about this policy to:

George Jenkins, CIO
Our Company, Inc.
2900 Corporate Drive
Columbus, OH 43215

Voice: 614-555-1234
Fax: 614-555-1235
E-mail: gjenkins@company.com

Revision #:	1.0	Supersedes:	N/A	Date:	03/18/15

§ 17.08   PROGRAM MAINTENANCE

[A]   Types of Program Maintenance

Program maintenance tasks, maintenance responsibility, and maintenance conventions are required for program maintenance.

    A. Program revisions are changes made that do not require a major logic change. Examples are:
       1. Updates of constants and other variables.
       2. Increases in dimensions of tables, arrays, or work areas.
       3. Implementation of hardware features.
       4. Inclusion of new software by recompiling a program.
       5. Correction of minor processing deficiencies.
       6. Conformation to programming standards.
    B. Program modifications are changes involving the redesign of program logic or the relationships of the subprograms or components. They are required to accommodate changes in input or output specifications.

[B]   Responsibilities and Controls

Policy should be developed that defines the responsibilities and controls of software in production. It should include the following items:

A. Testing or program maintenance will not be performed on any production software under the control of IT computers or workgroup systems. This will be done offline on a separate "test system," with no access to the production system software.

B. Testing or program maintenance should verify that changes have been made properly and that other sections of the program were not affected by the changes.

C. The programmer and program supervisor will review the final test output and documentation for correctness and completeness.

D. User management or IT computer operations management will require a sign-off before the modified software is placed into production. Once this occurs, the maintenance programmer will no longer have access to it. However, in case of an emergency the programmer may regain access under supervision and with the permission of user management or IT computer operations management.

[C]   Conventions

In addition to the conventions outlined below, those established for program development (as found in § 17.04[A], "Coding Conventions") should be followed in performing program maintenance.

A. **Changes to flowcharts.** Flowcharts should be modified in the following manner:
   1. A new chart is drawn using the software used to draw the original flowchart. The changes are noted on the new chart, dated, and initialed by the programmer. Both old and new charts are filed.
   2. Additional pages added to flowcharts because of changes require off-page connectors to direct the flow to the inserted pages.

B. **Changes to reports.** Always retain one copy of the original report layout in the documentation.
   1. Include in your documentation an example report that illustrates all of the totals derived.
   2. Include screen prints of options the business user has to select reports, such as by date range or other criteria.

C. **Changes in program coding and testing.**
   1. A source program is copied into a new file before extensive changes are made. After testing is complete and the updated program put into production, the old source program may be saved to an archive directory or erased after 90 days.
   2. When testing program changes, the entire program must be checked, not just the code that was inserted, deleted, or changed. Those segments not changed are tested to ensure the program will continue to function properly. The test data becomes part of the program documentation.

[D]   PC Software Developed by End Users

Personal computers have evolved from glorified calculators to powerful machines. Fueling this change is a wealth of powerful software that is easily customized by the person using it. This can lead a manager down a dark and slippery path. Amateur programmers lack the depth of experience to include safeguards of data integrity in their programs. They change them on a whim without adequate testing. They are even friendly to a fault and pass around copies of their handiwork without tracking versions or who has copies of the program. When bugs are repaired, only the programmer's copy is updated. In short, this can create havoc if it is not closely controlled. Policy must be created to keep this under control. See Chapter 28, "End-User Systems: Do-It-Yourself Computing" for policy suggestions.

[E]   End-User Testing Training

IT departments spend a considerable amount of time ensuring the accuracy of the reports and data issued to the business departments. Because of this, some people assume that any computer-generated report is accurate and do not question how it calculated the data or where the data came from. This can lead to faulty business decisions based on bad data.

If someone develops a spreadsheet or small database for his or her own use, it is his or her business. He or she knows where the data came from and how it works. But as soon as he or she begins using this report away from his or her own desk, you begin to see problems.

When training new users in the company, include instruction on data validation, editing, and how to cross-check results against samples of the input file. Most people care about the quality of their work and will appreciate this instruction.

[F]   Stealth Systems

It is rare an IT department can address every business user request for new software or additional features in existing systems. This sometimes leads to a well-meaning but hazardous growth of stealth systems throughout the company.

Stealth systems are applications written by someone for his or her own use to address a specific business problem. These will range from a department's homegrown vacation schedule to a Materials Management System. IT Managers cannot stop these systems from occurring. Instead, when it is reported that such a system has become an integral part of a department's operations, or has jumped to another department, the IT department must evaluate its validity. The IT Manager must decide if there is a compelling business case for supporting such a system. If so, then that system must be removed from end-user control and subjected to the IT validation checks and safeguards. It becomes a production system just like any other. Further user changes are not permitted.

[G] Hidden Programming Staffs

Sometimes, end users frustrated with attempts to obtain data processing support within their company will hire their own programming support staff under other titles. These might be college interns or others who are trained in the basics of PC programming. The problem is the loss of IT policy control of these people.

There are two basic approaches to this—accept it or kill it. Accepting this "secret IT staff" normally involves establishing the following policies:

A. The creation of a separate computing environment for these people to work in, typically on their own network and server. This reduces the likelihood that their efforts will bring down your more reliable production systems.
B. They are permitted to download data from the corporate files but never to upload anything to prevent them from adding back in bad data.
C. They are not permitted to write any software for anyone outside of their department and must adhere to IT policies concerning software piracy, antivirus protection, etc.
D. A requirement that all code be fully documented to the same standard as that maintained by the IT department. A copy of this documentation must be maintained in the IT library.

Quashing a secret IT staff means that the IT department must determine what business need this staff meets and then fulfill it. These people were brought in to meet a user requirement. If you take them away, the requirement is still there so IT must step up and fulfill it. The easiest way to do this is to take technical control of the people but leave their work assignments to the business department. The business department will continue to carry them under their budget. Since they are under your technical control, you can better ensure their code and data integrity meets your standards and can easily move the code around to other departments as required.

18

IT STAFFING: MEETING CUSTOMER SERVICE EXPECTATIONS

§ 18.06   TRANSLATING REQUIREMENTS INTO A STAFF LEVEL
    [A]   Overview
    [B]   Establish a Service Level Performance Goal
    [C]   Staffing Ratios
    [D]   Allocating the IT Staff

§ 18.01 OVERVIEW

[A] Purpose and Scope

IT departments have a problem. Their customer base is "captive" and generally forced to use their services. In a free market, inefficient businesses disappear since no one will pay for their services. Companies lack this ability of weeding out poorly performing departments. Too many IT departments blunder along as personal fiefdoms until they are outsourced by frustrated executives.

However, proactive IT Managers can address this problem head-on by constantly seeking their customers' feedback on the team's performance. Some managers even seek employees with reputations of complaining. These people will tell you what others are too polite to mention.

[B] Critical Policies to Develop Based on This Chapter

Using the material discussed in this chapter, you will be able to create the following policies:

A. Policy for establishing acceptable service levels.
B. Collection of service level metrics.
C. Identification of the service levels critical to quality factors.
D. Root cause determination of critical or systemic problems.
E. Establishment of staffing ratios.

Policies should always be developed based on the local situation. Successful managers cannot issue appropriate guidance if the policies are written with another company's situation or location in mind.

§ 18.02 WHAT IS THIS "THING" CALLED CUSTOMER SERVICE?

[A] Opinion vs. Fact

Customer service is a combination of opinions and facts. From the customer's perspective, the level of customer service is an opinion. From the service provider's perspective, the level of customer service is demonstrated by performance statistics. The trick is to align the two perspectives so that expectations equal performance.

The "opinion" perspective is whether the person receiving the service is "satisfied" with the end result. This satisfaction is very difficult to measure as it is affected by a wide range of factors from the day's weather to the number of other problems plaguing the person that day. Evaluating a series of events rather than a single occurrence provides a general perception of service. For example, we have all experienced the reliability of telephone and electrical service we use every day. Our experience has been that it seems to be always ready for use, so that the only times it is commented on is when it is absent.

We generally perceive it to be a high-quality service, yet we have all experienced times when these services were absent.

The "fact" perspective is represented in the performance statistics generated by the service provided. When confronted with complaints about poor service or when trying to add more staff members, the IT Manager will provide sheets of customer service statistics. These would include the average response time for a call, problem resolution rate, etc. Although these make a compelling, data driven statement, in the mind of end users, they rarely change a complainer's opinion.

[B]   Level of Service

An important factor in the size of an IT department is the level of service it provides to the company. Although a large staff does not automatically translate into a high level of service, it does indicate the potential. Service levels seek to provide the right number of workers, with the right mix of skills, available at the right time. Customer service is the single biggest determinant of IT staff size in most companies.

An IT department's customer service level is a collection of expectations by the various departments that it supports of how quickly the IT team can provide solutions to their technical problems. From the end user's perspective, customer service is everything that the end user expects the IT department to provide to them. The closer that this expectation matches reality, the higher the customer's satisfaction will be. Some of its components are:

A. How quickly a clear and accurate service request can be conveyed from the requestor to the IT department.
B. How promptly a solution is provided.
C. The correctness, completeness, and permanence of the solution.
D. Communications during the process of problem resolution and follow-up with the requestor after the solution is provided.
E. Reliable and predictable service from each of the IT areas.

Traditionally, IT departments led the way in introducing technology to the various business units. As computers became common home appliances, the need to drive technology into the workplace was greatly reduced. This, together with economic downturns, has evolved many IT departments into a "keep the lights on" mode rather than maintaining their leadership role. This follows the theory that IT is a utility and is expected to provide a service on demand. Such a passive stance results in executives noticing IT departments only when things go badly and not crediting things that go well.

To nurture or reestablish this leadership role, everyone in the IT department must work to establish and maintain positive working relationships with all areas of the business. In this sense, the IT department is a de facto member of each department's staff since most process changes require its involvement. This linkage will not occur by itself. It requires a consistent flow of communication between IT and each of the departments concerning expectations, service issues, and performance. This open channel of two-way information flow will positively enhance the perception of IT's service levels and contribution to the company's overall success.

This discussion is important to staffing and skills because service levels influence the number of people and the mix of skills required in an IT department. Given unlimited time, the staff would only need enough people to have a single expert for every technology. Each problem would be addressed in its own turn, depending on workload and the IT Manager's priorities. Anything occurring overnight would be addressed in its own good time. With only one expert per technology, some problems may wait weeks until they are addressed.

Unlimited time for a task is definitely not something IT departments possess. The level of skill a person possesses and applies has a direct impact on the speed of reaching the solution and customer satisfaction.

A comprehensive staffing formula that determines team size does not exist. A formula can only work with the factors that are provided to it. Miss a single factor and the answer will be wrong. Every company and every company branch has its own unique customer service requirements, and one size does not fit all.

When evaluating the quality of the IT department's services, consider this test. If the people calling for assistance had a choice to call the IT department or call anyone else, who would they call? If they had to write a check to the IT department every time they used it, would they do so or send the check elsewhere?

[C] Operational vs. Development Activities

An IT department provides two basic types of services: operational and developmental. Operational services are those activities used to sustain existing activities, such as printing reports, maintaining existing programs, or troubleshooting desktop computer problems. Developmental services are those one-time activities that require additional labor to complete, such as rolling out desktop software updates or writing new application programs.

Factors driving operational services:

A. Degree of standardization of IT products.
B. Number and dispersal of users and servers.
C. Number of sites supported.
D. Skill levels of end users.
E. Stability of the end-user workforce.
F. Stability of the business applications.
G. Age and stability of infrastructure.
H. Whether applications are developed internally or are vendor supplied.
I. Degree of automation installed.
J. Criticality of applications.

Factors driving development services:

A. Business growth rate.
B. Business environment stability.
C. Number, complexity, and urgency of pending projects.
D. Planned technology migrations.

[D] Perceptions Color Both Sides of the Issue

Customer service is a complex concept that means different things to different people. It has many different facets based on the person seeking assistance (perspective) and what he is requesting. To the IT Manager, it may mean responding to requests in a reasonable amount of time by applying the correct solution. Most business managers would agree with this on the surface. If only life were this simple.

Let's break this down further. In all companies, there are multiple users requesting a wide variety of services, from quick jobs to major efforts. They may request a new report, urgent program changes, a PC file restored, or a new user ID established. Some of these requests may be ill-conceived or a duplication of existing services. Others may lack approval of the department's manager or specify actions that are the wrong solution to the problem. The request may even be a tool in a departmental "power struggle" and not at all an important company task.

Complicating this situation are the people in the IT department who are delivering these services. Each has his own set of priorities, biases, skills, and product knowledge. Given these uncontrollable factors, providing a consistent level of service can be quite a challenge. Each IT support person has assigned tasks that are interrupted by service requests. He also has personal opinions or feelings about the requestor that may hinder the speed of his response.

[E] Communications

The key to managing expectations is communications. Customers must know that their issues are understood, being worked on, and what progress has been made. They should also understand the nature of the solution if it will require a change in their processes. Allow external time pressures to distract the IT support team from these important discussions and the customer's anxiety will rise and opinion of the group's service fall.

Ongoing communications allow the customer to shape the problem's description. If a particular deadline is missed, they may say that the urgency is now lessened until the next time the weekly program runs. They may explain a work-around they have used in the past or that they have used now, so again, the urgency is still high, but has dipped below the crisis level. They may even say that the problem has "gone away."

An important customer service communication is to alert end users of planned outages. Emergency outages can be very frustrating to the business units juggling their workload to meet deadlines. Most users can plan their work around a data system outage if they receive enough advance notice. Whenever possible, planned outages should be scheduled during the time of day and day of the week when the data systems are least required. If this is unavoidable, then ensure that everyone is provided at least one working day to reshuffle their work plans—or to suggest a less painful time.

A variation on planned outages is the early detection of a problem. Monitoring data systems availability and network performance can provide early warning of system components failure, such as a network circuit. Instead of waiting for someone to call and report a problem, valuable time can be saved by immediately dispatching the repair person and notifying the impacted departments of the problem. They will not welcome the news, but it is better to hear that IT is aware of the problem and work has begun to repair it rather than find out at an inopportune time that a critical system is dead.

[F] Voice of the Customer

It is easy to guess at what end users might be looking for in terms of customer service and just try to meet that. However, this could lead to wasted effort fulfilling low priority requirements while the true customer "needs" are left unfulfilled. Guessing is the fastest and easiest way to address the identification of customer service issues—and also the wrong way.

Everyone has some expectation of service when he or she conducts business. When entering a fast-food restaurant, each person has an expectation of how long it should take to receive the food, how warm it should be, its flavor, even the condiments like ketchup that should accompany it. All of these combine to create an overall experience of the transaction between the customer and the restaurant.

People who contact the IT department likewise have expectations about timeliness, accuracy, ease of communications, and a range of other things they expect to see when dealing with the IT staff. Taken together, they form a level of service in the eyes of the customer. To focus the IT team's customer service efforts, analyze the customer's expectations.

The "voice of the customer" is easy to find. Letters of complaint (or compliment) on the company's products and services, calls to the service desk, and the volume of services used or avoided are all signals by customers that they are satisfied or dissatisfied with what is being done for them.

§ 18.03 COMPONENTS OF IT SERVICE STAFFING

[A] Overview

Customer service is the single biggest determinant of IT staff size in most companies. IT departments tend to think in terms of positions such as the weekend network support person or the second shift service desk technician. Consider these same positions according to their contribution to the customer service efforts. Every position in IT has the following five characteristics to one degree or another.

[B] Standby

Standby—these persons sit and wait for something to occur. These are analogous to security guards. They may have other duties to perform, but if a problem arises, their top priority is to respond quickly. Examples of this are a service desk technician waiting for the telephone to ring or the person monitoring the flow of network traffic. Their primary responsibility is to be immediately available in case an event occurs. If nothing requires their attention, they provide value by their availability to respond.

Factors driving standby requirements:

A. Volume of calls for end-user support. Reduce this by increasing end-user training and repairing/replacing unstable technologies.
B. Desired speed of response for problem calls. For example, supporting a real-time securities sales and purchasing system requires instantly addressing problems during the hours that the stock market is open.
C. Correctly determining the urgency of the problem reduces the number of technicians that must be immediately available. If an issue can wait for an hour to be addressed, then the normal support staff can be assigned to it instead of requiring someone to stand by at all hours of the day, ready to act on a moment's notice.
D. The number of critical technologies requiring instant support. The impact of downtime must be evaluated for each system.

Undoing a well-thought-out standby strategy:

A. Upper management wants the fast response but has little tolerance for the sight of these expensive people sitting idle waiting for the telephone to ring. Often they will try to assign them to other tasks, thereby reducing their instant availability.
B. Technical people like to be challenged and will be bored during the slow work periods. They will appreciate the value of immediacy but find "excuses" for doing something other than sitting by the telephone. At times, the manager must personally enforce the scope of the work and the location of their place of work.
C. The law of inertia will take hold where objects (people) at rest tend to remain at rest. When the call volume again picks up (the whole reason they are all there), they will be slow to react. The authors recommend slightly understaffing to overcome this.

[C] Technical Experts

Technical experts—these folks are too difficult to find or pay for on a temporary basis. Often they are employees who were trained on the job. Examples of this are system administrators or network engineers. At a minimum, there will be one person assigned for each of the skill areas identified, even if they are not fully utilized.

Factors driving technical expert requirements:

A. The degree that the company's systems are standardized. If the company utilizes a wide range of vendors and technologies, then more experts are required since not all technology expertise is easily transferable.
B. The stability of the technology is a major factor in the number of experts required. Unstable hardware and software must be repaired or replaced. A variation is to provide standby equipment for critical hardware so that when a failure occurs, the alternate device is used until the primary unit is repaired by the expert (instead of the expert standing by to address failures).

C. There is a degree of "standby" for technical people such as a network expert always on station for companies that rely on the Internet for customer order entry.

Undoing a well-thought-out technical expert strategy:

A. Some executives feel that if they deny the funds for a sufficient number of experts, the IT Manager will be forced to find other ways to provide this service. Indirectly, this approach "wishes away" the offending technologies. Although there is some merit to this approach, the dark side is the failure of a major system with no one available to repair it for hours.
B. Introducing critical, non-standard technology without adding adequate resources or training to support it. This might be from an executive who purchased something at a "bargain" rate that no one knows how to repair.

[D]   Separation of Responsibilities

Sometimes it is not prudent management to place all of something into one person's trust. Checks and balances are essential inhibitors for removing temptation from the weak, for example, the security team that watches over confidential files and firewalls. It is important to separate the people who secure data from the ones who manipulate it. Otherwise there is a case of the fox guarding the henhouse. Security team members ensure that confidential data is identified, secured from unauthorized access, and that access is enabled as required.

Factors driving IT security requirements:

A. A security team requires a minimum of two people since someone must always be available in a crisis (covering vacations, sick days, etc.). Also, the more security staff that a company uses, the harder it is for a single security person to violate the security undetected.
B. The greater the number of technologies that must be protected (hierarchical databases, relational databases, different manufacturers, different OS architectures), the more experts that will be required. Standardization will minimize the staff requirements.
C. The greater the amount of data that is secured, the more staff that may be required. Break confidential data such as credit card numbers into linked tables and secure those tables, leaving the remainder of the fields with normal security.
D. The geographic dispersal of the facilities supported.

Undoing a well-thought-out security strategy:

A. A successful program will seem as if it is addressing a nonproblem since there are not any security breaches! If the time requirements permit, these people can work part-time in other areas as long as it does not compromise the separation of security and other IT functions, such as applications.

[E] Applications Support

Applications support—the classic IT position. These employees maintain existing data systems and develop new ones. Often they are grouped by their primary programming language skills, but are assigned to support entire application systems, such as accounts payable, EDI, etc.

Factors driving IT applications support requirements:

A. Dissimilar user interfaces require training classes for each application. It is unlikely that a single software package will suit all areas of the company (the secretaries will not want to use a spreadsheet for word processing), so standardizing on a single software package is unlikely. However, using an ERP with a standard user interface across multiple applications can ease customer training. If the underlying software likewise uses a standard set of software tools, then fewer technicians are needed.

B. Standardization of development tools such as programming languages, databases, operating systems, etc., will permit the IT Manager to rebalance work between the staff members.

C. The extent that end users can create or modify their own reports will decrease applications requirements.

Undoing a well-thought-out applications support strategy:

A. Non-IT executives "discover" new applications solutions that are inconsistent with the standard software tool set and implement them without the appropriate level of technical support training.

B. Rushing the development and implementation of new systems based on vague and shifting specifications.

C. Lack of clear, published, and enforced system development practices.

[F] Overhead

Overhead—the positions that drive up the IT head count. Overhead positions are the ones that facilitate the work of the other areas, such as specialized IT purchasing, contracts administration, and, of course, management. Overhead processes often seem to grow on their own into a paper-shuffling bureaucracy. IT Managers must avoid this as it decreases the department's flexibility.

Factors driving IT overhead requirements include:

A. Many IT departments approve the purchase of all computer technologies within the company. This contributes to standardization by guiding requests to approved products, but it takes a staff member's time. The more tasks such as this that the department takes on, the greater the staffing requirement.

B. The span of control for a manager is four to seven subordinates. If the subordinates are motivated toward the same goals as their leader, and if they are technically competent, then a larger ratio of workers per supervisor is possible. If they are new to the company or require considerable mentoring, then fewer workers can be effectively managed.

C. IT service contracts and their performance clauses are best administered by someone familiar with the technologies, department priorities, and support of end users rather than a distant clerk in the purchasing department.
D. The geographic dispersal of the facilities supported.
E. A well-thought-out, clear, and published IT strategic plan will broaden the span of control across the department.

Undoing a well-thought-out overhead strategy:

A. Previous management attempts at "flattening" an organization by removing middle management have reduced personnel costs but allowed the workers to inefficiently drift in whatever direction they wished.
B. Using an accounting clerk to administer IT contracts generally results in payment for a level of service that is never delivered since the accounting clerk lacks the knowledge or inclination to enforce the terms—thereby causing more work for the IT staff!

§ 18.04 METRICS—IT'S MEASURES OF SUCCESS

[A] Overview

IT staffing is driven by customers' service requirements. It is important to establish a process for gathering these requirements from the customers and measuring the team's performance at delivering them. End users exist in an ever-changing business environment. By periodically polling customers, the IT department's efforts can stay tuned toward the tasks most relevant to the company.

IT Managers are not unbiased judges of their service levels. They are too close to the efforts made by the department. Their view is colored by their intentions to provide a high level of customer service. However, a customer service level is not an intention. It is the opinion of the customer that counts (what was done—not what was meant). The best way to find out the customer's impressions is to ask them!

Identifying customer requirements is a five-step process.

A. Determine what the department's customer service levels are believed to be today.
B. Poll customers as to their opinion of the team's service performance. The difference between steps one and two often results in action plans to improve specific components of the service offering.

C. During the previous poll, ask the customers to determine the service levels they want to see.

D. Publish an improved service level goal for the department. This may not be all the customers want to see but is based on staffing and technical realities. This will establish an expectation in the minds of both the customer and the IT staff.

E. Draft a plan to focus the team and improve processes to achieve the new service goal.

To compare the different levels of customer service, a set of standard measurements is needed. These measurements, or "metrics," must be based on objective data. Customer service is very much a perception and we all perceive the same situations differently. Perceptions must be quantified by measuring their individual components.

[B] Critical to Quality

Customer service has many different aspects. Trying to track them all would be time consuming and not provide sufficient payback. The task at hand is to identify those aspects that are *critical* to the quality of the service offering.

Critical to quality (CTQ) characteristics are the most important parts of service. They are the basic elements of service offerings and vary somewhat between customer segments. In general, they follow the consumer CTQs characteristics of speed, cost, and quality. Changing any one of these changes the others. For example, increasing the speed (reducing the response time) costs more money for more people, or results in decreased quality.

A. Speed is how quickly something is delivered. In IT services, this might be how quickly a correct solution is provided, or how quickly someone answers the service desk phone. Lack of urgency is the most common IT services complaint.

B. Cost is something that all companies struggle with. Some companies use a direct chargeback for IT services while others use a simpler overhead allocation to all departments. Cost is also a consideration when the IT department estimates the cost of technical components for capital projects.

C. Quality is sometimes defined as conformance to specification. In customer service, this is how well the service conforms to what was wanted. For example, if an end user ordered software, just delivering the package to the requestor's desk fulfills what was asked for. Installing and configuring the software is implied since what the person actually wanted was use of the software. A high-quality delivery might additionally include an hour of desk-side assistance navigating through the product, assistance migrating files into the new format, and information on locally available training.

[C]   What to Measure

The trick to customer service metrics is to correctly identify what to measure. Gathering data takes time. A properly planned data collection effort minimizes this time. The management axiom that a manager gets what he rewards is very true. If the reward is for the number of calls closed, then the same problem report may be closed and reopened a number of times until a satisfactory conclusion is found. If the reward is for the speed with which calls are answered, then calls will be answered by inexperienced staff who will take messages for later action when the customer wanted the answer from the first person he spoke to.

Customer service factors are measured to demonstrate performance and to identify problems within the IT service offering for improvement. Performance factors might include the amount of time a call waits before it is answered, the elapsed time between when a problem is reported and when it is resolved, etc. Service offering problems are metrics gathered to uncover problems with technologies that cause these problems, such as an unstable program or piece of hardware. These metrics are used by the IT Manager to improve the data services offered. Each of these issues can be broken down into a number of smaller issues.

COMMENT

Uptime of 99.99 percent is worthless if the server crashes when it is needed most. Metrics must make sense and be relevant to IT's customers. Tracking the uptime during Saturday third shift when no one is around and the system is quiet is not something to crow about.

[D]   Typical Customer Service Metrics

If the service desk is already in place, metrics should be readily available. Ideally, this would include a problem tracking database that indicates who are calling, what they called about, when they called, and the time elapsed before the problem was resolved. These four key pieces of information will provide most of the data needed.

A. **Who is calling?** It is important to know who is using the service desk services. Some end users are more skilled than others. They call less frequently but the problems may be more difficult to resolve. Some end users are more inclined to call for smaller issues rather than try to figure them out themselves.

   Just as important as who is calling is who is not calling. Some departments have an official or unofficial person that everyone goes to with their technical problems before they call the IT department. In other cases, the departments have bypassed IT altogether by hiring such a person into a position with a clerical title but with actual responsibilities for IT support.

A large volume of calls from a department may also be indicative of its future requirements. If a project is under way to expand that group, then what does that add to the IT department's support requirements?

B. **What they called about.** The types of problems being serviced directly affect the staffing mix. Some problems are simply resolved such as resetting passwords for people with short memories. Others are more time consuming such as tracking down why a report has a given value in one of its fields. Repeated calls for the same problem point to unreliable equipment, unstable programs, or end users in need of further training. All of this is addressed by proactively identifying repeat issues and addressing them.

C. **The time of day and the day of week that they called.** Calls for help tend to come in waves and at about the same time of day every week. Many problems are first realized in the morning when workstations are restarted and people attempt to log into their applications. By tracking the time when calls come in, staffing levels can be augmented to ensure that someone can take the calls as they arrive. Comparing the type of problem to the time of day further helps to determine the skills required for these work surges.

D. **Time elapsed before the issue was resolved.** Simple calls can be quickly addressed where difficult problems may require days to address. Comparing this value to when a call was received indicates, from the customer's point of view, responsiveness of the IT department. The longer the interval between the report and solution, the more follow-up calls the team receives from the requestor urging quicker action.

If service requests are categorized according to the IT department it was assigned to, then an average resolution time per request to a department can be calculated. Is this average time satisfactory? The service desk is a logical place to gather data, but is there any other? If the department's data covers these four areas, the IT staffing and skills mix can be approximated. If so, then the service survey will validate and expand on the results. If the department lacks data on its IT support, then a process must be developed to consistently and accurately gather such data.

See Policy ITP-18-1 IT Staffing Metrics Collection Policy as an example.

POLICY ITP-18-1.   IT Staffing Metrics Collection Policy

Policy #:	ITP-18-1	Effective:	03/18/13	Page #:	1 of N
Subject:	IT Staffing Metrics Collection Policy				

1.0 PURPOSE

This policy mandates the metrics to be collected by IT to track the use and performance of the help desk.

2.0 SCOPE

This policy encompasses all calls made by users to the IT department for support. The IT Manager is responsible for implementing all aspects of this policy.

3.0 POLICY

The IT department must collect metrics on the operation and use of the IT help desk. These metrics must include:

A. Who is calling? This must be tracked by user and by department.
B. What the user called about. Calls must be tracked by system and application being used when the problem occurred.
C. The time of day and the day of week that the user called. The type of problem should be compared to the time of day to help determine the skills required for work surges.
D. Time elapsed before the call was resolved. This value must be compared to when a call was received to measure the responsiveness of the IT department.
E. The IT Manager who was assigned to resolve the problem. The average resolution time per request to a department is then calculated.

Help desk metrics must be updated monthly and made available on the corporate intranet.

4.0 REVISION HISTORY

Date	Revision #	Description of Change
03/18/13	1.0	Initial creation.

5.0 INQUIRIES

Direct inquiries about this policy to:

George Jenkins, CIO
Our Company, Inc.
2900 Corporate Drive
Columbus, OH 43215

Voice: 614-555-1234
Fax: 614-555-1235
E-mail: gjenkins@company.com

Revision #:	1.0	Supersedes:	N/A	Date:	03/18/13

§ 18.05 WHY USE A CUSTOMER SURVEY?

[A] Overview

The IT Manager may already have a clear idea of the department's service level, or may never have thought about it. After all, whenever executives call on anyone in the department, they always receive a prompt response. But are all callers treated with the same urgency as the IT Manager? Not likely! In this section we will establish the department's service level as seen by IT's customers.

Customer service exists to fulfill customer requirements. However, the business environment is constantly changing. As business shifts to keep pace with the competition, the mix and timing of IT services must also change. The survey is one tool for maintaining the alignment between the IT department and its customers. The survey indicates a general sense and not a statistical certainty. Therefore, it does not require a rigorous statistical sampling analysis.

[B] The Survey

The intent of the survey is to gauge the level of service provided by the department—based on the customer's point of view. Unfortunately, most IT Managers "guess" about their level of service and do not ask for their customers' opinions. They provide several unsatisfactory reasons for this.

A. Asking for an opinion resurfaces many of the customer complaints for actions denied due to company policy or lack of funding. This is an error since educating end users about department capabilities and limitations is important for setting expectations in their minds. Irreconcilable issues should be reevaluated for inclusion in the future service level.

B. The IT department is already overloaded with work requests and does not want to stimulate a new pile of work orders (the "let sleeping dogs lie" approach). Again, if the current IT Manager does not address these issues now, then the next IT Manager will! If there is an excess of pending work to be done, then the general service level will fall below customer expectations.

After reviewing the survey results, a desired customer service performance level is identified based on end-user expectations and funding. This desired level may include the IT Manager's perception that the team can achieve better results with the same resources. The performance metrics used for both the survey and the desired service level should be the same for easy comparison. The IT Manager's task is to develop a plan for moving the team's performance from the survey's baseline service level up to the desired level.

COMMENT

When someone picks up a telephone to dial it, there is an expectation, based on personal experience, of when to expect to hear a dial tone. After the number is entered, there is another expectation of when to expect to hear the telephone ring on the receiving end. When the time to hear the dial tone or the ring at the other end exceeds the customer's expectation, a problem is suspected.

The customer opinion survey will gather seven types of essential data, each of which drives customer service staffing levels:

A. Hours of operation, both normal and foreseeable additional hours. This is to validate alignment between customer work hours and IT support staff.
B. A detailed list of critical applications. This expands on the hours of service by assigning "experts" to specific support times.
C. A visual inspection of the hardware actually in use. During the interview, take a long look around. This is to uncover equipment slipped in without the IT department's knowledge or that was scheduled to depart, but never did. It would be valuable to also gather an inventory of software in use, but it would be very time consuming.

COMMENT

Several years ago, one of the authors was trying to drive out from the facility all of the old model workstations. New units were purchased and the service contract covering the old units was dropped. Meanwhile, a programmer at corporate headquarters was "saving" money by using the headquarters' old model workstations for a project to be installed in the same facility. Watch for someone else's junk slipping in the back door!

D. The department's staff turnover rate. New employees need some sort of orientation to the data systems. The higher the turnover, the greater the training need will be.

E. Any pending technical or process changes that impact IT's ability to support them.

F. Any ongoing IT problems. Some people hold back their frustration until they "explode." Find out if there are any simmering IT support problems and address them promptly. This one action will greatly enhance the perception of the service levels.

G. Collect a perception of service levels as they are delivered now, and how the customer would like to see them in the future.

COMMENT

Be wary of the "squeaky wheel," the person who attempts to dominate others through a stream of complaints and half-truths. Throughout all discussions, take care to educate managers and end users about the IT service priority system and why it is important to prevent low payback actions from delaying more important ones.

[C] Determining a Service Level Baseline

Surveys can be very time consuming to conduct. A 100 percent survey will allow everyone to contribute, but how much more will be learned than if only a sample of people were surveyed? The goal of the survey is to gather a general picture of the service levels. If there are complaints, now is the time to bring them out and address them. A sample service level survey is provided as Worksheet 18-1 Service Level Survey.

Who are the department's customers? This may sound like examining the obvious, but it helps to identify who the IT department is supporting. Sometimes, it may be more than the IT Manager has directed. A statement of the scope of work for the IT department anchors its service offering by establishing boundaries to guide the IT team. Trying to be all things to all people inevitably leads to failure as more and more work (and expectations) will be added to the workload without a corresponding increase in staff resources.

So who are the department's customers? Like many simple questions, the answers may be complex. Of course, customers are fellow workers within the company. These are the ones normally concentrated on. Other customers might be temporary workers or contract technical staff. This technical staff may be auditors, regulators, or contract technicians. Some companies provide equipment, software, and expertise to key suppliers or customers either to help them or to ensure they can keep up with the company's pace of operations.

WORKSHEET 18-1. Service Level Survey

Service Level Survey				
Department			Date	
Interviewed			Interviewer	
Number of workstations				
Normal workdays		Normal work hours		
Additional workdays		Additional work hours		
Critical Applications				
Application Name	Platform	Max Outage	Days of Week	Hours
Staff				
Turnover rate		Average longevity		
Department trainer		Super user		
Pending system changes:				
Ongoing problems:				
What would you like to see done differently:				

Side A

18-19

WORKSHEET 18-1. (Continued)

Service Level Survey Matrix							
	Operations	Programming	Desktop	Help Desk	Networking	Telephone	Applications
Availability to receive request							
Understand what is requested							
Accurate priority							
Promptness of solution							
Correctness/completeness of solution							
Follow Up							
Helpfulness							
Attitude							

Place these statements into a sequence of 1 to 10 with 10 being the most important and one being the least relative importance.

—Ease of contact—how easy it is to contact someone to report a problem.

—Hours of support—hours when support is available.

—Speed of first response—elapsed time to responder to call and discuss problem.

—Speed of solution—the elapsed time between first notice and providing solution.

—Correctness of solution—problem is solved and stays solved.

—Completeness of solution—problem is solved and cannot surface again.

—Follow-up call after solution.

—Courtesy—even in tense situations.

—Communications—listens politely and explains in non-technical terms.

—Understanding of the business environment surrounding the problem.

Side B

COMMENT

One of the authors managed a service desk for a large company and regularly explained to callers that the service desk was not a substitute for the facility's telephone directory and did not redirect calls from outside salespeople. This was especially a problem with outside calls routed to the service desk by other employees since the company lacked a telephone operator. If the service desk had accepted this work by servicing these calls as they came in, assigned tasks would have been delayed and a new expectation would have been established in the minds of the customers that this was a part of their job. The service desk also fended off calls for supporting employees' home PCs and dispatching the facility's maintenance staff.

Separate customers into support groups. There are several easy groupings for end users. From a staffing perspective, the easiest group is shifts. The requirements of the third-shift employees are typically different from the first shift, etc. It is a rare company that does not have someone in the facility at all hours of the day—often every day of the week. There are security guards, custodians, 24-hour call centers, off-hour teams for international, East Coast, or West Coast support, etc.

Another common grouping is company influence leaders. Not all customers are created equal, so the customer base should be segmented at least into priority customers and everyone else. All IT departments do this already. A request from the CEO is always treated as a high priority while a similar request from a clerk might wait several days until it rises to the top of the list. Aside from keeping their job, IT Managers do this because of impact. Most of the executive's actions impact a number of people, whereas the clerk's actions will impact a much smaller aspect of the company. Taken from another angle, an idle executive (no jokes, now) costs the company more per hour than an idle clerk. This may seem harsh in a society where everyone is considered equal, but it is true. From a survival standpoint, executives' opinions as to the IT department's service levels and competence have an impact on future funding and staffing.

Pros and cons of priority executive support. Arguments for executive priority service: Executives are paid more "per hour" than other workers. If they cannot complete their work due to a data system problem, then the company has lost more "labor expense" than if a clerk's system was broken. Executive systems should always work as fast as they can think so as to not hinder the forward movement of business. A disruption of work at the top ripples down through the organization, causing multiple delays for other workers. Also it is important for the IT department to generate "good will" with key decision makers.

Arguments against executive priority service: Since executives do not receive the same level of support as everyone else, they cannot appreciate the service level that others must live with. Priority treatment of executive requests presents an illusion that all is well when it is not.

To simplify the process, focus the survey on:

A. **Executives and department managers**. These are the influence leaders whose opinion counts more than that of others. Also, as a central point of contact for their teams, executives and managers can pass on any issues raised by their department in the past. Survey every one of these people.

B. **Key end users**. Usually more technically oriented than their peers, they would have a more realistic idea of the complexity of their requests. They often have insights into the true causes of long-term IT problems. Survey every one of these people.

C. **A random sampling of end users from each department and each shift**. Gather their perception since each touches the technology in different ways. Be sure to randomly survey at least 10 percent of this group. If the sampling is not random, then the results of the survey may be skewed.

D. **Vocal critics**. Survey every one of these people. Many people in our society feel it is rude to speak negatively of anything but the most serious of faults. The critics may point out areas of friction between IT and its users—and they won't be shy about telling the interviewer about it!

[D] The Survey Form

To consistently gather this data for later analysis, create a survey form that reflects the situation. An example form is provided to illustrate this discussion. This form is intended to gather a "broad brush" customer opinion and not a statistically rigorous response. That would require a different form and different sampling technique.

Forms allow for a consistent collection of data since each respondent is asked the same questions. This is important if more than one person will be conducting the data collection interviews. The sample form is a two-part document that should be copied to two sides of the same page to keep everything together.

A. **Front side of the form.** The first section is information used to verify for the service desk's records and the IT department's basic statistics.
1. **Number of workstations**. The more workstations in a department, the likelier that someone will call with an issue. This is normally provided by the department manager. Determine what will be counted as a workstation. Is it a terminal, a PC, a server dedicated to a single user, a smartphone, or tablet? Include work-from-home users.

2. **Normal workdays and hours**. The department's normal working hours must be covered by on-site IT assistance with the appropriate skills. This is the key to customer service. If the IT staff has the right skills at the wrong hours, service levels will be considered to be low.

3. **Additional workdays and hours**. Many departments schedule special days during the year when weekend or late evening support is important. Examples include inventory update counts, year-end closing for accounting, etc. These days and times also require on-site IT support, with the correct skill sets.

4. **Critical applications.** A critical application is any system that halts a company process that has been identified as critical to company operations. In a factory, this is a process that halts the assembly line. In a sales office, this might be an inoperable telephone system that prevents customers from calling in orders. This is important because the support of every critical application must be assigned to someone in the IT staffing plan. Some departments will claim that every system is critical, but this means that requests for new user IDs would be just as important as an inoperable payroll application. If the IT Manager cannot convince the customer to identify which systems are critical, then try ranking all of them on a list from 1 to whatever. Draw lines across the list to indicate which ones are critical, important, useful, etc. Critical systems should be between the top 10 percent and 25 percent of the applications. Fields on the form for critical applications:

   a. **Application name**—the name this application is commonly known by.

   b. **Platform**—does this application run on a server, a mainframe, or a workstation? If multiple critical systems are concentrated on a few platforms, it may be prudent to spread them around.

   c. **Max outage**—what is the maximum amount of time this application can be unavailable before the department's workflow is severely impacted? This is a key driver to staffing since a low value here means that a technical expert must be provided on standby during working hours.

   d. **Days of the week**—what days of the week is this process normally used?

   e. **Hours**—what hours of the day are most important for this process?

5. **Staff.** This section focuses on the department's staffing practices. Cheaper labor can be obtained if fewer skills are required. So while the hiring manager's budget looks good for hiring unskilled workers, their increased requests for technical assistance represent a cost shifted to the IT department. These workers will generate a greater number of support calls. Such workforces must be trained by either the IT department or the department hiring them, prior to providing them the IT support telephone number.

6. **Pending system changes.** If a department has major data systems or process changes near to implementation, the IT department should be alerted to shifts in support requirements. A chilling statement by an end-user department manager is, "Gee, I thought you knew. . . ."

B. **Back side of the form.** The reverse side of the form must be modified to reflect the department structure of the IT team. The intention is to elicit from the interviewee their opinion and impressions of the different IT groups' performance. Remember that someone calling the operations department to reset a user ID (perhaps requiring a few minutes) has a different expectation for task completion than they would for requesting a new business data report (probably requiring several days). Also, if someone is bypassing the service desk and calling their friend in IT operations for assistance, then the department's metrics would not reflect this.

Along the top of the matrix is a list of the various IT departments. Along the left side are a series of questions concerning this person's experiences working with these groups. A scale of 0 to 10 is recommended, where a 0 represents minimal or no contact with that IT team and 10 represents absolute perfection in all encounters.

A goal of this portion of the survey is to detect how often the various departments are contacted directly. Users should route their calls through the service desk. Secondly, a single IT team may be undoing all of the goodwill that the IT Manager is working hard to create. This may highlight who is doing this to which customer departments.

[E]   Evaluating the Survey Results

The results of this survey are evaluated in several ways.

A. **Total the number of workstations.** Assume that each one is loaded with the company standard software. The ratio of workstations to support persons is one gauge of IT efficiency and is useful when planning company expansions.

B. **Confirm hours of support to critical applications.** Service levels vary according to the hours of the day and the day of the week. During those hours when the majority of the workers are present, the service level should be at its optimum. During evening hours, weekends, and holidays, any workers on the job may have an expectation and a requirement for support.

Another issue for support times is special days when long hours are expected in the department. These might be during the annual reconciliation and closing of the accounting files, during a materials inventory verification, or to receive orders in support of seasonal sales (such as Christmas for a retailer). Each of these would change the normal support hours. A sample of hours or support matrix is provided as Worksheet 18-2.

WORKSHEET 18-2. Hours of Support Matrix

Weekday Processing

	00	01	02	03	04	05	06	07	08	09	10	11	12	13	14	15	16	17	18	19	20	21	22	23
Payroll									×	×	×	×	×	×	×	×	×	-	-					
Accounts Payable									×	×	×	×	×	×	×	×	×							
Accounts Receivable									×	×	×	×	×	×	×	×								
Materials—Inbound		×	×	×	×	×	×	×	×	×	×	×	×	×	×	×	×							
Shipping Notices																×	×	×	×	×	×	×	×	×
Production Schedule	×																							

Saturday—Weekend Processing

	00	01	02	03	04	05	06	07	08	09	10	11	12	13	14	15	16	17	18	19	20	21	22	23
Payroll																								
Accounts Payable																								
Accounts Receivable								×	×	×	×	×												
Materials—Inbound																								
Shipping Notices																								
Production Schedule																								

Sunday—Weekend Processing

	00	01	02	03	04	05	06	07	08	09	10	11	12	13	14	15	16	17	18	19	20	21	22	23
Payroll																								

Accumulate the list of critical applications identified by each department. When laid alongside the vertical axis of the desired support hours, it is easy to see the technical skills required to be on site for optimal support. The survey asked for the days of the week and hours of the day each application is needed, but the current support person can identify any behind the scenes action required for an application to be available for workers first thing in the morning.

The list of critical applications must be compared to the IT staff organization to ensure that every critical application has someone assigned to support it. While developing the skills database, the IT department offered what they thought the critical applications would be. The survey's intention is to ask the customers what they believe the critical applications are.

A. Critical applications in the database but not on the survey list should be evaluated to determine their current significance to the company. Their importance may have faded and IT did not realize it.

B. Critical applications on the survey list but missing from the database should be examined to determine their underlying technologies and added to the list. Someone in the IT department should then be assigned to support the application. (Will this identify further training requirements?)

Use a spreadsheet to track when critical systems need support. Use one column for each hour. Down the left column, list all critical applications. Place an "X" in the column for each hour that a particular critical application is needed based on the customer survey, and based on the IT Manager's knowledge of when critical systems and their supporting software run. Include overnight processing for these systems.

Compare the spreadsheet requirements to the staff's work hours. Should any of them begin their workday earlier to provide better coverage? The focus of customer service levels is on the availability of skills and timeliness of a solution.

A. **Turnover rate and planned system changes.** This will provide planning estimates for future service requirements. Both will temporarily require additional technical support. If a department experiences a high degree of turnover, then their data systems must be greatly simplified to reduce the amount of time expended on training. Another side of this is company "downsizing" where experienced users will be reassigned and suddenly using systems new to them.

B. **Pending system changes.** These are to catch any upcoming system or process changes that may require additional staffing support, usually temporary. These occur in branch offices when the corporate headquarters may be creating applications specific to a department. In some companies, communications between departments can be somewhat lax. Use this list to initiate discussions with each department to understand the impact of any change on IT support planning.

[F]   IT Team Performance

On the reverse side of the survey form are ratings for each of the IT teams. The goal of this matrix is not statistical. It is to uncover indicators of problems. The purpose is to:

A. **Identify which user departments are directly calling which IT departments.** In some cases, this may be appropriate. In other cases, it must be stopped and refocused through the service desk. Otherwise, the support and problem identification metrics will not be accurate.
B. **Identify any negative customer experiences with IT.** This will provide some idea of the type of problem and the department.

These questions could be further developed to obtain some clear statistical inference, but that is beyond the scope of this study.

§ 18.06   TRANSLATING REQUIREMENTS INTO A STAFF LEVEL

[A]   Overview

Many companies have a "head count" budget as well as a capital and an operating budget. This is one way that a large company seeks to control their employment benefits and pension expenses. The IT Manager has a responsibility to provide the optimum customer service for the minimal cost. The ideal trade-off is rarely achieved but managers try to do the most with the resources at hand.

[B]   Establish a Service Level Performance Goal

Once the department's baseline customer service level is established, the next step is to identify what the department's service level should be. The gap between reality and the goal identifies the staffing and skills necessary for the department to deliver this service. To identify the desired service level, use the same approach as with identifying skills by starting with nothing and imagine building the department from scratch. This helps to reduce the "filters" of corporate culture and a "business as usual" attitude.

Establish a level of service agreement with the executives for the responsiveness they require. (We exist but to serve!) Ensure that the proper number of people with the correct skill sets is available to meet that level. Keep in mind the previously discussed characteristics of standby, separation of responsibilities, etc. Note that staffing levels should be set to something less than peak requirements. (Otherwise, when a work surge arrived, there would be no "slack" time to address it.)

[C]   Staffing Ratios

Major IT industry pollsters have asked companies about the number of people they use to service a set number of end users. The ratios vary by many factors such as the industry, the technical sophistication of end users, etc. Companies of less than 500 people may have a ratio of 18 end users per IT person while companies with more than 10,000 people may have a ratio of 40:1. A part of this is the spreading of IT staff overhead. A small shop would need a minimum of one expert per major technology (network, programming, operations, systems administration, manager, telephone system, etc.). In a lean organization, the manager may be one of these experts as well as the team leader. Large organizations can spread their technical specialists over a wide range of equipment. To estimate the service desk size in a large environment, figure at least 30 minutes per desktop, per year, for support if upgrades are addressed centrally. Allow another half hour, per year, if upgrades are applied individually.

Some industries are more IT intensive and have a low tolerance for delays. For example, a stock brokerage may have a ratio of one IT person per 11 end users. In a manufacturing environment, the ratio may be 33 workers to one IT technician because shop supervisors are more than likely to be the only ones using PCs, and they require less support than most employees in the shop who do not have PC workstations.

Factors driving the staffing ratio:

A. Technology stability and reliability. Standardizing systems on proven technologies will require fewer support people rather than chasing the latest technologies—or limping along with the oldest ones.
B. An active preventative maintenance program that cleans, lubricates, and adjusts moving components on critical devices such as high-volume printers.
C. Timely replacement of obsolete equipment. Some companies purchase their technologies with three-year warranties and dispose of the equipment after the warranty expires.
D. Some companies will never upgrade their desktop units. New units are purchased with the latest software and peripherals which are expected to suffice until the hardware warranty expires. Then they are replaced with new units.
E. Variety of technologies being supported. It is easier for one person to support a large number of desktops with standard software than trying to support a few workstations with everything that anyone can install.
F. Frequency and complexity of technology refreshes. Variation in technology carries with it its own learning curve.

[D]   Allocating the IT Staff

There are three typical ways to determine the staffing organization and size of an organization: The "warm body" approach; the "magic staffing" formula; minimal staff, tweak and adjust. Each approach has its own merits and deep pitfalls—yet the IT Manager may recognize his own organization within one of these frameworks. The task at hand is to balance and periodically rebalance the work between the IT teams and the individual staff members so that the appropriate level of staff is present—but no extra. Remember, all decisions are driven toward improving customer service.

Expect considerable resistance to shifting work among the team based on current requirements. Over time, employees become familiar with their responsibilities and are loath to exchange them for the unknown. Work expands to fill the time allotted to it, so a vigorous program to root out low-value tasks is essential. Otherwise, everyone will state that they are too busy with this or that, and that the IT department does not understand their customers.

Also, remember that end users dwell in a dynamic business environment. To provide a high level of service, the IT organization must periodically reconfigure itself to meet changing requirements.

The warm body approach. One author spent a considerable amount of time in the Marines where the term "warm body" was used to indicate a "living, breathing" person of any type. The implication is that whoever was in charge of the task would ensure the person provided would know how to accomplish the task (usually something simple). The person in charge would further provide the "direction and motivation" to ensure it was properly accomplished. This rather direct approach to people management is common in most IT shops. A set number of people (warm bodies) are assigned to vaguely described staff positions and then expected to perform the work. This approach results in the assignment of people based on their primary skill and/or availability at the time the opening appeared—not on the total skills necessary.

The warm body approach begins with a nod toward customer focus but always ends with a focus on finding "a place" for the existing staff. Its essential elements are:

A. **Identify the major task assignments within the department.** This might range from watching a high-speed printer in the data center to development of systems enhancements for a major data system. Sometimes the task is just to be immediately available, such as answering calls at the service desk.

B. **Write job descriptions that describe the responsibilities as imagined by the IT Manager.** A set of job descriptions ensures that the department's work is accounted for among the various positions.

C. **Assign each job responsibility some general quantity of time required to perform it.** Use a weekly or monthly timeframe. This time may have some basis in history but we are estimating future requirements. The time is totaled until a full-time equivalent (FTE) of a person (40 hours in a week) is arrived at.

D. **Assign existing staff members to these positions.** Do this according to the best fit between their perceived skills and the estimated requirements for each position. This step is often complicated by in-process projects.

For example, the IT Manager assigns:

A. One programmer for each major business area supported to include all major and minor programs, reports, etc. This includes all end-user generated programs used within these departments. This is a general estimate that says each major system requires a full-time person. It does not address the full range of technologies those data systems depend upon.

B. One computer operator per shift, three shifts by five days per week. In this situation, a person must be standing by even if there is no work. Routine tasks could be shifted from someone else to this person, if they are technically capable of completing them.

C. One service desk person for first shift minus two hours, and another one for the second shift plus two hours. Computer operators handle the rest of the calls. This again indicates a "watch stander" who sits and waits for the telephone to ring. The job requirement is immediate availability. It also shows how routine tasks such as the third shift service desk can be shifted to operations since the call volume is low to none.

D. One network support person and one server administrator. These two people provide backup support for the other. In these cases, the skills required are so unique that it is cheaper to hire someone to perform them rather than to always bring in a consultant—even if they are idle from time to time.

One IT administrative manager should manage the IT budget, licensing, contracts, and any other paperwork.

The warm body approach is often used when reorganizing existing IT staffs to address existing requirements without hiring more people. In these cases, its focus is workload shifting. Some pitfalls of this approach include:

A. All workers are not equally productive as this approach assumes they are. Their inclination to work or learn new technologies varies widely among the group.

B. Few IT Managers have a clear idea of what is required for each position and how long each responsibility will require. Their guesses are normally too low.

C. Workers settle in the role they are assigned and are reluctant to "clean up" the tasks not completed by others.

The magic staffing formula. Many companies are intimidated by the amount of work required to conduct a detailed customer expectations survey and seek a mathematical approximation for a staffing level. Such a formula may provide a quick answer, but it does not address such essential elements as individual expertise level, dispersion of the work sites, complexity of tools, etc. It is called a "magic" formula since many IT Managers seek it but are never satisfied with the result. The best use of a staffing formula is as a guideline for a theoretical staffing level.

COMMENT

The magic staffing formula starts with an estimate of the work required, which in turn leads to the job descriptions. The warm body method approaches the issue from the other direction by building a task list with its implied work requirement as the job descriptions are built.

An example of a formula is provided. It requires the IT Manager to make assumptions about work requirements so that full-time equivalent positions can be determined. A quick glance at the formula shows that it must be adjusted to address local conditions. If multi-shift operations are supported then this should be accomplished for each shift, with likely different factors for each shift (assuming the majority of nonemergency support is completed on the first shift).

Calculate each of these points and add up the total number of people required.

A. **Desktop support.** The number of workstations in service divided by a factor representing the number of stations that a single person can support. This might be anywhere from 100 to 1,000, depending on the degree of hardware standardization and end-user technical sophistication.

B. **Server support.** The number of servers in service divided by a factor representing the number of stations that a single person can support. This might be anywhere from 10 to 100, depending on the degree of standardization. There should be at least two server support people (primary and backup).

C. **Network support.** The number of hubs and major network switching devices in service. Consider one person for every 20 devices. Add another person for backup support.

D. **Telephone service.** Typically two people can support a facility, with one acting as the backup. This has increased with the elimination of office switchboards and the shift to IVR technology for routing calls.

E. **Programming.** One person per major data system or customer department.

F. **Security.** Two or more people. This responsibility may be split among a part of the staff. More than one person reduces abuse, but too many people permit circumvention.

G. **Operations.** A minimum of one per person per shift. Add more based on specific workload. This may be the same person that works the service desk.

H. **Administration.** At least one supervisor for every ten IT people plus one department administrator.

The caveats to this model are the age of the equipment, how widely it is dispersed, the degree of standardization, and the technical sophistication of the users. These factors may vary the results of the formula by as much as 30 percent.

Minimal staff. The minimal staff scheme is to identify the bare minimum number of people required to achieve the desired level of service. Then as service deficiencies are identified, grow the staff slowly to cover them. This creeping approach will initially result in some customer dissatisfaction but will ensure that the IT staff is tightly focused on its goals. The steps are:

A. Establish an initial service level. If the service desk already has metrics for the number of calls and the response time by urgency level, track the number of calls over time, by priority to get the average response and resolution times.

B. Identify the minimal staff required to provide a basic level of customer service. This is generally someone to answer the phones during normal business hours and a single technical expert for each major technology supported. Staff to this level and monitor service level performance.

C. After a 60-day break-in period to allow the team to settle into their new roles and determine the fastest way to address problems, review service response and determine if additional staff are needed, and where.

D. Add new staff members incrementally and allow another 60 days to determine the impact before hiring any more.

The result of adding a new person (after the break-in period) should be an improvement in the service level statistics. If there is no change, then the problem is something other than the number of people assigned to customer service. The 60-day delay also allows time to absorb the person's efforts into the metrics before adding the next one.

The major drawback to this approach is that each person added requires some shuffling of responsibilities among the staff. Although this is manageable, it is disruptive to productivity until everyone settles into their new roles.

The level of customer service the IT department provides has a direct impact on the staffing of the department. Higher service requirements generally translate into more people. The trick is to provide an acceptable level of service with the minimal employee costs. Given that the service the department is providing is to meet ever shifting customer needs, good luck!

Flexible assignments make it easier to shift people to address work surges. If grocery stock clerks are called to the front of a store to run a cash register, this is flexible staffing at work. Instead of rigid job requirements, the entire staff should consider itself as a labor pool to assist wherever they have the skills to do so.

If the IT budgets limit the number or quality of the people that can be hired, then reduce the published service levels, usually by cutting support to lightly used systems, or systems with few users. This will focus the team on the mainstream requirements.

See Policy ITP-18-2 IT Staffing Levels Policy as an example.

POLICY ITP-18-2.   IT Staffing Levels Policy

Policy #:	ITP-18-2	Effective:	03/18/13	Page #:	1 of N
Subject:	IT Staffing Levels Policy				

1.0 PURPOSE

This policy mandates the staffing levels required to support each division with the organization.

2.0 SCOPE

This policy encompasses all divisions within the organization. The IT Manager is responsible for implementing all aspects of this policy.

3.0 POLICY

The staffing of IT personnel within each division of the organization will follow the formulas listed below.

    A. Desktop support—there will be one desktop support person for every 150 desktop workstations.

    B. Server support—there will be one server engineer for every 15 servers. There should be at least two server support people (primary and backup) for each server.

    C. Network support—there will be one network support person for every major network switching device in service. There must be at least two people in each division to allow for backup support.

    D. Telephone service—typically two people can support a facility, with one acting as the backup.

    E. Programming—one person per major data system or customer department.

    F. Security—two or more people. This responsibility may be split among a part of the staff.

    G. Operations—a minimum of one person per shift. Add more based on specific workload. This may be the same person that works the help desk.

    H. Administration—at least one supervisor for every 10 IT people plus one department administrator.

Exceptions to these staffing levels require approval of the division head and the corporate CIO.

4.0 REVISION HISTORY

Date	Revision #	Description of Change
03/18/13	1.0	Initial creation.

5.0 INQUIRIES

Direct inquiries about this policy to:

George Jenkins, CIO
Our Company, Inc.
2900 Corporate Drive
Columbus, OH 43215

Voice: 614-555-1234
Fax: 614-555-1235
E-mail: gjenkins@company.com

Revision #:	1.0	Supersedes:	N/A	Date:	03/18/13

19

SERVICE LEVEL AGREEMENTS

§ 19.01 OVERVIEW

[A] Purpose and Scope

IT management has long struggled with meeting the service expectations of its many customers. Many business departments do not understand the difference between a service desk technician, a network engineer, and an IT project manager. All they see is "someone from IT" when they need something done. There are also many complaints concerning how the IT department seems to consume an ever expanding piece of the company's budget.

From the IT Director's perspective, there is much to do and only so many people to do it. A steady stream of requests flow in, all demanding immediate service for issues that might be best categorized as routine or even of low importance. Yet at every staff meeting, someone is complaining about the "poor service" out of the IT department.

Over the years, companies have tried various solutions to providing service support. Among these are staffing ratios, outsourcing lower technology positions, and even on occasion, flooding the site with technicians. They have even occasionally tried assigning specific IT staff to support a department. (This sometimes resulted in technicians being hired into those departments in distinctly non-IT sounding titles but who were tasked with IT work.) Nothing seemed to mollify the critics.

Finally, someone used the analogy of paying for home services. If they called for a service technician, would they pay $500 per hour for a guaranteed half-hour response time, or $60 per hour for next day service? There are times when either would be appropriate, but the lower cost compensated for the longer wait.

Eventually IT departments settled on the idea that they provided a set of services to their customers. These services were time-based for response and for resolution. To describe their service offering to the company, they published a service catalog explaining the various services that they offer. Each service has a description, a process for completing it, and a service level agreement (SLA) for each major supported entity or critical IT system.

In its simplest sense, an SLA is a statement of expectations. It describes the service to be offered, how it is requested, hours of support, etc. SLAs can be short or long, vague or detailed. Most companies use a mix of the two. SLAs can be internally facing or used to describe support by external sources. In the IT Infrastructure Library (ITIL) sense, externally facing SLAs are called underpinning agreements. SLAs must apply to services that the IT department controls. Externally supplied infrastructure (such as electrical service) is beyond the department's control and should not be assured in an SLA.

IT's portfolio of SLAs needs to be kept current with emerging demands. For example, a new technology introduced to the company must be reviewed to see if it is covered under an existing SLA or if a new one is required. (This is often an SLA based on an external support company until the technology becomes a part of IT's standard product set.)

An SLA is supported by an internal process with promised results. If the process is properly designed, then it should provide predictable outcomes within a predictable amount of time. It is this predictability (with a small range of variation) that enables IT to validate whether it can fulfill its promises. Without predictable outcomes and process duration, IT will never be sure that its SLAs promise more than the IT department is capable of delivering.

An SLA must include a process for collecting data on its service delivery performance. Identify the critical few metrics to be collected and analyzed monthly. This enables both the IT team and the departments that it is supporting to focus on the facts of the service delivery incidents and less on the emotions of a failed incident.

Applying SLAs to the workplace is an IT culture change. IT technicians now must explain why they missed a service goal. This can be uncomfortable but helps to streamline IT processes. SLAs should be used as a tool to improve processes and not as a personal punitive tool.

COMMENT

One of the most valuable benefits of writing an SLA for a customer is how much the IT Director will learn about the business they support and the business manager will learn about IT's support challenges. The detailed discussion of IT needs and support available will be beneficial to both parties.

[B] SLAs as a Communications Tool

SLAs can be used anywhere. IT management is well familiar with the SLA concept. Their many service providers have used them for years. It is only a short step to apply them to internally provided services as well. The challenge is to obtain acceptance from their customers and the IT support team.

An approved SLA is a communications tool to the IT staff, to the various company departments, and even to the executive staff. The response times and procedures described in the SLA set expectations. From the customer's perspective, they have an idea of what to expect in response time to their problem. From the IT department's perspective, the SLA's approved priority helps to prioritize work based on management's intent. Instead of a customer expecting immediate response, they now know the time frame (within 1 hour, within 8 hours, etc.) when someone should respond. If it is within the SLA, then there can be no complaint about tardiness. From the technician's perspective, the decision on which call to address next is partially based on how close an SLA is to expiring.

In this sense, SLAs establish a minimum performance requirement. This time can be tracked to measure how well the IT team is fulfilling its service commitments. The result may lead to the purchase of better tools, hiring more people, or the replacement of some contracted services.

Performance measures do not try to track every movement in a process. Instead, they focus on key performance indicators (KPIs), which are like the vital signs of a human body. If these are in order then the rest should be okay. Collecting performance data takes time, analyzing it takes time, and then discussing the results with your customer takes even more time. Therefore, minimize the number of KPIs to the essential few. This focuses everyone's efforts on the significant few issues rather than the trivial many.

COMMENT

Every customer problem report is unique. The SLA strives to cover a high percentage of incidents within the promised time frame. The closer that IT support gets to responding to 100 percent of all calls within the SLA's response time, the higher the cost climbs. Most executives are content with a 90 percent response time metric score. To improve service for important processes, look at redundant systems, and proven manual workarounds to keep business moving until those rare but tough problems are resolved.

If your company issues SLAs to support external customers, then there is an additional challenge. Each external SLA must include a final review by the company's legal counsel prior to its authorization as it may obligate the company to an expensive course of action or include penalty provisions. To minimize the legal review, expense, and delay, pre-approved "standard" SLAs are used.

[C] Critical Policies to Develop Based on This Chapter

Using the material discussed in this chapter, you will be able to create the following policies:

A. Require that the IT department issue enterprise-wide service SLAs for approval by the company executives (as they apply to all departments).
B. Require that all critical systems as identified by the Business Impact Analysis (BIA) are supported by SLAs to recover them before the company suffers significant financial damage.
C. SLAs to support non-standard equipment and software at the benefiting department's expense.

Policies should always be developed based on the local situation. Successful managers cannot issue appropriate guidance if the policies are written with another company's situation or location in mind.

§ 19.02 TYPES OF SLA

[A] Overview

SLAs are one part of an overall solution. They mean nothing if there are not adequate resources available to fulfill them. These resources are a combination of equipment (spares and failover devices), trained and available team members, and support by the customers. If any of these is lacking, then the other components will be significantly overworked.

General types of SLAs include:

A. **Internal.** These are a statement of management intent. They direct the limited IT technical resources to what they should address next. If the stated response time is missed, the receiving department has no special recourse other than to complain to the IT management. However, the IT Director should understand why an SLA was missed to determine if the support process is capable of that level of support with existing staffing and tools.

B. **External.** Arranged with critical vendors of IT support. These vendors may be used to support non-standard technologies or infrastructure (such as network or telephone service). Their performance is normally beyond the IT department's control. Therefore, it is futile to promise its control to customers.

C. **Enterprise-wide.** Detail the services provided to entire company.

D. **Specific internal.** Typically tied to critical systems or devices. These are identified by the business impact analysis (BIA).

[B] Enterprise-Wide SLAs

An enterprise-wide SLA is an agreement between the IT department and all departments of the entire organization. For example, an SLA for the service desk response time to calls is an enterprise-wide SLA as it applies to all callers. However, an SLA to support the business critical accounting system is an agreement for a specific system.

Enterprise-wide SLAs often describe infrastructure connectivity, reliability, and availability. This might be the internal network, electronic mail, or desktop equipment support. It may also include the various routine IT support processes. For example, the time required for the completion of a new user ID, purchasing software, etc.

A typical enterprise-wide SLA might be for desktop support of typical office software. It might be for password reset or for assistance with a company written system. These are the sort of services that an IT department provides to all employees during its normal working hours. No special accommodations are included. These calls might have a one-hour response SLA with a four-hour target resolution.

[C] Critical Systems

For many IT departments, the identification of critical systems is based on historical experience or the loudest complaining business managers. Some

IT departments may have processes that they dread to support due to demanding users or impatient management. This ad hoc approach may seem adequate until you move to an SLA system where additional support beyond the enterprise level SLA may require the supported business function to pay for the additional staff. Moving from an ad hoc approach to a data driven prioritization system will focus the limited IT resources where it most benefits the company.

The IT systems that are critical to the company are identified by its BIA. The BIA is an analysis of the company's business processes by its executives down to the line managers. It determines the financial and legal impact to the company for the loss of a particular business function over time (one hour, one day, two days, one week, etc.). Then the IT systems that support that vital business function are identified and are prioritized for recovery.

There are always disagreements between what the BIA says and what a department may want for support. In those cases, the department can arrange for additional funds to pay for faster support. The challenge is that departments typically require services from a range of technical areas (network, programming, desktop, information security, etc.). Paying for an additional support person will likely not fulfill all of their requirements as a single person cannot resolve problems in all IT areas.

For many companies, their high priority systems are any that are used by company executives. Any calls from specific executive callers are always addressed as high priority problems. This may be good "politics" but it may cause executives to misjudge the level of service provided to the rest of the company.

COMMENT

Every critical IT system identified by the BIA must have its own SLA. This ensures that it will be adequately supported relative to its company approved business function priority.

[D] Special Service Level Support

There are times when a department needs special support beyond what is found in the enterprise-wide SLAs. Those departments should cover the cost for this support. Otherwise, the IT department responds according to the enterprise-wide SLA and provides best effort assistance.

Examples of special SLAs include:

- Better than enterprise-wide SLA support for an IT system that is not listed in the BIA as critical, yet is declared critical to a department's management.
- Support of non-standard software. For example, a computer aided design (CAD) software package purchased for the Facilities department. The IT

department may hire an external company to provide on-demand support under IT supervision rather than train a staff member on a sophisticated package only used by a few people.

- Support for non-standard equipment. Many companies use large (perhaps 46 inch) monitors to display information dashboards to departments or information for all employees. These large devices require two or more men to mount or dismount for repair and are more likely to be replaced rather than repaired. This may be contracted to a local company.
- Support for a department who is temporarily working weekends or evenings. For example, supporting a wall-to-wall materials inventory or moving a department to a new floor of the office building over a weekend.
- The expense for additional IT staff work hours is generally approved in the request used by that department to pay their own team to come in. The IT support may be lightly used so it is an opportunity for IT Managers to plan work on other things until they are called.
- Equipment or software brought on-site for a proof of concept. Support is by an external company at extra cost to the requesting department until it becomes a standard company offering.
- The expense of support for a non-standard device is easiest to arrange during the pre-purchase approval process. Requiring payment for an external support SLA before purchase helps to minimize the number of non-standard items brought into the company.

§ 19.03 DIMENSIONS OF AN SLA

[A] Overview

The IT department begins the process by creating a list of the many services that it provides. Making this list helps the IT department to identify the many technical skills and tools required to support all of the services that it offers. (The list also identifies services that will not be offered.) By cross-referencing the skills needed to the skills of the IT team, gaps can be identified to be filled in future training. Each significant service area needs its own SLA to include the steps to be taken, skills required, and the tools necessary to detail how that service will be provided. This list is presented to all IT customers as a catalog of services that the IT team provides.

Writing an SLA is a team effort. It must involve the people to be supported, the technicians who are providing the support, and the managers of both groups. The individuals discuss the details of the support needed and level of such support. The managers must agree on the metrics and any additional costs.

SLAs can be long and bulky or simple documents. SLAs are a communication tool for setting your customer's expectations. To minimize misunderstandings, it is best to keep them simple and easy for nontechnical people to understand. The agreement must be written in clear language with neither business nor technical jargon. It must be clear to those receiving the service as well as to those providing the service. It should describe what service is offered, when it is available, and some sort of measurement to validate that the SLA is being accomplished (also known as quality of service). Alternatively, this measurement may indicate that additional resources are needed.

Before submitting an SLA for consideration by others, always request a review from a technical, legal, and managerial perspective. If the SLA is with an external entity, then it must also be reviewed by the legal team.

Managing customer expectations can be tricky. Sometimes a dire emergency turns out to be a quick fix. They appreciate the quick response and the quick resolution to that incident. Unfortunately, the more often this situation occurs, the more the customer will expect every resolution to be just as swift. It may even lead them to delay calling for support since they believe that the solution will be swift when, in fact, the time to resolution depends on the situation.

COMMENT

The IT support needs of business departments are constantly evolving (with some departments like Engineering changing faster than perhaps the Accounting department). SLAs must remain relevant so include a change request process in your SLA management. This can be initiated by any stakeholder to update the agreement. Of course, these changes must be agreed to by the relevant stakeholders.

[B] SLA Creation Process

Creating a workable SLA can be very time consuming. If SLAs are new to your organization, creating the first one can be tedious. However, creating SLAs is a process and once the process is established, it can be improved and streamlined. Although it is a process, the creation of an SLA goes through the same steps as a small project and can be run as one. The steps are:

A. **Information gathering**
   1. Work with the customer to help them to identify their priorities. The BIA may help. These priorities are considered the "critical few" core business functions in that department. What days of the week and times of day need to be supported? What are the critical times of the year? For example, the Accounting Department may work weekends and long hours at the end of the fiscal year.
   2. Understand what the IT department can reasonably deliver, given its other commitments to company support. When reviewing the customer priorities, note the technologies that must be supported, the times and days of the week. Compare this to the team's expertise. It may be necessary to arrange for external support for less

common technologies, to alter IT support personnel hours, or to arrange for additional training.

3. Are there any constraints to be considered? For example, physical and logical security to access the technology for support. Is the hardware running in a heavily secured area where the technician must be escorted? Do all support personnel possess the appropriate level of server, application, and database access?

4. Who are the key stakeholders for this service? This includes the departments supported, the IT support team, plus anyone else impacted by the problem. At a minimum the IT team (not just the manager) and the supported department management must agree.

5. Who are the key stakeholders for that business function? Who must be notified of outages, and what is the escalation timeline for informing higher levels of that organization?

B. **Analyze the information**

1. Over the last several years, how many service tickets were recorded for this technology and department? What times of day and day of week were they reported? How long did they take to resolve? Were special tools or specific IT personnel required to resolve the issues? Could the resolution time have been shortened through the use of spare equipment, user training, or manual work-around processes?

2. Review the IT asset management records to identify any unsupported technologies in that department.

3. Check for any external support contracts that apply to this department.

4. Review system documentation for technologies specific to this department or tools required for support.

C. **Negotiate the agreement**

1. Based on what the IT team uncovered, describe what level of service can be reasonably expected. This is in terms of response times, times and days of the week coverage, and expected time to resolution.

2. List when unresolved issues will be escalated and the process for doing this.

3. Roles and responsibilities of the user and the IT team.

4. The process for metric collection and review.

5. Periodic review of SLA performance by the IT management and managers of that business function.

6. Review of the SLA change process.

D. **Presenting**

1. Review the SLA with representatives of the department being supported. Verify all of the assumptions used by the IT department to set the response and resolution times. Use this opportunity to educate the supported business function on their responsibilities for actions prior to calling for support. Carefully explain to them IT's true service support capabilities.

2. Solicit their suggestions for improving the SLA or for clarifying any aspect of it. Review suggestions for changes through the SLA change process.

COMMENT

A workable SLA must be a mutual agreement and carefully explained to all parties. This acts as a final quality check on the facts and assumptions on which it is based. Forced agreements face a constant struggle for credibility.

[C] Time

Time is a natural metric to monitor for SLA service performance. The first time metric to consider is the response time. How long should it take for the service desk to answer a call? This can be difficult because service desks have peak call times and the rest of the week significantly fewer calls come in. Staffing for peak support is expensive. The goal of answering the call is to resolve the issue before ending the call. However, the problem sometimes obviously requires a technician's support and a ticket is recorded.

Next is the time for the technician to appear on-site. If the call could not be resolved over the phone, then when the service technician arrives, they must first contact the person who called. If that person is not available, then they should notify the service desk. Of course, arrival time must be during the normal working hours for that department. Showing up after everyone has gone home increases the risk that the broken device or software may not be available for resolution.

Finally is the time to resolution. Of all the timing issues, this is the entire point of the SLA. Although the technician can declare that something is now functional, it is the customer who makes the final determination. Once the service ticket is closed, a follow-up is e-mailed to the person reporting the problem to ensure that they agree that the issue is resolved. Although this may seem time consuming, it can uncover instances of poor service.

The SLA must describe the days of the week and the normal times of day for service. This enables planning by the service desk manager. Many departments will have someone who comes in early or who stays late to complete something. If service desk staffing permits, always cover this hour before and the hour after. The hour before should be used to verify that all of the department's vital systems appear to be running properly. This catches problems before they are discovered by the customer and (in their eyes) speeds resolution.

There must also be a mechanism in the SLA program for requesting additional support for special business occasions. This is typically requested for weekend production, the company's busy sales seasons, etc. If the company uses an internal chargeback mechanism, this would be directly charged to that department. (The process for requesting special support might be a standard clause in all SLAs.)

[D] Scope

Every SLA has limits. The SLA document must describe the services it is intended to support, and to minimize confusion, it may need to specifically exclude what it is not supporting. This might be company locations, specific devices, specific software, or the general name of an IT system (collection of related hardware and software). Essentially, the scope says that under this SLA, we do this and we do not do that.

An SLA should be inclusive of all technology (hardware, software, and infrastructure) used by that IT service. Customers think in terms of the function that an IT system provides. They do not care if the IT function is not available due to a network problem, a software problem, or anything in between. The service (end to end) is either operating as needed or it is not.

For example, some companies provide cell phones or laptop computers to employees for company use. If they break while the employee is on vacation, the SLA might state that portable equipment must be brought to the IT Service desk for repairs. It may state that telephone support is only provided for company supplied hardware and software, and that telephone support is not to be used for personal devices. If company equipment used off-site is to be supported, then steps to do so must be a documented service desk procedure.

Over time, it is not unusual for SLAs to be changed as special circumstances occur. For example, if the company provides equipment for use by customers or suppliers, then some sort of support may be needed at their locations. Many times, the existence of this equipment is only known to a few people. As it is uncovered, the IT Director and the supported department must update the SLA and coordinate any additional expense.

COMMENT

An internal SLA is a sign of trust between two parts of the company. Both parties trust that the other is acting in good faith with every intention of fulfilling its part of the agreement. If this trust does not exist, then the SLA will be used as a weapon in internal battles and its value is minimal.

[E] Cost

Enterprise-wide SLAs should reflect the use of existing resources. This is useful data for discussing with company executives the appropriate staffing level for the IT department. Begin by obtaining agreement on the service catalog. Then lead the discussion to the level of support expected for each item in the catalog (most can be discussed as general groups). Wrap up the conversation with an explanation of how well the existing IT team can fulfill those desired service levels.

The point of the discussion is cost. Prompt service with technicians knowledgeable in every IT area is expensive and it is a rare IT organization who has all of their technologies adequately covered internally. At this point, the business executives can agree that the IT department must be staffed to provide the desired level of service or that the level of service described in the SLAs must be cut back to conform to current staffing and budget.

There are several tools that can be used to reduce the IT support costs:

A. Train end users to address basic problems on their own. Include self-help training aides. This may include pre-positioned spares for critical processes. It is a rare person who does not have at least one computer and printer at home. They can swap out devices like monitors and printers and address simple desktop software problems. Additional training and documentation can be provided for company unique software.

B. Use external IT services to supplement existing staff to fill jobs requiring difficult-to-find expertise or when additional people are needed for a limited time. These may be charged directly to the department who needs them. Meanwhile, the IT strategy should be to minimize the number of technologies in use.

C. Standardize hardware and software for company use. This is never accomplished for every piece of company technology. However, the closer that the company comes to 100 percent standardized hardware and software, the cheaper it is to support. Standardizing requires control of what is purchased and a strong program to migrate away from obsolete technologies as soon as they are marked for elimination.

D. Purchase spare equipment to swap in the event of a hardware failure. This is easiest when using standardized devices. Guard this equipment from unapproved use.

E. Create a lifecycle plan for each device based on the function it provides. The goal is to quickly eliminate it once it reaches end of life. A constant support problem arises from the last few of something lingering in use by a department years after the rest of the company has moved to other solutions. Use a lifecycle plan and asset management databases to locate and replace these lingering support requirements.

F. Manage the inflow of new technologies so they can be supported when embraced by the company. A great example is the emergence of "Pad" PCs. Many companies tried to stop them but all in vain. Instead, develop a process where the early adopters are allowed to try new things so long as they pay the additional cost of its support.

COMMENT

There are many simple IT support tasks that can be accomplished by the end user. At one time, laser printers were rare and expensive. A technician was dispatched to change every toner cartridge. Today everyone expects that the people using the printer will change their own cartridge. On the other hand, a persistent error message on the same laser printer is beyond the capabilities of a quick technician visit and may take additional time to resolve.

[F]   Assigned Responsibilities and Escalations

An SLA should include the essential steps for the troubleshooting process to support it. Each person involved in the incident has a role to play in its prompt resolution.

Typical participants in a service call are:

A. **Customer**. Responsible for immediate problem resolution action and work-around steps (anything to lessen the impact until the problem can be resolved, such as routing to a different printer until the desired printer is repaired).

B. **Service Desk**. Take the call promptly, verify the SLA that applies, walk the caller through the customer immediate action tasks and, if the issue is still unresolved, ask all of the pertinent questions for the problem ticket. Dispatch a technician to resolve the problem ticket. Follow up with the customer and technician until the ticket is closed.

C. **First response technician**. Review the ticket and the site's history. Take adequate tools and exchange parts. Notify the caller when you have arrived—do not go straight to repairing something. Address the issue and close ticket. If necessary, refer to a higher technical support. "Own" the call until resolved. Close the ticket when the problem is resolved.

D. **Supervisor response**. If additional support is needed, notify the technical supervisor that the SLA will be exceeded and why. Then notify the customer representative of the situation.

E. **Third-party service provider**. Called by the service technician if appropriate. They work under IT supervision and their performance is a component of the IT performance metric.

Responses to service calls are monitored by managers on both the customer side and the service provider side. They review performance statistics and are notified when a service call will exceed SLA limits. They are:

A. **Customer representative.** Usually a manager from that department—responsible for gathering local requirements and addressing day-to-day issues with the SLA. They report to and receive direction from the department's executives. They maintain their self-help instructions and train new employees in their department.

B. **IT Service Team Leader**. This is the first point of escalation from the service technician who cannot locate the correct support resources and who may miss an SLA. They monitor technician performance to ensure prompt response times and that all of the necessary tools are in place and in proper working condition for supporting a call.

At some point, there is a service issue that requires additional resources, prompt action, or where the customer feels additional effort is required. In those cases, the SLA should detail who is the escalation point for action all the way up to the IT Director, and how to contact them during normal working hours. (After-hours contact information must be closely held by the service desk.)

COMMENT

SLA service objectives must be realistic. For all but the most critical business functions, the service support goal is not 100 percent. That would mean a significant portion of the IT staff is sitting around waiting for the phone to ring. Instead, the company may determine that the acceptable service level of many SLAs may be somewhere between 80 percent and 95 percent. The fact is, if some IT support calls take a bit longer for response, it is annoying to the people involved but they can work on other things while they wait.

[G] Metrics for Measuring Performance

After describing in the draft SLA the service to be delivered, next explain how the performance of this service will be measured. SLA metrics will help both the line of business customer and the IT Director to gauge how well an IT service is being delivered. This provides data to consider whenever someone complains that service is "always late." Regular reports, based on data collected, enable its management like any other business process.

There are several challenges to note when working with metrics:

- You get the most of what is measured. Be sure to measure the right things or employees will emphasize the wrong ones.
- There is a cost to every metric measurement collected. It costs to collect, store, analyze, and review data.

Selecting metrics to follow is a joint decision. Customers will expect metrics to be meaningful and geared toward their view of IT service delivery. Each metric must be described in terms of what is to be measured, who collects it, why it is measured, how often, how the data is collected, how it is analyzed and what an acceptable level of performance is. (This sounds like a lot of detail but describing each step removes doubt and adds to the metric's credibility.)

Establishing a service metric requires several pieces of information:

- What is to be measured? Is it the time to respond, time to completion, customer overall satisfaction, how often the call is escalated, etc.?
- What period of time is measured? Is it every service ticket; is it system availability between normal working hours, etc.?

Service desk incident report tickets are an excellent source of historical data. They have the time of a call, its nature, who was dispatched, how it was resolved, etc. To keep this source of information reliable, take time to emphasize the value to the organization of honesty when entering or adding data to service tickets.

If someone goes through the effort to collect metrics, they should receive the courtesy of someone analyzing the information (or tell them to stop collecting). The result of the metrics might be that additional support is needed in an area to meet the promised time goals. It may also indicate a need to redesign the support process to streamline response time.

Metrics should be reviewed monthly between the parties to ensure that someone is addressing any problems they indicate. Over time, the metrics should trend toward improved performance. This is based on the experience curve, lessons learned from technicians, improved documentation, etc. If not, then the SLA process should be examined for areas to improve. SLA metrics provide a feedback mechanism to fine tune the IT processes for supporting its customers. Based on the number and severity of calls, some SLAs can be reduced to provide better support for others.

The IT team leader over that support function must explain any service problems where the SLA was exceeded. Even if no one has complained, out of SLA conditions should be addressed or the SLA metric considered for change. SLA metrics are an indicator of the IT team's ability to meet customer requirements. If these requirements are not being met then the data collected can be used to change the SLA time or to provide additional IT resources.

> ## COMMENT
>
> Delivery of the service is as important as the service delivered. The IT team must take time to communicate with the end users early in the process and throughout its resolution. There is nothing worse than to be sitting idle waiting for something to be repaired without knowing if the IT team is still working on it or not.

[H]   External SLAs

SLAs with external service providers will have everything mentioned so far, plus a more thorough legal review. This means that the service provider and receiver should work out all of the points prior to sending it to the legal department (which in many companies takes a long time to respond).

Some companies focus intently on the terms of the external SLA but it all comes down to whether the service provider is fulfilling your needs or is not. Penalty clauses sound good but are difficult to enforce. Hammering a supplier to minimize their price and then trying to force them to provide a high level of service will be a fruitless battle. SLAs are written to solve problems rather than to be the center of a long-running battle.

Instead of penalties, consider offering performance incentives to meet targets. Write the SLA to optimize the chances of receiving that service. If the service provider cannot fulfill the required SLAs then it is time to replace them.

> ## COMMENT
>
> Many vendors will offer a "standard" SLA. They do this because it is a form that covers their organization from all angles and is approved by their legal department. Use this document as a starting point and do not hesitate to change it to fit your local situation.

§ 19.04   SLA TEMPLATE

Each company determines what should be in their SLA. A lot of this depends on the culture's opinion of the IT services and its expectations for future service. No one likes to sit at home powerlessly awaiting a service call for a vital home service where there is no idea of when they will arrive. The same is true for business leaders. A written SLA provides a maximum time to respond with an anticipated time to resolve problems. It also carries a requirement for a monthly management review to address shortcomings.

Typical elements in an SLA may include:

A. **Description of the services covered.** This statement includes what is and is not covered by this document.

B. **Hours of the day, and days of the week, of coverage.** Typically this will be the company's normal business hours. However, some business functions keep very late hours and may be working on weekends on a regular basis. Expense for support outside of normal business hours may be charged to and spread among the requesting departments.

C. **Incident maximum response time.** This is typically how long the Help Desk has to connect with the person reporting the problem. During peak call times, the report may be recorded or received by e-mail. However, the service desk still must respond to the person reporting the problem within the SLA designated time.

D. **Incident maximum resolution time**. This is the typical maximum amount of time to problem resolution. There may be an instance where the problem exceeds this amount. The service desk must document what caused the delay and its periodic follow-ups with the technician and the person making the report until it is resolved.

E. **Escalation steps**. This is based on the incident's impact, to include IT and support department's management contact information.

F. **Special costs**. Any special costs to support this SLA that are charged to the business function (which may be spread among more than one department).

G. **Metrics for SLA performance**. Should include what to collect, who collects it, how it is collected, how often it is collected, how it is analyzed and who reviews it.

H. **Process for recommending changes.** This should be standard for all SLAs. Any SLA stakeholder should be allowed to submit changes for consideration by the IT and business function approvers. Proposed changes should be reviewed monthly.

I. **Periodic review process**. It is important to examine the performance history of the SLA and to reexamine the business needs to determine if the SLA has been effective, if it is still relevant and to review any recent proposed changes.

§ 19.05 PITFALLS

IT departments teach their customers how SLAs will be applied. If they permit customers to abuse them then they will. If they actively discourage this behavior, then it will be minimal. In the end, SLAs are for the support of people and business functions and not just equipment and software.

Some of the pitfalls of creating or using SLAs include:

A. Customers who confuse what they are paying for. An additional charge for fast response time for a specific function may be confused with having someone sitting around awaiting a call and the customer would then expect a prompt answer for any type of IT call to their department.

B. People who intentionally misrepresent a situation as a type of problem covered by a tight SLA to get someone on-site promptly only to realize it was something else all along.

C. Signing a service agreement without any service level measurements, and trying to add them on later when problems arise.

D. External SLAs without a clause explaining how the service may be transitioned to a different vendor.

E. Keeping the existence of the SLA quiet and not publishing the document where everyone can refer to it.

F. Transitioning the IT department to SLAs poorly, resulting in the SLAs being discarded at the first excuse. In this situation, the IT team fights any sort of accountability through the SLA metrics.

G. Expecting an SLA to repair poor communications with the customers. Clear up your relationship before implementing or the SLA will just be another point of argument. If there is mistrust and finger pointing before the SLA, it will still be there after the SLA is approved. This must be resolved first.

H. Ensuring that any internal or external support agreements supporting an SLA are workable. For example, ensuring that the shipping department will express-ship replacement equipment to a distant location within four hours or that your third-party support organization will adhere to the metrics you provide even though it was not in their original contract.

I. An SLA trying to detail every support item for a business function as the ongoing maintenance would be too much. SLAs are general documents. Too much detail makes them awkward, hard to manage, and quickly irrelevant.

J. SLAs applied to a service that the IT department does not control, such as long distance telephone, electrical power, or long distance network connectivity.

K. SLAs that do not clearly explain the roles and responsibilities of all parties.

§ 19.06 PERIODIC REVIEWS

Companies exist within a swirl of many environments—each of which directly affects their business. The marketplace may shift and products that were once mainstays of the business are no longer important. Customers with tight support requirements may have moved on and new ones with different needs are now in place. The business impact of various functions may have changed. New regulatory mandates may impact company operations. Any one of these could tighten or loosen SLA support requirements.

SLAs should be reviewed at least once per calendar quarter. While this can be time-consuming, the review can be combined with review of the performance measurements of each SLA's metrics. The goal is to ensure that the SLA is still providing a relevant level of support. It may be that the required response time and hours of coverage can be reduced or adjusted to better meet customer needs.

At some point, all SLAs must be retired. This usually occurs when a new IT system has replaced a previous one, or where resources used to support a specific customer are no longer needed since that customer has moved on. It may also be that the support for specific IT hardware items dictates that if it breaks it is automatically replaced with the new (and different) device.

Another good time to review SLAs is during annual budget planning. It may be that a department decides that it can survive with standard response times and wishes to drop the extra cost of special support agreements.

Periodic SLA reviews force stakeholders to consider what has changed in their environment. This is a good time to check for new technologies and changed business emphasis. Some companies require an annual SLA re-authorization. This ensures that it still meets the current business requirements or is checked for places to reduce service.

See Policy ITP-19-1 IT Service Level Agreement Policy as an example policy to establish an SLA.

POLICY ITP-19-1. IT Service Level Agreement Policy

Policy #:	ITP-19-1	Effective:	04/01/13	Page #:	1 of N
Subject:	IT Service Level Agreement Policy				

1.0 PURPOSE

This policy provides guidance for the establishment and operation of IT Service Level Agreements (SLAs).

2.0 SCOPE

The policy applies to all IT services provided to the company. Each IT service provided will be detailed in the IT department's Service Catalog and supported by an SLA. Any IT services required that are not in the Service Catalog and addressed by an SLA will be provided on a "best effort" basis.

3.0 POLICY

This policy applies to all IT services provided to the company. The SLA provides a description of what is provided so that the supported business units can determine if the level of IT services is being fulfilled or if there is a deficiency. The Service Desk is the Single Point of Incident Reporting Contact between the IT

Department and the business users it supports. All reports of incidents where IT services are not fulfilling its SLAs must be reported through the IT Service Desk.

3.1 Service Level Agreements

For every service in the Service Catalog, there will be either an SLA or a vendor underpinning agreement. In either case, the agreement will clearly describe the service to be provided, a set of operating parameters (measurements) that the service must fulfill, the days of the week and the times of service, and the planned response time.

One of the most valuable benefits from the creation of SLAs is how much the IT Director will learn about the business that is supported, how they use technologies, and how the IT department's service level is perceived. At the same time, the line of business manager can learn about the complexities and limitations of the IT department.

Each agreement will include:

A. Description of the services covered in this agreement
B. Hours of the day, and days of the week, of coverage
C. Incident maximum response time
D. Incident maximum resolution time
E. Escalation steps, based on the incident's impact, to include IT and support department's management contact information
F. Special costs to support this SLA
G. Metrics for SLA performance
H. Process for recommending changes
I. Periodic Review process and timing

3.2 Enterprise-Wide SLAs

General services provided to the entire organization are considered to be enterprise-wide services and covered under a general SLA. Examples of this include desktop equipment and software support. Enterprise-wide SLAs are negotiated with the top company executives.

Enterprise-wide SLAs are useful because company executives are determining what an acceptable level of service is. Based on SLA metrics, the IT department may need to hire additional staff or change staff working hours to meet them. As business circumstances require, this level of support can be increased and measured by SLA metrics.

3.3 Special Support SLAs

Every three years, the IT Business Continuity Team conducts a Business Impact Analysis to identify the company's critical few vital business functions. The absence of service from any of these functions will detrimentally impact the company's financial performance or expose it to significant legal liability. Every IT system required by the vital business functions must be supported by a Special Support SLA.

Special support SLAs must be designed to fulfill the vital business function's Recovery Time Objective. This is typically 20 percent of the IT systems.

For example, if the loss of the factory's air pollution tracking system for more than one hour exposes the company to significant legal liability then the SLA will mandate no more than a one-hour recovery time. It would also include escalation reporting times as that one hour runs out without a restored system.

SLAs are intended to guide IT support during normal business circumstances. SLAs do not apply during an IT disaster. In those cases, the business continuity recovery priority process establishes when a specific vital business function (and its IT systems) is to be restored.

3.4 Service Level Agreement Review and Changes

All new SLAs are reviewed after 30 days with the people who are supported by it and the Service Desk manager. This review is intended to identify obvious problems and opportunities for SLA process improvement.

Every month, the SLA metrics are reviewed by IT management and the supported business function with an eye on updating SLAs to fulfill shifting (perhaps seasonal) requirements. This is also the time to discuss the cause of any out of SLA performance.

Once a year, each SLA is reviewed from end to end by the IT Director and the business function supported (or the company executives for enterprise-wide support) to validate that it still meets current business needs. During this review, performance metrics are reviewed, out of SLA events discussed, and future requirements identified.

Every three years, a fresh requirements analysis verifies the current customer requirements, the current process capability to meet these requirements, and asks team members for their ideas on improving it. Also considered are best practices as lessons learned across the company.

3.5 SLA Metric Review Process

Each SLA contains a section describing performance measurements of the services that it provides. These metrics take time and incur cost to collect, analyze, and report. Therefore, these metrics must be reviewed soon after they are collected. If they are no longer relevant, then a change to the SLA should be initiated for approval by the supported entity and the IT Director to discontinue that metric.

Whenever SLA metrics exceed the SLA response or resolution times, an explanation of the circumstances must be recorded. The goal is to identify trends such as day of week, when specific support personnel are not available, etc., to assist in the improvement of staffing levels and staff training.

SLA trends are also examined to detect performance trending out of accepted service levels. SLA trends may also indicate a service whose demand is now minimal and may be a candidate for retirement. This is often accompanied with the retirement of specific models of hardware or software.

3.6 Responsibilities

IT Management is responsible for:

A. Implementing a system of SLAs that describe the various IT services provided to the company and, in some cases, to its customers. This includes:

1. SLA creation.
2. SLA negotiation and agreement with supported customers.
3. SLA annual review and updates.

B. Monitoring the performance metrics described in each SLA metric:
   1. Reviewing incidents that exceed the SLA maximum response and resolution times.
   2. Validating that the IT department is capable of fulfilling that service level.
   3. Recommending changes to staffing and support tools to fulfill the described service level.
   4. Negotiating a reduction in service level that the department is capable of delivering.

The IT Service Desk Manager is responsible for:

A. Identifying areas where an SLA might be appropriate.
B. Executing the SLA fulfillment processes.
C. Maintaining the IT Services Catalog.
D. Reviewing and responding to complaints about SLA violations.
E. Reviewing metrics and recommending changes.

4.0 REVISION HISTORY

Date	Revision #	Description of Change
04/01/13	1.0	Initial creation.

5.0 INQUIRIES

Direct inquiries about this policy to:

George Jenkins, CIO
Our Company2900
Corporate Drive
Columbus, OH 43215

Voice: 614-555-1234
Fax: 614-555-1235
E-mail: gjenkins@company.com

Revision #:	1.0	Supersedes:	N/A	Date:	04/01/13

20

CHANGE MANAGEMENT: KEEPING EVERYTHING UP TO DATE

§ 20.01 OVERVIEW

[A] Purpose and Scope

Managing change within the IT environment of an organization is critical to ensure that a high level of service quality is maintained. It is also important for ensuring compliance with various regulatory requirements such as Sarbanes-Oxley and for maintaining ISO certification. An effective change management policy can also reduce risk to the IT department and to the rest of the organization, as any change to the IT infrastructure introduces an element of risk. Items that must be included in a change management policy are:

A. **Defined approval process.** A formal, well-defined approval process is critical to ensure that changes are successful and do not cause disruptions.
B. **Up-to-date and accurate documentation.** This makes it easier to identify systems and processes that are affected by the proposed change.
C. **Scope.** Identify in the change management policy what areas the policy will cover. All major systems and processes that affect the organization's ability to perform its mission should be included.
D. **Oversight.** A Change Advisory Board (CAB) should be established to review all proposed changes. The CAB should include members from all critical areas of the organization.

Change management applies to changes to both hardware and software used to operate the organization. In this chapter, we discuss not only change management in general but also specific concepts that apply to the patching of the software applications used in the organization.

[B] Policy Objectives

The primary objective of a change management policy is to ensure that changes made to the organization's IT infrastructure do not interrupt the functions of the organization (i.e., do not make things worse than before the change!). It does this by providing a thought-out, standardized process and procedures for making changes. IT governance models such as IT Infrastructure Library (ITIL) and Control Objectives for Information and Related Technology (COBIT) require a defined change management process as a foundational element of the model. An effective change management policy also helps to satisfy Sarbanes-Oxley corporate governance audit requirements. Objectives for your change management policy include:

A. Reducing the risk associated with the introduction of changes.
B. Reducing the impact of changes on the organization.
C. Creating clearly defined best practices for introducing changes into the IT environment.
D. Defining a process for the approval of changes with multiple levels of review.

E. Improving communication about changes through notification and escalations, ideally through the use of automated tools.
F. Creating a central data repository for all changes and their effect on the IT infrastructure.

The strategic objective of a company's change management program is to create a consistently configured environment that is effective, meets the needs of the organization, and is secure against known vulnerabilities in operating system and application software.

[C] Critical Policies to Develop Based on This Chapter

Using the material discussed in this chapter, you will be able to create the following policies:

A. Change management policy
B. Patching policy
C. Policy mandating an asset inventory of all hardware and software
D. Policy for assignment of patch priority

Policies should always be developed based on the local situation. Successful managers cannot issue appropriate guidance if the policies are written with another company's situation or location in mind.

§ 20.02 CHANGE MANAGEMENT POLICY

[A] Overview

An organization's change management policies formalize the process of keeping its IT infrastructure up to date. That process starts when a request for a change is first made and ends when the change has been satisfactorily implemented. This request for change includes both planned changes, such as the implementation of a new software version, and unplanned changes, such as the patching of software to protect against a newly discovered vulnerability. Given the impact on the company and the urgent nature of some changes, its change management policy must have the endorsement and support of the CEO or head of the organization.

[B] Definition of Change Management

IT change management is the process of making any change to the organization's IT infrastructure. It typically includes the following steps:

A. A request for a change is made.
B. The change is analyzed for its potential impact on the IT infrastructure.
C. The change is approved or rejected by a change oversight committee (typically called the CAB or change advisory board).
D. If the change is approved, an implementation plan is created for the change. If the potential impact of the change is significant, the implementation plan should also be reviewed by the CAB.

E. The change is implemented.
F. The results of the change are documented.

The CAB should include members from all critical areas of the organization. Any area that has a stake in the functioning of the IT infrastructure should be represented. Members typically include:

A. User managers
B. Business manager to represent the organization's customers
C. IT Manager
D. Security Manager

Other individuals may be required to participate on the CAB for some changes; other possible members used as needed may come from the following areas:

A. Network infrastructure support
B. Customer support
C. Service desk
D. Applications development

The CAB is led by the Change Manager, who is responsible for managing the change management process. The implementation of each individual change is managed by the Change Coordinator. See Policy ITP-20-1 Change Advisory Board Policy as an example policy for creating a CAB.

POLICY ITP-20-1.   Change Advisory Board Policy

Policy #:	ITP-20-1	**Effective:**	03/18/13	**Page #:**	1 of N
Subject:		Change Advisory Board Policy			

1.0 PURPOSE

This policy authorizes the establishment of an information technology change oversight committee to be called the Change Advisory Board, or CAB. This committee is responsible for overseeing all changes made to information technology systems throughout the organization.

2.0 SCOPE

The Change Advisory Board authority encompasses all IT systems and technology that support critical business functions. The CAB operates under the authority of the CIO, and is responsible for any changes made to any of the following:

A. **Software applications.** Any changes to software used in production, such as installations, patches, and version upgrades. This includes operating systems, business applications, and device control software.

B. **Hardware.** Addition, removal, or relocation of computer hardware such as servers and desktops.

C. **Data.** Any changes to databases such as changes in the table structure or changes in source data, or changes to the database software.

D. **Schedule changes.** Any changes to the schedule of periodic or batch processes, such as backups, file transfers, accounting updates, etc.

E. **Telephony.** Any changes to the main telephone equipment such as relocating the PBX, adding new hardware, etc.

3.0 POLICY

The CIO will appoint a Change Manager, who is responsible for managing the change management process and heads the Change Advisory Board. The CAB will include members from all critical areas of the organization. The following areas must designate a member to serve on the CAB:

A. Administration
B. Production
C. Sales
D. IT Manager
E. Security Manager

Other individuals may be required to participate on the CAB for some changes; other areas to provided representatives as needed include:

A. Network infrastructure support
B. Customer support
C. Service desk
D. Applications development

4.0 REVISION HISTORY

Date	Revision #	Description of Change
03/18/13	1.0	Initial creation.

5.0 INQUIRIES

Direct inquiries about this policy to:

George Jenkins, CIO
Our Company, Inc.
2900 Corporate Drive
Columbus, OH 43215

Voice: 614-555-1234
Fax: 614-555-1235
E-mail: gjenkins@company.com

Revision #:	1.0	Supersedes:	N/A	Date:	03/18/13

[C]   Change Management Scope

It is important to define those types of changes that are covered by the organization's change management policy and those that are not. The organization's change management policy covers any change that can materially impact the ability of the organization to perform its mission. Changes to the following items are typically within the scope of the change management process:

A. **Software applications.** Any changes to software used in production, such as installations, patches, and version upgrades. This includes operating systems, business applications, and device control software.
B. **Hardware.** Addition, removal, or relocation of computer hardware such as servers and desktops.
C. **Data.** Any changes to databases such as changes in the table structure or changes in source data, or changes to the database software.
D. **Schedule changes.** Any changes to the schedule of periodic or batch processes, such as backups, file transfers, accounting updates, and so on.
E. **Telephony.** Any changes to the main telephone equipment, such as relocating the PBX, adding new hardware, and so on.

While there are no "insignificant" changes in an IT environment, there are a number of changes that do not require the full attention of the CAB. These are typically changes that are performed repeatedly during the course of operating the business and have established policies in place defining how these changes are to be performed. Changes outside the scope of the change management policy include:

A. Password resets
B. User adds/changes/deletions
C. System reboots
D. Security group changes
E. File permission changes
F. Changes to nonproduction systems
G. Disaster recovery plan updates

The CAB should periodically review production problem reports to see if items not currently within the scope of the change management policy should be within its scope. Special circumstances within the organization may require that seemingly minor changes be reviewed because of their potential impact on the organization.

[D]   Change Management Process

The organization's IT change management process must ensure that changes to the IT environment are done efficiently while minimizing the risk to the business. This is best facilitated by the use of a change management software application.

COMMENT

Change management software can be purchased from several vendors including SunView Software (*www.sunviewsoftware.com*), bmc software (*www.bmc.com*), and IBM's Rational Software division (*www-01.ibm.com/software/rational*).

No matter what system is used to document the change management process, the following steps are necessary:

A. **Enter change request.** All requests for changes to the IT environment must be made using the organization's change control system. The organization should have a Change Coordinator to work with the person requesting the change to bring some consistency to the process and to make sure all relevant information is captured. The Request for Change (RFC) should include the following information:
   1. **Contact information.** The requestor's name, position, and contact information.
   2. **Description.** A description of the change, including the nature of the change and a description of the item(s) to be changed.
   3. **Reason.** The reason for the change, including a cost-benefit analysis and any budgetary approvals required.
   4. **Priority.** A suggestion of the priority and category of the change based on the information currently available. Priorities for changes can vary between organizations, but typically include:
      a. **Emergency.** A change that will cause significant damage or risk of damage to the organization if not implemented immediately, such as major security patches.
      b. **High.** A change that is important and should be implemented soon, such as software changes required to meet regulatory requirements.
      c. **Medium.** A change that provides benefits to the organization, such as an enhancement financial planning system.

        d. **Low.** A change that is "nice to have" but not needed immediately and has a low impact.

   5. **Category.** A suggestion of the category of the change based on the information currently available. Categories for changes can vary between organizations, but typically include:

        a. **Major.** The change affects a large part of the organization, such as a department or division.

        b. **Significant.** The change affects a smaller portion of the organization, such as a group with a department.

        c. **Minor.** The change affects a small number of users.

   6. **Implications of not making the change.** Include financial impact and any impact on service level agreements (SLAs).

B. **Assess the change.** Someone from IT (the Change Coordinator if that position exists) assesses the urgency and impact of the change on the organization as a whole, considering the scope of the change and its impact on user productivity. This should include:

   1. Impact of the change, including how users and the organization will be affected.

   2. Risks involved in making the change.

   3. Risks of not making the change.

   4. Suggested implementation plan.

   5. Description of the change back-out plan.

   6. Impact of the change on disaster recovery plans.

C. **Approve the change.** For minor changes, approval is granted by the Change Coordinator or IT Manager; major changes are reviewed by the CAB for approval or rejection.

D. **Plan for the change.** This includes documenting the steps required to make the change, taking into account the technical requirements of the change. The plan should be optimized to minimize the impact on the IT infrastructure. For major changes the implementation plan should be reviewed by the CAB. The plan must also include steps required to back out or reverse the effects of the change if the change does not have the desired effect.

E. **Implement the change.** Implement the change following exactly the steps outlined in the implementation plan.

F. **Document the results.** A review should be made to determine if the change had the desired effect on the IT infrastructure or system changed. Document what went well and what did not; this will help in planning future changes.

See Policy ITP-20-2 Change Management Policy as an example.

POLICY ITP-20-2. Change Management Policy

Policy #:	ITP-20-2	Effective:	03/18/13	Page #:	1 of N
Subject:	Change Management Policy				

1.0 PURPOSE

This policy governs the process used to make changes to the organization's IT infrastructure and systems, and is designed to ensure that changes to the IT environment are done efficiently while minimizing the risk to the business.

2.0 SCOPE

The Change Management Policy encompasses all IT systems and technology that support critical business functions. This includes changes made to any of the following:

    A. **Software applications.** Any changes to software used in production, such as installations, patches, and version upgrades. This includes operating systems, business applications, and device control software.

    B. **Hardware.** Addition, removal, or relocation of computer hardware such as servers and desktops.

    C. **Data.** Any changes to databases such as changes in the table structure or changes in source data, or changes to the database software.

    D. **Schedule changes.** Any changes to the schedule of periodic or batch processes, such as backups, file transfers, accounting updates, etc.

    E. **Telephony.** Any changes to the main telephone equipment such as relocating the PBX, adding new hardware, etc.

3.0 POLICY

The following steps must be followed when making changes covered under this policy:

    A. All requests for changes to the IT environment must be made using the organization's change control system. A Change Coordinator will be assigned by the Change Advisory Board to work with the person requesting the change to bring some consistency to the process and to make sure all relevant information is captured. The Request for Change (RFC) must include the following information:

        1. **Contact information.** The requestor's name, position, and contact information.

        2. **Description.** A description of the change, including the nature of the change and a description of the item(s) to be changed.

        3. **Reason.** The reason for the change, including a cost-benefit analysis and any budgetary approvals required.

        4. **Priority.** A suggestion of the priority and category of the change based on the information currently available. The following priorities are to be used:

            a. Emergency. A change that will cause significant damage or risk of damage to the organization if not implemented immediately, such as major security patches.

b. High. A change that is important and should be implemented soon, such as software changes required to meet regulatory requirements.

c. Medium. A change that provides benefits to the organization such as an enhancement financial planning system.

d. Low. A change that is "nice to have" but not needed immediately and has a low impact.

5. **Category.** A suggestion of the category of the change based on the information currently available. The following categories are to be used

a. Major. The change affects a large part of the organization, such as a department or division.

b. Significant. The change affects a smaller portion of the organization, such as a group with a department.

c. Minor. The change affects a small number of users.

6. **Implications of not making the change.** Include financial impact and any impact on service level agreements (SLAs).

B. Assess the change. The Change Coordinator assesses the urgency and impact of the change on the organization as a whole, considering the scope of the change and its impact on user productivity. This should include:

1. Impact of the change, including how users and the organization will be affected.

2. Risks involved in making the change.

3. Risks of not making the change.

4. Suggested implementation plan.

5. Describe the change back-out plan.

6. Impact of the change on disaster recovery plans.

C. Approve the change. For minor changes, approval is granted by the Change Coordinator or IT Manager; major changes are reviewed by the Change Advisory Board (CAB) for approval or rejection.

D. Plan for the change. This includes documenting the steps required to make the change, taking into account the technical requirements of the change. The plan should be optimized to minimize the impact on the IT infrastructure. For major changes, the implementation plan should be reviewed by the CAB. The plan must also include steps required to back out or reverse the affects of the change if the change does not have the desired effect.

E. Implement the change. Implement the change following exactly the steps outlined in the implementation plan.

F. Document the results. A review must be made to determine if the change had the desired effect on the IT infrastructure or system changed. Document what went well and what did not; this will help in planning future changes.

4.0 REVISION HISTORY

Date	Revision #	Description of Change
03/18/13	1.0	Initial creation.

5.0 INQUIRIES

Direct inquiries about this policy to:

George Jenkins, CIO
Our Company, Inc.
2900 Corporate Drive
Columbus, OH 43215

Voice: 614-555-1234
Fax: 614-555-1235
E-mail: gjenkins@company.com

Revision #:	1.0	Supersedes:	N/A	Date:	03/18/13

§ 20.03   PATCH MANAGEMENT POLICY

[A]   Overview

A company's patch management policy formalizes the process of keeping software up to date. If these patches were merely to repair defects in programs, life would be much simpler. The existence of viruses and worms requires that software be patched on a regular basis to repair security vulnerabilities as they are discovered. The lack of an effective patch management process compromises corporate security and network integrity. It also leaves the company open to potentially damaging losses. Given the impact on the company and the urgent nature of some patching, this policy must have the endorsement and support of the CEO or head of the organization.

COMMENT

The most famous worm was the one created by Robert Morris at Cornell that shut down many Unix computers on the Internet in 1988. It successfully propagated itself on more than 6,000 systems across the Internet.

An operating system follows a predicable series of actions as it executes. It is this predictability that allows the smooth interface with other programs. It is also this predictability that allows a virus to insert itself and take control.

In the beginning, a virus was passed in an executable file format, so anti-virus programs were created to look for those file types. As defenses against this approach improved, viruses began appearing in macro files for word processors and spreadsheets. The "Winword Concept" was the first of the multiplatform viruses because it could infect any operating system that could run that word processing program.

COMMENT

An excellent source of information on computer viruses and how to address them can be found at the Symantec Web site (*www.symantec.com*). Symantec defines a computer virus as:

A computer virus is a small program written to alter the way a computer operates, without the permission or knowledge of the user. A virus must meet two criteria:

1. It must execute itself. It will often place its own code in the path of execution of another program.
2. It must replicate itself. For example, it may replace other executable files with a copy of the virus infected file. Viruses can infect desktop computers and network servers alike.

The best defense against the various forms of viruses is a vigorous prevention program. To defend against these types of attacks, software manufacturers analyze their programs and issue software patches to plug the gaps in the code. The problem is that, like any change to corporate software, it should be extensively tested to ensure that the cure is not worse than the disease. However, the longer the patch installation is delayed, the greater the likelihood that the company's computers will be infected. To address this, "Patch Management" has emerged as an IT process and, in some cases, its own IT team.

Patches themselves might involve only a few lines of source code. However, these few lines of code cannot be distributed by themselves. They must be compiled into the program in which they reside, and that entire module must be downloaded to correct the problem. At times, the patch may touch multiple modules. Therefore, in some cases, a single patch to a user's PC may require moving tens of megabytes of data to that machine. Multiplied over the number of units in service in a company, it is easy to see how a single patch can dramatically impact a company's workflow. Multiply this number again over the number of products supported in a PC, and it is easy to see how time-consuming the management of patches can become.

A company's patch management policy covers all types of hardware connected to the outside world through the Internet. The types of hardware might include:

- Workstations
- Servers
- Routers
- Switches
- Firewalls
- Smartphones
- Tablets

Any device connected to the network is a potential target of worms and viruses. While workstations and servers are the most frequent targets, future worms and viruses that may attack tablets, cell phones, or other network-connected devices should not be overlooked.

Many of these security flaws are identified and fixes developed before exploits are unleashed by virus creators. However, the time window available to apply and test patches is becoming shorter and shorter.

COMMENT

The Holy Grail for malicious program and virus writers is the "zero day exploit." A zero day exploit is an exploit that is created on or even before the same day as the vulnerability is discovered by the vendor. By creating a virus or worm that takes advantage of a vulnerability the vendor is not yet aware of and for which there is not currently a patch available, the attacker can wreak maximum havoc.

Also complicating matters is that workstations are now the targets of the attack as much as servers. Because workstations far outnumber servers, stamping out an infection becomes more difficult. In addition, when mobile users reconnect to the network, they are likely to become reinfected. Although Microsoft Windows gets much of the press, viruses and worms have also been known to target switches, routers, and firewalls. Unix and Linux systems are also not immune to virus infections. As Linux becomes more popular, expect to see more viruses targeted to these systems.

Unfortunately, patches can have bugs too. Many administrators are reluctant to apply new patches without learning—either by testing or by reports through informal sources—how they will affect systems. If the company can-not test adequately, make sure the vendor does.

[B] Policy Objectives

Most companies manage security patches in the same manner that they control other software upgrades—through their change management process. This allows for the orderly and controlled implementation of changes. The change management process ensures that quality verifications are performed by the appropriate teams before the patch is implemented. It ensures that patches are processed expeditiously while the potential for negative impact on the company is minimized. It is doubtful that a patch management system can be successful if it is not integrated into the IT department's change man-agement process.

The company's policy provides guidelines to ensure all software is up to date and has all known security vulnerabilities repaired. It must also ensure that existing applications still function properly after the patch is applied. Policy objectives should be flexible enough to cover new types of software that may become a target for viruses, worms, or other malicious code.

COMMENT

According to research by Eric Hemmendinger of Aberdeen Group, "[w]orldwide, enterprises spend in excess of $2 billion annually to investigate, prioritize, and deploy patches for security vulnerabilities. The trend is upward, with no end in sight for IS decision makers."

The strategic objective of a company's patch management program is to create a consistently configured environment that is secure against known vulnerabilities in operating system and application software.

[C] Asset Inventory

The first step toward a coherent corporate patch management program is an assessment of what the company has to protect. A comprehensive asset man-agement program can determine if all existing systems are accounted for and considered when processing patches. This requires a thorough inventory of all of the company's hardware and software.

The asset inventory should identify what is to be protected and where it is located. At a minimum, the inventory should identify:

A. All types of equipment in service.
B. All operating systems in service, their versions, and their patch levels.

C. All applications software installed, their versions, and their patch levels.
D. Where all equipment, systems, and software are located.
E. Who the primary user or primary support person is for each device.

Next, the current patch level recommended by the manufacturer for each of the operating systems and applications should be determined. Comparing this to the inventory results will indicate the company's current vulnerability to an external threat.

A side benefit of a company-wide inventory is to identify anyone who is already patching any of this equipment. Different subdivisions may be doing things differently—with uneven results. The contact information for each device will speed questions to the problem area.

What will undoubtedly become clear from the asset inventory is that patch management will be greatly simplified if software and equipment are standardized. The fewer the configurations to protect, the faster patches will be tested and the more stable the corporate technical environment will be. This implies that only standard company software should be loaded onto PCs as each additional product becomes another patch source to track—which is another reason companies should make their prohibition of unlicensed software clear to all users.

Another useful data application is "system discovery" tools. These programs help to identify when additional (rogue) equipment has been added to the network, often without prior approval. Once identified and located, the equipment can be checked for security compliance and brought up to date.

COMMENT

A source of inexpensive systems discovery tools is the System Center Tools Home page at *www.systemcentertools.com*. These tools work with Microsoft's Configuration Manager 2007 and MOM systems.

[D] Process Overview

An effective patch management process requires that the company has the following in place:

A. An asset inventory of all devices connected (or that might be connected) to the network.
B. An asset management process to collect changes as they occur.
C. Well-defined change management process.
D. Guidelines for prioritizing how critical each application is.
E. Communication plans to alert users of pending changes.

A well-defined change management process documents what was changed and how. Unless the company has the resources necessary to patch every system right away, a patch coordinator will need to determine which systems are most critical and deserve attention first. A good communications plan enables the IT team to efficiently use the resources available for applying the necessary patches.

The change management program must include a patch cycle for the application of routine patches. The routine cycle can be based on the calendar or on the release of an important update. Critical updates are processed differently and should be based on the company's exposure to the identified threat.

In either event, the process normally unfolds in the following manner:

A. **Identify a new patch requirement.** This can occur through notification by the software vendor or through the intelligence-gathering efforts of internal or external sources. The patch management policy must identify who is responsible for the identification of new patches.

COMMENT

Vendors of security vulnerability intelligence include:

Secunia	*www.secunia.com*
IBM Internet Security Systems	*http://xforce.iss.net*
Verisign	*http://www.verisigninc.com/en_GB/ products-and-services/network-intelligence-availability/idefense/ vulnerability-intelligence/index.xhtml*

B. **Assess exposure to the organization and risks involved.** The urgency for applying the patch should be determined by the level of exposure the security risk poses to the organization and the risks involved in applying the patch (see § 20.03[E], "Risk Assessment"). IT should determine the likelihood of a security breach if the patch is not applied versus the potential impact on mission-critical systems if applying the patch causes other problems.

C. **Determine whether patch should be applied.** Based on the potential threat and level of risk, IT must determine whether the patch should be applied immediately or during the next scheduled software update cycle.

D. **Create a plan to apply the patch.** IT should treat the application of patches like any other important project. Before rushing in to apply the patch, IT should take time to plan out the most effective steps to apply the patch and determine the impact it may have on other software applications.

E. **Test patch before it is applied.** New software is not installed without testing and neither should patches. IT should create a test environment that is isolated from the production network where workers can test for any unintended consequences. Again, there will be fewer configurations to test if the environment is standardized.

F. **Apply patch to systems.** Once satisfied with the testing, IT may apply the patch to the affected systems.

G. **Validate that patch was correctly applied.** Once the patch is applied, check the affected systems to ensure the patch was correctly applied.

H. **Document results.** IT must document lessons learned, problems solved, and unforeseen problems encountered so the next patch will go more smoothly.

COMMENT

The Gartner Group predicts a G20 country will be hit by major cyber-attack by 2015.

[E] Risk Assessment

To patch or not to patch, that is the question (apologies to Shakespeare). Many system administrators have bad memories of patches that caused more problems than they solved, especially with Microsoft Windows 2000. While vendors have gotten much better about the quality of the patches they release, they still cannot guarantee the patch will work with all possible combinations of hardware and software. The patch management process must include a thorough analysis of the risks involved in either applying the patch or not.

Before establishing a patch management plan, executive management must determine their corporate risk tolerance toward patching. Maximizing security might impact productivity if production systems are shut down every time a relevant patch becomes available. On the other hand, some patches may be so vital as to overcome objections. A policy guideline that addresses this situation will reduce the guesswork.

Of course, in practice such extreme measures are rare. The point is that patch management must be viewed as one component of the overall corporate risk management program.

To assess the risk of applying a patch, the following questions should be considered:

A. What is the probability of a vulnerability being exploited if the patch is not applied?

B. If the vulnerability is exploited, what is the probable severity of the damage? Consider the likelihood of physical damage to information, any legal ramifications, the possible financial impact, and how news of the incident will affect the company's reputation.
C. Which is the greater problem—downtime while applying the patch or security breaches from not applying the patch?
D. What effects will the patch have on mission-critical applications?
E. Is the patch really necessary for the company's systems?
F. What will indicate whether or not the patch was successful?

Some risks inherent in the patch management process include:

A. Missed patches.
B. The approval of risky patches.
C. A poorly designed patch application process.
D. A failure to perform adequate testing.
E. No identification of the issues created by the application of the patch.

To make a rough calculation of the severity of the risk involved with a patch, the following formula can be used:

$$\text{Risk Score} = \text{Threat Probability} \times \text{Criticality} \times \text{Effort Required}$$

Threat probability is scored from 1 to 10 and includes an assessment of the risk to the organization and the likelihood that the vulnerability will be exploited.

Criticality is scored from 1 to 10 and includes the importance of the system affected and the amount of damage that can be done.

Effort required is scored from 1 to 10 and is an estimate of the number of labor hours that will be required to complete the entire patch application process.

A very high-risk score indicates the need for an immediate patch, while a low score indicates the patch may be applied during the next change management process update. For values that do not meet either of these levels, the risk score should enable IT to prioritize when each patch should be applied.

[F] Patch Testing

All patches must be tested prior to installation to ensure that they will function as expected and be compatible with other systems. Patches must be tested for compatibility with the production operating system environment and with other applications. Testing must also be done to ensure that the patch does not expose vulnerabilities that were previously corrected or create new ones. A separate testing environment must be created for testing patches before patches are applied in the production environment.

The application of patches is similar to any other change made to production software and should follow the same change control procedures. Once a patch has been applied in the production environment, additional testing must also be performed to check for unanticipated problems.

The inventory of software systems must be kept updated with information about the latest patch level. A history of patches must be maintained to ensure that if a system has to be rebuilt, software patches can be reinstalled in the proper order. A backup of the patched software should be made after each patch is applied to facilitate rollback or recovery to a previous version if necessary. See Policy ITP-20-3 Patch Testing Policy as an example.

POLICY ITP-20-3. Patch Testing Policy

Policy #:	ITP-20-3	**Effective:**	03/18/13	**Page #:**	1 of N
Subject:	Patch Testing Policy				

1.0 PURPOSE

This policy is designed to ensure that software patches are properly tested before being released into the production environment.

2.0 SCOPE

This policy encompasses all IT systems and technology that support critical business functions.

3.0 POLICY

The IT Manager will designate a patch management coordinator who ensures that all software patches are handled as follows:

A. A separate testing environment must be created for testing patches.
B. All patches must be tested prior to installation.
C. New patches must be tested to ensure new vulnerabilities that were previously corrected are not exposed and that new ones are not created.
D. Patches must be tested for compatibility with the production operating system environment and with other applications.
E. Application of patches must follow the same change control procedures as any other change to the production systems.
F. An inventory of software systems must be kept updated with information about the latest patch level.
G. A history of patches must be maintained to ensure that if a system has to be rebuilt, software patches can be reinstalled in the proper order.
H. A backup of the patched software should be made after each patch is applied to facilitate rollback or recovery to a previous version if necessary.
I. Once a patch has been applied in the production environment, additional testing must also be performed to check for unanticipated problems.

4.0 REVISION HISTORY

Date	Revision #	Description of Change
03/18/13	1.0	Initial creation.

5.0 INQUIRIES

Direct inquiries about this policy to:

George Jenkins, CIO
Our Company, Inc.
2900 Corporate Drive
Columbus, OH 43215

Voice: 614-555-1234
Fax: 614-555-1235
E-mail: gjenkins@company.com

Revision #:	1.0	Supersedes:	N/A	Date:	03/18/13

[G] Capability Maturity Model as Applied to Patch Management

The Capability Maturity Model (CMM) was developed by Carnegie Mellon University in 1991 to measure the efficiency and effectiveness of organizations that develop software (see Exhibit 20-1). The CMM has been widely used and adopted to other technical areas, including patch management. The chart in Exhibit 20-1 can be used to determine which level the organization is at and compare it to the desired level for patch management. A comparison of where an organization is today versus where it would like to be will help IT to create an appropriate patch management process.

§ 20.04 PATCH MANAGEMENT TOOLS

[A] Overview

Patching software is a time-consuming process. In the past, a technician may have scurried around to each PC with a floppy disk loading the patch on machines. However, with the hundreds or thousands of devices in use by a typical company today, this is no longer practical. Manual patching is time consuming and error prone (due to missed devices). Given the time required to locate every device and then to load the patch, it is quite likely that a second patch will be required before the first patch is applied everywhere.

EXHIBIT 20-1. Capability Maturity Model for Patch Management

Level	CMM Attributes	Patch Management Attributes
1	Initial—the environment is unpredictable and reactionary.	Patches are not being applied.
2	Repeatable—controls are in place, but not used consistently; no formal training or communication processes in place.	No formal process in place or responsibility assigned for patch management; patches are downloaded directly from vendor Web sites; patches applied by hand using removable media.
3	Defined—controls are well documented and communicated; no monitoring of control activities.	Patches are obtained from known good sources; individual groups have assigned responsibility for patch management; patch process is documented but not consistent between departments; patches deployed using script files or Windows Update.
4	Managed—controls are standardized and tested on a regular basis; automated tools are not well integrated into the process.	Patch management is centrally coordinated and a common reporting process used; standard builds are updated with required patches; patch deployment is performed using software tools such as SMS or PatchLink.
5	Optimizing—an effective continuous improvement process is in place; integrated automated tools allow for quick action.	Patch deployment responsibility is centralized and fully automated; central responsibility is assigned for managing the patch management process.

The solution to this problem is the use of software tools that can distribute approved patches. These updates can then be controlled to be applied at the same time everywhere or selectively, and to confirm the installation was successful.

[B] Basics of Patch Tool Selection

A key consideration in developing a patch management program is the tools that are used to implement it. Many software tools are available to manage the patch application process. These tools follow one of two technological approaches:

A. **Agent-based.** Agent-based tools require that a software component be installed on each device to be managed. This can be a challenge due to differences in configurations and when a system administrator is

20-22

required to answer screen prompts during installation. In addition, the agent may require remote administrative rights.

The advantage of an agent-based approach is the speed with which patches can be applied. A single patch management server can service thousands of workstations at one time.

B. **Agent-less tools.** The agent-less approach is based on a patch management server that controls the network server to identify and push required patches. The success of this approach depends heavily on the network: pushing large patches to a number of units may swamp the corporate network.

The appropriate choice of patch management tools for an organization depends on a number of issues, including:

- The number of platforms supported
- The number of systems to be patched
- The existing expertise and amount of personnel involved
- The availability of existing system management tools

Portions of the patch management process may need to be automated because of:

- The increasing frequency of patches that are released and the systems they affect
- The complicated interrelationships among installed software, patches, and service packs
- The need for deployment speed

COMMENT

On average, Microsoft issues a new security patch every 5.5 days.

Patch management software should include the following features:

A. Identification of which patches are required. The software also should be able to determine which patches are required before other patches are installed.
B. Automatic deployment of mandatory patches.
C. The ability to roll back to the previous version of the software.
D. The ability to deploy multiple patches.
E. Comprehensive reporting capabilities that can identify which patches are needed by which systems.

    F. Patch compliance monitoring to ensure patches are not removed due to backup restoration or the installation of a new application.

    G. Secure patch delivery through encryption.

    H. Continuous enforcement of security policies to help ensure systems stay patched. Some patch management systems also can ensure that antivirus software is always running and that the virus definitions are current. Some also can check to make sure users do not make configuration changes that could make their PCs vulnerable.

    I. The ability to support all the platforms on the corporate network. (Many systems only support Microsoft Windows workstations and servers.)

    J. Accurate, up-to-date information and analysis of current security patches.

COMMENT

Patch management software vendors:

Lumension	*www.lumension.com*
IBM Tivoli Endpoint Manager	*www-01.ibm.com/software/tivoli/ solutions/endpoint*
Symantec	*www.symantec.com*

[C] Sources of Additional Information

Patch management depends on accurate, timely, and pertinent information to know what is needed, when, and why. Locating and assessing patches is a never-ending administrative challenge. The trick is to know all of the sources useful in gathering this information for evaluation.

The easiest information source to identify is the vendor that supplied the software or network components. These companies often have an invitation-only Web site to distribute updates to their customers. They also may include an automatic notification system to inform registered customers of a new release.

In addition to Web sites that provide information about security alerts, there also are lists of fake alerts. These bogus warnings are usually passed around in e-mails. Although harmless to the company's systems, it can require a considerable amount of patch management time to calm excited users. Some Web sites to monitor include:

§ 20.04[C]

Symantec Hoax List	*http://www.symantec.com/security_response/threatexplorer/risks/hoaxes.jsp*
Microsoft Security	*http://technet.microsoft.com/en-us/security/default.aspx*
McAfee	*www.mcafee.com*
Infraguard (an FBI/business consortium to address security threats)	*www.infragard.net*
Total Defense (formally CA)	*http://www.totaldefense.com*

21

THE INTERNET: MAKING IT PRODUCTIVE

§ 21.01 OVERVIEW

[A] Purpose and Scope

Policies that address the use of the Internet formalize standards for how the company connects to the outside world, and how these services are used by employees. While the Internet provides access to a wealth of valuable information and facilitates communication, it also exposes the company to a number of dangers. Some of the issues that cause problems for a company when employees use the Internet include:

- **Productivity.** Uncontrolled access to the Internet can drain away employee time and irresponsible use reduces network resource availability for critical business operations.
- **Inappropriate content.** Employees who view inappropriate content while on the job leave the company open to potentially damaging litigation.
- **Exposing proprietary information.** A connection to the Internet opens the potential for others to access the company's valuable proprietary information.

Internet usage policies cover all types of connections to the outside world through the Internet. The types of connections include:

- An individual computer using a Wi-Fi or cellular connection.
- A workgroup server using an ISDN, DSL, T1/T3, or cable modem connection.
- An organization-wide connection to the Internet.

The policies in this section cover basic activities performed while using the Internet, including but not limited to browsing (viewing Web pages), using e-mail, transferring files using file transfer protocol (FTP), and using hosted applications via the Internet.

[B] Policy Objectives

Policies developed for Internet use should provide guidelines to ensure the secure, proper, and reliable use of the Internet. Policy objectives should be flexible enough to cover new methods of Internet connectivity and technologies as they become available.

The company's Internet use policies should be part of the new employee orientation process. All new or existing employees should sign an acknowledgment that they have received a copy of the policies and that they will abide by them. The Internet use policies should also appear in the employee handbook. An online message, appearing when the user logs onto e-mail or the Internet, is helpful to remind employees of these policies. The company should offer training sessions on proper Internet usage.

COMMENT

The number of e-mails sent or received daily by the typical corporate employee is expected to rise to 136 by 2017 from 121 this year, based on projections released November 2013 by the Radicati Group, a Palo Alto, California, market-research firm.

[C] Critical Policies to Develop Based on This Chapter

Using the material discussed in this chapter, you will be able to create the following policies:

A. Internet Usage
B. Electronic Mail
C. Internet Security
D. Cloud Computing/SaaS/PaaS

Policies should always be developed based on the local situation. Successful managers cannot issue appropriate guidance if the policies are written with another company's situation or location in mind.

§ 21.02 METHODS OF INTERNET ACCESS

[A] Overview

There are several methods to connect to the Internet from an individual workstation or device. Each individual workstation or device might have its own connection to an Internet Service Provider (ISP) or be connected through the corporate network. The connection itself can be on-demand or continuously connected to the Internet. Each method has its own set of advantages and disadvantages. The IT Manager is responsible for developing policy on how corporate computer systems are connected to the Internet.

[B] Individual Access

The simplest method technically to connect to the Internet (usually done by the smallest organizations or by mobile workers) is for each individual PC to connect directly to an ISP via a public Wi-Fi or a cellular connection, or in increasingly rare cases by using a modem and a plain old telephone service (POTS) line. The user's PC connects to the local ISP and uses a Web browser to view content on the World Wide Web.

The IT technical support unit develops the procedure for connecting to the Internet through individual PCs. The technical support unit also determines the browser software used and may need to install the browser on the user's PC if not preinstalled.

An advantage of this method is there is less direct exposure of the network to the outside world if any existing network connection is unplugged. Another is the user's PC is exposed for only the time it is connected. This gives hackers less opportunity to gain access to the user's PC. Personal firewall software should be used as a form of protection while connected to the Internet.

A disadvantage of individual connections to the Internet is the lack of centralized monitoring or control. Usage standards cannot easily be enforced, and virus protection is left up to the user. Speed can also be limited when using a public Wi-Fi or a cellular connection. Anytime there is an Internet connection, that machine and any subsequent machine behind it are subject to unauthorized access.

Policies using the Internet via an individual connection should include the following procedures:

A. Personal firewall software must be installed and active.
B. Any network connections must be unplugged.
C. Virus-scanning software must be installed and active.

COMMENT

Examples of personal firewall software include ZoneAlarm and McAfee Internet Security. ZoneAlarm from Check Point Software Technologies costs less than $30; see its Web site at *www.zonealarm.com* for the latest information. McAfee Internet Security is a personal firewall product. They can be reached at *www.mcafee.com*.

[C] Corporate/Networked Internet Access

In most organizations, employees have access to the Internet from their workstations through the local area network. The network connects to the Internet through a router and/or proxy server; this acts as a firewall to protect the network from unauthorized access. The user's PC uses a browser to view content on the World Wide Web.

The IT technical support unit develops the procedure for connecting to the Internet through the corporate network. The IT technical support unit also determines the browser software used and may need to install the browser on the user's PC if not preinstalled.

An advantage of this method is Internet use can be centrally monitored and controlled. Also, a centralized firewall (either software or hardware) is used to protect the network from unauthorized access. Virus protection software is centrally installed and kept up to date.

A disadvantage of Internet access through the corporate network is there is a single point of failure protecting the network from the outside world. The connection is normally up 24/7, which gives hackers more opportunity to test your protection.

When using the Internet via the corporate network, the following procedures should be included in your policy:

A. Firewall software or hardware is installed at the point of connection to the Internet and updated daily.
B. Virus-scanning software is installed and updated daily. All downloaded files and e-mails are scanned for viruses.
C. The IT technical support unit generates a weekly report that shows the most frequently visited Web sites and total time connected to the Internet for each user.

COMMENT

Forrester, IDC, and the Yankee Group estimate that the cost of a 24-hour outage for a large e-commerce company would approach $30 million.

See Policy ITP-21-1 Internet Connection Policy as an example.

POLICY ITP-21-1.   Internet Connection Policy

Policy #:	ITP-21-1	**Effective:**	03/18/13	**Page #:**	1 of N
Subject:	Internet Connection Policy				

1.0 PURPOSE

This policy is designed to ensure that connections to the Internet by corporate computer systems are safe from intrusion by malware such as viruses that may be brought into the network by users using the Internet. It is also designed to prevent unauthorized and unprotected connections to the Internet that may allow a variety of unsafe content to enter the organizational network and compromise data integrity and system security across the entire network.

2.0 SCOPE

The policy applies to all corporate computer systems that are connected to the Internet. This includes connections made via the corporate network, modem connections using telephone lines, and wireless connections of any kind.

3.0 POLICY

All physical Internet connections or connections to other outside networks must be authorized and approved by your IT coordinator. Most users will access the Internet through the corporate network connection provided for their area by the IT department. Any additional connections must be approved by the IT department. These additional connections include but are not limited to:

A. Modem connection from a computer or communication device that may allow a connection to the network.
B. Any multipurpose printing or fax machines that have both a phone and network connection must be examined and approved for use by the IT department.
C. Wireless access points or devices with wireless capability are not allowed unless approved by the IT department. If any computers or other devices have wireless capability, the wireless capability must be turned off before connecting to the network unless it is approved for wireless operation by the IT department when connected to the network.

Any additional Internet connections not provided by the IT department must be reviewed and approved by the IT department. Typically, any additional connections from the corporate network to the Internet or other outside networks will require:

A. An IT department approved firewall operating at all times and properly configured.
B. Some communications through the connection may require encryption subject to a review of data to be transmitted by the IT department.

Any devices connected directly to the Internet without going through the corporate proxy servers must adhere to the following:

A. Personal firewall software must be installed and active.
B. Any network connections must be unplugged.
C. Virus-scanning software must be installed and active.

4.0 REVISION HISTORY

Date	Revision #	Description of Change
03/18/13	1.0	Initial creation.

5.0 INQUIRIES

Direct inquiries about this policy to:

George Jenkins, CIO
Our Company, Inc.
2900 Corporate Drive
Columbus, OH 43215

Voice: 614-555-1234
Fax: 614-555-1235
E-mail: gjenkins@company.com

Revision #:	1.0	Supersedes:	N/A	Date:	03/18/13

[D]   Wi-Fi Hotspot Internet Access

Most organizations have employees who work outside the corporate office for some period of the day. They might be salespeople who are on the road visiting clients and prospects or service personnel out in the field responding to customer issues. Whatever the reason, they will find it convenient to take advantage of Wi-Fi hotspots that are available in hotels, airports, cafes, libraries, and other areas to connect to the Internet. While connected they might be checking e-mail, or connecting to applications that are located back at the office using a virtual private network (VPN) or using services provided by a cloud computing vendor. In any case, it is critical to protect access to these applications and to ensure that all proprietary information is kept confidential, whether on the device being used to make the connection or on the network being accessed.

The IT technical support unit develops the procedure for connecting to the Internet using Wi-Fi hotspots when outside of the office. The IT technical support unit also determines the browser software used and any software and instructions needed to connect to the corporate network using a VPN.

The use of a Wi-Fi hotspot exposes the user to a number of security vulnerabilities, some related to the public nature of a hotspot and others to the use of airwaves for data transmission. These include:

- **Exposure to other devices using the hotspot.** A device connected to a hotspot is effectively on a local area network with all other users at that location, which makes it susceptible to many types of network attacks. These often involve probing for open, unprotected TCP or UDP ports and attempting to exploit vulnerabilities in the services running on them.
- **Interception of data by hackers.** Hackers have also discovered that Wi-Fi can be a convenient means of intercepting sensitive data from unwitting users by setting up rogue hotspots. These rogue hotspots can be in so-called man-in-the-middle attacks to capture all data, such as usernames and passwords, transmitted through them.

When using a Wi-Fi hotspot to connect to the Internet, the following procedures should be included in your policy:

A. Firewall software is installed on the device using a Wi-Fi hotspot to the Internet and updated daily. The firewall should support both inbound and outbound filtering.
B. Virus-scanning software is installed on the connecting device and updated daily. All downloaded files and e-mails are scanned for viruses.
C. All available patches for the device should be installed and up to date.
D. A VPN must be used when connecting to any company systems or applications.
E. Remind users to never leave a device unattended as mobile devices are easily stolen.
F. The wireless antenna should be turned off when not in use to avoid unintended connections.
G. The IT support unit generates a weekly report that shows the connections being made to internal systems and the length of time they are used.

COMMENT

According to a study performed in 2012 by iPass, a provider of enterprise mobility solutions, found that 29 percent of mobile employees have hijacked an unsecure Wi-Fi network, and that 88 percent stated that wireless access was as important to their lives as running water and electricity.

See Policy ITP-21-2 Wi-Fi Hotspot Internet Access Policy as an example.

POLICY ITP-21-2.   Wi-Fi Hotspot Internet Access Policy

Policy #:	ITP-21-2	**Effective:**	03/18/13	**Page #:**	1 of N
Subject:	Wi-Fi Hotspot Internet Access Policy				

1.0 PURPOSE

This policy is designed to ensure that connections to corporate computer systems and data using public Wi-Fi hotspots are safe and do not compromise proprietary corporate information.

2.0 SCOPE

The policy applies to any device using a public Wi-Fi hotspot to connect to corporate computer systems or data. This includes connections made using laptop computers, tablets, and smartphones. The policy applies to connections made to in-house systems as well as to systems hosted by a third party that contains corporate information.

3.0 POLICY

Connection to corporate systems or data using a public Wi-Fi hotspot is restricted to devices that have been approved and configured by the corporate IT department. The following procedures must be followed before a device is used on a public Wi-Fi hotspot:

    A. Firewall software must be installed on the device using a Wi-Fi hotspot to the Internet and updated daily. The firewall should support both inbound and outbound filtering.

    B. Virus-scanning software must be installed on the connecting device and updated daily. All downloaded files and e-mails must be scanned for viruses.

    C. All available patches for the device must be installed and up to date.

    D. A VPN must be used when connecting to any company systems or applications.

    E. Users must not leave a device unattended at any time as mobile devices are easily stolen.

    F. The wireless antenna must be turned off when not in use to avoid unintended connections.

    G. The IT technical support unit will generate a weekly report that shows the connections being made to internal systems and the length of time they are used.

4.0 REVISION HISTORY

Date	Revision #	Description of Change
03/18/13	1.0	Initial creation.

5.0 INQUIRIES

Direct inquiries about this policy to:

    George Jenkins, CIO
    Our Company, Inc.
    2900 Corporate Drive
    Columbus, OH 43215

Voice: 614-555-1234
Fax: 614-555-1235
E-mail: gjenkins@company.com

Revision #:	1.0	Supersedes:	N/A	Date:	03/18/13

§ 21.03   INTERNET SECURITY

[A]   Responsibility

The chief information officer should assign the responsibility for Internet security to the IT Manager. Internet security policies are critical for protecting corporate systems while connected to the Internet. The IT unit responsible for the corporate Internet connection develops and enforces security procedures protecting corporate systems while connected to the Internet.

A connection to the Internet not only connects a computer to systems all over the world, but also with all computers currently running on the company network. The Internet was not designed to be very secure, as open access for research purposes was a major design consideration. Other factors making an Internet connection a possible security problem include:

A. **Vulnerable TCP/IP services.** A number of the TCP/IP services are not secure and can be compromised by knowledgeable intruders; services used in the local area networking environment for improving network management are especially vulnerable.

B. **Ease of spying and spoofing.** The majority of Internet traffic is unencrypted; e-mail, passwords, and file transfers can be monitored and captured using readily available software. Intruders can then reuse passwords to break into systems.

C. **Lack of policy.** Many sites are configured unintentionally for wide-open Internet access without regard for the potential for abuse from the Internet; many sites permit more TCP/IP services than they require for their operations and do not attempt to limit access to information about their computers that could prove valuable to intruders.

D. **Complexity of configuration.** Host security access controls are often complex to configure and monitor; controls that are incorrectly configured often result in unauthorized access.

[B]   Firewall Usage

A firewall is a computer server providing security to a network. A firewall includes a number of technologies such as policy, network management, and technical controls and procedures. The firewall protects the network from probing by unauthorized users and allows only authorized access to the system.

Management first defines the type and level of security desired for the Internet connection for the protection of company information resources. Issues to consider for policies concerning firewalls include:

A. Dial-in policy.
B. VPN connections.
C. Which Internet services the organization plans to use (e.g., Telnet, FTP).
D. Assumptions about security versus usability (when does a service become too risky to use?).
E. Access to internal resources from the Internet.
F. Restriction of access to approved sites only or restriction of certain sites.
G. Use of chat programs such as AOL Instant Messenger and Windows Messenger.
H. Use of streaming audio and video.

There are two types of access control—explicit denial and explicit approval. Explicit approval restricts access to approved sites only and denies all other services by default. This is the more secure method, but more difficult to implement and maintain. Explicit denial restricts only certain sites and is easier on users, but new services that become available may expose the network to security problems.

The firewall installed should have the following features:

A. The firewall should be able to support a "deny all services except those specifically permitted" design policy, even if this is not the policy used.
B. The firewall should support the company's security policy, not impose one.
C. The firewall should be flexible and able to accommodate new services and needs if the security policy of the organization changes.
D. The firewall contains advanced authentication measures or contains the software hooks for installing advanced authentication measures.
E. The firewall employs filtering techniques to permit or deny services to specified host systems as needed.
F. The IP filtering network language should be flexible, user-friendly to program, and should filter on as many attributes as possible, including source and destination IP address, protocol type, source and destination TCP/UDP port, user, and inbound and outbound interface.
G. The firewall uses proxy services for Internet services such as FTP and Telnet, so advanced authentication measures can be employed and centralized at the firewall. If services such as NNTP, http, or gopher are required, the firewall contains the corresponding proxy services.
H. The firewall contains the ability to centralize SMTP access, to reduce direct SMTP connections between site and remote systems. This results in centralized handling of site e-mail.
I. The firewall accommodates public access to the site, so public information servers can be protected by the firewall but segregated from site systems not requiring public access.

J. The firewall should contain the ability to concentrate and filter dial-in access.
K. The firewall contains mechanisms for logging traffic and suspicious activity and contains mechanisms for log reduction, so logs are readable and understandable. Mechanisms for alerting someone when suspicious activity occurs are also important.
L. A firewall requires a secured version of the operating system, with other security tools as necessary to ensure firewall host integrity. The operating system should have all security patches installed.
M. The firewall is developed so its strength and correctness are verifiable. It should be simple in design so that it can be understood and maintained.
N. The firewall and any corresponding operating system are updated with patches and other bug fixes in a timely manner.

See Policy ITP-21-3 Firewall Usage Policy as an example.

POLICY ITP-21-3.   Firewall Usage Policy

Policy #:	ITP-21-3	**Effective:**	03/18/13	**Page #:**	1 of N
Subject:		Firewall Usage Policy			

1.0 PURPOSE

This policy is designed to ensure that connections to the Internet by corporate computer systems are safe from intrusion by unauthorized individuals from outside the organization. It is also designed to prevent unauthorized and unprotected connections to the Internet that may allow a variety of unsafe content to enter the organizational network and compromise data integrity and system security across the entire network.

2.0 SCOPE

The policy applies to all corporate computer systems that are connected to the Internet. This includes connections made via the corporate network, modem connections using telephone lines, and wireless connections of any kind.

3.0 POLICY

All networks or systems connected to the public Internet must be protected by a firewall that is configured using the following default settings:

A. All valid outgoing packets are let through regardless of their type.
B. All valid incoming packets "related" to the outgoing packets are allowed.
C. All outgoing TCP connections to port 80 (HTTP) are allowed.

D. All incoming ICMP packets of types 0 (ping response), 3 (MTU), 8 (ping), and 11 (TTL exceeded) are allowed.
E. All incoming packets from a trusted machine are allowed.
F. All other (incoming) packets are blocked.

All requests for modifications to the above default policy settings must be approved by the IT Network Administrator.

4.0 REVISION HISTORY

Date	Revision #	Description of Change
03/18/13	1.0	Initial creation.

5.0 INQUIRIES

Direct inquiries about this policy to:

George Jenkins, CIO
Our Company, Inc.
2900 Corporate Drive
Columbus, OH 43215

Voice: 614-555-1234
Fax: 614-555-1235
E-mail: gjenkins@company.com

Revision #:	1.0	Supersedes:	N/A	Date:	03/18/13

[C] Internet Usage Control

An Internet usage control system should be used to control access to inappropriate Web sites as well as to improve your network efficiency. It can also assist in enforcing your Internet acceptable usage policy and ensure relevant regulatory and legislative compliance by monitoring and controlling Internet content into and out of your organization. Features to look for in an Internet usage control system include:

A. Easy to use user interface.
B. Comprehensive reporting that allows you to easily and effectively monitor Web activity throughout your organization.
C. Allows you to identify sites to be avoided during key periods of the day.
D. Enforces policy through MIME and file types—manage/restrict access to different content types (e.g., video, music, images) and file types (e.g., MP3, ActiveX, MP4, and VBS).

E. Provides ability to configure the administrator e-mail alert policy.
F. Enforces URL and user management policy—controls access to Web-based e-mail, defines acceptable URL categories, protects against anonymous proxies that re-route traffic to inappropriate destinations, and controls access by unauthorized groups or users.
G. Configures the service with user and group level settings, using existing directory information on specific user level details.
H. Prevents accidental exposure—protects against inadvertent access to bad URLs and compromised sites.
I. Flexible user interface—creates different access policies, customizes block messages, and builds rules for recreational Internet access.
J. Support for multiple content categories.
K. Flexibility that allows and blocks lists.
L. Scalable across multiple sites.
M. Real-time advanced content analysis.

COMMENT

Suppliers of Internet usage control systems include Wavecrest Computing at *www.wavecrest.net*, and Websense Inc. at *www.websense.com*.

[D] Internet Training

Training for connecting to the Internet and for using the e-mail system should be provided by the information system's IT training unit. If the site does not have an IT training unit, training material can be made available by the local training unit. If unavailable, the company information systems organization can provide the training material.

Internet connection and e-mail system use training should be available as individualized training. The material should be loaned to the user and then returned to the unit that provided the material. The training provided should be in one of the following forms:

A. **Tutorial.** Users learn via a tutorial. This allows them to learn how to connect to the Internet and use the e-mail system at their own pace and as time is available. Users are provided with a learning guide with step-by-step instructions that assumes basic knowledge of the computer's operating system. After all items in the learning guide are completed, the tutorial is returned to the training unit.
B. **On-the-job training.** An experienced Internet user may be assigned to provide on-the-job training (OJT). The OJT instructor has a learning guide provided by the information systems organization. The IT organization provides the user with a copy of the learning guide via the instructor.

The OJT instructor follows the learning guide when working with the student. Training proceeds as time and the student's learning skills permit. A skill test is provided with the learning guide to gauge the student's mastery of the material.

§ 21.04 INTERNET USAGE

[A] Overview

Use of the Internet can make business and communication more effective. However, Internet service is a costly corporate resource. Irresponsible use reduces the Internet's availability for critical business operations, compromises corporate security and network integrity, and leaves the company open to potentially damaging litigation. An Internet usage policy defines how the Internet is used as a corporate resource.

COMMENT

According to a 2012 study by WorldPay, 29 percent of global online shoppers make purchases at work, with the peak time for purchases in the United States at 10:00 a.m.

[B] Tracking Internet Usage

The company should establish a mechanism for tracking all Internet usage by employees. Employees are notified of this policy through the use of an Internet/E-mail Acceptable Use Agreement (see § 21.06, "Acceptable Use Agreement"). This enables the company to manage its Internet and e-mail resources in a cost-effective manner and to manage its network more efficiently for future technology expansion.

COMMENT

Many states and the federal government are considering requiring firms to notify employees if their Internet and e-mail use is being monitored, with stiff fines imposed for not doing so.

The intention is to monitor the existence of the traffic being generated, much like a telephone bill tracks the calls made, the numbers called, the time of the calls, but not the content. In this manner the company will be aware of how its resources are being used, where they are needed, where new capacity is required, and other infrastructure management issues. Additionally, because of the vulnerability to litigation over inappropriate conduct in the workplace environment, it is the company's responsibility to ensure that its resources do not support inappropriate activities.

[C] Internet Use Guidelines

To ensure all employees understand their responsibilities, policies covering the use of the Internet should cover the following guidelines:

A. **Acceptable uses of company Internet access.** Describe what uses of the Internet are considered acceptable at your company.
B. **Unacceptable uses of company Internet access.** Describe what uses of the Internet are considered unacceptable at your company.
C. **Communications.** Remind employees that the Internet is just as serious a communication tool as is the printed page, and must not be treated lightly.
D. **Software.** Downloading of unapproved software poses a serious security threat.
E. **Firewalls and antivirus software.** These tools must not be tampered with or disabled for any reason.
F. **Copyright issues.** Transmission of company secrets is a serious violation of company policy.
G. **Security.** Make sure they understand how the use of the Internet affects network security for the company.
H. **Violations.** Describe the penalties for violating the policy.

See Policy ITP-21-4 Internet Acceptable Use Policy as an example.

POLICY ITP-21-4.   Internet Acceptable Use Policy

Policy #:	ITP-21-4	**Effective:**	03/18/13	**Page #:**	1 of N
Subject:	Internet Acceptable Use Policy				

1.0 PURPOSE

This policy defines the acceptable use for the company's Internet service.

2.0 SCOPE

The policy applies to all uses of company owned Internet access.

3.0 POLICY

3.1 Acceptable Uses of Company Internet Access
The company provides Internet access for business usage. Every staff member has the responsibility to maintain and enhance the company's public image and to use the company's access to the Internet in a responsible and productive manner that reflects well on the company. The company recognizes that there will be occasional personal use on lunch breaks and during non-working hours (with the approval of management), but this shall not be excessive or unreasonable.

3.2 Unacceptable Uses of Company Internet Access
The company Internet access may not be used for transmitting, retrieving, viewing, or storage of any communications of a discriminatory or harassing nature or materials that are obscene or "X-rated." Harassment of any kind is prohibited. No messages with derogatory or inflammatory remarks about an individual's race, age, disability, religion, national origin, physical attributes, or sexual preference shall be transmitted. No excessively abusive, profane, or offensive language is to be transmitted through the company's Internet system. Electronic media may also not be used for any other purpose that is illegal or against company policy, or contrary to the company's best interests. Solicitation of non-company business, or any use of the company Internet for personal gain, is prohibited.

3.3 Communications
Each employee is responsible for the content of all text, audio, or images that he or she places or sends over the company's Internet system. No electronic communications may be sent that hides the identity of the sender or represents the sender as someone else or someone from another company. All messages communicated on the company's Internet system should contain the employee's name.

Any messages or information sent by an employee to another individual outside of the company via an electronic network (e.g., blog, IM, bulletin board, online service, or Internet) are statements that reflect on the company. While some users include personal "disclaimers" in electronic messages, there is still a connection to the company, and the statements may legally be tied to the company. Therefore, we require that all communications sent by employees via the company's Internet system comply with all company policies and not disclose any confidential or proprietary company information.

3.4 Software
To prevent computer viruses from being transmitted through the company's Internet system, there will be no unauthorized downloading of any unauthorized software. All software downloaded must be registered to the company. Employees should contact IT if they have any questions.

3.5 Copyright Issues
Employees on the company's Internet system may not transmit copyrighted materials belonging to entities other than this company. Please note that non-adherence to this policy puts the company in serious legal jeopardy and opens the company up to significant lawsuits and public embarrassment. All employees obtaining access to other companies' or individuals' materials must

respect all copyrights and may not copy, retrieve, modify, or forward copyrighted materials, except with permission. Failure to observe copyright or license agreements may result in disciplinary action up to and including termination. If you have questions about any of these legal issues, please speak with your manager or IT before proceeding.

3.6 Security

The company routinely monitors usage patterns in its Internet communications. The reasons for this monitoring are many, including cost analysis, security, bandwidth allocation, and the general management of the company's gateway to the Internet. All messages created, sent, or retrieved over the company's Internet are the property of the company and should be considered public information. Notwithstanding comments above regarding our present intention not to monitor content, the company must reserve the right to access and monitor the content of all messages and files on the company's Internet system at any time in the future with or without notice. Employees should not assume electronic communications are totally private and should transmit highly confidential data in other ways. Electronic messages regarding sensitive matters should warn that such communications are not intended to be secure or confidential. This is just good business sense.

3.7 Violations

Any employee who abuses the privilege of company facilitated access to the Internet will be subject to corrective action up to and including termination. If necessary, the company also reserves the right to advise appropriate legal officials of any illegal violations.

4.0 REVISION HISTORY

Date	Revision #	Description of Change
03/18/13	1.0	Initial creation.
04/14/13	1.1	Modified to cover all Internet communications.

5.0 INQUIRIES

Direct inquiries about this policy to:

George Jenkins, CIO
Our Company, Inc.
2900 Corporate Drive
Columbus, OH 43215

Voice: 614-555-1234
Fax: 614-555-1235
E-mail: gjenkins@company.com

Revision #:	1.1	Supersedes:	1.0	Date:	04/14/13

[D] Peer-to-Peer Applications

Peer-to-Peer (P2P) applications are used to allow individual PCs to share files. These applications are mostly used for sharing music and video files. Examples include KaZaa, Morpheus, and Audiogalaxy. The use of these applications should be strictly forbidden on company-owned systems. P2P applications can present significant gaps into the corporate network, allowing viruses and worms to be introduced. P2P applications can be used to allow third parties to obtain the user's IP address, or allow access to data on the user's computer and the corporate network. Many P2P applications have been known to include "spyware" or "malware," which can allow others to monitor the user's Internet browsing or to take control of a PC's system resources.

P2P applications can also be a significant drain on the company's Internet bandwidth, especially when large files are downloaded. This problem is made worse when other users on the P2P network connect to the employee's PC and download files to their PC. This uses bandwidth that should be available for legitimate company purposes, such as e-mail, Web browsing, and e-commerce. Employee productivity also can be adversely affected by the use of P2P applications, as time is taken from business-related duties. Support costs may increase if the P2P application causes problems with business-related software on the employee's workstation.

§ 21.05 E-MAIL USAGE

[A] Usage and Retention

E-mail has replaced the printed memo as the business communication tool of choice. E-mail seems to be ubiquitous, and many employees avail themselves of free e-mail accounts for personal use. However, corporate e-mail service is a costly corporate resource that must be properly managed. Irresponsible use reduces its availability for critical business operations, compromises corporate security and network integrity, and leaves the company open to potentially damaging litigation. An e-mail usage and retention policy defines how e-mail is used and managed as a corporate resource.

To ensure all employees understand their responsibilities, policies covering the use of their corporate e-mail account should cover the following guidelines:

A. **Acceptable uses of company e-mail accounts.** Describe what uses of e-mail are considered acceptable at your company.
B. **Unacceptable uses of company e-mail accounts.** Describe what uses of e-mail are considered unacceptable at your company.
C. **Communications.** Remind employees that e-mail is just as serious a communication tool as is the printed page and must not be treated lightly.

D. **Privacy.** E-mails are not private. The company should reserve the right to monitor e-mail content ensuring that the e-mail system is used for appropriate purposes.

E. **Personal e-mail accounts.** Personal e-mail accounts should be prohibited as a potential source of viruses and as a potential compliance issue with government regulations for corporate recordkeeping.

F. **Spam.** While this should be obvious, remind employees that sending unwanted e-mails is not acceptable.

G. **Copyright issues.** Transmission of company secrets is a serious violation of company policy.

H. **Monitoring.** Let employees know that their e-mail may be monitored.

I. **Retention.** Company communications of any kind typically need to be retained as any other corporate document. See Chapter 38, "Document Management: Capturing Corporate Knowledge," for creating a document retention policy.

J. **Attachments.** Attachments with certain file extensions should be prohibited, as they are potential security and virus threats. Most organizations also limit the total size of attachments to 10MB.

K. **Confidentiality.** Any e-mail message that is meant to be confidential should be labeled as such in the subject line. Forwarding of confidential messages requires the permission of the original sender. Consider configuring your e-mail system to attach a confidential message notification to all e-mails that are sent to addresses outside the organization; here is an example:

> The information contained in this message may be confidential and is intended only for use by the intended recipients. If you received this message in error, please accept our apologies; you are hereby notified that any dissemination, distribution, or copying of this message is strictly prohibited. If you received this message in error, please return it to the sender immediately and delete it and any copies from your e-mail system. Please contact the sender if you have any questions about this message.

L. **Violations.** Describe the penalties for violating the policy.

See Policy ITP-21-5. E-mail Usage and Retention Policy as an example.

POLICY ITP-21-5.   E-mail Usage and Retention Policy

Policy #:	ITP-21-5	**Effective:**	03/18/13	**Page #:**	1 of N
Subject:	E-mail Usage and Retention Policy				

1.0 PURPOSE

This policy defines the acceptable use of the company's corporate e-mail system.

2.0 SCOPE

The policy applies to all uses of company owned e-mail accounts.

3.0 POLICY

3.1 Acceptable Uses of Company E-mail Accounts

The company provides e-mail accounts for business usage only. Every staff member has the responsibility to maintain and enhance the company's public image and to use the company's e-mail system in a responsible and productive manner that reflects well on the company.

3.2 Unacceptable Uses of Company E-mail Accounts

Company e-mail accounts may not be used for transmitting, retrieving, viewing, or storage of any communications of a discriminatory or harassing nature or materials that are obscene or "X-rated." Harassment of any kind is prohibited. No messages with derogatory or inflammatory remarks about an individual's race, age, disability, religion, national origin, physical attributes, or sexual preference shall be transmitted. No excessively abusive, profane, or offensive language is to be transmitted through the company's e-mail system. E-mail messages or attachments may also not be used for any purpose that is illegal or against company policy or contrary to the company's best interests. Solicitation of non-company business, or any use of the company e-mail system for personal gain, is prohibited.

3.3 Communications

Each employee is responsible for the content of all text, audio, or images that he or she places or sends over the company's e-mail system. All e-mails must contain the identity of the sender and may not represent the sender as someone else or someone from another company.

Any messages or information sent by an employee to another individual outside the company via an electronic network (e.g., blog, IM, bulletin board, online service, or Internet) are statements that reflect on the company. While some users include personal "disclaimers" in electronic messages, there is still a connection to the company, and the statements may legally be tied to the company. Therefore, we require that all communications sent by employees via the company's e-mail system comply with all company policies and not disclose any confidential or proprietary company information.

3.4 Privacy

E-mails are not private. The company reserves the right to monitor e-mail content ensuring that the e-mail system is used for appropriate purposes. Also, no security is 100 percent hacker-proof; someone outside the company may intercept and read e-mail. Routing of e-mail is not without errors; someone other than the intended recipient may receive the e-mail. Do not send anything by e-mail that should not be placed on the company bulletin board.

3.5 Personal E-mail Accounts

Accessing personal e-mail accounts is prohibited from company-owned computers, as they are a potential source of computer viruses. No company-related communication is permitted using personal e-mail accounts, as the communication may be subject to the company's communication retention policy.

3.6 Spam

Sending unwanted e-mail of any kind (spam) using a company e-mail account is prohibited.

3.7 Copyright Issues

Employees on the company's Internet system may not transmit copyrighted materials belonging to entities other than this company. Please note that non-adherence to this policy puts the company in serious legal jeopardy and opens the company up to significant lawsuits and public embarrassment. All employees obtaining access to other companies' or individuals' materials must respect all copyrights and may not copy, retrieve, modify, or forward copyrighted materials, except with permission. Failure to observe copyright or license agreements may result in disciplinary action up to and including termination. If you have questions about any of these legal issues, please speak with your manager or IT department before proceeding.

3.8 Monitoring

The company routinely monitors usage patterns in its Internet communications. The reasons for this monitoring include cost analysis, security, bandwidth allocation, and the general management of the company's gateway to the Internet. All messages created, sent, or retrieved over the company's Internet are the property of the company and should be considered public information. Notwithstanding comments above regarding our present intention not to monitor content, the company must reserve the right to access and monitor the content of all messages and files on the company's Internet system at any time in the future with or without notice. Employees should not assume electronic communications are totally private and should transmit highly confidential data in other ways. Electronic messages regarding sensitive matters should warn that such communications are not intended to be secure or confidential. This is just good business sense.

3.9 Retention

Company communications of any kind typically needs to be retained as you would any other corporate document. Certain e-mail communications must follow the requirements established in Policy ITP-38-1 Document Retention Policy depending on the subject or purpose of the e-mail. Please remember that e-mails deleted from your e-mail inbox are still saved on the company e-mail server. E-mail messages are automatically deleted from your inbox after 90 days and are archived. E-mails that are not managed as part of the corporate document retention policy are kept archived for seven years before being permanently deleted.

3.10 Attachments

Attachments with the following file extensions are prohibited, as they are potential security and virus threats:

.bat	Batch processing file used to execute system commands or programs.
.com	Windows command files.
.cpl	Control panel extension.
.exe	Windows binary executable files.
.js	Java script files.
.ocx	Object linking and embedding control.
.pif	Program information file used to tell Windows how to run non-Windows applications.
.scr	Screen saver programs; may include binary code.
.sys	System configuration files.
.vb	Visual Basic script files.

There is also a limit of 10MB of attachments for any e-mail message. Contact the IT Helpdesk if you have a need to transfer more than 10MB of files at any one time.

3.11 Confidentiality

Any e-mail message that is meant to be confidential must be labeled as such in the subject line. Forwarding of confidential messages requires the permission of the original sender. The corporate e-mail system will automatically attach a confidential message notification to all e-mails that are sent to addresses outside the organization. Do not attach your own individual confidential notice as this will be redundant and may be inconsistent with the official company message.

3.12 Violations

Any employee who abuses the privilege of company-facilitated access to the Internet will be subject to corrective action up to and including termination. If necessary, the company also reserves the right to advise appropriate legal officials of any illegal violations.

4.0 REVISION HISTORY

Date	Revision #	Description of Change
03/18/13	1.0	Initial creation.

5.0 INQUIRIES

Direct inquiries about this policy to:

George Jenkins, CIO
Our Company, Inc.
2900 Corporate Drive
Columbus, OH 43215

Voice: 614-555-1234
Fax: 614-555-1235
E-mail: gjenkins@company.com

Revision #:	1.0	Supersedes:	N/A	Date:	03/18/13

[B] E-mail Etiquette

As e-mail has not only replaced paper-based communication, but also become a substitute for having a conversation, the proper use of e-mail etiquette has become increasingly important. Communication received in an e-mail does not easily convey the mood and emotions of the communicator. Most messages come across harsher than intended. The following are useful guidelines for communicating by e-mail (most also apply when developing policies covering instant messaging (IM)).

A. **Be brief.** E-mail messages should be concise and to the point. It is helpful to think of e-mail as a telephone conversation that is typed instead of spoken. Always make the main point as quickly as possible (within the first two or three sentences). Many software programs used for reading e-mail allow for a preview mode, where only the first few sentences are displayed. Many people receive hundreds of e-mails a day and use this preview mode to determine which e-mails they will read completely. E-mails that take several sentences to get to the point may not be read at all.

COMMENT

Thank you for sending me a copy of your book—I'll waste no time reading it.
—Moses Hadas (1900–1966), book reviewer.

B. **Use the subject line wisely.** An accurate and specific subject line is helpful for determining which e-mails merit closer attention by those who receive mountains of e-mail, but be careful not to earn a reputation for over-hyping a message in the subject line; otherwise really important messages may not get read.

C. **Use grammar and punctuation correctly.** Poor grammar and punctuation reflect poorly on the sender. Do not overuse exclamation points (sometimes called "bangs") in an attempt to emphasize the importance of your message. If something is important, it should be reflected in the text, not in the punctuation.

D. **Use special formatting sparingly.** Avoid the use of fancy HTML formatting or "wallpaper" backgrounds. What looks great using e-mail client software may look like gibberish to the recipient. Stick to commonly available fonts, and realize that the spacing as displayed by the recipient may be different from that in which the message was sent, especially when displaying columnar data. Many users turn off HTML formatting to help prevent malicious code from being executed on their system.

E. **Abbreviations.** Abbreviation use is rampant with e-mail and IM. In the quest to save keystrokes, users have traded clarity for confusion (unless you understand the abbreviations). Avoid using abbreviations not normally used in paper-based communication.

F. **Salutations.** Each situation will be different, but in general, use the same salutation as you would in a business letter. Some form of salutation should be included in every e-mail as a common courtesy.

G. **Signatures.** Do not rely on the return e-mail address to inform the recipient who sent the e-mail. Sign e-mail messages in the same manner as a business letter. Include full name, title, company name, and telephone number and e-mail address. Avoid using quotes or images at the end of your e-mail.

H. **Printing e-mail.** Avoid printing a paper copy of e-mails received unless absolutely necessary. Most e-mail systems allow the creation of folders for storing old e-mails if a copy will be needed later.

COMMENT

According to a 2006 American Management Association survey, 26 percent of employers have terminated employees for e-mail misuse.

I. **Other.** Remember, all recipients may not read e-mail immediately. While the e-mail usually arrives quickly, this is not always the case. E-mail is not designed for immediacy (that is why people have telephones); it is designed for convenience. Do not use e-mail to schedule a meeting the same day or for anything requiring an immediate response. Other tips to keep in mind:

1. Avoid using e-mail to deliver bad news. Questions cannot be answered when a person reads the e-mail.
2. Do not include confidential or embarrassing information in an e-mail, as you have no control over someone forwarding it.
3. Avoid filling up other people's inboxes with "Thank You" or "You're Welcome" messages unless the sender requires an acknowledgement.
4. If an e-mail is received that causes a strong personal reaction, avoid responding to it immediately. Use the telephone to clear up any possible misunderstanding.
5. Make sure you have actually attached attachments when you say you have.
6. Using all capital letters in an e-mail is the equivalent of SHOUTING.
7. Never send a blank e-mail with attachments; make sure the subject line or body of the e-mail explains what the attachment is about.
8. When replying to an e-mail, either leave the old message as part of the new one or clearly reference your response. Do not assume the reader knows exactly what is being talked about.

COMMENT

The consequences of e-mail content were highlighted in the Microsoft antitrust trial, where the government used e-mails written by Microsoft executives to undermine their credibility. Statements made by executives in e-mails contradicted their public statements.

[C] E-mail Marketing

Although e-mail can be a cost-effective way for a company to reach existing and potential customers, the abuse of e-mail by "spammers" has caused an outcry against unsolicited e-mail. In response, Congress passed the Controlling the Assault of Non-Solicited Pornography and Marketing Act of 2003 (CAN-SPAM). This law, which took effect in January 2004, requires that companies maintain opt-out lists for people who do not want to receive e-mail from the company. The act allows for fines of up to $2 million against companies that violate the act. IT staffs will need to stay up-to-date on further CAN-SPAM developments and be attentive to the compliance efforts of the company, including the potential creation of a national "do not e-mail" list.

COMMENT

A 2011 FBI report showed that cost of spam and related scams to be $485.3 million. The figure includes both money lost to scam ridden spams like phishing attacks and Nigerian scams, and the costs involved in fighting spam with spam filters and other software.

According to the CAN-SPAM Act, spam is defined as any communication that does any of the following:

A. Accesses a protected computer without authorization and intentionally initiates the transmission of multiple commercial electronic mail messages from or through such computer.
B. Uses a protected computer to relay or retransmit multiple commercial electronic mail messages, with the intent to deceive or mislead recipients, or any Internet access service, as to the origin of such messages.
C. Falsifies header information in multiple commercial electronic mail messages and intentionally initiates the transmission of such messages.
D. Registers, using information that falsifies the identity of the actual registrant, for five or more electronic mail accounts or online user accounts or two or more domain names and intentionally initiates the transmission of multiple commercial electronic mail messages from any combination of such accounts or domain names.
E. Falsely represents the right to use five or more Internet protocol addresses and intentionally initiates the transmission of multiple commercial electronic mail messages from such addresses.

COMMENT

Also according to Nuclear Research, nearly 6 months after the passage of the CAN-SPAM Act, the costs of spam doubled from the year before: The average e-mail user received 29 spam messages daily, as compared with the average of 13 messages reported before the passage of the CAN-SPAM Act.

The IT department is responsible for developing policies and procedures to work with their marketing department to ensure compliance with CAN-SPAM.

§ 21.05[C]

All e-mail marketing sent out by the company must do the following in order to meet the requirements of CAN-SPAM:

    A. The subject line must be accurate.

    B. E-mail recipients who opt out must be removed from the e-mail list within 10 business days.

    C. The header information in the e-mail (originating e-mail address, domain name, and IP address) must be correct and accurate.

    D. The return e-mail address must be accurate and active for at least 30 days after transmission so recipients can opt out.

    E. The postal address of the sender must be included in the e-mail.

    F. The e-mail must be identified as an advertisement or solicitation.

COMMENT

Go to *http://thomas.loc.gov* and search for "S.877" and "108th Congress" to see the exact text of the CAN-SPAM Act.

While the CAN-SPAM Act does not prohibit the sending of unsolicited e-mail for marketing purposes, many organizations and individuals frown on the sending of unsolicited e-mails for any reason. Your marketing plan must weigh the ill will that could be generated by unsolicited e-mail against the value of using a purchased e-mail list for marketing purposes. See Policy ITP-21-6 E-mail Marketing Policy as an example.

POLICY ITP-21-6.   E-mail Marketing Policy

Policy #:	ITP-21-6	Effective:	03/18/13	Page #:	1 of N
Subject:	E-mail Marketing Policy				

1.0 PURPOSE

The company's relationship with its customers and prospective customers is one of its most important assets and must be protected from harm due to inappropriate or unwanted e-mail communication. Many of our customers spend a large amount of time and resources managing incoming e-mail, and they consider all unsolicited e-mail to be spam. This includes e-mails whose primary purpose is to market our goods and services. This policy provides guidelines for the use of e-mail for marketing purposes.

2.0 SCOPE

The policy applies to all e-mails sent to customers and prospective customers where the primary purpose is for marketing the company's goods and services.

3.0 POLICY

Marketing e-mails can only be sent to customers and prospective customers that have done business with the company or have agreed to receive marketing e-mails from the company through an opt-in process. In addition, all marketing e-mails sent out by the company must do the following in order to meet the requirements of the CAN-SPAM Act:

A. The subject line must be accurate.
B. E-mail recipients who opt out must be removed from the e-mail list within 10 business days.
C. The header information in the e-mail (originating e-mail address, domain name, and IP address) must be correct and accurate.
D. The return e-mail address must be accurate and active for at least 30 days after transmission so recipients can opt out.
E. The postal address of the sender must be included in the e-mail.
F. The e-mail must be identified as an advertisement or solicitation.

4.0 REVISION HISTORY

Date	Revision #	Description of Change
03/18/13	1.0	Initial creation.

5.0 INQUIRIES

Direct inquiries about this policy to:

George Jenkins, CIO
Our Company, Inc.
2900 Corporate Drive
Columbus, OH 43215

Voice: 614-555-1234
Fax: 614-555-1235
E-mail: gjenkins@company.com

Revision #:	1.0	Supersedes:	N/A	Date:	03/18/13

[D]   E-mail Archiving

With the ever-increasing amount of business communication being done via e-mail, it is critical that the organization has an effective and efficient process for archiving this communication. An e-mail archiving system can reduce the amount of active data stored on the network file system and can be important in satisfying regulatory and legal requirements for the retrieval of e-mails.

While e-mail archiving can be done manually, it is much more efficient to use an automated program. Consider the following when creating an e-mail archiving policy:

A.   How long should e-mails be retained?
B.   Should users be able to easily view archived e-mails?
C.   Can users delete personal e-mails before they are archived?
D.   Will other items such as tasks and calendar items also be archived?

See Policy ITP-21-7 E-mail Archiving Policy as an example.

POLICY ITP-21-7.   E-mail Archiving Policy

Policy #:	ITP-21-7	**Effective:**	03/18/13	**Page #:**	1 of N
Subject:	E-mail Archiving Policy				

1.0 PURPOSE

In order to manage the ever increasing volume of e-mail, calendar items and tasks, and to facilitate their retrieval, the company has implemented an enterprise-wide automated e-mail archiving system. The e-mail archiving system also reduces the amount of active data stored on the network file system and satisfies regulatory and legal requirements for the retrieval of e-mails.

2.0 SCOPE

The policy applies to all users of the company owned e-mail system. It applies to permanent and part-time employees, as well as contractors.

3.0 POLICY

This policy authorizes the implementation of an automated e-mail archiving system. The system automatically archives all company e-mail, calendar items, and tasks older than 90 days. All e-mails, calendar items, and tasks related in any way to company business must be archived. E-mail users are encouraged to delete personal e-mails from their mailbox before they are automatically archived after 45 days. Archived e-mail will be retained for a period of seven years.

4.0 REVISION HISTORY

Date	Revision #	Description of Change
03/18/13	1.0	Initial creation.

5.0 INQUIRIES

Direct inquiries about this policy to:

George Jenkins, CIO
Our Company, Inc.
2900 Corporate Drive
Columbus, OH 43215

Voice: 614-555-1234
Fax: 614-555-1235
E-mail: gjenkins@company.com

Revision #:	1.0	Supersedes:	N/A	Date:	03/18/13

§ 21.06   ACCEPTABLE USE AGREEMENT

[A]   Overview

An acceptable use agreement must be put in place ensuring all employees understand and agree to the company's Internet and e-mail use policies. The employee's immediate supervisor reviews the policy with the employee ensuring that the employee understands the seriousness of the policy.

[B]   Sample Acceptable Use Agreement

Worksheet 21-1 is a sample e-mail and Internet user agreement that is to be signed by all existing employees and by all new employees at orientation. The employee receives a copy and another copy is placed in the employee's personnel file.

WORKSHEET 21-1. E-Mail/Internet User Agreement

Employee Agreement:

I have received a copy of XYZ Company's E-Mail and Internet Acceptable Use Policy # _____, dated _____. I recognize and understand that the company's e-mail and Internet systems are to be used for conducting the company's business only. I understand that use of this equipment for private purposes is strictly prohibited.

As part of the XYZ organization and use of XYZ's gateway to the Internet and e-mail system, I understand that this Acceptable Use Policy applies to me. I have read the aforementioned document and agree to follow all policies and procedures that are set forth therein. I further agree to abide by the standards set in the document for the duration of my employment with XYZ Company. I understand that e-mail and Internet usage may be monitored by the company to ensure compliance with the Acceptable Use Policy.

I am aware that violations of this Acceptable Use Policy may subject me to disciplinary action, up to and including discharge from employment. I further understand that my communications on the Internet and e-mail reflect XYZ Company worldwide to our competitors, consumers, customers, and suppliers. Furthermore, I understand that this document can be amended at any time.

_____   _____
Employee's Printed Name   Date

_____
Employee's Signature

_____   _____
Manager's Signature   Date

22

WEB 2.0: THE NEXT GENERATION

§ 22.01 OVERVIEW

[A] Purpose and Scope

Web 2.0 refers to technology that is designed to facilitate creativity, information sharing, and, most notably, collaboration among users via the Internet. It enables people with elementary technical skills to easily find and share information. Organizations use Web 2.0 tools to facilitate team collaboration during project development, for the quick exchange of information and for building technical or business process documentation.

Web 2.0 describes a wide assortment of tools that can enhance the ability of people to collaborate, share ideas, or just socialize and network. Web 2.0 also describes trends in Web design and syndication of information, with software services delivered through the Internet, as opposed to purchasing individual software packages to run on a corporate server. Some of these services are free. In most cases, the same service provider will provide a range of enhanced services for a subscription fee.

The term "Web 2.0" does not describe any particular time period in the history of the Internet. While some tools are emerging, others have been around nearly since the Internet was created. Given this vague definition, defining exactly which tools and innovations are part of Web 2.0 and which are not is debatable.

Team members are likely familiar with Web 2.0 tools through their use of them in their personal life. These tools fall into three primary categories:

A. **Collaboration.** The chief collaboration tool is the Wiki. Where a Wiki might not be available, forums or mailing lists may be beneficial and require less work up front.
B. **Social Networking.** Instant messaging, if properly managed, is the most useful and simplest application of Web 2.0. Enhanced company directories are also very beneficial to a larger business. Virtual communities are potential time and dollar savers for training and for attending meetings.
C. **Syndication.** In the case of syndication, RSS (Really Simple Syndication) efficiently delivers information to team members.

These categories are not mutually exclusive. Both collaboration and social networking focused tools often feature syndication, and it is not at all difficult to link collaboration and social networking tools.

Each Web 2.0 tool addresses a specific problem. Some facilitate the sharing of information; others might provide instant communication. The key is to understand the benefits of each and select the ones that best suit your situation. There is also a cost in ensuring everyone knows how to use the tool and for administering its content. One community that has found Web 2.0 tools particular useful is virtual workers. Many of the collaboration and social networking tools enable virtual workers to make contacts, ask quick questions, and find internal assistance for issues as they crop up.

Large companies may bring these tools into their data center for better control. Examples are IBM's Sametime and Microsoft's Lync. Both provide instant messaging but enable the company to manage its own information security and, in some cases, to record traffic for legal compliance. Most Web 2.0 tools use PHP (a general purpose Web development scripting language) and one of the open source SQL databases such as MySQL.

Web 2.0 is based on the principle of "extreme trust" of users, which exposes it to malicious and criminal exploitation. Content can change quickly in real time. Current tools are not practical for filtering the text that people post. Java script encoding is flexible and attacks are difficult to detect.

COMMENT

In October 2005, a person who wanted to add 1 million "friends" to their MySpace site initiated the "Samy" worm, which exploited a cross-site scripting vulnerability. Although the effect on the users was benign, it illustrates how quickly a Web-based attack on a Web 2.0 application can occur.

There are some drawbacks to using Web 2.0 technology:

A. The Internet is in constant flux, with today's hot sites becoming tomorrow's unvisited orphans. Companies creating Web 2.0 tools rush their products to market. Information security aspects are sometimes saved for the next version. Companies providing Web 2.0 tools tend to come and go. If your service provider drops out of the marketplace, all of the time spent loading data and training the team may be lost.

B. Web 2.0 tools use the Internet, which is under constant attack. Web 2.0 tools are a two-way exchange of information subject to interception, fabrication, and interruption. There is always the possibility of data compromise.

C. There are some legal issues to consider. Text messages in many companies are considered to be official company communications and must be saved in the company's permanent electronic archives. Individuals, and in some cases companies, may be legally liable for the comments that are posted.

D. The freedom and openness provided by these tools can lead to unintentional consequences. Companies that use blogs as "open doors" to executives may expose company secrets and weaknesses to the public.

E. Anonymity is an issue because you cannot see who you are really communicating with. It may not be who you think it is.

Introducing Web 2.0 tools into a company requires updating the company's existing "Acceptable Use" agreement. These documents must now cover comments posted in blogs, documentation posted to Wikis, and all of the other Web 2.0 tools used by a company. Because most people already use these applications at home, it is very likely they have already found their way into your organization—so update that statement today!

COMMENT

New technologies bring new challenges. Always read the Terms of Service agreement closely for every Web site before rolling out any Web 2.0 tool to your team. You might be surprised at what you are being asked to agree to, as few people bother to wade through the text.

[B]   Critical Policies to Develop Based on This Chapter

Using the material discussed in this chapter, you will be able to create the following policies:

    A. Collaboration policy
    B. Use of instant messaging
    C. Guideline for blogging
    D. Social media usage

Policies should always be developed based on the local situation. Successful managers cannot issue appropriate guidance if the policies are written with another company's situation or location in mind.

§ 22.02   COLLABORATING USING WEB 2.0

[A]   Wikis

Wikis are probably the single most useful Web 2.0 tool. They have been around since the mid-1990s but took several years to reach any sort of popularity. A Wiki is a collection of Web pages centered on one topic per page. Each page of a Wiki can be edited by any user with permission to do so. Wikis create internal links to other pages. Some types of Wikis have discussion pages for each topic so users can propose changes to the page rather than making them outright.

COMMENT

The most famous example is Wikipedia, a free online ency-clopedia edited by anyone with access to a computer. Wiki-pedia posts over 3.6 million articles in the English section followed by over 1.2 million in German and 1.1 million in French. Wikipedia currently has articles in 271 languages.

A Wiki is useful for bringing team information into a single location. For example, as the team works on the project, members can record ideas, experiences, and design decisions for review by others later. IT projects benefit more from Wikis than perhaps any other Web 2.0 tool. A Wiki allows team members to easily record and access information. Later in the project when it is time to write the technical and end-user documentation, the Wiki can provide much of the source material. Wikis make it easy to:

A. Create a reference or how-to guide.
B. Exchange ideas, with each person contributing a portion of the solution.
C. Track the progress of a project and enable a supervisor to check up on the project without needing to directly contact team members.
D. Record the history of a project.
E. Give a biography for each team member.
F. Record a set of links to important information and maintain contact information for stakeholders.
G. Ensure that all of the Wiki data are safely backed up to off-line media.

To visualize the utility of a Wiki, consider this scenario:

A company needs to install antivirus software on all computers. Alex, an IT technician, goes around and installs the software on all computers that the company owns, or checks up on each machine after forcing a network download. He documents each problem encountered on the company Wiki. John, a new technician, is hired at a distant company site to also install the same antivirus software. John references the Wiki whenever his installation efforts encounter a problem. Because some computers are newer and have a different operating system, there are some new errors, and some errors that existed before have different solutions for that operating system. John logs in and updates patches for the old errors and posts the new ones.

Later, Alex checks the Wiki and notices that John erased his solutions. After discussing this with John, he is able to easily revert those segments back to the original content and add John's notes. When the next technician is hired, this guide is available to help train him or her. Additionally, users at remote locations installing this software to meet company requirements will be able to diagnose and remedy problems with their installation process thanks to the work of John and Alex.

A Wiki can also be used by team members to keep tabs on projects and to record information for later access. Because each team member is able to update the Wiki, it removes the bottleneck of just one person updating and distributing all of the information. Each team member is writing about what he knows best. The information is more accurate because it was not filtered through an intermediary. Each team member is keeping the Wiki updated, which reduces problems when a critical team member suddenly leaves the team. Instead of searching through the team member's file drawers, the information is already organized in the project's Wiki pages. It also enables stakeholders to check the status of a project. Wikis can be used to brief participants before a meeting to reduce the length of the meeting or to cut out regular meetings altogether.

Wikis come in multiple flavors. Many software packages are available, ranging from free and open source to proprietary. Some companies offer the software together with hosting services, which can include security measures. They can be either hosted on the Internet or run in-house. To locate an Internet-based Wiki site, use one of the common search engines to search for the term "Wiki." There are many out there.

COMMENT

To select the Wiki that's right for your project team, refer to Wikipedia's comparison of Wiki software chart at *http:// en.wikipedia.org/wiki/Comparison_of_wiki_software*.

For companies that wish to host their own Wiki site in-house, the software is available for free from Media Wiki (*www.mediaWiki.org*). This is the same software engine that powers Wikipedia. The Web site provides information on additional tools (all free) required to install this product. A dedicated server is recommended. In-house Wikis require Web server software, a SQL database capability, and usually PHP support. After the software is set up, potential users and clients need to be made aware of the URL and register as authorized users.

The third alternative is to hire an application service provider to host your Wiki. This provides a quicker start-up because the service provider has the technical expertise in Wikis that the in-house staff may lack. It is important to verify that the service provider ensures the confidentiality of your data.

Once a Wiki is set up, begin by editing a page. To add another page, create a link with the desired page name (such as "Welcome" or "ReadMe"), save the current page, then click on the newly created link to go to a blank version of a Wiki page to begin that topic. Most Wiki software provides on-screen basic instructions.

Like all technologies, Wikis have their problems. Some pitfalls to avoid include:

A. Before signing up for a Wiki, carefully review the terms of use from the provider to ensure that you own all of the content and that it does not become property of the Wiki provider.

B. Verify if your Wiki is open to the public or if you can control who sees it. Typically, public sites require a monthly fee to restrict access. Paid sites may also offer additional useful services.

C. Vandalism is easiest to prevent by requiring all users to register and receive permission, or by tracking IP or MAC addresses. This is more feasible within an in-house network than it is from an application service provider site.

D. Update your company policies on harassment to include postings to company-sponsored Wikis. A part of this update also identifies company confidential information that should never be posted— even on an internal Wiki.

E. Wiki postings are often unevenly developed, both in quantity and quality: one topic may have a large number of well-developed, well-proofread subsections, whereas another topic page may have only a few sentences in fragmented English.

F. It is easy for an author, even not deliberately, to introduce bias into an article, or to add something untrue.

[B] Forums

A simpler and more chronologically oriented tool for collaboration is the forum, which evolved from electronic bulletin board systems (BBS). Internet forums are also commonly referred to as Web forums, message or discussion boards, newsgroups, (electronic) discussion groups, discussion forums, or bulletin boards. A forum is a set of subject areas with subtopics, known as threads, where users can post comments on the subject. Forums often include a rating or tagging system used to hide unhelpful comments based on feedback from other users (such as I rate this formation as helpful, very helpful, etc.). Forums are moderated by administrators (Admins) or moderators (Mods). They have the power to create and close threads. They may also delete or modify existing posts.

Some companies utilize forums as a supplemental form of tech support, where interested users may help others before an official representative can answer the post. Note that such technical support may be both internal and external. Forums are of a semi-permanent nature, barring editing by moderators or the posters, as they are not edited by the community at large. They are organized as either a relational history, which forms a tree of replies, or strict chronological history, which is linear for each thread.

COMMENT

An excellent example of a forum is the Microsoft Developer Network (*msdn.com*). It allows users to post questions about errors they are receiving and get help from other community members. These members may not be Microsoft employees. Another example is *techsupportforum.com*, which provides open tech support on essentially any technical issue. The drawback is that not all posts are guaranteed to get an answer, and answers are not guaranteed to be correct or ideal. However, if you are totally lost in a problem, check here to get an idea.

Forums can help project teams and their managers in several key ways.

A. Forums do not require users to be online simultaneously. This facilitates collaboration among users working different shifts, in different time zones, or remotely. A team member can post a question to the forum, and then another teammate, many time zones distant, can post a response.
B. Forums provide a method for discussing ideas, problems, bug fixes, etc., that maybe are not worth discussing in large meetings, but that team members want to receive feedback on or to discuss in public.
C. Forums are excellent training tools. While it is desirable to have a lecture or notes-style method of training team members, real life simply can't be contained in a textbook. Forums, both in the company and externally, can be used to teach team members skills such as what a "LNK2019 error" means or how to troubleshoot a recurring "Blue Screen of Death." Inexperienced members can use these forums to post questions (as long as they try to resolve issues on their own for a few minutes) while experienced members answer questions to help them.

Forum software is available in PHP, Perl, ASP, and Java. One common version is an open source PHP BBS, which allows for password-protected user authentication along with requiring moderator approval to join and spam filtering. It also contains options for receiving updates via e-mail. An in-house forum system requires a server with PHP- (or other language-) enabled Web server with SQL database capabilities. The Web server stores information posted by various users as well as custom user settings, like forum display style and signature, which displays at the bottom of each post.

COMMENT

A forum site that describes other forum sites is *www .forummatrix.org.*

Once a forum is set up, each user needs to register. This involves providing an e-mail address and a display name, and setting a password, among any other preferences. The user will need to be confirmed—this can be done automatically, but it is a highly insecure procedure. Once this is done, the user can create threads and make posts. Also, users can subscribe to an RSS feed in most versions of the software or some other updater, which will deliver updates periodically regarding forum activity.

Forums are also a source of information on the Internet, even if not used internally by the company. They are a good place to find recommendations of hardware, software, or how to accomplish a given task. The open source community, particularly for Linux, makes good use of this type of tool. Forums are also good for researching such things as what computer server to buy or how to install Ubuntu on a hand-held computer. If no posts can be found on the topic, then register and start your own discussion.

Some guidelines and precautions for using forums:

A. Beware of the advice posted in forums. Forums (except for posts by admins) are generally open to anyone, from a know-it-all novice to a seasoned expert to a disgruntled anti (whatever) person, so the quality of information can vary. When researching such things as hardware or software recommendations, a consensus from several forums is prudent. Relying on just one or two forums may provide severely biased information. This is especially true when special-interest groups or vendors host the forum.

B. Most forums have a code of conduct or standard of etiquette and breaching these rules, whether written or unspoken, can lead to being banned from that forum. Be polite and refrain from jokes most people would not want their small children to hear.

C. Forums are generally vendor-neutral. While posting a recommendation is fine, or offering a product as a solution is acceptable, it should not be a blatant advertisement. While it is possible to make outright advertisements, there are often separate topic areas for this, and it is considered a breach of etiquette by most other users. Such postings are typically deleted and the poster warned or banned.

As useful as forums may be, they do have some drawbacks:

A. For this method of collaboration to succeed, it must be checked regularly. Users who don't receive feedback in a timely manner—say, a few days of their first few posts—are likely to abandon the forums, feeling they won't get helped.
B. Information can become duplicated—with conflicting versions! Someone competent in the forum's subject area must monitor postings and cull information that is no longer valid or pertinent to the topic.

[C]   Mailing Lists

Internet mailing lists have been around for many years as distribution lists in e-mail software. For Web 2.0, this basic concept is transformed into a massive service where individuals sign up to be e-mailed information as it is distributed—sometimes as a periodic newsletter or whenever something new is posted that you have previously expressed interest in learning about. The Web 2.0 mailing list is characterized as something a person can sign up for—or drop out of—all without administrator intervention. Often combined with forums, a mailing list is comprised of a root e-mail address that forwards a message or set of messages to all subscribers.

E-mails sent by mailing lists are generally managed by the community as threads. This is made possible by Web-enabled e-mail, which contains tags indicating any previous e-mails. It tracks when the "reply" or "forward" buttons were pressed—and so maintains a relational thread of e-mails.

Mailing lists are popular in the open source community because development tends to be very decentralized. They allow a question or development to be brought to the attention of many as often as they check their e-mail, as opposed to hoping they will check a forum or Wiki. One example of a mailing list used for software development is the four located at *kernel.org* regarding current Linux kernels and related issues. These lists help developers collaborate and to troubleshoot unusual issues.

A mailing list can help an IT project in several ways by:

A. Providing a means for group-wide communiqué, such as publishing project status reports or customer-approved scope changes.
B. Broadcasting information to team members or end users during a new product rollout, such as all employees must begin using the new payroll system two weeks from today.
C. Providing informal technical support. This is especially helpful when developing open source technology where the company does not wish to actively provide support. However, such lists can be discouraging to customers and clients if the product is supported solely by the mailing list.
D. Helping teach new team members. By forming a mailing list within a company, employees can seek, for example, technical help in software development.

E. Helping experienced members who may run across problems foreign to the department. Examples of this would be setting up unusual hardware or peculiar open source software that few others have any experience with. They could subscribe to a mailing list about that topic and get help through the list.

Most mailing lists have either written or expected rules of etiquette. Generally, these include:

A. Do not press "reply to all," unless there are recipients in the particular thread not normally part of the list; in this case, edit out the original sender so duplicates are not received (though some systems catch this).
B. Do not press "reply" to get the e-mail address, even if the original body text is deleted. The meta data in the e-mail header will still list the e-mail as part of whichever thread the e-mail being replied to is from. This is sometimes called thread hijacking. This makes a difference in Web sites that allow the mailing list history to be viewed, usually by thread tree.
C. Avoid sending mail to just one person, as if a specific question is asked. The community as a whole is more likely to have a solution than the specific person, and it helps to save time.
D. Do not send profane or harassing messages.

The Web site Nabble (*www.nabble.com*), among others, can be used to set up a forum/mailing list combination service free of charge. Remember that information on the public Internet is easily accessible by others.

As useful as mailing lists may be, they do have some drawbacks:

A. Overuse may result in blocking as "spam," keeping out the good with the bad.
B. Allow a way for people to opt out at any time.
C. Users "reply to all" are actions that will cause participants to drop off or block the list.
D. Someone must monitor who changes the messages and may be sending out spam.

[D] Tagging

When sifting through Wiki pages, forum posts, and old e-mail, it is helpful to have them labeled in a fashion such that searching for them goes quickly. A popular method for doing this is known as "tagging." Tagging is a way to organize and search information by applying various labels to places within the text. Tagging and similar concepts can serve many purposes, such as:

A. Tagging is a way to draw attention to your posts, such as when you need help for something or looking for your next billable internal assignment.

B. Tagging articles in a Wiki with various categories, such as "for beginners" and "linux" as well as "articles needing to be updated" and "articles being used by team x." Users can then search for all articles with that tag. Many Wikis refer to these tags as categories.

C. Voting on the quality of a forum post, usually by rating it as good or bad. These ratings then affect which forum posts show up by default. Less useful posts are collapsed to save time while reading a forum thread.

D. Recommending an article on a news or magazine Web site. The number of recommendations then affects which stories become headlines on a Web site to help bring more helpful articles to the attention of others. Some Web sites also use this as a way to personalize content for registered users.

Some examples of tagging: Wikipedia contains categories along the lines of "featured articles" as well as "computers" or "project management." Another example is the tags used by Gmail, called labels. Pandora is a free online music service that provides a form of good versus bad voting which will affect what types of music are played on a given personal channel.

Project managers utilizing Wikis, blogs, or other Web 2.0 tools will find tagging useful to quickly find relevant items. The results are more helpful than simply searching with a search engine. Externally, tags can be used for marketing. Tagging helps users find items because the terms one person uses to describe a system may vary greatly from the terms another may use. This helps the user find information more readily. Project managers can put tagging to work in several ways:

A. **Documentation.** For training and future reference, consider how such a system can be added to your project documentation, end-user, or help-desk instructions.

B. **Public relations.** Allowing visitors to recommend articles through an internal system or through a linker like Digg brings more attention to the company or team and its current work.

C. **Technical support.** Microsoft utilizes tagging and different forms of it in several places. In some help windows, it asks whether a solution is helpful or not. Solutions tagged as unhelpful often enough could theoretically be reviewed for potential removal. The more times a post is rated as being helpful, the more likely that post contains useful information about your project.

Getting started with tagging is usually fairly easy. A tagging capability is often included in a blog, Wiki, or forum software. Tags are often a part of social software, such as a custom company directory, Facebook, or Twitter. If they are not, then tagging can also be done by creating an account on *Del.icio.us* or a similar Web site and simply posting the link and a brief description. Tags are generally stored in the metadata of content.

While useful in many cases, tagging does have some drawbacks:

A. Finding good articles or being able to more quickly skim forum posts requires someone at some point to go through and make these recommendations. This means trusting the judgment of likely anonymous users.
B. The meaning of words can be ambiguous—and so are tags. Consider the word "draw." It may be used to mean to close or open something, to tie in a game, or to convey through some artistic means of thought, among other definitions. In this case, a search would need to be refined through other tags, if they are available.
C. Tags suffer from multiple (and incorrect) spellings, as well as plural form. Doughnut, donut, doughnuts, and donuts (not even counting misspellings like donot and douhgnut!) could all refer to the same set of information, but without venturing into misspellings, four different tags could be generated, each applied to different yet overlapping groups of articles! Ideally, the community would eventually fix this, but resolution may require actions by a moderator or not be fixed at all.

[E] Polls

A poll is a way to gather opinions or facts on any given topic. Polls can be found on many Web sites that seek to maintain an active user base. They are often found on magazine Web sites. Some polls are more for fun and morale, while most others are for gathering information. Polls could also be posted to gain feedback regarding how the employees feel the company is treating them or how well a project is progressing. These results can then be acted on by the appropriate company manager or leader.

The results of a poll can be used to make decisions when managing projects. Project managers can utilize a wide range of poll topics to accomplish a number of goals:

A. Performing risk assessments on aspects of the project or during critical decision points.
B. When a project is at a critical decision point, polls can obtain the consensus of the team.
C. Improving team morale—"Where should we hold the next team party?"
D. Providing a cost estimate for a client incorporating team expertise— "How long it will take for you to reach Milestone B?"
E. Getting feedback from a training session as to how well the trainees are learning—"How is the pace of the class?"
F. Obtaining user feedback on self-help instructions.

A common application of polling is the Delphi Method, which is used to gather time estimates from team members to predict how long it will take to develop a portion of software or complete the next landmark. This method is an iterative vote that solicits an estimate from each team member. The results are then presented and may or may not be discussed. The process is then repeated until most of the votes converge in close proximity to each other and the average remains consistent.

The easiest way to set up a poll is to use an online survey site. Two example sites are *www.surveymonkey.com* and *www.zoomerang.com*. A small survey can be built for free, which is a good way to determine if this tool is suitable for your project. In many cases, small surveys may be all that you need. However, if this tool is to be used to its full potential, then consider using the "paid" option.

Polls can be set up in several ways. Generally, polls are implemented on Web sites for easy aggregation of data. This probably only requires a basic Web server enabled with either Javascript or PHP. Alternatively, polls can be taken via some e-mail clients.

Microsoft Outlook allows for the insertion of votes in the form of a group of buttons, allowing a recipient to choose one and send back the results with names. Informally, an e-mail could be posted, or even something as simple as taking a vote at a meeting or posting paper in the office. However, the most benefit will be derived when polls are consistently and regularly featured on project and company Web sites, which can include forums and Wikis.

While useful in many cases, polls do have some drawbacks:

A. Too many polls will annoy recipients and they will quit responding.
B. Poll questions must not be obviously biased or ambiguous or they will lose their credibility.
C. Asking people their opinions implies that you will take action on their poll choices. It sets an expectation that something will be done. Always communicate back to the people involved with the poll results and actions that will be taken (and not taken).

See Policy ITP-22-1 Collaboration Policy as an example.

POLICY ITP-22-1.   Collaboration Policy

Policy #:	ITP-22-1	**Effective:**	03/18/15	**Page #:**	1 of 1
Subject:	Collaboration Policy				

1.0 PURPOSE

This policy defines the organization's position on employee use of web-based collaboration tools such as wikis, e-mail distribution lists, and forums for company business. While such tools can improve communication and productivity, they can also expose the company's information assets to competitors.

2.0 SCOPE

The policy applies to all technologies used to for sharing information amongst employees or with persons outside the organization.

3.0 POLICY

As collaboration tools are a communication medium that is covered under the general message retention requirements of the organization, the following guidelines have been established to protect both the company and the employee using such tools:

A. Use of collaboration tools is governed by the company's Internet Use policy.
B. Employees must carefully review the terms of use from the provider to ensure that the content does not become property of the tool provider.
C. Verify if the tool is open to the public or if you can control who sees the content.
D. Company confidential information must never be posted to a tool that is not hosted within the organization.
E. Company business cannot be conducted using non-company collaboration tools.
F. Be skeptical of information posted on collaboration tools that are accessible by persons outside the company.

4.0 REVISION HISTORY

Date	Revision #	Description of Change
03/18/15	1.0	Initial creation.

5.0 INQUIRIES

Direct inquiries about this policy to:

George Jenkins, CIO
Our Company, Inc.
2900 Corporate Drive
Columbus, OH 43215

Voice: 614-555-1234
Fax: 614-555-1235
E-mail: gjenkins@company.com

Revision #:	1.0	Supersedes:	N/A	Date:	03/18/15

§ 22.03 SOCIAL NETWORKING

[A] Instant Messaging

Instant messaging (IM or chat) is one of the most popular and most interactive services on the Internet. Using an IM program such as Windows Messenger, Trillian, or AOL Instant Messenger enables users to chat instantly with anyone anywhere in the world. Many companies find IM to be a useful tool for communicating with coworkers and customers. If someone is on the phone, a message can be sent that pops up instantly on his or her screen. IM has great potential for becoming an important business communication tool. It is a great tool for facilitating ad hoc discussions between workers in different locations.

But there are several negatives to IM. The capability to interrupt concentration—much like a ringing telephone—makes IM very disruptive in the office. Many IM programs will not work through a firewall and can be difficult to monitor. The use of external servers to distribute the messages can present a security issue, as no data security exists for consumer IM tools, nor are enterprise management tools available. The informal nature of IM encourages the creation of informal practices that are outside the formal communications channels of the firm. Key decision makers without access to IM may be left out of important discussions by users of IM.

Instant messaging has also been used for illegal or unethical actions. Because these actions sometimes occur during working hours and using company equipment, they become the company's business. To address these issues, large companies bring these same tools into their data center for better control. Examples are IBM's Lotus Sametime and Microsoft's Communicator. Both provide instant messaging but enable the company to manage its own information security and in some cases, to record all traffic for legal compliance.

The IT Manager is responsible for developing policies and procedures for using IM programs. All guidelines listed in § 21.04[C], "Internet Use Guidelines," apply to the use of IM. Additional guidelines to consider concerning IM include:

A. Employees must be specifically authorized to use IM.
B. Only company approved IM software should be used.
C. Employees will be assigned a unique IM identifier (also known as a nickname or handle) by the company. This identifier belongs to the company and its use by the employee is terminated when the employee leaves the company.
D. Company business cannot be conducted from non-company IM accounts.
E. As with e-mail, a retention policy for storing IM messages must be established.

COMMENT

The Securities and Exchange Commission's Rule 17a-4, which governs the financial services industry, requires companies to record, log, index, audit, and retrieve electronic communications. This includes IM messages.

If there are pockets of IM use already within the firm, consider using those groups as pilots for implementing an enterprise IM solution. Use the lessons learned in the pilot to develop enterprise-wide policies for IM use.

Because of the difficulty in verifying the identity of the person at the other end of an IM conversation, companies involved in financial services, health care, and legal services may want to totally ban the use of IM in their organizations.

Instant messaging carries a number of inherent risks. These include, among others:

A. Lost work time as employees engage in irrelevant discourse and sending messages for personal use.
B. Security violations, both deliberate and unintentional, as instant message clients provide an easy way to export information and an easy way to unintentionally acquire viruses.
C. "Lost" conversations.
D. Legal requirements for some industries to record and retain all messages. Some companies treat these messages just like e-mail for archiving and retention.

See Policy ITP-22-2 Instant Messaging Policy as an example.

POLICY ITP-22-2. Instant Messaging Policy

Policy #:	ITP-22-2	Effective:	03/18/13	Page #:	1 of N
Subject:	Instant Messaging Policy				

1.0 PURPOSE

This policy defines the organization's position on employee use of instant messaging (IM) technology.

2.0 SCOPE

The policy applies to all technologies used to send messages in real time to other employees or to persons outside the organization.

3.0 POLICY

As instant messaging (IM) is a communication medium that is covered under the general message retention requirements of the organization, the following guidelines have been established to protect both the company and the employee using IM:

A. Use of IM is governed by the company's Internet Use policy.
B. Employees must be specifically authorized to use IM.
C. Only company approved IM software can be used. Employees found using personal IM accounts on company equipment are subject to termination.
D. Employees will be assigned a unique IM identifier (also known as a nickname or handle) by the company. This identifier belongs to the company and its use by the employee is terminated when the employee leaves the company.
E. Company business cannot be conducted from non-company IM accounts.
F. The message retention policy in place for e-mail messages is to be followed for storing IM messages.

4.0 REVISION HISTORY

Date	Revision #	Description of Change
03/18/13	1.0	Initial creation.

5.0 INQUIRIES

Direct inquiries about this policy to:

George Jenkins, CIO
Our Company, Inc.
2900 Corporate Drive
Columbus, OH 43215

Voice: 614-555-1234
Fax: 614-555-1235
E-mail: gjenkins@company.com

Revision #:	1.0	Supersedes:	N/A	Date:	03/18/13

[B]   Blogs

Web logs, or blogs, have become a popular way to express personal opinions about current issues and subjects of general interest. Organizations and employees find blogs a very useful communications tool. Inside a company, posting about how projects are going allows your team to know you better and allows the project sponsor to keep tabs on the project. They have the potential to draw your team closer together, especially if team members are each keeping their own blogs. Blogs can also serve to record information so that the extended absence of critical team members doesn't shut down operations. Outside the company, blogs make an excellent marketing tool.

Blogs, like Wikis, can be very helpful at bringing new members up to date on a project. As an added bonus, dated blog entries are written and updates are made in separate entries. This allows a new team member to comprehend the product by watching its development over time throughout the blog history.

COMMENT

Blogs can be used to build credibility for a project and an understanding between the blog's author and readers.

Employees using blogs on company time, equipment, or connections must ensure that their comments adhere to the company's policies on electronic communications. Employees publishing blogs on their own time, using their own equipment and resources, should understand that their comments will still be constrained by the same electronic communications policies.

Free speech is a legal freedom in most countries. However, in business, it is difficult to call someone an imbecile in public and then expect that person to retain the same working relationship in the office. When a comment is published, it assumes a different character than when it is voiced to a small group. Companies do not want to assume liability for misplaced company remarks that may be attributed to an official company action or prevailing attitude. A blogging policy should outline clearly what the company's position is on the use of blogs by employees both at work and outside of work.

See Policy ITP-22-3 Blogging Policy as an example.

POLICY ITP-22-3.   Blogging Policy

Policy #:	ITP-22-3	Effective:	03/18/13	Page #:	1 of N
Subject:	Blogging Policy				

§ 22.03[B]

1.0 PURPOSE

This policy defines the organization's position on employee participation in the communication and sharing of information in the public Internet through such mediums as personal Web sites, Web logs (blogs), and networking sites.

2.0 SCOPE

The policy applies to all forms of information publication and communication via the Internet, including but not limited to Web logs (blogs), social networking sites such as Facebook and MySpace, and professional networking sites such as LinkedIn and Plaxo.

3.0 POLICY

While the company respects the right of employees to use personal Web sites and Web logs as a medium of self-expression, you must not be identified as an employee of the company while using such mediums without the prior approval of the corporate communications department. The following guidelines must be followed to ensure that readers will not view you as a de facto spokesperson for the company:

    A. You must make it clear to readers that any views you express are yours alone and that these views do not necessarily represent the views of the company. If there is any chance that you could be identified as an employee of the company when expressing personal views, you must provide the following notice in your communication:

> The views expressed on this Web site/blog/network are mine alone and do not necessarily represent the views of my employer.

    B. You must not disclose any information that is confidential or proprietary to the organization or to any customer or vendor that has disclosed such information to the company. Review the company's policy on confidential and proprietary information for guidance.

    C. Any communication occurring in a public forum such as those identified previously in this policy must be respectful to the company, fellow employees, our affiliates, and our business partners.

    D. As outlined in your employment agreement, any concepts or discoveries that you produce that are related to the company's business are property of the company and should not be discussed in a public forum without expressed written permission of the company. Consult your manager if you have any questions about topics that may be covered by this policy.

    E. The company may request at any time that you cease any communication concerning the company in a public forum or require you to block access to such communication if the company believes that such action is necessary to ensure compliance with government regulations or other laws.

F. Do not use the company's trademarks on any personal communication or reproduce any company material.

4.0 REVISION HISTORY

Date	Revision #	Description of Change
03/18/13	1.0	Initial creation.

5.0 INQUIRIES

Direct inquiries about this policy to:

George Jenkins, CIO
Our Company, Inc.
2900 Corporate Drive
Columbus, OH 43215

Voice: 614-555-1234
Fax: 614-555-1235
E-mail: gjenkins@company.com

Revision #:	1.0	Supersedes:	N/A	Date:	03/18/13

When you are ready to get started blogging, consider these things:

A. Read existing blogs to get a feel for what one looks like.
B. Blogs should be updated frequently. If not, the readership will drop off for more public blogs, or information gaps will develop in blogs used primarily for technical documentation and internal development.
C. Link to other sources—such as Web sites, blogs, etc.—as often as possible. In a similar vein, it is helpful to occasionally link back to older posts of your own, but not nearly as frequently as links to other Web sites or you will appear to be full of yourself (an arbitrary guideline might be no more than one link to your own posts to every 10 or 20 other links).

Project managers have found blogs valuable for:

A. Keeping notes on a project. At the end of the day, blogs are an easy and systematic way to record activities and thoughts on a project. Blog entries are sequential and show the evolution of the project. This sequential nature means the information is not categorized for easy searching (time for some tags).

B. Discussing current products and related topics: companies with products under constant development, such as Surveyor (*surveyor.com*), blog about recent developments in their robots and related software and hardware. This serves to inspire and help current users, bring in new customers, and keep interested persons aware of past and upcoming releases.

C. Providing a personal commentary, usually uncensored and with only basic guidelines, written by employees.

Blogs can be set up on free online services or on internal equipment. Many free blogs can be found by searching the Internet for "blog." Anyone providing a Web service has expenses, so a "free" site is advertiser supported, or of limited capabilities unless you upgrade to their paid service (which may be very worthwhile). Most blogs allow for the quick addition of images or text.

COMMENT

To establish an in-house blog capability, a server with Web software, SQL database capabilities, and PHP or other similar language support is required.

Some things to avoid while blogging:

A. **Using a public blog.** First determine if the entries are public or private. They should be private if individual user IDs are purchased.

B. **Editing once a post is made.** Not only will readers notice—especially because most software marks that a change has been made—but it seems more artificial and less personal. If you need to make a correction, do it in a later post.

C. **Employing ghost writers (having others write for you).** Bloggers must be writing their own blogs. This is as much a risk management issue as it is an integrity issue.

D. **Removing comments.** Many blogs allow for user-submitted comments. These can be very useful for the company as feedback; however, the comment section should not be pruned to only represent favorable views, as users will notice this. As a result, users will stop posting potentially useful feedback and also disregard existing comments as being biased. Use a spam filter to screen out obvious spam messages.

E. **Not having standards.** Because the blog will likely be affiliated with the company, some standards and policies should be made governing what may and may not be discussed on the blog. This will help reduce the disclosure of sensitive information.

F. **Not using an authentic voice.** If a blog reads like a brochure or a sales pitch, it is very likely to be substantially less successful than a blog written with an authentic voice. An authentic voice would sound like a person telling a friend about a project he is working on at work rather than a salesman telling a client why he should buy the product.

[C] Virtual Communities

Technology has now developed to the point where you need not leave your desk to attend a training session or meeting, even one that is several time zones away. One way this is done is by using a computer-based world known as a virtual community. Virtual communities allow people to interact by using avatars. An avatar is an object that represents a person—think of a person from the "Sims," or any program that allows the user to create a virtual person. These virtual people, each representing a person here in the real world, can then participate in meetings, give or take a lecture, or even socialize. The best-known program that allows this is called Second Life.

Because anyone with an appropriate workstation and high-speed Internet connectivity can participate in events in virtual worlds, even those in other countries, virtual communities give project managers several powerful tools:

A. **Conducting training from great distances.** Virtual communities allow people in distant locales to view PowerPoint slides while reading the text of a lecture. The avatars allow them to indirectly meet other team members and provide a much more personal touch than an independent study. In some cases, individuals can hear the lecture via a conference call while watching the virtual lecture.

B. **Crossing language barriers.** By using text-based communications as a primary or supplementary medium, international participants or participants with thick accents can take their time formulating and comprehending communications.

C. **Having meetings and conferences from great distances.** Much like training at a distance, having meetings in a sound-enabled virtual community is more personal than a teleconference call.

To get started, sign up for Second Life or a similar service, or create your own. Each of these will require a computer with network or Internet access, depending on the access needed, and a microphone or conference phone. Currently, Second Life registration can be found at *www.secondlife.com/join*. Second Life currently has a monthly fee for owning land, but none for just having an avatar.

An alternative to Second Life would be to create a custom world using Multiverse, a free MMO (massively multiplayer online game) builder. The world is as customizable as Java or Python and your hardware allows. This is a much more advanced solution than most other Web 2.0 tools, and unless the company has people with time to spare, this solution should be avoided.

Multiverse software is available for download at *www.multiversemmo.com*. Multiverse requires a server and a skilled programmer with enough time to implement all desired features.

For computer programs that manage voice chat, Skype is a VOIP (Voice Over IP) program that is free for Skype account to Skype account calls, but it tends to bog down a machine engaging in game-like online activities. Ventrilo has a modest monthly cost to have a server but is much gentler on machine performance. Additionally, some IM clients have voice chat capabilities.

There are two significant pitfalls to using a virtual community. First, ensure that company confidential information is not disclosed while traveling in the virtual world. You do not really know who you are talking to. Second, team members cannot spend so much time in the "fantasy" world that it hinders their work performance.

[D] Enhanced Company Directories

Everyone complains about a lack of communications in their company. In big companies, this lack is made worse because there are so many people that each person feels not only overlooked in communication but also insignificant as an individual. To enhance this sense of "self" and to improve the flow of information laterally, employees helping employees, company directories, and social networking sites are created.

Some of this structure is already in place. E-mail directories have long replaced printed telephone directories by including the employee's telephone number in his or her profile. It is the natural "go to" place for finding someone within the company. The next step is to expand this information base to include the data elements found in popular online tools.

Project managers use social networks to find personal information, such as pictures or even contacts from a friends list to assist when making hiring decisions. The contacts provide an unofficial extended reference list. The pictures posted are sometimes used to infer the personality of the person and some activities that might not be posted on a résumé. Like a blog, using such Web sites enables interested persons to relate more to an individual. From an internal perspective, such a site can improve the feeling of camaraderie in a group.

A successful implementation of an enhanced employee directory is Blue-Pages by IBM. It is utilized to send instant messages to a person and viewing tags created by him or her. This employee-edited tool allows customization of the appearance of the employee's page, such as what picture to show as well as the inclusion of a résumé. Project managers within the company can then use these BluePages to locate staff with the talents and skills they need to complete their projects.

Project managers can use social networks and directories to:

A. Help employees learn names through pictures.
B. Help managers in larger companies find the help they need within the company more easily via online résumés or similar listings.
C. Help employees see where they fit within a company through a set of links or a hierarchy diagram that is updated as changes occur.

The simplest way to set up an enhanced company directory is to utilize an existing company e-mail address book such as the one found in Outlook, and link to a Web page with all the necessary information. A Web 2.0 style directory reverses this with the Web page in the front and a link to the e-mail directory's data. However, this takes more effort to set up. It generally requires a Web site with a database back end located on the local intranet or approved public server. Employees are encouraged to add content, such as résumés, pictures, and even links to their own blogs or Web site bookmarks (see sections on blogs and tags).

There are several pitfalls to avoid when setting up an enhanced company directory. An employee-editable directory requires that employees are trusted and that there is a mechanism that unacceptable entries can be reported for management resolution. Because anyone can report unacceptable behavior, it should be rare. However, the acceptable use policy must be updated to identify those actions in a directory that would be considered undesirable and those that must not occur (typically a reflection of the company's standards of personal conduct).

People get bored with social network sites if the content becomes static. Although a personal Web page can inject some fun into the workplace, it must be guarded against hacking and require some measure of accuracy. (For example, it is unprofessional for employees to make unsubstantiated claims, such as they invented the Internet.)

[E] Twitter

Twitter is billed as a "social network" for staying in touch with friends and coworkers. It is a real-time short messaging service that asks one question, "What are you doing at this moment?" Answers must be 140 characters or less in length and can be sent via mobile texting, instant message, or the Internet. When you send a message using Twitter, it sends it out to your group of friends and posts it to your Twitter page.

Twitter's core technology is a message routing system that works with SMS (Short Message Service) from mobile devices, instant messaging, Internet, or from third-party APIs (Advance Power Interfaces). It acts as a rudimentary social networking platform for making it easy for people to stay connected.

Employees using Twitter on company time, equipment, or connections must ensure that their comments adhere to the company's policies on electronic communications. Employees using Twitter on their own time, using their own equipment and resources, should understand that their comments will still be constrained by the same electronic communications policies.

[F] LinkedIn

LinkedIn is the leading networking Web site for business professionals. LinkedIn allows professionals to stay in touch, get introduced to potential business partners, and share information about their areas of interest.

Employees using LinkedIn on company time, equipment, or connections must ensure that their comments adhere to the company's policies on electronic communications. Employees using LinkedIn on their own time, using their own equipment and resources, should understand that their comments will still be constrained by the same electronic communications policies.

Rather than ban the use of social networking tools at work, it is important for the organization to have a written policy that clearly defines how employees should use social networking Web sites such as LinkedIn, and also what, if any, information they can reveal about their employer on these Web sites.

COMMENT

According to most industry surveys, the average employee spends between one and two hours each day using the Internet for personal reasons.

[G] Facebook

Facebook began as a way for Harvard students to socialize and network using the Internet. It has since become the world's most popular social networking application with over 400 million users worldwide. Many adults are addicted to checking in on their Facebook friends and usage at work can cause many problems for an organization. Issues with Facebook usage at work include:

A. **Loss of productivity.** Time can slip away quickly while using Facebook, which means important work is not getting done.
B. **Bandwidth consumption.** While one person updating their status on Facebook is not going to bring down the corporate network, hundreds of people viewing pictures and using Facebook applications can consume precious Internet bandwidth.
C. **Spread of malware.** There are many third-party applications available on Facebook, some of which have not been verified to be free of malware.

COMMENT

According to a 2013 survey by Statista (*www.statista.com*), 29 percent of Americans use Facebook during work hours every day.

Of course, there are some legitimate business reasons for using Facebook. These include:

A. **Advertising.** Information about your products and services can be posted on your corporate Facebook page. People who love your products or services can become "fans," and spread the word to their network of friends.

B. **Background checks.** HR departments are increasingly using social networking applications such as Facebook to gather personal information about potential employees. If things you post on your Facebook page make the hiring decision makers uncomfortable, you are not likely to be hired.

C. **Recruiting.** Companies are using social networking tools such as Facebook to get the word out about what type of people they are looking to hire. Many times an online referral can be just as valuable as an offline one.

Organizations are also concerned about trade secrets and other confidential information being inadvertently disclosed on an employee's Facebook page. Hospitals are beginning to have issues with patients or their parents wanting to be "friends" on Facebook, which raises privacy and HIPAA issues. While many organizations are tempted to totally ban the use of Facebook at work, such a harsh policy could deter younger people from joining the company. It could also dispirit existing employees who are used to using these tools at home to communicate with peers.

Rather than ban the use of social networking tools at work, it is important for the organization to have a written policy that clearly defines how employees should use social networking Web sites such as Facebook, and also what, if any, information they can reveal about their employer on these Web sites. Such a policy should focus on how different groups of employees within the organization should use Facebook. For example, groups such as human resources and marketing might have complete access to Facebook, where other groups may have only limited access. Web filtering software is now available to control who can access Facebook and when access if available.

COMMENT

According to a 2012 regulatory filing, over 83 million Facebook profiles are fictitious. Facebook estimates that over 14 million have been setup for activities such as spamming.

See Policy ITP-22-4 Social Media Usage Policy as an example.

POLICY ITP-22-4. Social Media Usage Policy

Policy #:	ITP-22-4	Effective:	01/23/15	Page #:	1 of 2
Subject:		Social Media Usage Policy			

§ 22.03[G]

1.0 PURPOSE

This policy defines the use of social media on company time, as well as what can be said about the company on employee personal social media pages. While the use of social networking tools such as Facebook and LinkedIn can have important and legitimate benefits to the organization, abuse of such tools can also have a detrimental impact on productivity and can waste valuable corporate resources.

2.0 SCOPE

This policy applies to all employee personal social media pages or other social networking Web sites. It does not apply to corporate social media pages.

3.0 POLICY

The use of social media while at work for personal use must be restricted to break periods and lunch time. Avoid using social networking Web sites such as Facebook during normal work time. The company reserves the right to monitor use of social networking Web sites to check for abuse.

While the company respects the right of employees to use social networking Web sites at home, you must not be identified as an employee of the company while using such Web sites without the prior approval of the corporate communications department. The following guidelines must be followed to ensure that readers will not view you as a de facto spokesperson for the company:

A. You must make it clear to readers that any views you express are yours alone and that these views do not necessarily represent the views of the company. If there is any chance that you could be identified as an employee of the company when expressing personal views, you must provide the following notice in your communication:

> The views expressed on this networking Web site are mine alone and do not necessarily represent the views of my employer.

B. You must not disclose any information that is confidential or proprietary to the organization or to any customer or vendor that has disclosed such information to the company. Review the company's policy on confidential and proprietary information for guidance.

C. Any communication occurring in a public forum such as those identified previously in this policy must be respectful to the company, fellow employees, our affiliates, and our business partners.

D. The company may request at any time that you cease any communication concerning the company on social media Web sites or require you to block access to such communication if the company believes that such action is necessary to ensure compliance with government regulations or other laws.

E. Do not use the company's trademarks on any personal communication or reproduce any company material.

F. Do not use social media for communication with fellow employees or customers concerning business matters. Such communication must go through normal channels such as e-mail to comply with archiving requirements.

4.0 REVISION HISTORY

Date	Revision #	Description of Change
04/18/13	1.0	Initial creation.
01/23/15	1.1	Modified to cover all social media.

5.0 INQUIRIES

Direct inquiries about this policy to:

George Jenkins, CIO
Our Company, Inc.
2900 Corporate Drive
Columbus, OH 43215

Voice: 614-555-1234
Fax: 614-555-1235
E-mail: gjenkins@company.com

Revision #:	1.1	Supersedes:	1.0	Date:	01/23/15

§ 22.04 SYNDICATION

[A] RSS Feeds

Various stakeholders wish to receive different types of communications. The method of distribution varies from manager to manager, from team member to team member, and from recipient to recipient. One way Web 2.0 tools can simplify this information flow is by using Really Simple Syndication (RSS). RSS is software that publishes, organizes, and delivers blog posts, news articles, and Wiki modifications. They can also do simpler things such as deliver traffic and weather reports. Delivery can be event-by-event or digest-form e-mail, depending on how a user subscribes.

COMMENT

Netscape first developed RSS in 1999. The RSS symbol is 🔊, which was first used around late 2005 by Mozilla Firefox.

RSS tools can distribute just about anything that can be received by a computer, such as:

A. News releases
B. Updates to a Wiki or blog
C. New articles in a favorite magazine
D. Webcasts

An RSS feed is essentially an XML document formatted so that it is ready for use by the aggregator. Ideally, a project creates its own Web page using RSS feeds to significant information sources. This mash up combines services or information from multiple Web sites into one that is pulled down to your workstation.

RSS can be used to keep the project manager apprised of changes in the environment. For example, if materials must arrive at a certain time, the project manager might choose to monitor suppliers, West Coast longshoreman unions, and anything else that might impede the delivery.

To begin using RSS, download aggregator software to your workstation. Customize it to search for content using specific keywords. The Web site *www.whatisrss.com* provides links to Web sites for a number of platforms that are feed readers, such as Yahoo (My Yahoo), Bloglines, and Google (iGoogle). Mozilla Firefox contains an in-browser reader that allows a Web site's recent RSS content to be viewed by clicking the RSS symbol in the address bar.

To publish using RSS, go to *www.rss-specifications.com* and select Creation Software to acquire syndication software. Many Wiki and blog hosts automatically format the content for syndication, so no extra work is required in this case. Also, some blog software enables reformatting the blog into an RSS feed.

There are several pitfalls when using RSS feeds:

A. Too much data takes too much time sifting gems from gravel.
B. RSS can perform unattended downloads and make unattended connections.
C. An exploit could infect you through an update.
D. Malicious code may be hidden inside of XML.
E. JavaScript malicious code is difficult to detect.
F. Weak programming standards have resulted in weak security.
G. RSS readers are susceptible to attack browsers.

[B] Photo and Video Sharing

It is true that a picture is worth a thousand words when explaining something to someone. Photo and video sharing Web sites provide a way to publish and share your pictures movies, animations, and other graphics. There are several types of hosting sites, but the main two divisions among free sites are those that are ad supported and those that are photo finishing sites trying to sell services.

Photo and video sharing can be used to:

A. Reveal a new product.
B. Store images and movies for linking from blogs or Wikis.
C. Introduce team members and encourage them to share pictures and possibly home videos with one another to help remove anonymity in the company and improve morale.
D. Reduce company need to print photos and other graphics, allowing it to be hosted/shared/published. One way in which this differs from e-mail is that it doesn't consume space in the user's inbox.
E. Distribute tutorials.
F. Record anything else that may be of interest to anyone within the company or to customers.

Flickr, Photobucket, and similar Web sites allow free posting of pictures and other images. To engage in photo sharing, all that is really needed is a server or other computer to store the images and a way to allow users to view them. Depending on the level of security needed, this can be on a company hosted server or a more public place such as Flickr or Photobucket.

The most popular example of video sharing is YouTube. The main page provides links to featured and promoted videos. A search can be done to find videos, and when one is being watched, a panel containing related videos is shown for easy access to others. Videos are hosted without cost. The posts track the number of views and allow comments to be left by viewers. The author is also allowed a title block containing a title, a short description, any public messages, and contact information. Navigate to *www.youtube.com*, create an account, and post away. Be sure that you have rights and permission to post any content.

A very helpful feature often implemented with photo and video sharing, usually included in the host Web site, is tagging. As mentioned above, tagging serves to help individuals find what they are looking for more efficiently.

An alternative to posting on these Web sites would be to use RSS to distribute videos, but the ideal would be to use RSS to distribute text-based media with links to these items.

Some downsides to photo and video sharing include:

A. These photos and videos still take up space on a server somewhere, and they will either take up extranet bandwidth to download or they will take up internal server space.
B. The possibility of not being able to use your photos and videos if an external site is used! Be aware that many companies block YouTube to ensure proper use of company resources; however, this would not prevent sharing through alternative means, such as through a company-sanctioned blog or company Web site.

23

AGILE PROJECT MANAGEMENT: SOFTWARE AT THE SPEED OF BUSINESS

§ 23.01 OVERVIEW

[A] Purpose and Scope

Project management and software projects go together like oil and water. Companies invest millions of dollars in software development projects and need a project management framework to ensure the team stays focused on the project. The traditional methods do not always work.

If you are building a bridge, then you must design the entire structure from end to end before beginning. This ensures that the foundations will be able to support the weight of traffic and the bridge itself. Developed over the millennium (since the pyramids), what we now think of as traditional project management has worked well. However, for some reason, many software projects were failing using the same methods.

The traditional project management model emphasizes planning up front what will be done and when it will be accomplished. Buyers can see buildings and bridges—tangible objects. They have a good idea of what they want and can even watch them go together. Software is different. Each software system is unique. Where an architect may spend many months preparing and analyzing a construction site, the software customer cannot "see" software assembled and they want work to begin now.

Project sponsors only have a vague idea of what they want and have no idea of how it goes together. For a multiyear programming project, this means looking ahead to guess what the software will look like after a long period of development. This approach is not responsive to a changing, dynamic environment. These projects frequently run over schedule and over budget—if they complete at all. When they finish, it often is not what the client needs today.

To address these shortcomings, some creative IT Project Managers tried focusing on the end goal: developing working software that provides the functions that the client actually wanted. Their work began a new style of IT Project Management known as "Agile."

Agile simplifies management activities and eliminates much of the built-in delays found in traditional project management. It emphasizes face-to-face communication among the team members, the Project Manager, and the customer. Often the entire project team is located in the same open work area.

Agile is less susceptible to the problems that plague traditionally managed projects, such as:

A. **Inflexible plans.** Making a budget and plan before the project begins hinders its ability to quickly respond to changes in customer requirements. Every proposed change requires time for negotiation and approval. Agile develops software iteratively and tests frequently. This prompt feedback resolves problems early in the process when they are least expensive.

B. **Inaccurate estimates.** Traditional projects make time estimates based on initial planning. Agile uses an overall rough estimate for the project. Each task's duration is estimated immediately before execution. Simple metrics provide the team feedback on estimate accuracy.

C. **Issues with integration.** Software and hardware systems rarely come together without a hitch. By catching issues early, these problems can be preempted before they become larger problems.

COMMENT

An analogy of Agile project development is creating a spreadsheet. Consider two approaches:

1. Create a detailed design of all rows and columns. Document the permissible content of the cells and all functions to be used. When the design appears to be complete, then the work can begin.
2. Begin with a vague idea of the desired final product. Start creating rows and columns. Insert formulas as you go and check with some data. If something does not seem right—just change it. When the final product provides sufficient value, end the task. Every so often, save the work in a backup so a known good older version can be reverted to.

The first approach is the traditional project management approach of knowing where you are going before you begin. The second is the Agile approach where you have a general idea of where you are going and refine that vision as the project executes.

[B] Defining Agile

Agile is a project management technique for software development through simplicity. According to the Manifesto for Agile Software Development (*www.agilemanifesto.org*), the Agile philosophy includes:

A. **Favoring individuals and interactions over processes and tools.** Processes and tools add a significant amount of overhead, which often exceeds the value added. Agile simplifies processes to the minimum effort required.
B. **Working software over comprehensive documentation.** Agile strives to minimize complications. This frees the development team to focus on the project. Often documentation is generated because the process says to do it rather than due to a customer request.

C. **Customer collaboration over contract negotiation.** Most customers have only a general idea of what they want. Locking their first thoughts in a detailed project requirements document guarantees failure because the customer may get exactly what was asked for but not what was wanted. Timely customer collaboration means that the development team will have more feedback sooner, so discrepancies are realized promptly.

D. **Responding to change over following a plan.** Planning gives a path forward, necessary to schedule work, but being inflexible in the plan is frustrating and unfruitful.

[C]   Comparing Agile with Traditional Project Management

Traditional project management has its roots in the creation of physical objects. Pyramids, skyscrapers, and large ships are complex things. Their creation is well suited to traditional project management. A thorough understanding of the customer's requirements is necessary before any work begins. Otherwise, extensive reworking may be required to accommodate changes, or the required changes are never made. In both cases, the customer will not be satisfied.

This problem, identifying all of the requirements before work begins, is at the heart of customer dissatisfaction with software development. Few customers fully understand what they want or the implications of later changes. As the product begins to take shape, new ideas spring to the customer's mind. The business climate might shift and open new opportunities or challenges arise from competitors. Depending on customers to identify what they need in advance, and anticipating only minor changes before completion of the project, is not realistic.

Another driver is the company executive's desire of "when" and "how much." To establish a completion date and final project cost, a clear set of specifications is required. Any changes to these requirements will impact the cost and completion date.

Agile changes these basic project management assumptions. Now a project is roughly estimated based on a vague scope that describes the final product based on the current vision. A budget is approved and work begins. The overall project is worked in small pieces. At any point (usually at the end of a "Release"), the project can be declared as "done" enough.

IT Managers have long struggled with this dilemma. The customer demands a firm budget and schedule for the project to begin but only vaguely knows what they want. The result is ongoing conflict with the customer about paying for new features. A project team may even hide problems from the customer to complete the project on time (you get what you reward). However, this focuses on time and cost rather than on customer satisfaction. See Exhibit 23-1 Traditional vs. Agile Project Management.

EXHIBIT 23-1. Traditional vs. Agile Project Management

Application	Traditional Project Management	Agile Project Management
Overall Strategy	Disciplined planning Focused on ceremony	Just-in-time planning Focus on coding, testing, and software delivery
Organizational Structure	Static, hierarchical organization Team members are like interchangeable parts Team members are generally one-area experts	Interaction-oriented Tasks arranged to fit individuals Team has redundant skill sets, which boosts efficiency
Planning	Intensive up-front planning Is tied to a schedule that is awkward to adjust to unforeseen necessary changes Plans are rarely good enough to mitigate unpredictable problems	Just-in-time approach to planning Never assumes schedule is good past the current iteration, but provides an overall estimate Planning is flexible enough to handle problems beginning no later than the next iteration
Change	Minimizes change through a rigid process Making value-added changes is difficult Time lost waiting for customer approval	Adapts to change, using it as an opportunity rather than a roadblockValue-added changes are cost-effective due to the nature of iterations Customer representative empowered to act, sits with team
Addressing Risk	Attempts to mitigate risk through up-front planning	Iterations builds risk management directly into the development cycle
Maintaining Order	More control through rigid instructions	Basic rules that are just enough to set limits without suffocating the team
Information Flow	Centrally located, distribution varies Code owned by individuals Customer communication intense up front, minimal throughout	Open access Collective code ownership On-site customer or at least very regular personal interaction

[D]   Critical Policies to Develop Based on This Chapter

Using the material discussed in this chapter, you will be able to create an Agile projects policy that includes:

A. Work area
B. Team responsibilities
C. Artifacts to be created and retained when no longer required
D. Metrics to collect and post
E. Estimating projects

Policies should always be developed based on the local situation. Successful managers cannot issue appropriate guidance if the policies are written with another company's situation or location in mind.

§ 23.02   CULTIVATING AN AGILE CULTURE

[A]   Getting Started

Agile project management is different from traditional project management. Agile believes in the contributions and insights of the individual team members. Converting a project team to an Agile mindset may require up to a year before the group functions smoothly together. The Agile work environment plays a key role in team development and project success. Agile tries to:

A. Encourage creativity and flexibility when approaching a problem. Listen to everyone's ideas. This shows respect to the team member and raises morale.
B. Remove distractions and obstacles from the physical and computing environment.
C. Improve communication by placing the entire team, as well as the Project Manager and the client, in the same open room.
D. Encourage collaboration by providing white boards and shared table space.
E. Ensure that the team is not competing to score higher on whatever job grading curve they perceive exists in regard to their job status. This builds trust and more open communications.

[B]   Simplicity Saves Time

Simplicity reduces unnecessary work in a project. The unnecessary work is wasted labor. Simplicity also reduces risk by reducing chances for a failure to occur. The fewer the steps in a process, the fewer are the opportunities to make an error. Further, simplicity enhances communications to allow all stakeholders to better understand the project progress. Agile does this by:

A. Conveying progress and tasking assignments using easy to read visual tools. At any time, a stakeholder can see the current project status.
B. Utilizing a small set of metrics based on key qualities of the project for clear communications.
C. Creating tasks of small, easily estimated activities.
D. Focusing on a small subset of requirements at each iteration. This quickly provides something substantial.

COMMENT

This is similar to the Japanese manufacturing process of "lean" manufacturing. Lean identifies seven types of waste to identify and drive out of processes. Whenever possible, completely eliminate the process step.

[C]   Mitigate That Risk

Risk mitigation guards against potential problems. Agile does this through flexibility. A sudden adverse change such as a team member absent for a week does not halt the progress. A measure of this agility is the project's "truck number." The truck number is how many members of the team would need to be hit by a truck during lunch to severely hamper a project.

One way to increase the truck number is to develop cross-functional teams. An Agile project management concept is collective code ownership and cross-functional teams (where each team member has multiple duties regarding documentation, testing, and writing code). In projects where each developer is an expert on one type of activity or one piece of the code, the absence of one team member can hamper or threaten progress on the project. The most agile teams keep their truck number as high as possible.

Another way to increase the truck number is to prevent one person from becoming the sole expert on a piece of code. Different team members will all work on or with a piece of code over time to ensure multiple people understand its inner workings.

Agile combats risk by developing software iteratively. Some risk mitigation techniques that are enabled by iterative development include:

A. Focusing on developing functioning software. Testing early and often to develop a stable, stand-alone version with specific features.
B. Developing tests for features first, and then developing the feature.
C. Only engaging in tasks that add value in the eyes of the customer.
D. Soliciting feedback from the customer on a frequent basis. This allows the project manager to adjust the course of the project or to fix mistakes before they become ingrained in the code.

E. Investigating and exploring features shortly before implementation. This allows the feature to be revised based on the client's current requirements.

[D]   The Role of the Agile Project Manager

In a traditional project, the Project Manager "drives" the team forward, urging, nudging, cajoling, bribing, pleading, demanding, threatening—whatever is required to keep the team members focused on the goal. This is not the Agile way.

A successful Agile Project Manager is also a good leader. In traditional project management, it is much easier to follow a process from beginning to end, step by step. Agile methodologies free the Project Manager to focus on leadership. An Agile Project Manager's responsibilities include:

A. Monitoring team progress. Knowing where the team is succeeding and where it is lagging or failing.
B. Identifying and removing obstacles.
C. Facilitating discussions rather than dictating instructions.
D. Setting appropriate guidelines for team dynamics. Monitoring how the team interacts, and if necessary, intervening. Encouraging the team to organize themselves in the way most helpful for them while making sure no one is shut out or that cliques are formed.
E. Continually refocusing the team on the vision. Informing the team of the project's intent, and then letting them run with it. At every plan meeting, reminding them of the project's vision.
F. Ensuring the team feels comfortable telling the project manager when something is wrong, sub-optimal, or just when the team member disagrees with them.
G. Facilitating collaboration and communication. Breaking down information barriers. Providing white boards. Setting up Wikis and other Web 2.0 tools. Ensuring everyone has a chance to speak.

[E]   Team Member Responsibilities

Agile team members perform many duties:

A. **Implementing a feature.** Creating project deliverables desired in the finished product.
B. **Testing.** A feature cannot be completed until it has been tested. Agile requires writing a feature's test prior to creating it.
C. **Fixing a bug.** Testing finds defects in the code. Bugs are tracked via a prioritized list.
D. **Documenting the project.** Create value-added documentation.
E. **Refactoring code.** Through reuse, code frequently becomes bloated. Take time to identify and remove excess from the code.
F. **Accommodating customer requests.** Anything the client wants done is assigned as a task. This creates the risk of scope creep. It is the customer's responsibility to ensure that all requests add value.

§ 23.03 AGILE FEATURES

[A] Managing Progress Through Features

Project sponsors rarely know exactly what they want. They have a vague idea but until they can see the software in action, cannot tell you specifically what they need. However, programming languages are very long on specifics and short on vagueness. Programmers need to know the data entry field, the edits, the storage, how fields are combined or referenced, how the system interfaces with other software and so on—and all of it specific. It has been this disconnection between the customer vagueness and the software specificity that has led to so many project failures.

Agile projects ask clients to describe projects as a story. Software requirements derived from the story are broken down into smaller units of individual features. A feature is a unit of functionality that adds business value to the project. Features are the main planning unit and describe the value to be created. Characteristics of a feature include enough detail to estimate the work and a defined set of tests to verify its completion.

Any stakeholder can suggest a feature. Features are described in more detail through discussions with these stakeholders, the testers, and developers. One team member is responsible for managing the list and avoiding duplication. To keep everyone involved, the feature list manager cannot refuse to add any features to the list. However, features that add excessive risk with minimal value continually percolate to the bottom of the priority list and will likely never be implemented.

Every feature on the list needs an estimate of how long it will take to complete it and how much value is expected to come from it. The entire list is prioritized in one ranking to avoid ambiguity. The work involved and the return on investment estimates can help in this ranking. When in doubt, keep the prioritizing process simple.

Each feature on the list is described with:

A. **Description.** What the feature will accomplish. This helps tests to be developed and estimates to be made.
B. **Tests for Acceptance.** Tests that demonstrate that the feature is "done." Leave these vague until the iteration for which the feature is scheduled.
C. **Return on Investment (ROI).** How much value is being gathered.
D. **Ultimate Priority.** The importance assigned to completing the feature. Consider sorting primarily by customer identified ROI and secondarily on risk.
E. **Category.** Sometimes features are somewhat similar or are coded within the same area. This may enable grouping features together for efficient creation.
F. **Effort Estimate.** A descriptive term chosen by the team to represent the complexity and difficulty of the feature.

[B] Planning Poker—Estimating Agile Time

Agile teams describe progress and work remaining in terms of the assigned effort estimate. This gives a clearer picture of what has been accomplished or what will be accomplished. Explaining progress in terms of features and tasks is not as meaningful because not all tasks and features require the same effort or provide the same benefit. Past team estimates form the basis for improved estimation over time. This is a big benefit of Agile.

Estimates by their nature are not exact. Issues that interfere with our ability to create good estimates include:

A. Individuals by themselves rarely have adequate knowledge to consistently produce accurate estimates.
B. Team estimation can be tricky as one individual can easily influence individuals in the group.
C. Anchoring can occur when the first person to offer an estimate impacts the thinking of the rest of the team.

One of the more popular techniques used by Agile teams to determine feature estimates is to play Planning Poker. The method was first described by James Grenning in 2002 and later popularized by Mike Cohn in his book *Agile Estimating and Planning*. Planning Poker is based on the Delphi method, where participants vote and the results are presented immediately. In Planning Poker, each person on the team is given a deck of cards. The values on the cards represent a sequence of numbers that represent values that the team uses for estimation. Units typically used for estimation can include:

A. Actual days.
B. Ideal time (no interruptions, fast computers, no bugs).
C. Relative difficulty (easy, average, hard, very hard).
D. Story points, which is a relative indication of how long it will take a programmer to implement the feature or story.

The cards are marked with increasing values, typically using the Fibonacci sequence including a zero (0, 1, 2, 3, 5, 8, 13, 21, 34, 55, 89) or some other progression of values.

For each feature or story, the following sequence is followed:

A. The Product Manager provides an overview of a feature.
B. The team discusses what is required to code the feature, without expressing any time or number values.
C. Each team member lays a card face down, with everyone turning them over at the same time.
D. Team members whose values are significantly different than the average are asked to explain their estimates. This may be a sign that the task is not defined well enough or is too large to be accurately estimated. It could also be a sign of significant optimism, pessimism, or naiveté.
E. The vote is recast until the results converge on one value.

Other significant factors in building estimates are:

A. Those who do the work set the time estimate (not managers). The worker has the best feel for their own capabilities.
B. Smaller tasks are easier to estimate accurately. If a task is too large, there are too many variables in it to begin to formulate a reasonable estimate. In such a case, break it up into smaller portions.

The most popular approach is to estimate tasks in terms of ideal hours (no interruptions, fast computers, no bugs). The team is not held strictly to these hours for scheduling, as they are ideal hours. For example, after an iteration with 400 man-hours, perhaps only 100 ideal hours' worth of features were delivered. The ideal hours number can be used to predict time required for future iterations. In this case, the Project Manager knows the team can accomplish 100 ideal hours of work in an iteration. Therefore, if the total backlog has 560 ideal hours of work remaining, the Project Manager can estimate that the project will likely require another six iterations.

COMMENT

An excellent source for Planning Poker playing cards can be found at *store.mountaingoatsoftware.com*.

§ 23.04   AGILE METRICS

[A]   Fundamental Metrics

Project Managers are asked a number of questions by both clients and management. How much will all of this cost? When will the project be done? How many bugs are there? Agile methods have a set of metrics that help answer each of these questions, which call for various estimates or summaries. Well-defined measurements help to standardize communication and make planning easier. Metrics can help do things such as:

A. **Assigning the expected ROI on work completed or pending features.** The ROI estimation is provided by the customer with input from other stakeholders.
B. **Designating how much work a feature is expected to take.** A rough estimate is provided at the project inception and then more carefully when the feature is chosen for inclusion in an iteration.
C. **Determining how much work can be reasonably attempted during an iteration.** This is based on past recent team history and the estimations for each feature selected. This is represented as a velocity.

    D. **Projecting a completion date.** This can also be done by looking at prior velocity and applying it to the remaining features.

Agile metrics provide basic, significant information about the project that are simple to collect and easy to understand:

    A. **Tasks Completed.** This is a helpful metric to present, because it does not encourage the team to concentrate on pumping out the maximum number of features while neglecting bugs and choosing not to re-factor code.

    B. **Known Bugs.** How many tests are currently being failed and/or how many defects are known.

    C. **Features Remaining.** Look at the feature list to determine this.

    D. **Task Size.** This can be as "small-medium-large," "4, 8, or 16 hours," or a label such as "need time to learn" or "too large to reliably estimate."

    E. **Elapsed Time.** This can be in hours, man-hours, or days.

    F. **Risk.** This estimate can be in terms of value and/or estimated time. Risk should be considered whenever a new bug is discovered. Some bugs may not be worth fixing in the eyes of the customer.

    G. **Resource Cost.** Monetary and other resources consumed. This should be figured for each development cycle.

[B]   Derived Metrics

Metrics can be combined into new measurements called "derived metrics." An example of a derived metric or unit is speed. A car's speedometer shows how many miles or kilometers per hour a car is traveling. A mile or kilometer is a metric for distance and an hour is a metric for time. They are combined to give speed. When combined with a direction, it gives velocity. The same applies to metrics used with Agile project management. Useful derived metrics for Agile include:

    A. **Velocity.** How much the team accomplishes in an iteration. This is found by dividing the total work done by the length of the iteration. The total work done is the sum of the effort estimates of all completed tasks. All estimates should be converted to one type (such as three large is the same as nine small).

    B. **Resource burn rate.** How much of a given resource is being consumed by the project. This is the total resource cost divided by the length of the iteration.

    C. **Task burndown.** How many tasks the team is completing. This is shown very well in a burndown chart (shown later in this chapter). The task burndown is simply how many tasks were completed each day, or in each iteration.

    D. **Value delivered.** The sum of the values assigned to each feature accepted by the client.

    E. **Defect rate.** The number of bugs being discovered per iteration or per feature completed.

[C]   Guidelines for Using Metrics

Some guidelines to enhance the effectiveness of the metrics are:

A. **Use simple metrics.** Complicated metrics add overhead both during collection and when explaining them.

B. **Only use metrics that add value.** The value added by the metric must be greater than what it cost to gather the data. If a metric has not added value after a few iterations, scrap it.

C. **Minimize the number of metrics collected.** Adhere to the principles of value-added and being simple to collect to pare down the number of metrics to a minimal useful set.

D. **On occasion, change your metrics.** People tend to focus on what is measured and neglect the rest. For this reason, it may be useful to change which metrics are being used from time to time.

E. **Metrics are only meaningful when used relative to one team.** Different people approach problems differently. For this reason, the numbers for one team cannot be compared to another team for the same reason.

The goal is to reach the optimal velocity, not the maximum. Maximum velocity does not necessarily imply maximum productivity. Refactoring, testing, and debugging may not occur if a team is only rewarded or recognized for the number of features they complete.

[D]   Analyzing Metrics

The goal of collecting metric data is to use it for some purpose. (Otherwise, why spend the effort?) With all of the metric data collected, it is important to utilize the information. Here are some key ways to examine metrics:

A. **Present metrics within context.** The most obvious way to present a metric is to say "The team has completed 50 features,"—that is, to give one number by itself. However, that doesn't really tell anything useful. A more useful statement is to give a baseline, "The team has completed 65 features, 50 of which are from the original 300. The scope has increased to include a total of 320 features."

B. **Examine trends.** A team may have had no new bugs last week but suddenly they have 10 new bugs this week. This is less troublesome in context in that, on average, the team has been finding about five bugs per week over the last six weeks. Notice how multiple metrics are combined here—Known Bugs and Elapsed Time.

C. **Compare apples to apples.** Only compare values for a team with values from the same team. Another team of the same size, in the same amount of time, may have completed twice as many features but have five times as many bugs. Then consider that each team has a different meaning for "bug" and that they can hardly be compared to each other at all.

D. **Represent data visually.** Visual tools provide insight into the progress of a project. When posted in a public location, they also provide motivation for the team to make the chart look good (i.e., make steady headway). One good tool is the Burndown Chart, shown in Exhibit 23-2.

[E] Burndown Charts

Metrics should be presented graphically and posted in a prominent place for the team to review them. This shares information on project progress and enhances team ownership of their project's results. Two types of burndown charts are the Iteration and the Release. In general, the top part of the column is work accomplished in that period, and the lower part is work remaining. The next entry begins with work remaining, but its total also adjusts for any work added or removed.

Refer to Exhibit 23-2 Iteration Burndown. In iterations, the team is focused on accomplishing the tasks at hand, whether feature implementation, refactoring, or testing. Accordingly, the iteration burndown is in terms of the number of tasks remaining.

EXHIBIT 23-2. Iteration Burndown

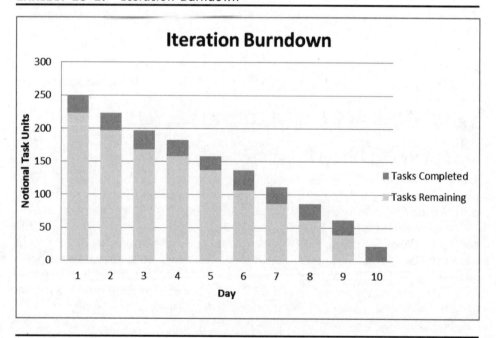

In the Release Burndown chart in Exhibit 23-3, each iteration is designated by its release followed by which iteration it is in that release (the third iteration in the second release is 2-3). Notice that the units have changed to being in terms of features. Acceptable units include value, number of features, requirements, feature size or complexity, along with any other unit that represents features.

The chart is in terms of features because true project progress is measured by value delivered. Coding, testing and maintenance are all essential

EXHIBIT 23-3. Release Burndown

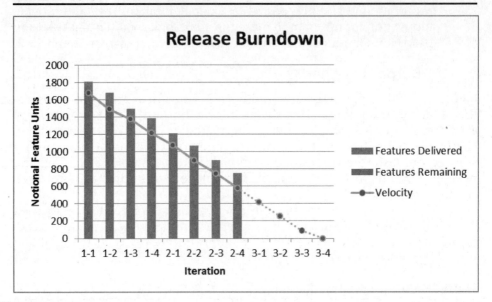

development tasks, but none of them individually deliver value. Value has only truly been delivered when the client accepts a feature as being complete.

§ 23.05 THE AGILE DEVELOPMENT CYCLE

[A] The Agile Product Life Cycle

Much like traditional project management, Agile projects go through life cycle phases. They also go through the same steps as a traditionally managed project only with a different order and with different emphasis at each point.

An Agile development cycle is just that—a cycle. It is broken into mini-projects called "iterations." The entire project is not attempted in a single iteration. Rather, each iteration should be just long enough to accomplish something useful. The first iteration builds a basic version of the desired product. The customer inspects it, and then adds features to the requirements list for the next iteration. Every few iterations perform a product release.

The differences between the life cycles are:

A. The up-front requirements development in Agile is focused and brief. Where traditional project management attempts to define everything up front in substantial detail, Agile defines everything up front with just enough information to help the team understand what is going on and to pick out a starting point for the first iteration and first release.

B. Agile performs a mini-waterfall cycle over and over again, once for each requirement, in a just-in-time manner. Requirements are only analyzed and discussed in thorough detail when they are selected for an iteration. The meeting for the start of an iteration should generally only last two to four hours. Any less time and details are probably being skipped. Any longer time and the task is probably being over-killed. Imagine the process shaped as a spiral. With each turn of the spiral, more of the solution is uncovered.

C. Agile delivers software at the end of every release, which can be as often as the team would like. This allows for mutually beneficial feedback from the customer and other stakeholders before beginning the next release.

Planning is accomplished on two levels. The iteration level involves choosing features to implement and defining them in greater depth. At the release level, the goal is to determine what the customer needs, would like, and can do without at the end of the release when the next functioning version of software is released.

Agile saves detailed planning for just before the information is needed. This permits including the project knowledge to date as well as the customer's current requirements. Just-in-time planning provides a systematic way to accommodate changes requested by the customer.

These four phases occur over the lifetime of the Agile project as well as each release and iteration. Each of these phases ends with a re-synchronization of user expectations and a decision point to continue or kill a project:

A. **Project Inception.** Definition and agreement of all stakeholders as to scope. The scope of the project is determined by many examples that define required functions. Initial systems architecture is developed. Cost, schedule, and risk are estimated.

B. **Elaboration.** Project engineering encompassing the details of the problem and possible solutions are formed. Time, cost, and risk estimates are refined. A prototype is constructed.

C. **Construction.** A working system is built.

D. **Transition.** The product now has sufficient business value to be turned over to the customer.

[1] Project Inception

Project inception is similar to starting any other type of project. Requirements are gathered, risks are evaluated, a business case is assembled, and technical feasibility is checked. These are all of the usual project start-up actions. The Project Manager ensures that all the time spent adds value to the project. Project requirements are combined to create a project vision statement. The vision statement describes what the finished product will look like and how it will perform. It also includes measurable performance criteria.

COMMENT

Inception (and all other phases) lacks many of the traditional tools, which are not perceived as value-adding in Agile. One traditional tool that is still useful is the critical path, which defines which features have others as a prerequisite. This is done at a high level, so as to not be caught off guard when the customer wants to finish in one iteration, and the last crucial feature depends on many things not currently completed.

At the beginning, there needs to be enough definition and clarity that the team can begin with the (somewhat hazy) big picture in mind. This provides a foundation vision that gradually becomes clearer as more work is accomplished. Just enough planning should be done to get started with the first iteration and lay out a high-level release plan. The first feature list is like a napkin sketch or a rough draft and reflects the potential result of the project, given enough time. There is no need to wait until every detail has been added to the list.

The customer provides a representative on-site to serve as the Product Owner. The Product Owner plays a crucial role in development, bearing the responsibility for choosing which features are next for development. The Product Owner must be available on-site as much as possible—ideally all day, each working day. This way, when a feature has been selected that has inevitably been described in ambiguous terms, the team can consult the Product Owner and get an answer immediately, or at least get the question to and through the customer's proper channels with the help of the Product Owner.

Once requirements have been gathered and the business case has been made, the project is declared to be technically feasible and the basic architecture for the product is proposed. The customer agrees to the project definition (scope, vision, and measurable success criteria). The schedule and costs are approved, which includes approved plans for the elaboration phase.

[2] Elaboration

The elaboration phase is similar to the typical project design phase. It creates a tested technical design that forms the basis for the final product. During this phase, the requirements and features are analyzed further to identify architecturally significant requirements. The high-level architecture is developed and tested to ensure it can provide the technical performance required by the specifications. Sometimes this may require building a prototype to validate the architectural design. Ensuring that the architecture can support the desired construction is a key risk mitigation action.

COMMENT
Failure to adequately design and test the architecture is a common cause for failure during the development phase.

At the conclusion of this phase, the risks have been updated, as are the appropriate mitigation actions. This is accomplished through extensive use of case analysis plus architecture testing. The project's business case is updated and enough information is made available for a decision by the customer. If the project is to proceed, the project plan and budget for development are then approved.

[3] Development

Development entails the actual coding activity and anything that adds value, such as light documentation, routine testing, and maintenance. During development, the specification of the features derived from requirements during elaboration is formalized and coding begins. This formalization only happens once a feature is selected for implementation for the next iteration.

As the coding progresses, the results are tested extensively. The product is compared to the desired outcomes described in the use cases. Product testing verifies component performance, as well as conformance, to requirements. Time is set aside to create the user documentation and technical support manuals. The project plan and budget for the transition phase are approved.

[4] Transition

When the project is nearing completion, it needs to be transitioned to the customer. Extensive acceptance testing is now performed. The continuous testing performed throughout the project should have reduced the remaining problems to minor performance and functionality issues. Technical efforts in this phase concentrate on promptly resolving defects. Data may require migration prior to testing the new system. In some cases, the new technology must also run parallel to the current system. The product is checked against the promised product quality described in the inception phase.

The future support team is now trained on the technical aspects of the product. They verify that the technical support manual created in the construction phase is acceptable. Training is provided to end users so that they can understand how to use the product features. At the end of this phase, a customer satisfaction survey is provided to those who participated in the use case development effort to fine-tune future efforts.

It ends when the customer accepts the final product and their technical maintenance team takes responsibility for ongoing support. At the end of the transition phase, the project is administratively closed and preparations begin for the next project.

[B]   Releases: The Macro Cycle

Agile projects are developed in high-level cycles known as releases. The goal of a release is to have stable, integrated, and tested software. At the start of the project, a release plan is developed which applies to all releases. This is a game plan that gives guidance on how to handle problems as they arise. Like other Agile plans, this one is not set in stone. To maintain agility, if one or more of the project releases determine something else is required, then the plan is changed.

Releases should be stand-alone products. At the beginning of the project, a release product may be a very empty shell, but it should begin to mimic the form of the vision that is being tended and grown as the project progresses through successive iterations. The release plan considers the overall effort and breaks the project down into smaller projects. The macro cycle for releases follows the following steps:

A. **Release Plan** When setting the scope for the current iteration the following actions should be taken:
   1. Establish a business model. The framework of expectations for both the customer and the development team are defined for the project.
   2. Gather core requirements using a function and feature list. This is usually accomplished through the development of use cases.
   3. Craft a high level outline of the releases and iterations. With this information in place, an iteration plan can be developed. The key points to an iteration plan are:
      a. A list of requirements for the entire project. Each requirement should have the information listed earlier, including a priority and estimation of size.
      b. A work breakdown structure. This enumerates which personnel are assigned to which tasks, and in what order the tasks should be handled.
      c. A critical path or similar diagram, showing the tasks that must be completed and/or are underway before another task can either begin or be finished.
      d. A schedule based on the previous information that will be followed during the iteration.
      e. A risk management process for identifying, assessing, and assigning responsibility for mitigating risks. The individual iterations will use this guidance to address their risks.
      f. A problem resolution plan (commonly known as an issues list) to track problems that arise and to assure that someone is assigned to resolve them.
      g. A product acceptance process to describe the types of tests that the customer requires.
         A release is typically between one and six months in length. The proportion between the release and iteration length should be between 2:1 and 8:1. Releases need not be the same length; though keeping a similar length is easier to manage.
B. **Feature Selection** Usually, the features chosen are the highest priority features, but do not forget that tasks (testing, documentation, etc.)

should be included as well. If features come up that seem like they will be too large to fit in an iteration or too large to be estimated, they should be broken down further. The smaller units are coding tasks that can be tested easily and correspond to one check in using revision control software.

Feature selection is based on the amount of work the Project Manager believes can be accomplished given the team's prior velocity. The release plan should be revised after each iteration to reflect reality and the new knowledge gained by the team.

C. **Wrapping up the Release** Finally, the closing phase is when the customer determines whether or not to proceed with an additional iteration. The product may now be deemed to be up to specifications, or it may be deemed to have made insufficient progress to continue. If the customer decides to continue, the next iteration plan must be approved and the project continues.

[C] Iterations: The Micro Cycle

Within the framework of releases are a series of smaller projects known as iterations. Each of the iterations is itself a small and complete project. The micro cycle for releases follows the following steps:

A. **Iteration Plan** An iteration plan plots a course of action for meeting the goals for the current or upcoming iteration. At any time, there are usually two iteration plans being referenced and/or written: the plan for the current iteration, and the plan for the next iteration. In earlier stages of an iteration, more focus will likely be placed on adhering to the plan for the current iteration. Later on, the iteration plan for the next iteration will become more important.

This is the time to assess the customer's comfort level for each defined function. Any perceived problems expressed by the customer should be resolved.

COMMENT

Iteration-based metrics such as velocity are very hard to measure if the iteration length changes or if the team composition changes. Iterations are very controllable, and unlike most things in Agile development, these should probably seldom change, except to perhaps accommodate a holiday. Most teams use an iteration length of one to six weeks, with two or three weeks being the most common.

When setting the iteration length, consider the following:
1. An iteration should be just long enough to produce something useful.

2. When the iteration is over, it is time to seek feedback and begin another iteration. By keeping the length short, the risk that a single lurking issue can threaten the project is averted.

3. Many teams avoid starting on Monday and ending Friday to prevent motivation challenges.

4. The team's style.

B. **Feature Selection** At the beginning of each iteration, features that are selected for implementation should be elaborated upon until they are sufficiently clear to the developers. The time estimates should be updated according to those changes and any new knowledge the team has gained since then.

Iterations need not add up to exactly the prior or average velocity. This is one of Agile's strong points—continuous refinement based on current knowledge. Were all of this predicted up front, the estimates would be worthless three months into the project.

As a safe guard, every feature selected should not come from the highest priorities in the list. While most of them should come from there, it is good to pick a few lower priority features that make sense to implement in the iteration. This prevents team members from being held up because a necessary component is not ready, and it also makes it easy to choose which features to cut to complete the iteration on time if necessary.

C. **Wrapping Up the Iteration** At the end of an iteration is the assembly of pertinent documentation and software. It includes organizing the distribution of the product. Since each iteration is like launching a new project and includes an entire project life cycle, the project should be able to stand alone at this point.

At the end of each iteration, several evaluations need to take place:

1. The team should make a final run of all tests for that iteration to build a list of known bugs and incomplete features.

2. The product owner should evaluate the direction of the project and affirm or reject it.

COMMENT

Different Agile methods emphasize different things, but all have the same goal of delivering value. The main focuses of various paradigms of Agile methods include the following:

- *Team Organization* styles form a framework for holding the team together.
- *Systems Development* styles describe the mechanics of the product life cycle and what to do along the way.
- *Best Practice* focused styles present strategies for the integration of the two and ways to improve risk mitigation.

§ 23.05[C]

See Policy ITP-23-1 Agile Project Management Policy as an example.

POLICY ITP-23-1. Agile Project Management Policy

Policy #:	ITP-23-1	Effective:	03/18/13	Page #:	1 of N
Subject:	Agile Project Management Policy				

1.0 PURPOSE

Software development projects require more flexibility than is provided by traditional project management. This policy provides guidance on the use of Agile project management processes to help ensure the successful delivery of software that meets the customer's needs.

2.0 SCOPE

This policy applies to all software development projects developed using in-house resources, whether by IT or by end users.

3.0 POLICY

All software development projects are required to follow the Agile development processes outlined below.

   A. **Managing progress through features.** At the start of each project, the stakeholders in the project will develop a list of features desired in the application. The stakeholders are responsible for prioritizing the list of features at the start of each iteration.
   B. **Designation of Product Owner.** The stakeholders must designate a Product Owner that will be the on-site representative on the development team. The Product Owner must be available on-site as much as possible—ideally all day, each working day.
   C. **Estimating using Planning Poker.** The development team will estimate each feature using Planning Poker.
   D. **Development using iterations.** The development team will establish the iteration length for the project and the amount of work that can be completed per iteration. Functional software must be delivered to the customer at the end of each iteration.
   E. **Development team metrics.** The development team will report the following metrics to the customer at the end of each iteration:
      1. **Tasks completed.** This is a helpful metric to present, because it does not encourage the team to concentrate on pumping out the maximum number of features while neglecting bugs and choosing not to re-factor code.
      2. **Known bugs.** How many tests are currently being failed and/or how many defects are known.

3. **Features remaining.** Use the feature list to determine this.
4. **Velocity.** How much the team accomplishes in an iteration. This is calculated by dividing the total work done by the length of the iteration. The total work done is the sum of the effort estimates of all completed tasks.
5. **Resource burn rate.** How much of a given resource is being consumed by the project. This is the total resource cost divided by the length of the iteration.
6. **Task burndown.** How many tasks the team is completing. This is clearly shown in a burndown chart (shown earlier in this chapter). The task burndown is simply how many tasks were completed each day or in each iteration.
7. **Value delivered.** The sum of the values assigned to each feature accepted by the client.

F. **Project completion.** The project is complete once the stakeholders determine that a sufficient quantity of features has been completed.

4.0 REVISION HISTORY

Date	Revision #	Description of Change
03/18/13	1.0	Initial creation.

5.0 INQUIRIES

Direct inquiries about this policy to:

George Jenkins, CIO
Our Company, Inc.
2900 Corporate Drive
Columbus, OH 43215

Voice: 614-555-1234
Fax: 614-555-1235
E-mail: gjenkins@company.com

Revision #:	1.0	Supersedes:	N/A	Date:	03/18/13

24

VENDORS: GETTING THE GOODS

§ 24.01 OVERVIEW

[A] Purpose and Scope

Problems! An IT Manager's desk is covered with problems. Fortunately, for every problem at hand, there is a long list of vendors standing by to help solve them. The key is to locate and engage the vendors who provide the right product, at the right time, and at a fair price.

When properly selected and managed, purchases will solve problems. Poorly selected and unmanaged purchases will create far more problems than they solve. However, IT Managers do not have time to sit and entertain every salesperson who wishes to visit. It is essential that the company identify those vendors who are the most important to its ongoing success and develop them as valuable members of the team.

Some IT technologies represent long-term investments for the company. The IT department normally directs the purchase of servers, major software packages, and desktop units. The IT department's future success depends on the success and direction of future products of these companies. The IT Manager must include the plans of these vendors into the department's budget to minimize "surprises."

A positive working relationship between IT and the purchasing department is important. Both groups want what is best for the company. A positive working relationship will allow members of each department to address issues as they arise and minimize battles over "turf" and personalities.

COMMENT

All companies are buyers of goods and services—and all companies are vendors. Treat vendors with the courtesy that you hope your own company receives from its customers.

The best policy for dealing with outside vendors is exercising good business practices based on sound moral and ethical codes. Depending on its dealings with vendors, a company can lose or gain respect from other vendors, employees, and the industry at large. Remember that the company needs reliable suppliers and suppliers need reliable customers.

[B]   Critical Policies to Be Developed Based on This Chapter

Using the material discussed in this chapter, you will be able to create the following policies:

A. Vendor management
    1. Non-disclosure agreements
B. Vendor selection
C. Temporary workers

Policies should always be developed based on the local situation. Successful managers cannot issue appropriate guidance if the policies are written with another company's situation or location in mind.

§ 24.02   VENDOR MANAGEMENT

[A]   Overview

The second most important task an IT Manager faces is the timely purchase of high quality goods at a fair price. (The most important IT Manager task is the leadership and care of the IT staff.)

Vendors can be a time saver or a source of constant irritation. In most cases, this reflects their relationship with the IT Manager. If the IT Manager's attitude (or the company's culture) is to "beat up vendors," then vendors will be defensive and passively resist concessions. Pressing vendors may bring results in the short-term but will create long-term animosity if the treatment persists. An aggressive approach may result in the IT Manager not knowing how badly the vendor takes revenge in pricing and delivery or the IT Manager may be forced to spend a considerable amount of time researching technology to ensure the vendor cannot push back on price or features.

Such adversarial relationships are unnecessary and wasteful. If the IT Manager lacks trust in a key vendor, then that vendor should be replaced. Key vendors should be treated as partners who are looking out for their own interests. However, they also may be allies who will work hard to protect a valuable business relationship. The trick is to keep them close enough to benefit the company, but distant enough that they keep working to earn the company's business.

Not all vendors are of equal importance to the company. Some vendors provide critical technology whose well-being is vital to the IT department's success, while other vendors are only needed occasionally. Most IT Managers make this distinction subconsciously.

Good vendor management is a key to successful IT management. Vendors can be a source of information about technologies and their industries. They can provide quick solutions to vexing problems and make a manager's job a lot easier. They can also get a manager fired.

Vendor management is managing the relationship between the IT department and its vendors to the company's long-term advantage. Long-term advantage means that the IT Manager protects the company by driving down the vendor's prices, and increasing the vendor service levels. However, vendors that lose money to a customer cannot afford to do so for long. They cease to either sell to that customer or become insolvent. Therefore, the IT Manager must keep prices down while allowing for a fair return to the seller.

The buyer-seller relationship is an agreement between two consenting parties to exchange one thing for another. In this case, the exchange is money for goods or services. The amount of money exchanged for goods depends on the relative power of the two parties:

A. **Power of the Purchaser** is most evident when acquiring goods and services that are commonly available. The purchaser has multiple sources readily available to provide the desired materials. This increases competition and drives down prices. Examples are paper for printers, network cables, and long-distance carriers.

B. **Power of the Seller** is when there is a single or very few suppliers. This occurs often in IT when there is a unique product such as a major database package or specific network equipment. The seller dictates the price and the buyer must accept it or go through greater expense to implement an alternative (which may also be a competing unique product). The IT Manager selects products that, wherever possible, avoid this situation. Examples of products where the seller has a great deal of power to set the price are enterprise resource planning (ERP) software systems and local telephone companies.

In the end, the IT Manager needs the vendor as much as the vendor needs the IT Manager. The vendor wants to sell and the IT Manager wants to buy. The key is to find the middle ground that meets the requirements of all parties concerned. IT Managers most appreciate the vendors who solve problems and do not create any new ones.

[B] Vendor Selection

How can an IT Manager select a supplier who will actually deliver what is wanted, when it is wanted, and at the agreed upon price? Acquire vendor services based on the optimal solution for the IT department and not just on price. To avoid any form of collusion that would influence selection or inflate price, there must not be any familial or close personal relationships between a vendor and person with selection authority within the company. Never accept gifts from a vendor as they imply a favor to be reciprocated later.

Steering the company through the minefield of vendor incompetence is only half of the challenge; the other half is to understand the purchasing company's culture. An unrealistic internal culture can spell disaster for any undertaking even when employing the most competent service organization.

COMMENT

What is wrong with buying from the lowest bidder? Nothing—if the item is a commodity that is exactly the same no matter where it is purchased. However, consider specialty and build-to-order items. Once airborne, cynical military transport pilots like to remind their passengers that their aircraft was built by the lowest bidder.

An IT Manager should take care not to create enemies when negotiating vendor services. Information systems personnel are mobile; their paths cross in unexpected ways. Today's salesperson may be tomorrow's boss. While a person may try his or her best to avoid problem situations, many discoveries emerge only after the contract is signed.

[C]   Personnel Augmentation

IT departments typically hire the services of two types of outside personnel—consultants and temporary workers. Hire consultants to work on a specific project. They may work off-site and only appear for meetings. Temporary workers may be on the job indefinitely.

The key to hiring consultants is to have a clearly defined objective for them. Vague objectives may consume the IT budget before the work is completed. Recriminations may pass back and forth, but the project is still incomplete. A clear vision of the scope and deliverables in the beginning will provide the most efficient use of consultants.

Another important task is to assign someone on the IT staff to work closely with consultants to ensure they understand what is being done and why. Otherwise, all of the knowledge required to support the final product may walk out of the door in the consultant's head!

Unlike consultants who are on-site for the duration of a project, temporary employees are just that—workers acting like employees for a limited amount of time. Temporary workers are assigned tasks in the same manner as regular employees, but serve at the convenience of the company. Some people support a short-term surge in work while others may linger for years. When their contract expires or when the company no longer requires their assistance, they can be terminated on short notice.

A variation on this is bringing in prospective new employees on short-term contracts. This permits the managers to evaluate the employees' performance before hiring them.

[D]   Acquiring Goods and Services

IT uses a variety of materials to support its operations. This runs the gamut from laser printer toner to network cables, workstation repair parts, monitors, paper for printers, and software manuals. Most IT materials are commodities purchased based on price and supplier reliability.

Companies closely watch their cash outflows. Acquisition of material is made through the purchasing or supply management departments. These departments ensure all purchases adhere to company policies and accounting rules. Where possible, IT should funnel their purchases through the same few purchasing agents. This will save time by eliminating the need to explain the same basic requirements for every purchase.

The purchasing department will provide information about vendors with which the company deals and verify the financial health of key suppliers. (What good is a warranty if the company has vanished?) Purchasing also will check with other customers to ensure the vendor fulfills its promises.

The legal department will review all contracts before approval. Just as the IT staff is expert in building and delivering quality service, the company's legal team is expert at monitoring current legal developments and protecting the company's interests in its agreements.

A critical management maxim is to "inspect what you expect." Even the most honest vendors sometimes make mistakes and the dishonest ones will consistently try to bid low and then deliver less. Most companies have a procedure to confirm upon receipt that an item meets purchase order requirements and to start the payment process for the invoice or bill received. A delay of payment can force an obstinate vendor to be cooperative in meeting contract obligations.

[E] Purchasing—The Magic Three Factors

The magic three factors in purchasing a product are how well it meets the need, the promptness of delivery, and its price. A product that meets the need but is not available when needed is not of much use. On the other hand, if it is available but highly priced, then questions also will be raised as to the wisdom of completing the purchase.

A. **Fits the need.** To purchase the right product, the buyer must have a clear understanding of what is wanted. Often this is not the case. The IT Manager may want to buy a certain item (e.g., LTO2 tape drive) but does not have the detailed understanding of all of the options available, the trade-off between these options, and which one best fits immediate and anticipated requirements. Further, the IT Manager rarely knows the same information about leading competitors of the technology.

It is always prudent for the IT Manager to check with several organizations that review the performance and features of the types of equipment in question. Many of these resources are available online, but may be biased. However, to save time, most companies align with their key vendors to provide these specifications and solutions. This is a lot like "the fox watching the hen house" since the vendor can specify items far more expensive than required. This is where the long-term key vendor approach comes in. The trade-off is a bit of money lost to a less-than-optimal price against time saved by the company.

The IT Manager can reduce the vendor's temptation to overcharge by spreading the business among several similar companies. In this way, the threat of further competition will help to keep them focused on the account. It also provides multiple viewpoints about the same problem. Lazy IT Managers who hand blank checks to vendors will eventually be disappointed and probably replaced by the company.

B. **Can I have it when I need it?** The timing of product delivery is important. Companies do not want to pay for equipment before it is ready to use. On the other hand, they do not want workers to be idle while waiting for a key component to appear. It is important, when ordering complex material or hiring skilled temporary workers, that the vendor identify an expected delivery date. The purchase should be contingent on the vendor meeting that date.

Some IT Managers wait until the last minute to push through purchase requests for vital goods and services. They expect the salesperson to scramble and deliver the material on time. The miraculous delivery may not seem so when charges for express shipments appear on the invoice. (This would be where the vendor quotes the purchase price plus shipping.) If an urgent purchase is anticipated, the IT Manager should ask the desired vendor about availability. The vendor may order the required item and hold it at the warehouse until receiving the order.

Delivery also depends upon the goods ordered. While a factory may be able to afford to keep machinery in a finished goods warehouse for a while, it is difficult to do the same with people. Unlike equipment sitting in a warehouse, qualified personnel are rarely sitting around doing nothing. Lead-time is essential for locating and hiring skilled temporary workers. This becomes more complicated when hiring a large number of skilled people.

As with all things, there is a twist to the timing of purchases. It pays to know the vendor's fiscal cycle. Most sales forces strive to meet a sales quota. Accelerating a major purchase to fall within the current sales year may help the sales representative (and his manager) to meet sales objectives and possibly secure bonuses. In this situation, the IT Manager will gain additional price and feature advantages by accelerating the purchase.

COMMENT

The biggest cost driver in IT is standardization. It reduces the costs of support, training, and price per unit. Wherever practical, IT Managers should "fit" requests into the context of a standardized product before considering a different technology. However, a square peg is still square and a round hole is still round. If a standard product does not meet the requirements, the manager should not waste hour after hour trying to force the square peg into the round hole.

C. **How much will it cost?** Acquiring goods or services "at a fair price" requires an understanding of the suppliers' costs for what is being purchased. This is easier for commodity items than for specialty items. Determining the "fair" price begins with a comparison between products supplied by different companies. Calculate costs over a five-year useful life span. This includes the cost of a maintenance agreement, the cost of materials and consumables, and the expense of any required supporting devices.

A caveat of this is the "spot" market. Sometimes vendors carry much more inventory than their financial condition will bear. They may occasionally run a "sale" with special pricing to cut their inventory in a short time. Low-volume vendors generally offer these deals. Vendors of premium priced goods would rather scrap them than admit that they could have sold them at a lower price. Therefore, if there is flexibility in the goods or services wanted, and if the item will not significantly alter efforts to standardize products, the IT Manager should check the spot market before making a purchase.

IT Managers must take the time to learn about the things that motivate the vendor. Is it volume? Is it maintaining an ongoing sales relationship? Is it the protection of existing service contracts? Knowing what the vendor prizes most will provide the buyer with a negotiating advantage. Another important thing to understand is the vendor's cost structure. Ask the vendor what aspect of a purchase is driving its costs. They cannot sell goods at a loss unless they expect to recoup those funds later. Forcing a vendor into a money-losing situation will hurt the buyer in the end.

The lowest price is not everything. It is advantageous for the company to deal with the fewest number of vendors possible. It also is ideal for IT staff to have as few products as possible to learn and support. Therefore, if one of the company's "key vendors" is within 10 percent of the lowest price, buy it.

On the other side, vendors will reduce their marketing expense if they know they can pitch their best price up front. Vendors save time and labor haggling over pricing. Their understandings of the purchaser's company will help them to understand what is required to fill the company's needs.

[F] Recognizing the Key Vendors

Key vendors are those who provide critical technology to the company. This could be the supplier of the "standard" IT server or network hub. It could be the company that provides the database management software, the operating system, or even the standard programming language.

Another way to identify a key vendor is one that is allotted a large portion of the IT budget. This might be any company that provides more than $1 million in goods and services or that is assigned more than five percent of the budget. Key vendors for an IT department rarely number more than a dozen. Keeping this number low is important because the IT Manager will spend time working with these companies to ensure their alignment with the department's direction.

IT Managers have a responsibility to train their critical vendors in how the company purchases materials or services. They need to understand such processes as the paperwork flow of purchases, who to call for accounts payable questions, and the name of the buyer for IT. This will allow them to address their own problems rather than pass them on the IT Manager. Some steps to take when working with key vendors include:

A. **Letting them in on the company's plans.** Key vendors are long-term partners. This creates an opportunity to work together and strategically align the company's IT plans with their product offerings. To some extent, this reduces the IT Manager's negotiating power, but it also increases price reductions and improves service since the seller spends less time on "selling" and more time on "servicing" the account.

Before exchanging insights into strategies, both companies should enter into a non-disclosure agreement (see Worksheet 24-1 Mutual Non-Disclosure Agreement as an example). This document (approved by the legal department) assures the parties that neither will disclose to anyone else the confidential insights provided to the other. The vendor wants to keep its product changes under wraps and the company does not want the vendor to disclose its plans to competitors.

With the non-disclosure agreement in hand, the IT Manager can share the company's three-year technology strategy with key vendors to explain the direction of the IT department and its anticipated requirements for goods and services. Often the vendor can provide explanations of technical trends that will work with the company's plans and indicate areas of technical opportunity.

In turn, the vendors should share with the company their technical directions over the next several years. This might alert the IT Manager as to when the vendor intends to drop support for an old technology or make a change in pricing. The vendor also may provide some recommendations and cost estimates when the IT Manager is creating the annual budget.

WORKSHEET 24-1. Mutual Non-Disclosure Agreement

MUTUAL NON-DISCLOSURE AGREEMENT

THIS NON-DISCLOSURE AGREEMENT (this "Agreement") is entered into this _____ day of _____, 20 _____ and made effective the _____ day of _____, 20 _____ by and between XYZ Company, Inc., a [name of state] corporation ("First Party"), and [name of client] ("Second Party"), an [type of entity] with offices at [address].

A. **Purpose.** Both parties, during the term of this agreement, will have access to and become familiar with various trade secrets, confidential and proprietary information, technology, data, computer source code, designs, development concepts, plans, and know-how of the other party and heretofore known only to its employees, agents, and independent contractors. These trade secrets and confidential or proprietary information, including without limitation, client data, client information, company data, software, related products, information relating to software or technology provided by first party to second party for use in consultation regarding and in the design and development of the software and/or related products, first party's operations or the financial conditions or results of its operations, its marketing or business strategies or plans, the names, addresses, case histories or specifications of any of its customers or prospective customers, the types of goods or services sold or proposed to be sold to any customers or prospective customers of first party, the names, addresses, training, background or information regarding any person who is or was an employee, agent or independent contractor of first party and other compilations of information, which are owned by first party and which are regularly used in operation of its business (all of the foregoing shall be referred to collectively as "confidential information"), are the result of large amounts of time, effort and expense of first party in developing such information and in recruiting and training such employees, agents and independent contractors and are essential to the success of first party.

B. **Covenants of Non-Disclosure.** Absent receipt of express written consent from the other party, each party shall:

1. Not use any confidential information for his own purposes other than in connection with his activities for or on behalf of the other party and shall refrain from, either intentionally, directly or indirectly, during the term of this agreement or after termination of this agreement, using, disclosing, disseminating, or publishing, to or with any person, firm, company or entity, or knowingly making available to any others, for any use other than in connection with the transactions contemplated hereby, any confidential information; and

2. Restrict disclosure of such confidential information only to others as may reasonably be necessary in the conduct of the other party's business; and

3. Advise all such persons of the strict obligations of confidentiality hereunder; and

4. Take such steps to protect the confidentiality of confidential information as required by the other party's policies and procedures and such additional steps as would be taken by a reasonably prudent person to protect confidential materials.

C. **Public Knowledge.** Notwithstanding the foregoing, information provided to the undersigned shall not constitute confidential information if such information (i) is or becomes generally available to the public other than as a result of a disclosure by or through the undersigned or the undersigned' partners, directors, officers, employees or affiliates in contravention of this agreements, (ii) was already available to, or in the possession of, the undersigned prior to its disclosure by, or at the direction of, the Second Party in connection with the undersigned's evaluation of a possible transaction, or (iii) is or becomes available to the undersigned from another source.

This Agreement shall be construed in accordance with [name of state] law. The parties hereto agree that any action concerning, relating to or involving this Agreement must be filed in [name of county] County, [name of state] and the parties hereby consent to the jurisdiction of the courts in [name of county] County.

First Party: XYZ Company, Inc.	Second Party:
Signature	Signature
Title	Title
Print Name	Print Name
Date	Date

B. **Negotiating a national pricing agreement.** The sales process is very expensive for vendors. Vendors closely aligned with the company may offer a national pricing agreement. This is a schedule of the company's best price based on the company's historical purchasing volumes. A price list reduces costs for the vendors and allows the buyer to compare prices without calling for quotes.

C. **Reviewing their business continuity plans.** Once a vendor becomes an important part of the company's future success, it may be important to inspect its business continuity plans. Close alignment means that if the vendor has a problem, the IT department also has a problem. Written and tested business continuity plans demonstrate a corporate commitment to minimize the impact of disasters on the vendor-company and therefore on its customers.

D. **Being careful not to trust too much.** The IT Manager must always be on guard against allowing the convenience of a critical vendor relationship to overshadow good business decisions. Vendors definitely watch out for their own interests. They may attempt to preempt IT's purchase of a competitor's product by alluding to a nonexistent product or features on a product (commonly known as "vaporware").

A recurring sales pitch vendors make is that they want to be the company's sole supplier of a given product or service. Of course they do! They want to inflate their prices! *Sole suppliers are never a good idea.* Whenever they exist due to unique products, consider adding similar technologies or moving to a commodity technology. Although key vendors are convenient, compare their prices to their main competitors to ensure they are not slowly inflating their prices.

E. **Monitoring the financial health of key vendors.** Companies need their key vendors to be financially healthy and to remain in business for as long as the IT department needs them. The company's purchasing agent must periodically verify the financial viability of key vendors to provide early warning of a collapse or serious problems. If problems are detected, the IT Manager should create a plan of action to implement if the supplier is in danger of insolvency.

COMMENT

An awkward situation is the "captive" customer where a sister company provides goods or services. One author worked for a company that owned a chain of PC stores. Every purchase was required to pass through them; however, the sales representative was not paid any commission for these sales. Other companies were anxious for the business, but the company was forced to use this "in-house" supplier. Consequently, prices were high, service was poor, and deliveries late.

[G] Commodity Vendors

A commodity is an item that is essentially the same no matter where it comes from. A sealed copy of Microsoft Windows is the same no matter where purchased, yet prices may vary. Items identified by the IT Manager as commodities can be procured through the normal purchasing processes since where it is purchased is primarily a matter of price and delivery.

The goal of the purchaser is to drive for products that are commodities. Commodities markets are highly competitive and the prices tend to be cost based. Commodity suppliers strive to drive down their costs since margins are already thin. In a commodity market, the company with the best managed supply chain will typically be the lowest cost supplier.

The goal of a commodity vendor is to establish that its product is somehow not a commodity and superior to other like items. The intention is to widen margins. The vendor achieves this with a high level of customer service, product "branding," or the additional features.

[H] Low-Volume Vendors

Low-volume vendors provide small quantities or on-demand materials. They are not welcome to "drop in and chat" with the IT Manager. Low-volume vendors make up the bulk of the IT department's vendors. Typically, the IT Manager will not spend a lot of time cultivating the relationship.

The advantage of low-volume vendors is that they will work to become key vendors. This may naturally occur when the company migrates from one technology to another. The vendor also may provide special pricing in the "spot" market—when a company must unload some of its inventory and is willing to do so at a reduced price.

See Policy ITP-24-1 Vendor Management Policy as an example.

POLICY ITP-24-1. Vendor Management Policy

Policy #:	ITP-24-1	Effective:	03/18/13	Page #:	1 of N
Subject:	Vendor Management Policy				

1.0 PURPOSE

IT spending represents a large portion of the company's annual expenses. This policy provides guidance on the development of positive vendor relationships. It is a supplement to existing company policies covering the purchasing of goods and services, and for the payment of invoices.

2.0 SCOPE

This policy encompasses all IT purchases of materials and services, from the recognition of a procurement need through the delivery of the final product.

3.0 POLICY

A. The IT department will provide the technical requirements to the purchasing department. The designated company purchasing agents will conduct all price and terms negotiations with vendors.

B. The goal of the IT vendor policy is to ensure the department obtains the best quality and delivery at the lowest practical price. To accomplish this, the department will divide its materials into:

 1. Critical materials and services—essential for continued critical IT operations, or consumes at least 10 percent of the IT annual operating budget.
  a. Cultivate at least two primary vendors.
  b. Maintain close strategic alignment through annual discussions of mutual strategy and non-disclosure agreements.
  c. Annually compare prices to alternative vendors.

 2. Non-critical materials and services.
  a. Provide specifications for acquisition by Purchasing department.
  b. Assist in the evaluation of products by new vendors.

C. The IT Manager will work closely with the Purchasing department to qualify reputable vendors for use by the IT department. As technologies change and new companies enter markets, it is beneficial to understand the materials and prices available in the marketplace. Based on IT trade information, the IT Manager may recommend new vendors for qualification by Purchasing.

D. All vendors will be selected in a fair and public manner. When submitting the purchase request to Purchasing, the IT Manager will:
   1. Disclose family or business connections with the requested vendor by *anyone* in the IT department.
   2. Disclose any gifts from that vendor to any IT employee during the previous 12 months.

E. The Legal department will review all agreements with external organizations prior to submitting them to executive approval. This includes:
   1. Non-disclosure agreements.
   2. Terms of purchase.
   3. Ownership of intellectual property.

F. When time permits all major purchases will be conducted through the Request for Proposal process.
   1. A clear and technical description will be provided to a list of at least five qualified vendors for their bid.
   2. Conduct a bidders conference to clarify the requirements and hear objections to specifications.
   3. Predetermine a scorecard for evaluation proposals prior to receiving the proposals.

4.0 REVISION HISTORY

Date	Revision #	Description of Change
03/18/13	1.0	Initial creation.

5.0 INQUIRIES

Direct inquiries about this policy to:

George Jenkins, CIO
Our Company, Inc.
2900 Corporate Drive
Columbus, OH 43215

Voice: 614-555-1234
Fax: 614-555-1235
E-mail: gjenkins@company.com

Revision #:	1.0	Supersedes:	N/A	Date:	03/18/13

§ 24.03   PLAY BY THE RULES

[A]   Overview

Every company has its own processes for spending money. The purchasing of materials should not be the IT Manager's responsibility. It should be the province of the company's purchasing or supply management department. Leave it this way. Otherwise, the IT Manager will drown in a raging sea of administrative detail. To minimize the amount of time spent in this area, the IT Manager should learn all facets of the company's purchasing processes, policies, and procedures to ensure the smoothest flow of requests. It is easier to learn the purchasing department's processes than it is to fight a losing battle against them.

COMMENT

It is far cheaper for a vendor to "wine and dine" an IT Manager than it is to lower its prices. This could include expensive dinners, free tickets to sports events, occasional gifts, or even paid vacations. IT Managers may feel that it is just a perquisite of their position. Such a rationalization is wrong and unethical. Vendors only spend this money in the expectation of future favorable treatment. IT Managers know that the "gifts" will stop if purchases cease. It is the vendor's way of bypassing the company's safeguards against wasting money.

Some companies have a policy that prohibits the acceptance of gifts from vendors (including free meals) over a certain amount (often $20). Other companies only require the prompt reporting of these activities. Otherwise, the purchasing agent may find the IT Manager demanding a high-priced item from a specific vendor for "technical" reasons.

[B]   Maximizing the Purchasing Department's Expertise

The purchasing department ensures that the company obtains the best goods, delivery, and price combination for all procurement. Just as IT Managers are the experts in their field, treat the purchasing department likewise. After sending the appropriate paperwork to the purchasing department, the IT Manager should relax and wait for the goods to appear.

Although everyone has been cheated by someone at some time, employees in the purchasing department have likely encountered it much more often. Their procedures weed out fraudulent vendors before the company's funds are at risk. They go through several steps to qualify vendors, including:

A. Confirming the financial "health" of the vendor through a financial rating review.
B. Verifying the status of the vendor in the community, through such things as the Better Business Bureau and customer referrals.
C. Drafting the purchase order, which will include the company's standard terms and conditions for purchasing goods. Modifications to these terms are between the purchasing department and the vendor—and not the concern of the IT Manager.

Due to the complexity of the specification for purchasing IT products, most companies leave it to the IT Manager to select the desired product and vendor. While this may save time, IT-controlled purchasing decisions may be reviewed by internal auditors.

Purchasing departments must not succumb to sales representatives bypassing the IT department. Just because they claim their product is a low-cost alternative to the item specified by the IT Manager, it does not make it true.

[C]   Legal Review of Contracts

IT Managers will encounter several vendor management documents on a regular basis. The first is the company's purchase order. A purchase order is a legally binding document. The company's legal team carefully reviewed the terms in these documents. The IT Manager must never alter them. Vendors who have any complaints must work them out with the purchasing department.

For example, before a temporary worker can work on-site, a workers' compensation insurance policy is required, usually for a set amount. This will be included in the terms of the purchase order but rarely discussed during negotiations between the IT Manager and the employment agency. Large companies routinely provide this, but small companies cannot—especially on short notice. Only the company's purchasing agent can approve exceptions to required terms.

Another legal document is a service contract. These can run the gamut from repairing servers to staffing the service desk. The terms of the agreement may drive up the vendor's cost, which in turn will drive up the price to the company. When negotiating these agreements, request only the minimum services. However, once approved by all parties, never excuse the vendor from performing to the level specified in the agreement. If the vendor promised to provide something at a set price, then it must deliver or renegotiate the contract at a lower price.

The company's legal team should always review contracts for goods or services. Agreements may seem straightforward until added clauses contradict the contract's original intent. The company's attorneys can make sense of these complex documents and protect the company.

COMMENT

When hiring consultants or temporary employees, IT should always review the agreement with the human resources department to ensure adherence to all relevant laws and company policies.

[D] Receiving the Goods

Many things can go wrong with an order, and the receiving dock is the company's first line of defense against incorrect shipments. Materials can be damaged in transit or even the wrong item shipped. The receiving dock clerk should be required to match the purchase order to the item received to ensure that the correct item has arrived before accepting the material.

In most companies, materials must be "properly received" before an invoice can be paid. This provides a "check and balance" because the payment cannot be processed until the person who ordered the materials approves the receipt. In a crisis, IT materials and parts might come in the front door by express delivery and bypass the receiving clerk. In those cases, the IT Manager must properly submit the paperwork so the vendor can be paid.

For services, the IT Manager must verify to the accounts payable department that the services billed on the invoice are correct. Compare copies of contractor and temporary worker time sheets to the invoice to validate the expense.

[E] Accounting's Role in Positive Vendor Relations

Once the correct goods arrive, the IT Manager should timely pay the vendor. This is one area IT Managers often overlook because they do not consider it to be their responsibility to ensure prompt payment. Yet, this action can greatly raise their value in the vendor's eyes. Orders are nice to receive, but all vendors need a cash flow to remain in business. Do not let the company's Byzantine accounts payable processes ruin a carefully nurtured vendor relationship.

Sometimes paperwork gets lost, is incomplete and shuffled into a pending basket, or held by an accounts payable clerk for other reasons. IT Managers can pass the invoice off to a faceless clerk or help the clerk to work through issues that arise. Just as a high level of service is expected within the vendor's organization, the vendor will be pleased to receive the same courtesy.

[F] Budgets Drive the Purchases

Budgets are a company's way of projecting costs against anticipated revenues. The drawback is the need to forecast major purchases far in advance of their actual purchase (if they are even purchased at all). The challenge for the IT Manager is to predict what will be needed and the price of each component.

Before the annual budgeting cycle for the upcoming year, the IT Managers should visit with each of the key vendors. Ask them what products will come to market in the next year. Ask them about prices for the new technology and projected price reductions for existing equipment. If this is a true partnership, they can provide most of this information. All of this is fodder for assembling a budget.

§ 24.04 CONSULTING AND TEMPORARY PERSONNEL SERVICES

[A] Overview

IT departments occasionally require the services of nonemployees. This may include supplemental technical support for a specific project or temporary staff augmentation. In either case, temporary technical workers are an expensive purchase. Unlike a machine that delivers something tangible, much of an IT worker's output is intangible. The IT Manager ensures that these workers deliver the value for the price the company is paying.

A distinction is drawn here between consultants who are brought in to assist with defined tasks of a fixed duration and temporary employees (temps) who are integrated into the department and assigned tasks like any other team member. Temps may work on a range of assignments and remain on-site for an indefinite length of time.

Consulting services are often justified because in-house skills are unavailable, extra personnel are required, or the firm is seeking an unbiased, objective opinion. Many of these personnel are well-paid, ambitious individuals who enjoy the variety of challenging assignments that a consulting firm offers.

Outside consultants can be objective because they are not embroiled in the organization's political struggles. They should render professional judgments based on the facts. Unfortunately, whoever hired the consultant may have influenced the selection of a "cooperative" consultant, thereby losing objectivity.

Sometimes the workload is such that the company will arrange for temporary workers to supplement the staff. Unlike consultants who are engaged for the duration of a project, temporary employees are just that—workers acting like employees for a limited amount of time. "Temps" can be very useful during seasonal workload surges. They are useful during the long-term absence of an employee.

Highly skilled temps are similar to contractors except their tenure is not tied to a contract. In some cases, they linger for years. Some companies use highly skilled temporary employees on a large scale to push the responsibility of maintaining a workforce onto the employment agency (e.g., service desk, PC repair). Based on their agreement with the employment agency, this allows the company to rapidly scale back the number of temps on-site. (Rapidly scaling up the workforce is difficult due to finding and training a large number of people at the same time.)

It is a good management practice to locate and prequalify consulting services before the company actually needs them. In some cases, the agreements and pricing can be determined far in advance. Later, if a staff increase is required on short notice, the agreement can be referenced, which will shorten the acquisition cycle.

Referrals are the best way to find reliable contractors. The IT Manager should maintain memberships in IT professional organizations to develop these contacts. By discussing the performance of various vendors with peers, the manager can learn which ones to avoid as well as which ones to hire.

[B] Types of Temporary Personnel Organizations

Consulting firms can provide a range of services or focus on a select few. Choosing the right organization to supplement the IT department is a very important task. Often the size of the company selected depends on what is needed. Companies tend to fall into the general categories of small and large.

Small organizations are usually local and may have some idea about the buyer's company and its services. They will work hard to build a long-term relationship with their customers. Small companies typically focus on a single technology (such as UNIX) or are broad-based but technically shallow.

Small companies may be financially unstable and no longer in business when needed problems arise—even if under a warranty period. The loss of one large customer can force some small companies to fold.

Large professional services organizations try to provide "one-stop shopping." In a sense, the IT Manager drops the staffing problem on their door step and they provide all of the answers (for a fee). If the large company does not have the required expertise on hand, it will sub-contract it to someone who does.

The dark side to large companies is that, from time to time, they have workers not currently hired out to customers. These "off-the-bench" workers are sent to customers as experts in something they know little about. To prevent this, IT Managers must personally interview and approve every consultant assigned to a project.

In addition, contract workers might make work for themselves to extend their employment. The old saying that good contract workers must be dragged kicking and screaming from the building is not too far off the mark. Always document contract workers' exit plans before hiring them.

[C] Utilizing Temporary Personnel

Many of the reasons for acquiring contracted temporary personnel are the same as for contracting a consultant. In addition to being less expensive than consultants, temps offer other benefits to the company.

Because employers compete in a market for skilled talent, it is best to avoid designation as a company that hires and quickly fires. Just as the firm compares job candidates when hiring, job seekers compare the merits of different employers. One of the major reasons that job candidates do not accept positions is a company's unstable employment profile.

> ## COMMENT
>
> Some companies use temporary technical staff as a "try before you buy" approach. Prospective employees are hired through an agency as temporary employees for a set period—usually six months. At the end of that time, the company can hire them as regular staff or release them with no further obligations.

On the other hand, there are some valid reasons for not employing temporary workers. One involves the learning curve—the time needed to master a job or learn a firm's processes. The more complex the job is, the larger the learning curve will be. When a temp leaves the company, the time spent training that person will be lost.

Another reason is that temps may not be very loyal. If a better opportunity arises, they will leave, and all of their training time is lost. While this is a valid concern, many contract workers are comfortable with temporary employment and commit to the task. The more professional the responsibility, the greater the loyalty that person will exhibit to the profession than to the firm. This may account, in part, for the turnover of skilled personnel who feel their employers are not giving them opportunities to gain professional maturity.

[D] Ground Rules for Engaging Temporary Staff

Consultants can be valuable assets if a proper relationship is established. It is imperative to maintain proper conditions for maximum benefit while minimizing the cost. There are several procedures to follow when acquiring the services of an outside consultant.

A. **Define specifications and scope.** This will give the consultant a clear understanding of what to do and what not to do. The IT Manager should clearly state what is expected as far as specifications and have this confirmed in writing. A major mistake when using a consultant is to hire the consultant before clear specifications are developed and then complain about the cost. If the IT Manager cannot clearly articulate which services are required and the desired product to be created, then how can the consultant provide an accurate price? Any wasted effort will be included in the bill even if the firm does not get what it wanted. Imagine a giant taxi meter sitting on the consultant's desk. As long as the consultant is on-site, the meter runs whether the taxi is moving or not. IT Managers should manage consultants just as any other employee—except that they should be used for the expertise for which they were hired. Do not drop them at a desk and walk away without instructions or there will be a bill for a lot of wasted time!

B. **Clearly define what is needed.** The IT Manager should provide a written job description to the contracting company whenever requesting workers. This helps them to establish the appropriate billing rate for each level of expertise. Whoever works on the project, the IT Manager should ensure that person remains on it for its duration. The consulting company should not be allowed to change personnel without IT's approval.

C. **Required documentation.** The documentation left behind after the completion of a project may be the only future source of reference for that job. Documentation is expensive and often ignored to save time or money. This type of savings will only create more expenses later. When defining documentation requirements, the IT Manager should make certain the consultant adheres to the company's standards.

D. **Monitor the consultant's progress.** Outline a monitoring procedure for the consultant in the contract. Obtain feedback on the status of the consultant's work at predetermined time intervals by defining efforts in the smallest measurable units and relating them to percentages of the total time. As progress is reported, the cumulative percent of progress completed can be compared to the cumulative dollars spent. These two values should be in accord to ensure dollars budgeted will not be depleted before the project is completed. Use a Gantt chart to compare these values. The effectiveness, or lack thereof, of the consultant's performance should not be a surprise at the end of the project. Consultants are self-directed persons; they must be to survive in the profession. However, they may be sidetracked by extending their scope or misinterpreting directions received from more than one source. As with any newly employed person, do not leave consultants alone for long periods. Nor should there be any misunderstanding as to the status of an in-process project. Document this in a clear, easy-to-understand, written, dated, and signed report.

E. **Always pair a consultant with an employee for development projects.** If consultants work alone, when they walk out of the door, all of the project knowledge will go with them. True, there may be system documentation, but experience provides so much more. Pairing an employee to work alongside the consultant builds in-house expertise. Additionally, it is a good way to infuse a different technical perspective into the IT staff. Ignoring this step may require the company to have to rehire the consultant for a high fee to provide ongoing system maintenance.

F. **Know who is being hired.** When hiring a consultant, the services of a company or a specific individual are employed. When hiring a specific individual, it is easier to estimate the time and cost for a project based on that person's proven expertise. However, will that person be available when he is needed? This is difficult if the purchasing paperwork is held up by budget politics. If a large number of people are required, then a consulting company will select and "validate" the credentials of the people provided.

G. **Ensure that intellectual property remains the property of the company.** All contract employees must sign an agreement that all intellectual property created while contracted by the company is the property of the company (see Policy ITP-24-2 Ownership of Intellectual Property Policy).

POLICY ITP-24-2. Ownership of Intellectual Property Policy

Policy #:	ITP-24-2	Effective:	03/18/13	Page #:	1 of N
Subject:	Ownership of Intellectual Property Policy				

1.0 PURPOSE

It is critical to protect the intellectual property rights of the company. This policy provides guidance on protecting the intellectual property of the company when engaging outside IT consultants.

2.0 SCOPE

This policy encompasses all work performed by IT personnel that are not employees of the company. This policy shall apply to intellectual property of all types, including but not limited to any invention, discovery, trade secret, technology, scientific or technological development, research data, and computer software regardless of whether subject to protection under patent, trademark, copyright, or other laws.

3.0 POLICY

All services provided by outside vendors shall be considered "work for hire," and all intellectual property rights that may apply to that work shall belong to the company. All vendors will be required to sign an intellectual property rights agreement before any work can be done for the company.

4.0 REVISION HISTORY

Date	Revision #	Description of Change
03/18/13	1.0	Initial creation.

5.0 INQUIRIES

Direct inquiries about this policy to:

George Jenkins, CIO
Our Company, Inc.
2900 Corporate Drive
Columbus, OH 43215

Voice: 614-555-1234
Fax: 614-555-1235
E-mail: gjenkins@company.com

Revision #:	1.0	Supersedes:	N/A	Date:	03/18/13

[E] Outsourcing

At some point, a company may decide that an outside company can more effectively manage a portion of its IT operations. The idea is that a company focused on a single aspect of IT, such as PC repair, can do it better than a company that does it as one small part of its operations. Some IT Managers believe contracting for this service is similar to contracting for electricity or other essentials that a company could but does not provide for itself.

Outsourcing agreements typically provide for a company to deliver a specific service for an extended period such as:

A. Service desk services
B. Database operations
C. Hardware maintenance
D. Network operations
E. Training
F. Web site operations
G. Programming
H. IT computer operations
I. Systems analysis
J. End-user computing support

Replacing an existing business function brings with it major training issues about local processes, personal contacts, local technical issues, etc. To overcome this, the outsourcing company normally hires the employees whose function is being outsourced. This presents several opportunities as well as problems:

A. It reduces operating cost through (hopefully) better management. Outside management with no internal loyalties may be needed to make necessary staffing changes.

B. Consider using outsourcing to start up a new operation. Once a professional facilities management service starts up an operation, the department can be turned over to internal operations management. The outside service can stay on temporarily to ensure everything is up and running, while permanent employees have a chance to develop skills necessary to run the department.

C. It can be a step toward avoiding unionization or for breaking up a union shop. Using an outside management service or outsourcing will convert the facilities to a nonunion operation without going through a difficult decertification process. If this is the company's intent, it must consult with legal counsel prior to proceeding.

D. Outsourcing may provide temporary technical services where no in-house talent is available, such as to conduct an asset inventory.

There are some issues to be aware of when using an outsourcing service operation. The operating responsibility shifts away from the firm's own controlled management, and the outside management may not understand the firm's particular needs. Also, implementing an outsourcing agreement may impact employee morale. Information systems personnel may resent reporting to an "outsider." This can be a greater problem when there is an expected reduction in the workforce. Problems can escalate to sabotage.

The IT Manager should never enter into this type of arrangement without an agreed-upon exit plan for the contractor. Relationships can sour over time and once a contractor has all of the expertise in its control, it may be very expensive or difficult to eliminate. The agreement should allow that, at a minimum, the company can hire the contractor's on-site employees for no penalty.

Outsourcing to offshore companies introduces other complications. Areas with low labor costs tend to be in developing countries. The technical infrastructure in these places is less fault-tolerant, civil order is more fragile, and the company may lack an adequate, tested business continuity plan. Once these and other factors are considered, the IT Manager should be able to determine whether the benefit of the low-cost service outweighs the potential loss of service to the company's customers.

§ 24.05 REQUESTS FOR PROPOSAL

[A] Overview

Selecting vendors for major purchases can be a tedious process. Like any large endeavor with many details, it is best managed as a project. Few people begin a major purchase with crystal clear ideas of what is needed down to the fine details. They begin with a general idea, such as to hire a vendor to provide on-site workstation support. The request for proposal (RFP) process can help clarify many of the lesser details through discussions with the vendors. In this sense, the vendors help shape the solution as they bid for the business.

The RFP process is normally run by the purchasing department with technical advice from the IT Manager. However, in some companies, the responsibilities are switched with IT running the process under the purchasing department's guidance. In either case, purchasing is the team that should oversee the final selection.

A well-run RFP process is a tedious process for both the company and the bidders. It should only be used for major purchases of services or technology.

[B] Project Startup

As with any major endeavor, a well-executed start is critical to the project's success. The following steps will help ensure a good start to any project:

A. Conduct a kick-off meeting with the project team.
B. Confirm project plan, scope, approach, and schedule.
C. Identify and schedule key interviews with staff and management.
D. Collect, review, and summarize background materials.
E. Identify project templates to be used.

[C] Preparing Requests for Proposal

To begin the process, a formal RFP letter should be sent to all possible candidates. The RFP should define the format of the proposal to ensure a responding vendor can be evaluated and compared with others.

The RFP must contain several essential elements:

A. Technical specifications of the hardware, software, or services desired. This may include CPU speeds, disk capacity, or working hours for contract personnel. These details will drive the cost of goods and services, so they must be clear and request the minimum reasonably required. Any unstated (but necessary) specification provides an opportunity for the bidder to underbid the price knowing that a later expansion will be required.
B. Mandatory requirements should be clearly separated from the "nice-to-have" requirements. Vendors must know early in the process the minimum qualifications for the bid.
C. A statement that selection will not be based on price alone and that the company has the option to reject all bids.
D. Any required terms and conditions for the purchase. This should be the same as the boilerplate on the back of a purchase order.
E. The due date for submitting all proposals. This is normally 30 to 60 days after the bid is published.
F. The date of the bidder's conference.

COMMENT

One author bid a workstation support agreement for three full-time PC technicians to support a major factory. Bringing in a substitute technician to cover vacations was awkward because the facility encompassed several buildings and 2 million square feet. Instead, the vendor was required to schedule technician vacations during the factory's annual summer maintenance break when the workers were away. This negated the need for trained vacation substitutes and lowered the vendor's cost.

About four months into the agreement, the vendor pushed hard to be relieved of some of the required deliverables. This is a form of bait and switch where the vendor bids low to gain the business with the intent to reduce service after a settling-in period. After several calls to the vendor reminding them they must fulfill what they agreed to, the purchasing department gave the vendor 30 days to fully comply or the agreement would be terminated.

Never write an RFP that is clearly skewed toward a single vendor or when the vendor has already been selected. Either action will tarnish the company's reputation leading fewer vendors to bid in the future.

When writing specifications for the bid, it helps to understand what drives the vendors' cost. If an optional item is identified as a mandatory requirement, the price might be driven higher. One way to understand the vendor's cost structure is to look at it from their point of view. What material needs to be purchased to meet the agreement? How many skilled people need to be involved to fulfill the agreement and for how long? What should they cost? If you were the bidder, what sort of budget would you need to fulfill these customer requirements?

[D] Developing RFP Evaluation Criteria

After the RFP is approved by the company and before submitting it to vendors, the evaluation criteria for bids should be determined. An easy way to accomplish this is by assigning one of two value types to each specification:

A. A mandatory requirement without which the bid will be automatically rejected. This might include a required service level, a minimum CPU speed, or a firm delivery date.
B. Optional-but-important factors. Each of these should be assigned a weight to indicate which specifications are more important than others.

Evaluate the costs and expandability of hardware and software purchases over a three-year period. This should include mandatory supplies (some companies sell the equipment cheap and then overcharge for expensive supplies), service contracts, and service level agreements.

Training, documentation, conversion, performance, and acceptance are all optional items that can be included in the bargaining process. Some general items to consider include:

A. Delivery or start dates.
B. Finish or completion dates.
C. Vendor responsibilities vs. customer responsibilities.
D. Pricing methods for purchase, lease, or rent.
E. Annual cost escalators for multi-year contracts.
F. How and when the vendor will bill.
G. Removing the vendor's disclaimers.
H. Provisions for equipment, software, and personnel backup.
I. Emergency and preventive maintenance.
J. Provision for detailed specifications for hardware, software, or service performance.
K. Realistic launch dates for implementations.

In addition, IT should avoid long-term contracts with new or unproven vendors. All contracts also should include performance clauses and penalties for nonperformance or late delivery times.

The compilation of weighted factors is best done using the Delphi method. The IT Manager should have seven people who are familiar with the proposal independently list those factors important to the purchase and their corresponding weights. Then those seven send the lists to a person who was not involved with the selection to compile. This person will make a list of all the factors and return the new list to the seven participants. They will once again go through these factors, choosing and weighting their choices, and new lists will go back to the person to compile the list of most prevalent factors and their weights. Those items assigned low-weight values or only mentioned once should be discarded. This process should continue until a general consensus is reached.

COMMENT

An important mandatory requirement for any long-term agreement is that the vendor possesses a documented, tested business continuity plan. An IT Manager does not want someone else's disaster to impact local operations. The continuity plan of the successful bidder should be reviewed and approved before placing an order.

[E] Bidder's Conference

A bidder's conference is a meeting between the company and all vendors bidding for the contract. This important meeting helps to identify overlooked specifications and may drive the price. The open forum allows all bidders to hear the same answer to questions. The purchasing department normally conducts the bidder's conference.

The format for the meeting should be as follows:

A. All bidders sign in as they enter so they can later receive an updated RFP that includes changes made during the meeting.

B. All representatives of the company introduce themselves and explain their roles in the RFP development.

C. A representative of the company reads the RFP line by line. At the end of each section, the company representative asks the bidders if there are any questions or suggestions for improving it.
   1. Every suggestion or question is written down for later evaluation.
   2. Clarifications can be agreed to on the spot.

D. A representative of the company asks the bidders if there are any specifications in the RFP that prevent them from bidding on the proposal. If there are, the company should consider whether that item is essential to the bid or can be moved to the optional category.

E. At the end of the reading of the RFP document, open the meeting for questions from the bidders.

F. Within a week, the updated RFP is reissued to all bidders.

[F] Evaluating the Bids

Reject all submissions received after the cutoff date for submitting bids. This is only fair to the companies who submitted bids on time.

Review bids as a team, which should include at least one IT person familiar with the technology and a purchasing agent. The team should begin with the completeness of the bids. Remove from consideration any bid that does not fulfill all of the mandatory requirements. If the bidder's response to a mandatory item is ambiguous, the company may choose to ask for a clarification or not. Use a form similar to Worksheet 24-2 Bidder Analysis to help you rank the bidders objectively.

Vendors who provide clear and complete information asked for in the RFP and meet preliminary evaluation standards should be selected for more detailed analysis. Those who do not should be removed from further consideration. Bids should address the specification elements noted in the RFP. The goal is to narrow the field to the final five candidates for close evaluation.

The final vendors may be required to demonstrate their ability to perform as promised in the bid. This includes demonstrations of equipment, customer recommendations, and specific tests used to prove performance benchmarks. Validate every critical requirement in the RFP by testing or through a performance demonstration.

If the bid includes a service agreement, the bidders should present the resumes of the people they are proposing for the assignment. Each person should be "locked in" to the account for at least one year to stop the vendor from presenting top-notch people and switching them for novices.

WORKSHEET 24-2. Bidder Analysis

Bidder Analysis							
Good and Services			Bidder 1	Bidder 2	Bidder 3	Bidder 4	Bidder 5
Mandatory Requirements	**Meets**						
Deliver 20 units by April 1							
3 GHz CPU							
1 TB Disk							
Optional Requirements	**Rating (1 to 10)**	**Weight**					
Expandability – Technical							
Expandability – Price							
Training Cost							
Training Availability							
Service Agreement							
Financial Analysis							
Purchase Price			8				
Service over three years			8				
Materials over three years			8				
Training			6				
Installation			8				
Vendor Analysis							
Customer References			10				
Dun & Bradstreet Report			10				
Better Business Bureau search			8				
Internet search			6				

The company should keep all bids and notes pertaining to the evaluation process. Unhappy bidders who did not win the contract may file complaints about the process later. All records should be stored by the purchasing department and available for review by the company's auditors. The legal and accounting departments will determine the ultimate retention period for this material.

An evaluation of the vendor is just as important as the response to the RFP. Is it financially viable enough to deliver as promised? Is it known for ethical business practices or just the opposite? Verify this in several ways:

A. Financial health.
B. Annual 10-K reports for publicly held companies.
C. Ethical business practices.
D. Customer reports (ask for and verify references).
E. Web searches for "I hate" Web sites.
F. Searches of news archives for published problems.
G. Local Better Business Bureau reports.

COMMENT

The IT Manager should contact the vendor's customers to make a final evaluation before signing an agreement. Ask if they would recommend the vendor's product or service. If they do, set up a site visit. Be sure to talk to the project manager who would be familiar with the details—not the upper executives who do not hear about the routine problems.

Visit the operation to see anything reflecting the vendor's accomplishment. Since most people are reluctant to offer negative information, ask the following:

A. Would you use the same vendor again? If so, why? What has been the major problem with the vendor? Do you know other users of the vendor's product? Are they generally happy? If so, why? Who are the other users? What are their names and telephone numbers?
B. How long does it take for the vendor to respond to issues? Are the people who respond knowledgeable and friendly? Has the vendor ever lied? Has the vendor had the resources to resolve your problem(s)?
C. Does the hardware/software satisfy your needs? Follow up with questions about how long they have had the system and how often it has gone down. Ask about its expandability and upgrading possibilities.

D. Do the users like the system or service? Ask to talk to users to confirm this. Ask users their likes and dislikes about the system or service and why.

E. Ask how long it took to put the hardware/software into operation. Did they receive adequate training? Are the user manuals easy to understand and follow?

F. Is the operation or service provided better than what they could do themselves? If so, why? Is the service worth the cost?

G. Were there any unexpected or hidden costs? What was the nature of these costs? Were the costs reasonable? Was the vendor confronted? If so, what was the reaction?

H. Were the vendor's employees easy to work with? Did their salesperson follow up after the sale? Does the vendor exhibit a genuine interest in the success of the service or product?

I. If you were starting all over, what would you do differently?

Part III

MANAGING AND OPTIMIZING INFRASTRUCTURE

25

SERVICE DESK SUPPORT: HANDLING DAY-TO-DAY HASSLES

§ 25.05   THE SERVICE DESK IN A DISASTER
    [A] Overview
    [B] The Service Desk's Role in the Crucial First Few Hours
    [C] The Service Desk as the Emergency Command Center

§ 25.01 OVERVIEW

[A] Purpose and Scope

Most IT departments have established a service desk to support their user communities. A service desk acts as a lightning rod to attract all of the calls for IT assistance into one central point and away from the rest of the department. The service desk is where users of the company's technology assets can turn for help.

In times gone past, whenever someone wanted support from the IT department, they would call whomever in IT they worked with last. This was a positive thing since in times of trouble they were falling back on the people who had helped them before. It represented a relationship based on confidence in that person's expertise (or else they would not call them). Often the user took pains to maintain a positive one-on-one relationship with these secret contacts.

There were just a few flaws with this approach. First, what would they do if the person that they were looking for were absent or ill? The caller would leave a message and wait for a response. They had no way of knowing how long their wait would be unless they walked over looking for them. What if the person they called was not inclined to help that day? In addition, there is not a record made of each call so persistent problems were not visible to IT management. Without this critical feedback, the manager might be sitting in the midst of a crumbling house and not even know it. In addition, most of the support calls were about very basic issues. These calls pulled expensive IT staff away to handle simple tasks. These interruptions prevented the manager from focusing the staff on the most pressing business issues.

So over time, service desks evolved as a tool that kept all of the good in the previous example and addressed all of the bad in a positive way. Service desks function as a single point of contact for anyone calling with an IT question or problem to report. Instead of "knowing who to call" and hoping they will be available, people seeking assistance can call the service desk and be sure of obtaining a prompt answer. The service desk in turn takes ownership of reported problems until they are resolved.

[B] Critical Policies to Develop Based on This Chapter

Using the material discussed in this chapter, you will be able to create the following policies:

A. Creating a service desk
B. Service desk operations

Policies should always be developed based on the local situation. Successful managers cannot issue appropriate guidance if the policies are written with another company's situation or location in mind.

§ 25.02 ROLE OF THE SERVICE DESK

[A] Voice of the Customer

The service desk receives calls from a wide range of people. It is the IT Director's "public face" to the company. The folks answering the service desk telephones will spend far more time talking to the end users than the director will. If they present a positive, helpful attitude, then the IT department's image will shine. If they are impolite and cannot communicate effectively, then the department's reputation will suffer accordingly.

In their conversations with the service desk, callers will also provide valuable feedback on the service the IT organization is providing. Sometimes they may say this is a repeat call because the problem persists. Sometimes they may say "Please don't send so-and-so over from IT because they are rude, incompetent, etc." There is a lot of valuable information coming across these lines so IT Managers should periodically take turns on the phones. Always act on complaints. The old rule is for every complaint made, 10 more were never reported.

Encourage a constant flow of customer feedback on the service desk's services. Ensure customers know they can call the service desk manager or the IT Manager if they experience any problems with the service desk staff. It is better to hear a bit of bad news from them than to have it amplified by flowing through the executive channels. In casual conversations with end users, ask them specifically about their experiences with the service desk. Some people are too polite to call the IT Director about a problem but may raise the issue if prompted. Managers may also hear some good things that can be opportunities for publicly praising or rewarding the staff.

[B] Staffing

When staffing the service desk, select people carefully for attitude and patience as much as for technical knowledge. During its busy times, the service desk is a hectic place. Patience is essential to calm down a situation while the problem is resolved. Often callers are in a panic and can at times be quite brusque. Cool-headed service desk personnel can defuse the heated emotions and work toward the technical solution. Hotheaded ones will get the IT Director in trouble as well.

Before extending an offer to a service desk applicant, always run a background check. Service desk technicians will soon find their hands deep in a broad range of tools. If this person is to hold a position of trust, they must be of sound character. A criminal background check is essential if they will be responsible for changing user passwords and setting up accounts.

[C] Service Desk Manager

The service desk manager's attitude, work ethic, and demeanor will establish the tone of the service desk staff. Choosing the right person makes all of the difference between a successful service desk and a mediocre one. The service desk manager should plan from the beginning to be a hands-on leader who pitches in when the telephone queue gets too long. He must be dedicated to customer service and ensure that everyone connected with the service desk is likewise minded.

The service desk manager must have the authority to drive calls to completion within the IT department. He personally follows up on calls that are unresolved after 48 hours. Usually, these were escalated to a programmer or network technician to address. If they are unresolved for a second 48 hours, escalate them to that person's manager. This action will not gain them any friends, but a truly service oriented service desk manager would not trust this task to anyone else.

The service desk manager is the "lightning rod" to take all of the complaint calls about the service desk. Sometimes the caller just wants to unload his frustrations onto someone. Sometimes he has a valid point that will improve the service desk's service. Other times the service desk manager must educate him as to why his request violates company policy. Taking these calls and listening carefully is important. Otherwise, they will flow through the management chain, growing ever uglier until surfacing in an executive staff meeting.

The manager represents the service desk at IT change control meetings. As new systems roll out, the service desk manager ensures that developers provide the end users with training and documentation. (This is a defensive move since, without something to refer to, end users will all call the service desk with the same questions.) The service desk manager further ensures that the developers provide adequate desk support documentation and reviews it for adequacy. Proofread all documentation for clarity, accuracy, and pertinence to the support the service desk will be providing. It is important that the service desk be informed in advance about any impending changes so they can answer user inquiries about changed screens or know who to call if the change is failing.

COMMENT

If the service desk knows a data system change has been implemented, they can judge from their calls if the change has failed and can provide the programmer with a quick "heads-up" about the problem.

The manager also acts as the service desk "tool master" by reviewing problem resolutions entered in the problem tracking system. These resolutions are candidates for the service desk knowledge base. Search this repository when confronted by tough problems. Offer the same knowledge base for user self-help through the service desk's intranet Web site.

Another important task is to assemble metrics of the problems encountered during the previous reporting period. Use this to uncover trends, identify marginal equipment, and even users who need further training on their software. Metrics are valuable tools for the IT Director to demonstrate the high quality of support they are providing to the company.

[D]   Service Desk Technicians

Most service desks employ at least two technicians to cover the telephones— one to come in early and one to stay late. These technicians should be very patient people who can sympathize with the caller while calming them down and gathering the pertinent information.

The early shift person begins work at least one hour before the bulk of the employees arrive. This person uses a start-of-day checklist to verify that the network and servers are functioning properly. This allows a bit of time to address any system problems and to call for technical support on the problems before they are uncovered by the users.

Accompany start-of-day checklist by a list of action steps required to check each device and explaining what the proper response would be. Sometimes this involves linking to each server to verify they are operational. It also requires checking each print queue to detect printer jams or other problems.

COMMENT

Just as some people are slow to wake up in the morning, so are some computers! Calls seem to peak sometime before the morning break and then slack off until almost quitting time when they make one final surge. Of course each site is different but the morning seems to be when most calls come in. Adequately cover the telephones during this peak time.

The late shift person covers from some point later in the day until about an hour or so after normal business hours. This provides help assistance for people working late. If additional hours of coverage are required, schedule them through the service desk manager in advance. This reduces the likelihood of abuses. The service desk manager can carry an after-hours pager if night coverage is required, or this pager can be rotated through the IT staff. Many companies cover their third shift service desk with the late night computer operators.

During normal business hours, make sure the service desk staff takes their breaks. They should leave the telephones behind and walk around. They should not be visiting users during their breaks. Breaks allow them to mentally decompress and be ready to jump back into the fray!

COMMENT

Encourage the service desk staff to take their breaks away from their workstations. Visiting users will not understand that a technician is reading the newspaper while the telephone is ringing. The technicians should relocate to the company break area, or to a designated spot in the office.

[E] Working Under Pressure

Sometimes the callers are so angry that they take out their frustrations verbally on the technician. Although this may give them some measure of personal satisfaction, it is not acceptable business practice. Everybody has the right to respect and human dignity, both the caller and the service desk technician. The goal is to defuse the situation, identify the facts, and quickly move the problem to resolution. If achieved, then these callers can turn into appreciative customers. There are some basic steps the service desk can take for addressing abusive callers.

In both types of calls, record the facts as they unfold. If the caller makes specific insults or accusations, then record them. When the call ends, immediately pass on notes of the discussion to the service desk supervisor who can determine if there is sufficient cause to complain through the Personnel Office channels. It is a violation of human resources policy in most companies to verbally abuse an employee with references to their gender, their race, etc. People who call in anger may find themselves in a company disciplinary situation if their remarks are not business-like and focused on the issues.

Angry callers are disturbed about something and rarely was it caused by the service desk. Something set them off before they called and as unfair as it sounds, the service desk technician was just the first person they could unload it on. These callers feel compelled to share their frustration verbally, and often forcefully, with the service desk. Angry callers spew out their complaint and usually run out of steam. They then settle into asking for help with a problem.

Steps for addressing this type of call:

A. Try to separate the facts out of the midst of their emotion. A small bit of information here and there gradually turns the conversation toward the problem at hand.

B. Overlook the angry words (if they are not abusive) while shaping the problem definition.

   C. Slow down the tempo of the call. If necessary, apologize, make an excuse, and quickly put the person on hold for 15 seconds or so to let them cool down.

   D. Empathize, agree with them that the situation is regrettable, and ask for their help in resolving it.

Abusive callers are an entirely different matter. They gain some sort of personal gratification from the exchange. Abusive callers are as much (or more) interested in irritating or intimidating the service desk technicians as they are in having their problem resolved. A call is abusive if the language and word selection of the caller are personally derogatory or make the service desk technician feel uncomfortable.

Steps for addressing this type of call:

   A. If they get the service desk technician angry or argumentative, then they have achieved their personal goal. Give them a few moments to run out of steam and always respond calmly to their tirade. Remember, the service desk technician is in control and can end the call at any time. Answering angrily or meekly encourages more of the same caller behavior.

   B. If the telephone has caller ID, call the person by name, which may slow him down (unless he is using someone else's telephone).

COMMENT

Never argue with a fool. They will drag you down to their level and beat you with experience.

   C. Take charge of the calls. No matter what they are focusing on, bring the conversation back to the issues at hand—a description of the problem, when it first began, etc. Keep the tone of the call firm, even tempered, and unflappable.

   D. Whether it is true or not, inform the caller that all calls into the service desk are recorded.

   E. If the abuse does not stop, tell the caller that either the abuse ends or the call does. Only state this once and feel free to hang up if they continue their abuse. Immediately report the situation to a supervisor.

§ 25.03 ESTABLISHING A SERVICE DESK

[A] Overview

There are at least six major decisions to make when establishing a service desk. Some of them, like staffing, cannot be determined until all of the questions have been addressed and a picture emerges of what the service desk service offering will look like. If a service desk is already in place, consider how these factors stack up against local operations:

A. Establish a service level.
B. What products will the service desk support?
C. Building a service desk team.
D. Service desk problem tracking database.
E. Communicating with IT customers.
F. Other handy service desk tools.

COMMENT

ITIL provides an excellent model for a service desk. However, it requires executive commitment to be put in place. An ITIL based service desk creates a catalog of services based on negotiated service level agreements, providing specific services (and resolution times) for specific customers (usually an entire department). If a customer wants a higher level of service, then they must fund it. For example, the service desk may offer a four-hour resolution for password resets on Monday through Friday. If a department requires a one-hour resolution, then they must fund staff for that additional service.

See Policy ITP-25-1 ITIL Service Desk Policy as an example.

POLICY ITP-25-1.   ITIL Service Desk Policy

Policy #:	ITP-25-1	**Effective:**	04/01/13	**Page #:**	1 of N
Subject:	ITIL Service Desk Policy				

1.0 PURPOSE

This policy provides guidance for the establishment and operation of the IT Service Desk.

2.0 SCOPE

The policy applies to all call centers and contacts for reporting disruption of IT services outside of the SLA (Incidents). The Service Desk is to be the Single Point of Incident Reporting Contact between the IT Department and the business users it supports.

3.0 POLICY

All reports of incidents where IT services are not fulfilling an SLA must be reported through the IT Service Desk.

3.1 Normal Service Desk Operation

The IT Service Desk will be staffed on each working day from at least one hour before the start of the business hours and two hours after the end of business hours. Support for other days and times is arranged by the business managers through the IT Service Desk Manager.

The IT Service Desk uses the service incident report ticketing system to gather information from anyone reporting an incident. Calls resolved while the person reporting the incident is still on the phone are recorded on a tick sheet according to the call's functional support area.

The IT Service Desk technician receiving the call will attempt to resolve the problem while the caller is still on the line. If this cannot be accomplished within three minutes, then the Incident ticket is recorded and assigned to a service technician.

The Service Desk technician refers to the Configuration Management Database to review the relevant SLA. The SLA response and resolution times are recorded on the ticker for the service technician's reference. If the requested IT Service is not covered by an SLA, then the ticket is noted as a "best effort" response and resolution time.

3.2 Service Catalog

Every IT service provided is recorded in the service catalog in the configuration management database. For each service, an SLA between the IT Management and the supported business function describes the level of service for a particular business function. The SLA describes what IT is to provide (for example, response time on a screen), during which days and hours, and how quickly a reported incident will be addressed.

Services not described in the service catalog will be performed only as a last priority, "best effort" response. Services that are not appropriate to an IT service desk will not be provided. For example, the IT Service Desk does not provide directory assistance. If someone is calling from inside the company, then he or she must use the in-house directory. If someone is calling from outside the company, he or she must contact the company's general contact number. Also, the service desk does not provide the correct time. If someone needs the time of day, he or she should call the public telephone service.

3.3 Service Level Agreements

For every service in the service catalog, there will be either an SLA or a vendor underpinning agreement. In either case, the agreement will clearly describe the service to be provided, a set of operating parameters (measurements) that the service must fulfill, the days of the week and the times of service and the planned response time.

Each agreement will include a RACI chart indicating who is responsible for delivering what portion of the SLA. Each SLA must be signed by the business function to be supported, the IT Director, and the Service Desk Manager.

A. **Service Level Agreement (SLA).** An SLA is between the IT department and the supported business function. It describes the services to be provided, measurements of performance, and the maximum time to respond. Based on what is requested, the supported business function may be required to provide additional funding to the IT department.

B. **Underpinning Agreements (UA).** A UA is between the IT department and an external service provider to fulfill a service in the service catalog. For example, this might be manufacturer provided service for servers, high capacity laser printers, support for system software, etc. In some cases, the IT department has little influence on the performance of these services, such as telephone or electrical service.

C. **Approvals.** Every SLA must be approved by the manager of the supported business function and the IT Director. At least once per year, every SLA is reviewed by this same group to determine its continued relevancy and to evaluate its performance.

3.4 Service Level Maintenance and Sunset

All new processes are reviewed after 90 days with the people who use it or are affected by it. This review is intended to identify obvious problems and opportunities for improvement.

Any stakeholder can suggest a modification to an SLA. These are normally reviewed during the monthly discussion of SLA performance.

Every three years, the process is completely redesigned. The analysis verifies the current customer requirements, the current process capability to meet these requirements, and asks team members for their ideas for improvement. Also considered are best practices as learned across the company.

3.5 Reporting Process

The incident reporting ticketing system holds a wealth of information about IT service performance. Once per week, the Service Desk Manager will statistically analyze the previous week's tickets to identify equipment, software, or other service offerings as to which incident reporting is increasing. This report will also help Problem Resolution identify circumstances (date, time, and other reported aspects of the issue) that may cause the problem.

3.6 Responsibilities

IT Management is responsible for:

A. Implementing an incident reporting ticket system
B. Implementing a Configuration Management Database to hold all IT information in a single repository

The IT Service Desk Manager is responsible for:

A. Enforcing application of this policy

4.0 REVISION HISTORY

Date	Revision #	Description of Change
04/01/13	1.0	Initial creation.

5.0 INQUIRIES

Direct inquiries about this policy to:

George Jenkins, CIO
Our Company, Inc.
2900 Corporate Drive
Columbus, OH 43215

Voice: 614-555-1234
Fax: 614-555-1235
E-mail: gjenkins@company.com

Revision #:	1.0	Supersedes:	N/A	Date:	04/01/13

[B]   Establish a Service Level

Once a decision is made to establish a service desk, the first thing is to determine what level of service is to be offered. This translates directly into how much user assistance the service desk will provide before the call is escalated up the IT support chain. This decision will drive the size and expertise level of the service desk staff.

A. **What days of the week and hours of the day will the service desk be manned?** An office that runs from 9:00 a.m. until 5:00 p.m., Monday through Friday, may want a service desk available from 7:00 a.m. until 7:00 p.m. That allows time for the service desk technicians to change the backup tapes, verify that the network and servers are ready for the day's work, etc. If there is enough of a need for Saturday support, staff that day also. Always bring in the service desk early enough to verify that critical systems are operational before the bulk of the employees arrive. This allows time to address system problems before the employees arrive.

> ## COMMENT
>
> Publish the service desk's normal hours of service. It sets an expectation in the users' minds so they will not be shouting because no one answered the telephone on a Sunday morning.

Some departments will appreciate extra support at different times of the year. The accounting department will work late when they are closing the fiscal year books. The materials department may need help during a weekend inventory count, etc. The IT Director must understand the events scheduled in the facility and provide the appropriate level of service desk support. Eventually, the other departments will see the benefit and notify the service desk of upcoming events.

Another staffing issue will be the peak times of the day. After a few weeks, the peak demand times will be obvious. There will also be peak days of the week. During those times, extra help answering the telephones is always appreciated. During times of peak demand, rotate the rest of the IT staff through the service desk a few at a time. Taking service desk calls from time to time might open their eyes a bit.

B. **Time to answer incoming calls.** How long is too long for the telephone to ring? Thirty seconds may seem like eternity if the person is calling with an urgent request. It takes people to answer a surge in incoming calls. The service desk's telephone equipment must allow multiple calls into the same telephone number so others can answer the phones.

However, when the calls drop off or there is a lull before the next barrage, the service desk staff is just sitting and waiting. This is the difficult part of staffing, balancing between enough people to answer the telephone and people sitting around since the phones are quiet.

Tracking the time to answer and the number of calls that give up and stop waiting are both important metrics to track. They will be useful for identifying peak times and shifting the service desk's staff around to meet it. If possible, provide a way for people to leave a voice-mail message when the call wait times are high.

C. **Call to resolution time.** How much time will elapse between receiving a call and the resolution for an average request? The more skilled the service desk staff is, the more calls they will address while the customer is still on the line. We all would like to have our issues resolved with a single call. It is a helpless feeling when a caller is told that "someone" will call us back "later." Not everyone can remain chained to a telephone waiting for "someone" to call back at some vague point in the future.

COMMENT

Resolution time, by product, is another metric to track. When analyzing the service desk performance data, this will indicate which devices on the primary support list take longer per call to support.

D. **Substitutes.** A trained substitute must be on hand to cover the service desk while the usual people go to lunch, take restroom breaks, are absent due to illness, etc. Do not just park someone in front of the telephone to answer it. It is unfair to them and the callers will not receive the level of service they have come to expect. The trained substitute should also be available to handle call volume surges. These usually come at the beginning of the day with a smaller surge toward the end. In most cases, the service desk manager sits in during the breaks and to cover sick days.

[C] Which Products Will the Service Desk Team Support?

What technologies will the service desk support? Even if the service desk staff is skilled, there is a limit to what can be supported. Use a copy of the last hardware and software asset inventory list. Mark each item that will be fully supported as "Green," each item that assistance can be somewhat provided as "Yellow," and those items that you will be helped with as time permits as "Red." Publishing this list is an important part of the IT department's stated service level.

Just as important as determining what the service desk will support, the service desk staff must clearly understand what they will not support. Beware of people dumping their support responsibilities onto the service desk. Good service desk technicians hate to not provide assistance with anything that they can. Do not become the facility's source for telephone numbers. They need to get directory assistance elsewhere. Understand where the other points of dispatch are within the facility, such as facility maintenance and the security office. Refer callers to them. If the questions do not involve IT, do not try to help. Ensure that the service desk technicians understand that only the service desk manager can approve taking on any additional support tasks.

COMMENT

Make a policy to cover the items the service desk will support and to what level. Changes to this list are up to the IT Director (typically quarterly). Otherwise, the IT Director will one day find the service desk staff supporting the televisions in the cafeteria!

Typically, "Green" level items are the IT standard products. This should be the majority of the calls. This also implies that as new items are added to the "standard" list, the service desk must be among the first to be trained. Copies of these products should be available on the service desk computers so they can see what the caller sees. In addition, classify any item that is a component of a critical business function as "Green."

Green items have additional value to end users. These are the ones the IT department will hold training classes on, provide tips on their use in the company newsletter, and provide third-party books on how to use them. This positive approach strategy is intended to "pull" users toward the standard items instead of "pushing" them off the Red ones.

The "Yellow" items are usually the previous standard items. Over time, the staff can easily handle these calls also since they previously supported them as Green. The Yellow list tends to hold all of the legacy equipment that just keeps on running despite its age. Every year at capital budget time, be sure to propose eliminating these technologies.

Red level items are items the team gives their best effort to support after all of the Green and Yellow level calls are resolved. Some sites disavow any help for this category, but the company has already spent the money to buy them so the service desk may as well try to keep it going—after the other categories are addressed. Red level items often require picking up a manual and trying to determine how something works. Red items are those that are too old to repair or "renegade" systems that somehow appeared in the facility despite all policies against them.

COMMENT

Try as it might, the IT department will never be able to fulfill all of the demand for data processing services. Renegade (or "stealth") systems can pop up in any department. Eventually, someone finds a way to circumvent the IT acquisition policies. This can be by political strength or by finding a way around controls of the purchase of hardware and software. They may even have a vendor that rents them hardware and software to support their products.

Some people will never give up their tried and true hardware and software, but these same people are the ones still driving their old brown Studebaker to work. A few people may be emotionally attached to something but what they value most is its predictability. A few may be afraid of change but if the IT department makes it easy for them, and proves that the new system is reliable, then most people will cooperate. Make the transition easy by loading their data into the new software, and providing training and support until they settle in with the new products. Important (business-wise or politically) Red level items can also be supported by arranging for third-party support. Be sure to make the requesting department pay for this. If they feel the pain, they will be interested in replacing it and will be reluctant to do this again in the future.

COMMENT

At one time, one of the authors had a public affairs team that demanded to use a specific brand of software to create the facility's newsletter. "Politically," this purchase could not be blocked. Technically, there was not anyone on the staff who knew how to support it. The expense to train someone to answer the occasional question was not cost justified. Instead, a company was contracted to provide on-site training and support for the product, and the cost was billed to the user's budget.

Hardware—End-user hardware is usually supported by dispatching repair technicians to the users' site. In the case of small items, such as keyboards or bar-code scanner guns, end users may also bring broken items to the service desk to exchange for working units. Resolving hardware issues takes time, so consider how many devices there are out there that could break. Also, the service desk needs documentation on what to ask and what to do when troubleshooting each class of item. Clear, complete documentation will help to determine the proper person to dispatch and the tools they should bring along.

Green level hardware items should have a pool of on-site spares. When one of these items breaks, the spare unit is exchanged for the broken one. The broken unit is sent out for repair and, on its return, becomes the new spare. This provides a high level of support and the least downtime. If the hardware is too large to exchange, then a service contract and "work around" contingency plans must be set in place.

Typically, Yellow level items are not repaired unless they would be expensive to replace. Yellow items will use up their spares until they are gone and then be replaced by equivalent Green level units.

Red level hardware items are not supported. If they can be replaced by a Green or Yellow item, they should be. But if they must be repaired, then send them out for repair or have an on-site repair technician called in. However, if the item is that critical, then it shouldn't be in this category.

Software—there is a wide world of software on the market. However, most companies focus their efforts on a carefully selected list of products. How much help should the service desk provide before dispatching someone to address the problem? Software problems can often take a considerable amount of time to address. Some users cannot adequately (or truthfully) explain what they did that led up to the problem. It can try the service desk's patience to dig out the facts without making a desk-side visit.

Unlike hardware, software lives in a "matrix" world. The operating system interacts with the network on different levels and the many applications running on a PC interact with both. The fewer variations there are the better. To avoid the subtle problems that can be caused, most companies configure their workstation operating systems to restrict users from loading their own software.

Network devices—the service desk supports network availability by watching a network monitor. This monitor indicates when traffic ceases in a network segment or is excessively high. In either case, they immediately notify the network manager to investigate.

Telephones—telephone adds/changes/removal requests are often controlled through the service desk. Telephone instruments sometimes break, employee offices are moved, and voice-mail accounts must be established. All are routine requests for service. The service desk adds value by asking the next set of questions. In the case of a departing employee, where should their calls be routed to? (Usually this is whoever is taking on that job responsibility or his or her supervisor.)

For departing employees, the same questions apply to their e-mail and data files. The service desk can dispatch one request to close someone's accounts and ensure the flow of information is picked up by their department.

Servers and mainframes—usually this involves user IDs and passwords. The service desk either sets up new users or collects incoming ID applications and passes them to the appropriate system administrator. Another routine request is for access to specific files or databases. These requests must be checked against a table that details who can authorize access to whom and then the access request can be passed on to the appropriate person.

The service desk may also monitor the mainframe systems to ensure availability. If a user calls in and says he cannot connect to an important system, this might indicate that for whatever reason the specific mainframe capability has ceased to function.

Web-enabled cell phones and tablets—many sites support these units in the same way as they do PCs. Medical staffs depend on the portability of RF-connected devices to provide information as they roam through the hospitals. Smartphones and tablets can provide Web access from any location. These devices have also replaced internal radio and pager systems for locating key staff anywhere in the facility.

[D] Building a Service Desk Team

With a list of the products that the service desk will be supporting and how well it will be supported, decide what sort of people will be answering the telephones. The skill level of the service desk staff depends on the level of service these individuals are expected to provide. Whatever they cannot answer must be passed up to the next level of expertise. Meanwhile, the customer is still waiting for an answer.

On one end of the support scale is the person who answers the phone and always dispatches someone to fix the problem. These people are cheap but do not save the IT department much time since they cannot fix anything and probably do not understand the business environment. On the other end is the highly paid technical person who can answer most questions but is bored because the work seems "easy."

With that trade-off in mind, consider these three general levels of service desk support.

Level I support takes the message and dispatches someone to address the problem. The advantage of this approach is that it is cheap to staff. It provides the immediacy of someone answering a call. Since they do not know how to repair anything, they refer to their list of who is available to address that type of issue at that moment. However, there is still a training issue. To know whom to dispatch, this person must know the proper questions to narrow down the problem. Using Level I support means the caller can always expect a delay in obtaining results, even in an "emergency." The first call resolution rate will be very low.

A user stating, "the third-floor computers are down," might mean that there is a power outage or that the network connection for these devices has been broken. They may also be exaggerating the problem (imagine that!). Instead of sending an electrician to check the power grid, or instead of dispatching the network technician, the service desk staff must know the sort of questions to ask. In this example, the caller's PC could not start the desired program and was the only one that had a problem. In the caller's mind, the entire enterprise had stopped even though his problem was local and minor.

Level I support is often outsourced. The users call a toll-free number and have no idea where it is answered. The experience may seem familiar when trying to call a public utility. They cannot check anything while the customer is on the line and always dispatch someone to call the customer back and to look into the problem. A disadvantage of an outsourced service desk is that they will never learn much about how the facility is laid out or the internal terminology the company uses daily. This becomes frustrating to users when describing an urgent problem.

Some outsourcing arrangements involve sending the caller to an "off shore" company. This is done to save on labor costs. Companies have experienced mixed results when customers have difficulty understanding the technicians' questions and directions.

Level II support is similar to the mainframe console operators of days gone by. Level II service desks require a higher level of technical expertise and on-site training. Like Level I, they take the call but they can also resolve common problems while the customer is on the line. A common example is to reset passwords. This implies providing the service desk with security authorizations to set up accounts and change passwords (background checks are essential!).

Level II support handles routine questions for computer operations. They may include kicking off or killing mainframe jobs and monitor the running of critical jobs. They can check to see when long-running jobs have completed and the status of reports being printed. At some sites, Level II support may also be permitted to change the priority of mainframe jobs.

Providing Level II support implies that the service desk manager must establish a training outline when hiring new technicians. Level II technicians work on mainframe problems, simple network problems, and PC software issues—truly a wide range of issues. Few people walk in the door with this level of understanding, especially of site-specific tasks. The service desk manager must develop a documented training program to ensure the new employee can learn to answer questions like the rest of the staff.

Level III service desk support normally cannot be reached directly by the end users. This small group supports the Level I or Level II service desk by taking calls they cannot resolve. Level III support might include such things as resolving network device problems, rebooting a server, or replacing a PC hardware component. It might also include the person who makes changes to the PBX (adds/deletes). Level III support can also be contracted through a third-party service. The IT department's service contracts typically provide Level III support. They require that only a few skilled IT staff named on a list can call them for help. Be sure to include the service desk staff on this list, or at least the service desk manager. The key to faster training is carefully documented procedures and technical documentation.

[E] Service Desk Staffing Issues

One of the more valuable aspects of the service desk to the IT Manager is how it handles all of the routine calls that flow in. The service desk is a natural place to store forms for requesting user IDs and for later creating the new ID/passwords. Requests for user IDs, office moves (PCs and telephones), and all of the other routine paperwork can flow out from and into the service desk. The service desk staff must of course be trained in this and have guidelines to follow, but overall, this is routine work to fill their off-peak hours. Requests for security access to sensitive data or software will flow through the service desk but is handled by the IT staff as before.

Resetting passwords can be time consuming. If the company's security software forces periodic password changes (as it should), then the service desk staff will be called on to assist the people who forget them. The trick is to ensure that no one fools the service desk technicians into letting them into another person's account. An identity authentication procedure is essential.

COMMENT

Step-by-step work instructions are needed that will closely control who can reset a password and how they will authenticate who is calling. The service desk technician is not permitted to deviate from these steps.

Another time killer for the IT staff is restoring files that the user has deleted. The service desk can pick this task up and, depending on their size and complexity, run the reloads in their off-peak hours.

The industry standard for staffing service desks is roughly one technician per every 75 users. The size of the staff also depends upon other factors:

A. The expertise of users is a big driver for staffing. If the team is supporting a large number of novices, they can flood the service desk with many basic questions. This is more typical in sites that experience a lot of employee turnover or who hire seasonal workers. On the other hand, if the team is supporting a large number of engineers running high-powered workstations, a low-tech service desk is not of much use to them.

B. The stability of the systems being supported can also be a factor. If the systems are stable and behave in predictable ways, then it is easier to train the staff. If they employ cutting edge technology, then the staff must have the technical background to isolate the problems.

C. The number of technologies to support may guide staffing plans. The wider the range of technologies or things there are to know, the more likely that the staff will specialize or take longer to train.

D. In the long run, staff size can be reduced if the service desk manager proactively chases down recurring problems. This will result in fewer repeat calls (and happier users).

[F] Service Desk Problem Tracking Database

Sometimes the service desk is quiet as a summer afternoon at the fishing lake. Other times it is a boisterous, hectic madhouse. In both cases, there is a common problem of how to ensure that "no request is left behind." A very important service desk tool is a problem tracking database. As these calls are received, they are entered into a problem tracking and reporting database. The database will provide many essential functions:

A. Move problem tracking off a notepad and onto a shared database. This provides visibility of the problems encountered to the service desk manager and the potential for a wide range of management reports. Problem reports are less likely to be lost.

B. The tracking database keeps track of which IT person the call was escalated to, and when. The service desk manager will use this to follow up with the assigned IT person to ensure they complete the tasks.

C. The database tracks calls based on their priority. Each site devises their own scale for prioritizing problems. A priority system can be as complex as desired.

Some sites find a five-level system adequate:

1. **Critical.** This involves a system that prevents a critical business process from functioning. Assigned IT technicians drop what they are doing and help resolve this issue. An example would be if the facility's data network died. Notify the service desk manager immediately.

2. **Important.** This is an issue that impacts a number of users but the facility's critical functions are still operating. An example might be a failure in the e-mail system.

3. **General support.** A problem affecting a single user. This will be the majority of the calls.

4. **Routine.** Typically, this is for new user IDs, office moves, etc. These requests need to be assigned and scheduled, but their urgency depends on how close they are to becoming due.

5. **Information.** These are questions that are escalated in a non-urgent fashion to the appropriate IT support person. An example would be a question as to how to build a pivot table in Microsoft's Excel. This type of question would be passed on to the software trainer.

COMMENT

Many companies automatically apply a "critical" priority to problem calls from top executives no matter how trivial the issue.

So how would a typical problem call database work? Starting at the beginning, the telephone rings! The technician sees who the caller is in the telephone instrument's caller ID window. He initiates a new problem report and answers the call. If the call involves an appropriate service desk issue, the technician decides if it is a "quick hitter" or a problem to be tracked. Sometimes the call involves a question such as how late the service desk will remain open that evening, the status of an open call, etc. These types of calls are recorded on a tick sheet, as they take longer to add to the database than they do to resolve. It is useful to track overall call volume but entering these calls into the database would not serve any purpose.

If the caller has a problem to be tracked, their contact information is entered into the database. This can be read directly from the caller ID display. Most sites preload customer information that is automatically pulled into a new problem ticket based on the telephone number. More sophisticated sites also tie in their asset database so the service desk technician knows exactly what the caller is supposed to have on their desk.

Next, the service desk technician asks the pertinent questions that will narrow down the issue to hardware, software, or user training. As he discusses the problem's symptoms with the user, the service desk technician enters notes in a problem description field. Don't be surprised if the user categorizes it as one thing and, upon questioning, the service desk technician concludes the cause is something else.

If the service desk technician escalates the call to the IT staff, he selects the appropriate person based on the chart of the primary and secondary support person for each technology. When the ticket is saved, copies are e-mailed to the requestor and the person assigned to the call. If the problem is urgent, the service desk technician will also call the IT support person to dispatch him directly to the problem site.

Most service desk databases use e-mail to notify the requestor whenever anything on their call ticket changes. The tickets typically maintain a history of date/time stamps so the responsiveness of the IT staff can also be monitored. This can be an important management metric for evaluating responsiveness and productivity. Sometimes technicians close a problem ticket even though the customer says the problem still exists. E-mailing a confirmation catches many of these discrepancies before they explode into larger issues.

[G] Communicating with Customers

Customers contact the service desk several ways. Some will send e-mail for non-urgent requests and a few will walk over and knock on the door. However, most will call on the telephone which can provide some powerful management tools. Giving priority to callers over walk-ins will reduce the number of people hanging around to chat with the service desk staff.

The first thing the service desk needs is a single number that all service desk calls funnel into. The number should be catchy and easy to remember. One company used a four-digit extension that spelled out HELP (4357). When that number rang, it could be picked up by any of several adjacent telephones. Each telephone could handle numerous calls all made into the single number.

On the telephone was an internal caller ID function. This provided the answering service desk technician a quick heads-up of who is calling. (Of course anyone could call from any unused telephone and the best joke was calling from the facility manager's phone.) The caller ID was also used to screen calls. Political reality is that the top executives approve the IT budget. If they call, they are usually answered first.

> # COMMENT
>
> End users run the gamut from "I'm an expert," to the quiet ones who are afraid they will break the PC and be forced to pay for it. In between is the curious person who tinkers, the know-it-alls, and the ones "documenting everything that happens to them to cover their backsides." Unfortunately, every in-house lunatic feels it is their duty to call the service desk and offer their services for resolving problems!

If it is difficult to adequately staff to cover peak periods, provide callers with the choice of holding or leaving a voice-mail message. This allows those people with routine requests to leave their message and move on instead of endlessly waiting on hold.

It is essential that someone monitor the voice-mail box and begin addressing these calls in the order they were left (oldest first). If customers perceive that these voice-mail messages will not be answered in a reasonable time period, they will stop using this service. Consider a guideline that every message will be answered within two hours. Again, this is a matter of staffing during peak periods.

Spending the day with a telephone pressed against an ear can become quite uncomfortable. Equip each service desk person with his or her own telephone headset. This also reduces background noise and improves his or her ability to hear a faint voice over the hubbub around the service desk.

Another useful telephone tool for the service desk is to broadcast a system-wide announcement via voice mail to all telephones. Unfortunately, the message may not be relevant to all users, so use this sparingly. However, if a major component is broken and will remain so for some time, it will reduce the number of calls the service desk receives about it. The message should acknowledge what is wrong and a conservative time estimate of when it will be resolved.

[H]   Other Handy Service Desk Tools

The service desk staff needs tools close at hand to do their job. During busy times, the calls can come in fast and furious. Ready access to tools will increase the number of calls they can resolve without escalating the issue to the IS staff.

A. **Reference manuals.** When the phone rings, there is no time to go searching for manuals to research questions. The service desk staff needs a set of technical manuals close at hand to investigate questions that arise. In addition to technical manuals, they need a complete and current set of end-user instructions in both printed form and electronic form (to e-mail to new users). This will allow them to assist users of in-house developed systems with operational questions.

It is amazing how many users cannot read or refuse to follow instructions. Often a substitute worker in a department is not provided with adequate instruction so the service desk ends up walking them through the process. Before escalating a problem to a programmer, the service desk will walk them through the appropriate steps to ensure the user is correctly using the product. The service desk library might include a set of PC manuals for standard software. The service desk manager must set a limit for how much time they can afford to give one caller. At some point, these questions must be referred to the training staff to address.

During slack times, the service desk technicians can review this documentation to improve their skills. They can also review technical manuals of their key products.

B. **Asset lists.** A list of the assets assigned to each user is helpful. This gives the technician an idea of the type of workstation, the operating system, and the standard software loaded on it. It would also detail any unusual peripherals. If the IT department has a current asset inventory, identified by user, it may be possible to connect it with the client database and whenever a user's telephone number is entered, both their contact information and their asset information becomes available.

C. **Recall lists.** A matrix is needed that describes who on the IT staff supports what technologies. This list, in technology order, identifies the primary and secondary support person to call. The third one on the support list is always the IT Manager. Typically this list would include all known hardware and software. It would include back room technical staff such as the network team and the database administrators. When a problem occurs that must be escalated to the IT staff, the corresponding name is selected from this list. A second list is referenced for the contact information for that person. This includes their office telephone number, cell phone number, and home telephone number. It should have everything the service desk technician needs to know about contacting this person. When calling someone for a problem, make a note on the problem report of when they were called and if a message was left. Wait about 15 minutes and try again. After another 15 minutes, call the next level of support.

COMMENT

The service desk policy must include instructions that the technicians never provide anyone's home telephone number to anyone from their recall rosters. This violates the privacy policy in most companies. If a call is essential, they should dial it and then patch the requestor through to the person they want to call.

EXHIBIT 25-1. Critical Process Impact Matrix

Critical Process Impact Matrix									
Date:		Normal Operating		Critical Operating		Support		Customer Contacts	
System	Platform	Days	Times	Days	Times	Primary	Backup	Primary	Backup

D. **Critical process matrix.** An important tool for the service desk is a matrix of which processes are critical, and the time of day they are most important to be operational. This matrix is normally maintained in a spreadsheet. This sheet combines critical processes and times they must be available (see Exhibit 25-1 Critical Process Impact Matrix).

Fields on the matrix:

1. **System name.** This is the official and/or common name this system is known by.
2. **Platform.** The server or primary hardware platform this system normally runs on. If a problem requires that the AS400 be rebooted during the day, sort the list to bring all of the AS400 systems together and quickly see which customers must be notified when it is to go down, and when it is restored.
3. **Software.** This is the name of the software system as known to the IT staff. This may or may not be the same as the system name.
4. **Priority.** This is how important this device is to restore to service. Consider using the Green/Yellow/Red ratings. Use the "Critical" rating for all critical business function components.
5. **Critical availability.** The times this system must be available to support the facility. For example, if the order-entry staff only works Monday through Friday, and if this system died on a Saturday, the downtime is not a critical event. The problem still needs to be worked but no one will miss it until Monday.
6. **Time of day.** Use the 24-hour clock format.
7. **Day of week.**
8. **Support.** When a problem occurs, the service desk must quickly determine who to notify.
9. **Primary.** Who on the IT staff is called first for a problem?
10. **Secondary.** Who on the IT staff is called second for a problem? Remember, the third level support is always to call the IT Manager.
11. **Customer contacts.** If the system must be brought down, who must be notified? When service is restored, who should be told first?
12. **Primary.** Which customer is to be notified first of a problem?
13. **Secondary.** Which customer is to be notified second of a problem?

    To make this matrix even more powerful, add to the bottom of the spreadsheet all of the contact information for each person on the list. Individually highlight each cell in the Support and Customer contact columns and establish a hyperlink between the name and their telephone number. Of course, this adds yet another list that must be maintained when telephone numbers change, but on a day-to-day basis, it is faster.

E. **Big marker board.** Most service desks maintain a large marker board within sight of the service desk technicians, which contains current information.

1. Calendar of availability—rather than fumble through the support list leaving messages that may never be returned, the service desk can refer to the board to see which IT technical staff members are scheduled to be out of the building that day. Staff members that call in sick can also be added to this list.
2. Scheduled system activities—sometimes the only way to clear a system problem is to reboot the server. This might be held off until late hours or set up to occur during lunch. The service desk is informed but the note is also posted on the board. Also posted are notices of

system/software upgrades scheduled with the date and time of planned implementation.

3. Telephone numbers for reaching key support staff not in the facility or at home. Examples might be visits to other company sites, or attending seminars.

F. **Tools.** The service desk can be a busy place and sitting all day answering the telephone can be tedious. Ensure the service desk technicians have comfortable, adjustable chairs. Lighting can be a problem in many offices so ensure there isn't glare on their screens for quick reference. Desktop space is important for spreading out manuals and for taking notes. The temptation is to fill all space with dedicated monitoring equipment and more PCs. Leave some room for reading and writing.

§ 25.04   THE PROACTIVE SERVICE DESK

[A]   Overview

Service desks tend to fall into one of two operating philosophies: reactive or proactive. Reactive service desks pride themselves on how fast they can answer a call. When no one calls, they sit and pass the day doing whatever they are inclined to do. However, when the calls come in again they are slow to react since their focus is on however they are passing the day—not on their customers. Reactive service desks will rise to a basic level of competence and go no further. Their outlook is entirely defensive, and as any military strategist can explain, defensive tactics may prevent defeat but will not win the war.

Proactive service desks address the calls as they come in. But when the call volume slackens, they shift their focus to identifying common problems and eliminating them before they result in a call to the service desk. The difference between reactive and proactive is like sitting in a fire station. A reactive fireman waits for an alarm before doing anything. A proactive fireman also inspects buildings and stops situations before they turn into fires.

Service desk staffs are organized to provide a certain level of service during busy times. Providing enough people to handle calls during the busy time will result in staff members sitting around during the slack periods. This need not be! The laws of physics apply to objects as well as to people. People at rest tend to remain at rest. But, if these same people are taught to remain in motion then they will automatically remain in motion. During these slack periods, assign tasks for the service desk to perform.

Service desk managers must address this problem early and decisively. If executives see the service desk team lounging at their desks or wandering around the facility they will be quickly marked for staff reduction. What a pity. The service desk is uniquely situated to make a major improvement in the IT department's service level—if they are properly led!

The real power of the service desk is to identify marginal processes or emerging systemic problems and focus the IT team on their prompt resolution. From its central point of problem collection, the service desk can "see the big picture" of what is happening with the facility's technology.

It is often the first person to detect a problem-reporting trend that indicates a computer virus. He needs to know what signs to look for and what damage containment actions to take until the IT staff swings into action. Fast action here saves a lot of work later.

[B]   Managing by Metrics—Nothing but the Facts!

Some managers blunder through their business day by day. They lack vision, imagination, and are probably already promoted beyond their level of competence. These people consider it a bad day when the telephone rings a lot and a good day when things are quiet. They do not manage their work—their work manages them!

Others recognize that to take control of their work environment, they need to measure it. Measurements provide early indications of problems before they explode! A true saying is that managers cannot manage what they cannot measure. Are call volumes increasing or decreasing? Why? Has a department just skipped training their seasonal workers and told them to call the service desk for every minor question? Are there any departments or users who never call the service desk? Why? What products or departments or users or time of the day are causing the most calls? Is there more than one cause at play here? Take care, though. Managers will find that they will get what they measure, whether the end result is what was wanted or not.

Metrics can build a case for more staffing, perhaps based on the number of callers who hang up before someone can get to them. They can build a case for better tools, such as a network monitoring system to detect when segments are becoming overloaded or RF nodes blink off. Metrics can show which categories or specific items of equipment are causing the most problems so they can be targeted for replacement. The performance functions the service desk manager measures can tell a lot!

In addition to measuring the IT systems it supports, the service desk must also measure its own performance. Services provided by the service desk must be measurable and regularly analyzed. Measuring without analyzing is just going through the motions. The time to answer calls and the overall level of service desk performance will be a constant issue with customers. Some will complain if the telephone is not answered on the first ring and others will try to cut the "over-staffed" service desk!

There are two tools readily available to the service desk manager for capturing data on the team's operations: the telephone system and the problem tracking database.

  A. **Telephone system metrics.** Most telephone systems will allow the service desk software to capture usage characteristics for calls. These telephone metrics are a useful complement to the problem database metrics. If the telephone system does not support these features, consider adding them during the next capital budget cycle. Common telephone systems statistics are:
  1. **Average time to answer.** On the average how long, is it taking the service desk staff to respond to an incoming call? This shows

how well the service desk is meeting its published service level standard.

2. **Average talk time.** How long is the tech spending on the call? Are they talking too long? Chatting with users is an important part of relationship building, but it should be confined to slack times. During busy times, this could add an intolerable wait to incoming calls.

3. **Number of calls received after working hours.** Do the service desk hours need to be extended? Based on automated caller ID, who and which departments are calling, at what times and day of the week?

4. **Abandonment rate.** This is for people who gave up waiting for the service desk to answer and hang up. There is always the odd call where the user's problem resolved itself while waiting for the service desk to answer the telephone, but this may also be an indication that staffing during this time period is too light.

B. **Problem tracking database metrics.** Most problems are reported to the service desk via telephone. However, there is still a small but steady flow of walk-in requests, e-mail, and voice mail requests that are missed in the telephone metrics. The big picture for this is the problem tracking database. Trends might include:

1. **Identifying troublesome hardware and software.** Are there a lot of calls for problems with a particular printer? Does a particular network device cease working every time a thunderstorm rolls in? Identify equipment for additional maintenance or replacement.

2. **Identifying troublesome users.** Is there someone who calls the service desk a lot? Does he have legitimate questions or is he lonely and wants to chat with someone? If he is lonely, ask his supervisor to talk to him. If he has ongoing problems, could they be addressed with further training?

[C] One Call—One Success

An important service desk metric is the number of problems resolved during the first call. The greatest customer satisfaction is derived from one request—one resolved problem. When you consider the time to record information, dispatch someone to assist them, to return calls, etc., resolving problems at the first call is a money saver for the company. There are a number of things that affect this:

A. **Technical expertise of the service desk technicians.** IT departments everywhere are under pressure to reduce their costs, and workforce expense is a major part of this. Highly skilled service desk technicians can use their experience and training to resolve calls quickly. Unfortunately many calls are for basic questions and do not require a lot of skill to resolve. This leads to boredom and high employee turnover.

Most service desks follow a model of technicians skilled in addressing the basic issues. These people can address many of the calls without passing them on. But to address the more difficult issue, the next level technician is standing by to receive calls transferred to them. This hand-off is done with the customer still on the line so they are not lost in the shuffle, and a call back is not necessary. A second level technical staff can hang on to the first call and improve the statistics.

B. **Technical difficulty of the call.** The first call metrics not only depend on the expertise of the service desk technician, but also depend on the technical difficulty of the problem. These calls are quickly passed on to second level support since the service desk technician lacks the expertise to address them.

C. **Time available to work through the issue.** In busy times, the phone calls seem to roll in constantly. It is not possible to spend much time resolving the call instead of passing it on. The longer time spent on working a single call means that many more people are sent to voice mail or give up waiting. In this sense, trying to improve the first call statistics will hurt the metric for the average number of minutes that an incoming call must wait.

D. **The service desk manager must regularly review the problem tracking database to identify the types of problems referred to the IT staff.** Then develop a strategy to train the IT staff, or acquire the tools so the service desk technicians can address these problems—if appropriate. To address this, the service desk manager examines the statistics of the types of calls and when they are reported. The types of calls are further broken down into the symptoms and solutions. Working with the second level technicians, the manager can develop a series of questions that can be used to localize problems and recommended solutions. Additional training by the IT technicians is also helpful. In the case of common problems, the solutions can be provided without passing the call on to the next level.

[D]   Training End Users

The service desk is uniquely situated to identify end users who require additional training in using a product's basic functions. Most people would prefer to address their own problems rather than call for help. When the call volume slackens, the proactive service desk can take positive steps toward increasing user satisfaction while reducing call volumes.

A. **Refer people to the training staff.** If someone is struggling to learn the use of a product one command at a time (and calling the service desk each time), then refer them to the training staff for assistance. The trainers can schedule some desk side support on basic product usage until that person can sit through regular training. The service desk could also provide by e-mail or through their Web site, information on training classes available. An alternative trainer is that department's power user.

B. **Conduct mini-training courses.** Mini-courses are a chance to present and discuss one aspect of a product to a small group of people. Mini-courses can be over lunch (or as a special, focused training orientation session for a department). Typically, the approach is a lecture with a set of written instructions on how to perform that specific function (such as pivot tables in Excel, formatting text and pages in Word, or how to write a very basic database report).

C. **Create self-help sheets.** Volume software licensing saves companies money by providing a single copy of the software along with the right to make a specific number of copies. However, this means that printed user manuals will not be provided. The manuals are only available electronically. Yet the user must have a grasp of the product's terminology before the electronic document's topic search can be successful. To assist end users, the service desk can create self-help booklets and guidelines. After assisting a user with the electronic manuals, the service desk can send a follow-up copy of the help sheet for future reference. The service desk may keep a supply of help sheets for basic functions, such as electronic mail practices, a list of standard company word processing templates, and using voice-mail accounts. There may also be easy to follow pictures for how to use various telephone features. These tools will increase customer satisfaction and reduce the volume of trouble calls. These sheets are e-mailed or sent out via interoffice mail on request.

D. **Issue end-user documentation for in-house created systems.** Sometimes new or transferred employees are thrust into a job without adequate training. To ease this transition (and to reduce the volume of calls), the service desk can maintain an online library of end user documentation that can be issued via e-mail to employees. These may also be available on the intranet (if they do not involve confidential data systems).

E. **Compose a list of the best third-party self-help books for each of the standard products.** Often these books provide a clearer explanation of a product's features than do the manufacturer's manuals.

[E]   Carry the Message to the Masses

A problem with the service desk is that it appears to the caller as a faceless voice—almost a non-person. Of course this is not true, but matching a face to a voice to a name helps to build personal credibility with end users. To do this, during the slack work times, the service desk staff must leave its back room and mingle with the masses in the facility.

The service desk manager has a responsibility to explain and promote the service desk to other departments. One way is to attend their staff meetings and provide a short overview of the service desk, how it conducts business, and what it is and what it is not. Take time to educate these people about the IT world while learning about theirs. As time permits, bring along available service desk technicians. These meetings allow the users to match a face to a voice. They also are useful for setting an expectation in the users' mind of the services they can expect from the service desk. Make clear to everyone that the service desk manager is always open to any questions or criticisms of the service desk operations. This provides a ready outlet for customer complaints and suggestions for improving service.

Discussion points at these meetings might include:

A. **Visit the various departments carrying the word.** Use these conversations to raise any problems they have had with the service desk in the past.
   1. Explain to people that denied requests are the result of good policy—not the service desk (don't shoot the messenger!).
   2. Hours of operation—does this cause them any problems?
   3. Staffing levels—do they have problems getting through to the service desk? Is it worse at certain times or days of the week?
   4. Are the answers provided by the service desk technicians clear and understandable?
   5. What are supported products and how are they selected?
   6. What should the service desk do differently?
B. **Publish articles in the facility's newsletter and on its general information Web page.** Profile a service desk staff member. Keep each article nontechnical, brief, and focused on a single topic.
   1. Frequently asked questions.
   2. Most common problems reported for the past month.
   3. News of impending upgrades.
   4. Security practices.
   5. Company policies on end-user computing responsibilities.
C. **Posters.** Posters are another communication tool for the service desk to keep its message in front of its customers. Posters should focus on a single message. The message should teach the reader about something new or remind them of something they should be doing.

   Posters have a useful life of about two weeks. At that time, rotate the posters among locations and introduce new ones. Otherwise, they become a fixture on a wall and their message is no longer reviewed in passing.

   Examples of poster topics include:
   1. Service desk hours of operations and services offered.
   2. Information to capture before reporting a problem to the service desk (error number, actions that lead up to the problem, etc.).
   3. How to sign up for training.
   4. URL for the service desk Web page.
   5. Company policy on security and safeguarding passwords.
D. **Establish a service desk—with links to:**
   1. Online manuals for company developed software.
   2. Self-help guides for standard products.
   3. User FAQs.
   4. Company policies concerning IT and end-user computing.
   5. Information on scheduled system outages.
   6. IT forms.
   7. Software vendor sites.
   8. Third-party product use sites.

E. **Speak to training classes.**

Computing training sessions are excellent times to spread the service desk's message. Recently graduated students are likely to call for help. A few minutes discussing tips for reporting a problem can make their next call to the service desk far more productive. Explain how to identify error messages, how important it is to write them down, and how to describe the steps leading up to a technology failure.

A standard part of this presentation is a recap of the service desk service level goals—hours of operation and services offered. Other basic information of interest includes the process for ordering new equipment or software, anti-piracy policy, and good data backup practices.

[F] Hail and Farewell

In large companies, there is a steady trickle of employees joining the company and departing for other opportunities. Each group will place a set of demands on the service desk technicians that are easily organized into checklists that can be provided to the appropriate managers.

A. **New employees.** New employees arrive full of enthusiasm and more than a touch of apprehension. Each company has their own twist on how e-mail, voice mail, etc., is implemented. Instead of responding to the same series of requests floating in one at a time, the service desk can collect the most common new user setup issues into a single form. Time spent working with new users will reduce their frustration and the number of elementary calls made to the service desk.

The first sign of a new employee is a user ID request. This might trigger an e-mail memo (which they cannot see until the account is created) that will contain pointers to the knowledge base and specific documentation of immediate interest.

Stop by on an employee's first day and provide him or her with a user ID and password. Walk the employee through setting up voice mail and logging into the e-mail system for the first time. This is another opportunity to spread the good word of the service desk's stated service level and hours of operation.

New employees often take on responsibilities of a person who has departed the company. They may require access to electronic records and department specific systems. Include on the checklist questions about who this person is replacing and what systems they will require access to (and training for).

B. **Departing employees.** Employees leaving the company must have their user IDs disabled promptly. This protects the company against any departing mischief and the employee from unfair accusations.

An important part of disabling the user IDs is to identify who will be provided access to the e-mail, voice mail, PC files, and server files. Often this is the supervisor of the departing person. Later when a replacement appears, some of these may be shifted to the incoming worker. The idea is to capture this information early and have it ready to act on instead of requests dribbling in from the department as they think of things. This sheet provides a basis for setting up the file shares and permissions of their replacement.

[G]   Knowledge Base

Over time, service desks become a major storehouse of information on problems and their solutions. So why not share it? A knowledge base is a powerful tool for capturing the successful resolution of problems and saving time when a similar issue arises. As problems are resolved, their solution is recorded in the service desk-tracking database. The trick is to make this information available in an easy to search and understand format, usually accessible from the service desk's Web page. The result is a self-help tool for end users as well as the service desk staff.

During times of slack service desk demands, assign a technician to review the problem description and resolution. Clean up both (grammatically and factually) and add them to the knowledge base. Extraneous notes entered during the debugging process should be removed so that when someone searches for a problem, only the successful solution is presented. Before adding an entry to the knowledge base, it is important to ensure that its solution does not contradict an existing article. Knowledge bases can be internal or external. An internal knowledge base would only be accessible to the service desk staff. It would include topics such as working with company confidential systems and other security issues. An external knowledge base is for general company self-help. A knowledge base can also be purchased from a third party or accessed via the Internet. This is a tool for the service desk staff to use until their own knowledge base is brought up to snuff.

[H]   Power Users—The Service Desk's On-Site Helpers

Every service desk has to contend with end users who are skilled in some aspect of data processing. They may have held a data processing position in a previous company or may be a skilled hobbyist. Some departments create "stealth" data processing staffs to fill their requirements that the IT department cannot or will not meet. These people can ask some very detailed questions when requesting support. In general, these people are referred to as power users.

Power users handle their own simple problems themselves. They like to tinker with things and teach themselves about technology by reading books. They can be dangerous, ignorant know-it-alls, or very intelligent, knowledgeable people. In some cases, they can even be malicious. Power users are easier to manage if the IT department works with them instead of against them.

Power users scare some IT departments. They see them as an uncontrolled threat to their systems' stability. They publish piles of rules to curtail their activities and inevitably lose the fight. It is far better to reach out and make these skilled people an extension of the IT staff than to try and rub them out.

Most departments have someone on their team they normally turn to when they have system problems. As can be seen from the service desk logs, many of these questions are basic and easy to answer. Let the power users do this! Help them to reduce the service desk's workload and free them for seeking out the root cause of the more serious problems.

Power users are still restricted from doing certain things, but give them the freedom to handle simple issues. Things to do to promote their use:

A. Consider giving them their own service desk telephone number. Give them priority service for their routine requests. Many of the people in the user departments will see this and go to them with questions, most of which the power user could possibly answer.

B. Use them to review software and process changes for their department before they are implemented. They can also sign off on the adequacy of end-user documentation.

C. Provide them with priority seating for training classes pertinent to their area.

D. Consider forming a user council to provide feedback from the departments.

E. Consider hiring them into the IT department!

[I]   Customer Surveys—Closing the Feedback Loop

Customer feedback is an important tool for improving the service desk's products and services. Sometimes the feedback is freely offered, such as in formal complaints or compliments. Sometimes, the feedback is indirect by departments no longer calling for assistance. Many people are reluctant to suggest things that may be viewed as criticism so they will not offer anything. Instead of waiting for people to speak up, the service desk manager can institute an ongoing program of customer satisfaction survey. These surveys are a series of open-ended questions that try to understand how the team's performance is viewed by its customers.

Surveys have two general goals. The first is sent randomly to anyone with a user ID. This is to solicit general comments. The other is as follow-up to service desk calls. This would provide information about the quality of the technician's response and the customer's service desk experience.

§ 25.05   THE SERVICE DESK IN A DISASTER

[A]   Overview

In an emergency, there is a lot of chaos. Imagine if the electricity went out in the building at this moment. The IT Manager may have some idea of what to do but the dark can be disorienting. Other people may not be so cool-headed and add to the confusion of all. Where should the IT staff go? What should they be doing? No one knows when a short-term calamity will strike. A proactively managed service desk will have predetermined actions developed and published so that in an emergency, the IT staff knows where to go, what to expect, and what to do until the IT Director can form a plan of action.

Containing and recovering from major disasters is covered in a later chapter. In this section actions will be described for addressing short-term disaster containment and recovery efforts that typically last four hours or less. This category of business disruption requires a concerted effort to address but is typically resolved before the full IT disaster plan can be implemented.

[B]   The Service Desk's Role in the Crucial First Few Hours

Companies occasionally struggle with short-term disruptions to their operations. Power outages or brownouts, loss of data communications, loss of telephone communications, or a small fire in the facility are examples of interruptions that are usually resolved within a few hours. Meanwhile the company's workers need a central place to contact and be contacted from until the emergency is resolved.

During their normal workday, whenever people have a technical problem, they call the service desk. In a crisis, they will instinctively fall back on previous actions to cope with the situation. With some prior preparation, the service desk will be ready to handle this influx of traffic. These actions are not intended to replace the facility's security or maintenance coordination. They are to provide guidance to the IT staff and information for end users.

Each type of emergency calls for its own response. Examples of this are:

A. A power outage will require someone to help recover unattended computers when they restart. Those systems on mini-UPS systems must be monitored or gracefully shut down. Does the service desk have a list of these machines and where they are located?

B. Network outages may require that the facility switch to manual processing until the network is restored. The loading of this paper-coded data may be tedious and IT assistance important. For example, in a factory, materials will still be accepted and issued during the network outage but the inventory will be out of sync. Does each department have manual procedures for continuing work and collecting data until service is restored? Does the service desk have copies of them?

C. During a telephone service outage, the company may ask employees to use cell phones to notify key customers of the problem and to provide company cell phone numbers for critical incoming calls. Some companies depend heavily on the ability to respond to customer requests instantly. For others, the telephone is a useful tool that they can work without. If the facility is a just-in-time supplier to another factory, loss of telephone communication may unnerve the customer. Have an alternate plan for establishing communication of all critical information.

D. During a fire, the network and asset management team tries to determine what is in the affected area and stages repair materials for use in an area where those workspaces will be recovered and where rewiring will be required. A fire may burn wires and destroy equipment. It may be hours before that portion of the facility can be entered. The team could while away their time waiting for admission to the burned area or it could estimate what is damaged and begin assembling materials for the repairs.

With just these four examples, it is easy to see how useful the service desk will be. As a command center and place for all to meet, it reduces chaos so that plans can be made and action begun. The response to all emergencies is essentially the same:

A. Determine the scope of the problem.
B. Determine the impact of the problem.
C. Implement containment actions to prevent it from spreading.
D. Implement recovery actions to restore everything to full service.

General emergency actions for the IT staff and the service desk include:

A. All IT Managers report to the service desk to provide status reports and to formulate an initial plan of containment/recovery action.
B. Everyone in the IT department, excluding the service desk and the IT Managers, will report to a central area to provide a workforce pool for addressing the issue. The central area should be equipped with emergency lighting and be in the proximity of the service desk.
C. The IT Director will pre-designate one manager to oversee the service desk area and one to oversee the personnel pool.
D. Pre-designate teams for:
   1. Network and telephone system support.
   2. Systems recovery (after the emergency passes) to catch up data files, restart systems, and whatever else is required based on the emergency.
   3. End-user notification of the problem, suggested work around actions and for when the issue is resolved.
E. Report the dispatch and return of all teams to the service desk.
F. Report the status of each team's efforts to the service desk on the hour.

[C] The Service Desk as the Emergency Command Center

To carry out this mission, the service desk must have more than adequate emergency lighting. Emergency lighting is battery driven and comes on when electrical power is lost to the building. In addition, the service desk equipment must be on a UPS system to maintain its PC and mainframe connections.

Finally, the IT management team must have a standing order to automatically report to the service desk when a crisis erupts. This saves valuable time and reduces chaos.

The service desk has the tools in place that are essential for coordinating an emergency:

A. Communications—telephones set up to handle a rush of calls into a single number. Also the ability to broadcast messages over e-mail and telephone voice mail. Two way radios and company provided cell phones provide links between recovery crews and the service desk.

B. A status board—the white board used to post absences, etc., is perfect for posting problem status. The service desk usually has a large marker board that can be used to indicate the progress of the recovery. This provides the same message to all readers.

C. A team accustomed to working under pressure—on-site and ready to act.

D. System and department information—staff recall lists, system documentation, copy of the full disaster recovery plan, etc.

E. Emergency power and lighting to continue operations during outages.

F. An emergency supply of flashlights, batteries, and extra two-way radios.

The service desk is most suited to short duration, contained problems. Most IT crises last less than four hours. For example, how many electrical blackouts has your site experienced and how long did they last? Fires can be major disasters but most are contained within a portion of the facility, and out within an hour.

In a large emergency, the IT Director would shift his command center function to the facility identified in the company's disaster plans.

26

MANAGING IT ASSETS: IDENTIFY WHAT YOU HAVE

§ 26.01   OVERVIEW

[A]   Purpose and Scope

Asset management policies address both hardware and software. Well-defined and maintained asset management policies and procedures are financially rewarding, will fine-tune the company-wide information systems operations, and help avoid embarrassing litigation.

IT assets are poorly managed in most companies. An IT Manager looking for a way to reduce the department's costs without firing anyone should always look here first. Most IT people take their equipment for granted and neglect the administrative side of their business. Typically, the asset manager position is assigned based on personnel availability rather than aptitude.

IT management must formally direct the IT asset management policies and procedures throughout the organization. To be successful, IT management should:

A. Assume the stewardship of all IT assets in the company.
B. Inform all employees of the directives.
C. Explain the need for the policies and procedures.
D. Mandate that all employees use only company-owned hardware and software. Even if their intentions are honorable, no one is to bring in their own hardware or software.
E. Never permit the downloading of company-owned software to privately owned computers or secondary storage in any form.
F. Note infractions in the employees' records.
G. Emphasize that serious or repeated violation of asset management policies will be grounds for dismissal.

Bygone mainframe computing days seldom had asset management problems. Capital expense budgets funded new hardware and the software was developed in-house. The hardware was unique and bulky and depreciated over time. All of this activity came under the domain of the data processing department. Today, computer hardware is found throughout the company. Often there are no controls over purchase, standardization, or use. Software is even more problematic. It can originate from legitimate in-house development or purchase, or from questionable or illegal sources. This anarchy can appear insignificant because of undocumented direct expense, but the indirect repercussions can be great and the cost astronomical.

[B]   Critical Policies to Develop Based on This Chapter

Using the material discussed in this chapter, you will be able to create the following policies:

A. Asset management program for the IT department.
B. Tagging equipment.
C. Collection of idle assets.
D. Personal assets.

E. Consultant and visiting technician assets.
F. Scrapping hardware.
G. Software assets.
H. Install/Move/Add/Change (IMAC).

Policies should always be developed based on the local situation. Successful managers cannot issue appropriate guidance if the policies are written with another company's situation or location in mind.

§ 26.02 LAY THE GROUNDWORK

[A] Overview

Counting all of the IT devices and software packages in even a small company is a tedious and time-consuming task. In a large company, it seems like an insurmountable assignment. This is why most IT departments do not want to tackle the job. IT Managers know there is excess technology in the company but feel it is cheaper to leave it alone than to pay for the labor of a wall-to-wall count. Such managers work day to day and are not in control of their department.

This section explains the careful preparations that can reduce the cost of counting equipment. A sharply defined project scope identifies what to count and what to pass by. Each item has its own characteristics. Which ones should be gathered? What is the best way to tag assets for later database updates? All of these questions depend on the local situation, but must be locked in before proceeding with the count.

COMMENT

Test the technology counting process on the IT department first. This should work out the obvious defects in the process.

[B] Asset Management Project Scope

The first step in asset management is to identify what is to be managed—the scope of the project. There are many different IT assets to manage and it might be easier to tackle them separately. Also, be prepared for resistance, as some people will believe this is the first step in taking away their equipment. The types of assets to manage may include:

A. Workstations and peripherals
B. Company-owned PCs in employees' homes
C. Network devices
D. Desktop telephone instruments and add-on devices

E. Servers in computer room and business departments
F. Data collection devices, such as bar-code scanners
G. Data output devices such as bar-code printers, CD writers, etc
H. Mainframe and server software
I. PC software
J. Tablets
K. Company-sponsored smartphones

This list can go on and on. The point is that there is a lot to look at. Each type of device has its own unique data elements to collect so identify these before starting. Examples of unique data elements might be the size of the monitor screen, the firmware revision level of network devices, or a workstation's CPU speed. For most companies, the main effort centers on workstations since there are so many of them, they cost so much, and they are very visible to executives.

COMMENT

Using the 80/20 rule, an IT Manager can save time by only tracking the major items such as desktop units. Rapidly evolving technologies such as tablets may not be worth the effort to track unless widely used.

Exclude some things from the project. Keyboards and PC mice are generally disposable and not worth the expense to track. Consider setting a lower limit based on cost, such as hardware under $100 is not worth the effort to track. (Due to software licensing issues, track all software.) Typically, all software is tracked because a single package has the potential to interrupt the operation of a wide range of systems.

[C] Asset Manager Appointment

Asset management is a major IT responsibility. The company depends on the IT Manager to identify requirements, to redeploy idle assets, and to save the company money. Yet when it comes to getting purchase orders signed, all the executives see is a never-ending stream of requests for expensive new equipment. If an IT Manager has problems getting purchase requests approved, it is because the executives do not believe that IT is a good steward of the company's assets. Establishing an asset management program can be a step in the right direction.

To establish an asset management program, appoint someone as the asset manager (or coordinator). This can easily become a full-time job. In some companies this function resides in the IT operations team since it is a part of IT's routine efforts. In smaller companies, it is an additional duty for the PC Support Manager. An asset manager should be someone good at paperwork and who pays attention to details. They should have a broad business and technical background so they know the difference between a terminal, a PC, and a network router.

To begin, the asset manager should:

A. Inventory assets (what's out there?).
B. Tag assets (easy identification in the future).
C. Establish and maintain an asset database (management reports).
D. Develop a three-year workstation planning strategy (what should we buy or retain?).
E. Control all future purchases (adhere to strategy).
F. Reevaluate asset repair (when to scrap the old?).

There are many benefits to doing this:

A. Use the data to develop a long-term asset strategy to drive out variation and focus on "standard" equipment. Standardization saves money in training, staffing, and reduced operational complexity. Standardization may seem a simple dream with rapidly changing technologies, but the department can drive in that direction.
B. Evaluate the equipment repair strategy to move some categories to less expensive approaches.
C. Collect idle equipment for redeployment or disposal.
D. Provide management with asset data for informed decisions.

See Policy ITP-26-1 Asset Manager Assignment Policy as an example.

POLICY ITP-26-1. Asset Manager Assignment Policy

Policy #:	ITP-26-1	Effective:	03/18/13	Page #:	1 of N
Subject:	Asset Manager Assignment Policy				

1.0 PURPOSE

This policy assigns the Information Technology Manager as the company's custodian of all technology owned by the company.

2.0 SCOPE

This policy governs all technology owned by the company, to include (at a minimum):

A. Telecommunications (telephones systems, cell phones)
B. Data network
C. Smartphones and tablets
D. Desktop equipment (computers, monitors, personal printers, scanners)

E. All network attached devices
F. Mainframe computers and peripherals
G. Servers and peripherals
H. All software

3.0 POLICY

The Information Technology Manager is assigned as the company's Technical Asset custodian of all technology owned by the company.
The Technical Asset Custodian will:

A. Standardize hardware and software to minimize complexity.
B. Reallocate equipment and/or software for company benefit irrespective of the budget that originally purchased it.
C. Administer service contracts to provide an acceptable level of support for both hardware and software.
D. Analyze, publish, and follow a five-year technology strategy to guide purchases and identify technologies for retirement. This plan is to be updated semiannually.
E. Plan and manage the migration of all software (both purchased and in-house developed) to new versions.

4.0 REVISION HISTORY

Date	Revision #	Description of Change
03/18/13	1.0	Initial creation.

5.0 INQUIRIES

Direct inquiries about this policy to:

George Jenkins, CIO
Our Company, Inc.
2900 Corporate Drive
Columbus, OH 43215

Voice: 614-555-1234
Fax: 614-555-1235
E-mail: gjenkins@company.com

Revision #:	1.0	Supersedes:	N/A	Date:	03/18/13

[D]   Asset Information Database

In its simplest form, an asset inventory count could just be a count of what you have. To move this forward into managing your assets, you need to gather descriptive information as to what you have, where it is, and how it is being used.

If IT has service desk problem-tracking software, it may already have an asset management module. Service desk software uses a key, such as the user's telephone number, to bring up a description of that person's workstation to assist in the troubleshooting process. If such a module already exists, examine the data fields it captures to see if it is adequate. Once the asset database is populated with data, the service desk will be its biggest customer.

COMMENT

Data collection and maintenance is expensive. While it only takes a moment to jot down a serial number or other characteristic, it takes more time to enter the data, update it, etc. Justify every data element collected to avoid gathering useless data.

For every field in the asset database, create a validation table of correct entries. This minimizes the number of free form fields and makes counting text fields easier.

An asset management database can be as detailed as the IT Manager wants to make it. However, the more fields there are to track, the more time will be required to keep it current. Track only those data elements that need reporting. The best place to start is an outline of the reports the IT Manager might use. Such reports might be:

A. Total number of devices, subtotaled by model.
B. Number of workstations, subtotaled by processor speed.
C. Number of network devices, subtotaled by model and where they are located.
D. Number of devices per department.
E. Breakdown of processors by user type.
F. When each item was purchased.
G. Length of warranty (save in a date field indicating when it ends).
H. Operating system (type, version, and service pack level).
I. Hardware characteristics such as CPU type, RAM, and disk space.

COMMENT

How powerful is an asset database? If today a requirement came down to install software in all desktop units (and not notebook PCs), and this package required a minimum of 10 GB of disk along with 1.5 GHz processors and 512 MB of RAM, how quickly could a cost estimate be determined? How accurate would it be?

Each of these reports brings its own data collection requirement—and each could be quite useful. The more successful the asset management efforts are, the more the accounting department will ask for data—especially data elements that were not collected during the inventory count!

Below are examples of how data tables might look for tracking assets.

In Exhibit 26-1, users are identified by their telephone extensions and names. The department code is necessary if the report is to detail the amount of equipment in a given department. Other things to add might be the location by office number or factory column identification. The telephone extension number can be used to link to the equipment table. If the telephone is shared over multiple work shifts, this may not be a problem since the workstation usually is also shared. The database may track it under the first shift owner's name or allow for multiple owners.

EXHIBIT 26-1.

Data Table 1. User Information

User		Dept.
Telephone	Name	Code

In Exhibit 26-2:

User phone #:	This ties to the user name table.
ID tag:	Used if placing a company asset tag on the device.
Device type:	PC, network hub, AS400 terminal, etc. Pick from a list to ensure consistency.
Serial number:	Essential for tracking movement and for some service contracts.
Maker:	IBM, Dell, Cisco, HP.
Model:	Gives some idea of what is in it.
CPU speed:	Important when estimating cost of upgrading software.
Hard disk size:	Not so important with 100+ GB drives.
RAM:	Important when estimating cost of upgrading software.
CD RW:	May or may not be important—great for making data backups.
DVD:	May not be important.
OS:	Type and version number are very important when planning software upgrades.
Monitor size:	Or any other relevant fields.

To this, add any number of other fields such as date purchased, warranty expiration date, date information was last verified, etc. Warranty is a nice way to reduce hardware repair costs, but requires time for record maintenance. Further complicating this—if a new motherboard is installed in an old PC, does the IT department need a mechanism to track its parts warranty separate from the PC's?

EXHIBIT 26-2.

Data Table 2. Equipment Tracking

User Phone #	ID Tag	Device Type	Serial #	Maker	Model	Workstation Specific						Monitor Size
						CPU Speed	Hard Disk Size	RAM	CD RW	DVD	OS	

COMMENT

Warranty support usually requires shipping the unit back to the manufacturer for repair. Workstations cannot leave the premises for repair because of data security issues. Consider negotiating a no-warranty purchase. Usually, this covers the unit for the first 30 days (to address out-of-box failures). Beyond that, repair the unit as usual.

Depending on how sophisticated the asset-tracking system will be, consider linking the asset record to a repair record for any updates or to a table listing every item in the machine. Although this example used personal computers, this is equally useful for network equipment, printers, bar-code scanners, etc. The result is useful for identifying problem units and problem vendors.

[E]   Asset Tagging

Many companies have a capital item asset-tagging process in place. It is intended to deter theft, help keep track of asset location, and allocate overhead budget based on material used to support a department. Asset tagging is something to do correctly or not at all. It is a major labor investment to establish and maintain. If the resources to do this or the benefits derived are not present, then do not start it.

COMMENT

Asset tagging is a poor theft deterrent. One of the authors worked at a company that always stamped their name and logo on their hand tools. So many tools were stolen that it became something of a point of pride to have a complete set of tools at home with the company imprint on them. The removal of asset tags can mar the surface of an item that may reduce its resale value—but not by much. Stolen goods are usually sold cheaply.

Most equipment comes with a serial number from the manufacturer. However, these numbers vary widely in length, composition, and attached in some of the most inconvenient places. In addition, the longer the serial number, the greater the chance of incorrectly keying it into the database. Therefore, most companies attach their own asset number to expensive equipment. This makes it easier to track individual items.

The most basic asset-tracking numbering system starts at 000001 and increases by 1 from there. Other approaches use the first two digits to identify the class of item and the remaining numbers to identify the individual item. Typical groups might be workstations, network hubs, printers, monitors, etc. Embedding a "device group identifier" in the serial number reduces the likelihood of someone swapping asset tags on equipment. The service desk also has an idea of what the device is by the serial number.

The general costs for asset tagging are:

A. Expense of printing or buying preprinted tags.
B. Expense of portable tag readers (if using RF-ID or bar codes).
C. Time to expand the database to accept the tag ID.
D. Time to gather information on each item and to attach the tag.
E. Time to update the asset database every time a tag moves.
F. Interruption of new equipment delivery to attach a tag.

The three most important things to consider are:

A. **What to tag.** What needs tracking? Someone must decide what is going to be tracked. Do not attach tags unless the IT department is committed to tracking equipment. There is a labor cost for every device tagged and tracked. Base this decision on what will be done with the information. Is equipment tracked to maximize warranty coverage? Is the goal to gather capital item depreciation for accounting? The IT department may want to manage certain classes of equipment such as network cards or workstations. Anything the IT department wants to track the location of is a good candidate. Disposable items such as keyboards and computer mice are not worth the effort. Perhaps the decision of what to tag may be driven by its cost, whether it is leased, or under a service contract.

B. **How to tag.** The purpose of a tag is to read it later. At the same time, the less obtrusive it is, the less likely the operator is to remove it. After determining what to tag, establish a procedure of where to attach the tag. For example, the back of a PC is difficult to read since some PC system units are tucked deep under desks and held in place by too-short wires. A suggested place to tag PCs is near the bottom of the case on the side, such as the front lower corner of the right side of the case (when facing the unit). Network hub cards are usually in a rack in a locked closet. Attach the tag to the front panel if there is space.

For items that can only be reached by technicians (usually in locked cabinets), the asset tag can be attached to a paper tag which is tied to the device. However attached, take some pictures of the tagging points to standardize where it goes. Document the tagging procedure for each major type of equipment. Different devices may have different attachment issues, but always tag workstations in one general area, printers in another, and so forth.

Asset tags, by their nature, are permanent. Using an adhesive to attach them requires an idea of the object to which they will be stuck. The more permanent the glue, the fewer chances there are to attach it! All adhesives have solvents that will remove them (even if they seriously mar the surface at the same time). In some cases, attach tags with screws, but this is a bit of overkill for electronic equipment.

C. **Which tag is best?** The best tags have an RFID chip embedded in them. This way, the chip reader only needs to get close to the device and there is no need to move equipment during an inventory count. A less expensive approach is to use bar-coded labels. In both cases, when conducting subsequent item counts, a portable reader can quickly collect information.

Along with the bar code, include the same number in human readable format, in case equipment is moved without access to a bar-code reader. Also, include on the label a request prohibiting its removal, along with the company name. It may not stop everyone, but it will slow down the more honest ones. Bar codes and RF-ID chips pay off in subsequent inventory counts. They allow the IT asset manager to move quickly through a department scanning bar codes instead of reexamining every device to discover whose it is. Without bar code, someone must write down every tag number and even careful people make data transcription mistakes. See Policy ITP-26-2 IT Hardware Asset Management Policy as an example.

POLICY ITP-26-2.   IT Hardware Asset Management Policy

Policy #:	ITP-26-2	Effective:	03/18/13	Page #:	1 of N
Subject:	IT Hardware Asset Management Policy				

1.0 PURPOSE

This policy provides guidance for the proper management of computer hardware assets. Its purpose is to minimize costs, drive out obsolete technology, provide the ready location of assets, and ensure that obsolete devices are disposed of properly.

2.0 SCOPE

This policy applies to all employees, contractors, and visitors. It covers all electronic hardware assets purchased or created by the company, to include:

A. PCs, servers, network devices, printers, monitors, Memory sticks.
B. Computer workstations of all sizes to include both fixed and portable, to include tablets and other mobile devices.
C. Computer servers in any location on company property.
D. Company-owned workstations and servers at employee homes, for use while traveling, at vendor sites, or at customer sites.
E. Video cameras except for combination camera/cellular telephones, which are considered to be primarily cell phones.

Excluded from this policy are:

A. Telecom devices and cell phones.
B. Devices purchased by employees with their own funds for their personal use, such as smartphones, tablets, and music players not connected to the corporate network, are excluded from this policy.

3.0 POLICY

The following guidelines are established for using company hardware and software assets.

A. **Appointment of an IT Hardware Asset Manager.** The IT Manager will appoint a member of the Information Technology (IT) department as the company's IT Hardware Asset Manager. This person has the authority for implementing this policy.
B. **Acquisition.** The IT Hardware Asset Manager is responsible for selecting and acquiring computer hardware for use by the company. This person will:
   1. Publish a quarterly list of standard hardware approved for use.
   2. Coordinate with the hardware repair and support organization to ensure it can support changes to the standard hardware list.
   3. Review and approve all IT hardware purchase requests to ensure they conform to the approved standard equipment list.
   4. Review and recommend approval or denial to the IT Manager for the purchase of any non-standard devices.
   5. Maximize redeployment of idle equipment prior to purchasing new devices.
C. **Strategic planning.** The IT Hardware Asset Manager will monitor company asset usage and IT strategic plans and will annually develop a Three-Year Hardware Asset Roadmap that:
   1. Includes industry projections of new hardware technology releases for planning changes to the standard unit list.

2. Synchronizes future requirements with the Software Asset Management Three-Year Roadmap to identify required hardware upgrades.
3. Identifies the number of devices, by type, expected to achieve obsolescence for budgeting replacement purchases.

D. **Maximize utilization.** The IT Hardware Asset Manager identifies, collects, and safeguards idle IT hardware assets.
1. The IT Hardware Asset Manager has the authority to confiscate idle IT hardware assets even if they were purchased with a different department's funds.

E. **Disposal.** The IT Hardware Asset Manager ensures that all pertinent corporate policies for the proper disposal of assets are followed. The IT Hardware Asset Manager:
1. Creates and maintains a process for removing data from disks and persistent memory prior to the scrapping, sale, or donation of equipment.
2. Coordinates with the company's environmental management department to ensure that all equipment and supplies declared as scrap are disposed of in accordance with current environmental regulations.
3. Updates the appropriate accounting records concerning capital assets.

F. **Tracking database.** The IT Hardware Asset Manager creates and maintains an asset-tracking database. This database will provide the essential data for tracking equipment from purchase to obsolescence, locating specific devices, and providing information for warranty or insurance claims. The IT Hardware Asset Manager will:
1. Conduct an initial asset count and periodic department asset verification audits throughout the year.
2. Report monthly to the IT Manager on the number and location (by department) of all IT hardware assets.
3. Attach an IT asset tag to all hardware assets.
   a. Promptly tag new equipment entering the facility.
   b. Idle assets recovered and lacking a tag receive a reissued or new tag.
4. Update the asset database whenever tracked assets are relocated.

G. **Security.** The IT Hardware Asset Manager safeguards company assets from theft.
1. An equipment pass recorded with the facility security team must accompany all assets leaving the premises.
   a. The IT Hardware Asset Manager provides passes for equipment leaving the premises for repair.
   b. Issues a permanent pass to Notebook PC users.
2. Assets owned by another company and used on the company's premises must be clearly marked as to their owner. The company's security team must check this equipment in and out of the premises, by serial number.
3. Employees taking assets off-site are responsible for their safe return.
   a. Damaged items will be investigated by the IT Hardware Asset Manager to determine if neglect caused the damage. If so, the report will be turned over to the IT Manager for resolution.

b. Employees whose borrowed items are stolen must provide a copy of the police report or repay the company for the borrowed but never returned item.

H. **Acceptable uses of company computer network, workstations, and servers.** The IT Hardware Asset Manager publishes guidelines for the appropriate use of IT hardware. These assets are to be used solely for company use. Personal use is prohibited.

I. **Personal assets.** Employees are prohibited from bringing into the facility personal hardware assets such as PCs, peripherals, or any other hardware devices.

1. The IT Hardware Asset Manager may confiscate personally provided assets since only company property is permitted on the premises except where written permission is provided by the IT Hardware Asset Manager and the device has been checked onto the premises by the security team.

2. Devices purchased by employees with their own funds, and for their personal use, such as mobile phones and tablets, are excluded from this policy.

J. **Violations.** Any employee who abuses the use of company-owned assets is subject to corrective action including termination. If necessary, the company reserves the right to advise appropriate legal officials of any illegal violations.

4.0 REVISION HISTORY

Date	Revision #	Description of Change
03/18/13	1.0	Initial creation.

5.0 INQUIRIES

Direct inquiries about this policy to:

George Jenkins, CIO
Our Company, Inc.
2900 Corporate Drive
Columbus, OH 43215

Voice: 614-555-1234
Fax: 614-555-1235
E-mail: gjenkins@company.com

Revision #:	1.0	Supersedes:	N/A	Date:	03/18/13

[F] Idle Equipment Collection

During the course of an asset inventory, someone will undoubtedly come across small stockpiles of equipment. Some of this equipment does not work. Some of it will be obsolete. Some is new and never been plugged in. Now is the time to set aside an area to receive this material.

Idle material is the result of a number of things. Usually, someone had a system problem and a replacement unit was installed. However, no one ever came back for the old device so it was shoved into a closet or under a desk in an empty office. Most companies are littered with disconnected keyboards, monitors, and computer mice. Walk around with a large cart and pick up all the obvious material. If the facility has a newsletter, encourage people to call the service desk to arrange for a pick up.

Another type of idle equipment is the private stashes of spare equipment. These are computers, scanners, network cards, monitors, and a wide range of devices that are in working order but kept hidden away as spares. (This is an indicator that people lack confidence in IT's ability to support them!) Expect considerable political pressure not to pick up these piles. Once identified, the company's accounting manager will be the IT Manager's biggest ally in confiscating this equipment. The problem is that all of these stashes cost money to establish. By consolidating these stashes into one place, the company saves money since fewer spare parts are needed. These types of stashes often contain new in-the-crate equipment. The warranty clock is ticking! Over time, these new items are worth less and less as better technology becomes available.

Idle equipment must be stored in a locked room. Do not permit people to freely walk in and take whatever they want. Remember, IT is now controlling the assets, not just shuffling them around. If the asset room is viewed as a candy store, then the best equipment will quickly migrate to newly reestablished department stashes. In this room, install a large worktable, shelving for the equipment picked up, and a cabinet for individual circuit boards. A file cabinet for keeping records will be useful as will a kit full of basic tools. Ensure only a few people have keys to the doors. Establish a sign-out sheet for equipment taken from the room. (All devices can enter but few can leave!) The IT Manager must establish guidelines for removing equipment.

Purchase three types of colored tags (or stickers): green, red, and yellow. Also, obtain a stockpile of cleaning supplies. If using stickers, the attachment point must be clean. Attach a yellow tag. Yellow is for caution, that the device has not yet been checked. Imagine a technician's feelings if he trucked a large monitor up 10 floors only to see that it does not work! Assume all incoming equipment is broken until proven otherwise.

Once all of the technology orphans have been collected, test every item to see if it works. Sort the equipment into piles according to its value (very old workstations versus newer technology). Test the obviously new items first. Old equipment may not be worth the time. It is difficult to thoroughly test every item. In most cases, just turning it on and trying to use it is test enough.

The best time to attach the yellow tag is when picking up the device. Write on the tag where it came from. This is most important for workstations that may hold important data on the hard disks.

Every item that seems in workable order should have a green tag attached. The tester should write his name and the date on the tag. This provides some traceability. Items that do not work get a red tag. Place them in one of two piles. One pile is the to-be-scrapped items. The other is the to-be-repaired items. Note on the red tag in which pile they belong.

COMMENT

When preparing a workstation disk for redeployment or scrapping:

- Set the unit aside for two weeks to see if someone wants a file from it.
- Make a full backup of the disk.
- Repartition and perform a sector by sector reformat for at least three passes.

The company's accounting department will provide guidelines to follow for scrapping equipment. They will need to know the asset tag number, serial numbers, make, model, etc. In most states, businesses pay a "property tax" on their assets and the accounting team will want to remove these items from the books. If the company has an environmental department, they can advise the safest way to dispose of the devices. There are other possible disposal outlets:

A. Call the company used to repair that type of device. They might buy the old equipment for use in their repair operations. This is the most common source of spare parts for old technologies.
B. Call a local vocational school to see if they want them for their students to dissect and/or repair.
C. Offer them to the local computer repair shop that might be able to reuse some of the parts.
D. If the equipment is still usable, consider a donation.

When scrapping PCs, most companies overlook recovering the software licenses. The rights conferred on the purchaser by each software company's license are different, but they typically allow a company to use one copy of a program on one machine. The right to use that program may be transferable within the company after discarding to PC. However, the company will need to show proof of a license, which is why the license notices of incoming software are collected and filed as "IT Vital Records."

Collect items needing repair in one place. If the pile is high enough, the repair service may come in to work on them rather than requiring the IT

Manager to send them all out. Manufacturers often offer a flat rate repair for some items, such as bar-code scanners. The biggest problem will be the data on workstation hard drives. Track down the last owner if possible or ask the manager of the department to look at the data to see what they want to keep.

COMMENT

Never send out a workstation for repair with the hard drive still installed. If this is done, the company just lost security over that data. If necessary, install another hard drive in the unit before shipping it out for repair. (With a spot of luck, this might fix the problem!)

When redeploying PCs, reformat the hard disk and load it with the company's basic software load. Most people are reluctant to delete old programs and data off their disk. This can make for a surprisingly complex set of software baggage that builds up but never gets used. Users also will expect support for these obsolete "drag-along" programs. Reformatting removes the accumulated program fragments and DLLs. It also will improve the unit's performance.

Provide a list of working equipment to the IT Manager. Consider this equipment for redeployment whenever someone calls for a new purchase. Another use is to begin migrating older working equipment out of the offices by installing newer equipment from the idle equipment room. Who gets the best of the redeployable equipment is another political battle. In this way, the IT department can quietly exchange idle assets for the most difficult to maintain units.

Justifying taking equipment out of this room for an installation is the same process as for purchasing a new device. This equipment is not for providing "favors" to someone.

[G] Data Collection Forms

The last step before beginning an inventory count is to create a data collection form to gather equipment information as the inventory team moves through the facility. The form should include all of the data elements in the database table. There are also some decisions to make:

A. Will PC software be counted and tracked? Which ones? How is it recognized?
B. Will circuit boards within PCs be counted?
C. What about PCs with locks or passwords that prevent anyone from checking them unless the assigned operator is present?
D. Is there anything else to do during the count, such as detect illegal copies of software?

For the machine count, use a form to record idle equipment uncovered for later pickup. A floor plan is useful if there is a lot of area to cover. As rooms are completed, color them in on the floor plan. Use a sheet of small colored dots to mark the doors of completed rooms.

COMMENT

If the company has previously standardized one model, then by capturing the model name of the desktop units it is possible to fill in the hard drive, CPU, etc. from the standard equipment for that model.

§ 26.03 CONDUCTING THE INVENTORY

[A] Overview

Finally! It is now time to begin the inventory count. The goals here are to uncover idle assets, find hidden equipment stashes, and tag all hardware assets and to gather data on what is present in the facility. This is a lot of work, but for a big payback.

A technology count touches employees across the organization from the executives to the custodians. When it is finished, how will IT be perceived by the employees? Before launching this effort, debug the process first on the IT department and then on at least one more department.

Throughout the process, continuously communicate with everyone. Tell departments what will happen before arriving for the count. Tell departments already counted just what was found. As the database is populated, constantly monitor for problems in the data entry and readability of the data collection sheets to ensure high quality in the data.

[B] Conducting the Count

Take some time to get (almost) everyone on IT's side. Meet with the facility staff and explain the process. Issue a schedule of when the inventory team expects to visit each area. This might be over a weekend so that equipment is not moving around during the count. Schedule days and times after a department is counted for the employees to bring over their notebook PCs and tablets for tagging.

Before the count begins, issue an announcement to the "target" department several days in advance. The IT Manager and that department's manager should both sign and acknowledge it. It should explain the material counting process. This is a good time to remind the department why this is good for the company. Ask people to remove any material they have placed around their equipment so its serial number can be checked. Also, ask everyone to put idle assets outside their office door. Pick these up before the count to save and count them later.

During the count, be sure to look in every closet and large storage cabinet. If locked, ask security to open them. Ferret out stashes of good equipment and forgotten broken equipment. Be very thorough. Look into large boxes, drawers of empty desks—anywhere keyboards, mice, modems, scanners, etc., could be stuffed.

COMMENT

Enter data sheets into the asset database *as soon as they are turned in*. A problem reading the data may require someone to revisit some areas to verify information. It is best to catch this problem early in the process.

Once the count and tagging is complete, run some summary reports. Provide these to the IT Manager and the accounting manager. After the data appears to be clean, provide business managers with a recap of tagged material in their department. Exhibit 26-3 is an example of a report that includes some accounting allocation assigned to each device. Some companies would use an asset report such as this to assign depreciation expense to their budget. The value of each unit may be a flat amount based on equipment type.

[C]   Set a Hardware Strategy

The first step is to identify a minimum workstation configuration. Examine the total equipment counts by category. Clean up any data classification inconsistencies. Let us use personal computers as an example. Report them by category. What are the current operating system hardware requirements in CPU, RAM, and disk space? Does each of the workstations meet the minimum configuration? How about the recommended configuration? Look on the vendor's Web site for this information. Some example products are:

> Microsoft Windows 8.1 sets its hardware minimum as:
> CPU: minimum 1 GHz
> RAM: 1GB (32-bit) or 2 GB (64-bit)
> Hard disk space: 16 GB (32-bit) or 20 GB (64-bit)
> Adobe Photoshop CC for Windows
> CPU: Intel® Pentium® 4 or AMD Athlon® 64 processor (2 GHz or faster)
> RAM: 1 GB
> Hard disk space: 2.5 GB for installation, additional space required during installation
> Operating System: Windows 7 with Service Pack 1 or later
> Microsoft Office 2013
> CPU: minimum 1 GHz
> RAM: 1 GB (32-bit) or 2 GB (64-bit)
> Hard disk space: 3 GB available

EXHIBIT 26-3. Asset Report by Department

Date: 9/11/2004

Dept. Name: Tech Support

PCs	$95,950	< 1 GHz	1–2 GHz	2–4 GHz
		62	8	18
Notebook PCs	$6,969		2	
Monitors	$24,240	15"	17"	19"
		21	47	20
Inkjet printers	$2,345	HP 932c	Canon 5100	Epson Stylus 740
		7	3	12
Laser printers	$3,214	LJ 5000	Lexmark 1855	LJ 1100
		2	1	1
AS 400 printers	$2,780	4224	4230	
		1	1	
Telephones	$24,240	Lucent 6224	ATT 7406	
		69	23	
Fax machines	$1,295	Intellifax 1550		
		1		

Total Assets	$161,033
Monthly Charge	$4,473

These of course are the manufacturer's minimal configurations required for the product to run. Consider doubling these requirements if users want it to run with acceptable response times. Using the survey together with the hardware capabilities recommended by the company's standard software, a minimal standard workstation configuration can be selected. Do not bother to repair workstations with less than this minimal configuration. Any equipment in the idle assets room that falls below this must be either upgraded or scrapped.

COMMENT

Some companies never upgrade hardware or software. Every three years (about when the hardware warranty ends), all of the hardware is replaced along with the latest version of software.

Based on the hardware survey, the IT Manager can now estimate the cost to raise all of the existing workstations to the recommended hardware capability. As new software upgrades are contemplated, there is now a data-driven basis to identify workstations in the business departments that are below the minimum; these are prime candidates for replacement by any of the more capable equipment recovered. Most companies have at least three desktop minimum configurations. Some workers use their equipment lightly and only need a minimal configuration. An office worker spends more time using a keyboard but his programs do not tax the equipment. The engineering team will often exercise every megahertz of their equipment with newer and more complex software. Consider establishing categories of capability for workstations. Some examples might be:

A. **Minimal User.** E-mail, Internet communications, runs basic software.
   - **Minimum configuration.** 1-GHz processor, 250-GB hard drive, 20-in monitor.
B. **Office Worker.** E-mail, word processing, spreadsheet, database.
   - **Minimum configuration.** 2.5-GHz processor, 500-GB hard drive, 24-in monitor.
C. **Engineer.** CAD, e-mail, word processing, spreadsheet.
   - **Minimum configuration.** 3.0-GHz processor, 1-TB hard drive, dual 24-in monitors.

COMMENT

Hard disk storage space is cheap. However, some companies keep user disks small to force storage of files on the file servers, which are then backed up.

The second step is to identify candidates to eliminate. Are there any pockets of very old technology to eliminate? Electronic technologies of all types seem to reinvent themselves every two years. If there are clusters of very old equipment, spare parts to repair them may no longer be available. If the company waits until they break, the IT Manager must make a decision during a crisis instead of at leisure today. However, before announcing the scrapping of someone's "old faithful" terminal, find out if there is a special requirement for that specific device. The older the technologies, the more likely it is that a specific device must be used to support a business function.

Another type of device to eliminate is anything on a lease. Some leases allow the early return of leased equipment—some are just disguised time-payment purchases. If the equipment can be returned, it will lower IT's monthly costs a bit (assuming they can be replaced with equipment from the idle asset room). If the equipment cannot be returned early, at least now the IT department knows where it is. Document a procedure for returning "scrap" devices that are on lease.

Make a projection of the hardware minimums anticipated for the next several years. This forms an important part of the Desktop Computer Three Year Plan. Assuming the company staffing levels remain the same during this time, how many units will become obsolete.

COMMENT

There are many things the asset database can be used for. An easy benefit is to develop a roadmap for replacing and upgrading the desktop and notebook units in the company. By sorting the computers according to their CPU (assuming it was a data element that was captured for each unit), then the number of units to replace every year can be estimated.

Use the same process for servers, network cards, and any other hardware device. Look at what the company has, estimate what may be needed next year and the year after, identify the weak, and project the capital needs to replace them.

The primary driver for upgrading hardware is a new software version. A close relationship with critical software vendors will provide substantial advance notice of expanded hardware requirements, in time to include them in the upcoming year's budget.

[D] Determining the Number of On-Site Spares Required

The following steps will help you to set the correct spare equipment stocking level:

A. Look at the total number of machines in each class.
B. Determine how long it would take to get one repaired. Are they sent away for repair? Does the service person come into the building to fix them? Are they common items or rare?
C. Estimate how often this device seems to break down.

Calculating the number of spares:

A. How many devices of this type are in service?
B. How many workdays between failures?
C. Typically, how many days does it take to get that type of device repaired?
D. How many workdays in a year (roughly)?

E. Determine the mean time between failures.
F. Determine the number of machines/days in week.
G. Divide the number from Step D by the number in Step E.

Example:

Say the company is using 200 PCs. The IT Manager estimates one hardware problem per unit, every two years. History shows that it typically requires five working days to get a PC repaired. Given vacations and holidays, a PC is in use 48 weeks per year times five days per week or 240 days per year. Therefore, if the company works 240 days per year, and a PC fails every two years, there is a mean time between failures (MTBF) of 480 days. In a given week (five days), if there are 200 machines running, the result is 1,000 machine/days per week. Divide the MTBF by the number machine/days in a week to see if the IT department needs to keep a bit more than two spares on hand. Round this number up to three as the minimal stocking level.

If there is less than the minimal stocking level on hand, order some equipment today! If there is more than the minimal stocking level, then redeploy that equipment in place of purchasing new equipment. Another option is to scrap broken machines instead of paying to repair older equipment to deplete the idle assets. Once the emergency spares stocking level is on hand, lock it up! People with marginally financed projects will try to use this equipment to make their projects look less expensive than they are. Do not use these machines for anything other than spares.

[E] Developing a Service Strategy

Let us return for a minute to the equipment count. The first step in a service contract strategy is to identify which equipment is vital to the organization. Some machines must be operational at all times. If practical, store the spare parts for those machines next to that device. However, most machines can wait for an hour or so for repair. The operator may not think so, but it is usually true.

Ideally, critical machines have their backup device always online and in parallel with the primary unit. This allows for a quick changeover. No matter how stable the existing process is, never let the users convert the backup unit to any other purpose. If a process is not critical enough to protect the spare machine, then it really isn't that critical at all.

Service contracts are another area where an asset management program shows its power. Compare the equipment totals with the company's service contracts:

A. Evaluate the company's coverage. Is everything on the contract that should be on it?
B. Is the company paying for service support for hardware that is gone? Is every serial number on the contract still in-house? Before canceling anything here, make another pass or two through the area to look for it.

C.   Look at each device separately. Is the company paying for the proper level of service? Is that expensive 24/7 support still required? Always check with the users before lowering the service response time.
D.   Evaluate the list of critical equipment. Is it properly covered? This is not the place to cut corners!

Look for ways to lower cost. If there are plenty of spares for a particular device type, consider establishing a quick swap/service center. In this approach, exchange one of the spares for the broken item to restore service.

The repairperson only needs to come in weekly to work on the accumulated broken equipment. Do service contracts cover any of the older technologies? How much is it costing per device? Often the older hardware is the most expensive to support. This helps to justify the expense to eliminate older technology.

[F]   Ongoing Asset Management (IMAC)

After tagging and counting, maintain a vigorous effort to keep the database current. This requires updating the asset database anytime that equipment moves out of the idle assets room. Anything moved back to storage also is noted. Depending on their workload, the service desk can keep this up to date. Every time someone reports a problem, take a moment to verify the asset information. Technicians who move equipment can also update the asset records. Use Worksheet 26-1 Install, Move, Add, Change (IMAC) Form to help control the movement of IT assets.

Think for a minute about how far the asset management program has come! From running the business using "tribal knowledge," the IT Manager can now proceed based on the facts! When the annual budgeting cycle comes around, the IT Manager can better estimate equipment needs for the upcoming year. When software conversions become necessary, a data driven estimate of required hardware upgrades can be created.

As is apparent, conducting a full asset count is very time-consuming. Instead of doing this every year, audit one department every month since there are now bar codes or RF-ID tags on all of the machines. This plus other steps maintain the accuracy and usefulness of the database.

To ensure that your asset inventory database is kept current, it is important to have a policy for tracking changes to deployed equipment. All changes should only be made by qualified technicians after being approved by both the user's manager and the IT department. This policy should cover:

A.   Installing new equipment such as a PC and printer for a new or existing employee.
B.   Moving equipment to another location.
C.   Adding or removing hardware or software from an existing system.
D.   Creating or disabling a network, e-mail, or voice-mail account.
E.   Adding or removing a service from an existing employee's account.
F.   Changing an employee's name or other personally identifiable information.

WORKSHEET 26-1. Install, Move, Add, Change (IMAC) Form

Install, Move, Add, Change (IMAC) Form			
Please complete this form and fax to x1234 or e-mail it to imac@ourcompany. com. One form must be completed for each affected device. Incomplete forms or requests that do not comply with relevant IT policies will be returned for revision.			
Date Requested:		Department:	
Name:		Extension:	
Date Required:		☐ Install ☐ Move ☐ Add ☐ Change	
Current Location:		New Location:	
Hardware			
☐ Desktop	☐ External Speakers	Other Approved Hardware:	
☐ Laptop	☐ Desktop Printer		
☐ Monitor	☐ Memory		
☐ Keyboard	☐ Hard Disk		
☐ Mouse	☐ External Hard Disk		
Software			
☐ Windows 7	☐ Visual Studio	Other Approved Software:	
☐ Windows 8	☐ Active Sync		
☐ Microsoft Office	☐		
☐ Microsoft Outlook	☐		
☐ Adobe Reader	☐		
Computer Replacement			
Current Computer		**New Computer**	
Computer Name:		Computer Name:	
Model:		Model:	
IT ID:		IT ID:	
Service ID:		Service ID:	
Approval			
Supervisor:		Date:	
IT Manager:		Date:	

Your policy should cover the following:

A. Lead time required to schedule a change.
B. What approvals are needed.
C. How to handle the user downtime while the changes are being made.
D. Letting users know that other IT emergencies may take precedent over the scheduling of their changes.

See Policy ITP-26-3 Install/Move/Add/Change Policy as an example.

POLICY ITP-26-3. Install/Move/Add/Change Policy

Policy #:	ITP-26-3	Effective:	03/18/15	Page #:	1 of 2
Subject:	Install/Move/Add/Change Policy				

1.0 PURPOSE

This policy provides guidance for the proper management of modifications to desktop or mobile computer equipment. This includes requests from users for the initial install of the system, relocation of desktop equipment, and adding to or changing the system's configuration.

2.0 SCOPE

This policy applies to all employees and contractors using computer assets owned by the company. This policy applies whenever a change is made to company owned equipment, such as:

A. Installing new computer equipment.
B. Moving a desktop system to another location.
C. Removing old equipment.
D. Disabling an employee account (e.g., network access, e-mail, or voice mail).
E. Modifying existing equipment (e.g., adding RAM or installing software).
F. Changing an employee's name or other personally identifiable information on a system.

Excluded from this policy are:

A. Equipment purchased by employees with their own funds for their personal use, such as for smartphones, tablets, or personal music devices and that are not used on the corporate network.

3.0 POLICY

To ensure all employees understand their responsibilities, the following guidelines are established for the relocation or modification of company IT assets.

§ 26.04[A]

A. Complete the approved Install, Move, Add, Change (IMAC) form.
B. Forward the signed IMAC form to the IT Help Desk at least 3 days in advance of when the change needs to be made. The more notice that the IT department is given the greater the chance that the change will be completed when desired.
C. As most moves or changes involve system downtime for the user, outage windows will be minimized as much as possible. Users will be notified as to the estimate downtime so that appropriate arrangements can be made.
D. All approved changes will be made as scheduled whenever possible; there may be a delay in the event of an IT-related problem or emergency.

4.0 REVISION HISTORY

Date	Revision #	Description of Change
03/18/15	1.0	Initial creation.

5.0 INQUIRIES

Direct inquiries about this policy to:

George Jenkins, CIO
Our Company, Inc.
2900 Corporate Drive
Columbus, OH 43215

Voice: 614-555-1234
Fax: 614-555-1235
E-mail: gjenkins@company.com

Revision #:	1.0	Supersedes:	N/A	Date:	03/18/15

§ 26.04 SOFTWARE ASSET MANAGEMENT

[A] Overview

When most people think of asset management, they think in terms of physical property. For a long time, this was true of IT systems also. Software was expensive but the hardware cost much more. With improvements in manufacturing and lower prices, companies now have more money invested in software than in the equipment to run it. Software asset management is quite different from hardware management yet it also can be a place to save money in the IT budget.

[B]   Lay the Groundwork

Expand the asset database. The software asset database table is typically linked to the hardware table since software exists to support a hardware device. In addition to the user information collected during the hardware inventory, it is useful to know the software's version number.

What information to collect?

A. **Purchased Software—PC**
   1. Software name
   2. Manufacturer's name
   3. Version
B. **Purchased Software—Server/mainframe**
   1. Software name
   2. Manufacturer's name
   3. Version
   4. Annual maintenance fee
   5. Number of simultaneous users licensed
   6. Restriction on the license, such as CPU size, number of CPUs, etc.
C. **In-House Developed Software**
   1. Software name
   2. Programmer's name
   3. Version

The difficulty in collecting software information is in deciphering which EXE is which program. An automated inventory program will know. There is software available that will check the networked PCs overnight or the next time they log onto the server. A nice feature about this type of software is that it can be set to re-inventory PCs at programmed intervals. There is also software on the market that will use the network to "visit" each workstation on the network. In addition, by catching units as they log on, it can capture data from notebook PCs when they return from the field.

COMMENT

Examples of this class of products are Lansweeper at *www. lansweeper.com* and Express Metrix at *www.expressmetrix.com*.

The Business Software Alliance (*www.BSA.org*) has three evaluation tools available for download that can audit Windows and UNIX based systems to identify what programs are present in those systems.

A major benefit of this class of automatic software auditing is when preparing to roll out new software. It is easy to assemble a list of who might need the new version, and who might still be running an old OS version and require a double version upgrade.

[C]   Unauthorized Software

The inventory team will likely find unauthorized software during their count and must be ready to address it. Searches of user hard drives may turn up anything from the company bowling team scores to pornography. Be sure everyone on the team understands what the company will permit before proceeding. Based on the company's policy on unauthorized software, copy the offending files to a secure library on the server and then delete them from the PC. Leave the offending operator with a copy of the policy.

Remove illegal software and report to the IT Manager. The problem with removing it is that the longer it is in place, the more ingrained in that department's operation it may become. Removing it is the right thing to do but, in the short-term, it may hurt that department's operations. In that case, immediately purchase the necessary number of copies and assign the cost to that manager.

An exception would be computer games. Most companies have a policy of "death on sight" for computer games loaded onto their company PCs. Make sure of what is being deleted before erasing it.

COMMENT

Disk checks performed during a software inventory may uncover other unauthorized files on the PC such as gambling pools and pornography. Before beginning the inventory count, work with the Human Resources department to determine:

A. Exactly what is a violation.

B. How (and to whom) to report these violations.

C. How to gather and secure the "evidence."

D. Rules of conduct for the technicians during and after any incidents.

Draft written instructions for what to do and train the team on what to do. A similar set of instructions should govern unauthorized software.

[D]   Conduct the Inventory

Making the rounds of all of the offices for the software inventory is just like the one for the hardware count—only more tedious. If an automated software inventory system is used, then compare its results to the hardware list to determine who was missed. The inventory must include every workstation, every server, and do not forget the all-important network software versions. Remember that notebook PCs and tablets may not show up on the automated software count—or they may pop up over time as they reenter the facility and attach to the network. Schedule times with each department to bring in their machines for evaluation.

Although PCs have been used throughout this chapter as an example, it is important to know information about IT's other software. Typically, each IT section handles their own. They can continue to do so but including them in the database allows some upper management visibility. For example, the software on network devices does not change very often but, without an accurate list of what is there, there is no management oversight. Often the network manager does not know what is there either.

[E]   Crunch the Numbers

Roll up the numbers after the inventory is completed. Compare this number with the number of software licenses the company can prove it has purchased. Report the results to the IT Manager. Purchase needed copies immediately.

Now look for traces of "homegrown" department-written software. If someone writes a program for his own use, that is one issue. But if someone has written such a program and now it is in widespread use, then the IT department must step in and ensure it follows good data processing procedures (like all of the numbers add up), etc.

[F]   Ongoing Software Asset Management (IMAC)

Cleaning illegal software one time is a good first step, but unless the employees believe that IT is now monitoring their systems, it will all be back. Publish a clear policy explaining that installation of software not purchased by the company is forbidden and that people doing so will be disciplined.

See Policy ITP-26-4 Software Asset Management Policy as an example.

POLICY ITP-26-4.   Software Asset Management Policy

Policy #:	ITP-26-4	Effective:	03/18/13	Page #:	1 of N
Subject:	Software Asset Management Policy				

1.0 PURPOSE

This policy provides guidance for the proper management of computer software assets. Its purpose is to minimize costs, drive out obsolete technology, provide the ready location of assets, and ensure that obsolete assets are disposed of properly.

2.0 SCOPE

This policy applies to all employees, contractors, and visitors. It covers all software assets purchased or created by the company, to include:

A. Software purchased for use by employees.
B. Software created by employees to include (at a minimum):
1. Programs of all types written by employees on company equipment, whether on premises or during off-site business.
2. Programs of all types developed during paid working hours.
3. Spreadsheets, document templates, personal databases, etc.
C. Company-owned software at employee homes, for use while traveling, at vendor sites, or at customer sites.
D. Personal software installed on company equipment.

Excluded from this policy are:

A. Software purchased by employees with their own funds for their personal use, such as for smartphones, tablets, or personal music devices and that are not used on the corporate network.

3.0 POLICY

To ensure all employees understand their responsibilities, the following guidelines are established for using company software assets.

A. **Appointment of an IT Software Asset Manager.** The IT Manager will appoint a member of the Information Technology (IT) department as the company's IT Software Asset Manager. This person has the authority for implementing this policy.
B. **Acquisition.** The IT Software Asset Manager is responsible for selecting and acquiring computer software for use by the company. This person will:
1. Create and publish quarterly a list of standard software approved for use by the company.
2. Coordinate with the server support team and desktop support teams to ensure they can support any changes to the standard software list.
3. Review and approve all IT software purchase requests to ensure they conform to the approved standard equipment list.
4. Review and recommend approval or denial to the IT Manager for the purchase of any non-standard software.
C. **Strategic planning.** The IT Software Asset Manager will monitor company asset usage and IT strategic plans and will annually develop a Three-Year Software Asset Roadmap that:

    1. Includes industry projections of new software technology releases for planning changes to the standard unit list.

    2. Synchronizes future requirements with the Hardware Asset Management Three-Year Roadmap to identify required software upgrades.

    3. Identifies the number of software products, by type, expected to lose technical support for budgeting replacement purchases.

D. **Maximize utilization.** The IT Software Asset Manager identifies, collects, and safeguards idle IT Software assets. Collecting idle assets makes them available for redeployment.

    1. Prior to reuse, verifies each product's license to ensure it can be legally transferred from one machine to another.

    2. The IT Software Asset Manager has the authority to confiscate idle IT Software assets—even if purchased with a different department's funds.

E. **Disposal.** The IT Software Asset Manager follows all pertinent corporate policies for the proper disposal of software. The IT Software Asset Manager:

    1. Updates the appropriate accounting records concerning capital assets.

    2. Creates and maintains a process for removing data from disks and persistent memory prior to the scrapping, sale, or donation of equipment.

    3. Coordinates with the company's environmental management department and outside sources to ensure that all equipment and supplies declared as scrap are disposed of in accordance with current environmental regulations.

F. **Tracking database.** The IT Software Asset Manager will create and maintain an asset-tracking database. (Potentially incorporate this into the Hardware Asset Management database.) This database will provide the essential data for tracking software from purchase to obsolescence, locating specific products, providing information for support or insurance claims. The IT Software Asset Manager will:

    1. Conduct an initial product count and periodic software verification audits throughout the year.

    2. Report monthly to the IT Manager on the number and location (by department) of all IT managed software assets.

    3. Promptly add software entering the facility to the asset database.

G. **Security.** The IT Software Asset Manager safeguards company assets from theft. Software is a unique product because it can be stolen while the original product remains intact.

H. **Personal assets.** Employees *are prohibited* from bringing into the facility personal software, whether purchased or acquired through the "public domain."

    1. The IT Software Asset Manager may confiscate personally provided software. Only company property is permitted on the premises except where written permission is provided by the IT Software Asset Manager.

2. Software contained in personal devices such as smartphones, tablets, and music players not connected to the corporate network are excluded from this policy.

I. **Violations.** Any employee who abuses the use of company-owned assets is subject to corrective action including termination. If necessary, the company reserves the right to advise appropriate legal officials of any illegal violations.

4.0 REVISION HISTORY

Date	Revision #	Description of Change
03/18/13	1.0	Initial creation.

5.0 INQUIRIES

Direct inquiries about this policy to:

George Jenkins, CIO
Our Company, Inc.
2900 Corporate Drive
Columbus, OH 43215

Voice: 614-555-1234
Fax: 614-555-1235
E-mail: gjenkins@company.com

Revision #:	1.0	Supersedes:	N/A	Date:	03/18/13

[G] Using Computers to Solve Computer Problems—Automated Asset Detection

Asset management is a time consuming process—finding things, counting them, categorizing them, and then totaling them. It is boring and time consuming. Time is required for the original count and then to keep it current. Consequently, it tends to be a special occasion when a count is taken and considerable effort expended. This "snapshot" is useful in the short-term but, as time goes on, is less and less reliable. Since IT is in the automation business—of converting tedious manual effort into quick machine based tasks—why not use computers to do the work? How would such an automated solution work? Is it confined to servers and mainframes, or does it reach down into PCs, tablets, smartphones, and other devices? How low will it go? As always, before selecting a solution, clearly define the problem.

There are several problems with attempting to manage software assets. Asset management often focuses on physical objects. Controlling physical objects is important but somewhat easier since they can be seen and counted. However, even the sharpest IT technician cannot look at a server and say what software is loaded on the disks. To identify the software, directories must be searched and someone must know what package each of the executables represents. Again, this approach is only suited to an inventory snapshot.

An automated tool can quickly pay for itself just through the efficient management of software licenses. Most IT shops are a jumble of old and new versions—heavily used software and "residual" packages that were just copied over from the old server. An automated tool can determine:

A. How many copies of software are on the many servers and workstations? This number is essential for:
    1. License compliance reporting.
    2. Estimating vendor maintenance costs.
    3. Has someone recently loaded a non-standard package?
B. Is this software still needed?
    1. Can any of the software be turned off? Existence of software may create maintenance costs for something that no one uses. This is tricky when some packages run in the background to support other applications. In many situations, it is so difficult to establish true need that system administrators leave these tools in place "just in case" they are needed. An expensive insurance policy.
    2. How much is something being used? Can some of the light users share fewer licenses?
C. What version and patch level are the various packages?
    1. How does a company ensure that all copies of a particular software package are at the same patch level? Sometimes a package supporting other software cannot be upgraded. For example, if software used SQL Server 2000, it may not be able to use SQL Server 2005.
    2. How does a company detect when an older version of a package has been recently loaded "somewhere"? The financial payback from a successful tool may be immediate. Turning off unneeded licenses can halt monthly maintenance expenses for services not needed. Further, this savings compounds over time. An automated check also reduces the likelihood of being caught "under-licensed" for a product.

The central problem is how to search through the various devices to collect what is there. This is accomplished by collecting the various directories and system files that detail hardware and software installed. The tools selected must accommodate all of the various technology types in a given IT department. Typically, this is Windows Server OSs, UNIX, Linux, Solaris, mainframe, and workstation operating systems.

> ## COMMENT
>
> The content of the inventory database is highly confidential to the company. Some software has known vulnerabilities. If a hacker knows that a particular server is running behind on its patches, his focused attack will have a greater chance of success.

Automated inventory tools use a central collection server, and some way to gather the information. Gathering falls into agent based and agentless systems. Whichever approach is used, the primary obstacle is navigating through the company's data security processes so that all devices can be examined.

A. **Central Collection Server.** The central server receives inventory information from the various workstations and servers. The information is compared against a database of known applications to identify which software they represent, and which entries are data files. The result is a database of hardware and software detected in the IT system.

   There may be a set of rejected entries that are either data files or unknown software, such as homegrown programs. These must be added to the recognition database to avoid flagging them as unknowns in the future. The remaining unknown entries must be researched. This effort is heaviest when the software is first set up.

   The database of known software is ever changing. As software vendors add versions, patches, etc., this information must be updated. Typically, automated asset reporting vendors will provide a weekly download. It may be easier for the collection server to connect to the vendor and request the file instead of permitting the vendor to directly send it down through the firewall.

B. **Agent based.** Agent based asset information collection installs a piece of software (the agent) on each device where data collection is desired. The agent collects data throughout the day (especially on software usage). Once per day, this data is sent to the central server and the local file is purged. Overall, the agent and file place little burden on the server or workstation.

   The primary complaint about agent based systems is the cost of the agents plus the fact that a different agent must be purchased to execute on each of the various technologies supported (workstation OSs, server OSs, etc.).

C. **Agentless.** Agentless data collection uses the central collection server to check the many devices and collect the data. The collection server checks the various devices at a pre-set rate to collect the data. This works best in a small to medium sized environment. Large environments running an agentless system must tier their collection servers since a single server may lack the capacity if usage data is also collected.

Life being as it is, every time something is saved (by not loading an agent), something else is increased—in this case, the complexity of data security. Security is more of an issue with the agentless approach. Where an agent based system is sending data out of a server, security is less of a hurdle. However, for the central server of an agentless server to "touch" so many devices requires opening a lot of security doors that may be difficult to maintain.

D. **Reporting.** Once the automated inventory system is complete, the reporting part is easy. IT Asset Managers can now detect when something is loaded onto a server or workstation. They can provide a count of how many copies of a software package are installed and compare it to their license count. When a software package is eligible for an upgrade, an estimate of the work required and sites affected can be made.

This reporting is valuable for tying asset use to those who benefit from it. It may be that a product is so little used that it does not justify the cost of its monthly maintenance. Reporting is also valuable for providing ad hoc information about software usage so often requested out of the blue by company executives.

§ 26.05 SOFTWARE ASSETS

[A] Overview

The IT Manager will keep current with software developments in the IT profession and proprietary software development. If there is (IT or user) beta testing, the status and results will be reported to the members of the committee.

A. **Approved software.** Approved software sanctioned by the IT Manager will be found on the approved computer software list. The software has been used, tested, and approved by the IT programming unit and the information systems software committee. Being on the approved computer software list means it will be available to users or information systems staff. The only question is whether to charge the software to the information systems budget or a user budget. This question will be addressed by corporate policy.

B. **Requesting software.** Software licenses cost money to purchase, to support and sometimes in monthly licensing fees. The IT Manager must safeguard the company's interest and prevent casual purchases. The unit manager requesting the software sends a request to install the software on an identified computer or computers. Typically, requests for exemption are for:

1. **Other software.** If software is not on the list and is needed, look for it on the asset management software database. If the software is

available and approved to be used, it will be installed on the end user PC.

2. **Special software needs.** There can be a special need for software that is neither on the approved computer software list nor on the asset management software database. The end user is required to resolve any software problems with the vendor. If the software gains acceptance, it is placed on the approved computer software list and the service desk will support the software.

C. **Unauthorized software.** Employing unauthorized software can be a very expensive experience for the company. The IT Manager is responsible for policing all company computers for any unauthorized software whether it is in use or not. Just the software's presence on the hard drive can create a problem.

D. **Antivirus procedures.** To start an antivirus procedure, no software will be brought into the firm that does not belong to the firm. Even authorized disks will be checked for viruses before they can be brought into the firm's work area. This includes newly purchased software prior to its release to the users. The antivirus device will contain the latest version of virus protection. Downloading of any Internet information without specially granted permission is absolutely prohibited.

E. **Approved computer software list.** The approved computer software list contains software approved for user acquisition, including approved software operating systems and company-developed software. To discourage the use of any unapproved software, service desk support will not provide support to any unauthorized computer or user.

The asset management software database lists all software that is permitted to be in use and by whom. Proprietary software can be on the asset management software database (i.e., software developed by members of the firm and owned by the firm). Users who may have a problem with this software will contact the person(s) who developed it.

[B] Software Copyright Compliance Planning

Software not in compliance with the authorized ownership puts the company in jeopardy of lawsuits by the manufacturer of the software and/or its distributor. It is imperative the IT organization has the full support of top management to develop and maintain a policy of software copyright compliance. Document and publicize the plan throughout the company. This in itself will provide credibility; the company has a policy in place and will not tolerate any infraction. Maintain records of employees punished for knowingly violating the policy. Always hold offenders liable for costs incurred by their actions.

The IT software asset manager has responsibility for enforcing the unwarranted use of copyrighted software used illegally within the company. There are software packages on the market that can assist this process, and vendors who will undertake a continuous or one-time contract.

One easy way to control the number of copies of software is to retain the disks after loading the programs. Tag them with the name of the person whose machine they were installed on, along with its asset tag number.

COMMENT

Sometimes it is difficult for IT Managers to draft a policy that clearly states the company's position on unlicensed software. The fear is always that an audit will find the policy to be inadequate and little better than no policy at all.

The Business Software Alliance (*www.BSA.org*) provides sample policies covering this area that address *all* of the important points. It is found at *http://www.bsa.org/anti-piracy/tools-and-resources*.

A companion document is a memorandum for employees reminding them of the company's policies on unlicensed software.

27

PERSONAL COMPUTERS: MANAGING USER DEVICES

§ 27.01 OVERVIEW

[A] Purpose and Scope

Personal computers and related devices make up a major share of today's IT assets. In most offices, there is at least one computer per person and more when including mobile devices and laptop computers. The cost of personal computer software and the data within it now overshadows the cost of the hardware. The proper management of these assets is critical if companies are to gain maximum benefit. The responsibility for maximizing the utilization of these assets falls squarely on the information services department.

Current technologies make PCs seem like a series of interchangeable building blocks to be mixed and matched at will. This is definitely not true. Internal software drivers, ROM-based software, design assumptions, and interactions with other software make introducing new components a tedious task. The PC Support Manager will carefully select hardware components that are compatible with the installed base to ensure that they will work as envisioned.

To maximize the company's benefit and minimize its cost, the PC Support Manager will recommend to the IT Manager a series of policies governing the purchase and use of personal computer assets. These policies will reduce the variation in personal systems making their support and repair possible for lower cost and with fewer people.

[B] Critical Policies to Develop Based on This Chapter

Using the material discussed in this chapter, you will be able to create the following policies:

A. Duties of the PC Support Manager.
B. Acquisition policies.
C. Operations policies.
    1. Acceptable use of computer equipment.
    2. Daily operations procedures.
    3. Backup procedures.
    4. How accessories and supplies are managed.
    5. Managing mobile devices.
    6. Managing mobile networks.
    7. Managing employee-owned devices.
D. End-user computer committee.
E. End-user technical support.
    1. Hardware and software support policy.
    2. Network support policy.
    3. Maintenance contracting.

Policies should always be developed based on the local situation. Successful managers cannot issue appropriate guidance if the policies are written with another company's situation or location in mind.

§ 27.02 PC SUPPORT MANAGER

[A] Overview

The PC Support Manager's duties and responsibilities will vary from one location to another, depending on needs. Whatever title this person has, the objective is to ensure that policies covering personal devices meet existing business needs and are enforced. Many companies create this assignment to provide a single point of contact for all activities and information pertaining to PCs and other personal devices; this includes desktops, laptops, tablets, and smartphones. This provides a "single voice" that consistently issues the same information. The PC Support Manager recommends policies relating to personal computers to the IT Manager for approval.

[B] Responsibilities of the PC Support Manager

The PC Support Manager ensures that the company's investment in personal computers achieves its full potential. The person assigned the position of PC Support Manager will have a wide range of responsibilities, including the following:

A. Recommends a list of hardware and software for the company to standardize on based on its existing assets, its current business needs, and the strategic business direction of the company. Accompany each item with a note of why it was selected. All existing items in the same product class (such as printers) will be grouped together with the recommended replacement. The narrative also should state which existing items in the company assets inventory it replaces.

B. Creates and maintains a three-year strategic direction list for hardware and software migration. The IT Manager approves the final list. Base the recommendation on the existing asset inventory, emerging technologies, and emerging business requirements. Update the plan annually.

C. Processes requests for new hardware and software in a timely manner. (If the PC Support Manager's review becomes a major delay in the process, people will find ways to avoid it.)

D. Keeps abreast of the latest hardware and software technologies and problems through review of trade press and by attending trade shows.

E. Provides an ongoing hardware and software troubleshooting service for users to handle day-to-day operating problems. This includes management of outside hardware repair services.

F. Provides informal and formal training assistance for users.

G. Enforces policies regarding hardware and software operations, to include actively seeking out and deleting unauthorized software.

H. Provides backup service for critical data.

I. Provides LAN service and/or supervision.

J. Works closely with the service desk to detect systemic problems with devices, processes, and software.
K. Publishes a newsletter detailing user successes, known problems and their workarounds, and tips for easier computing.
L. Assists the IT Manager in identifying end-user applications for conversion into IT applications.
M. Identifies critical end-user files that must be moved to the server for data backups.

[C]   In-House Consulting Service

The PC Support Manager is the in-house consultant for users of personal computer hardware and software. The person in this position assists users in understanding the capabilities of their systems and advising them how to use them for maximum performance. In this role, the PC Support Manager constantly strives to demystify the technology by using nontechnical terms to describe technical functions.

The Network Manager identifies the standard for PC and network communications to ensure continuity and compatibility of the PC systems. The PC Support Manager ensures that all devices connected to the network are approved by the Network Manager.

Access to mainframe databases should require approval by the PC Support Manager before contacting the database administrator and/or data manager. The PC Support Manager should try to match requests to existing data views. End users should only access corporate databases in a read-only mode and are rarely allowed to directly update corporate databases.

The PC Support Manager should maintain a daily log, which is the data source for monthly activity reports. Depending on cost accounting practices, users may be charged for the time they use. The daily log should record, by user charge code, time spent on the following items (travel time also will be included):

A. Device troubleshooting
B. Software troubleshooting
C. Informal and formal training assistance
D. User consulting service
E. The PC Support Manager's indirect (administrative cost) time can be kept in the following categories:
   1. Reading and other education methods used to keep up with current technology.
   2. Communication network services.
   3. Web site use and maintenance.
   4. Publishing newsletters and other information.
   5. User education and training preparation when not charged to a given department.
   6. General administration duties, etc.

COMMENT

Most sites use trouble tickets issued by the service desk instead of an activities log. Both serve the same purpose. This data can be used to demonstrate service levels, measure workload, detect problem trends, etc.

[D]   Training

The PC Support Manager arranges for training on all company standard end user hardware and software. The goal of this training is to raise user productivity and satisfaction with the tools provided to them. It is a waste of company resources to drop off a new device loaded with software on someone's desk and hope he can master it on his own. Training leverages the equipment investment by showing the basic as well as advanced features to all employees. Offer training on the standard products in three levels:

A. **Basic.** How to start and navigate through the basic features of the product.
B. **Intermediate.** How to manipulate data, import, export, and build complex reports. Most users stop at this point.
C. **Advanced.** A thorough explanation of all product features for those users who are constantly running this software.

Training is a time-consuming process. Not everyone is suitable as a trainer. Many people lack the patience to work through the issues with users who do not seem to understand the technology. Those people who do have the patience often find this position very rewarding. To accommodate employees' busy schedules, provide training in several ways:

A. **Online Help.** Software today rarely comes with a printed manual. Make sure that users can access any help functions included in the software, and make any user guides or manuals available on the corporate Intranet.
B. **Self-paced.** Some companies purchase self-paced software that users use to walk through the product at their own pace. This may be available to them in a central "walk-up" facility or they might access the software from their own device. There is the same issue of who to ask specific questions about the product.
C. **Classroom.** This is the best way to instruct a group of people over a short period, but there is the added expense of an equipped classroom and an instructor.

> ## COMMENT
>
> A fully equipped training center has many other uses. It can provide a test area for new software since the testers are within earshot. With additional network and telephone jacks, it can provide an emergency operations center for disaster recovery.

D. **One-on-one.** Personal tutoring is the typical way that executives learn how to use the features of their devices. This is the most time-consuming method, but the PC support staff often provides personal mentoring on specific issues.

A major tool in the training program is a dedicated training room. This room should be equipped with one PC per student, plus a PC for the instructor. The instructor will require a projector to display the PC screen on the wall where all can follow along. The classroom should be isolated from the production network to prevent accidental corruption of corporate data. Reload the training room PC hard disks to the basic configuration at the end of every class, or use virtual images that can easily be reloaded for each class.

Whenever the training room is not in use, anyone should be able to walk in and access self-paced training. However, the ideal way to access self-paced training is from the individual's own device. This way they can do small portions of the training throughout the day. However, if there are too many interruptions throughout their day, they could use the PCs in the classroom.

The PC Support Manager should manage the PC training room schedule. Anyone wishing to use the room for any purpose should schedule it through the PC Support Manager. This avoids conflicts with scheduled classes.

> ## COMMENT
>
> A training center attracts strange classes. One author's training center was used for self-paced training for volunteer firemen!

Offer PC training in a variety of ways:

A. Purchase blocks of "tickets" to a local training facility and distribute them to people who require training. This has the added benefit of getting them off-site and away from distractions. This is the best path for supporting non-standard products.

B. Hire a full-time training company. This works if there are many people to train, an equipped training room is available, and the training company has a pool of instructors who can cover all of the company's primary products. When the instructors are not in class, use them for one-on-one instruction. They may also develop courses on in-house developed software.

C. Hire college teachers on an as-needed basis. Most college instructors are available on an hourly basis for work outside the college. For most end user products, these people can teach the material they have already developed for use at the college! They may also develop training sessions for in-house-developed software or new software upgrades. Again, an equipped training room must be available to do this.

D. Promote training provided in the evenings by local colleges on the standard software tools. Make schedules available and assist employees in filing claims for tuition reimbursement.

A major issue for providing training is when people reserve seats in a class and then do not show up. This prevents others from scheduling to attend training. Establish a training policy such that anyone who makes a reservation and does not show up (and stay for the class) still pays for their portion of the instructor's expense.

COMMENT

For training conducted on-site, half-day classes seem to work best as it allows time for the students to address pressing matters in their normal jobs.

Training is the IT department's best tool for raising user productivity and satisfaction. Good training is the number one defense against a deluge of simple questions to the service desk. In addition, after the service desk solves a problem, they may recommend to the PC Support Manager that specific people receive additional training or that specific topics need better coverage in class.

To back up the training, the PC Support Manager should maintain a library of reference material available on the corporate Intranet. This allows the IT staff and end users to investigate issues and find better ways to do a task. This library should include a complete set of manuals or user guides for every approved product (past and present).

The PC Support Manager's office should be near the training center and easily accessible to all users. It is important that users feel comfortable in approaching and discussing issues at any time during business hours. Obtain basic support equipment for a technical training operation:

- Whiteboard, which can double as a projection screen.
- Video projector.
- Tabletop lectern.
- Flip chart (floor model).
- DVD player and monitor.
- Supply items: nonpermanent color markers, flip chart paper, and erasers.

[E]   Newsletter

Most companies still create and distribute company newsletters. Most of the paper newsletters have shifted to a Web-based format, which is cheaper to distribute. PC Support Managers must maintain an open communication channel with users. This makes them more approachable by the "shyer" users.

A newsletter is a great place to spread the good news about maximizing end-user tools. It is also a valuable communications tool for the service desk to explain ways to address common and systemic problems. If many users experience the same problem, workarounds can be detailed here. This is a great outreach tool for proactive issues, such as pending upgrades. Let everyone know what is coming and when. Publish the training schedule so everyone knows what is available. Remember the target audience and keep the style conversational; stay away from technical jargon. If a dedicated newsletter is too burdensome, add articles to the facility's newsletter. In any event, keep the flow of communications consistent.

§ 27.03   ACQUISITION PROCEDURES

[A]   Scope

PC Support Managers are responsible for the inventory control of all hardware (desktop, laptop, tablet, and smartphone) and software acquisitions. They also assist users with all future hardware and software requirements.

Forward purchase requisitions for hardware, software, and service or consulting contracts to the information systems department's PC Support Manager who approves the purchase requisitions, then forwards them to the purchasing department. Use purchase requisitions only for approved budgeted expenditures.

[B]   Hardware Acquisition

The information systems manager sets the standards for PC hardware acquisitions. The fewer the variations in personal computer hardware there are in the company, the easier it is to maintain the existing base and to test new items for future use. The PC Support Manager recommends to the IT Manager a list of hardware and software that meets the company's needs in the most reliable and cost-effective manner. Create a policy stating that all PC purchases must conform to the approved products list.

An approved products list allows companies to focus their buying power on a few products and drive down the price. It also simplifies support requirements since there are fewer products for the IT support staff to master and eases the testing and rollout of new products since the devices are similar.

To ensure that purchases adhere to the list, the purchasing department should forward to the PC Support Manager any requests for devices they receive. Once the PC Support Manager verifies that the product is on the approved list, return the purchase request to the purchasing department for processing.

There are many valid business reasons for deviating from the approved list. If a requested item is not on the list, the PC Support Manager should call the requestor for an explanation. Sometimes there is a valid reason to purchase very old hardware or software if the migration to newer technology is too expensive. Some departments, such as engineering, may require unique products to achieve their business goals. The approved products list is a guideline that should restrict the majority of users with the option that the IT Manager can make exceptions to meet business needs. Before approving an exception, the PC Support Manager should explore standard solutions with the users to see if they fully understand the capabilities of approved products. All deviations to the list must include a plan for providing ongoing training and support for that item.

Hardware that deviates from the list must include an explanation of who will repair it and how much it will cost. If the device will support a critical function, then the user must pay for an on-site spare machine as a quick backup (a function that the PC Support Manager provides for standard units). Once IT approves the purchase of non-standard hardware, they assume responsibility for maintaining it just like any other device.

Some PC Support Managers take the stance that since they are unfamiliar with non-standard hardware they should not support it. This sounds like a spoiled child. The PC Support Manager exists to support the customers in satisfying *whatever* might be their business needs. If their needs are for an unusual item, then the local IT staff should make a "best effort" to support that item and know who to call for help if the problem is beyond their technical abilities.

Suggested procedures for hardware acquisition include:

A. **Approved hardware purchases.** Departments with budget approval for hardware expenditures complete a purchase requisition and forward it to the PC Support Manager, who checks the equipment against the approved hardware listing. If the equipment conforms to the current standard, the purchase should be approved. (Refer to Policy ITP-26-2, IT Hardware Asset Management Policy.)

If it is not on the approved list, the PC Support Manager should contact the requestor for clarification as to why an exception is needed (often they do not realize what is available). If the requestor cannot provide a satisfactory explanation and is adamant about the equipment desired, then the purchase requisition is forwarded to the IT Manager with a note explaining the problem.

B. **Hardware loans.** It is very handy to have equipment to loan as needed. It is a very unpopular job holding borrowers to their commitments to return it on time, and with all of its pieces. If departments frequently need to borrow equipment for things such as road shows, temporary offices, etc., then consider establishing their own pool of equipment. It is usually more cost effective to maintain a company owned equipment pool than it is to rent equipment.

Departments requesting a loan of hardware from the PC idle assets room should send a memo or e-mail to the PC Support Manager with the following information. (In the event of an emergency, a telephone call will do.) The memo must include:

1. What is to be loaned? Include a checklist of accessories (consider a laptop PC and its power supply cord as one kit), such as cables and power supplies that must come back with the unit; otherwise, there will be a delay before loaning it again. Be sure to include any important software beyond the standard office tools.
2. Expected length of time for the loan. A firm return date is critical.
3. Reason for the loan.
4. The department and person requesting the loan.
5. Where the equipment will be used.
6. The person who will be using the equipment.

The person to whom the equipment is released should complete an "out card" that shows the date, time, equipment loaned, serial number, and to whom it is loaned (this can be an online form). This card should be signed by the receiving person and filed, by date, under the requesting department. When the item is returned, the card should be signed and dated by the person returning the item. The "out card" file should be reviewed once per month. Delinquent borrowers should be contacted. Cards for returned items should be held on file for one year.

If the item is damaged, it should be noted on the card, which will become the source for a damage memo report completed by the PC Support Manager. This memo should be sent to the department manager of the borrower. Arrangements should be made to repair or replace the piece of equipment. The PC Support Manager should decide the cost, if any, that will be charged to the borrower's account for the repair or replacement and ensure borrowers have removed their data and reload the system's standard configuration promptly on its return before shelving it.

See Policy ITP-27-1 Hardware Loan Policy as an example.

POLICY ITP-27-1. Hardware Loan Policy

Policy #:	ITP-27-1	**Effective:**	03/18/13	**Page #:**	1 of N
Subject:	Hardware Loan Policy				

1.0 PURPOSE

This policy provides guidance for the proper management of computer hardware assets that are loaned to employees for temporary use. It is usually more cost effective to maintain a company-owned equipment pool than it is to rent equipment. The purpose of this policy is to ensure that such devices are most effectively utilized and properly tracked.

2.0 SCOPE

This policy applies to all company-owned hardware that is loaned on a temporary basis to employees, contractors, and visitors. This includes:

A. PCs, servers, network devices, printers, monitors, USB flash drives, and tablets.
B. Computer workstations of all sizes to include both fixed and portable systems, to include smartphones and tablets.
C. Company-owned workstations and servers at employee homes, for use while traveling, at vendor sites, or at customer sites.

3.0 POLICY

Departments requesting a loan of hardware from the PC idle assets room will send a memo or e-mail to the Desktop Support Manager with the following information. (In the event of an emergency, a telephone call will do.) The memo must include:

A. What is to be loaned? Include a checklist of accessories (consider a laptop PC and its power supply cord as one kit), such as cables and power supplies that must come back with the unit; otherwise, there will be a delay before loaning it again. Be sure to include any important software beyond the standard office tools.
B. Expected length of time for the loan. A firm return date is critical.
C. Reason for the loan.
D. The department and person requesting the loan.
E. Where the equipment will be used.
F. The person who will be using the equipment.

§ 27.03[B]

The person to whom the equipment is released must complete an "out card" that shows the date, time, equipment loaned, serial number, and to whom it is loaned. This card must be signed by the receiving person and filed, by date, under the requesting department. When the item is returned, the card is to be signed and dated by the person returning the item. The "out card" file should be reviewed once per month. Delinquent borrowers will be contacted. Cards for returned items should be held on file for one year.

If the item is damaged, it should be noted on the card, which will become the source for a damage memo report completed by the Desktop Support Manager. This memo will be sent to the department manager of the borrower. Arrangements should be made to repair or replace the piece of equipment. The Desktop Support Manager will decide the cost, if any, that will be charged to the borrower's account for the repair or replacement, and ensure borrowers have removed their data and reload the system's standard configuration promptly on its return before shelving it.

4.0 REVISION HISTORY

Date	Revision #	Description of Change
03/18/13	1.0	Initial creation.

5.0 INQUIRIES

Direct inquiries about this policy to:

George Jenkins, CIO
Our Company, Inc.
2900 Corporate Drive
Columbus, OH 43215

Voice: 614-555-1234
Fax: 614-555-1235
E-mail: gjenkins@company.com

Revision #:	1.0	Supersedes:	N/A	Date:	03/18/13

C. **Laptop PCs and mobile devices.** Company-owned laptops and mobile devices are useful because they allow a user to take the computer to the problem. As prices have dropped and computing power increased, laptop PCs are now considered as alternatives to desktop units in many offices. Companies spend a considerable amount of time maintaining security on their premises. Once a laptop PC or mobile device leaves this shelter, it becomes highly vulnerable to theft and damage.

Before allowing laptop PCs or mobile devices to leave the premises, determine whose insurance covers loss or damage. If a device is stolen from someone's car, whose insurance covers the theft? If a device is damaged (and they are quite fragile), who covers the repairs? How much responsibility does the user have for safeguarding the unit?

Besides the loss of the hardware, laptop PCs and mobile devices also contain company data. This hits the company in two ways. Before a laptop or mobile device leaves the company premises, a safety copy of the data should be made and left inside the facility for the following reasons:

1. The loss of use of data will delay whatever work was being done.
2. Company-confidential data can be compromised. What seems to be a random theft may have actually been industrial espionage. Why break into a building with all of its guards and security cameras when the most sensitive files can be read by stealing the CEO's laptop PC or tablet at an airport?

COMMENT

There is security software (sometimes as part of the operating system) available for the most sensitive laptop PCs and mobile devices that encrypt everything on the hard disk every time a file is saved. This extra layer of software may slow system performance but keep the company's secrets off the front page of the newspaper.

D. **Mobile Device Acquisition Procedures.** The policies and procedures for the acquisition of mobile devices should give clear guidance on how these devices are brought into the organization. Areas that should be covered by such policies include:

1. **Budgeting procedures.** Specify the budget from which these devices are to be purchased. How are repairs and replacements handled?
2. **Requisition procedures.** How are requisition requests handled?
3. **Purchasing procedures.** Document the procedures for making the actual purchase.
4. **Receiving procedures.** How are the devices received in the organization and placed into inventory?

See Policy ITP-27-2 Mobile Device Acquisition Procedures as an example.

POLICY ITP-27-2.   Mobile Device Acquisition Procedures

Policy #:	ITP-27-2	**Effective:**	03/18/12	**Page #:**	1 of N
Subject:	Mobile Device Acquisition Procedures				

1.0 PURPOSE

This policy defines the process for the acquisition of non-PC electronic mobile devices.

2.0 SCOPE

The policy applies to all portable mobile devices that interface in any way with the corporate systems. This includes smartphones, tablets, USB flash drives, pagers, and any other device capable of storing corporate data.

3.0 POLICY

The following guidelines will be followed for managing mobile data devices:

3.1 Budgeting Procedures
Mobile devices are budgeted as part of each department's budget. Each department submits its expected needs for the following year's budget. This is based on the prior year's budget plus inflation, replacement of old equipment, and new needs. It is supported by the use of the current equipment and forecasted use for the next budget year.

Budgets must be created for supplies and replacement of current equipment. Departments with their own hardware for one-of-a-kind use will require a budget for maintaining the equipment.

The information systems department will create a budget for general corporate support. This department creates a budget for capital expenses benefiting the whole company plus a replacement parts budget. In addition, a vendor service budget is required.

3.2 Requisition Procedures
Budgeted items must have a requisition issued. The requisition goes to the IT asset manager to confirm it meets standards or requires a standards waiver. The need for the device is evaluated just as any new device that has access to the corporate network.

The requisition is approved and sent to the budgeting department so it can adjust the records. It is then sent to the purchasing department.

3.3 Purchasing Procedures
Purchasing receives the approved purchase requisition. If needed, it will take care of the competitive bids for the item. After the purchase order is sent to the vendor, a copy is sent to receiving and accounts payable.

3.4 Receiving Procedures

The agent for the asset manager or a special order item representative inspects the item for approval. After it is approved, a receiving notice is sent to accounts payable.

The asset manager's agent affixes a tag to the device and records the information. The information is sent to the asset manager.

4.0 REVISION HISTORY

Date	Revision #	Description of Change
03/18/12	1.0	Initial creation.
02/12/13	1.1	Modified section 3.4 Receiving Procedures

5.0 INQUIRIES

Direct inquiries about this policy to:

George Jenkins, CIO
Our Company, Inc.
2900 Corporate Drive
Columbus, OH 43215

Voice: 614-555-1234
Fax: 614-555-1235
E-mail: gjenkins@company.com

Revision #:	1.1	Supersedes:	1.0	Date:	02/12/13

COMMENT

The research firm IDC estimated that the number of mobile workers reached nearly 1.2 billion worldwide in 2011.

[C] Software Acquisition

It should be company policy that information systems management has control over all company software. To ensure system compatibility and to avoid interoperability problems, purchase all software from a list of approved products. The PC Support Manager drafts the list for approval by the IT

Manager. A standard software products list enables the support staff to focus on a few vendors for better price and support.

Unlike most hardware, software typically requires training for users to become productive with it. Standardize on a few software packages. This eases both training and employee mobility within the company since all departments use the same basic tools.

Larger companies may purchase a software license for a certain number of machines. A variation is purchasing a "site" license for unlimited copies at a single site. The PC Support Manager will administer any per-seat or site-licensed software according to the terms of license, to include loading software on the appropriate systems and tracking the number of copies installed.

Departments must not bypass this process by purchasing their own software. Doing so introduces new support costs that were not apparent when the purchase was first considered. Controlling the purchase of software is an important part of a company's software license compliance (antipiracy) program.

Software may be developed in-house or acquired from an outside source. Only consider in-house software development if commercially available software cannot be found for less than the in-house cost. The availability of in-house programming personnel is also a consideration. The PC Support Manager, who decides whether the actual programming effort is done in-house or contracted out, makes arrangements for any in-house-developed software. Charge the cost of this effort to the requesting user's department budget.

Software can be purchased for multiple users or a single user. Most software is purchased from vendors for a one-time cost, while some is only available for an annual fee. In addition, upgrades are generally available for a single user or multiple users. Purchased off-the-shelf software is available in two forms. One is for the horizontal market, for widespread use across many different kinds of firms. Examples would be word processing or spreadsheet software. The other is for the vertical market, that is, for applications pertaining to given industries. This kind of software may be more flexible because, in some cases, the source code is available, making it possible to alter the program to meet the user's own needs.

It is the PC Support Manager's duty to seek newer and better software. (Refer to Policy ITP-26-4 Software Asset Management Policy.) Maintain a published list of approved software, continually updated with software newly approved to respond to new needs. Only approved software may be used.

A part of the PC Support Manager's technical advisor role is to include a budget for training, especially if software is for several people. It reduces the number of service desk calls, raises user satisfaction, and ensures the company's investment returns benefits as quickly as possible.

Suggested software acquisition procedures are as follows:

A. **Specially developed software.** A user requiring software that is not available by purchase works with the PC Support Manager to define the needs. The PC Support Manager then submits a memo to the person responsible for PC programming systems and provides enough information so that a project proposal can be developed and the cost estimated. Project proposal information is reviewed with the user requesting the program. If time and money are available, a written request is issued by the user management. Program development is handled using the standard procedures for information systems program development. As long as no security problem exists, the new software is made available to other PC users.

B. **Purchased software.** The user sends a memo requesting the approved software to the PC Support Manager who reviews the request and, upon approval, sends the software to the requesting party. An internal charge is made to the requesting department's account. If the software license is not available for reuse in the idle assets stock, the PC Support Manager will issue a purchase requisition on behalf of the requesting department, which is forwarded to the purchasing unit. When the software is ready to install, send a copy of the class schedule to the requesting department along with a link to any manuals or user guides available on the corporate Intranet. Since this is from the approved software list, a class should be available. If no local classes are available, see if local colleges offer continuing education classes and forward their schedule and registration forms.

It is critical that the PC Support Manager maintain software licenses in a fireproof file cabinet, preferably off-site. In case of a disaster, those copies can be used as authority to reload software into replacement devices without repurchasing it (often the manufacturer will even send a "gold" disk if there is adequate documentation). This license file is a primary company defense in case of a software audit. It is evidence for buying upgrades instead of purchasing new software.

C. **Software registration.** All software registration will be collected, completed, and submitted by the PC Support Manager in the company's name.

D. **Software library.** Copies of in-house-developed PC programs and the original licensed software, as well as backup copies of other purchased software, are maintained in a software library. Users with one-of-a-kind software are encouraged to store backup copies here as well. All software will be the most current version in use. Disks out of the shrink-wrap may require bug fixes. The library ensures the latest stable version is provided. The same applies to manuals' errata sheets. The library is under the control of the PC Support Manager.

E. **Software demo disks.** Software demo disks will be provided to users requesting them. These can be provided by vendors or developed in-house, and are not charged to the user's account. Preferably, these will run on a dedicated PC, as demos may introduce subtle configuration problems and not all software uninstalls cleanly.

The software library may provide an opportunity for potential users to try software before obtaining their own copies. The library also contains proper documentation and user instructions so that software may be tested. The PC Support Manager may be called on to demonstrate software or demo programs to potential users.

[D] Database Access Acquisition

Database access is an important part of personal computer management since most end-user-written PC programs are for report writing or accessing data. Arrange database access through a database administrator to ensure the query is efficiently coded. All corporate database updates must be by way of IT developed or approved programs.

The PC Support Manager also arranges for new PC users to access the database and provides them with training and an operations manual that explains the programs being used and what each of the data elements represent. Normally, database access front-ends are provided to prevent the uneducated user from "dimming the lights" with poorly designed queries. Including a data dictionary explaining the contents of a field will improve reporting. Ambiguous field names should never be used.

§ 27.04 OPERATIONS PROCEDURES

[A] Overview

PC (desktop, transportable, laptop, and mobile) operations use recommended manufacturers' operations instructions as outlined in the manufacturers' manuals. These manuals should be supplemented with those provided by the information systems PC Support Manager, which can be purchased or written in-house.

[B] Acceptable Use

Acceptable use policy explains the appropriate use of company assets. A personal computer is an incredibly versatile thing. It can be used to draft documents, add numbers, draw pictures, surf the Web, and on and on. A company's acceptable use policy outlines the activities that the company identifies as acceptable uses of its equipment. It also details activities it specifically forbids.

Acceptable use policies are an extension of the pre-computer days. In those times, gambling pools were kept on a pad of paper, pornographic pictures hung on the walls, or piles of personal catalogs might be on a desk. All were forbidden on company property as distracting employees from work.

Today, a PC can do all of that and much more. Companies must publish a policy to remind employees of the ways this tool can be used that are acceptable to the company's management. Publishing this policy and ensuring all employees read and understand it provides a tool in the event that abusing employees need to leave the company.

See Policy ITP-27-3 Acceptable Use Policy as an example.

POLICY ITP-27-3. Acceptable Use Policy

Policy #:	ITP-27-3	Effective:	03/18/13	Page #:	1 of N
Subject:	Acceptable Use Policy				

1.0 PURPOSE

This policy describes the acceptable use of company computer equipment.

2.0 SCOPE

This policy applies to all users of information technology within the company.

3.0 POLICY

Employees are responsible for exercising good judgment regarding reasonable personal use.

- A. Physical security.
    1. Employees are required to safeguard all company equipment assigned to their exclusive or shared use, and all company equipment within their work area.
    2. Employees traveling with mobile computers will always carry them in carry-on baggage and not in checked baggage.
- B. Information security.
    1. Data created on company systems remains the company's property. The company cannot guarantee the confidentiality of information stored on any network device.
    2. Any information considered sensitive or vulnerable must be encrypted.
    3. For security and network maintenance purposes, individuals authorized by the IT Manager may monitor equipment, systems, and network traffic at any time.
    4. Secure all PCs, laptops, and workstations with a password-protected screensaver with the automatic activation feature set at 10 minutes.
- C. Self-help. All users of company equipment are expected to take charge of their own training:
    1. Attend in-house classes provided by the IT department.
    2. Review and become familiar with software documentation.
    3. Take night classes at the local college on software use (reimbursable through the company's tuition assistance program).
- D. Unacceptable use.
    1. Employees are never authorized to disable the antivirus software on their workstation.
    2. Hacking systems and databases or acting to disrupt systems or cause unnecessary network congestion or application delays.

3. Use of remote control software on any internal or external host personal computers or systems not specifically set up by the IT staff.
4. Any use of computer equipment that violates state or U.S. law and regulations.
5. Creating or forwarding of chain mail regardless of content, sources, or destinations.
6. Posting company information to external newsgroups, bulletin boards, or other public forums without authority.
7. Using company equipment for personal profit, political fundraising, gambling activity, non-business-related instant messaging, or chat room discussions, and downloading or display of offensive material.

4.0 REVISION HISTORY

Date	Revision #	Description of Change
03/18/13	1.0	Initial creation.

5.0 INQUIRIES

Direct inquiries about this policy to:

George Jenkins, CIO
Our Company, Inc.
2900 Corporate Drive
Columbus, OH 43215

Voice: 614-555-1234
Fax: 614-555-1235
E-mail: gjenkins@company.com

Revision #:	1.0	Supersedes:	N/A	Date:	03/18/13

[C] Bring Your Own Device—BYOD

It was not long ago the companies did not allow employees to use devices not purchased by the company on the corporate network. While this policy helped keep the corporate network secure, the proliferation of consumer purchased smartphones and tablets has made enforcing this policy more and more difficult. Employees are finding that these devices are an increasingly important tool for both personal and professional productivity. In addition, there is an increasing need for contractors, clients, guests, and others working temporarily on-site to access the corporate network. IT managers can either do their best to keep these devices off the corporate network, or they can embrace the "bring your own device" (BYOD) concept and develop appropriate policies and procedures to support this concept.

Some guidelines to consider when creating a BYOD policy include:

A. **Give employees clear guidelines on what will be supported.** Allow them to choose between a company-issued device and using a company-provided allowance to purchase an alternative. These alternatives must meet certain standards, but allow the employee some flexibility in what device they use to do their job. Consider who is responsible for supporting these alternative devices—it is usually best to require the employee to obtain support from the device provider.

B. **Consider installing a digital certificate on each device.** This allows the company to authenticate each device and record user behavior.

C. **Specify the state of the device.** Specify in your policy that any devices connected to the organization's network cannot have been rooted or jailbroken.

D. **Limit login attempts.** Consider locking the user's account after some number of consecutive failed login attempts.

E. **Specify password requirements.** Proper password requirements are even more important on mobile devices. Create strong password requirements that are practical for the devices employees might use.

F. **Virtualize key applications.** Allow employees to access important applications and data on a virtualized machine, without any data being stored on the mobile device. This eliminates issues with sensitive data being stored on a device that is easily lost or stolen.

G. **Require employees to agree to install remote wiping software.** This software can then be used if the device is lost or stolen, if IT detects a virus or data breach, or if the employee leaves the organization.

H. **Create a segmented network.** Most organizations already have a network for internal use and another for guests, clients, and contractors; create a separate virtual network for mobile devices. This allows the company to control access to important systems and also control the amount of bandwidth used by these devices.

See Policy ITP-27-4 Bring Your Own Device (BYOD) Policy as an example.

POLICY ITP-27-4. Bring Your Own Device (BYOD) Policy

Policy #:	ITP-27-4	Effective:	03/18/13	Page #:	1 of N
Subject:	Bring Your Own Device (BYOD) Policy				

1.0 PURPOSE

As mobile devices become an increasingly important tool for both personal and professional productivity, the company recognizes that employees may wish to

§ 27.04[C]

use their personally owned devices to perform their job. This policy defines the acceptable use of mobile devices not purchased by the company within the organization, specifically the use of these devices on the corporate network. The organization reserves the right to revoke the privilege of using personally owned devices if a user does not follow this policy.

2.0 SCOPE

The policy applies to all mobile devices used by employees that are not company issued devices. This includes laptop computers, tablets, smartphones, and portable data devices owned by the employee. The policy covers employees of the company and any contractors that are working at company-owned facilities requiring access to the corporate network.

3.0 POLICY

The user of the mobile device will accept responsibility for taking reasonable precautions in protecting the data on the mobile device and the security of the corporate network. The following guidelines must be followed when using a personally owned device on the corporate network:

A. Employees not using company-provided devices must either use a device on the approved device list or obtain support directly from the vendor for the device.

B. The device must be used in the manner intended by the manufacturer; it cannot have been rooted or jailbroken.

C. An employee's user account will be locked after five consecutive failed login attempts.

D. IT will install a digital certificate on the device to allow access to critical applications and to allow the company to record user behavior.

E. The employee must agree to install remote wiping software so that the company can delete important corporate data if the device is lost or stolen. IT will also wipe the device if a virus or data breach is detected, or if the employee leaves the organization.

F. IT will provide a virtual network for employee-owned devices to access the corporate network.

G. All employees desiring to use a personal device on the corporate network must have read and signed the corporate computer acceptable use policy, and agree to follow all requirements of that policy.

4.0 REVISION HISTORY

Date	Revision #	Description of Change
03/18/13	1.0	Initial creation.

5.0 INQUIRIES

Direct inquiries about this policy to:

George Jenkins, CIO
Our Company, Inc.
2900 Corporate Drive
Columbus, OH 43215

Voice: 614-555-1234
Fax: 614-555-1235
E-mail: gjenkins@company.com

Revision #:	1.0	Supersedes:	N/A	Date:	03/18/13

[D]   Bring Your Own Network—BYON

Just as employees increasingly want to use their own devices at work, there is a growing trend toward also bringing their own networks. Employees are finding it increasingly convenient to access the Internet or other online resources using their own network, usually in the form of wireless mobile hotspots. In addition, there is an increasing need for contractors, clients, guests, and others working temporarily on-site to access cloud-based services in addition to the corporate network. In some organizations, corporate restrictions on the access to social media or shopping Web sites cause employees to create an ad hoc network in order to be able to access these types of sites.

A big concern with these ad hoc networks is that employees will use corporate applications on the corporate network at the same time that they are connected to the network they created. Any corporate data that might pass through the ad hoc network cannot be monitored by the company network administrators and is not likely secured. Malware threats can also be introduced through the ad hoc network and place other corporate data at risk. IT managers can either do their best to keep these networks away from the corporate systems or can embrace the "bring your own network" (BYON) concept and develop appropriate policies and procedures to support this concept.

Some options to consider when creating a BYON policy include:

A. **Prohibit employees from using personal networking devices with company-owned equipment.** Using this approach requires that this restriction be clearly spelled out in the corporate acceptable use policy along with the consequences for violating the policy.
B. **Create a secondary wireless network for use with personal devices.** Most organizations already have a network for internal use and another for guests, clients, and contractors; create a separate wireless network for personal devices. This allows the company to

control access to important systems and also control the amount of bandwidth used by these devices.

C. **Allow use of ad hoc networks but hold employees responsible for any lost data or security threat created.** While this approach may not hold up to a legal challenge, it does reinforce to the employee the seriousness of the issue.

See Policy ITP-27-5 Bring Your Own Network (BYON) Policy as an example.

POLICY ITP-27-5. Bring Your Own Network (BYON) Policy

Policy #:	ITP-27-5	Effective:	03/18/15	Page #:	1 of 2
Subject:	Bring Your Own Network (BYON) Policy				

1.0 PURPOSE

As mobile networks become an increasingly important tool for both personal and professional productivity, the company recognizes that employees may wish to use their personally owned networks in the performance of their job duties. This policy defines the acceptable use of ad hoc networks not provided by the company within the organization, specifically the use of these networks using company-owned devices or accessing corporate data. The organization reserves the right to revoke the privilege of using personally owned networks if a user does not follow this policy.

2.0 SCOPE

The policy applies to all mobile networks used by employees that are not part of company-managed networks. This includes networks that are used with a cellular data provider or any other form of access outside the corporate network. The policy covers employees of the company and any contractors that are working at company-owned facilities requiring access to the corporate network.

3.0 POLICY

The user of the mobile network will accept responsibility for taking reasonable precautions in preventing any company data from being accessed on the ad hoc network. The following guidelines must be followed when using a personally owned network:

A. Employees using personal ad hoc networks must not use these networks for accessing corporate systems.
B. Ad hoc networks cannot be used to access cloud-based applications that contain non-public corporate data. Such networks can only be used to access corporate Web sites that are accessible to the general public.

C. All employees desiring to use a personal network on the corporate network must have read and signed the corporate computer acceptable use policy, and agree to follow all requirements of that policy.

4.0 REVISION HISTORY

Date	Revision #	Description of Change
03/18/15	1.0	Initial creation.

5.0 INQUIRIES

Direct inquiries about this policy to:

George Jenkins, CIO
Our Company, Inc.
2900 Corporate Drive
Columbus, OH 43215

Voice: 614-555-1234
Fax: 614-555-1235
E-mail: gjenkins@company.com

Revision #:	1.0	Supersedes:	N/A	Date:	03/18/15

[E] Device Security

Theft of hardware is bad, but the cost to reproduce the data lost with the unit could be more than the value of the equipment. Locate desktop PCs or any stationary PC in a secure environment. Employees assigned mobile equipment assume full responsibility for safekeeping both the hardware and the software. Preventing unauthorized access to any PC system should be of utmost concern to all employees.

Due to their light weight and small size, laptop PCs and mobile devices are very vulnerable to theft. A special pass should be attached to laptop PCs with the owner's photograph on it so guards can easily check them out of the facility. Consider the following to keep your devices secure:

A. **Physical location.** The room where computers are kept should be locked when not in use. If not possible, seriously consider employing a cable lock to deter any removal of the desktop computer hardware. Keep portable computers in a safe place at all times, including when the hardware is in transit. Handle all portable computers as "carry-on luggage" while on public transit.

   If a desktop PC is moved to a new permanent location within an area under the jurisdiction of the PC Support Manager, they should be informed in writing within 24 hours of the move. If the new area is not under the jurisdiction of the current PC Support Manager, they must approve the move before it takes place and inform the asset manager and the new area's PC Support Manager. The PC Support Manager ensures there is adequate electrical and network connection available in the new location prior to moving the equipment.

B. **Access security.** Stationary PCs with a network connection and/or hard drives with any restricted information should be required to have one of the following:
   1. A lock.
   2. An access security board with a lock-slot so the board can use a cable security system.
   3. Personal access code software (in the event the PC does not have an available slot for an access security board) or use of a screen-saver password.

C. **Software and data security.** Software disks held centrally should be stored in a locked place. Data disks and backup tapes and disks should be stored in a PC media safe or other such comparable device if so warranted by the data administrator or the PC Support Manager. Where practical, data backups should be stored off-site for protection. Encourage users to back up their data directories to the network, which will in turn be backed up daily and the media stored off-site.

[F] Operation Rules and Procedures

The following are rules and procedures that apply to the operation of all PCs and mobile devices:

A. Devices should be rebooted at least once a week for reliable operation. Daily rebooting is recommended for critical systems.
B. In areas with a higher than normal amount of airborne dust, dust covers should be used for PCs, keyboards, monitors, and other attached devices when not in use.
C. No food or beverages on or near the hardware or software.
D. No smoking near the hardware or software.
E. A clean, cool, and dry air-working environment is recommended for the computer.
F. Keep magnetic devices away from the computer, disks, and tapes.
G. Plug all computers and mobile equipment into a surge protection unit. Do not permit other electric devices to be plugged into the surge protection outlet or into the same wall plug with the surge protection device. Use only grounded electrical outlets. Plug company-critical equipment into an uninterrupted power source (UPS) with a signal to shut down the PC before the UPS batteries die.

H. Illegal copying of software is never permitted.
I. No hardware or software may be removed from the firm's premises without the PC Support Manager's written permission for each occasion. Portable computer systems used outside the workplace require a permission letter or ID card signed by the manager to be kept with the system at all times. The permission letter/ID card identifies who has permission to use and carry the authorized equipment and software. It also will contain the serial numbers of the units authorized and identifies the software contained in the system.
J. No hardware (including portable equipment) or software will be loaned to non-company persons.
K. Removable media will be kept in their disk containers or storage unit when not in use.

[G]   Backup Procedures

Backup procedures may vary within the same company. Not all data and software have the same value (although it is better to be safe if not sure). The following procedures are recommended:

A. **New software.** The PC Support Manager who retains all the original media and keys should manage the installation of newly purchased software. If subsequent upgrades require access to the media, they must be coordinated with the PC Support Manager. This step is to reduce the company's liability of someone making illegal copies of the software that it owns.
B. **Hard drive backup procedures.**
   1. At the end of each workday, all new data should be backed up onto network drives or tape. Some active transactions (e.g., word processing, billing) will need to be backed up more often.
   2. A backup copy of the hard drive data should be maintained on the network disk or tape.
C. **Removable media data.** When data is kept on removable media (e.g., flash drives, portable drives, CDs) and not on a hard drive, the disk is copied for backup. The two copies of the data are never stored together. It is recommended that the backup copy be write-protected.
D. **Storage.** All data copies will be stored securely as soon as they are made.

COMMENT

The U.S. Post Office in Washington backed up its PCs daily. But when the ninth floor of the building burned, so did its PCs and the backups that were stored in the desks under the PCs.

[H] System Crash

In case of a device system crash, the user writes down what occurred just prior to the crash and the time of the crash, and then calls the service desk for assistance. The device should be left on, ideally with the error message displayed. If the device is a desktop PC, post a sign on it stating that the system has crashed and it is not to be used. Mobile devices should be taken to the PC Support Manager or service desk.

[I] Mobile Device Operations Procedures

Mobile devices cover a wide range of applications and complexities. The total investment in these devices can be difficult to track and is not known in most companies. More important, the data kept on these devices is difficult to track and control. Meanwhile, most of these devices operate without a central sense of direction. Without the orchestration and guidance of information systems, their costs continue to grow while their efficiency diminishes. A major part of controlling these devices is the procedures set forth by an IT department within well-thought-out policies.

COMMENT

According to a June 2013 report by ITU, there are 2.1 billion active mobile broadband subscriptions worldwide. This number grew 40 percent annually over the previous 3 years.

Information systems is responsible for maintaining and enforcing a company-wide software application policy for all supported devices. The acceptable application software list should be maintained in the asset management software database and updated monthly by the information systems software committee. Installation of unauthorized application software should not be permitted. The jailbreaking of any mobile device owned by the company should be prohibited, as well as the use of personally owned devices that have been jailbroken. Devices altered in this way are more susceptible to viruses and malware. Service desk support should not be provided for unauthorized application software or for devices that have been jailbroken.

Most devices are configured by default to power on with no security. If supported by the device, a password must be entered when the device is powered on. The password should be the same as the password used by the user when logging into his personal computer or corporate network domain. Make sure the data is encrypted if supported by the device.

COMMENT

Roughly, one out of three users had lost or had stolen a mobile device, according to a report published by Norton in 2011.

See Policy ITP-27-6 Mobile Device Usage Policy as an example.

POLICY ITP-27-6. Mobile Device Usage Policy

Policy #:	ITP-27-6	Effective:	03/18/13	Page #:	1 of N
Subject:	Mobile Device Usage Policy				

1.0 PURPOSE

This policy defines the acceptable use of mobile devices within the organization, specifically the protection of important corporate data stored on such devices. This policy is also designed to protect the corporate network from being infected by any hostile software when the mobile computer returns. This policy also considers wireless access.

2.0 SCOPE

The policy applies to all mobile devices used by employees that are at any point connected to or share data with the corporate network. This includes laptop computers, tablets, smartphones, and portable data devices.

3.0 POLICY

The user of the mobile device will accept responsibility for taking reasonable precautions in protecting the data on the mobile device and agrees to adhere to this policy. The mobile device user will not be allowed to have administrative rights on the network unless granted special exception by the network administrator. The user of the mobile device agrees not to use the mobile device for personal business and agrees to abide by the organizational computer usage policy. Any device that is connected at any time to the corporate network must adhere to the following:

A. Devices connected to the corporate network must be determined to be a benefit to the organization rather than a convenience by the designated IT Manager.

B. Any mobile device that can store corporate data must support encryption of the data; corporate data on mobile devices must be encrypted at all times.
C. It is never permitted to jailbreak a corporate owned mobile device, or use such an altered device on the corporate network.
D. All mobile devices owned by the organization or allowed on the organization network must be identified by their MAC address to the IT department before being connected.
E. The mobile device operator must be identified by name and contact information to the IT department.
F. The mobile device operator must be familiar with the organization's acceptable use policy.
G. Devices not owned by the organization are subject to a software audit to be sure no software that could threaten the network security is in operation. All computing devices are subject to a software audit at any time.
H. Mobile devices capable of taking pictures are not allowed in sensitive areas of the company.

4.0 REVISION HISTORY

Date	Revision #	Description of Change
03/18/13	1.0	Initial creation.

5.0 INQUIRIES

Direct inquiries about this policy to:

George Jenkins, CIO
Our Company, Inc.
2900 Corporate Drive
Columbus, OH 43215

Voice: 614-555-1234
Fax: 614-555-1235
E-mail: gjenkins@company.com

Revision #:	1.0	Supersedes:	N/A	Date:	03/18/13

> **COMMENT**
>
> Not just PCs are vulnerable to hackers. A 2011 report by Lookout from their Mobile Threat Network found that three out of ten Android phone users are likely to encounter a Web-based threat on their device each year.

While many best practices apply to all mobile devices, there are issues specific to each type of mobile device that must be considered. These include:

A. **Tablets.** A tablet is a small hand-held computer used to write notes, track appointments, contacts, and otherwise keep your life in order. Most can also be used to send and receive e-mail and browse the Internet. Information in the tablet can be synchronized with data in server-based applications such as Microsoft Exchange.

   Information systems is responsible for determining the manufacturers and models of tablets that should be supported. At no time should personally purchased tablets be allowed to be used and supported due to security concerns.

> **COMMENT**
>
> According to a 2011 survey by Gartner, only 3 of 70 organizations contacted had formal policies in place covering the use of personal devices on the corporate network.

Information systems is responsible for maintaining and enforcing a company-wide data synchronization policy for all tablets. A standard synchronization package should be selected that supports all the different tablets in use at the company. The applications and data to be synchronized must also be determined. It is desirable to use synchronization software that can be administered from a single server to control what is being transferred to and from the tablets.

The use of tablets makes good data backup procedures even more critical, as there are more opportunities for data to be changed inadvertently. Verified backups before the first synchronization are very important in case there is a problem during the synchronization process.

Tablet users are notified that the data on the tablet is valuable and sensitive company information, and must be protected. All tablets should be password-enabled with encryption turned on, if available, to prevent unauthorized access to the data if the tablet is lost or stolen. Some tablets with remote access capability can be erased remotely if lost or stolen—check to see if your devices support this feature. Other items to consider include:

1. **Filtering of data**. Information systems must determine what subset of data records is to be synchronized with the tablet. Filter setting can protect sensitive data that should not be synchronized and can be used to save time by transferring only data that is actually needed.

2. **Field mapping**. This is used to map fields from the server application to the tablet application. Information systems must create standards for which data fields can be synchronized and where they map between the server and the tablet.

3. **Conflict resolution.** Data kept on both a server and a tablet have conflicts when data is changed in one or both places. Establish policies to resolve these conflicts.

4. **Control at the server.** Some synchronization products allow settings to be controlled at a central server. This also makes it possible to synchronize over the LAN.

B. **Smartphones.** An Internet-enabled cell phone allows users to access the Internet using their cell phones. Information systems is responsible for maintaining and enforcing a company-wide usage policy for all smartphones. Use should be monitored periodically to ensure the phones are used for business-related purposes.

Smartphone users should be notified that the data on the smartphone is valuable, sensitive company information, and must be protected. All smartphones should be password-enabled (if possible) to prevent unauthorized access to the data if the smartphone is lost or stolen.

Another issue to consider is the proliferation of smartphones that are capable of taking and transmitting pictures. These phones can be a huge security risk, especially in sensitive areas of the company. You may need to ban the use of smartphones in sensitive areas to protect against unauthorized images being taken using these devices.

COMMENT

PICpatch offers an inexpensive camera phone label that can be used to cover the camera lens of a cell phone when the phone is carried into sensitive areas. The labels change when they are removed to alert security personnel that the camera lens was exposed, and is easily detached and leaves no residue once the phone is removed from the secure area. More information about their products can be found on their Web site at *www.picpatchlabel.com*.

C. **Wearable Computers.** A wearable computer is a small computer that is designed to be mobile. The system is worn. This differs from a tablet or laptop, which are designed to be carried and used by being held in the hand. A wearable computer is normally worn on a belt, with optional peripherals including a wrist-mounted touch-screen display, voice-enabled headset, and a head-mounted monitor. They are sometimes integrated into a person's clothing. Wearable computers are especially useful for applications that require computer support while the user's hands, voice, eyes, or attention are actively engaged with the physical environment. Such applications include presentation of information to mechanics, military or paramilitary personnel, path-finding for the blind, real-time translation from one spoken language to another, and continuous medical monitoring.

Information systems is responsible for maintaining and enforcing a company-wide use policy for all wearable computers. Wearable computer users should be notified that the data on the wearable computer is valuable, sensitive company information and must be protected. All wearable computers should be password-enabled to prevent unauthorized access to the data if the wearable computer is lost or stolen.

Information systems is responsible for setting up processes for backing up data on all wearable computers. Procedures include standards for use of docking stations, connections to the LAN, and backing up data to a server. A directory on a server that is regularly backed up should be created for storing data and applications from the wearable computer. Instructions for backing up data and applications are created by information systems and provided to all users of wearable computers.

COMMENT

IBM's Almaden Research Center is working on personal area network (PAN) technology, which uses the natural electrical conductivity of the human body to transmit electronic data. In the future, a user of PAN technology will be able to transfer information via touch rather than issuing typed commands or pressing buttons. For example, your computer might recognize you when you simply touch the keyboard. This capability could yield significant benefits in the areas of access control and data privacy.

D. **USB Flash Drives.** USB Flash drives have replaced the once ubiquitous floppy disk as the most common tool for copying and transporting files.

They are inexpensive, easy to use, easy to transport, and hold large amounts of data. These attributes not only make them attractive to end users for legitimate transportation of computer files, but also cause a security headache for the security personnel responsible for protecting the organization's important data. The same device that allows a user to easily transport Word documents or PowerPoint files for work at home can also be used to carry viruses back to the office, or used to steal valuable corporate data.

Just as it is impractical to search everyone's lunch box as they exit a factory, it is impossible to search every employee and visitor as they leave the office. It is critical that the organization establish policies on the approved use of these devices to keep this risk to a minimum. These policies should include at least the following:

1. Define who is permitted to use flash drives and what types of data are permitted to be stored on these devices. Many organizations go so far as to prohibit the use of personally owned flash drives with corporate-owned computers.
2. Restrict access to flash drives using Group Policy in Windows.
3. Procedures for copying files to and from flash drives.
4. Develop rules for vendors and visitors who want to use flash drives during presentations or visits to the organization.
5. Backup procedures for any data that is updated while on a flash drive.
6. Cover the use of flash drives as part of your virus and spyware policies for employees who use home or off-premise computers.
7. Create password and data encryption standards for flash drives. You may want to consider using biometrically protected flash drives for extremely sensitive data.
8. Institute a reporting procedure for notifying security in the event that a flash drive is lost or stolen.
9. Ensure that PC and laptop systems are configured so that AutoRun features are disabled, as this is a popular method of spreading malware and viruses. Also, consider disallowing some or all executables from running on portable devices.
10. Limit the use of flash drives and other USB devices to only certain registered devices to better control how these devices are used.

Strictly enforce proper security measures on PCs and other network endpoints such as requiring timely installation of security updates, use of proper, up-to-date anti-virus and firewall usage, and enforcing the use of strong passwords. Measures such as these can prevent malware and viruses from spreading to other devices on the network.

See Policy ITP-27-7 Flash Drive Usage Policy as an example.

POLICY ITP-27-7. Flash Drive Usage Policy

Policy #:	ITP-27-7	**Effective:**	03/18/13	**Page #:**	1 of N
Subject:	Flash Drive Usage Policy				

1.0 PURPOSE

USB flash drives have replaced the once ubiquitous floppy disk as the most common tool for copying and transporting files. They are inexpensive, easy to use, easy to transport, and hold large amounts of data. These attributes not only make them attractive to end users for legitimate transportation of computer files, but also cause a security headache for the security personnel responsible for protecting the organization's important data. This policy defines the acceptable use of USB flash drives within the organization, specifically the use of these devices on the corporate network.

2.0 SCOPE

The policy applies to any USB storage device used with any other device that is connected to the corporate network. This includes flash memory devices, external magnetic hard drives, external optical drives, digital cameras, portable media players, and mobile phones.

3.0 POLICY

The user of the USB storage device will accept responsibility for taking reasonable precautions in protecting the data on the mobile device and the security of the corporate network. The following guidelines must be followed when using a USB storage device on the corporate network:

A. IT will control what USB devices can be used on computers they manage using Group Policy in Windows.
B. No company confidential material may be copied to a USB storage device.
C. Devices may only be used on PC and laptop systems that have had AutoRun features disabled.
D. Employees must report immediately the loss of any USB storage device.
E. All employees desiring to use a USB storage device on the corporate network must have read and signed the corporate computer acceptable use policy, and agree to follow all requirements of that policy.

4.0 REVISION HISTORY

Date	Revision #	Description of Change
03/18/13	1.0	Initial creation.

5.0 INQUIRIES

Direct inquiries about this policy to:

George Jenkins, CIO
Our Company, Inc.
2900 Corporate Drive
Columbus, OH 43215

Voice: 614-555-1234
Fax: 614-555-1235
E-mail: gjenkins@company.com

Revision #:	1.0	Supersedes:	N/A	Date:	03/18/13

COMMENT

Reviews of biometrically protected flash drives can be found on the Web at *http://fingerprint-usb-review.toptenreviews .com/*.

Another thing to consider to help support the use of mobile devices is to take advantage of power users. A power user is a person who uses a particular device on a regular basis (usually daily) and becomes very knowledgeable about its operation. This person usually enjoys sharing information about using the device with others in the organization. Ask power users if they could be contacted if a new user needs assistance. If they agree, their names should be listed as power users with the instructions given to new users.

Power users should be able to operate and perform minor device adjustments. They should know how to replenish expendable stock items and perform standard housekeeping and preventive maintenance procedures. A power user can be walked through some of the malfunctions by the service desk or a maintenance person over the telephone. At the service desk, there should be a power user's location book with the power user's name, telephone number, and location listed. A second listing by location, with the power user's name and telephone number listed, is also helpful. This can be used to contact another power user who is close by for assistance when the nearer power user is not available.

It is critical that operating procedures be furnished to all device users. The IT service department or the systems and procedures department should furnish the operator procedure manuals. The manuals provide operator instructions, minor maintenance instruction, backup procedures, and procedures for troubleshooting. Minor preventive maintenance procedures should also be provided. If practical, the manual should be available on the company's intranet site.

The procedure manuals contain any manufacturer's furnished material helpful to clarify the device's operation. The illustrations used by the manufacturer could be beneficial to the operator. Close-up and wide-view photographs are helpful if included in the operator procedure manuals. A prototype manual should be developed and tested before it enters service. Use an unskilled person for the test. This should be done with more than one person. Avoid the brightest person in the area and any experienced operator for debugging the procedure manual.

[J]   Accessories and Supplies

Accessories can improve productivity, reduce fatigue, and improve morale. These accessories and supply items are on a "recommended" or "approved list" provided by the PC Support Manager. The approved vendors will carry listed items. This information helps when ordering through the purchasing department. The approved list will be published, updated, and distributed by the PC Support Manager.

PC supplies and minor accessories can, over the course of a year, amount to a large expense. Still, given the size of the items and the volumes, it is much easier to treat them as you would the pens and pencils in the office supplies. The PC Support Manager should identify what items are acceptable (e.g., inkjet refills, toner cartridges) by brand and model, and purchasing will provide these items through their office supplies program.

Supply items can be purchased with the user's department petty cash fund or a budget requisition. They are requisitioned from the unit responsible for office or computer supplies according to standard operating procedure.

Accessories are classified in two groups: ergonomic devices and productivity aids. (The following items are not identified by brand name.)

A. **Ergonomic devices.** Ergonomic devices are to help the human body interact with the PC system and function with the least amount of fatigue, error, and bodily harm. The following types of ergonomic devices are available on the "recommended list" provided by the PC Support Manager:
    1. Keyboard wrist rest
    2. Mouse wrist rest
    3. Tablet docking stations
    4. Footrest
    5. Ergonomic keyboard
    6. Arm support
    7. Ergonomic, adjustable chair
    8. Adjustable workstations for special employees
    9. Glare monitor screen

> ### COMMENT
>
> Remember to consider the requirements of the Americans with Disabilities Act when developing policies concerning ergonomic devices.

B. **Productivity aids.** The following, if used properly, have been known to increase productivity:
   1. Tilt-and-turn monitor stand
   2. Copyholder (flex arm, attachable, or standard)
   3. Copyholder light
   4. Diskette storage devices
   5. Cartridge storage devices
   6. Desktop printer stand and/or organizer
   7. PC rollout keyboard system
   8. Keyboard with mouse
   9. Keyboard labels for F keys and/or other keys

[K] Disposal of Excess Equipment

Office computer and other electronic devices contain hazardous materials such as lead, mercury, and cadmium. Old CRT monitors are the worst offenders, containing up to five pounds of lead. With computer obsolescence accelerating, the volume of waste from discarded computers is growing at three times the rate of any other type of waste. It is projected that as many as 500 million computers were taken out of service between 2000 and 2007.

The Resource Conservation and Recovery Act (RCRA) was updated in 2004 to include guidelines regarding the disposal of computer monitors. The RCRA rules only apply if the equipment is disposed of in a landfill; they do not apply when recycling, donating the equipment or trading the equipment in when buying new.

> ### COMMENT
>
> Environmental regulations on disposal of computer equipment should not be taken lightly—in 2000, AT&T agreed to pay a penalty of $195,000 for not properly responding to an agency request for information about its computer-disposal practices.

Policies covering the disposal of surplus computer equipment should mandate that all such equipment be disposed of properly. Computer equipment may no longer be needed for a variety of reasons:

A. Worn out or damaged
B. No longer utilized
C. Technical obsolescence
D. Maintenance costs are excessive
E. Replaced with a newer model

These policies should cover all computer equipment that is capable of storing data. This includes PCs, tablets, external hard disks, cell phones, etc. The policies should also outline the approved processes for disposal of the equipment. Possible disposal options include:

A. **Redistribution.** Every effort should be made to redistribute the equipment to another use within the organization. This may require minor upgrades to the equipment such as additional memory or hard disk capacity.
B. **Recycling.** Some computer equipment can be recycled or disassembled for parts for reuse in other equipment.
C. **Disposal.** Equipment must be disposed of in compliance with local and federal regulations.

Procedures must also be developed when equipment has been identified for disposal. The procedures should provide for consistent tracking and handling of the equipment. Before any computer equipment leaves the control of the organization, the procedures must ensure that all company software and data has been removed from the system. If any licensed software is eligible for use on another device, the software license inventory should be updated to reflect the availability of the license for use on another device. The software and data on any physical storage device must be destroyed using a method appropriate for the type of hardware, operating system, and the sensitivity of the data.

See Policy ITP-27-8 Computer Equipment Disposal Policy as an example.

POLICY ITP-27-8.   Computer Equipment Disposal Policy

Policy #:	ITP-27-8	Effective:	03/18/13	Page #:	1 of N
Subject:	Computer Equipment Disposal Policy				

1.0 PURPOSE

This policy mandates that all surplus computer equipment be disposed of properly. Computer equipment may no longer be needed for a variety of reasons:

§ 27.04[K]

A. Worn out or damaged
B. No longer utilized
C. Technical obsolescence
D. Maintenance costs are excessive
E. Replaced with a newer model

2.0 SCOPE

This policy covers all computer equipment that is capable of storing data. This includes PCs, tablets, external hard disks, cell phones, etc.

3.0 POLICY

There are three approved processes for disposing of excess computer equipment listed below. They are listed in order of preference:

A. **Redistribution.** Every effort should be made to redistribute the equipment to another use within the organization. This may require minor upgrades to the equipment such as additional memory or hard disk capacity.
B. **Recycling.** Some computer equipment can be recycled or disassembled for parts for reuse in other equipment.
C. **Disposal.** Equipment must be disposed of in compliance with local and federal regulations.

The following procedures must be followed when equipment has been identified for disposal:

A. The department with the surplus equipment will notify the help desk and schedule a time for the equipment to be picked up.
B. The help desk will assess the condition of the equipment and determine the appropriate means of disposal.
C. Based on the disposal process selected, the help desk will:
  1. Notify the appropriate department that the equipment has been removed from inventory.
  2. Arrange the transfer of the equipment to inventory if it is being redistributed.
  3. Arrange for the equipment to be picked up by the approved disposal vendor if it being recycled or disposed of.

Before any computer equipment leaves the control of the organization, the help desk must ensure that all company software and data has been removed from the system. If any licensed software is eligible for use on another device, the software license inventory must be updated to reflect the availability of the license for use on another device. The software and data on any physical storage device must be destroyed using one of the following methods:

27-41

A. Windows provides a mechanism for repartitioning and formatting the original hard drive before installation.
B. Utilize a Department of Defense approved data destruction software application following DOD guidelines.
C. Destroy the hard drive in a manner that does not allow the drive to be rebuilt. Options include crushing or shredding of the disk drive.

4.0 REVISION HISTORY

Date	Revision #	Description of Change
03/18/13	1.0	Initial creation.

5.0 INQUIRIES

Direct inquiries about this policy to:

George Jenkins, CIO
Our Company, Inc.
2900 Corporate Drive
Columbus, OH 43215

Voice: 614-555-1234
Fax: 614-555-1235
E-mail: gjenkins@company.com

Revision #:	1.0	Supersedes:	N/A	Date:	03/18/13

§ 27.05   END-USER TECHNICAL SUPPORT

[A]   Overview

End-user technical support is available in several forms. The information systems organization provides some forms of support. Different vendors provide other end-user support.

Payment for support services depends on company policies. The payment can come from one central source and/or department budgets. Whichever method is used, a record system will be maintained. The following sections cover the various types of end-user support available in most organizations.

[B]   The Resident Expert

Every business department seems to have at least one person with an aptitude for all things technical. This person is usually looking over a technician's shoulder whenever they come to resolve a problem or to tune a system. Early on the PC Support Manager can choose to fight this person (and lose) or enfranchise them as an extension of the IT staff. The resident expert concept means that they will be asked to handle all of the simple problems that arise in a department. They probably already do so. In exchange, they will be given priority service, first chance at new software classes that open, ready access to the technical library, and help with tougher problems. A thorough resident expert program will reduce the volume of simple user error calls and open a wide channel of business user feedback.

[C]   Computer Technician

Computer technician is the title of the IT person who provides desk-side help with end-user computer and equipment problems. PC technicians work under the direction of the PC Support Manager. In either case, the person in charge of this unit reports to the manager of information systems. The service desk contacts this unit when they cannot solve a PC problem. The problem may be with hardware, software, or a supply item.

The computer technician is always dispatched by the service desk (users are never given their direct telephone number). The problem-tracking database provides utilization tracking. The computer technician should carry a cell phone so they can proceed to their next call without always returning to their desk first. This communications path also allows them to "drop and run" when critical systems are having problems. If there are multiple PC technicians, consider assigning them to the primary support of specific areas to better understand the users' needs. They can still support other areas but will have deeper knowledge of specific departments. Another way is to assign them by technology but this will confuse users. By nature, a PC technician is a generalist.

Computer technician skill requirements. The computer technician has general knowledge of the users' PC hardware and/or software uses, including supply items. The hardware and software are identified under their respective approved lists. For large, complex organizations, there are specialists for lesser-used equipment. The computer technician is called by the service desk if the computer operator has a problem the service desk cannot walk them through. It could be a problem where the computer technician requested a call to them the next time it happened.

It is important that computer technicians have a good understanding of their users' business to recognize a priority call. This helps them focus on critical issues and less on "squeaky wheels." The technicians need patient temperaments so they can help users through basic and embarrassing mistakes without alienating them. Computer technicians are IT's primary trainers since they can provide a steady stream of tips to users with whom they are constantly in contact. The technicians who run calls must have a quick connection to someone they can refer to for priority resolution (who do I see next?) and for backup in a crisis.

Computer technician resource requirements. The computer technician will be provided with a toolkit to cover the kind of hardware they will need to resolve problems. This will be carried in an attached case provided by the company. There will be a minimum of space for spare parts. Supply items that are often used should be stored close to the computer operation. Other items needed may be obtained by someone else, from the source, to save the technician's time. The computer technician also will be provided with a mobile phone.

Computer technician's responsibilities. The technician will maintain a daily activity log. The computer technician should perform the following computer tasks at the user's site:

A. Replace faulty computer parts.
B. Perform hardware upgrades.
C. Check connection cords.
D. Run a virus check and remove any viruses.
E. Check operation of the network connection.
F. Reformat hard drive.
G. Reload operating system.
H. Load new software and confirm it is operational.
I. Install hardware accessories.
J. Perform routine diagnostics.
K. Remove any unauthorized software from computer.
L. Disconnect and/or remove unauthorized hardware. Turn over the unauthorized hardware device to the PC Support Manager.

At times there may be hardware problems requiring the user's computer or attached devices to be taken back to the repair area. If the time the equipment is away from its operating area becomes a problem, the computer technician will arrange for a loaner unit to be provided. The loan will be only for the time the user's equipment is not available. If the loaner is the functional equivalent to the old one, then leave it. Expect loaners that are superior to the old unit to be difficult to get back. Given the time necessary to copy files from the loaner back to the old unit, it may not be worth the fight.

The computer technician's work log. While working on any device, the technician should look for any illegal software. Any such software found is deleted and recorded in the log. Unauthorized hardware attached to the desktop computer will be confiscated and delivered to the PC Support Manager. It also will be recorded in the daily log sheet. The PC Support Manager acknowledges acceptance of the equipment by signing the computer technician's daily log sheet.

Weekly computer technician's report. The charge time will be portal to portal. The charge time is summarized by user, user's unit, and other duties not charged to a user. Any administration or other nonuser charge time is prorated to service calls. If the company has an interdepartmental charge system, the end-user's department is charged for the service time for the maintenance. How these costs are handled will depend on the company's accounting practice.

The computer technician writes a short weekly report to the PC Support Manager. The report notes any special hardware or software problems occurring during the week. Any operator problems needing resolution will be recommended. Can the operator problems be remedied with operator training, new operation manuals, or equipment? If the operator problem deals with an ergonomics issue, state what the problem is in the report.

[D] Software Support

There will be software that is not on the current approved computer software list, but is in the asset management software database. Some of the end users using software will be assigned to a computer technician if the service desk cannot be of assistance. The technician will pull the software file folder for the programs and review the documentation before going to the end user's workplace.

Computer technicians are not expected to solve all the end-user problems they encounter. There will be special hardware and/or software technicians who are not generalists. When the service desk contacts the IT unit for computer support, they will provide information to have the proper technician answer the service call.

COMMENT

Consider an outside support contract for critical software the team cannot support. For example, two vocal users needed PageMaker to build company newsletters. It was not feasible to train or hire a support person for them. Instead, an open purchase order was arranged for outside support as needed.

The asset management software database has the inventory information of legally owned company software. All software on the approved computer software list is on the asset management software database. Not all asset management software database programs will be found on the approved computer software list. The technician will not resolve all software problems for these programs.

A. **End-user computer software.** The software for end users is found on the approved computer software list. The service desk and the IT technical support unit support this software.

B. **IT computer software.** The software for the IT units is on the approved computer software list. The IT programming unit supports this software. Obviously, games, football pools, questionable photographs, etc., are not a part of the company's business and can be removed.

C. **Company IT unit's computer software.** Other IT units using purchased packaged software may call on the IT technical support unit for assistance. If the IT programming unit developed the software, it should be contacted for support. This software is in the asset management software database but seldom found on the approved computer software list.

D. **Special computer software.** All software is required to be in the asset management software database. This software can include several types of programs and may be supported by information systems. The question will be asked: How did the user come into possession of the software? Some special computer software, not on the approved computer software list but on the asset management software database, can be identified as follows:

1. **End-user software still in use.** End users can use software that is no longer available but is still supported. The software may no longer be available on the market or is about to be replaced. Often this software was on the hard drive of the last PC which was on the hard drive of the PC before it. Users do not know why it is there but are afraid to remove it.

2. **Software for special applications.** This software is purchased for specially approved application and/or hardware. The department that arranged to acquire the software is responsible for obtaining the needed support.

3. **Software testing.** Software purchased by end users for testing will not be supported. The person who acquired the program(s) will seek support from the vendor.

4. **Turnkey software operations.** The vendor will support contracts drawn for vendor-developed turnkey-operated systems.

[E]   Computer Ergonomics Support

If the company has an environmental ergonomics unit, it should be available to assist the information systems department. If the service is unavailable, consulting firms are available for this kind of support. Most ergonomic problems do not require a consultant. Someone is selected in the end-user technical support unit and trained. College courses and short commercial programs on ergonomics are now available. Books and periodicals also are available.

COMMENT

The Human Factors and Ergonomics Society is a national organization with local chapters. They can be reached at *www.hfes.org*. AliMed publishes an excellent ergonomics and occupational health catalog. They can be reached at *www.alimed.com*.

[F]   Service Desk

A service desk provides a central point of contact for all users who are experiencing a problem. A well-run service desk is critical to user satisfaction.

§ 27.05[F]

In years gone by, users "just knew" who to call. If they had a computer problem, they left a message on a specific person's phone (usually a programmer) and waited for that person to call back. If that person was on vacation or out sick, they had no way of knowing. If that person did not know how to solve the problem, it did not matter, as they would find someone for the user who did. This was very personal customer service but with hit-or-miss results.

A service desk acts as a buffer between the users and the IT department. The service desk should be informed who will be out of the office, and when. They should have a matrix of who to call for support for each system first, who to call next, etc. The service desk technicians should resolve all of the simple calls that used to interrupt the kindly but very busy programmer. In an emergency, such as a network outage, all users call the service desk to get updates instead of each user calling his favorite programmer.

An early decision is the level of service the service desk is to provide. Its staffing level will determine how quickly a call will be answered. Certain times of the day will be busier than others so use a call-tracking database to chart the time of day and the day of week when call volume peaks. The larger the staff, the quicker the telephone can be answered and problems addressed.

The second decision ties closely to the first in that now that the phone is answered promptly, can the technician resolve the call? How much technical depth should be required of a service desk technician? One strategy is to use nontechnical (low-paid) people to answer the telephone, ask a few questions to identify whom to refer the call, and then pass on the message. In this model, the customer twiddles their thumbs and awaits a call from a technician. Another approach is to use technical people to resolve the questions as they come in and refer difficult problems to the appropriate technician. Both approaches work but which one is right for the facility?

Another question is if the service desk resides in the local facility or is provided by an outside company. The advantage of the inside service desk is that the people learn about the facility's operations, insider jargon, who works where, and allows the technicians an opportunity to be on a more personal basis with end users. The service desk also can take walk-up requests. Using an outside provider allows them to staff for the peaks and valleys but the company loses a great deal of control over who is answering the telephone.

With this trade-off in mind, consider that the person answering the service desk telephone will have more one-on-one contact with IT users than anyone else in the department. A bad experience calling the service desk will translate into a black mark on the entire IT department no matter how many times it is explained that these people are a contracted service.

Service desk calls tend to come in waves. During the quiet periods, the technicians can get a bit of rest and monitor vital system activities. This monitoring of network volumes, mainframe job flows, and the pattern of incoming calls provide the IT Manager with some early warning of data system problems.

Some companies rotate their programmers and PC technicians through the service desk during peak periods so they can listen to some of the user calls. This is a valuable opportunity for the service desk staff to learn more about their systems and for the programmers to hear some of the problems their systems cause end users.

A key cost driver for contracted service desk services is the level of service provided. If all that is expected is taking a message and asking a few scripted questions, then just about anyone—anywhere—can take the call. The result is to dispatch a technician. This is the model used by most public utility companies. This approach is synonymous with a simple answering service. Another cost driver is the required response time—how many rings before the call must be picked up?

But, if service desk staffers are expected to provide some level of problem resolution during the initial contact, they need the ability to access data systems for troubleshooting. This may require an on-site office or a dedicated high-speed data line.

Security also is a major concern. High-volume calls for service desks are password problems. Since the service desk technicians need access to change these, they may pose a security risk.

Vendor contracting. After the bid proposals are received, they are compared with each other. Lowest bidders do not always provide the best service. Beware of startup companies without verifiable experience. Calculate the costs for providing the service in-house. This provides a baseline to evaluate the bids.

Write a short-duration flexible contract when beginning a relationship with a new vendor. This provides information to both the vendor and the company about the contents of the final contract. The company's legal representatives review the contract and make recommendations before it is signed.

In-house service desk. An in-house service desk often starts as a pilot project. As the bugs are worked out, it can accommodate more internal customers. Start an in-house service desk with a lump-sum budget. Record the number of contacts by unit and the time spent per contact. This will be helpful for future planning.

There are several ways to operate an in-house service desk. The one best method depends on corporate culture, union concerns, etc. The following things should be considered when operating an in-house service desk:

A. **Operations.** Record conversations to provide an audit trail of the dialogue between the user and the service desk technician. This reduces and simplifies note-taking by the service desk staff. Use a voice-mail system to avoid busy signals or no answer when calling the service desk.

B. **Facility.** The service desk work area provides rapid access to information needs. It is ergonomically suitable for the tasks of the service desk staff. The job is confining and any ergonomic assistance would help reduce the burnout rate for this job. A regular change or rotation of duties also would prolong the life of the service desk technician.

A service desk is a built-in feedback mechanism for finding out how the company's systems perform. Use the data!

The service desk's demeanor is critical. Users' opinion of the department will be greatly shaped by the service desk; they are the ones users talk to most. The service desk staff must be able to work under pressure. Abusive callers should be forwarded to the service desk supervisor.

[G] Maintenance Contracting

All hardware may not be maintained in-house. In some instances, vendor equipment service contracting for some devices might be a better solution. Some mobile devices are best maintained using vendor contracts. Some leased items include service agreements. Contracts can specify an unlimited number of service calls or charges on a by-call basis. Contracts can provide for spare parts or parts can be charged as installed. Some vendors can offer an array of equipment they can service. Service can be provided for normal working hours or around the clock.

There can be one or more service vendors. There are firms providing a full-service blanket for most hardware. Other firms service one or more machines. Consider these options when deciding the service best for the company.

Before any maintenance contracts are signed, the legal representative of the company reviews them. Upon approval, the authorized management personnel sign them. Purchasing is contacted regarding such contracts. The procedure followed will be the corporate procedure for contracting services.

Some things must use outsourced repairs:

A. Parts availability—they will not sell them to anyone.
B. Technical expertise.
C. Warranty work—usually only good if the equipment is packed up and delivered back to the factory or to a salesperson. This may not be worthwhile in the case of PCs unless they can be removed from service and sent away.

Equipment with moving parts (like printers) has a higher ongoing maintenance cost than solid-state devices.

Using an asset database, compare the cost of a maintenance contract to the cost of buying several spare devices. Use spare devices to replace broken equipment and then send the damaged material out for service on a time-and-materials basis.

A key component of maintenance contracts is the hours of coverage. Normal working hours coverage is cheapest and "24/7" is very expensive. Keep in mind that this is response time—not maximum resolution time.

28

END-USER SYSTEMS: DO-IT-YOURSELF COMPUTING

§ 28.01 OVERVIEW

[A] Purpose and Scope

End-user computing is the creation or use of software applications by someone internal to the company without the involvement of the IT department. These applications can be developed in a wide range of computer language formats, from traditional languages such as C or Visual Basic to the embedded formulas in spreadsheets. They can be created in-house or purchased from an app store such as Apple iTunes, Google Play, or the Windows Phone Marketplace. The challenge to the IT Manager is to ensure that those who create or use such applications understand and adhere to good data processing practices using effective policies and procedures.

Long have end users complained about the slowness of traditional IT application development. In their view, simple requests to the IT department take weeks or months. As personal computers became more powerful, software became easier to use. Non-IT employees knew how to use them both, and end-user computing emerged as a force. Today personal computing classes are routinely required throughout the national education system.

Initially managers of the various departments thought they now had a quick way to develop or purchase their own applications. They gradually came to realize that they had grabbed the proverbial tiger by the tail and could not let go!

The individual department managers were relearning the lessons painfully learned by IT over the years. End-user computing policies must be in place to ensure that end users do not create more problems than they solve when they take matters into their own hands.

[B] Critical Policies to Develop Based on This Chapter

Using the material discussed in this chapter, you will be able to create the following policies:

A. Permissible end-user systems
B. IT involvement

Policies should always be developed based on the local situation. Successful managers cannot issue appropriate guidance if the policies are written with another company's situation or location in mind.

§ 28.02 THE PROBLEMS WITH END-USER COMPUTING

[A] Overview

The IT staff works with technology every day. They likely have several years of technical college training as well as years of experience designing, implementing, and supporting data systems of various types. During this time, some basic principles of the art of data processing became ingrained in their actions and work plans. In short, they do things automatically that will ensure their systems are reliable, efficient, and always available.

Business managers focus on the problems found in their own department. End-user programming for them is something of a diversion. If something provides the results they seek, then it is a success. Little time is wasted polishing the code or checking results. That work is for another time.

Most end-user problems result in subtle errors. A slightly inaccurate total here, a missing record there, slightly out of date tables used, etc. If a value is blatantly incorrect, then something is done about it. However, if the numbers appear to be plausible then the application is used to help run the business.

Regardless of the source, end-user computing generated data are relied upon by management for decisions that impact corporate strategies, regulatory compliance, and customer relationships. The integrity of the data and the accuracy of this processing are no less important than that provided by the IT department.

[B]   The Evolution of End-User Computing

In times long gone by, punch cards were the primary tool for controlling computers. Each card held an 80-character line of data or programming code. Developing programs was a tedious process involving the building, debugging, and maintaining of sequences of punch cards in a series of trays.

Around the late 1970s, from the ranks of electronics hobbyists emerged personal computers. These machines could perform simple tasks but were mainly a curiosity. Sometime around 1978, the early personal computers emerged. Among these machines were the Commodore PET, TRS-80 Model I, and the Apple II. An important feature of these devices was that they contained a small version of the BASIC programming language on an 8K ROM. BASIC was easy to learn and could perform simple tasks. Data was stored on cassette tapes and later on floppy disks.

These devices initially lacked powerful, easy-to-use software. As the software emerged, so did demand for the machines. Word processing programs drove early demand. Up to this point, professionals used typewriters to create lengthy documents or paid someone to type them. Back and forth went draft copies with pen changes until finally the document reached its final form. Each document revision required typing the entire text from the beginning, which introduced more errors. The productivity improvement justified the purchase of computers for many secretaries' desks, although the printers that were used closely mimicked electric typewriters.

A popular package of this early era was WordStar, which provided many formatting features. Limited as it seems today, this package encouraged more people to buy PCs for home and the office. Still, PCs were a novelty the users thought of as playing with an oversized calculator.

COMMENT

Around this time special-purpose word processing worksta-
tions appeared in many secretarial areas around companies.
The refinements made to this software made their way into
PC software and these stations disappeared.

In 1981, IBM introduced their first personal computer. This greatly increased the credibility of PCs as office tools and opened the gates to purchase by large corporations. Along with the new computer came a new type of software called VisiCalc. This product introduced the concept of an electronic spreadsheet and, together with new word processing software, spurred the widespread use of office personal computers—and along with it end-user computing.

The combination of word processing and spreadsheet programs provided sufficient value to move PCs from secretary stations onto managers' desktops. Now, instead of asking a secretary to type a simple memo, they did it themselves. (Many of their peers would sniff that they do not want to learn how to use a PC as "they do not type.")

Up to this point, end-user written programs in BASIC or Pascal were primarily for engineering purposes. Saving programs and data to cassette tapes was quite slow. Although the IBM had a tape storage option, it was rarely seen as everyone used the 160K, single-sided floppy disk drive (power users had *two* floppy drives). PCs were still expensive and only found on selected desks.

Most company data was in the form of reports. These reports display the summation of the individual data elements but the elements themselves and the calculations used to create them are not visible to the reader. Reports compiled in an office included the names of the people creating and typing them. Mainframe-generated reports were meticulously developed. However, VisiCalc spreadsheets allowed anyone to create financial reports that appeared like the tediously created, manually assembled reports.

Soon, the first end-user introduced problems appeared. These reports depended on the accuracy of the formulas embedded in the spreadsheet cells, and the data that was entered. They were recognizable by the simple dot matrix printers that created them. Still, the strong reputation of mainframe-generated reports gave these documents unwarranted respect.

In a short time, easy-to-use database packages, more programming languages, and faster hardware rolled in. Desktop units gradually contained as much raw computing power as mainframe computers. Windows with its GUI interface shielded users from the coldly impersonal DOS and provided a visually attractive interface for programmers. Merge this with recent college graduates who worked with computers in school and the mix was right for business departments to write their own data systems.

Aware of the benefits and tired of delays in getting needed systems from IT, end-user departments began to establish "shadow" data processing operations. Programmers hid behind titles like "data coordinator" with a job description that read like something right out of the IT department. "Power users" emerged as recent college graduates, familiar with personal computing tools, entered the offices. Some offices began to resemble PC repair stations complete with stacks of spare parts and piles of tangled cables. Today, with the proliferation of tablets and smartphones in the workplace, you do not even need to know the basics of programming—just download an application from the app store and off you go.

COMMENT

One author worked for a company whose IT Director routinely sidelined program requests and bragged of the money saved by not performing "low value" work. Unfortunately, the only person whose value judgment he listened to was his own.

So here we are today. In every business department are users with enough technical sophistication to create complex data systems, write reports against major databases, develop sophisticated spreadsheet analysis, and purchase applications all without IT involvement. Is this a good idea or are there problems lurking under the surface?

[C] Reasons End-User Computing Is Popular

Personal computing, as its name implies, is computing done by and for a single person. Although playing a game is a form of personal computing, this term usually refers to programming "something" to do work. In a home setting, personal computing is not much of an issue. If a student's spreadsheet has an error, then their grade suffers. If their database search of an encyclopedia fails, then they reap the consequences.

In an office setting, end-user computing can be more rewarding or create its own consequences. End-user computing—the creation of data systems (big or small) by others than the IT department—carries with it far more responsibilities than most people are aware of, or are willing to take on. Regardless of the source, the information generated by end-user computing tools are made for decisions affecting corporate strategies and customer relationships. The integrity of the data in these applications is no less important than the data stored in the corporate databases.

The widespread use of end-user computing attests to its popularity. Some of the reasons end-user computing remains popular include:

A. **Productivity.** Documents of all types are created and stored electronically. Changes are quickly made and printed. Word processing allows typing memos instead of writing them out and sending them back and forth for revisions.

B. **Agility.** In a fast-paced business environment, there is no time to wait for a bureaucratic IT department to waddle through their justification processes simply to estimate the cost of a request. By then, the opportunity is gone.

C. **Timeliness.** Small requests take far longer to explain than for a trained user to create or purchase them.

[D] Examples of End-User Programming

End-user developed programs primarily automate the tedious and repetitive tasks on a worker's desk. Examples of this are:

A. **Reporting.** Roughly half of the requests to IT involve developing new reports or modifying existing ones. Many requests are for single use reports where the end user only has a vague idea of what he or she wants. Rather than perform exhaustive data systems analysis and design process, IT should provide easy-to-use tools to allow end users to create their own reports. These tools must have limits to prevent a poorly written database query from dragging down the entire server. A common check is to limit end-user queries to a maximum of 5,000 records.

COMMENT

End-user computing has long been a mainframe function. Some programs such as QlikTech'sQlikView and SAP Business Objects Crystal Reports have provided the tools for generating reports from the core mainframe databases with a minimum of keystrokes.

B. **Web pages.** This powerful communications medium is useful for internally publishing information. Rather than print reams of paper and then walk around distributing it, a department can post the information on a portal using tools such as Microsoft SharePoint. Examples of information include daily reports, business performance metrics, policy manuals, etc. IT limits are usually to publish a policy about acceptable content in a department's Web page. IT also locks the page to internal usage only while policing all pages to keep confidential data off the Web.

C. **Spreadsheets.** A great tool for listing and totaling numbers for budgets, expense tracking, quality statistical analysis, etc., spreadsheets manage very large lists through sorting and pivot tables. The rapid graphing of data (instead of tediously graphing by hand) is also a great tool for quickly examining data. The text formatting capabilities of spreadsheets make them a quick way to develop simple forms.

D. **Word processing.** Many programs provide a capability to create data entry forms which only allow data to be entered into specific fields. People who complain about the time it takes to perform basic work in a word processing program never had to suffer through the various tab settings, line spacing settings, and other mechanical aspects of setting up an electric typewriter to build a document. Not only is the software easier to use, but it makes the creation of newsletters with graphics and pictures an easy desktop task.

E. **Database.** Great for collecting data or reporting from lists too large for a spreadsheet. All end-user created databases must be maintained on the department's server file share to ensure they can be backed up. Multi-user databases (except for read only) must be created and managed by the IT department.

F. **Graphics.** Computer-aided design (CAD) software did for draftsmen what spreadsheets did for accountants. It has taken the engineering world from drafting tables to the desktop and saved countless hours redrawing and copying blueprints and component designs.

[E] Some of the Pitfalls

A long list of problems can arise from end-user computing. They are quite familiar to IT workers who have been struggling with the same issues for years. The key to end-user computing is to identify the risks from these issues at the local site, to educate end users on how to minimize the risk, and to support them in these mitigation efforts. IT Managers have found that addressing the issues in advance is far easier than "firefighting" the problems as they arise.

End users do not always differentiate between sensitive company data and all of the other data they work with. "Sensitive data" requires protection due to the risk and magnitude of loss or harm which could result from inadvertent or deliberate disclosure, alteration, or destruction of the data.

Some of the end-user computing pitfalls include:

A. **Data.** Data, the object of end-user computing, is also its central point of failure. End users do not apply the necessary controls to ensure data accuracy going in and its correct summation coming out. The result can damage a company in several ways.

   1. Incorrect management decisions, based on incorrect outputs.
   2. Improper disclosure of information, due to poor security.
   3. Fraud, since the person controlling the data can also control changing it.
   4. End users who create their own database systems risk the data being out of date with the rest of the company's data.

> ## COMMENT
>
> One author worked at a company where the freight traffic manager kept detailed records of all shipments in a spreadsheet. It included items such as what was sent to where, how much it weighed, the amount bid by the carrier, the class of service ordered, etc. The following month when the freight bills were submitted, this sheet was validated to reconcile the bills and stop numerous attempts at overcharging. It also provided data for filing missing freight claims.
>
> This spreadsheet automated a routine task that concerned no one else. However, the data was critical to protecting the company from freight overbillings and enhanced their ability to file successful claims. Overbillings frequently ran $10,000 per month or more. To protect this important company information, the file moved from the creator's never-backed-up PC to a computer file server.

The problem arises when departments create their own set of data parallel to the IT databases. These files and databases are beyond the standard IT data integrity safeguards. Although quick to report from and easy to manipulate, these parallel data stores may provide misleading results. IT should develop department databases to ensure they contain accurate data. On request, IT can reload the database with the latest data. Problems that may arise with end-user created data files include:

1. The corruption of data due to a lack of program edits for data entry or correction.
2. Errors may take a long time to become apparent with bad output embedding into other files.
3. A loss of critical company data can occur due to poor program controls, lack of storage management, or poorly written programs that corrupt files.
4. Failure to retain data according to regulatory requirements places the company at legal risk. This is true even if the end user created the file solely for his personal use. Since these files are out of the IT department's sight, their existence may not be known to the company until an inopportune moment.
5. When an end user downloads corporate data or builds his own database, he assumes personal responsibility for its security. This is something that few users think about since IT has always handled this quietly in

the background. The simplest way to protect data is to store it on a network server where the user accesses it through his or her own user ID security access. Unfortunately, with the proliferation of notebook PCs, tablets, and smartphones, this has become more of a challenge.

6. In a report, old data often looks just like new data. To ensure that the data in the file is the current version, consider displaying the latest date in a data field on the report, reading the directory for the file creation date.

7. Notebook PCs, tablets, and smartphones present double problems since both hardware and data can be lost at the same time. Portable computing devices should contain a minimal amount of sensitive data. If used for data collection, periodically copy the information to a server for protection.

Another issue surrounds who "owns" the data. If an end user creates a file or database from scratch, then, in his mind, he controls use of this file. Of course, the company owns all data and the IT Manager represents the company in all technical matters. Still, some users use databases as part of their ongoing turf battles.

COMMENT

Managers be warned. Spreadsheets and other end-user developed software used in the preparation of company financial information may be audited under the Sarbanes-Oxley Act. IT Managers must find these programs and bring them under IT quality control. Controlling these programs includes controlling access to them and locking cells to prevent unauthorized changes. Be sure to keep an adequate number of data generations in archive.

B. **Software.** Unlike hardware problems, software defects have no physical appearance. They require tedious effort to identify and resolve. Sometimes the problem only occurs in that rare moment when several circumstances converge at once and may be very frustrating to figure out. Normal IT testing uses a wide combination of data and logic branches to test for such errors.

End-user programs employ a wide range of languages. The most common type of programming is the formulas embedded in spreadsheets. Each formula in a spreadsheet represents another opportunity for an error. Problems with end-user coding include:

1. Managers do not thoroughly question the code developed by their clerks as they lack coding skills themselves (the danger of managing

what someone does not know). However, they can cross-check the totals on reports with reports from other sources to see if they are consistent.

2. If a program problem arises after an employee leaves the company, then managers are on their own to address it. Yet they often lack the technical skills to review or update the code. In a crisis, expect a call to the IT department requesting a bail out. This is caused by:

   a. Employees leaving the company.

   b. Consultants or college interns writing something and then leaving.

3. Programs often lack a clear identification or version number. As copies float about, no one knows who has what code. Often the various copies look the same but are actually different versions and provide different results. Updates are not carefully distributed. Consequently, in the eyes of the users, the same programs are giving different results for the same data!

4. End-user programmers often lack a standard naming convention for programs, files, or program variables, which make them difficult to track or debug.

5. Half-hearted programming attempts that are pressed onto IT a half-built program for upgrading as a production system. This circumvents the cost/benefit analysis that screens out the low value work.

C. **Lost productivity.** A business manager writing his own programs is similar to the IT department hiring their own accountant instead of using the accounting department. A few people thrive on writing their own programs. They find it a useful outlet for their talents and gradually spend more and more of their workday (and personal time) writing and supporting these programs. Gradually, their regular job suffers and they realize that this new "hobby" is ruining their normal work performance. At this point, their supervisor often steps in and reminds them that their assigned work always takes precedence over their optional (computer) work. Although they may entertain notions that IT will "discover" them and hire them as a programmer, this very rarely happens. Problems that occur include:

1. These programs are not free. The ratio of maintenance time to development time is approximately 10 to 1. Every program that is created and used adds an ongoing time burden to that department.

2. End users generally underestimate the complexity of a task and time required to develop the programs. They save time by skipping such things as data entry edits.

3. Time is lost to the company when employees build parallel databases that may be out of sync. If the data exists in the data center, that is where to use it. Assuming responsibility for a database containing the same data doubles the cost to the company.

4. Similarly, data downloads are a one-way trip. Never send a download back to the main corporate database. This would bypass the edits buried in the data entry screens and could result in corrupted files.

[F] Sharing

A single application used by its author is not the problem. This person knows the underlying assumptions and can correct code errors as they move on. In its truest sense, this is "personal" computing. The problem is when friends share applications and the code seems to take on a life of its own. The more useful the application, the faster it moves from hand to hand through the organization. As defects are uncovered and repaired, no one knows where all of the copies are. The original author is held responsible for any problems that arise and calls are made to his desk expecting support for the program, just as if IT provided it. After a few weeks of fending off calls and complaints made to their boss, most end users learn their lesson and never share code again!

COMMENT

The authors have seen homegrown code seemingly proliferate all by itself. An example of this was a complex spreadsheet built to track overtime hours for union members in a large factory. This was a very useful tool for each department. The IT department snubbed the spreadsheet as "too controversial and low payback." Yet each end user saved a considerable amount of time every day using these sheets. The result was a lack of management for an important plant application. As different versions of the same sheets floated around, the union members were paid on grievances for improper solicitation of overtime.

[G] IT Strikes Back!

From IT's point of view, all of this end-user computing amounted to unnecessary chaos. IT occasionally receives panicked calls to figure out why an important program did not work that was used to generate critical data. Sometimes this involved languages that were far different from the IT standard and no one knew where to begin. Also, "foreign" hardware appeared connected to standard workstations that were also dumped on IT to support. To deflect criticism and avoid future problems, IT took the offensive!

The first stage is denial. The IT department denies any obligation to support these technologies and tells the user he is on his own. This lasts as long as it takes a complaint to reach the executive level and then some poor soul in IT is dispatched to "figure it out before going home tonight." Denying a department support for its homegrown systems may be the fair way to treat the problem but the company is stuck in the middle. On one hand, they have paid for this "nonstandard" system and need it to work. On the other hand, IT has worked diligently to standardize units to save money and now someone is demanding support for something else. If the floodgates were opened, the IT department would be required to support every rickety amateur system cobbled together on obsolete or oddball hardware by anyone whose intentions far exceeded his abilities.

The second stage is locking down the operating system on everyone's workstation to prevent anyone from adding software or hardware tools to their devices. Supplement this barrier by terse company policies forcing all hardware and software requests to flow through the IT department, which lacks the resources to answer any request in a timely manner. A common action is to establish a system administrator account on each workstation and to severely limit user rights, such as:

A. The system administrator locks down the operating system stopping the installation of driver programs without IT involvement. Non-standard hardware is forbidden.

B. Restrict end-user computing by "outlawing" most programming languages. Remove software development tools from all workstations. Lock the operating system so that only the system administrator can load software.

C. Only the IT Manager can grant exceptions to this policy, and the answer is always a terse but polite "no."

D. Issue an executive directive that department managers are responsible for the accuracy of end-user computing created and used in their departments. The IT department will only assist with debugging it on an as-available basis.

E. IT will confiscate any non-company computing hardware that appears.

F. Data may not be taken to use on home computers outside of IT control, since data security may be compromised.

The second stage of reaction solves IT's problem of support requests for strange technologies at all hours, but it deprives the company of the productivity gains of these tools, reducing the value of personal computers to that of stand-alone word processing stations. As a department, IT lacks the time to support all of the service requests as it is. After locking down the workstations, expect the number of requests to rise since users can do little themselves. In a short time, IT will be viewed as more of the problem than a solution.

To gain executive support for locking down workstations, the IT Manager will list all of the problems and service calls that will go away since users can no longer cause these types of problems. This often accompanies a promised reduction in IT staffing with fewer calls anticipated. What they fail to realize is that all of the small things that the "well behaved" users did for themselves now become urgent requests for IT support. IT becomes a broken record repeating this or that cannot be done—or that it is not allowed. Instead of saving the company money, it adds another level of complexity. IT becomes the place that all departments love to hate.

The second stage only lasts as long as it takes the company's executives to realize that IT is the problem and not the solution. The next IT Manager will focus on the company's greater interests, and end-user computing policies will move on to the next stage.

The third stage strikes a compromise between the open environment and the totally closed environment. In this situation, users are "certified" as competent by attending specific training classes (typically two hours in length or less) that explains the IT development standards for testing, documentation, exchange of software, why standards are a benefit to them, etc. After this, they are free to use approved software tools to develop systems for their own use or use in their departments, so long as they adhere to the company policies for end-user computing.

In the third stage, IT's cost of supporting an expanded tool set is balanced against the productivity gains for the company from using these tools. The IT team facilitates the proper use of technology by making it the easiest path to follow.

See Policy ITP-28-1 End-User Computing Policy as an example of an end-user computing policy.

POLICY ITP-28-1.   End-User Computing Policy

Policy #:	ITP-28-1	Effective:	03/18/13	Page #:	1 of N
Subject:	End-User Computing Policy				

1.0 PURPOSE

This policy provides guidance for the proper development and management of software created outside of the IT department. It is intended to ensure that all software used by more than one person, or software that provides a critical company function, adheres to good programming practices. The result will be software that operates in a predictable manner and consistently provides correct calculations.

End-user programming refers to any software developed by someone who does not work in the IT department. Software developed within the IT department is subject to the IT department's policies for software quality, documentation, change control, and testing.

2.0 SCOPE

This policy applies to all employees, contractors, and visitors. It pertains to software developed outside of IT to support critical business functions or that is shared among two or more employees. At a minimum, it includes:

A. Programs
B. Spreadsheets
C. Databases
D. Document templates
E. Report queries

§ 28.02[G]

Excluded from this policy is software developed by an employee to assist in his or her work duties, and that is not required to perform a critical business function, and that is not shared with other employees.

3.0 POLICY

Computers can be found in every work area of the company. An important component is the software that runs inside of them to perform work. Often this software can be used to organize or automate daily office tasks. This is the "personal" in personal computing. Examples are spreadsheets, single user databases, or even document templates. Some of this software can also be used to build complex programs.

The problem arises when this software is used to build software that becomes critical to a department or that is used to provide data for use in executive decisions. Where the IT department will extensively test and validate the output of its software, programs developed by non-IT employees may not be as rigorously proven accurate or reliable. In some cases, they may provide inaccurate data that will be used as the basis for management decisions.

3.1 Employees
Employees are permitted to use software provided by the IT department to develop programs for use in their normal duties. They are not permitted to purchase software for developing programs without IT management approval.

A. Employees may not distribute copies of software that they have created to other employees unless it has been validated by the IT department.
B. Personally developed software used in their normal work tasks must be documented for use by others in their absence. One time use software is excluded.
C. As described in the Software Management Asset Policy, employees may not bring in software from home or other sources to develop personal use software.

3.2 Managers
Managers are required to safeguard the company's continued effective and efficient operation by ensuring that all software developed by end users is properly managed. They will:

A. Monitor the work tasks for critical company tasks to ensure that any software developed for them will be properly documented and, where appropriate, submitted to the IT Manager for review.
B. Identify and submit to the IT Manager employee developed software candidates for shared use.
C. Keep employees focused and not permit their responsibilities to evolve into a full-time software developer or maintenance function.
D. Require reports generated by personally developed software to include a notation in the heading indicating the person creating the document.

3.3 IT Manager

The IT Manager will:

A. Annually inform all business managers concerning this policy.
B. Provide ongoing advice to all company departments on managing end-user computing to the maximum benefit of the company.
C. Identify a standard set of software for use by end users to develop software.
D. Promptly respond to requests to review locally developed software.
E. Provide team members to advise all departments on the proper use of end-user programming tools, and to answer technical questions as they arise. These people are not provided to write code or to debug programs.
F. Maintain an online catalog of locally developed software supported by the IT department.
G. Ensure that the data output of any end-user developed programs may not be loaded back into any corporate database.

4.0 PROCEDURES

Software deemed of value to other departments or that is critical to the operation of the company must be validated by the IT department. Candidates are forwarded to the IT Manager for consideration after the end user inserts all of the updates and features that they require in the final product.

This review is not a bypass of the company's normal software development qualification process. Software is evaluated and accepted on an "as is" basis. Mandatory updates and additional features will be processed through the normal software upgrade request process.

The originating department manager will provide:

A. One copy of the software and any required data files.
B. A verbal description of the software's function, to include its inputs, outputs, frequency of use, and any situational variables required for the software to function.
C. Examples of correct input files and reports and/or output files.
D. Name of the person who wrote it and his or her contact information.
E. List of data that feeds the program and where the output is used.
F. Assurance that no changes are made to the software during the review process.

The IT Manager will assign a Business Analyst to:

A. Communicate with the manager who submitted the code and keep him or her apprised throughout the evaluation process.
B. Review the code and provide an estimate to bring it up to IT standards.
   1. If more than 20 hours of code re-work is required, then the evaluation is passed over to the new development review process.

28-16

  2. Additional work may be required by the requesting department in the area of user documentation.
 C. Ensure that the software does not duplicate an existing function.
 D. Validate that all outputs are correct given the data input.
 E. Review all code to ensure it conforms to standard IT naming conventions.
 F. Estimate the resources required to bring the code up to IT standards.

After acceptance of software by the IT department, the original author can no longer change it. All changes must be made by the IT department through its change control process.

5.0 REVISION HISTORY

Date	Revision #	Description of Change
03/18/13	1.0	Initial creation.

6.0 INQUIRIES

Direct inquiries about this policy to:

George Jenkins, CIO
Our Company, Inc.
2900 Corporate Drive
Columbus, OH 43215

Voice: 614-555-1234
Fax: 614-555-1235
E-mail: gjenkins@company.com

Revision #:	1.0	Supersedes:	N/A	Date:	03/18/13

§ 28.03 PERSONAL COMPUTING vs. CORPORATE COMPUTING

[A] Overview

At some point, someone is going to want to borrow a copy of a program that an office worker has written. In exchange for the program, the borrower promises to accept it "as is" and never call for assistance in using it. Perhaps it automates some sort of tracking database. Perhaps it generates reports on some department metric. Whatever it is, end-user programs are shared and control of versions has just been lost. The person who "borrowed" the program may later provide it to another person and on and on. Meanwhile the original author has found and repaired several bugs in the code (one of them critical) and added more features. However, to the casual observer, there is no identifiable difference as the interface screens look the same in both the new and old versions. Since the program is written for his or her own use, the office worker has not mentioned these changes to anyone else.

[B]   When End-User Programs Should Fall Under IT Control

End-user programs are those that have impact on a single person—truly personal computing. An end-user developed program becomes corporate computing and may fall under IT control if the program crosses any of these "lines in the sand":

A. The application uses or creates sensitive data as described by the company or government regulatory agency. To protect the company against government actions, the IT department must take immediate control of the program and data. The user still has access to it, but any software changes must pass through the IT department and the data must be stored on a server managed by IT.

B. All multi-user systems or multi-user files are corporate systems due to their complexity and impact on operations. For end users, this usually involves many people sharing the same data file.

C. All company applications or data files must be under the control of the IT department. Each company creates their own criteria for what a critical system is, but in general, it is any application that impacts the company's cash flow or regulatory compliance.

[C]   Moving End-User Authored Programs to Production

Just because the idea and design for a program originated outside of the IT department is no reason to invoke the "Not Invented Here" response. There are many advantages of starting programs in user departments. The program already has:

A. Proven worth so a cost-benefit analysis is quickly completed.

B. The end-user developed program acts like a prototype. The basic logic flow has already been defined and there are committed users ready and interested in the finished products.

C. Much or all of user-developed code can be included in the final product.

Moving an end-user program into normal corporate production involves running it through the same development process as with other programs. The time savings comes from the portions of the work already done by the original developer. All of this assumes that the production version will have essentially the same features as the end-user developed version.

Of course there are some pitfalls in this process:

A. End users will want IT to add features and functions that were never in the original design.

B. The end user will be impatient and not understand the complexities or delays. He or she may even try to pull the program back from the IT developers.

C. The end user will chafe at the questions asked to build the project scope and system design documentation. They may mistake these questions as criticism, so phrase them carefully.

D. The program is now locked and the source code maintained by IT, and the end user has lost the freedom to change it at will. He or she may try to circumvent the IT change control process by not deleting all copies of the program.

E. End users may try to circumvent the normal software development process by creating a half-baked program and use this conversion process to have it more quickly completed. Only working programs should be considered and the production version should have the same features as the original.

Procedures for moving end-user programs to IT control should include the following:

A. Software deemed of value to other departments or that is critical to the operation of the company must be validated by the IT department. Candidates are forwarded to the IT Manager for consideration after the end user inserts all of the updates and features that they require in the final product.

B. This review is not a bypass of the company's normal software development qualification process. Software is evaluated and accepted on an "as is" basis. Mandatory updates and additional features will be processed through the normal software upgrade request process.

C. The originating department manager will provide:
   1. One copy of the software and any required data files.
   2. A verbal description of the software's function, to include its inputs, outputs, frequency of use, and any situational variables required for the software to function.
   3. Examples of correct input files and reports and/or output files.
   4. Name of the person who wrote it and his or her contact information.
   5. List of data that feeds the program and where the output is used.
   6. Assurance that no changes are made to the software during the review process.

D. The IT Manager will assign a Business Analyst to:
   1. Keep the manager who submitted the code apprised throughout the evaluation process.
   2. Review the code and provide an estimate to bring it up to IT standards.
      a. If more than 20 hours of code re-work is required, then the evaluation is passed over to the new development review process.
      b. The requesting department may be required to provide or rewrite end-user documentation.
   3. Ensure that the software does not duplicate an existing function.

4. Validate that all outputs are correct given the data input.
5. Review all code to ensure it conforms to standard IT naming conventions.
6. Estimate the resources required to bring the code up to IT standards.

After acceptance of software by the IT department, the original author can no longer change it. The IT department through its change control process will manage all future changes.

[D] Managing App Store Applications

With rank-and-file employees as well as executives becoming accustomed to downloading easy-to-use applications for their smartphones and tablets, the demand for the same convenience in the workplace grows. Much to the dismay of most IT departments, users are expecting to have convenient access to applications for their mobile devices to do their job.

There are two options for employees to obtain applications for their mobile devices: the device maker's public app stores such as Apple iTunes, Google Play, or the Windows Phone Marketplace, or an in-house corporate app store.

A. **Public app stores.** Public app stores give users access to thousands of applications, some of them useful in performing their job. Just as you would manage what a user can do on the corporate network from their home computer, mobile applications must be managed to ensure that enterprise resources and data are protected. Some of the challenges of public app store applications include:
   1. Downloading of malware-infected applications.
   2. Control of data as it moves between the mobile device and the corporate network.
   3. Storage of confidential data on the device.

COMMENT

In 2010, Apple rolled out the iOS Enterprise Developer Program that allows organizations to host and distribute iOS apps using a corporate-branded storefront. The program costs $299 a year, and gives the organization access to technical support from Apple engineers.

B. **Corporate app stores.** In response to demands from users to access their data and applications from their mobile devices, many organizations are developing their own in-house app store for use by employees.

While this affords the organization greater control over applications being used, it does not solve issues such as:

1. Employees can still visit malware-infect Web sites and download malicious applications from public app stores.
2. Expanding access to corporate resources increases the possibility of an employee leaking confidential information.
3. Applications must still be vetted for malware whether written in-house or by third parties.

Policy elements to consider, whether applications are downloaded from public or private app stores, include:

A. Should users be required to authenticate before the application launches?
B. Can you restrict network access of the application to specific servers, IP addresses, and/or ports?
C. Determine the local storage rules for the application; is the application allowed to write data to the local device and, if so, is the data required to be encrypted.
D. Determine whether the application can be accessed offline, and if so, whether PIN access is required for authentication.
E. Will document sharing from within the application be allowed?
F. Are specific API's, such as copy/cut/paste and open URL, allowed?

COMMENT

The research firm Gartner predicts that by 2014, 60 percent of corporate IT will deploy their own in-house app stores.

To manage the use of applications, whether downloaded from a public app store or a private one, consider using a mobile application management (MAM) solution. Look for a solution that allows you to do the following:

A. Integrate with public app stores such as Apple iTunes, Google Play, or the Windows Phone Marketplace to allow users access to public applications.
B. Create group policies to secure the distribution of applications.
C. Provide a catalog of approved applications and have the ability to blacklist publicly available applications.
D. Require users to authenticate before allowing them to view and download applications.
E. Monitor and enforce compliance with corporate application policies at the device level.

F. Receive alerts when an unapproved application has been installed by a user.

G. Create privacy policies for any application data that is collected.

H. Disable corporate applications if a user loses the device or leaves the organization.

See Policy ITP-28-2 App Store Application Policy as an example of an app store policy.

POLICY ITP-28-2. App Store Application Policy

Policy #:	ITP-28-2	**Effective:**	03/18/13	**Page #:**	1 of N
Subject:	App Store Application Policy				

1.0 PURPOSE

This policy provides guidance for the management of applications downloaded from a public app store, such as Apple iTunes, Google Play, or the Windows Phone Marketplace. It is intended to ensure that all software downloaded for use on mobile devices does not harm the corporate network or cause the disclosure of confidential information.

2.0 SCOPE

This policy applies to all software downloaded onto a mobile device such as a smartphone or tablet that can connect to the corporate network.

3.0 POLICY

In order to properly manage the use of applications on mobile devices, the company requires that any mobile device that can connect to the company network be managed by our selected mobile application management solution. This solution allows IT to manage the device by allowing it to:

A. Create group policies to secure the distribution of applications.

B. Provide a catalog of approved applications and be able to blacklist publicly available applications.

C. Require users to authenticate before allowing them to view and download applications.

D. Monitor and enforce compliance with corporate application policies at the device level.

E. Receive alerts when an unapproved application has been installed by a user.

F. Create privacy policies for any application data that is collected.

G. Disable corporate applications if a user loses the device or leaves the organization.

Date	Revision #	Description of Change
03/18/13	1.0	Initial creation.

5.0 INQUIRIES

Direct inquiries about this policy to:

George Jenkins, CIO
Our Company, Inc.
2900 Corporate Drive
Columbus, OH 43215

Voice: 614-555-1234
Fax: 614-555-1235
E-mail: gjenkins@company.com

Revision #:	1.0	Supersedes:	N/A	Date:	03/18/13

§ 28.04 MANAGING A PROACTIVE END-USER COMPUTING PROGRAM

[A] Overview

It is difficult to resist an idea whose time has come. End-user computing is one such idea. The key for the IT Manager is to maximize the good that the company derives from this idea while minimizing its costs. It is also an opportunity for the IT Manager to show some leadership. This end-user computing thing is not going to go away. The best course of action is to shape the course of events for maximum IT benefit at minimal cost.

It is said that "nature abhors a vacuum." If the IT Manager does not take the initiative to control events, then the events will control the IT Manager! By providing leadership in this area, IT is seen as a facilitator of technology instead of a spoiled child who must be dragged into the modern era, kicking and crying every step of the way.

The IT Manager is ultimately responsible for the company's end-user computing program. They see a clear distinction between corporate computing and personal computing. However, if the IT Manager were to ask any executive about this, he will find that supporting *any* technology in the company is the responsibility of the IT department. In most cases, it is better to step forward and take up the assignment than wait until it is a mess and be told it was the IT Manager's job all along!

Never lose sight that IT provides a service to the company by supporting their fellow employees in the various departments. If this linkage is enhanced, then the status of the IT department, in the users' opinion, will be enhanced. If IT becomes irrelevant to their efforts, they will find less and less support for their activities—and IT will never have a clue why!

Managing the efforts of so many end users can be akin to herding cats. Focus the IT support team's energies on managing a few of them closely and the rest of the herd will drift off in all directions. End users cannot be kept tightly together but at least they can be moved in the same general direction. With a well-thought-out and properly supported program, the IT Manager can shape an end-user computing environment that is controlled, consistent, and secure and that will enhance the productivity of end users.

[B] What to Do?

The IT Manager can take some basic steps to energize and focus the company's end-user computing efforts with these simple actions:

A. Develop guidelines for users to follow. Most employees will strive to do things "the right way"—if they know what the "right way" is. These guidelines are usually stated as company policies. People cannot be faulted for breaking rules that do not exist. Craft a set of clear expectations of what end users and their managers should be doing to ensure data accuracy and security. Then begin an employee awareness program to explain these policies to them. The sooner this begins, the fewer bad habits that will need to be broken later.

B. Educate users, managers, and IT staff members on their respective roles. End-user computing is just like anything else in a company. Whether it is filling out an expense statement or scheduling vacation, there is a right way and a wrong way to do it. But just like filling out an expense statement, the IT Manager can make it easy to comply or difficult to understand, resulting in an ongoing stream of questions from frustrated users. Education is an ongoing process to make people aware of the policies and then to periodically remind them what should be done. It is far easier and cheaper to work with people than to police them. The policing still needs to be done, but fewer problems will be uncovered.

C. Provide software training and support for end users on the tools the company wants them to use. The IT staff must understand its role in providing this support. In some companies, end-user support groups allow employees to help their coworkers and cut down on IT support requirements. The IT Manager's goal is to make it easier for end users to comply than to go their own way.

D. Appoint one or more IT staff members to assist users in program development and management. This group must not write programs. They help end users over the "rough spots" in their own code. These must be patient people who can explain complex issues in easy-to-understand terms.

E. Develop a "power user" program to help users to help themselves. These people act as a "force multiplier" for the IT staff by addressing many of the simple issues in their department without calling IT for help.

   F. Periodically solicit employees for end-user developed applications to consider converting into company systems. A part of their cost/benefit analysis will be how widespread the application's applicability is.

   G. Monitor workstations to ensure the company is in compliance with its software licenses. If employees are free to load anything they want to—they will! If an IT staff member is asked to assist on an unlicensed program, he or she must immediately take firm action to remove the offending software.

   H. Every IT team member acts as the enforcer of company computing policies. Any time he or she encounters a violation, he or she must make an on-the-spot correction. The explanation can teach the user and eliminate the problem. Although an unpopular task, this will be accepted by end users if it is applied in a tactful, fair manner.

   I. Work with the company's internal audit department to conduct periodic reviews of departments to ensure that policies and procedures are adequate to properly control the environment and that all end users consistently follow them.

[C] End-User Development Training

Time spent training end users will save much more time later undoing their poor work because no one told them how to do it any differently. The following people should be trained:

   A. **Train the users.** Some IT workers get a sort of thrill in making computing appear as something just shy of magic. Although entertaining, an effective end-user computing program requires just the opposite approach. IT processes work the way they do for a reason. Often they are the result of a specific problem that was found to be avoidable. When working with end users, take every opportunity to demystify IT practices. Point out why each policy exists and how adhering to them will reduce the likelihood of problems later.

      All employees will benefit from end-user computer training. For most, this is just basic word processing and spreadsheets. Others will want more technical training on databases and mainframe reporting tools. All classes should include a section to increase employees' awareness of data security risks, vulnerabilities, and the appropriate preventive controls. An understanding of the "big picture" will help the details in the IT policies to make sense.

      Some companies provide end-user training in an internal facility which allows full control of the class environment and curriculum. A training facility is an expensive investment since it ties up a number of desktop units (usually 12 to 15). However, the classroom provides other capabilities for the IT department such as a disaster recovery command center and a place to test software.

      An important adjunct to formal classes is to make self-help material readily available. This includes manuals, related third-party "how-to" books, and self-paced instructional materials. The cost of books can be lowered by bulk purchases. Many companies provide third-party books to anyone who attends a class, as the employee may reach for the book in the future instead of calling IT for basic problems. Often these books are easier to understand than the manufacturer's manuals.

B. **Train the department managers.** The key to controlling end users is through their supervisors. Few managers will admit that their departments are so over-staffed that they have time to develop their own programs. Create a training session that explains to these managers the pitfalls of end-user computing and the negative side of minor software development in their department. The better that these managers understand the issues involved in managing technology, the fewer problems that IT will be called in to clean up.

Much of this information is common sense. The manager of each business department is responsible for ensuring that all of his employees know, understand, and adhere to all company policies governing end-user computing—just as he ensures his employees follow the policies issued by human resources, accounting, etc. In this sense, end-user computing is the same as any other office process he oversees.

Manager training is important since they are the ones who stand to lose the most from a poorly run program. Inaccurate reports will be angrily tossed back by executives. Disgruntled employees may leave on short notice leaving the manager to figure out a way to update programs that no one else knows how to read.

The department managers should conduct their operations as if the company's auditor may walk in the door tomorrow—as well he may! Even if an audit is scheduled, there may be considerable effort required to "clean up" the end-user systems. The easier task is to ensure that all systems adhere to company policies as they are being developed instead of delaying this work until later.

COMMENT

One author worked for a major manufacturer who decided to outsource their materials warehouse. The materials director carried end-user computing to a different level by negotiating the outsourcing contract that included warehouse management software without involving the IT department in the discussions. They then ordered almost a quarter of a million dollars of custom program modifications (which they thought the outsourcing partner would absorb but did not), only to find out after the money was spent that they had not even purchased the base software license. The software and the changes all belonged to the programmer!

[D] Cultivate the Power Users

Every department has at least one person that all workers come to with their computing problems. This local computing expert is often known as a "power user." Power users are recognized by their supervisors as master PC tool smiths and may evolve into full-time support for that department. Managers like this since they can control their priorities and align the power user's support efforts to the department's priorities. Part of their value is their understanding of the department's processes and how to apply technology to address their issues. In short, it places a small "IT shop" under the department manager's control.

The IT Manager should encourage this process by providing a high level of support to power users. Power users must understand that this is a two-way street. In exchange for them addressing simple issues in their departments, the IT department will support them with a full set of reference materials and priority support from the service desk.

Being power users does not exempt them from the limitations placed on end-user computing. They still are restricted on the types of tools that can be used and must document all of the code they develop. In a sense, they are held to a higher standard than other users since their coworkers may violate a rule out of ignorance, whereas the power user would have known better.

[E] Appoint IT Staff Members to Mentor End Users

Appoint one or more IT staff members as internal computing consultants. This team provides instruction on proper computing practices and technical advice for end users of computing equipment and software. The role of internal computing consultants includes advising end users on the true capabilities of equipment and helping them match business needs to the appropriate, cost-effective equipment.

An internal computing consultant's responsibilities might include:

A. Helping people through the IT bureaucracy. IT procedures have a purpose, but to outsiders prone to fast action, they may appear as worthless obstacles. The internal computing consultants can assist with this paperwork by ensuring the forms are correctly filled in and sent to the right person. They must not, however, shortcut the IT process or assume the role of filling in requests for end users. They are to help the process to work, not teach people how to cheat it.

B. Providing informal and formal training for end users. Often these are 30-minute one-on-one sessions addressing a single issue, for example, how to debug a spreadsheet or create a pivot table.

C. Coordinating with the service desk to identify problem areas for pro-active problem solving. Again, this team helps end users with service desk issues and demonstrates how to work through the "IT system."

D. Maintaining a Web site for end-users' self-help, to share tips and success stories, and to record their concerns with the end-user computing program. Often, the most effective teachers are coworkers.

E. Coordinating formal training on standard software tools. Ensure that classes are "tuned" to include local issues and working preferences.

COMMENT

End User's Computing Pledge

- I will use personal computing tools to automate the routine tasks on my own computing devices.
- I will keep all company assets and data safe from theft and secure from unauthorized access.
- I will not copy for others software or sensitive company data files.
- I will only use software authorized and installed by the company.
- I will back up the routine files on my devices to the network server at least once per week.
- I will maintain all critical data on the server, and make copies daily if it is on a notebook PC or other mobile device.
- I will safeguard all user ID and password codes and never divulge them to others—to include writing them down in an easily accessible place.
- I will be patient and understand that major IT problems take a long time to resolve.
- I will not bring home computing questions to work as this takes time away from the company's business.
- I will identify all critical applications on my devices so they can be included in the department's business continuity planning.
- I will develop user documentation for all applications I create that are routinely used or that are critical to my work assignments.
- I will identify all applications that I create with version number and "last changed" dates according to IT guidelines.

§ 28.05   END-USER POLICIES

[A]   Overview

The "personal" in personal computing implies a great deal of autonomy from the central IT organization. However, this autonomy does not allow end users the freedom to create unreliable or inaccurate code. They must follow the company's policies and procedures to reduce the likelihood of misleading information, avoid lawsuits, and avoid public embarrassment.

Department managers are responsible for all aspects of their operations including end-user computing. The needs of each department vary as does their ability to support independent data systems. A wise manager follows IT policies governing this area to avoid many of the problems that may arise.

A successful end-user computing program is a team effort. Team members contribute according to their skills and abilities. Use end-user computing policies to educate both the end users and the IT department about how both parties can work together for the company's benefit.

End-user responsibilities echo standard IT practices for good computing. This is a two-step process. First, make each standard as simple to understand and easy to comply with as possible. The second step is to convince users that these actions are in their own self-interest. The easier a task is to perform and the more that the participant believes in the value of the outcome, the less enforcement that will be required. Enforcement takes valuable IT time and usually results in ill feelings. If a good reason for an end-user policy cannot be explained in simple terms, then it is likely that the policy is not needed.

COMMENT

Make good computing practices a habit in your organization. Military uniforms in all countries include hats. Yet the prevailing fashion in Western countries for decades has not included hats. Is the military that far behind in its fashions? The answer is that aside from fashion, military uniforms are built for utility. They include a hat because the military wants to *ingrain* in its members to always put something on their head whenever they venture outside. In a war zone, this would be a helmet for their protection. The goal is to make that action habitual.

[B]   End-User Software Policies

End-user policies are a way for the IT Manager to identify and communicate specific actions to ensure the security of data and that all programs follow prudent IT practices. Phrase end-user policies in a nontechnical, straightforward fashion that details what is to be done, as well as why it is important. Base policies on existing IT policies. Polish the language to improve clarity for the intended audience.

    A. **Data security.** When data is stored in the data center, the IT organization controls who can access it. This not only safeguards it from competitors, but ensures the company is in legal compliance with a wide range of government regulations from such agencies as the Securities and Exchange Commission, Internal Revenue Service, and a wide range of federal laws governing personal data privacy. The protection of data stored on a user's PC becomes that person's responsibility.

B. **Information contained in computer files is to be accessed or used for authorized business purposes only.** Casual browsing through computer servers for personal reasons is strictly prohibited. This policy reminds users that rummaging through files is like rummaging through someone's desk and not permitted.

C. **Asset protection.** Hardware, software, and data are all company assets and must be safeguarded. The first line of defense is the person using the equipment. Losing a notebook PC is a double hit—loss of the hardware and loss of the data in the unit.

D. **Ownership of software.** Software created using company time or equipment belongs to the company and not to the person who wrote it. It may not be removed from the premises or sold by its author. Many companies require that a copyright notice be added to all software created by end users.

E. **Anti-piracy.** It is illegal and against company policy to create unlicensed copies of software. In some cases, this may include the libraries used to develop the code. End-user computing developers must be aware of the license restrictions of any purchased modules incorporated into their systems. For example, a compiled program may require a run time module to execute. It may or may not be permissible to distribute this with copies of the compiled program.

COMMENT

A published policy and documented enforcement is a company's best defense against lawsuits for software piracy.

F. **Software forms a large part of IT's initial and ongoing expenses.** Most companies delegate the authority to control the purchase of *all* software to the IT department. This allows for the management of software licenses, upgrades, and a measure of cost control. Departments may purchase their own software but only if it is on the list of software the IT department supports.

G. **Data backup.** It is the responsibility of the device user to make safety copies of the unit's data whenever it has changed significantly. This is typically accomplished by copying the data to the network server, or copying it to a CD, which is stored in a place far removed from the unit.

1. Storing critical files on a server. It is the end user's responsibility to store the primary or backup copy of their critical data on network-attached servers. This provides a safety copy to restore inoperable machines. Backups must be accomplished based on the volatility of the data, but usually daily.

2. Data backups from devices should be automatic and completed without end-user assistance. However, this will require preparation. The goal is to only back up data and not a copy of every device's operating system. This also implies checking periodically to see if a device's backup is not occurring and find out why.

3. Provide storage space on the network for personal files and department data sharing. Educate and periodically remind end users why this is in their own self-interest.

COMMENT

One author worked with a freight traffic manager who created and maintained detailed shipping records on an extensive set of spreadsheets. All of this data resided on his PC. Its existence only came up in casual conversation and the user never thought about saving the data on a network server. Yet the loss of this data would seriously damage the company's ability to audit its extensive freight bills—and cost it valuable cash.

[C] System Documentation

System (or user) documentation is an explanation of how to use a particular program. It includes such simple things as how to start it, the data to enter, types of results to expect, options to select or commands to issue, etc. In essence, it tells "the story" of the software.

System documentation is not written for the people who wrote the software. They already know all of this stuff. It is written so that others can use the program. Therefore, it must be straightforward with sufficient visuals so that someone familiar with the department but relatively unfamiliar with the program can run it and correctly use its options.

System documentation is required in ISO compliant shops. All experienced managers require it since every employee takes vacations, has the occasional sick day, or leaves the department. Good documentation provides a way to train new employees and/or allow a substitute to stand in during an absence. Without documentation, the manager is faced with a period of time without the benefit of that program until someone can figure out how to use it.

Therefore, it should be an IT end-user computing policy that every end user who develops software for company purposes provide a written explanation of the system before it is deployed. The documentation must be simple enough to understand so that the system may be run by anyone familiar with the general business function but unfamiliar with that program.

An electronic copy of all end-user system documentation (and subsequent updates) must be filed with the IT service desk. This will provide a reference file in the case of future problems. The service desk will not provide copies of this documentation to anyone outside of the originating department without the IT Manager's permission.

At a minimum, system documentation should include the following elements:

A. An author's identification section to include the author's name, date of the program's last update, and the date of last update to the documentation. (Some sites prefer to use version numbers instead of the last date of update.)

B. The program's name (or identifier) and a brief description of its purpose.

C. An explanation of any assumptions used when developing the code. This will be useful when researching a problem.

D. A list of all edits applied against incoming data.

E. The details of every formula and data transformation used in the code.

F. A list of error messages generated by the program and what may cause them. Exclude error messages generated by the software tool (such as programming language) since these are included in that product's manual.

G. The series of commands to initiate the application, to include the path and filename.

H. An explanation of the data sources used or referenced, such as electronic downloads, data entered, validation tables, database files, etc.

I. Samples of output documents such as forms, reports, and data entry screens. Any formulas used to create these documents must be explained.

J. Schemas of the database file structures to include the name of each field and the data type and length. Also, include access keys for each table along with their relationships to other tables.

K. The developer will display a version number somewhere on the program's first screen so that a user can readily identify which version of the program he is using.

See Policy ITP-28-3 End-User Systems Documentation Policy as an example.

POLICY ITP-28-3.   End-User Systems Documentation Policy

Policy #:	ITP-28-3	Effective:	03/18/13	Page #:	1 of N
Subject:	End-User Systems Documentation Policy				

1.0 PURPOSE

This policy provides guidance for the proper documentation of software created outside of the IT department. It is intended to ensure that all software used by more than one person, or software that provides a critical company function, is well documented so that the system may be run by anyone familiar with the general business function but unfamiliar with that program.

End-user programming refers to any software developed by someone who does not work in the IT department. Software developed within the IT department is subject to the IT department's policies for software quality, documentation, change control, and testing.

2.0 SCOPE

This policy applies to all employees, contractors, and visitors. It pertains to software developed outside of IT to support critical business functions or that is shared among two or more employees. At a minimum, it includes:

A. Programs
B. Spreadsheets
C. Databases
D. Document templates
E. Report queries

Excluded from this policy is software developed by an employee to assist in his or her work duties, and that is not required to perform a critical business function, and that is not shared with other employees.

3.0 POLICY

An electronic copy of all end-user system documentation (and subsequent updates) must be filed with the IT service desk. This will provide a reference file in the case of future problems. The service desk will not provide copies of this documentation to anyone outside of the originating department without the IT Manager's permission.

At a minimum, system documentation should include the following elements:

A. An author's identification section to include the author's name, date of the program's last update, and the date of last update to the documentation. (Some sites prefer to use version numbers instead of the last date of update.)
B. The program's name (or identifier) and a brief description of its purpose.
C. An explanation of any assumptions used when developing the code. This will be useful when researching a problem.
D. A list of all edits applied against incoming data.

E. The details of every formula and data transformation used in the code.

F. A list of error messages generated by the program and what may cause them. Exclude error messages generated by the software tool (such as programming language) since these are included in that product's manual.

G. The series of commands to initiate the application, to include the path and filename.

H. An explanation of the data sources used or referenced, such as electronic downloads, data entered, validation tables, database files, etc.

I. Samples of output documents such as forms, reports, and data entry screens. Any formulas used to create these documents must be explained.

J. Schemas of the database file structures to include the name of each field and the data type and length. Also, include access keys for each table along with their relationships to other tables.

K. The developer will display a version number somewhere on the program's first screen so that a user can readily identify which version of the program he or she is using.

4.0 REVISION HISTORY

Date	Revision #	Description of Change
03/18/13	1.0	Initial creation.

5.0 INQUIRIES

Direct inquiries about this policy to:

George Jenkins, CIO
Our Company, Inc.
2900 Corporate Drive
Columbus, OH 43215

Voice: 614-555-1234
Fax: 614-555-1235
E-mail: gjenkins@company.com

Revision #:	1.0	Supersedes:	N/A	Date:	03/18/13

29

TECHNOLOGY RELOCATION: SUCCESSFULLY MOVING YOUR IT OPERATIONS

§ 29.01 OVERVIEW

[A] Purpose and Scope

Relocating a modern office is fraught with challenges. The infrastructure that supports the modern office worker is usually built up over a long period of time. Many firms have not relocated their offices for 10 or 20 years, which means that most of the technology being used in the office has been added over that period. Since the office was first established, new workstations have been purchased, new servers installed, network and communication cabling run and rerun, and phone systems installed and upgraded.

In an ideal world, each new addition or modification to the office infrastructure would be clearly documented. Each new system or upgrade would be seamlessly integrated with the existing technology. Unfortunately, what we normally end up with is a collection of technologies that are jury-rigged together and poorly documented. As long as the technology works, no one pays much attention to it, and as time goes on, the person who implemented the system moves on to another firm. This can happen with networks, servers, telephone systems, and cable and wiring. Worse yet, the configuration information that is part of the computer infrastructure is not always backed up as part of the backup process and often is not documented elsewhere.

Adding to the challenge of office relocation is the infrequency of such a project. Because moves are so infrequent, there is rarely someone on staff who has been through the relocation process.

Without proper planning, a relocation project will cause mission critical disruption in business services. In addition, hundreds of detailed tasks must be done properly in order to give you the amount of time you need to make the move a success. All of these tasks need to be executed *in addition* to all of the current daily requirements of keeping the business functioning.

If you have an existing disaster recovery plan (DRP), it can often times be extended to your relocation plan. It is often an excellent opportunity to test your DRP. If you do not have a DRP (shame on you!), then a relocation project provides an opportunity to collect the information needed to prepare one.

[B] Critical Policies to Develop Based on This Chapter

Using the material discussed in this chapter, you will be able to create the following policies:

A. When to outsource a relocation project
B. Selecting a Primary Move Coordinator
C. Relocation processes
  1. Planning requirements
  2. Design requirements

Policies should always be developed based on the local situation. Successful managers cannot issue appropriate guidance if the policies are written with another company's situation or location in mind.

§ 29.02 BUSINESS ISSUES

[A] Overview

When faced with a technology relocation project, there are several issues to consider:

A. **Resources.** What resources are currently within the organization that can be used on this project? Are there enough people to perform all of the tasks required leading up to and including moving day? Who will be available at both the new and old locations for follow-up post move?

B. **Experience.** What level of experience do people within the organization have with a project of this type? Have they relocated a business prior to this move? Do they understand the move process? Can they think about the overall business process?

C. **Downtime.** A relocation project will be disruptive to operations. What are the company's vital processes and how long can it afford to have them unavailable? How much will it cost your business to be non-functional or impaired for one hour? For one day or longer?

D. **Cost.** There are numerous costs to be considered in a relocation project. In addition to the cost of the physical move, costs for outside resources, temporary furniture, last-minute glitches, etc., must be included.

Worksheet 29-1 is a questionnaire that can help during the planning process of a relocation project. The questionnaire can help the IT Manager determine the readiness of the organization for the move and highlight areas where outside support may be needed.

[B] What Can Go Wrong

Like most projects, a relocation project consists of many small tasks, most of which must be done correctly if the project is to be successful. You will of course want to have help in physically moving the furniture and equipment, but what else do you need to worry about? As you begin your planning for this project, think about the following aspects of the relocation process:

A. **Disruption of ongoing business.** In addition to employees having to pack and unpack their own belongings and personal contents, someone has to pack file cabinets, common areas such as kitchens and conference rooms as well as supply and storage areas. Someone also has to plan the physical move of such contents and infrastructure requirements such as telephones, local area network, and connectivity to the outside world.

B. **Relocation learning curve.** You have probably never managed a relocation project before, so you will be learning as you go along. The learning curve can be steeper than it looks. Organizing existing contents, furniture, and technology and placing them properly onto new floor plans can be a highly complicated process.

WORKSHEET 29-1. Relocation Information Questionnaire

Relocation Information Questionnaire

1. What is the impact of this project to the success of the organization?

   ☐ Mission Critical
   ☐ Very Important
   ☐ Somewhat Important
   ☐ Not Very Important

2. What is the reason the company is considering the move?

   ☐ Current facility too big
   ☐ Current facility too small
   ☐ Consolidation of facilities
   ☐ End of lease
   ☐ Improved location
   ☐ Cost reduction
   ☐ Acquisition
   ☐ Other

3. Are you moving or renovating into the following:

   ☐ Constructing a new building
   ☐ Existing site no renovation
   ☐ Existing site with renovation
   ☐ Renovation of your current site

4. Location information if moving:

   Moving from:
   Address: _____
   _____
   Sq. footage: _____

   Moving to:
   Address: _____
   _____
   Sq. footage: _____

5. Will this relocation affect daily operations?

   ☐ Yes
   ☐ No

6. Will this relocation affect critical projects?

   ☐ Yes
   ☐ No

7. Will this relocation affect the company's computer technology?

   ☐ No
   ☐ Yes
   　　☐ Workstations
   　　☐ Servers
   　　☐ Infrastructure
   　　☐ Internet connectivity
   　　☐ Other

8. Will other technologies will be affected by this relocation?

   ☐ No
   ☐ Yes
   　　☐ Telephones
   　　☐ Building security
   　　☐ Time clocks
   　　☐ Other

9. What dependencies exist?

   ☐ Construction schedule
   ☐ Equipment schedule
   ☐ Lease expiration
   ☐ Personnel resources
   ☐ Communications connectivity
   ☐ Utilities connectivity
   ☐ Other

WORKSHEET 29-1. (Continued)

Relocation Information Questionnaire

10. Has a budget been established?

    ☐ Yes
    ☐ No

11. Has a schedule been established?

    ☐ No
    ☐ Yes
        Start date: _____
        End date: _____

12. Who is responsible for coordinating the move?

        Name: _____
        Title: _____
        Phone: _____

13. Has a project team been created?

    ☐ Yes
    ☐ No

14. How are current IT needs supported?

    ☐ Internally
    ☐ No support currently maintained
    ☐ Outsourced to a third party
        Who: _____

15. Do you have enough internal staff to provide follow-up support after the move?

    ☐ Yes
    ☐ No

16. Do you have people on staff experienced in managing relocation vendors (construction/utility/movers, etc.)?

    ☐ Yes
    ☐ No

17. Have you addressed any of the following?

    ☐ Choosing vendors
    ☐ Vendor management
    ☐ Communication to employees
    ☐ Establishing timelines
    ☐ Allocating resources
    ☐ Preparing the project plan
    ☐ Identifying the risks
    ☐ Controlling the budget
    ☐ No decisions have been made

18. Is the documentation of all the company's technologies current and complete?

    ☐ Yes
    ☐ No

29-6

C. **Downtime costs.** Just what are the costs you will incur if users are down after the move? What if they cannot use their workstations, or there is no connection to the Internet, or the telephones do not work and customers cannot reach you? What is the cost to your organization if one or all of these problems occur?

D. **Day-to-day work.** While you are planning for the move, employees still have their day-to-day tasks to perform. Does the IT staff have extra time to plan for the connectivity required at the new location and to work with all the service providers involved? Do your executives and department heads have time to manage additional responsibilities associated with the move?

E. **Other projects.** What other projects are planned that could be impacted by the move?

F. **Things that can go wrong.** Many things can go wrong during the relocation. Some things to consider include:
   1. Internet or phone systems are not working and your customers cannot reach you.
   2. No one is managing the old site and you get charged with a clean-up bill.
   3. Telecommunication lines stay connected at hundreds of dollars per month in the old empty building.
   4. Improper installation of furniture, carpet, cabling, electric—pick your poison.
   5. Loss of productivity while looking for workstation or server parts.

COMMENT

The biggest problem areas in most moves are telephones and connectivity. Most of the problems are caused by language and timeline expectations. Start early, confirm repeatedly, and if necessary, respectfully demand resolution. If you can't speak the language, find someone who can as soon as possible!

[C] Benefits of Outsourcing

There are many reasons why the IT Manager may want to consider outsourcing the management of a technology relocation project. Using a relocation expert can have the following advantages:

A. **Ability to focus on task.** As a Project Manager at your organization, you probably have multiple projects for which you are responsible at any one time. An outside person can focus 100 percent of his or her time on the relocation project, without the distractions of other activities within the organization.

B. **Availability as needed for project.** An outside Project Manager can more easily dedicate time to the relocation. Internal Project Managers still have other responsibilities, and have trouble dedicating the required time. Like many projects, technology relocation can take more time than originally estimated.

C. **Service provider connections.** Does any one person within the organization have connections with all of the service providers required to successfully complete the move? These service providers may include:

1. Movers
2. Security/safety teams
3. Property manager
4. Technical furniture/cabinets specialists
5. Equipment disposal companies
6. Temporary office space
7. Electrician/heating, ventilation, and air conditioning (HVAC) professionals
8. Voice/data/video cabling
9. Utilities
10. Internet service providers (ISPs)
11. General contractor
12. Architects/space planners/interior designers
13. Off-site storage and alternative storage solutions
14. Office furniture
15. Hazardous waste removal
16. Electrostatic
17. Painters

D. **Availability of qualified resources.** Do you have the necessary expertise in-house to assist with the relocation? You will need to work with multiple outside service providers for many of the required tasks and it helps to have experience working with these service providers. Experience has shown it takes an average of 8 hours per external vendor to coordinate a move. For complex systems (such as phones), it is not uncommon to spend over 160 hours with a vendor to guarantee services at the destination.

E. **Communications.** A central point of contact is integral to the success of the move. In addition, having the right person available, one who understands the escalation process of your vendors and suppliers and can speak their "language," may be the difference between service and no service come Monday morning.

F. **Can scale to meet needs of the project.** When it comes time to make the move, an outside service provider can bring the extra resources needed to help complete the project on time. Internal employees will be focused on getting back to the deadlines to take care of your customers and conduct "business as usual." External resources can supplement as needed.

G. **Past experience.** The organization does not move very often, so it is not likely there will be someone on staff who has experience with a project of this type. External relocation specialists will bring experience to your table and will benefit you in many ways.

H. **Facility planning.** Do you have someone who understands the construction and infrastructure of building as well as your business? Having someone with building experience in the pre-construction phase will help you plan your space more effectively and avoid many expensive change orders—often at $250 or more. This applies to cabling, telephone, plumbing, electric, etc.

I. **Understanding end-user requirements.** An internal resource may make assumptions about the end-user requirements that an external person would not make. An external person can ask the "dumb" questions that ensure that everything is covered.

COMMENT

I have experienced moves with two different corporations. The first chose to use a professional relocation firm. I left on Friday at my regular time and arrived at my new office Monday morning, sat down and began working immediately. *I didn't know how amazing that was until I experienced a move without a relocation team.*

My new employer did not outsource our relocation. Our business operations were significantly impaired for a full week. Amidst the file and content wreckage, PCs were in disarray, the phone system did not work correctly, and our nuclear camera as well as several printers were offline for weeks. I will not choose to go it alone again.

—*A Medical Billing Director in Columbus, Ohio*

[D]   Primary Move Coordinator

One of the most important tasks of a relocation project is the selection of a Primary Move Coordinator (PMC) by the Executive Move Committee. It should be someone with a broad knowledge of the company's operations. Even if an outside service provider will perform most of the relocation effort, there must be an internal person responsible for making sure the firm's objectives for the project are achieved. If this job is relegated to a person with low status within the organization, the relocation is guaranteed to be plagued with problems. The PMC should be someone who can gain the willing cooperation of the team members and their supervisors. The type of person selected to lead this project will signal to everyone else in the company how serious the relocation project is.

The PMC should be publicly assigned to this task with management's unqualified support. This is essential to overcome internal politics and to let everyone know their assistance is important and required. As the project moves forward, regular public displays of support are required if the project is to result in a smooth and trouble-free relocation.

Except in the smallest of companies, no one person knows all aspects of the operation. Supporting the PMC will be a team of representatives from the various business units within the organization. These representatives, usually referred to as Department Move Coordinators, are critical to building a viable relocation plan, and are the source for the expertise needed to keep their area functioning and running efficiently before, during, and after the move. To a great degree, a team's success will depend on who is selected as the PMC and how well he or she works with the team. The PMC should be someone with good analytical, communications, and leadership skills that can keep the project focused. Therefore, the PMC must be a skilled negotiator and able to reach consensus with the various company departments to gain the use of their key people.

The Primary Move Coordinator policy must spell out the responsibilities of the position:

A. Creates and maintains the master move plan, communication plan, and budget.

B. Accepts total responsibility for the relocation. This should be his or her main responsibility for the duration of the project.

C. Creates documentation. It is critical to document every aspect of the project. If the current environment is not well documented, the PMC must lead the effort to get it updated. The layout of the new facility must be documented, as well as the move from the current facility to the new one.

D. Maintains service provider relations. Working closely with all of the various service providers is critical. This might be simply working with the outside relocation service provider or managing all the individual service providers if the project is managed in-house. A good rapport must be established with each service provider to ensure its cooperation as the project progresses. You never know when you will need one of them to put out some extra effort to get something completed on time or to accommodate last-minute changes.

E. Serves as the central point of contact for all communications. The PMC should be the central source for information concerning the project. A relocation project requires the coordination of the services of multiple service providers and task requirements with the organization.

F. Provides leadership and direction. The PMC must keep everyone involved focused on the successful completion of their tasks.

G. Has the authority to make quick decisions. No matter how complete the planning and attention to detail, many tasks will require last-minute adjustments or change orders. The PMC must have the task and budget authority to get these things done in a timely manner to keep the project on schedule.

H. Works closely with IT to meet the objectives of the relocation.

§ 29.02[D]

See Policy ITP-29-1 Primary Move Coordinator Policy as an example.

POLICY ITP-29-1. Primary Move Coordinator Policy

Policy #:	ITP-29-1	**Effective:**	03/18/13	**Page #:**	1 of N
Subject:	Primary Move Coordinator Policy				

1.0 PURPOSE

This policy mandates that a project coordinator be appointed for any technology relocation that includes more than 25 users.

2.0 SCOPE

This policy encompasses all IT systems and technology that supports critical business functions.

3.0 POLICY

The Executive Move Committee will designate a Primary Move Coordinator (PMC) for any technology relocation project that includes more than 25 users. The PMC has the following responsibilities:

A. Creates and maintains the master move plan, communication plan, and budget.

B. Accepts total responsibility for the relocation. This should be his or her main responsibility for the duration of the project.

C. Creates documentation. It is critical to document every aspect of the project. If the current environment is not well documented, the PMC must lead the effort to get it updated. The layout of the new facility must be documented, as well as the move from the current facility to the new one.

D. Maintains service provider relations. Working closely with all of the various service providers is critical. This might be simply working with the outside relocation service provider or managing all the individual service providers if the project is managed in-house. A good rapport must be established with each service provider to ensure its cooperation as the project progresses.

E. Serves as the central point of contact for all communications. The PMC should be the central source for information concerning the project. A relocation project requires the coordination of the services of multiple service providers and task requirements with the organization.

F. Provides leadership and direction. The PMC must keep everyone involved focused on the successful completion of their tasks.

G. Has the authority to make quick decisions. No matter how complete the planning and attention to detail, many tasks will require last-minute adjustments or change orders. The PMC will have the task and budget authority to get these things done in a timely manner to keep the project on schedule.

4.0 REVISION HISTORY

Date	Revision #	Description of Change
03/18/13	1.0	Initial creation.

5.0 INQUIRIES

Direct inquiries about this policy to:

George Jenkins, CIO
Our Company, Inc.
2900 Corporate Drive
Columbus, OH 43215

Voice: 614-555-1234
Fax: 614-555-1235
E-mail: gjenkins@company.com

Revision #:	1.0	Supersedes:	N/A	Date:	03/18/13

[E]   Partners

Few companies will have all of the resources required to successfully complete a relocation project. Most will require the assistance of several different service providers that specialize in some aspect of the project. As much as possible, IT should try to find service providers that have experience with technology relocation projects. The moving of servers and other delicate equipment is not the same as moving household furniture. These service providers may include:

A. **Movers.** No matter how sophisticated the technology, there will still be plenty of heavy lifting that needs to be done. These people have the skill, training, and muscle to get your equipment moved to the new location with a minimal amount of damage. That said, the "mover's" job is to move product from Point A to Point B. You need to fully understand your risk in this process.

B. **Security/safety.** The service providers should have security plans in place to ensure the equipment arrives safely and is not damaged or compromised during the move. The IT Managers must ensure access to corporate data is not compromised due to poor security during the relocation.

C. **Technical furniture/cabinets facilities.** New furniture and equipment cabinets may be required due to differences in the layout of the new facility as compared to the old one. Specialized HVAC, fire suppression, and electrical requirements need to be planned and ordered 90 to 180 days in advance of the move.

D. **Equipment disposal.** A relocation is the perfect time to dispose of equipment that is no longer being used. Many areas have restrictions on placing old computers and monitors into the normal trash due to the high concentrations of toxic material within this equipment; therefore, a special disposal service may need to be contacted. Look for recycling companies that have verifiable processes for disposing of equipment in an environmentally sound manner and for the destruction of any data left on devices.

E. **Temporary office space.** If new construction is not completed when the move date arrives, you may need temporary office space for affected personnel.

F. **Cabling.** The new office will of course need network cabling installed to company specifications. Cabling is the least expensive component in the technology network, yet is expected to last the longest. Do you have engineers who have the talent to run new cable? Do they have the time and quantity of labor needed to complete the task? Consider how many drops you need for both voice and data.

G. **Utilities.** Companies require electricity, water, heating, cooling, etc., to operate a modern office. Independent contractors install most of these items and will require a central point of contact to coordinate their efforts.

H. **ISPs.** A corporate or department connection to the Internet will more than likely need to be up and available on day one. Dedicated connections to a cloud services provider also may be required if the company uses software applications delivered in this manner.

I. **General contractor.** Some businesses work with a general contractor who will ensure all the service providers can complete their tasks on time and on budget. When it comes to crunch time and the flooring guy is holding up the furniture guy who is holding up the cabling guy who is holding up the new phone system from being installed, the general contractor can keep the project moving along.

J. **Technology SPACE Planner.** If the new location requires extensive remodeling, an architect will be required to ensure the new facility is properly designed. Most architects and space planners do not normally deal with technology-specific issues. Therefore, IT should work with someone who understands and can identify the company's technology SPACE requirements for the new location. SPACE stands for:
- **S**tructure and layout of your technology rooms and closets.
- **P**athways to deliver and support technology throughout the facility.
- **A**ir conditioning/humidity and other environmental concerns for sensitive electronics.
- **C**abling and wiring.

- Electrical and lighting (many times the existing power and configuration is not adequate to support company-specific needs).

K. **Off-site storage.** Off-site storage may be required for certain equipment that cannot be immediately installed in the new facility.

L. **Office furniture.** System furniture (cubicles) needs to be ordered in advance of the installation date, which then needs to be coordinated with cable and electrical vendors. During a move, it is not uncommon for businesses to paint or reorganize file cabinets to make them all match within a department. Now is a great time to get rid of old, worn furniture rather than move it.

COMMENT

Firms that specialize in technology relocation are usually a division of a moving company or a technology consulting company. When using outside help, make sure they specialize in technology relocation. Don't forget to ask for success stories and testimonials!

---

§ 29.03   RELOCATION PROCESS

[A]   Benefits of Planning

Just like any other major project, a relocation benefits greatly when it is well planned. Some of the benefits of planning include:

A. Resource needs are known ahead of time.
B. Problem areas are identified.
C. Follow-up support costs are lower.
D. Environmental problems are identified and cleaned up.
E. Other resource-intensive projects are consolidated.
F. Asset management can be initiated.
G. Project management is more efficient.
H. Disaster recovery/site guide can be developed.
I. Stress on employees is minimized.

As noted in Exhibit 29-1 by The Knowledge Group, a Columbus, Ohio–based consulting firm that specializes in planning integrated building technology, the earlier in the process decisions are made, the higher their value and lower the cost. If the IT Manager waits to make decisions, values diminish and cost rises sharply. A little pre-planning can result in huge savings.

EXHIBIT 29-1. Planning Cost/Benefit Analysis

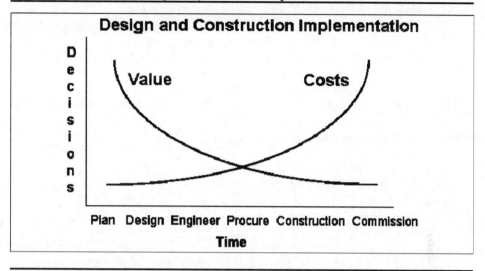

The results of not planning can include the following problems:

A. Lack of testing
B. Vendor overlap
C. Loss of business continuity
D. Loss of clients
E. Longer project duration
F. Poor use of personnel
G. Missed process changes
H. Reduced time for daily support and other business projects during the relocation project
I. Lost opportunity to save by shopping for services (especially local Internet providers)
J. Lost chance to upgrade or replace technology

Numerous things can go wrong on this kind of project before, during, and after the move. Most, if not all, of them can be prevented with careful planning. Common omissions prior to move include:

A. Forgetting to arrange copier (or other special equipment) move
B. Not having updated floor plans
C. Not having accurate inventory of furniture
D. Non-networked equipment not accounted for
E. Networked equipment inventory is incomplete

During the move, problems that may crop up include:

A. Theft due to improper security
B. No power at new location

C. No access or limited access to elevators
D. Telecommunications lines not installed as needed
E. Unorganized activities that can make work very inefficient

After the move is complete, some problems that may occur include:

A. Critical supplies missing
B. Haphazard disconnect/reconnect process causes extra unneeded help-desk tickets
C. PCs cannot connect to network
D. Old telecommunications lines not cancelled
E. Lack of supplies in new facility
F. Security systems do not work
G. Pictures need hanging
H. Loss of critical employees

A well-planned relocation project managed by an experienced Project Manager will take much less time and resources than a relocation managed by someone without experience. Exhibit 29-2 shows the results of research performed by Franklin Moves, a technology relocation firm, comparing moves managed by experienced versus inexperienced Project Managers. Franklin Moves' research shows that, although the experienced manager

EXHIBIT 29-2. Experienced vs. Inexperienced Coordinator

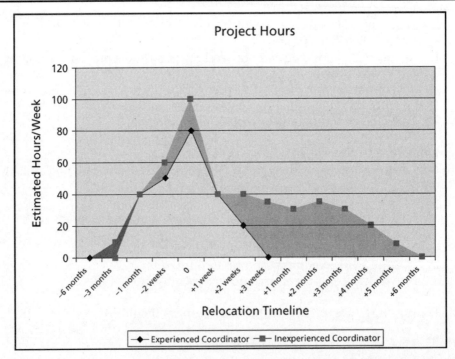

spends a little more time up front, this planning time pays big dividends later in the project. The small shaded area on the left side of the chart in Exhibit 29-2 shows the extra time spent by the experienced manager. The shaded areas at the top and right portion of the chart show a dramatic increase in the amount of hours spent by the inexperienced manager versus the experienced one. Proper planning allows the experienced Project Manager to complete the project more quickly, with fewer fires to fight after the move has taken place.

[B] Design Phase Activities

Once the initial planning is completed, the IT Manager can begin designing the logistics of the relocation project:

A. **Select tracking tools.** Determine what set of tools and software will be needed for project tracking, budget tracking, and implementing the communications plan.

B. **Create a communications plan.** This will include a central repository for communications such as meeting minutes, budget status, and scheduled items to which both internal and external contacts can refer. A good communications plan will reduce miscommunication and the workload of the project coordinator.

C. **Develop a budget.** IT must have the necessary budget resources to complete the project effectively. Make sure there is a contingency fund for unexpected items that pop up at the last minute. This fund should be approximately 10 percent of the total budget.

D. **Collect data.** IT will need data on many areas of the organization in order to get it moved to the new location. Look for office diagrams, review floor plans, and develop checklists to make sure you have covered everything. Some areas requiring special attention include:

1. General
   a. Room dimensions and location of outlets and ports
   b. Power and lighting
   c. HVAC
   d. Security
   e. Floor coverings
   f. Dedicated spaces for technical equipment
   g. Backup batteries for computer and phone equipment
   h. Identify equipment needing separate moving company or shut down procedures

2. Networks
   a. Document and assess current network architecture and applications
   b. Review technology standards, policies, and procedures
   c. Interview affected employees
   d. Create a list of reusable equipment
   e. Determine a budget for new local and wide area networks
   f. Develop new local and wide area network architecture designs
   g. Issue request for proposals (RFPs) if outside service providers are required

      h. Review RFP responses and provide recommendations if necessary
      i. Coordinate with network service providers (wide area network only)
      j. Decide a salvage plan for unneeded equipment

3. Voice systems
      a. Document and assess current voice communications architecture
      b. Review technology standards, policies, and procedures
      c. Interview affected user groups
      d. Determine a budget for voice system
      e. Develop a new voice network plan and specifications
      f. Issue RFPs if outside service providers are required
      g. Review RFP responses and provide recommendations if necessary

4. Data centers
      a. Audit existing equipment to determine what can be used at new location
      b. Define equipment layout and cabling floor plan
      c. Issue RFPs if outside service providers are required
      d. Review RFP responses and provide recommendations if necessary

5. Business continuity plan
      a. Develop a business continuity plan for move
      b. Determine possible points of failure and develop prevention and restoration plans
      c. Coordinate design of all systems to ensure connectivity
      d. Develop technology delivery schedule for new location

E. **Confirm lead times.** Many of the tasks that will be performed for the relocation must be done in a specific order. For example, cubicles cannot be placed until the carpeting is completed, inter-cubicle voice/data/electric cannot be run until the cubicles are in place, and computers cannot be reconnected on the desktops until all of the previous steps are completed. If one falls out of place, the whole schedule slides. There are typically 30- to 60-day lead times for many types of phone services.

F. **Review new space.** IT should walk through the new facility and compare what is there to the diagrams the company was given. Special attention should be paid to wiring, door locations and swing, furniture size, and how the furniture will be delivered. Make sure the doorways are wide enough for the company's equipment and the equipment that will be used to move it. Hallways and elevators also should be noted.

G. **Identify resources required.** Different types of resources will be required during the relocation project. Without the required resource levels and skill levels available, the project will suffer.

H. **Finalize employee locations.** It is critical to know where everyone will end up at the new location and what infrastructure requirements they have. When planning for network drops, plan to have extra drops in case there are last-minute changes.

I. **Develop timeline.** Work your way back from the relocation date to make sure there is enough time to complete the project.

J. **Create and resolve post-move punch list.** This is the step that always gets dropped first and costs companies thousands of dollars. It is critical to address all remaining details to successfully complete the move.

K. **Lease issues.** Identify items in the lease concerning the removal of old cabling, furniture, etc. You may be responsible for removing anything added to the building after you moved in.

L. **Confirm project closure across all areas.** This includes facilities, technology, and internal employee communication. Once in the new facility, internal employees will be focused on meeting deadlines and taking care of customers. If project closure is not confirmed, there may be items that remain unresolved that can cause problems when addressing customers' needs.

Other items that need to be accounted for include:

A. Business cards.
B. Letterhead and envelopes.
C. Marketing materials (use up old stuff before the move; have new stuff delivered to new location).
D. Business contact notification (e.g., customers, service providers, partners).
E. Having calls automatically transferred to the new number.

If new construction is involved, work closely with the contractor. Be available to answer questions at any time during the project.

[C] Implementation Phase Activities

Once IT has planned and designed how the relocation will be executed, the plan can be implemented. The following are some of the tasks performed during the implementation phase:

A. Updating and maintaining project plan and schedule.
B. Managing the purchase, delivery, integration, installation, and configuration of equipment.
C. Defining labeling standards for new building.

COMMENT

The importance of labeling cannot be overstressed. Label computers, peripherals, boxes, binders, etc., with some kind of identification of the new location. In addition, designate a location to serve as a holding area for miscellaneous IT items.

D. Reviewing network and telecommunications plans.
E. Managing inventory logistics plan.
F. Managing change management system.
G. Managing project budgets.
H. Creating acceptance test plan.
I. Conducting quality audits.
J. Facilitating project status meetings.

Other things to consider during this phase include:

A. Packing nonessential items early and identifying temporary storage locations.
B. Making sure plenty of moving materials are available (e.g., boxes, packing material).
C. Checking employee vacation schedules and other reasons to be absent.

COMMENT

It is a good idea to give every user two keyboard or equipment bags for all the smaller items, such as phones, cables, and mice. Have the users label the bags and their equipment with the location of their new desks.

Hiring a qualified company to do the disconnect/reconnect will allow your IT department to focus on escalation and critical equipment.

[D]   Relocation Phase Activities

Finally, the company is ready to move. The following tasks are performed during the relocation phase:

A. Developing a final relocation plan.
B. Developing a relocation contingency plan.
C. Confirming vendor availability during the move.
D. Establishing a relocation service desk.
E. Managing and coordinating the relocation of systems.
F. Conducting acceptance testing of new and relocated systems.
G. Completing final documentation of new facility.
H. Creating and resolving a post-move punch list.
I. Confirming project closure across all areas.

Follow-up support after the move is critical to success. No matter how well-planned the relocation, minor issues are sure to pop up that will need attention. A quick resolution of these items will ensure that everyone affected by the relocation is back to work and productive as soon as possible.

COMMENT

Do not forget to have phone services, T1 lines, etc., disconnected at the old location after the move is completed. Forgetting to do so simply wastes money.

30

COMPUTER SECURITY: PRACTICE SAFE COMPUTING

§ 30.01 OVERVIEW

[A] Purpose and Scope

A company's computer systems are the lifeblood of its ever-changing, complex operations. The investment in computer systems is more than a question of resources and cost. It also is a question of remaining competitive. Properly implemented and secured computer systems can give a company a competitive advantage by multiplying the effectiveness of its workforce. Poorly designed systems act as a drag on the business. To protect this investment, the company must have clearly defined policies to stipulate that all computer systems are properly secured and protected from improper use. A well-implemented security system provides integrity, confidentiality, and availability.

Implementing and supporting computer systems is expensive, and a company that employs its own support staff has invested a considerable amount of money into processes to support its business. All of this is lost if confidential and critical company and customer data is compromised to the world. If you have internal staff or hire a computer security consultant, insist on a CISSP certification. This certification proves a well-rounded scope of knowledge and knowledge of current new threats.

[B] Security Objectives

Computer security is often perceived as elusive and costly. The reality is that true security is a myth. Any security system will yield at some point if the attacker has unlimited time, money, access, and intellectual capacity. So the magic question that every CIO wrestles with is how much security do we need? How much money, manpower, and time should be committed to security?

The answer: A company only needs to buy one second of security. The challenge is to invest enough to exceed the tenacity, creativity, and resources of an attacker plus a safety factor of that one second. All information systems will yield under varied, sustained, and tenacious attacks. The ideal system will protect unauthorized use of information systems for one second longer than the maximum limits of frustration and tenacity of the worst hacker or until the information is no longer of value. The "art" part of security planning is in choosing the correct time when your protective systems will yield. All information has a "value lifespan," which is the point where its value reaches zero. For example, the combination to my middle school locker was 24-18-46. This information no longer has any value to anyone.

So, how do you get to that second? The answer is to go through a three-step process that looks under all of the rocks, fills in all of the potholes, and paves the road to remaining employed and sleeping well at night.

A. Step One. Identify the protection needed and for how long.
B. Step Two. Select the methods to protect.
C. Step Three. Pre-plan detection, recovery, and response.

Make time your ally!

Step One. This is often the hardest step because it requires senior management to acknowledge they are willing to sacrifice certain areas of their business to focus maximum protective activities on the most critical assets to the business. Often these can be identified by legal requirements, contractual requirements, trade secrets, patents, research and development, brand protection, sensitive materials, or other items that if compromised, altered, or stolen would have a significant impact on the business. Examples include:

- Banks. Transaction queues, accounts payable, accounts receivables, and securities records.
- Hospitals. Medical records, accounts receivables, accounts payables, and logistics.
- Manufacturing. Processes, marketing, accounts payables, accounts receivables, and logistics.
- Retail. Client information, marketing plans, accounts payables, accounts receivables, and logistics.

Step Two. The key to selecting the most appropriate and cost-effective methods to protect the critical assets is to create a fabric with a diverse multi-dimensional framework. Four areas that must be considered:

A. Internal personnel and profiles of external attackers
B. Operational procedures
C. Electronic barriers and honey pots
D. Time

Step Three. The final step is to carefully pre-plan a response to an attack. This planning can be the most important part of successfully defending the entire organization. A plan must be developed for three things:

A. Detection and identification of the intent of the attacker
B. Recovery
C. After-an-attack response

An attack can be detected in many forms, including poor network performance, altered information, deleted information, or public disclosure of internal documents. Recovery may be as simple as restoring information from a backup or as complex as comparing a production database with a backup copy table by table, record by record, field by field, and then manually identifying and correcting any fraudulent entries.

COMMENT

The IT staff should be trained on providing an immediate response to an attack. One company used red cable for their interconnection to the Internet and had a relay so they could interrupt the connection remotely from various locations. One large company used an inline intrusion detection system (IDS) that would automatically detect many types of attacks and block those attempts while simultaneously allowing normal traffic to flow.

Remember, time is an ally. The longer the system can withstand an attack, the more likely it is to exceed the patience or resources of an attacker. Many companies like to buy all of their network hardware from one manufacturer because it reduces the amount of spare parts that they must keep on-site and reduces the amount of training for their support personnel. The problem with this is that once a hacker penetrates the network, he or she will know where a weakness exists that will allow them free access to the entire network. By using equipment from more than one manufacturer, time is gained and an attacker is frustrated.

[C]   Critical Policies to Develop Based on This Chapter

Using the material discussed in this chapter, you will be able to create the following policies:

A. Proper actions to protect systems against people.
B. Security must be integrated into your business processes.
C. Guidelines on who should have local admin rights to desktop systems.

Policies should always be developed based on the local situation. Successful managers cannot issue appropriate guidance if the policies are written with another company's situation or location in mind.

§ 30.02   PEOPLE SECURITY

[A]   Internal Threats

Companies employ many people. The issue is: can these people be trusted? Nontechnical employees perform 85 percent of all fraud using authorized systems. This internal fraud costs businesses worldwide an estimated $3.5 trillion a year, according to the Association of Certified Fraud Examiners (2012). Does the company employ anyone who has been convicted of embezzlement or blackmail? Are the employees loyal to the company and its leaders? Was anyone discharged from the military with anything other than an honorable discharge? Are there any employees who maintain close personal contacts with employees at competitors? Is anyone exhibiting signs of financial trouble, such as gambling, working multiple jobs, abusing alcohol or drugs, or spending well beyond his or her salary? Is anyone taking judgment altering prescription drugs?

COMMENT

One employer noticed that the administrative assistant to the vice president of sales, a single mother of two, began driving a new Porsche to work and then asked for vacation time so she could vacation in the Cayman Islands with her new boyfriend. Upon further exploration, it was discovered that her boyfriend was connected to a major competitor.

Policies to protect against employee security threats include:

A. Having all employees sign a confidentiality and "non-compete" contract. This at least gives legal recourse to recover the economic cost of damages. Labor laws of your country or locale may restrict the structure or scope of what you can include.
B. Running routine security checks on all company officers every year or two to make sure there are no significant changes in their background.
C. Running routine security checks on critical technical people.
D. Developing a written policy on automatic prosecution of anyone caught in the theft, unauthorized destruction or unauthorized use of company data.
E. Limiting who has access to very sensitive information, such as mailroom workers, administrative assistants, file clerks, marketing staff, and external printers.
F. Compartmentalizing sensitive information so that few employees know the entire picture until it is about to become public knowledge.
G. Having all systems administrators and key network people write down their passwords and provide them to a trusted party in sealed envelopes. One company used a safe with two locks to secure the passwords so it required two officers of the company to access the information. An alternative to this elaborate procedure is to make sure that you have fully qualified and cross-trained key staff members who have fully equal capabilities.

H. Ensuring that all contracts with external companies include confidentiality and non-compete clauses and assign ownership rights to the
company.

Another area that is critical to the protection of computer systems from
internal threats is computer and network account management. Always
ensure the number of people that have the authority to grant access to IT
resources is small and that there are routine audits or cross checks. Disable
guest accounts on all systems. Make sure the number of accounts with full
control is limited to a small number of people that is proportional to the size
of the organization.

COMMENT

One company had production programs and databases
located in individual personal accounts. When one systems
administrator left the company, no one could delete or disable the account because of the number of production processes that were running there. Separate development, test,
and production accounts that mirror each other should be
created and the number of IT people with access to the
production accounts restricted. One company even had a
completely independent group that just handled the deployment of software changes and thus no developers were
allowed direct access to production systems.

Separations can be a major source of computer security issues. When an
employee leaves the company, it can be a challenging experience for everyone
involved. Are there clear written procedures on the actions to take when an
employee leaves the company? Are there additional steps if the person is an IT
person, such as inventorying all of the systems he or she had access to and
transitioning all in-progress work to knowledgeable staff? Are there clear written procedures on the actions to take when temporary employees or contractors leave the organization? Are e-mail accounts reviewed for improper activity
and future traffic rerouted to a successor or manager?

Keys to managing internal threats from people include:

A. Management at all levels must be aware of IT security risks and procedures. Security should be a mandatory requirement in every person's
job appraisal.
B. Eternal vigilance by everyone.

C. Training should be periodic and updated. Small training sessions every month or two will keep security fresh in everyone's mind. By covering a different topic each time, the training can be made comprehensive and relevant.

[B] Social Engineering

Social engineering is the use of nontechnical means to get information about a company or computer system that allows unauthorized access. Movies often show a female spy extracting secrets from a scientist. While such scenarios are fictional, true sting operations like this are performed every day. It usually involves the use of interpersonal telephone skills to convince unsuspecting victims to provide sensitive information over the telephone. These "social engineers" can be hackers, prison inmates, or someone from the competition. The most common scheme is for the caller to call in to a receptionist and ask for someone in technical support. When connected to that person, the caller gets a name and then claims that the receptionist has sent him to the wrong number. He then asks the person to transfer him to his intended victim, and then proceeds to convince the victim that he is from tech support and needs his password due to a system problem. Once he has the password, all he needs is an external connection to the network and he is in.

Malicious attackers know that the easiest way to break into a system is through the people that use it. Important information can be found in the trash (Do you know who empties your trash?), in e-mails (many login IDs are the same as a person's e-mail prefix), and by just asking. Social engineering depends on the ability to persuade people to divulge information that is useful to the attacker. Many times each piece of information by itself seems harmless, but put together can give attackers the tools they need to get into your system. An old invoice or company directory can give the attacker enough information to convince his victim that he is part of the team. Much of the information needed is available on the Internet or in company brochures and other publications.

Attackers use the following general steps in performing their attack:

A. **Gather information.** There are many sources of information that can be used to develop a relationship. These include old phone lists, company documents such as invoices, the Internet, trash bins, eavesdropping at social events, etc.

B. **Develop a relationship.** Once the attacker has enough information, he or she can then begin to develop a relationship with someone at the target company. This can be done in one day with a single phone call or over the course of several weeks. The attacker exploits the natural tendency of most people to be trusting.

C. **Take advantage of the relationship.** Once the attacker has gained the person's trust, he or she can trick them into revealing additional information needed for the attack.

D. **Attack.** Now that all the needed information has been collected, the attacker proceeds with the attack.

So how do you protect your company against social engineering attacks? It starts with a clear, comprehensive, and communicated security policy. The security policy must be trained, enforced, and compliance monitored regularly. The policy must be relevant and easy to use by the employees. A policy that is hard to follow and not clear gets in the way and encourages employees to work around it. Other guidelines to protect your company include:

A. Forbid the exchange of passwords between employees for any reason. A technical support person should never ask an employee for his password. Use automated password reset tools to eliminate human intervention in changing passwords.
B. Use password authentication questions to ensure that requests to reset passwords come from authorized users.
C. Avoid using password authentication questions that are easy to answer with just a little research. Mother's maiden name, children's names, addresses, pet names, etc. can all be found without too much difficulty.
D. The use of biometric devices or security tokens can significantly reduce the chances of a successful attack using social engineering.
E. Background checks of all employees with access to sensitive systems can identify employees who might be susceptible to divulging information in exchange for money.

While you cannot and do not want to turn your company into Fort Knox, securing the information inside your company may just be the most important job in your company. This information in most cases is the most important asset in your company. Securing your systems from internal and external threats is not a one-time activity, but requires continuing vigilance and commitment to keeping your data safe.

§ 30.03 PROCESS SECURITY

[A] Threat Analysis

Conduct a vulnerability analysis to determine how the company's systems may be attacked and when they may be attacked. When studying how the company's systems may be attacked, the IT Manager must consider internal threats, external threats, accidental disclosures, deletions or alterations, and denial-of-service attacks. One technique is to take the perspective of one of the company's competitors and write a plan on how they would take apart the company. This can provide great insight into the company's weaknesses. Look for the holes in people, processes, and technology. Review the audit checklist in Worksheet 30-1 and customize it for your company.

WORKSHEET 30-1. Security Audit Checklists

SECURITY AUDIT CHECKLISTS—DESKTOP

1. Do you have multiple layers of security including several layers of door locks (keyed differently) as well as network and application passwords?
2. Do you have limits on who gets CD-RW or DVD-RW drives?
3. Do you disable USB ports where not needed so that memory stick devices cannot be used?
4. Is antivirus software kept current mechanically?
5. Is another brand of antivirus software on hand to be used in the event of failure of the primary?
6. Is Internet access limited?
7. Do you limit employee's ability to download and run executable files over the Internet?
8. Do employees understand that they should treat company data the same way they would treat cash?
9. Are screens viewable from open doors, windows, or common areas?
10. Are screens that are visible by non-company employees maintained to the highest level of security?
11. Are passwords changed frequently?
12. Are passwords required to be strong (i.e., composed of A–Z, a–z, 0–9, $.:;*^#@!)?
13. Are common area computers disabled when not in use?
14. Are the owners of notebook computers, smartphones, and tablets taught to carefully guard them?
15. Is the loss of a notebook, smartphone, or tablet immediately reported, removed from network access lists, and have all security privileges been revoked?
16. Is the amount and sensitivity of information stored on notebooks, smartphones, or tablets limited to the minimum necessary?
17. Do people know how to encrypt files and are the proper tools available for use?
18. Do people know to never share their passwords with anyone including internal staff and technical staff?
19. Do you have testing criteria, procedures, and equipment to evaluate any new software and upgrades for malicious activity?
20. Are all systems maintained with a secure version of the operating system and all necessary security patches applied?
21. Are computers turned off during evenings, weekends, and holidays?
22. Is a hardware key or user authentication required?
23. Once a user is authenticated, how is access to authorized materials contained?
24. Does the operating system provide the necessary secure environment?
25. Does the operating system keep each application in restricted memory space?
26. Does the operating system purge passwords from memory?

27. Does the operating system wipe files that are deleted?
28. Does the operating system lock the screen and keyboard when not in use?
29. Do you use terminal servers instead of PCs?

SECURITY AUDIT CHECKLISTS—NETWORK

1. Do you still have hubs or mini-hubs on the network or have they all been replaced with switches?
2. Does the number of wired connections in switches match the number of devices? Are spares bundled and disabled?
3. Are there nonsecure wireless network access points?
4. Is dial-in access used? Does it require VPN software to function? Can dial-back modems be implemented?
5. If modems are on the network, are they separated from the network by a firewall device?
6. Is sensitive information being sent over the Internet unencrypted?
7. Are network cables properly labeled and bundled?
8. Do routers block unauthorized traffic?
9. Do you have a firewall to block unauthorized access attempts?
10. Do you restrict who can send data to outside destinations (FTP)?
11. Are all satellite offices given the same level of attention and protection as the home office?
12. Do satellite offices use the home office firewall security for Internet access?
13. Are there limits on who has dial-out modems on the network?
14. Are there tools that can identify all equipment on the network?
15. Are network cables bundled separately from telephone cables and clearly marked?
16. Do trustworthy personnel install network cabling?
17. Is fiber optic cable used where possible?
18. Do other trading partners who provide data have the same emphasis and level of commitment to security?
19. Do you have two telephone truck cables providing service to the building via different routes and telephone exchanges (POP)?
20. Have the points or equipment in the network where a failure of that one item would disrupt service been identified? Is there an alternate route or stand-by equipment plan?
21. Are encryption devices necessary and, if so, are they in use?
22. Is there an intrusion detection system in-line with the Internet interface?
23. Are intrusion detection systems logically located immediately before the servers with no routers between them?
24. Has the network been reviewed by a certified ethical hacker for security holes?
25. Are server logs checked on a regular basis for security violations?

26. Are all system administrators and network people trained that in the event of a successful attack they are to capture all evidence to CD-ROM as soon as possible?
27. If cryptography is used, are the people using it properly trained in its use?
28. Is there a honey pot system to automatically attract attacks?

SECURITY AUDIT CHECKLISTS—COMPUTER ROOM

1. Are your major systems on an uninterruptible power supply (UPS) system and not on a stand-by (SPS) system?
2. Does a stand-by generator back up your UPS?
3. How long can you go without commercial power?
4. Is maintenance routinely performed on the UPS and generator? Are they tested regularly?
5. Are backups performed routinely?
6. Are your computer room people happy?
7. Are the working conditions safe and comfortable?
8. Do you have a fire suppression system?
9. Does your fire suppression system work automatically?
10. Does your fire detection system automatically report it to the fire department?
11. Does the air conditioning system automatically shut down when a fire is detected to deprive it oxygen?
12. If you have a Halon system, do your people understand how it works and the dangers of it?
13. Is the computer room door locked, with a limited number of people having access?
14. Are computer rooms located in the core of a building with no outside windows?
15. Does the computer room have emergency lighting?
16. Are there flammable materials in the computer room (including carpet)? What about adjacent rooms?
17. Are all cables routed overhead or under the floor?
18. Can servers detect unusual activity during evenings, weekends, and holidays and page someone?
19. Can servers track unusual activity and provide a complete log?
20. Can unusual activity be reversed?
21. Who has night, weekend, and holiday access to the computer room and why?
22. Is the location of all keys known?
23. How long has it been since the locks were changed?
24. Is a hardware key or user authentication required?
25. Once a user is authenticated, how is his or her access contained to authorized materials only?
26. Does the operating system provide the necessary secure environment?
27. Does the operating system keep each application in restricted memory space?

28. Does the operating system purge passwords from memory?
29. Does the operating system wipe files that are deleted?
30. Does access to the main system consoles provide extra physical security?
31. Do your systems have remote control software such as PC Anywhere?

SECURITY AUDIT CHECKLISTS—PEOPLE

1. Can your people be trusted?
2. Has anyone been convicted of embezzlement, theft, or blackmail?
3. Are your people loyal?
4. Has anyone received a discharge from the military with anything other than an honorable discharge?
5. Are your people motivated and do they have goals that are consistent with the company's?
6. Do you employ anyone who is working multiple jobs and may be in financial trouble?
7. Do you employ people who maintain close personal contacts with employees at competitors?
8. Do you employ people that gamble a lot?
9. Do you employ any alcoholics or illegal drug users?
10. Do you employ anyone on prescription drugs that could alter their judgment?
11. Do you employ anyone that is spending well beyond his or her salary?
12. Do you employ confidentiality contracts with all employees?
13. Do you limit who has access to very sensitive information?
14. Do you take good care of your systems administrators and network engineers?
15. Do you have a policy to refer for prosecution anyone caught in the theft of company data?
16. Are routine security checks run on all VPs and above and critical technical people every year or two to verify that nothing has significantly changed?
17. Is new account creation limited to a small number of people and cross-checked?
18. Are guest accounts removed from all systems?
19. Is the number of accounts with full control limited to a number of people that is proportional to the organization's size?
20. Do your system administrators and key network people write down their passwords and provide them to a trusted party in sealed envelopes?
21. Is security a mandatory requirement in every person's job appraisal?
22. Do your employment agreements with software developers assign ownership rights to the company for anything developed on company time or with company assets?
23. Do you have clear procedures on the actions to take when an employee leaves the company? What if he or she is an IT person?

24. Do you have clear procedures on the actions to take when temps or contractors are used and then leave?
25. Are your service desk person and other technical people trained to detect social hacking?
26. Are sensitive documents shredded beyond recovery?

SECURITY AUDIT CHECKLISTS—PROCESSES

1. Do you have policies regulating games, freeware, and shareware?
2. Are sensitive documents shredded beyond reconstruction?
3. Is internal code thoroughly tested before it is moved into the production environment?
4. Are there periodic code reviews that examine all custom source code for potential damaging problems?
5. Is code scanned for future dates, login IDs, passwords, copy, or FTP commands?
6. Are there safeguards in place to preclude wrongful alteration of data?
7. Do you have a response plan to address hacking attempts? Does it include contact phone numbers for technical and law enforcement resources?
8. Are your network people trained on identifying a denial of service attack? How fast can they isolate and thwart the access route?
9. Do you have a response plan for a virus attack?
10. Are standard software products pre-selected and their use enforced?
11. Is the security impact given consideration with all technology purchases?
12. Do you keep a list of the security risks that have been considered and approved with the approval manager's name and date?
13. Do your e-mails and faxes have confidentiality footers?
14. If you have security people, do they have clearly written instructions? Do they include inspecting outgoing boxes?
15. When new equipment is purchased, does it come from a trusted source?
16. Is new computer equipment locked up until it is placed in service?
17. Is access to mainframe Open Database Connectivity (ODBC) datasets read-only and password protected?
18. Is access to mainframe ODBC datasets limited to a need-to-know basis?
19. Are common passwords blocked from usage?
20. Does someone maintain a notebook of all of the software license numbers and the agreements? Is there a periodic internal audit to verify that no unauthorized copies have been made and that all licensing requirements are met?
21. If unauthorized copies are found, are they immediately removed or purchased?
22. Are the company's intellectual property rights guarded on internally developed software and products?
23. Is a standard security checklist (ISO 17799) used and maintained?

24. Are there built-in mechanical checks of financial data to detect alterations or out-of-tolerance numbers?
25. Is there double entry of critically important pieces of information?
26. Is there an audit trail that can detect all adds, changes, and deletions?
27. Do your people know how to search the audit trail?
28. Does the audit trail assign responsibility for the action to a person or unique process?
29. Can the auditing be disabled? Who knows how to do it?
30. Is company-confidential information clearly identified or marked? Do screens have the word "Confidential" on them?
31. Is sensitive information on your Web site? Who checks your Web site and how often?
32. If competitors wanted to find out information about your company, how would they do it?
33. How do you deal with data integrity issues? Who is responsible for correcting them and identifying their point of origin?
34. Do you have a feedback mechanism that blocks the reoccurrence of data integrity problems?
35. Are remote control applications used such as PCAnywhere or VNC? Are they properly secured?
36. Do the introduction screens of all systems clearly state ownership and confidentiality of the information they contain and the prosecution policy?
37. Is there a diversity of equipment and operating systems so that a successful penetration into one machine does not allow access into other more secure machines?
38. Do your internal Web applications use CGI instead of Java?
39. If you supply sensitive or proprietary data to other companies, do they have the same level of commitment to security that your company does?
40. Do your contracts with suppliers or third-party companies provide recourse if their network is hacked and the hacker gains access to your data?
41. Do you periodically physically inspect your trading partners that handle sensitive information?
42. Do your trading partners have any personnel problems that could compromise your data?
43. Have you ever had your main conference rooms, boardroom, HR, marketing, purchasing, and executive offices checked for unauthorized clandestine listening devices?

SECURITY AUDIT CHECKLISTS—RESOURCES

Hacking Exposed
www.hackingexposed.com

AntiOnline
www.antionline.com/index.php

Yahoo! Security and Encryption
http://dir.yahoo.com/computers_and_internet/Security_and_Encryption/

CERT Coordination Center
www.cert.org

Center for Information Technology, National Institutes of Health
cit.nih.gov/Security/

National Institute of Standards and Technology, Computer Security Resource Center
csrc.nist.gov/

U.S. Department of Energy, Office of Cyber Security
http://energy.gov/cio/office-chief-information-officer/services/incident-management

ICSA Labs
https://www.icsalabs.com

ITSecurity.com
www.itsecurity.com/

Security Intelligence Technologies
www.spyzone.com

A threat analysis should answer three major questions: Who, what, and why? Who the attacker is may include U.S. competitors, foreign competitors, foreign governments, disgruntled employees, or independent attackers. What the attack may target includes critical assets such as financial and logistical systems; business functions required to sustain normal operations; business assets that are valuable, rare, and difficult to imitate; customer and medical information; and future business plans. Key IT resources also can be targets. Why the attacker does it usually involves a transfer of wealth, denial of service, retaliation, fun or challenge, or corporate espionage.

In thinking about when the company's systems might be attacked, consider the following.

A. U.S., foreign, and religious holidays.
B. Significant dates in history in this country and others.
C. Peak business hours locally and in time zones where competitors are located.
D. After-school hours (3:00 p.m. EST).
E. Foreign governments that may be interested in your company's protected assets, trade secrets, or future research.

F. After significant corporate events such as:
  1. Layoffs.
  2. Outsourcing.
  3. Mergers and acquisitions.
  4. Public knowledge of increase in liquid assets.
  5. Shortly after a new operating system is released.
  6. When key people are traveling.
  7. Corporate events (social hacking).
  8. Happy hour.
  9. Right after a patent is issued.
  10. Right after a joint venture or partnership is formed (bleeding through).
  11. After implementation of new hardware, software, or applications.
  12. Retirement of senior security personnel because junior staff may not detect the attack.

A threat analysis should answer three major questions: Who, what, and why? Who the attacker is may include U.S. competitors, foreign competitors, foreign governments, disgruntled employees, or independent attackers. What the attack may target includes critical assets such as financial and logistical systems; business functions required to sustain normal operations; business assets that are valuable, rare, and difficult to imitate; customer and medical information; and future business plans. Key IT resources also can be targets. Why the attacker does it usually involves a transfer of wealth, denial of service, retaliation, fun or challenge, or corporate espionage.

[B] Process Security Planning

Once the threat analysis is completed, the IT Manager should have a clear understanding of the security risks so the following questions can be answered:

A. What needs to be protected?
B. Who does the protection?
C. When should it be protected?
D. How is the best way to protect it?
E. What should be in the response plan?

In the IT world, key resources such as passwords, laptops, servers, networks, databases, and proprietary information often require protection. The IT Manager should clearly assign responsibilities to design and implement security to protect the company's critical assets. Any company person that is traveling must be aware that he or she becomes a moving target and any information on a laptop computer can be stolen.

COMMENT

All employees must be taught to treat sensitive company information like it was cash!

When should security be considered in the design process? Any time new IT equipment is being selected, security should be considered. Any time new applications are designed or significantly altered, security should be considered. Security should be reviewed in response to new threats. When new employees are hired, security access should be reviewed. Mergers, acquisitions, or the sale of a division of the company provide significant holes where sensitive company information can grow feet.

The security plan must:

A. Be in writing.
B. Be taught to all employees.
C. Require when and who has received the training to be documented.
D. Outline the IT Manager's accountability for accepting all known risks.
E. Ensure quality, focused time be set aside on a periodic basis to develop and review the plan.

In addition, the security plan must include:

A. Prevention
B. Detection
C. Recovery
D. After-action response
E. Criminal prosecution

The response plan must be a written document! Detection and how to develop an audit trail for evidence collection and preservation should be included. It should focus on recovery and the uninterrupted continuance of business operations. It should include the phone numbers of technical personnel and law enforcement officials.

[C] Software Development

Just like any software development product, it should be built to last the first time. Too many applications are written as one-time, short-lived projects that seize roots and last forever; security was rarely considered in the initial design. Security should be considered on every project no matter how small. A one-time application that is left on the production system can accidentally be executed again at some point in the future by someone on your staff or a hacker.

COMMENT

Could It Happen to You?

Overvalued house goofs up city's budget.

Value erroneously changed to $400 million may lead to municipal layoffs.

The Associated Press Updated: 5:42 p.m. ET Feb. 10, 2006

VALPARAISO, Ind.—a house erroneously valued at $400 million is being blamed for budget shortfalls and possible layoffs in municipalities and school districts in northwest Indiana.

An outside user of Porter County's computer system may have triggered the mess by accidentally changing the value of the Valparaiso house, said Sharon Lippens, director of the county's information technologies and service department. The house had been valued at $121,900 before the glitch.

County Treasurer Jim Murphy said the home usually carried about $1,500 in property taxes; this year, it was billed $8 million.

Lippens said her agency identified the mistake and told the county auditor's office how to correct it. But the $400 million value ended up on documents that were used to calculate tax rates.

Lippens said the outside user changed the property value, most likely while trying to access another program while using the county's enhanced access system, which charges users a fee for access to public records that are not otherwise available on the Internet.

Lippens said the user probably tried to access a real estate record display by pressing R-E-D, but accidentally typed R-E-R, which brought up an assessment program written in 1995. The program is no longer in use, and technology officials did not know it could be accessed.

URL: *http://msnbc.msn.com/id/11278451/*

When developing software, use the model and process shown in Exhibit 30-1. Each developer should write new code in his own personal account space. If he is modifying code, then he should check out the most recent version from a code library. There are many code library management systems. If the company does not have one, buy one. The code library should have source code and compiled code. It also should be used to move commercial code to the production environment. Once the code is developed and tested at the individual level, the developer should move the code to the acceptance testing area. This allows it to be tested for interactions with code and environment that replicates the production system. Once it passes testing, then it should be moved into the code library. Operations personnel should be informed by an approval document that testing and management have completed. Operations personnel should then move the code from the library to a staging area. A mechanical process will then move the code to the production area during a quiet period in operations, usually early morning or on a weekend.

Some key points to keep in mind:

A. Shred sensitive scrap documents beyond reconstruction.
B. Thoroughly test code before it is moved into a production environment.
C. Periodically review all custom code for potential damaging problems.
D. Scan all code for future dates, login IDs, passwords, copy, or FTP commands.
E. Always have a rollback plan.
F. Implement safeguards that will preclude wrongful alteration of data.
G. Make all ODBC and OLE access to your critical databases read-only and password protected.
H. Designate one person to maintain a notebook of all software license numbers and agreements. Systems should be audited periodically to

Exhibit 30-1. Software Development Process

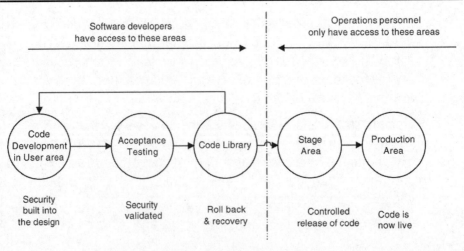

identify any unauthorized copies. Read and have legal staff approve all license terms and agreements before integrating commercial software into your business processes. Make sure that your company owns all work products developed using commercial or open-source products.

I. Protect internally developed software as intellectual property just like a patent or copyright.

J. Clearly mark screens, documents, and e-mails as confidential if they contain sensitive information.

K. Implement a feedback process that identifies data integrity issues and traces them back to their points of origin.

A company has the most control over internally developed software, but it also offers the greatest possibility of containing defects that can improperly alter data or allow a hacker to access data. Databases that provide data to Web screens is best served from a replica of the production databases. Any data entry from the Web can be fed as transactions to the production database, so they can be logged, validated, and reversed if necessary.

[D]   Network Design

In the ideal network, every authorized user can access what they are authorized for and the other three quadrants of possibilities are blocked and attempts logged. The company should have a single portal to external data sources that is guarded by an inline intrusion detection system, while all internal systems should be masked and invisible to outside sources. Servers such as Web servers are placed in a middle controlled-access zone sometimes referred to as the DMZ. Satellite offices should be given the same level of security attention as the home office.

COMMENT

Automatic discovery tools should be used to identify all the devices on the network. You will probably be surprised at what you will find at some point, especially evenings, weekends, and holidays. This brings up a key point; if a server containing sensitive information is not needed during non-business hours, it should be disconnected from the network. The software that manages sensitive data should record unusual activity and alert the proper individuals. When diagramming a network, any place where the failure of one piece of equipment can disrupt operations should be identified. Alternative methods, routes, or equipment should be planned to mitigate these single points of failure.

One of the most common errors in network design is to look beyond the touch points with your business-trading partners. If their network is hacked, then your interconnection can become compromised. Even if you only send them a data file, if their system is compromised then your data file can be stolen. Make sure that your trading partners have at least the same level of commitment to security as your company.

[E] Passwords

The most common approach to securing data systems access is through a User ID/Password combination. A "User ID" is a name for identifying to the computer the person (or entity) who is seeking access. Authentication is the method to prove to the computer system that the user is one and only correct user with that ID. The best authentication uses at least two of three techniques: something that someone knows, possesses, or a personal physical characteristic, such as biometric measurements. A password is one of the most commonly used methods because it is the least expensive to implement and, when paired with a user ID, authenticates that the person requesting access is really that user. Passwords are an important aspect of computer security. They are the front line of protection for user accounts. A poorly chosen password may result in the compromise of the entire corporate network.

The choice of rules for passwords that people are required to follow is significant in blocking unauthorized access. If you look at Exhibit 30-2, you can see that the longer the password and more options that can be used to construct it, the longer it will take to break the password using brute force attacks. For example, the move from seven to nine characters dramatically improves the protection level. Note that the time to crack is based on a single computer attempting the attack. Attackers now resort to hijacking a grid of computers

Exhibit 30-2. Password Security

Number of characters in password	Possible Combinations A–Z	A–Z, 0–9	Estimated time to crack 1.5 GHz PC
1	26	36	
2	676	1,296	
3	17,576	46,656	
4	458,976	1,679,616	
5	11,881,376	60,466,176	
6	308,915,776	2,176,782,336	5.8 hrs
7	8,031,810,176	78,364,164,096	8.8 days
8	208,827,064,576	2,821,109,907,456	321 days
9	5,429,503,678,976	101,559,956,668,416	31.4 years
10	141,167,095,653,376	3,656,158,440,062,980	

Exhibit 30-3. Encryption Key Security

Power/Cost–Time for brute force attack	40-bit key	56-bit key	64-bit key	128-bit key
$2K – 1PC	1.4 min.	73 days	50 years	10^{20} years
$100K – Company	2 sec.	35 hours	1 year	10^{19} years
$1M – Government	0.2 sec.	3.5 hours	37 days	10^{18} years

to conduct an attack and thus may harness 1,000 or 10,000 computers to break passwords. There also are most frequently used word lists that yield a useful password much faster than running through all possible combinations sequentially.

If encryption is used for network traffic, the largest key possible should be used. For example, in Exhibit 30-3, the use of a 128-bit key to encrypt communications would require a significant amount of money and resources that would normally only be available to a government. If your company operates completely inside the United States, you are highly encouraged to use 128-bit encryption with one of the high security algorithms that are available in the United States. If your company does business inside and outside the United States, then you have to consider and comply with the laws, including import and export laws, in all of the countries in which the company operates. This makes choosing a security product a challenge.

COMMENT

InfoSysSec is a good Web site to explore for help (*www.infosyssec.net/index.html*).

Sometimes it is advantageous to choose a standard that is in use in the countries outside the United States and then implement it in the United States. The reason is that the United States has restrictions on exporting some encryption products, but no limits on importing them.

Your password policy should require the use of strong passwords, and give guidance to your users for keeping them secret. You should also establish a time limit for how long a password can be in use before requiring it to be changed. Some suggested guidelines for creating good passwords include:

A. Passwords for typical user accounts should be at least eight characters in length; administrative passwords should be at least 15 characters in length.

    B. A password cannot be a word or phrase that can be found in any dictionary or a word spelled backwards.

    C. It should contain at least three out of four from the following: lower case letters, upper case letters, numeric character, and special character (e.g., !@#$%^&).

    D. Must not be a common pattern found on a standard keyboard or any other common pattern of letters or numbers.

    E. It should not be based on personal information such as birthdays, addresses, names, etc.

Of course, it does no good to have a well-formed password that is discovered through non-technical means. To protect the secrecy of passwords include the following guidance in your policy:

    A. Passwords can never be written down anywhere that is not under lock and key (no sticky notes!).

    B. All user account passwords must be changed every six months and cannot be reused. All administrative passwords must be changed every three months.

    C. Passwords can never be included in unencrypted e-mails or other form of electronic communications.

    D. Users must have different passwords for each system that does not use some method of single sign on.

    E. Never reveal your password to anyone over the phone, including help desk personnel.

    F. Do not share your passwords with assistants, coworkers, family members, or friends. All passwords must be treated as company confidential.

    G. Do not use the "Remember Password" feature of any application.

    H. Do not store your passwords in any portable electronic device such as tablets or cell phones.

    I. Tools used for password management complexity checking must be enabled when available.

See Policy ITP-30-1 Password Policy as an example.

POLICY ITP-30-1. Password Policy

Policy #:	ITP-30-1	Effective:	03/18/12	Page #:	1 of N
Subject:	Password Policy				

1.0 PURPOSE

The purpose of this policy is to prevent the unauthorized use of company-owned computer workstations and servers by establishing standards for strong passwords and the protection of user and system passwords.

2.0 SCOPE

The policy applies to all corporate computers and devices that store corporate information. It applies to all users of the organization's network, using any device that has access to the network.

3.0 POLICY

All company-owned workstations and servers must be protected using a user ID and password combination. Passwords are used for user accounts, servers, e-mail accounts, routers, Web applications, screen savers, etc. Users of any company-owned systems that require a password must follow the guidelines below for creating passwords:

A. Passwords for typical user accounts should be at least eight characters in length; administrative passwords should be at least 15 characters in length.
B. A password cannot be a word or phrase that can be found in any dictionary or a word spelled backwards.
C. It should contain at least three out of four from the following: lower case letters, upper case letters, numeric character, and special character (e.g., !@#$%^&).
D. Must not be a common pattern found on a standard keyboard or any other common pattern of letters or numbers.
E. It should not be based on personal information such as birthdays, addresses, names, etc.

It is important to protect the secrecy of passwords. The following guidelines must be followed when handling passwords:

A. Passwords can never be written down anywhere that is not under lock and key (no sticky notes!).
B. All user account passwords must be changed every six months and cannot be reused. All administrative passwords must be changed every three months.
C. Password can never be included in unencrypted e-mails or other form of electronic communications.
D. Users must have different passwords for each system that does not use some method of single sign on.
E. Never reveal your password to anyone over the phone, including help desk personnel.
F. Do not share your passwords with assistants, coworkers, family members, or friends. All passwords must be treated as company confidential.
G. Do not use the "Remember Password" feature of any application.
H. Do not store your passwords in any portable electronic device such as tablets or cell phones.
I. Tools used for password management complexity checking must be enabled when available.

Any exceptions to this policy must be approved in advance by the corporate IT security department.

4.0 REVISION HISTORY

Date	Revision #	Description of Change
03/18/12	1.0	Initial creation.
04/06/13	1.1	Added requirement for use of password management complexity checking.

5.0 INQUIRIES

Direct inquiries about this policy to:

George Jenkins, CIO
Our Company, Inc.
2900 Corporate Drive
Columbus, OH 43215

Voice: 614-555-1234
Fax: 614-555-1235
E-mail: gjenkins@company.com

Revision #:	1.1	Supersedes:	1.0	Date:	04/06/13

[F]   Physical Security

Physical security is simple but often overlooked. A lost notebook, smartphone, or tablet should be reported immediately so that it can be locked out of the network and any passwords changed. All key security patches should be checked for updates daily, automatically if possible. The amount of information stored on smartphones, tablets, and notebook computers should be maintained at the minimal level necessary, and notebooks should be backed up to a protected server. There are security devices that encrypt the contents of a notebook computer or destroy sensitive files when hacking attempts are detected. Some high-end devices can read a fingerprint to verify owner identity before granting access. If your building has security guards, they should have written instructions on identifying packages and identifying data theft methods.

Many executives and managers love to have windows in their offices. If their computer screens can be seen through the window, then they can be read from a distance. Reflective window coating and polarized screen filters can limit outside observation. If you have any computers in an area accessible to nonemployees such as a public lobby, they should be given intensive security protections.

COMMENT

When Holiday Inn centrally computerized their reservations, they were so proud of their computer system that they built a round building with floor-to-ceiling glass on all sides in front of their corporate headquarters to show it off.

[G] Disaster Recovery Planning

All businesses should have a written disaster recovery plan (DRP). It can be as simple as a couple of pages for a small company to several hundred pages for a large multi-national corporation. One way to determine how much effort should be invested in the DRP plan is to determine the cost per minute of total loss of a company's computing capacity. This should include the salaries of idle employees, average revenue, and a projection of lost customers and the gain to your competitors.

COMMENT

One very common mistake is not having your backup data far enough away from the primary site. If you think about drawing a circle around each site at the maximum range that a disaster could reach from that site, the circles should not touch between your primary and backup site. Some major companies have put their backup sites in the same city with the primary site to share training; however, the entire city was in an earthquake fault zone. Earthquakes, hurricanes, and volcanoes can cause damage up to 300 miles away.

Organize the DRP so that selected parts can be implemented if required. Keep it rich in details on key contacts, decision makers, and phone numbers—especially after hours. If the plan calls for augmentation by contractors, ensure that the vendors are preselected and prequalified. Some contingency contracts may need to be in place before a disaster, since several companies may be demanding the same support resources at the same time. Get first priority. Have a contingency fund or quick access insurance plan in place. Finally, test your plan!

COMMENT

Security policies written with teeth are legally defendable. Some companies have a notebook with more than 20 one-page policy statements that every new employee must read and sign. Policies need to address people, processes, and technology issues. Training time should be used to refresh people about policies. Great policies are one of the layers in designing a secure, multi-layer fabric to protect corporate assets and your job.

[H] Testing

This is the one area where you really want to be from Missouri—Show Me! Testing software to validate that it does what it was designed to do is frequently done; testing software to verify that it does nothing else is rarely done. Test commercial hardware and software for malicious activity before it is allowed on your production network. Internally developed software testing should include a code review for dates, passwords, account names, and copy or FTP commands. You might consider a special "firewall" that will allow any program to read from the database but log all write attempts without committing the transactions. This technique allows a review to verify transactions before they are allowed in the production environment.

What questions should I be asking my technical staff? The best questions are: Where are the holes and weaknesses in our organization? How can scams, spoofing, viruses, and worms damage our company? How can an attacker disrupt or deny our ability to use our computing and network resources to conduct normal business? Do we have multiple and diverse protective barriers? Do you have an inline intrusion detection and prevention system that alerts your technical staff when specific attacks or attempts occur? Do these systems automatically adapt and respond to different attacks? Do they detect unauthorized locations, activities, connections, and IDs?

[I] Malware Protection

Malicious software programs such as viruses, Trojan horses, and worms pose a threat to the security of the organizations computer systems. Any of these types of attacks can compromise data integrity, cause a loss of productivity, disclose valuable company trade secrets, and have a potential negative impact on the reputation and credibility of the organization.

Any computer system or device that is connected to the corporate network or the Internet is vulnerable to attack. It is therefore critical that all such systems and devices must have current approved malware protection measures in place.

§ 30.03[I]

It is critical that your policy requires that all corporate computers and devices that store corporate information and that at any time connect to the corporate network must have approved and supported malware protection software correctly installed, configured, activated, and updated with the latest malware definitions. Any devices infected with a virus or other malicious code (collectively referred to as "malware") must be immediately disconnected from the corporate network until the infection has been removed. Directions for procuring, installing, configuring, and using malware protection software should be posted on the corporate intranet.

If a particular operating system or computing platform does not have malware protection available, use of a device using such an operating system should be approved by corporate IT security, who can determine the operating procedures necessary to minimize the possibility of malware infecting the corporate network. If malware protection software becomes available for an operating system or computing platform previously lacking such software, it should be installed as soon as possible on all such devices.

Users should be instructed to not disable or bypass malware protection on any device or system they access, and are responsible for ensuring that updates to malware detection are received in a timely manner.

When an enterprise-wide malware attack is in progress, corporate IT security must notify all corporate users via the best available method. Such notifications are to be made only to users within the organization, and are not to be forwarded or shared outside the organization except by officials approved to do so. After such an attack has been identified, all storage devices must be scanned using the latest malware definitions available.

Any exceptions to this policy must be approved in advance by the corporate IT security department. See Policy ITP-30-2 Malware Protection Policy as an example.

POLICY ITP-30-2. Malware Protection Policy

Policy #:	ITP-30-2	Effective:	03/18/12	Page #:	1 of N
Subject:	Malware Protection Policy				

1.0 PURPOSE

The purpose of this policy is to prevent the infection of company computers, computer systems, and other digital devices by computer viruses and other malicious code. This policy is intended to prevent major damage and loss of information to hardware, applications, and user data.

2.0 SCOPE

The policy applies to all corporate computers and devices that store corporate information. It applies to all users of the organization's network, using any device that has access to the corporate network.

3.0 POLICY

All corporate computers and devices that store corporate information and that at any time connect to the corporate network must have approved and supported malware protection software correctly installed, configured, activated, and updated with the latest malware definitions. Any devices infected with a virus or other malicious code (collectively referred to as "malware") must be immediately disconnected from the corporate network until the infection has been removed. Directions for procuring, installing, configuring, and using malware protection software are posted on the corporate intranet.

If a particular operating system or computing platform does not have malware protection available, use of a device using such an operating system must be approved by corporate IT security, who shall determine the operating procedures necessary to minimize the possibility of malware infecting the corporate network. If malware protection software becomes available for an operating system or computing platform previously lacking such software, it must be installed as soon as possible on all such devices.

Users must not disable or bypass malware protection on any device or system they access, and are responsible for ensuring that updates to malware detection are received in a timely manner.

When an enterprise-wide malware attack is in progress, corporate IT security must notify all corporate users via the best available method. Such notifications are to be made only to users within the organization, and are not to be forwarded or shared outside the organization except by officials approved to do so. After such an attack has been identified, all storage devices must be scanned using the latest malware definitions available.

Any exceptions to this policy must be approved in advance by the corporate IT security department.

4.0 REVISION HISTORY

Date	Revision #	Description of Change
03/18/12	1.0	Initial creation.
04/06/13	1.1	Added prohibition on disabling malware protection

5.0 INQUIRIES

Direct inquiries about this policy to:

George Jenkins, CIO
Our Company, Inc
2900 Corporate Drive
Columbus, OH 43215

Voice: 614-555-1234
Fax: 614-555-1235
E-mail: gjenkins@company.com

Revision #:	1.1	Supersedes:	1.0	Date:	04/06/13

Have you tested your plan to recover from a malware attack? Do your systems produce audit logs and if so, how are they reviewed? Is your staff trained on how to respond to intrusion activity involving theft, alteration, deletion, or insertion of Trojan horses? Review the audit checklists in Worksheet 30-1 and customize them for your company.

If you are the victim of an attack, it is critical that you and your staff collect the information you need to identify the attacker and prevent future attacks. Is your staff trained in legal evidence collection requirements? Some things you and your staff should know include:

A. Evidence should be collected as soon as possible after an attack.
B. Evidence must be preserved in a permanent form (e.g., printed, CD ROM).
C. Collection and preservation of evidence should be witnessed by more than one person.
D. Evidence must be maintained in a pristine, unaltered state.
E. Evidence should be collected by trained experts.
F. Original evidence should be surrendered to law enforcement officials while copies should be maintained by corporate attorneys.
G. A log must be maintained identifying the chain of custody of all evidence materials.
H. Each person involved should write a memorandum outlining dates, times, and activity as soon as possible.

COMMENT

Prosecution of security violations is necessary!

[J] Local Administrator Access

One source of potential security problems on user systems is the use of local administrator access (local admin). There are two main levels access to a typical workstation:

A. **General.** This access level allows the users to make minor changes to their workstation. Installation of new hardware or software that makes changes to the workstation's operating system will require the assistance of the help desk. Having this level of access will generally ensure that your workstation is stable and secure.

B. **Local Admin.** This access level gives the users complete and unrestricted access to their workstation. This includes the ability to install any software or hardware, edit the registry, change file level permissions, and manage the default access accounts. Making these kinds of changes can cause serious security and stability issues.

Users that do not have local admin rights are protected from making many common mistakes that can cause security issues, such as installing unsecure software or incorrectly editing the registry. Therefore, many IT departments restrict the use of local admin rights by individual users. Many users however feel that they need local admin access to their workstation for the following reasons:

A. **Software installation.** Users do not always plan ahead and want the flexibility to be able to install software needed to do their job without waiting on IT. Any software that installs into the Windows or Program Files directories needs local admin rights to do so.

B. **Software updates.** Updating the software already installed on the workstation typically requires admin rights.

C. **Device drivers.** Installing device drivers for new hardware requires admin rights to the workstation.

D. **System settings.** System settings such as network configuration require admin rights.

For these and many other reasons, users ask for local admin access so that they do not have to wait for the help desk to update their workstation. An important function of IT is to provide workstations that are stable, managed, and secure. Giving users local admin rights to the workstations has the following potential risks:

A. **Malware.** Giving users local admin rights allows them to disable the security applications that protect their system, such as virus protection and firewalls. This makes it easier for malware to be introduced to their system.

B. **Productivity.** Having a standard operating environment for all users makes it easier for IT to support a stable system. Creating non-standard operating environment by individual users makes it much more difficult for IT to provide prompt and efficient support when problems arise.

C. **Licensing.** If anyone can install any software at any time onto their workstations, it becomes more difficult to ensure that all users are in compliance with licensing agreements. This can expose the company to potential legal liability if licensing agreements are violated.

In situations where employees believe that they cannot perform their jobs without having local admin rights to their workstations, consider implementing the following approval process:

A. The employee must ask his or her immediate supervisor to submit a formal request to the head of IT justifying the need for the employee to have local admin rights to the employee's workstation.

B. The request must include the business impact of not having local admin rights as well as the duration that local admin rights are needed. A duration of 1 year or less is recommended.

C. All requests should be reviewed by the head of IT as well as the organization's chief security officer.

D. All approved requests should be reviewed annually to ensure that all grants of local admin rights are still required.

Your policy for managing the user of local admin rights must take these factors into consideration. See Policy ITP-30-3 Local Administrator Access Policy as an example.

POLICY ITP-30-3. Local Administrator Access Policy

Policy #:	ITP-30-3	Effective:	03/18/15	Page #:	1 of 2
Subject:	Local Administrator Access Policy				

1.0 PURPOSE

This policy provides guidance on the user of local administrator rights (local admin) on company owed workstations. Giving a user local admin rights allows the user to have complete and unrestricted access to the operating system on their workstation.

2.0 SCOPE

The policy applies to all corporate computers and devices that store corporate information. It applies to all users of the organization's network, using any device that has access to the network.

3.0 POLICY

Granting local admin rights to user workstations introduces the following risks to the organization:

A. **Malware.** Giving a user local admin rights allows them to disable the security applications that protect their system, such as virus protection and firewalls. This makes is easier for malware to be introduced to their system.

B. **Productivity.** Having a standard operating environment for all users makes it easier for IT to support a stable system. When individual users create non-standard operating environment is makes it much more difficult for IT to provide prompt and efficient support when problems arise.

C. **Licensing.** If anyone can install any software at any time onto their workstations, it becomes more difficult to ensure that all users are in compliance with licensing agreements. This can expose the company to potential legal liability if licensing agreements are violated.

By default, only IT staff will have local admin access to their workstations. In situations where employees believe that they cannot perform their jobs without having local admin rights to their workstations, the following approval process must be followed:

A. The employee must ask their immediate supervisor to submit a formal request to the head of IT justifying the need for the employee to have local admin rights to their workstation.

B. The request must include the business impact of not having local admin rights as well as the duration that local admin rights are needed. The duration must be for 1 year or less.

C. All requests will be reviewed by the head of IT as well as the organization's chief security officer.

D. All approved requests are reviewed annually to ensure that all grants of local admin rights are still required.

4.0 REVISION HISTORY

Date	Revision #	Description of Change
03/18/15	1.0	Initial creation.

5.0 INQUIRIES

Direct inquiries about this policy to:

George Jenkins, CIO
Our Company, Inc.
2900 Corporate Drive
Columbus, OH 43215

Voice: 614-555-1234
Fax: 614-555-1235
E-mail: gjenkins@company.com

Revision #:	1.0	Supersedes:	N/A	Date:	03/18/15

§ 30.04 LEGAL ISSUES

[A] Overview

The data stores of companies have long been under siege by people who wish to exploit them for criminal purposes. Over the years, the repeated loss of data by various companies has led to a series of regulations that directly affect the daily efforts of IT departments. It is essential that IT Managers know about these legal issues as they may become personally liable for failing to follow these laws.

As with all legal questions, IT Managers must refer to their company's legal counsel for *written* guidance on what they must do to comply. Furthermore, IT Managers must monitor changes in the legal landscape to ensure their policies, procedures, and strategies do not lead the department into activities outside of the limits of these laws.

In general, recent laws address:

A. Ready availability of critical information such as medical records. This has required moving some archived data from tape (stored off-site) to online disks.
B. Records availability through data retention. These laws mandate how long specific data elements must be retained. The complexity is that data is often mixed up on storage devices, forcing the retention of entire pieces of media (such as an entire backup tape) for as long as the longest period for each data element on that media.
C. Data accuracy through software controls. Companies must now identify their internal control processes and verify that they provide adequate safeguards for the accuracy of financial reporting. These controls must be in place and monitored regularly to identify tampering.
D. Security of data records. Companies must safeguard from disclosure specific types of data. This data has long been protected by companies but now there is a legal requirement to ensure compliance. Examples are customer data and health records.

[B] Health Insurance Portability and Accountability Act (HIPAA)

The Health Insurance Portability and Accountability Act (HIPAA) requires securing and maintaining personal health information (PHI) for specific retention periods (depending on the type of information). While organizations possess this data, they must safeguard it from unauthorized access. Although this information may be on a wide range of media (x-ray photographs, paper records, electronic records), the primary challenge to the IT Manager is electronic availability, security, and retention.

Consideration for implementing HIPAA is similar to any other data security issue. Common practices include:

A. Password protection and authorization controls.
B. Hierarchies of security based on need to know. A doctor might need different information than a nurse.
C. Backup and retention of data and ensuring 100 percent data reliability.
D. Forms and releases must be scanned, saved, and available.
E. Health records must be retained for at least six years.
F. Automatic audit trail.
G. A business continuity plan is mandated as necessary to ensure records are readily available.

The process for safeguarding data is moving toward the increased use of fixed disks. DVDs and CDs create a security and control problem both because of the nature of the media and the ease of copying it. Such portable technologies bypass physical and electronic security measures. This will drive up online storage costs over time.

HIPAA's reach is long. Many professionals believe it extends to electronic mail and IM communications that discuss patient conditions or that include other medical data. Such messages must use encrypted communications to avoid interception. These communications, in turn, must match the retention levels for that type of information.

A good place to start researching a compliance program is the National Institute of Standards and Technology's (NIST) HIPAA Resource Guide. These standards provide a general requirements framework that should be a part of any compliance program.

[C] Sarbanes-Oxley Act (SOX)

Several cases of major corporate accounting fraud have led to the enactment of the Sarbanes-Oxley Act (SOX) requiring the safeguarding of sensitive corporate data. The act contains many sections. The part generally applicable to IT Managers is Section 404.

Section 404 requires that the Securities and Exchange Commission (SEC) publish rules governing internal controls to ensure that a publicly traded company's financial data is accurate. Since all companies rely on information technology to create this data, IT falls squarely in the middle of this law. Companies must now be able to certify IT processes annually as secure, comprehensive, and repeatable.

Rather than fight SOX-required changes, implement them as part of an overall IT process improvement initiative. Well-run IT shops have many of these safeguards already in place such as change management and information security, so the task is to identify and plug the gaps. IT must demonstrate that it has emplaced appropriate internal controls to manage any changes to software that play a significant part in financial controls or reports.

Special attention must be paid to:

A. Financial record retention systems and policies that manage them. They affect information collection, validation, analysis, and storage.
B. Data mining, scrubbing applications, and analysis systems because they jeopardize data integrity.
C. Data and systems security, because unauthorized access could severely and negatively impact the quality of reported information.
D. Ensure that all IT policies and procedures are documented and current. Include an annual review plan for all.

SOX constantly refers to "controls." A control is a checks-and-balance process ensuring that new systems or changes to existing systems function properly. This is present in most companies as their change control process. However, in most companies, there is a way to bypass the process or it is just an automatic approval. Correctly done, the change is properly tested, verified by others, and then verified again after implementation.

SOX requires an annual audit of all controls to verify their effectiveness. This implies keeping records during the year. Common control concepts encountered when implementing a SOX program include:

A. Documentation of each control and how it is supposed to work. IT Managers can perform their own audit and regularly compare how the documented process compares to reality. For example, the software development process, from inception to development standards to testing program to finally change control of installed modules.
B. The separation of responsibilities between the person requesting a change and the one approving it. People cannot approve their own documents. A list of who is authorized to approve what changes must be published.
C. The most common approval control points are change prioritization, test result approval, and rollout. All approvals must be written and recorded. Keep these records in a safe place. In most cases, there will be multiple people authorizing changes (IT Manager, IT quality technician, requestor, manager of department affected, etc.).
D. Audit and verify that controls are still in place and effective. The details are important. Event logs, audit trails, and reporting are key to meeting this goal.
E. Periodically test critical financial business processes to ensure they still work as planned. Keep records of all such checks along with what was checked, how it was verified, who did it, when, etc. Use a formal test plan and record the results.

COMMENT

SOX compliance does not end at the four walls of the company's offices. They include any outsourced functions as well. Be sure that any outsourced support (or contract labor) that touches any of the company's controls or controlled objects, also is compliant with the company's SOX program.

Key indicators of a well-run SOX compliance program are:

- Repeatable processes
- Change management
- Consistency of control testing and documentation throughout the organization
- Ongoing management emphasis through employee training and refresher training
- Proper authorization of changes

There are several models to choose from when selecting a roadmap for compliance. Each has its own strengths and costs. All models overlap in important areas.

- ISO17799—international standard for information security
- COSO—an SEC approved internal controls framework
- COBIT—a business focused framework based on COSO

COMMENT

An ironic twist is that SOX Section 404, the one that causes IT management the most problems, has the same identifier as the HTTP 404 error.

[D] Gramm-Leach-Bliley Act

The Gramm-Leach-Bliley Act covers any business significantly engaged in financial activities. It addresses the confidentiality of customer data. Responsibility for protecting the data from disclosure remains with the company even when the data is passed to a third party for use. Ensure all third parties are required by contract to secure the data at all times.

The Gramm-Leach-Bliley Act has two areas of emphasis:

A. The financial privacy rule governs collecting of customer's personal and financial information. It also applies to companies who receive this information.
B. The safeguards rule requires the design, implementation, and maintenance of safeguards to protect this data.

The act encourages the encryption of data in storage and in transit. It also recommends destroying data that is not needed, since this ultimately protects it from disclosure.

A criticism of the Gramm-Leach-Bliley Act is that it is more descriptive than prescriptive. The act leaves the definition of "protecting the security and confidentiality of information" up to each company.

COMMENT

More information is available from the Federal Trade Commission at *www.ftc.gov/privacy/privacyinitiatives/glbact .html*.

[E] SEC Rules

SEC rules have long mandated the collection and retention of financial records and anything pertaining to a securities transaction. More recently, the rules were updated to include electronic mail and instant messaging. The SEC found that these communications were involved in communicating to customers and between securities employees and yet the records of these communications were not made or retained.

Specifically, SEC Rules 17a-3 and -4 have implications for IT Managers and for IT securities team members. Companies now require comprehensive, auditable, and legally credible policies, practices, and systems to manage e-mail. Typically, these records must be retained for six years.

[F] Committee of Sponsoring Organizations (COSO)

In 1992, the Committee of Sponsoring Organizations (COSO) established a framework for the proper authorization, recording, and reporting of transactions. The SEC officially recognizes the COSO framework as adequate for establishing internal controls over financial reporting. COSO is also the basis for COBIT's professional standards for internal controls and auditing.

In the COSO framework, an internal control is a process—a way to approach an issue. It is about what people do, not what manuals say they ought to do. Internal controls only provide some assurance that something will occur, and not an absolute guarantee. Each internal control addresses a specific objective.

COSO identifies internal controls as processes designed to provide reasonable assurances regarding objectives in three areas:

A. Effectiveness and efficiency of operations.
B. Reliability of financial reporting.
C. Compliance with applicable laws and regulations.

The COSO framework measures five internal controls for each of the three areas:

A. Control environment—processes for managing and developing people in the organization and delegation of authority systems.
B. Risk assessment—identification and analysis of risks to achieving assigned objectives.
C. Control activities—policies and procedures for execution of management directives.
D. Information and communication—effective communication for running and controlling the business.
E. Monitoring—ongoing activities or separate evaluations.

[G] Control Objectives for Information and Related Technology (COBIT™)

COBIT was created by the Information Systems Audit and Control Association (ISACA) and the IT Governance Institute (ITGI). It describes a set of control objects for maximizing the benefits derived from the use of IT. It also describes appropriate IT governance and control. (COBIT is a trademark of the Information Systems Audit and Control Association and the IT Governance Institute.)

COBIT uses COSO definitions as the basis of its control objects, but extends the notion of control throughout the enterprise. It also makes the COSO principles and objectives applicable to the IT function. The COBIT control objectives provide a working document for IT management and staff, the control and audit functions, and business process owners. The conceptual framework includes:

A. Information criteria
B. IT resources
C. IT processes

The COBIT framework focuses IT process on the company's business. It strives to ensure IT resources are used responsibly and appropriately. IT Managers appreciate COBIT because it helps them to understand their IT systems and decide on the level of security and control necessary to protect their companies' assets through the development of an IT governance model.

§ 30.04[H]

While the full COBIT framework exceeds SOX Section 404 requirements, companies should consider customizing the applicable portions of COBIT for their own compliance requirements.

COMMENT

The IT Governance Institute (ITGI) advances international thinking and standards in directing and controlling an enterprise's information technology. It can be contacted at *www.itgi.org*.

A criticism of COBIT is that it describes what needs to be done, but never states how to do it. COBIT helps define processes for identifying and managing IT risk. Other existing standards must take up where COBIT leaves off. While every control objective is applicable to every organization, few companies are able to implement the entire COBIT process.

[H] Personal Information Protection and Electronic Documents Act (PIPEDA)

Canada has enacted the Personal Information Protection and Electronic Documents Act (PIPEDA). Among other things, this legislation governs the collection, use, and disclosure of information in commercial activities. Personal information is factual or subjective information in any form about an identifiable individual.

PIPEDA addresses ten principles for protecting gathering, retaining, and destroying information about people.

A. Accountability—an organization is responsible for protecting both personal information in its possession or that it transfers to a third party. Accountability for PIPEDA rests with individuals designated in a commercial enterprise.

B. Identifying purposes—an organization must identify the reasons for which personal information is collected either prior to or at the time of collection.

C. Consent—an organization is responsible for collecting, using, or disclosing personal information only with the individual's knowledge and consent. This requires an organization to document and retain all consent given and withdrawn.

D. Limiting collection prohibits organizations from collecting personal information indiscriminately or through deception. Each data element must have an identified purpose.

E. Limited use, disclosure, and retention means organizations must use or disclose personal information only for the purposes for which it was collected. Retain personal information only as long as necessary to fulfill the identified and consented-to purpose.

F. Accuracy—organizations must ensure that personal information is correct, complete, and up-to-date. The validity of the data is the commercial enterprise's responsibility. Implied is a process for identifying and correcting errors, and cross validating data.

G. Personal information must be secured against loss, theft, or unauthorized access. Safe destruction of the data is required when it is no longer needed. Always document destroyed data.

H. Organizations must publish their information management policies to employees and customers. Make it easy to find and understand.

I. Individuals can request access to their personal information, determine its appropriate use, and learn the names of third parties to whom it will be disclosed.

J. Legal guidelines exist for challenging a company's compliance with this act. Individuals dissatisfied with a company's collection or use of their data have a legal process to correct it.

[I]   Fair and Accurate Credit Transactions Act of 2003 (FACTA)

FACTA (Fair and Accurate Credit Transactions Act of 2003) governs records disposal. Consumer information is any record about an individual (paper or electronic) such as credit worthiness, reputation, characteristics, etc. It applies to companies that possess or maintain consumer reports for business purposes, regardless of industry.

FACTA reduces the risk of consumer fraud created by improper disposal of any consumer report record. FACTA requires that anyone that possesses or maintains covered consumer information take reasonable measures to protect against unauthorized access or use in connection with its disposal.

[J]   ISO 17799

ISO 17799 is the International Standard Organization's standard for information security. It is an adaptation of an earlier British Standard BS-7799. In the future, ISO will change the numeric designator to ISO-27002 as the ISO-27000 series has been set aside for information security.

ISO 17799 provides best practice recommendations on information security management for initiating, implementing, or maintaining information security management systems. The 2005 version of the standard contains the following 11 main sections:

A. Security policy
B. Organization of information security
C. Asset management
D. Human resources security

E. Physical and environmental security
F. Communications and operations management
G. Access control
H. Information systems acquisition, development, and maintenance
I. Information security incident management
J. Business continuity planning
K. Compliance

[K] Canadian Budget Measures Act (Bill 198)

Drafted in response to major corporate accounting scandals in the United States, the Canadian government enacted a law similar to the U.S. Sarbanes-Oxley Act (SOX). The Budget Measures Act increases the level of executive responsibility and accountability in Canadian companies. The law describes certification requirements, disclosure controls, and internal control requirements.

The law requires an annual certification by executives that their filings are true and do not omit facts. Like the SOX legislation, this means that the IT processes that contribute significantly to these reports must be tightly controlled to avoid accidental or purposeful manipulation. Internal controls must be established, tested, and used. Controls encompass the collection of information, its processing and summation.

These controls will significantly impact the design of data management systems. Records retention, security and overall management will force IT Managers in Canada to examine all of their existing systems for gaps.

A legally defensible records management system is an important part of a Budget Measures Act compliance program. Consistency in process across all IT systems is essential. This includes procedures, data retention schedules, policies, data disposal methods, etc. An important tool in consistency is clear documentation explaining what to do, how to do it, and when deviations are permitted.

31

DATA BACKUPS—THE KEY TO A PROMPT RECOVERY

§ 31.07   DATA RETENTION AND LEGAL MANDATES
      [A]   Overview
      [B]   Legal Mandates
      [C]   Do Not Overdo It

§ 31.01 OVERVIEW

[A] Purpose and Scope

Data can be stored on a range of media. Paper, CD, and magnetic tape all hold data of some sort. Data backups are "safety" copies of data for use if the original data medium is destroyed or damaged. A backup can be a copy made on carbon paper, copy machine, or more typically, a nonvolatile storage disk. The potential cost to the company if data was lost justifies the time and expense that goes into making and handling backup copies of computer data.

The IT world handles massive amounts of data. Where even 30 years ago the bulk of the company's data was stuffed in file cabinets and dusty boxes, it is now spread across a wide range of computers and servers. The task of the IT Manager is to ensure that data is safeguarded, available, and readable in the event that the company requires it again.

Computers are rather fragile devices. Environmental factors—such as extreme temperatures, dust, magnetic radiation, and moisture—can cause them to fail suddenly. Add to this the chance of hardware failure such as a disk head crash or even a stray voltage surge that disables some components and it is easy to see the harsh climate in which computers exist.

To protect computers, or at least the larger, less portable ones, secured and filtered rooms called data centers are built. These rooms have filtered air, filtered electricity, thick walls, a secured entry, and a long list of safeguards to protect the equipment.

As a further safeguard, copies of the data should be periodically made and stored off-site in a secure location. This off-site storage should be updated often (usually daily). Once the data departs the cozy safety of the data center, it must again be protected from threats to its integrity until it is safely and properly stored at the off-site facility.

Data backups are the key to any disaster recovery plan. Equipment can be replaced. Buildings can be leased. However, the expense of recreating corporate data from scratch is far more than most companies can support. If an IT Manager misses this point, his or her long-term employment outlook is bleak.

The challenge for the IT Manager is to find the best way to ensure this is done properly. In the past, data was stored in a computer room on the mainframe computer and IT had complete control to shut it down (usually on Saturdays at midnight) to make full backups. For some companies, this is still the best method.

Most companies however cannot backup their data this way. Their customers expect around-the-clock service every day of the year. This includes hospitals, Web-based enterprises, and virtual companies whose employees are located around the world. Web applications must be available 24 hours per day—every day of the week. This means those files can never be closed.

Complicating matters is that data is collected and distributed among a variety of locations. The increased use of notebook PCs means important company data is floating around and probably not being backed up regularly, if at all. Consider for a moment the company CEO's PC. What might be stored in it? How well protected from theft or a harsh environment is it, and how likely is it to have a daily data backup stored safely away?

[B] Critical Policies to Develop Based on This Chapter

Using the material discussed in this chapter, you will be able to create the following policies:

A. Mandate a program for data backups.
B. Workstations, notebook PCs, and other data-creating/retaining devices.
C. Off-site storage.
D. Data retention.
E. Legal mandates.

Always develop policies based on the local situation. Successful managers cannot issue appropriate guidance if the policies are written with another company's situation or location in mind.

§ 31.02 DATA RECOVERY

[A] Types of Backups

The frequency of data backups depends on how much the data changes over time. Files containing purchase orders and employee attendance records probably change daily, while files supporting end-of-the-year accounting reports probably only change once per year. Rather than tediously evaluating and tagging each file, most data backups copy the entire contents of a disk volume to tape.

Typically, companies make many types of data backups:

A. Weekly (or full) backups are time consuming but everything on every server or mainframe disk is copied to the backup media.
B. Daily (or incremental) backups copy only those files where something has changed since the last full or incremental backup.
C. Mirrored disk where a copy of the data is always up to date and available. A variation is for the mirrored data to reside in a distant data center.
D. Journaling transmits transactions to an off-site storage facility as they occur. This is also known as a continuous backup.
E. Create special backups when specific files must be transported.

COMMENT

Although this chapter refers to backups as copied to magnetic tape, they can just as easily be stored on any other nonvolatile media such as optical disk or a disk pack located a significant distance away.

[B]   The Data Backup Lifecycle

An interesting aspect of data backups is the belief that once the backup media is full, the job is done. The purpose of data backups is not to make copies. The goal is to have something readily available and technically readable when needed. Therefore, the task of making a backup does not end until that copy is reused for a future backup or destroyed. The implication is that the person responsible for creating the data backups is responsible for it throughout its "life cycle," including transportation for off-site storage and its safekeeping in the facility. This requires establishing a chain of custody throughout the media's "lifetime."

Once filled with data, move the media promptly off-site. Data backups sitting in the data center will protect the company against damaged files, but if the data center is destroyed, the company will not be protected. To achieve its full potential, the backup must be transported to the off-site storage facility and securely locked.

Inspect the off-site facility periodically. Take nothing for granted. Companies change, priorities shift, and new people come onto the job. What was well done in the past may now be in a shambles. Verify that the climate control of the vehicle transporting the media keeps it within an acceptable range. Ensure that media is closely protected during transit. Verify these same issues inside the storage facility itself.

COMMENT

IT Managers in small companies sometime take their backup tapes home for safekeeping. Although these people mean well, this does not address the issue of protecting the tape while in transit and storage. Few houses or cars are climate controlled or as physically secure as a data center. A backup only has to fail once—and can do so at the worst possible time.

[C]   Recovery Time Objective (RTO)

One of the critical considerations for data backup planning is the company's recovery time objective (RTO). RTO is the cornerstone of a disaster recovery plan. The RTO identifies how long the company can afford to wait after a disaster to recover its critical data systems. (See Exhibit 31-1.) This time includes locating a facility, obtaining equipment, preparing it for use, and recovering the data/software from the media. In the meantime, money will be flowing out of the company with very little flowing in. Few firms can survive this for long.

EXHIBIT 31-1. The Recovery Time Objective Identifies How Long a Company Can Afford to Wait to Recover Its Data Systems

Instant Failover   1 Minute
Data Shadowing
Journaling
Hot Site Recovery
Quick Ship
Mobile Data Center
   1 Week +

Because the RTO identifies how long the company can wait for the backup data to be restored, by implication it determines the backup strategy. A company that can afford a long-term outage (such as a Minnesota golf course in the dead of winter) can wait for as long as it takes (well, at least a few weeks) until alternate equipment is installed and the backup tapes methodically loaded. A company that cannot tolerate anything but the briefest outage might demand instant recovery. Instant recovery requires an always-on remote data center that mirrors the active data center's activity. When the primary data center fails, then the back-up operation kicks in. However, this means twice the cost (dual servers, dual disks, and redundant high speed data connection between them). Instant recovery requires a "hot" backup with the alternate servers always on and data mirrored from the primary system. As is obvious, the faster the data recovery, the more expensive it is.

Magnetic tape can only spin so fast; it takes time to restore servers. To shorten this time, some companies establish shadowing data centers, use hot site contracts, or disk-to-disk backups. The solution selected will often be as unique as the company's data requirements. RTO should be a major consideration whenever evaluating any data backup changes.

COMMENT

The Recovery Time Objective focuses on the recovery of critical files, not everything in the data center. (Critical files are identified by the Business Impact Analysis.)

[D] Recovery Point Objective (RPO)

The recovery point objective (RPO) is the amount of data that must be added to the recovered files to bring the business records back up to date. For example, in a company that only operates from Monday through Friday, a full data backup is made every Saturday and stored off-site. Incremental backups are made each workday night of any files changed that day. If the data center was destroyed on a Sunday, then no data would be lost because the full backup was made on Saturday and no files had been changed since. However, if the disaster struck on late Monday afternoon, then all of the data that was added to the files that day would be lost (anything changed between the Saturday morning full backup and the point of incident).

Consider what this data might be: online transactions, data keyed from documents, or real-time database corrections. What could be used to recreate these adds, changes, and deletes? Think of a company with 100 people in the accounting department and all of the data they change in a day. Would it be possible to recreate all of their work from a single day? How much of a data loss can the company survive?

RPO is important because it indicates the tolerable time between data back-ups. After the backup is restored, the data lost from the Monday transactions must somehow be recreated. If this loss is not tolerable, then a real time backup strategy may be required. Source documents are rarely retained and many transactions are now entered online without a paper trail. One solution to this is to "journal" or record every transaction that occurs throughout the day and then discard the file after the next good backup. However, this may only cover a small part of the many transactions that pass through a data center in a day.

COMMENT

The Recovery Point Objective determines the frequency and type of data backups. For example, medical records or stock transactions cannot lose many hours of backups so a mirroring solution is required. However, a grocery store's inventory can lose point-of-sale connection for several hours. The cost of recounting the shelves once every several years is less than paying for real time data mirroring.

[E] Recovering Data

Backups are only made so that, if needed, the data on them can be reloaded onto another machine. Typically, this means recalling the backup media from off-site storage and then reloading the file. Of course, this means the support person must know which tape holds the desired file. Often the software that manages the backup provides this file list.

A problem with this scenario is that users seldom want to wait to recall a tape from off-site storage. Many people think "When was the last time the data center was flattened?" and consequently do not send their backup tapes off-site until the next backup is made. However, this means the tapes going off-site are at least one week old. While this method provides a higher service level, it pushes the RPO to at least one week—which is too much time for any company to recover from.

COMMENT

Few IT Managers personally verify their data backup and off-site storage process. Never take for granted this is exactly as it should be. Pull out the documented backup and off-site storage process and walk through it.

Some companies reach a compromise by making two copies of the weekly backups. One set is stored off-site the next day and the other set is retained for prompt file restores. See Policy ITP-31-1 Data Backups and Retention Policy as an example.

POLICY ITP-31-1. Data Backups and Retention Policy

Policy #:	ITP-31-1	Effective:	03/18/13	Page #:	1 of N
Subject:	Data Backups and Retention Policy				

1.0 PURPOSE

This policy guides the frequency and type of data backups. It also addresses the length of time that backups must be retained.

2.0 SCOPE

The policy applies to all devices that hold or accumulate data in the support of company operations, to include telecommunications, network applications, desktop units, notebooks, tablets, etc.

3.0 POLICY

The IT Manager is responsible for making and retaining an adequate number of data backup "safety" copies. To accomplish this, the IT Manager may create further policies and procedures and delegate authority to implement them.

3.1 Devices. Data backups will be made of all devices that contain or collect data, to include at a minimum:

    A. Servers and their internal disks
    B. Storage Area Networks
    C. Telecommunications switches (PBX)
    D. Network Controllers
    E. Desktop PCs
    F. Notebook PCs
    G. Programmable Logic Controllers

3.2 Types of Data

    A. Personal data is not to be stored on company equipment.
    B. Legal compliance data—must be identified. The label on the backup media must include what data it contains and the appropriate retention period. Care must be taken to ensure the data is securely stored.
    C. Business critical data—must be identified. The label on the backup media must include what data it contains and the appropriate retention period. Quick access to this data is required in the event of a disaster.
    D. Non-critical data—must be identified. Non-critical data is not legally required to be retained for a period of time. Typically, this data is deleted after 13 months. The label on the backup media must include what data it contains and the appropriate retention period.

3.3 Data Backup Frequency. The frequency of data backups is determined by how frequently and how much a data storage element changes.

    A. Full backups weekly—*all* data is backed up weekly and retained for 13 months.
    B. Incremental backups daily for changing data. These are retained for 30 days.
    C. Off-site journaling is used for immediate backup of critical data that cannot be reconstructed from daily backups.

3.4 Data Retention
The company's Records Management Office determines data retention. The retention period is determined by the data element with the longest required retention period on that backup media. If the contents of the media are not known, then the media must be retained for a minimum of seven years.

3.5 Off-site Storage

    A. Data backups will be transported off site every morning after the backups are created.

B. Once every calendar quarter, the IT Manager will audit the off-site storage process to ensure that:
1. Media is kept in a climate-controlled environment during transit.
2. The storage facility is secure.
3. The storage facility is climate controlled.
4. The data center security is appropriate for media going out and for media coming in.
5. There is a documented chain of custody for backup media from the point it leaves the data center until it is returned.

3.6 Data Destruction

Data that has outlived its usefulness to the business, and whose age exceeds the legal limits for retention, must be properly destroyed.

A. The media must be rendered permanently unreadable. This is primarily accomplished through physical destruction. Paper documents are shredded, burned, and the ashes pulped. CDs and magnetic media are shredded.
B. When data is destroyed, it must be documented as to whom, by what means, when, and what the data consisted of.

3.7 Legal Mandates

A. SEC Rules 17a-3 and -4. Brokers and dealers must retain records for 6 years.
B. Gramm-Leach-Bliley Act—financial institutions must ensure confidentiality of customer data.
C. HIPAA—health records must be retained for a minimum of 6 years.
D. Sarbanes-Oxley—public company accounting records must be retained for 7 years.

4.0 REVISION HISTORY

Date	Revision #	Description of Change
03/18/13	1.0	Initial creation.

5.0 INQUIRIES

Direct inquiries about this policy to:

George Jenkins, CIO
Our Company, Inc.

2900 Corporate Drive
Columbus, OH 43215

Voice: 614-555-1234
Fax: 614-555-1235
E-mail: gjenkins@company.com

Revision #:	1.0	Supersedes:	N/A	Date:	03/18/13

§ 31.03   DATA BACKUPS—MAJOR RESPONSIBILITIES

[A]   Overview

A basic management rule is that if no one is responsible for an action, then nothing will happen. The policy for data backups must clearly identify the person responsible for ensuring that all data backups are properly made, transported, and stored off-site. Delegate this person authority to ensure the cooperation of all IT staff. In most companies, the person appointed to this responsibility is the IT Operations Manager.

A comprehensive data backup program encompasses many areas such as:

- Telecommunications switches are simply special-purpose computer servers. Should the voice-mail system be backed up? How often should this be done and would the recovered data be worthwhile?
- Network devices take time to configure and are set to specific firmware versions. Yet in the end, is it easier to spend the time periodically backing it up rather than recreating the data?

Each of the IT Managers should have a role to play in a successful backup program. Any one of the individuals could inadvertently undermine what the company believes to be a comprehensive and reliable program.

[B]   IT Operations Manager

Traditionally, the data center operations manager is responsible for managing the company's data backups. This is an outgrowth of the old data center days when all of the company's computer data was stored in the fixed disks drives in "the glass house." Over time, the world has changed from a single mainframe to multitudes of servers proliferating across the company. What was once nearby and manageable is now spread out of sight and in some cases, its existence known only to a few.

COMMENT

Like all IT processes, backing up data to tape can create a log of errors that must be monitored and investigated to avoid partially backing up—or skipping—critical files during a backup.

Appointing the IT Operations Manager to manage backups is easy since most of the disk and tape backups still reside in the data center. Once appointed, make sure the person appointed is clearly responsible for the success of the *entire* program. This person must create policies and procedures to ensure safeguards are followed. He must then drive these processes throughout the company to ensure they are followed.

Responsibilities for this position might include:

A. Ensuring that all data center disks are protected with off-site data backups. It is possible to rationalize which parts of which disk volumes should be backed up, but the time saved would be more than lost in the ongoing management of such an arrangement.

B. Educating the company on the importance (and limitations) of data backups and the many places they need to be made (e.g., network devices, telephone PBX, voice mail, PC, remote servers).

C. Contracting for an off-site data backup storage facility or arranging for storage at a distant company-owned facility. This includes a secure courier service to protect media en route.

D. Periodically inspecting the security, handling, and storage of media stored off-site. Document each inspection for later reference.

E. Validating that media returning from the storage facility is still readable. Often testing is not necessary as it is accomplished with every successful file restore. The Operations Manager must ensure that all media types are verified, not just the troublesome few.

F. Establishing and publishing standards for marking backup media. A consistent naming approach makes media management much easier.

G. Establishing a program to "retire" media that has been used so many times that it may be unreliable. This ensures the media is properly destroyed and not just tossed in the trash (where it might be read by an enterprising thief).

H. Actively seeking out and ensuring that company servers located outside of the data center are properly backed up.

I. Ensuring that a copy of all company software (written in-house and third party) is maintained off-site. As software is patched, this must be kept current. (In some environments, software must be reloaded and cannot be directly restored from media.)

COMMENT

One of the authors was the Operations Manager at a data center but was locked out of the data management functions of one section of the servers. They were managed by one of the systems administrators. That person decided, without telling anyone else, that it was not necessary to back up some of the servers since they were for reference and never changed. Over time, the backup tapes for these servers rotated through and were overwritten with a different backup. When a disk crashed on one of the "reference" servers, active production files were discovered running on that machine. There was no way to recover either the files or the production data.

[C] Database Manager

Not every backup is a simple copy out and then back in. Some database systems will not work this way. The method for making database backups depends on how the data will be later reloaded, such as a dump/rebuild or a direct copy. An important person in the development of a backup program is the database administrator (DBA). With around-the-clock service now the norm, the DBA must ensure that the architecture of the systems enables the timely backup of all databases and supporting files.

In addition to being backed up, the database must be able to be recovered quickly. Often this exercise is performed during version upgrades or during a small crisis. Approach each database management system separately as each may have its own unique recovery requirements.

[D] Software Manager

Wages for software developers are expensive. The loss of code created by a major development effort can not only set back a company's progress but also create a major financial loss. Software managers must ensure that the data backup strategy is considered for each new system developed.

COMMENT

Sometimes applications servers are not backed up regularly, as they are constantly changing the code. This is wrong. If that server disappeared tomorrow, how many man-hours of labor are lost, and how much more is required to recreate the code. Always back up development servers by the same schedule as the production data—even if they are located on a server disconnected from the main network.

There are files other than databases that support applications. Parameter files and other fixed reference files may be essential to software operation. These files must be closed or copied for backup. In addition to copies of source code, software often depends on third-party programs. The source code and license keys for these programs must also be stored off-site for recovery during a disaster.

COMMENT

One of the major problems with updating software for Y2K compliance (converting year fields to four digits) dealt with lost source code. Many programs could not be updated because no one knew where the original code was. Some companies felt it was cheaper to simply upgrade to a new system.

Also, store a copy of each purchased software package off-site along with the licenses proving the number of copies purchased.

[E] Network Manager

Network devices are essentially special-purpose computers. They contain configuration and software versions that are important to the company's continued operation. If a firewall, router, or bridge were physically damaged, it could be replaced and reconfigured. However, once the replacement device is in place, where are the configuration data and logic rules to reload? If this information must be reconstructed from memory or old documents, how long will this prolong the outage? With backups and documentation (paper backups) of configuration information, network devices can be recovered more quickly.

The network manager must identify all devices that contain data and arrange to back them up. Network data is not normally large. For disaster recovery purposes, it is usually printed in documents for reference in rebuilding the network. For recovering individual devices, it is often backed up to the data center—over the network! Sending the data to the data center allows it to be backed up along with the normal systems backups and the network team avoids handling tapes. Paper copies of network configuration information should be maintained in the off-site storage facility and updated as devices change or at least monthly.

[F]   Shop Floor Systems Manager

Servers spring up like weeds in the most unusual places. Time and attendance servers may be found in a payroll office cabinet. Servers controlling electronic locks may be under a desk in the security office. Shop floor monitoring servers may be cached away all across a factory. Each of these represents important company information that should be copied and stored off-site.

Sometimes these orphan servers are isolated from the corporate network. Locating them is the first challenge. Backing them up is the next one as the users may resist anything that threatens their total control. This is where the company policy is handy to establish the requirement for backups. The key is to teach them how an IT backup protects them. Often this will deflate most of their arguments.

The first option is to back these devices up over the network. This will eliminate the handling of media by the users. If that is not possible, then it may be necessary to purchase additional hardware. Leave nothing to chance. Provide preprinted labels using the company's standard media marking format along with a supply of the media. Create a time-controlled program that will automatically make the backup during a scheduled quiet period. A process for delivering the backups to the data center for inclusion in the off-site storage containers must be provided.

Some servers, such as shop floor control servers, only need the software backed up. The data can be reloaded from the main computers. However, if the server collects historical data that is essential to the company, then that data must also be backed up.

[G]   Telecommunications Manager

Telephone switches and their supporting devices are special-purpose computers. They use configuration files for switching, voice-mail files for holding messages, and automated attendant files for routing calls. All of these should be carefully recorded on backup media and, where appropriate, in print.

Some data systems do not recover well. Installing a new telephone switch may take just as long as configuring the backup. It all depends on if a small part of the switch was damaged or the entire telephone switching room is gone.

Voice-mail systems and automated attendants are good candidates for restoring from backups. Current and old voice-mail messages may be important to conducting the company's business. They also may fall under the legal data retention of such laws as the Sarbanes-Oxley Act or various SEC regulations.

(When in doubt about data retention, always consult the company's legal advisor as requirements vary based on the industry the company serves.)

§ 31.04 DESIGNING FOR BACKUPS

[A] Overview

Designing for backups balances the competing requirements of several groups—each with a legitimate business concern. It sounds simple, yet it is quite complex. Consider these three contending parties:

A. **Operators.** Operators are pressed by management to minimize the number of tapes used and the amount of time required to make backups. Tapes are expensive, so the fewer that are used, the lower the cost. From a labor perspective, this translates into fewer tapes to handle. Operators will use software to compress data onto tapes and use a backup method that selects volumes for backups based on how quickly they can be backed up.

B. **System administrators.** They are most interested in the availability of files for restoration when they need them. Decompressing a tape to find the desired files takes time, so they prefer uncompressed media. Also, they might prefer the tapes to correspond to disk volumes rather than from across a variety of storage devices. Further, they want the tapes to remain readily available on-site for prompt file recovery.

C. **Disaster recovery managers.** Their major concern is that critical files are segregated from the rest of the files so that in a disaster, only the files required for a recovery are on the tapes to be loaded. This greatly reduces recovery time and helps the company to meet its recovery time objective. In addition, tapes must be *immediately* moved off-site after backups are completed.

COMMENT

A complicating factor is the legal retention for a piece of data. A piece of backup media must be retained (and not reused) for as long as the longest legal retention time for a single data item. Therefore, it may save a company some expense by separating data into long-term and short-term retention when creating backups instead of mixing them.

This illustrates just three of the primary contending groups who use data backups. Three different requirements, three different technical strategies, and all address some business requirement. It is up to the IT Operations Manager to determine which approach is best suited for the company.

If the equipment allows, two copies of the full backups can be made. This requires a tape loader with sufficient capacity to hold the media or someone to refill it. In this case, one set of tapes should be retained on-site for use in recovering files and the other copy is promptly sent off-site for disaster recovery.

Backing up an open file can be a challenge. Backup software typically skips an open file since it is possible that an update will occur halfway through the copy, which would make the file unreadable later. Yet if the file is critical to the company, it is all the more important to make a backup of it. Software developers must ensure they do not design their systems so files cannot be backed up. If 24/7 availability is required, an alternate backup strategy must be in place prior to the "go live" date.

[B] Data Mirroring

Data mirroring is a set of on-site disks that are exact duplicates of the primary production file. The process for keeping the two copies in sync vary, but the idea is that as updates are made to one file, it is reflected in the other almost instantaneously. When it is time to back up the database, the mirror connection is "broken" leaving the primary database to continue running while the mirror becomes a snapshot of the database at the moment the connection was shattered. The tape backup is made of this snapshot. After the backup is completed, the mirror is reconnected and reconnected with the primary disk bank. Of course, like all technology-based solutions, this approach depends on expensive hardware to implement.

There are several issues with this approach:

A. Expense—since the amount of disk required will be double.
B. Data mirroring addresses high availability but not disaster recovery. Backups must still be made and moved off-site.
C. A corruption in the primary file will likely be reflected in the mirror, making them both unusable.

A variation on this is data vaulting where the "mirror" is maintained in a distant off-site, secure facility. This provides several advantages to the company. It eliminates the need to make backups for emergency recovery since the data is already loaded off-site and ready to attach to a recovered server. (However, this does not fulfill legal data retention requirements since the mirror is always changing and sometimes backup media is retained as a data "snapshot" for many years.)

Vaulting requires a high-speed data line from the data center to the vaulting site. An alternative is to send it through a virtual private network (VPN) over a high-speed Internet line. The transmission media selected will depend on the size and frequency of transactions to be recorded.

[C]   Journaling

Some companies have a very tight recovery point objective. They cannot recreate or afford to lose any of their data. Examples include stock trading, banking, and credit card transactions systems. For these companies, restoring to yesterday's backups is not an option.

To support these environments, a journaling process can be used. This records every transaction onto a backup system, often located off-site. These micro-incremental backups can be used to recreate all transactions up to the point of failure.

[D]   Data Retention

How long should data backups be kept? It depends on what they are being made for. If the backups are made for local business reasons, then they are kept for as long as they satisfy these reasons. If they are kept for legal reasons, then the laws will say how long to keep them.

To build a history, a series of archives was established. Daily backups (incremental) were kept for seven days and then recycled. Weekly backups were retained for a month. The last weekly backup of the month was retained for 12 months as the monthly backup. The last monthly backup was retained for seven years as the annual backup. At that point, seven years was how far back a tax audit could reach.

In times long past, backups were made so that files could be restored. Once per week, a full set of backups was made. Every weekday after that, incremental backups were made. Incremental backups only copy files that were changed that day. At the end of the week, usually on Saturday night, the next set of full backups was made.

Of course, there are gaps here. If a file is created one day and deleted the next, it would never show up on the annual backups. Some companies addressed this by keeping weekly backups for a year. This still did not fully address the problem, but it was a compromise between coverage and the cost of the tape media.

Those days are gone. We now live in the world of Sarbanes-Oxley, HIPAA, and others. It is now imperative that the IT Manager obtain from the company's legal advisor a written statement of how long to keep each type of data to fulfill legal mandates.

COMMENT

Some companies strive to maintain the smallest amount of backup data possible. The less data there is available to search, the less the company must provide for a litigant during legal "discovery." This is especially important for e-mail and instant messaging archives.

§ 31.05   MEDIA HANDLING, TRANSPORTATION, AND STORAGE

[A]   Overview

It is always interesting to watch people unfamiliar with backups. They believe the job is done once the tape is filled. That is only the beginning. The backup media must be properly stored in shipping containers and safely conveyed to the storage site. The vehicle transporting them must be climate controlled and protected from dirt, magnetic influences, etc. It would not be appropriate for the tapes to sit in the back of a car while the driver stops for lunch in the middle of the Arizona summer (or the depths of a Montana winter). Throughout its "life" (from creation to its later reuse in the data center), the media must exist in the same type of secure environment as found in the data center.

To ensure that this is the case, the courier service used to transport the media must be evaluated periodically to ensure it correctly handles the media both going to the storage facility and returning from it. Tapes must be climate controlled and controlled through a "chain of custody" to avoid compromise.

A further check is to verify the extent of the courier's liability if the data is lost. If the courier is reputable, this potential loss helps to sharpen their attention for proper handling of backups. If the courier service is the "low bidder," then it may be the weak link in the data security chain.

COMMENT

In April 2005, the Associated Press reported that a major discount broker lost one of its backup tapes while in transit. The company began informing 200,000 people of the potential data compromise.

[B]   Marking Media for Ready Identification

If there were only a single tape to send off, life would be simple. In most companies, there is a series of tapes to store. Clearly identify each of these. In some manner, this identification must be cross-referenced to a list of the files on the media. Files should be able to be located both electronically (the fast way) and manually (visually scanning a list of which files are on which tape).

Data centers using automated tape loaders take advantage of bar-coded serial numbers on the tapes. The operator loads the machine full of tapes and returns when they are full. The media management software (which controls the tape loader) keeps track of which file is on which tape.

However this is done, a standard process for marking media should be included in the data backup policy. This will allow the media for remote sites, telecommunications, network and any other users to be readily identifiable as to where it came from and when it was made.

COMMENT

When writing the policy, develop a set of markings and where the label should go for all types of media used. The telephone system may use one type, the network machines another, etc. Typically this includes tape cartridges (each type may be different), CDs, floppy disks, etc.

[C]   Periodic Inspection

IT Managers spend a considerable amount of effort establishing and maintaining a secure environment for their equipment. Snug within this cocoon sits the company's data. Once that data is copied to backup media, effort must be made to ensure it stays safe. As the media is handed over for transportation to the storage facility, ensure it is guarded every step of the way. Follow a package through the entire process from end to end. Critical areas include things that would make the data less secure and things that would harm the media, making it less reliable to read.

COMMENT

The data Operations Manager should audit the off-site storage process at least twice per year. Visit the storage space and look for lax security, structural problems, etc. Be sure to stand in front of the company's containers on the rack and then look around. Don't accept a tour through "the nice section" and not see where the company's valuable data is actually kept.

The policy for data backups should include mandates for the IT Operations Manager to verify the security of backups. This includes ensuring:

A. Media is delivered for off-site storage in a locked, labeled container.

B. The media leaving the data center is handed directly to the courier. (Identification is required—every time.)
C. The courier does not make unauthorized stops along the way.
D. The media is secured in a controlled climate during the entire trip.
E. The media is received at the storage facility and promptly locked away.

Things to look for include:

A. Media is not kept in a climate-controlled environment during transit. This might mean tapes deforming in a hot car trunk while the courier takes a leisurely summer lunch break. The same would be true for a bitterly cold day while the media is left in an unheated space.
B. The storage facility security is insufficient.
C. The storage facility is not climate controlled.
D. The data center security is lax for media going out and for media coming in. Examples would be unattended data containers lying about or containers sent to the wrong customer.

[D] Destroying Old Media

At some point, backup media may be damaged, no longer usable, or needed. These items cannot be casually tossed into the trash as some enterprising thief may still read them—even if the data is past the legal expiration date. Media must be destroyed in a controlled manner.

COMMENT

The custodian of the backup media may be legally liable if data is willfully destroyed to obstruct an investigation.

Most companies use a third-party service to shred or burn expired media. Before the media is shipped off-site, it should be logged as to what items were shipped for destruction and when. The third-party company should provide a report detailing which items were destroyed, on what day, by whom, and the method used. Refer to the company's legal advisor for how long to keep data destruction records.

Why is this important? If a court order arrives for a legal "discovery" and specific data files are included, a list of destroyed media will identify which items are no longer available. Otherwise, the company will be uncertain as to what is available and spend a considerable amount of time chasing down something that may no longer exist. In addition, the researching party may suspect that any media that is not produced may have been hidden.

COMMENT

Some companies offer on-site destruction. The IT Manager can carry the container of obsolete media to the truck and watch its destruction to be sure it is unreadable.

§ 31.06 WORKSTATION, NOTEBOOK PC, AND DATA COLLECTION STATION BACKUPS

[A] Overview

Workstations, notebook PCs, and other data collection devices, by their nature, create, process, and collect data from many sources. This data may be of great value to the company. It also may be difficult or impossible to recreate. The problem is how to capture this data and back it up.

Making a data backup is not that hard. Connect the PC to the company's data network and copy everything from the disk to the data center. At some later point, copy this data to backup media. Take a moment to consider what data has been copied. How much space was required to copy the operating system (which is not needed for a recovery)? How much space was required to copy the application programs, which likewise are not necessary? All that is needed is the data! How can it be separated?

[B] Identifying the Problem

The issue is how to back up the data without also copying the programs. Microsoft's Windows program is on most corporate PCs. It requires about 2 GB of storage to run. Copying this over to backup media not only wastes time but also creates unneeded copies of software.

Over the years, many ways to accomplish this have been attempted.

A. In the early days of PCs, companies tried backing them up to a roaming tape drive. This unit sat on a cart and stopped by to back up the PC's disk while the owner went to lunch. However, the cost of the tape controller cards (required for each PC) kept the number of users small.

B. Another way was to minimize the hard disk size on the workstation to be just sufficient to support the software thereby forcing users to save their data on network drives. These drives would be backed up along with the rest of the company's data. The problem was that network storage was much more expensive than desktop storage so the company ended up buying additional PC disks.

C. More recently, notebook PCs and desktop units have come equipped with CD writers. On the surface this seems like an easy way for individuals to back up their own data. The problem is that data that was secure behind passwords and other security devices is now floating around on uncontrolled CDs that are stuffed into drawers or lying on desktops.

[C]   Separating Data from the Software

The first step is to separate the data from the software. Most PCs are backed up to a server in the data center over the corporate data network. Although not a big deal for one unit, it can stress the network if 500 PCs all dump at the same time on a Friday afternoon.

Copying files can take one of two approaches: inclusive or exclusive. The inclusive approach copies all of the files. It is simple to implement and trades ease of administration for a heavier load on the resources.

Exclusive copying examines the file suffix of every file being copied. It excludes copying any file with an .exe or .com suffix. Other file types also can be added to the "stop list." A variation on this is to not copy any files from specific directories that are found in the company's standard PC image, such as the operating system or applications software.

Another approach is to require all users to store their PC data in one master directory, such as "My Documents." Anything in this directory is backed up and everything else is not. This can be implemented with a bit of user training. Also, any software installed by the company that saves files should be set to default their storage somewhere under the data directory.

§ 31.07   DATA RETENTION AND LEGAL MANDATES

[A]   Overview

Companies retain data for their own historical uses. Beyond that, from a business standpoint, this media can be recycled or destroyed. In reality, it passes from data retained for a business need to data retained for legal purposes. Many laws dictate the length of time certain types of data must be retained. During this retention period, the data must be safeguarded in the same manner as any other important, confidential data.

[B]   Legal Mandates

Legally, different types of data have different retention periods. Legal mandates must be based on opinions provided by the company's legal representative. Legal requirements must be written and included in the backup policy. This will prevent people along the chain of custody from claiming ignorance. These legal mandates should be reviewed and updated at least annually.

The longer media is retained, the greater the storage costs will be. Backup media equipment evolves. It requires the company to retain old media reading equipment or to contract with a company that can provide this service.

This is complicated by how the media backup was made. If all of one type of data was saved on one backup device, that retention period is based on what the data is. Since most companies mix all of their data together, all of the media must be kept for as long as the retention period of the data with the longest time.

The balance to this is to keep no more data on hand than is necessary. In a legal investigation, there is no need to leave pieces of information that may inaccurately paint a picture of something illegal. When media has passed its legal expiration date, it should be properly destroyed, and that destruction recorded for future reference.

A list of legal mandates and how they apply to a company should be provided by its legal advisor. With the fast pace of technical innovation, these laws are somewhat open to interpretation. Some of the current laws that impact the retention of data include:

A. The Sarbanes-Oxley Act of 2002 (SOX), which applies to publicly traded companies. The Act requires IT, accounting & finance, and legal to collaborate on the implementation of a published records management program.
   1. Section 404—discusses internal controls on information technology for financial control.
   2. Section 302—effective internal controls are designed and maintained to ensure officers are aware of all material information.
B. The Health Insurance Portability and Accountability Act (HIPAA), which details how personal health information can be electronically maintained or transmitted.
C. The Gramm-Leach-Bliley Act, which protects consumers' personal financial information being held by financial organizations.
D. Various tax and accounting rules, which require the retention of accounting data for seven years.

[C]   Do Not Overdo It

A fool's approach to data retention is to try and keep everything and in that way hope to miss nothing. This is foolish because storage requirements would grow and grow until the expense bankrupts a company. Data retention is a cost like any other and appropriate strategies are required to meet all legal and business purposes for data retention and then to properly dispose of it.

A. Make an inventory of the data created by the company (yes, it is a big task).
B. Categorize the data into groups of the longest retention time. When in doubt about which category to use, choose the one that has the longest retention period.
C. Review this plan with legal counsel since one of its primary purposes is legal compliance. Be sure to obtain a written answer.
D. Publish these guidelines to all employees.

32

GREEN COMPUTING: EARTH FRIENDLY IT

§ 32.01 OVERVIEW

[A] Purpose and Scope

Climate change is a socially disruptive issue. Many people have opinions as to whether it is caused by or is accelerated by human activities. One of the significant questions involves the emission of greenhouse gases that are a result of fossil fuels burned to create electricity. The concept of Green Technologies begins with the responsible use of electrical energy. However, as more companies explore how they use energy, they see that from their perspective it is more about the cost-efficient use of resources.

A key resource used in the modern office is electricity. If you think of it as a material, much like steel or plastics, then it is easier to understand material waste. Imagine buying a small tree just to create one wooden pencil. Imagine buying half of a cow just to eat one steak. These may seem like exaggerations, but they are not far off. Consider the desktop workstation that is never turned off. It runs 24 hours per day seven days per week (including vacations and holidays). For all of that electricity purchased, it is used about 25 percent of the time. The rest of the time is wasted running and contributing nothing to the company's profits.

Another issue is the proper disposal of obsolete electronics. Old computers, printers, cell phones, network devices, telephone instruments, and so on require proper disposal. Improper disposal may result in companies paying for expensive landfill clean-ups. There is also an emerging body of laws governing how electronic devices may be scrapped.

[B] Critical Policies to Develop Based on This Chapter

A Green Technologies policy is both an opportunity to save money and necessary to avoid legal entanglements. It explains how the company will reduce the amount of energy it consumes while maintaining its current level of service. It also details the approved process for disposal of obsolete electronic assets.

This policy will also identify by position title required actions by IT Managers. This clarifies who must complete what actions and at what time. A series of periodic reports provides executive management with assurance that the savings gained through a well-considered Green Technologies strategy are not lost through staff inattention.

Using the material discussed in this chapter, you will be able to create the following policies:

A. Purchase of New Electronic Equipment
B. Utilization of Data Center Assets
C. Equipment Disposal

Policies should always be developed based on the local situation. Successful managers cannot issue appropriate guidance if the policies are written with another company's situation or location in mind.

§ 32.02   A TIME TO STOP

[A]   What Is Green?

Green Technologies are the efficient use of computing resources in an environmentally friendly manner. They provide economic savings, demonstrate corporate social responsibility, and minimize environmental impact. Green Technologies also reduce energy consumption. Given the rising cost of energy of all types, these savings can be significant. Green Technologies are a collection of things:

A. **They are the efficient use of electricity to support computing.** Efficient use minimizes wasted energy that does not contribute to a company's business. Typically this is energy lost through heat to power equipment no one is using and the use of inefficient electronic devices. Green Technologies also encompass using energy sources with a minimal environmental impact, such as solar or wind power.

B. **They maximize existing equipment utilization.** For many years, it was far easier to add another server and more disks than it was to properly manage system capacity. As existing systems became more powerful, yet more lightly used, their hardware was rarely swapped out for something smaller. Another issue was the many copies of large databases and files kept online "just in case" they are needed. All of this added up to high energy usage to power and cool servers and disk drives that added nothing to the bottom line.

C. **We live in a throwaway society.** Many things we use, especially electronic devices, are cheaper to discard than to repair. A repair is minimally one-half hour of bench time (technician and tools at about $100 per hour) plus parts. Given the amount of surface-mounted components used on electronic circuit boards, a repair may not be practical. Entire circuit cards must be exchanged. This may lead to a multi-week delay. Given the time delay, labor, and price of a replacement, it is often cheaper to buy a replacement and discard the old item.

Climate change is a socially disruptive factor. As nations search for ways to reduce their greenhouse gas emissions, they are turning their attention toward the carbon footprint created by modern technology. There is no need to wait for this unwanted governmental interference. Green Technologies do not require that companies sacrifice performance or features. It is just a different way to provide the same things.

[B]   Stop Wasting Energy

Computing equipment is the main user of energy in most companies. There is a desktop workstation for every office worker. Data centers are always "on." Servers are running and disk drives are spinning even during holidays and weekends when no one is around. Many applications are only used occasionally, but the equipment still draws power around the clock. All of this adds up to a large amount of electricity that is spent "just in case" something is needed.

This is compounded by the number of desktop units that run around the clock, even when no one is present to use them.

Think about it. Are your office lights left on around the clock, every day of the year? Is the heat or air conditioning for the offices always held at the most comfortable temperature over long winter weekends? You carefully manage the other electrical wastes, why not this one? How about saving some money? Consider:

A. Reduced energy to power IT equipment has an immediate financial payback to the company.
B. Reduced power usage will reduce the amount of air conditioning required.
C. Cooler-running equipment extends its useful life.
D. If no one is present to use the computer, then who is inconvenienced?

[C] Stop Wasting Equipment

Over the years, companies kept adding technology but not managing its efficiencies. It is far easier to add a new server and slap in additional disk drives than it is to rebalance the load across existing units. Equipment is plentiful and becoming more powerful with every new model. Disks regularly drop in price, and there was plenty of storage to support the sloppiest system design. It was much easier to purchase new equipment than to argue with someone.

Purchasing a new server for each application meant that some applications, though important, only ran for a short time every day. The rest of the day, that server and its disk drives were powered up but idle. Eventually, data centers began to fill up. This idle equipment used electricity and generated heat that had to be cooled, requiring even more energy.

Another waste of equipment is through online storage. Everyone wants all of their files, along with their many versions, to be available online all of the time. This is a waste of energy and resources. Some databases keep multiple copies of the same data online for recovery and to potentially ease trouble-shooting later. All of this takes disk space, energy, and cooling. Most of it is never accessed.

[D] Stop Polluting the Planet

Large companies often follow a three-year equipment refresh cycle to match the manufacturer's warranty coverage. Items older than three years are replaced with newer and faster units. These old components are either sold on the used-equipment market or sent away as scrap. Consider the pollution this still-useful equipment creates in a landfill, and the additional pollution produced while creating its replacement.

Electronic equipment usually includes small amounts of toxic materials. Old hardware improperly thrown in landfills may release toxic elements into the environment. This can be addressed by purchasing equipment that does not include toxic materials, by using electronics longer than a few years, and by proper disposal. Of course, to buy equipment without these toxic materials, manufacturers must first offer it at a reasonable price.

COMMENT

The transition from traditional IT processes to Green Technologies has its roots in the chemical industry. Over time, chemicals have been reformulated and manufacturing processes modified to reduce the amount of toxic materials used and discarded. Many newer chemicals are now biodegradable or recyclable.

[E]   Policies Implement Strategies

A Green Technologies policy must explain to all employees the company's executive guidance for implementing the Green Technologies program. The policy must address every area of the company involved. Some companies focus on electronic devices while others also include paper recycling and waste water management. Manufacturing facilities should not combine their Green Technologies and manufacturing environmental programs to avoid confusion.

A company's Green Technologies policy must reflect its strategy. Companies approach this issue various ways. A common theme is that this is an issue that must be addressed for economic and social reasons. Before drafting a policy, select the strategy you intend to implement. The different strategic approaches are:

A. The "From Here on Out" approach is to apply the policy to future purchases where practical. This can be implemented as an official purchasing policy or even quietly by the person specifying which new equipment to purchase. This may also be attached to a company's social responsibility initiatives. This approach takes time before it can show any measurable results. The cost of energy and equipment disposal is added to the company's normal ROI calculation.

B. The "Company Differentiator" approach is for organizations that want to use their Green credentials to differentiate their company and attract or retain customers. They see it as a way for their business to stand out as more socially responsible than those of competitors. Rather than wait for equipment to expire, this organization seeks out and replaces the most inefficient offenders. The principles of Green Technologies are applied across the organization to include all sources of energy waste and disposal concerns such as copiers, fax machines, refrigerators, vehicles, etc.

C. "Thoroughly Green" seeks to reorganize the way that technology is used in a company from top to bottom. Over the years, many companies have rushed to automate everything without a full understanding of what is needed—or if something else is already in place to do that function. Eliminating low value or duplicate systems reduces the need for equipment (which is better than using it efficiently). Examples of this are multiple copies of mirrored data, insistence on keeping rarely used data in online storage instead of offline, and maintaining a larger number of generations of online data than needed (need is determined by the frequency of access). Thoroughly Green encompasses new building construction using on-site, nonpolluting renewable energy sources. Social factors are on an equal level to financial considerations.

See Policy ITP-32-1 Green Computing Policy as an example.

POLICY ITP-32-1.   Green Computing Policy

Policy #:	ITP-32-1	Effective:	03/18/13	Page #:	1 of N
Subject:	Green Computing Policy				

1.0 PURPOSE

This policy requires employees to consider all significant environmental and cost factors in the purchase, use, and disposal of electronic equipment. It ensures the consistent, efficient, and effective implementation of environmentally friendly operations across the organization.

2.0 SCOPE

The policy applies to all technology devices and their operation within the company. Specifically this includes all equipment purchased for the collection and processing of data throughout the organization as well as all telecommunications devices to include telephones, cellular telephones, and fax machines.

3.0 POLICY

This policy provides for the efficient use of electronic equipment in terms of energy management and fuller utilization. It applies to all employees and identifies specific duties for the IT Manager, Facilities Manager, IT Desktop Support Manager, Data Center Manager, and Purchasing Manager. This policy applies to the:

A. **Purchase of new electronic equipment.** The purchasing manager will ensure that all technology hardware purchases include an energy usage comparison between the new item and the item it is replacing—or the last similar item purchased. The power supply of new equipment must have an Energy Star Plus 80 rating. If the price difference between the "Plus 80" item and least cost alternative is within 10 percent, then the Plus 80 item will be purchased.

Incoming equipment must be compliant with European Union's directives 2002/95/EC (Restriction of Hazardous Substances directive, or ROHS). This will ease the disposal of equipment at the end of its useful life.

The Vice President of Technology is authorized to approve any deviations to this policy.

B. **Utilization of data center assets.** The following individuals are responsible for managing the utilization of all data center assets,

1. The data center manager will semiannually review equipment utilization for the previous 12 months and report:
   a. Review all databases in the data center and submit a report that the minimum number of data copies are maintained in online storage, or identify the excess number of copies in use.
   b. Verify that all data in online storage is accessed at least once every three months or is moved to offline storage media.
   c. Create a baseline report of estimated electrical usage (or request a special meter to monitor data center use) for the data center. Provide a comparison of electricity used over the past 12 months and detail specific actions to reduce it.
   d. Identify servers that are not required for 24/7 operations and the impact of shutting them down on evenings, weekends, and holidays.
   e. Identify batch reports suitable for conversion to online review instead of printing the entire document.
2. The data center manager will create and maintain a document:
   a. Detailing the electrical utilization of each piece of data center equipment as a cost factor used for calculating when to replace existing equipment.
   b. Listing efforts to reduce the amount of cooling required.
3. The System Administrator will review all servers and identify units that could be combined using virtualization. A proposal and action plan for migrating servers used less than 30 percent during working hours to a virtual environment.
4. The Desktop Support manager will create and maintain a document detailing the electrical utilization of each model of desktop and portable computing items used in the company. The amount of energy required for a particular piece of equipment will be considered as a cost factor used for calculating when to replace it.
   a. Create a baseline report of estimated electrical usage for the desktop equipment to include shared printers. Report semiannually on estimated power usage.
   b. Ensure all power converters are on a power strip so they can be turned off.
   c. Remind users to turn off equipment when leaving for the night.
   d. Turn on and prevent user changing of power saving options on each company computer, monitor, and printer.
5. The Facilities Services Manager will create and maintain a document detailing the electrical utilization of each model of copier and fax

machine. The amount of energy required for a particular piece of equipment will be considered as a cost factor used for calculating when to replace existing equipment.

C. **Equipment Disposal.** The IT Manager is responsible for the proper disposal of all electronic devices from the desktop, the data center, telecommunications systems, and company-owned telephones. The Facilities Services Manager is responsible for the proper disposal of all copiers and fax devices.

The first choice for technology disposal is resale or donation to someone who can continue its useful life. If that is not an option, then return it to the original manufacturer for disposal. If a third-party company is used to manage equipment disposal, then the IT Manager and the Facilities Manager must visit the disposal facilities every six months to ensure the equipment is properly broken apart and toxic materials are sent on for proper disposal or recycling.

4.0 REVISION HISTORY

Date	Revision #	Description of Change
03/18/13	1.0	Initial creation.

5.0 INQUIRIES

Direct inquiries about this policy to:

George Jenkins, CIO
Our Company, Inc.
2900 Corporate Drive
Columbus, OH 43215

Voice: 614-555-1234
Fax: 614-555-1235
E-mail: gjenkins@company.com

Revision #:	1.0	Supersedes:	N/A	Date:	03/18/13

§ 32.03   PUT ENERGY-HOG EQUIPMENT ON A DIET

[A]   Overview

Green Technologies focus on hardware. The amount of energy it demands every day and generally around the clock is substantial and ever increasing. If someone offered to sell you a new computer server for 20 percent more cost than everyone else was paying, would you buy it? If the taxes on data centers went up 20 percent, would your company react? If the price of gas for your car went up 20 percent, would you be angry? When will energy prices level off? Isn't it time to take a fresh look at your organization's energy usage and eliminate areas of waste?

Computing equipment wastes electricity. It wastes a lot of electricity, and that translates into money spent for doing nothing. Green Technologies is about minimizing the amount of energy that is wasted by computing hardware that is doing . . . nothing.

Have you ever seen coworkers who never turned off their workstation—even before leaving on vacation, because they did not want to wait while it started from a power-off state? If you asked this person why, he or she will provide a long list of reasons—none of which compares to the money lost for powering unused equipment. Funny thing is, this same person will likely turn out the office lights every night . . . to save electricity.

The traditional reason given for not turning off equipment is that the spike of electricity when it is turned back on slowly wears down the electronic components. This is true, but the impact is minimal. It would take so many more years of daily off-and-on switching to cause a failure that the equipment would not still be in service.

A similar situation occurs in data centers. In this case, it takes time to power down and then restart servers. Many system administrators fear (no better word describes this) that if turned off, they will not restart properly. Given the amount of time required to power down and restart the many servers, does it make sense to even look here for savings?

COMMENT

When you drive your car to work, you stop to put gas into it. You see how much it costs and how the price has risen, so you adjust your driving habits and usage accordingly. Data center managers rarely see a company's electric bill. While the facilities manager strives to reduce usage, the IT Manager's goals are maximum availability. A company's reward system and feedback system need to change.

Computing equipment is powered by electricity. To create this energy, power companies use coal-fired plants, nuclear energy, and hydroelectric power generation. Each of these has its own drawbacks. As the world's requirements for electrical energy increase, so does the number of power plants, which further adds to greenhouse gases in the atmosphere, which some people believe increase the natural cycle of global warming. As nations strive to fulfill their treaty promises to reduce greenhouse gases, businesses can expect increased governmental pressure to use less energy.

§ 32.03[B]

Government initiatives have emerged over time to encourage various aspects of Green Technologies. Often these guidelines overlap or are based on previous standards. Government initiatives are either guidelines to be followed voluntarily or legal mandates.

[B] Energy Star

Electronic devices that plug into a wall outlet use a "power supply" module to connect to a power source. This device filters line noise and power fluctuations, and converts the incoming power to the voltage levels required for that device. A typical power supply is about 70 percent efficient. For example, it takes 100 watts of incoming power to provide 70 watts of usable power in the device. The rest of the energy is lost as heat.

In 1992, the U.S. Environmental Protection Agency (EPA) created "Energy Star" as a program for promoting energy-efficient technologies. It began as a voluntary labeling program to promote energy-efficient computers and monitors and later expanded to encompass office equipment and residential climate control equipment. Over the years, Energy Star has contributed to the use adoption of (light-emitting diode) LED traffic lights, power management for office equipment, and minimal standby power usage for a wide range of devices.

In 1996, the Energy Star program was extended to encompass major appliances, lighting, home electronics, new homes, and commercial and industrial buildings. Today, Energy Star is a joint effort of the EPA and the U.S. Department of Energy.

COMMENT

Obtain the latest information about Energy Star at *http://www.energystar.gov*.

Energy Star was revised in 2007 to tighten efficiency goals and introduce a tiered rating system. Existing equipment designs can no longer use the logo unless they are requalified. Energy Star's latest specifications for computers apply to a variety of products, including desktop and notebook computers, integrated computer systems, desktop-derived servers, and workstations.

The latest Energy Star version introduced a power supply certification called "80 Plus." This means that a power supply has 80 percent or greater AC power supply efficiency at rated power. Qualified products must now meet energy use guidelines in standby, sleep mode, and while computers are being used:

A. Desktops, integrated computers, and desktop-derived servers must use less than 2 watts of power when the device is switched off, and no more than 4 watts when in sleep mode.

B. Notebook PCs must use less than 1 watt of power when the device is switched off, and no more than 1.7 watts when in sleep mode.

C. Internal power supplies must switch to sleep mode within 15 minutes of inactivity.

D. External power supplies must switch to sleep mode within 30 minutes of inactivity.

The new computer specification is expected to save consumers and businesses more than $1.8 billion in energy costs over the next five years and prevent greenhouse gas emissions equal to the annual emissions of 2.7 million vehicles.

Power management of monitors is an easy place to save money. The older cathode ray monitors (non-flat panels) use a lot of power. Even the newer flat-panel models need power to operate. A popular notion is that turning a monitor off and on several times a day (through power management) will damage it. The power surge on startup does wear on the components, but problems will take about 20 years before they are apparent.

The first step in power management is to place the monitor in sleep mode. This is a reduced power consumption state ordered by the computer. The screen wakes up when a key is pushed or some other recognized user interaction occurs.

The least power is used when the monitor is turned off. Typically, this means the monitor is still drawing a small amount of power. To stop this power leak, plug the monitor into a power strip and turn it off at the power strip and not the monitor power switch.

COMMENT

Screen savers do not save power because the program running to display the image requires CPU resources.

[C] Electronic Products Environmental Assessment Tool™ (EPEAT™)

EPEAT™ is a tool that evaluates how "green" a product is prior to its purchase. It was created by the Green Electronic Council in cooperation with major electronic component manufacturers. EPEAT™ provides an independent standard for purchasers of electronic devices. It includes self-declaration of equipment conformance to the standard. These claims are randomly audited. EPEAT™'s criteria are based on the EPA's Energy Star requirements for PCs, IEEE 1680 Standard for Environmental Assessment of Personal Computer Products, and the "sensitive material" criteria requiring companies to meet the European Union's tough standards for limiting the hazardous chemicals and components used to make them.

COMMENT

Obtain the latest information about EPEAT™ at *http:// greenelectronicscouncil.org/*.

Executive Order 13423 requires all U.S. federal agencies to use EPEAT™ when purchasing computer systems. Ninety-five percent of electronic products procured by federal agencies must meet EPEAT™ standards, as long there is a standard for that product.

EPEAT™'s 23 mandatory and 28 optional evaluation criteria cover such things as:

A. Energy conservation
B. Recycling and disposal
C. Packaging materials
D. Reduction of environmentally sensitive materials
E. Design for end of life

EPEAT™ evaluates electronic products according to three tiers of environmental performance—bronze, silver, and gold. A product must meet all the required criteria in order to qualify for EPEAT™ bronze. Manufacturers may pick and choose among the optional criteria to boost their EPEAT™ "score" to achieve a higher level.

A. Bronze—meets all 23 required criteria.
B. Silver—meets all required criteria plus at least 14 optional criteria.
C. Gold—meets all required criteria plus at least 21 optional criteria.

[D] Advanced Configuration and Power Interface (ACPI)

ACPI was developed in 1996 by a group of major hardware and software manufacturers as an open industry standard. It defines the hardware and software interfaces that enable operating systems to configure and manage a device's power usage. Previous standards used the hardware to determine power management switching, and the results were sometimes unpredictable.

ACPI uses the Basic Input Output System (BIOS) chip on a computer to control the low-level hardware details under the control of the operating system. ACPI first appeared in Windows 98. An example of this is the "Power Option" module in the Windows™ Vista™ operating system. ACPI is also found in Linux and FreeBSD.

ACPI's power management language called ACPI Machine Language (AML) is embedded in the BIOS's firmware. It includes power event interruptions that are controlled by the operating system. The goal is to provide code that will run in all operating systems. However, ACPI must run with full privileges. This means that buggy or hacked code can easily damage a computer's data. Two power management modes are supported:

A. **Sleep mode.** A Windows PC can be set to sleep mode (or standby mode) after a period of inactivity. In this condition, the disk drives are stopped and the system state is maintained in RAM by a small amount of electricity. Take care! If total power is lost, so is everything in RAM. While in sleep mode, your monitor draws about 5 watts and your PC about 2 watts. The savings are about the same as if the equipment was turned off for the night. The advantage is that when you wake it up, the machine is ready for work much faster than starting it from a cold state as everything is already in RAM.

B. **Hibernate mode.** Hibernate mode copies the computer's state to disk before shutting down. This is commonly used in notebook PCs. However, it takes noticeably longer than sleep mode to recover to full readiness. It also requires the same amount of free disk space as it has RAM. If a hibernating PC loses power, everything is still safely stored on disk for recovery.

[E] Restriction of Hazardous Substances (ROHS) Directive

Among the strictest regulations on the computer industry is the European Union's Restriction of Hazardous Substances directive, or ROHS. This directive covers hardware sold in the European Union countries, although many other countries have also adopted it. ROHS restricts the sale of equipment with more than the permitted levels of:

A. Lead—found in solder, printed-circuit foil, and rechargeable batteries.
B. Cadmium—found in rechargeable batteries.
C. Mercury—found in high-intensity light bulbs, batteries, and high-voltage rectifier tubes.
D. Hexavalent chromium—found throughout electronic circuitry.
E. Polybrominated biphenyl (PBB)—a flame retardant.
F. Polybrominateddiphenyl ether (PBDE)—flame retardants used in plastics.

In the United States, ROHS is a component of the EPEAT™ standards. The United States competes in global markets, and meeting global standards ensures that its products will be welcome in those markets.

[F] Virtualization

Past practice has been to purchase a new server to support each new application. This created more heat in the data center and consumed floor (or rack) space. This server also consumed electricity around the clock. In many cases, a server was used for less than an hour a day. This was compounded when servers were replaced with newer and more powerful equipment during the typical three-year equipment refresh cycle. Old servers that were lightly used are updated to even more powerful servers, which resulted in yet more idle time per day.

A popular solution is to let a collection of small applications share the same server. This reduces electrical usage because fewer servers are in operation. Consequently, this reduces energy required for cooling and frees floor space in the data center. This is accomplished by moving small applications on physical servers to virtual servers.

Virtualization is not new. It originated in mainframe computers decades ago and was more recently reintroduced into servers (themselves much more powerful than the long-gone mainframes). Virtualization creates a set of virtual machines within the operating environment of a server. Each virtual machine thinks that it is a physical device when it is actually a partition in RAM. If a virtual server needs to be restarted, just that partition is initialized while the rest of the physical server keeps running.

The cost of the software to create and manage these virtual environments is offset by the savings on buying servers and their licenses. There are additional savings on energy and cooling over what would have been the server's service life. Additionally, there is the energy savings.

COMMENT

For every watt of power used to power something in the data center, another watt is expended to cool it.

[G]   Is Thin Client the Answer?

Another power-savings approach is the use of "thin client" devices instead of personal computers on desktops. The term "thin client" can mean many things. It is easier to explain by first describing a "fat client" device.

Basically, a fat client is a full-function personal computer. It pulls data out of the data center as needed and then processes it. A fat client has a hard drive for storing data and programs, etc. The problem with a fat client is that data on its drives are not backed up to offline media. A disk crash means data are lost. If software must be patched, then the changes must be tested against a wide range of applications and local operating system settings. Also, they must be scheduled around each end user's schedule. Also, if a fat client PC is broken, that worker is hindered until it is repaired, as his or her workspace is stored on the device.

A thin client contains just enough software to interact with a server that performs most of the processing. A thin client device is rather small and may be included in the same case as the monitor or the keyboard. If it breaks, then it can be easily swapped out because no data are stored within it.

With their smaller size and lack of a hard drive, thin clients need much less power than a PC. Some operate on as little as 5 watts. Part of this is due to the absence of a hard drive. Also, because the data are in the data center, there is no need for CD drives, floppy drives, and so on. A thin client usually has an embedded operating system stored in flash memory. Most offices have one PC per desk. Many of these have 300- to 500-watt power supplies in them. Consider the savings in energy usage by swapping them all for 5-watt units.

Of course, this only shifts the load from the desktop to the data center. Thin clients require a significant server support and a robust network along with space in the data center. There are many advantages to thin clients, notably the amount of control over programs run on the equipment. However, from a Green Technologies perspective, running a few servers requires less electricity than powering hundreds of PCs that spend much of their day idle.

§ 32.04   WHAT CAN YOU DO?

[A]   The Basics

Sometimes companies are slow to act. There are things that you can do with your own desktop or department, ranging from the simple to the extreme. The tipping point is where more time is spent saving energy than is saved by reducing power usage. Also, few companies can afford to swap out all of their power hogs, so improvements are made one step at a time.

Energy waste is sometimes easy to spot. Power adapters attached to electrical outlets continue to draw electrical power even if the attached device is turned off. It seems like anything you use outside a PC's chassis has yet another power transformer. Each of these continues to draw power even when the device is turned off.

Another sign of waste is heat. Devices that are warm to touch indicate a loss of energy converted to heat. Not only does the heat represent wasted electricity but it increases the building's cooling load.

[B]   Create a Power Usage Baseline

A clear baseline or starting point is important to show the progress you will make in your conservation program. It is difficult to use the company's electric bill to show less usage because so many things impact it, such as seasonal highs and lows of heat or air-conditioning use, addition of new equipment, and so on. It is easier to claim savings based on the power rating of devices and hours of nonuse saved.

Begin by gathering the power rating of each device in use. Yes, this will take a long time, but the Internet can speed this along. Also, there will be many devices that are the same (such as standardized purchase of PCs from one manufacturer), which minimizes the number of devices to research. This baseline is a measurement of where you are today. It will allow you to demonstrate the benefits provided by your Green initiative. Otherwise, the disconnect between the one who pays the bill and the ones who use the electricity will continue. Also, as you reduce, other departments may be piling on. Take the following steps:

A. Obtain an inventory of all equipment in the data center, on the desktop, and in between on the network. If such a list does not exist, then create one.

B. After you know what is in service, look up the devices on the manufacturer's site or e-mail them for the devices' rated power consumption, standby power usage, and cooling requirements. Note next to each item on the list its rated usage.

C. Identify the biggest electrical and cooling users. It is not always the biggest physical devices. These devices are warm to touch when in operation. These are targets for elimination.

D. Identify the cost per kilowatt for your facility.

E. Estimate the cost of cooling to be the same wattage as used to operate something. If you have doubts as to how much heat a personal computer generates, shut off the ventilation to a closed training room for a few hours and then step inside.

With this information in hand, you can now compare future purchase requests to existing usage to ensure the energy needed goes down with each purchase. Also, as you evaluate devices for updating your standard equipment list, you can select those with the smallest requirements.

[C]   Telecommuting

Telecommuting, or working virtually, is where office workers do their work from home. Now that high-speed networks are generally available, people can sit at home and do most of their daily work. Some companies offer their employees the chance to work from home one or two days every week.

Company savings from telecommuting include reduced electricity and cooling (because you are not there and your desktop unit is off). However, the savings to the environment are significant. Imagine the amount of air pollution saved if no one drove to work for two days per week! Employees with company-provided notebook PCs and cellular telephones can work from nearly anywhere.

Many people welcome the opportunity to work from home one day per week. Just the time saved from not commuting to work is reward enough! Companies that depend on a primarily virtual workforce can reduce their expensive office space and bring in each team for meetings one day per week. This maintains personal contact while dramatically reducing pollution from long commutes to work.

[D]   Enable Software-Controlled Power Management

Something you can do today is to turn on the power management settings on as many devices as possible. Operating systems include a Power Management module. This software sets a timer and, after a specified period of inactivity, will place the device into "sleep" mode. After an additional length of time, the device is completely turned off. As a way to save power, many companies set the sleep and power-off timers and then lock that module so only system administrators can change it.

COMMENT

Setting power management timers to a low value is a sure way to gain enemies. Be sure that the power settings take into account the length of a typical lunch break or office meeting.

Power management can be enabled on many different office devices. Printers, copiers, and fax machines typically have their own sleep mode and power-off settings. Take the time to learn about each to set them, or require the company supplying them to set it for you.

In many cases, if a device is to be idle for more than 16 minutes, it should switch to sleep mode. At that point, it costs less energy to turn something back on than is used for it to consume electricity doing nothing. Consider how much your time is worth. If it takes a long time to shut down the computer and then restart it later, the value of your time will probably be much greater than the value of the amount of electricity you will save by turning off the computer.

COMMENT

Modern PCs are solidly built. They will become obsolete long before the effects of being switched on and off multiple times cause noticeable damage. Also, electronic devices produce heat, so turning them off reduces building cooling loads.

[E] Buy Some Power Strips

Many devices arrive with a power transforming device that is plugged into the wall. Cell phone chargers are a good example. These devices remain active and drawing electrical power even when the device they are attached to is turned off. The amount of power consumed may be significant. Some larger devices also have a similar arrangement where they continue to consume electrical power even through the power switch is off.

Where possible, connect all of these devices to a power strip and then connect that power strip to the wall. At the end of the day when this equipment is no longer needed, turn off the power strip. That will completely disconnect everything from the power grid. If this is done for all desktop computers across the company, the savings will be noticeable. Refer back to your equipment inventory and add up the standby power that is no longer drawn by these devices.

[F]   Save Trees and Toner

An ongoing tragedy is the trash cans sitting outside a data center. Some people have mounds of paper printed and then use it little or not at all. Reports are picked up and much of the paper simply tossed away. Sometimes it is printed "just in case" the data center has a problem and then tossed at the end of the day. This can be reduced by providing reports online to everyone, and on CDs for those who "must" have a hard copy.

Printing is expensive! Printers use a lot of energy. They are physical devices with many moving parts. Add to that the ink or toner that hits the paper. Finally, there is the cost and time to dispose of the now unneeded paper. Because it is hard to tell what might violate security guidelines, many companies hire someone to come in and shred it all before disposal.

Therefore, online viewing of reports is an all-around time and money saver. Users receive their reports through e-mail or pull them out of an online directory. Report-viewing software permits selected pages to be printed or saved on a local hard drive.

[G]   Substitute One Piece at a Time

When compiling the energy usage baseline list, some of the devices will stand out as significant electrical consumers. Liquid crystal displays (LCD) use less than half of the electricity consumed by old, bulky cathode ray tube (CRT) monitors. However, select replacement models carefully. Sloppy design can result in a sleek-looking LCD using almost as much power as the CRT it replaced. The most efficient LCD monitors are those that use LED for backlighting.

Watch the trade press for technology trends toward more efficient equipment. For example, in notebook PCs, flash memory is becoming (an expensive) substitute for fixed disks. This lightens the weight and reduces battery drain. Solid state electronics are also more reliable than mechanic disk drives. As the cost for large-scale flash memory comes down, this will become more common.

Power stepping enables a CPU to adjust its power consumption based on demand. If there is less computing demand, the power used may drop by 30 percent. In some units, if the processor detects excessive heat, it will automatically switch to low power instead of damaging itself.

COMMENT

AMD's "PowerNow!" technology allows operating systems to dynamically adjust processor power states, voltage, and clocking frequencies depending on workload. Tests indicate this can reduce up to 75 percent of the CPU's power consumption.

Some devices just need to be available all of the time, such as network components (hubs, switches, etc.). In these cases, the goal is to replace existing devices with more energy-efficient equipment. Review all aspects of the network design to remove layers that may no longer be necessary. In most companies, networks have grown over time. Adding people here, moving departments there, and even work areas temporarily created may have left underutilized components strewn about.

§ 32.05   SAFE DISPOSAL

[A]   Overview

Companies declare equipment to be surplus for a number of reasons. Some companies dispose of servers and desktop units when the three-year warranty expires. This way they hold down their repair costs. Also, the older the device, the more frequently its hardware will fail. The belief is that the newer hardware is significantly more powerful and reliable.

There are three categories of disposal: reuse elsewhere, recycle, or scrap. Each of these options has many variations. The key is to minimize the company's expense in proper disposal while ensuring that toxic materials are not introduced into the environment.

COMMENT

California's Electronic Waste Recycling Act of 2003 established a statewide recycling program for obsolete computer and consumer electronics equipment. Retailers collect an electronic waste recycling fee at the point of sale of certain products. Distribution of recovery and recycling payments to qualified entities covers the cost of electronic waste collection and recycling. This law further recommends environmentally preferred purchasing criteria for state agency purchases of certain electronic equipment.

[B]   Reuse Surplus Equipment Elsewhere

A part of your company's Green Technologies policy must include the collection of surplus electronic devices for disposal. Establish a collection point where everyone can drop off surplus items. Provide a set of tags that can be attached as they are dropped off. Usually this is a green tag for known good, yellow if it works but has minor problems, and a red tag for known bad.

Much of this hardware has plenty of useful life remaining in it. Where possible, it should be sold on the used-equipment market or donated to local charities. Technical schools can use older equipment to illustrate lessons on how to repair hardware. Used equipment vendors will snap equipment up for resale as a unit or to sell the individual parts.

[C]   Recycling Old Technology

Recycling generally means to overhaul and then reuse something again (e.g., rebuilding a car engine is expensive but cheaper than purchasing a new one). The same is true for recycling printer supplies. Inkjet printer cartridges, laser printer toner cartridges, toner cartridges for copiers, and other devices can often be recycled. In many cases, a company will purchase the old cartridge from you. Some companies sell their empty cartridges to finance their annual Christmas party.

Computing hardware, such as monitors and personal computers, may have traces of valuable materials, but for the most part, the best way to recycle them is to assign them to a new purpose through donation or sale on the used equipment market.

[D]   Tossing Equipment onto the Scrap Heap

If the device cannot be reused in this way, then disposal must be properly handled. Green Technologies ensures that electronic components, with the toxic substances used to create them, are properly disposed. Surplus equipment that is of no further use to the company (including defective circuit cards and components) must be properly broken apart through verifiable channels. This fulfills the company's responsibility to ensure the environmentally friendly demise of equipment.

There are various places that accept computing equipment for disposal:

A. Manufacturer sites
B. Local government collection sites
C. Private disposal companies

Design for end of life is a concept in which the original design of a piece of hardware acknowledges that the item will someday become scrap. It minimizes the amount of toxic materials used in the manufacture of the equipment. Further, those toxic materials that are used will be easy to isolate from the nontoxic parts of the item.

So how big an issue is this? Computing equipment contains leads (in the solder), cadmium, mercury, hexavalent chromium, and polybrominated fire retardants. These serious pollutants must be excluded from the normal waste stream. Up to 50 million tons of surplus computing and cellular telephone equipment are dumped annually across the globe.

COMMENT

Proper disposal of nonvolatile memory, such as disk drives and static RAM storage, is important to ensure the security of company data. Companies must ensure that the data on all equipment leaving for disposal or reuse is properly deleted according to Department of Defense standards.

Many major manufacturers have long recognized the problems with improper disposal of equipment. Two of the popular programs are:

A. Hewlett-Packard accepts equipment from consumers no matter what brand it is. It sorts incoming devices for reuse or to recapture materials used to create it. The latest information and guidelines for HP's extensive program can be found at *www.hp.com/hpinfo/globalcitizenship/index.html*.

B. Dell computers offers the "Dell Earth" program, which provides consumers free recycling of Dell-brand computer equipment. You may also recycle the computing equipment from other manufacturers if it is together with the purchase of a new Dell computer. Dell offers its Asset Recovery services to companies for recycling their old equipment at *www.dell.com/assetrecovery*.

33

OPEN SOURCE: MANAGING ISSUES

§ 33.01 OVERVIEW

[A] Purpose and Scope

Freeware—just the sound of it rings with cost savings. After all, free is always cheaper than paying for something. Instead of an endless series of administrative hassles, writing requests, justifying a purchase, and multiple rounds of debating the cost, new software is available after a short Internet download. Something that is "free" might have fewer features than the bloated commercial products who try to please everyone, but that is OK. Most software has far more options than you will ever use.

To clarify some terms:

A. **Freeware** is software that is available for use at no cost. It is only the executable code.
B. **Open source** is both the source and executable code. It is also available at no cost.

The term "free software" refers more to your license rights than to its price. It means that you can run it, copy it, pass it on to others, and read the source code to learn from it, or to help to patch its bugs. Also, just because something says that it is free, does not make it so. "Free" software only pertains to its original purchase. This is only one of the many costs to consider. Someone must know it well enough to patch it and to validate performance after the patches are made. There are issues involving training, ensuring the license is not violated, etc.—so many things that must be considered beyond just the initial purchase price.

Some companies try to ban all free or open source software from their company. This sounds nice but is usually defeated by several factors. First, individuals (usually in the IT department) know how to bypass the network firewalls and will download and use what they wish. There are ways to enforce this but they are all policed by the same IT department. Second, when technicians are working under tight deadlines, it is faster to pull in a freeware product than to suffer through a tedious approval process. Finally, executives focus entirely on the "free" aspect and overlook the inconvenient truth of support costs.

Freeware and open source have much in common. Both are general terms applied to a category of software distribution. However, within these broad categories are many variations on the theme which require close attention when using these products. The "free" and "open source" software movement will continue to grow. Downloading server software tools that perform a single function very well has long been a staple of system administrators. The key is for IT executives to implement the proper policies and procedures that will protect the company (and the IT executives) in the event that problems arise.

A company policy forbidding free or open source software is not practical. It is likely that some of it already exists in your data center. The best defense is a formal policy controlling its acquisition and use. A well-written policy that is properly distributed may reduce a company's legal liability in the event that an employee oversteps a license's limitation.

[B]   The "Free" Software Movement

Companies require their IT systems to be stable and reliable. They expect them to be instantly available and to function in a predictable manner. Any disruption to this forces workers to reschedule department workflows and threatens their ability to predict when specific tasks will be completed, often forcing them to work extended hours. Therefore, the selection of software must include a careful consideration of the threats to its stable, predictable operation.

Freeware is a software distribution solution that is the convergence of several movements. The first is from individuals who have written a piece of software that they feel could be very useful to others. However, the process of packaging it, distributing it through sales channels, collecting funds, providing installation support, etc., is too much for a one-man operation. Therefore, to gain positive publicity (and perhaps some career improvement), the product is offered to the public for free. A second movement is a personal desire to break the grip of the major software houses. These companies have been accused of ignoring defects and charging high rates for their products because there are few viable alternatives. Their copyrights and patents are used to stifle creativity. These feelings run higher in foreign markets, but this opinion is not unusual. Products like UNIX originated with a few people creating an operating system to meet their own needs. Over time, it ended up in the academic world where many people developed add-ons and utility programs. Eventually someone tried to pull back the license rights to provide the traditional support services. To fill the need for a truly free product, Linux emerged and is now a common tool in most data centers.

A third driving force for freeware is its use as a competitive weapon. Most people only use the basic features of a product. However to provide a "full featured" solution (and to improve sales), commercial packages provide many additional features. Some of the major software companies will therefore issue a "free" basic product that just happens to provide the same features as the main selling product by a competitor. The result is positive publicity for the open source provider and diminished revenue for the competitor.

Another force is from small companies depending on open source to reduce their IT costs. As these companies grew, they leveraged their experience with this type of software to minimize their expansion costs. Over the years, this demand for open source software has steadily grown. Even large companies use some of the open source software tools as the right tool to perform a particular task.

> ## COMMENT
>
> Shareware is a software distribution license where the product is provided free to the user under certain license conditions. Essentially this is a "try before you buy" approach. The license for some of these programs solicits payment if you like the software or use it for an extended period of time. Others permit personal use but require payment if it is used by a company.

[C] Critical Policies to Develop Based on This Chapter

Using the material discussed in this chapter, you will be able to create the following policies:

A. Software selection criteria.
B. Tying the product to a business requirement and business function. How will the software be supported?
C. Automated software monitoring for license management.
D. Employee education on the proper use of open source software.
E. Using open source software on company equipment.
F. Creating a procedure for reviewing requests.

Policies should always be developed based on the local situation. Successful managers cannot issue appropriate guidance using policies written with another company's situation or location in mind.

§ 33.02 CONSIDER ALL OF THE COSTS

[A] Overview

In most companies, obtaining approval to purchase software is a tedious, frustrating experience. Writing requests, making presentations to executives, and other acts of justification seem like a lot of wasted technical time. The hurdles to obtain a simple signature for something you feel is essential to your success seems to be such a waste of time. Why not just download the freeware version and move on?

Unfortunately, doing so removes management oversight from the process. Company strategies to minimize the number of different software packages that they support are bypassed. A short-term gain in time and cost is overshadowed by the ongoing expense of support. The primary barrier to the influx of unmanaged software licenses is a clear and consistently enforced IT governance policy.

COMMENT

The IT department is not the only culprit of sneaking in software. Most office workers were exposed to open source code while in college. They know where to find it and how to download it into the servers. If done quietly enough, by the time anyone knows it is there, the software is already a key part of a critical IT system!

[B]   Look at the Big Picture

When someone thinks of the "cost" of something, he or she generally refers to the purchase price. In the case of server software, this is often a significant sum. If something is purchased and immediately consumed, then that is likely its only cost. Software is different. It is purchased and must be maintained (defects repaired as they become known) to keep its usefulness.

The purchase price is only one component of the cost of buying and using something. We purchase something because we need to use it. But what does it cost to use it? Think about your car. It costs a lot of money to purchase it, then more money for insurance, fuel, and maintenance. Then there are also legal expenses for the title, license plates, and taxes. Some of these fees are infrequent while others are based on how much the car is used.

Think about how much money would be saved if you performed your own car maintenance? This exchanges your time for money savings. Of course, you must purchase tools and take the time to learn how to repair it. So, even if the car was provided for free, there is a considerable expense in its ongoing use.

Freeware and open source software have a lot in common with your car. They require maintenance, tools, and a lot of time. The primary difference is that the purchase price is zero. When considering freeware and open source software, always consider the ongoing usage expenses. They can easily exceed any savings realized.

[C]   Cost of Ownership

The cost of ownership is a way to calculate the total costs involved with using a piece of software. It includes all the money and labor used to acquire, install, maintain, and then retire a product. The use of freeware or open source software only changes one of these costs to zero. The rest of the expenses remain and in some cases, increase. These costs include:

A. The purchase cost
   1. Identifying a business need, which includes specific functions that the solution must perform.
   2. Examining the marketplace to identify possible solutions and their cost.

3. Selecting a product and examining its licensing limitations.
4. Negotiating a purchase price.
5. Legal advice while negotiating license restrictions.
B. Internal support costs
   1. End-user staff training (or self-training) in its use.
   2. Technical support staff time to install and test the product and validate its actual function.
   3. Time to review proposed patches, examine them, test, and install.
   4. Adding recovery of the software to the appropriate business continuity plan.
   5. Any required data conversions.
C. Vendor support costs for ongoing support
   1. Enables vendors to retain a staff with expert understanding of the product.
   2. Identification and repair of product defects (testing, documentation, training) and information security issues.
   3. Response to customer inquiries for support and optimal product use.
   4. Creation of training materials.

COMMENT

The annual maintenance fee for commercially provided software is calculated as a percent of its retail price. This fee varies but is typically 15 percent of the retail purchase price. If internal support costs exceed this amount, then consider hiring an external support company.

[D] Information Security and Patching

IT professionals have long complained about the performance, features, and stability of commercial software. Commercial software companies depend on the goodwill and individual recommendations of customers to spread their sales to other sites. This desire for additional sales motivates the seller to constantly improve the product to maintain customer approval.

However, imagine a product whose acquisition cost is zero. No one is concerned with selling more of it. Patches are developed according to the whim of someone who uses it. If taken from a public Internet site, a company has little idea of who is offering patches or enhancements to them. Those who patch it may be very conscientious or quick hitting and careless. These changes may also (accidentally or intentionally) implant breaches to your information security defenses. The news media is full of stories about information security breaches from poorly written software or code with a "back door" that lets malicious people into your data systems.

COMMENT

A properly written open source software license should never expire or be limited to a set number of computers. This reduces the need for license audits or maintaining proof of purchase documents for the many years the software is in service.

Before celebrating your savings, consider what the software support that costs money provides you. First, there is the certainty of where the software came from. If you send money to an established company for software, then it is likely not planted online as a free product by someone who may have inserted something unethical inside of it. Commercial software is in business for the long run. A well-publicized security breach would quickly close their doors.

Second, after the software is in service, you have an expectation of someone providing tested security and defect patches to the product. Again, a commercial software company has a keen interest in detecting and promptly patching any security vulnerabilities that arise in its product. Like any other patch, this requires someone who is intimately familiar with the code to analyze the issue, propose changes, implement and test the changes, and then prepare the patch for distribution. With freeware or open source software, this work falls on the entity using the product.

Patching (to correct defects or to patch security holes) is the same thing every company does today with code that it writes for its own use. The difference is that the code that originated within the company itself is not well known outside its walls. Unless that organization is targeted, it is unlikely that a hacker will spend the time penetrating it. However, if the company is using generally available code patches, then it may be easy enough to penetrate and is worthwhile to try.

Third, if you modify the open source code to meet local requirements, then it becomes an ongoing maintenance challenge to keep the program patched. Even the changes published by the product's users' groups will require additional analysis before installation.

[E]   Software Selection

Software only exists to fulfill a business need. The selection of software must focus on fulfilling that business need. The use of freeware or open source software is only one aspect of the overall selection process and should not be the make-or-break selection issue. Unfortunately, this is precisely the reason some products are selected and it represents a loss of management control of the IT department. The process of approving the purchase of new software acts as a brake on the chaotic acquisition of programs. Each of these programs represents an ongoing company commitment to keep it patched and operational, and to provide trained support technicians or to purchase a support service.

Selecting a freeware product is the same process as selecting a commercial product. The criteria must answer:

A. What business problem are you solving?
B. How will the business process be improved?
C. What is the product's minimal footprint?
D. What is the implementation timeline and checklist?
E. What is the product's acceptance testing?

§ 33.03 LICENSING

[A] Overview

A software license is permission to use a product under certain circumstances. It describes, among many other things, the number of copies permitted to use, how they may be used, and in some cases on which specific machine they are to be used and the rights of the users and the supplier. Software licenses were born out of the unique character of software. First, software is not depletable. Make five copies and the original software is still the same as before—not smaller or less in any way. Second, the purchaser can easily make many more copies for practically no cost at all. This diminishes the software's value in regard to the company that originally created it. Third, some companies price their product proportionally to the customer's benefit. The more powerful the server is that it runs on, or the more processors that it has, the higher the license fee.

Whenever someone loads new software onto his or her computer, typically, a license notification pops up and the operator cannot proceed until the "I agree" button is pressed. If you do not agree, then the installation is halted. It is truly a rare person who takes the time to read the licenses and determine if the restrictions meet his or her business objectives. Objectionable clauses are never at the beginning or end of the text. They are usually buried in mid-paragraph about two-thirds of the way through the verbiage. Hidden there may be permission to use data gathered through the product for public uses, to provide free access to a server, to monitor usage, and on and on. Each license is different and another opportunity to create problems for a company. There is no "standard" commercial software license (although they all seem to include the same basic clauses).

In recent years, open source software license violations have been challenged in court for a wide range of issues. Because most of these challenges have been settled quietly out of court, it is difficult for companies to identify pitfalls to avoid. Further complicating the issue is the nature of the complaint, as some of these challenges have involved patent rather than copyright issues.

[B] Every License Is Different

A software license states the conditions under which the software supplier provides its product. It describes how the product may be used and additional limitations on the user. Given that few people bother to read the license, companies often impose any sort of requirement they wish. This is the primary tool that software distributors use to prevent the unauthorized copying of their product.

By default, software is covered by an implicit copyright. This protects the author but does not describe how the product can be used. Software without a clear license should never be used as the author may later assert his or her rights and require that you immediately cease using it.

COMMENT

A license is a legal document. Therefore, the appropriate person to examine it is either someone skilled in software licensing and law or your company's legal advisors.

Common license terms include:

A. **Copyright.** Explains the limitations that the software owners impose on anyone who licenses their product for use.
B. **Copyleft.** Sort of the opposite of copyright. This type of license includes a minimum of restrictions while permitting maximum distribution and use of the product. Its application varies among licenses. Copyleft is intended as a whimsical "anti-copyright" term.
C. **Embedded code.** This is where a piece of open source licensed code is used as a part of a larger software product. Under most open source software licenses, the embedded code license forces the software in which it is embedded to also be open source (governed by the same freedoms and restrictions)—or that license is revoked.
D. **Public domain.** Software offered to humanity for whatever use they wish to make of it. In essence, every right held by the author is freely given up. However, this permits anyone to take the same code and sell it for a profit with nothing owed to the original author—not even acknowledgement of the person who created it. Therefore, few authors follow this path.

COMMENT

Never take anything for granted when examining a software license. The single sentence inserted into the middle of the long and tedious text can easily change a happy purchase into an obnoxious cash drain.

[C]   Common "Free" or Open Source Licenses

By default, all software is covered under copyright law as an original work. This provides certain rights to the author. Before someone can use that code, the author must describe under what conditions the code is made available. This is the "license." A commercial software license is full of detailed restrictions on the user. A commercial license is written to protect the rights of the author and deny many rights to the purchaser.

What if your goal was a license that instead of forbidding many things, spent most of its verbiage explaining the many things you can do? Early open source authors used "copyleft" as a term to indicate the opposite to "copyright." The goal was to assure the world that a piece of software that the author had written was available to all. In the beginning, open source licenses suffered from many well-intentioned people crafting a legal document without the benefit of legal training—and it showed.

To facilitate the proper open source licensing, several companies developed and distributed (as open source of course) standard licenses that guaranteed the user many rights, and still held a few for the author. (The primary difference between the many open source licenses is the degree of rights withheld by the software authors.) These licenses regularly evolve to ensure that they cover the latest legal interpretations.

Earlier open source licenses were based on U.S. copyright law. In more recent times, the licenses have been updated to ensure they also conform to the European Union and international statutes. One example of this is the GNU GPL. This license is provided by "The GNU Project," which is a free software, mass collaboration project. This license offers your code as open source with the restriction that it can never be used in a commercial product. The GNU GPL guarantees your freedom to share and change all versions of a program. Some of its key features include:

A. The source code must be available.
B. The source code can be copied and freely modified. However, if any of the code is used in a product that you create, the entire resulting product is considered to be open source and subject to the same license.
C. No royalties may be charged but someone may charge a distribution fee.
D. A warranty disclaimer must be included.

Imagine working so hard to create and debug a program only to later find it for sale by someone who did nothing more than the legal paperwork to take ownership? The GNU GPL addresses this by requiring that all improved versions also be free software. In this way, authors exercise their licensing rights to prevent others from financially gaining from their work.

An essential part of open source is that users are free to cooperate and share ideas. This enables people to share bug fixes and improvements with others and acting as a whole, make the product even better for everyone.

COMMENT

The Free Software Foundation (FSF) promotes the rights of everyone to use, study, copy, modify, and redistribute computer programs. It holds the copyrights for a significant portion of the GNU operating system. It uses these rights to defend free software from companies seeking to turn it to proprietary. More information is available at *www.fsf.org.*

Another emerging challenge to open source licenses is in the area of patents. Some companies have asserted patent rights for their software, which raises legal challenges to open source code that used the same general approach to doing something.

Software is covered as intellectual property under both copyright and patent law. Copyright law prevents someone from copying your software. However, the same result can be created by other technicians who code it completely from bottom to top. Patents are different. They also cover the function that something does as well the exact way the patent holder implemented it. So if your program provides a unique function, a patent prevents anyone else from doing that, no matter how it is coded.

As with all legal issues, there is always a caveat. The European Patent Convention excludes patents on computer programs. The hope is that U.S. law will be changed to conform to this international standard. Most of the large technology companies do not know how many software patents they have or what exactly they cover. Therefore, how can an open source developer working alone identify and avoid these pitfalls? The result is a distinct chill on the creation and distribution of open source software. In addition, if a company contributes a patch to a piece of open source software, how can the company be sure that it did not violate some other company's patent rights in doing so?

In recent years, software license holders have been suing companies under patent (rather than copyright) law. This has decreased the adoption of open source systems as companies cannot figure out what is and what is not legal. Newer versions of open source licenses have been modified to guarantee patent rights will not be asserted and that the product is offered royalty free.

COMMENT

Freeware/open source software is always provided without any warranty. Commercial companies bake into their price some money for potential returns and lawsuits arguing warranty issues. Open source code has no such bucket of money to draw on, so let the buyer beware! If it does not work, or includes components that expose your company to license or patent violations, you have limited recourse.

[D]   Sometimes Payment Is Expected

There are companies that provide services around open source software. These companies provide tested versions of the product to customers. As a part of their ongoing efforts, they act as a "trusted source" of software that is free of known issues. Companies that support open source software charge a subscription fee for their services such as telephone support and the prompt distribution of tested patches. In essence, this is the same support as provided by a commercial product, without the product's initial purchase price.

Some of these companies will also offer for sale proprietary products created by their staff that are complementary to the open source code. Many companies find these arrangements give them the best of both the open source and commercial worlds.

[E]   Embedded Code

When developing software, take care that freeware or open source licensed software is not included inside your product. Although once it is compiled, a company may feel that it is successfully "buried" and that no one can determine what the internal components may be. However, the press is full of legal suits and counter suits between the major software companies over who has used portions of whose code inside their products. To avoid license disputes, it is recommended that your IT governance policy forbid the inclusion of open source code within any company software.

Some open source licenses will permit the embedding of their code inside a larger product under certain conditions. These are spelled out in the license agreement. However, most open source licenses require that the larger product that contains open source software must carry the same limited restrictions as in the included open source module.

§ 33.04 SERVER SYSTEMS

[A] Overview

Computer servers, by their nature, run software that is shared by many users. Therefore, if the server has a software problem, then multiple users cannot do their work. This is one of the risks that a company assumes if it uses freeware or open source software.

All software has a situation in which the right combination of events will lead to incorrect results, or will cause the software to stop working. When this occurs in commercial software, there is a company standing by to address the problems through maintenance. The support organization is intimately familiar with the code and how it is supposed to work. However, in a free software situation, this is not the case.

Freeware or open source software is maintained by the open source community at large. If the company that uses this software cannot wait then it creates its own patches. This means that when a software error arises, someone must sift through the code and try to figure out what has happened. In addition, that person can check the Internet for resolution ideas and post the problem on electronic bulletin boards where someone might provide the answer.

COMMENT

Operating system code is complex and massive. No one has the time to read and study it thoroughly. Therefore, it must come through a trusted source.

[B] Free Operating Systems

The most famous open source operating system software is Linux. Linux is based on the idea that the fundamental program on a computer is its operating system. If a free operating system could be provided then it would break the lock that the major software companies hold on the market.

Before bashing the big software development companies for their hold on the market, please understand the value that this provides to everyone. Companies want a no-worry operating system to run their software. Software companies want a stable and universal platform that their products can run within. Operating systems are very complex programs and require a large staff to keep them in repair (repairing bugs, adding features, and plugging information security leaks). As much as people love to gripe about the major companies, organizations of this scale are needed to support full-time technical staffs.

Three examples of open source operating system software are:

A. **Linux.** Linux originated with a young college student in Finland. A long and complex design and programming effort resulted in an operating system kernel, which he called Linux. The Linux kernel is available to everyone under the GNU GPL. Over the years, many companies have based their own versions of the operating system on this kernel. Today Linux-based software is widely used on servers and desktop computers, and has been embraced by the large commercial software companies.

Although Linux is "free," it is rather large to download. Typically, a Linux distribution site will charge a distribution fee to package the code onto CDs and ship it. This is permissible under the license because the code is available for a (massive) download and even from friends.

B. **Open Solaris.** Open Solaris is a UNIX-based operating system from Sun Computing. Open Solaris is free, but the license restriction must be read carefully.

C. **Berkley Software Distribution.** Berkley Software Distribution (BSD) is the basis for many open source operating systems. BSD is UNIX based and compatible with most hardware. Variations on this code usually contain "BSD" in their name.

COMMENT

How wrong they were! Throughout its early years, many technical "experts" derided Linux as a hobbyist's toy. Now it is a mainstream product that is used in practically all large companies (especially in the area of Web support).

[C]   Utility Programs

Utility programs were likely the original open source category. Whenever some technically minded person created a single-purpose program that was handy to use, it would end up as freeware or open source. Of all areas of open source code, this is the most popular. Many people have created software that performs specific tasks for them from converting file formats to complex network monitoring services. Whenever someone writes and perfects something of this sort, there is little market for selling it, so it is often offered for "free" distribution.

§ 33.05   APPLICATIONS SOFTWARE

[A]   Overview

All companies use the same basic software—word processors, spreadsheets, databases, and presentation software. They do so because these products are so very useful and well understood by employees. The issue is cost. At hundreds of dollars per license times the number of office workers in company, this is expensive. As with desktop operating systems, a few companies provide all of the products—when they wish and how they wish. This is counter to open source thinking where everyone is a part of the development and sharing.

One reason that companies standardize on the desktop software market leaders is that they can exchange data with other companies. Unless a customer can read the document you send them, the less common programs would be of low value. However, regulatory organizations are forcing support for a common file format to exchange data. This both opens the marketplace to competitors and enables the use of open source desktop software.

[B] Open Office

Operating systems are very complex to create. Yet, Linux and others have managed to do just that and provide the result to the open source community. The next major challenge in breaking the grip of the major software companies was to bring a complex desktop suite of tools to the open source community. Sun Microsystems accomplished this significant achievement when it published its StarOffice™ desktop software as OpenOffice™. The software is now distributed by the Apache Software Foundation, and can be found at *www.OpenOffice.org*.

OpenOffice uses XML-based file formats for storage and data interchange. This file format is supported by the major proprietary desktop products so that files can be exchanged between them. Even though most people only use a few of the many features in their desktop programs, it is useful to have the other functions available. OpenOffice provides the many features you would expect in expensive desktop software. The six OpenOffice modules are:

A. Writer—full-featured word processing program. It includes spell checking, table of contents creation, tables, etc.
B. Calc—an easy to learn yet powerful spreadsheet program.
C. Impress—creates multimedia presentations.
D. Draw—creates graphics and diagrams.
E. Math—for creating mathematical formulas.
F. Base—a relational database program with wizards, forms, reports, etc.

[C] Mozilla's Firefox

Windows-based PCs are typically delivered with Internet Explorer installed. This proprietary Web browser is easily the most popular one in the world. However, an open source alternative is available in Firefox (available at *http://www.mozilla.com/en-US/firefox/*). This software provides all of the major features found in other browsers. It also has other features that many users feel make it a superior product, such as less memory usage and faster speed.

> ## COMMENT
>
> A listing of free software is found at *directory.fsf.org*.

§ 33.06 MANAGE THE PROCESS

[A] Overview

To ensure the best use of open source software, you must carefully manage its use within the organization. An important part of this process is to consider the risks involved. Some important risks to using open source software to be wary of include:

A. **Examine the source code.** Examine the source code carefully to ensure that nothing malicious is contained in the program. Ideally, this is done for you if the code was obtained from a reputable distributor. Nonetheless, all freeware or open source code is provided without a warranty so this is still your responsibility. (After all, would you eat a sandwich provided by a stranger without looking at it first?) However, in most cases, this is not practical.

B. **Be aware of jurisdiction restrictions.** Open source and freeware licenses are based on U.S. law. Restrictions contained within them, and permissions given to users, may not be valid in all jurisdictions.

C. **Liability issues.** Companies that contribute a patch to a piece of open source software may open the organization to liability for accidentally violating some other company's patent rights.

D. **License issues.** Open source software that does not use one of the free, standard licenses may include whimsical clauses that could lead a company to accidentally default on the license. These licenses may also omit a key clause that grants all privileges to the user that could, again, lead to a license violation.

E. **Code defects.** Examine the code for inaccuracies. Even commercial codes have bugs and who knows what minor changes have been made to your code without updating the version information.

F. **Applying patches.** The code must be kept patched. This means to either blindly apply patches as they become available (see the first bullet point about this) or understand the code thoroughly enough to analyze potential changes before installing. This requires someone skilled in all programming used by the software plus a thorough understanding of how the code is structured.

G. **License restrictions from included code.** Open source software is developed by individuals who may have incorporated a number of other open source packages within the main program. Each of these programs or code-bites may have unique license restrictions in them from the restrictive to the whimsical.

H. **Maintenance of extensions.** Any extensions that you code for the software may not be adopted by the overall community for that software and rejected for inclusion in the project. These become your responsibility to maintain them.

I. **Review patches.** Code patches depend on individuals and volunteer groups to promptly patch them. If interest wanes, then patches may be slow in coming. Also, the patches received may be highly tuned to that company's applications—not necessarily toward the way you use it.

[B] License Auditing

Companies must be in control of their operations, but most are not. Employees purchase software or wireless access points on their own and bring them to work. Software (and other things) are downloaded over the Internet and installed on company computers. The list goes on and on. Some of these actions can open the company to extensive legal sanctions. One of the first defenses that a company must employ is an audit of all software installed on all of its computers.

A software audit collects information on all of the software installed on the company's disk drives (it may not detect software on removable storage). The best way to collect this information is through an automatic discovery program, which regularly checks all storage. In this way, the company can see what is in place. The next step is to eliminate all software that does not conform to its standards.

With this slightly slimmed down inventory, the next step is to determine how often these programs are used. It is not unusual for an IT technician to download a copy of an open source product just to see what it does. It may only have been executed once but lingers in storage "just in case" it is ever needed.

If the company is later sued for using a product that copyright of patent protects, it can now provide data on what is installed and when it was last used (but perhaps not how many times it was run). Plaintiffs will try to demonstrate (or imply) that a company uses an offending piece of code extensively. These inventory logs will minimize the amount of the award.

The second software inventory step is to identify any company software that may have incorporated open source programs into its products and if any of these systems have been passed on to customers. The license for each of these packages must be examined to ensure that the license restrictions were all followed.

The third step is to ensure that all license requirements for open source software selected for use by the company are fulfilled. If not, then that software must be eliminated and a commercial product provided in its place.

Open source software can originate from anywhere and may have passed through several sets of hands before you received it. This means that you may not be able to identify its original author. The result is that the license is "take it or leave it." Negotiations over specific terms are not possible.

[C]   Educate Everyone

Policies provide guidance—but only if employees are aware of their existence and content. Given the expense of a single license lawsuit, it is far cheaper to ensure that all employees are made well aware of the open source policy. Some companies provide this as training in small groups. Training includes a list of the policy's guidelines and an explanation of each point as to why it is important. The training session should not only inform them what is expected but also work to gain their willing conformance with an understanding about the legal issues that can be created.

At the end of the session, require each employee to sign a statement that he or she understands the policy and will comply with it. This step is to protect the company from someone who breaks the policy. With a signed acknowledgement, it is much easier to discharge the person. This may also ease legal penalties as the company can demonstrate that it took good faith measures to avoid problems. As with all legal questions, consult your company's local counsel.

For a policy to be effective, it must be clearly and regularly communicated to all employees. Licensing is a legal issue. Issues with open source licensing are very similar to a company's anti-piracy program. This policy not only passes on guidance to employees but also protects the company against license infringements for unauthorized use. Consider providing each employee with a personal copy of this policy, post it on company bulletin boards, and recap it in the company newsletter. Document all company efforts to inform and remind employees of this policy. See Policy ITP-33-1 Use of Open Source Software on Company Equipment as an example.

POLICY ITP-33-1.   Use of Open Source Software on Company Equipment

Policy #:	ITP-33-1	Effective:	04/01/12	Page #:	1 of N
Subject:	Use of Open Source Software on Company Equipment				

1.0 PURPOSE

This policy guides the selection and use of open source or "freeware" software on company equipment to ensure that the rights of the license holder are respected and that the company does not enter into obligations that it is not prepared to fulfill. It also ensures that the information security aspects and long-term product support are addressed.

2.0 SCOPE

The policy applies to all users of information technology and authors of software within the company. It also applies to the engagement of external organizations that create software for the company.

3.0 POLICY

The CIO establishes and enforces governance for the selection, introduction, and ongoing support of open source software used by the company.

A. Software Selection

The selection process is designed to pick the best tool for the task to be accomplished. Open source software selection competes with commercially available software in the process. Selection is based on alignment with desired function and the five-year total cost of ownership. All open source software used on company equipment must be approved by the Open Source Review Board.

Free software (where only the executable code is provided) is never to be used on a company-critical server or data system. The potential for information security breaches is too great. Open source software can only be used as a component of a company-critical data system if an outside organization can provide a prompt level of support, judged by the CIO to be adequate.

All software selected is subject to a license evaluation by the legal department to ensure that the company is able and willing to meet all of its restrictions. The check also ensures that no permission is given to access, review, or publish company data or the company's use of the product.

Open source software selected for use must also address:

1. Selection of the version to be used. Popular open source products are available in many different variations and some may be more troublesome than others.
2. Stability of the product in industry. The length of time that this product has been in use and user comments on its reliability. All software has defects but type and severity of problems should be noted.
3. Data storage follows an internationally recognized open format that permits data exchange with other products.

   Open source software provides its source code on request. This code must be checked for breaches in the company's information security defenses. After the product is installed, someone in the IT department, or a hired service provider, must be able to analyze, test, and implement code patches to the software. The code check may be bypassed if the source code was provided by a trusted source (a commercial company who charged for its review of the code).

B. Installation & Support

All software, whether open source or commercially obtained, must be tested in isolation to validate its performance, functions, and security characteristics. Test data sets must be applied to validate that the expected results are provided for all data manipulations. This testing also validates installation steps. (If ongoing support is provided by a commercial enterprise, then these steps can be skipped.)

The IT department must train at least one primary and one alternate support person to address support issues that may arise with each product. In some cases, this support may be provided by an outside organization.

Internal support for open source software requires a source of information on the availability of patches. A real-time source of patch information is essential to maintain information security. Most open source software has a community of volunteers to promptly address program problems. These communities must be identified and monitored for the latest product information.

As patches become available, their source code must be evaluated for security breaches and to ensure that it does not alter the critical function of the program. All patches must be verified in a test environment prior to installation.

C. License Monitoring

The IT department gathers licensing requirements for all installed software into one location to ensure compliance. This complex task is made easier by separating the "standard" compliance issues (do not make unauthorized copies, etc.) from the special clauses which may be unique to each license.

An unusual aspect of open source software licensing is that because the author receives no money for his or her work, the author will sometimes insert whimsical clauses into the license. To minimize potential problems and the time required to manage a wide range of license requirements, only software whose license conforms to the GNU GPL (General Public License) will be accepted for use.

The CIO must ensure that an automated software inventory tool is used to identify all software stored or in use on company servers, desktops, notebook, programmable drives, and portable computers. Those products identified as open source must be compared to the approved list. Any product that is recognized as open source but is not on the approved software list will be automatically deleted. The person using this unauthorized software product will receive a formal caution from the Human Resources director, and retraining on the Corporate Acceptable Use policy.

D. Inclusion of Open Source in Company Software

Open source software must never be incorporated inside a company-created product for any reason. If a particular function is required and that software is neither available for purchase nor practical to purchase, then the entire product will be purchased.

All consulting services companies must certify that they will not create any software for use by a customer, or that is owned by a customer, that contains any open source or "freeware" software. This statement must be included on the approved statement of work and included in the standard clauses of all purchase orders.

E. Risks to Monitor

Information security of the company's data systems requires constant vigilance. Every software package and every software change introduced into the computing environment must be carefully examined to ensure that it does not open unauthorized access to malicious users, or threaten the integrity of the company's data through sloppy code.

Open source license has the potential to introduce its own unique licensing requirements. The company may find these requirements difficult to fulfill or to prove it has met them. This exposes the company to liability claims from the license holder. The company must implement a process for ensuring that all license requirements of all open source licenses are followed.

F. Employee Education

Every employee and contract worker in the company must understand and comply with this policy. To do so, everyone must know that it exists and what it prohibits. The CIO will include an explanation of this policy during the Acceptable Use orientation provided to all employees and reviewed by them again annually. The key element is to ensure that no one loads any software on company computers without approval by the CIO.

Every year, following the Acceptable Use orientation, each employee will sign a statement acknowledging his or her agreement to follow the open source policy. These statements must be securely stored and reviewed in all internal audits.

G. Participation in Open Source Projects

Written permission must be obtained from the manager of any employee that wants to participate in an open source project. Organizations desire to participate in such projects must first review their participation with the Open Source Review Board.

4.0 REVISION HISTORY

Date	Revision #	Description of Change
04/01/12	1.0	Initial creation.
03/16/13	1.1	Added reference to Open Source Review Board.

5.0 INQUIRIES

Direct inquiries about this policy to:

George Jenkins, CIO
Our Company, Inc.
2900 Corporate Drive
Columbus, OH 43215

Voice: 614-555-1234
Fax: 614-555-1235
E-mail: gjenkins@company.com

| Revision #: | 1.1 | Supersedes: | 1.0 | Date: | 03/16/13 |

[D]   Open Source Review Board

To protect the organization and to drive consistency in how open source software is used within the organization, many organizations create a committee or group, commonly called an "Open Source Review Board" to evaluate and approve the use of open source applications. This board establishes a formal review process and creates a list of acceptable open source applications. Requests for open source software not already on the list must be first approved by the board before being installed on company equipment. Typical questions to determine if software must be approved by the board include:

A.   Will the software ever be distributed outside the organization?
B.   Will the software be imbedded within a product sold to customers or used in a consulting engagement?
C.   Does the software include any proprietary modules or drivers?
D.   Are you contributing software to an existing open source project or creating a new one?
E.   Are you considering contributing to a project on your own time, or just joined the company and are already contributing to a project?
F.   Does the license contain any restrictions on the use of the software?

If the answer to any of these questions is yes, then a review by the board should be required before the software is installed. A typical review process consists of the following steps:

A.   **Proposal Owner.** The business unit creates and submits a proposal to the review board. The proposal should include:
  1.   A complete explanation of why the open source software is being considered for use.
  2.   The name and description of the software.
  3.   A description of how the software will be used.
  4.   A copy or a link to the license terms and conditions.
B.   **Legal Team.** The legal team reviews the proposal and the licensing terms. The legal team may approve the proposal, approve with conditions, or reject the proposal.
C.   **Review Board.** The board reviews the proposal to determine if the use of the open source software is appropriate. The board may approve the proposal, approve with conditions, or reject the proposal.
D.   **Proposal Owner.** The proposal owner receives the findings of the review board and determines if any conditions placed on the use of the software make the use of the software prohibitive.

See Policy ITP-33-2 Open Source Review Board as an example.

POLICY ITP-33-2.   Open Source Review Board

Policy #:	ITP-33-2	**Effective:**	03/16/13	**Page #:**	1 of N
Subject:	Open Source Review Board				

1.0 PURPOSE

This policy mandates the creation of an Open Source Review Board to manage the use of open source software within the organization. The board will establish a formal review process and create a list of acceptable open source applications. Requests for open source software not already on the list must be first approved by the board before being installed on company equipment.

2.0 SCOPE

The policy applies to all users of information technology and authors of software within the company. It also applies to the engagement of external organizations that create software for the company.

3.0 POLICY

All open source software must be approved by the Open Source Review Board before being installed on company equipment. The board will maintain a list of acceptable open source software, and meet once per month (or as needed) to review new requests. Any group with the organization considering the use of open source software must consider the following questions:

A. Will the software ever be distributed outside the organization?
B. Will the software be imbedded within a product sold to customers or used in a consulting engagement?
C. Does the software include any proprietary modules or drivers?
D. Are you contributing software to an existing open source project or creating a new one?
E. Are you considering contributing to a project on your own time, or just joined the company and are already contributing to a project?
F. Does the license contain any restrictions on the use of the software?

If the answer to any of these questions is yes, then a review by the board is required before the software is installed. The review process consists of the following steps:

A. **Proposal Owner.** The business unit creates and submits a proposal to the review board. The proposal must include:

1. A complete explanation of why the open source software is being considered for use.
2. The name and description of the software.
3. A description of how the software will be used.
4. A copy or a link to the license terms and conditions.

B. **Legal Team.** The legal team will review the proposal and the licensing terms. The legal team may approve the proposal, approve with conditions, or reject the proposal.

C. **Review Board.** The board reviews the proposal to determine if the use of the open source software is appropriate. The board may approve the proposal, approve with conditions, or reject the proposal.

D. **Proposal Owner.** The proposal owner receives the findings of the review board and determines if any conditions placed on the use of the software make the use of the software prohibitive.

4.0 REVISION HISTORY

Date	Revision #	Description of Change
03/16/13	1.0	Initial creation.

5.0 INQUIRIES

Direct inquiries about this policy to:

George Jenkins, CIO
Our Company, Inc.
2900 Corporate Drive
Columbus, OH 43215

Voice: 614-555-1234
Fax: 614-555-1235
E-mail: gjenkins@company.com

Revision #:	1.0	Supersedes:	N/A	Date:	03/16/13

34

VIRTUALIZATION: OPTIMIZING RESOURCES

§ 34.01 OVERVIEW

[A] Purpose and Scope

The exponential growth in applications and systems required to support today's Internet-enabled business has created an explosion in the amount of hardware resources in most businesses. As each new application is brought on line, it is typical to dedicate hardware to the care and feeding of the new application. As the cost of hardware has declined, most organizations install each application on its own separate physical server. Doing this also prevents a misbehaving application from affecting other applications and helps to ensure the desired level of performance, as the application does not have to share resources. Data storage is also typically dedicated to an application, which makes it easier to ensure that the application will have the data storage space it needs when needed. All of these new servers and data storage devices require an ever increasing amount of IT resources, personnel, and energy to keep them running.

Application and storage requirements are not evenly spread out over time. Many applications sit idle for long periods of time, and storage is allocated for applications that may never need it. This wastes valuable corporate resources in the form of both hardware and the energy required to operate the devices. One answer to this problem is virtualization. Virtualization is the concept of sharing hardware resources among the services and applications that use the resources. It allows you to use software to take a single hardware resource and turn it into multiple resources from the application's point of view.

For example, a single physical server can be transformed into multiple "virtual" servers, each with its own central processing unit (CPU), memory, disk drive, and network controller that are not connected to each other except that they all run on the same physical server. This allows multiple applications to now run on a single server without the possibility of them interfering with each other. Server virtualization is the most common form of virtualization, and is what most people think of when they hear the term "virtualization." Other resources that can be virtualized include disk storage, memory, network resources, and applications. By virtualizing physical resources, you can save energy and money and make it easier to reposition these resources as the needs of the business change.

COMMENT

The market-research firm IDC estimates that the typical server spends 85 percent of the time waiting for a user request and not performing any useful activity.

[B] Critical Policies to Develop Based on This Chapter

Using the material discussed in this chapter, you will be able to create the following policies:

A. Server virtualization policy
B. Desktop virtualization policy
C. Application virtualization policy
D. Storage virtualization policy

Policies should always be developed based on the local situation. Successful managers cannot issue appropriate guidance if the policies are written with another company's situation or location in mind.

§ 34.02 SERVER VIRTUALIZATION

[A] Overview

When most people hear the word "virtualization" they think of server virtualization. As with many "new" computer technologies, it is based on concepts and practices that date back to the 1960s, when expensive mainframe computers were designed so that several copies of the operating system could run at the same time. As the power of Intel-based servers have increased in step with Moore's Law (which states that the number of transistors on a chip doubles every 24 months, and with it computing power), they are more than capable of handling today's server applications. For most servers today the average processor utilization rate is 10 to 15 percent, which means that they are mostly sitting idle. Server virtualization allows us to put that idle time to good use running additional applications, which lowers both our capital investment in machines and our cost for energy.

A server virtualization solution can be implemented through specially designed hardware or implemented through software. Either method makes use of a layer of software called a hypervisor, which acts as a gatekeeper between the different operating systems running on the server and the underlying hardware.

Software virtualization is most commonly implemented in one of two ways: full virtualization or paravirtualization. Full virtualization is where the hypervisor is independent of the operating system(s) and sits between the hardware and operating systems to make virtualization possible. The advantage of full virtualization is that it makes it possible to virtualize any operating system. The disadvantage is that the hypervisor needs to be much more sophisticated to be able to handle anything an operating system might want to do. Because of this, overall performance is also negatively affected. In the other software-based virtualization technique, paravirtualization, the operating system is modified to be aware of the fact that it is being virtualized. This requires a much lighter and less complicated hypervisor because the operating system is more cooperative, easier to implement, and better performing than a full virtualization implementation.

§ 34.02[B]

Hardware-based virtualization takes advantage of recent virtualization technologies that are being added to the CPU itself by both Intel, which began offering its Virtualization Technology (VT) product in 2004, and AMD, whose Virtualization (AMD-V) product was released in 2006. By having the CPU designed with virtualization in mind, the job of the hypervisor becomes much easier and results in improved performance of the systems being virtualized.

[B] Possible Benefits

Using virtualization to consolidate servers in the data center provides numerous benefits not just for IT but also for the entire organization. These benefits include:

A. **Reduced hardware and personnel maintenance costs.** Consolidation of servers means less physical hardware to maintain, reducing both the cost of maintenance contracts and the cost of personnel required for support. Disposal costs are also reduced.

B. **Higher investment utilization.** Consolidating many virtual servers on fewer physical machines increase the utilization of your investment in hardware.

C. **Increased space utilization.** Reducing the number of servers can reduce the amount of space needed, or at least allow you to use the space more efficiently.

D. **Lower energy costs.** Less physical hardware means that less energy is required to both power and cool the servers.

E. **Faster deployment of new servers.** By having a standard virtual server built you can quickly and easily deploy new servers.

F. **Support multiple operating systems on a single hardware platform.** With virtualization you can support various versions of Windows, Linux, and other operating systems on a single piece of hardware.

G. **Easier disaster recovery.** Virtualization technology makes it easy to create a snapshot of a production environment that can then be restored onto a different piece of hardware if the original machine fails or is destroyed. The snapshot image can be stored off-site along with backups of changes to the data for easy restoration after a disaster.

H. **Eliminating application conflicts.** With virtualization it is easier and cost-effective to run each server application on its own server, which prevents a misbehaving application from impacting another application.

I. **Support for testing environments.** You can easily load a copy of a production virtual image for testing software changes or new software in a production environment. Testing can be done without worrying about impacting other application or systems.

[C]   Potential Issues

Using virtualization to consolidate servers in the data center can create issues that must be managed not just by IT but also by the entire organization. Issues to watch out for include:

A. **Increased complexity.** Virtualization is a technology that requires experience and expertise to manage properly. It adds a layer of complexity to the standard server environment that must be managed properly.

B. **Resource requirements.** When looking at servers to virtualize you need to look not only at CPU utilization but also at other resources such as memory, storage, and network bandwidth. You may need to increase the quantity of these other resources in order to run multiple virtual machines on a single piece of hardware.

C. **Server sprawl.** Without careful planning you could find yourself with an unmanageable number of virtual servers.

D. **Single point of failure.** If the server hardware fails you now impact each virtual server running on that machine. This multiplies your disaster recovery problem as it affects multiple applications and possibly multiple areas of the organization. You may want to consider using a cluster over different physical servers or some other failover technique.

E. **Licensing issues.** As with any newer technology, you must pay careful attention to licensing issues that might arise. Software vendors can be very aggressive in enforcing licensing violations, even those that might be unintended.

COMMENT

The cost of not carefully monitoring software licensing was over $250,000 to one organization when a normal hardware refresh added additional CPUs to the server. While the organization did not perform the hardware upgrade to increase performance or add additional users, the additional CPUs caused the organization to be out of compliance with its CPU-based licensing with the vendor. While there was no intention to defraud the vendor, the organization was technically out of compliance and had to pay the vendor the full list price of the additional CPU licenses under threat of legal action.

F. **Hardware compatibility.** Not all application/hardware combinations can be easily virtualized. Some specialized applications such as point-of-sale systems may not work correctly in a virtualized environment.

[D]   Policy Considerations

For most organizations the benefits of virtualizing servers demand that the IT organization have a policy in place to begin making use of this technology whenever possible. IT should evaluate all existing server applications for reinstallation on a virtual server. It is important for gaining the acceptance of the business that all existing service level agreements with the business units for server applications be met in a virtualized environment. If the business believes that an application cannot be moved to a virtual server, their reasons must be documented and a report submitted to the CIO for review by executive management. All applications that cannot be moved into a virtual environment should be considered for replacement.

The server virtualization policy should not mandate the use of a particular virtualization technique or vendor; directions for specific technologies are better dealt with in a procedures document. The policy should, however, specify the requirements for any server virtualization software that is to be used. The selected technology should support:

A. Industry-wide standards for server virtualization.
B. A centralized management console.
C. Multiple operating systems.
D. Live migration, which enables the moving of a running virtual machine from one physical server to another.
E. Industry standard x86 hardware and standard storage devices.
F. Industry standard backup and recovery tools for disaster recovery.

See Policy ITP-34-1 Server Virtualization Policy as an example.

POLICY ITP-34-1.   Server Virtualization Policy

Policy #:	ITP-34-1	Effective:	03/18/13	Page #:	1 of N
Subject:	Server Virtualization Policy				

1.0 PURPOSE

This policy defines the requirements for the acquisition, use, and management of server virtualization technologies. Server virtualization allows for the consolidation of multiple applications onto a single server, while still providing the separation of resources needed by these applications.

2.0 SCOPE

The policy applies to all new and existing server applications supported by the organization's IT department or located in the data center.

3.0 POLICY

All existing server applications must be considered for reinstallation on a virtual server. All existing service level agreements with the business units that use a server application must still be met in the virtualized environment. Reasons why an application that cannot be moved to a virtual server must be documented and a report submitted to the CIO. All applications that cannot be moved into a virtual environment should be considered for replacement.

This policy does not mandate the use of a particular virtualization technique or vendor; however, the selected virtualization software must support the following:

A. Industry-wide standards for virtualization.
B. Centralized management console.
C. Multiple operating systems.
D. Live migration, which enables the moving of a running virtual machine from one physical server to another.
E. Industry standard x86 hardware and standard storage devices.
F. Industry standard backup and recovery tools for disaster recovery.

4.0 REVISION HISTORY

Date	Revision #	Description of Change
03/18/13	1.0	Initial creation.

5.0 INQUIRIES

Direct inquiries about this policy to:

George Jenkins, CIO
Our Company, Inc.
2900 Corporate Drive
Columbus, OH 43215

Voice: 614-555-1234
Fax: 614-555-1235
E-mail: gjenkins@company.com

Revision #:	1.0	Supersedes:	N/A	Date:	03/18/13

§ 34.03 DESKTOP VIRTUALIZATION

[A] Overview

The maintenance of applications running on desktop PCs consumes a huge amount of time and resources from the IT support department. It is difficult to keep track of what versions of each application are on each desktop, and users are inclined to download and install the latest cool flash games. Conflicts can occur between incompatible versions of different applications, making the entire desktop unstable.

Two popular environments for providing a better managed and more stable desktop environment are Citrix XenApp (formally Citrix Presentation Server) and Microsoft Remote Desktop Services (formally Microsoft Terminal Services). Desktop virtualization takes this one step further by giving the user a virtualized full client environment using a server-based hypervisor. This gives the user full administrative control over the desktop environment and applications, without the worry of problems caused by conflicting applications.

Virtualized desktops can be either client-based or centralized on servers in the data center. Virtualized desktops running on servers are referred to as a virtual desktop infrastructure (VDI). Client-based desktop virtualization allows legacy or otherwise non-compatible applications to operate in their native environment on another possibly more current operating system. This also allows two or more operating environments to run on a single desktop. VDI delivers the desktop experience over the network by communicating with a client device that supports remote desktop protocols (RDP).

[B] Possible Benefits

Some of the possible benefits of desktop virtualization include:

A. **Easy to deploy.** Standard desktops can be quickly rolled out to new users by either copying the virtual desktop file to the client or pointing the client to the desktop server.
B. **Lower costs.** Desktop machines can be less expensive PCs or thin client devices. Support costs are also reduced.
C. **Mobility.** Desktop virtualization gives you the ability to use your desktop environment from any PC with network or Internet access.
D. **Fully functional.** You still have access to typical desktop features such as multiple monitors, USB devices, etc.
E. **Disaster recovery.** Recovery of the desktop is simplified as a new device can be quickly installed to use the virtualized image on the server. Backups can be managed at the server level.

Desktop virtualization also creates the opportunity to have desktops provided via the Internet, much like many vendors are doing with applications using the "software as a service" (SaaS) model. For desktops, this is sometimes called "desktop as a service" (DaaS).

[C] Potential Issues

Some issues to be aware of when considering desktop virtualization include:

A. **Initial higher costs.** Your "per seat" cost may be initially higher due to the cost of the servers, virtualization software, and Windows licenses.
B. **Different licensing requirements.** The OEM version of Windows that comes with most new PCs cannot be used in a virtual environment; new licenses must be purchased.
C. **User resistance.** Many users will resist giving up their full client PCs.

[D] Policy Considerations

For most organizations, the benefits of virtualizing the desktop suggest that the IT organization have a policy in place to begin making use of this technology whenever possible. IT should evaluate all existing desktop applications for reinstallation onto a virtual desktop. It is important for gaining the acceptance of the business that all existing service level agreements with the business units for desktop applications be met in a virtualized environment. If the business believes that an application cannot be moved to a virtual desktop, their reasons must be documented and a report submitted to the CIO for review by executive management. All applications that cannot be moved into a virtual environment should be considered for replacement.

Another issue the policy should address is the level of support for legacy desktops. Consider making it policy that the user must choose either a laptop computer or a virtual desktop on a standard workstation. Consider eliminating support for legacy desktops and replace them upon failure with either of these options. You should also consider limiting the amount of time that will be spent on support issues for legacy desktops before one of these options are required.

To get the most benefit from desktop virtualization, create a universal corporate desktop image with separate customizations for each business unit. If support for a legacy configuration is required, create a separate legacy desktop image that has no upgrade path and that contains only the bare minimum drivers to function.

The desktop virtualization policy should not mandate the use of a particular virtualization technique or vendor; directions for specific technologies are better dealt with in a procedures document. The policy should, however, specify the requirements for any desktop virtualization software that is to be used. The selected technology should support:

A. Industry-wide standards for desktop virtualization.
B. A centralized management console.
C. Flexible desktop policy management.
D. Live migration, which enables the moving of a running virtual desktop from one physical server to another.
E. Industry standard x86 hardware and standard storage devices.
F. Industry standard backup and recovery tools for disaster recovery.

§ 34.03[D]

See Policy ITP-34-2 Desktop Virtualization Policy as an example.

POLICY ITP-34-2.   Desktop Virtualization Policy

Policy #:	ITP-34-2	**Effective:**	04/18/13	**Page #:**	1 of N
Subject:	Desktop Virtualization Policy				

1.0 PURPOSE

This policy defines the requirements for the acquisition, use, and management of desktop virtualization technologies. Desktop virtualization improves IT's ability to manage and support applications running on individual workstations.

2.0 SCOPE

This policy applies to all new and existing desktop applications and virtualization technologies supported by the organization's IT department that are run on a user workstation (desktop or laptop).

3.0 POLICY

All existing desktop applications must be considered for reinstallation on a virtual desktop. All existing service level agreements with the business units that use a desktop application must still be met in the virtualized environment. Reasons why an application that cannot be moved to a virtual desktop must be documented and a report submitted to the CIO. All applications that cannot be moved into a virtual environment should be considered for replacement.

This policy does not mandate the use of a particular virtualization technique or vendor; however, the selected virtualization software must support the following:

- A. Industry-wide standards for virtualization.
- B. Centralized management console.
- C. Multiple operating systems.
- D. Live migration, which enables the moving of a running virtual desktop from one physical server to another.
- E. Industry standard x86 hardware and standard storage devices.
- F. Industry standard backup and recovery tools for disaster recovery.

4.0 REVISION HISTORY

Date	Revision #	Description of Change
04/18/13	1.0	Initial creation.

5.0 INQUIRIES

Direct inquiries about this policy to:

George Jenkins, CIO
Our Company, Inc.
2900 Corporate Drive
Columbus, OH 43215

Voice: 614-555-1234
Fax: 614-555-1235
E-mail: gjenkins@company.com

Revision #:	1.0	Supersedes:	N/A	Date:	04/18/13

§ 34.04 APPLICATION VIRTUALIZATION

[A] Overview

The traditional client/server model allows data to be managed at the server level, and requires an application running on a client of some kind (usually a desktop PC). The client is required to have its own operating system and licenses and be updated on a regular basis. Few clients or servers run only one application, so multiple applications are installed, potentially causing conflicts between applications or problems due to a buggy application affecting the entire system. This negatively impacts the productivity of the users of the system and adds to the IT support workload.

Application virtualization allows you to separate a software application from the underlying operating system. It can be used at the desktop or server level. This makes it easier to manage and update the application without affecting other applications that might be in use on the same hardware. Applications become a single file on the operating system that can be moved or copied from one system to another and backed up for archival purposes. Client applications can be streamed to the client on demand and are encapsulated so that they cannot interfere with other applications.

Application virtualization is similar in concept to server virtualization, but instead of having separate isolated copies of operating systems sharing resources, you have separate isolated copies of several applications sharing resources. The physical hardware is hidden from the application as it is in server virtualization, but in addition, the operating system is also hidden. This allows a virtualized application package to be copied to a machine and the application is run as if it had been installed directly on the machine.

[B] Possible Benefits

Using virtualization to manage and distribute applications provides numerous benefits for not just IT but for the entire organization. These benefits include:

A. **Reduced personnel maintenance costs.** Virtualized applications require less support from IT personnel because worries about incompatible drivers or libraries go away. Patches and upgrades are also easier to deploy.

B. **Ease of deployment.** Virtualized applications can run on a machine without installing device drivers or making registry entries, which means you do not have to have administrative rights to deploy the application.

C. **Ease of maintenance.** Because virtual applications exist as a single file, they can be easily removed from a system when no longer needed. They also allow you to migrate to a new operating system without having to upgrade or replace legacy applications.

D. **Eliminates application conflict.** Applications that would be incompatible with each other if installed directly on a single machine can be safely run virtualized on the same machine.

E. **Portability.** Virtualized applications can be executed from portable media such as memory sticks or USB drives on any machine regardless of the operating system.

F. **Improved security.** Because the application is isolated from the underlying operating system security is improved. You can also lock down corporate endpoints by running applications in user mode without having to lockout users.

G. **Fewer resources required.** A virtual application requires fewer resources than creating an entire virtual machine.

H. **Instant-on failover.** Virtualized applications can be managed just like any other enterprise data, allowing replications to support instant-on failover of applications.

[C] Potential Issues

There are a few issues to consider when virtualizing an application. These issues include:

A. **Not all applications can be virtualized.** Specialized applications such as virus protection or some older applications that require unique device drivers or use memory in an unsupported way may not run in a virtual mode.

B. **Setup tools required.** To virtualize an application it must be packaged using a virtualization tool such as VMware ThinApp or Microsoft Application Virtualization.

C. **Increased network traffic.** Streaming virtualized applications to machines on the network place an additional burden on your network bandwidth.

D. **Client requirements.** Although any virtualized application can be streamed to any client machine, the receiving client must still be powerful enough to run the application.

[D] Policy Considerations

For most organizations, the benefits of virtualizing applications suggest that the IT organization have a policy in place to begin making use of this technology whenever possible. IT should evaluate all existing applications for virtualization. It is important for gaining the acceptance of the business that all existing service level agreements with the business units for applications be met in a virtualized environment. If the business believes that an application cannot be virtualized, their reasons must be documented and a report submitted to the CIO for review by executive management. All applications that cannot be virtualized should be considered for replacement.

Another issue the policy should address is the level of support for legacy applications. Consider eliminating support for legacy applications and replace them when possible. You should also consider limiting the amount of time that will be spent on support issues for legacy applications before they will be replaced.

The application virtualization policy should not mandate the use of a particular virtualization technique or vendor; directions for specific technologies are better dealt with in a procedures document. The policy should, however, specify the requirements for any application virtualization software that is to be used. The selected technology should support:

A. Industry-wide standards for application virtualization.
B. The ability to centrally deliver and manage a single instance of an application.
C. Performance monitoring and measurement to ensure that SLAs are met, as well as compliance with corporate security requirements.
D. Flexible application policy management.
E. Local peripherals such as printers and USB ports.
F. Industry standard x86 hardware and standard storage devices.
G. Industry standard backup and recovery tools for disaster recovery.

See Policy ITP-34-3 Application Virtualization Policy as an example.

POLICY ITP-34-3. Application Virtualization Policy

Policy #:	ITP-34-3	**Effective:**	04/18/13	**Page #:**	1 of N
Subject:	Application Virtualization Policy				

1.0 PURPOSE

This policy defines the requirements for the acquisition, use, and management of application virtualization technologies. Application virtualization improves IT's ability to manage and support applications running on servers and individual workstations.

2.0 SCOPE

This policy applies to all new and existing applications and virtualization technologies supported by the organization's IT department that are run on a user workstation (desktop or laptop) or on servers.

3.0 POLICY

All existing applications must be considered for virtualization. All existing service level agreements (SLAs) with the business units that use an application must still be met in the virtualized environment. Reasons why an application that cannot be virtualized must be documented and a report submitted to the CIO. All applications that cannot be virtualized should be considered for replacement.

This policy does not mandate the use of a particular virtualization technique or vendor; however, the selected virtualization software must support the following:

A. Industry-wide standards for application virtualization.
B. The ability to centrally deliver and manage a single instance of an application.
C. Performance monitoring and measurement to ensure that SLAs are met, as well as compliance with corporate security requirement.
D. Flexible application policy management.
E. Local peripherals such as printers and USB ports.
F. Industry standard x86 hardware and standard storage devices.
G. Industry standard backup and recovery tools for disaster recovery.

4.0 REVISION HISTORY

Date	Revision #	Description of Change
04/18/13	1.0	Initial creation.

5.0 INQUIRIES

Direct inquiries about this policy to:

George Jenkins, CIO
Our Company, Inc.
2900 Corporate Drive
Columbus, OH 43215

Voice: 614-555-1234
Fax: 614-555-1235
E-mail: gjenkins@company.com

Revision #:	1.0	Supersedes:	N/A	Date:	04/18/13

§ 34.05 STORAGE VIRTUALIZATION

[A] Overview

Storage is another IT resource that is underutilized. Disk storage is wasted on applications that reserve a minimum amount of storage for their use, but which in many cases just sits unused. Storage virtualization allows the physical storage from multiple storage devices to appear to be a single storage device to the operating system or application. The storage can then be allocated as needed for use by users, applications, and servers. Just as with server virtualization, storage virtualization can increase utilization to 75 percent or better.

There are three basic technologies used for virtualizing storage:

A. **Storage area network (SAN).** This is the most common method for virtualization storage. It starts with a SAN that connects several storage devices using a high-speed Fibre Channel network. Software on a storage virtualization device or host server is then used to provide an abstraction layer between the host performing the I/O and the storage controllers that provide the storage capacity.

B. **Host-client.** This method uses software that runs on file and application servers to detect available storage and maintain the necessary metadata for storage management.

C. **In-array or embedded functionality.** This method uses a special network controller and management software to allow different physical storage systems to be used as one large resource.

[B] Possible Benefits

Virtualization of your storage resources provides a number of benefits, which include:

A. **Easier administration.** Virtualized storage can be managed from a single administrative console. Tedious and time-consuming storage administration tasks can be automated.

B. **Improved storage management.** Storage growth can be closely monitored and managed, making upgrade planning easier.

C. **Vendor independence.** Some storage virtualization technologies allow for homogeneous storage to live behind the virtualization engine. You are not locked into one vendor which allows for a more competitive price point.

D. **Disaster recovery.** Disaster recovery is improved as storage can be more easily moved around or backed up to other locations.

E. **Easier migration.** Data can be migrated to new storage devices without disrupting the application, because the physical storage is not directly tied to the application. This makes it easier to swap out end-of-lease equipment or to refresh old storage with newer devices.

[C]   Potential Issues

Issues to be aware of when considering storage virtualization include:

A. **Compatibility.** If you have heterogeneous storage devices, are they all compatible with the virtualization technology you're considering? Most of the major enterprise storage vendors now offer virtualization technologies that allow for heterogeneous storage devices to live behind them.
B. **Metadata management.** You must ensure that the storage metadata is protected and backed up.
C. **Vendor lock-in.** Be aware that whichever option you choose, you may be locked into a particular vendor.

COMMENT

At one company, storage virtualization made disaster recovery testing much more efficient (and therefore more likely to be done) by allowing storage to be mirrored across distances. With this ability, they were able to mirror the data needed by the applications to the disaster recovery site and then point the servers to the disaster recovery site data when needed. To perform the disaster recovery test, they simply had to stop the mirroring, make the target storage writeable, and then reboot the disaster recovery servers to point to the disaster recovery site storage. It took the process from 4 to 6 hours each way to 1 to 1.5 hours each way and it reduced the amount of IT staff needed to make the failover process work. Overall, this was a savings of 3 to 4 hours and a reduction in the staff required to perform the test.

[D]   Policy Considerations

For most organizations, the benefits of virtualizing storage suggest that the IT organization have a policy in place to begin making use of this technology whenever possible. IT should evaluate all existing storage requirements for virtualization. It is important for gaining the acceptance of the business that all existing service level agreements with the business units be met in a virtualized storage environment. If the business believes that their storage cannot be virtualized, their reasons must be documented and a report submitted to the CIO for review by executive management. All storage that cannot be virtualized should be considered for replacement.

The storage virtualization policy should not mandate the use of a particular virtualization technique or vendor; directions for specific technologies are better dealt with in a procedures document. The policy should, however, specify the requirements for any storage virtualization software that is to be used. The selected technology should support:

A. Industry-wide standards for storage virtualization.
B. Automation of data and storage management, including data migration, replication, backup, recovery, and retention.
C. Universal access to storage using standard interfaces and protocols.
D. Performance monitoring and measurement to ensure that SLAs are met, as well as compliance with corporate security requirements.
E. Industry standard x86 hardware and standard storage devices.
F. Industry standard backup and recovery tools for disaster recovery.

See Policy ITP-34-4 Storage Virtualization Policy as an example.

POLICY ITP-34-4. Storage Virtualization Policy

Policy #:	ITP-34-4	Effective:	04/18/13	Page #:	1 of N
Subject:	Storage Virtualization Policy				

1.0 PURPOSE

This policy defines the requirements for the acquisition, use, and management of storage virtualization technologies. Storage virtualization improves IT's ability to manage and support the data storage requirements of the business.

2.0 SCOPE

This policy applies to all new and existing storage virtualization technologies supported by the organization's IT department.

3.0 POLICY

All existing data storage being used must be considered for virtualization. All existing service level agreements with the business units that use data storage must still be met in the virtualized environment. Reasons why business unit's data storage that cannot be virtualized must be documented and a report submitted to the CIO. All applications whose data storage cannot be virtualized should be considered for replacement.

§ 34.05[D]

This policy does not mandate the use of a particular virtualization technique or vendor; however, the selected storage virtualization software must support the following:

A. Industry-wide standards for storage virtualization.
B. Automation of data and storage management, including data migration, replication, backup, recovery, and retention.
C. Universal access to storage using standard interfaces and protocols.
D. Performance monitoring and measurement to ensure that SLAs are met, as well as compliance with corporate security requirements.
E. Industry standard x86 hardware and standard storage devices.
F. Industry standard backup and recovery tools for disaster recovery.

4.0 REVISION HISTORY

Date	Revision #	Description of Change
04/18/13	1.0	Initial creation.

5.0 INQUIRIES

Direct inquiries about this policy to:

George Jenkins, CIO
Our Company, Inc.
2900 Corporate Drive
Columbus, OH 43215

Voice: 614-555-1234
Fax: 614-555-1235
E-mail: gjenkins@company.com

Revision #:	1.0	Supersedes:	N/A	Date:	04/18/13

35

CLOUD COMPUTING: INFRASTRUCTURE ALTERNATIVES

§ 35.01   OVERVIEW

[A]   Purpose and Scope

Policies that address the use of cloud computing services formalize how and under what circumstances the company will make use of these services. While the use of cloud computing services can provide many benefits to the organization, there are numerous issues that must be addressed by having the appropriate policies in place. Some of these issues include:

    A. **Security.** Applications and data that are in the cloud are not under the direct control of the organization.

    B. **Latency.** Will the performance of applications not located on the corporate network satisfy the needs of the users?

    C. **Auditability.** Can the cloud computing solution be audited to satisfy regulatory requirements?

Cloud computing policies cover all types of applications, services, and data that are not hosted on equipment under the direct physical control of the organization. The types of services covered include:

    A. **Software as a Service (SaaS).** This refers to applications that are provided by the cloud vendor.

    B. **Platform as a Service (PaaS).** The cloud vendor provides the platform that runs applications created by the customer.

    C. **Infrastructure as a Service (IaaS).** Here the cloud vendor provides processing, storage, network capacity, and other computing resources to be used by the customer.

The policies in this section cover any situation, in which applications, services, and/or data are used by the organization, which is not under the direct physical control of the organization.

[B]   Policy Objectives

Policies developed for cloud computing use should provide guidelines to ensure the secure, proper, and reliable use of the applications, services, and data hosted in the cloud. Policy objectives should be flexible enough to cover new methods of cloud computing and technologies as they become available.

COMMENT

Research firm Gartner expects spending on IT cloud services to reach $210 billion by 2016. Much of the growth will be adoption by small- and medium-sized businesses.

[C] Critical Policies to Develop Based on This Chapter

Using the material discussed in this chapter, you will be able to create the following policies:

A. Cloud computing/SaaS/PaaS/IaaS options
B. Management of cloud computing vendors
C. Selection of cloud computing vendors
D. Guidelines for the types of services that can be in the cloud

Policies should always be developed based on the local situation. Successful managers cannot issue appropriate guidance if the policies are written with another company's situation or location in mind.

§ 35.02 CLOUD COMPUTING

[A] Overview

Cloud computing is the use of software and IT services on an as needed basis, typically provided via the Internet. Cloud computing can augment or replace services that have traditionally been performed in-house. It is typically a pay-per-use model that makes it possible for an organization to have access to a shared pool of computing resources (servers, storage, applications, etc.) on demand. The term comes from the common use of the "cloud" metaphor to describe the Internet. The term encompasses the concepts of Software as a Service (SaaS), Platform as a Service (PaaS), and Infrastructure as a Service (IaaS).

A. **Cloud Software as a Service (SaaS).** Applications provided by the cloud vendor are accessed by the customer via the Internet.
B. **Cloud Platform as a Service (PaaS).** An entire platform of IT-related services is made available via the Internet for the deployment of customer-created applications to the cloud.
C. **Cloud Infrastructure as a Service (IaaS).** The customer rents processing, storage, network capacity, and other fundamental computing resources from the cloud vendor.

Cloud computing is becoming a significant component of managing an organization's software infrastructure. With the increasing shortage of skilled workers to operate software systems in-house, more companies turn to cloud computing to manage and maintain their software infrastructure. It is critical that the information systems group manage the selection and use of cloud computing applications and platforms, ensuring the company receives the value the cloud computing vendor was hired to provide. Cloud computing policies formalize standards for how these vendors are used and managed within the organization.

The most likely software applications to outsource to a cloud computing vendor are everyday applications that every organization in an industry uses, or functions such as security that require specialized personnel to support properly. Such services are also appropriate when an organization does not have the time, technical resources, or money to buy, build, maintain, and support a software application. Requirements for future scalability can also be a consideration, as a cloud computing vendor can usually scale up more quickly if additional resources are required to support more users.

COMMENT

In a 2013 Gartner survey, customer relationship management (CRM) continued to be the largest market for SaaS applications, with the highest growth being in Office Suites and database management systems.

[B] Definition

A cloud computing vendor is a supplier that makes software applications or an IT services platform available over the public Internet, usually on a subscription basis. The cloud computing model has grown out of the ashes of the ASP offerings during the dot-com bubble and works similarly to the time-sharing systems used in the 1960s and 1970s. Cloud computing vendors typically provide access to the following types of applications and services:

- Supply chain management
- Storage
- Voice-response systems
- Virus protection on a VPN
- Hosted contact center
- Enterprise resource management
- Security
- Business process management and workflow
- Data warehousing
- Industry specific vertical applications
- E-purchasing
- Human resources
- Recruiting
- E-mail
- Document and workflow management
- Customer relationship management
- Group scheduling
- Service desk
- Secure collaboration communities

A cloud computing vendor can also combine service offerings traditionally not offered by one company. The four primary ingredients are the following:

A. **Packaged software applications.** Licenses to products developed by ISVs are sold for a sizable up-front fee, on a subscription basis or on a per-use basis.
B. **Data centers and connectivity.** Data-center services are offered by hosting companies (e.g., DataCenter.BZ, Ecommerce), hardware companies (e.g., IBM, Dell), and telecom providers (e.g., CenturyLink, Verizon, AT&T). Telecom and business Internet service providers (ISPs) provide connectivity.
C. **Application monitoring and ongoing support.** Firms such as Infocrossing and Verizon typically offer application monitoring. System integrators (SIs) or ISVs typically provide second-level support.
D. **Systems implementation and integration.** Systems integrators (SIs) or the service arms of ISVs traditionally offer these services.

The cloud computing vendor is used to provide access to a single application or can be used to replace the entire user desktop.

COMMENT

The research firm IDC expects spending on IT cloud services to account for 9 percent of revenues in five key market segments. More important, spending on cloud computing will accelerate throughout the forecast period, capturing 25 percent of IT spending growth in 2012 and nearly a third of growth the following year.

Corporate and IT management must have a clear set of long-term goals and objectives for the outsourcing of applications and IT platforms. Cloud computing vendors can be used:

- For operations difficult to manage and staff. Cloud computing vendors can reduce headcount needs.
- To avoid hardware and software obsolescence.
- To improve focus on core competencies. Most companies do not include IT as part of their core competency.
- To supply talent and/or resources unavailable in the organization.
- To reduce internal operation costs.
- To make applications available to a mobile, distributed workforce.
- For their ability to scale rapidly.
- To make IT costs more predictable.
- For turnkey solutions. The role of general technology contractor shifts from the company to the cloud computing vendor.

- To free resources for other efforts.
- To bring systems up and running faster. Cloud computing vendors can generally deliver software to a customer more rapidly than in-house resources or an external software developer can.

[C]   What Should Be in the Cloud

The most important decision to be made is what applications, services, and data are appropriate for the organization to move to the cloud. Several factors need to be considered when performing this evaluation. Some factors that would make a move to the cloud appealing include:

A. **Services with scaling issues.** The cloud might be a good option for services that need to scale up infrequently or at certain times of the year. For example, an e-commerce site that does most of its business over the holidays could use services from a cloud vendor to cover its peak times, without having to invest in infrastructure year-round just to cover the holiday rush.

B. **Applications that need to be up quickly.** This might be for a new department or service that needs to be up and running quickly, and cannot wait to go through the normal IT procurement channels. Using the cloud, a new service can be up and running and tested to see if it is a candidate for being a permanent part of the organization's service offering.

C. **Ease of desktop support.** No bulky applications have to be installed and maintained on user machines, as only a Web browser is required.

D. **CAPEX vs. OPEX costs.** Building out a system internally requires sometimes scarce capital, where a pay-as-you-go cloud solution can be incrementally expensed.

Not all applications are suited for the cloud. Issues that might prevent you from moving applications or services to the cloud include:

A. **Latency.** Applications on the cloud will never be as fast as those hosted on your own physical network.

B. **Bandwidth.** If your users move around large amounts of data, the cost of the required bandwidth to connect to the cloud vendor could eliminate any cost savings.

C. **Sensitive data.** With governments becoming ever more strict about the governance of financial, health, and other sensitive data, you should carefully consider moving sensitive data outside of your direct control.

D. **Too big to scale.** If your organization is extremely large, you may not see an enormous savings in outsourcing to the cloud. You may find that you can achieve better economies of scale by doing your own cloud rather than outsourcing to someone else.

E. **Custom requirements.** If your organization requires extremely customized applications or services, you might not be able to find a cloud vendor that can meet your needs.

§ 35.03 CLOUD COMPUTING VENDOR SELECTION PROCESS

[A] Overview

Selecting a cloud vendor to provide application and IT-related services requires the use of stringent evaluation procedures. Not only must the applications and services themselves be evaluated, but hosting facilities, bandwidth, and support capabilities must also be carefully considered. The relative newness of the cloud computing market and the volatility of the stock market upon which they rely for funding make the selection of the right cloud computing vendor extremely important. Betting an organization's technology infrastructure on a company that may experience a sharp drop in its stock price may cause trouble. If its stock price drops, the company may not have the money to invest in research and development, which may impact its ability to service its customers.

In addition to technical considerations, constantly reevaluate with whom the company does business in this area. Have a company-wide agreement on the criteria for choosing a technology vendor. Get involved in a professional network of chief technology officers (CTOs) who can meet on a regular basis to discuss technology providers' performance. Bet the infrastructure on a combination of established and newer companies. The best cloud computing companies, and the ones most likely to stay in business, are those that have formed a technology and business alliance with an established company such as IBM, Microsoft, or Oracle. These more established companies have done their own evaluation of technology providers and found them credible partners. A small sample of cloud computing vendors is listed below:

Company	Product	Web site
Amazon	Resizable compute capacity	*aws.amazon.com/ec2/*
Google	Various applications	*www.google.com*
Microsoft	Various applications	*www.microsoft.com/cloud/*
Sage	Customer relationship management	*www.sagecrmsolutions.com*
Salesforce.com	Customer relationship management	*www.salesforce.com*
Smart Online, Inc.	Small business software	*www.smartonline.com*
Zimbra, Inc.	Enterprise messaging and collaboration	*www.zimbra.com*
Zoho.com	Office Suite and business applications	*www.zoho.com*

[B]   Request for Proposal

When IT management is ready to receive vendor proposals, a formal request for proposal (RFP) letter is sent to all possible candidates. The RFP defines the format of the proposal ensuring that a responding vendor can be evaluated and compared easily with others. The RFP should cover the following items:

A. Information about the project
1. Type of applications and/or services to be outsourced
2. Minimum performance requirements and evaluation criteria
3. Reliability level required
4. IT contact person
5. Level of integration with other systems required
6. Any required reporting capabilities
7. Ownership of data
B. General information about the vendor
1. Vendor contact person
2. Vendor maintenance, training, and operation support
3. Credentials of firm
4. Former and current customer references
5. A copy of their Business Continuity Plan along with a log of when and how it was tested
6. Quality of support (credentials of staff, average length of service, etc.)
7. Compliance with government regulations
C. Services information
1. Service volume expandability
2. Operating systems available options
3. Availability of a virtual to physical server conversion option as a migration safety net for virtual machines
4. Availability of full copies of data and applications
5. Documentation clarity and completeness
6. User-training and implementation resources available
7. Process to ensure data security and availability
8. Reliability of service
9. Scalability of service
10. Availability of support
11. Security of connection
12. Physical security of data center
13. Next expected release of software
14. Types of reports issued detailing application access and use statistics
15. Management of software upgrade process
16. Dedicated or shared server
17. Storage space available per user and cost
18. Backup and redundancy resources available
19. Migration of virtual machines
20. Customization options available, if any

The RFP is for an ongoing service contract with a given time limit. The service is billed monthly at a flat rate or prorated by transaction or user volume.

All items in the contract with the cloud computing vendor are negotiable. A 3- to 5-year contract is typical. Standard support is usually 12/5 (12 hours a day, 5 days a week) with 24/7 support available at an additional cost. Systems with a small number of users are typically placed on a shared server with other customers of the cloud computing vendor. Dedicated servers are available for an additional cost. The base fee per user normally covers the infrastructure at the cloud computing vendor (but not the cost to connect) and any software licenses required. A fixed amount of hard-disk storage space is usually included, with 1GB–10GB per user typical. Carefully evaluate what users need and try to ensure as much as possible is covered in the standard agreement. As with any major purchase, add-ons can significantly add to the cost of the service.

The method by which the company connects to the cloud computing vendor is also an important consideration. A dedicated frame relay connection to the cloud computing vendor is the most secure and reliable, but more expensive than connecting over the public Internet. A connection over the Internet can be much less reliable, as overall Internet traffic can impact your performance. Using a dedicated frame connection, a good rule of thumb is 10 users for a 64K line, 20 users on a 128K line, and 50 to 60 users on a full T1 connection. For the same connection over the Internet, about one-half to two-thirds as many users can be supported as on the frame connection.

For each vendor selected to receive a copy of the RFP, assign an internal IT person the task of liaison between that vendor and the company. That person's job is to manage the communication between the vendor and the company and to encourage the vendor to provide its best response to the RFP. Encourage the vendor to put the maximum effort into its response, especially if the vendor suspects that a competitor may have an advantage. Even if another vendor is selected, any attractive items in the losing vendors' proposals can be used as negotiating points with the vendor ultimately elected.

[C] Evaluating Cloud Computing Vendors' Proposals

All proposals received should be analyzed using a predetermined set of criteria. The elements compared should be in the same sequence on each proposal. Copies are given to each evaluator, and a date and time are selected to meet and discuss them.

Vendors providing clear and complete information requested in the RFP and meeting preliminary evaluation standards are selected for more detailed analysis. Those who do not will be removed from further consideration.

Current and former customers should be contacted to discuss their experiences with the vendor. The following questions are helpful for obtaining useful information:

A. Would you use the same vendor again? If so, why? What has been the major problem with the vendor? Do you know other users of the vendor's product? Are they generally happy? If so, why? Who are the other users? What are their names and telephone numbers?

B. How long does it take for the vendor to respond to problems? Are the people who respond knowledgeable and friendly? Has the vendor ever lied? Has the vendor had the resources to resolve your problem(s)?

C. Does the application satisfy your needs? Follow up with questions about how long they have had the system and how often it has gone down. Ask about its expandability and upgrading possibilities.

D. Do the users like the service? Ask to talk to users and confirm this. Ask users what they liked and disliked about the service and why.

E. Ask how long it took to put the application into operation. Did they receive adequate training? Are the user manuals easy to understand and follow?

F. Is the service provided better than they could do themselves, and if so, why? Is the service worth the cost?

G. Were there any unexpected or hidden costs? What was the nature of these costs? Were the costs reasonable? Was the vendor confronted about this? If so, what was the reaction?

H. Were the vendor's employees easy to work with? Did their salesperson follow up after the sale was made? Does the vendor seem to have a genuine interest in the success of the service?

I. If you were starting all over, what would you do differently?

COMMENT

"This coming 'services wave' will be very disruptive ... Services designed to scale to tens or hundreds of millions will dramatically change the nature and cost of solutions deliverable to enterprises or small businesses."

—From an internal memo from Bill Gates, Microsoft Chairman, October 30, 2005.

§ 35.04 CLOUD COMPUTING VENDOR MANAGEMENT

[A] Overview

Managing a long-term cloud computing project is not an easy task. Some of the reasons for difficulty include:

A. Pricing and service levels established at the beginning of the contract do not contain meaningful methods for measurement and improvement of service.

B. Expectations and assumptions of both parties change over time. Most contracts cannot anticipate changes in technology, personnel, and business processes, etc.

C. Cultural differences between the two companies can cause misunderstandings and mistrust.

D. Differences in the goals and objectives of the two companies can cause problems.

E. Lack of management oversight may cause priorities to become out of sync with the reasons for entering into the contract in the first place.

[B] Service Level Agreement

Information services and affected business units must work together to determine the service level requirements for the applications that are outsourced to the cloud computing vendor. These service levels must be determined at the outset of the agreement and used to measure and monitor the supplier's performance. The service levels are written in a service level agreement (SLA). The SLA defines the consequences for failing to meet one or more service levels.

The SLA should include the following sections:

A. A precise definition of key terms

B. Specific service levels for all key categories (e.g., system availability, service desk responsiveness, security administration, change management)

C. Frequency of service level measurement (usually monthly)

D. Guarantee that all security breaches are reported

E. Responsibility for sensitive data

F. Weighting by importance of key service levels

G. Calculation of credits for missing service levels

H. Calculation of credits for frequency of missing service levels (increased frequency of missed service levels might increase the service credit by some predetermined factor). The performance factors specified in the SLA not only provide an objective measure of the vendor's performance, but can serve as a basis for termination of the service if threshold service levels cannot be met. Other non-key performance levels can be specified to add to the case for termination if warranted.

Typical credit for failure to meet routine service levels ranges from 5 to 15 percent, with penalties for severe service failures reaching 20 to 25 percent. Force majeure clauses excuse a party's failure to perform if the failure resulted from an act of nature, such as an earthquake or other natural disaster beyond the party's control. The cloud computing vendor will attempt to include as much as possible in this category; the IT Manager will define it as narrowly as possible. Under no circumstances should a force majeure clause absolve the vendor completely from its responsibilities.

The SLA might also include provisions for vendor rewards for any additional value-added services provided. Make sure these services will really add value before agreeing to payment.

§ 35.04[B]

Negotiating and designing an SLA is difficult and time-consuming, but a fair and comprehensive SLA is critical for a successful cloud computing relationship. During the negotiation, both parties learn a lot about how their future partner approaches various aspects of their relationship.

Establish guidelines for how the organization's relationship with cloud computing vendors is to be managed. See Policy ITP-35-1 Cloud Computing Vendor Management Policy as an example.

POLICY ITP-35-1. Cloud Computing Vendor Management Policy

Policy #:	ITP-35-1	Effective:	03/18/13	Page #:	1 of N
Subject:	Cloud Computing Vendor Management Policy				

1.0 PURPOSE

This policy defines the framework by which cloud computing vendors will be managed. Cloud computing vendors are any vendors of software where the software and data is stored by the vendor, with access provided via the Internet.

2.0 SCOPE

The policy applies to all software applications and IT services that are managed and hosted by a third-party provider.

3.0 POLICY

The following guidelines will be followed for managing a cloud computing vendor:

A. The areas for which a cloud computing vendor is used will be budgeted annually.
B. Contracts that expire within the next budget year require a new contract proposal 3 months before the cut off for budget consideration.
C. If the current cloud computing vendor's performance or new proposal is not satisfactory, an RFP will be sent to no fewer than two other vendors.
D. Cloud computing vendor proposals must include the following items:
   1. A copy of their Business Continuity Plan along with a log of when and how it was tested
   2. Compliance with government regulations
   3. Credentials of firm
   4. Former and current customer references
   5. Documentation clarity and completeness
   6. User-training and implementation resources available
   7. Process to ensure data security and availability

8. Reliability of service
9. Scalability of service
10. Availability of support
11. Quality of support (credentials of staff, average length of service, etc.)
12. Security of connection
13. Physical security of data center
14. Next expected release of software
15. Types of reports issued detailing application access and use statistics
16. Management of the software upgrade process
17. Dedicated or shared server
18. Storage space available per user and cost
19. Backup and redundancy resources available
20. Customization options available, if any

4.0 REVISION HISTORY

Date	Revision #	Description of Change
03/18/13	1.0	Initial creation.

5.0 INQUIRIES

Direct inquiries about this policy to:

George Jenkins, CIO
Our Company, Inc.
2900 Corporate Drive
Columbus, OH 43215

Voice: 614-555-1234
Fax: 614-555-1235
E-mail: gjenkins@company.com

Revision #:	1.0	Supersedes:	N/A	Date:	03/18/13

Part IV

BUILDING AND SHARING KNOWLEDGE

36

DOCUMENTATION: GETTING EVERYONE ON THE SAME PAGE

§ 36.01 OVERVIEW

[A] Purpose and Scope

The purpose of documenting IT processes and procedures is to save money. When installing or creating processes, programs, and hardware, someone analyzed the requirements, planned the solution, and created it. This analysis, creation, and implementation all took a considerable amount of time, thought, and planning. Yet, often this knowledge is not captured and slips away into distant memory. IT Managers have the choice between paying a bit more to capture this information during implementation, or paying someone else later to go through the same tedious process of analyzing and learning about a process so they can address a problem. When the next problem occurs, they will again pay someone to analyze and learn about the process, and on and on.

Why is this lesson so difficult to learn? Well-written reference documentation for all IT processes pays for the time required to develop it, over and over again. The IT Manager's task is to provide policies and processes to make this documentation easy to write and yet capture the essential information useful in the future. To accomplish this, they must publish a policy guiding when to document a process and the information this document should contain.

Processes that must be documented include business critical systems, processes where no deviation is permitted (such as data backups and security measures), and processes that rarely fail. Omit from this requirement processes that are one-time data systems and ad hoc reports.

The quality and comprehensiveness of IT reference documentation is an important determinant in the size of an IT staff. If all technical knowledge is in the head of a programmer, then how many systems can that person adequately support? If that person left the company or even took a vacation, then what materials are available to train the next person? A thorough program of IT technical documentation allows a smaller staff to support more technology than maintaining a larger staff of experts with the details locked inside their heads.

It is rare to encounter an IT Manager who does not believe in good system documentation, but it is just as rare to find one that consistently ensures its completion in a timely manner. A management maxim is that "You get what you reward." Management support is the key to this program. Without the visible and ongoing management support of a documentation program, it will quickly fade. Make the team believers and the IT Manager will not need to nag them—they will do it on their own!

Creating reference documentation, like anything else in the IT department, is a matter of time and labor. Often it requires the involvement of some of the department's more expensive technicians. A standard format focuses the writers on providing the essential information without losing time determining how to organize it. Standard document formats become simple fill-in-the-blank answers to a series of questions. Whoever a document's target audience may be, the text must answer the "5 Ws& H": Who, What, Where, When, Why, and How. By keeping these in mind at all times, the reference material will always be on target.

[B]   Critical Policies to Develop Based on This Chapter

Use the material discussed in this chapter to create the following policies:

A.   Determine what should be documented and what can be ignored.
B.   Standardize documentation overall formats.
C.   Develop a policy guiding document version controls and retirement.
D.   Develop a policy guiding the development of standardized flowcharts.

Policies should always be developed based on the local situation. Successful managers cannot issue appropriate guidance if the policies are written with another company's situation or location in mind.

§ 36.02   DEVELOPING A REFERENCE DOCUMENTATION POLICY

[A]   Overview

This chapter identifies the essential elements of IT documentation and formalizes them into a policy to guide the department. A key consideration in the development of any document is how the reader will use it. For example, technical documentation is for quick reference. The reader will scan it in an emergency for the essential information. End-user documentation tends to be step-by-step actions that are explained in terms and in relationship to the end user's processes—not IT jargon.

IT documentation policy formalizes the requirement and format for the various types of reference materials. Among the benefits:

A.   Minimize the time lost reanalyzing processes when troubleshooting or during new development. Technical documentation of a system's internal workings is the starting point for programmers to investigate problems or to make system changes.
B.   Reduce IT staff training costs since knowledge is available when needed.
C.   Reduce the number of service desk calls by providing users of IT processes with clear, adequate instructions on how to use the systems and what to do if specific error conditions appear.
D.   Standardize reference document formats to ease cross training and to allow a wider range of people easier access to technical details.
E.   Standardize storage and handling of reference documentation to ensure that the current version is always available.

COMMENT

Developing and maintaining accurate and complete systems documentation is an important part of a company's disaster recovery and business continuity plan. Over the long run, the identification of obscure or unstable technologies can lead to capital spending to replace them.

Good data systems documentation makes everyone's job easier. The cost of document development is "up front" in technician time building the documents. Payoff occurs repeatedly whenever someone needs to research the features of a system or to address problems in a crisis.

How often does a data system fail while the primary support person is on vacation? Has an important system failed at night when the after-hours support staff must be called on to address the issue? Has a key employee ever departed from the company taking all of the knowledge of the system along with him?

A consistent documentation program helps an IT Manager to provide guidance to employees. It reduces the variations in customer service from "the way we have always done it" to a well-considered approach. In essence, it details how to implement processes and then audits performance to enforce compliance.

COMMENT

Does your IT department support a complex system that is critical but stable? In the beginning, the person who developed it knew how the technology worked. However, since this application has not failed in years, the next time it had a problem, they had to start over from the beginning since the knowledge of the data flows has faded. Good documentation in this case would serve as a refresher when isolating a problem. Be sure that the documentation includes *all* technology in the system chain, including hardware and software.

Some managers require a review of system documentation before implementing routine changes or new systems. Another procedure is to schedule an annual management review of system reference materials for those "stable" systems that never seem to need changes. Do not be afraid to audit. A principle of sound management is to "inspect what you expect."

Documenting data systems highlights the chain of technology that is critical to the application's operation. From a business continuity planning standpoint, documentation helps to identify process weaknesses and single points of failure. The identification of a single point of failure calls for several immediate actions by the IT Manager—all aimed at better serving the customers:

A. Document any actions that would work around the problem until it can be resolved. Often these are manual processes.
B. Install duplicate equipment, if possible, so that the process can be shifted to the alternative hardware and work can promptly resume.
C. Ensure that all technical documentation pertaining to the process is current and understandable.
D. Ensure that personnel assigned to support that process are properly trained and aware of all of the aspects of the process.

[B]   Policy Objectives

The IT documentation policy has several objectives. It mandates compliance, provides some measures of what adequate reference documentation is, and provides guidance for a department librarian to ensure the availability of the latest versions. The IT documentation policy objectives include:

A. The IT documentation policy is all-inclusive of processes and technical systems supported by the department.
B. IT documentation will follow specific standards defining the content, approach, and objectives. Standard formats allow all readers to focus on the content of the document and not waste time trying to decipher different document layouts.
C. The IT librarian maintains all reference documentation in the appropriate format.
D. All documentation will be updated whenever a system change or enhancement is implemented.
E. Every year, each IT supervisor will review, update, and certify the accuracy of the documentation that supports their operations.
F. Submit technical, end user, operations, and service desk instructions prior to the rollout of all new systems or updated processes.

See Policy ITP-36-1 IT Documentation Policy as an example.

POLICY ITP-36-1.   IT Documentation Policy

Policy #:	ITP-36-1	Effective:	03/18/13	Page #:	1 of N
Subject:	IT Documentation Policy				

1.0 PURPOSE

This policy identifies the essential elements of IT documentation and formalizes them into a guide for the IT department. Well-written reference materials communicate a clear, accurate picture of the process or system. This policy mandates the creation and maintenance of reference materials, and provides guidelines on what they should contain.

2.0 SCOPE

This policy encompasses end-user instructions, technical flow explanations, project documents, systems analysis studies, and all of the various reference documents created to provide ongoing support to an IT activity. Excluded from the policy are typical memorandums and e-mails.

IT functions requiring policies and procedures documentation include, but are not limited to:

A. Software development
B. IT internal processes
C. End-user instructions
D. Help desk troubleshooting steps
E. Systems analysis and reports
F. Project plans and supporting historical documents
G. Disaster recovery actions
H. Security procedures
I. Network logical and physical architectures

3.0 POLICY

3.1 Know Your Audience

Write all documentation to a specific audiences' background. Technical documentation assumes that the reader has a fundamental understanding of the technology. End-user documentation assumes they know the basics of using the equipment.

A. **Technical reference documents.** Use technical references to locate a piece of information. What information elements would you want to see in a document if tasked to fill in for an absent programmer? At a minimum, it should include an overall diagram of the system modules and data flows; a list of all file layouts; a list of where major inputs come from, what the primary outputs look like, such as reports; and a narrative of how it all fits together.
B. **End-user documentation.** End-user reference material follows the process flow from the user's perspective. It includes the screens they would step through, the menus, and an explanation of all options. Use this type of reference for training and for looking up answers. The text of each section will be narrative but there should be an outline format

table of contents along with an index—both of which are easily created using the tools in most word processing programs.

3.2 Types of Documentation

A. **Informational documents.** Detail all of the steps in performing a function that allow latitude on the part of the operator. For example, if an overnight process normally ends by 4:30 a.m. and it is still running at 5:00 a.m., the instructions may require the operator to call the supporting programmer. However, if the operator is aware of earlier issues with the overnight processing that delayed the start of this program for two hours, provide the option to exercise judgment and wait before calling.

B. **Directive document.** Follow these steps exactly. The process steps are a directive from the IT Manager. An example might be a step-by-step process to be followed by the help desk technicians to verify a caller's identity before resetting a password. No one may deviate from this process. Another directive type process is a precise explanation of the proper handling, shipping, and storage of data backups.

3.3 Text Standards for All Documents

A. Use 12-point type using an Arial or Times Roman font.

B. Each document should read from major topic to minor topic—or broad view to narrow view. The beginning of the document deals with actions that would affect the entire process, and then deeper into the document addresses specific issues.

C. On the first page, include a brief narrative of the business function that this particular process supports.

D. Be concise. Limit each sentence to less than 25 words, each paragraph to one topic, and each sentence to a single idea. This avoids swamping a person's short-term memory. Concise text respects the reader's time and reduces ambiguity.

E. Write in a neutral tone and avoid humor, personal opinion, inspirational statements, and popular slang.

F. Define any unusual technical or business terms that are used. Reader comprehension is improved by writing longer statements that work around "insider" code words. Common technical or business terms are acceptable.

G. Use graphics to provide supporting information, not to repeat what was already written.

H. Always write in the active voice. It is easier to understand than the passive voice.

Use simple, direct sentences and leave the large words for the dictionaries. Simple sentences are not an insult to anyone's intelligence. No one looks to IT documentation as a source of fine literature; they appreciate finding what they want to know as quickly as possible.

3.4 Document Identification

A. Set the page footers to include a page number in the center, and the current date in lower-right corner. This date will help to indicate which files are the latest.

B. Include the phrase "Company Confidential" in the heading for every page along with a small version of the company logo.

C. Every page must have the date approved in the lower-left corner. When updating individual pages and sections, this date will change, so there may be more than one "approved on" date in the same document.

D. Every document more than five pages long shall have a table of contents. This should include all section headings in the document for quick reference.

E. Section headings group together similar information and assist the reader with quickly locating the topic he or she seeks. Use these guidelines when writing section headings:

   1. Use a "level-one" heading to start a broad subject area. Level-one headings are typically generic titles, such as "Hardware," "System Justification," or "Immediate actions for system crashes." Level-one headings should contain one distinct type of information subdivided by lower level sections.

   2. Use level-two, level-three, and level-four headings to progressively subdivide information into easy-to-identify sections. The titles should succinctly summarize the information contained in that section.

   3. Do not use more than four heading levels. Instead, subdivide the level 0 (zero) section into its major sections.

4.0 REVISION HISTORY

Date	Revision #	Description of Change
03/18/13	1.0	Initial creation.

5.0 INQUIRIES

Direct inquiries about this policy to:

George Jenkins, CIO
Our Company, Inc.
2900 Corporate Drive
Columbus, OH 43215

Voice: 614-555-1234
Fax: 614-555-1235
E-mail: gjenkins@company.com

Revision #:	1.0	Supersedes:	N/A	Date:	03/18/13

§ 36.03   DOCUMENT FORMATS

[A]   Overview

Documentation is institutional knowledge, permanently recorded for ready reference. It includes procedure development, design, implementation, operation, and revision data that successors can follow. It incorporates policies, rules, and information for distribution to all users associated with information systems operations.

Documentation tells a story about how something works or how to use it. It is a shame to spend days writing a document that is useless to the intended audience. One of the problems is the variety of writing styles and formats used by various people. People write in the way most comfortable to them. Some seem to get quickly to the point and some explain every small action in tedious detail.

However, each type of document requires its own format. Technical documents are for troubleshooting, so highlight the essential facts in the front, and do not bury them deep in the text. Examples of this might be the name of the server, software, and various technologies used. End-user documentation would skip all of this as the customer does not care if hub #7 supports a particular peripheral. Something works or it does not. Therefore, end-user documentation looks at the same process, but from the end-user's perspective. Technically, this is only as deep as their desktop monitor will reach. Beyond that, the end user's interest is minimal.

Creating documentation, like anything in the IT department, is a matter of time and labor. Often it requires help from the department's more expensive technicians. The establishment of a standard format helps to focus their efforts to provide the essential information in a minimal amount of time. No time is lost trying to discern the layout of a document. All effort focuses on locating what was wanted. Technical documentation that follows a standard format will ensure that whoever is called up to address a problem will at least not waste time fumbling through page after page looking for basic details. The information will be in the same place in all documents.

The manager's task is to remove the roadblocks (real and imagined) and develop an easy to follow writing methodology for the staff to use. This should include standard document formats, naming conventions, and word processing guidelines.

Many technicians will tell you they are not "writers." (Of course, they were not technicians until they learned what to do, either.) Like any technical skill, it needs a bit of explanation, a few examples to demonstrate the basics, and a lot of practice.

Writing good reference documentation is no more difficult than telling a story to someone. Good documentation is easier to read when written conversationally. Start at the beginning (where the process originates) and then explain the flow of data through to the end. Use simple, direct sentences and leave the large words for the dictionaries. Simple sentences are not an insult to anyone's intelligence. No one looks to IT documentation as a source of fine literature; they appreciate finding what they want to know as quickly as possible.

[B]   Know Your Audience

Before writing the first word, consider who will be reading this document and how they will use it. Each audience has its own set of requirements and expectations. Documentation is useless to a technician if it is too wordy, useless to end users if it is too technical, and useless to the service desk if it is too long. If the authors focus their efforts on how the audience will use the document, they can save themselves a lot of time writing it.

When writing the technical explanation, a general rule is to assume the reader understands the basics of the technology. Likewise, when explaining an accounting program, it is unnecessary to explain the accounting rule as to why to debit to a particular account.

The best judge of the usefulness of documentation is the people who will be using it. Often, developers write the documentation for code they have personally written. In general, the technical explanation they write is not for them; it is for their supervisor and their backup person. The supervisor and backup support person should judge whether it is appropriate to the requirements. Likewise, the end user for that document should approve it. Otherwise, it is likely to be set aside and the users will call for every small problem.

A. **Technical reference documents.** Use technical references to locate a piece of information. Everyone approaches technical debugging in his or her own fashion. What information elements would you want to see in a document if tasked to fill in for an absent programmer?

At a minimum, it should include an overall diagram of the system modules and data flows; a list of all file layouts; a list of where major outputs come from, such as reports; and a narrative of how it all fits together. The section of the policy covering technical reference documentation should require that an explanation of a data system's use and internal workings be an integral part of any new system implementation.

Funds for the development of reference materials are a part of each project. Write technical and end-user reference materials during system implementation to capture a fresh understanding of how the system works. See Exhibit 36-1 as an example.

EXHIBIT 36-1. System Document Format

Process Title: Bill of Lading System	
Written by: Larry Mosshammer	Approved by: Jim Webber
Document Number: S-13-001	Date Approved: April 1, 2014

System Objective:

To provide accurate Bills of Lading so that finished goods are routed to the correct destination with the correct optional accessories.

Work-Around Steps in an Emergency:

This system is classified as <u>CRITICAL</u> to this facility. If it totally fails, then the shipment of finished goods from the factory is halted.

    A. <u>If the scanner gun fails</u>, then use the keyboard at the shipping office to enter the job number into the workstation. This functions the same as the scanner and creates a Bill of Lading. It is important to enter the correct job number. A spare scanner gun is located in the office.

    B. <u>If the scale or its interface fails</u>, continue shipping and call for service by the scale company.

    C. <u>If the data download from the mainframe fails</u>, continue shipping until it is resolved. The workstation has 48 hours of shipping information stored on it, but any corrections to this information will not be included on the Bills of Lading.

    D. <u>If the workstation fails</u>, replace it with the stand-by unit sitting in the office. Download the data from the mainframe and continue shipping. The download may require an hour to receive and load the database.

    E. <u>If the printer fails</u>, a spare printer is located in the shipping office.

    F. <u>If the "product shipped" transaction to the mainframe fails</u>, then the job number's status remains built-not-shipped until it is scanned by the receiving warehouse.

Process Steps During Normal Operation:

    A. The day before a product is scheduled to be assembled, the shipping information is extracted from the mainframe's Production Master Table and copied into a generation dataset called "aaa.bbb.HeresYourStuff(0)." Changes to the shipping information fields on the Production Master will flag that record for the next download. Extracts are scheduled to run at 0530, 1130, 1730, and 2330.

    B. At 0600, 1200, 1800, and 2400 the shipping office workstation automatically requests a copy of the mainframe extract.

    C. This file is loaded into the SQL database called ShippingData.sql. The job number is the record key and is unique to each finished product. If the record exists, it is replaced. Otherwise, it is added.

    D. When a finished item is ready to ship, its ticket is scanned to obtain a Bill of Lading. The job number is looked up in the database. If it exists, then Crystal Reports is used to format a Bill of Lading and print the document. If the job number is not found, then Crystal Reports formats and prints a rejection ticket.

E. After a Bill of Lading prints for a job, it is flagged as shipped in the PC's database and a single transaction file is sent to the mainframe to change the job's status.
F. This file is sent as xxx and is picked up by the mainframe program xxxx, which executes every 90 seconds.
   a) <u>Production Scheduling</u> for reporting actual versus scheduled built.

Technologies Used:

A. Hardware.
   a) PC at shipping station
   b) Special serial interface board connecting to scale
   c) Personal UPS on shipping PC
   d) IBM Mainframe
   e) Bar code scanner gun
   f) Scale Interface Box
   g) HP LaserJet
   h) Internal facility network
   i) External network to data center
B. Software.
   a) Visual Basic version 7
   b) Crystal Reports 7
   c) SQL Server version 7.1

Files and Interfaces:

A. Mainframe.
   aaa.bbb.HeresYourStuff(0)
B. Workstation.
   ShippingData.sql

Operator Routine Maintenance Actions:

A. Properly shut down and reboot the shipping workstation once every workday.
B. Once per week, run the database cleanup function using the process outlined in the operator procedure.
C. Clean the printer per the manufacturer's instructions every time the laser toner cartridge is replaced.

B. **End-user documents.** End-user reference material follows the process flow from the user's perspective. It includes the screens they would step through, the menus, and an explanation of all options. See Exhibit 36-2 as an example.

People will read this type of documentation to gain some overall understanding on how the system works or to look up solutions to problems. The better the user instructions are, the fewer the calls for help! Use this type of reference for training and for looking up answers. The text of each section will be narrative but there should be an outline format table of contents along with an index—both of which are easily created using the tools in most word processing programs.

User instructions should include illustrations of screens, reports, and lists of valid edit codes. Explain any error messages used by the program that the end user may see. This is true even if the response is to report the error to the service desk since end users often are the first to encounter software problems.

An important factor in end-user materials is to avoid the use of technical jargon—unless it is in common use in that department. In this case, the text should avoid bits and bytes discussion about network devices but would appropriately include business terminology used within that department such as scrap reporting and automated shipping notices.

EXHIBIT 36-2. End-User Document Format

Process Title: Creating New User Accounts Written by: Larry Mosshammer	Approved by: Jim Webber
Document Number: P-13-001	Date Approved: April 1, 2014

Process Objective:

This procedure is for approving and creating new user IDs. User IDs are the first line of security defense against unauthorized access to company data. This process assures that only authorized personnel are provided user IDs.

Responsibilities:

A. Service Desk Technician—ensures the form is properly and completely filled in, creates the new account, and stores forms in the file.
B. Service Desk Supervisor—works with other departments to obtain advance notice of major changes that would require the creation of new user accounts. Ensures that this procedure is followed by training new technicians in its use and by periodically monitoring the creation of new accounts.

Supporting Materials:

A. New User ID request form #F-0100-001.
B. Restricted supervisor authority to create new accounts.

References:

A. Process P-0100-020 for background checks on all personnel able to create new user accounts.

Technologies Used:
A. Hardware.
    None
B. Software.
    None

Process Steps:

1. The Service Desk Technician verifies at the beginning of each shift that there is an adequate supply of new user ID request forms in the hopper outside of the Service Desk Door.
2. New ID request forms are sent through the interoffice mail or picked up from the hopper outside of the door.
3. Forms are completed according to the instructions on the back of the form.
4. Completed forms are sent to the Service Desk via interoffice mail or dropped off at the Service Desk window.
5. The Service Desk technician reviews incoming forms for completeness, ensuring that both the employee and supervisor signature blocks are completed.
6. A call is logged in the Service Desk trouble tracking system to set up the user ID.
7. The Service Desk technician uses the AS400 xxx to establish a user ID following the company's ID pattern.
8. A standard password of "Christmas" is set for the account. The account is set to require that the password be changed the first time it is used.
9. The Service Desk calls the user based on the telephone number on the application to inform the user of his or her new account ID and password.
10. The ID request form is filed in the Service Desk cabinet under "User ID Requests," in alphabetical order of the user's last name.
11. The trouble call to set up the ID is closed.

C. **Service desk or operations documents.** Service desks are often an extension of the data systems operations team. Both sit in Service back rooms and address routine issues that arise. The documentation needs for both are similar. Service desk and operations documentation comes in two basic forms, informational and directive. Each is appropriate in certain circumstances.

1. **Informational documents.** List the steps that allow latitude on the part of the operator. For example, if an overnight process normally ends by 4:30 a.m. and it is still running at 5:00 a.m., the instructions may request the operator call the supporting programmer. But if the operator is aware of earlier issues with the overnight processing that delayed the start of this program for two hours, he or she will have the option to exercise judgment and wait before calling.

2. **Directive documents.** Follow these steps exactly. The process steps are considered a part of a directive from the IT Manager, for example, a step-by-step process to be followed by the service desk technicians to verify a caller's identity before resetting a password. Deviation from this process is not permitted. Another directive type process is a precise explanation on the proper handling, shipping, and storage of data backups.

[C] Readability

There is a "score" that can be determined for a document that indicates its readability called a "fog index." Most word processors include some sort of reading level gauge to identify the audience's difficulty in understanding a document's text. IT documents are dry and definitely not recreational prose. At least try to make them easy to read.

A fog index for technical documentation is somewhat skewed by technical terms. Technical writing should be simple and easy to understand. Readers have a responsibility to understand the common technical terms used in their specialty and by the company. If in doubt, add a glossary to the document. Rather than repeat glossaries in every document, consider establishing a single library-wide glossary of technical and company-unique terms. To calculate the fog index:

A. Count the number of words in the document or passage under review.
B. Count the number of sentences.
 1. Divide the number of words by the number of sentences and save this number.
C. Count the number of words with three or more syllables.
 1. Divide the number of words into the number of big words to obtain a percentage. Treat this percentage as a whole number and save it.
D. Add the two saved numbers together (as whole numbers) and multiply the results by 0.4. The result is the fog index.

Most IT documents will have an index rating of between 11 and 13, but the lower the rating is, the easier the information is to read.

§ 36.04 DOCUMENT MANAGEMENT

[A] Overview

Every IT department keeps some sort of reference library. In some cases, it is in a dusty bookcase. More often, manuals and system documentation are scattered around the various work areas and programmer cubicles. All of these documents vary in how current they are. In many cases, no one knows what material a coworker may have on the shelf and must search around the department looking for an old manual.

A well-maintained reference library will provide an IT Manager with ready access to the latest information, savings on storage space since so many copies of so many things are not floating around, and greater agility for responding to user problem reports. Most hardware and software vendors would be very happy to provide their documentation electronically (on a disk or via an Internet link) since printing mounds of manuals only distracts them from what they do best.

> ## COMMENT
>
> Well-written software documentation is a service-desk's most valuable tool. When users call, service-desk analysts can answer most questions if they have access to current user documentation and can look up detailed questions in the technical reference materials. The more information the service-desk has, the fewer distractions passed on to the technical staff. Oh yes, and the callers appreciate the quick answers to their questions!

An IT reference library is a tradeoff between restricting the flow of materials and widely dispersing them. Its goal is to ensure that current information is readily available when needed. An IT library should use a variety of methods to provide information to those who need it.

For reference material generated by the IT department, or provided electronically by vendors, the library should use an intranet Web page. This reduces the number of paper copies and the likelihood of using obsolete information.

Using an outdated document may hinder or misdirect troubleshooting efforts and deepen the crisis of the moment. The IT librarian ensures the latest version of all documents is readily available.

Some technicians find it easier to purchase new books instead of checking into what is already in the IT library. Perhaps they feel more secure if they possess their own copy or they are casually interested in something new and would like to research it further. The IT library's inventory provides the IT Manager with data for controlling this cost.

[B]   Enforcing Quality

The librarian establishes a schedule that spreads the revalidation of documents throughout the year. This minimizes the workload on the IT staff and allows them to schedule this task into their slack periods. The librarian ensures the annual audits are performed on each document and follows up with supervisors for document reviews that are past due.

> ## COMMENT
>
> To minimize the drain on the librarian's time, consider using an electronic document management system, such as Microsoft SharePoint software (*www.microsoft.com/sharepoint/*).

[C] Storage and Access

The librarian must devise a filing system to readily identify documents. Often this involves using the names and code numbers already assigned to the various data systems. Most IT staff members think of the various data systems by their common names. Use these when possible.

IT reference material is normally stored in one of three places.

A. **Materials needed at the workplace to accomplish the job.** These reference materials are what a worker needs immediate access to in the normal performance of his job. Individuals may keep essential reference materials by their workstations. Examples are programming language reference materials at the desk of each programmer. Keep a copy of documents that must be readily available in the individual work areas. In most companies, each developer has basic manuals at his desk. Work should progress as fast as the developer can think so a basic set of manuals should be readily available in his work area.

   A computer operator might need step-by-step instructions for performing a specific action, etc. Material such as this should be available at his point of application. For example, attach the documentation explaining the operation of a tape backup device to its side.

B. **Electronic materials.** Much of an IT department's technical documentation is developed locally. Rather than print and track who has copies, a central location for review is needed. Reference materials created by the IT staff should be stored on a shared network drive that is accessible through a secured intranet Web page controlled by the librarian. Read access to this directory is generally available to the IT staff while write access is restricted to the librarian.

   Whenever publishing a newer version, the intranet link points to the newer version. As problems arise, the troubleshooter looks up the documentation on the network instead of searching for his (possibly outdated) copy of the documentation. For this reason, printing copies of reference documentation off the network is discouraged, but not prohibited.

COMMENT

Several software vendors provide tools that make it easier to collect policy and procedure information and make it available over the corporate intranet. Some packages to check out include Zavanta from Comprose, Inc. (*www.comprose.com/zavanta-software*) and onGO DMS from Uniplex Software (*www.uniplex.com*).

C. **Physical reference materials stored in the central library.**
To save on storage space and to minimize the cost of lightly used manuals, many companies collect them into a central library for review (or borrowed for a short time). The intention is to make documents and manuals available for use and yet minimize floor space requirements. These resources are accumulated into a central location and loaned as needed. Log in a "due back by" date so that the next person requiring the material will not need to search for it. Few materials are required beyond a week, so this encourages storing them in the library instead of on a cubicle shelf.

Previously, manuals were purchased as desired with no control over versions, location, or verification that the book was not already on the premises. A central repository saves on shelf space and ensures the maximum benefit from the company's investment in manuals. The trick for the librarian is to ensure the materials get maximum use while maintaining control over their location. In a pinch, it is better to lose track of a book for a short while than to hinder the troubleshooting of a critical issue.

COMMENT

Librarians must balance the savings realized by reducing the number of manuals floating around against ensuring they are readily available for use. Do not let the library become a place where manuals enter and never see the light of day again! Make it easy to take out books and gently remind people to return them.

[D] Version Control

Reference materials have a problem. How can the support staff determine if they are reading the latest information on the topic? Some data systems are in constant flux while others may remain static for years. A document may be four years old but still be the latest word—or one week old and obsolete. It is difficult to keep current multiple copies of documentation. Page replacements, pen changes to text, and maintaining a locater of each document can be a massive undertaking. Multiply this by the number of systems in a large company and it is easy to see why some companies do not even bother to try.

There are several ways to address version control. The first is that only the current documentation is available via the Web page. Printing personal copies is discouraged. Second, the "date approved" provides an indication of currency. Finally, if the data system uses a version number in its name, then that can be included in the document title. Although a large IT shop may devise some sort of version or serial number for documents, many companies will find this more effort than required.

A goal of version control is for the librarian to weed out and destroy obsolete manuals. "Obsolete" is a strange term in IT since there may still be hardware and software in operation that might be considered long past its prime yet the company still depends upon it for daily service. It does not matter how old a document is, only whether it is the best available reference for that technology. Tracking manuals eases the problem of gathering up old manuals when a newer version is issued. See Policy ITP-36-2 IT Documentation Management Policy as an example.

POLICY ITP-36-2. IT Documentation Management Policy

Policy #:	ITP-36-2	Effective:	03/18/13	Page #:	1 of N
Subject:	IT Documentation Management Policy				

1.0 PURPOSE

This policy establishes a central repository of technical information in the IT department to ensure that the latest version is readily available to the IT department. It also provides guidance on ensuring the current version of documentation is readily available when needed.

2.0 SCOPE

This policy includes the management of all IT documents, whether purchased, received from outside organizations, or originated within the department. Documents supplied by other company departments, such as Human Resources, are excluded.

3.0 POLICY

3.1 Central Repository of Reference Material
All IT manuals, technical instructions, process instructions, etc., are to be managed centrally. IT reference material is normally stored in one of three places:

A. **At the point of application.** Reference materials required frequently will be stored at their point of use. Examples are reference materials for programming languages at the desk of each programmer or systematic instructions for a Help Desk technician.
B. **Electronic materials.** The IT librarian will establish a network file share and a collection of manufacturer provided CDs for ready use by the department. Reference materials created by the IT staff are to be stored

on a shared network drive accessible through a secured intranet Web page controlled by the librarian.

C. **Central library.** To save on storage space and to minimize the cost of lightly used manuals, they are to be collected into a central library for review as needed or short-term borrowing.

D. **Purchasing new manuals and reference material.** The IT librarian will check the list of existing documents to ensure that the manual requested is not already on the premises.

3.2 Restricted Access

A. **Company confidential materials.** Some of the department's technical documents could be used against the company. Examples are documentation of security systems, manuals detailing the accounting and payroll systems, etc.
   1. The IT librarian will safeguard these materials and only permit access by those whom the IT Manager approves.
   2. The IT librarian will segregate these materials so that access is only granted to the appropriate information. For example, the IT security team does not need access to the payroll system documentation, etc.

B. **Monthly access list review.** The IT librarian will submit to the IT Manager a list of employees that have access to the confidential documentation. The IT Manager will note any changes, approve, and return it for the IT librarian's file.

3.3 Document Management

A. **Department librarian.** The IT Manager will assign a member of the IT department as the official keeper of all reference materials. This person will be referred to as the IT reference librarian. Before adding anything to the library, the librarian will ensure:
   1. The documents conform to department policy for reference materials.
   2. The documents are stored in the proper location. This may include archiving old versions on the same subject.
   3. Authorized personnel have the appropriate security to access or update confidential material.
   4. The documentation custodian should maintain a copy of all documents on CDs for times when the online system is not available.

B. **Document's author.** A process's developer is responsible for writing the documentation and providing it to the librarian in an acceptable format. If the document conforms to the reference documentation policy, it should contain all of the required information. The librarian will reject vague or poorly written documents.

C. **Author's supervisor.** The developer's supervisor ensures the documentation is technically correct and reviewed annually to ensure it is still relevant.

3.4 Version Control

Version control is a process for ensuring that the department uses the most current information. The IT librarian will maintain a list of all library controlled documents along with their version numbers. The librarian will also include the location of each document, such as those kept at the workplace (programming manuals).

The IT librarian will weed out and destroy excess copies of obsolete manuals (always keeping at least one on-site).

A. **Electronically stored reference material.** Only the current version of documentation is available via the Web page. Print copies as needed.

B. **Central library.** To save on storage space and to minimize the cost of lightly used manuals, collect them into a central library for review as needed or short-term.

C. **Old versions.** The IT librarian will maintain a storage area with older versions of manuals. The IT librarian will also maintain an online storage area for older versions. In both cases, the IT librarian controls access to older versions.

3.5 Annual Documentation Review

Every month, the IT librarian will check through the locally created IT technical and end-user documentation for documents not updated in the past 12 months. The IT Manager responsible for that system must validate that the documentation is still correct.

4.0 REVISION HISTORY

Date	Revision #	Description of Change
03/18/13	1.0	Initial creation.

5.0 INQUIRIES

Direct inquiries about this policy to:

George Jenkins, CIO
Our Company, Inc.
2900 Corporate Drive
Columbus, OH 43215

Voice: 614-555-1234
Fax: 614-555-1235
E-mail: gjenkins@company.com

Revision #:	1.0	Supersedes:	N/A	Date:	03/18/13

COMMENT

End users tend to keep printed copies of documentation for quick reference. Use a different color of paper for the different versions of end-user documentation (or at least for the cover). This will make it easier to spot out-of-date copies.

§ 36.05 SYSTEM REFERENCE INSTRUCTIONS

[A] Process Overview

Most data processing systems will require the same major sections in their documentation. In essence, each section is like a chapter of a book since each addresses a different audience. Each section tells the story of the same system or process from the perspective of the various groups. Write sections to stand on their own without reference to the others. Insert a "page left blank" page in the place of unneeded sections. This demonstrates that the section is not missing, just not required. Most systems documentation will follow the format outlined in the following sections.

The narrative section should briefly explain the business context of a process and, in general, how it functions. It should describe the benefits provided by the process to the company and its day-to-day business/technical environment.

The narrative should identify the upstream and downstream data flows as well as the primary intended functions of the process.

[B] End-User Reference Documentation

Most departments experience some measure of employee turnover and absence. Well-written end-user documentation is useful for training new employees or as a valuable reference for occasional users. It provides the reader with a "big picture" perspective of a system. The weakness of pop-up help screens is that they are context sensitive. They may be used for support or training.

Write this stand-alone section for printing and for use in the end-user's department. User procedures should be easy to read and follow (written at an eighth-grade level for nontechnical personnel).

On-screen help and tips pop-ups can be a source of helpful instructions as they provide assistance in context of the problem. They are a valuable supplement, but not a replacement for end-user documentation.

Well-written end-user documentation should contain:

A. Program or hardware operating instructions
B. Corrective action for error messages
C. The texts of all on-screen help messages and when they can be invoked
D. Steps for accessing tutorial information

[C] Operations Reference Documentation

The operating procedures include everything necessary to initiate, schedule, process, control, and restart all phases of the system(s) while it is in operation. An operator may need to monitor the job's progress, set up high speed printers for special jobs (like printing customer bills for a utility company, or payroll checks), or restart failed programs.

The types of information to be included are:

A. Input/output requirements.
   1. Scanning instrument instructions
   2. Removable disk and/or CD instruction
   3. Special printer setup instructions
   4. External labeling
B. Data management is an important part of operations. Files must be mounted, broken programs restarted at the correct file generation, and a wide range of actions required in given circumstances. Operations data management actions include:
   1. Data retention period.
   2. Data security level.
   3. Number of backup generations required. If more than one, they should not all be stored in the same location.
   4. Any special recovery instructions to ensure data consistency.
   5. How to verify that recovered data is properly in place and the program is processing it.
C. Program job instructions should include the following:
   1. Job setup instructions
   2. Sources of originating data
   3. Report setup and disposition
   4. Sample output forms
   5. Corrective action to take for error messages
   6. Expected job run time
   7. Process restart procedures

[D]   Service Desk Reference Documentation

Service desk technicians refer to the reference materials provided by the other IT departments. Sometimes end users "forget" to read their documentation and the service desk walks them through a system action. Sometimes the service desk uses the technical documentation to see if a reported problem indicates a more serious issue or is something they can resolve.

The service desk requires access to the instructions provided to all departments (except for information held back for security reasons). In some cases, they will need a subset of the instructions to address frequently asked questions.

[E]   Technical Reference Documentation

Maintain information about hardware and software for each data system. They contain:

A. **General information.** This section identifies the technology and its objectives. Each program and major hardware device should have a unique identification number or name.

B. **General objectives.** The general objectives include a brief narrative statement of each program's purpose or use. It also addresses what passes data to it, how the data is transformed, and what passes out of it.

C. **Program's systems specifications.** Vendor-supplied information also will be included.

D. **Program flowcharts.** Flowcharts will be drawn using American National Standards Institute (ANSI) symbols.

COMMENT

Visio from Microsoft is a popular program for creating a wide range of business and technical drawings. Contact Microsoft at *www.microsoft.com*.

E. **Written program documentation.** Software reference documentation serves various functions. Pay back for the time and expense required to document software includes reduced maintenance costs, faster response to user requests, and possibly management job security.

COMMENT

A key aspect of object-oriented programming is the reuse of code. If the purpose, inputs, and outputs of a software object are vague, then how can someone reuse it? Establish a standard format for all reusable objects as soon as possible and ensure all future documentation conforms to it.

Software reference documentation should include:

A. Overall flow of program showing data going in, how it is transformed, and to where it is passed.
B. Source code listings.
C. Source and format of input data, to include all combinations of data strings into and out of each module.
D. System naming conventions—needed for variables, database, inputs, outputs, and controls.
E. Report layouts.
F. Screen layouts displaying control buttons, text boxes, and screen labels.
G. List of all validation edits and tables used by the program.
H. List of error messages that can be generated by this code and what causes them (do not include ones generated by the operating environment).
I. Formulas used in any critical calculations.
J. Index of table field names—names used in databases, programs, and input/output locations (useful when programming and doing maintenance later).

[F] Program Testing Reference Documentation

The proper testing of software is a formalized process. Test data takes considerable effort and time to develop. Always retain test data and scripts along with a narrative explaining how it exercises the program. Keep it in a CD attached to the technical documentation. Test data will require modification to follow changes to the programs; it will save the developer a considerable amount of time if it remains in sync with the programs.

Keep listings of input used for testing and the resulting outputs in the program test file. Screen-print or draw screen displays for documentation.

§ 36.06 PROJECT DOCUMENTATION

[A] Overview

The history of previous projects, both successful and incomplete, provides invaluable assistance in gauging the risks, costs, time duration, and task identification of future ventures. Important project documents are the initial plans (which are estimates for work) and the project's results (actual task duration, actual resource utilization, etc.). Project documentation also includes instructions, charts, correspondence, and other material dealing with a specific project. It provides a permanent record of the decisions made, along with a short list of the problems encountered and the methods used to resolve them.

Create a project binder at the start of a project to provide an ongoing record of pertinent information. It should include all related material throughout the life of the project. It is important to know which document supersedes another, so date each one before placing it in the binder.

[B] Identification and Responsibility

Project managers are responsible for initiating and maintaining their project binders. Binders can help ensure the required documents are accumulated and forwarded to the IT library. Do this at the conclusion of every project milestone.

The IT librarian is responsible for ensuring that all of the project documents are collected at the various stages of the project:

A. Initial plan when the project begins.
B. An in-progress "snapshot" of the plan at each milestone.
C. Final results at the end of the project.

The librarian organizes all materials to facilitate future reference. Typically, a project's materials are stored in a hard copy filing system.

See Policy ITP-36-3 Project Documentation Policy as an example.

POLICY ITP-36-3. Project Documentation Policy

Policy #:	ITP-36-3	Effective:	03/18/13	Page #:	1 of N
Subject:	Project Documentation Policy				

1.0 PURPOSE

The purpose of this policy is to collect documents used for managing a project for use in later review and analysis. These documents can be reviewed for information on improving the quality of the project management effort. It also provides insights into design tradeoffs and the logic behind them for team members later supporting that system.

2.0 SCOPE

This policy encompasses documents used in the management of a project. It excludes routine memos and working papers not directly related to the project analysis.

3.0 POLICY

3.1 Project Binder Contents
The project binder will contain any analysis used to justify the project plan. The size and complexity of these documents will vary according to the size and complexity of the project. The project binder should contain:

A. **Table of contents or index.**
B. **Basic project documents.** The basis for the project may be in the form of a feasibility study or a systems design. The project proposal should include:
   1. **Project charter.** A document describing the project's scope and key objectives. It also provides the authority for the project manager to commence the project. This should include the project's criteria for success.
   2. **Major project tasks.** An outline of the steps necessary to complete the project.
   3. **Estimated costs and benefits.** Compute estimated costs for each major task and/or material. Identify costs as "estimates" obtained at the time the proposal was written and subject to revision. List all assumptions made in determining these costs.
C. **Project plan.** The schedule includes:
   1. Systems concept. A brief narrative written for nontechnical, management-level personnel that provides a detailed overview of the project objectives.
   2. List of tasks, and their sequence.
   3. State all assumptions made about resources, features, and timelines made during the planning process.
   4. Risk assessments.
   5. Stakeholder analysis.
   6. Communications plan.
   7. Initial budget.
   8. Resource list and work calendar.
   9. A copy of the feasibility study is included if available.

3.2 Project Progress Folders
Project progress documentation, maintained during the life of the project, contains the history of the project and copies of all relevant correspondence

filed by date. These documents provide a source of information when writing the project completion report, and should reflect any agreements between the project group and users or vendors. These documents include:

A. **Minutes of project status and problem-solving meetings.**
B. **Labor utilization record.** Post the estimated "hours per task" versus the "actual hours per task" to the project schedule.
C. **Project documentation checklist.** To ensure that documentation for the in-progress project is fully collected, refer to the project documentation checklist (Worksheet 36-1).
D. **A final report that illustrates the actual course of the project.** Compare this to the initial documents to improve task identification and estimates of budget and time duration.
  1. Final project plan showing the actual duration and sequence of tasks.
  2. Final budget, indicating the actual project expenses.
  3. Final risk assessment plan along with a list of mitigation actions taken during the project.
  4. Scope change log detailing all proposed and accepted changes to the project scope.

4.0 REVISION HISTORY

Date	Revision #	Description of Change
03/18/13	1.0	Initial creation.

5.0 INQUIRIES

Direct inquiries about this policy to:

George Jenkins, CIO
Our Company, Inc.
2900 Corporate Drive
Columbus, OH 43215

Voice: 614-555-1234
Fax: 614-555-1235
E-mail: gjenkins@company.com

Revision #:	1.0	Supersedes:	N/A	Date:	03/18/13

Use Worksheet 36-1 Project Documentation Checklist to track project costs and progress.

WORKSHEET 36-1. Project Documentation Checklist

Project Documentation Checklist			
Description of Project			
Major Project Tasks (Use only those applicable to this project.)			
	Start Date	Finish Date	Estimated Cost
Preliminary Analysis	MM/DD/YY	MM/DD/YY	$999,999
Systems Analysis/Design	MM/DD/YY	MM/DD/YY	$999,999
Programming	MM/DD/YY	MM/DD/YY	$999,999
Data and File Conversion Costs	MM/DD/YY	MM/DD/YY	$999,999
System and Program Testing			$999,999
Training Costs			$999,999
Hardware Purchase			$999,999
Software Purchase			$999,999
Administrative Costs			$999,999
Miscellaneous			$999,999
TOTAL COST			$999,999
Estimated Annual Operation Cost			
Data Entry			$999,999
Processing			$999,999
System/Program Maintenance			$999,999
Administrative			$999,999
Other (specify)			$999,999
TOTAL ESTIMATED ANNUAL OPERATIONS COST			$999,999
Project Staffing (Name the project leader and state the estimated number and competence level of personnel assigned to work on the project.)			
Personnel to Contact (List names of people best able to answer pertinent questions about the various tasks within the project.)			

§ 36.07 SYSTEMS ANALYSIS DOCUMENTATION

[A] Overview

Systems analysis is the technical and business review of a proposed change or addition to a data system to determine the extent of the time required and the approximate cost. IT Managers use the results of the study to establish the cost to benefit ratio of the proposed changes. The documents also provide much of the initial information.

A systems analyst establishes a scaled down version of a project plan to ensure that the true impact of the request is considered. The analyst formalizes the request's scope and reviews the technical and business processes involved to identify all of the tasks required to make the change. The result is a time and direct cost estimate for management consideration. If the proposal is accepted, the systems analyst's report will provide the basic information for the project's charter.

Include rejected proposals in the library. Business conditions may change on short notice and yesterday's "nice to have" request becomes tomorrow's urgent requirement.

[B] Systems Documentation Binder

Maintain a systems documentation binder for each assignment. This is a scaled down version of a project plan. Combine some of these items onto the same page depending on the complexity of the issue. All binders should include:

A. **Title page.** The title page contains the project name and identification number, effective dates, and the lead analyst's name and title, names and responsibilities of all other persons assigned to the project on the second page.

B. **Table of contents.** This reflects the specific contents in the systems binder.

C. **Revision sheet.** Included in every systems binder (see Worksheet 36-2), it contains columns for:
1. **Number of revisions.** Revisions are numbered sequentially starting with 1.
2. **Revision date.** Effective date of the revision.
3. **Portion revised.** The specific part of the system under revision, including all areas of documentation such as procedures, flowcharts, reports, etc.
4. **Name.** The name of the systems analyst making the revision.
5. **Authorization.** The name of the person authorizing the revision.

WORKSHEET 36-2. Revision Sheet

Revision Sheet				
Project Name:			Project Number	
Revision #	Date	Item Revised	Revised By	Approved By
Project Leader:				Date:

[C] Scope

The scope of the assignment is the boundaries of the request. Vague requests result in vague estimates. It is the analyst's responsibility to translate the business-based request into a succinct technical description. The scope anchors the analysis to minimize drift. On occasion, the analysis is broken into several requests and may require several different scope statements.

Expand the succinct scope statement by listing the criteria for determining if the change has been successful. This is where the specific requirements are detailed, such as items to be added to reports, required validations, etc. This section also includes a statement on the business issues that justify the request.

[D] Product Specifications

What is to be created or changed because of this activity? Will it be a new report or a new database? Perhaps a new subsystem added to an existing function. Systems specifications provide a means of communication between the designer and the implementation team, who may be in-house programming staff or outside contract workers. The systems specifications provide a record of the structure, functions, flow, documentation, and control of the system and include:

A. **System narrative.**
   1. Descriptive title of system.
   2. Source, expected schedule, and volume of input data.
   3. Size and characteristics of the data.
   4. Sample exhibits of input documents.
   5. Outputs indicating volume and due dates. (This may be a monitor display or hard copy.)
   6. Sample exhibits of outputs.
   7. References to material or organizations that may furnish additional information. (This may include vendor-supplied information.)
   8. Samples of interactive screens.
B. **Data system and business process flowcharts** identifying the steps in the processes performed and illustrating their sequence.
C. **Program specification requirements** defining the environment within a system in which a subsystem or a single program operates. They describe the data inputs and outputs, including source, format, disposition, and retention method. They include the time when the process will run, process controls, functions, and limitations. The specifications include any security issues that may arise.
D. **File/database specifications** used in the system are identified.
E. **A test plan** based on existing test data and previous test plans for this process.

[E]   Schedule

To determine the cost and timeline of a system change, the analyst should develop a basic project plan. This plan should list the tasks involved and apply time and cost estimates to each task.

All plans are projections of the future and created in the context of assumptions. There is an assumption that all of the required people will be ready, willing, and able to perform when called upon. There is an assumption that the computers and network will be operational, provide adequate response times during development, etc. Trying to build a schedule without making assumptions is not practical. An assumption list, however, should skip basic items such as the example about system performance and identify other assumptions that are essential to the schedule.

One result of the task breakdown is a resource plan that identifies all of the people and special equipment required to make the change. This might be additional workstations, new software packages, etc. This breakdown helps to identify costs and the lead time for ordering materials and services from outside of the company.

[F]   Risk Assessment

Even small changes have risks and a brief risk assessment will detail the potential problems with the change. At a minimum, every item on the assumptions list should be on the risk assessment sheet along with its mitigation actions. Potential problems include:

A. End-user resistance
B. Incorrect specifications
C. Critical days to avoid due to the business cycle (in the end-user's department or in IT)
D. Unproven technologies
E. Planned changes to upstream systems
F. System performance from existing poor design

[G]   Stakeholders

It is important to identify all of the groups involved with the change so they can assist in its development and approval. The systems analyst would likely have interviewed each of them during the analysis, and this is a good place to capture who they are, their attitude toward the changes, the abilities or inclination toward helping to develop, test, or implement them, etc. This is also the place to identify those against the changes. Typical stakeholders include:

A. Requestor
B. Users
C. Union officials

D. Business department manager
E. Network analyst
F. Systems security analyst
G. Service desk
H. Operations

[H]   Recommendations

After the analysis is completed, make recommendations both in summary and in detail. The summary recommendation includes a recap of the request, major time and cost drivers uncovered, and a total requirement in time and money.

The detailed report would provide all of the supporting information that totaled to the time and cost estimates. The detail is important in case any assumptions were flawed. If a proposed project is rejected, always record who denied the request and why.

§ 36.08   FLOWCHARTING STANDARDS

[A]   Purpose

Flowcharts pictorially explain how data flows through a system. They illustrate the relationships between modules and decision points and make it easier to understand its accompanying narrative. Flowcharts perform several functions in the systems investigation, analysis, design, development, and installation phases. They provide a visual overview of a process so that you can quickly locate the part of the process of greatest interest. There are several good software flowcharting programs available for PCs. Using a software package to draw flowcharts allows them to be easily and neatly changed.

Flowchart diagrams range in complexity from global system flowcharts to procedure step detail. Often software flowcharts begin with a "big picture" view and then display finer levels of details on additional charts.

The flowchart exhibit(s) should be on a single page. The manner in which the flowchart is illustrated will depend on the IT technical skills of the viewers. Such charts are most valuable when rendered in the simplest terms for the whole group.

[B]   Global System Flowcharts

A "global system" is an interaction of systems, with one or more systems outside the organization. One example would be a travel agent's system, interacting with both an airline ticket reservation system and the various credit card systems. The reservation and cost information must be approved before the travel agent can issue a ticket and charge the customer's credit card account.

[C]   Enterprise System Flowcharts

An "enterprise system" is an interaction of two or more data systems within the organization, which requires all participating systems to function. One example occurs when the production control system interacts with the incentive payroll system of manufacturing, which then interacts with the inventory system for inventory control. The payroll is affected by the worker's scrap rates, which affects inventory and scrap rate report counts. The production unit count credits the worker's pay, but also affects the preventive maintenance schedule, etc.

[D]   System Flowchart

The system flowchart shows how the information flows through a data system or process. It is all on one page. If greater detail is required for any area of the system, a subsystem or lower-level flowchart, which illustrates only the desired detail, is drawn for that purpose.

System flowcharts are not governed by any national standard. Intended for a diverse audience, from top management to programmers, flexibility is necessary to be able to target a presentation appropriately. While programmers can follow a system flowchart drawn for top management, top management may have a problem with one drawn for a project team of systems analysts and programmers because it will often utilize standard programming flowchart symbols.

[E]   Procedure Flowchart

Procedure flowcharting is useful for illustrating manual office procedures and is easy to follow, even by people outside the data-processing area. It confirms to the operations personnel that the systems analyst has recorded the procedure correctly. It also gives the systems analyst an easy-to-follow source of information when writing procedures.

Six symbols are used to draw the procedure flowchart. They represent:

1. Original information placed on document
2. Addition of information to document
3. Physical handling of document
4. Document inspection to render a decision
5. Document holding or storage
6. Document leaving procedure area

These are illustrated in Exhibit 36-3. A sample procedure flowchart is shown in Exhibit 36-4.

EXHIBIT 36-3.   Procedure Flowchart Symbols

Process or Element	Symbol
Original operation, the first time information is placed on a document.	◎
Adding information to a document in a later procedure step.	(hatched circle)
Handling the document, such as sorting, matching, separating, or stapling.	○
Inspection of a document for a decision to be made. Two or more courses of action will follow.	□
Storage of document(s) as inactive, delayed, filed, or held. Also used as a destroy symbol.	▽
Sending or moving the document from one area to another. Also used to show document being sent outside.	○

EXHIBIT 36-4. Sample Procedure Flowchart

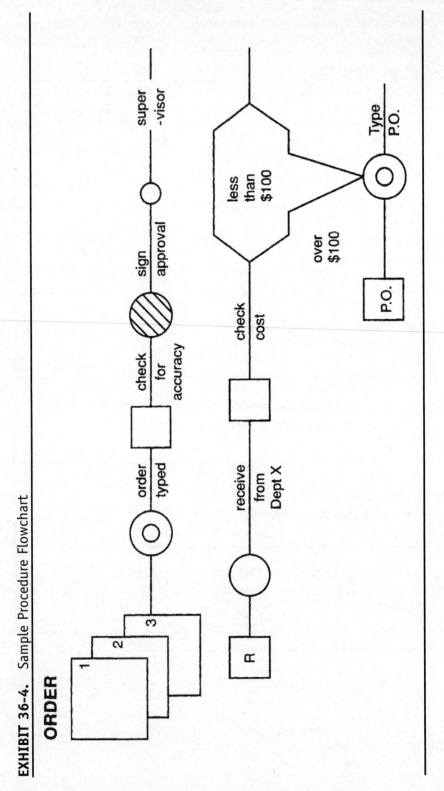

If a new, changed procedure contains manual operations, draw it as a procedure flowchart. When preparing a procedure flowchart, consider the following:

A. The direction of flow is left to right—and from top to bottom.
B. Identify the procedure flowchart in the lower left-hand corner with the following:
    1. Project name
    2. Project number
    3. Date
    4. Name of person who produced flowchart
C. All input documents have a receiving point, a starting point, and a disposition. Documents may be sent to a file, disposal, or to someone else.
D. Each line represents a data element flow.
E. Describe process steps briefly by printing the information to the right of the symbol.
F. When a multiple copy form, the parts are illustrated by the inspection symbol and the form title or number is printed inside the square.
G. When the same activity affects two or more documents simultaneously, it is shown by drawing a vertical rectangle around a symbol indicating the activity. Draw the flow lines to meet the rectangle.
H. Indicate the charting of one document affecting or creating other documents on the line of the affected action. A "V" line coming from the original document is dropped or inverted to meet the affected document line. After the action shown by a symbol is completed, the last leg of the "V" returns the document to its original level.

[F]   Dataflow Diagrams

Dataflow diagrams are replacing the more traditional systems flowchart. Like the systems flowchart, they have not been guided by any one national standard. There is more than one proposed set of symbols, but all share the same concept and objective. The four diagramming symbols used in this text are based on work by C. Gane and T. Sarson. Their book, *Structured Systems Analysis and Design Tools and Techniques*, is the source of the concept and symbols represented here.

Dataflow diagrams, which have been around for some time, are familiar in the academic environment. They have many advantages over traditional systems flowcharts when presenting graduated levels of overviews for both current and proposed systems. Because the documentation system is so simple and employs so few rules and symbols, there is little variation between textbooks illustrating its use. Its simplicity provides for a uniform pictorial presentation of systems by systems analysts, programmers, operations personnel, and most users.

Refer to Exhibit 36-5 for the dataflow symbols. The standard programming flowcharting template may be used with some minor substitutions. The auxiliary operation symbol can replace the dataflow environmental element symbol. The process symbol can replace the dataflow process or procedure symbol. Use the programming or procedure flowcharting templates to draw the data storage symbol.

EXHIBIT 36-5.   Data Flowchart Diagram Symbols

Process or Element	Symbol
Entity, an environmental element, can be the source or destination of data to or from the system or subsystems.	
Process system or procedures that act on data being received from an external source or an internal file (hard copy or computer database or file).	
Data storage. This can be a computer file or database, hard copy, microfilm or COM, reference lists or tables, even the back of a tablet.	
Data flow. This can be in many forms, such as LAN or WAN systems, direct computer communications, the U.S. mail, UPS, courier, or what have you, between the process system (symbols) and data storage or external source. An arrow will be drawn at the contact point of the receiving symbol to denote the recipient of the data.	

The diagramming symbols used for data flow diagrams are based on work by C. Gane and T. Sarson, *Structured Systems Analysis and Design Tools and Techniques,* Prentice Hall, Englewood Cliffs, NJ, 1979.

§ 36.08[F]

The dataflow diagram illustrates the system's flow and transformation process all on one page. Draw subsystems requiring more detail at the next level, also in their entirety, one per page, with an identification number linking them to their source. This is shown in Exhibits 36-6, 36-7, and 36-8. Repeat this procedure until the final, lowest subsystem level. The complexity and number of subsystems within the undertaking determine the number of levels that may be "exploded." The dataflow diagram levels may be defined as follows:

    A. **Context diagram.** The total system concept is the "large picture," illustrating all data flows into and out of the system. The processes themselves remain unnumbered and not described in this general overview. The context dataflow diagram would be the one most likely considered for use in a management presentation (see Exhibit 36-6).

EXHIBIT 36-6. Context Dataflow Diagram

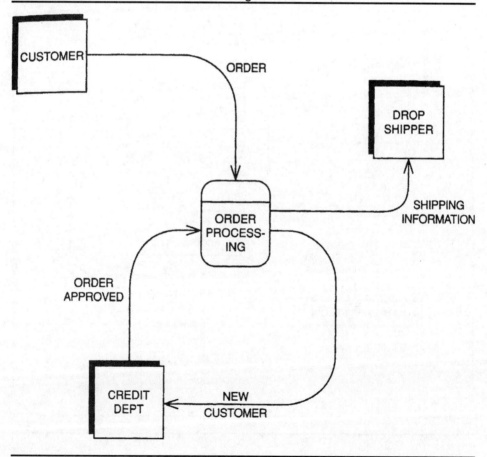

B. **Level 0 (zero) dataflow diagram.** This level represents the total system, numbering and describing each process. Data storage symbols depict the movement of data to or from storage (see Exhibit 36-7).

C. **Level 1 dataflow diagram.** This level represents one of the processes or procedures found at the zero dataflow level exploded into its own subsystem detail (see Exhibit 36-8).

D. **Level 2 dataflow diagram.** This level represents the further exploding of a given process found at level 1 into its own subsystem detail.

EXHIBIT 36-7. Level Zero Dataflow Diagram

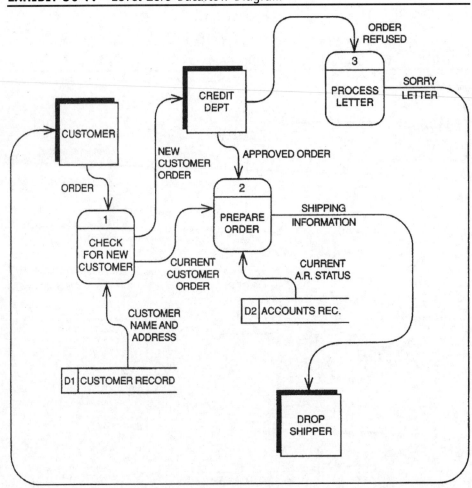

EXHIBIT 36-8. Level 1 Dataflow Diagram

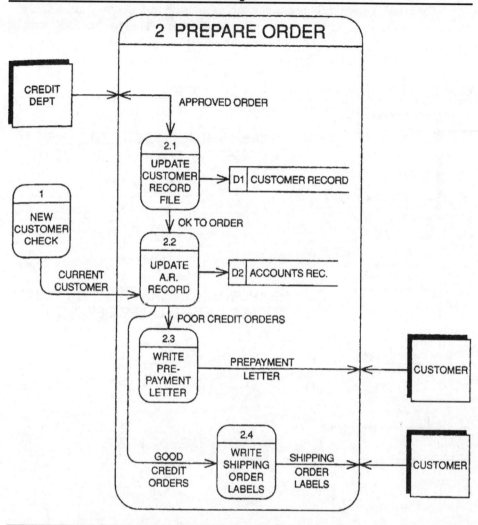

[G] Supplemental Dataflow Conventions

The dataflow diagramming procedure can get complex with successive levels of explosions. To help clarify the diagram, each of the four symbols employed can use supplemental conventions. Refer to Exhibit 36-9. Following are additional conventions that may be of help:

A. Duplicated entity symbols contain a diagonal slash in the bottom right corner. This can reduce the complexity of dataflow lines.

B. Process symbols contain the process number in the top part of the symbol. When a diagram is exploded, append a decimal representing the current level to the process number to provide for an audit trail of the related detailed processes (see Exhibit 36-9).

EXHIBIT 36-9. Supplement Dataflow Conventions

SLASH IN THE LOWER RIGHT-HAND CORNER TO INDICATE A DUPLICATE ENTITY.

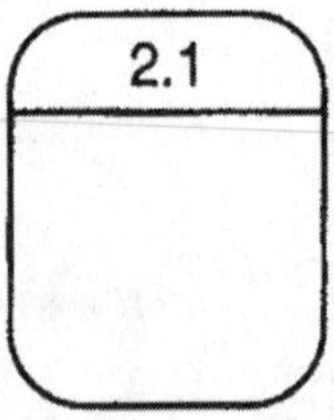

2.1

EXPLODED DIAGRAMS USE DECIMALS TO INDICATE RELATED DETAILED PROCESS.

D1

DATA STORAGE NUMBER.

D1

USE A LINE TO INDICATE DUPLICATE DATA STORAGE.

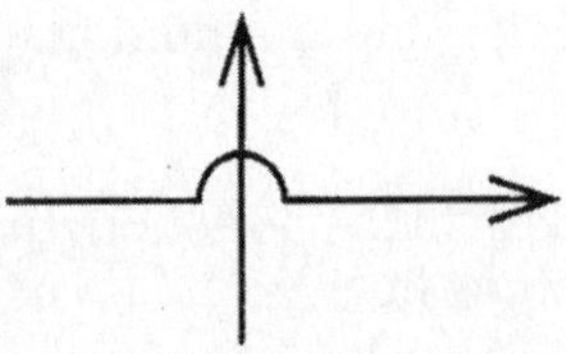

USE A CROSS ◯ OVER BRIDGE FOR LINES THAT DO NOT INTERSECT.

C. Data storage symbols have a boxed area on the left side of the symbol in which to write the data storage ID. A vertical line drawn to the left of the ID indicates a duplicate data storage location.

D. When dataflow lines cross each other, one of the lines may use a small crossover bridge to illustrate that the lines do not intersect.

Using dataflow diagrams is good for both documenting a current system and developing a proposed system.

A. Develop a freehand context diagram. This can start with on-hand user input.
   1. List external entities, data flows, and processes.
   2. Determine scope of system being charted.
   3. Draw context diagram.
B. Develop a level 0 (zero) dataflow diagram.
   1. Apply detail to each process or procedure.
   2. Identify and post data storage. Note data storage types such as hard drive, tapes, optical disk, file drawer, etc.
   3. Identify process exceptions and post to diagram.
   4. Draw the diagrams with the aid of a template. Relabel any symbols requiring meaningful text and clean up the arrangement of the symbols.
   5. Explode to the next level and repeat 1, 2, and 3 above.

[H]   Program Flowcharts

A program flowchart shows operation steps and logic decisions followed by the computer for a given program in the processing sequence. All the symbols employed should conform to the ANSI standards. Refer to Exhibit 36-10. Follow these rules in preparing the flowcharts:

A. The general direction of flow is top to bottom, and left to right.
B. Whenever increased clarity is desired, use arrows to indicate the direction of flow.
C. Identify each page with:
   1. Project name
   2. Project number
   3. Name of person who produced the flowchart
   4. Date
   5. Page X of Y
D. Identify the terminal connector showing that a line continues to a following page with an uppercase alphabetic character in the center of the connector symbol. The line continued on the following page starts with a connector symbol and the same character in its center as the departing connector. If that line does not continue on the following page, post the page number to the right of the connector symbol and post the departing page number to the right of the receiving connector.

E. Describe process steps briefly by printing the description within the symbol. If necessary, print additional information next to the symbol to clarify a step.

F. Later, when changing the flowchart, updates should be noted, dated, and signed by the person making the change.

EXHIBIT 36-10. Common Flowchart Symbols

Data Store Used for hard disk storage.	
Process Represents a processing function or activity.	
Decision Represents a decision step, with one or more alternative paths to be followed.	
Preparation Represents the modification of a program.	
Document Represents a printed document input or output (i.e. reports).	
Sequential Data Used for sequential data, such as tape input or output.	
Manual Operation Shows a manual operation which is limited to the speed of a human being.	
Data Represents data that is available for input or resulting from processing.	
Off Page Connector Used to indicate that the flow continues on another page. The page number is written inside the symbol.	
On Page Connect Used to indicate that the flow continues elsewhere on the page. A number is written inside the symbol to match up with the target connector.	
Flow Lines Used to connect the symbols and show the process flow.	

EXHIBIT 36-10.   (Continued)

Annotation Used for adding comments to an operation step.	
Predefined Process Used to illustrate a process that is defined elsewhere.	
Display Used to show output on a display (looks like a CRT screen).	
Manual Input Used from manual input (i.e. keyboard input).	
Terminal Point Used to start or stop a flowchart.	
Online Storage Represents any type of storage that is directly accessible by the system.	

[I]   Unified Modeling Language™

The latest method being developed for documenting object-oriented systems is the Unified Modeling Language™ (UML). Rational Software Corporation (now part of IBM) developed UML, with contributions from other leading methodologists, software vendors, and many users. UML is based on extensive use of the Booch, OMT, and Jacobson methods to document business processes and objects, and for component modeling. UML provides the application modeling language for:

A. Business process modeling with use cases
B. Class and object modeling
C. Component modeling
D. Distribution and deployment modeling

The Object Management Group (OMG) is developing UML into an industry standard. OMG is an open membership, not-for-profit consortium that produces and maintains computer industry specifications for interoperable enterprise applications. This standard is still in the process of being developed; for the latest information on UML, go to the OMG Web site at *www.omg.org*, or the IBM Web site at *www-306.ibm.com/software/rational/*.

[J]   IDEF

Integrated Definition, better known as IDEF, was originally created by the U.S. Air Force as a series of modeling methods that can be used to describe operations in an organization. It is now being further developed and maintained by Knowledge Based Systems. IDEF was originally developed for use in manufacturing environments, but has been adapted for wider use and for software development in general.

There are 16 different modeling methods, each of which is designed to capture a particular type of information through the modeling process. IDEF methods are used to create graphical representations of various systems, analyze the model, create a model of a desired version of the system, and to aid in the transition from one to the other. The following is a list of IDEF methods either currently used or in development. IDEF0 through IDEF4 are the methods most commonly used.

A. **IDEF0**—Function Modeling
B. **IDEF1**—Information Modeling
C. **IDEF1X**—Data Modeling
D. **IDEF2**—Simulation Model Design
E. **IDEF3**—Process Description Capture
F. **IDEF4**—Object-Oriented Design
G. **IDEF5**—Ontology Description Capture
H. **IDEF6**—Design Rationale Capture
I. **IDEF7**—Information System Auditing
J. **IDEF8**—User Interface Modeling
K. **IDEF9**—Scenario-Driven IS Design
L. **IDEF10**—Implementation Architecture Modeling
M. **IDEF11**—Information Artifact Modeling
N. **IDEF12**—Organization Modeling
O. **IDEF13**—Three Schema Mapping Design
P. **IDEF14**—Network Design

More information about the IDEF methods can be found on the Internet at *www.idef.com.*

See Exhibit 36-11 for sample of common IDEF symbols.

EXHIBIT 36-11.   Common IDEF Symbols

Process Represents a processing function or activity.	Process Name A0
Label Used to label an input, output, control or mechanism.	Label $\mathcal{N}$
Connector Used to connect processes.	

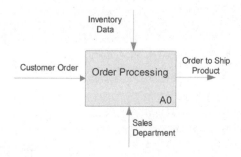

IDEF0 Example Process

37

DATA MANAGEMENT: TAKING CARE OF YOUR INFORMATION

§ 37.01   OVERVIEW

[A]   Purpose and Scope

Data is a critical corporate resource that must be managed properly as well as protected from unauthorized disclosure or modification. Corporate data must be managed in a controlled environment to ensure the integrity and accuracy of the data. As new systems are developed or purchased, they should be integrated into the existing corporate data environment and not implemented as standalone systems. The sharing of data in a secure environment requires that the appropriate policies and procedures be in place.

Data management policies cover all data created and used by the organization. This data includes, but is not restricted to:

A. Human resource data
B. Customer data
C. Memos
D. Strategic plans
E. Planning data
F. E-mails
G. Financial data
H. Best practices
I. Facilities data
J. Employee data
K. Policies and procedures
L. World Wide Web pages

All of this information must be protected and managed properly; the appropriate policies and procedures help ensure that each employee understands his role in protecting the organization's valuable data.

[B]   Critical Policies to Develop Based on This Chapter

Using the material discussed in this chapter, you will be able to create the following policies:

A. Define system of record.
B. Define ownership of data.
C. Define the roles and responsibilities of those who create or have access to sensitive data.
D. Protecting sensitive employee information.

Policies should always be developed based on the local situation. Successful managers cannot issue appropriate guidance if the policies are written with another company's situation or location in mind.

§ 37.02 ISSUES RELATING TO DATA

[A] System of Record

Data is factual information, in particular, information organized for analysis or to make decisions. Organizations create a tremendous amount of data, all of which must be managed properly just as you would any other valuable asset. Data includes every piece of factual information created by the organization. There are numerous systems within the typical organization that create and manage this data. These systems include:

A. Accounting/finance
B. Customer relationship management (CRM)
C. Enterprise resource planning (ERP)
D. Order entry
E. Human resources
F. Customer service
G. Intranet/extranet
H. Document management

In an ideal world, each data element used by the organization would only exist in one place and would not be duplicated in different systems. The reality is that specialized systems from various vendors are implemented in most organizations that require copies of different data elements. For example, your CRM system may not interface with your Accounting system, so you end up with customer information in both systems. The larger the organization, the more likely you are to have multiple special-purpose systems that require their own copy of important data. It is critical to identify which system will be the definitive source of important information.

A "system of record" is an information storage system (usually a computer system) which is the definitive data source for a given data element or piece of information. We go to the system of record when we need to know the "truth" about a particular item of data. All other systems are considered incorrect if their copy of the data does not match the system of record. Ideally, these secondary systems do not edit the data for which they are not the system of record, but instead receive updates from the system of record for these data elements. For example, you may determine that the CRM system is the system of record for basic customer information such as name, address and contact information. This basic contact information is also needed by your Accounting and Customer Service applications. Any changes necessary to basic customer information should be made only in the CRM system. The Accounting and Customer Service applications should receive updates on a regular schedule of this basic customer information.

In selecting which system should be the system of record for a particular data element, consider the following criteria:

A. **Scope.** How widely is the system used throughout the organization?
B. **Value.** How much impact does the system have on the core economics of the business?

C. **Influence.** How important is the sponsor of the system within the organization?

D. **Activity.** How much raw data is being fed into the system by high-volume, mission-critical transactions?

The higher a given system rates using the criteria listed above, the more likely it is to be a good candidate for being the system of record for the data elements used within the system. A system of record policy is necessary to ensure that a single "version of the truth" exists for all important data used throughout the organization. See Policy ITP-37-1 System of Record Policy as an example.

COMMENT

According to a 2012 study conducted by research firm IDC for information infrastructure company EMC Corporation, the digital universe will reach 40 zettabytes (ZB) by 2020, resulting in a 50-fold growth from the beginning of 2010.

POLICY ITP-37-1.   System of Record Policy

Policy #:	ITP-37-1	Effective:	03/18/13	Page #:	1 of N
Subject:	System of Record Policy				

1.0 PURPOSE

The company views corporate data as an asset of the company to be managed and protected. While multiple versions of data may necessarily exist due to the existence of specialized computer systems, this policy mandates that a system of record be identified for all data created and maintained within the organization. The system of record is to be considered the definitive and authoritative source of truth for a given data element.

2.0 SCOPE

This policy encompasses all data in all its forms and throughout its lifecycle. The IT Manager is responsible for implementing all aspects of this policy.

3.0 POLICY

The IT Manager is responsible for defining a system of record for all corporate data. In addition, the IT Manager is also responsible for the following:

A. All points of data collection for the system of record must be defined and documented.
B. Data entered into the system of record must be accurate and timely.
C. Systems that capture data that update the system of record must include the appropriate validation and security to ensure the integrity of the data.
D. Processes used to update the system of record must be documented and auditable.

Users of copies of data from a system of record are responsible for managing the refresh of the data copy from the system of record to ensure that accurate information is used in all systems.

4.0 REVISION HISTORY

Date	Revision #	Description of Change
03/18/13	1.0	Initial creation.

5.0 INQUIRIES

Direct inquiries about this policy to:

George Jenkins, CIO
Our Company, Inc.
2900 Corporate Drive
Columbus, OH 43215

Voice: 614-555-1234
Fax: 614-555-1235
E-mail: gjenkins@company.com

Revision #:	1.0	Supersedes:	N/A	Date:	03/18/13

[B]   Ownership of Data

Your data management policies should make it clear that all data created by the organization is owned by the organization, and not by any individual within the organization. This includes both structured and unstructured data, and any metadata about that data. Structured data is data that is formatted in an organized way for easy retrieval from computer systems, such as data in a database or in an XML file. Unstructured data is typically data created by a human being for personal use, such as word processing documents and spreadsheets. Metadata is information about the data, such as field names, file layouts, version control information, etc.

The Data Custodian (see § 37.03[A], "Data User Roles" for a definition of Data Custodian) is responsible for ensuring that the appropriate policies and procedures are in place to protect the data under his stewardship. These policies must document how access to the data is obtained, who has access to the data, and the retention period for the data.

[C]   Legal Obligations

There are several federal and state laws and regulations such as the Family Rights and Privacy Act (FERPA), the Sarbanes-Oxley Act (SOX), the Health Insurance Portability and Accountability Act (HIPAA), the Electronic Communications Privacy Act (ECPA), the Gramm-Leach-Bliley Act and the Freedom of Information Act (FOIA) that affect various aspects of data within the organization. These laws are quite complex and have been modified from time to time. It is critical for the organization to ensure that the legal obligations with respect to the organization's data are kept current. These obligations require the following actions:

A. All managers are expected to stay informed on any local, state, and federal laws and guidelines that affect how the organization's data is stored and managed. This can be done through participation in professional organizations, subscriptions to appropriate periodicals, or thorough participation in Internet listservs. Where appropriate, this can be delegated to members of their team. Processes must be in place to disseminate important changes to others within the organization that may be impacted.

B. Senior staff meetings should include on their agenda a discussion of recent changes to laws and regulations that affect the handling of data within the organization.

C. All managers are responsible for ensuring that their staff members are informed about changes in the legal environment and that corporate policies on the handling of data are being followed.

D. Employees are responsible for staying current on applicable laws and policies that affect their job. They must attend any training opportunities that apply to the handling of data in their area of responsibility.

§ 37.03   ACCESS TO DATA

[A]   Data User Roles

To ensure that everyone understands their role in the proper management of data, your data management policies should outline the different roles associated with the handling of data and the responsibilities of the people in those roles. These roles and their responsibilities include:

A. **Data Owner.** The organization is the owner of all data that originates within the organization.

B. **Data Custodian.** A member of senior management of the organization who is ultimately responsible for ensuring the protection and use of the organization's data. His responsibilities include:
   1. Identifying what data belongs to the organization and determining the system of record for the data.
   2. Identifying and documenting what roles are allowed access to the data and the level of access they have.
   3. Determining and documenting the process for authorizing individuals to access the data.
   4. Implementing processes that maintain the integrity and accuracy of the data.
   5. Ensuring that the data is protected and that applicable laws are followed concerning handling of the data.
C. **Security Administrator.** This role is responsible for the security of the data and systems that store the data. The responsibilities of this role include:
   1. Providing access to the users that are approved by the data custodian.
   2. Protecting the data from unauthorized users.
   3. Ensuring that appropriate disaster recovery procedures are in place.
D. **Data User.** This role is designated by the data custodian to have permission to access and use the data. The responsibilities of the data user include:
   1. Being accountable for all data access made with his user account.
   2. Ensuring that all use and distribution of data is only for approved purposes.
   3. Not disclosing data to unauthorized people.
   4. Keeping his password secret.
E. **IT Department.** This role is responsible for supporting the data systems infrastructure. The responsibilities of this role include:
   1. Documenting and supporting the structure of the organization's data.
   2. Supporting the use of standard data definitions throughout the organization.
   3. Facilitating the sharing of data and integration of data between the organization's systems.

[B] Data Retention

It is important to establish a data retention policy for all data in your organization for two reasons: to meet legal and business requirements, and to prevent data overloading your storage systems. Various state and federal regulations require data to be retained for some minimum period of time; some examples include:

A. Information relating to the manufacture, processing, and packaging of food—two years.
B. Patient medical records—up to two years after the patient's death.

C. Information relating to the manufacture, processing, and packaging of drugs—three years.
D. Information relating to the manufacture of biological products—five years.
E. Records relating to the audit process, including e-mails—seven years.
F. Trading account records—six years after the termination of the account.

Some organizations will want to save virtually every bit of data they create to be on the safe side; others will weigh the expense of storing all of this information with the possible costs of legal action caused by data not being available. The organization's legal department and senior management are responsible for creating the data retention schedule; it is then up to IT to enforce and conform to the policy in the most efficient way possible.

[C]   Handling of Restricted Data

While all data is important, special care must be taken when a user is in possession of data that is confidential or restricted in some way. Restricted data is data whose use is restricted by law, is confidential to the organization, or data that has been designated as protected from general access or modification. Types of restricted data include, but are not limited to, personnel data, financial data not for use outside the organization, and data to which unauthorized access, modification, or loss could seriously or adversely affect the organization, its partners, or the public.

COMMENT

The cost of lost data is high: in early 2006, one IT worker at Providence Health System in Portland, Ore., was fired and three others quit following the theft of computer tapes that held sensitive patient information, including addresses, phone numbers, and social security numbers. Employees at Providence routinely brought home tapes used to back up the data on systems there. Predictably, the tapes were stolen from a van parked outside one of their homes. A company official told the local paper that the loss was expected to cost the company more than $7 million, not including any costs of litigation.

The following are basic practices that employees must follow when handling restricted data:

A. **Systems should not include restricted data unless absolutely necessary.** Examples of restricted data include social security numbers, employee personal information, financial information such as credit card numbers or bank account numbers, and responses to a Request for Proposal (RFP) before a decision has been reached.

B. **Restricted data should not be stored on workstations, laptops, or other portable computing and storage devices unless absolutely necessary.** Restricted data should only be retained on a temporary basis on such devices. Protective measures such as encryption must be used to safeguard the confidentiality or integrity of the data in the event of theft or loss of the equipment. Permanent copies of restricted data should never be stored for archival purposes on workstations or portable equipment.

C. **Avoid transferring or storing restricted data.** Proliferation of data greatly increases risks of unauthorized access, particularly when the data is stored in ad hoc analysis tools such as spreadsheets and desktop databases. When data is copied for analysis or research, restricted data should be deleted whenever possible. When use and storage of restricted data must occur, provide appropriate security, following the organization's security protocols and the security requirements.

D. **Never e-mail restricted data.** Since e-mail is not a secure form of communication, restricted data should never be part of an e-mail, either in the body of the e-mail or in an attachment.

E. **Do not leave restricted data on a printer unattended.** Documents printed with restricted data must be removed immediately from the printer.

F. **Printed documents with restricted data must be shredded when no longer needed.** Never dispose of restricted documents in the regular trash.

G. **Delete personal information.** Any personal information such as gender, ethnicity, credit card numbers, etc., must be deleted from all systems when there is no longer a business need for the information.

H. **Make sensitive data easily identifiable.** When designing data structures, use naming conventions that make it easy to identify sensitive information.

§ 37.04 PROTECTING EMPLOYEE DATA

[A] Overview

While all data is important to the organization, data concerning the employees of the organization is of a special nature. The handling of employee data is indicative of the relationship between the organization and its employees, and establishes the level of trust the employee has in the organization. It is critical that this trust be maintained by protecting the privacy of personal data about the employee and his/her family that is collected by the organization from any source before, during, and after employment.

Your policy for the management of employee data should include the following:

A. Define the personal data the company collects from the employee and from other sources.
B. Describe how the data is used and disclosed.
C. Document the security measures used by the company to protect the employee's information.
D. Define who has access to the employee's information and the purposes for which it will be used.
E. A process for access by the employee to his personal information and how corrections can be made.
F. Procedures for notifying the company of possible improper disclosures of personal information.
G. How and under what circumstances an employee can opt out of disclosing certain personal information and the consequences of doing so.

The policy should also state that it applies to all entities controlled by the organization, and to any subcontractors that receive personal information. The policy does not imply any privacy rights for communications by the employee using company resources, such as e-mails, instant messages, telephone calls, etc.

[B] Privacy Officer

A member of senior management must be designated as ultimately responsible for the protection of personal employee information. This is usually the head human resources person with the organization. The person will be responsible for the following:

A. Ensure that all systems and processes comply with the employee data privacy policy.
B. Assess on a regular basis (at least annually) the compliance status of all systems with applicable laws and regulations.
C. Report to senior management the results of each assessment in writing.

[C] Collection of Personal Data

Personal data about employees is typically collected during the application and hiring process, and during their term of employment. This information may include:

A. Background checks.
B. Results of personality tests.
C. Drug test results.

D. Medical insurance enrollment information.

E. Applications for participation in certain benefit programs.

Personal employee data that is collected may include, but may not be limited to, the following:

A. Individual information such as name, gender, date of birth.

B. Contact information such as home address, phone numbers, e-mail addresses.

C. Identification numbers such as driver's license number and social security number.

D. Background information such as education, work history, military status, and criminal record.

E. Work history and training attended.

F. Medical and health information.

G. Compensation information such as salary, commissions, stock options, and 401K plan account information.

[D]   Use of Personal Data

The personal information collected is to be used only for the purpose required, and may be shared with service providers or other organizations where required. Personal data may be disclosed under the following situations to:

A. Internal personnel who need to receive the information to perform their jobs, such as managers and finance personnel for budgeting purposes.

B. Service providers of benefit programs, such as health plans and 401K plans.

C. Potential buyers of the business unit that the employee is a part of.

D. Customers to whom the organization is providing services.

Personal information is disclosed only to the extent necessary to perform the activity. Home addresses and personal contact are typically not disclosed, without the prior approval of the employee except in emergency situations. Outside firms that are given access to personal employee information are required to sign a written confidentiality agreement before the personal information is disclosed. Employee personal information is never disclosed or sold for marketing purposes.

Employees should also be aware that the company may be required to disclose personal data by law in situations such as the issuance of a search warrant, a court order or subpoena, or for other legal reasons by government agents or agencies.

[E]   Security of Personal Data

The company will maintain reasonable and appropriate physical, electronic, and procedural safeguards to protect the personal information of its employees. Personal data will be protected against misuse, modification, unauthorized access, and improper disclosure. Each employee of the company is required to sign an employment agreement that contains an obligation to protect the confidential information of the company, which includes personal information of fellow employees. Employees in the Human Resources department may be required to sign an additional confidentiality agreement before gaining access to sensitive personal data. All new employees are required to attend a training course within the first 30 days of employment that covers their obligations to protect company information.

[F]   Access to Personal Data

All employees will have access to personal data that is stored by the company to ensure the accuracy of the information. Access is available during regular business hours, and notice must be given at least 24 hours in advance to allow Human Resources to schedule access to the information. Each member of the employee's immediate family will also be allowed access to any information stored about them (but not the employee) during regular business hours, with at least 24 hours notice.

If the employee or family member feels that the data stored by the company is inaccurate, a request can be made in writing to have the information changed. The appropriate data custodian (usually the Human Resources Manager) must respond within 48 hours confirming that the information has been changed or explaining why the change will not be made. If the change is not made, the employee may submit written information to be stored with the data in question explaining why he feels the data is inaccurate; this most commonly occurs in the case of information concerning performance reviews.

See Policy ITP-37-2 Employee Data Management Policy as an example.

POLICY ITP-37-2.   Employee Data Management Policy

Policy #:	ITP-37-2	**Effective:**	04/18/13	**Page #:**	1 of N
Subject:	Employee Data Management Policy				

1.0 PURPOSE

This policy defines how data about each employee is managed within the organization.

2.0 SCOPE

This policy applies to all employee personal data collected and stored by the organization and to any subcontractors that receive employee information. This policy does not imply any privacy rights for communications by the employee using company resources, such as e-mails, instant messages, telephone calls, etc.

3.0 POLICY

The organization collects the following types of information about each employee:

A. **Personal information.** This is the employee's home information and personal contact information that is used by the HR and Payroll departments. It consists of basic employee data such as name, address, telephone number(s), title, marital status, credit report, Social Security Number, etc. Any changes to this information can only be made by these departments.

B. **Work information.** This includes data describing the employee's office, work address, and work contact information.

C. **Disaster recovery information.** This includes employee personal emergency contacts as well as information about the employee that is important to the organization's disaster recovery plan, such as an employee's current skilled licensing and certification status.

An employee data administrator is to be appointed by the IT department to ensure that employee data can only be accessed and modified by the appropriate parties. This employee data administrator will provide access rights to the appropriate personnel for access to this data. An employee's personal data can only be viewed by the employee, the employee's immediate supervisor, and the appropriate HR personnel via the corporate Intranet. Work information can be accessed by anyone in the organization.

To ensure that employee data is kept up-to-date, there are four levels of employee data access available on the corporate Intranet. These levels are:

A. **My Profile.** This is where every employee can manage his or her information. At this level, the employee can update his or her personal information, the emergency contact and disaster recovery information, and search other employee's work-related information.

B. **Department Access.** Department managers can modify the information of the employees in their department and run department reports.

C. **Division Access.** Division vice presidents can modify the information of the employees in their department and run division reports.

D. **HR Access.** The appropriate HR personnel can modify the information of all employees and run corporate reports.

Each employee is responsible for ensuring the accuracy of his or her information. The employee Intranet is to be used by the employees to keep the information they can update current, and to report to HR any incorrect data that they cannot directly modify. Employees must also notify HR immediately if they suspect that there has been an improper disclosure of personal information.

§ 37.04[F]

4.0 REVISION HISTORY

Date	Revision #	Description of Change
04/18/13	1.0	Initial creation.

5.0 INQUIRIES

Direct inquiries about this policy to:

George Jenkins, CIO
Our Company, Inc.
2900 Corporate Drive
Columbus, OH 43215

Voice: 614-555-1234
Fax: 614-555-1235
E-mail: gjenkins@company.com

Revision #:	1.0	Supersedes:	N/A	Date:	04/18/13

38

DOCUMENT MANAGEMENT: CAPTURING CORPORATE KNOWLEDGE

§ 38.01 OVERVIEW

[A] Purpose and Scope

While the paperless office has not yet arrived, document management solutions available today are a big step in making the paperless office a reality. An appropriate document management system will not only reduce the number of trees killed to support your business but will also help you to meet legal requirements, such as Sarbanes-Oxley and HIPAA, and support your disaster recovery plan.

A document stored electronically has many advantages over a printed piece of paper. The advantages include:

A. A single copy is available to more than one person at a time without physically making copies.
B. Backups of the document are easy to create and retrieve if needed.
C. Electronic documents are harder to lose—they cannot easily be lost by misfiling.
D. They can be found using computerized search technologies.
E. They can be processed by a workflow system and quickly routed to the appropriate person.
F. They are much cheaper to store than paper.

Document management encompasses all systems and processes used to capture, store, manage, and print information that either originates physically on paper or that is created using document-creation software such as Microsoft Office. This includes the storage of paper or microfiche in file cabinets and the storage of documents in electronic formats on a computer system. When evaluating an existing or proposed document management system, consider the following questions:

A. What are the documents that are critical to my business?
B. What is document collaboration?
C. Why not just put documents in a file cabinet?
D. What about my off-site storage?
E. How much can we afford to spend?
F. What regulations do I have to follow?
G. How long do I need to keep documents?
H. Can I incorporate my existing documents into this system?
I. Is the system easy to use?
J. When can I get started?

[B] Critical Policies to Develop Based on This Chapter

Using the material discussed in this chapter, you will be able to create the following policies:

A. Document Management Policy Scope
B. Document Retention Policy

C. Document Capture Procedures

D. Document Management System Implementation Procedures

Policies should always be developed based on the local situation. Successful managers cannot issue appropriate guidance if the policies are written with another company's situation or location in mind.

§ 38.02   CAPTURE AND STORAGE

[A]   Capture Options

A document management system must make it easy for documents to be captured and stored in the system. For paper-based documents, the capture process must be a fast, simple, and reliable way to capture the valuable information stored on paper and convert it into a digital format that can be efficiently stored and made available to those who need it.

Source documents come in many flavors. They might be on paper or stored in a computer using the native file format of the application that created the document. Paper documents come in many different sizes, including (in inches) $8\frac{1}{2} \times 11$, 11×17, 17×22, 22×34, and 34×44. The International Organization for Standardization (ISO) has created a standard paper size system specifying a number of formats; the most common formats and their uses are:

A. A0, A1—technical drawings, posters.

B. A1, A2—flip charts.

C. A2, A3—drawings, diagrams, large tables.

D. A4—letters, magazines, forms, catalogs, laser printer, and copying machine output.

E. A5—note pads.

F. A6—postcards.

G. B5, A5, B6, A6—books.

H. B4, A3—newspapers, supported by most copying machines in addition to A4.

Of course, most documents created in the modern office start out as an electronic file; many never see physical paper. Popular electronic file formats include:

A. .doc—Microsoft Word 2003 and earlier.

B. .docx—Microsoft Word 2007 and later.

C. .epub—an open standard for e-books.

D. .html—Web page.

E. .pdf—Adobe portable document format.

F. .rtf—rich-text format.

G. .tiff—used for images.

H. .txt—plain-text file.

I. .xml—Extensible Markup Language; a standard for creating markup languages that describe the structure of data.

Documents can also arrive at the organization through e-mail attachments or via a network fax server. When reviewing document capture options, consider the following:

A. How many documents will you need to capture?
B. How often will the system be utilized?
C. What condition are the documents in? Documents in good condition can be scanned using an automatic document feeder; older or worn documents may have to be scanned by hand on a flatbed.
D. What are the dimensions of the documents? Larger documents such as blueprints or architectural drawings may require a large flatbed device.
E. Can the system be centrally administered? Centralized administration can lessen the burden on the service desk by reducing configuration errors caused by users in remote locations.
F. How well the system scale? As your needs change and increase, will the system be able to handle future volumes?
G. Does the system support batch processing of documents? Batch input of documents is important when source documents arrive in batches.
H. Can documents be easily grouped together?

Most organizations will want to consider using a scanner with an automatic document feeder. This allows a stack of documents to be scanned at one time, rather than having each page placed by hand on the flatbed of the scanner. The most important consideration is that the scanner be able to handle the size and condition of the majority of paper documents to be scanned by the organization.

[B] Storage Options

Two questions need to be addressed concerning document storage options: how will original paper documents be stored and how will electronic documents be stored? There are basically three options for dealing with original paper documents:

A. **Store in file cabinets.** You may need to store the original documents in a readily accessible location if quick access to the original is a business requirement. The main disadvantage is the cost of file cabinets and storage space required.
B. **Use a professional document storage company.** This option eliminates the need for on-site storage but does come at a cost. Access to the physical document may require several hours for the document to be retrieved and delivered. This is a good method for storing e-mail if the SEC is a potential auditor.
C. **Shred documents after scanning.** For most documents, the original copy is not required, so the paper can be shredded and recycled. Shredding can be done on-site or the documents taken off-site to be shredded.

COMMENT

Companies that provide off-site storage include Fireproof Records, Global Relay, and Iron Mountain.

There are several options for the storage of digital documents:

A. **Magnetic media (hard drives).** This is the storage media used by the typical computer. This type of storage is becoming increasingly cheaper and allows for fast access to digital documents. Technologies such as storage area networks (SANs) and network attached storage (NASs) support scaling your storage requirements to whatever is needed. Its main drawback is that it contains a large number of moving parts that are subject to failure.

B. **Compact disks (CDs).** These are small disks used to store digital information. Their main advantages include low cost, durability, and ubiquitousness. The CDs main disadvantage is the limited amount of storage available per disk (650 MB).

C. **Digital video disk (DVDs).** A DVD is essentially a larger CD. Like a CD, it is very durable and ubiquitous but holds up to eight times as much information as a CD.

An electronic document management system must not only reliably store digital documents today but must also support new technologies developed in the future. To increase the chances of the system supporting future technologies, nonproprietary file formats for both scanned documents and documents created by software applications should be used. This will help ensure that a move to a new and improved system in the future will not require documents to be converted from a no-longer-supported file format. The two most common and oldest standard file formats are ASCII for text and TIFF for images. It is a good bet that future systems will continue to support these formats.

[C] Indexing

Indexing of documents when they are captured make it easier to find the document later. Common indexing processes include:

A. **OCR/pattern matching.** OCR (optical character recognition) translates printed characters into alphanumeric characters recognized by a computer. This allows the document to be stored not just as a picture but as the words in the document. OCR cannot usually translate handwriting or characters created with ornamental fonts. Pattern matching provides the capture of data on a form based on a desired pattern. For example, a Social Security number is in the pattern of xxx-xx-xxxx.

Pattern matching will look for this pattern and translate the result (using OCR) into an index field.

B. **Full-text indexing.** Full-text indexing is used in conjunction with OCR to allow the entire text of a document to be searched. The usefulness of full-text indexing depends upon the accuracy of the OCR process and the power of the search logic. There are several search options that make full-text indexes more useful:

1. Soundex. This is a phonetic algorithm for indexing names by their sound when pronounced in English. This allows for words with the same pronunciation to be encoded to the same string so that matching can occur despite minor differences in spelling.

2. Fuzzy logic. Allows for minor differences in spelling of words to still return a match during a search. The helps compensates either for words that were misspelled in the source document or for errors in the OCR process.

3. Wildcards. Allows for the use of special characters in a search to match portions of a word. Common wildcard characters are the asterisk (*), used to match any character or characters ("comp*" would find the words "computer" and "company"), and question mark (?) for matching any single character ("d?g" would find the words "dig," "dog," and "dug").

4. Proximity. Used to find occurrences of words used within a specified number of characters or words from each other.

C. **Metadata.** Metadata is the use of index field information stored about a document that makes a search quick and easy. For example, you might associate in an index the date the document was created, the author, a subject, etc. You can then use this metadata index to quickly find the document. This is especially helpful if the metadata does not occur within the text of the document.

D. **Electronic folders.** By creating electronic file folders, search time can be reduced by only searching specific folders. It also allows users to browse a folder that contains documents of the type they seek. A flexible electronic folder system also eases the transition from a paper-based file system to an electronic one by having the electronic folders mimic the paper-based system.

[D]   Electronic Discovery Requirements

The Federal Rules of Civil Procedure (FRCP), which are the rules governing civil procedures in U.S. district (federal) courts, were amended in 2006 to address the discovery of electronic information. "Electronically stored information" is now specifically defined in the FRCP and includes "writings, drawings, graphs, charts, photographs, sound recordings, images, and other data or data compilations stored in any medium from which information can be obtained." What this means is that electronic information does not just include asking for the other party to provide copies of their e-mails. The new amendments, for example, allow a party to inspect the other party's computer system, including hard drives, and obtain copies of hard drives among other things. Performing searches of the other party's electronic information will allow the discovery of deleted e-mails and other documentation that may not have been produced.

As the IT Manager, this means you need to track and manage all electronic documents (as defined by the FRCP) stored by the organization, which makes the implementation of a document retention policy even more important. If your organization is sued, and in some situations even before a lawsuit is commenced, you may be asked to discuss the location of all electronically stored information and your document retention policy with your organization's attorneys. You may also be asked to preserve any existing documents that might be considered evidence and to document what kind of electronically stored information the other party and even non-parties may have that were sent from your organization.

In addition to a specific definition of electronic documents, there are also special provisions incorporated in the rules governing interrogatories, which are requests for production of documents and subpoenas to obtain electronically stored information. If there is concern about your organization withholding electronic information, the other side might obtain an expert to inspect, search, and sample your information. The other party must specifically request what form the discovery should be produced in (Word, PDF, etc.). Otherwise, the party receiving the request may produce the information in any reasonable form. While there is a specific provision for sanctions related to electronic discovery, the rule is limited due to a computer system's constant change of stored information. The general discovery provisions in Rule 26 of the FRCP are:

A. A party must disclose electronically stored information in its initial disclosure by category or type and include sources potentially responsive that the party is not searching or producing.

B. A party should produce relevant, not privileged, and reasonably accessible electronically stored information.

C. If a party asserts privilege or protection, written notice must be provided.

D. Electronic Discovery Topics for Parties Conference to include: forms of producing electronically stored information; preservation of electronically stored information, and whether the parties can agree on approaches for asserting claims of privilege or work product inadvertently produced.

Rules 33 and 34 of the FRCP covering interrogatories and requests for production state that:

A. Electronically Stored Information is DEFINED under Rule 34 and not to be included under the definition of documents.

1. Electronically stored information is defined to include writings, drawings, graphs, charts, photographs, sound recordings, images, and other data or data compilations stored in any medium from which information can be obtained, or translated, if necessary, by the respondent into reasonably usable form, or to inspect, copy,

test, or sample any designated tangible things which constitute or contain matters within the scope of Rule 26(b) and which are in the possession, custody or control of the party upon whom the request is served.

B. Rule 33: A party may substitute access to documents or electronically stored information for an answer to an interrogatory if the burden to answer is substantially the same for either party. Another party may have to provide technical support, software information, or other assistance to comply.

C. Rule 34: Parties may test or sample materials sought in addition to copying and request preferred form of electronic discovery, or producing party may produce in their preferred reasonable form. Electronically stored information is to have its own definition—do not define under "documents."

[E] Retention Policy

Most documents have a shelf life. Few documents need to be kept forever, so it is important to have a document retention policy to provide guidance on when a document should no longer take up valuable shelf or disk space. A document retention policy should make your organization more efficient while avoiding litigation due to the improper destruction of documents. Federal and state laws dictate how certain documents should be handled and stored, and the method of their destruction.

It is vitally important to follow the document management process that you have put into place. If a scanning solution is implemented but the paper document is retained, a court of law may ask for the original paper-based document. In this case having the electronic document does you no good. But if your process is to scan the paper document then destroy the original, a court of law must recognize the electronic document as the best evidence. In this case the metadata and index search become more powerful.

COMMENT

The trial and collapse of Arthur Andersen made clear the importance of a well-thought-out document retention policy.

Your document retention policy should address the following:

A. What documents will be maintained?
B. How long should each type of document be kept?
C. What process should be used to destroy each type of document?
D. Who is ultimately responsible for retention activities?
E. When and how will retention policies be tested.
F. How is the destruction of documents to be tracked?

The following types of documents should be covered in your document retention policy:

A. **Accounting documents.** This includes gross receipts, expense receipts, and other business transactions. Often this is the most paper-intensive area in a business.

B. **Business records.** This includes articles of incorporation, bylaws, capital stock, copyrights, and trademark registration and patents.

C. **Tax records.** This includes any documentation to support deductions and well as federal, state, and local tax returns.

D. **Personnel records.** Employment records are critical for dealing with lawsuits from current and former employees. This includes resumes, applications, performance reviews, and employment contracts. Employee records should be kept at least five years after the employee leaves the company.

E. **Legal records.** Documents such as customer and supplier contracts, intellectual property, and corporate records must be retained.

F. **Electronic records.** E-mail is becoming a critical means of business communication and is subject to discovery in legal proceedings. Other forms of electronic communication such as instant messaging and Web pages may also need to be retained.

Exhibit 38-1 lists the generally recommended retention period for different types of documents. These are only guidelines; please consult the advice of your organization's legal and accounting advisors for specifics that may apply to your type of business and your legal jurisdiction.

EXHIBIT 38-1. Generally Recommended Document Retention Period

Type of Document	Retention Period
Most financial records	4 years
Auditor's reports	Permanent
Annual financial statements	Permanent
Payroll records	6 years
Business records	Permanent
Insurance records	6 years
Tax records	Permanent
Pension and profit sharing records	Permanent
Personnel records	6 years
Press releases	Permanent

§ 38.02[E]

Type of Document	Retention Period
Legal documents	10 years
Sales and marketing documents	3 years
E-mails	Depends on subject

All paper documents are to be destroyed at the end of the retention period using a licensed and bonded third-party document destruction company that can bring the destruction equipment on-site. This will allow the destruction of the documents to be monitored.

COMMENT

The latest information on tax record retention can be found at the IRS Web site at *www.irs.gov*.

See Policy ITP-38-1 Document Retention Policy as an example.

POLICY ITP-38-1. Document Retention Policy

Policy #:	ITP-38-1	Effective:	03/18/13	Page #:	1 of N
Subject:	Document Retention Policy				

1.0 PURPOSE

The company views documents created and received by the company as an asset of the company to be managed and protected. The law requires that certain types of documents be maintained for a specified period of time; failure to do so may subject the company and any responsible employees to lawsuits and fines.

2.0 SCOPE

This policy encompasses all documents in all their forms and throughout their lifecycle. This includes documents such as memos, contracts, account information, e-mails, instant messages, etc. The following types of documents are covered by this policy:

- A. **Accounting documents.** This includes gross receipts, expense receipts, and other business transactions.
- B. **Business records.** This includes articles of incorporation, bylaws, capital stock, copyrights, and trademark registration and patents.

C. **Tax records.** This includes any documentation to support deductions as well as federal, state, and local tax returns.

D. **Personnel records.** Employment records are critical for dealing with lawsuits from current and former employees. This includes resumes, applications, performance reviews, and employment contracts. Employee records should be kept at least five years after the employee leaves the company.

E. **Legal records.** Documents such as customer and supplier contracts, intellectual property, and corporate records must be retained.

F. **Electronic records.** E-mail is becoming a critical means of business communication and is subject to discovery in legal proceedings. Other forms of electronic communication such as instant messaging and Web pages may also need to be retained.

The CEO will appoint a person to be responsible for implementing all aspects of this policy.

3.0 POLICY

The company has established a retention and destruction policy for documents received or created by the company to ensure compliance with legal requirements and to protect the company's intellectual property. The retention policy for each type of document is listed below:

Type of Document	Retention Period
Most financial records	4 years
Auditor's reports	Permanent
Annual financial statements	Permanent
Payroll records	6 years
Business records	Permanent
Insurance records	6 years
Tax records	Permanent
Pension and profit-sharing records	Permanent
Personnel records	6 years
Press releases	Permanent
Legal documents	10 years
Sales and marketing documents	3 years
E-mails	Depends on subject

§ 38.02[F]

All paper documents are to be destroyed at the end of the retention period using a licensed and bonded third-party document destruction company that can bring the destruction equipment on-site. This will allow the destruction of the documents to be monitored.

4.0 REVISION HISTORY

Date	Revision #	Description of Change
03/18/13	1.0	Initial creation.

5.0 INQUIRIES

Direct inquiries about this policy to:

George Jenkins, CIO
Our Company, Inc.
2900 Corporate Drive
Columbus, OH 43215

Voice: 614-555-1234
Fax: 614-555-1235
E-mail: gjenkins@company.com

Revision #:	1.0	Supersedes:	N/A	Date:	03/18/13

[F] Security

Security is critical to the success of a document management system—you don't want the wrong document to fall into the wrong hands at the wrong time. In addition, the system's security should ensure that legitimate users are able to do their job and not compromise the integrity of the underlying database, file system, and network. The document management system should provide multiple levels of security, including the authentication of users, the proper assignment of what the user is authorized to do, and the logging of activity in an audit trail.

The system must balance access and security through the control of access to the system and control over what each user is able to do once in the system. Access to the system is done through some sort of authentication process, which might include any combination of the following:

A. **Username/password.** The user gains access by providing a username and password.
B. **Login levels.** Access to certain features and functions is based on the user's login level.
C. **Biometric.** Access is controlled by scanning a fingerprint or by voice recognition.

Once authenticated into the system, the user is allowed to perform activities based on the rights set up by the system administrator. There are several basic types of rights that the system should support:

A. **Individual/group rights.** Rights can be assigned to each user individually or as a member of a group.
B. **Access rights.** Rights are assigned to specific objects in the system, such as folders and documents.
C. **Feature rights.** Determines what actions a user can perform, such as view or read/write.

The security system should also support the logging of all system activity and the generation of audit trails. It should include who used the system and when and what actions were performed. Especially important is logging unsuccessful attempts to access content or to make unauthorized changes to documents.

§ 38.03   RETRIEVAL AND COLLABORATION

[A]   Document Access

Access to the right information stored in the right document by the right person at the right time is the ultimate purpose of any document management system. Another strength of a document management system is the ability of multiple users to access a single document at the same time. The system should support the following process for getting documents into user's hands:

A. **Online access.** Most document management systems include an application that is run on the user's workstation to support searching and managing documents.
B. **Intranet and Internet.** This allows the user to access documents using a Web browser on the organization's intranet or via the public Internet.
C. **Print and fax.** The system should support common printers and fax systems.
D. **CD and DVD.** CDs and DVDs are common ways to send large volumes of documents that might be too much for other methods.
E. **E-mail.** E-mail has become the most common form of communication in business today; e-mail makes it possible to distribute documents widely at a very low cost. The system should allow the e-mailing of documents such that the recipient does not require any special software to read the document.
F. **Portable folders.** This allows users to synchronize important documents between their laptop and the document management system, so that they have copies when needed on their laptop when they are not connected to the system.

[B]   Annotation and Redaction

Annotation is the mark up of documents without altering the original. Common annotations include highlighting a portion of text, using special stamps such as "draft" or "secret," and adding comments and redaction (using blackout or whiteout to hide text). A document management system's security should allow the administrator to control who can annotate documents and what annotations are visible to what users. All annotations should be overlays that in no way alter the original document. In this way, the original document can still be printed or viewed by those with the proper security.

[C]   Workflow

Workflow can have a major impact on the efficiency of an organization by automating the routing of work documents from one person to another. An example is a purchase order that is created then routed to the appropriate people for approval and payment. Rules can be created so that the purchase order goes through one series of steps if the amount is below a certain threshold, and a different series of step if it is above a specified amount. Workflow can be of two different types:

A. **Serial or linear.** The document flows in a single path from one person or department to another until the workflow is complete. At a single step, only one person can route the document to the next task.
B. **Parallel or group.** The document can be routed to the next step by more than one person. For example, a purchase order is approved for payment if any one of three different accounting clerks approves it for payment. Or a proposal may require the approval of two different managers in a single step before going on to the next step.

A workflow system also helps to eliminate bottlenecks by giving management visibility into the status of any document at any time. The system can also notify users if a document has been waiting for some action past an acceptable amount of time.

§ 38.04   PRINTING AND ARCHIVING

[A]   Legal Requirements

As regulatory requirements continue to increase, a document management system becomes an increasingly critical tool to ensure the organization is in compliance with regulations at the local, state, and federal level. A properly implemented system can help ensure compliance by enforcing the consistent application of document policies and procedures and by providing a verifiable audit trail of all actions taken surrounding a document.

While legal requirements will differ in the details, two major features must be supported to fulfill the basics requirements of most regulations:

A. **Storage media cannot be altered.** All activities performed on a document from creation to destruction must be tracked in a way that cannot be altered.

B. **Information must be set in time.** All activities performed on a document from creation to destruction must be time-stamped in a way that cannot be altered.

In addition to the items above, other features that the document management system should support to meet legal requirements include:

A. Documents can be retrieved and printed as needed.
B. Indexes should be used to allow for quick retrieval.
C. Documents are stored on appropriate media.
D. Documentation on how the system works must be available and up to date.
E. Cross-referencing of other systems should be allowed.
F. Controls should be in place to detect and prevent the deterioration of documents.

While following the processes just listed should keep you in compliance with most legal requirements, a local attorney should be consulted for any specific local requirements.

[B]   Long-Term Storage

All document management systems do a good job of storing documents for today's software and hardware environment, but what about long-term? Many vital records must be kept in perpetuity; will you have the hardware and software available to retrieve these documents 50 or 100 years from now? There are several issues to consider that can affect your ability to access documents in the future:

A. **Media failure.** All media will eventually fail; hard drives, CDs, DVDs, and tapes do not last forever. The only way to avoid media failure is to periodically read and refresh the data to new media.

B. **Software failure.** All software has bugs; it is possible that a bug in the software could damage a document.

C. **Obsolete data formats.** Software for creating documents gets updated to "new and improved" file formats or may at some point be no longer available.

D. **Site failure.** If all your documents are stored in one place, will they survive a fire or natural disaster?

E. **Organizational failure.** If an organization ceases to exist, what happens to the important documents being stored?

> # COMMENT
>
> While the tapes containing the data on how to build a Saturn V rocket still exist, there are no longer any machines available to read the data. And even if you could read the data, the software to turn that data into useful information is no longer available!

[C] Disaster Recovery

One of the most important aspects of a document management system is its support for your disaster recovery plan. The digital archiving of documents simplifies the disaster recovery planning by making it easy to store important documents offline in a secure location. Backups of entire document repositories can easily be made to portable media such as CD, DVD, and tape and stored in a secure location. The documents can then be easily restored if the active documents are lost. The document management system should provide software to allow viewing of the documents stored on the backup media.

§ 38.05   DESIGNING A SOLUTION

[A] Gathering Business Requirements

The first step required in a document management project is the documentation of all of the business reasons for doing this project. As cool as the technology might be, it only exists to help us meet one or more requirements of the business. This is true not just in document management projects, but for any project that will change how the organization functions. This activity will include the following steps:

A. Determining the primary business objective.
B. Documenting the secondary business objectives.
C. Determining the financial value of meeting the business objectives.
D. Understanding your organization's technical and user environments.

There are always more projects than there are funds available in almost any organization. Your document management project is just one of many projects that management will be asked to fund.

The first step in designing a document management system is the determination of the business objectives of the project. There are many good business reasons why an organization would consider implementing a document management system. Maybe the organization is looking to implement a disaster recovery plan. Maybe there is some regulatory compliance issue related to your industry that requires you to be able to efficiently retrieve documents. Your employees might be asking for a better way to share documents. Or maybe it's just that the number of filing cabinets is overwhelming and there is no end in sight to the growth. It seems that every new business day we discover that another document or set of documents is lost or missing.

All of these business needs are found throughout every conceivable type of business, whether your business is one person in your basement or a Fortune 500 corporation with operations in several countries. Everyone deals with paper and filing paper and the problems that paper generates.

So the issue here is that one of these needs or maybe several of these needs are the reason why a company would want or need to implement a document management solution. Defining the most critical needs is to define your business objectives.

Business objectives will vary from organization to organization. But the primary function of a document management system is to store information in an organized fashion and to make that information available to end users in such a manner that they are able to enter key points or indexes about the document, and the result is what they need to work with. The information must also be sharable across the network or maybe even the entire world if the information is public in nature. The document management system end user must also be able to print any document on demand or have the ability to e-mail or distribute the document if the need arises. Additionally, the document management system must be able to accommodate multiple file types and the existence of electronic files along with digital images.

All of these aspects are and will be business objectives that need to be met in order for a document management system to be implemented. A particular business may have only one of these items as its objective, or a business may have all of them. But at least one of the mentioned items will be present in order for a document management system to be necessary.

While there are usually many objectives for a project, the primary business objective oftentimes is the only reason for purchasing and implementing a document management solution. Once the primary objective is met, then and only then will you be able to move on to secondary and ancillary business objectives. However, often we find that multiple objectives are met because of the overlapping nature of documents.

As an example, ABC Company was having a hard time storing dispatch records. A technician would complete work at a customer's site and the ensuing record or document would be stored in a traditional steel filing cabinet. With the ever-growing set of documents to track service technicians' hours, it was time to digitize the documents and store them electronically. This electronic storage of the documents was the primary business objective.

A secondary business objective was discovered at the same time. Once the documents were electronic, searching for a particular item was shortened often from days or weeks to seconds. Once an operator knew what he or she needed to search for—technician name, ID number, or a word-text search—the result was displayed on the computer screen in seconds.

This secondary objective was discovered only after the initial objective had been met. The financial windfall was that both objectives were met with the same initial investment in the application.

Determining financial benefits is a very complex process, and it is very often difficult to get an exact answer. If a company or department is doing research, then the paper copy is invaluable and a price cannot be put on pre-serving the data forever. In a real estate environment where many different parties have a copy of the same document, it might be a matter of simply making an electronic copy and moving on. The cost to have someone photocopy the document and ship a new version is considerably lower than having to re-create a research document from scratch.

Financial benefit is determined by the value of the data on the paper and what goes into storing the ever-growing amount of paper. Here are some items to consider when evaluating financial benefit of a document management solution:

A. What is my current cost to store paper?
B. What is the long-term storage requirement?
C. What is the relative value of the data on the paper?
D. Can I easily recreate the paper?
E. Does someone else own a copy of the paper document?
F. Is there some regulation forcing me to preserve the data?

At this point in the discussion, you must stop and ask yourself: how do I store paper for my office? Several questions come to mind when determining the current physical storage and also determining the eventual physical storage once you start to store some or all of the documents digitally:

A. What is the physical environment available to house all of the docu-ments that are used during the normal course of business?
B. How many pages need to be stored (weekly, monthly, and annually)?
C. What sizes of documents need to be stored?

Remember to consider different sizes of documents used in various depart-ments, such as small invoice documents in accounting. Accounting depart-ments are full of many different sizes of paper—check stubs, invoices, receipts, cash register receipts, etc.

Part of the discussion must also be centered around documents that are never on paper. Accounting applications can print reports to an electronic file. Resumes are routinely written and then e-mailed from recipient to recipient until they are either eventually printed or stored electronically. A good, usable document management application should be able to have electronically cre-ated documents stored right alongside scanned paper documents.

[B] Technical Requirements

Once the business requirements are understood, the requirements can be com-pared against available hardware and software to design a solution that fits the organization. A document management system will require at least a personal computer. In many cases, the system will be installed on a network file server and then be distributed to end users by way of their personal workstation. A workstation can be directly connected to the file server either by way of a network cable or over a connection through the Internet.

The most important aspect of the technical environment is the amount of hard disk space that will be required to store the paper images. What a document management system will do first and foremost is store electronic images of paper documents. Vast amounts of paper documents exist in today's business climate, and this usually makes up the bulk of the information that will be stored in the system. So we need to be aware of the number of pages and take into consideration size of paper and whether any of the documents need to be scanned in color.

Another issue of a technical nature is what different types of systems will be delivering information into the system. This includes scanners, AS400 mainframes, digital copiers, existing PDF images, and business software applications such as AutoCAD and accounting and practice management applications.

Network infrastructure is vitally important to the end users who are using the document management system. A good infrastructure is necessary to move the large amounts of data that are found within a document management system. If the network infrastructure is not adequate, once a large number of documents are scanned the whole system will begin to run slower and or halt business productivity. One of the many reasons to implement a document management system is to increase productivity. If productivity is diminished because of poor execution of the network infrastructure, then you are not better off. This argument is true of any software application but is even more important for a document management system due to the nature of a scanned image. In a pure database application a weak network infrastructure may be usable for several years because the data being entered are placed within a database. A document management system uses the database as well, but the existence of the image magnifies the weak network infrastructure and a network slowdown or failure will be imminent.

Workstation and server hardware should be fairly new and robust. Many document management systems require the use of a fat client. A fat client is software loaded on the local workstation that connects with the server component. Other document management systems will store the documents on an Internet-connected server and only require a Web browser to attach to the server. This will allow older equipment at the workstation or even appliance terminals to be used as the client workstation. However, with newer software it is advisable to stay current on the workstation hardware. Upgrades to hardware and software should be considered every year and completed when productivity begins to decrease due to old or outdated hardware and software.

The same discussion about the workstation is also true of the server. Servers purchased from most hardware suppliers and manufacturers usually carry a three-year warranty. The hard drives in the server may have a five-year warranty. The technology is upgraded so fast that more often than not the server will need to be upgraded at every three years, and it is advisable to upgrade at least within five years of purchase.

§ 38.05[C]

Of equal importance with computer hardware is the scanning hardware used to convert paper documents into digital ones. Devices used to scan paper documents fall into the following categories:

A. **Scanner only.** Scanning is the only function the device performs.
B. **Multifunction devices.** The device performs functions besides scanning, such as copying and printing documents.
C. **Desktop scanners.** A small device that sits on a desktop and is typically used by a single user at a single workstation.
D. **Workgroup scanners.** A larger device that is connected to multiple users via the local area network.

[C] Planning for Implementation

Implementing a document management solution is similar to any other IT project. An internal project leader must be assigned to see the project through to completion. The project leader will also be responsible for managing the activities of outside vendors used, especially the selected document management solution vendor. Planning is critical for the success of the project and should include the following:

A. **Organize the project team.** The team should include representatives from the user community as well as IT.
B. **Develop a detailed work plan.** Break the project down into manageable phases with clear deliverables at the end of each phase.
C. **Hold regular status meetings.** Review project progress on a regular basis.
D. **Develop a communication plan.** Be sure to keep all important stakeholders informed of progress as well as any issues that come up.
E. **Develop a support plan.** The long-term success of the project will depend on the quality and level of support available to users. The plan should include service level agreements and how issues are to be handled.

End-user training is critical for the success of a document management solution. Training should be performed on-site if possible so that the users' training experience is as close to what they will experience on the job as possible. Make sure that all end users understand the following:

A. How does a user get access?
B. What is the scan procedure?
C. What is the retrieval procedure?
D. How is tech support supplied?
  1. Via Web site?
  2. Via telephone?
E. Who is the on-site expert?
F. Is follow-up training available?

39

IT TRAINING: BUILDING THE RIGHT SKILLS

§ 39.01 OVERVIEW

[A] Purpose and Scope

Information technology is an ever evolving field. Every day new hardware and software arrive in the marketplace. Every day new versions of software seem to appear in the data center. Keeping pace with all of these changes is a challenge to IT departments everywhere. Keeping pace is also a personal challenge. IT professionals, who lose their technical "edge," may find their careers slowing or stagnating.

Training is the way we all learn new skills. Some training is formal such as in a classroom. Some training is informal, such as learning by reading a book, or try-and-fail. Some people will quickly grasp new concepts while others struggle to absorb the lessons. Each person learns at his or her own rate and is best taught in his or her own way.

COMMENT

"Force has no place where there is need of skill."—Herodotus (484 BC–430 BC), The Histories of Herodotus

---

It is the IT Director's responsibility to ensure that the limited number of people in their department possess the adequate skills to the needed level of expertise to support customer requirements. Given the evolving nature of technology, this is an ongoing task. The easiest way that an IT Director can ensure the IT team keeps its technical edge is through a formal training program.

A formal IT training program is an often neglected task. The assumption is that the people were hired for their skills, so what is there to train? Training someone rarely provides immediate results. Instead, it is an investment for the future. This investment is in providing additional skills to the company, and an investment in the individual, which is always appreciated by the staff.

Training is a long-term investment because there is a difference between familiarity with a subject and expertise. Training provides familiarity to the subject. It passes through the various pertinent topics and tries to link them together. However, expertise, the full understanding of how the training subject works together, only comes from practice. This is why in elementary school you were drilled in mathematics tables for multiplication, division, addition, and subtraction. This was to move you from familiarity to expertise in basic mathematics.

COMMENT

U.S. Marine Corps basic training is about 13 weeks long. However, it only provides familiarity to its many subjects. Typically, a Marine infantryman requires several years to master all of these same subjects.

Some companies use training classes as a reward. The individual benefits from the training, but the trip can be scheduled during the times of the year that the spouse can (at her own expense) accompany the team member on the trip.

[B] Management Excuses

For some reason, the first thing that executives attack in a budget reduction is the money allocated to training. The argument is that the department can skip additional training for one year with minimal harm. Unfortunately, the training budget is often cut or eliminated again in following years. The result is a staff with stagnating technical skills. As the company wishes to move to new technologies, new people must be brought into the organization. This introduces an unnecessary level of tension into the department as the "old people" seek to protect their jobs, pay increases, and promotion potential. Also, it forces a reduction of current staff with outdated skills to make room for the newcomers.

Another issue is that some IT Managers can see no further than their own self-interest. Since the training budget does not directly benefit them or advance their career, it is considered an optional expense. Their feeling is that training takes time away from work that could advance their career and provides little in immediate return. Another excuse against training is that the people they have in place now are fully utilized. New technologies should be assigned to new hires who already have developed expertise.

[C] Critical Policies to Develop Based on This Chapter

Using the material discussed in this chapter, you will be able to create the following policies:

A. Policy requiring that all documented processes include verifiable measurements of effectiveness before implementation, to include:
B. Policy for the collection and tracking of reported defects and early detection.
C. Policy for reporting compliance to approved process.
D. Root cause determination of critical or systemic problems.

Policies should always be developed based on the local situation. Successful managers cannot issue appropriate guidance if the policies are written with another company's situation or location in mind.

COMMENT

"Divide each difficulty into as many parts as is feasible and necessary to resolve it."—Descartes

---

§ 39.02   TRAINING FOR IMMEDIATE REQUIREMENTS

[A]   Overview

Immediate training requirements are those for maintaining current service levels. These are short-term (less than one year) plans. It involves identifying what skills are needed, reviewing the skills inventory currently in the department, and then training team members to cover any gaps. Sometimes, it is not practical to support every technology with in-house staff. It may be prudent to contract for support requiring a high level of skill that is rarely needed. Over the long-term, work to eliminate this technology from the company.

Training for immediate needs or short-term changes may be in response to a staff departure or to a recent lapse in service support. It may also provide a greater depth of expertise or reflect a desire to return outsourced services to an internal support group.

Most IT departments slap together their annual training plans based on recent events or to support an upcoming technical migration. Instead, these plans should be based on data that is available to the IT Director in several forms. The steps to building the annual training plan are as follows:

A. Make a list of all technologies used in the company: hardware, software, and IT processes.
B. Identify the ones whose support is outsourced (usually hardware).
C. List who is the primary, secondary, and tertiary support for each (yes, three deep).
D. Identify each person's current level of expertise for each technology.
E. Identify the desired level of expertise for each level of support.
F. Bridge this gap with a training program.

Technologies and processes are identified so we can determine the skills needed by the IT team. Skills are broken into six separate categories for easier administration. To some degree, each person in IT touches on every area. The categories are:

A. **Hardware.** This list includes every hardware item supported by the IT staff from the major to the minor. In most cases, we deal with the significant end item, such as a server or a workstation, and do not dig down into their optional components.

B. **Software Tools.** This list includes the basic tools used to build applications or to provide utility services to end users. This would include software such as COBOL, C, operating systems, and programming utility programs. Some tools, such as Microsoft Windows, use a single entry to include all of the programs that accompany it (Internet Explorer, Outlook, etc.).

    Other tools have multiple skills associated with them, such as SQL Server. One person may have the skill of system administrator where most of the staff would have the skill of accessing the data without the skill or security permissions to establish new tables.

C. **Applications.** A list that includes every in-house developed or purchased software technology that supports a business function. This might be payroll, warehouse and inventory management, general ledger, shipping/receiving, etc. Each program uses hardware components and software packages in the background to make it run, such as a credit card reader or SQL Server.

D. **Business Understanding.** Technology is easier to support if you can understand the customer's environment. This list is often organized by the department it supports. Within the department are subcategories that require specific understanding. An example would be an overall understanding of accounting principles for a small team. In a larger IT team, this would be broken into knowledge of accounts payable, accounts receivable, etc.

E. **Security Items.** Make a list of every sensitive technology or data system that requires reliable people. This might be the administration of passwords, the payroll database, e-mail system, etc.

F. **IT Operational skills.** Essential expertise for using the processes that keep an IT department moving forward. Examples are: rebooting a server, contract administration, license management, maintaining the technical library, knowledge of the Business Continuity Plan, actions necessary during an emergency, etc. Each of these skills is essential for a smooth running IT department. Just because someone is aware of them doesn't mean they know how to properly use them.

COMMENT

Unsupported Hardware

Checking through the various departments, you will inevitably come across some hardware or software that is not supported by your department. These devices fall into three categories:

Special Purpose Equipment

An example of special purpose equipment might be machine control of automated manufacturing systems. These devices use personal computer hardware but their physical configuration and the software languages used are nothing like what the IT department is skilled to handle.

These devices should be listed separately and a support plan developed for them. Often the department who uses them also supports them. The IT Manager's goal is to ensure they follow basic IT principles such as an adequate program of data backups (stored in your vault), documented systems, cost effective hardware support, etc. If the using department does not have adequate skills to support the equipment, they must either plan to build these skills or contract for someone else to provide them.

Old and Lingering Devices

This category includes obsolete equipment that is still used by someone even though its replacement is on-site. This equipment is usually expensive to repair and should be replaced as soon as possible. The risk is that it may break at an awkward time forcing an unplanned upgrade or an expensive repair bill.

Unauthorized Equipment

Well-meaning people will sometimes bring into the facility hardware or software they have personally purchased or sneaked through a gap in the purchasing process. This is a major problem for the IT department. This requires several steps, all of which must be paid for by the guilty department. First, they must pay to upgrade the hardware to your current standard even if it means that the unauthorized hardware is far from the end of its useful life. Second, a training program on the replacement system must be documented and conducted. Third, the gap in the purchasing process must be plugged to prevent more of this from occurring.

[B] Identify Current Assets

The first step is to identify what the IT department is currently supporting. This is broken down into hardware, software, and processes. Next you identify those technologies and processes that you will support and those that will be supported by outside companies. These are typically technologies that rarely fail, that are so few in number that it is difficult to maintain a reasonable level of staff expertise, or whose technologies would be too difficult to learn. The IT department has to support:

A. Hardware is the physical equipment to maintain. Few IT shops possess a soldering iron or the skill to use it. In some cases, spare devices are kept on-site and the broken units are shipped away for service, such as scanner guns and printers. The skill required is to troubleshoot down to the device, recognize the potential defect and to ship it off if repairs must be made off-site. The service company is called on-site to repair larger devices.

B. Software requires understanding how the tool works and how to troubleshoot problems. Well-written software will provide meaningful error messages when it fails. Poorly written software will simply stop working making it difficult to determine where the failure occurs. Most software is somewhere in between the two.

C. Processes are the many procedures and actions performed within the department to keep business moving forward. Typically, they apply to administrative tasks but are also used throughout technology support. From purchase requests for new equipment, to new user IDs to monthly budget reports—the smooth operation of processes is essential.

COMMENT

The author was tasked to support a sophisticated desktop publishing application unfamiliar to anyone in the IT department. Since the purchase of this non-standard technology was pushed heavily by executives, we managed to include a service contract in the purchase. The user calls for service as needed, and the IT department managed the agreement to ensure the vendor did not take advantage of unsophisticated users.

Obtain a list of the hardware and software in use by the company from the asset management database. If one is not available, then an inventory is necessary. An asset inventory is time consuming but is also useful for forming strategic plans for the managing of assets. Most importantly, it can be used to manage the retirement of very old and non-standard assets which will reduce the demands on the IT training program.

Also, create a list of the processes used to run the IT department. Process support is more likely to cause a problem than technology support. For example, if the primary technician supporting the Accounting software is on vacation, the software may operate satisfactorily during the absence. However, the process of creating new user IDs cannot wait weeks until the process support person returns from time off. Where the Accounting software runs automatically, processes stop if no one is executing them.

[C]   Create a Rating Scale

Rating a technical person is a lot like rating a chef or a lawyer—just about impossible! What we call "skills" are a combination of talent, training, experience, attitude, motivation and the current situation; all converging at a point in time. Many a famous battlefield general was considered "skilled" and yet still lost battles. How many baseball players were known as "home run kings" yet still strike out? It is an extremely rare person who has mastered every facet of their vocation and can "bat 1000." Long before arriving at that point, the challenge of the job would have been lost and the worker would have moved on to more interesting work.

So how can something as intangible as technical skills be evaluated? The answer depends on how finite of a skills assessment you are looking for and what will be done with it once it is completed. Some skill assessments are focused on productivity ratings. Their goal may be to weed out the people who contribute the least or to reward those who help the most. A person's productivity is not directly correlated to his or her knowledge of the subject. They can be very knowledgeable but lack the motivation to be productive. In this sense, replacing the employee does not address the skills issue since the negative environment will likely sour the incoming person as well.

Employees can be rated in many ways, each approach with its own trade-offs in terms of finite accuracy, time required to perform the assessment, and the usefulness of the results. Several of these ratings scales might be:

A. **Subjective.** Express an opinion as to their skills concerning a particular technology on a scale from 0 to 5.
B. **Experience.** Based on years of experience.
C. **Examination.** Ratings based on a skills examination.

A subjective scale is simple to understand and explain. Ratings reflect experience with a person's work. Subjective ratings can be swayed by the rater's bias, their attitude the day the rating is assigned, or by a recent event involving the person being rated. The following is an example of a subjective rating scale:

A. *"No experience"* at all with this tool. This category can include casual contact but essentially the person would have no idea where to start. They may have read a trade magazine story about the technology or looked over someone's shoulder while they worked with it. This person would require training, mentoring, and a considerable amount of time to become proficient with this technology.

B. *"Trained,"* but lacking experience applying the product. The person knows where to start but would need to review reference materials before beginning. Often this occurs when someone attends school too far in advance of applying the technology for the first time. Another example of this is where someone has a business degree but no experience supporting a Finance department's data systems. This person would require mentoring and perhaps refresher training to perform a task proficiently.

C. *"Familiar,"* but would need time to better understand the technology before becoming proficient. This is a common rating for the many products we have all previously mastered but not used in several years. A "familiar" rating is common for reliable technologies that rarely have problems. Someone with this rating should be able to address routine questions without a significant delay. The backup support person for each data system should, at a minimum, possess this rating.

D. *"Skilled"* would indicate that the person is experienced enough with this tool to sit down and immediately apply the technology. They could also act as mentors to less skilled coworkers. "Skilled" people can answer most questions about a technology without referring to manuals and can promptly address common problems. The primary support person for each data system should possess this rating for each technology that the system uses.

E. *"Expert"* would indicate that the person is highly skilled in many (but not necessarily all) aspects of the product—typically the ones that relate to their current responsibilities. This person understands the product's capabilities and can apply this tool in the optimal fashion. The skills staffing goal is for every critical technology to have at least one "expert" on the IT staff, or a vendor identified that can provide expert support on short notice.

F. *"Master"* indicates that the person is the master of the tool. Even if they do not have direct experience working every aspect of the tool, their understanding is such that if the technology is capable of doing something, they can make it happen. Rarely achieved, this rating is most common in the specialized skills where the person has taken a technology-mastery career path rather than a management track.

As is obvious, these categories are very broad. When presenting this rating scale to someone, be prepared for an argument! Where someone falls within this score, range depends on what they may be thinking about at the time. If they are thinking about how they used that technology in a successful task, then they may feel like an "Expert." If they recall the one time in ten that the technology totally stumped them, the same person may feel as if they are only "familiar" with it.

Not everyone needs to be considered an Expert in at least one area. Look for a mix of experts to skilled personnel. If everyone is an expert, then the scoring is too low or your department is overstaffed in expertise and likely has a larger salary budget than necessary.

[D]   Evaluate Team Members

Before rating anyone, establish a baseline of the skills someone in their position should know. Obtain a set of all approved position descriptions in the IT department from Human Resources. Use whatever they have, even if it is out of date. The job descriptions should detail the technology, management, and business expertise that this person is expected to possess.

Detailed and specific duties outlined in a job description make it easier to identify skills required and where in the organization these skills should reside. Vague job descriptions may be easier to write but are of no use to anyone. Accurate job descriptions are important. When the Human Resources department assesses the appropriate salary range for an employee, they use the job description to determine a typical salary in the local market.

Scales of this sort must be carefully explained to the people under evaluation. Some of the people may be more modest while others may overrate themselves out of pride of their previous accomplishments. An adequate response is in the ratings of "3" or "4," although a "2" is a common answer if the person had not recently worked with the technology.

Having your skills evaluated can be an emotional experience. A common approach is for the supervisor and individual to start with a list of supported technologies and business processes for the department. Then in different rooms, each rates the individual in those knowledge areas. A meeting is held to compare the supervisor's and individual's evaluation.

Out of this meeting, the supervisor will likely learn that the individual is skilled in more areas than they have recently worked in. In the end, it is the supervisor's evaluation that sets the skill level, based on the worker's performance. The gap between the actual skill level and the desired skill level is filled by training.

Understanding the competencies of your team members is a leadership principle. If they have skills developed at other employers, from hobbies at home or even from previous assignments, they should use this opportunity to educate the supervisor about them.

Some of the skills they present may not, at first glance, appear to be relevant to the IT department. Possessing a forklift license may be useful somehow if supporting a warehouse. However, if that person is only supporting accounting systems then the skill although real, is not relevant as it does not contribute to the IT department's success. It is the IT Director's responsibility to maximize the team's contribution and should not leave useful skills idle.

A major issue in evaluating employee skills is the attitude and degree of resistance of the employees under evaluation. If the assessment is viewed negatively, employees might intentionally distort it in an effort to protect themselves from perceived threats to their employment. Some people will see this as yet another management attempt to pile on more work for no more money or to reduce the size of the IT staff.

In a sense this is true because the study will likely result in a re-leveling of responsibilities and workload. It may highlight people who are drastically underutilized and whose current skills do not fit in the organization. A good manager will address the people issues during this phase but the intent of this study is to improve the service level of the organization while also improving its cost structure. In most cases, time freed from the redeployment of work can be absorbed by addressing issues in the department's work backlog or on new systems development.

A potential skills assessment form is found in Worksheet 39-1 Skills Assessment Form. Each item on the matrix has space for three ratings in the format of "//." The left most space is for the required skill level per the job description or the IT Manager's determination. The middle space is for the technicians self-evaluation score. The right most space is for the supervisor's score of that person's skill level

For example, a task that has a job description value of "4" or expert would be recorded as "4//." If that person rated himself or herself as a "3" or skilled, the score would become "4/3/." If the supervisor agreed with that score, the final notations would be "4/3/3."

WORKSHEET 39-1. Skills Assessment Form

Individual Skills Assessment: Randy Mosshammer	Computer Operations Analyst
Unix Servers	
Boot and shutdown	4/4/4
Start, run tape backups	4/2/4
ID hardware problems—call for support	4/2/2
Load new software	3/3/4
Troubleshoot network problems	4/4/4
User IDs	
Establish new IDs/password	4/4/4
Reset passwords	4/2/3
File ID requests	4/4/2
Queue Management	
Reset queues	4/3/3
Add new printers/devices	3/1/1

[E]   Identify Pending Requirements

Based on approved or pending IT Department requirements for the upcoming year, identify the additional technical skills that may be required. This would also include personnel whose skills are no longer needed as that technology is retired. Plan ahead for these people's transition to a new position. Examples of future requirements include:

- Pending retirements of people or technologies.
- Major projects in support of line of business departments.
- Major IT product upgrades by vendor.
- Scheduled hardware refresh.
- New IT business processes.
- Corporate mergers and acquisitions.

[F]   Mandatory Company Training

Mandatory training is usually required by the Human Resources department for all employees. As with all training, this takes time away from productive uses. Where possible, obtain advance scheduling information from Human Resources and add it to the IT annual training calendar. This may trigger a reschedule request to the Human Resources team if it conflicts with a planned major IT activity such as the roll out of a new ERP version.

Training sessions required by the Human Resources department are typically to ensure that all employees know the company's policies and laws pertaining to the company. Then if an employee action triggers a law suit, the company can demonstrate that the employee knew better and should shoulder all of the blame. Examples of this include:

- Sexual or racial harassment.
- Financial disclosure and potential conflict of interest.
- OSHA right-to-know safety training.

IT may also initiate annual mandatory training for employees. These sessions raise individual awareness of technical issues across the company, such as:

- Information security policies and procedures.
- Physical security of IT assets.
- Business Continuity Planning.
- Maximizing the benefit of the IT Help Desk.

COMMENT

Many companies use self-paced video training modules for mandatory training. This enables everyone to hear the same message and to schedule the session to fit their work load.

[G] Ongoing Training

Training is a tool for implementing a change. However, it is also a method of repeating to the IT team information or processes they must understand to be successful. Ongoing training is training that is scheduled, usually on-site, to refresh individual skills. These are usually general classes applicable to large segments of the IT department. It might include basic areas as conflict management, time management, continuous improvement workshops, or how to use basic IT tools.

[H] Understanding Your Customer's Business

It is one thing to write programs and quite something else to understand enough about the customer's business to make an educated guess when working on their systems. People who work closely with their end users will understand not only what a software program should be doing but also what the customer is expecting to see. They understand the department's workflows and the types of information they need.

Business knowledge skills involve an understanding of the business function the data system is supporting. Data systems exist only to support the business departments yet it is sometimes difficult for the business managers to express their full requirements for an application. An understanding of the business processes required in that department (accounting, inventory management, human resources) greatly increases the IT support's ability to understand requirements, identify errors, and anticipate future requirements.

This knowledge originates from several sources. Some comes from business classes taken during college. Such classes do not impart a deep expertise but they do provide an understanding of major requirements and a solid introduction to their business terminology. Another source is from professional certifications studied to better understand the business department. These are common in the insurance and materials management industries. Of course, over the years, the best teacher is experience working in the department supporting their applications.

[I] Preparing for the Future

The IT Director must look ahead to the next several years to ensure that today's IT training aligns with the department's (and company's) long-term goals. This can be challenging since many of the IT department's goals depend on service requests from the business departments it supports. Trying to estimate future training requirements is tough. IT departments service business departments some of whom may not plan beyond next week. However, for a small investment of time, a long-term training program can be outlined which can guide training provided.

> # COMMENT
>
> Eliminating non-standard technologies requires analysis as to what functions that particular technology provides. Elimination is a long-term strategy but saves time in reduced maintenance expense and eliminates the need for an IT staff member's expertise to support it.

Hardware and software manufacturers (usually) have a long-term plan for their products. Of course, a technology breakthrough can scuttle the best plans, but such a plan provides the development teams goals to work toward. Often, they will share these plans with valued customers in exchange for signing a non-disclosure agreement. They may not explain all that they intend to do but it will be enough for you to plan future training programs.

Another long-term intention can be found in your company's three-year business plan. This might indicate if acquisitions or mergers are in the future. It will also indicate if significant future business initiatives will require the introduction of new technology.

§ 39.03 TRAINING THE CREW

[A] Overview

Selection of a training strategy is a long-term action. It is not practical to pull the majority of an IT staff out of service to attend training. Therefore, training assignments are spread over time based on required skills and how urgent their needs are to acquire them. There are seven general solutions to the skills gaps:

A. **Ignore it.** The technology list was intended to be all inclusive but that does not mean that every technology is critical to the facility's operation. If the technology is not associated with a critical business function and if the data application can wait several days until someone can be found to repair it, then we can assign someone to support it and explain to them their support task is to supervise someone from the outside to repair it.

B. **Outsource it.** Some technologies are automatically outsourced. Very few companies repair the hardware on their mainframe computers. This is outsourced to the manufacturer. Other technologies typically outsourced are the major software tools which are maintained by the company that published them. Some technologies are too difficult to find someone to support them and are often outsourced. The flip side of this is training to bring an outsourced technology back under in-house support.

C. **Training in and out of house.** Training for every technology is tough to find. Sometimes all that is needed is an hour or so of explanation and an hour of working with it to be proficient. Other technologies will require weeks of off-site training at expensive schools. Training is expensive and most IT department spread it around the staff over the course of a year.

D. **Eliminate it (a long-term strategy).** All non-standard technologies should be slated for replacement. Elimination is a long-term strategy that removes the non-standard item and the need to support it.

E. **Re-assign staff.** The easiest approach is to shuffle the staff's assignments until you reach the optimal mix of skills required and skills available. However, excessive shuffling will disrupt productivity (and morale) so shuffling or responsibilities should be accomplished in small increments.

F. **Mentor it.** Mentoring someone through a technology is a variation on in-house training, except it is usually on a one-on-one basis. This is where the team's "experts" can step forward. However, not every technical person is cut out to be an instructor so the results of this approach will be uneven.

G. **Depend on available support documentation.** If the technology is highly stable, then training someone to support it won't help much since by the time they need the expertise, the training is long forgotten. Instead, focus on detailed troubleshooting documentation that can be reviewed whenever an emergency occurs.

COMMENT

Many people take advantage of their employer's offer for tuition reimbursement program. This is a government sponsored program where workers can expand their employability and career advancement through attending college classes on their own time. However, the classes must pertain to their employment and lead to a college degree.

College classes may provide a broad view of business. Working toward a college degree is a long-term commitment and tuition reimbursement does not cover all expenses. The personal benefit is significant. Unlike a technical certificate, a college degree does not go out of date. No matter when it is earned, it fills a qualification on job applications throughout the individual's lifetime.

[B]   Types of Training

Training requires four elements to all be ready at the same time: money for the training, time for training, student availability and an available training medium. The typical sequence is for the IT Director to designate the student and then tell them when the training must be completed. If there is a budget limit, then the class may be held to "local only—no travel" or "do it on line." If the company is paying for the training then they can control the training approach, the timing, and the cost.

Sometimes training is simply "recommended" to an IT technician, such as to qualify for a promotion. In this case, this training approach and cost is controlled by the individual. The time is implied to be outside of normal work hours.

People learn in different ways. Some prefer for someone to explain everything to them while others are content to read the book and experiment with the technology. Matching training to people is usually a matter of asking them for their preference. Typical IT training approaches are:

A. Focused class that only addresses the main topic. This approach is the most expensive. It also requires that the student must find an open date for such as class. It may be out of town adding travel expense to the tuition cost.
B. Attend a college class. Some college classes now teach technologies such as Oracle database management, Microsoft products, Cisco certification, etc. These classes require 8 to 12 weeks to complete and usually include hands-on labs.
C. Online lecture courses address the problem of finding an open class. They run frequently. The students can be located anywhere in the world and still sit in on the lecture. However, they may be conducted during the work day taking time away from the normal job. These are less expensive than a sit-in-the-room class, and also save on travel time.
D. Online, self-paced courses accessible via the Internet at any time. These are similar to self-training by reading a book except that the online exercises may include feedback from an instructor and possible links to the correct answers.
E. How-to technical books accompanied by a DVD of lecture material enable the student to study at home at their own pace.
F. On the job training is a common approach where the expert teaches the student. The advantage is that the lessons are on the actual equipment to support. The disadvantage is that many technicians make poor teachers. They cannot organize the material coherently and tend to jump from one partially explained topic to another. They may also digress to unrelated topics based on what pops into their head. This approach works best if there is well-written technical documentation. If not, then the student should write it as they touch on various points to reinforce the concept and to provide later reference notes.

[C]   Validate Training

Training is expensive and time consuming. It rarely provides a tangible result. For the time and money spent, how can the benefit be demonstrated to skeptical executives? This may be through an end of course exam, attendance feedback sheets, or evaluations of skill improvement from the person's supervisor. The most common is an end of course survey on the class and its presentation. These can be collected at the end of the session or e-mailed to the participant's supervisor. If the questions involve rating scales (such as from one to five), then statistical recaps and trending can be reported. A monthly recap of course evaluations should be provided to executives to demonstrate effectiveness.

End of course exams should be announced at the beginning of the session and reflect the key points of the training. If printed training materials are provided, the exam can be "open book" and reinforce where in the material to find certain answers. If the exam requires a demonstration of some sort such as to write a short piece of code, then individual evaluations and follow up with the students will be required.

[D] Cross-Training Is a Workforce Multiplier

Cross-training is the development of technical skills in the IT department so that multiple people can perform the same function. Cross-training is an essential requirement to maintain an acceptable level of customer service and achieve key process indicators (KPIs). Without it, the department experiences occasional lapses of service where a technology (hardware, software, or business process) fails and no one is available with the skills to promptly restore it.

Cross-training takes time and patience. Time is required to teach someone a different technology. It requires both the skilled technician and the student to set aside productive work to train over a period of time. This may be difficult to do if the department has a large work backlog. However, cross-training pays for itself through reduced time spent scrambling when a problem occurs. It reduces the stress on the staff from fighting incidents with unfamiliar technologies as there is always someone assigned to cover an absence.

COMMENT

Cross-training is an important feature of Agile software development. Cross-functionality is important because it increases the team's "truck number" (how many team members would have to be hit by a truck during lunch to make the project fail) and because it gives team members insight into other products. Skills that should be possessed by multiple team members include programming, quality control or assurance, architecture or user interface design, and business analysis. To emphasize cross-functional behavior, no Agile team member may have a title to reflect a certain skill.

§ 39.03[E]

No one can afford to have a department full of one-trick specialists. These are people who specialize in a single or a few related technologies. They are very knowledgeable but then who can support their technology when they are absent for illness or vacation? Practicing their individual skill often occupies less than a full workday so they make work or act busy. Cross-training enables the IT Director to level some of the team's workload.

Some IT people will resist this additional assignment. They are comfortable with what they do and are not interested in learning something different. There may also be personality friction between the primary and secondary support personnel. However, there are times when the IT Director must be firm with the staff. Cross-training is essential for providing a high level of customer service. Refer to Worksheet 39-2 Cross-Training Matrix.

An essential tool of cross-training is technical documentation. Even when someone is trained to support something on a backup basis, they lack the day-to-day interaction with it to build a high level of expertise. Well-written technical documentation will help. It jogs the memory and provides trouble-shooting steps.

When the primary support person is preparing for a scheduled absence, require the backup support person to perform during primary support person's absence. Include a brief refresher training session before departure.

IT team members' efforts at providing backup support should be an important part of their performance annual review. This will encourage them to manage their time to learn about their additional support areas and to gain some level of expertise.

COMMENT

Cross-training the staff can be a challenge. Some technicians make poor teachers. Not everyone can clearly explain something to someone else. Also, the material is not organized for a logical flow. This requires that the trainee connect the various pieces of what is being presented.

[E]   Value of Institutional Knowledge

Some business managers look at their payroll to identify high paid personnel to cut so they can bring in a much cheaper replacement. This is many times a false economy. The new person may not be as technically skilled as the person they replaced and their productivity will be lower for a long time. The new person needs time to be trained on the department's processes and workflows. This can be addressed through classroom instruction and a review of technical documentation. The short-term payroll numbers may look better but the effectiveness of the IT department has been diminished.

WORKSHEET 39-2. Cross-Training Matrix

	Applications			System Administration			Operations			Outsiders	
	Randy Mosshammer	Rob Wallace	Karen Goff	James Foster	Linda Laughlin	Kim Owens	Leih Weasley	Marv Lindmark	John Ratzenberger	Contractor	Corp Headquarters
Mainframe											
Syncsort	X										
COBOL	X	X	X								
TSO	X	X	X								
ISPF	X										
SQL	X		X								
Server											
SQL Server – App Dev			X								
SQL Server - Admin										X	
UNIX - User		X	X	X	X	X	X	X	X		
UNIX - Admin				X	X	X					
Workstations											
Windows XP				X	X						
Windows 7				X	X						
MS Word	X	X	X	X	X	X	X	X	X		
MS Excel	X	X	X	X	X	X	X	X	X		
MS Project			X	X		X				X	
Lotus Notes						X					X
IT Processes											
Asset Management	Y			Y			Y				
Materials Purchasing	Y			Y			Y				
Monthly KPI Reports	Y			Y			Y				

WORKSHEET 39-2. (Continued)

	Applications			System Administration			Operations			Outsiders	
	Randy Mosshammer	Rob Wallace	Karen Goff	James Foster	Linda Laughlin	Kim Owens	Leih Weasley	Marv Lindmark	John Ratzenberger	Contractor	Corp Headquarters
Mandatory Training											
Sexual Harassment	Z	Z	Z	Z	Z	Z	Z	Z	Z	Z	
Information Security	Z	Z	Z	Z	Z	Z	Z	Z	Z	Z	
Environmental Compliance	Z	Z	Z	Z	Z	Z	Z	Z	Z	Z	
X — Critical Systems Y = Mandatory Department Skills Z = Mandatory Team skills											

Technology is fine but IT is a service department to a larger entity. Institutional knowledge is acquired through long and often painful experience. It includes knowing who is really calling the shots in various departments and for what types of issues. It includes knowing who is most knowledgeable about some aspect of the business and establishing a working relationship with that person to share his or her knowledge. None of this is written in a book or available in a class. Even if it was, it changes over time.

COMMENT

Technicians often wonder why the departments they support resist using technology as it was designed or are constantly dissatisfied with IT services. Customer service is about relationships between the service provider (IT Department) and the customer (the rest of the company). This relationship is built on trust from individual to individual. An IT professional who has supported the Accounting department for many years builds this relationship. Discarding the old worker and replacing him or her with a new person creates animosity toward the new person and a breakdown in the relationship that will take a long time to repair.

Another nontechnical area of expertise is in the detailed understanding of the workflows and priorities of the people that they support. It takes time for the IT team to understand specifically what the business departments expect from them at different times of the year and to provide it the way they need to see it. The supported department expects the IT department to know and understand these things and is reluctant to train the IT team (as they are busy also).

The value of institutional knowledge (sometimes referred to as "tribal knowledge") is a significant reason why training is needed to retain existing IT staff. Otherwise, the department will be forced to discharge long-term employees to make way for team members with the latest technical skills. Each of these staff reductions diminishes the amount of company knowledge and reduces the effectiveness of the department. Also, the relationships built by the departing team may not be easily transferred to the new people. For these reasons, companies should provide an ongoing training program for their IT departments.

§ 39.04 MANAGING TRAINING

[A] Training Records

Managing the IT training program ensures that the limited training budget is spent where it will provide the greatest benefit. This benefit is based on the analysis of current and future needs. However, as funds and time permit, the desires and career goals of individuals can also be accommodated.

Training records are a way to record who attended, what training, and when. The creation and maintenance of training records are a requirement of ISO and other quality programs. For each individual this will include their current position description, information on their cross-training assignments, and the results of any end of course exams. It will also indicate previous positions held in the company and other skills not relevant to IT support.

COMMENT

Some companies require employees who attend employer paid training to remain with the company for a set period of time or to repay the cost of the training. On one hand, it ensures that the company recoups the cost of training investment. However, if an employee is unhappy and unproductive, how much benefit is there to retain them on the payroll?

[B] Team Career Planning

A career is an individual thing. Most people only vaguely plan their future since it evolves so slowly. This is usually one step at a time. Others will have plotted their timeline to a corporate vice-presidency before they turn 30. Career planning is a one-on-one conversation between the IT specialist and the IT Director. The goal is to understand each person's goals and desires so that as opportunities arise for staffing new projects or training for new technologies, personal desires will coincide with assignments. This conversation can also update the job description to reflect current requirements.

Some people do not want additional training. They feel comfortable applying their hard-won expertise. Their plan is to leave the company if the technology is discontinued. They do not wish to transition from an expert on one thing to a novice being trained on another. One way to break down this barrier is to assign them to cross-train on a different support role. This may open their eyes to a new and interesting challenge or confirm that when their technology leaves, they must be discarded.

Team career planning is a part of most companies' quarterly or annual performance reviews. It provides a positive discussion point in the midst of an uncomfortable time for the employee. During this session the employee is asked to explain their short- and long-term career goals and identify some training that they are interested in taking.

[C] Timing Is Everything

Training should be completed no earlier than 30 days before it is to be applied. This is based on the "use it or lose it" principle. Training only provides familiarity with a subject and unless this expertise is exercised, it may be soon lost. Assign newly trained staff members to work on a series of small projects immediately after training to build a deeper understanding.

Repetition aids retention. Ask an IT professional to list the many technical skills they have acquired over the years and the list can be long. Then ask them to highlight the ones for which they still retain a basic mastery and the list shrinks quickly. This is because they no longer have access (or time) to refresh their skills on each one. Remembering what was taught varies by person. Some people will say that no matter how long ago you learned to ride a bicycle, you never lose the skill.

[D] Measuring Effectiveness

Training can be a major investment for the organization. As such, it is important that the value of all training activities be measured and tracked. The most popular model used for measuring the effectiveness of training was developed in the 1950's by Donald Kirkpatrick. The Kirkpatrick Model uses four levels to evaluate the outcome of training:

A. **Level 1—Reaction.** Measures the student's reactions to the training. This should include the student's overall reaction to the training as well as specific components of the training (e.g., the instructor, handouts, exercises, schedule, audiovisuals, etc.). If a student does not have a good reaction to the training, he or she is less likely to achieve the other three levels. Measuring Level 1 effectiveness is best done using a survey at the end of the training.

B. **Level 2—Learning.** Measures what the student learned as a result of the training. The student should be required to demonstrate that the learning objectives of the class were met. This might be done using a written test or by having the student demonstrate mastery of the skills taught in the training.

C. **Level 3—Behavior.** Measures the change in the student's behavior as a result of attending the training. The student must be able to apply what was learned to his or her job. It is important for management to encourage the application of new skills on the job, and to make this part of the evaluation process. Also recognize that behavioral changes take some time to develop.

D. **Level 4—Results.** Measures the business improvements that resulted from the training. Ideally you will want the training to have a positive effect on the organization's bottom line. Depending on the nature of the training, you can measure this by observing an improved quality or quantity of work, less wasted resource, increased sales, higher morale, lower absenteeism, and increased profits. Results at this level are the hardest to measure.

Results in each of these four areas should be evaluated to determine the overall value of the training to the organization. It is critical that performance standards for each of the four levels are established so that an evaluation of the value of the training can be made. These evaluations must be communicated to management to assist in determining the most effective training and to improve future versions of the training program.

See Policy ITP-39-1 Training Effectiveness Measurement Policy as an example of training measurement policy.

POLICY ITP-39-1. Training Effectiveness Measurement Policy

Policy #:	ITP-39-1	Effective:	01/01/13	Page #:	1 of N
Subject:	Training Effectiveness Measurement Policy				

1.0 PURPOSE

Training is a major investment that the organization makes in the skills of its employees. As such, it is important that this investment be made as efficiently and effectively as possible. To meet this objective, it is important that the value of all training activities be measured and communicated to management.

2.0 SCOPE

This policy applies to all training received by employees. This includes both in-house and training done outside the organization.

3.0 POLICY

All training received by employees must be measured in the following four areas:

A. **Level 1—Reaction.** Measures the student's reactions to the training. This should include the student's overall reaction to the training as well as specific components of the training (e.g., the instructor, handouts, exercises, schedule, audiovisuals, etc.). If a student does not have a good reaction to the training, the student is less likely to achieve the other three levels. Measuring Level 1 effectiveness is best done using a survey at the end of the training.

B. **Level 2—Learning.** Measures what the student learned as a result of the training. The student should be required to demonstrate that the learning objectives of the class were met. This should be done using a written test or by having the student demonstrate mastery of the skills taught in the training.

C. **Level 3—Behavior.** Measures the change in the student's behavior as a result of attending the training. The student must be able to apply what he or she has learned to his or her job. It is important for management to encourage the application of new skills on the job, and to make this part of the evaluation process. Also recognize that behavioral changes take some time to develop.

D. **Level 4—Results.** Measures the business improvements that resulted from the training. The training should have a positive effect on the organization's bottom line. Depending on the nature of the training, you can measure this by observing an improved quality or quantity of work, less wasted resource, increased sales, higher morale, lower absenteeism, and increased profits. Results at this level are the hardest to measure.

Results in each of these four areas should be evaluated to determine the overall value of the training to the organization. Managers must develop performance standards for each of the four levels so that an evaluation of the value of the training can be made. These evaluations must be communicated to management to assist in determining the most effective training and to improve future versions of the training program.

4.0 REVISION HISTORY

Date	Revision #	Description of Change
03/18/13	1.0	Initial creation.

5.0 INQUIRIES

Direct inquiries about this policy to:

George Jenkins, CIO
Our Company, Inc.
2900 Corporate Drive
Columbus, OH 43215

Voice: 614-555-1234
Fax: 614-555-1235
E-mail: gjenkins@company.com

Revision #:	1.0	Supersedes:	N/A	Date:	03/18/13

GLOSSARY OF IT TERMS

802.11 An evolving family of specifications for wireless local area networks (WLANs) developed by a working group of the IEEE.

ACTIVEX This Microsoft-based technology is designed to link desktop applications to the World Wide Web from within a browser. ActiveX allows software developers to create interactive Web content for their applications.

ADWARE A software application that can display advertising banners while the program is running or via some other triggering mechanism. This is sometimes installed as part of a free program as a way to generate advertising revenue for the creators of the software.

AMERICAN NATIONAL STANDARDS INSTITUTE (ANSI) Organization devoted to the voluntary development of standards. It has worked with the computer industry to develop standards for languages such as FORTRAN and COBOL.

API (APPLICATION PROGRAM INTERFACE) A method of allowing an application to interact directly with certain functions of an operating system or another application.

APPLET A software component that runs within another program; most commonly a Java program that can be embedded in a Web page.

APPLICATION A term referring to a software program that accomplishes a certain task.

APPLICATION LAYER The layer of the OSI model concerned with application programs such as electronic mail, database management, and file server software.

APPLICATION STORE (OR APP STORE) A service which allows users to browse and download applications from a centralized marketplace. Made popular by Apple by its iTunes store for the iPhone, iPod Touch, and iPad.

APPROVED LIST A list of computer software and/or hardware for which the IT department provides user support.

ARCHITECTURE A system's architecture is described by the type of components, interfaces, and protocols it uses and how these elements fit together.

ARCHIVAL BACKUP A procedure to back up or copy files in secondary storage onto another secondary storage device.

ASCII (AMERICAN STANDARD CODE FOR INFORMATION INTERCHANGE) A standard for encoding characters (including the upper- and lowercase alphabet, numerals, punctuation, and control characters) using seven bits. The standard set is 128 characters; IBM expanded this to 256 by adding an eighth bit to each existing character. This expanded set provides graphic, mathematical, scientific, financial, and foreign language characters.

ASP (ACTIVE SERVER PAGE) A Web page that has one or more ASP scripts embedded in it.

ASP (APPLICATION SERVICE PROVIDER) An older term for SaaS.

ASP.NET A set of Web development tools offered by Microsoft.

ASP SCRIPT A small computer program that runs when an ASP-based Web page is accessed.

AUDIT TRAIL A means of locating the origin of specific data that appears on final reports.

BACKUP A copy of a file, directory, or volume placed on a separate storage device for the purpose of retrieval in case the original is accidentally erased, damaged, or destroyed.

BAR CODE A printed pattern of vertical lines used to represent alphanumerical codes in a scannable reading form.

BENCHMARK A standard measurement used to test the performance of hardware or software.

BETA TESTING Using and testing software not yet put

on the market by the vendor.

BI (BUSINESS INTELLI-GENCE) A broad category of application programs and technologies for gathering, storing, analyzing, and providing access to data to help enterprise users make better business decisions. BI applications include the activities of decision support, query and reporting, online analytical processing (OLAP), statistical analysis, forecasting, and data mining.

BIA (BUSINESS IMPACT ANALYSIS) A systematic analysis of a company or business unit to identify its critical business functions and the impact to the company if these functions ceased to function. These business functions are linked to the IT systems that support them (lose the IT system, and that function cannot continue). Risks to the most valuable processes are identified along with mitigation actions to reduce the likelihood or impact of these risks. In the event of a disaster, the BIA indicates how much is lost per hour or per day for the length of the outage.

BIT A binary digit; must be either a zero (on) or a one (off). The smallest possible unit of information in a digital system.

BLACK SWAN EVENT A significant event that appears out of nowhere and changes everything. A term used in risk management; these events are rare and difficult to predict.

BLOG A short form for weblog.

BLUETOOTH A wireless technology that enables communication between Bluetooth-compatible devices; used for short-range connections between two electronic devices.

BRIDGE A device used to connect LANs by forwarding packets across connections at the media access control sublayer of the data link layer of the OSI model.

BROADBAND Refers to high-speed data transmission in which a single cable can carry a large amount of data at once.

BROWNOUT A period with low voltage electric power because of increased demands.

BROWSER A program used to access the World Wide Web. It interprets HTML code including text, images, hypertext links, JavaScript, and Java applets. Also referred to as a Web browser.

BUG A programming error causing a program or a computer system not to perform as expected.

BYTE Eight continuous bits representing one character in memory.

CALENDAR TIME The actual duration of a project, from the date it starts to the date it is completed. This includes both work and non-work days.

CAPTCHA Strings of letters and numbers used to attempt to verify that a Web page is being accessed by a person and not an automated program. It is an acronym that stands for "Completely Automated Public Turing test to tell Computers and Humans Apart."

CHANGE ADVISORY BOARD (CAB) A committee tasked with reviewing changes to be made to an IT system.

CHANGE COORDINATOR An individual designated to oversee the management of the change control process.

CHANGE MANANAGE-MENT A general IT term that under ITIL identifies the process for ensuring changes do no harm on installation.

CHAT Another term for instant messaging.

CLIENT A computer that accesses the resources of a server. See CLIENT/SERVER.

CLIENT/SERVER A network system design in which a processor or computer designated as a server, such as a file server or database server, provides services to clients' workstations or PCs.

CLIP ART A collection of graphic images available for use with desktop publishing.

CLOUD COMPUTING A concept where IT-related resources are provided as a service via the Internet. See PAAS, SAAS, and PRIVATE CLOUD.

COBIT™ (CONTROL OBJECTIVES FOR INFORMATION TECH-NOLOGY™) A framework of IT management best practices that assists companies in maximizing the business benefits of their IT organizations.

COMPILER A program that reads high-level program coding statements (source code) and translates the statements into machine executable instructions (object code).

COMPUTER STORE An IT support unit of information systems providing company employees with the opportunity to view and try out approved hardware and software.

CONTROL OBJECTS Used to maintain control of some aspect of IT. It might be security access to customer data; it might be read access to the payroll file, ability to manipulate data before or after processing, or even the ability to intercept data that should be confidential. COBIT has 215 specific control objectives.

COOKIE A small text file sent to your computer by a Web site you have visited. This allows the Web site to recognize you when you return. While cookies can be useful, they can also be used for targeted advertising which is not always welcome.

COPY PROTECTION The inclusion in a program of hidden instructions intended to prevent unauthorized copying of software.

COST-BENEFIT ANALYSIS A projection of the costs incurred in and benefits derived from installing hardware, software, or a proposed system.

CPM (CRITICAL-PATH METHOD) A process used in project management for the planning and timing of tasks relying on the identification of a critical path. The time needed for the series of tasks along the critical path determines the total project completion time.

DAT (DIGITAL AUDIO TAPE) A popular tape backup format.

DATA DICTIONARY A list of data elements used in database management programs. Each data element contains information about its use, its size, its characteristics, who can use it, who can alter it, who can remove it, and who can only view it.

DATA ELEMENT A field containing an element of information used in records

found in database management systems. Examples would be FICA number, name, part number, etc.

DATA INDEPENDENCE Data stored in such a way that users can gain access to it in a database system without knowing where the data is actually located.

DATA MANAGER A person responsible for the management of all corporate data. The database manager may report directly or indirectly to this person.

DATA PROCESSING The preparing, storing, or manipulation of information within a computer system.

DATA RECORD A complete addressable unit of related data elements expressed in identified data fields used in files and database systems.

DATA REDUNDANCY The same data stored in more than one location.

DATABASE An organized collection of information, in random access secondary storage, made up of related data records. There can be more than one database in a computer system.

DATABASE MANAGEMENT PROGRAM A data application program providing for the retrieval, modification, deletion, or insertion of data elements. Database systems tend to reduce unnecessary "data redundancy" by providing a central location for accessing data.

DATABASE MANAGEMENT SYSTEM (DBMS) The operating software system that provides for the access and storage of data.

DATABASE MANAGER The person responsible for managing the corporate IT database. This person reports to the manager of

corporate information systems, but can report to the corporate data manager, too.

DATABASE SERVER The back-end processor that manages the database and fulfills database requests in a client/server system.

DATAFLOW DIAGRAMS A method of showing data flows all on one page. It starts at the lowest detail level, which is the system level. Corresponding process parts are all shown in more detail, each on its own page. Dataflow diagrams have their own flow-charting symbols.

DDOS (DISTRIBUTED DENIAL OF SERVICE) Denial-of-service attacks are attacks whereby a hacker floods a network server with data in an attempt to crash the system. A distributed denial-of-service attack uses multiple computers to attack at the same time.

DEBUGGING The procedure of locating and correcting program errors.

DECISION TREE A graphic representation of all possible conditions or processing alternatives and end results. It resembles the branches of a tree growing out from the main trunk.

DEDICATED FILE SERVER A file server that cannot be operated as a user's server work station. See FILE SERVER.

DE FACTO STANDARD A standard based on broad usage and support.

DEFAULT A value or option that is chosen automatically when no other value is specified.

DEFECT RATE In Agile project management, the number of bugs being discovered per iteration or per feature completed.

DESKTOP SUPPORT MANAGER A person responsible for managing and providing support to and training for end users and their devices. This person reports to IT management.

DINGBAT Stock symbol, such as a star, triangle, dot, or arrow, usually used for visual emphasis.

DISK DUPLEXING A method of safeguarding data whereby the data is copied simultaneously to two hard disks on separate channels. If one channel fails, the data on the other channel remains unharmed. When data is duplexed, read requests are sent to whichever disk in the pair can respond faster, decreasing the file server's response time.

DISK MIRRORING A method of safeguarding data whereby the same data is copied to two hard disks on the same channel. If one of the disks fails, the data on the other disk is safe. Because the two disks are on the same channel, mirroring provides only limited data protection; a failure anywhere along the channel could shut down both disks and data would be lost. See also DISK DUPLEXING.

DNS (DOMAIN NAME SERVICE) A service on the Internet that translates a Web site name (e.g., www.microsoft.com) into the actual IP address for the Web site (e.g., 207.46.19 .190).

DOCUMENTATION The instructions and references providing users with the necessary information to use computer programs and systems or alter them at a later date.

DOCUMENT FLOWCHART A flowchart constructed all on one page showing the flow of documents used in a given system. It shows the documents traveling from left to right across a page from one user to another. Each user is in its own vertical column.

DOMAIN NAME The name that identifies a Web site (e.g., Microsoft.com).

DOMAIN NAME SERVICE HIJACKING A hack in which inquiries seeking one domain are routed to another domain without the user's knowledge. Such attacks on the Internet's control structures could make packets of information undeliverable, quickly snarling traffic on the network.

DSL (DIGITAL SUBSCRIBER LINE) DSL is a modem technology that transforms ordinary phone lines (also known as "twisted copper pairs") into high-speed digital lines for ultra-fast Internet access.

DVD (DIGITAL VIDEO DISK) A high-density compact disk for storing large amounts of data, especially high-resolution audio-visual material.

ELECTRONIC MAIL (E-MAIL) A network service enabling users to send and receive messages via computer from anywhere in the world.

EMOTICON Common name for the small text-based symbols, such as the familiar smiley: :) used in e-mail to represent emotions.

EMULATOR A computer program that makes a programmable device imitate another computer, producing the same results.

ENCRYPTION The scrambling of information for transmission over public communication systems. The receiver requires the same technology key to unscramble the coded information.

END USER A person who benefits directly or indirectly from a computer system.

ENTERPRISE ARCHITECTURE (EA) An enterprise's architecture is described by the type of components, interfaces, and protocols it uses for management, information, and computing systems, and how these elements fit together.

ERGONOMICS The science of designing hardware, tools, and the working environment taking into account human factors so as to enable people to interact more comfortably and more productively.

ERP (ENTERPRISE RESOURCE PLANNING) A software application that integrates departments and functions across a company into one computer system.

EXPERT SYSTEM A computer program containing the knowledge used by an expert in a given area that assists non-experts when they attempt to perform duties in that same area.

EXTREME PROGRAMMING A lightweight programming methodology that focuses on frequent testing, integration, and user review.

FAILURE MODE AND EFFECTS ANALYSIS (FMEA) A tool that examines a process in detail to identify potential problems and their resolutions.

FAULT TOLERANCE Resistance to system failure or data loss.

FEASIBILITY STUDY A study to determine the

possibility of undertaking a systems project.

FEATURE In Agile project management, a feature is a unit of functionality that adds business value to the project. Features are the main planning unit and describe the value to be created. Characteristics of a feature include enough detail to estimate the work and a defined set of tests to verify its completion.

FILE A name given to a collection of information stored in a secondary storage medium, such as a tape or disk.

FILE ALLOCATION TABLE A table on a disk recording the disk location of all the file parts.

FILE SERVER A computer providing network stations with controlled access to shareable resources. The network operating system is loaded on the file server and most shareable devices, such as disk subsystems and printers, are attached to it. The file server controls system security. It also monitors station-to-station communications. A dedicated file server can be used online as a file server while it is on the network. A non-dedicated file server can be used simultaneously as a file server and a workstation.

FILE SHARING The ability for multiple users to share files. Concurrent file sharing is controlled by application software, the workstation operating system, and/or the file server/database server operating system.

FLASH DRIVE Also called a USB FLASH DRIVE, it is a storage device that is made up of flash memory and an integrated USB interface. Storage capacity of up to 1 terabytes is available.

FLOWCHART Analysis tool consisting of a diagrammatic representation of a system process or abstract relationship, normally made up of labeled blocks or keyed symbols connected by lines.

FREEWARE Software that is available for use at no cost. Only the executable code is supplied and no changes can be made to the program by the user.

FTP (FILE TRANSFER PROTOCOL) A protocol used to transmit files between computers on the Internet. An anonymous FTP is a file transfer between locations that does not require users to identify themselves with a password or log-in. An anonymous FTP is not secure, because it can be accessed by any other user of the Internet.

GAGE REPEATABILITY AND RELIABILITY (GAGE R&R) A process for validating the process and measurement data collection tools.

GANTT CHART A project scheduling tool using graphic representations to show start, elapsed, and completion times of each task within a given project. It can also show the planned scheduled (S) time and the actual completed (C) time. The Gantt chart indicates the status of a given project at any point. A Gantt chart employing dollars can also illustrate money budgeting for given tasks vs. money spent.

GATEWAY A device providing routing and protocol conversion among physically dissimilar networks and/or computers.

GIGABYTE (GB, G-BYTE) A unit of measure of memory or disk storage capacity; two to the thirtieth power (1,073,741,824 bytes).

GREEN IT (OR GREEN COMPUTING) The use of IT resources in an environmentally sustainable manner. Typical areas of concern are electrical power usage by IT-related equipment, such as servers and printers, power usage in cooling data centers, environmental impact of manufacturing electronic equipment, and the environmental impact of disposing electronic devices at end of life.

HACKER A technically knowledgeable computer enthusiast who enjoys programming but is not usually employed as a programmer.

HOTSPOT See WI-FI HOTSPOT.

HTML (HYPERTEXT MARKUP LANGUAGE) The authoring software language used on the Internet's World Wide Web. HTML is used for creating World Wide Web pages.

HYPERVISOR A layer of software used in server virtualization that sits between the operating systems running on the server and the underlying hardware.

ICANN (INTERNET CORPORATION FOR ASSIGNED NAMES AND NUMBERS) A nonprofit corporation that is responsible for allocating IP addresses and managing the domain name system.

IDE (INTEGRATED DEVELOPMENT ENVIRONMENT) An interface from which you can edit, browse, compile, and debug a software application.

IDE (INTEGRATED/INTELLIGENT DRIVE ELECTRONICS) The most common disk interface for hard drives, CD-ROM drives, etc.

IEEE Institute of Electrical and Electronics Engineers, Inc. Develops standards for the design and use of technology, including computer-related technology.

IM (INSTANT MESSAGING) A form of communication over the Internet which involves immediate messages between two or more users who are online simultaneously.

INCIDENT MANAGEMENT An ITIL term for a controlling the resolution of a service disruption.

INFORMATION SYSTEMS The department within a company that is responsible for computer information systems processing and the storage of all centralized data.

INFORMATION TECHNOLOGY (IT) The different techniques required to perform the task of information systems processing. The technology units within the information systems organization are required to be orchestrated by the information systems manager.

IN-HOUSE Denotes that the task is done within the company by company resources.

INPUT DEVICE Peripheral hardware that inputs data into a computer system.

INTELLIGENT WORKSTATION A terminal containing PC processing capability that runs independently or in conjunction with a host computer.

INTERFACE A shared boundary between two systems, such as between data communications (terminating) equipment and data terminal equipment (DTE). Also a boundary between adjacent layers of the ISO model.

INTERNAL IT AUDITOR A person representing the company with internal information technology auditing. He/she follows the guidelines provided by the CPA firm's auditors. He/she is concerned with computer systems audit trails and the security of the hardware, software, and data.

INTERNET The largest network in the world. Successor to ARPANET, the Internet includes other large internetworks. The Internet uses the TCP/IP protocol suite and connects universities, government agencies, businesses, and individuals around the world.

INTERNETWORK Two or more networks connected by bridges and/or routers; a network of networks.

IP ADDRESS A code made up of four numbers separated by three dots that identifies a particular device on the Internet. Every device on the Internet requires an IP address to connect.

ISO 20000 The international standard for IT governance, based on ITIL.

ISP (INTERNET SERVICE PROVIDER) An ISP is used as your local connection to the Internet. It provides other companies or individuals with access to, or presence on, the Internet.

ITERATION In Agile project management, an iteration is a development cycle where completed code is delivered to the customer. An Agile project will consist of numerous iterations, each adding more value for the customer.

ITIL (IT INFRASTRUCTURE LIBRARY) An integrated set of best-practice recommendations with common definitions and terminology. ITIL covers areas such as Incident Management, Problem Management, Change Management, Release Management, and the Service Desk.

JAILBREAKING The altering of the operating system of a smartphone or other mobile device to allow the user full access to the operating system (also known as root access). This allows the user to perform actions and run applications that have not been approved by the manufacturer.

KED (KNOWN ERROR DATABASE) A database where information for all known errors is maintained.

KEY PERFORMANCE INDICATORS (KPIs) These are the vital signs of an IT team, or a set of values used to measure or compare performance against.

KNOWN ERROR An ITIL term for a known IT service problem that will be repaired later, and where the customer has a documented work around to maintain service.

LASER PRINTER A high-resolution printer that uses electrostatic reproduction technology, like electrostatic copy machines, to fuse text or graphic images onto plain paper.

LEASED LINE A full-time link between two or more locations leased from a local or inter-exchange carrier.

LIBRARY A collection of programs and data files for a computer system's offline storage.

LOCAL AREA NETWORK (LAN) The linkage of computers within a limited area so users can exchange information and share peripherals. This linkage can be wired or wireless.

MAINFRAME A large computer, generally with high-level and multiprocessing power and the capacity to support many users at once.

MALVERTISING (MALWARE ADVERTISING) The use of online advertising to spread malware, especially to mobile devices.

MALWARE (MALICIOUS SOFTWARE) A generic term covering a range of software programs and types of programs designed to attack, degrade, or prevent the intended use of a computer or a network. Types of malware can include viruses, worms, Trojans, malicious active content, and denial of service attacks.

MASHUP A Web application that combines data from more than one source into a single application.

MEGABYTE (MG, M-BYTE) A unit of measure for memory or disk storage capacity; two to the twentieth power (1,048,576 bytes).

METADATA Data about data. It may describe how the data was created, who created it and why, how it can be modified and accessed, and how it is formatted.

METRIC A measurement that describes some characteristic of something; it measures a process's performance and can help identify areas for improvement.

MILESTONES Used with Gantt, CPM, and PERT charting to show when measurable units of task(s) have been completed. With Gantt charts, the actual milestones can be drawn on the charts.

MMO or MMOG (MASSIVELY MULTIPLAYER ONLINE GAME) A computer or video game that is capable of supporting hundreds or thousands of players simultaneously.

MOBILE APPLICATION MANAGEMENT (MAM) The managing of mobile device applications, including the development, procurement, securing, deploying, updating and removing of applications from mobile devices used within the organization.

MODELING An analytical process based on mathematical network behavior formulas called models used to predict the performance of product designs.

MODULAR PROGRAMMING A style of programming requiring that program functions be broken into modules. It is a form of program segmentation and is the correct way to code procedural programs. This is also a good way to write reusable code. Quick BASIC and Visual BASIC programming require this type of program coding.

MSP (MANAGED SERVICE PROVIDER) Another term for a SaaS vendor.

NETWORK A series of points connected by communications channels. Public networks can be used by anyone; private networks are closed to outsiders.

NETWORK ADMINISTRATOR A local area network manager who is responsible for maintaining a network.

NETWORK INTERFACE CARD (NIC) A circuit board installed in each network station allowing communications with other stations.

NONDEDICATED FILE SERVER A file server that also functions as a workstation.

OBJECT CODE The machine-readable instructions created by a computer or assembler from source code.

OBJECT-ORIENTED PROGRAMMING A type of programming in which the data types and the allowed functions for a data type are defined by the programmer.

ONLINE DEVICE A peripheral device externally attached to a computer or available to other computers on a network.

OPEN SOURCE Free software that includes both the source and executable code. The purchase price is free but there will be license restrictions that control how the product is used.

PAAS (PLATFORM AS A SERVICE) Builds on the concept of SaaS to allow organizations to build entirely new applications directly on the Internet.

PARAVIRTUALIZATION A server virtualization technique where the operating system knows it is running in a virtual environment and is designed to cooperate with the hypervisor.

PASSWORD A security identification used to authorize users of a computer system or given program.

PC (PERSONAL COMPUTER) Smaller computers employing microprocessor chip technology. These can come in various configurations, such as PDAs, mini-notebooks, notebooks, laptops, transportable desktop workstations, and microcomputers.

PDA (PERSONAL DATA ASSISTANT) A small hand-held computer used to write notes, track appointments, and otherwise organize your life. Today almost all devices used as PDAs are smartphones or tablets.

PEER-TO-PEER A network design in which each computer shares and uses devices on an equal basis.

PERFORMANCE MANAGEMENT The activity of ensuring that technical resources in the organization's infrastructure provide the maximum return on investment and that they are functioning as originally intended.

PERIPHERAL A physical device (such as a printer or disk subsystem) that is externally attached to a workstation or directly attached to the network.

PERT (PROGRAMMED EVALUATION REVIEW TECHNIQUE) A planning and control tool for defining and controlling the tasks necessary to complete a given project. The PERT chart and CPM charts are one and the same. The only difference is the manner in which task time is computed. The CPM chart uses only one expected time. With the PERT system, the time required for each task is computed as follows: The longest expected time, the shortest expected time, and four times the expected time are totaled and divided by six. This gives the expected time needed.

PHISHING A form of identity theft in which an authentic-looking e-mail is used to trick recipients into giving out sensitive personal information, such as credit card, bank account, or Social Security numbers.

POTS Plain old telephone service.

PRINCE 2™ A project management technique developed in the UK. PRINCE2 is a highly structured "gate" approach good for large or complex projects but a bit too administrative for smaller efforts.

PRINT SERVER A device and/or program for managing shared printers. Print service is often provided by the file server, but can also be provided from a separate LAN microcomputer or other device.

PRIVATE CLOUD A type of cloud infrastructure that is operated solely for a single organization. It may be managed by the organization or by a third party and may exist on premise or off premise.

PROGRAM RUN BOOK Operating instructions for the benefit of those who run a given program, including any restart procedures in case of program failure. Most often used by mainframe computer operators, but can also be provided for minicomputer operators and PC users.

PROJECT SLIPPAGE Occurs when a project's critical path milestone finish date is not met. The critical path of a PERT or CPM chart determines the project completion time. Projects that are not using PERT or CPM technology can have project slippage, too. It is first recognized when it becomes obvious that the project finish date will be later than planned. See CPM.

PROTOCOL A formal set of rules setting the format and control of data exchange between two devices or processes.

RDP (REMOTE DESKTOP PROTOCOL) A multi-channel protocol that allows a user to connect to a networked computer.

RECOMMENDED LIST A list of software that the IT department recommends and for which it provides user support. The list can also contain recommended IT hardware for users.

RECORD LOCKING A data-protection scheme preventing different users from performing simultaneous writes to the same record in a shared file, thus preventing overlapping disk writes and ensuring record integrity.

RELEASE MANAGEMENT An ITIL term for the area that controls the release of approved changes.

REQUEST FOR CHANGE (RFC) The process of proposing a modification to any component of an IT infrastructure or any aspect of an IT service.

RESOURCE BURN RATE In Agile project management, how much of a given resource is being consumed by the project. This is the total resource cost divided by the length of the iteration.

ROUTER Hardware and software routing data between similar or dissimilar networks at the network layer of the OSI model.

RPO (RECOVERY POINT OBJECTIVE) The point where data was last backed up. The time between that point and the point of a disaster indicates how much data may be lost. This is determined by a BIA.

RSS (REALLY SIMPLE SYNDICATION) An XML-based system that allows users to subscribe to their favorite blogs and Web sites.

RTO (RECOVERY TIME OBJECTIVE) The amount of time that a company can be out of service due to a disaster before its survival is threatened. This is determined by a BIA.

SAAS (SOFTWARE AS A SERVICE) A process where software is deployed, hosted, and managed for multiple parties from a centrally managed facility. The applications are delivered over networks on a subscription basis. This delivery model speeds implementation, minimizes the expenses and risks incurred across the application life cycle, and overcomes the chronic shortage of qualified technical personnel available in-house. Sometimes referred to as on-demand software.

SAO (SELECTIVE APPLICATION OUTSOURCING) See SAAS.

SCANNER A PC input device that copies documents into computer memory.

SCHEMA Schema and subschema are the tools used to define the structure of a database.

SERVER A network device providing services to client stations. Servers include file servers, disk servers, and print servers. See CLIENT/SERVER.

SERVICE LEVEL MANAGEMENT The primary interface between the customer and IT. It negotiates cost effective service level agreements with customers and then works within the IT organization and external vendors to ensue the desired level can be provided. The agreed services and support levels are detailed in the service catalog which is created and maintained by Service Level Management.

SHAREWARE A term for try-before-you-buy software. Shareware comes in a wide variety of marketing models. Some ask the user to pay for it; others only require payment if the product is used in a company. Others may place an expiration date on the license (such as 45 days) and then disable the software if it is not purchased.

SHIELDED TWISTED-PAIR CABLE Twisted-pair wire surrounded by a foil or mesh shield to reduce susceptibility to outside interference and noise during network transmission.

SIMULATION A technique for evaluating the performance of a network before downloading it. Simulation employs timers and sequences as opposed to mathematical models to reproduce network behavior.

SITE LICENSING Procedure in which software is licensed to be used only at a particular location.

SIZE SNOWBALL EFFECT The larger the project size and/or the longer the required project calendar time, the more likely that additional time and effort will be needed to complete the project. As more time and effort are required, these snowball, which in turn extends the finish date and increases the final cost. The user's needs change over time. The longer a project takes, the more the user can justify changes to the final product, and the number of changes will snowball. In addition, the changes that are required for a useable product also take even more time to install, which can justifiably require more changes.

SLA (SERVICE LEVEL AGREEMENT) A formal agreement between a service provider (external or internal) and customers to provide a certain level of service. Penalty clauses typically apply if the SLA is not met.

SMS (SHORT MESSAGE SERVICE) A communications protocol that allows the sending and receiving of short text messages between mobile telephone devices.

SOA (SERVICE-ORIENTED ARCHITECTURE) A collection of services that communicate with each other. The services are self-contained and do not depend on the context or state of the other service. They work within a distributed system's architecture.

SOCIAL ENGINEERING A means of manipulating people into divulging confidential information or performing other actions that compromise the security of a system.

SOCIAL NETWORKING A means of communicating and sharing information between individuals with similar interests on an online community. Popular examples include Facebook, LinkedIn, and Twitter.

SOURCE CODE Written program code before the program has been compiled into machine instructions.

SPAM Common term for unwanted or unsolicited

e-mail. To 'spam' someone is to send massive amounts of unwanted e-mail.

SPYWARE A general term for a class of software that monitors the actions of a computer user. It is usually installed without the user's knowledge, typically as part of software that the user downloaded from the Internet.

SURGE PROTECTOR An electrical device that prevents high-voltage surges from reaching the computer system.

SYSTEM OF RECORD The data source for a given piece of information. The system of record for any given data element is the single "version of the truth" for that data element.

TABLET A portable personal computer that uses a touchscreen as a primary input device and is designed for individual use. The Apple iPad, Samsung Galaxy Tab, and the Motorola Xoom are popular examples.

TASK BURN DOWN In Agile project management, how many tasks the team is completing. Task burn down is simply how many tasks were completed each day, or each iteration.

THIRD-PARTY VENDOR A firm marketing hardware for manufacturers.

TOTAL QUALITY MANAGEMENT (TQM) A broad-based program where quality is instilled in an organization from the top down.

TRUCK NUMBER In Agile project management, the truck number is how many members of the team would need to be hit by a truck during lunch to severely hamper a project.

TURNKEY SYSTEM A system in which the vendor takes full responsibility for complete system design and provides the required hardware, software, operations manual, and user training.

TWISTED-PAIR CABLE Wiring used by local telephone systems.

UNDERPINNING AGREEMENT Used in ITIL to denote an externally facing SLA.

UNSTRUCTURED DATA Data that is typically created by a human being for personal use, such as word processing documents and spreadsheets.

UPS (UNINTERRUPTED POWER SOURCE) A device providing electric backup power to a computer system or other devices when the normal electric power fails. This occurs so quickly that the operation of devices that depend on electricity is not interrupted.

URL (UNIFORM RESOURCE LOCATOR) Web browser addresses of Internet pages and files used instead of the actual IP address.

USB (UNIVERSAL SERIAL BUS) An industry communications standard for connecting computers with other electronic devices. It has replaced serial and parallel ports, and is also used for charging portable devices.

USB FLASH DRIVE See FLASH DRIVE.

USE CASE A description of how end-users will use a software application. It describes a task or a series of tasks that users will accomplish using the software, and includes the responses of the software to user actions.

USER-FRIENDLY A computer system easy for persons with no computer experience to use, causing little or no frustration.

VALUE DELIVERED In Agile project management, the sum of the values assigned to each feature accepted by the client.

VDI (VIRTUAL DESKTOP INFRASTRUCTURE) A form of desktop virtualization that emulates the PC hardware environment of the client by delivery to a thin client from a server.

VELOCITY In Agile project management, how much the team accomplishes in an iteration. This is found by dividing the total work done by the length of the iteration. The total work done is the sum of the effort estimates of all completed tasks. All estimates should be converted to one type (such as X large is the same as Y small).

VIRTUALIZATION The concept of sharing hardware resources among the services and applications that use the resources. It allows you to use software to take a single hardware resource and turn it into multiple resources from the application's point of view.

VISUAL BASIC A third-generation event-driven programming language and associated development environment (IDE) from Microsoft.

VPN (VIRTUAL PRIVATE NETWORK) A network connection that uses the Internet to transfer information using secure methods. For example, you could set up a VPN between your laptop and your corporate network using security and encryption and the Internet as your transfer pipe.

WALK-THROUGH A technical review of a newly designed program or system. The review is conducted by interested parties such as programmers, systems analysts, users, and/or auditors. Program walk-throughs are conducted by peer programmers to detect program errors. In a walk-through, people play the role of devil's advocate in reviewing another person's/team's effort.

WAN (WIDE AREA NETWORK) Any network extending more than a few miles. It can use more than one form of message carrying.

WAP (WIRELESS APPLICATION PROTOCOL) A standard used by mobile phones and other hand-held devices to access the Internet.

WEB BROWSER See BROWSER.

WEBLOG A journal stored on the Internet that is frequently updated and available for public access. Usually referred to as a blog.

WEBMASTER The person in charge of maintaining a Web site.

WEB PAGE An HTML document that is designed to be read by a Web browser.

WEB SITE A collection of Web pages.

WEP An acronym for "Wired Equivalent Privacy." WEP is a security protocol designed to create secure wireless (Wi-Fi) networks. It was the first widely used security protocol for Wi-Fi networks and has declined in use as more secure protocols have become available.

WI-FI Refers to wireless network components that are based on the IEEE 802.11 specifications.

WI-FI HOTSPOT A publicly available connection to the Internet using a Wi-Fi modem. Typically available at hotels, cafes, and libraries.

WIKI A Web site that allows users to add and update content on the site using their own Web browser.

WIRELESS NETWORK A LAN system that does not require physical connections—information is transmitted through the air. Commonly referred to as a WLAN.

WLAN See WIRELESS NETWORK.

WORK SAMPLING Consists of a large number of random observations of predetermined tasks that an employee or group of employees perform. Data collected by the work sampling observations identifies the amount of time spent on each task.

WORM A program that replicates itself repeatedly. A worm capable of penetrating networks could quickly overload the Internet.

WPA An acronym for "Wi-Fi Protected Access." WPA is a security protocol designed to create secure wireless (Wi-Fi) networks. It is similar to the WEP protocol but offers improvements in the way it handles security keys and the way users are authorized.

WWW (WORLD WIDE WEB) A subset of the Internet that consists of HTML pages that can be accessed using a Web browser.

XML (EXTENSIBLE MARKUP LANGUAGE) Used to define documents with a standard format that can be read by any XML-compatible application.

ZERO DAY EXPLOIT A malicious computer attack that takes advantage of a security hole before the vulnerability is known. So called because the software developer has zero days to fix the security problem before the first attack is made.

INDEX

References are to sections, exhibits and policies.